*American Society*

CONSULTING EDITOR
CHARLES H. PAGE
THE UNIVERSITY OF MASSACHUSETTS

# American Society

## A SOCIOLOGICAL INTERPRETATION

### by *ROBIN M. WILLIAMS, Jr.*

*Cornell University*

THIRD EDITION

*Alfred A. Knopf*  *New York*

*For*

*Marguerite, Bob, Nancy, and Susan*

# Preface to
# the Third Edition

The eventful years since the publication of the first edition of this work in 1951 make up a very short period in the great sweep of history but a long enough span in an average lifetime to give some perspective and sense of both the continuity and change in society. When an author comes back to take a fresh look at a book written at an earlier time, he must wonder what it still has to say to a new time; he knows that the book will stand in great need of agonizing reappraisal. He must ask himself what really needs to be changed, for there surely is no virtue in sheer tinkering for the sake of change itself. But he must ask even more insistently of every statement in the work: Is *this* still true? Is *that* really worth saying? Are there subtle sins of omission that are masked by an overlay of valid assertions? Are the fundamental assumptions of the work a viable base for continuing analysis? More specifically, have the social and cultural changes of the 1950's and 1960's made necessary a new estimation of the main character and thrust of American society?

Some readers of the second edition have asked why it did not contain more analysis of racial and ethnic relations. Aside from the fact that not everything could be put between two covers at once, the reason lay primarily in the fact that the author already had published and intended to publish other, specialized works in intergroup relations.[1] Yet it is a valid criticism that the two earlier editions did not give a very extended discussion of this subject. Accordingly we have added relevant materials on this crucial topic, especially in the chapters on stratification, religion, education, values, and social organization.

Friends and critics (sometimes the same persons) have suggested that earlier versions of this analysis did not sufficiently emphasize the importance of two conspicuous features of the modern world: first, the vast development of science and technology; second, the changing character and pervasive effects of military institutions and organizations. Clearly anyone in reasonable command of his faculties, observing the world around him today, must quickly acknowledge the importance of careful analysis of these aspects of life in the late twentieth century; we hope that the present text at least indicates our awareness of the specific importance of these matters.

It has never been our intention to make *American Society* an encyclopedia; our main aspiration always was to participate with the reader in a selective and focused review and analysis of a national social system. It was not easy to leave out so much. And we often have regretted the fact that, under self-imposed restrictions of scope, almost nothing could be done with the large, diffuse, and complex field of expressive culture, including both the classic or academic and

---

[1] For example, *The Reduction of Intergroup Tensions* (New York: Social Science Research Council, 1947); Chapter 10 in Volume II of Samuel A. Stouffer, *et al.*, *The American Soldier* (Princeton, N.J.: Princeton University Press, 1949); Chapter 13 in Joseph B. Gittler (ed.), *Review of Sociology* (New York: Wiley, 1957); *Strangers Next Door* (Englewood Cliffs, N.J.: Prentice-Hall, 1964).

the popular activities and products in literature, music, sculpture, dance, theater, and painting, as well as sports and organized recreation and all manner of informal diversions and consummatory symbolizations. The present edition was planned to include an extended discussion of expressive culture and the organization of expressive behavior; but the materials that were urgently required to deal with topics already present were so abundant they crowded out the intended addition. But hope springs eternal, and we already are looking ahead to treating the expressive sector of the society in the *next* edition.

The Preface to the First Edition said: "Solid work on a *comparative* sociology of the major cultures and national systems is, of course, greatly needed. As such studies appear, the present work will be seen in proper perspective as a single case study." It is now especially gratifying, at long last, to note the substantial beginnings of the accumulation of such national studies; present or projected from various people in the field are fairly comprehensive sociological analyses of Australia, Brazil, Canada, France, Germany, Great Britain, Israel, Italy, Japan, the Netherlands, Norway, Poland, and Sweden. Systematic compilations of cross-cultural data have appeared, and several sophisticated works in comparative sociology already are at hand. Sociological science cannot be provincial; its future contributions increasingly will be placed in a context of international studies in a world that we now are forced to visualize as a spaceship destined to become more crowded in the years just ahead.

ROBIN M. WILLIAMS, JR.
*Ithaca, New York*

# *Preface to the Second Edition*

In the years since the first publication of this book, our society has experienced many important changes. During the same period, research in social science has revealed much new information and has clarified numerous points which in 1951 were obscure. Meanwhile the author has become aware of shortcomings in the original text. Although it is gratifying to find that the main theses of the book do not require basic alteration, it is also gratifying to be able to revise the entire work in the light of new data and in terms of the substantial progress in fundamental theory which has been achieved during the past decade. The present volume also has benefited from the careful criticism of the original work by many colleagues, both in the field of sociology and in other social science disciplines.

The revised version differs from the first edition in several respects. Wherever available, updated facts and figures have been supplied. The findings of new research have been woven into the text throughout the book. Revised theoretical formulations have been incorporated at several points, most notably perhaps in Chapter 11, "Value Orientations in American Society." An attempt has been made to clear up some particularly murky passages, and, in general, to communicate as simply and directly as possible. As in the first edition, however, we have not hesitated to use technical terms whenever they are needed for clarity and precision of statement.

As the social sciences show increased maturity, they receive increased public attention and recognition. The new situation calls for the most careful self-criticism and for the continuous revision of our ideas in terms of new and more penetrating research and theoretical reflection. There is no longer any question that the scientific study of society is possible and that such study can contribute to the clarification and enrichment of human experience. The task before us is to build on the solid foundations already laid.

*Ithaca, New York*

# Preface to
# the First Edition

This book is intended to provide a reasonably compact survey of the main cultural and social structures of American society. It is hoped that such a provisional synthesis will be of use not only in sociology and anthropology but also in related fields of economics, history, political science, and social psychology. The work has grown out of five years' experience at Cornell University in the development and teaching of a course on the structure and functioning of American society. Such a synoptic course was first suggested to the writer by Leonard S. Cottrell, Jr., who foresaw at the close of the Second World War a growing need for an analysis that would attempt to grasp and integrate the broad outlines of the society as a whole. Initial experiment showed that students of the most varied backgrounds and academic interests were eager to gain some systematic view of the total social structure. From the criticisms and suggestions of hundreds of these students the present work has immeasurably benefited.

The volume was designed originally to include a rather full consideration of social change in the United States. As the work developed, however, it became clear that more than a minimal analysis of the institutional structure and social organization would itself exceed the limits of a single volume. Accordingly, the present treatment is largely, though by no means entirely, restricted to a cross-sectional view of the social structure. We are, of course, acutely conscious of the need for a comprehensive and rigorous analysis of the *processes* that are so rapidly transforming our institutions. Some hints regarding the social dynamics of our society are to be found here, especially in the last three chapters, but the exceedingly difficult analyses needed for an orderly synthesis must be reserved for a later time. Our more modest aim is to look at American society through the "wrong end of the telescope"—to make the main contours of its social topography appear in something like full perspective.

Every decision has its costs, and our attention to salient structures has meant a heavy loss of detail. The student is therefore urged to make full use of the supplementary readings suggested by footnote references and by the lists at the end of each chapter, as well as of other references suggested by his instructor.

Such concentration upon America, it is true, might encourage myopia about other great societies of the West and East. Surely, however, one does not need in these times to stress the interdependence of our society with other national systems nor to deliver dicta concerning the hazards of extreme cultural parochialism. Solid work on a *comparative* sociology of the major cultures and national systems is, of course, greatly needed. As such studies appear, the present work will be seen in proper perspective as a single case study. In any event, it is surely worthwhile to seek now all possible clues as to what America is and what it may become.

*Ithaca, New York*

# Acknowledgments

This book, like any other, is a social product to which many have contributed. Footnote acknowledgments indicate the writer's awareness of numerous specific influences on his thinking, but such citations do not indicate all the contributions to this volume. I am, of course, indebted to my former teachers. C. Horace Hamilton of North Carolina State College showed me that sociology could mean empirical research and hard thinking, and gave reality to the vision of a scientific sociology. As a student at Harvard University I acquired lasting obligations to Gordon W. Allport, John D. Black, Robert K. Merton, Talcott Parsons, Pitirim A. Sorokin, and Carle C. Zimmerman. My colleagues in the departments of sociology and anthropology at Cornell University have contributed heavily to this book, although perhaps they will not always recognize their ideas here. Discussions with other members of the Cornell faculty have profoundly affected my thinking. In particular, Chapter XI bears various marks of the discussions of the Cornell Values Study Group (Urie Bronfenbrenner, Stuart M. Brown, Jr., Leonard S. Cottrell, Jr., Mario Einaudi, Robert B. MacLeod, Morris E. Opler, Edwin P. Reubens, Edward A. Suchman, Gregory Vlastos, Robin M. Williams, Jr., and A. D. Woodruff).

A special word of appreciation goes to Melvin L. Kohn for his competent research assistance and perceptive criticism in the development of the first edition. I also wish to thank Mrs. Allen Clark and Miss Ruth Almond for their indispensable editorial assistance, and Mrs. Katharine Riegger and Mrs. Margaret Anagnost for secretarial aid in preparing a somewhat difficult manuscript for publication.

To my wife, Marguerite York Williams, who contributed so greatly to the original edition. I am deeply appreciative for patient encouragement, sensitive evaluation, and many major insights during the years in which we have tried to understand human society.

During the years in which the materials for the third edition have been undergoing what sometimes seemed to be endless revisions, several persons made major direct contributions to the work. I am indebted for secretarial aid to Valerie Mould, Maxine Topik, and Virginia Glickstein. Valuable research and editorial assistance and advice were given by James E. Curtis, Janice Willis, Kathleen Rosendahl, and Gary D. Bouma. Finally, the whole manuscript benefited greatly from a sensitive and skilled editorial review by Charles H. Page. At Alfred A. Knopf-Random House, the editorial work of Theodore Caris and Sybil Elman Maimin lightened the author's load—and improved the book. The fact that some of the suggestions made by these several friendly critics were not followed is entirely my own fault.

# Contents

## I

Introduction  3

## II

Geography, Resources, and Population  6

GEOGRAPHY  6
RESOURCES  8
TECHNOLOGICAL RESOURCES  10
POPULATION  12

## III

The Problem of Analysis: Basic Approaches and Concepts  21

THE BASIC APPROACH  22
CULTURE  25
INSTITUTIONS  36
STATUS AND ROLE  41
SOCIAL ORGANIZATION AND GROUP  44

## IV

Kinship and the Family in the United States  47

"KINSHIP" AND "FAMILY" DEFINED  47
THE LEGAL NORMS OF THE AMERICAN KINSHIP SYSTEM:
    AN ILLUSTRATION OF EVIDENCE  51
MAIN STRUCTURAL FEATURES OF THE KINSHIP SYSTEM  56
EXTENDED KINSHIP RELATIONS  62
PATTERNS OF EQUALITY  68
FAMILY STATUSES AND ROLE PERFORMANCES  70
MATE SELECTION AND ROMANTIC LOVE  90
FAMILY STABILITY AND INSTABILITY  92

## V

Social Stratification in the United States  99

INTRODUCTION  99
MAJOR CONCEPTS AND PROBLEMS  100
THE AMERICAN CASE  114

## VI

## American Economic Institutions  *166*

THE NATURE OF ECONOMIC INSTITUTIONS  166
TYPES OF SOCIAL MECHANISMS CONTROLLING ECONOMIC ACTIVITY  171
MAJOR STRUCTURAL CHARACTERISTICS OF THE AMERICAN ECONOMY  177
NATURE OF THE CORPORATION AND ITS ORGANIZATION  192
THE PROFIT MOTIVE  208
LABOR RELATIONS AND LABOR ORGANIZATIONS  211
SECURITY, RIGIDITY, AND POSSIBLE NEW DIRECTIONS  224

## VII

## Political Institutions of the United States  *231*

THE NATURE OF POLITICAL INSTITUTIONS  231
THE STRUCTURE OF THE STATE IN AMERICAN SOCIETY  242
THE POWER ELITE  262
THE CIVIL AND THE MILITARY POWERS  264
THE RIGHTS AND DUTIES OF CITIZENS  269
POLITICAL PARTIES AND THE VOTERS  273
SOCIAL ORGANIZATION AND LOCAL POWER STRUCTURE  289
INTEREST GROUPINGS  292
THE SYSTEM AS A WHOLE  300

## VIII

## American Education  *305*

EDUCATION AS AN INSTITUTION  305
PRINCIPLE CHARACTERISTICS OF AMERICAN EDUCATION  311
CULTURAL THEMES  334
COLLEGES AND UNIVERSITIES  338
CULTURAL GOALS AND EDUCATIONAL CREEDS  351

## IX

## Religion in America  *355*

INTRODUCTION: RELIGION AND SOCIETY  355
DISTINCTIVE FEATURES OF AMERICAN RELIGIOUS INSTITUTIONS  370
RELATIONS OF RELIGION TO OTHER INSTITUTIONS  402
RELIGION AND THE STRUCTURE OF AMERICAN SOCIETY  407

## X

## Institutional Variation and the Evasion of Normative Patterns  *413*

INTRODUCTION  413
SPECIFIC EXAMPLES OF PATTERNED EVASION  421

CULTURAL FICTIONS 431
CONCLUSION AND IMPLICATIONS 436

## XI

### Values in American Society 438

AN ANALYSIS OF VALUES AND VALUE-ORIENTATIONS 438
WHAT ARE "DOMINANT VALUES"? 448
WHAT ARE VALUE SYSTEMS? 450
THE PROBLEMS OF CONSISTENCY, INTEGRATION, AND LEVELS OF
    VALUATION 451
MAJOR VALUE ORIENTATIONS IN AMERICA 452
CONCLUSION 500

## XII

### Social Organization in the United States 505

THE NATURE OF SOCIAL ORGANIZATION 505
MAIN TYPES OF SOCIAL ORGANIZATION 510
GENERAL CHARACTERISTICS OF SOCIAL ORGANIZATION IN THE
    UNITED STATES 523

## XIII

### Interrelations of Major Institutions and Groupings 547

INTRODUCTION: SOME GENERAL CONSIDERATIONS 547
HOW INSTITUTIONS ARE INTERRELATED 551
SELECTED CASE STUDIES OF INSTITUTIONAL INTERRELATIONS 556

## XIV

### The Integration of American Society 580

INTEGRATION AND CHANGE IN SOCIAL SYSTEMS 580
FACTORS IN THE COHESION OF AMERICAN SOCIETY 588
CONFLICT AND INTEGRATION 607
INTEGRATION, ANOMIE, AND ALIENATION 609

## XV

### Social and Cultural Change 620

A REVIEW 620
SOME GENERAL THEORIES 621
TRENDS—PAST AND CURRENT 625
THE FACTORS SUPPORTING CHANGE IN AMERICA 630

### Indexes FOLLOW PAGE 640

*American Society*

# Introduction

There are so many excellent books about
the people and society of the United States that a new one should aspire to
be of more than topical interest. A work on American society must aid our
understanding by presenting either new information, a new or more
complete analysis of established facts, or a new synthesis and integration of
the countless facts and interpretations that lie at hand.

The present work is a study in sociology, a survey of our society that
uses the data, methods, concepts, and theory characteristic of one particular
field of the social sciences. It is not a study in economics, although it often
touches upon matters popularly termed "economic." Nor is it a historical
work, although all of its data are in some sense "historical." It deals at times
with political institutions, but it does not lay claim to the historically
distinct field of political science. It recognizes the basic conditioning factors
of biological and physical nature: man is a warm-blooded, mortal creature,
sensitive and vulnerable to a world in which he lives within narrow margins
of survival. He is by no means a basically serene or placid form of living
organism. We cannot ignore his remarkable biopsychic capacities, both for
creation and for destruction. But neither biology nor physical science,
fundamental as each is, deals directly with the central content and interest of
a sociological exposition.

This book draws upon all areas of study of human behavior for data
and principles that will help to describe and explain its own proper field:
the social relations and concomitant beliefs and values that characterize the
people of the United States. Many things very important from other points
of view are omitted or given only passing attention. But every treatment
of any subject is inherently selective; we never analyze all of the indefinite
number of aspects that conceivably could be treated. And this is not a cause
for regret. On the contrary, such selectivity is not only inevitable but also
one of the main roads to more useful knowledge of human society.

Since our present task is an exercise in applied sociology, in that we shall
apply sociological concepts and principles to a specific national society as a
whole, we must use the fundamental method of understanding any human
society: the practice of repeated, questioning observation. If we want to
comprehend how and why men behave as they do, we must look at what
they do (and do not do), listen to what they say (and do not say). We must
observe persistently, be alert to recurring patterns and far-from-obvious
causal connections. The main focus, however, will be upon analysis rather
than description. In other words, we shall be interested primarily in *why*
American society is the kind of society it is, rather than simply in a detailed
description of its present characteristics. Therefore, the only descriptive
material presented is that which seemed indispensable to a sociological
analysis. There are available numerous excellent descriptive accounts. What

is urgently needed is a more complete analysis aimed at summarizing at least part of the existing body of scientific knowledge about the culture and social structure of the United States.

A study such as this necessarily has a certain detachment. Actually, there would be great advantages in having it done by an observer from a radically different culture. It is impossible for a person brought up in a given society to get entirely outside all the presuppositions of that society and culture: there will always be blind spots in observation and analysis, and there will always be particular perspectives and evaluations implicit in the selection and interpretation of data. It does not follow, however, that everything is merely "a matter of opinion." There are facts about our society that can be agreed upon by all those who accept scientific criteria of fact. Furthermore, it is a cardinal principle of the professional ethics of social science that the data included and the conclusions derived be based upon scientific relevance alone, not on personal wishes, political inclination, ideological sympathies, and the like.

Perhaps we shall never attain the objectivity of the hypothetical "man from Mars" in looking at our own society, but we can temporarily suspend our tendency to describe human conduct with praise or blame. By refraining from judgments of desirability or undesirability we can make a disciplined attempt at scientific understanding of such matters as the regularities in social behavior, the interdependence of actions within a social system, the causes and consequences of observed behaviors. Such will be the basic aim of this book. The analyses undertaken here are guided in part by the belief that much of the public and private action in our day is taken without consideration of the repercussions that may arise out of the total social system within which the actions take place. And often even a systematic analysis of various isolated parts of the social structure turns out to be highly unrealistic, if not actually fallacious, by reason of this same neglect of context. In this age of shrunken distances and planetary problems we must see things clearly and see them whole. America, with its varieties of national origins, climate, and cultural traditions, is a good place to start. The present work is an attempt to sketch the broad structural features of American society in such a way that the total system can be visualized as a going concern.

On the face of it, such an attempt is difficult. Indeed, if one wished to go into any really considerable detail, such a picture could not be drawn within the limits of any one work, no matter how extensive. Obviously, it is necessary to be ruthlessly selective and parsimonious of detail. American social structure can be treated in only its broadest outlines; only the most significant elements of structure and interrelationships can be touched upon. And not only will the analysis be in these general terms, but it will be incomplete as well, for many vitally important questions simply cannot be answered yet for lack of reliable data or adequate theoretic and analytic tools. Nevertheless, these disadvantages may not outweigh the value of this modest foundation for later, more thoroughgoing analysis.

Finally, a warning is necessary. Many readers will find parts of the subsequent discussion deceptively neat and simple. Because the exposition focuses on substantive content—not questions of underlying theory and methodology—many conclusions may wear an appearance of self-evident reasonableness or plausibility. It is a safe generalization to say that in every such instance, a penetrating inspection will reveal implications and questions of considerable intellectual challenge. A useful counterbalance to easy acceptance of first impressions from reading the text may be to pay special attention to the way in which questions are raised and problems posed. Close observation will show that the analysis has its own systematic way of asking questions; this way of asking questions and then going about an analysis probably will be the most lasting contribution of the chapters that follow.

Here is the basic problem: there are approximately 200 million people inhabiting a vast territory and considered to constitute a nation. This collectivity has territories, outposts, and spheres of influence around the planet. For some purposes, the nation is thought of and treated as if it were an integral unit: in its name wars are fought, treaties concluded, agreements made; and its citizens abroad find that the label "American" means something to persons in other nations. But internally it is evidently quite heterogeneous: the people are categorized into many occupational, racial, ethnic, and religious groupings; there are diverse interests; there are competing and conflicting groups of many kinds; there are marked regional and local differences in typical behaviors and values—and so forth. Yet for a social system to exist, for the word "nation" to have a concrete meaning, the behavior of millions of individuals in the bewildering network of crisscross group affiliations must somehow show considerable regularity and coordination. How is that possible? This is our bedrock question. How is it possible—concretely and in detail—that so many diverse human individuals manifest the predictability necessary for the existence of a society? The *fact* of this regularity can be documented as we proceed, but we shall also keep returning to the question of its *causes*.

We must also raise a second question. If there is an American social system, or a congeries of "systems," how and why does it change or remain the same through time? What significant changes in structure are discernible? How can we account for the changes we observe?

We thus have to study *structure*, the relatively definite and enduring social relations; and we have to study *change*. We shall begin with the most obvious influences upon this society, as upon all others, its location, its land and physical resources, its geographic habitat, and its population. Following this, there will be a brief analysis of certain major institutional patterns, groups, and other structural complexes of the society. Once this "morphological" description has been recorded, the analysis will turn to the functional interrelations of structural elements, or, to continue the analogy, the "physiology" of the system. Last will come a consideration of the changing structure of American society in a changing world.

With a task of such magnitude before us, this is perhaps enough of a preamble.

# Geography, Resources, and Population                II

We start with the realities of the land and the people. We are seeking a sociological portrait of America. The facts of central interest here are therefore facts about human relations. Yet human relations do not occur in a vacuum; and if we are to grasp the nature of American society, we will do well to glance briefly at the geography, the resources, the technology and "material culture," and the gross population characteristics of the modern United States.

## GEOGRAPHY

The history of the United States and the nature of its present culture and social structure are the result, in part, of a unique combination of geographic circumstances. In the first place, the North American continent is a great land mass bounded to east and west by the great expanses of the Atlantic and Pacific oceans. Especially in earlier days of slow overseas communication and transportation, the distance between the Atlantic seaboard and Europe was of momentous consequence. For example, it made possible, although it certainly did not completely determine, the emergence of a national consciousness out of an aggregation of varied and poorly integrated colonial provinces. It permitted, under the conditions of the times, the growth and organization of independent tendencies, culminating in the revolution that split the colonies from the British Empire. It interposed a formidable barrier to extensive *direct* contact with European cultures and power struggles during the formative years of the nation. It minimized for most of the nation's history the danger of large-scale invasion by major foreign powers. It thereby indirectly contributed to a certain fluidity and "openness" in social relations and to the development of a decentralized, nonsecretive, nonmilitary governmental structure. Furthermore, the ocean barrier undoubtedly encouraged the feeling of alienation from Europe and attention on American rather than European matters. The newness of the New World and its consciousness of being somehow quite different from Europe, instead of a transplanted part of Western European culture, rested to an appreciable degree upon the consciousness of the Atlantic barrier.

With the work of Frederick Jackson Turner and his followers before us, we are no longer likely to ignore or minimize the significance of the frontier in American history. "Frontier," of course, has had a meaning radically different in the United States from that which is taken for granted in Europe. The frontier meant danger, hardship, grinding toil, and privation; it also meant expansion, opportunity, economic growth, social mobility. The con-

6

quest of the frontier gave new equalitarian meanings to political democracy. It lent added force to a sense of progress. It gave birth to distinctively American legends, myths, and heroes. We must also emphasize, however, the oceans and what they meant in military security and economic advantage. From 1607 to World War I, the Atlantic served as a shield—partly in actual fact, partly in feeling—behind which a Monroe Doctrine could be promulgated, national leaders could speak of avoiding "entangling alliances," and an infant republic could dare to limit its standing army to eighty men.[1]

The barrier was, of course, also a highway. Although Americans could believe in their military security because of their distance from the great powers, the waters were potentially an unobstructed road for immigrants, soldiers, and goods. Much of the security attributed to the ocean distances in our early history was perhaps a matter of the preoccupation of European powers with intramural conflicts. When the social and economic situations permitted, the "barrier" teemed with the movement of men and trade. Thus, the same geographic fact takes on sharply contrasting implications as circumstances change. Perhaps we could ask no better example to illustrate the role of geographic conditions as passive agents, limiting or facilitating but not determining social behavior.

The United States, as eventually constituted, has had the great advantages of possessing ice-free ports on two oceans. Given the social and economic conditions of the nineteenth century, the possession of such ports meant that the country had a prime requisite for development as a maritime power—and this without the heavy cost of conquest that many other nations have incurred in the attempt to gain access to the sea.

From the beginning, the bays and rivers insured that America, for all her vast heartland of arable plains, would not be a land-locked society. From the beginning, she was geographically accessible. Even in early colonial days, Americans began to utilize not only ocean ports but also extensive inland waterways. The first settlements reached inland along the coastal indentations and the rivers; and when the footholds had been won, the rivers and their valleys formed the channels for the vanguards moving toward the mountain barriers.

A second prime geographic feature of the United States is the great expanse of contiguous land mass. The thirteen colonies that originally federated under the Constitution established a kind of beachhead on the fringe of a continent. Settlement could proceed as an advance on a broad front; and the continental mass offered the possibility of establishing an enormous contiguous area of free trade, mobility, and communication.[2] In early periods, the varied geographic characteristics of different areas and the distances separating them contributed to provincialism and sectionalism

[1] This was the total regular Army at its lowest strength, in 1784. See James Ripley Jacobs, *The Beginning of the U.S. Army 1783–1812* (Princeton, N.J.: Princeton University Press, 1947), pp. vii, 14.

[2] In this as in many other instances, geography played the role it did only because of definite social conditions. One of the more important was the absence of well organized, powerful, and technologically advanced peoples in possession of the territory. The settlers drove out or exterminated the American Indians (who would not take kindly to enslavement); they did not have to subjugate thickly settled peoples.

and in other ways gave a loose and amorphous quality to the total society. But the political unification of the nation preserved the continental expanse as an enormous free-trade area for an expanding and developing industrial order.

The idea of apparently unlimited lands in the New World had powerful social and psychological effects upon the American. Even a cursory reading of early American history tells of the preoccupation with the land, which went along with a vivid sense of room, of expansion, of great territorial sweeps to be mastered. Very early indeed, the Americans began to act as if they had decided that this land was somehow *meant* for them to possess. And the sheer fact of the vastness of the land resources was highly significant in the early differentiation of American society from its European origins. Immigrants from tight, localistic, feudally tinged societies met here abruptly with empty lands, with space, with abounding resources. What this experience did to the typical personality structure and social relations of the Americans is inevitably a main theme of any adequate social history of this country. For the society of Western Europe from which the American settlers came in the early seventeenth century was still fundamentally rural; and the United States at the time of its emergence as an independent political entity was overwhelmingly agrarian. In such a society, the whole organization of human relations is closely bound up with the extent of land resources and the social conditions under which they are utilized.

### RESOURCES

Thus, among all resources that of the land was first seized upon and became decisive for national development.[3] Within the present boundaries of continental United States are approximately 3 million square miles—an area exceeding that of all Europe. The successive waves of settlers from the first landing to the official closing of the frontier in 1890 were always pushing on to new lands. And these were lands so varied as to support nearly every major type of valuable plant and animal; they were largely fertile lands, unexhausted by exploitative tillage, relatively free from entrenched proprietorship. They worked a deep ferment among the land-hungry peoples and the venturesome promoters of Europe; and they furnished the foundation for that free-farmer society that Jefferson idealized and that was for so long a major theme of the American ethos.

Even today the United States, although it seems to many of its inhabitants to be densely settled, is a relatively empty area in terms of ratio of population to both total and agricultural land. This characteristic it shares with the U.S.S.R., as well as with Canada and Australia; such nation-societies stand in sharp contrast to the very heavily populated lands of many other societies. In the United States for every ten persons there are 61.7 acres of agricultural land; in Taiwan, for every ten persons there are 2.3 acres. Further illustrations of similarities and contrasts are shown in Table 1.

---

[3] "The expanse of ocean and the expanse of land in the west have been two of the greatest geographical factors in molding the thought as well as the character of the American." James Truslow Adams, *The American* (New York: Scribner, 1943), p. 227.

TABLE 1 • *Population Per 1,000 Hectares\* of Agricultural Land for Selected Countries†*

| COUNTRY | POPULATION PER 1,000 HECTARES |
|---|---|
| Soviet Union | 339 |
| United States | 399 |
| Spain | 1,347 |
| United Kingdom | 2,677 |
| Japan | 7,563 |
| Egypt | 9,282 |
| Taiwan | 10,446 |
| South Korea | 11,185 |

\* 1 hectare = 2.471 acres.
† Figures are for various years between 1956 and 1959.
SOURCE: Adapted from Bruce M. Russett, et al., World Handbook of Political and Social Indicators (New Haven: Yale University Press, 1964), pp. 146–147.

But land was only the first and most obvious of the natural resources that the territory offered to a people equipped to utilize it. The ocean, the land, and the forests could furnish the basis for an agricultural and trading society. The industrial civilization of the nineteenth and early twentieth centuries, however, was based directly upon two prime minerals—coal and iron. The United States had both, in easy proximity, together with the limestone for processing the ore into steel. The later hegemony of American industrialism was conditioned also by the emergence of petroleum and electricity as additional sources of vast inanimate energies. The United States now uses inanimate energy on a scale never before attained in any other society. The total horsepower of all prime movers in the nation had reached by 1940 the imposing figure of 2.8 billion; by 1964 the total had soared to the nearly incomprehensible level of 14.2 billion.[4] This enormous output of energy continues to increase. Yet most of mankind even today must depend upon human muscles and draft animals for production. The tremendous utilization of energy from mineral resources in the United States is unique to a degree not always understood by its own people.

The resources available to this society are utilized by a relatively young and vigorous population, equipped with highly developed skills and technical knowledge and organized for effective economic production. One consequence is a level of material well-being above that of most areas of the world. Although international or crosscultural comparisons of levels of living are notoriously difficult and treacherous, there is no question that with respect to food, clothing, shelter, transportation, and other physical

[4] United States Bureau of the Census, *Statistical Abstract of the United States, 1965,* 86th ed. (Washington, D.C.: 1965) p. 529.

necessities and comforts American society as a whole is more favored than that of any other contemporary national area.[5] Income levels as measured in the market economy are very high. For example, the standard estimates of Gross National Product (in United States dollars) per capita for selected countries in 1957 were as follows:[6]

| | |
|---|---|
| Mainland China | 73 |
| India | 73 |
| Haiti | 105 |
| United Arab Republic | 142 |
| Japan | 306 |
| Poland | 475 |
| Argentina | 490 |
| Italy | 516 |
| Soviet Union | 600 |
| Switzerland | 943 |
| France | 1,428 |
| Canada | 1,947 |
| United States | 2,577 |

Although the Gross National Product may not accurately represent "real" personal incomes, the general orders of magnitudes among nations are reasonably dependable. Other indices give similar results.

## TECHNOLOGICAL RESOURCES

To this panoramic view of the geography and natural resources of the society one must add a very highly developed technology and technological apparatus. America's giant industrial plant is the epitome of the application of scientific technology to production, and even its agriculture is mechanized and technically rationalized to a degree not yet approached even in modernized Europe.

The bare descriptive facts regarding the technological resources of the society would fill volumes; we will present a few salient characteristics most relevant to the analysis developed in the present volume. The structure and functioning of the social system as such are basically affected by:

1. The presence of the elaborately developed industrial and agricultural technologies and apparatus;

[5] By the end of the eighteenth century, "The American mind turned to the then new and daring proposition which it has never abandoned: that common prosperity, by giving every individual a growing stake in the national society and making his economic interests a cementing link in the new national loyalty and self-awareness, was the safest foundation for the Union, and, in fact, for every modern nation." Hans Kohn, *American Nationalism: An Interpretive Essay* (New York: Macmillan, 1957), p. 41.

[6] Data from Russett, *et al.* (eds.), *op. cit.*, pp. 155–157.

2. The existence of an extraordinary set of transportation facilities, providing for extensive and rapid mobility of materials and persons;
3. the highly developed networks of facilities for both mass communication and point-to-point communication.

For illustrative purposes, the last two items may be used to suggest the sociological importance of the character of technological development.

The functioning of the contemporary United States as a social system is greatly dependent upon the remarkable set of facilities for transportation and communication. The network of railroads, airlines, water routes, and improved highways makes feasible the unprecedented ease and speed with which people and goods can circulate over a large territory. For example, more than half of all motor vehicles in use in the entire world (about 150 million) are in the United States (over 80 million). Approximately eight of every ten families in the nation own one or more automobiles. As of 1960 it was estimated that the number of persons per motor vehicle here was only 2.5, which means that every man, woman, and child could simultaneously sit in the front seat of a vehicle, with room to spare. The remarkable character of this statistic may be appreciated by comparison with the mean number of persons per motor vehicle in other societies, for example: Sweden, 6.3; France, 6.3; United Kingdom, 7.5; Japan, 52.6; Brazil, 77.0; India, 1,000.0.[7] As we shall see later, the great mobility of the American population is one of its most marked characteristics and is intimately related to many other features of American behavior. From earliest colonial days, this has been a nation perennially on the move. It is a society with a rich store of vehicles[8] for the interchange of populations, communications, and goods.

Along with highly developed means of transportation, there are, of course, very elaborate and active communication systems. Telephones, telegraph systems, and the postal system are facilities most Americans take completely for granted; yet the development of such a point-to-point communication system has never existed before over such a large area within a single political collectivity. The same can be said, perhaps with even more force, of the development of mass communication: radio, television, newspapers, magazines—one or more of these reaches nearly everyone. Again, comparisons among selected countries, as presented in Table 2, help to place this situation in appropriate perspective.

The entire society is continuously being crisscrossed by streams of letters and telephone calls (over 250 million a day). The proportion of telephone calls that are long-distance is increasing. Domestic travel is increasing, and fast air transportation links major centers into one vast "village" in terms of time required for personal contact. And the American population is con-

---

[7] Calculated from data presented in Hans L. Zetterberg and Murray Gendell, *Sociological Almanac for the United States* (rev. ed.), (Totowa, N.J.: Bedminster Press, 1963), p. 74.

[8] "Vehicle" has been proposed by Pitirim A. Sorokin as the generic term to designate all means for externalizing and communicating social values and meanings. See his *Society, Culture, and Personality: Their Structure and Dynamics* (New York: Harper & Row, 1947), esp. pp. 48–63.

TABLE 2 · *Indices of Communication for Selected Countries, 1960 (number per 1,000 population)*

| NATION | TELEPHONES | RADIOS | NEWSPAPERS | TELEVISIONS |
|---|---|---|---|---|
| United States | 411 | 941 | 328 | 297* |
| Sweden | 347 | 360 | 462 | 133 |
| United Kingdom | 156 | 290 | 514 | 211 |
| France | 97 | 242 | 243 | 42 |
| Japan | 59 | 157 | 397 | 64 |
| Soviet Union | N.A. | 190 | 172 | 24 |
| Brazil | 14 | 65 | 60 | 17 |
| India | 1 | 5 | 11 | N.A. |

* As of 1962, TV sets were in 90 percent of all households; and 13 percent had two or more sets.

SOURCE: Adapted from Hans L. Zetterberg and Murray Gendell, Sociological Almanac for the United States (rev. ed.), (Totowa, N.J.: Bedminster Press, 1963), p. 74.

tinually exposed to mass stimuli that simultaneously present to large numbers of individuals the same items of information and similar interpretations of the world.[9]

Clearly the social structure of the United States has a *permeable character*. Our society is very far removed indeed from the isolation of local communities that has been typical of most human societies throughout history until the last few decades.

### POPULATION

Any comprehensive survey of the population of the United States would require more space than is available in this entire book; and the reader who is interested in securing a full population analysis will find available a number of excellent works. Fortunately, the most essential facts regarding population can be summarized quite briefly.

First of all, the total population of the United States is only about 6 percent of the world total of over 3 billion human beings. The population of the world is now increasing at a rate of just less than two percent per year, representing a fantastic growth in absolute numbers.[1] Barring truly massive catastrophes, and allowing for the lowest birth rates that can be reasonably expected, the world's total will be well over 6 billion persons by the year 2,000. Nothing like this has ever happened before. In the two centuries from 1650 to 1850 the world's population doubled; it doubled again in the single

[9] Although the mass media show much more diversity of views than can be found in societies with highly centralized governments. Cf. Alex Inkeles, *Public Opinion in Soviet Russia* (Cambridge, Mass.: Harvard University Press, 1950).

[1] See United Nations Department of Economic and Social Affairs, *World Population Prospects as Assessed in 1963* (New York: United Nations, 1966), p. 134.

century 1850–1950; it now is doubling in about thirty-five years. There must be limits somewhere.

Perhaps the most striking demographic characteristic of the population of the United States is its ethnic and racial heterogeneity. America is a land of minorities; or as the title of Louis Adamic's book put it, "a nation of nations." To ethnic and racial heterogeneity must be added the varying religious affiliations of the people, since these affiliations often index more broadly cultural as well as purely creedal differences.

This mixture of peoples has been the result of three great waves of immigration occurring after the formation of the nation as an independent political unit. The first, during the 1840's and 1850's, drew chiefly upon the British Isles and northwestern Europe, including Germany; Irish immigrants, were, of course, prominent in this phase. The second occurred during the post-Civil War period of industrial expansion; it continued to draw heavily from northwestern Europe, but increasingly brought southern and eastern Europeans as well. The third wave, centering in the enormous influx of 1900–1910, was made up largely of persons from southern and eastern Europe. Since the passage of restrictive immigration laws following World War I, a large proportion of immigrants has come from Canada, Mexico, our own commonwealth of Puerto Rico, and other parts of the Americas. Since the early 1930's, numerically small but culturally important increments to the national population have been added by refugees from totalitarian regimes. Altogether, during the years 1820–1961, approximately 42 million immigrants entered the country, and some 35 millions, or over 80 percent, remained here—the largest voluntary population movement in all history. Even under the greatly reduced immigration quotas now in effect, the nation is receiving some 3 million immigrants in a decade.

The successive "geologic deposits" of population have created a multi-culture society in which nearly every nationality, race, or creed can be found. "The American, that new man" of whom Crèvecoeur spoke, is a composite product of over three centuries of contact and intermingling of diverse cultures within the same country. Again and again in later chapters, the multiple implications of this central fact will enter into our analysis. Even though the 1920's marked the end of relatively unrestricted immigration, nationality and ethnic identifications and sociocultural characteristics persist as important influences in present-day American life.[2]

The population of the United States is now *urbanized*. Most of the peoples of the earth in all eras have lived under "rural" conditions; and in America many of the most important attitudes and customs of the cultural heritage were formed in periods when the majority of the inhabitants lived on farms or in villages and small towns.[3] Perhaps in part because of a certain

[2] Excellent studies of this subject include George E. Simpson and J. Milton Yinger, *Racial and Cultural Minorities* (New York: Harper & Row, 1965); Nathan Glazer and Daniel Patrick Moynihan, *Beyond the Melting Pot* (Cambridge, Mass.: The M.I.T. Press, 1963); Milton Gordon, *Assimilation in American Life* (New York: Oxford University Press, 1964); Stanley Lieberson, *Ethnic Patterns in American Cities* (New York: Free Press, 1964).

[3] For the important place of the small town in American history see Page Smith, *As a City Upon a Hill* (New York: Knopf, 1966).

nostalgic appeal lingering around the rural tradition, it is not always fully realized how completely the United States has become an urbanized nation. The society that had counted 5 percent of its people as "urban" in 1790 found by 1960 that 70 percent lived in urban areas.[4]

By 1960 the actual farm population had declined to just over 7 percent, and in three geographic divisions (New England, Middle Atlantic, and Pacific) was 3 percent or less. In contrast, 63 percent lived in the massive concentrations of population represented by 212 standard metropolitan statistical areas.[5] This development is especially impressive when we recall that extensive urbanization and the growth of really large cities are quite recent historical events. As late as the beginning of the nineteenth century, less than 2 percent of the world's population lived in cities of 100,000 or more.[6]

The merging of vast urban conglomerations into continuous urbanized belts, constituting "continental cities" or "megalopolitan areas," is a process already far advanced in the United States along the East Coast from Massachusetts to Virginia,[7] around the Great Lakes, on the West Coast, in Texas, and in several other emerging areas. The rapid, sprawling, uncoordinated growth of these giant conurbations, with their burgeoning outer rings and their crowded, blighted inner cities, creates dislocations, social tensions, and conflicts of great magnitude and difficulty.

In the second half of this century, the character of urban organization represents the outcome of trends that had been discerned much earlier.[8] The highly concentrated central city has given way to a sprawling network of cities, suburbs, satellite cities, rural urban fringes, highway-corridor settlements, and heavily settled open country areas. The new population aggregates as well as lines of functional interdependence cut across a profusion of political and administrative units.

The census classification is based on residence; and no doubt the percentage classified as urban underestimates the proportion of the population that is sociologically urban. For instance, a large proportion classified as "rural nonfarm" by the census has many of the essential social and economic characteristics of urban populations. Even the population residing in strictly open country is increasingly subject to urban influences; the line between city and country becomes more and more difficult to establish.

Variation in the percentage of population classified as urban from one

[4] Change in the pattern of urban settlement resulted in a new and more inclusive census definition of "urban" between 1940 and 1950. Cf. Warren S. Thompson and David T. Lewis, *Population Problems* (5th ed.) (New York: McGraw-Hill, 1965), pp. 129–135.

[5] *Ibid.*, pp. 139, 145.

[6] Amos H. Hawley, "World Urbanization: Trends and Prospects," in Ronald Freedman (ed.), *Population: The Vital Revolution* (Garden City, N.Y.: Anchor Books, 1964), p. 73.

[7] Jean Gottman, *Megalopolis: The Urbanized Northeastern Seaboard of the United States* (New York: Twentieth Century Fund, 1961).

[8] The shift from central city to metropolitan area was seen by R. D. McKenzie in the early 1930's [*The Metropolitan Community* (New York: McGraw-Hill, 1933)], and the tendency for the well-to-do to move to the suburbs had been observed and noted prior to World War I.

state to another is very great, ranging from 86 percent in Rhode Island to 38 percent in Mississippi. The great region north of the Ohio and east of the Mississippi contains the most highly urbanized sections of the country. There are massive concentrations of population in cities like New York, which are centers of economic and social influences that set their stamp upon the entire national life.[9] The United States is very far indeed from the agrarian society that in its first census recorded that only 5 percent of its less than 4 million people lived in centers of 2,500 or more.

It is a useful reminder of cultural persistence, however, to note that even in a society so highly urbanized as that of the United States, highly important social differences remain between rural and urban populations.[1] For example, compared with the urban population the rural-farm population is more often characterized by residential stability, low education, large families, lower incomes, less unemployment, and higher fertility ratios.

We have, then, a heterogeneous people, an urbanized people. It is also a *mobile* people. The continent has been peopled by immigration and the long-continuing westward movement. More recently, there has been an enormous farm-to-city movement: from the time when reasonably dependable data were first made available in 1920 to 1959 the sum of departures from farms is estimated to have been over 68 million persons. For the same period, the total migration *to* farms was about 41 million persons. Thus, a ceaseless interchange of farm and city population occurs, in which there is a large net balance in favor of the urban areas. In addition to rural-urban and urban-rural migrations, there is extensive mobility of residence within both urban and nonurban areas. The percentages of the population that changed residence annually as of the early 1960's were: 20 percent in urban centers, 22 percent in rural nonfarm areas, and 14 percent in rural-farm areas. And there are several hundred thousand agricultural workers who live a precarious existence as migratory laborers. Overall, about one-fifth of the people change place of residence each year. Since 1860, each census has shown about one-fourth of the population living outside the state of birth; and the percentage has increased slightly over recent decades. The American people have become, if anything, more rather than less responsive through mobility to differences and changes in economic opportunity and other advantages in areas somewhat distant from their initial location.

Mobility of families from one community setting to another forces changes in work associates, family visiting circles, children's school and play groups, participation in organizations, and relationships with kin. Mobility of individuals affects psychosocial control over behavior by exposing the person to varied values and practices, by removing him (temporarily) from the pressures of close social circles, by offering opportunities

[9] In 1960, five cities in the United States had a population of more than a million, sixteen others, more than 500,000. The vast urbanized area of New York-Northeastern New Jersey alone contained over fourteen million persons. From Boston to Washington, D.C., urban concentrations flow into one another, constituting almost a "continental city."

[1] Leo F. Schnore, "The Rural-Urban Variable: An Urbanite's Perspective," *Rural Sociology*, 31, 2 (June 1966), 135–137.

for relatively anonymous actions. Thus, mobility often has been seen as a process that frees the individual from social control, encouraging anonymity and independence. But only certain kinds of mobility have such effects. Much of the geographic mobility in American society is that of nuclear families (composed only of parents and their children—see Chapter IV) changing residence as they rise in income and occupational rank. Such families typically appear to be quite sensitive to the sociocultural characteristics of neighborhoods and sensitive to the values and norms of the groupings to which they aspire.[2] The social and psychological impacts of mobility appear to be minimized by an elaborate stock of economic and social devices, ranging from credit cards or letters of introduction to informal patterns of etiquette. Furthermore, most moves are for relatively short distances. Nevertheless, the rates of movement shown by the data cited above are high enough to have enormous effects upon a great many important aspects of the present social system.

The *age distribution* of a society's population may have crucially important implications for its economic development and political stability, as well as for the functioning of other major institutional sectors. For example, a very high proportion of young children may overburden limited educational and health services.

Compared with nonindustrialized countries, the population of the United States has a relatively advanced age distribution; compared with northwestern Europe, a relatively young population. Although higher birth and lower death rates since World War II increased both the proportions of very young and of elderly persons, the United States for many years enjoyed a fortuitous "unearned increment" in the form of an age distribution favorable to economic productivity—relatively few dependents and many persons in the vigorous working years of life. As of 1960, children under ten years comprised 21.7 percent and adults aged sixty-five and over 9.2 percent of the total population.[3] Obviously an important characteristic of any population is the ratio of the working-age population to the number who are likely to be economically inactive because they are too young or too old to work. Demographic studies conventionally calculate a total dependency ratio by combining those under fifteen and those over sixty as "dependent," dividing this figure by the number aged fifteen to fifty-nine and multiplying by 100. The United States has the high ratio of 80 percent, whereas the ratios for Western Europe are lower, for example, 75 percent for France, 67 percent for the United Kingdom, or 64 percent for Sweden.[4] The ratio for the United States is rising, as a consequence of a rapid rise in the proportion of children and youths and a smaller increase in the proportion of persons in the older brackets.

2 For example, see Ruth Hill Useem, John Useem, and Duane L. Gibson, "The Function of Neighboring for the Middle-Class Male," *Human Organization*, XIX, 2 (Summer 1960), 68–76.
3 Bureau of the Census, *1960 Census of the Population*, Vol. I, Characteristics of the Population, Part 1, Table 47, p. 153.
4 Thompson and Lewis, *op. cit.*, p. 90.

Another important demographic characteristic of the American population is the *high proportion of married persons*. The proportion of single persons is lower than in other nations for which we have reliable data; in 1960, only about 8 percent of those who had reached the age of seventy-five had never married. Furthermore, Americans marry at an earlier median age (in 1965, twenty-three years for men, twenty-one years for women) than in most of the major countries for which data are available; and, despite high divorce rates, the married state is the normal condition for the great majority of adults.[5] For example, in 1964, 92 percent of all women aged thirty to thirty-four were married. As we shall see below, even if many American marriages dissolve, the individuals typically lose little time before reentering the married condition.

The establishment of urbanism as a way of life in the Western world was associated with declining *birth rates*, and the United States was no exception to the general tendency. By the 1930's the average net reproduction rate for the entire United States was too low for replacement requirements (1934–1940); the urban rate in 1940 was such that with a continuation of the given birth and death rates for a period of a generation, the city population would decrease to about 74 percent of its then current size. A net urban deficit in reproduction had existed for a long time, the growth of the cities having been accomplished by immigration.

Until the end of World War II, birth rates had been falling continuously in this country for a century. After World War II there was a reversal of the trend, although really large families are no more popular now than in the previous period of generally low birth rates. The increase came about largely through a decrease in the families with no children or with only one or two. The size of the upturn in birth rates in recent years is indicated by the contrast between the rate of 18.4 in 1933 and rate of 24.4 for the decade 1945–1954. In the years 1935–1944 there were 26.4 million births; in the following decade there were 36.8 million births.[6] Although these rates were low in comparison with those prevailing a century ago, the short-run increases were impressive. As compared with the preceding two decades, the increased fertility of the American population from the end of World War II into the 1960's reflected high rates of marriage, younger age at marriage, and earlier and more closely spaced births,[7] as well as a moderate increase in the size of completed families. Undoubtedly, economic prosperity, as well as changes in expectations and values, favored these developments. However, the re-

[5] The low proportion of single persons in the United States is shown by comparison of its 25 percent with 29 percent in France, 33 in Sweden, 37 in Italy, and the extraordinary 53 percent in Ireland. (Thompson and Lewis, *op. cit.*, p. 233.)

[6] Cf. T. Lynn Smith, *Population Analysis* (New York: McGraw-Hill, 1948), p. 210. Whereas a net reproduction rate of 100 is necessary to maintain population numbers, the rate for the United States in 1950 was 96 and for urban areas, 74.

[7] "Not only does the United States have one of the highest marriage rates in the West, but the low average age at marriage (around twenty for women and twenty-two to twenty-three for men) is virtually unparalleled among industrialized nations." (Charles F. Westoff: "The Fertility of the American Population," in Freedman (ed.), *op. cit.*, p. 113.)

search evidence we have does not support the notion that a radical shift toward large families has occurred or will soon occur. As mentioned above, the change in size of completed families has been due primarily to a shift from the childless or one-child marriage to the family with two, three, or four children, not to the large nineteenth-century model.[8] And indeed, the 1960's brought stabilization and slight decline in crude birth rates, for instance, from 23.7 percent in 1960 to 21.7 percent in 1963. However, all indications are that birth rates are likely to remain at levels high enough to produce very substantial increases in the total population during the remaining decades of this century. Indeed, concern for crowding and overtaxing of the society's facilities—education, health services, transportation, and the like—has largely replaced the prior generation's apprehensions about a "twilight of parenthood" that never materialized.[9]

The mortality and morbidity rates prevailing in any society are crucial indicators of that society's adaptative capacities to cope with problems of survival in its environment. The low levels of mortality and illness in America reflect comparatively adequate nutrition, sanitation, public health measures, and direct medical care, although some health conditions here do not compare favorably with those of such countries as Sweden: in 1960, infant deaths per 1,000 live births numbered only 17 in Sweden but 26 in the United States. The latter rate had fallen to 23 in 1966. The "expectation of life" at birth is an index that summarizes the cumulative impact of mortality rates; and the United States exhibits a relatively high expectation of life, although the record is startlingly less favorable for the Negro population. At the beginning of the twentieth century, one-half of the infants born could be expected to survive to approximately age fifty-eight; the corresponding figure by the mid-1960's was about seventy-three.[1] Infant deaths per 1,000 live births were 64 in 1930 but had dropped to 26 in 1956, remaining at about that level during the ensuing decade. Maternal deaths, which were 67 for every 10,000 live births in 1930, had fallen to the negligible level of 4 by 1956.

Even within a single generation, the advances in the control of deaths from communicable diseases have been dramatic. For example, if we take four great killers of yesterday—smallpox, diphtheria, whooping cough, and typhoid and paratyphoid—the combined annual deaths occasioned in 1930 per 100,000 population were 250; by 1956, the corresponding figure was 25, or just one-tenth of the earlier rate. Together with other protections, the combination of improved medical science and technology with public meas-

[8] To maintain a constant size of population requires approximately 2.4 children for every woman who has children. (Thompson and Lewis, *op. cit.*, p. 271.)

[9] We are also reminded now by economic analysts that rapid population growth, other things being equal, tends to reduce savings and to absorb resources that otherwise could be used to increase per capita physical and personal capital. On this theme, see Joseph J. Spengler, "Population and Economic Growth" in Freedman (ed.), *op. cit.*, esp. pp. 66–67.

[1] Expectation of life, 1963: white females, 74.4; white males, 67.5; nonwhite females, 66.5; nonwhite males, 60.9. (*Vital Statistics of the United States*, Vol. II, Section 5, Table 5-5.)

ures and relatively adequate levels of nutrition has greatly reduced the incidence of premature death or disability.[2] Furthermore, American society has not been forced to undergo the devastations of periods of mass deaths from famines, epidemics, and wars that have repeatedly swept over most settled societies with long histories in Europe and Asia.[3]

In summary, then, the salient demographic characteristics of our population include its cultural heterogeneity, high mobility, urbanization, high marriage ratios, relatively low but recently increased fertility, and low mortality. Many other characteristics, including the relatively high educational status of the population, have been analyzed by students of population. It is not necessary to go into any further details, however, in order to recognize the outlines of a composite, industrially advanced society. The United States contrasts sharply with the great agricultural populations of the technologically undeveloped regions of the world. To try to understand what kind of society has shaped and has been shaped by these characteristics is our difficult and challenging assignment.

## SUGGESTED READINGS

GOTTMAN, JEAN. *Megalopolis: The Urbanized Northeastern Seaboard of the United States.* New York: Twentieth Century Fund, 1961. The title has added a word to our vocabulary, and the book presents a detailed portrait of one of the world's great conurbations or "continental cities."

HAUSER, PHILIP M., and LEO F. SCHNORE (eds.). *The Study of Urbanization.* New York: Wiley, 1965. Well-selected essays provide varied introductions to the complex tasks of analyzing processes of urbanization.

LIEBERSON, STANLEY. *Ethnic Patterns in American Cities.* New York: Free Press, 1963. Fine example of sociological induction from meticulous analysis of available statistical data on changes in "ethnic" distribution of urban populations.

MARSH, ROBERT. *Comparative Sociology.* New York: Harcourt, Brace & World, 1967. Advocates and develops an approach for systematic cross-cultural analysis and gives important illustrations of studies which successfully detect regularities that transcend particular times and places.

MERRITT, RICHARD L., and STEIN ROKKAN. *Comparing Nations: The Use of Quantitative Data in Cross-National Research.* New Haven, Conn.: Yale University Press, 1966. Companion work to Russett, *et al.*, noted below. Represents the growing emphasis upon use of objective data and systematic analysis in cross-national studies. Rich source of important ideas. Useful bibliography.

MOORE, WILBERT E. *Social Change.* Englewood Cliffs, N.J.: Prentice-Hall, 1963. Tightly packed survey of nearly all the major ideas, with substantial original contributions. Best introduction to the subject.

---

[2] "The recent advances in death control have been almost equivalent to the elimination of all mortality before the age of 40." William Petersen, *Population*, 2nd ed. (New York: Macmillan, 1969), p. 270.

[3] Cf. Thompson and Lewis, *op. cit.*, Chapter 14 and references listed there.

PETERSEN, WILLIAM. *Population.* New York: Macmillan, 1961. Excellent textbook. First rate technical analysis enlivened by sense of social relevance and crisp style.

RUSSETT, BRUCE M., *et al. World Handbook of Political and Social Indicators.* New Haven, Conn.: Yale University Press, 1964. Comprehensive source of critically selected data on seventy-five variables for over one hundred nations. Gives classifications, correlations, and substantial analysis. Valuable aid to comparative study of modern complex societies.

TAEUBER, KARL E., and ALMA F. TAEUBER, *Negroes in Cities.* Chicago: Aldine, 1965. A pioneering work in sophisticated use of census data; applies quantitative methods to analysis of massive changes in contexts of "race relations." Conclusively shows that racial segregation cannot be explained by economic factors. Demolishes mistaken beliefs underlying some public policies.

THOMPSON, WARREN S., and DAVID T. LEWIS. *Population Problems.* 5th ed. New York: McGraw-Hill, 1965. A standard work, repeatedly revised. Combines skillful demographic analysis with interesting social commentary.

# The Problem of Analysis: III
# Basic Approaches and
# Concepts

This, then, is the setting within which American society has taken its present form. No matter how much weight we must give to other elements in later analysis, we must never forget the factors of a high ratio of resources to population, a geographic and climatic setting and technology favorable for industrial and commercial development, and the fundamental demographic characteristics of the people.

Although American society cannot be well understood without considering these factors, they alone cannot explain even the most elementary sociological problems. From them we cannot predict very specifically about such matters as the American language, the forms of family life or economic organization, the nature of religious beliefs or political ideology, or most of the other facts men wish to know about their society. For this reason we must begin to deal with factors that require sociological concepts for analysis. Ultimately, these concepts rest on the belief that human societies as they actually exist are not fully explainable by any sort of physical or biological determinism. On the contrary, societies are systems of human behavior fairly independent of their biophysical environments except when these conditions press too severely upon human biological requirements for survival. Within the very broad limits of these requirements, there is wide variation in human customs and beliefs—a fact noted by observant "tourists" from the most ancient times to the present. It has remained for social science to develop concepts for grasping more precisely and expanding this basic insight; generations of workers have shaped the ideas and methods we need for understanding society today.

By now there is general recognition of the complexity of social behavior; but this awareness is not enough to alert us to the necessities of valid analysis of social systems. Difficult as such analysis is, the results of the study of total social systems already are impressive; and the prospects are excellent for rapid advances in knowledge, especially through cumulative comparative study of the structure and dynamics of well-defined systems and subsystems.

The scientific analysis of societies is a feasible task because the basic variables are limited in number, in range of variation, and in possible workable combinations. It is not true that social arrangements are indefinitely plastic, "limited only by the creativity of the human mind." Numerous types of relationships, groups, or societies can be imagined that are not viable as continuing arrangements. Not anything that is conceivable can become the basis for group life. Many combinations of factors that could occur as sheer logical possibilities are extremely rare or do not occur at all in actual societies. There really are only a few main ways of organizing marriages, reckoning descent, or selecting leaders.

The enormous specific complexity of all social life has been so often noted and is so obvious to every person's own observations that this talk of limits, implying some underlying simplicity, may seem strange if not preposterous. But there is no paradox between the observed complexity and the scientific possibility of finding relatively simple descriptive and explanatory principles. Biological variations among the billions of human beings now inhabiting the earth are fantastically great. Yet the genetic laws governing the variations are elegantly simple as compared with the bewildering profusion of *phenotypic* (immediately observable) diversity. Genetics would never have been born as a science had it not by-passed the surface elaboration by finding (actually, constructing as hypothetical units) a limited number of invariants whose combinations predictably generated the phenotypes. Similarly, were sociology to try to describe every concrete detail or nuance of everyday social interaction, its task would be hopeless. Its rapid progress in the present generation has occurred in those fields and problems in which an analogous, if still often imprecise, procedure has been employed —as, for example, in the analysis of organizations, in controlled studies of small groups, in social demography, and in analysis of processes of conflict.

### THE BASIC APPROACH

In the remaining chapters recur such terms as "cultural structure," "social structure," "patterned behavior," "structural interrelations," "system," and the like. All such terms imply that social behavior is not purely random or without regularity. Those who think of human behavior as changing, highly variable, unpredictable, or "individualistic" may find it difficult to grasp this focus on *structure*. Hence, at the outset, we shall outline briefly what structural analysis implies.

The basic logical and methodological questions on this point are similar to those found in the various physical sciences. In any field of inquiry a "structure" is a relatively fixed relationship between elements, parts, or entities (as, for example, the structure of a house, an animal, or a plant) containing gross, observable parts that maintain a fixed relationship to one another for an appreciable time. We can easily see that some structures endure for very long periods, others are highly evanescent. Yet a simple organism with a lifespan of a few seconds has a structure, even as does the planet itself.[1] The ease or difficulty of observation is not an essential criterion of structure: biology has no hesitation in ascribing structure to a cell that no one can observe directly by his unaided senses. The structure of social action is no mere analogy, but a strict parallel. To demonstrate structure one need only show a recurrence of elements related in definite ways. In the interests

---

[1] Cf. Charles E. Merriam's paraphrase of Sherrington's conclusion from the study of cells: "Thus he arrives at the view that the only difference between structure and function in the constitution of the human organism is a difference in the speed of change." *Public and Private Government* (New Haven, Conn.: Yale University Press, 1944), p. 40.

of realism it is best to speak of the structure of social phenomena only where there is an *important* degree of continuity, where human activities are so patterned (recurrent) that we can observe a group standardization persisting, although changing, over a considerable time.

The criterion usually brought to bear when we want to say whether something does or does not have a structure is the presence or absence of a continuing pattern, an ordered set of relationships among parts. By this test, human societies certainly are structured. Another criterion, although much more rarely invoked, is the extent to which the existing arrangements are resistant to alteration—whether energy is required to change them. By this criterion also, societies are structures. They are not easily altered, nor are they indefinitely plastic; change does not proceed without limit in any direction. If anyone doubts these propositions he can convince himself of their truth by attempting to alter in an important way an established set of social relationships or a widely accepted norm of conduct. (The attempt may very well be costly and painful, but that is another matter, and is of course part of the proof of the propositions.)

Human beings in society do exhibit complexes of action, thought, and emotion (1) shared by many individuals, (2) repeated in many successive situations, and (3) definitely related to *other* patterns in the same social aggregate. This is essentially what is here meant by "structure:" an appreciable degree of regularity and relationship.[2] There is, thus, nothing obscure or mystical about the concept, and the question of how definite and enduring the structure is in any particular case is left open for empirical study. The question cannot be answered satisfactorily by speculation.

Examples of structure in the present sense are not difficult to find. Perhaps the aptest instance for college students is the social structure of a university, a very elaborate patterning and coordination of the actions of many individuals. Streams of people move from room to room and building to building at appointed hours. Professors meet their classes, often with incredible regularity. Books are ordered and delivered, buildings lighted and heated, food served at cafeterias. Masses of people appear at athletic events scheduled months in advance. Beneath this surface level of regularity, order and predictability take much more subtle forms. There are classroom rituals and subtle stereotypings of student-teacher relationships. Students form cliques and friendship constellations; they are graded in "generations" from freshman to senior; there are Greeks and "independents." The university has a system of formal rules and expectations concerning the behavior of faculty and students and informal codes that supplement, modify, or counter the official structure.

The often-repeated question of whether or not human conduct is "really predictable at all" is answered every day that a society exists. Without some rough predictability as to what other people will do under given circum-

---

[2] Again, we must be careful: the regularity does not have to be uniformity of observed specific behaviors in particular situations; such behaviors may be quite varied even while being shaped or controlled by highly structured "codes" or "maps." Cf. Claude Levi-Strauss, *Structural Anthropology* (New York: Basic Books, 1963) for a provocative discussion of structure considered in this way.

stances, there could be no continuing human association, no adjustment, no cooperation—that is, no society.[3] To complement the undoubtedly essential and valuable conception of social structure, it long has been conventional practice to counterpoise to it the notions of change and evolution. Change, like structure, has often been conceived in ad hoc terms of discrete variables, or clusters of variables. It now seems increasingly likely that new power in societal analysis can be gained by thinking of structure in terms of systems and subsystems and of change as sets of processes involving sequences within and among subsystems.

The importance of bringing in the notion of *systems* may not be immediately obvious. The great potential scientific advantages are twofold: (1) more accurate and comprehensive description is made possible when we can locate specific variables in actual functioning systems where their connections make sense—not merely as "clusters" of variables that in some unexamined way "just happen" to fall together; (2) greater economy of explanation is gained whenever we can show the flow of inputs and outputs among connected systems, for then it may be possible to explain many important social processes without requiring impossibly elaborate knowledge of all the *internal* processes of each and every subsystem.

Along with the development of precise concepts, all science rests upon observation. Since sociology studies the behavior of human beings in association with others, its data consist of observations of what people say and do; and it assumes that it can infer certain predictabilities from the data. This assumption is tested by acting upon it; that is, by making predictions and then discovering the degree to which they accurately predict behavior *under specified conditions*. The relevant conditions are of several different kinds.

The total field of "causes" or "forcings" within which human social behavior occurs consists of five continuously present, simultaneous, and interacting groupings of systems: (1) the physical and biopsychical environments (*ecosystems*), (2) the human organism itself, (3) the psychological systems of personality, (4) cultural systems, (5) social systems. Every social act is the act of a social actor, who is also personality-in-organism; interactions occur through communication by means of culturally derived symbols. Every such act accordingly is at once physical, biological, psychological, cultural, and social. The behavioral sciences gain dependable knowledge of social behavior not by asserting claims for the general "priority" or "dominance" of one or another of these aspects but by cumulative analysis of specific relationships of elements among the systems through repeated empirical studies. The linkages often occur in lengthy chains or loops of antecedents and consequences—as, for example, when external social conditions generate a severely punitive system of child-rearing disciplines, which leads to psychological mechanisms that eventuate, on the one hand, in psychosomatic disorder and, on the other, in patterns of social distance and withdrawal, and are also expressed in particular types of literature and plastic

---

[3] Of course, large-scale and long-term predictions are very different from the common-sense anticipations upon which we act from minute to minute in ordinary daily life.

arts. To be able to trace such networks of influences is extremely difficult, of course, but when successful, the effort can give us findings that are important and often surprising.

One additional consideration is crucial for understanding the actual functioning of all social systems from the two-person group to the largest possible total society. Social systems operate under *constraints*. They are not indefinitely plastic, free to assume any conceivable form or to accept any imaginable norms. They always exist under definite limitations of physical environment, of natural resources and technology, and are affected by relations with other social systems. Furthermore, every social system is shaped by *scarcity*, not only in the means of subsistence but also in the energy and the cognitive, affective, evaluative, and communicative capacities of individual persons. Even in societies of relative material affluence there is never enough time for mortal men to do well all the things that an ideal society might need or desire. The things which men desire that are in short supply include not only food, clothing, sexual gratification, housing, transportation, and other creature comforts but also education, recreation, adornment, affection, prestige, social approval and respect, beauty, intellectual stimulation, religious expression, and many other gratifications, fulfillments, and challenges. These many good things are in competition for limited attention, energy, and resources. Finally, the specific character of any social system is affected also by functional compatibilities among the various components of interaction and culture.[4] Some things simply will not easily fit together in the same set of social arrangements. For example, if one wants a stable extended family system and, at the same time, rapid technological innovation, high occupational specialization, and great geographic mobility, then some very special mechanisms, to say the least, will be required if a workable total system is to be maintained.

Two crucial propositions have been asserted: (1) societies are not explicable solely in terms of biophysical environment; (2) human interactions show structure; that is, they are in some degree recurrent or predictable. If these are so, it becomes fruitful to consider what conceptual tools are most useful in analyzing social phenomena.

## CULTURE

The first main concept is culture. Most inclusively, culture is social heredity —the total legacy of past human behavior effective in the present, representing the accumulation, through generations, of the artifacts, knowledges, beliefs, and values by which men deal with the world. It is the precipitate of *learned* human adjustments to the physical environment and to society. Thus, according to the famous enumerative definition of E. B. Tylor, culture is "that complex whole which includes knowledge, belief, art, morals, law, custom, and any other capabilities and habits acquired by man as a member

---

[4] All together, the above sets of constraints enormously reduce the unimaginably large number of conceivable kinds of social behavior. Cf. George J. McCall and J. L. Simmons, *Identities and Interactions*, (New York: Free Press, 1966), pp. 14–38.

of society."[5] A way of visualizing American culture in this broad sense would be to answer the question: What is available to be learned by all the infants born in the society today? This would emphasize (1) that culture comes down from the past, is not created by any one person or generation, and continues beyond the individual lifespan and (2) that culture is learned—it is no automatic or instinctive heritage but must be won anew by each succeeding generation. Culture points to those common elements in behavior that are derived from individuals' having been reared in the same tradition.[6]

This inclusive definition of culture is very useful in giving us a fundamental perspective on behavior: once the idea is grasped, one always sees behavior in relation to the pervasive social inheritance. Once its full implications are seen, it destroys the naïve reliance on "instinct" theories of human behavior, explodes the myth of a highly specific, fixed "human nature" apart from culture, and sensitizes the observer to aspects of social life he otherwise might not notice.

For this book, however, a more specific concept of culture is useful: culture as a normative structure, a system of what Linton has called "designs for living."[7] In this sense, culture is the "blueprint for behavior," relatively standardized prescriptions as to what must be done, ought to be done, should be done, may be done, and must not be done. Every day we face an elaborate network of "rules" saying that some behaviors are obligatory, some approved or permitted, and some disapproved or positively forbidden. "Rules" is in quotation marks because it includes not only the *how* of behavior but also the *what*; that is, culture includes a system of goals and values. Certain things are emphasized as preeminently worth striving for, others are matters of relative indifference; some possibilities of experience and behavior are ignored, others are defined as valueless, inappropriate, or evil.

In a very broad and loose sense we might say that culture is to social behavior as gene pools are to living organisms. Both are "heritages," or "precoding." Both contain the potentiality for enormously large numbers of unique combinations of basic elements, hence, the potentiality for great variation in individual outcomes. Neither is specifically deterministic of the total sequences that follow from the initial coding; both genetic and cultural specifications are inadequate to control detailed development; but both carry a set of rules that guide processes which, in turn, can generate the requisite detail through the *interactions* of initially defined units, such as

---

[5] Most readers of this book already will be familiar with the uses of the term in its technical senses. "Classic" references include: Edward Burnett Tylor, *Primitive Culture* (London: J. Murray, 1871); Alexander A. Goldenweiser, *Early Civilization* (New York: Knopf, 1922); Robert M. MacIver, *Society: Its Structure and Changes* (New York: R. Long and R. R. Smith, 1931); Ralph Linton, *The Study of Man* (New York: Appleton-Century-Crofts, 1936).

[6] No complex culture is completely integrated. "In any total culture there is always a coexistence of several different cultural systems subordinated to, coordinated with, neutral, and contradictory to each other, and a coexistence of many cultural congeries within the systems and outside of them. In highly integrated total cultures, there may be one or two dominant or main supersystems, several other systems or minor supersystems, and a multitude of congeries." Pitirim A. Sorokin, *Sociological Theories of Today* (New York: Harper & Row, 1966), p. 157.

[7] Cf. Linton, *op. cit.*

proteins, enzymes, cells, tissues, words, beliefs, items of knowledge, values, norms.

What we are calling the normative aspects of culture include knowledge, beliefs, technology, values, and norms. *Knowledge* may be considered, for present purposes, as that which is reliably certified as true of the empirical world. Best illustrated by the highly developed modern sciences such as physics and chemistry, it also includes various kinds of empirical knowledge that fall short of the highest scientific accuracy and generality but are still sufficiently dependable for many practical purposes. *Beliefs*, which in many cases shade into empirical knowledge, are illustrated by concepts of deities, afterlife, spirits, and the like, as well as by many ideas about the nature of society[8] and the physical world. By the tests of scientific verifiability[8] these cognitive beliefs fall into two categories: (1) those not yet fully tested but nevertheless subject to scientific tests and possibly refutable by those tests; (2) those outside the domain of empirical verification by any presently known scientific procedures (for example, the existence of heaven and hell, the superiority of American society to any other). *Technology* consists of the application of knowledge and beliefs in action that aims to transform material things, or psychological states, or social phenomena. (There is a technology of psychotherapy as well as a technology of making automobiles.)

Knowledge and belief have to do with what *exists* or is supposed to exist. *Values*, on the other hand, concern standards of desirability; they are couched in terms of good or bad, beautiful or ugly, pleasant or unpleasant, appropriate or inappropriate. One can be quite sure that disease exists without regarding it as desirable, and one may regard as desirable conditions that do not yet exist anywhere. *Norms*, to which we will return in detail later, are rules of conduct; they specify what should and should not be done by various kinds of social actors in various kinds of situations.

Taken all together, then, these normative aspects of culture make up an impressive set of guidelines by which people regulate their own behavior and that of their fellows. The present work deliberately concentrates on those parts of culture that regulate *social relations*. Only limited attention will be given to the portions of culture concerned exclusively either with the relations of man to nature and to the supernatural or with the expression of beliefs and feelings in recreation, art, literature, drama, and other aspects of expressive culture.

In the analysis of societies and their subparts, it is simple but essential to recognize one basic proposition: causal interdependence does not necessarily imply normative order. There will be a causal order in any social aggregate, no matter how filled with conflict, disagreement, or confusion. And even the most completely norm governed societies, possessed of highly integrated cultures, will contain conflicts of psychobiological needs and drives with social requirements, disjunctions between ideological aspirations

---

[8] This is, of course, an assumption that raises difficult philosophical questions. A work of the present character cannot deal at all competently with them. It is perhaps enough to say that for present purposes the distinction between positive scientific knowledge, ignorance and error, and nonempirical beliefs is a heuristic one—utilized because of practical convenience and claiming no "ultimate" validity.

and actual behavior, opposition of individuals and of collectivities, and so on. There is causal order in a mob, a disintegrating empire, a world war, a catastrophic economic depression. The student of man's social behavior can avoid much confusion (and unproductive controversy) by recognizing at the earliest possible moment that to describe causal or functional orderliness is not to assert that the order is one of conformity to norms nor, certainly, to claim that the orderliness is ethically desirable.

Another elementary but basic fact about culture must be emphasized in the beginning. It is a common misunderstanding to suppose that unless one is *aware* of cultural factors one is not influenced by them. Nothing could be further from the truth. Participants in social groups are seldom fully aware of what determines their behavior or of what results from it. Usually we do not fully know what we are doing until after we have done it, and often we remain unaware of causes and consequences even then. Probably no individual ever "knows" the total culture in which he is immersed. Most American parents, for example, certainly do not usually think of themselves as doing anything so formidable as transmitting culture when they deal with their children. They just act. But their actions constitute, in fact, an important part of the transmission of culture. When little Johnny is told that it is not polite to hit the guest over the head with his baseball bat, or is admonished, "Don't be a bully," he is being introduced to the norms of his culture. Thousands of specific experiences with specific persons in particular situations comprise the socialization process. The individual eventually learns a complex and fairly standardized system of rules, perspectives, and valuations common to many other individuals in the society.

Culture, then, has these characteristics:

1. It is inferred from observation of behavior.
2. It exists prior in time to any given individual and continues beyond one's lifespan.
3. It is *acquired* by individuals and manifested in their behavior.
4. It includes rules or designs for obligatory, approved, permitted, disapproved, and forbidden actions.
5. It is never completely static and uniform.

### Cultural Norms and Sanctions

It has been emphasized that culture includes definitions of events, objects, or behaviors as "good" or "bad;" it marks off the things to be sought or avoided. Certain goals or ends are thus prescribed as worthy of pursuit and others are discouraged or ignored. The core of any culture consists of those values and ideal patterns widely regarded as obligatory. The term "cultural norm" refers to a specific prescription of the course that action *should* (is supposed to) follow in a given situation. Cultural norms, therefore, include both cultural *goals* and the approved *means* for reaching those goals. To be *cultural*, the norms have only to be acquired by learning and to be shared by individuals. But norms shade into one another in many complicated nuances. There is a continuous gradation from almost purely technical or cognitive norms (how to boil an egg, the most effective way to manufacture nuclear weapons) to moral norms (thou shalt not kill). At the intermediate steps, one finds, among others, conventional norms (custom, etiquette, and so on) and esthetic norms (standards of taste, beauty, and so on). Any one of these types of norms may be further specified according to the degree to which it is actually widespread and obligatory in a given society or community or group—in Linton's usage, whether it is a universal, a specialty, or an alternative.[9] Some norms simply indicate what must not be done; they *proscribe* certain kinds of behavior. Other norms *prescribe* what should be done or must be done. Although by the present definition norms always carry some prescriptive or proscriptive quality—some one of the many qualitatively different kinds of "shoulds" or "oughts"—there is an enormous variation in the *kind* of normative emphasis, ranging, for example, from the conformity accompanying fashions and fads to the most deeply ingrained taboos and ethical precepts.

Upon first inspection, the enormous variability in the cultural norms that exist and have existed in different societies may create an impression of arbitrary or capricious development. Closer analysis indicates that although many norms surely are "arbitrary," "unreasonable," or "wrong" from the standpoint of some individual or collectivity affected by them, a social rule is never wholly divorced from the actual conditions of human interaction in which it emerged. Norms are not simply invented as sheer mental creations, nor do they appear in the absence of some real problem in social intercourse. Typical problematic situations from which new norms develop are failures of desired coordination of activities, deficiencies in efficiency of performance, conflicts of interests and values, overlapping claims to authority, threats to social order or to other valued conditions. However, this is not to say that norms always, or even usually, are fully accepted by everyone to whom they apply. For one thing, a norm would not be necessary if everyone spontaneously and willingly did what the norm would enjoin: the presence of a norm is a sign that somebody does not want to do the required action or wishes to do the forbidden one. For another, norms often are made by the more powerful for the less powerful and enforced by the former upon the latter. When this is the case, rarely are norms merely neutral with regard to advantage and disadvantage; and the resulting inequalities are not always welcomed by those who get least. Many norms thus reflect some "balance of power" and are maintained only so long as they serve the interests of those who had the edge in bargaining. It is a plausible hypothesis, for instance, that where women are not dependent upon husbands for status and security, the premarital sexual code will be more permissive than where the wife is more dependent.[1]

It is evident also that a very substantial amount of social control and standardization of behavior is not achieved by socialization into specific norms of proscription and prescription but rather is derived from *lack of*

[9] Linton, *op. cit.*, chap. 16.
[1] James Coleman, "Female Status and Premarital Sexual Codes," *American Journal of Sociology*, 72, 2 (September 1966), 271.

*k of*
*perceived*
*alternatives*

*never*
*ceases to*
*reasons to*
*differently*
*Primitive*
*Societies]*

*means of*

*covering*
*-orms;*
*-STIMONY*
*OSERVED*
*BEHAVIOR*

*) OR*
*MENSIONS*
*variation*
*NORMS:*

*perceived alternatives.* The individual does not do a great many things that he conceivably might do, primarily because he is actually ignorant of the possibilities or because his attention is regularly focused elsewhere. Therefore it never occurs to him to try out a course of action not coded into the cultural repertory at hand.

In empirical research, cultural norms are discovered in two main ways. Norms are inferred from *testimony*; that is, people either explicitly state the norms, or from their description of the approved and disapproved conduct for certain situations one can clearly infer implicit norms. Aside from testimony, cultural norms may be discovered by observing spontaneous behavior in real-life situations, for example, the meting out of socially supported rewards and penalties (social sanctions).

Thus, cultural norm is a category that includes a very diverse universe of social prescriptions. Like culture itself, it points to an important *area* of interest but requires further clarification in application to particular problems. Some major dimensions of variation in cultural norms, which are the subject of extensive sociological and anthropological investigation, are sketched below.[2]

A    DISTRIBUTION

1. *Extent of knowledge of the norms*, both by those who apply the norms and those to whom the rules are applied.
2. *Prevalence of acceptance of or agreement with a norm*—again, both by the subjects who "send" and the social objects who "receive" the prescriptions.    *(universal < persons / circumstances) ref non- universal*
3. *Prevalence of the actual application of a norm*, for example, whether it is applied to everyone or only to people in particular social positions and whether it is applied under nearly all conditions or only in highly special circumstances.

B.    ENFORCEMENT

1. *Punishment vs. reward:* whether enforcement is mainly by punishment for nonobservance or by reward for observance.
2. *Severity of punishment*, ranging from extremely heavy to very mild, or *magnitude of reward*, ranging from great to small.
3. *Enforcing agency*, for example, enforcement by a designated and specialized formal agency or office or enforcement by a diffuse, universal responsibility within an entire group or community.
4. *Consistency of enforcement*, varying from slack and episodic to strict and continuous.
5. *Source of authority for enforcement:* enforcement may be justified as rational, expedient, or instrumental; or it may be believed to be based on authority that is divine, absolute, inherent, magical, and the like.
6. *Internal vs. external enforcement:* the degree to which the norms are enforced because people have made them a part of their own consciences

2 There definitely are other modes of differentiation. See chaps. X and XI.

or ideals; the degree to which the norms have been "internalized" as an emotionally significant part of individual personality.

C TRANSMISSION

*(primary from relations)(a)*

1. *How the norms are learned* (the socialization process), whether early in life, from family, friends, and intimate groups, or later, from occupational associates, teachers, mass media, and so on (secondary relations). *(b)*
2. *The degree to which those who teach or impose norms reinforce the learning* of those who are expected to conform, for example, a parent giving warmth and approval when the child behaves as desired.

D CONFORMITY TO NORMS

1. *Amount of conformity attempted* by persons who are supposed to conform; nearly everyone may really try or only a few may make a realistic effort. *(How many try to conform)*
2. *Amount of deviance or nonconformity*—ranging from very rare to very frequent. *(How often)*
3. *Extent of deviance*—ranging from (a) hardly noticed individual variations, to (b) patterned evasions accepted by many people,[3] to (c) systematic and drastic violations (as in organized crime).[4]

To say that in societies and groups as going concerns there are always norms and that these norms constitute a structure is not to say that norms are static or that they must be taken simply as given facts. Norms have origins. They arise out of problematic situations: for example, they give temporary or long-lasting resolutions to conflicts of claims among persons and collectivities. All norms are continually subject to reinterpretation and reappraisal in their specific application in the daily life of imperfect men. Norm making and norm enforcing are *activities*, carried on by complexly motivated men, usually under pressing immediate circumstances.[5] Once a rule has somehow been formulated and accepted it represents a *settlement*. Like all settlements, a norm will favor some interests and values and will work against others. In this sense there is no such thing as an unbiased rule or a neutral law.

Social norms, by definition, always involve at least two persons as actors, ego and alter (other). Generally we are not fully assured that a norm is involved until we see support by a third party or have evidence that the dyad (two interacting persons) is oriented to external standards; for example, as Simmel suggested, there are three parties in every marriage: the husband, the wife, and the marriage. At any moment of interaction, one

---

[3] See chap. X.

[4] The above classification is freely adapted from Richard T. Morris: "A Typology of Norms," *American Sociological Review*, VII, 5 (October 1956), 611–612. The continuity of work in social analysis is illustrated by the fact that this article drew, in part, upon the formulations of the first edition of *American Society* and improved upon them.

[5] For an analysis consistent with this view, see Lon L. Fuller, *The Morality of Law* (New Haven, Conn.: Yale University Press, 1964).

actor is a norm sender and the other is a norm receiver; and at any earlier or subsequent instant sender and receiver may reverse places.

The prevalence of any particular norm within a given social aggregate depends in the first place upon *how universally the norm is accepted as a valid guide to conduct*. It may be accepted by everyone or only by a very small, idiosyncratic sector of the population. The effective constraint of many highly prevalent norms derives partly from their near universality. Thus, in an English-speaking society if one wishes to be understood, he must speak English; and his use of that language rather than another defines his social world in a particular way.

The extent of acceptance (consensus) is not identical with the *universality of application* of the norm. Certain norms are applicable only to special subsegments of the society, even though universally recognized as valid and binding. There may be high consensus upon the norms governing the status of parent and child, yet the norms for parents clearly do not apply to children. Special occupational codes—say, of a judge, a chief, a merchant —are widely accepted but are binding only upon those occupations.

Furthermore, norms vary widely in their *modes of enforcement* and in their sources of authority. The source of authority has been variously imputed to divine revelation, the wisdom of ancestors, ideas of natural law and inherent rights, the magical or charismatic quality of a leader, and social expediency in terms of a taken-for-granted framework of ultimate values. Often the question of final legitimacy is simply not raised at all; a norm has authority from widespread practice, or "because it has always existed." Observe again the striking variation in the details of normative structure: many norms are axiomatically accepted—by "absolute social logics" (W. Lloyd Warner); others claim various kinds of derivative and elaborately rationalized justifications. Furthermore, the most immediate source of authority is often some definite social organization; and the purposes of the organization lend authority to the rule. Thus, the modes of imputed legitimacy are related to the mechanisms of enforcement.

An important distinction between norms enforced by the diffuse pressure of the total community and those enforced by specifically designated and publicly acknowledged functionaries is shown in the contrast between a small town (where nearly every member of the community may act to penalize violations) and the specialized and limited functions of the policeman, the military officer, or the bureaucrat. Between extremes, of course, lie many shadings.

Norms may be normative, that is, carry a controlling or regulating influence upon behavior, in either a psychological or a social mode, or in both simultaneously. When a conception of the course that action should follow (under a given set of circumstances, or unconditionally) is fully accepted by the individual, it is *psychologically* normative. The psychological states that lead to acceptance are numerous and varied. The norm may be an unconscious component of personality, laid down early in childhood. It may be part of an ideal self or ego ideal, genuinely integrated with the mature ego. The amount of conviction or psychological energy attached to the norm may be great or only very moderate.

The *social* character of a norm, on the other hand, can be observed only in interaction; and its first sign is the appearance of approval or disapproval. We have suggested that rules often, if not universally, emerge from some opposition or conflict of interests or values. We suspect, subject to modification by better evidence than is now available, that the most frequent initial process, at least in groups that have developed any marked structural differentiation, is not one of general consensus arising from discussion and persuasion but rather of the formulation by one social unit and the enforcement of the rule upon the members of another—by faculty for students, by parents upon teen-agers (or vice versa), by doctors for nurses, or by executives upon workers. However, enduring social rules rarely remain purely unilateral. If we have a clear case of an obligatory norm, approval and disapproval will be accompanied by definite sanctions, that is, by generally recognized rewards or punishments. And the final sign of a genuinely social norm is that the sanctioning is approved (accepted as legitimate) by relatively disinterested parties.

When we see one person react to another's conformity with or violation of norms by rewarding or punishing him, we can speak of "sanctions."[6] But a sanction need not be intended as such. One may punish another person who has violated a norm even if one does not have any conscious intention of trying to "bring him back into line." Indeed, just the spontaneous disapproval of our behavior by someone whose respect we cherish is often a severe sanction and may be sufficient to induce us to alter our conduct. And a person may be rewarded by inner satisfactions, such as having a quiet conscience, even if no one intends to reward him. Norms become fully institutionalized when they are tied to definite social positions and when conformity to them is directly gratifying to the individual and at the same time brings forth favorable responses from others. Social control is no problem when people find it a pleasure to "do their duty" and when they spontaneously approve others who do the same; in fact, a perfectly integrated society (an unrealizable, or utopian, state of affairs) may be defined as one in which everyone would want to do what he had to do. Short of that perfect integration, however, norms are supported by many specific rewards such as wealth, power, and social esteem and prestige. Similarly, violations of norms are met with an impressive array of penalties that vary in intensity from such conditions as socially disgraceful death, extreme physical torture, or complete social ostracism and condemnation, to various minor deprivations, mild ridicule, or group disapproval.

It may seem self-evident that negative sanctioning (punishment) is necessary to maintain norms, especially if one reasons that norms are rarely produced unless there is some important motivation to behave in ways other than those specified by the norm. Yet there is a striking lack of clear evidence that punishment actually is necessary for the maintenance of many par-

[6] The behavior referred to by the term "sanctions" may be highly diverse. For a clarification of much of the actual complexity, see Jack P. Gibbs, "Sanctions," *Social Problems*, 14, 2 (Fall 1966), 147–159. The clearest ideal type of sanctioning is that of a socially approved response to norm violation or norm conformity, intended to punish or reward that behavior, by an agent who is accorded a right thus actively to sanction.

ticular norms. Alleged deterrent effects are difficult to demonstrate; for example, homicide rates are not greater in states that have abolished the death penalty; various other crime rates do not seem to correlate at all highly with the severity of penalties.[7] Deviance may be treated either as "crime" or "illness" for reasons that do not follow from scientifically validated evidence.[8]

Thus, the effects of positive and negative sanctions upon social behavior are neither self-evident nor easy to ascertain. Whether some particular kind of interaction or transaction is actually experienced as positive or negative is not obvious—whether the recipient will find the act or object to be rewarding or punishing, fulfilling or depriving depends upon his system of values, his beliefs and expectations, his needs and motives, and upon many variable features of the situation of action. We know that punishment may be desired and actively sought, that some individuals are frightened by success and made guilty by gratifications, that the responsibility one man energetically seeks is shunned by another.

There is substantial evidence that under many conditions punishment strongly reduces the likelihood of the punished behavior—typically with important side effects, many of which may be undesired (for example, a child learns to be aggressive by being punished, or becomes overly constricted and rigid). On the other hand, severe punishment for strongly condemned actions often does not seem to deter the forbidden behavior; thus, as noted above, the abolition of the death penalty for murder in a number of states has not resulted in any increase in the homicide rate. Furthermore, it is known that certain kinds of negative sanctioning actually set up a vicious cycle in which the punishment increases the rate of deviant behavior and accentuates alienative and rejecting psychological mechanisms; this pattern often appears to be important in the development of alcoholism and of juvenile gang delinquency.

On the other side, some social transactions commonly conceived as rewarding may not always be so regarded. Thus it is often assumed that social approval is rewarding and this assumption undoubtedly is correct for a very high proportion of ordinary social interactions. Yet two important qualifications are immediately apparent. First, individuals may differ greatly in the need for and sensitivity to social approval, as a consequence of differences in temperament and life history; some people need very little approval. Because of differences in socialization of children it is quite likely that there are substantial differences in this respect as among major strata and subcultures within our society. Second, the influence of approval is not equal for every source of such approval. One has to ask always, "approval from whom?" It is the person's "significant others," or reference groups

---

[7] Cf. Jackson Toby, "Is Punishment Necessary?" *Journal of Criminal Law, Criminology, and Police Science,* 55, 3 (September 1964), 332–337; Jack P. Gibbs, "Norms: The Problem of Definition and Classification," *American Journal of Sociology,* 70, 5 (March 1965), 586–594.

[8] Thomas J. Scheff, "The Societal Reaction to Deviance: Ascriptive Elements in the Psychiatric Screening of Mental Patients in a Midwestern State," *Social Problems,* 11, 4 (Spring 1964), 401–413.

and reference individuals, whose approval, respect, esteem, or love is consequential; outside of a fairly well defined and limited universe of such meaningful individuals and groupings it often is the case that the individual "couldn't care less" whether or not others approve of what he does.

To analyze adequately the possible effects of sanctions upon conduct, therefore, it is necessary to have empirical specification of *what* constitutes reward and punishment and of how strong (intense, important, central) a particular type of sanction is to the recipients; and it is further necessary to know the fine structure of significant social referents who are or may be sources of sanctions.

But this is not the end of the matter, for the control of social behavior is not merely confined to a simple meting out of direct, conventional rewards and punishments. Of course, anything that an individual experiences may have a rewarding or punishing aspect. But many of the more complex and subtle forms of behavior control are not *primarily* organized around *immediate* gratification-deprivation or pleasure-pain dimensions. Effective psychotherapy, for example, often reflects a continuous and delicate interweaving by the therapist of permissive receptivity to socially disapproved expression of feelings and evaluations, limited reciprocity in affective exchange, confronting the patient with realities not previously understood or accepted, approval of insight and reevaluation, questioning of assumptions and expectations, supplying information about probable consequences of various kinds of behavior, and many other similarly complex modes of attempted influence. More generally, such processes illustrate the possible importance of *cognitive* and *evaluative*, as well as *affective*, aspects of interaction as behavior control. Moreover, behavior may be affected by changing the situations within which persons must act without directly altering the structure of rewards as such—for example, high grades may be retained as an academic reward but awarded primarily for research accomplishments rather than for performance on examinations.

In view of all these considerations, one may wonder how the concept of sanction has turned out to be as useful as it unquestionably is in social analysis. A primary reason evidently lies in the important degree of uniformity in the preferences men develop for various kinds of experiences. In spite of all exceptions and complexities, most people find it rewarding to be healthy rather than ill, free rather than imprisoned, reasonably well nourished rather than starving, respected by other people rather than held in contempt, free from pain rather than undergoing torture, partly self-directing rather than totally dependent, and so on. These broad uniformities of values and motivations provide a kind of commonsense first approximation, permitting initial description and analysis. Beyond such preliminary study, the notion of sanctions serves primarily as a sensitizing concept that continually calls attention to the possible effects of the rewarding/punishing *aspects* of any social interaction. We are thereby reminded to watch always for the "control" implications in all social interchanges, recognizing that a very great deal of social control is an unplanned, diffuse consequence of countless ordinary interactions that are not explicitly or primarily directed toward the goal of control.

Besides the modes of variation already mentioned, there are great differences in the formal characteristics of concrete social norms. First, norms may vary in *explicitness* from those implicit rules or understandings (rarely, if ever, verbalized) constituting the norms "everybody knows" or unconsciously accepts to the vast body of verbalized (spoken or written) norms embodied in law, regulations, precepts, codes, and so on.

Distinct from explicitness is a second dimension, *specificity*. A norm may be quite explicit though highly general and vague: love your neighbor as yourself. A norm may be implicit but definite: do not criticize the behavior of your host's children in his presence. Any society or group will have specific, minutely detailed norms as well as those highly generalized imperatives that apply to particular situations only by implication.

Finally, norms vary in *rigidity or flexibility* from the requiring of exact conformity to the permitting of wide latitude. Approximations to both of these extremes can be observed in our own society. Of course rigidity-flexibility is intimately related to other qualities. For example, it is easier to see violations of a specific rule than of a generalized precept—indeed, the certainty, promptness, and intensity of sanctions provide a practical definition of rigidity. An implicit norm is easier to modify or evade. Nevertheless, normative rigidity is to some degree an independent variable. Most of us have experienced the flexibility of norms between friends in contrast to the exacting regulations of military organizations or highly developed industrial, governmental, or educational bureaucracies.

Because, as the preceding discussion emphasizes, there are so many different kinds of norms,[9] no brief formal definition is likely to specify successfully all the characteristics that may be of interest to us in considering some *particular* norm. Therefore, the best strategy is to specify the relevant characteristics of any type of norm that is the focus of attention in a particular analysis. In this book our central interest is in *institutional* norms.

## INSTITUTIONS

Our next important concept is the central sociological idea of *institution*.[1] Among the various norms of a given society, those that are "institutional" for any particular person are, for him, moral imperatives closely identified with his sense of self-respect; violations of them usually result in his feeling guilt, shame, horror, self-deprecation. Full internalization of an institutional or moral norm may be identified by these tests: (1) the social actor conforms in a situation in which violation of the norm would be advantageous

[9] This observation has been repeatedly made in sociological writings. Cf. Gibbs: "Norms: The Problem of Definition and Classification," *op. cit.* Gibbs correctly insists on clear distinctions among three generic aspects of norms: (a) a shared *evaluation* of behavior in terms of what it ought to be or ought not to be; (b) a shared *expectation* as to what behavior will occur; (c) *reactions* of a positive or negative kind to particular behaviors (p. 589). His approach generates a potentially valuable typology of norms, specified in a manner suitable for use in empirical research.

[1] It is advisable to defer any further discussion of the modes of relations among various types of cultural norms to later chapters dealing with institutional interrelations, the problem of societal integration, and the analysis of sociocultural change.

in terms of his known interests and in which no risk of external sanctions would be incurred; (2) questioning and indirect inquiry fail to find evidences that the individual was acting in response to expected reactions of other persons specifically known to him. For a whole group or society, probably the best index to an institutional norm is the occurrence of severe penalties for violation. Such penalties are truly institutional, however, only if supported by an effective consensus of the society. When severe sanctions are imposed by a small but powerful minority upon an unwilling population, that which is institutional for the ruling group may not be institutional for the others. In addition to the test of social sanctions, therefore, evidence of the degree of consensus with which the sanctions are accepted and supported is required. Institutional norms usually tend to be relatively stable, although permanence is a correlative rather than a defining criterion of their institutional character. They also tend to prescribe reciprocal rights and duties and to be enforced through designated social functionaries; however, there are many exceptions.[2]

In summary, institutional norms differ from other cultural norms primarily in the intensity of social sanctions and in the degree of consensus with which they are supported and applied. In other words, cultural norms are institutional insofar as they are made *obligatory* by effective social agreement.[3] In operation, institutional norms are also likely to be persistent, enforced through definite social organs, and reciprocally binding on the occupants of designated social positions. In the fully developed case, institutional norms are: (1) widely known, accepted, and applied; (2) widely enforced by strong sanctions continuously applied; (3) based on revered sources of authority; (4) internalized in individual personalities; (5) inculcated and strongly reinforced early in life; and (6) objects of consistent and prevalent conformity. For example, there would be no doubt whatever that judged by these criteria the prohibitions of murder, treason, cannibalism, and rape represent institutional norms in American society.

The various specific "rules" of any society are related to one another, not at random, but in definite patterns, which can be usefully classified and analyzed in several different ways. The approach followed here is to classify norms according to the major needs or value centers with which they are most closely associated, for example, economic, political, religious, and so on. Thus, the term "institution" refers to a set of institutional norms that cohere around a relatively distinct and socially important complex of values. American society, for instance, like any other, must somehow deal

[2] See Pitirim A. Sorokin, *Society, Culture, and Personality: Their Structure and Dynamics* (New York: Harper & Row, 1947), pp. 69–91. Sorokin establishes the valuable concept of "law-norms," which are obligatory norms defining the rights and duties of the parties in a definite social relationship. Law-norms are both imperative and two-sided. Unlike a moral norm, which recommends but does not require a certain course of conduct, a law-norm, on the one hand, establishes a *right* to demand the specified behavior, and on the other, imposes a corresponding duty. In the most fully developed instances, law-norms specify the subjects and objects of both rights and duties, the source of the norms, the details of the required actions, and the sanctions involved.

[3] William J. Goode, "Norm Commitment and Conformity to Role-Status Obligations," *American Journal of Sociology*, 66, 3 (November 1960), 246–258.

with sexual activity, the care of dependent children, and the social relations established by sexual unions and the birth of children. The institutional norms concerned with these matters constitute the familial or kinship institutions of the society. Similarly, there is in every society a set of functional problems centering around the coercion of some individuals by others. The problem of power is a central fact of political life; and it is convenient to group together the norms regulating power as the *political institutions* of the society.

Institutions regulate the modes of meeting important recurrent situations such as birth, death, marriage, acquiring economic goods, dealing with power relations, maintaining social consensus, and training the young, and at the same time help ensure that these situations will recur. By defining problems and approved solutions in certain ways, any particular institutional structure channelizes human experience along certain lines and ignores or prohibits other possibilities. It is a truism that the problems or evils of any society result partly from its most venerated institutions.

To say that institutions are made up of norms is true; but the statement is incomplete, and sad experience shows that it is open to remarkable misunderstandings. For the norms typically are not static, formalistic, arbitrarily imposed rules (although, indeed, some may be) but rather represent standing bargains that have been hammered out in the incessant struggles of men to realize their vital interests and values. The limiting case of perfect integration between duties and rights, burdens and gratifications, is precisely a limiting case; most institutionalized rules represent partial accommodations and contain unresolved tensions. It is a great mistake, therefore, to imagine that the presence of even the most completely institutionalized social order is any automatic guarantee of stability.

The main sets of institutions analyzed in this book differ in their modes of organization—in their *social* structures. The norms of kinship are diffusely enforced and applied to many millions of small groups (families) and systems of relationships (kinship). Economic institutions are embodied in such organizations as the corporation, the trade association, the labor union, the stock exchange. Political norms appear in such concrete structures as governments, parties, factions, lobbies, pressure groups. To find "education," one examines schools, colleges, universities, institutes. Religious institutions also may be approached, as a first approximation, through observation of delimited and named organizations. But stratification appears to have no organizational counterpart similar to the unit structures of other institutionalized sectors of social life. Instead the phenomena of allocation of scarce values and the ranking of positions and social units in scales of invidious evaluation appear throughout the social system. There is stratification in the business firm, the university, the church, the army, and so on, as well as the more diffuse, inclusive stratification of concrete individuals and family units in the total-community setting.

Do these considerations mean that stratification is not an institution, in the sense of our definition? Clearly not, for institutions as here analyzed consist entirely of functionally interrelated sets of institutionalized norms— and many of the norms of stratification have the necessary qualities of consensus, obligatory force, sanctions, pervasive application, and others already mentioned above. It is true that stratification is more diffusely organized than the other main institutions. Yet, it is an institutional subsystem; and it is not entirely lacking in specialized organizational forms, for example, the exclusive club, the honorific society, the exclusive association based on ancestry (Daughters of the American Revolution, Sons of the Golden West). In its diffuse and decentralized characteristics, stratification resembles the institutions of recreation; but it derives more closely from the basic realities of political and economic structure.

Is science an institution? Quite evidently, yes. It is possible to treat science as a subaspect of other institutions, primarily of education, economy, and polity. Yet the special norms of science fully justify its separate analysis, and we shall devote a section of a later chapter to a brief review of its distinctive institutional qualities.

As will appear in more detail in Chapter X, in a large and complex society the overt, publicly supported institutions fall far short of accounting for the facts of actual behavior. Cultural norms, as discovered by research, are statistical entities; that is, there is not a sharp line between normative and not normative but a gradual shading from norms intensely supported by nearly everyone to those only casually accepted by a relatively few. Within such complex aggregates as modern nations many norms are effective only within limited subcultures; and there are wide differences in individual conformity and conceptions of the normative structure. Furthermore, minority power groups can force certain standards of behavior upon dissenting groups. Finally, some publicly ignored or disapproved norms are actually followed by considerable portions of the society. Some causes for these latest or counterinstitutional patterns will be discussed in Chapter X. Here it suffices to note that an analysis of the publicly approved institutions gives a selective and incomplete picture of a society. It is a necessary first approximation, but it requires supplementation to avoid oversimplifying the total social system.[4]

Many of the so-called contradictions in a large, complex, heterogeneous society reflect diverse levels of sociocultural regulation. Especially in societies with highly explicit ethical systems derived from religious authority, there is always a set of moral norms and values representing the highest aspirations of the moral culture. Such norms and values ordinarily are fairly loosely and

[4] Students are occasionally disturbed by finding the term "institution" used in different senses by different writers. Although the variant usage is perhaps unfortunate, there are several useful ways of defining institutions; and the particular concept chosen is largely a matter of convenience for the purposes at hand. "Institution" is sometimes defined not as a complex of norms but as a concrete social organization (church, school, etc.) or as a broad field of activity ("making a living"). The present usage has been chosen both for theoretic consistency and because it facilitates the analysis of similarities and differences in various types of social organizations, for example, the similarity of "bureaucratic" principles in business and in government. Other usages are explained in the following references: F. Stuart Chapin, *Contemporary American Institutions* (New York: Harper & Row, 1935); Talcott Parsons, *The Social System* (New York: Free Press, 1951); Sorokin, *Society, Culture, and Personality* (New York: Harper & Row, 1947); A. L. Kroeber, *Anthropology* (New York: Harcourt, Brace & World, 1923); Walter Buckley, *Sociology and Modern Systems Theory* (Englewood Cliffs, N.J.: Prentice-Hall, 1967).

unstably related to daily social action. First, they are heroic in their demands —are so difficult of actual attainment as to result in considerable nonconformity and in erratic movements, now toward rigor, now toward laxness. To love one's enemies, to turn the other cheek, to follow the golden rule, to be chaste, charitable, forgiving, and honest, taken literally, are aspirations difficult to attain under the realities of living in most societies past or present. These imperatives are axiomatic, unconditional ideals of behavior. Even if the norms form a consistent, coherent system embedded in a stable social order—and these are stringent conditions—complete conformity of actual behavior to all norms is impossible, at least in a complex, rapidly changing society such as the contemporary United States. The cultural blueprint itself lacks unity and consistency. There are many varied, and often opposing, subcultures. Furthermore, the internal variety and the rapid change weaken the power of ideals to control conduct. Such influences are added to the inherent tension between the social action and ideals, which by definition are standards of conduct more difficult to actualize than the ordinary accepted patterns.

In addition, ideal norms are typically plastic and vague; they state a very general principle without specifying its detailed application. Where cultural prescriptions are so general, there can always be countless variant interpretations. Often the norm becomes largely symbolic: what is enjoined is a state of mind (love thy neighbor as thyself) rather than a specific set of overt acts. Each group or individual can project its own needs and presuppositions into the rule and thus draw from it rather diverse implications for specific acts. In short, the meaning of the norm shifts according to numerous variations in time, place, emotional needs, intergroup and interpersonal relations, and situational pressure and interests of the most diverse kinds.[5]

Even when there are many relatively definite norms, substantial portions of the society's population may be in a condition of normlessness (anomie) because in their immediate experience there is not a clear and consistent set of social requirements. And even when there is what the most powerful elements in the society regard as a clear, consistent, and morally valid system of norms, other elements of the body politic may be specifically alienated, that is, in a variety of ways psychologically detached from, repelled by, or hostile to the nominally established rules.

If we thus avoid thinking that the easy formula of "institution" is enough to explain all behavior, we certainly should not fall into the opposite error of assuming that institutions are fictional and make no difference as to what actual individuals do.[6] The obligatory norms centering around major

[5] We are not speaking of norms as clinically ideal states from a psychological standpoint nor as statistically modal forms of behavior, but rather as approved modes of conduct. Cf. Elizabeth Bott, Family and Social Network (London: Tavistock Publications, 1957), p. 193: Norms are "people's ideas about what behavior is customary and what behavior is right and proper in their social circle." Bott points out that there are the social norms that individuals believe to be current, the norms of common consent on which there actually is agreement, and the personal norms which individuals hold but believe that others do not share.

[6] The latter unwarranted assumption was common in much American social thought prior to the last few decades. Even as late as 1933, a prominent psychologist could write

social needs constitute the essential structure by which human behavior is channelized and given order and coherence. Society does not have definite institutional regulation of all activities; but society without some common institutional regulation would be a mere aggregate of human individuals and not society as we know it. And, as later chapters will show, one can describe institutional norms from specific and objective data and systematically trace institutional interrelations.

There are three main problems in the study of social institutions. First, one must describe and analyze the normative structure itself: the existing patterns, their causes and interrelations, the sources and mechanisms of institutional integration, and consequences of the norms. Second, one must discover the processes of change in institutional patterns: their causes, mechanisms and results. Third, one must study the relation of individual personalities to the normative structure; this is the area of social psychology dealing with culture-and-personality problems and facing the complexities of social control and of motivations for conforming, innovating, or dissenting.

In most of this book we shall deal mainly, although not exclusively, with structure and structural interrelations, focusing on these three questions: What institutional structures can be discerned in American society? What accounts for their characters, differences, and interrelationships? What consequences ensue for the total social life of the people? These questions are made scientifically meaningful only by asking what *difference* does it make that the institutional pattern is X rather than Y? All societies have institutions; the crucial question is, how do they differ? And this question can be answered only by comparison either with other societies, or American society itself at some past period, or with some hypothetical standard. Thus, any statements about institutional variation always imply a standard of comparison, explicit or implicit. If, for example, one says the separation of church and state is an institutional pattern in American society, one implies a comparison with some society lacking this separation. The relations of individuals to their institutions can be studied intensively in small communities, but a broad comparative perspective is essential for adequate understanding of the institutions themselves.

## STATUS AND ROLE

Two other crucial terms remain to be explained: "status" and "role." Many different definitions of these terms have been developed, and a clear consensus on usage does not now exist. The words have been taken from ordinary speech and given special meanings in anthropology, sociology, and social psychology. As used in a variety of research endeavors and theoretical

---

in terms that essentially denied the reality of institutions in the present sense. See Floyd H. Allport, *Institutional Behavior* (Chapel Hill, N.C.: The University of North Carolina Press, 1933). And a kind of reductionism in which institutions almost disappear by fiat is close to the surface in some contemporary analyses of elementary social behavior and exchange theory. (Cf. George Homans, "Bringing Men Back In," *American Sociological Review*, 29, 6 (December 1964), 809–818).

formulations they have acquired (inevitably) a rather large set of different specific meanings. In future work, it is likely that a number of new terms will be needed to deal properly with the actual empirical complexity thus revealed. Consensus on usage can only emerge gradually. In the meantime, the appropriate procedure is to make explicit one's own definitions and to indicate that other legitimate and workable definitions are employed elsewhere. For example, William J. Goode has proposed that a status be regarded as that special class of roles which is "institutionalized," in which role relationships are themselves normatively defined, where there are mutual expectations, supported by sanctions. Status, then, is a matter of degree: the more fully institutionalized (normatively obligatory and sanctioned) a relationship is, the more closely it approximates a status relationship.[7]

For present purposes, we consider status to be a position or place in a set of relationships among people. Statuses are polar or reciprocal: any particular status always implies at least one other to which it is related, for example, mother-child, employer-employee, doctor-patient. The entire set of statuses of a society constitutes a kind of map that identifies labeled positions and shows the complex relationships among them. Along with every status goes a set of norms that defines the expected and approved behavior for the occupant of the status. In other words, every status carries with it a set of rights and duties in relation to other statuses; these rights and obligations represent the normative demands and expectations that pour in from other people upon the incumbent of a status; for example, the prescriptions for the proper behavior of a male parent toward his children give us the social meaning of the status of "father." The position is initially identified by the minimal specifications—a mother is a woman who has borne a child, a judge makes legal decisions in a court, a soldier fights in war.[8] The full status is specified by description of all the applicable norms and their interrelations.

This seems to be a reasonably clear way to answer the question Does a status exist except as defined by a particular set of rights and duties? For instance, does it make sense to talk about a social position of father apart from the norms that define fatherly behavior? Taken quite literally, there is no social position if there are *no* norms that define the position's behavior. However, there is a minimal generalized definition of a position, in terms of activities or attributes, that does not directly specify obligatory norms; thus, a father is a male progenitor of a child, a teacher lectures and advises, a leader initiates action for followers. Close examination is likely to show that such positions generally are regarded as carrying implied duties and rights. Perhaps the best solution for simplicity and clarity in usage is to

---

[7] Goode, "Norm Commitment and Conformity to Role-Status Obligations," *op. cit.*

[8] The minimal description of a status always has to tell us something about the activities that partially define the position. Either implicitly or explicitly any particular status is further defined by the rights and duties, privileges and disabilities, immunities and obligations that inhere in the position and apply to any occupant of that status. "Inhere in" means "enforced on the basis of some social consensus among other relevant actors." In other words, every status entails a set of rights and duties in relation to at least one other position.

think of status as any *specifiable cluster of rights and obligations socially defined as a unit* so that exercise of any one implies access to exercise of the others. The most important distinction among statuses, then, would be between generalized statuses—such as those of sex, age, and social rank—whose rights and duties are created by diffuse consensus, and specific statuses (offices, occupations) that are defined within a segmental set of interactions (as in a business firm).

Role, also, has come to be a sponge word that has soaked up far too many meanings. Among its main usages are these:

1. Role often is treated as the *total* behavior of an incumbent of a status while he is socially defined as acting in that status. Thus, a father's role would consist of everything he does when other relevant people are treating him as a father. This is a global and unsatisfactory usage that fails to note that the father is simultaneously occupying *other* statuses (of age, occupation, religious communicant, and so on) as well as engaging in personally idiosyncratic behavior.
2. Role sometimes is conceived of as the *full set of actual behaviors* that represents specific performance of the rights and duties of a status. This is *role performance* in the sense of full enactment of status prescriptions.
3. Role may be thought of as the *minimal performance* necessary for an incumbent to continue to hold a status.
4. Role is regarded as the set of *expectations for behavior* that is attached to a status. (This, of course, is a partial description of status itself.)
5. Role consists of the actor's conceptions and evaluations of the status norms that apply to him. This is *perceived role*, or *psychological role*.[9]

Anyone is free, of course, to attach any of these or other meanings to the term. In this study we shall use "role" to mean "role performance"—that is, behavior in direct response to status norms. Such performance may vary greatly in style (and in motivation and other psychological accompaniments); but the crucial characteristic is its direct orientation to the norms of a status. The role consists of the performance elicited by some reference to rights and duties, resulting from the application of a set of evaluative standards to an incumbent of a particular position. In the fully institutionalized case, the role prescriptions will not be merely external demands but will be accepted by the status incumbent as personally obligatory.

Each status represents a social identity in the sense that an occupant is expected to behave in given ways in certain types of situations and is expected to have certain associated values, beliefs, sentiments, and symbols. Other identities represent *social types* or *social categories* rather than fully developed statuses, for example, flappers, do-gooders, hippies, Uncle Toms, smart operators, squares, and the like. These diffuse and variable categorizations represent particular combinations of statuses, together with dis-

9 For a comprehensive review of concepts of role, as well as of norm, sanctions, and status, see Bruce J. Biddle and Edwin J. Thomas (eds.), *Role Theory: Concepts and Research* (New York: Wiley, 1966).

tinctive styles of life, and include newly emerging and noninstitutionalized behavior.[1]

Statuses and roles tend to occur in organized sets, not merely as isolated units.[2] Everyone is male or female and of a certain age; and, therefore, every other status of a person is inevitably compounded with sex and age statuses. Thus, the status of mother in our society typically goes along with the statuses of woman, adult, wife, daughter-in-law, homemaker, and other positions (for example, member of the Parent-Teachers Association). In the same way, there are role sets associated with a particular status: a school superintendent must relate himself to school board members, teachers, other superintendents, parents, and so on.[3] The patterned character of status and role sets is vividly shown by the rarity and difficulty of certain combinations, such as a Negro woman becoming a medical doctor in general practice.

To recapitulate briefly, we have seen that culture in the most inclusive sense includes knowledges, skills, artifacts, symbols, technologies, beliefs, and values, as well as norms for conduct. Among the conduct norms, we have concentrated on these regulating social relationships (rather than, for instance, the relationship of man to nature or to the supernatural). Finally we have examined briefly the special class of norms we call institutional, and the concepts of status and role.

## SOCIAL ORGANIZATION AND GROUP

So far we have discussed only the cultural structure, the normative patterns, but have not made explicit the idea of social organization as distinct from culture. The distinction arises from the fact that culture is not concrete behavior itself but contains the normative standards for behavior. The embodiment of cultural norms in concrete social relations marks the area of social organization. Social organization is not to be identified with any particular social groupings nor with highly formalized organization. Social organization refers rather to the actual regularity of human interaction, no matter what specific form the interaction may assume. (See Chapter XII.) There is organization precisely to the degree that the actions of individuals toward other individuals are recurrent and coordinated by the orientation of the acts of each to those of others. A newly formed unit of military conscripts will be oriented to a definite culture considerably before its actual social organization has come into conformity with the rules that are supposed to apply. The practical test of organization is always predictability, and hence involves social relationships. A social relationship exists to the extent that the interaction between two or more individuals is recurrent by virtue of the mutual

[1] Orrin E. Klapp, Heroes, Villains, and Fools: The Changing American Character (Englewood Cliffs, N.J.: Prentice-Hall, 1962); and Symbolic Leaders: Public Dramas and Public Men (Chicago: Aldine, 1964).

[2] Robert K. Merton, "The Role-Set: Problems in Sociological Theory," The British Journal of Sociology, 2 (June 1957), 106–120.

[3] For a specific analysis of the whole problem of studying statuses and roles, see Neal Gross, Ward S. Mason, Alexander W. McEachern, Explorations in Role Analysis: Studies of the School Superintendency Role (New York: Wiley, 1958).

orientation of the acting individuals to one another. The coordination of interindividual action through mutual concerns and expectations is precisely the measure of social organization.

Organization in this generic sense is clearly distinguishable from any specific organized group. A group is a specific aggregate of persons within which there is organization; it exists only to the extent that the specific persons are in fact organized. A proximate, although inadequate, clue to the existence of a group is a greater frequency of interaction within the aggregate than occurs in outside relations; a group is an aggregate within which there is a "special density of interaction," to use the phrase with which Chester I. Barnard has characterized "informal organization." A formally organized group is a specific aggregate of persons carrying out interrelated roles in explicitly defined positions. Actual social aggregates range from relatively unstructured, casual, and transient systems of interaction to the most highly formalized and enduring groupings; and it is essential to know the relative importance of various kinds of formal and informal groups in attempting to describe any society.

We now have in hand the basic concepts necessary to begin our substantive analysis: structure, culture, cultural norm, institution, status, role, and social organization. Our approximate and incomplete model for the analysis of American society now includes the organized activities of a population that interacts in terms of a particular culture as it attempts to realize certain normative goals in relation to other societies and its physical and biosocial environment. All the terms in this statement are essential in the approach we shall employ. For the translation of these terms into useful analytic tools many diverse sets of data will be utilized. Every scientific fact is a statement about phenomena in terms of a particular set of concepts. Our facts must be objective, that is, the operations by which they are derived can be described and publicly communicated so that ultimately they can be replicated and checked by any competent observer. At the same time, the multitudes of heterogeneous facts must be ordered and analyzed in concepts that are as clear and invariant as possible. The sources of information that supply our factual observation are initially illustrated in the following chapter on American family and kinship. They include statistical compilations, law codes, judicial decisions, historical records, observational reports, specialized research reports, and a variety of other materials. The present chapter supplies a minimal framework within which such data can be clearly arranged.

## SUGGESTED READINGS

BIDDLE, BRUCE J., and EDWIN J. THOMAS (eds.). *Role Theory: Concepts and Research*. New York: Wiley, 1966. Surveys and critically interprets a vast amount of research and theoretical work. This volume is the definitive summary of the main literature, especially in social psychology, up to the time of publication.

GROSS, NEAL, WARD S. MASON, and ALEXANDER W. MCEACHERN. *Explorations in Role Analysis*. New York: Wiley, 1958. Another ground-breaking work.

Intensive study of school superintendents in Massachusetts led to development of complex sets of concepts necessary to grasp the interplay of demands and expectations actually present in so-called role-behavior. Shows the sad inadequacy of "common sense" for understanding what really goes on in "occupying a social position."

HOMANS, GEORGE C. *Social Behavior: Its Elementary Forms.* New York: Harcourt, Brace & World, 1961. Points to social psychological sources of normative patterning and advances testable hypotheses concerning emergence of "social control" in noninstitutionalized interaction.

LINTON, RALPH. *The Study of Man.* New York: Appleton-Century-Crofts, 1936. Astonishingly fresh a generation after its publication, this anthropological excursus gives clear conceptions and vivid examples of many forms of cultural and social structure and of changes in them.

MARCH, JAMES G. (ed.). *Handbook of Organizations.* Chicago: Rand-McNally, 1965. Encyclopedic collection of writings on social organization, with special focus upon large, complex formal structures. A gold mine of data, concepts, methods, and ideas for further study.

PARSONS, TALCOTT. *The Social System.* Glencoe, Ill.: Free Press, 1951, especially Chapters I–IV. A classic work. Presents a comprehensive set of concepts and schemes of classification for studying total societies and nearly all their main components. Studded with hundreds of astute insights and proto-hypotheses. Sometimes difficult reading, but well worth the effort.

SOROKIN, PITIRIM A. *Society, Culture and Personality.* New York: Cooper, 1947. The best single source for gaining a view of the main outlines of Sorokin's vast body of writings. Do not be put off by the terminology or the opinionated style, but look for the sophisticated conceptions of norms and institutions. The concept of "law-norms" goes to the heart of the matter.

THIBAULT, JOHN W., and HAROLD H. KELLEY. *The Social Psychology of Groups.* New York: Wiley, 1949, especially Chapters 8 and 13. A pioneering synthesis, concentrating upon experimental research but making excellent use of observational and historical data. Was at least a decade "ahead of its times" in its grasp of the phenomena of power, norms, and status-role structures in group processes.

# Kinship and the Family in the United States    *IV*

S ome kind of institutionalized *family group* is
found in nearly all societies and is fundamental to their social systems. In
this chapter, we shall look at the American family and kinship systems as
though we had never seen them before. Americans tend to regard the
relatively isolated small conjugal unit of husband, wife, and children—
characteristic of our society—as perfectly natural; but it is quite special. In
many historical, as well as preliterate societies, the kinship unit has been a
larger group, often including several generations and various collateral
branches and having much greater family continuity than in our society.
Again, Americans take for granted various distinctive patterns of dating and
courtship; but these depend upon rather unusual features of our society.
We observe Mother's Day or joke about in-laws often without realizing
how such behavior relates to our basic kinship system.

Kinship relations can be analyzed on two different levels: (1) institutional patterns (structure) and changes in them and (2) the individual's
relation to these patterns and to the associated personal and social relationships. In this chapter we shall focus mainly upon the system of kinship
positions (statuses) whose reciprocal cultural prescriptions define required,
recommended, permitted, discouraged, or forbidden sentiments or feelings
and behavior. Later, we shall examine some important types of deviant
behavior. And toward the end of the book we shall discuss changes in the
basic structures themselves.

## ''KINSHIP'' AND ''FAMILY'' DEFINED

Since this is an institutional treatment, our subject should be defined in
terms of norms. By "kinship system" we mean a *pattern of social norms
regulating those relationships that are directly based on the facts of birth
and the birth cycle.* A society is perpetuated only by new births; and the
prolonged human infancy requires extended adult care, the central fact
of all kinship systems. The social relations based on actual or potential
births fall into four main categories: (1) the selection of marriage partners
(courtship, arranged marriage, and so on); (2) the marriage bond—the
relatively enduring, socially accepted sexual and social union of one or
more men with one or more women; (3) the immediate conjugal (nuclear)
family of husband, wife, and children; and (4) the extended kinship relations beyond the immediate conjugal unit. Our analysis centers on the last
two categories, those fundamental to the social character of marriage and
courtship.

*[handwritten margin notes: Kinship system; 4 main categories of social relations]*

47

In analyzing any kinship system we always have to take into account both age and sex categories. Norms differ for young and old, for males and females. Age and sex thus are important for many social relationships outside of the kinship system but also enter into the definition of kinship statuses and roles.

Our primary interest here is in kinship structure, the system of norms that defines kinship positions and the relationships among them. When we speak of "the family" we refer to the structure of institutionalized norms that prescribe familial statuses in an indefinite number of particular family units. A (particular) family is an actual group whose members are united by kinship ties and by actual or potential common residence; often, also, the group as a whole engages in economic production as well as consumption, carries on religious activities, and is a unit in recreational activities. Particular families may come and go while the basic form of the family and of its relations to other kinship groupings (for example, clans, lineages) remains the same. Indeed, this basic stability was preserved for many centuries in China and in several other major historical societies.

We can see, then, that it is necessary to distinguish between (1) the total *kinship structure* (the inclusive network of kinship norms) and (2) the *family system* (the form of the basic kinship unit—for example, polygamous or monogamous, patriarchal or matriarchal) and (3) particular *family groups*.[1] American society has a very simplified kinship structure. But even in this society the kinship system includes much more than just the family system. The latter consists merely of a collection of discrete nuclear families. The wider kinship structure includes the relationships among family units as well as the norms for roles within these units.

Kinship relations are by no means a simple reflection of blood relationships. The biological basis for kinship is, of course, the fact that relationships are established among persons by their being born of certain parents or by the possibility of births resulting from marriages. Imagine how different our reactions to marriages would be if no children were ever expected to result from them. The seriousness with which the marriage bond is regarded is fundamentally affected by the anticipation that a marriage will eventually become a family group. The birth of a human being is always an imperative social event. Infants must be cared for if they are to survive, and that care must be of a very special kind if the infant is to develop into a normal adult. All societies have formed durable kinship units that provide for infant care and child rearing.

Restraints upon sexual behavior do, indeed, vary greatly among different societies; but the norms certainly are not, as is sometimes thought, arbitrary. As a general tendency, the punishment of sexual relations outside of marriage tends to be more severe when physical aggression is involved, when there is the likelihood that a child will be born without provision for regularized nurturance, socialization, and status placement, or

[1] The fruitfulness of a clear distinction between kinship and family is shown by Maurice Freedman, "The Family in China, Past and Present," *Pacific Affairs*, XXXIV, 4 (Winter 1961–1962), 323–336.

Kinship relat.
are based
1) Birth
2) Sex-diff
3) Birth-Or
4) Sibling gp

when an existing marriage or set of family relationships will be disrupted.[2] Clearly the maintenance of stable arrangements for child rearing is a different matter from sexual regulation as such, but the two are not likely to be completely independent.

Birth, then, is the primary biological point of reference for kinship. But there is the further criterion of sex: the fact that the two parents are of opposite sex produces other highly significant relations, especially if both parents nurture the child. Third, there is birth order; if older and younger children remain together for years, age tends to define relationships among them, and between them and other relatives. Seniority also influences the relations between an individual and his relatives outside the immediate family. Thus, as Ralph Linton has pointed out, the culturally ascribed roles for various kinship statuses will be filled from a certain age-sex category: "Note the impossibility of adhering to the formal roles for an uncle-nephew relationship when the uncle is a child and the nephew is an adult."[3] Finally, several children from the same parents make the sibling group a potential subunit of the system: there are societies in which the group formed by brothers and sisters is a basic unit of social life.

These several biological reference points combine to give each individual a different social position. "Children" are not merely children; they are male or female, older or younger, with siblings or without. The sister of one's father is not in the same biological category as one's mother's sister, but both in our society are "aunt." Because of the complexity of the biological categories, no summary categorization of the social kinship system is adequate. This is clear for the American system, and anthropological observations demonstrate it in various other societies.[4]

Some of the simplest facts of human relations are the most fundamental. For instance, all known societies, past and present, have (or had) an incest taboo: all forbid sexual relations between persons in certain kinship positions. Some systematic prohibition of this kind is universal, and violations of it typically arouse strong repugnance or moral revulsion. *But the line of prohibited intermarriage is drawn at very different points in different societies.* Even for the nuclear family, some societies have had fairly extensive exceptions to the general rule against within-family marriages.[5] Apparently many such marriages occurred among commoners, not just among royalty and the nobles. Such arrangements violate both the principle of maintaining clearly differentiated roles within the nuclear unit and that of securing cooperative alliances with other families.

All societies prohibit incest · but degree of relation involved = various

In the traditional clan system of China, on the other hand, the prohibition nominally extended to a very wide group of relatives, many of whom

---

[2] Cf. Julia S. Brown, "A Comparative Study of Deviations from Sexual Mores," *American Sociological Review*, 17, 2 (April 1952), 135–146.

[3] Ralph Linton, "Age and Sex Categories," *American Sociological Review*, 7, 5 (October 1942), 590.

[4] A classic summary of anthropological evidence is given by George P. Murdock, *Social Structure* (New York: Macmillan, 1949).

[5] Russell Middleton, "Brother-Sister and Father-Daughter Marriage in Ancient Egypt," *American Sociological Review*, 27, 5 (October 1962), 603–611.

were quite distant kin by contemporary American standards. Some societies prohibit the marriage of cousins to the sixth degree;[6] in other societies the intermarriage of one type of first cousin is mandatory (cross-cousin marriage). There are many such detailed variations, each of which is considered right and proper in the society in which it occurs.

The various prohibitions against intermarriage of kin do not seem to be fully explicable on purely biological grounds. The notion of instinctive aversion ignores such evidence as inbreeding among animals, the widely varying degrees of kinship permissible for intermarriage in different societies, the actual occurrence of incest, and the frequent intermarriage of fairly close blood relatives in societies that do not forbid it. A second biological explanation rests upon the allegedly harmful results of inbreeding. But the scientific evidence concerning the biological effects of human inbreeding is by no means clear-cut; in general, it seems to bring out genetically recessive traits, good or bad. Yet all known societies unequivocally prohibited marriage of close kin long before any definitive scientific evidence was available. Finally, Freud's contention that the taboo is necessary to repress sexual desires within a kin group, although partly true, seems inadequate. Prohibitions against sexual relations with relatives seem in general to be more preventive than repressive; that is, they ensure that certain persons simply will not be regarded as potential sexual or marriage partners.

More promising is an explanation of the incest taboo as preventing potentially disruptive conflicts within the kinship group. If family groupings are to exist at all—and there are important reasons for their universal presence[7]—internal conflicts must be kept within some restricted ranges, and positive cooperation or solidarity must be maintained at some minimal level. The expression of solidarity may take the form of prohibiting divisive alliances within the unit.[8] Exogamy (marriage outside the kinship unit), furthermore, links together a series of internally solidary groups that would otherwise constitute a "mosaic" society of relatively small, closed segments. This function is especially striking in American society. Our society is made more diffuse and mobile by a marriage system tending to establish kinship relations cross-cutting segmentary local groups.

One more point should be made before we turn to the specific features of the American system. Kinship relations are among those learned earliest and most thoroughly. We learn them at first unwittingly, and they become integral to our personalities very early in life. They are implicit in the very language we are taught and are impressed upon us by countless experiences and injunctions throughout the most formative years of childhood. So

[6] For example, see David F. Mandelbaum, "The Family in India," in Ruth N. Anshen (ed.), *The Family: Its Function and Destiny* (New York: Harper & Row, 1949), pp. 167–187.

[7] We have noted the helplessness of the human being at birth and the prolonged period during which the infant needs adult care for survival. Recent research has shown that diffuse social stimulation, physical contact, and generalized emotional support and responsiveness of the kind supplied in "usual" families are important in normal personality development.

[8] Frank W. Young, "Incest Taboos and Social Solidarity," *American Journal of Sociology*, 72, 6 (May 1967), 589–600.

completely and so early do we learn the system that we are seldom aware of ever having learned it. It seems completely natural and is taken for granted as a part of a fixed order of the universe. For this reason, and because we often have deep emotional blockages regarding some aspects of family and kinship relations, we often tend to make two untenable assumptions: (1) that the kinship system is simple—easy to describe by untutored common sense without rigorous analysis (actually, some features of our kinship system are so far from obvious that even prolonged and systematic study leaves many gaps in knowledge); (2) that American family-roles reflect a constant human nature and, hence, that our unanalyzed concepts of "father," "mother," "uncle," and so on, are directly applicable to other societies. Anthropology has shown, however, that kinship statuses vary widely between cultures; a "father" in the Trobriands is certainly not the "father" of Freud's central Europe.

In America, a number of rather divergent family types are often found even within the same region, so we must proceed cautiously. Unless otherwise specified, "the American kinship structure" will refer to that prevailing among urban, middle-class groups, which tend to embody the ideal patterns toward which most other population elements are oriented. As we examine the kinship structure of urban, middle-class America, however, we can consider also its modifications among rural groupings, upper-class or lower-class groups,[9] ethnic, racial, or religious minorities,[1] and in other divisions of the society.

We turn first to American family law for certain clues about the basic structure of the kinship system.

## THE LEGAL NORMS OF THE AMERICAN KINSHIP SYSTEM: AN ILLUSTRATION OF EVIDENCE

Though in detail complex, vague, and various, American family law still exhibits a rather clearly defined core of principles about which the kinship system is built. The greatest uniformity and antiquity mark the following as key points:

1. Violation of the incest taboo, which applies to the immediate biological family and to certain other relatives by blood descent or marriage, is one of the most fundamental breaches of the regulative order.

[9] Cf. Lee Rainwater, *And the Poor Get Children* (Chicago: Quadrangle Books, 1960); Daniel R. Miller and Guy E. Swanson, *The Changing American Parent; A Study in the Detroit Area* (New York: Wiley, 1958); Mirra Komarovsky, *Blue-Collar Marriage* (New York: Random House, 1964); William J. Goode, "Family and Mobility" in Reinhard Bendix and Seymour Martin Lipset (eds.), *Class, Status and Power: Social Stratification in Comparative Perspective*, 2nd ed. (New York: Free Press, 1966), pp. 582–601.
[1] Jessie Bernard, *Marriage and Family Among Negroes* (Englewood Cliffs, N.J.: Prentice-Hall, 1966); George E. Simpson and J. Milton Yinger, *Racial and Cultural Minorities*, 3rd ed. (New York: Harper & Row, 1965). For a comparative view across nations: William J. Goode, *World Revolution and Family Patterns* (New York: Free Press, 1963).

*[margin: bigamy]*

2. Marriages must be monogamous. All states prohibit bigamous marriages.

*[margin: civil contract]*

3. Marriage is more than an ordinary civil contract; it contains an element of *status* in the legal sense.

> *Marriage clearly differs from an ordinary contract, in that: (1) it cannot be rescinded or its fundamental terms changed by agreement; (2) it results in a status; (3) it merges the legal identities of the parties at common law; (4) it is not a contract within the Fourteenth Amendment, United States Constitution, forbidding legislation impairing the obligation of contract; (5) the tests of capacity differ from those applied to ordinary contracts.*[2]

*[margin: assumption of validity]*

4. Legal tradition gives the benefit of doubt as to validity to marriages that are marriages in social fact, although they might otherwise be null, void, or voidable on technical grounds of law.[3]

*[margin: divorce—difficult]*

5. There are many specific barriers to the dissolution of marriage; these reflect the basic presumption that a valid marriage should be maintained unless there is clear and crucial ground for its dissolution.

*[margin: kinship → legal obligations]*

6. There are definite legal obligations incumbent upon individuals as a consequence of their kinship relations, regardless of their personal wishes or "contractual" agreements.

*[margin: man = most powerful partner]*

7. There are vestiges of a surviving legal "double standard" that indicate an underlying conception of the male (husband or father) as the more powerful, responsible, and independent party to a marriage.

*[margin: atomism; women's equality (individualism)]*

8. Women have a high degree of legal autonomy and freedom in marriage and kinship obligations; there is a strong tendency toward husband-wife equality. In some respects this represents marked individualization or "atomization" of the kinship unit.

*[margin: family authority regulated by state]*

9. Familial authority is specifically limited by the state in a variety of ways; the kinship unit is extremely open to external political authority —compulsory school attendance, regulation of child labor, juvenile courts, military draft.

*[margin: "unwritten law"]*

10. Court decisions seem in many instances to reflect certain customary norms that are not a formal part of the statutory or common-law systems, for instance, the "unwritten law" that sometimes exculpates a husband who kills his wife's paramour.

Among the characteristics of norms, two are essential in defining the socially obligatory force we call "institutional:" (1) the existence of a high degree of consensus in a defined population that the norm exists and should be followed and (2) the reliable application of strong restitutive or retributory sanctions to violators of the norm. Unnecessary confusion can be avoided simply by the recognition that both characteristics exist in varying degree and may vary independently, thus:

[2] An early but still useful digest of American family law is contained in the series of volumes produced under the direction of Chester G. Vernier. The above passage is reprinted from Chester G. Vernier and Fred A. Weller, *American Family Laws: Introductory Survey and Marriage*, Vol. I, (Stanford, Calif.: Stanford University Press, 1939), p. 51, with the permission of the authors and of the publishers.

[3] *Ibid.*, pp. 102–103.

| | | *Normative violation is:* | |
|---|---|---|---|
| | | STRONGLY SANCTIONED | NOT STRONGLY SANCTIONED |
| *Norm is supported by:* | HIGH CONSENSUS | Institutional norm | "Folkways;" "ideal" (lip-service) norms |
| | LOW CONSENSUS | Imposed rule; unpopular law | Matters of taste; personal preferences |

Strictly speaking, there is an ethical view in which a "violation" in a *moral* sense is not wrong merely because it does not conform to the rule as such but rather because it is an action damaging to the vital values and interests of others or oneself. In this sense, "wrongness" consists of a breach of faith, commitment, or trust that has harmful consequences; in these terms "moral norms" would have to be more than specific rules for particular actions—they would have to include obligations for seeking justice, using good judgment, showing consideration, and the like. Nevertheless, as a matter of the actual operation of social institutions, it is the prescriptive or proscriptive norms that are the *immediate* referents of consensus and sanctions, and it is, therefore, to the networks of norms that institutional analysis continually refers in locating its objects of initial analysis.

The marriage contract is the first tangible evidence of the *institutional character of the family.* Most civil contracts may be broken by mutual agreement of the contracting parties. But in the case of a marriage contract, American law generally regards mutual agreement not only as an inadequate ground for divorce but as a specific bar to divorce. Mutual agreement to contrive a divorce is collusion, which the law at least nominally regards as fraud and as a sufficient basis for denying a divorce. Evidently, marriage is not an ordinary civil contract. American family law treats marriage and kinship relations in terms of status rather than contract. When one contracts to have a house built, the agreement affects only specified rights and obligations; but marriage involves blanket obligations (to "love, honor, and obey"), not a specific limited sector of life. A person does not merely enter a contract by marrying; he becomes a different legal person. There is a new status that cannot lawfully be nullified merely by a change in sentiments or by mutual agreement.

Furthermore, the tests of capacity to make marriage contracts differ from those of ordinary civil contracts. The courts have often held, for example, that a marriage illegally entered upon by minors is valid if there is a child or if the wife is pregnant. There is thus a general tendency to recognize as legal and binding those marriages that are marriages in social fact, even if the parties were originally not technically competent to contract marriage.

The divorce laws are especially instructive as to the peculiar nature of marriage. Though with much variation from state to state, the majority of jurisdictions, even those with liberal divorce laws, give marriage a status radically different from other contracts.[4] Historically, the rule of recrimination applies in divorce proceedings: divorce is denied when both parties are guilty of behavior that would justify divorce if only one partner were guilty. Mutual violation could thus result in the court's refusal to grant a decree. This situation is just the opposite of the rule in ordinary contracts, where mutual breach of contract rescinds the agreement. Furthermore, most jurisdictions deny absolute divorce where connivance is proved—that is, when one spouse consents to, accepts, or aids in acts that would otherwise be valid grounds for the decree. Divorce is supposedly denied for collusion —agreement of husband and wife to "impose upon the court." More striking is the denial of a decree because the plaintiff has condoned offenses that would otherwise entitle him to divorce.[5] So far does the legal system go in trying to preserve marriages that at one time thirty-two states explicitly provided that a divorce could not be granted solely on the basis of the uncorroborated testimony, admission, or confession of the parties.[6]

Such examples could be multiplied, but these perhaps illustrate that marriage—and kinship relations generally—are, in law, relatively durable and productive of a far-reaching change in the status of a person.[7] The law seems to regard these statuses and relationships as valid unless proved otherwise; the burden of proof is upon the one who would terminate a relationship or avoid a responsibility. These norms are detailed, relatively permanent, and of basic structural importance. The legal structure thus reflects the moral consensus of the society that fulfillment of marriage and kinship obligations is highly important.

On the other hand, recent years have brought a marked relaxation of the old "adversary theory" of divorce (one party is innocent, the other has offended). Three jurisdictions (New Mexico, Alaska, the Virgin Islands) now even include incompatibility among the grounds for divorce; six states permit divorce because of voluntary separation and eleven more for protracted separation. More strikingly, forty-two states allow divorce for cruelty, usually including mental cruelty. In effect, the law is coming to permit divorce by mutual consent.[8]

The legal order thus both reflects and helps to create a given family system. Much of family law—including statutes, enactments, common law, and judicial precedents—simply summarizes or codifies current social

---

[4] See Chester G. Vernier and Benjamin C. Duniway, *American Family Laws: Divorce and Separation*, Vol. II (Stanford, Calif.: Stanford University Press, 1932).

[5] *Ibid.*, p. 79.

[6] *Ibid.*, p. 141.

[7] Obviously, actual social practice may not be in accord with the official norms; for the moment, however, let us consider only the nominally dominant rules.

[8] See Kingsley Davis, "Divorce and Its Effects," in Morris Fishbein and Ruby Jo Reeves Kennedy (eds.), *Modern Marriage and Family Living* (New York: Oxford University Press, 1957), pp. 100–113.

practice. Much law, however, tangibly influences marriage and kinship relations, even where it does not unequivocally reflect public opinion. (At the time of enactment, the requirement of medical certificates, waiting periods, and the like for couples wishing to be married must have been considerably ahead of popular thinking.) On the other hand, marriage and family law that runs counter to popular beliefs and well-established behavior tends in the long run to be modified, formally abolished, or tacitly ignored. Nevertheless, such adjustments are usually slow, and many divergencies between law and practice typically exist at any given time.

Of course, law seldom perfectly embodies the current social practice, still less the current wishes, aspirations, and dissatisfactions of the people. There are invariably maladjustments or areas of tension and confusion at the growing points of the law, partly because a main formal function of law is to provide security by ensuring a general predictability in recurring situations. The major basis for predictability is the fact that previous cases have been decided in certain ways. There is great judicial emphasis upon precedent, general rejection of retroactive legislation, and a pervasive conservative tendency in the legal system. In periods of rapid social change, problems arise that the law cannot cope with except in a way that no longer accords with the beliefs and desires of most members of the society. Legal norms, then, can never be safely taken as adequately descriptive of actual social relations. Not even the most astute legislator or judge can foresee all the varied situations that will eventually complicate the application of a particular statute or decision. Exceptions, peculiar cases, and unusual circumstances are especially numerous in kinship relations and, therefore, never completely covered by the explicit provisions of the law.[9] In general, the more detailed regulation of the kinship system is left for diffuse cultural standardization, not enforced by a formal social organization. The legal net is too wide meshed to catch the smaller variations.[1]

Equally important, the family is hard to regulate from outside. If it is to have any real existence it must have some autonomy. Otherwise it becomes merely a nominal group or an appendage of some other organization. In America, the privacy, inviolability, and independence of the family household still have deep cultural roots, although it is no longer true that "every man's home is his castle." Family behavior is hard to reduce to rule, for diffuse symbolisms and personal motives may decisively influence the social meaning of acts. Often more important than a specific overt act, an act easy to identify objectively, are the imputed motives and meanings from a long series of subtly interrelated actions. Apparently identical acts may have exactly opposite meanings for different members of the family.

[9] Indeed, the legal structure is itself forced to set up an elaborate series of social mechanisms for fitting the law to the unusual situation. Equity proceedings provide the clearest explicit instance; but much the same purpose is served by jury trial, by wide statutory leeway for administrative or judicial discretion, by the right of appeal, by advisedly vague legal language, and by many other means.

[1] "In the great interstitial areas of life where institutional controls cannot easily reach, particularly in the primary group, control will be determined by the interplay of personality." Jessie Bernard, *American Family Behavior* (New York: Harper & Row, 1942), p. 428.

Therefore, evidence about American kinship structure must include more than law. The following synthesis draws upon law, statistical records, literature, and the substantial body of sociological and psychological research.

### MAIN STRUCTURAL FEATURES
### OF THE KINSHIP SYSTEM

The American kinship system is marked by the following characteristics: First, the incest taboo everywhere forbids a person to marry father, mother, child, grandparent, uncle, aunt, niece, or nephew.[2] In twenty-nine states intermarriage of first cousins is forbidden; intermarriage of blood relatives is seldom otherwise limited. Second, marriage is monogamous, and there is no prescriptive pattern for kinship marriages. Third, no discrimination is made between paternal and maternal relatives for marriage purposes. Fourth, although the family name descends through the male line, there is little other emphasis upon the male line of descent. The descent system tends to be bilineal or, more strictly, multilineal.

These four characteristics indicate a highly dispersed system of intermarriage and kinship.[3] From any given individual the ancestral lines can fan out indefinitely into the past, so that any one of many lines of heredity may be emphasized for some purposes. Similarly the lines of descent are dispensed among a large number of kin-name groupings.

Thus, fifth, there is an emphasis on the immediate conjugal family.[4] In a highly developed consanguine kinship-system, by contrast, the tightest unit is the descent group of siblings, a group of brothers and sisters whose spouses enter as strangers and remain always somewhat so. In America, the solidarity of spouses is stressed, to the exclusion of in-laws. We really have nothing comparable to the corporate kin-groupings of some historical societies. For instance, under the laws of the last hundred years of Imperial China, an official who lost a parent was supposed to retire during his mourning, certain relatives could legitimately conceal the offenses of one

[2] See Vernier and Weller, *American Family Laws: Introductory Survey and Marriage,* Vol. I, *op. cit.,* pp. 173 ff.

[3] Talcott Parsons, "The Kinship System of the Contemporary United States," *American Anthropologist,* 45, 1 (January–March 1943), 22–38. We know more about the kinship systems of dozens of tribal societies than we do of our own. Even such essential elementary facts as the actual use of kinship terms have been studied only rarely in the United States; see David M. Schneider and George C. Homans, "Kinship Terminology and the American Kinship System," *American Anthropologist,* 57, 6 (December 1955), 1194–1208; Lionel S. Lewis, "Kinship Terminology for the American Parent," *American Anthropologist,* 65, 3 (June 1963), 649–652.

[4] Margaret Park Redfield, "The American Family: Consensus and Freedom," *American Journal of Sociology,* LII, 3 (November 1946), 175. "The American family—parents and children—appears on the surface as a simple conjugal type with no important or formal connections with remoter kin, no rituals of ancestor worship (except, perhaps, in the case of the D.A.R.'s), and no intricate economic ties. It is a small, compact group of two generations, bound together by ties of affection and functioning to care for the young until they reach years of maturity and can repeat for themselves the process of family rearing."

another, and it was an offense for close relatives to bring even just charges against one another. Lineages periodically became strong centers of local power.[5]

The contrast is clear. The emphasis in modern, urban, middle-class America upon the marriage pair is bound to result, insofar as it is actually carried out, in a greatly simplified kinship structure of nuclear families.[6] This has profound sociopsychological implications, to be examined later.

Sixth, the immediate family of father, mother, and children tends to be the effective residence, consumption, and social unit. No extended kin-groupings are of more than secondary importance in these respects, except among a few relatively small population-elements. The doubling-up of families in the same household ordinarily occurs only under economic depression, housing shortage, or extraordinary family circumstances. In 1960, only 2 percent of married couples were without their own household. Even grandparents in the home, once more or less taken for granted, has become unusual.

The relatively independent conjugal unit is regarded as desirable, right, and proper by social consensus. It is felt that each family (typically this is simply assumed to mean "immediate family") *should* be an autonomous group. It is considered unfortunate if for any reason other relatives have to reside in the household. Except in extraordinary crises parents are expected not to interfere with the families of their children.

Seventh, in urban communities, which are increasingly representative of the country as a whole, the family group is typically a consuming rather than a producing unit. Kinship units as work groups and productive organizations have largely disappeared except in farming and certain types of small retail businesses. The family producing-unit characterizes societies with relatively little industry and economic specialization. The family farms and the small shops and stores of earlier America combined functions that have been separated in an age of giant corporations, mass industry, and highly specialized occupations. The cooperation of all family members in a common economic enterprise made for a kinship grouping quite different from that of the modern urban family. Contrary to some impressions, however, the unity of the old style rural family did not rest exclusively on *shared* activities (for example, men's and women's work were sharply segregated) but rather on the fact that the activities of each member were family centered and did not involve potentially disruptive extrafamilial associations.[7]

Eighth, because the nuclear family is the unit and the kinship system is multilineal, American society places relatively little emphasis on family

[5] Freedman, *op. cit.*, pp. 324–325.

[6] Cf. Margaret Mead's statement: "A primary stress upon the husband-wife relationship results in a bilateral kinship-system and a very simple kinship-structure which lacks the continuity of descent-groups . . . the family founded upon the husband-wife relationship is too unstable and discontinuous a form of organization to provide the type of firm structure which is given by social groups based on blood relationship." *Encyclopaedia of the Social Sciences*, Vol. VI (New York: Macmillan, 1931), p. 67.

[7] Cf. William J. Goode, *After Divorce* (New York: Free Press, 1956), p. 93.

tradition and family continuity. Of course the "old society" families of Charleston, South Carolina, or Beacon Hill of Boston, for example, put considerable stress upon lineage and collateral kinship. However, such groups are commonly regarded as so exceptional as to be ready subjects for comment. Among many wealthy, "upper-upper" groups there has developed a marked concern with family continuity and tradition; but they are neither types nor models for the society as a whole. Significantly also, families wishing to emphasize continuity and tradition often have a difficult time doing so. A thriving business is done in ferreting out genealogies, tracing descent from notable persons, discovering (or inventing) coats of arms, and so on. One does not need a specialized search for traditions, genealogies, and symbols where these things are a solid part of actual family life. Again, however, continuity is not an all-or-none matter; and some effort to maintain kinship linkages is quite widespread. For example, the retention of considerable symbolic emphasis on kinship is shown by the finding of a study in the Chicago area that 62 percent of children were named after a particular relative, and that only 16 percent did not have any child named for a relative.[8]

Ninth, there is comparatively free choice of mates. In fact, American mate selection is to a considerable extent an application of free competition in the institution of marriage. The unique, detailed system of dating has changed considerably from the "open market" described by Willard Waller for the 1930's,[9] but the independence from kinship controls remains and may have increased. Within certain legal barriers[1] the choice of spouses is purely personal; the kin of the prospective mates have no right to interfere. Parents are usually asked to sanction the marriage choice, but this convention is residual. The free choice of mates is made possible by the autonomy of the marriage unit. The married pair do not have to fit into an established kinship unit with consequent important and complex repercussions upon many other individuals. This autonomy in turn rests upon geographic and occupational mobility. Arranged marriages typify social systems where the new couple will reside near one or both of the in-law families, maintaining intimate association with a continuous and extended kinship group; a marriage is a sort of treaty between groups, as well as a personal contract between individuals.

*Social systems in which a considerable number of individuals are in a complex and delicate state of mutual interdependence tend greatly to limit the scope for personal emotional feeling or, at least, its direct expression in action. Any considerable range of affective spontaneity would tend to impinge on the statuses and interests of too many others, with disequilibrating consequences*

[8] Alice S. Rossi, "Naming Children in Middle-Class Families," *American Sociological Review*, 30, 4 (August 1965), 503.

[9] Willard Waller, "The Rating and Dating Complex," *American Sociological Review*, 2, 5 (October 1937), 727–737.

[1] The most important legal barriers concern "race," degree of consanguinity, age, and physical or mental health. Thirty-one states require a physical examination; twenty-five have a waiting period.

*for the system as a whole. This need to limit affective spontaneity is, fundamentally, why arranged marriages tend to be found in kinship systems where the newly married couple is incorporated into a larger kin group.*[2]

The individualistic system of mate choice is favored by the autonomous conjugal unit, the discontinuity of generations, the deemphasis of kinship, and the extensive geographic and social mobility found in American society.

Either a matrilocal or a patrilocal rule of residence concentrates a solidary kin group into which new nuclear families must be incorporated. As the wider kin-group preponderates, marriages tend to become arranged unions serving group interests rather than personal affinity alone.[3] Our own "neo-local" system of residence in which a new household is located independently of either family of orientation frees mate choice from many restraints of the locality-kin grouping and at the same time works toward bilateral descent.[4]

Geographic immobility is a massive factor affecting the total character of a kinship system. When each party comes to the marriage with a close-knit circle of friends and relatives who have long lived in association and who realistically expect to do so in the future, the marriage has to fit into social networks already firmly established.[5] Prior relations of kinship and friendship involve strong emotional ties, reciprocal relations of support and exchange, and interlocking agreements upon social norms. The obvious path of least resistance (and least disruption) is for the new marriage to be, in effect, negotiated, and for husband and wife to maintain the segregated (although somewhat overlapping) circles of associates that they had before marriage. Both geographic and social mobility tend to reduce the support and constraint of a closed social network, thereby affecting mate choice, sex-role segregation, child rearing, and many other aspects of family structure and process.

Tenth, linked to the father-mother-children unit and free marriage-choice is the tendency for adult children to disperse from the parental household. This geographic dispersion of children has reached extraordinary breadth in America.[6] As we shall see later, it is directly tied up with vertical mobility between social classes.

Briefly, then, these are the main structural features of the dominant kin-

---

[2] Parsons, *op. cit.*, p. 30.

[3] Mandelbaum, *op. cit.*

[4] Murdock, *op. cit.*, p. 209; "The final result of neolocal residence is thus always bilateral descent."

[5] Elizabeth Bott, *Family and Social Network* (London: Tavistock Publications, 1957). This study demonstrates that tight social controls and extended kinship-relations exist in an industrial setting in one of the largest cities in the world.

[6] Cf. Linton, "The Natural History of the Family," in Ruth Anshen (ed.), *The Family* p. 45. "The outstanding feature of this [the current family] situation is the almost complete breakdown of the consanguine family as a functional unit. . . . This breakdown seems to be directly correlated with the increased opportunities for both spatial and social mobility which have been created by the current technological revolution."

ship system in the United States. The interrelations of these features warrant further examination.

Already it seems clear that the major rules of kinship and marriage do not constitute a mere aggregate of separate, discrete norms. On the contrary, the rules of marriage, descent, residence, division of authority and obligations, and inheritance are systematically related to one another in such a way that a change in any major set of norms is likely to result in changes in others. Indeed, kinship systems are sufficiently determinate that some conceivable combinations of rules never, or only very rarely, occur. For example, there is no known instance of a society in which there is patrilineal transmission of authority but matrilocal residence at marriage: this conceivable combination raises so many practical difficulties that no permanent system of this kind can be found.[7]

A kinship system is a set of interdependent social relationships involving strong interests and emotions, urgent problems of authority and order, and many reciprocal bonds of dependence and support. Its internal organization is not likely to be capricious or haphazard. Evidence from many societies shows great regularity even in kinship arrangements that may seem exotic and inexplicable at first glance. Thus, as George C. Homans and David Schneider have shown, in societies that have only one preferred or favored form of cross-cousin marriage (for example, marriage of a male Ego with father's sister's daughter, or with mother's brother's daughter), the opposing systems go along with different systems of familial authority. When Ego before marriage is primarily disciplined by the father or other older males of the father's lineage, cross-cousin marriage is almost always with mother's brother's daughter. When jural authority over Ego is vested in mother's brother or mother's brother's lineage, cross-cousin marriage tends to be with father's sister's daughter. To take one other example, in the overwhelming majority of societies for which we have adequate data, the roles of father and mother are functionally different; and it is the father who is primarily responsible for the instrumental and executive tasks that relate the family to the larger social environment.[8]

As an obvious consequence of the prohibition of intermarriage among members of the nuclear family there is created a division between what W. Lloyd Warner has usefully termed the family of orientation and the family of procreation. The family of orientation is the family of father, mother, brothers, and sisters into which a given individual, Ego, is born; the family of procreation is established by Ego's marriage and consists of his spouse, sons and daughters. Ego is the only common member of the two families; and in the American case each member of the two families is typically linked by marriage to one other previously unrelated nuclear family. Thus, the two families typically link outward to as many previously

[7] See George C. Homans and David M. Schneider, *Marriage, Authority, and Final Causes* (New York: Free Press, 1955), pp. 53–55.
[8] Morris Zelditch, Jr., "Role Differentiation in the Nuclear Family: A Comparative Study," in Talcott Parsons and Robert F. Bales, *Family, Socialization and Interaction Process* (New York: Free Press, 1955), pp. 307–352.

unrelated families as there are individuals who marry, and this widening web extends backward and forward indefinitely. The end result is a kinship system structured on an "onion" principle, with successive "layers" arranged symmetrically around the two nuclear families at the center.

Thus, the core of the kinship system from any given individual's point of view consists of the seven kinship positions of father, mother, brother, sister, spouse, son and daughter. Each of these positions is specifically distinguished from any relatives outside the two nuclear families—a situation radically different from any kind of clan system. As one looks backward in time, the first ascendant layer beyond this central core consists of the families of orientation of Ego's parents, his grandfathers, grandmothers, uncles, and aunts. Except for the patrilineal inheritance of the family name, no further terminological distinctions are made within this group of kinsmen. Looking forward the same principles apply: in the first descendant families (those established by Ego's children) children's spouses are assimilated to the status of son or daughter, as the case may be, and the offspring are simply grandchildren. The same undifferentiated symmetry holds for the first collateral families established by Ego's brothers and sisters; both terminologically and in social fact they are not differentiated by the sex of the sibling or of Ego, and the children of these families are impartially nephews and nieces.

In the fully developed case, therefore, the main structure of the American system is found in these six types of interrelated nuclear units: Ego's family of orientation, his family of procreation, his in-law family, and the first ascendant, descendant, and collateral units. Within this structure, the three major bases of classification utilized are sex, generation, and affinity (relationship through marriage). Beyond this inner circle of relations, there is only the undifferentiated collateral category of "cousins," without distinction by sex or line of descent, and the successive ascendant and descendant relatives distinguished only as "great-grandfather," "great-great-grandfather," and so on. In both the ascendant and the collateral directions the socially effective relations tend to fade out rather quickly.

Thus, there are forces in the system that tend to place special importance upon the nuclear family unit and to isolate it from an extended kinship grouping and, therefore, to make the marriage bond the keystone of kinship structure. A series of further consequences and implications follow from the interrelated structural characteristics already outlined. For example, the social isolation of the nuclear family is reinforced to the extent that there is an effective norm against discussing marital or family problems with relatives or friends. Apparently, this kind of barrier against revealing family secrets to others is fairly common among middle-income strata. It may be much less frequent in lower-income families. One study of blue-collar marriages suggests that wives in particular often discuss their problems with friends and relatives and appear to receive considerable help and support in so doing.[9]

Quite clearly, there are great variations within our society in the degree

---

[9] Komarovsky, *op. cit.*, p. 10. For other data on lower-class families, see Rainwater, *op. cit.*

to which nuclear family units are freestanding or embedded in a network of solidary kin-relations. We have seen that there are many indications of autonomy of nuclear units. Yet, the accumulated research of recent years leaves no doubt that certain kinds of extended kinship relations continue to be pervasive in urban America; indeed, improved transportation and communication may actually have led to some increased interaction among some types of relatives. Patterns of communication, visiting, family gatherings, and various kinds of influence, support, and aid are widespread and intensive enough to show that the kinship system is not merely a collection of completely self-contained nuclear families.[1] This fact requires close examination.

## EXTENDED KINSHIP RELATIONS

Kinship systems vary dramatically in the structural place of the nuclear family. It is useful to think in terms of four generic types: (1) traditional extended family systems (China, the Balkans); (2) modified extended kinship structures; (3) isolated nuclear family systems; (4) weak or dissolving nuclear families.[2] In the most highly developed systems, the newly formed nuclear families are subordinate units within large households, highly dependent upon the superior unit economically and socially. At the other extreme, isolated nuclear families lack any external social support from kinsmen and show high rates of dissolution. Between these extreme forms are two main types. In one—the modified extended family system—kin-related nuclear families maintain considerable interaction and carry out substantial exchanges of gifts, services, and other scarce values but at the same time retain separate residences and a high degree of autonomy. In the other intermediate type, the nuclear units have relatively few interactions or exchanges with kin-related families but nevertheless maintain themselves and carry out a continuing series of important group activities. Both in the recent literature of family sociology and in the sometimes acrimonious discussions of policy concerning public assistance to families much disagreement has been revealed concerning the actual importance of these four types.

The evidence indicates that the relatively autonomous but stable nuclear family is both the normative ideal and the most common form, with the modified extended-kin network closely following. The really strong and self-sufficing extended family units are exceedingly rare; even the small proportion of joint households are not really "extended families" in the classic sense. On the other hand, in spite of a comparatively high divorce rate, most nuclear families do survive until broken by the death of one spouse. The

[1] See Marvin B. Sussman and Lee Burchinal, "Kin Family Network: Unheralded Structure in Current Conceptualizations of Family Functioning," *Marriage and Family Living*, 24, 3 (August 1962), 231–240.

[2] Eugene Litwak, "Extended Kin Relations in an Industrial Democratic Society," in Ethel Shanas and Gordon F. Streib (eds.), *Social Structure and the Family: Generational Relations* (Englewood Cliffs, N.J.: Prentice-Hall, 1965), pp. 290–291.

most numerous type of nuclear family maintains a moderately active kinship net of interactions—mostly between households of parents and children and among households of siblings—and is able to give or receive some financial aid or services in high-priority situations such as illness, accident, fire, legal trouble, getting jobs, residential moves, sending children to college.

From all the vast, if diffuse, evidence available on variations in kinship and family arrangements in many societies, past and present, it seems quite clear that it is useful to regard most of the known instances as constituting definite social subsystems. This means that both the kinship norms and the prevailing practices are relatively enduring, interconnected, and sufficiently autonomous to maintain a boundary against environmental changes. There is an internal causal network that results in some constancy of internal states even though conditions affecting the system change; and this in turn means that there are feed-back mechanisms that maintain within a range of variation these relatively stable features. Thus, monogamous marriage and relatively autonomous nuclear family units have been prominent continuing features of American society from its beginnings. Beyond question, these structures have been exposed to severe strains as a consequence of changes in other aspects of kinship and in the environing social structure.[3] Yet these particular marriage and family forms have not given way to polygamy, extended families, communal child rearing, or any of many other conceivable alternatives.

Family organization is reciprocally related to the involvement of family members in interaction *outside* the family unit, that is, the internal structure is partly determined by the external relationships and, in turn, helps to determine those relationships. More specifically, the involvement of spouses in separate, tightly knit interaction networks outside the nuclear family tends to be associated with segregated and traditionalized sex roles within the family unit. Furthermore, such external involvement produces a tendency for wives (and probably husbands as well) to rely on friends and relatives for primary group support and to deemphasize the affective-companionate aspects of marriage.[4] It appears that both the frequency of extrafamily interaction and the open or closed character of the social networks are weighty factors affecting the internal structure and functioning of the nuclear kinship units.

The inconclusiveness of much discussion of the modified extended family versus the isolated nuclear family has derived simply from the lack of clear reference to an ordered set of defining characteristics. It seems likely (and it would be quite feasible to test the idea) that there is a single dimension of structural extendedness that includes some such pattern as the following:

[3] Murdock (*op. cit.*, p. 32) found in his sample of 187 societies for which acceptable data could be compiled that only 24 or 13 percent were characterized by monogamous, independent-nuclear families.

[4] See data and references given in Joel I. Nelson, "Clique Contacts and Family Orientations," *American Sociological Review*, 31, 5 (October 1966), 663–672.

## Connections Among Nuclear Units

| Structural Type | SIMPLE AWARENESS | RITUAL GESTURES OF SOLIDARITY | FREQUENT INTERACTION | SUBSTANTIAL ECONOMIC AID | RECIPROCAL SERVICES | NEAR DWELLING | COMMON RESIDENCE |
|---|---|---|---|---|---|---|---|
| ISOLATED | X | | | | | | |
| QUASI-ISOLATED | X | X | | | | | |
| LINKED AUTONOMY | X | X | X | | | | |
| MODIFIED EXTENDED TYPE I | X | X | X | X | | | |
| MODIFIED EXTENDED TYPE II | X | X | X | X | X | | |
| KIN-NEIGHBORHOOD SOLIDARITY | X | X | X | X | X | X | |
| JOINT OR CORPORATE EXTENDED UNIT | X | X | X | X | X | X | X |

The classic types of extended families, although varying in many ways, have in common the characteristics of joint households or near dwelling, strong authority over subordinate nuclear families, occupational nepotism, and, frequently, close cooperation or coordination in work and economic dealings. Families of this kind are, indeed, difficult to maintain under conditions of industrialized and commercialized urban life, with high mobility both geographically and occupationally. However, extended kinship-relationships of a modified kind open up other possibilities. A series of two or more nuclear families may be linked together by relatively frequent communication and by mutual or unilateral aid.[5] Such a familial network often can mobilize greater financial resources and a more extended and effective system of communication than a nuclear family standing alone.[6] Under present-day conditions of relatively easy and inexpensive communication and transportation, such linked families also can maintain fairly strong sentiments of solidarity and a sense of common membership and (limited) obligations. The organization of such linkages appears to be loose and relaxed but capable of mobilization to meet unusual or emergency needs of member units. Arrangements of this kind need not retard occupational or geographic mobility and may actually facilitate them.

Although the available data leave much to be desired, they suggest that the larger and more intensive extended networks are found in certain ethnic or religious groupings[7] (for example, Italian-Americans, Jews of East European Orthodox backgrounds, Protestant whites from the Appalachians), in some upper-class lineages, and in rural areas that retain considerable geographic clustering of kinsmen.

Under the conditions of life in most human societies before the days of modern science and medicine and high material productivity, death rates were high. Infants were subject to enormous mortality, as were many weakened, disabled, or over-strained individuals. Under such conditions, orphans were frequent; and many elderly persons could not survive without close care. There were no adequate hospitals or nursing homes, and governmental and private philanthropic care frequently was almost entirely lacking. Impersonal systems of effective insurance for the overwhelming bulk of the population were unknown.

Under these circumstances, an extended family and strong kinship system were important survival aids. Even in modern India there is evidence that the probability of survival for any member of a family is closely correlated with the survival of other members. More than half of the marriages are broken by the death of the husband or wife before the wife reaches the age

[5] Eugene Litwak, "Geographic Mobility and Extended Family Cohesion," *American Sociological Review*, 25, 3 (June 1960), 385–394, and "Occupational Mobility and Extended Family Cohesion," *American Sociological Review*, 25, 1 (February 1960), 9–21.

[6] Michael Young and Peter Willmott, *Family and Kinship in East London* (London: Routledge and Kegan Paul, 1957).

[7] See Nathan Glazer and Daniel Patrick Moynihan, *Beyond the Melting Pot* (Cambridge, Mass.: The M.I.T. Press, 1964); Milton M. Gordon, *Assimilation in American Life* (New York: Oxford University Press, 1964).

of forty-five.[8] Massive disruption of extended kinship ties through rapid industrialization and urban growth is especially marked in a context of individual social mobility and an individualistic value system. When such disruption is abrupt and pervasive, it necessarily leads to instability of the nuclear family itself. As a society reaches an advanced stage of urbanism and industrial and commercial development, forces tending to reintegrate a modified kinship system come into play, for example, relatively quick and easy transportation and communication, increased importance of affectional interdependence, and the reduced disadvantages and constraints of remaining kinship ties—ties that are now more equalitarian, relaxed, flexible, and optional. The kinship network remains highly open and dispersed—it is a federation of allied nuclear families rather than a tightly organized consanguine system—but the extreme isolation and fragmentation of the transitional generations is reduced.[9]

Because of the historical coexistence of industrialism and the small, nuclear family system in Western Europe and the United States, it has been assumed by many observers that industrialism produces (or requires) such a family system. As comparative evidence has been analyzed, it has become plain that nuclear family systems can exist in nonindustrial societies and that industrial societies can operate without extreme development of the nuclear family system.[1] The causal hypothesis that remains is much more modest than earlier claims; it asserts only that (1) an industrial system tends to favor universalism and specificity in performance, and geographic and social mobility of individuals; (2) these conditions are less easily met by rigid extended kin groups than by smaller and more flexible units; hence (3) industrialism favors a reduction in the scope of solidarity kinship units, approaching the nuclear family.

Even if nuclear families were completely separated from any frequent direct contact with relatives, this would not necessarily mean that such families were socially isolated. Although little systematic information is available, there are many interesting indications that functional analogues to extended-kin relations have developed to some extent. The pattern of baby-sitting generally involves local girls or women who are regarded as trustworthy, and this probably means that the relationship is more than strictly commercial; it is likely that the baby-sitter often is a member of a family with whom ties of at least mild friendship or regular acquaintance have been established. Perhaps more important is the existence of cliques or networks of unrelated nuclear families who establish relationships of mutual trust, aid, and support; many of these relationships seem to have a quasi-kinship character, even to the extent of mutual use of kinship terms ("cousin," "sis," "uncle").

Diagnoses of changes in American kinship patterns and family norms and behavior have been tempered and refined in recent years by more com-

[8] Andrew Collver, "The Family Cycle in India and the United States," *American Sociological Review*, 28, 1 (February 1963), 86–96.

[9] Wilbert E. Moore, *Social Change* (Englewood Cliffs, N.J.: Prentice-Hall, 1963), p. 107.

[1] Sidney M. Greenfield, "Industrialization and the Family in Sociological Theory," *American Journal of Sociology*, LXVII, 3 (November 1961), 312–322.

plete data on the current situation and by better cross-cultural and historical analyses. As these materials have been assimilated, it has become clearer that the American family system today does not differ so radically as sometimes depicted from its forms in the nineteenth century[2] and that many non-Western systems have much in common with our own.[3] Further, the relative autonomy of the family system from many gross changes in other institutions, for example, industrialization, is now more clearly seen, as is the part that can be played in turn by familial institutions in influencing other parts of the social order, for example, permissive child-rearing and occupational mobility. Evidences from other urbanized Western societies point to the retention of kinship ties to a marked degree through prolonged experiences of rapid social change.[4]

Geographic mobility is a fundamental influence upon kinship relations, even given the ease of long-distance telephoning and the speed of automobile travel. Extended kinship relationships may be expected to be most active either when kinsmen live in close proximity or when they are wealthy enough to be able to disregard the costs of frequent visits or other communications. The extent to which kinship networks are subject to possible influence from mobility varies greatly among different income strata and specific occupations. Especially influential in accenting the nuclear family and deemphasizing other kinship ties is likely to be the high rate of relatively long-range mobility among professional, technical, and kindred workers.[5]

In summary then we find that:

1. Married couples maintain their own separate households; in 1960, this was true in 97.8 percent of the cases.[6]
2. Obligations to the nuclear family typically take precedence over claims of other kinship relations.
3. But, most nuclear families do maintain relations with an extended set of kinsmen, through visiting, mutual or unilateral economic aid, and exchange of other types of help and support.
4. The amount of contact among relatives varies directly with the closeness of the relationship and the closeness of geographic location of the units.
5. No extended kinship unit acts as a unit of economic sharing and social solidarity to anything like the same degree as the nuclear family.

Thus, we may say that the system is one with an important degree of kin relatedness, centered upon links among relatively autonomous nuclear-

[2] Frank F. Furstenberg, Jr., "Industrialization and the American Family," *American Sociological Review*, 31, 3 (June 1966), 326–337.

[3] W. J. Goode, *op. cit.*

[4] See K. Ishwaran, *Family Life in the Netherlands* (The Hague: Van Kevlen, 1959); Johan Goudsblom, *Dutch Society* (New York: Random House, 1967).

[5] James D. Tarver, "Occupational Migration Differentials," *Social Forces*, 43, 2 (December 1964), 231–241.

[6] United States Bureau of the Census, *United States Census of Population: 1960*, Vol. I, *Characteristics of the Population*, Part I, United States Summary, Table 79 (Washington, D.C.: Government Printing Office, 1961).

family households. This relative independence is connected with certain equalities in kinship and marriage relations.

## PATTERNS OF EQUALITY

### In-Law Families

First, the autonomy of the nuclear family not only makes loyalty to that unit more important than loyalty to in-laws, but it also tends to place both in-law families in the same relation to the married couple.

> *The strong emphasis for ego as an adult on the marriage relationship at the expense of those to parents and siblings is directly correlative with the symmetrical multilineality of the system. From the point of view of the marriage pair, that is, neither family of orientation, particularly neither parental couple, has structurally sanctioned priority of status. It is thus in a sense a balance of power situation in which independence of the family of procreation is favored by the necessity of maintaining impartiality as between the two families of orientation.*[7]

The husband's family has no superiority—of authority, for instance, over the conjugal unit—nor does either line have a clearly preferred claim to distribution of gifts, favors, visiting time, and other evidences of concern, respect, or affection. Just as parents are not supposed to show favoritism to any particular one of their children and are supposed to show the same regard for the latter's spouses as for the children themselves, so the married children in their turn are not expected to discriminate in favor of either the husband's or wife's family. When a husband or wife insists upon ignoring the wife's (husband's) family, there will probably be tangible social repercussions.

### Sibling Equalities

A second equality is that of siblings in inheriting property and enjoying parental favor.[8] American law generally makes siblings equal heirs to intestate property.[9] A parent may favor one child rather than another; but if

---

[7] Parsons, *op. cit.*, p. 30.

[8] One may be allowed to suspect that in many kin groups in all cultures there is a strong pressure in actual personal-social relations toward equality of parental affection and concern for the children. Sibling jealousy, protests against "favoritism," and demands for equality of placement in the immediate family group are by no means confined to the United States. The point here, however, is that this may or may not be institutionalized, in the sense of general social sanction of equality or of birth-order preference, and that the fact of institutional sanction or the lack of it makes an important difference in what does happen in fact.

[9] A good example is supplied by the inheritance law of New York State, which contains the following provisions. "The real property of a deceased person, male or female, not devised, shall descend, and the surplus of his or her personal property, after payment of debts and legacies, and if not bequeathed, shall be distributed to the surviving spouse, children, or next of kin or other persons, in manner following:

1) One third part to the surviving spouse, and the residue in equal portions to the children, *and such persons as legally represent the children if any of them have died before the deceased.* (Italics added)

the parent actually makes a very unequal bequest, except under very special circumstances, the action is likely to seem arbitrary. This fact alone tells us that there is no generally approved principle of inequality.

In spite of considerable divergence among subgroups, in American society as a whole parents are expected to treat their children impartially in other ways. Neither sex nor age sanctions unequal affection. Of course, duties and privileges differ with sex and age, but only as formal requirements for adapting the child to the general age-sex patterns of the larger society, and are not considered to represent favoritism. The very fact that favoritism is disapproved shows the acceptance of impartiality as a norm. Furthermore, parents are expected to accept their children's spouses without discrimination. Thus, children-in-law are assimilated to the family pattern of symmetrical equality.

### Husband-Wife Equalities

Both of the features just described relate to the statuses of the husband and wife. The impartial treatment of in-law families is favored by the equality of husband and wife, which rests partly on the isolation of the nuclear family; both of these facts foster equality of status between respective in-law families. This equality leaves the ties of the nuclear families to be determined by the detailed variations of particular situations. The pattern of in-law equality is the favored resolution of the bargaining possibilities. The structural bipolarity probably results in continuing pressures for reciprocities. Thus, one study has shown that in the naming of children the tendency in the most recent years has been toward a decrease in the linkage of sons to paternal relatives and of daughters to mothers' kin. In short, the changes in the naming pattern suggest that "while a structural symmetry has long existed between the nuclear family's two families of origin, an affective social symmetry between them is only now in the making."[1]

Of course, equality is only relative or comparative. There is not exact equality, and certainly not identity, of rights and duties. Many current discussions of the "democratic" American family suggest that all family members are almost completely equal in capacities, rights, and duties. But obviously an infant is not "equal" in these respects to the parent who cares for and disciplines him. Family statuses differ and have different values. Family organization must have some division of labor and differentiation of authority among the various members so long as any coherent group exists at all. Nevertheless, institutionalized rights and obligations are differently distributed among the pivotal family statuses in different societies and are differently valued. For instance, the formal authority of the father

---

8) Where the distributees of the deceased, entitled to share in his estate, are all in equal degree to the deceased, *their shares shall be equal.* (Italics added)

11) *Relatives of the half-blood shall take equally with those of the whole blood in the same degree.* (Italics added)

14) The right of an adopted child to take a share of the estate and the right of succession to the estate of an adopted child shall continue as provided in the domestic relations law." *New York, Decedent Estate Law, Sec. 83.*

Note that the equality principle is specifically extended to descendants by affinity.

[1] Rossi, *op. cit.*, p. 499.

is certainly no less in contemporary American society than in the European tradition. The wife and mother has correspondingly greater rights in certain respects.[2] These are not accidental variations but rather derive from the basic kinship pattern we have been examining.

## FAMILY STATUSES AND ROLE-PERFORMANCES

### The Roles of Women and Men

As the marriage pair, rather than a more extended family unit, becomes the crucial link in the kinship system, the roles of husband and wife become correspondingly separated from wider kinship-rights and obligations. Neither partner has immediate recourse to a solidary group of kinsmen. Their relative isolation, especially in a mobile and competitive society, tends to concentrate into the marriage relationship the partners' emotional needs for security and affection. This situation in itself tends toward husband-wife equality. For these needs are not easily met except on a basis of intimate congeniality that is difficult to achieve in formally inequalitarian relationships. The equality of spouses is clearly encouraged also by the lack of strong priority of either line of descent. (Note that we are still speaking of norms —social prescriptions—not of psychological states of dominance and submission and the like. Even under commonly accepted norms of equality, the henpecked husband and the masculine autocrat of the breakfast table are familiar figures.)

Since husband and wife constitute what is in several ways the most basic solidary group in the kinship order, they must, partly because of peculiar features of the social stratification system,[3] be treated by the wider community as a unit and thus as social equals in important respects. Were this not the institutional pattern, ordinary social intercourse between the individual family and outside groups would certainly put such strain upon the marriage bond as to threaten it. It is not a trivial matter of mere convention or manners that in the typical middle class, urban community, if either spouse is invited to a mixed social gathering, the other spouse must be likewise invited. For any aggregate of persons becomes a real social group only by being identified as a unit, by sharing a common set of experiences, and hence by sharing a common universe of meanings and symbols.[4] This kind of solidarity is, of course, quite compatible with marked differentiation of sex roles and with inequalitarian husband-wife relationships; but once we are given a kinship system of dispersed, multilineal nature built around

---

[2] For the historical legal background see, for example: Chester G. Vernier and John B. Hurlbut, *American Family Laws: Husband and Wife*, Vol. III (Stanford, Calif.: Stanford University Press, 1935). Beyond the minimal legal framework, important variations and ambiguities in norms and beliefs concerning parenthood are brought out in sharp outline by common responses to adoptive parents and children. See H. David Kirk, *Shared Fate* (New York: Free Press, 1964).

[3] See Chapter V.

[4] Another indicator of kinship solidarity is the prevalence of various types of family reunions: Millicent R. Ayoub, "The Family Reunion," *Ethnology*, 5, 4 (October 1966), 415–433.

the marriage bond, the pressures to treat the nuclear family as the primary unit are bound to work toward equalities between husband and wife. And still other social conditions, external to the husband-wife relation itself, affect the roles of husband and wife. Sharp segregation of role activities within the family probably will be found to be at a maximum when there is a combination of low physical mobility, low social mobility, extended kinship connections in the area of residence, high birth rates, and certain types of occupational demands upon the husband. When each of the married partners brings to the marriage a previously established set of social relationships with a tight knit social circle of friends and relatives, the roles of husband and wife probably will tend to be clearly segregated, at least when both of the antenuptial social circles remain highly accessible, supportive, and demanding.[5]

The much-discussed emancipation of women in Western societies often is presented in an exaggerated and distorted way. Thus, the percentage of women employed for pay outside the home sometimes appears to be cited as if it constituted evidence of sex equality or feminine emancipation. In point of fact, from the very beginning of the Industrial Revolution, most women who worked for pay did so as a matter of economic necessity; it was only the middle- and upper-class women who were confined to the home in the Victorian sense.[6] In the United States, nearly a century of change and agitation culminated in the emancipated American woman of the 1920's.[7] Since that time, no clear unilinear trend toward further emancipation has existed. Although the proportion of women in the labor force has increased, few women are in the most prestigious and highest-paid occupations in business and the professions. Yet there is no doubt that women in the United States have a relatively great amount of freedom. The disappearance of formalized chaperonage is in itself an important indication of emancipation. Our statutory laws have greatly modified the older common law conceptions in the direction of equalizing the formal rights of husband and wife. The modifications did not come without effort, and they involved strong sentiments, values, and vested interests. Thus, the first nineteenth-century movements to secure new legal and economic rights for women (usually dated from the 1848 Seneca Falls Conference) had close connections with the abolitionist movement. (Some of the parallels between inferior ascribed status based on race and that based on sex were perceived at an early stage.) Similarly, later resistance to the claims of women for the right to vote was strong, organized, uncompromising, often bitter, and prolonged.[8]

Eventually, however, the legal autonomy of women in most areas of life

[5] For illustrative data see Bott, who has suggested that "The degree of segregation in the role-relationship of husband and wife varies directly with the connectedness of the family's social network" (*op. cit.*, p. 60).

[6] Viola Klein, *Britain's Married Women Workers* (New York: Humanities Press, 1965).

[7] Carl N. Degler, "Revolution Without Ideology: The Changing Place of Women in America," *Daedalus*, 93, 2 (Spring 1964), 653–670.

[8] See the vivid documentation in Eleanor Flexner, *Century of Struggle: The Women's Rights Movement in the United States* (Cambridge, Mass.: Belknap Press, 1959).

was established. Married women came to have the capacity to make contracts, own property, make wills, and sue or be sued in their own right. Some court decisions now even affirm that the husband and wife may sue each other. The legal status of such husband-wife suits is still confused and ambiguous; but they mark a radical move not only toward equality of rights in law but also toward an individualization (atomization) of the legal structure of the family.

Besides legal rights, American wives hold a remarkable set of customary or conventional intrafamilial rights that, although perhaps less rigid and explicit, are hardly less common or less important socially and psychologically.

Conceptions of the behavior appropriate for married women vary greatly among socioeconomic strata. In general, the upper and middle strata are more likely to accept and approve individualized and equalitarian patterns—economic independence, careers, active participation in civic and political affairs,[9] and a relatively high degree of personal autonomy. Not even in theory is the wife expected to render unquestioning obedience to her husband, much less in actual practice. The marriage relationship most commonly held up as a model is one in which joint decisions are reached. It remains true that general consensus still holds that the husband should be head of the house; but it is felt that only in rare circumstances will patriarchal rather than democratic processes be desirable.

Many discussions of the position of women in our social order have failed to make certain essential distinctions. Probably the most frequent and important source of confusion is failure to distinguish among the *evaluation of women as persons*, the *legal rights* of women, and the *role performances actually expected of women*. It is possible to have a society in which women are highly valued yet do not share many of the formal rights exercised by men or play masculine roles. In early America, for example, women did not lack a place of high honor and esteem, although they were confined to distinctly feminine roles and were without many legal rights that have been since acquired. Similarly, formal equality of legal rights turns out to be a question-begging term unless distinguished from the broader patterns of sex status. Thus, the failure of the husband to provide economic support for the wife is a criminal or quasi-criminal offense nearly everywhere in this society. Under a principle of strict equality, the wife would bear a corresponding obligation; and seventeen jurisdictions have specified that the wife is required to support the husband under certain circumstances. Nevertheless, that the law presupposes differential sex-roles is clearly demonstrated by the legal status of alimony, which generally is still considered to be a continuation of the husband's obligation to support the wife, an assumption that obviously does not correspond to the facts in a great many contemporary divorce cases.[1]

---

[9] E.g., Carol Slater, "Class Differences in Definition of Role and Membership in Voluntary Associations Among Urban Married Women," *American Journal of Sociology*, LXV, 6 (May 1960), 616–619.

[1] Vernier and Duniway, *American Family Laws: Divorce and Separation*, Vol. II, *op. cit.*, pp. 259 ff.

Probably the most obvious change in the general social position of women has been a shift of expected and accepted feminine behavior in the masculine direction. Some specific evidences may be briefly enumerated:

1. *Legal rights:* women vote, hold public office, practice professions, hold and dispose of property.
2. *Occupational role:* women participate in paid work outside the home on a large scale: they have entered traditionally male occupations.
3. *Educational participation:* there are coeducational school systems, colleges, and universities; graduate studies are open to women.
4. *Recreational patterns:* women participate in active sports, patronize drinking places.
5. *Courtship behavior:* women have a kind and degree of freedom and initiative in courtship that was not sanctioned before.
6. *Symbolic evidences:* women emulate men's clothes in their slacks, tailored suits.

Perspective on this well-known set of facts may be gained by recalling the status of women in traditional China where as late as 1919, "in a case arising from a man's selling his wife, the Supreme Court ruled that the 'purchase of a woman for the explicit purpose of begetting children is justifiable and not invalid.' "[2]

Nevertheless, women's role performances remain clearly distinguished in a number of ways. Housekeeping and the care of children are still primary responsibilities of adult women. In 1960, only 31 percent of all married women were reported to be working outside the home. The percentage of all women gainfully employed is nearly twice as great in the Soviet Union as in the United States; about 80 percent of Soviet women between ages twenty and twenty-nine are so employed.[3] In the American case, the percentage of married women in the labor force is highest among younger women, urban women, those with no children under ten years of age, and those whose husbands' incomes are in the lowest brackets. Paid employment (or subsistence upon so-called welfare payments) is no freely chosen luxury for the nearly 12 million women who were sole heads of households in 1966, constituting 20 percent of the total of 58 million households; females headed 26 percent of the nonwhite but only 7 percent of white households.[4]

In the higher income levels, the working wife seldom has a job equal to that of her husband in status or pay. Despite long agitation for the principle of equal pay for equal work, it is difficult to find evidence of husbands and wives competing on an equal basis and in large numbers in precisely the same occupations;[5] when women work in wage-earning oc-

[2] Freedman, *op. cit.*, p. 330.

[3] Norton T. Dodge, *Women in the Soviet Economy; Their Role in Economic, Scientific, and Technical Development* (Baltimore: Johns Hopkins Press, 1966).

[4] United States Bureau of the Census, "Households and Families by Type; 1966," *Current Population Reports*, Series P-20, No. 152 (Washington, D.C.: Government Printing Office, 1966).

[5] The practice of equal pay for women and men in the same jobs has undoubtedly gained

cupations, it is usually out of the presumed necessity of supplementing the husbands' incomes, and the career jobs (white collar, professional, and business) of married women will typically not be in direct competition with men in their husbands' occupation.

Evidences thus abound of the persistence, well into the second half of the twentieth century, of traditional, family centered behavior of American women.[6] Although the proportion of women working for pay outside the home has increased, the proportion in professional and technical occupations has not increased over the last generation. In education the proportion of higher degrees awarded to women has not increased since the termination of upward trends around 1930. In the United States, 6 percent of physicians are women; in the U.S.S.R., the figure is 75 percent. Of the professional staffs in institutions of higher education in the U.S.S.R., 47 percent are women; in the U.S.A. only 20 percent. The proportion of women teachers in colleges and universities is declining; actually the peak in the proportion of the faculties who were women was reached in the year 1879.[7] Women constitute just 8 percent of persons enumerated in the National Register of Scientific and Technical Personnel.

Much of recent discussion of women's roles appears to be dealing with the problems of the last generation, not this one. The problem of the working wife, for instance, is no longer a major issue in most families. It is now widely taken for granted that married women will work for pay outside the home if necessary, for example, to supplement the family income, to use special training in the period before children arrive, to fill the days usefully after the children no longer require continual care. The question has shifted from whether wives or mothers should be in the labor market at all to when, how, and under what specific circumstances such employment is justified or desirable. Although only a minority of women work, the crucial point is that the opportunity exists and, hence, the possibility of choice.

Married women are now generally entitled by law to their earnings for services rendered to third parties outside the household. Nevertheless, "In the main, the courts have jealously guarded the right of the husband to the wife's services in the household. Even in jurisdictions in which the spouses may freely contract *inter se*, the wife cannot contract for services to which the husband is entitled as implied in the marital relation."[8] Furthermore,

ground in recent years, partly under the influence of the industrial labor unions. However, as late as 1933, the comprehensive survey of the President's Research Committee on Social Trends complained that "it is almost impossible to secure wage data for both men and women doing precisely the same tasks, even within the limits of a single occupation." *Recent Social Trends*, Vol. I (New York: McGraw-Hill, 1933), p. 736.

6 Many studies agree that the central orientation of girls in our society is toward marriage, with only a secondary orientation to jobs—and mostly to "feminine" occupations at that. Cf. Hyman Rodman (ed.), *Marriage, Family, and Society* (New York: Random House, 1965), p. 5 and references cited there.

7 For these and other uncommon facts, see Jessie Bernard, *Academic Women* (University Park, Pa.: Pennsylvania State University Press, 1964).

8 Vernier and Hurlbut, *American Family Laws: Husband and Wife, op. cit.*, p. 195. Incidentally, this passage is a tribute to the individuation of the modern family as well as to the persistence of traditional family rights. It is significant that this legal question can ever arise on a scale worthy of comment.

women working in paid jobs outside the home are typically concentrated in occupations most closely allied to traditional homemaking roles: in domestic service, teaching, nursing, laundry service, needle trades, as waitresses, hairdressers, dieticians, social workers, and so on. Because women are employed in the less well paid jobs and because there is a widespread tendency to pay women less than men even within what is essentially the same occupation,[9] the average income of working women is considerably below that of men. Although the ratio has been increasing, in 1959 the median earnings of employed women were still not quite one-half those of men. Clearly women are not employed on the same basis as men, and in times of economic depression there has been a strong tendency to discharge women workers first; in any severe economic crisis there is vigorous agitation to send women back to the home.

Marriage and family still come first for most American women, even though most of them at some time do work for pay outside the home. Although the career woman is an important social type, the percentage of women who follow continuous careers is very small. Few women hold administrative or executive positions; for example, in the field of education only about 8 percent of high school principals are women. Few women attain high political office. And established conceptions of the feminine role exert widespread and powerful influences in many subtle ways. If a woman becomes a doctor, she is likely to specialize in dealing with women and children. If she becomes an electrical engineer, she may be advised (as in an actual case known to the author) to specialize in the design of household appliances. Even the political issues concerning which women have been most active have been closely associated with the traditional feminine functions of nurturance and protection—schools, juvenile delinquency, mental health, protective legislation, child labor, and the like.

In short, even in our "emancipated" society there remain persistent and important pressures tending to preserve the statuses of women as mothers and homemakers. These pressures are neither wholly arbitrary nor a simple matter of social inertia and the survival of traditional prejudice. If women were to compete for jobs on an equal basis with men, drastic changes would be necessary in the family system, or in the occupational structure, or in both. So long as women bear children, who must be cared for and trained during the extended period of dependency, there must be some social arrangement to ensure that the necessary functions are performed. We can imagine a situation in which men, children, and retired elders might take over the major part of child rearing; or, we can conceive of homemaking and child-rearing functions being performed by professional workers operating through new forms of social organization. *Complete* freedom of occupational competition for women would certainly involve one or both of these paths, or the disappearance of stable family units as we know them. At present, the family system is made partly compatible with the employment of many married women by: (1) low birth rates and small families, (2) ex-

[9] A not uncommon practice is to give women and men slightly different specific job-designations even when the actual work is practically identical.

trafamily service agencies providing certain household aids and child care, (3) the tendency not to employ women in jobs that compete with those of men in the same socioeconomic class.

At the same time, however, the family structure does help to establish equality of the sexes and removes many elements of psychological dependency in the feminine role.[1] Feminine roles are, therefore, often not clearly defined; and the fundamental choices that women make are frequently complicated by insecurity, vacillation, and cross-purposes.[2] Parsons has pointed out three broad patterns of adjustment: (1) the "glamor girl" role, which emphasizes personal attractiveness; (2) the "domestic" role, which maintains the older pattern of the wife and mother; (3) the "good companion" role, in which the wife tries to balance the obligations of home and family against her desire to accept wider social responsibilities and participate equally with her husband in many activities.[3] The first pattern is inherently unstable and nonfamilistic. The forces tending towards equality and the cult of individual personality (which is itself reciprocally related to the small-family pattern) militate against the second; so does the great emphasis upon romantic love, even after marriage. Thus the multilineal kinship-system, the small family, and the patterns of free mate choice and romantic love all favor a role for the married woman as an equal partner.

At the same time, as we have seen, there are many restrictions on women's careers outside the home. Since it is largely through success in such careers that an individual's prestige rank is established in our society, many modern women do experience internal conflicts. Their search for an equivalent for the male's occupational role has led to a striking participation in culture (art, literature, and so on), in philanthropic and community-service work, and in many other broadly humane activities. The extraordinary development of women's clubs provides a good illustration of this attempt at deflected achievement. In all this it cannot be forgotten, of course, that the sexes do differ not only biologically but also in many social and psychological characteristics.[4] Abundant evidence shows widespread, marked, and persisting differences between men and women in our society in important values, interests, aspirations, and behavior patterns. The differences are not merely quantitative—for example, that women are less likely to have high occupational aspirations or to be aggressively competitive in games—but extend into complex qualitative differences. Thus, girls and boys about to graduate

---

[1] The new economic bases of family life are of particular importance, especially "the progressive diminution of the economic dependence of spouses upon each other." Ralph Linton, "The Natural History of the Family," in Anshen, *The Family, op. cit.*, p. 47.

[2] Compare the statement by Margaret Redfield (*op. cit.*, p. 182): "Although American women are freer than most other women, they have often not known what to do with their freedom. This seems to come from the fact that beyond the roles of glamor girl and nursemaid, the part to be played by women is vaguely defined in our society."

[3] "Age and Sex in the Social Structure of the United States," *American Sociological Review*, VII, 5 (October 1942), 610–613. There are certainly other patterns, e.g., the unmarried "career woman."

[4] Eleanor E. Maccoby (ed.), *The Development of Sex Differences* (Stanford, Calif.: Stanford University Press, 1966).

from high school show markedly different kinds of aspirations for education and economic success.[5]

Finally, it is important to note that the roles of wives and mothers always imply the roles of husbands and fathers. Men have their problems, too; and there are ambiguities and conflicts in either sex role whenever these complications exist in the other. In longer perspective many of the present problems undoubtedly will turn out to be passing phenomena of transformations in familial and occupational systems. We may be sure, in any case, that for both social and psychological reasons relatively clear and commonly shared definitions of sex-linked roles will be continually sought and often achieved.

### Status and Role Performances of Children

European observers of the American scene seem to be almost universally impressed by the freedom of children in their relations to parents and other adults. They note that at an early age children begin to be treated as individuals who are entitled to be consulted, to state their wishes, to ask the "reason why" for orders or requests.[6] They are struck by the lack of severe authoritarian relations between parents (or teachers) and children and by the way in which children enter into adult conversations and "talk back" to adults. To many observers from other cultures, the urban middle-class child appears to be overly assertive, undisciplined, lacking in respect for his elders —in short, a "spoiled brat." The pervasive emphasis upon freedom of expression for the child is often noted as a further indication of lax discipline.

What do these appraisals suggest about patterns of child-adult relations? There seems to be little doubt that on the whole American children have extraordinary freedom in certain respects and develop, at an early age, patterns of independence that differ from the roles of children in corresponding social and economic classes in nearly all the major cultures of Europe, Asia, and Latin America. It is certain that in the past the ideal patterns for children's roles were more nearly reflected in such maxims as "spare the rod and spoil the child" and "children should be seen and not heard."[7] There are tendencies toward the gratification of children in their wishes—so much so that American sociologists and psychologists can speak seriously of the filiocentric, or child centered, family. Unquestioned obedience is usually not required of children.

This summary appraisal is necessarily oversimplified and couched in advisedly general and qualified terms. There are enormous variations in child-rearing patterns among various classes and subcultures within the United

[5] Ralph H. Turner, "Some Aspects of Women's Ambition," *American Journal of Sociology*, LXX, 13 (November 1964), 271–285.

[6] See, for example, Kurt Lewin, "Some Social-Psychological Differences between the United States and Germany," *Character and Personality*, IV (1936), 265–293.

[7] It is impracticable here to detail the mass of diverse historical evidence bearing on the above statements. Some of the pertinent facts and interpretations may be found in the following references: Anshen (ed.), *The Family*; Bernard, *American Family Behavior*; Arthur W. Calhoun, *A Social History of the American Family* (New York: Barnes and Noble, 1945); Willystine Goodsell, *A History of Marriage and the Family* (New York: Macmillan, 1934); Bernhard Stern, *The Family: Past and Present* (New York: Appleton-Century-Crofts, 1938).

States;[8] there is nothing like complete uniformity in the use of corporal punishment, nor in the kinds of demands made upon the child as to toilet training, punctuality, cleanliness, aggression control, nor in the extent to which parents require affection rather than simple obedience or respect from the child.

Research findings over the past twenty-five years show parents in the middle classes to be consistently more accepting and equalitarian in their child-training practices than are working-class parents.[9] Middle-class parents now tend to combine free emotional expression and tolerance of the child's impulses and needs with high expectations for independence, responsibility, and achievement on the part of the child. Working-class parents more frequently rely on physical punishment; middle-class parents tend to use reasoning, conditional love, and appeals to guilt and other methods that rely on the child's emotional attachment to the parents. In all social classes, there is evidence of greater flexibility in regimes of infant feeding and weaning in the more recent years.

The sheer fact that child-rearing practices do vary with social class is well established, although the reported differences are variable and not always consistently patterned. What has been less often analyzed is the exact nature of the links between class and child-rearing patterns and the parent-child relationships that these patterns partly express. One important linkage is the chain of effects that runs from class position to values to parent-child relationships. Middle-class occupations less often require strict conformity to requirements laid down by persons in positions of authority. In turn, middle-class parents seem to be more likely to regard child rearing as problematic, to seek expert advice and opinion, to discuss the matter. Consistent with the value requirements of their occupational world, middle-class parents tend to cater to the child's emotional and developmental needs and to encourage independence and initiative, whereas working-class parents more often seek obedience and conformity to external standards of overt conduct.[1]

Thus, there do seem to be broad tendencies toward permissive discipline

---

[8] See, for example, Allison Davis, Burleigh B. Gardner, and Mary R. Gardner, *Deep South* (Chicago: University of Chicago Press, 1941); Arnold W. Green, "The Middle Class Child and Neurosis," *American Sociological Review*, 11, 1 (February 1946), 31–41; Martha C. Ericson, "Child-rearing and Social Status," *American Journal of Sociology*, LII, 3 (November 1946), 190–192; Allison Davis and Robert J. Havighurst, "Social Class and Color Differences in Child-rearing," *American Sociological Review*, 11, 6 (December 1946), 698–710; Robert Sears, *et al.*, *Patterns of Child Rearing* (Evanston, Ill.: Row, Peterson, 1957).

[9] An excellent summary of the evidence may be found in Urie Bronfenbrenner, "Socialization and Social Class Through Time and Space," in Eleanor E. Maccoby, Theodore M. Newcomb, Eugene L. Hartley (eds.), *Readings in Social Psychology*, 3rd ed. (New York: Holt, Rinehart and Winston, 1958), pp. 400–425. See also Melvin L. Kohn, "Social Class and the Exercise of Parental Authority," *American Sociological Review*, 24, 3 (June 1959), 352–366.

[1] Melvin L. Kohn, "Social Class and Parent-Child Relationships: An Interpretation," *American Journal of Sociology*, LXVIII, 4 (January 1963), 471–480; Leonard I. Pearlin and Melvin L. Kohn, "Social Class, Occupation and Parental Values: A Cross-National Study," *American Sociological Review*, 31, 4 (August 1966), 466–479.

in certain respects and toward an idealization of childhood in middle-class populations. The sources of these tendencies are very complex indeed and cannot be treated adequately in a work of the present character. In part they stem from the high evaluation of individual personality and from the cultural emphasis upon the future. The confusion of standards of conduct in a complex, heterogeneous, rapidly changing culture and the effect upon the child of subjection to multiple and divergent social authorities in the persons of parents, teachers, social workers, play groups, and so on, both play a part. Furthermore, the urban child cannot easily be directly initiated into the standards of the adult culture, because the occupational and residential patterns do not permit, for example, the social apprenticeship of sons to fathers that occurs so easily in stable agricultural societies. The exact effects of differing socioeconomic contexts upon personality still are largely uncharted. Although studies have shown that there are some correlations between measured personality characteristics of children and the socioeconomic position of their families of origin, the relationships shown by available research are not close.[2]

The segregation of the immediate conjugal family from a wider kinship group probably does have highly significant effects upon the child. Instead of developing diffused emotional ties to a large group of adults, the child must manage his needs for dependence and growth in relation to a few persons—chiefly his father and mother. Parents thus necessarily play a two-sided role in relation to the child, ministering to his wants and gratifying his demands for care, security, and affection but also thwarting him in various ways. Insofar as the nuclear family is the prime socializing group during the early years of life, the inevitable ambivalences of the child toward the agents of socialization are focused upon the parents. This tendency is to some degree offset by play groups, nursery schools, kindergartens, adult neighbors, and friends who play a part in the child's emotional world. At the same time, however, in the American school or play group the child must compete for place and is thus thrown back upon his one ascribed group—the tiny circle of the family—for reassurance and security.[3] Thus, we have the curious fact that as the effective kinship unit has become smaller, the importance of the immediate family has in some respects become enhanced.

As in most other societies, the early socialization of children is largely carried out by the mother; but in urban America, especially in the middle and upper classes, her role tends to bulk larger and to extend to later years of childhood and youth. The father's place in the home often is residual and tends to be heavily encroached upon by the demands of his job.[4] Thus, he

[2] See the judicious summary in William H. Sewell, "Social Class and Childhood Personality," *Sociometry*, 24, 4 (December 1961), 340–356.

[3] This is one of the ways in which parents "capture" the child; note the concept of "personality absorption" suggested by Arnold W. Green, "The Middle Class Male Child and Neurosis," *American Sociological Review*, Vol. 11, 1 (February 1946), 31–41.

[4] The central role of the mother appears to be most marked in the "commuter family," in business and professional families, and in certain unstable family groupings of working-class populations, e.g., the "mother centered" urban Negro family. The father still plays

sometimes must appear to the children as a somewhat harassed man who passes briefly through the home at evening and on weekends and holidays. Since the segregated nuclear family is the emotional center of the child's life, the mother plays a part unlike that of any other adult member of the child's social circle. Her importance to the child is all the greater insofar as the child is expected to love, as well as to obey and respect, his parents. Some writers have contended that because American women are the prime socializing agents for boys as well as girls, the male identifies women with morality, with far-reaching consequences in sexual adjustments, standards of masculinity, and attitudes toward many moral standards.[5] The overweening role of the mother, they suggest, lays the basis for many of the difficulties that plague the male adolescent in his attempt to establish an adult, masculine role. These problems demand additional research;[6] but it does seem clear that the contentions just mentioned are considerably exaggerated: the unresolved Oedipal situation is not unique to the United States nor is there clear evidence that American women are more active and vigilant guardians of the behavior of children than mothers in many other societies. Certainly, the relationships of both father and mother to their children differ profoundly as between sons and daughters. It is a commonplace observation that in our culture there are many similarities in the values parents attempt to develop in boys and girls, for example, independence and social maturity. But there are important differences also. Girls are more likely than boys to emphasize being well liked; to value interpersonal harmony and success; to stress the "tender virtues" of kindness, consideration, sympathy, and understanding; to attach great importance to moral values and aesthetic considerations.[7]

An important hypothesis derives from the idea of socialization by legitimation, that is, the processes in which an adult interprets or translates his reactions to a child's behavior into an explicit abstraction or principle that is communicated to the child. Such general rules or principles furnish the child with a code for interpreting probable adult responses in broad classes of circumstances. If adult behavior is then fairly consistent in terms of such principles of orientation, rapid learning can occur and be reinforced. Children in social environments with minimal development of this mode of socialization must learn complex social patterns by a slow process of encountering particularized angry or otherwise punishing responses in a succession of concrete situations. An important and plausible hypothesis, therefore, is that socialization by legitimation is a necessary condition for development of the capacity for a wide range of complex moral judgments.[8]

a more positive role in much of rural society, in some ethnic groups having a "patriarchical" tradition, and in established upper-class lineages.

[5] Philip Wylie, *Generation of Vipers* (New York: Farrar and Rinehart, 1942).

[6] Geoffrey Gorer, *The American People: A Study in National Character* (New York: Norton, 1948).

[7] Morris Rosenberg, *Society and the Adolescent Self-Image* (Princeton, N.J.: Princeton University Press, 1965).

[8] Cf. Glen H. Elder, Jr., "Parental Power Legitimation and Effects on Adolescents," *Sociometry*, 26, 1 (March 1963), 50–65.

In America there appears also to be relatively great stress upon rational methods of rearing the young. Though most marked in urban and well-educated groups, there is a very general disinclination throughout the society to advocate child-training methods merely on grounds of tradition. Furthermore, American parents seem avidly to seek scientific information and the advice of experts or pseudoexperts; they very often are preoccupied with problems of child rearing;[9] they often show definite signs of uncertainty and insecurity as to how to bring up their offspring. There are a multitude of magazines, bulletins, pamphlets, newspaper articles, columns, and so forth, dealing with how to treat the child; and there is considerable instability in the popularly accepted recommendations in these matters. For example, the bulletin *Infant Care*, published by the United States Children's Bureau, went through ten editions from 1914 to 1955; and 36 million copies were distributed. An analysis of its content from edition to edition shows drastic changes. In 1914, parents were told that masturbation would "wreck" a child for life and were advised to use forcible restraint; thumb-sucking was also to be stopped by mechanical means. By the 1950's, both problems had come to be regarded as petty nuisances that might well be ignored. In recent years, flexibility and permissiveness have been advocated in weaning and toilet training.[1] At some periods, all babies must be fed on rigid schedules; they must be handled as little as possible; they must be allowed to "cry it out;" overprotection and spoiling are avoided with something approaching moral horror. Within a few years, the tenor changes: the despised rocking chair is back in psychiatric favor, mothers are told to indulge their propensities to hold and cuddle the child, rigid schedules for feeding and sleeping are modified in the interest of "fitting the regime to the needs of the child." In short, fads and fashions characterize popularly accepted dictums on child care and training.

Can such variable and subtle patterns be dependent in any way upon the rather gross structural features with which we have just been concerned? We contend that these sociopsychological conditions are in part direct consequences of the structural emphasis upon the marriage bond and thus, upon the isolated conjugal family unit. Of basic importance is the lack of inter-generation continuity resulting from the isolation of the conjugal unit. This isolation is, in turn, largely, although by no means entirely, conditioned by the geographic dispersion of adult children. An extreme case might be that of an urban middle-class family unit of husband, wife, and one child living two thousand miles away from the rest of their kin. Under circumstances like these, which are certainly more or less approximated by millions of American families, the immediate family is almost entirely cut off from authoritative guidance by the older generation. The young mother faces child-training problems as an individual, without that stabilizing continuity of contact with elders and the wider kinship group that has been typical throughout the history of the human race. She is equipped with whatever

[9] Witness the incessant discussion of this topic so typical in middle and lower-upper class urban groups.

[1] Robert R. Sears, Eleanor E. Maccoby, Harry Levin, *et al.*, *Patterns of Child Rearing* (Evanston, Ill.: Row, Peterson, 1957), pp. 9–10.

memories she may have of her own childhood and with her observations of the socialization of other children; but this experience is often inadequate as a guide to the highly specific and pressing problems she confronts in rearing her own children. The father is in a similar, although perhaps even less fully informed position. Both have absorbed something of the general ethos of respect for rationality, practicality, scientific methods; and thus they tend to seize upon the latest pronouncements of the presumed experts in order to gain some sense of dependability and security.

Parental influence upon children may be expected to decrease as the parents' share of all the child's social interactions decreases. *Between some limits*,[2] the less time parents spend in interaction with their children, as compared with the child's exposure to teachers, other adults and peers, the less is likely to be the parents' effectiveness as models and authorities. Further, it is a plausible hypothesis, supported by considerable evidence, that the greater the number and the reward value of the child's alternatives to interaction with parents, the less will be the parents' potential influence. To the degree that parents do not actually control the child's life chances (which may be determined instead by teachers, counsellors, peers, and others), the child, sooner or later, is likely to become aware that crucial sanctioning power lies outside the family. At the same time, if interaction with parents is situationally segregated so that the child fails to experience the parent in a variety of realistic adult roles and settings, the possibility of full identification with the parent as a model for future behavior is likely to be reduced. As parents' and children's activities become segregated, interdependence diminishes, which implies further loss of parental control over interactions and sanctions.

As these interrelated developments occur, the child is rendered dependent upon extrafamilial mentors and models, first, other children or youths; second, sanctioning adults who control avenues of access to desired goals. The child learns that the parents' capacity to intervene at school is severely limited, that the father will not be able to place him in a definite job, that his peers' ability to make daily life miserable or gratifying far exceeds that of his parents.

Thus, both the loss of common participation and of interdependence tend to lead to diminished control and influence. Loss of influence means loss of capacity to set limits, to guide, to help the young person in his or her own efforts to define and gain self-mastery of his own impulses and needs. The child or youth (who *always* will have problems of *desired* self-control) then inevitably will feel "they cannot (or will not) help me." And, all together, these events lead toward differentiation of interests, beliefs, knowledge, and values between parents and their offspring. It is this complex pattern—rather than merely some inevitable generational gap—that seems most important in accounting for alienation between generations in late twentieth-century America.

[2] This qualification is necessary because parental interaction must reach some minimal level before it will exhibit any important effect, and it may be that beyond a certain high level no additional increments of influence can be detected, or a reversal of effects may occur.

*Many ties across generations are maintained i Communicate : Financial aid ; Advice*

Yet we must not overstate the case. Evidence is accumulating which suggests that ties between the generations are maintained to an important extent even in urban areas.[3] Studies of samples of American males of retirement age indicate that patterns of close communication and financial and emotional assistance are maintained between older parents and their adult children.[4] Support and advice in child rearing must be fairly common in these circumstances.

## The Roles of Elders

Reverence for the old was a phase of a society that placed strong emphasis upon family life. . . . A society that has shaped its ideals about progress can never place its affairs in the hands of the old and give them the reverence that a society does that lives in the past. . . . The decline of ancestor worship, the competitive character of modern economic life, democratic government, individualism, and the cult of progress, have thus all conspired to reduce to a marked degree the functions and rank possessed by the aged in earlier society.[5]

This quotation suggests that American society may have little place for the aged person. Yet persons of sixty-five years of age and older constitute 18.5 million persons or 9.4 percent of the total population. It seems important to appraise carefully the status of the aged person in the family system. There is a common impression that elderly persons have little place in the system, that they are left isolated and functionless. To what extent is this true? What features of the family system affect the roles of the aged?

In comparison with past periods of our own society and with traditionalized rural societies (for example, old Ireland, China, India, or central Europe), the elders in America have a more restricted functional place in the kinship system and occupy a position of relatively lower prestige. The pattern of the modern urban family does not strongly support the traditional roles of the elders. There is resistance to sharing the household with aged parents or other relatives; physical facilities tend to be designed for the small family. Urban life, on the whole, favors the active adult; industry, on the whole, has favored the younger worker. Although employer-initiated early retirement of industrial and business employees was practically unknown

*U.S. aged less respected + less powerful > Trad. rural societies*

*Urban life favors active adult*

[3] Evidence on the retention of kinship ties within as well as outside the nuclear family in modern society is accumulating. Cf. Bott, *op. cit.*; Floyd Dotson, "Patterns of Voluntary Association Among Urban Working-Class Families," *American Sociological Review*, 16, 5 (October 1951), 687–693; R. Albrecht, "Relationships of Older People with Their Own Parents," *Marriage and Family Living*, 15, 4 (November 1953), 296; R. Albrecht, "The Parental Responsibilities of Grandparents," *Marriage and Family Living*, 16, 3 (August 1954), 201; R. Firth (ed.), *Two Studies of Kinship in London*, London School of Economics Monographs on Social Anthropology, No. 15 (London, 1956); M. B. Sussman, "The Help Pattern in the Middle-class Family," *American Sociological Review*, 18, 1 (February 1953), 22–28; M. B. Sussman, "Family Continuity: Selective Factors Which Affect Relationships Between Families at Generational Levels," *Marriage and Family Living*, 16, 2 (May 1954), 112.

[4] Gordon F. Streib, "Family Patterns in Retirement," *The Journal of Social Issues*, XIV, 2 (1958), 46–60. Fully 50 percent of the persons studied say that all their children live close enough to make it possible for parents to see them whenever desired.

[5] Cecil C. North, *Social Differentiation* (Chapel Hill: University of North Carolina Press, 1926), p. 84.

before the late 1950's, the practice appears to be spreading rather rapidly. Both optional and compulsory early retirement programs may be used to reduce the labor force, in response to technological change, as well as to eliminate workers judged to be inefficient.[6]

The obligation of children to aged and needy parents is still recognized by the legal system but often does not have full social acceptance.[7] The 1960 United States census showed that only 10 percent of households with both husband and wife present contained persons other than their own children.[8] Of such households, just over 4 percent contained any parents of either the husband or the wife. The desirability of separate living accommodations continues to be strongly emphasized. In 1960, of nearly 40 million husband-wife households, less than 2 million contained parents of the spouses. In popular literature, songs, movies and the like, youth is represented as the ideal time of life. A culture that glorifies youth, action, strength, and competitive success, a culture that prides itself upon being modern, up-to-date—this kind of culture is not likely to accord age the immediate respect that it can command in more highly traditionalized social structures. Where social change is slow, the elders are the great repository of knowledge and lore; but in rapidly changing societies like modern America, derogatory terms like "old fogy" can become common. The intergeneration cultural gap resulting from rapid social change, discussed below, thus turns out to have as its reverse side a certain social isolation and loss of firm, institutionalized status and esteem for aged parents.

Working in the same direction are at least two other major extrafamilial influences. First, for several generations many millions of American children learned to deprecate in some measure the culture of their immigrant or second-generation parents. In the attempt to become "American" the classic second generation rejected much of the culture with which their elders still identified; thus they have tended to ignore, scoff at, or openly rebel against the ways of the elderly family members, and the authority and social esteem of the elders consequently has diminished. By midcentury, however, this particular source of generational cleavage had become of secondary importance.

Second, vertical social mobility has inevitably affected the status of parents of adult children. The small farmer or worker whose son has become a businessman or professional worker will typically not have the same position in the family structure as he would had his son been his apprentice in a stable occupational system. Rapid upward social mobility thus appears to deprive elderly parents of an important social function. Here again, how-

[6] *Cf.* Otto M. Reid, "Aging Americans: A Review of Cooperative Research Projects," *Welfare in Review*, 4, 5 (May 1966), 7.

[7] Few systematic studies have been reported. One bit of supporting evidence is supplied by Robert M. Dinkel, "Attitudes of Children Toward Supporting Aged Parents," *American Sociological Review*, 9, 4 (August 1955), 370–379. On the other hand, Streib (*op. cit.,* p. 55) reports that offers of financial help by children exceed parental expectations.

[8] United States Bureau of the Census, *United States Census of Population: 1960, Families*, Final Report PC (2)—A4 (Washington, D.C.: Government Printing Office, 1963); calculated from Table 44, page 354.

ever, our conclusions must not be taken to imply too much. Although on net balance vertical mobility is not fully compatible with the type of parent-child solidarity found in stable, landowning farm families, it does not necessarily result in marked alienation or a rupture in communication. One important study shows, for example, that "where all the children have been more successful than their parents, they are more likely to keep in close touch with them and to form a close-knit family than those families in which the children have been less successful 'in getting ahead.' "[9] The potentially disruptive effects of mobility are weakened, or avoided altogether in many cases, partly because parents and children strongly agree in placing a high value on occupational achievement and derive many major satisfactions from it.

It still remains true that older parents' roles cannot be understood without taking into account the central importance of the nuclear family unit in the kinship system.[1] The emphasis upon the marriage pair inevitably means less stress upon the parent-child bonds. The independence of the households of married children is in part simply another way of stating the minimal role of parents. Census data for 1950 showed that less than 7 percent of married couples were without their own households; by 1960 only 2 percent were so classified. With wide geographic dispersion of children and with relatively high mobility—in 1950, one-fifth of the population had changed residence during the preceding year—one could say that the elders often have little authority in the kinship structure simply by virtue of having no family group in which authority can be exercised.[2]

There are, of course, variations in subcultures of the United States. Highly stable, rural landowning families, certain families with long-established wealth, and some closeknit ethnic and religious groups give greater place to the aged. As a general principle, however, it can be predicted that a "vestigial" role for the elders will be most conspicuous in those population segments in which the nuclear-family pattern is most strongly developed.

There is considerable indirect evidence that social strains have developed around the roles of the aged. From their origins in commercial promotion schemes, Mother's Day and Father's Day have proceeded to rapid institutionalization largely because we have a society in which grown children are typically separated from their parents. The enormous vogue of various kinds of family greeting cards is another evidence of attempts to maintain symbolic, "long-distance" solidarity in a social structure that tends to render a more tangible solidarity impossible. Probably there are important elements of overcompensation in these efforts. For example, there is widespread concern over old age as a "social problem" and agitation concerning old-age

---

[9] Streib, *op. cit.*, p. 51.

[1] The American case is best seen in contrast with kinship structures in which old age is highly esteemed and the authority of elders is great. See Francis L. K. Hsu, "The Family in China," in Anshen, *The Family, op. cit.*, pp. 123–145; Olga Lang, *Chinese Family and Society* (New Haven, Conn.: Yale University Press, 1946); F. L. K. Hsu, *Americans and Chinese* (New York: Henry Schuman, 1953).

[2] Cf. Paul C. Glick, "The Family Cycle," *American Sociological Review*, 12, 2 (April 1947), 171.

pensions and retirement plans. As Parsons has suggested in discussing the Townsend program and the widespread attention it aroused, more than mere "economic security" is involved in the agitation for old-age pensions.[3] The most fantastic schemes have received a wide hearing, partly because the whole old age problem becomes the object of strong emotions: on the one hand, because of the social isolation, insecurity, and sense of futility that beset functionless elders and, on the other, because of the guilt feelings of young adults over their own reluctance to accept the support of aged relatives. A striking omission in much of contemporary comment on old age is the lack of thorough discussion of the facts of natural and inevitable death and the connection between approaching death and the experiences and behavior of older persons.[4]

A somewhat more specific piece of indirect evidence is the existence in our society of "pools" of elderly persons living in certain urban centers. In some communities, such as Long Beach, California and St. Petersburg, Florida, there are great numbers of retired individuals or elderly couples living apart from their relatives and associating chiefly with others in a similar situation. Indeed, of the 1960 population in these two cities, 13 and 28 percent, respectively, were sixty-five or over. By contrast, in centers of industry there are smaller proportions of older persons, for example, in the steel town of Gary, only 6 percent are sixty-five or older. Although the situation is less striking for villages and small towns, both census statistics and monographic studies show that village populations tend to include disproportionately large numbers of elders; and it is possible to identify a fairly distinct social type of village that has as one of its main characteristics a concentration of retired persons, especially widows and widowers from farm areas.

Some of the important social and psychological implications of the marked development of the independent nuclear family for the position of aged persons thus seem to be identifiable and subject to at least a broad structural analysis. One other extrafamilial factor of great significance remains to be emphasized: the prevalence of abrupt retirement in our occupational system. In most past societies, the active adult only gradually relinquished his occupational responsibilities as he approached the end of his life.[5] Even in the United States this pattern remains important for landowning farmers and some business proprietors and professional persons. However, the dominant patterns for urban occupations have come to be either retirement at a fixed age (common among government workers, white-collar businessmen, hired professionals, and so forth) or simply discharge

---

[3] However, even in pressure-group movements for benefits to the aged, integration between generations is not totally broken. In the Townsend Movement for old-age pensions in the 1930's, as many as one-third of the members were under sixty years of age. Abraham Holtzman, *The Townsend Movement: A Political Study* (New York: Bookman Associates, 1963).

[4] See the suggestive comments of Robert Blauner in reviewing recent books on this topic in the *American Sociological Review*, 30, 6 (December 1965), 979.

[5] This pattern is certainly typical of contemporary agricultural societies. In some hunting and military societies, the active adult role was terminated rather abruptly, but usually with provision for respected substitute functions.

and inability to get another job (although less frequent among wage earners than in the past). Where these conditions prevail, the elderly person is left doubly bereft of social function and life rationale; he has no occupation and little place in the families of his children or in any other kinship grouping. However, the whole situation of retirement is quite complex and seems to be changing rapidly. It is possible, for example, that the status "retired person" may be increasingly recognized as a definite and respectable position, particularly when the retiree continues to be active and useful in various ways.

No doubt the thesis that aged persons in America occupy an unusually difficult status, as compared with past times or other societies, contains elements of stereotyping and exaggeration. Norms of respect for old age probably always have elicited less than full conformity; and not all old people even in stable agrarian societies enjoyed prestige and power.[6] On the other hand, there is completely decisive evidence that in our present society a socially isolated and impoverished older person experiences a difficult situation. With the growth of systematic retirement provisions in industry and government, the extreme cases of economic distress in later life may be expected to decrease. And it is possible that shifts already under way in prevailing attitudes may eventually restore to the aged in America some of the quality of social dignity which once appeared to be irrevocably lost in our industrial society.[7]

*Margin note: change is underway*

## Position and Role Performances of Youth[8]

*Margin note: U.S. culture — high value on youth; but adolesc = great period of strain; Youth = "social problem"; adolescen problems due to transition from depen-dent sta to adu...*

It seems clear that American culture places a strikingly high value on youth. Yet, in this same culture, adolescence tends to be a period of relatively great stress and strain; and the problems of youth are the objects of widespread discussion and concern. Certain features of the kinship system can be shown to be directly related to this seeming paradox.

The problems of adolescence arise in the transition from one social status to another—from the dependent status of "child" to the responsibility and autonomy attributed to the mature adult. In a great many societies this transition is clearly defined by public rites or ceremonies and by a variety of other means that have in common the definite signalizing of a well-under-

---

[6] Bernice L. Neugarten, "The Aged in American Society," in Howard S. Becker (ed.), *Social Problems: A Modern Approach* (New York: Wiley, 1966), pp. 172–174.

[7] Cf. Wayne E. Thompson, "Pre-retirement Anticipation and Adjustment in Retirement," *The Journal of Social Issues*, XIV, 2 (1958), 35–45.

[8] Pioneering analyses were contributed by Kingsley Davis, "Adolescence and Social Structure," *The Annals of the American Academy of Political and Social Science*, Vol. 236 (November 1944), pp. 9–11 and "The Sociology of Parent-Youth Conflict," *American Sociological Review*, 5, 4 (August 1940), 523–535. Recent syntheses summarize a vast amount of research, for example: S. N. Eisenstadt, *From Generation to Generation: Age Groups and Social Structure* (New York: Free Press, 1956); David Gottlieb and Charles Ramsey, *The American Adolescent* (Homewood, Ill.: Dorsey Press, 1964); David Gottlieb, Jon Reeves, and Warren TenHouten, *The Emergence of Youth Societies: A Cross-Cultural Approach* (New York: Free Press, 1966). See also F. Musgrove, *Youth and the Social Order* (Bloomington: Indiana University Press, 1965); Kenneth Keniston, *The Uncommitted: Alienated Youth in American Society* (New York: Harcourt, Brace & World, 1965).

*S. society*

*rights of passage*

stood transition from one status to another. In American society, there are only a few equivalents of such rites of passage, such as the "coming-out party" of upper-class girls. For the vast majority of the population, the transition from child to adult is institutionally recognized by disparate events (high-school graduation, getting a full-time job, marriage, and so on) that are not closely integrated into a pattern. The lack of clear structuring varies, of course, with region, social class, ethnic group, and rural or urban residence as well as with sex; probably it is at a maximum among the culturally marginal and mobile elements of our large cities.

*less supervision more 'mixed' company delay of marriage*

Boys and girls face qualitatively different ambiguities and uncertainties; but both often find it difficult to tell when and how adult behavior is expected. Thus, the monitoring and guidance of interaction between adolescent boys and girls clearly tends to become less as extended kinship relationships attenuate, as young people are more often intensively involved in peer groups, and as the nuclear family comes to have fewer resources to support its own efforts to counsel and control.[9] The extended period of formal education tends to defer marriage well beyond the age of full biological maturity. Yet premarital chastity continues to be emphasized, though decreasingly, at the same time young men and women are permitted and encouraged to associate closely.[1] The resulting strains and difficulties are themselves enhanced by an appreciable lack of clarity in de facto social codes. The adolescent has to deal with these biosocial problems for several years while he or she anticipates full emancipation from parents, mate selection in a relatively competitive marriage market, and the eventual establishment of a separate and independent household.

*not struct pre-marital chastity*

*process of emancipation from nuclear family cleanly structured*

We have seen that the family system is organized in such a way as to require the emancipation of young people from the family. In general, the children of the parental household are expected, and thus feel obligated, to leave home, get a job, and establish their own families, especially in the socially mobile groups in which the children are expected to move up in the social and economic scale. Because our occupational structure is still one of rapid change, competitive placement, and high specialization, the tendency is to defer final occupational choice until after childhood. Yet, if the young person is to enter a "good" occupation, he is likely to need an extended period of specialized training. Thus, among the middle-class groups, at least, he must choose his occupation as an adolescent, but without clear and institutionally stable guiding definitions and prescriptions. The lack of arranged marriage and of hereditary occupational placement gives him great freedom at the very time that the parental family is in the process of relin-

*competition for job a spouse; early choice of occupation required by schooling; but not channeled.*

[9] Cf. Ira L. Reiss, "Some Comments on Premarital Sexual Permissiveness," *American Journal of Sociology*, 72, 5 (March 1967), 558.

[1] Decreasing emphasis on premarital chastity is shown in studies of college students and their parents. See Mervin M. Freeman, *The College Experience* (San Francisco: Jossey-Bass, 1967), chaps. 6 and 7. Note the relevance of John F. Cuber and Peggy B. Harroff, *The Significant Americans: A Study of Sexual Behavior Among the Affluent* (New York: Appleton-Century-Crofts, 1965). For a review of data concerning frequency of premarital sexual intercourse, see Robert R. Bell, *Premarital Sex in a Changing Society* (Englewood Cliffs, N.J.: Prentice-Hall, 1966).

quishing its control over him; but because the emancipation process is not clearly structured, this release from parental control often is halting, erratic, and ambiguous. The exact nature and timing of his assumption of adult privileges and responsibilities are left to be settled by a "bargaining struggle."

Of course, the fact that the family system itself does not provide clear and strongly supported definitions of the attainment of adulthood does not allow us to conclude that no regularized forms of transition exist for American adolescents. Many of the procedures and relationships that can provide for gradual and orderly movement from the statuses of childhood to those of adulthood are now in the educational system and the associated informal peer-groupings. Yet it is just the relationship between the family unit and outside social formations that generates many felt problems.

Thus, the influence of extrafamilial factors is conspicuous in the changing relationship of adolescents to their parents. As a consequence of technological and occupational changes, the father no longer works with his sons or can be closely associated with them throughout the day and year; at the same time, increasing proportions of mothers work outside the home. Concurrently, the extension of compulsory school attendance, the rise in the demand for education as a prerequisite for employment, and the enforcement of child-labor laws, have insured that youths spend a major part of their waking hours outside the family. The growth of commercial recreation and the reduction in the frequency of whole family relationships with neighbors have worked in the same direction. The inevitable consequence is an increasing proportion of time spent by young people in association with their peers. Frequent interaction and similarity of condition have the predictable consequences of creating relatively distinctive norms, values, beliefs, and patterns of interaction—in short, a "youth culture." It has been observed that youth movements—concerted political or nonpolitical action apart from or opposed to adult leadership and norms—are most likely in societies in which the family unit cannot insure (and may even impede) the attainment of full adult social status by its younger members.[2] Social solidarity in all kinds of groupings is facilitated by rewarding interdependence under a set of mutually accepted norms. If interaction decreases and consensus decreases, the remaining interdependencies are likely to be less often rewarding and more often felt as frustrating and burdensome.

Small wonder, then, that parent-youth relations in our society often have a special emotional intensity. Furthermore, the adolescent deals with a small family, not with an extended group of kinsmen. Instead of diffused emotions and the unanimity of authority, there is a focus upon the parents —who may or may not be supported by the larger consensus of the community. Furthermore, even while the youth is casting off parental guidance and control, he is likely (for reasons suggested above) to be in special need of security and emotional support. The small island of the immediate family is frequently his only dependable support in the surrounding sea of competition and instability. Out of this changing balance of dependence and independence, needs and claims, comes much of the adolescent behavior

[2] See Eisenstadt, *From Generation to Generation, op. cit.*

described by exasperated or concerned adults as vacillating, erratic, chaotic, or strange.

We have seen that relatively extreme alienation of youths from adults and adult standards undoubtedly is an important part of the orientations of a minority of American adolescents. But it is not the dominant pattern of response among the majority.[3] Children still are strongly influenced by their parents; and adolescents are concerned with adult approval and disapproval, not merely with the reactions of peers.[4] Differing research findings and interpretations concerning the existence of adolescent subcultures partly result from the two basic facts of, first, pervasive ambivalence among youths and, second, great variations in different segments of the society (racial, ethnic, class, and rural-urban). From just the basic institutional structure of our society, one can confidently predict considerable continuity between youths and adults in basic orientations[5] but also very important reactions of rebellion and alienation.[6]

A certain amount of conflict between parents and youth is to be expected in any society because of intergeneration differences in interests and perspectives and the correlative differences in social rights and responsibilities. Some disagreement and opposition between parents and children, or between older and younger persons more generally, is not a new human condition. What seems more noteworthy in our times is a kind of alienation or noncommitment of youths whose parents have been highly permissive and indulgent. In many cases, the father has largely withdrawn from exercising firm authority or giving clear guidance, whereas the mother has reacted by efforts to capture and control through manipulation of love and fear. Meanwhile, the authority of the parents in this type of situation is continually challenged by other vested authorities as well as by youth. This clash of authorities is a specific manifestation of the broader problem of cultural conflicts and lack of integration.

Thus, it is partly the institutional characteristics of the American family, not particular personalities nor a generalized human nature, that give rise to certain typical "problems" of adolescence.

## MATE SELECTION AND ROMANTIC LOVE

The great emphasis in American culture upon the idealization of romantic love is closely associated with certain features of the basic family system. With the diminution of the extended family and the correlated loss of many

---

[3] Cf. Marie Jahoda and Neil Warren, "The Myths of Youth," *Sociology of Education*, 38, 2 (Winter 1965), 140–144.

[4] D. C. Epperson, "A Reassessment of Indices of Parental Influence in *The Adolescent Society*," *American Sociological Review*, 29, 1 (February 1964), 93–96; Frederick Elkin and William A. Westley, "The Myth of Adolescent Culture," *American Sociological Review*, 20, 6 (December 1955), 680–684.

[5] High school youths essentially replicate the political orientations of adults. See H. H. Remmers (ed.), *Anti-Democratic Attitudes in American Schools* (Evanston, Ill.: Northwestern University Press, 1963), p. 62.

[6] Erik Erikson, *Identity: Youth and Crisis* (New York: Norton, 1968); Nevitt Sanford, *The American College* (New York: Wiley, 1962), esp. chaps. 13–15 and 24–25.

*Margin notes (handwritten):* chief function of family today providing affection + security / "Romantic Love" = causal key / to fulfill need for dependence + overcome resistence to marriage etc. / children from small families — tendency to rely on one/few persons / Impersonal society / Family relation can carry heavy emotional load / Rom. love = widespread / Choice of mate: restricted by Residence Social class [Race] [Religion] etc. / 1000 social pressure

previous functions of the nuclear unit, the family's chief function has come to be that of providing affection and security. When choice of mates is relatively free, personal attraction bulks larger in marriage than it could under any system of arranged marriages; it is a commonplace hypothesis in the sociological literature that our emphasis upon romantic love is in part an equivalent for the group support and regulation of marriage in the less diffuse and mobile systems of many other societies. At the usual age of first marriage, the young person is still acquiring emotional independence from the parental family, under the multiple stresses just discussed. The need for dependence is strong, and the institutional demand for independence is strong. Under these circumstances it is necessary to break through complex and deep-seated resistances to marriage and its responsibility and emotional independence without the help of a clearly defined system of mate choice based upon status and wider kinship regulation.[7] An almost compulsive emphasis upon romantic love emerges in part from this situation.

Furthermore, young people who have been brought up in the relatively isolated and autonomous small family unit probably bring to a marriage a tendency to depend emotionally upon one or a very few persons, and, in the extreme cases, after marriage are almost completely thrown back upon one another for full emotional response and basic psychological securities. In a mobile, competitive world, so largely dominated by relatively impersonal and segmented social relationships, the courtship process and the marriage relation can thus come to carry a kind of intensity and importance not typical of societies lacking these characteristics. The ideals of premarital chastity and lifelong fidelity in marriage, insofar as they are socially effective, increase this intensity.

It is clear, of course, that romantic love is not confined to America nor to modern times. It is potentially universal, and actually very widespread in time and space.[8] But nowhere is it completely released from social control. In fact, the greater the emphasis upon freedom of personal choice of mate, the more likely it is that there will be other ways of restricting the field of eligibles[9] within which young people may choose. Residential separation, restricted social circles, and a thousand social pressures, both the obvious and the subtle, combine to insure that socially capricious final choices will be quite rare. This result derives partly from preference, partly from conformity, partly from opportunity. Thus, the well-known tendency for persons to marry partners who live in close geographic proximity is certainly

[7] For a summary of research on processes of mate selection see Robert R. Bell, *Marriage and Family Interaction* (Homewood, Ill.: Dorsey Press, 1963), chaps. 4–6.

[8] "love relationships are a basis of the final choice of mate among a large minority of the societies of the earth." W. J. Goode, "The Sociology of the Family: Horizons in Family Theory," in Robert K. Merton, Leonard Broom, Leonard S. Cottrell, Jr. (eds.), *Sociology Today* (New York: Basic Books, 1959), p. 194.

[9] Numerous studies have shown these facts: "spouses tend to be alike in those status characteristics that are structurally central for their society, such as race, religion, rank, education, and income." Goode, *op. cit.*, p. 23. See evidence of educational congruity in mate choice in Charles B. Nam, "Family Patterns of Educational Attainment," *Sociology of Education*, 38, 5 (Fall 1965), 399. For example, of husbands who did not graduate from high school, 74 percent marry women who are not high school graduates, and only 5 percent have married women who attended college.

not a simple result of conformity to a norm that stipulates "you should marry someone who lives near you." In addition, propinquity typically is confounded with social and cultural similarity: for example, because of de facto residential separation, persons residing in the same section of a city are especially likely to be similar in race, religion, ethnic origin, and social class. In the second place, physical propinquity maximizes sheer opportunity for contact. And, third, propinquity makes for economy of time, effort, and money in courtship.[1] Abundant opportunity and rewarding similarities thus combine with low cost and with social inducements and pressures to generate attraction, for the most part, among those within a restricted field of eligible partners.

All the indirect influences or secondary institutions that operate to encourage romantic love are at work in a family system that has already freed the spontaneous affective inclinations of the young couple from elaborate restrictions.[2] In proportion as marriages are not arranged, they are left to the choice of the potential partners; and, as institutionalized status (such as social class or caste) is less important, the choice rests more on individual qualities and achievements. Given the fact that American society has come to permit considerable personal choice, the pattern of romantic love is encouraged both by the family structure and by a series of indirect consequences of that structure. Of course, the extreme stereotype of romantic love is partly a cultural fiction. Marriage partners available to any given individual are severely limited in practice by race, religion, social class, propinquity, and so on. Nevertheless, our culture continues to idealize romantic love.

## FAMILY STABILITY AND INSTABILITY

Despite many cultural prescriptions supporting the permanence of the marriage tie and the solidity of the nuclear family, American society is characterized by what are commonly regarded as high rates of divorce and other forms of family dissolution. The atomization of the family into separate legal personalities is far advanced; the family is extremely open to external agencies and influences, from nursery schools to radio and from the social worker to the truant officer, the military draft, and even the political party. Kinship obligations sometimes are not strongly upheld, and many of these have been taken over by the state.[3] The effective family unit, therefore, is

---

[1] William R. Catton, Jr. and R. J. Smircich, "A Comparison of Mathematical Models for the Effect of Residential Propinquity on Mate Selection," *American Sociological Review*, 29, 4 (August 1964), 522–529. This study of marriages in Seattle showed that a formula using distance alone was a better predictor of marriages than a formula based on number of "intervening opportunities" in relation to number of potential partners at a given distance.

[2] Ira L. Reiss, "Social Class and Premarital Sexual Permissiveness: A Re-Examination," *American Sociological Review*, 30, 5 (October 1965), 747–756; Ira L. Reiss, *Premarital Sexual Standards in America* (New York: Free Press, 1960); Winston Ehrman, *Premarital Dating Behavior* (New York: Holt, Rinehart and Winston, 1959).

[3] For the wide variety of specific connections between governmental actions and familial norms and behavior see the special issue: "Government Programs and the Family," *Journal of Marriage and the Family*, 29, 1 (February 1967), 5–205.

usually a small permeable group, often not supported by the surrounding society. This generalization, as noted before, is subject to many detailed qualifications. For instance, there are indications from local studies that sibling solidarity, which diminishes after later childhood and adolescence, is reasserted in the later years of life (after ages forty-five through fifty). The sibling relationships provide equalitarianism, sociability, and freedom of choice and thus seem to fit well with the collateral emphasis and loose structure of the basic system.[4]

Family instability or disorganization means some disruption in performance of the various statuses. Even within a system of nuclear families, instability is constituted by a set of events much broader than divorce or separation. The major kinds of disruption are: (1) incompleted family unit (that is, illegitimacy); (2) willful separation of one spouse: annulment, divorce, separation, desertion; (3) failure of one or more members to give adequate socioemotional response and support (the "empty shell" family); (4) disruption through external events, such as the involuntary absence of a member because of imprisonment, death, military conscription; (5) "internal" sources of role-failure, for example, psychosis, physical illness, mental retardation of a child.[5] Although divorce rates frequently constitute the only reliable and comprehensive indicators of instability or disruption, the other types are evidently of substantial importance.

Increasingly, it has come to be recognized that the family unit is an open system which is profoundly influenced in its *internal* structure and processes by influences from its external social relations. There are strong indications that rates of marital stability or instability are closely related to the extent of common or overlapping group affiliations of the spouses. For example, among preliterate peoples, stability of marriage is highest when the spouses in bilateral systems either come from the same village or marry their cousins; or, in unilineal systems, when the wife is decisively separated from her kin group of origin and is socially incorporated into the kin group of her husband.[6] In our own society, nuclear units apparently are most stable when surrounded by a social circle of families committed to similar norms and values.[7]

In the United States, in recent years, the ratio of divorces to marriage has been approximately one to four. Based on the experience of the middle decades of this century, between one-sixth and one-fifth of adults who live out an average lifetime will experience divorce.[8] In addition, the number of marriages broken by separation, desertion, and near desertion probably equals the number dissolved by divorce. The divorce rate per one hundred

[4] Elaine Cumming and David M. Schneider, "Sibling Solidarity: A Property of American Heritage," *American Anthropologist*, 63, 3 (June 1961), 498–507.

[5] William J. Goode, "Marital Satisfaction and Instability: A Cross-Cultural Class Analysis of Divorce Rates," *International Social Science Journal*, XIV, 3 (1962), 507–526.

[6] Charles Ackerman, "Affiliations: Structural Determinants of Differential Divorce Rates," *American Journal of Sociology*, LXIX, 1 (July 1963), 13–20.

[7] See the data in Carle C. Zimmerman and Lucius F. Cervantes, S.J., *Successful American Families* (New York: Pageant Press, 1960).

[8] Cf. William J. Goode, *After Divorce* (New York: Free Press, 1956), p. 11.

marriages, which was sixteen in 1930 and twenty-one in 1940, climbed to the all-time high of forty in the postwar year of 1946. By the mid-1950's, however, the rate had dropped back to the prewar levels and since has remained relatively stable on a high plateau. Divorces per one thousand married females fifteen years of age or older were 8.8 in 1940, rising to 17.9 in 1946, then dropping to 10.3 in 1950 and 9.2 in 1960, with a slight increase in the 1960's.[9]

The ratio of divorces in a given year to the average number of marriages in each year of the preceding decade is a good index of marriage instability, since most divorces occur within ten years after marriage. This ratio rose from 6 percent in 1890 to about 40 percent in 1947. From 1867 to 1932, divorce occurred in increasingly earlier years of marriage: during 1867–1886, a marriage was most likely to break up in its seventh year, but by 1922–1932, in its third and fourth year, and today before the third year.[1] Although divorce rates are higher in urban than in rural areas, even before World War II divorce had come to the open country; for example, there was about one divorce for every four marriages even in the most rural counties of Ohio in the period 1939–1947.[2]

Until recent years at least, most divorces dissolved marriages rather than families; most divorce couples were childless; in 1922 only 34 percent of divorce actions involved minor children, whereas by 1959, slightly over half involved such children.[3] In desertions and informal separations, on the other hand, it appears that there is a smaller proportion of childless couples than in the total population. Through a lack of data concerning desertion and nonsupport, however, we must rely chiefly upon divorce as an index of family instability. Judged by divorce alone, the United States certainly has a high rate of family dissolution. Differences among national divorce laws and customs make strict comparison very dubious; but without doubt, family breakup is very frequent in our society, by any standard of comparison.[4]

How is this family instability to be explained? Full causal analysis is impossible here, since a thorough treatment would deal with all of American civilization. However, the preceding discussion has provided important clues. The question partly reduces to another: Why do persons stay in a particular family rather than leaving to join some other unit or to live outside any family group at all? In the most general terms, they remain as

[9] See Ralph Thomlinson, *Population Dynamics* (New York: Random House, 1965), p. 462, and Bureau of the Census, *Pocket Data Book, U.S.A., 1967* (Washington, D.C.: Government Printing Office, 1966).

[1] William M. Kephart, *The Family, Society, and the Individual* (Boston: Houghton Mifflin, 1961), p. 616, 631.

[2] A. R. Mangus, "Marriage and Divorce in Ohio," *Rural Sociology*, XIV, 2 (June 1949), 132.

[3] Kephart, *op. cit.*, p. 631.

[4] Paul H. Jacobson, *American Marriage and Divorce* (New York: Holt, Rinehart and Winston, 1959); William J. Goode, "Family Disorganization" in Robert K. Merton and Robert A. Nisbet (eds.), *Contemporary Social Problems* (New York: Harcourt, Brace & World, 1961), pp. 411–412.

members of particular family groups because they find there acceptable rewards or are constrained by penalties that would be incurred by loss of membership. Anything that makes life in families more rewarding, or alternatives less so, presumably induces stability.

Now, as a general rule, family units become more complex, larger, and more stable as one goes up the scale of social strata. With more economic resources and power, the family's control over its younger members is enhanced; and the authority of the dominant or leading parent (usually the father) is strengthened. Conversely, at the bottom of the economic and social scale, the family tends to have a simple and loose structure. As Freedman has pointed out for the case of Imperial China:

*Poverty and powerlessness produced, instead of a strong patriarch, a weak father. He could rally no support from outside to dominate his sons. He had few resources to withhold from them. . . . Demography, economics, and the power situation at this level of society ensured that families of simple structure were a constant feature of the landscape.* [5]

In our own society, family stability is least in the lower economic strata. Specifically, the rate of divorce is negatively related to occupational level, being lowest in professional, managerial, and proprietorial occupations and highest among operatives and laborers.[6] It is similarly negatively associated with income and with education.[7] As Goode suggests, it is highly likely that forces making for total instability generally have their greatest prevalence in lower socioeconomic strata. Whether the divorce rate, as a specific indicator of instability, also will be higher depends upon the permissiveness or ease of divorce: when divorce is legally difficult or otherwise costly, it will be relatively higher in the upper classes. In countries moving from a restrictive to a permissive situation, the class differentials tend to become reversed as members of the upper strata begin divorcing at high rates. After such a transition, the differentials tend to revert to the model of low divorce/ high status. In the United States, the high-divorce pattern is widely accessible, and the strains of lower-class marriages frequently result in marital dissolution.

It is plausible to hypothesize further that the higher the divorce rate over a period of years, the lower the level of internal strain required to induce the dissolution of marriages. When divorce is objectively easy and when high rates in the immediate past have intensified the force of example and have reduced the social stigma and other disadvantages, the partners who find their relationship difficult are likely to be more disposed to terminate it. Use of the conceptions of *availability* of divorce (permissiveness) both in law and in informal social norms and expectations and of *alternatives* to divorce (as remedies for marital disharmony) may help us to under-

[5] Maurice Freedman, "The Family in China, Past and Present," *op. cit.*, p. 327.

[6] W. J. Goode: "Marital Satisfaction and Instability," in Reinhard Bendix and Seymour Martin Lipset (eds.), *Class, Status and Power: Social Stratification in Comparative Perspective*, 2nd edition (New York: Free Press, 1966), pp. 381–383.

[7] Except that among nonwhites, high education goes with a high incidence of divorce.

stand differences in frequency of divorce among modern national societies.[8]

Popular explanations of "the divorce problem" commonly stress the alleged personal incompatibility of the spouses. Yet plainly personal incompatibility by itself explains very little; one still wants to know why the incompatibility ever arises, why it sometimes leads to divorce, and why some families often endure even in the face of severe interpersonal tensions. There are structural factors far more basic than the reasons commonly advanced for family breakdown. Marriages dissolve because (1) divorce or separation is permitted, (2) there are few strong internal bonds holding the marriage together, and (3) the marriage pair or family unit is not well supported by the surrounding social structure. Modern America combines all these features. It permits divorce far more readily than formerly. At the same time the American family has lost many of its former functions— the multiple activities that once centered in and around the home. The family as an almost purely consuming and affectional unit contrasts sharply with the old style "trustee family," which was practically a self-contained social system combining economic production, education, "government," religious functions, and "social security," including several generations, and comprehending nearly all phases of the individual's life. The sharing of common tasks in a collective enterprise in such families was one manifestation of the close economic and social interdependence of family members.

Modern family instability is often blamed directly upon the loss of multiple functions. It is more accurate to say that the remaining family bonds bear too heavy a load and break under it. As the family has become less important, it has also become more important; as the scope of family activities has narrowed, the emotional significance of the surviving relationships has, in one sense, increased. High expectations are imposed upon a relatively vulnerable structure. For instance, the ideal of perfect husband-wife compatibility in romantic love conflicts with the fact that many families have few common activities and institutional supports.

From considerations of this kind it is easily possible to build up the impression of extreme fragility in American families. This impression would not be entirely accurate. The high divorce rates of the years immediately following the turmoil of World War II have declined. Even at the peak of the divorce rate in the United States, higher rates had been found in many nonliterate societies as well as in major political societies (Japan, Russia, Palestine, Egypt, at various periods).[9] Furthermore, most divorced persons rather promptly remarry—in fact, about 94 percent of women divorcing at age thirty will eventually remarry. And it appears that the remarriage rate of divorced mothers is not much lower than that of female divorcees generally.[1] To an appreciable extent, we have developed a largely unrecognized

[8] Cf. Lincoln H. Day, "Patterns of Divorce in Australia and the United States," *American Sociological Review*, 29, 4 (August 1964), 509–522.

[9] George P. Murdock, "Family Stability in Non-European Cultures," *The Annals*, 272 (1950), 195–201.

[1] Goode, *op. cit.*, p. 207. A basic point in this connection is made by Goode (p. 216): "Although the rate of divorce is high the existing kinship institutions indirectly move both

subsystem of tandem monogamy—or sequential polygamy[2]—in our complex efforts to deal with the new as well as the permanent aspects of the relations of men and women and children in families.

And we must remember, as suggested in passing at several points in earlier discussion, that the image of the relatively autonomous and isolated nuclear family does not accurately describe all of American society. Both in rural and in urban areas, extended kinship relations retain an importance not obvious to superficial inspection. Despite high geographic mobility, most families of procreation retain meaningful relations with their families of orientation. Even in the seemingly impersonal and turbulent metropolitan areas, patterns of visiting and of mutual aid in crises govern relations with kinsmen who are socially accessible.

The American family is not a dying institution. It already has been strengthened by new forces. Although it is subject to stresses within the kinship structure as well as to multiple strains from other institutions, for example, an occupational system that interferes in many ways with stable family life—such signs as higher birth rates and renewed emphases on family values attest to the continued tenacity of this basic social unit.

## SUGGESTED READINGS

BERNARD, JESSIE. *Remarriage: A Study of Marriage.* New York: Dryden Press, 1956. Exemplary analysis of a topic of special interest in a society with many divorces—and few permanently divorced persons.

CHRISTENSEN, HAROLD T. *Handbook of Marriage and the Family.* Chicago: 1964. Comprehensive and authoritative compilation; highly useful for reference and selective reading.

EISENSTADT, S. N. *From Generation to Generation: Age Groups and Social Structure.* New York: Free Press, 1956. Important study of structural and dynamic significance of age groupings in relation to other aspects of total societies.

GOODE, WILLIAM J. *World Revolution and Family Patterns.* New York: Free Press, 1963. Achieves a carefully reasoned appraisal of vast quantities of data. Shows the unevenness of change and the evidences that family systems often have substantial autonomy from external forces.

JACOBSEN, PAUL H. *American Marriage and Divorce.* New York: Holt, Rinehart & Winston, 1959. Valuable synthesis of data available at the end of the 1950's, giving essential background and trends.

KEPHART, WILLIAM M. *The Family, Society, and the Individual.* Boston: Houghton Mifflin, 1961. Highly successful textbook; well-balanced review of evidence and thoughtful discussion of hypotheses, findings, and social implications.

---

child and mother back into relatively well-defined statuses, thus fixing responsibility for maintenance, status placement, and socialization of the child.

2 Jessie Bernard, *Remarriage: A Study of Marriage* (New York: Dryden Press, 1956), p. 46: "probably more persons practice plural marriage in our society today than in societies that are avowedly polygamous." About one out of every eight married persons has been married more than once.

KOMAROVSKY, MIRRA. *Blue-Collar Marriage*. New York: Random House, 1964. Sensitive and careful theoretical interpretations, based on intensive interviews with a small number of families. Questions certain stereotypes and provides a rich set of hypotheses.

MURDOCK, GEORGE P. *Social Structure*. New York: Macmillan, 1949. Pioneering analysis of kinship systems, with systematic effort to use cross-cultural evidence to appraise major theories. Provides valuable comparative perspective on the American case.

RAINWATER, LEE. *And the Poor Get Children*. Chicago: Quadrangle Press, 1960. Landmark study of husband-wife relations, sex, and contraception among families at low levels of income.

SHANAS, ETHEL, and GORDON F. STREIB (eds.). *Social Structure and the Family: Generational Relations*. Englewood Cliffs, N.J.: Prentice-Hall, 1965. Challenging set of essays and research interpretations. Refutes some popular certitudes, demonstrating once more the hazards of believing what "everybody knows."

# Social Stratification in the United States

*V*

**A**s our survey of kinship and the family has suggested, the separation of different institutional areas for purposes of analysis is somewhat artificial; in concrete social life there is no sharp line separating one institution from others, and actual social situations represent a most complex crisscrossing of numerous normative systems. Thus, the full extent of institutional interdependence cannot be seen until all the major institutional complexes have been described. It follows that no one institution can be adequately analyzed until we have some understanding of all the others; yet one must have some information about each institution in order to comprehend the actual functional interconnections of all of them. Therefore, we will first present a provisional and incomplete analysis of each institution, reserving to a later chapter the more complicated problems of interrelation of institutions and other structures in the total society.

The consideration of kinship structures leads us quite easily into an analysis of social stratification. For example, it has already been observed that the emphasis in American society on "moving up in the world" is of great importance in explaining the diminished importance of extended family ties and that social stratification is related to problems of solidarity of the nuclear family itself. As a matter of fact, some of the crucial questions we have to ask in diagnosing any society concern the extent to which, and the specific ways in which, kinship plays a part in the systems of stratification of that society. Is family or kinship a main criterion of allocation or ranking? Is the unit of stratification an individual person, or a kinship group, or something else? To what extent is family membership an advantage in maintaining or attaining a given position in the stratification order? To move toward answers to questions of this character we have first to consider what we mean by words such as "social stratification," "class," "caste," "ranks," and "prestige." There are great variations in the meanings commonly attached to such terms; and the formal definitions that have been set forth often do not fit the available facts. Therefore, we must be explicit about our own concepts in the present analysis.

Much terminological discussion has marked the efforts to describe the main kinds of *social formations* in which social stratification occurs. Sometimes the term "social class" is used to refer to any locally ranked clique or congeniality circle; sometimes any group conflict within a social organization is interpreted as class conflict.[1] Such vagueness is unnecessary and may be avoided by concentrating upon *specific combinations* of the major elements of stratification. For example, the most highly developed forms of caste are marked by endogamy, hereditary occupation, fixed relations to other castes, prescribed social distance expressed in degrees of ritual purity, an elaborate system of religious-ideological justification, and local corporate caste organization. At the theoretical extreme of a completely "open-class" system, all structural units of stratification would be lacking. There would be only individuals possessing different amounts of scarce values and receiving continually changing evaluations from others.

### MAJOR CONCEPTS AND PROBLEMS

*Stratification*

"Stratification" of society, whatever else it may mean, certainly denotes some way whereby *some* kinds of units are arranged in *some* kinds of strata. Conceivably the units might be nations, religious organizations, castes, military groups, "races," or any other social categories into which human individuals are placed. We are interested here primarily in two kinds of units: (1) the individual person and (2) the kinship group.

What is "stratification"? Every classification of human beings is also a potential ranking, and the number of possible classifications is indefinitely large. We might stratify people according to their emotional stability, their ability to play badminton, their knowledge of medieval Latin, the color of their hair, the number of friends they have, the reputation of their ancestors. Actually, only a few of the qualities of individuals or groups are seized upon as either criteria or symbols of their station in society. Nevertheless, all known societies have some system of ranking their constituent members or groups along a superiority-inferiority scale. Theoretically, all individuals might be seen as unique persons, or they might be placed into categories valued *equally*. But in no large-scale or long-continued social grouping have they been equal; the differential valuation of men as individuals and as members of social categories is a universal, formal property of social systems.[2]

One main aspect of stratification is evaluative social ranking—the ordered arrangement of social units along a scale or scales of superiority-inferiority-equality according to some commonly accepted basis of valuation. An ordering according to such differential esteem constitutes *prestige-ranking*. The second main aspect of stratification is the distribution or *allocation of rewards and facilities*: primarily income, wealth, authority, and power.

[1] Cf. Ralf Dahrendorf, *Class and Class Conflict in Industrial Society* (Stanford, Calif.: Stanford University Press, 1959).
[2] Of course, the extent and kind of inequality varies tremendously from one culture to another. For some purposes it is useful to distinguish between "ranking" as the sheer ordering of units along some dimension of magnitude from "ranking" in some evaluative sense of goodness or desirability: see Melvin M. Tumin, *Social Stratification* (Englewood Cliffs, N.J.: Prentice-Hall, 1967), pp. 24–33.

Clearly it is scientifically legitimate to focus upon any one of the several main kinds of stratification; but there is no clear evidence that the study of one such criterion is always more productive of scientific understanding than the others, although some investigators may indeed believe that power is more important than prestige, or vice versa. Similarly, a full treatment of stratification will deal both with its causes and with its consequences, as well as with the processes of maintenance and change. Furthermore, attention may be focused on structure (strata, classes, castes) or on processes (mobility, distribution, or flows of scarce values.) Different students will elect to study different phenomena; for example, Gerhard Lenski explicitly chooses to emphasize the causes of stratification rather than its consequences, to analyze power and privilege rather than prestige, and to be concerned with processes more than with structures.[3]

A first step toward clarity in considering stratification is to distinguish it from social differentiation. The latter is simply the classic "division of labor," in the broadest sense: the separate organization of activities into specialized positions called *statuses*. Stratification consists of the allocation to these special positions of varying unequal amounts of prestige and of the other scarce values. Yet a third phenomenon is distinct from these two, namely, enduring *social classes* or *strata* that are carried across generations by inherited position or differential opportunities associated with kinship or birth in a particular family unit.[4]

Stratification as an institutionalized structure emerges from two primary social processes: (1) differentiation and (2) evaluation. The first two sources of differentiation within and between societies are biological variability among individuals and physical variability in environments. Both singly and in combination, variations in genetic inheritance and in physical environments permit an indefinitely large number of distinctive individual combinations. Given the initial development of human culture, further differentiation of individuals and collectivities arises from the adaptative maneuvers elicited by varying environmental pressures, challenges, and opportunities. Both technological effectiveness and economic efficiency in the use of scarce resources have competitive survival value. Differing ecological niches (rain forest, Arctic margin, desert, seacoast, mountains) favor differing technologies and economic activities. Within each relatively homogenous zone of adaptation, subgroups and individuals vary in effectiveness and efficiency. In general, it seems reasonable to suppose that the greater the range of differentiation within a society the greater the range of stratification. The more the prevailing value-system emphasizes scarce and distributive values (rather than common values accessible through participation) the greater the range of stratification.

All continuing social collectivities develop standards of evaluation and make judgments of desirability in terms of them. Given such values and the specific norms related to them, and given social differentiation, it follows

[3] Gerhard E. Lenski, *Power and Privilege: A Theory of Social Stratification* (New York: McGraw-Hill, 1966), pp. ix–x.

[4] Cf. Dennis H. Wrong, "The Functional Theory of Stratification: Some Neglected Considerations," *American Sociological Review*, 24, 6 (December 1959), 772–782.

that collectivities and individuals will be differentially evaluated; the probability that all would be judged as of identical worth is extremely slight. And if there is consistency in recurring differential evaluation of the same set of units, there is ranking.[5] If rankings, then, are relatively stable over time and if substantial numbers of social units come to be grouped or categorized as belonging to certain common rank-positions, the ranked categories may be called *strata*. Note that the term "stratification" is commonly used to refer both to the fact that such strata exist and to the processes by which they are formed.

We are interested not in any and all varieties of stratification but rather in *institutionalized* stratification; a system of allocations and rankings is institutionalized just to the extent that it is generally accepted as right and proper by the groups within which it operates.[6] By no means is all stratification of this nature. Many kinds of rankings are based largely on power alone. A small-scale instance is provided by the ranking according to physical strength and fighting prowess found in boys' gangs, a ranking somewhat analogous to the pecking order observable among animals. In society at large, an individual or a group may use coercion to gain or maintain station, even though the methods may run counter to many of the major institutionalized values nominally accepted in the society. Furthermore, in a large and complex social aggregate there are wide variations in the degree to which the legitimacy of a given system of stratification (or of the positions occupied by various individuals within it) is accepted by various groups or subsystems of the collectivity.

### Varieties of Rankings

The term "ranking" seems at first glance to carry a fairly clear meaning, perhaps because of our familiarity with military hierarchies. Actually, several specifications are necessary to make the term analytically useful. In the first place, *the accurate ranking of individuals is possible only within a given scale of valuation.* The accepted scales of valuation of different societies, or even of subgroups in the same society, often have little in common. How, for instance, does one judge accurately the relative standing of a Spanish bishop of the Roman Catholic Church, a Brahmin, a French general, an American millionaire, a Russian commissar, a Swedish scientist, a member of the English nobility? Individuals occupying these positions have high rank in their respective social systems, but what common denominator would permit precise ranking of each position relative to the others?[7]

[5] However, not all social distinctions become objects of ranking, nor are all ranked social objects precisely ordered into unitary hierarchies.

[6] This conception has been developed by Talcott Parsons, "A Revised Analytical Approach to the Theory of Social Stratification," in Reinhard Bendix and Seymour Martin Lipset (eds.), *Class, Status and Power: A Reader in Social Stratification* (New York: Free Press, 1953), pp. 92–128.

[7] As Speier has correctly emphasized, no single objective basis for stratification is determining for all societies; institutionalized stratification is a matter of reciprocal evaluations, and the privileges or disadvantages of different social positions are to be understood as "the objective manifestation of social evaluations which are implied in the way the individual

In less marked degree, the same difficulty characterizes a complex and dispersed collectivity such as the United States. The Nob Hill society of San Francisco may be in some ways similar to the Beacon Hill society of Boston, but it is difficult to compare the rankings of the two local systems. Furthermore, the stratification that prevails within specific social organizations such as churches, armies, factories, governments, families, criminal gangs, schools, and so on (segmental stratification), must be distinguished from caste and class arrangements, which crosscut communities and the more inclusive society.[8] Segmental stratification is most conveniently studied as a part of *social organization,* class or caste stratification as a part of the broader *institutional systems* of a society. Our present interest is thus in the second type, by which persons are summarily given a station[9] in a scale of objective privilege and responsibility and in a correlative scale of invidious prestige and deference. An individual's position on this scale is in part, however, a weighted sum of his positions in the various segmental orders to which he belongs. In American society, these orders include specific religious groups, families, cliques, formal associations, residential groupings, ethnic or racial categories, and occupation; a person's occupation and his rank within it are primary influences upon his rank on the scale that stratifies the whole society.[1] The ranking of persons into broad strata for the whole society is much less precise and specific than the ranking that occurs in a small community, or segment of a community; and most individuals probably are not nearly as much concerned with the former as with the latter.[2] In the local area, characteristics of individuals and families often are widely known in great detail; in the larger social arena judgments are more broadly categorical and tend to focus on wealth, authority, occupation, publicized achievement, and outstanding family reputation. In actual behavior, a person's standing or prestige rank varies from group to group and situation to situation; and even the prestige of occupations is differently rated in different parts of the society. To speak of a scale of stratification for

---

and his external qualities are typically treated by men of different positions and in the way that men of different positions are typically treated by him." Hans Speier, "Social Stratification in the Urban Community," *American Sociological Review,* 1, 2 (April 1936), 194–195.

[8] W. Lloyd Warner and Allison Davis, "A Comparative Study of American Caste," in Edgar T. Thompson (ed.), *Race Relations and the Race Problem* (Durham, N.C.: Duke University Press, 1939), p. 220.

[9] Kingsley Davis, "A Conceptual Analysis of Stratification," *American Sociological Review,* 7, 3 (June 1942), pp. 309–321.

[1] Always, of course, a given individual's summary rank is influenced by the age and sex categories to which he belongs. Thus, in certain situations, a lower-class adult may have age prerogatives that override class distinctions in dealing with an upper-class child or youth. Similarly, occupation may be a primary criterion of stratification only within racial or ethnic categories.

[2] "There are probably two kinds of class order in the United States: (1) a number of separate class structures in small communities all over the country—structures seen and agreed upon only by certain members of those communities, and (2) nationwide classes, perceived vaguely by about three-quarters of the population." Richard T. Morris, *et al.,* "Social Stratification," in Leonard Broom and Philip Selznick, *Sociology,* 3rd ed. (New York: Harper & Row, 1963), p. 197.

a whole nation, therefore, is to make a generalization that may not exactly fit any particular situation.

There is little doubt that stratification in small and moderately sized communities, at least, is a system. There are bounded interdependence and specific causal connections among its elements. There is more doubt as to whether there is anything that could properly be considered a national system. Certainly, translocal stratification lacks the concreteness of the total interpersonal rankings of the local community. Nevertheless, in other respects, there is a system of national stratification. It exists, first, in the enduring objective differentials of income, wealth, authority, and power. It exists also in the relatively high degree of consensus about categorical rankings of occupational prestige, extending even to fairly definite evaluations of specific conspicuous positions. It exists in the interpersonal knowledge, mutual acquaintance, and intimate association among persons in "elite" circles of upper strata.[3] Finally, it has reality in the web of communication and mobility that links together, in a great variety of ways, persons in similar rank positions in different regions and localities.

Ranking in a hierarchy of prestige carries with it many and diverse kinds of permitted, forbidden, and enjoined behaviors, and various degrees of privilege and power. In the diverse universe of prestige rankings, for example, are included those based on age, seniority, and sex. In general older persons are ranked over younger; those senior in years of service, residence, or membership take precedence over their juniors; in some respects, men outrank women. Individuals are also ranked on a large number of personal characteristics of mind, body, and personality; on their sociometric positions in a network of interpersonal attraction; on their memberships in social categories and groupings. The ways in which these several criteria are invoked vary from one situation to another, and the distinctions are often subtle and changeable.

However, the more enduring and structurally significant rankings are those that are: (1) total rather than segmental or specific to particular situations, (2) decisive for the position of at least a nuclear family unit rather than a single individual. Such rankings involve primarily the main socially recognized *positions* occupied by the family head, usually the husband-father, and most importantly, occupation and standing within it.

Thus, the "elite" strata are in part defined as elite by the deference that they receive from others. Deference may take an almost indefinite number of forms: acquiescence in material advantages or other objective privileges, tones of voice, ritualized salutations and leave takings, use of honorific titles, order of precedence, and so on. The pervasive elaboration of symbols of rank and honor in all complex societies is repeatedly noted in sociological observations. Men often are powerfully moved by these symbols: titles; insignia; medals; distinctive clothing, housing, automobile; terms of address; letterheads; type of office and furnishings. Almost any item in a style of life

[3] E. Digby Baltzell, *Philadelphia Gentlemen: The Making of a National Upper Class* (New York: Free Press, 1958), and *The Protestant Establishment: Aristocracy and Caste in America* (New York: Random House, 1964); C. Wright Mills, *The Power Elite* (New York: Oxford University Press, 1956).

can become associated with a ranked position: foods eaten, heirlooms, magazines and books read, music heard, place of residence, favored kinds of sports, schools attended, drinking patterns, pronunciation and accent, gestures, religious affiliation, recreational activities, and so forth.[4] Whatever the specific behavior and symbols, their common element is their generally recognized social meaning as deferential. The elite groups may be further defined by their share of various kinds of tangible privileges and immunities—for example, high income, possession of valued material goods, exemption from burdensome tasks, special immunities (from taxes, for instance, or from jury service, military service, prosecution for various misdemeanors, crimes), access to the person and goods of others, specific power and authority. Thus, prestige is the "subjective" aspect, and *wealth* (command over purchasable goods and services) and *power* (ability to control the acts of others), important "objective" aspects of station.

Much confusion in the consideration of stratification can be avoided by holding fast to the following elementary distinctions.

1. Stratification refers to the existence of a rank order. Such an order *can have a unique meaning only within a given social system,* but the ranking orders of different societies may be compared in several important respects.[5]
2. Any given ranking system can be analyzed in terms of:
   a.) The *distribution of objective privileges,* for example, income, wealth, safety (health, crime rates), authority, and so on;
   b.) *Rankings* by members of the society (prestige and esteem);
   c.) The *criteria of rank,* whether personal qualities or achievements, family membership, possessions, authority, or power;
   d.) The *symbols of rank,* for example, style of life, clothing, housing, organizational membership, and so on;
   e.) The *ease or difficulty and frequency of changes in rank position;*
   f.) The *solidarity among individuals or groups* sharing a similar position in the system:
      (1) *Interaction patterns* (clique structures, common organizational memberships, intermarriage, and so on;
      (2) *Similarity or dissimilarity of beliefs, attitudes, values;*
      (3) *Consciousness of stratification position shared with others;*
      (4) *Concerted action as a collectivity*—for instance, "class warfare."

The nature of many controversies current in the literature on social stratification can be clarified by reference to these basic elements of the problem.[6] For instance, the Marx-Engels theses distinguish classes according to relations of individuals to the means of economic production—in our

[4] Cf. Harold M. Hodges, *Social Stratification: Class in America* (Cambridge, Mass.: Schenkman, 1964), chaps. VII–VIII.

[5] For examples of useful studies of this kind, see Reinhard Bendix and Seymour Martin Lipset (eds.), *Class, Status and Power: Social Stratification in Comparative Perspective,* second ed. (New York: Free Press, 1966), pp. 149–199, 309–321, 561–615.

[6] T. B. Bottomore, *Classes in Modern Society* (New York: Pantheon Books, 1966).

terms, according to the objective distribution of one special privilege. The possession of rights over the means of production is regarded as carrying with it intrinsic social power, including that of legalized coercion. Eventually class solidarity develops out of similar objective position (f-2), leading to class consciousness (f-3), and finally to concerted action (f-4). These different aspects of Marxian theory are often commented upon as if they constituted a single, unitary conception.

In current studies of stratification, the accumulated reworkings of data and theories permit intellectual resolution of many of the heated controversies generated by Marxian theory. It is easy now, especially in the American setting, to criticize Marx for obvious errors and limitations—communism did not come first to highly industrialized countries, the progressive splitting into proletariat and bourgeoisie has not occurred in the way anticipated, and so on. Yet hardly any serious analyses of stratification can afford to neglect Marx's pioneering recognition of the pervasive importance of control and power, his perception of how the consequences of productive arrangements spread through the social system, the problem of class consciousness, the built-in sources of opposition of interests, the role of ideologies, and the conditions for class solidarity and class action. The comprehensiveness and scope of Marx's analysis cannot just be set aside in favor of studying local prestige-cliques in small American communities.[7]

What is called for in this situation is a clear recognition that the total set of phenomena we call social stratification includes both a structure of power and a system of prestige ranking, both diffuse strata and highly organized class units, both militant class consciousness and apolitical status-envy, and so on. The really important and interesting questions are not the old global polemics but precise inquiries into the actual relations among different aspects of stratification—power and prestige, mobility and political orientations, occupation and style of life—and between stratification and other aspects of society and culture.

### Occupations and Stratification

In part because of the availability of the data, a great many investigations have utilized occupation as the defining mark of class. The usefulness of this approach is apparent; in our modern society a person's occupation is one of the most important determinants of his whole way of living. Occupation alone, however, will not identify social class position. Unfortunately, data corresponding to the elements affecting stratification outlined above are as yet extremely scanty; and accordingly we shall be forced to rely heavily upon occupation as a rough index of social rank. Interpreted with care, however, the available information about occupational groupings throws a great deal of light on the stratification systems of our society. For example, it can be used to indicate, at least crudely, the relation of individuals to the means of production (Who controls the means of livelihood?) and the way this

[7] For a quite different kind of analysis, see W. Lloyd Warner and Paul S. Hunt, *The Social Life of a Modern Community* (New Haven, Conn.: Yale University Press, 1941); W. Lloyd Warner, Marchia Meeker, and Kenneth Eells, *Social Class in America* (Chicago: Science Research Associates, 1949).

relation affects their social and political attitudes. Occupational categories serve as well as they do as indices of stratification because there is a relatively high degree of consensus concerning the prestige of various occupations.

Not only is some set of rated or ranked evaluations of social position always present in continuing total societies, but in the specific case of occupations a considerable body of data for different nations indicates marked similarities in ratings.[8] The source of this convergence of evaluations across East and West, communist and noncommunist, and industrialized and nonindustrialized countries is open to debate.[9] Judging from one limited sample, ratings in a nonindustrialized society (Indonesia) are very much like ratings in the industrialized nations (U.S.S.R., Japan, Great Britain, New Zealand, United States). If this is the case, industrialization cannot be the common factor leading to similar average rankings. A possible explanation is that members of those complex societies that contain specialized institutional sectors and a fairly elaborate division of labor use common standards to evaluate occupations. In all cases there appear to be tendencies to rate highest those occupations that involve the exercise of power, high financial return, high education, mental-verbal activities, dealing with crucial values in personal crises (doctors, lawyers, priests), and "service to society."[1] The exact significance of these possible criteria remains unknown and is the object of much critical discussion. Whatever the explanations that may be developed out of later research, it is necessary to include at least four sets of factors, namely: (1) the social value attached to the activities represented by a given occupation or position; (2) the scarcity of qualified personnel; (3) the power of the incumbents in a given occupation to control their remuneration, conditions of work, and style of life; (4) the prestige-relevant attributes of persons practicing the occupation, apart from direct evaluation of occupational activities themselves. These aspects of occupational ranking are correlated but do vary independently to an important extent.

The ranking of individuals according to occupational activity is affected by two main considerations: the prestige of the occupation itself and the evaluation of the individual's position and performance within it. An activity of high importance, or even indispensability, may not be highly ranked or otherwise rewarded if persons willing to adequately perform it are available in abundant supply and if the occupation has little power or authority. An occupation may be raised or lowered in prestige by the extraneous social characteristics of its practitioners (for example, upper-class persons, women, foreigners). Maximum prestige may be expected for an occupation of crucial social value, monopolized by a powerful social group or association

---

[8] Alex Inkeles and Peter Rossi, "National Comparisons of Occupational Prestige," *American Journal of Sociology*, LXI, 4 (January 1956), 329–39.

[9] R. Murray Thomas, "Reinspecting a Structural Position on Occupational Prestige," *American Journal of Sociology*, LXVII, 5 (March 1962), 561–565.

[1] Cf. Archibald O. Haller and David M. Lewis, "The Hypothesis of Intersocietal Similarity in Occupational Prestige Hierarchies," *American Journal of Sociology*, LXXII, 2 (September 1966), 210–216.

that dictates entrance requirements and conditions of work and manned by persons of upper-stratum origin. To some degree this characterization might be applied to a considerable proportion of medical doctors in the United States, to Junker officers in 1914 Germany, or to *fin de siècle* university professors in Europe.

This formulation avoids the indeterminant argument of "functional" versus "power" interpretations. The functional view holds that differential reward is necessary if the socially important and difficult tasks are to be performed. The power interpretation is that occupants of controlling positions are effectively able to compel the remainder of the population to grant rewards and privileges. The first view focuses upon supply and demand, the inducements that elicit varying supplies of performances; the second points to coerced advantage. Certainly both interpretations have some validity, and the exact importance of each differs in various kinds of social structures.

In American society, broad occupational groups are evaluated according to a definite pattern that places at the bottom of the prestige scale manual labor[2] and unskilled personal service involving direct personal dependence upon superiors. Above this level the prestige of occupations seems to follow roughly the degree of skill presumed to be entailed and the size of the income derived. The authority over persons inherent in a given occupation further modifies the rank order; for example, factory foremen, policemen, or judges seem to receive an added increment of prestige on this ground.

The distribution of occupational prestige suggests the hypothesis that deference tends to flow to those positions that are perceived as (1) potentially having vital consequences for the most important values and interests of individuals—for their physical survival, health, safety, economic position, social standing, peace of mind, or total spiritual destiny; (2) "autonomous" or "voluntaristic," in the sense that the practitioner is thought to be relatively free to give or withhold goods, services and sanctions.[3] Of course, the average ratings of the prestige of occupations represent the aggregation of many complex judgments, based on greatly varied amounts and kinds of information.[4] There is some evidence to suggest that generalized prestige ratings may not be based on an estimate of the specific valued characteristics of an occupation and of its practitioners so much as upon a judgment that other people accord the occupation a certain degree of prestige or that it "belongs" to (as explained below) a certain cluster of other occupations, for example, professions.[5]

[2] See the early report in Cecil C. North and Paul K. Hatt, "Jobs and Occupations: A Popular Evaluation," *Opinion News* (September 1, 1947).

[3] Louis Kriesberg, "The Bases of Occupational Prestige: The Case of Dentists," *American Sociological Review*, 27, 2 (April 1962), 238–244.

[4] For example, persons in lower, as compared with those in higher socioeconomic strata, have less information about the whole set of occupations and tend to make judgments in primarily economic terms.

[5] Edward O. Laumann and Louis Guttman, "The Relative Associational Contiguity of Occupations in an Urban Setting," *American Sociological Review*, 31, 2 (April 1966), 169–178.

The universal existence of stratification of some kind in self-subsistent societies is beyond dispute. Very disputable indeed, however, is the adequacy of conceiving of occupational positions as layered within a single unidimensional scale of generalized prestige. Not at issue is the fact that broad categories of occupations can be ranked in a single order. The point, rather, is that such an ordering (apart from its possible multidimensional character) does not exhaust the important generalized ordering of occupations; in particular, it ignores the possible significance of *situs*,[6] the horizontal clustering of occupations. Certain sets of occupations may belong together by virtue of common contribution to a certain societal activity or function, such as legal authority, manufacturing, entertainment, education, health, commerce. Such clusterings may be actual in the sense that (1) each constitutes a necessary functional unit (without the total combination the tasks do not get done); (2) the occupants of the set share common beliefs, values, and behavioral patterns—they constitute a subculture; (3) persons outside the situs and those within it conceive of it as a unity and attribute common characteristics to incumbents of occupations within it. Initial attempts to develop a classification of situses suggest that analysis in these terms may add importantly to the understanding of complex occupational structures.[7]

Popular evaluations of occupations, at least at the level of abstract stereotypes, seem to be highly crystallized and have remained stable over a considerable period of time.[8] In some twenty studies of the social prestige ranking of occupations that have been made during the last twenty-five years in the United States, there is remarkable consistency in the rankings reported.[9]

A recent and comprehensive review of all main studies reaches the conclusion that the ordered ratings of prestige of major occupational titles is "remarkably stable through time as well as space."[1]

Individuals are also judged according to their prominence, ability, or reputation *within* a specific occupation. The individual's rank (his standing) is dependent not only upon his occupation but upon his success in it; he is "the best doctor in town," "a leading lawyer," "the top salesman in the eastern district," and so on. These evaluations play a complex role in establishing an individual's class position. Within a specialized occupational field, the social evaluations especially important to him are those of his

---

[6] The term is from Emile Benoit-Smullyan, "Status, Status Types, and Status Interrelations," *American Sociological Review*, 9, 2 (April 1944), 151–161.

[7] Richard T. Morris and Raymond J. Murphy, "The Situs Dimension in Occupational Structure," *American Sociological Review*, 24, 2 (April 1959), 231–239.

[8] W. H. Form, "Toward an Occupational Social Psychology," *Journal of Social Psychology*, XXIV, First Half (August 1946), 87.

[9] See the summary and bibliography in Maryon K. Welch, "The Ranking of Occupations on the Basis of Social Status," *Occupations*, XXVII, 4 (January 1949), 237–241. Cf. also the two articles by Raymond B. Cattell in *Journal of Social Psychology*, XXI (February 1945), 3–55.

[1] Robert W. Hodge, Paul M. Siegel, and Peter H. Rossi, "Occupational Prestige in the United States, 1925–1963," *American Journal of Sociology*, LXX, 3 (November 1964), 286.

peers—of other people who are technically competent to judge his performance. These informed valuations, however, are only loosely correlated with broader reputation in the total community. In a highly specialized occupational structure, competence in occupations requiring complex technical knowledges and skills can be accurately judged only by other experts in the special field. General community reputation is only in part established on the basis of strict technical competence; it is also affected by a wide range of irrelevant factors. For instance, most people are necessarily not competent to judge the skill of a medical doctor; yet their ignorance is no bar to the establishment of his definite reputation. The "best doctor in town" might owe his ranking in large measure to a good bedside manner, the "right social connections," and a variety of other extramedical factors. There is, indeed, an observable tendency in such instances for reputation to become cumulative, in part just because there is both a strong need to get the best doctor and a lack of the technical knowledge for making a selection.

We must consider also the definiteness of the stratification structure. On the one hand, we have the sharp delineation of specific positions within a definite formal organization; within a modern army, for example, there are clear-cut ranks, each of which carries defined rights and duties along with a specific "package" of claims to prestige and deference. The army has a hierarchy of institutional office. The positions are explicit and the stratification is to an important degree "objective"—a matter of directly observable privileges and responsibilities. At the other pole of organization, we have the local community, where the individual's station is determined by the judgments of a loosely defined aggregate of associates, acquaintances, and other local residents. Although the position of citizen "No. 1" may be unmistakably clear, he holds it by a diffuse cultural consensus; it is not explicit and carries no definite body of duties and privileges. One has to know the community attitudes to define the individual's position; whereas in the organized hierarchy, such knowledge is not necessary: a commanding general is a commanding general so long as he holds this position within the organization, regardless of the diffuse valuation of soldiers and other citizens.

Thus, the station of any individual may always be in part described by pointing to his *objective privileges,* his *general prestige* in the total relevant community, or his *specific position within an organized group.* What, then, are the *criteria* by which individuals or groups are evaluated or placed in any given position in a stratification system?

### Criteria for Stratification

To begin with, we know that different cultures emphasize different criteria. In some societies at some periods we find a rigid inequalitarian system in which an individual's position is determined for life by *birth into a family of a particular category or grade.* The theoretical ideal type of such a caste society would exclude every consideration for placement save birth.[2] Other

---

[2] See Gerald D. Berreman, "Stratification, Pluralism and Interaction: A Comparative Analysis of Caste," in A.V.S. de Reuck and Julie Knight (eds.), *Ciba Foundation Symposium on Caste and Race: Comparative Approaches* (London: J. A. Churchill Ltd.,

*"class"* *(wealth*

cultures emphasize *possessions:* not birth, but the fact of wealth becomes primary in invidious social evaluation. Still other cultures may attribute high *Personal* position to individuals on the basis of certain *personal qualities:* beauty, wit, *quali* social wisdom, physical strength, religious piety, possession by spirits, or *Achievem* whatnot. This kind of evaluation merges into that based on the criterion of *achievement:* if personal qualities designate what the person is considered to be, achievements identify what he does. The acts that are valued highly are very different in various cultures; the range includes ascetic achievements (of monks, hermits, saints, and so on), military prowess, scientific work, commercial success, and artistic accomplishments. Finally, there is con- *Authorit* siderable intercultural variation in the use of *authority* as a criterion of rank. Authority exists in all societies; that is, there is some form of recognized (legitimate) right by which some individuals control the acts of others, even when the control may conflict with the immediate wishes of those subject to it. Again, however, the social evaluation of authority has a wide range; some societies make the exercise of authority the main criterion of general social rank, whereas others deprecate it. Authority shades off into the sheer exercise of nonlegitimized *power,* that is, the purely coercive control of others, without support by social consensus. Of course, authority often emerges from illegitimate seizure of power, and sheer power some- times commands a grudging admiration and ambivalent prestige even in *Six class* our own society. *criteria*

Six classes of criteria of evaluation have now been outlined:[3] (1) birth (or more broadly, membership in kinship unit); (2) possessions (wealth and income); (3) personal qualities; (4) personal achievement; (5) author- *distingu* ity; and (6) power. The nature of the differential valuation of individuals *intrinsic* is clarified by the distinction drawn by E. T. Hiller between intrinsic and *extrinsic* extrinsic valuations.[4] Perhaps this distinction comes out most clearly when *valuation* authority is vested in formal organizational status. Here, the valuation of *ie –* the *office* may diverge rather widely from the valuation of a *specific person* *personal* *occupying the office.* If the office carries great authority within a social *qualities* complex itself receiving high social valuation, it must by that fact receive *prestige* a measure of respect and prestige. This prestige tends to be transferred *of* to the person occupying the status. The minister receives deference because *office* of his institutional function; only gross failure or misconduct can prevent any individual in such a position from receiving at least a minimum of in- stitutionalized deference. Similarly, respect is required for the symbols of legitimized authority, regardless of the intrinsic qualities of a particular officer. It may be said that there are "good" leader-follower relations when

1967), p. 51: "An interactional definition of a caste system might be: A system of birth- ascribed groups each of which comprises for its members the maximum limit of status- equal interaction, and between all of which interaction is consistently hierarchical."

[3] This classification is taken from Parsons, "An Analytical Approach to the Theory of Social Stratification," in Reinhard Bendix and Seymour Martin Lipset (eds.), *Class, Status, and Power: A Reader in Social Stratification* (New York: Free Press, 1953), pp. 848–9.

[4] E. T. Hiller, *Social Relations and Structures* (New York: Harper & Row, 1947), pp. 191–215.

the followers respect both the office and the person occupying it. There is then an integration of the two types of valuation. Of the several bases of valuation outlined above, only personal qualities and achievements are intrinsic—and the latter only insofar as achievements are taken as indices of the quality, nature, or character of the person. The other main criteria of ranking—possessions, group membership, power, and authority—are extrinsic.

Social differentiation permits an extended range of extrinsic rankings. This is not to imply that social differentiation is a process imposed upon interaction solely by the functional efficiencies of division of labor in tasks nor that it is derived exclusively from power and coercion. Rather, differentiation initially is intrinsic to the rewarding or punishing qualities of interaction itself, insofar as individuals differ in their capacities to give rewards. For the evaluative standards that always develop in social experience render it inevitable that a person who gives disproportionate rewards builds up claims against those benefited—and these unreciprocated net balances constitute potential power—hence, social differentiation. Any social network quickly becomes differentiated in this way. And because such differentials are always *evaluated*, the differences become the basis for prestige rankings, and thus, stratification.

Social stratification typically focuses upon extrinsic criteria; for it is these that largely permit an extended scale of ranking. The intrinsic valuations appear more often as *prerequisites for consideration of the individual on the legitimate rank-order scale;* for instance, only individuals who are "persons" fall into the major ranking system. Others are in some sense "outside" the structure—slaves, foreigners, heathens, untouchables, excommunicates, lumpen proletariat and the like. They are considered to belong to another social system, to be "outside the pale," or even in an entirely different category of being.[5] The distinction between intrinsic and extrinsic valuations is closely related to the distinction between esteem and prestige. A good servant may be held in high esteem but be invested with very little prestige. The first is a valuation of his personal qualities or his performance of an accepted role; the second is a valuation of his functional position in the social system.[6]

Intrinsic valuations tend to be equalitarian. For instance, the religious concept of the person as having an inviolable soul accountable only to God, a concept current in our culture, gives *everyone some* positive value. It establishes a floor below which invidious devaluation of the human in-

[5] Cf. James West, *Plainville, U.S.A.* (New York: Columbia University Press, 1945), pp. 125–126, on the "people who live like animals."

[6] See Kingsley Davis' analysis "Prestige, Esteem, and Rank" in *Human Society* (New York: Macmillan, 1950), pp. 93 ff. Compare Runciman's discussion of "praise" as over against "respect": there is a vital difference between deference based on admiration for merit and for social contribution, on the one hand, and deference based on categorical positions of power, authority, and group memberships. The first establishes a *pro tem* "aristocracy" of excellence, the second perpetuates an institutionalized stratum of privilege. (W. G. Runciman, *Relative Deprivation and Social Justice: A Study of Attitudes of Social Inequality in Twentieth-Century England* (Berkeley and Los Angeles: University of California Press, 1966) pp. 274–284.)

dividual cannot go. In contrast, by the criteria of extrinsic valuation there are persons and groups that are valueless, or of negative value.

In principle, we can show with great precision the distribution of scarce values, the allocation of privileges, among the individuals of other social units within any given social system. It can be expressed in objective, statistical terms once we know what the relevant privileges are. Groupings or strata derived from such measurements are not necessarily real social groups, however, but may represent simply the more or less arbitrary classification of the investigator. The distribution of privileges (the criterion of extrinsic evaluation) begins to take on full sociological meaning only when it is related to *prestige rankings, social-interaction groupings,* and *beliefs and values held in common.* We shall use the term "social class" to refer to an aggregate of individuals who occupy a broadly similar position in the scale of prestige. These rankings can then be analyzed according to their sources and supports in economic position and political power, and in terms of their relations to attitudes and social organization. There is no doubt that the several major bases for stratification tend to go along together. Power or authority can bring wealth; wealth is often associated with power; high income frequently means also high prestige. But we must not make the elementary mistake of confusing correlation with identity. Many prestigious occupations do not pay particularly well. A general with a moderate income may have vastly more authority than a wealthy stockmarket operator. History is full of impoverished aristocrats, as well as of the new wealth that does not yet command high prestige. As a matter of fact, some of the most interesting problems in the analysis of stratification have to do precisely with the *relations* among the various types of rank orders.

### Ideal Types of Stratification

In approaching American society, we shall have to locate its particular system of social classes with reference to three ideal types of stratification structures. The first, that of *caste,* is a system in which an individual's rank and its accompanying rights and obligations are *ascribed*[7] on the basis of birth into a particular group. In the theoretical, fully developed system, birth alone determines the person's class; no change is possible because of personal qualities or achievements. In the second type, that of *estates*—a form approximated in some parts of Europe during feudal times—classes (nobles, clergy, and commoners, for instance) are rigid; and transmission of position is largely hereditary. However, some limited upward mobility is permitted: the exceptionally gifted and energetic peasant lad can on occasion enter the priesthood or the military services and advance to high rank. There is likewise some restricted opportunity for interestate marriages, the prototype being the marriage of the commoner girl to a man of a higher estate. Finally, the third ideal type of stratification is the *open-class* system. Here

[7] See Ralph Linton, *The Study of Man* (New York: Appleton-Century-Crofts, 1936), pp. 115 ff., for the distinction between ascribed and achieved status. Hiller, *Social Relations and Structures,* has added a category of assumed status for those positions that are not "achieved" but are entered on a basis other than that of birth.

the various strata are highly permeable; there is a great deal of rising and falling in the scale. At the theoretically conceivable extreme, "classes" would be merely those temporary and nominal aggregates of individuals who happened at any particular time to receive about the same evaluation. Birth into a particular family of a particular group would be formally irrelevant to the later class position of the individual. Obviously such a society is highly competitive. Individuals must compete for status on the basis of personal qualities and achievements.

## THE AMERICAN CASE

### An American Ideal

In a caste or castelike society, the upper groups control the criteria for ranking and successfully impose their standards upon the whole society. To take an American example, in plantation areas of the Old South the dominant white upper classes defined not only their own position but that of lower-class whites and of the Negro population as well.[8] In a long established castelike order, at least under the conditions of a stable agricultural society, a justifying ideology can come to be so widely accepted that even in the lower castes the standards of the dominant orders become the criteria of ranking.[9] In an open-class society, on the other hand, there is no single accepted standard; each group or stratum tends to have its own perspective. Presumably those who in their own eyes are upper class will always attempt to set the scale for the entire population; but in a highly mobile, competitive system there may be considerable and effective disagreement. Differently located strata will emphasize different criteria of ranking. Thus, in our own society the upwardly mobile middle classes tend to stress competitive occupational achievement and respectability, whereas the newly arrived members of the upper strata emphasize wealth, and the established upper-upper groups give disproportionate weight to lineage ("purity") and to certain symbols of secure status.[1] If a society is to function, of course, there must be some minimal consensus as to the criteria for the social distribution of rewards and for the assignation of prestige rankings. However, as the United States demonstrates, there is room for much variability and inconsistency in the criteria for determining class membership in a complex open-class society. By "American" ideals, *position should be based*

---

[8] Wilbert E. Moore and Robin M. Williams, "Stratification in the Ante-Bellum South," *American Sociological Review*, 7, 3 (June 1942), 343–351. For evidence on the importance of the middle classes in that society, see Frank L. Owsley, *Plain Folk of the Old South* (Baton Rouge: Louisiana State University Press, 1949).

[9] This does *not* mean necessarily that members of the less privileged strata are content with their lot. Discontent and suppressed resentment are often endemic among lower castes. Reexamination of the case of caste in India suggests that even there the deprived strata have seldom been fully satisfied with their position.

[1] These different perspectives and evaluations are more than "mere rationalization." Undoubtedly each grouping tries to establish a moral claim to esteem and prestige on the basis of the attributes it has in largest measure. Nevertheless, these variant perspectives prevent upper-class standards from dominating the system, that is, from "closing" it.

*upon personal qualities and achievements.* With one important exception to be discussed later—that of discrimination against minority groups—it is held that our society is and *should be* one in which the individual is free to move into those positions in the society that he has earned by ability, effort, and moral worth. He is supposed to rise or fall according to his own merits: his position is determined by what he is and does or can do *as an individual.* In its logically developed form, this conception of the stratification process becomes an internally consistent scheme that satisfactorily explains and justifies the entire system. It runs as follows:

1. This is a society of equality of opportunity and free, competitive placement. ("Anyone who has it in him can get ahead.")
2. Hence, success is solely a matter of individual merit.
3. Hence, those who are at the top deserve to be there; and those at the bottom are there because of lack of talent or effort: it is "their own fault."
4. Thus, the placement of individuals could not be otherwise without violating the value of individual achievement.

It takes no great acumen to see that actual equality of opportunity does not exist for a very great many individuals; nor is it difficult to show that inherited position, social connections, and a variety of circumstances essentially irrelevant to strictly personal qualities and achievements help place individuals in the stratification order. The more difficult and significant task is to go behind these rather obvious discrepancies and analyze the specific interplay of *different* institutional principles that operate in the stratification system. Of course, the main characteristics of stratification in the United States are by no means unique. Although the situation here does have important distinctive features, it has much in common with other industrialized societies, for example, a complex occupational hierarchy, great differentials in rewards, similar evaluations of occupations, and class differences in satisfaction or discontent.[2]

### Objective Stratification

We may begin by briefly documenting some of the objective facts about stratification in the United States. We know that there are marked differentials in the distribution of scarce values. In 1959, the top 4 percent of families received 18 percent of the total income; on the other hand, the bottom 31 percent of families—those receiving less than $4,000 per year—had to do with 10 percent of the total distribution.[3] Although American average incomes are relatively high, in comparison with other nations, the average figures are not highly illuminating. Few people live on a "median income"; and it is the differentials that tend to command attention. Between the top levels of affluence and the bottom strata of deprivation and poverty are great differences in total life-situation in terms of medical care

[2] Cf. Alex Inkeles, "Industrial Man: The Relation of Status to Experience, Perception and Value," *American Journal of Sociology*, LXVI, 1 (July 1960), 1–31.

[3] Herman P. Miller, *Rich Man, Poor Man* (New York: Thomas Y. Crowell, 1964), pp. 1–13. The relative proportions have not changed greatly since the end of World War II: in 1946, the top 5 percent of *individuals* received 18 percent of total income, after taxes.

and health, food, clothing, shelter, education, recreation, and general access to the comforts and amenities of life in our culture.[4]

In the absence of a single universal, or even generally accepted, principle for allocation of rewards, actual distributions of scarce values often represent mixtures of diverse criteria and give rise to considerable resentment and potential conflict. Confrontations of anomalies tend to be avoided in operating systems by physical isolation, by systematic ignorance and secrecy, by ideological diversions, and a variety of other means by which direct comparisons of highly unequal rewards are rendered infrequent and difficult. Specifically those of great wealth, authority, power, and prestige are separated from those possessing little of these characteristics in residence, work place. places of dining and recreation. The amounts, kinds, and modes of acquisition of advantages are often carefully guarded secrets. (Vicarious participation in luxury, however, often is encouraged.) The starkness of inequality is often clothed in mystification.

At the same time. we have a highly differentiated occupational structure, in which approximately 19 percent of employed persons are laborers or service workers; another 19 percent are operatives and kindred workers; 14 percent are craftsmen, foremen, and kindred workers; 23 percent are in clerical and sales occupations, 12 percent in professions and technical pursuits and only 13 percent are independent proprietors, farmers, managers, and officials.[5]

Self-employed workers who were 23 percent of the labor force in 1910 constituted 15 percent by 1960, and the decline continues. Over half of the present labor force are employees of quite large organizations. The proportion of workers who are in "white-collar" occupations has been increasing rapidly since about 1920.

In the most recent years, especially since the end of World War II, the stratification structure has been greatly affected by major changes in income levels and income distribution. Real incomes have risen sharply and the income of those at lower levels has increased more rapidly than the average. Between 1939 and 1956, the real weekly wages of factory workers increased by more than 50 percent. As total real income has increased, the command of consumers' goods has tended to become more evenly distributed[6]—with exceptions to be noted below.

Moreover, the occupational distribution and the social evaluation of various occupations have worked in the same direction. The proportion of occupations that are poorly paid, heavy, hot, dirty, and of low prestige has decreased; the expanding occupations are those that ordinarily have been thought to be more desirable and of higher rank. And the college

---

[4] And through these differentials, income is a primary determinant of generalized ranking; cf. Wilbert E. Moore, *Industrial Relations and the Social Order* (New York: Macmillan, 1947), pp. 483–484.

[5] United States Bureau of the Census, *United States Census of Population: 1960*, Vol. I, *Characteristics of the Population* (Washington, D.C.: Government Printing Office, 1964), p. lxxvii.

[6] Seymour Martin Lipset and Reinhard Bendix, *Social Mobility in Industrial Society* (Berkeley and Los Angeles: University of California Press, 1959), p. 108.

teacher who realizes that a plumber receives an hourly wage above that which he himself enjoys might on occasion begin to revise his image of occupational ranking. It has become increasingly difficult to identify the economic position of individuals by such symbols as clothing, automobile, or recreational patterns. The mass diffusion of standardized goods under conditions of high and continued prosperity results in increasing uniformity in styles of life. The great variability and vagueness in people's conception of stratification partly derives from the wide distribution of standardized symbols of a "respectable" mode of living.

Nevertheless, there is considerable consistency in generalized ratings of the prestige of occupations—ratings that are not greatly affected by the rater's sex, occupation, economic level, education, region, or size of community.[7] In general the high prestige occupations are those that require high education, yield high income, have low rates of unemployment, and include few nonwhites; however, there is no one single-dimensional scale that accounts for the ratings.

Changes in occupational structure since the turn of the century reflect changes in basic technological, economic, and educational conditions. Farmers and farm managers decreased from 20 percent to 4 percent during 1900–1960, whereas professional, technical, and kindred workers increased from 4 to 12 percent, and the clerical force grew from 3 to 15 percent.[8] As the nation shifted from agriculture and primary manufacturing to service employments, the demand increased for highly trained white-collar workers and decreased for unskilled workers. The net effect has been widespread upgrading in wealth, income, education, and other generally valued characteristics, although as noted earlier, the ranking of occupations according to general prestige has remained largely stable for the period of nearly half a century covered by more or less comparable studies. Few important changes have been recorded since the first studies in 1925. However, comparison of the nation-wide studies conducted by the National Opinion Research Center in 1947 and in 1963 does show some increase in the prestige of scientific and artisan occupations.[9]

The role of differentials in wealth and income in our stratification system is complex and varies greatly in different occupations and communities. Wealth serves as the base for supporting a style of life considered to symbolize class position, and people with money attempt to buy the *symbols* thought to index high status. The proverbial conspicuous consumption of the newly rich is merely a salient instance of the purchased badges of rank.[1]

---

[7] Albert J. Reiss, *et al.*, *Occupations and Social Status* (New York: Free Press, 1962). (This work contains a useful objective occupational index, developed by Otis Dudley Duncan, based on a corrected and weighted combination of education and income.)

[8] Cf. Warren S. Thompson and David T. Lewis, *Population Problems*, 5th ed. (New York: McGraw-Hill, 1965) pp. 184–193.

[9] Hodge, Siegel, and Rossi, *op. cit.*

[1] Thus, Warner found that the highest proportionate expenditures for automobiles and household maintenance occurred in the lower-upper class, among those families just on the margin of acceptance into the upper-upper elite. *The Social Life of a Modern Community*, *op. cit.*, p. 299. It should be noted that this study is based on research undertaken in the 1930's.

Wealth, furthermore, gives its possessor greater educational, occupational, and general cultural opportunity. In the race for achievement, those who start without wealth have difficult hurdles to clear before they can reach equality with their more favored rivals. In addition, wealth is very frequently interpreted in our society as an index of achievement: he has money, therefore he must be successful; and to be successful he must have achieved something. For the primary status-giving positions throughout most of our history have been in business, where the orientation to profits has made achievement subject to the common measure of money; and in our complex society, in which judgments of achievement have to span very diverse and specialized occupations, the difficulty of finding a basis for comparisons leads to concentration on some obvious and universal signs of status. Wealth, as the most universal and easily recognized mark of occupational success, has thus been a convenient symbol of achievement.

The data on income and wealth are extremely complex, subject to diverse errors of reporting and to ambiguities of definition, and not always well adapted for the uses to which we wish to put them. Nevertheless, we must do the best we can with the information we have. The critical and ingenious work of such specialists as Simon Kuznets, Herman Miller, Gabriel Kolko, and Robert Lampman insures that the major sources of possible misinterpretation are at least taken into account.[2] Drawing together a composite of the findings of several major studies, the central conclusions seem to be these:

1. There is great inequality in the distribution of incomes.[3]

2. Although international comparisons give somewhat varying results depending upon the particular data and methods used, it appears that the income distribution in this country is quite similar to that in Sweden, Denmark, and Great Britain, and is substantially less inequalitarian than in many so-called underdeveloped nations.[4]

3. In terms of personal income before taxes, the share of the wealthiest tenth of the population has decreased only very slightly since 1910; nominally, the decrease was from 34 percent to 29 percent, but "hidden" understatements may be sufficient to account for the seeming decrease. On the other hand, the poorest half of the population received a smaller proportion of total income in 1959 than in 1910: a decrease from 27 percent to 23 percent. The only significant increases in income shares have been in the strata just under the top level—strata largely made up of professions, small businessmen, high clerical occupations, and lesser managers.[5]

[2] Simon Kuznets, "Quantitative Aspects of the Economic Growth of Nations," *Economic Development and Cultural Change*, XI, 2 (January 1963); Herman P. Miller, *Rich Man, Poor Man*; Gabriel Kolko, *Wealth and Power in America: An Analysis of Social Class and Income Distribution* (New York: Praeger, 1962); Robert J. Lampman, *The Low-Income Population and Economic Growth*, Study Paper No. 12, Joint Economic Committee, 86th Congress, 1st Session (Washington, D.C.: Government Printing Office, 1959).

[3] Miller, *op. cit.*, p. 35.

[4] Kuznets, *op. cit.*, Table 3.

[5] Gabriel Kolko, *Wealth and Power in America*, *op. cit.*, pp. 14–15. Documentation is given by Kolko of considerable understatement of income actually received by the richer strata (pp. 16–45).

4. Much the same general conclusion holds for the distribution of wealth, as distinct from income. Contrary to some popular opinions, the best available studies suggest that there has been no really important change over the last forty years in the inequality of ownership of wealth, including ownership of stocks in corporations.[6]

However, attempts to use wealth as the sole criterion of stratification set up powerful strains. Much wealth is known to have been acquired by morally disapproved means; much wealth is inherited or acquired in other ways that can hardly be regarded as "achievement." In a dynamic and violently oscillating economy, there are such rapid changes in the income and wealth of large numbers of individuals that widespread doubt is created as to the correlation of wealth with achievement or personal qualities. Finally, the occupational structure is so complex that income or wealth clearly does not form a single scale for evaluation of movie stars, business executives, ministers, athletes, university scientists, and so on indefinitely.[7] In some occupations, especially the salaried professions, it is not even supposed that income is a measure of the "worth" of a man's contributions; salary is supposed to represent recognition and to be adequate for the style of life expected of a certain occupational status.

Equality of income or wealth has never been a major objective of national policy. For example, national legislation dealing with taxation has not envisaged any substantial equalization of incomes. It was only under the pressing need for revenue in World War II that personal income taxes were raised to levels that really made a difference in the higher brackets. The consequence was that high-income strata sought and found a large number of ingenious ways of avoiding the burden of a sharply progressive tax. Particularly important has been the shift in incomes in the business community away from the highly vulnerable fixed salary to tax-free interest, capital gains, and other exempt or low-tax forms.[8] So effective have been these devices that the distribution of income *after* federal income taxes is practically the same as the distribution before taxes. Meanwhile, the middle- and low-income groupings are subject to effectively unavoidable and substantial income taxation. Furthermore, most other taxes are regressive, bearing most heavily upon the low-income family; sales taxes are notorious in this respect, but social insurance taxes are also highly regressive. Although it is extremely difficult to estimate the total tax burden by income levels with any great precision, available studies suggest that low-income families and individuals pay nearly as large a proportion of their small incomes in taxes as high-income persons do; and the loss of the low-income family is

[6] In addition to Kolko, *op. cit.*, and Miller, *op. cit.*, see Edward B. Cox, *Trends in the Distribution of Stock Ownership* (Philadelphia: University of Pennsylvania Press, 1963), and Robert J. Lampman, *The Share of Top Wealth-Holders in National Wealth, 1922–1956* (Princeton, N.J.: Princeton University Press, 1962).

[7] For all these reasons, the notion that wealth and virtue are synonymous has lost some of its force in American culture. Nevertheless, there is still some allegiance to the older system of belief. See Moore, *Industrial Relations, op. cit.*, p. 487.

[8] Kolko, *op. cit.*, p. 32. Other devices include deferred income stock options, expense accounts, company automobiles, free vacations, and other expensive "fringe benefits."

undoubtedly greater in terms of the needs unsatisfied by reason of the heavy tax payments.[9]

## The Rediscovery of Poverty ( 1960's )

After decades of inattention, public discussion of poverty and the poor was reopened and focused during the 1960's by actions of the President and the Congress. These political developments had been preceded by several volumes that rediscovered for middle-class audiences the persistence of economic and social deprivation.[1] This new concern was not merely for the relatively small (although important) populations of the Skid Rows of the cities,[2] but dealt broadly with unemployment, partial unemployment, low wages, and consumer "exploitation"[3] among able workers who wished to work and tried to work to support their families.

Such refocused attention suggested to many observers that the so-called "levelling up" resulting from rising national real income had been exaggerated. The symbols of respectable well-being, such as good houses, automobiles, and major household appliances are indeed widely distributed. But systematic and conspicuous differences remain and are obvious to inspection.[4] Although much of the most extreme poverty is hidden away—in segregated slums, back streets, isolated rural areas—its continued presence is inescapable; and evidences of the conspicuous consumption of the very rich permeate the mass media and are accessible to public scrutiny.

Individuals and family units may be poor primarily because their whole society is poor. This is currently true of most of the so-called underdeveloped countries: it was true of the United States at the depths of the Great Depression of the 1930's. On the other hand, poverty in the midst of a society of great average affluence derives from a combination of "social" (or structural) and "individual" causes. Because of differentials in economic development in conjunction with relative immobility of population, certain localities and regions are much poorer than others. For example, families in the South are more than twice as likely to be poor as families in the remainder of the nation. Pockets of poverty exist in many local areas of declining economic opportunity, for example, in coal-mining localities. Massive poverty is associated with membership in social categories subject to sys-

[9] Contrary to many opinions, the return flow of "welfare" payments does not offset the tax payments. Cf. *ibid.*, p. 39.

[1] Lewis A. Coser, "The Sociology of Poverty," *Social Problems*, 13, 2 (Fall 1965), 140–148; Michael Harrington, *The Other America: Poverty in the United States* (New York: Macmillan, 1962); Robert H. Brenner, *From the Depths: The Discovery of Poverty in the United States* (New York: New York University Press, 1956); Herman P. Miller, *Income of the American People* (New York: Wiley, 1955).

[2] Donald J. Bogue, *Skid Row in American Cities* (Chicago: University of Chicago Press, 1963); Samuel E. Wallace, *Skid Row as a Way of Life* (Totowa, N.J.: Bedminster Press, 1965).

[3] David Caplowitz, *The Poor Pay More* (N.Y.: Free Press, 1963).

[4] Cf. Kolko, *op. cit.*, p. 126: "Differences in modes of living and consumption, dictated by differences in income, create a sharply stratified social order and a distinct class structure. Although absolute consumption may increase on every income level as real income gradually expands, the inequalities of income and consumption remain. This, at least, has been the pattern in the United States."

tematic discrimination: although most of the poor are whites, nonwhite persons are more than three times as likely to be poor as white persons.[5] Still others are poor by reason of structural dislocations such as the sudden destruction of a skilled occupation by new technology. In addition to all such structural sources of poverty are those that derive from individual or familial characteristics that preclude effective competitive activity in full-time occupations; these disabilities or quasi-disabilities include physical handicaps, ill health, advanced age, low education, excessively large families, and the situation of female household heads with young children to support.

These considerations gain additional implications when put alongside a revised appraisal of insurance and subsidy programs, governmental and private. Analysis of actual effects indicates that many of the security and welfare innovations since 1932 have provided little real protection to the most disadvantaged strata. Minimum wages generally are set below prevailing market levels. Unemployment compensation leaves a large proportion of workers completely unprotected, and levels of compensation are very low in relation to wages or to subsistence needs. Old age insurance benefits are too low to support the level of living most recipients had previously maintained. Health insurance, even after medicare provisions, is not sufficient to protect persons in the lower half of the income distribution from financial catastrophe in the case of major and prolonged illness or disability.

There appears to be growing acceptance as desirable national goals of the aims of the reduction of unemployment to minimum (frictional) levels, the maintenance of some adequate subsistence income for all families and individuals, and the avoidance of rapid inflation. It is clear that the measures required to attain these general objectives are more than narrowly "economic." Much unemployment and low income is structural—due to social and political factors that prevent the needed economic activities and adjustments, such as racial discrimination; lack of training; barriers to employment of the aged, youth, the handicapped; or diverse social barriers to mobility of workers.

Although many of the basic conditions that tend to produce both militant protest and sporadic mass outbursts of expressive violence had long been known to social science,[6] the waves of urban riots that swept the nation, beginning in 1964 and continuing through the decade, were not expected by many of the more affluent white Americans. Both structural barriers to communication (for example, segregation) and wilful or opportunistic ignorance were involved.

Thus, all political rhetoric to the contrary notwithstanding, both income (or wealth) and occupation are central criteria of stratification; and there

[5] Of the 34.1 million persons classified as "poor" by criteria of the Social Security Administration in 1964, 10.5 million were nonwhite (almost entirely Negro). (Mollie Orshansky, "More About the Poor in 1964," *Social Security Bulletin*, 29, 5 (May 1966), 18.)

[6] Lewis A. Coser, *Continuities in the Study of Social Conflict* (New York: Free Press, 1967); Robin M. Williams, Jr., *Strangers Next Door* (Englewood Cliffs, N.J.: Prentice-Hall, 1964), and *The Reduction of Intergroup Tensions* (New York: Social Science Research Council, 1947).

are sharply unequal distributions of the objective privileges offered by both in the American population.[7] Differences in these respects are closely related to a series of specific behavior-patterns that together make up recognizably different, class-typed ways of living. To take only one example, the correlation of economic and occupational levels with participation in formally organized associations has been demonstrated in a large number of studies. For instance, Mirra Komarovsky found that in a sample of 2,223 adult residents of New York City, the percentage of persons belonging to formal associations was invariably larger the higher the occupational status.[8] Warner and associates reported that in "Yankee City" the percentage of persons who were members of some formal associations increased from only 22 in the lower-lower class to 64 in the upper-middle and 72 in the upper-upper class.[9] Even in the small town and rural areas, research has consistently shown different patterns of social participation among persons on different economic levels. The pattern is that participation in the family and in informal neighborhood relations makes up a larger part of all social participation for the poorer groups than it does for the wealthier, although a larger proportion of persons in the lower occupational categories report having no close friends.[1] The upper economic groups are more likely to belong to segmental, special-interest associations.

There are other social effects of economic stratification in our society. In spite of the remarkable public school system and provisions for economic assistance in securing college training, economically upper-class persons can most easily secure an education. Persons in the lower income and occupational strata read less, travel less, are less active in political affairs. Their social horizons are constricted.[2] Furthermore, evidence consistently shows that mortality and morbidity rates vary inversely with income. Casualty rates in recent wars have been higher among the lower-income families.[3] Sickness and health, death and life are thus to an appreciable degree functions of economic position.

Objective evidence of stratification in the United States is to be found not only in the differences in occupation and income but also in the great differentials of authority and power. The growth of large, centralized economic and political associations has meant the emergence of hierarchical

[7] Cf. John Porter, *The Vertical Mosaic: An Analysis of Social Class and Power in Canada* (Toronto: University of Toronto Press, 1965).

[8] Mirra Komarovsky, "The Voluntary Associations of Urban Dwellers," *American Sociological Review*, 11, 6 (December 1946), 686–98; see also Leonard Reissman, "Class, Leisure and Social Participation," *American Sociological Review*, 19, 1 (February 1954), 76–84.

[9] Warner, *The Social Life of a Modern Community, op. cit.*, p. 329.

[1] Joseph A. Kahl, *The American Class Structure* (New York: Holt, Rinehart & Winston, 1957), pp. 137–138; Peter H. Rossi, *Why Families Move* (New York: Free Press, 1955), pp. 34–40.

[2] Genevieve Knupfer, "Portrait of the Underdog," *Public Opinion Quarterly*, XI, I (Spring 1947), 103–114; Albert K. Cohen and Harold M. Hodges, "Characteristics of the Lower Blue-Collar Class," *Social Problems*, 10, 4 (Spring 1963), 303–334.

[3] Albert J. Mayer and T. F. Hoult, "Social Stratification in Combat Survival," *Social Forces*, 34, 2 (December 1955), 155–159.

organizations of sweeping power; in these structures it is possible for a few individuals to exercise quite comprehensive authority over large numbers of employees, union members, or citizens of the state. The military services, of course, provide the outstanding examples.

Finally, although the data are scanty and unsystematic, there are many converging indications that immunities and disabilities in the face of the law and penal system are correlated with class position. Sutherland's studies of "white-collar crime" have shown that many business practices that are legally punishable offenses are either not detected or not severely dealt with when committed by middle- and upper-class persons.[4] John Useem, in his study of a small South Dakota town, reports a tendency in the same direction.[5] August Hollingshead shows how in a midwestern town the system of discipline in the school is adjusted to favor the upper-class child.[6] Class discriminations in the administration of justice sometimes take the form of greater leniency in dealing with intragroup offenses of the lower classes. As Myrdal has shown, this leniency results in lack of legal protection for the law-abiding members of the lower stratum. On the other hand, the lower-stratum individual who commits an offense against a member of the upper groups may be treated with unusual severity.[7]

In short, detailed study of stratification considered as a *distribution of objective privileges* clearly demonstrates the presence in American society of marked differentials in wealth and income and in social participation, authority and power, education, health, safety, and legal protection. *This* kind of stratification, then, is an important reality. Our next question is: To what extent do persons sharing objective positions have common attitudes and ideas; and to what extent do those in dissimilar positions differ in their interests, beliefs, and values?

### Interstrata Differences in Attitudes

The broad answer to this question is that on a wide variety of political and economic issues and topics the culture orientations of individuals are definitely associated with their occupational position and their income level, although the latter are not adequate to predict an exact pattern of ideology.[8]

[4] Edwin H. Sutherland, "White Collar Criminality," *American Sociological Review*, 5, 1 (February 1940), 1–12; "Crime and Business," *The Annals of the Academy of Political and Social Science*, 217 (September 1941), 112–118; "Is 'White Collar Crime' Crime?" *American Sociological Review*, 10, 2 (April 1945), 132–139. See also James S. Wallerstein and Clement J. Wyle, "Our Law-Abiding Law-Breakers," *Probation* (April 1947); Marshall B. Clinard, *Sociology of Deviant Behavior* (New York: Holt, Rinehart & Winston, 1957), chap. 9.

[5] John Useem, Pierre Tangent, and Ruth Useem, "Stratification in a Prairie Town," *American Sociological Review*, 7, 3 (June 1942), 341.

[6] August B. Hollingshead, *Elmtown's Youth* (New York: Wiley, 1949), esp. chaps. 6 and 8.

[7] Gunnar Myrdal, with the assistance of Richard Sterner and Arnold Rose, *An American Dilemma*, Vol. I (New York: Harper & Row, 1944), chaps. 24–27.

[8] Cf. this statement: "Occupation provides income, influences the location of residence, develops working habits, and makes associations and companionships." (Dewey Anderson and Percy E. Davidson, *Ballots and the Democratic Class Struggle* (Stanford, Calif.: Stanford University Press, 1943), p. 106. It is through the *similarity of circumstance*

Whether or not one wishes to consider objectively defined income and occupational strata as "classes," it remains true that different aggregates of persons classified in these terms do show great differences in beliefs or attitudes.

The findings of one of the most comprehensive studies of opinion data, analyzed by Centers, may be summarized in support of this contention. The main conclusions of this study included the following:

1. *Characteristics of various strata:* Persons who identified themselves as upper class make up 3 to 4 percent of the population; they think of the upper stratum as being composed largely of big business owners and executives and certain "higher" profession groups. Those persons who claimed to be middle class (some 40 percent of the population) think of the middle class as made up principally of business owners and managers; however, substantial numbers of urban manual workers and farm tenants and laborers also claim to be middle class (rather than working class). Individuals who said that they themselves belonged to the working class defined the stratum mainly in terms of factory workers, laborers, farmers, service workers, and servants. Somewhat less than one-half of those claiming working class affiliation were office workers. Finally, the small proportion of the population identifying itself as lower class did so largely by the criterion of poverty.

2. *Sociopolitical attitudes:* In general, the more conservative opinions were held by persons from occupations popularly judged to be in the upper levels of an occupational hierarchy. Both objective occupational position and expressed class-affiliation worked in the same direction.[8]

The general findings of this study have been supported and qualified by several other important investigations.

Even under conditions of economic depression in the 1930's, as the data assembled in Arthur Kornhauser's work indicate, between the ideological extremes represented by the small group of wealthy and powerful individuals on the one hand and the disaffected among manual workers on the other, there was a large and inchoate aggregate of diverse groupings characterized by "moderate" attitudes.[9] The entire range of income and occupational levels represented a continuous gradation of attitudes with no sharply defined cleavages at any one point and with great overlapping of opinions as between any two adjacent income levels. Middle-income groupings are heterogeneous in occupational composition and in attitudes; ideologically they constitute no definite class but stand rather as a diffuse cushion between the wealthy top strata and the more militant sections of the wage earning worker populations.[1] The closest approach to a definable gap in political and

---

and through the *interaction* this occasions that both occupation and income level tend to evoke and index similar cultural characteristics among persons of similar objective condition.

8 Summarized from Richard Centers, *The Psychology of Social Classes* (Princeton, N.J.: Princeton University Press, 1949), pp. 206–219.

9 Arthur Kornhauser, "Analysis of 'Class' Structure in Contemporary American Society—Psychological Bases of Class Divisions," in George W. Hartmann and Theodore Newcomb (eds.), *Industrial Conflict* (New York: Dryden Press, 1939), p. 241.

1 This conclusion was supported by another depression-era study: Alfred Winslow Jones,

economic attitudes occurs between the small segment of high-income people and the remainder of the population. At every income level, however, the connection between attitudes and objective economic position is attenuated and complicated by the influence of ethnic background, racial category, regional culture, religion, education, and a variety of other cultural and personal factors.

Research summarized by Herbert Hyman documents the persistence of the situation just described into the 1950's.[2]

We may infer from the information reviewed thus far that:
1. There are large and consistent differences in attitude or ideology between persons differently circumstanced in income and occupation.
2. The attitudes of these various groupings nevertheless overlap; and a common value-system seems to extend quite widely through disparate economic levels.

These broad conclusions have been further verified and specified by many studies since mid-century. In spite of strong influences tending to differentiate the values and interests of strata and of status groupings,[3] the ideological conservatism of the center has been maintained.[4] The relative weakness of class position as a determinant of political orientations in the United States is shown by the low correlation between class and voting for left or right parties, as compared, for example, with Great Britain. The net proportion voting for the left is less closely tied to class than in either Great Britain or Australia (although more class linked than in Canada).[5]

Even while ideological influences have reduced the sharpness of political opposition, social mobility has worked in the same direction. The available research indicates that persons who rise and fall in stratification position tend to be politically apathetic nonvoters. Even the persons who have been downwardly mobile into manual occupations—who might be expected, on first thought, to be discontented and receptive to political dissent—are less likely than manual workers who inherit their class position to identify with unions or with working-class political organizations.[6]

It is a merit of good research that it often shows us the limitations of our unexamined assumptions and commonsense clichés. It is no surprise to be

*Life, Liberty, and Property* (Philadelphia: Lippincott, 1941), pp. 318 ff. Even in a strike-torn industrial city, Jones' study showed that "The central morality is humanitarian and approves of acts in the interest of human welfare and alleviation of suffering even if they entail the infringement of corporate property. It approves of trade unions, and would like to see a well-led, unified, strong, labor movement, but one that refrained from violence." *Ibid.*, p. 339.

[2] Herbert H. Hyman, "The Value Systems of Different Classes," in Bendix and Lipset (eds.), *Class, Status, and Power*, 2nd edition, *op. cit.*, pp. 488–499.

[3] We refer both to the sources of political extremism in the changing positions of occupational and income strata and, especially, to the convergence of class conflict and racial and ethnic militancy centering upon the aspirations and demands of black Americans.

[4] See the reviews of the research literature in Hodges, *op. cit.*, pp. 195–242; Suzanne Keller, *Beyond the Ruling Class* (New York: Random House, 1963), pp. 198–226, 259–326.

[5] Robert Alford, *Party and Society* (Chicago: Rand McNally, 1963), pp. 102–106.

[6] Lipset and Bendix, *Social Mobility in Industrial Society, op. cit.*, pp. 68–70.

told that successfully upwardly mobile persons tend to become politically conservative; but it is arresting to discover that Swedish workers who move into nonmanual occupations tend to move to the left politically.[7] Similarly, we may not initially find it plausible that downwardly mobile American workers would be more often ideologically conservative than persons who have not lost position. Yet, at least one careful study shows that "skidders" are more conservative in their values and beliefs regarding the stratification system (adhering essentially to a belief in opportunity in a free-mobility system) and tend to emphasize aspirations for escape from their present position.[8]

### Variations in Stratification Within the Society

Although available studies of class ideology are subject to important criticisms because of theoretical and methodological gaps or deficiencies, there can be little doubt that there is a substantial correlation between *occupation* and *expressed class affiliation* and between each of these and patterns of opinions on social, economic, and political issues.

Although the existence of these differences in outlook among various occupational groupings is thus confirmed by a considerable body of consistent data, it must be stressed at the same time that the strata in question are in large measure statistical aggregates rather than *crystallized social groups*. Occupational classes constitute a rather irregular continuum rather than a series of clearly separate categories of stratification. If a statistically defined stratum, such as families receiving a certain level of income, is homogeneous in other major characteristics that serve as criteria for social ranking, the likelihood is increased that the stratum will become a real social entity. Recognizing that others in the stratum are "our kind of people," class consciousness is likely to appear. On the other hand, if each of various strata of wealth, income, authority, and occupational prestige is highly heterogeneous in ethnic origin, style of life, education, religion, place of residence, and the like, then awareness of class and the development of class solidarity will be minimized. A system in which there is rapid social mobility tends to create large numbers of varied and inconsistent combinations of ranked statuses.[9] Both the complexity of the income and occupational distributions and the relatively great amount of interstrata mobility, together with other factors to be examined later, work in the direction of blurring rigid distinctions. Although there are definite and remarkably stable stereotypes concerning the social ranking of occupations[1] the net result is

[7] *Ibid.*, pp. 66–68.

[8] Harold L. Wilensky and Hugh Edwards, "The Skidder: Ideological Adjustments of Downwardly Mobile Workers," *American Sociological Review*, 24, 2 (April 1959), 215–231.

[9] Hodges, *Social Stratification: Class in America*, *op. cit.*, p. 13.

[1] Cf. North and Hatt, "Jobs and Occupations"; Maethel E. Deeg and Donald G. Paterson, "Changes in Social Status of Occupations," *Occupations*, XXV, 4 (January 1947). The latter study repeated a test used by Counts in 1925; ratings assigned to broad occupational groups by a sample of 475 students in 1946 were not very different from those reported twenty years earlier. Such stable rankings contrast with actual diversity within

that the precise rank of any particular individual is frequently ambiguous and that the entire stratification system is differently perceived by persons located at various positions within it.[2]

A system of stratification may be characterized by discrete and clearly discontinuous layers or classes, or by a continuous gradation in which no clear separations or breaking-points appear. Boundaries between strata or classes[3] may be identified in several different ways, namely (1) discontinuities in the distribution of such scarce values as income, wealth, education, authority, or power; (2) discontinuities in attributed prestige; (3) use of categorical ascribed position as the basis for prestige ranking; (4) discontinuities in style of life (clusters of consumption patterns, living arrangements, recreation, manners, speech, and so on); (5) intermarriage. At one extreme, there would be a continuous smooth distribution of the specified scarce values, prestige ratings, ascribed positions, and styles of life; and the web of close social contacts would be seamless throughout. At the other pole, there would be definite clusterings of all the elements, with clear separations between each cluster and others.

From the various sets of data already reviewed here, it is evident that many of the boundaries between strata in the United States are indefinite and that large sections of the ranking system are continuous. As noted above, the middle ranges of occupation and income do not seem to be sharply segmented at any point. However, our diagnosis of a relatively clear boundary at the top of the scale is supported by Werner Landecker's Detroit data, which indicate that the top strata are divided from the remainder by a major boundary.[4] These topmost strata are characterized by college graduation, professional or executive positions, and incomes in the highest 7 percent of income earners. Not investigated in this study are differences in life styles, ideologies, or patterns of social interaction. The exact relationships between the different major aspects of stratification need further research; but it is likely that the future evidence will show that discontinuity is especially great at a very high upper boundary and at a boundary separating "respectable working-class" from lower and déclassé elements.

As Sorokin has shown in a criticism of definitions of "social class," it is necessary to remind ourselves continually that a nominal aggregate of persons occupying similar occupational positions, or receiving similar incomes, or enjoying equivalent prestige is not necessarily a unitary group nor a self-conscious stratum.[5] Recognizing this reservation, however, we can still show

---

occupations; see, for example, the description of "lower-class" lawyers given in Jerome E. Carlin, *Lawyers on Their Own* (New Brunswick, N.J.: Rutgers University Press, 1962).

[2] Cf. the suggestive diagrams and discussion in West, *Plainville, U.S.A., op. cit.*, pp. 116–133.

[3] Werner S. Landecker, "Class Boundaries," *American Sociological Review*, 25, 6 (December 1960), 868–877. Landecker contrasts the conception of "class structure" with that of "status continuum."

[4] *Ibid.*, p. 877.

[5] Pitirim A. Sorokin, *Society, Culture, and Personality* (New York: Harper & Row, 1947), pp. 256–275.

that occupational position carries with it a characteristic economic position: for example, all unskilled wage workers face the problems presented by relatively low income, lack of capital, and the necessity of earning a living from the sale of their labor in an uncertain market. Similarly, the full social significance of affluence is not found if persons become dependent upon *specific* employers. But economic abundance when coupled with free access to alternative jobs enormously reduces personalized deference, diminishes suppression of grievances, and enhances a sense of autonomy. Over a period of time, such similar objective conditions tend to create—slowly or rapidly—certain broad similarities in culture within a given stratum.[6]

This generalization needs to be translated into specific facts concerning the American scene. Fortunately, the findings of many intensive community studies are available as a check against the data from extensive surveys. Monograph after monograph has shown that in American communities (1) those in different income and occupational strata consistently differ in behavior and attitudes, (2) different occupational positions are given definite social evaluations, (3) consciousness of stratification is highly variable but is universally important.

It would be fruitless to review all the specific studies of named and anonymous communities that have contributed to this richness of data, from "Middletown,"[7] "Yankee City,"[8] and Greenbelt (Maryland)[9] to Philadelphia[1] and Skid Row.[2]

As such studies have accumulated, their findings have given specific content to the conclusion that the nature of the stratification system varies greatly from one part of the United States to another and takes on special colorations in different types of communities. The range of objective stratification is certainly very much greater in the large urban centers than in the smaller towns and rural areas; it is probable that cleavages in belief and values are likewise greater in the larger centers, although precise comparisons on this point cannot be made from the available research evidence. In the smaller communities and in areas of static or declining economic opportunity, especially in the older settled regions of the Northeast and South, highly developed local systems of ranking have become established; and

[6] Cf. Pitirim A. Sorokin, *Social Mobility* (New York: Harper & Row, 1927); Cecil C. North, *Social Differentiation* (Chapel Hill: University of North Carolina Press, 1926); H. C. Lehmann and P. A. Witty, "Further Study of the Social Status of Occupations," *Journal of Educational Sociology*, V (1931).

[7] Robert S. Lynd and Helen M. Lynd, *Middletown: A Study in Contemporary American Culture* (New York: Harcourt, Brace & World, 1929), and *Middletown in Transition* (New York: Harcourt, Brace & World, 1937).

[8] W. Lloyd Warner and Leo Srole, *The Social Systems of American Ethnic Groups* (New Haven, Conn.: Yale University Press, 1946); Warner and Lunt, *The Social Life of a Modern Community, op. cit.*

[9] W. H. Form, "Status Stratification in a Planned Community," *American Sociological Review*, 10, 5 (October 1945), 605–613.

[1] Baltzell, *Philadelphia Gentlemen: The Making of a National Upper Class, op. cit.*

[2] Samuel E. Wallace, *Skid-Row as a Way of Life* (Totowa, N.J.: Bedminster Press, 1965); Bogue, *Skid Row in American Cities, op. cit.*

under these conditions relatively heavy weight is given to lineal principles—to membership in the "right family," to inherited wealth and position, to long residence in the community, and to such symbols of status as manners, education, and place of residence.[3] These economically static areas are typically areas of heavy emigration in a society characterized by long-run expansion and movement; and the local stratification system tends to be stabilized by the departure of youths who are ambitious beyond the scope of their opportunities in the area or who for various reasons do not find it easy to accept the rigidity of the local system. To the degree that local business and job opportunities become "appropriated" by specific families and cliques there develops a continuing structure of control by which the dominant strata, utilizing economic and political mechanisms (including local government and education), are able to perpetuate existing stratification differentials. With the passage of time, distinctive behavior patterns and social perspectives come to characterize different strata; and the more privileged portions of the community build ideologies buttressing this quasi-estate system.

Thus, John Useem and associates found in a midwestern town of 3,500 people that the "elite" was marked off from the "bottoms" by clear-cut differences in the total manner of living.[4] Persons in the locally recognized upper strata, as compared with persons from the levels of least prestige, were (1) more mobile and engaged in a wider range of social interaction; (2) more "secularized," in a variety of ways; (3) less likely to exchange aid and advice among families; (4) less likely to make the family the center of their attention and social participation; (5) more likely to attribute high rank to personal excellence and to give quasi-biological explanations for the existence of low-status groupings. The detailed articulation of such a rigid local stratification structure is likely to be most marked in long-settled communities or regions that combine a static economy and emigration with considerable objective differentials in wealth and power. Other conditions being the same, the sharpness of divisions between strata or classes tends to be the greater the longer individuals remain in a given position and the less interstratum mobility there is.[5]

The distinction we have used between local and translocal stratification, similar to the "inclusive" and "segmental" types used by Warner, helps to account for the great variations from community to community recorded in specific studies. To some extent each local system has a distinctive, particular mode of allocation and ranking. At the same time, there is an important degree of national similarity in prestige rankings of occupations, in criteria of position, in evaluation of styles of life, in norms of class-related behavior,

[3] Florence Rockwood Kluckhohn, "Dominant and Substitute Profiles of Cultural Orientations: Their Significance for the Analysis of Social Stratification," *Social Forces*, XXVIII, 4 (May 1950), 376–393.

[4] Useem, *et al., op. cit.*

[5] Cf. Sorokin, *Society, Culture, and Personality, op. cit.*, p. 274. A good example of how criteria of stratification may shift as a community becomes stabilized is supplied in Form, "Status Stratification in a Planned Community," *op. cit.*

and in general ideology of stratification. And there clearly are national elites. The reality is that both the generalized and the particular systems exist and mutually influence one another.[6]

In the large centers of industry and commerce, finely meshed stabilization of a ranking system is difficult to maintain, especially when economic opportunities are increasing and thereby attracting an influx of persons from other areas. Industrial or commercial expansion opens up the possibility of rapid occupational shifts, and geographic mobility tends to cut through the rigidifying factors of kinship affiliations and other established group memberships and identifications. The very fact that economic relations in the larger centers tend to become impersonal and narrowly specific in nature frees the individual from the lineal transmission of established status and permits him to compete for placement. At the same time the urban center in our culture fosters great inequalities of wealth and power. Thus, conditions are created favorable to emphasizing individual achievement, as well as wealth, conspicuous consumption, power, and office (especially offices of authority). Insofar as there is rapid social change and marked oscillations in economic conditions, the tendency to freeze clear-cut lines of stratification is continually being countered; and to the degree that economic positions of individuals change rapidly, the ranking system exhibits a vague and shifting character. Rank tends to be conceived of in more abstract and categorical terms than it is in the smaller communities: persons become "working class" or "business class" rather than members of the "Smith family" or "the Tops." Among the studies already cited, those reported by the Lynds and Jones have depicted in particular the categorical cleavages that grow out of the occupational structure of industrial cities. These considerations are enough to show why it is that no one local community can represent or reflect the stratification system of the whole society. The national system includes high governmental officials, religious leaders, industrialists, labor union leaders, financiers, publicists, and so on; these "elites" of influence, wealth, and power cannot be found by studying only local systems. It is undoubtedly important to Jonesville that John Jones is its leading citizen; but that community is not Washington, New York, or Detroit. Studies of stratification in small communities have enriched our understanding; but they do not touch the higher reaches of wealth, authority, influence, and prestige at the main centers of decision making in the United States.

Considerable debate has gone on among students of social stratification as to whether there is in fact a "single system" of prestige classes (or strata) in the nation as a whole. The answer delivered by the available research is yes and no. The "yes" means, first, that there is, indeed, a single national set of ratings of occupations and that these ratings do not depend closely upon the criteria people say they use in making them. In the second place, there clearly is a national system of political and economic power and reward—a system that is widely recognized and acknowledged. On the other

---

[6] Cf. Thomas E. Lasswell, "Orientations Toward Social Classes," *American Journal of Sociology*, LXV, 6 (May 1960), 585–587.

hand, the "no" means that, first, specific local rankings form local systems that always have unique features, and, second, there are subcultural differences in the criteria of ranking. A specific example of the last point is the special importance education apparently has as a criterion of prestige among Negro Americans.[7]

In the past, the high vertical mobility of American society has prevented the formation of well defined social classes. We have now seen that the society is nevertheless stratified in terms of the objective distribution of privileges and have reviewed some data suggesting that attitudes, values, and other cultural characteristics are appreciably related to objective position. We may now raise some additional questions for more systematic attention.

### Stability of Occupational Position: Transmission of Position

Analysis of intergeneration transmission of occupation in the United States has to reckon first with the change from an agrarian and trading society to a mass-production industrial economy, especially since about 1870. The proportion of the gainfully employed male workers who were working in agriculture and allied extractive occupations declined from slightly over 50 percent in 1870 to less than 20 percent in 1940 and to approximately 5 percent in the 1960's.[8] (The significance of these figures may be appreciated by recalling that in large parts of the world today three-fourths of the workers are in agriculture.) The proportion of workers employed in manufacturing and mechanical industries has remained practically constant since 1910, whereas the proportions employed in trade, public service, clerical, and professional pursuits increased greatly; for instance, of the total working population in 1910 approximately 36 percent were in service industries; but by 1950, the figure had risen to 53 percent. These trends have continued. Actually, from 1947 to 1963 blue-collar jobs were but 3 percent of the increase in total employment in the American economy. Blue-collar employment decreased in absolute numbers in such major mass-production industries as motor vehicles, iron and steel, textiles, and tire manufacturing.

These drastic shifts from the primary extractive and processing occupations to employment in secondary and tertiary industries signify that a high degree of precise occupational continuity from father to sons is not to be expected. The primary industries—farming, forestry, fishing, mining—have tended to use large proportions of manual workers. The rapidly expanding industries require higher proportions of skilled, clerical, technical, managerial, and professional workers. Of macroscopic proportions has been the attrition of the "old middle classes" of independent farmers and small manufacturers and the emergence of an as yet amorphous congeries of "new

[7] We say "apparently" because the determination of relative importance of education versus other factors such as occupation and income is a difficult and uncertain task with the existing limited data. See Norval D. Glenn, "Negro Prestige Criteria: A Case Study in the Bases of Prestige," *American Journal of Sociology*, LXVIII, 6 (May 1963), 645–657.

[8] See the convenient table in Everett K. Wilson, *Sociology: Rules, Roles, and Relationships* (Homewood, Ill.: Dorsey Press, 1966), p. 543. In 1960, the percentage in agricultural occupations was 6.5.

middle classes" composed of clerical, technical, managerial, and professional groups. These new middle classes are diverse in social origins, in specific economic interests, in political inclinations, and in general style of life. Since the occupations represented in the new middle classes *are* new, the personnel has necessarily been drawn in large part from other older employments.

For the past three centuries or so, the long-run trend in Western countries undergoing industrialization and urbanization has been apparently toward a decrease in hereditary transmission of occupation.[9] The increase in urban at the expense of rural employments, the incessant subdivision and specialization of jobs, rapid technological changes, and the rise and decline of industries have all contributed.[1] The entire economic system of our own society has been continually reshaped in quite drastic ways over the comparatively brief period of national existence. In consequence, every major occupational category contains recruits from a variety of other occupational backgrounds. The United States is thus very far indeed from the model of a pure caste system in which the occupations of the fathers are, for good or ill, visited upon the sons for generation after generation. Nevertheless, our society is at the same time far from the opposite pole of zero occupational transmission. We must locate it between these two extremes.

A comprehensive review of those studies of occupational transmission that were available in the late 1920's indicated that "in the majority of cases the sons enter the occupation of the father in a greater proportion than any other one; . . . each of the occupations is recruited principally from the sons of the fathers who have such an occupation."[2] This same review showed, furthermore, that occupational shifts typically do not represent sudden jumps from occupations very low to those very high in income or prestige or vice versa; shifts are rather to roughly adjacent occupations. Except for periods of mass social upheaval, vertical occupational movement largely occurs step by step—unskilled to skilled laborer, clerk to manager, and so forth—rather than by the spectacular ascent of the Horatio Alger myth or of the latter-day Hollywood success story.[3]

In terms of the intergenerational movement from manual to nonmanual occupations, the United States shows approximately the same proportion of upward mobility as France, Great Britain, Sweden, and Japan. In terms of

[9] See the summary and evaluation of evidence in Sorokin, *Social Mobility, op. cit.*, pp. 421–424.

[1] "Widespread social mobility has been a concomitant of industrialization and a basic characteristic of modern industrial society." Lipset and Bendix, *Social Mobility in Industrial Society, op. cit.*, p. 11.

[2] *Ibid.*, p. 438.

[3] Cf. Leo C. Rosten, *Hollywood* (New York: Harcourt, Brace & World, 1941): "One reason for Hollywood's stars becoming national idols is that they represent a new type of hero in American experience. Hollywood's children of fortune are not the thrifty newsboys of the Horatio Alger stereotype—honest, diligent, pure of heart; here, instead, are mortals known to be spendthrift and Bohemian. . . . They represent a new type of folk-hero in a society whose ethos rests upon hard work and virtuous deportment" (pp. 12–13). And again: "Hollywood means Luck" (p. 15). Reprinted by permission of Harcourt, Brace & World, Inc.

*[handwritten marginalia: U.S. - Same? Shift (manual to non-manual) as most Industrial C less down than other Industrial C]*

the opposite shift (manual sons of nonmanual fathers), the United States appears to have less downward mobility than any other nation for which data are available. In terms of the ratio of those upwardly mobile to those who are stable in nonmanual positions, the United States is more open than Italy, Hungary, Finland, West Germany but less so than France and Great Britain. Although these indexes are crude and the comparisons gross, it is reasonable to conclude that the amount of social mobility into higher strata is not conspicuously greater in this country than in several other industrial or industrializing societies.[4]

*[handwritten marginalia: Rates of vertical mobility due to:]*

Rates of vertical mobility are compounded of (1) pure mobility, (2) changes in the proportion of the population in each stratum, (3) changes in the rank order of each stratum or substratum, (4) differences and changes in birth rates in different strata, and (5) changes in population growth.[5] Pure mobility represents the rising and falling that would occur even when the strata do not change in size or in position in the hierarchy. It is generally quite small in comparison with the mobility generated by changes in the character of the stratification system itself. As already noted, much of the transfer to higher occupational groupings has simply represented changes in the basic economic structure and in the income distribution, resulting in an increasingly middle-class society. Fertility differentials in the past, as well as the large-scale immigration of unskilled workers, have contributed also to vertical mobility.

*[handwritten marginalia: "pure" mobility = small compared to other-caused mobility]*

Some examples from monographic studies will help us to visualize in concrete terms the stability of occupational placement.[6] In the study of "Central City,"[7] it was found that nearly three-fourths of the small business-men came from the upper half of the occupational-income scale; and no free professionals or big businessmen were derived from backgrounds of low-income, white-collar, or wage-worker occupations. Of the higher white-collar category, 61 percent derived from the upper half of the income hier-archy; of the lower white-collar grouping, 49 percent were of upper-half extraction. In terms of job histories, both the stratum of small businessmen and of lower white-collar workers show extensive upward mobility: only 1 in 5 of the small businessmen were in an occupational-income level so high at the time of marriage; two-thirds of foremen were wage workers at marriage. On the other hand, professional workers were overwhelmingly at that category by the time they married. The same is true at the bottom of the income-occupation scale; about 90 percent of all categories of labor were wage workers at marriage. In Mills' words, "There is rigidity at the bottom and at the top—except among small businessmen who, relative to com-

*[handwritten marginalia: C.W. Mills rigidity at bottom & top]*

---

[4] See the data presented by W. J. Goode in Bendix and Lipset, (eds.), *Class, Status, and Power*, 2nd ed., *op. cit.*, pp. 585–589.

[5] Ralph Ross and Ernest Van Den Haag, *The Fabric of Society: An Introduction to the Social Sciences* (New York: Harcourt, Brace & World, 1957), chaps. 11 and 12.

[6] These studies are few, scattered, and difficult to compare; but their findings can be checked to some degree against census data and against the cumulative picture derived from more general historical and sociological studies.

[7] C. Wright Mills, "The Middle Classes in Middle-Sized Cities," *American Sociological Review*, 11, 5 (October 1946), 520–529.

parable income groups, have done a great deal of moving up the line."[8] Findings consistent with Mills' conclusions have been reported by several other local studies. In a study of Greenbelt, Maryland, for example, it was found that 71 percent of manual workers had been engaged in manual labor as their first job and 82 percent of persons in white-collar occupations had started as white-collar workers.[9] These data refer to *career mobility*, that is, the movement of individuals during their own working lives. Available studies seem to support the conclusion that this kind of mobility is less in the top and the bottom strata than in the middle ranges.

Improved methods of analyzing both intra- and inter-generational mobility recently have given a more exact picture of the extent of vertical movement. Thus, using socioeconomic status (SES) ratings of specific occupations, Duncan and Hodges have shown for a Chicago sample that no more than 10 percent of workers have SES scores identical with those of their fathers and that there is much regression toward the mean—that is, sons of low SES origin tend to have upward mobility, whereas those of high origin tend to experience downward mobility. However, sons of high occupational origin do have an advantage over those of lower origin, particularly through the higher level of education they attain.[1]

Career mobility and *intergenerational* mobility may not always follow the same pattern. The Occupational Mobility Survey of six large cities, in 1951,[2] showed that sons do, indeed, tend to follow their fathers' occupations but that the proportion who do so is less in the higher and the lower occupations than in the middle categories of white-collar and skilled workers. Although the data are complicated by the factor of age (sons are in the early stages of their careers and, obviously, their eventual occupational placement is not known) as well as by the changing size of the groups from which the sons derive, there is evidence of much mobility, both upward and downward, but of substantial recruitment of middle-class workers from middle-class backgrounds.[3]

It must be noted, however, that the findings of studies that have relied upon comparisons of occupations of fathers with those of sons cannot be taken as pure indications of actual intergenerational mobility, even when the two populations are standardized for age. If, for example, one takes the 47 million members of the 1960 male labor force, it turns out that of the 32 million who had not been in the labor force in 1930, there were 13 million

---

[8] *Ibid.*, p. 523.

[9] Form, "Status Stratification in a Planned Community," *op. cit.*

[1] Otis Dudley Duncan and Robert W. Hodges, "Education and Occupational Mobility: A Regression Analysis," *American Journal of Sociology*, LXVIII, 6 (May 1963), esp. 634–637. Note also "The data are consistent with the supposition that education was becoming a more important determinant of occupational status, in terms of both its net influence apart from level of origin and its role as a variable intervening between origin and destination" (p. 644).

[2] Gladys L. Palmer and Carol P. Brainerd, *Labor Mobility in Six Cities* (New York: Social Science Research Council, 1954); Miller, *Income of the American People, op. cit.*

[3] See also the data from a period of economic depression reported in Percy E. Davidson and H. Dewey Anderson, *Occupational Mobility in an American Community* (Stanford, Calif.: Stanford University Press, 1937).

whose fathers were still working or seeking work in 1960. Thus, there is hardly a complete turnover of the labor force in a period of 30 years. Hence, comparisons of cross sections at two such points in time will always involve a very substantial overlap or duplication.

The stability of strata in modern society is profoundly affected by the educational opportunities available to youth. Our society has succeeded to an extraordinary degree in approaching formal equality of opportunity for elementary and high-school training, but the higher reaches of the educational ladder are less equally accessible. There is evidence that even among boys of the high IQ level, fathers' occupational position is highly correlated with college attendance.[4] Since a college education is increasingly a prerequisite for entrance into middle- or upper-strata occupations, it is a key influence upon the fixity or mobility possible in the stratification system. For, as Elbridge Sibley has aptly noted, "Not universal equality of status but a high rate of vertical mobility has been the most important demographic basis of this nation's tradition of classlessness."[5] Educational achievement is a major factor in determining occupational careers. In general, children from the lower economic strata have less opportunity to stay in school, receive less encouragement to advance to higher levels of training, and, in many instances, are not surrounded by the social conditions making for high motivation for educational and occupational advancement.[6] There undoubtedly is a tendency for strata to perpetuate themselves. There are other complicated relationships between and among the social opportunities, economic advantages or disadvantages, intelligence, motivation, and values of persons differently located in the occupational and social-prestige structure. Important as these relationships are, they can not be adequately examined in the present broad institutional analysis. The highly interesting technical analyses now available are summarized in several important works dealing with social stratification. It is enough here to note that the stabilizing cycle of stratification, which can make the transmission of class position a closed circle, starts with the fact of initial economic position, power capacities, and prestige rank of a family. Assume that on all three counts the

*[handwritten margin note: much educational opportunity but — Father's status plays a role]*

[4] Elbridge Sibley, "Some Demographic Clues to Stratification," *American Sociological Review*, 7, 3 (June 1942), 322–330.

[5] *Ibid.*, p. 322.

[6] For example, the influence of family and friends, close association with adults rather than peers, "conditional" parental approval. Achievement motivation seems to be highly developed by the affective relationships and methods of child rearing most characteristic of middle-class, especially upward-aspiring, groups. Where high motivation for achievement develops, it is likely that there is parental pressure for early independence, and that the child is somehow convinced that love comes in the form of approval which is contingent upon mastery of tasks and acceptance of future-oriented restrictions. See Melvin L. Kohn, "Social Class and Parent-Child Relationships: An Interpretation," *American Journal of Sociology*, 68, 4 (January 1963), 471–480; Leonard I. Pearlin and Melvin L. Kohn, "Social Class, Occupation and Parental Values: A Cross-National Study," *American Sociological Review*, 31, 4 (August 1966), 466–479; Bernard C. Rosen, "The Achievement Syndrome: A Psychocultural Dimension of Social Stratification," *American Sociological Review*, 21, 2 (April 1956), 203–211; and Bernard C. Rosen, "The Achievement Syndrome and Economic Growth in Brazil," *Social Forces*, 42, 3 (March 1964), 341–354.

position is low. This means that opportunities for education and initial occupational placement will be limited. It tends—with many exceptions—to be associated with a type of socialization of children that does not strongly inculcate achievement values and motivation for achievement. The resulting lack of certain knowledge and skills, as well as the consequent personality characteristics, may reduce the likelihood of occupational advancement. Since initial occupational entry is so often crucial for a later career, the early acceptance of a manual job or "dead-end" business occupation often perpetuates the class level from which the individual originally came.

To what extent are the upper occupational strata self-perpetuating and closed groupings tending toward a real social class of aristocratic inclination? Clearly, aristocracy of the European pattern was very early destroyed by the conditions of American life; and no important hereditary upper "estate" survived the fluidity of eighteenth- and nineteenth-century society in the United States. Out of the reshuffling and turmoil of our dynamic economy, however, there have emerged new strata possessing concentrated control of wealth and power.[7] The social origins of the top occupational strata obviously are a matter of prime significance to an appraisal of the extent of closure of the stratification system.

Taussig and Joslyn showed from a sampling of business leaders just prior to the depression of the 1930's that higher business positions were occupied by persons drawn mainly from business and professional strata rather than from the ranks of farmers and laborers. Of the 8,749 persons responding to a questionnaire sent to 15,101 directors, officers, partners, or owners of business organizations judged to be of major importance in the national economy, 50 percent were sons of major executives or owners of businesses. Yet businessmen constituted only 7.4 percent of the married males in 1880.[8] Furthermore, almost one-half of the sons of large owners and major executives were connected with the father's business; and of those probably three-fourths possessed substantial control of the business.[9] The greatest continuity was found among major executives and large owners; fathers of important businessmen were less likely to have followed their own fathers into farming, clerking or selling, or positions as minor executives.[1] These findings for a loosely defined top stratum of businessmen are consistent with Sorokin's results from a study of American millionaires and multimillionaires.[2] Sorokin showed an even greater closure of occupational origins among the very wealthy than was found among the less affluent business leaders.

More recent studies show that since the beginning of the nineteenth cen-

---

[7] See Anderson and Davidson, *Ballots and the Democratic Class Struggle, op. cit.*, p. 230.
[8] F. W. Taussig and C. S. Joslyn, *American Business Leaders* (New York: Macmillan, 1932), p. 88.
[9] See *ibid.*, pp. 112 ff.
[1] *Ibid.*, p. 139. It is to be noted that since these data concern the ancestors of present business leaders, a high degree of occupational transmission of the lower positions could not occur—only continuity or upward mobility is to be expected in the nature of the data.
[2] Pitirim A. Sorokin, "American Millionaires and Multimillionaires," *Social Forces*, III, 4 (May 1925), 627–640.

tury, American business leaders have come for the most part from economically well off families and that the proportion so derived has remained fairly stable (between three-fifths and three-fourths) for a long time. Less than one-fifth of the business elite come from the ranks of laborers, craftsmen, small entrepreneurs, lower white-collar employees, or farmers.[3] In the instance of high ranking political officials, similar tendencies exist; for example, 95 percent of United States senators have fathers who were professionals, proprietors, officials, or farmers.[4] That a "national" upper class is to an important extent a reality in America seems to have been well documented.[5]

The very, very rich generally were so to begin with: over half inherited their wealth,[6] and most of the others started with substantial advantages and gained the top brackets in speculative or especially favored routes. For the broader business elites of top executives, owners, and managers, the data consistently show—not surprisingly—that business and professional origins are disproportionately represented. However, the most plausible conclusion is that mobility into business elites has not changed greatly during this century but that some net increase probably has occurred.

The recruitment of elites in most of the other main institutional sectors of our society is also disproportionately from business and professional backgrounds. However, such data as are available indicate some increase during the twentieth century in the proportions rising to high positions from lower-class backgrounds. The openness in this respect appears to be greatest in religion and education, although eminence achieved without higher education is proportionately most frequent in business, journalism, and in some segments of mass entertainment.[7] Few of the present families even in the economic and political elites have been there for several generations. And there is little convincing evidence that class lines are freezing: vertical mobility appears to be at least as frequent now as it was fifty or twenty-five years ago. Comparing business leaders in 1928 and in 1952, Warner and Abegglen conclude that movement from lower origins into the top stratum has increased. Mobility undoubtedly differs greatly in various other strata.

Few studies of small businessmen have been made. In one local study (Lexington, Kentucky), businessmen were found to be better educated than males in general and disproportionately from business or professional origins but, more often than big business leaders, began in manual occupations, had

---

[3] Lipset and Bendix, *op. cit.*, pp. 122–127.

[4] Evidence from studies by Donald R. Matthews and C. Wright Mills summarized by Bernard Barber, *Social Stratification* (New York: Harcourt, Brace & World, 1957), pp. 410–411.

[5] Cf. E. Digby Baltzell, *Philadelphia Gentlemen: The Making of a National Upper Class, op. cit.*; W. Lloyd Warner and James C. Abegglen, *Big Business Leaders in America* (New York: Harper & Row, 1955), p. 14: "two of every three leaders of American business come from families whose economic and social positions were well above the average for the nation."

[6] Richard Austin Smith, "The Fifty-Million Dollar Men," *Fortune* (November 1957).

[7] Suzanne Keller, *Beyond the Ruling Class: Strategic Elites in Modern Society* (New York: Random House, 1963), pp. 292–312.

lower education, and more often received financial aid from parents or kin.[8]

Natalie Rogoff found that when corrected for changes in the occupational structure, occupational mobility rates in Indianapolis were about the same in 1910 and 1940.[9] Taking into account the expanding economy and the growth of middle-level occupations, it is even possible that total upward mobility is somewhat greater than a half-century ago. At any rate, there certainly was no trend during the period studied toward a more rigid structure. An ingenious and rigorous analysis of more recent data indicates that upward mobility, especially into salaried professional and technical positions, has increased and that downward mobility, into blue-collar and farm occupations, has decreased over the decades since 1932.[1] On the other hand, there is much stability of position, most movement is in small steps, and common beliefs greatly exaggerate the frequency of spectacular ascent.

### Stratum Solidarity: Patterns of Interaction

The materials so far reviewed certainly show that American society is marked by a wide range of objective stratification and of prestige rankings. Stratification is not a clear, unitary system, however, but is rather a loosely articulated series of ranking systems, varying from one sector of the society to another and changing through time. Vertical mobility is still great, blurring rigid class distinctions and diversifying and shifting the patterns of ranking. Nevertheless, pervasive forces are working in the direction of stabilizing objective privileges, creating ascribed statuses and hereditary positions, stabilizing class-typed values and beliefs, and separating various strata from one another by differences of culture and by closure of social interaction.

To what extent, however, are aggregates of persons possessing similar positions with regard to wealth, income, authority, power, or prestige being transformed into *status groups*, marked off by differences in interpersonal associations and in style of life?[2] In what measure do objective strata and prestige categories constitute real social groupings rather than arbitrary statistical aggregates or points on a continuous scale? Are there any clearly discernible breaks in the structure of stratification that mark off one class from another?

The internal solidarity of status groupings can be provisionally tested by discovering the extent to which their members associate intimately or intermarry. Visiting together and eating together are universal symbols of solidarity and usually imply approximate equality of status, at least in the immediate social context. Some American students of stratification have

[8] Gordon F. Lewis, "A Comparison of Some Aspects of the Backgrounds and Careers of Small Businessmen and American Business Leaders," *American Journal of Sociology*, LXV, 4 (January 1960), 348–355.

[9] Natalie Rogoff, *Recent Trends in Occupational Mobility* (New York: Free Press, 1953), p. 106.

[1] Otis Dudley Duncan, "The Trend of Occupational Mobility in the United States," *American Sociological Review*, 30, 4 (August 1965), 491–498. A comprehensive analysis of national data substantiates these conclusions: Peter M. Blau and Otis Dudley Duncan, *The American Occupational Structure* (New York: Wiley, 1967).

[2] Kurt B. Mayer, *Class and Society* (New York: Random House, 1955), pp. 24–25.

used intimate social interaction as a criterion for identifying social classes; although this procedure is inadequate, such interaction still serves as one important index of stratum solidarity. If persons of like economic circumstances associate among themselves, interact frequently, intermarry—and do not interact frequently on an intimate basis with persons of a different economic level or occupational grouping—in all likelihood over a period of time these persons will become increasingly bound together by cultural consensus, awareness of common interests, interpersonal attachments and understandings, and an increasingly shared total pattern or style of living. The development of a web of social relations within a stratum of like-circumstanced people is, accordingly, one of the most significant signs of the emergence of true status groupings from what may formerly have been diffuse prestige strata, occupational categories, or simple aggregates of separate individuals and groups possessing the same share of the scarce values of the society.

The formal associations of American communities, of course, often crosscut a wide range of strata—as Warner, for example, has shown in "Yankee City." Formal organizations of a community-wide nature serve to link together in the prosecution of common purposes very diverse segments of the community and to this extent militate against the separation of strata and the cleavage of the community into disparate status groupings. On the other hand, less impersonal, less segmental, and less functionally specific social relations are more likely to reveal the presence of detailed prestige distinctions and segregated intimate social interaction.[3]

Prior to the 1960's, most research on the relationship between occupational prestige position and stratified social interaction used relatively simple assumptions and methods of analysis that failed to show the fine-grained texture. More recent work shows that the structure of social relationships (with kin, close friends, and neighbors) is indeed segmented according to occupational prestige, that is, persons in a given occupational rank tend to associate with others of similar rank.[4] However, associational groupings by occupations are also determined by other important factors that are independent of occupational prestige. For example, there is a clear segregation of a middle-rank grouping of bureaucratic occupations from a grouping of entrepreneurial occupations.[5]

For the time being we shall leave aside the very sharp insulation of ethnic and racial groupings that characterizes American social structure. Although ethnic, racial, and religious distinctions are obviously related closely to stratification and social class, the two are different. Ethnic and racial factors help to fix the ranking of individuals; class distinctions stratify ethnic groupings internally. But individuals may belong to the same stratum and be

[3] Although as W. Lloyd Warner and Paul S. Lunt, Vol. II, Yankee City Series, *The Status System of a Modern Community*, Appendix 2, Table 20 also show, some informal social relations in "cliques" do cut across social-class lines; see *op. cit.*, Vol. 2, Appendix 2, Table 20.

[4] Edward O. Laumann and Louis Guttman, "The Relative Associational Contiguity of Occupations in an Urban Setting," *op. cit.*

[5] *Ibid.*, pp. 177–178.

divided by ethnic or racial lines, and stratification occurs where no ethnic or racial distinctions exist. The two systems thus crisscross while remaining analytically separate. The ethnic and racial factors are of importance to us here only insofar as they blur potential class solidarity. The diversity of racial stocks, ethnic categories, and religious affiliations in the United States has hindered the development of unitary class groupings: every separation or distinction on these grounds throws together persons of dissimilar objective position or prestige and divides groups having similar economic and political interests and characteristics. The result is a *segmentation* of potentially solidary classes—a segmentation simultaneously favored by other factors such as the relative weakness of kinship structures, the complexity of the occupational system, the geographic dispersion of the society, and the varying incidence of social privileges (for instance, legal equality versus great economic inequalities). In short, the influence of categorization by religion, race, and nationality provides a specific illustration of the general fact that a pluralistic society does not favor the crystallization of clear cut, unitary classes. Thus, as Sorokin has indicated: "at the end of the nineteenth century and the beginning of the twentieth, there was no American 'aristocracy of the aristocracies.' . . . Its [America's] aristocracy was a composite, mosaic aristocracy. . . ."[6]

In the very top ranks, however, a small segment of wealthy, powerful, or otherwise important individuals and families do form "an informal but real multibonded upper stratum . . ."[7] With the consolidation of wealth and power into certain hereditary "dynasties," common association, intermarriage, and awareness of class interests tend to consolidate a true upper estate.[8] Even in relatively small cities and local communities, this interweaving of multiple ties among upper economic strata has been well documented.

Other students of stratification, with access to the same facts, have reached the conclusion that there is no one ruling stratum or elite but rather a pluralistic conglomeration of "strategic elites," each representing a special area of competence, authority, valued achievement or qualities, and style of life. Pushed to an extreme, this line of thought would suggest that no one set of decision makers exercises focal power and perpetuates its position through time. Rather there is a continually shifting interplay among a large number of loose aggregates of individuals who exert leadership by reason of special accomplishment or power. Such elites—economic, political, scientific, educational, military, entertainment, religious, and so on—are not thought to constitute a uniform ruling class.[1]

In Kaufman's study of a small rural community, the heads of the 455 family units were ranked by local raters into prestige classes on the basis of the "standing," "respect," or "reputation" of these families in the commu-

[6] Sorokin, *Society, Culture, and Personality, op. cit.,* pp. 302–303.

[7] *Ibid.,* p. 293.

[8] Cf. Ferdinand Lundberg, *America's 60 Families* (New York: Vanguard Press, 1937). See also Ferdinand Lundberg, *The Rich and the Super-Rich: A Study in the Power of Money Today* (New York: Lyle Stuart, 1968).

[1] The fullest development of this thesis is Keller, *Beyond the Ruling Class, op. cit.*

nity; and the extent of intimate association among these families was then ascertained. When each mutual visiting relationship was defined as a bond between families, over three-fourths of the bonds had a range of one-half a prestige class or less.[2] The summary finding was that "prestige class was related to informal association in two ways. First, the number of associates that an individual had was correlated with his prestige rank. Second, the intimate associates of a community member were very likely to have a prestige rank the same as, or similar to, his own. This latter finding lends support to the hypothesis that the smallest class unit is the friendship group or clique."[3]

James West's study of "Plainville" observed that stratification could be most clearly discerned in intimate visiting and "social" activities. In the more impersonal and restricted interactions outside the context of family and clique, the associations of male groups freely crossed lines of stratification.[4] On the other hand, churches, clubs, and visiting cliques were definitely status-bounded units, composed of persons of the same prestige class.[5]

In both of the studies just reviewed, the identification of prestige classes on the basis of rating assigned by local informants probably results in accenting the amount of class-bounded interaction. Nevertheless, the data still show that relatively intimate types of social interaction tend to be closely bounded by the lines of local prestige classes. Moreover, this structural constriction is not peculiar to rural communities but is found in such large cities as Detroit.[6] Also, preferences, as well as actual social relations, are stratified. Thus, one study shows that among urban white males there is a marked tendency to prefer intimate social relations with persons of comparable occupational prestige and that they prefer such relations with persons in occupations of higher rather than lower prestige. The latter ordering of preferences is the dominant one: regardless of the occupational rank of the respondent, the preferences are directed toward high-prestige occupations.[7]

Studies of the marriage patterns in a number of American communities indicate similar class boundaries.[8] Mills, in his study of a medium-sized city, shows that it is most usual that marriages are made between stratum equals but that enough cross-stratum marriages occur to prevent "social

[2] Harold F. Kaufman, "Prestige Classes in a New York Rural Community," *Memoir 260,* Cornell University Agricultural Experiment Station, p. 14.

[3] *Ibid.,* p. 15.

[4] West, *Plainville, U.S.A., op. cit.,* p. 198. See also Art Gallagher, Jr., with Foreword by Carl Withers (James West), *Plainville Fifteen Years Later* (New York: Columbia University Press, 1961).

[5] *Ibid.,* p. 134. It should be kept in mind that the locale of this study is a village (population: 275) and its rural hinterland, and that out-migration of young people is heavy. (Cf. p. 24: "The outside world absorbs about half of all who are born in and around Plainville.") See also Hollingshead, *Elmtown's Youth.*

[6] Richard F. Curtis, "Differential Association and the Stratification of the Urban Community," *Social Forces,* 42, 1 (October 1963), 68–77.

[7] Edward O. Laumann, "Subjective Social Distance and Urban Occupational Stratification," *American Journal of Sociology,* LXXI, 1 (July 1965), 26–36.

[8] Mills, "The Middle Classes in Middle-sized Cities," *op. cit.,* pp. 523–526.

*much intra-shahen*
*marriage*
*too much*
*into strata*

closure" of income-occupation strata, at least at the broad intermediate levels of the hierarchy. Among small businessmen, slightly more than one-half had married women whose fathers were in the upper half of the income-occupation distribution; and 40 percent had married the daughters of wage workers. In the higher white-collar occupations, about one-half of the men studied had married into families in the upper half of the hierarchy. Other studies have shown similar findings.

The "assimilation" of different ethnic segments into a single stratification order has proceeded at very different rates *in its two main aspects:* (1) access to occupational positions that are high in income and prestige and (2) reduction in social distance, resulting in increased social acceptance across ethnic lines.[9] Sharp value-conflicts have been generated when barriers to social acceptance have been maintained on the ascribed bases of religion, race, or national origin in the face of substantial occupational achievement and economic up-grading. In summarizing evidence on class endogamy in the United States, Kingsley Davis has concluded that "social background and the social limits to competition mean that most Americans marry within their own social class."[1] The exact proportion of marriages that are class bounded depends, of course, upon how one defines the limits of "class"; however, the general tendency for like to marry like—economically, occupationally, and culturally—is well established. Since marriages create families and children initially absorb the culture of their parents, and since the initial status of the child must be that of his parents, class endogamy necessarily generates forces tending toward the emergence of recognizable status groupings from aggregates of objectively similar persons. It is in this way that the apparently discrete facts of occupation, income, residence, visiting, intermarriage, and child training are woven into the pattern from which definite status groupings can emerge. That the crystallization of such social "estates" in the United States is far from complete is testimony to the dynamic forces of an open-class structure that still work against the numerous pressures toward formation of closed-status groupings.

### Congruities in Distribution and Ranking

Indices of "class" used in research on stratification have included occupation, income, education, self-identification, style of life, local prestige-rating. We have seen that such attributes tend to be positively correlated—high position on one tends to be associated with high positions on others. Yet many exceptions are apparent; and systematic evidence shows that the various main attributes commonly regarded as factors in general social ranking (income, education, residential area or type of dwelling, race or ethnicity) ac-

9 "There are two ways of looking at a stratification system: (1) as a system of differential access to status symbols as objects, as measured by economic and educational correlates, and (2) as a system of norms of social distance that determine equal status contacts of which intermarriage is the most crucial for the future state of the local system." (James M. Beshers, Edward O. Laumann, and Benjamin S. Bradshaw, "Ethnic Congregation-Segregation, Assimilation, and Stratification," *Social Forces*, 42, 4 (May 1964), 486).

1 Kingsley Davis, Harry C. Bredemeier, and Marion J. Levy, Jr. (eds.), *Modern American Society* (New York: Holt, Rinehart & Winston, 1949), p. 611.

tually are only loosely correlated.[2] Yet, whatever it is that Americans rate when they evaluate occupations according to "general standing" (usually interpreted as "generalized prestige"), the actual ratings can be very closely predicted from the income and educational attainment of those practicing the occupation.[3]

There is some evidence consistent with the view that the most marked effects of inconsistencies in the positions occupied by individuals may appear in cases in which the rights and privileges of achieved positions are divergent from those associated with the ascribed positions occupied by the same individual, for example, a university educated, high income, professional person who is a Negro in a racially discriminatory community; an impoverished member of an aristocratic lineage. On the other hand, persons with widely different combinations of the rewards of achieved positions, for example, high income-low education, low income-high power, high occupational prestige-little authority may not regard the status combinations as stressful, or even as inconsistent. Indeed, we would expect that as the number of qualitatively different distributive scales and rankings increases, and as varying combinations increase in proportional frequency, the significance of *generalized* ranking would decrease—and with it, the significance of status inconsistency.

Thus, quite important possibilities are apparent in the further investigation of status consistency and status crystallization. What are the kinds and degrees of association between various sets of criteria and symbols of ranking? How do these differ in different economic and political strata? In different types of communities? What changes or trends can be discovered? More fundamentally, what are the social and psychological correlates and consequences of status-inconsistency? And underlying this query are questions concerning the sources of pressures or demands for consistency, the degree of looseness or variation acceptable under varying circumstances, and, indeed, the very meaning of "consistency" itself.

All these questions are more complex than they appear to be upon first inspection. Very little is yet known about the necessary and sufficient conditions for a particular degree and kind of clustering of ranking attributes, and perhaps even less as to why particular combinations come to be normatively defined as proper and obligatory.

### Class Consciousness and Awareness of Stratification

To what extent is there awareness of classes and class membership in contemporary American society? To what extent has this awareness developed into "class consciousness" in the Marxian sense? How does consciousness of stratification vary among the various classes, strata, and other segments of the society? What are the more important factors that accentuate or

---

[2] Charles B. Nam and Mary G. Powers, "Variations in Socio-economic Structure by Race, Residence, and Life Cycle," *American Sociological Review*, 30, 1 (February 1965), 97–103.

[3] Duncan and Hodge, *op. cit.*, p. 631. (For forty-five occupations rated in the 1947 study by the National Opinion Research Center, the multiple correlation coefficient between ratings and education and income indexes was +.91.)

deemphasize awareness of class? Questions of this order are of prime significance for understanding the possible implications of objective social differentiation. There is no warrant for assuming in advance that objective stratification automatically and inevitably leads to a particular state of class consciousness.[4] Possibly the fairly widespread reluctance in American society to recognize or admit that there are social classes helps to prevent the crystallization of invidious distinctions. For lack of awareness of class, or resistance to such awareness, means that in ordinary person-to-person social interaction the symbols of prestige are not given maximum stress; there is instead a certain pressure toward informality and "democratic manners." The minimal use of honorific titles, for example, contrasts with the meticulous use of them in certain European cultures; the old style German use of the husband's title in addressing a married woman (Frau Doktor Schmidt) typically impressed Americans as being pretentious or absurd. Great men are expected to be simple and "folksy" in their personal dealings. In relations between persons of unequal position, ritual signs of deference are often resisted by those of lower position, who tend to take pride in rejecting others' claims to symbols of superiority. In particular, there is special resistance to privileges and demands for deference based solely upon formal position or rank rather than upon demonstrated personal qualities and achievements.

One of the most comprehensive compilations of systematic evidence on these points has come to us from studies of American soldiers in World War II. Extensive research demonstrated that soldiers wanted privileges to be "earned" rather than to be categorical and that the rigidity of military deference requirements was probably a major cause of the resentments of enlisted personnel toward officers and toward the system of military rank.[5]

> *Civilian society in America is not a classless system. . . . But, at least, within white civilian American society, there is no such yawning social chasm as that separating enlisted men and officers in the Army. Civilians might complain that they cannot afford the Waldorf-Astoria or abstain from going there because they would feel uncomfortable about their table manners, but they have the right to go there, whereas enlisted men do not have the right to venture into relatively commodious establishments reserved for officers only. And the officers' superior status was openly asserted and had to be continuously acknowledged by a host of acts symbolic of deference—such as saluting and the use of "Sir." The nearest analogy in civilian life would be that of the social relations of whites and Negroes, especially in the South—witness the often used phrase "caste system" to describe the Army.[6]*

[4] ". . . it is the social status structure rather than the economic or political power dimensions which plays the largest immediate role in producing those social divisions, shifting and amorphous as they may be, of American communities which center around intimate friendships, clique life, association membership and participation, and intermarriage." Milton M. Gordon, *Social Class in American Sociology* (Durham, N.C.: Duke University Press, 1958), p. 249. See the classic statement on differences between classes and status groupings by Max Weber (H. H. Gerth and C. Wright Mills, trans.), *Max Weber: Essays in Sociology* (New York: Oxford University Press, 1946), pp. 180–195.

[5] For the detailed findings see Samuel A. Stouffer, *et al.*, *The American Soldier* (Princeton, N.J.: Princeton University Press, 1949), Vol. I, chaps. 2 and 8; Vol. II, chaps. 3 and 6.

[6] *Ibid.*, Vol. I, p. 56.

*U.S. Military class awareness enforced* (handwritten margin note)

The military service in wartime elicited a very marked and widespread consciousness of differential ranking; the change from civilian position was usually abrupt, ranks were conspicuously symbolized, differences in privilege were explicit and universally known, and frequent promotions emphasized tantalizing rewards for the able or fortunate. Military doctrines often clashed with ideologies of democracy and equality. There was, officially, little flexibility in the patterns of authority and deference; but in practice, the influence of the wider culture softened the inequalities of the hierarchical system. Indeed, the strength of the modifying tradition was dramatically symbolized when an official War Department board (headed by General James Doolittle) made this statement: "Americans look with disfavor upon any system which grants unearned privileges to a particular class of individuals and find distasteful any tendency to make arbitrary social distinctions between two parts of the Army."[7]

Clearly the awareness of social class differentials is by no means fully correlated with objective differences. Such awareness is facilitated or hindered by other definite features of the society and culture. Awareness tends to be increased by rapid changes in the relative position of strata, by intensive communication within strata coupled with slight interpersonal communication across strata, by marked differences in style of life, by inter-strata differences in racial, ethnic, or religious memberships, by minimal occupational differentiation within each major stratum, by sharp discontinuities in income and wealth, by blockages to expected individual advancement, and by discrepancies between aspirations and actual position.

*class-awareness increase: e.g.—endogamy, communi..., rapid chan in strata, prestige etc.* (handwritten margin note)

In the wider civilian society of the United States, consciousness of class differences is minimized by (1) the tendency in our culture not to give clear recognition to invidious distinctions; (2) the rather marked diffusion of equalitarian social manners through a wide range of occupations, income levels, and positions of authority; (3) the wide accessibility of such commonplace symbols of "respectable" position as automobiles, the less costly versions of fashionable clothing, or even the occasional opportunity to attend commercial amusements carrying prestige; (4) the many legal or political rights that are nominally universal: the franchise, the right to hold public office, the equal responsibility for military service and jury duty, the right to a public school education and the accessibility of college training, the availability of a wide variety of public services open to all citizens,[8] and (5) the persistent dissemination of the ideology of equal opportunity and a classless society.

*minimizing class-awareness* (handwritten margin note)

Active consciousness of a definitely stratified order is further checked by (6) relatively high social mobility—both horizontal and vertical—and the consequent fluidity of strata; (7) the complexity of the occupational structure; (8) the crisscrossing of diverse criteria and symbols of position, such as income, residence, religion, ethnic background, education, family prestige, organizational affiliations, and manners.

---

[7] Cited in *ibid.*, Vol. I, p. 379.

[8] As always, subject to the major exceptions still represented by ethnic or especially racial, discrimination.

In the second half of the twentieth century, public discussion of class has become more widespread, and acceptance of the basic descriptive facts of unequal allocation and differential ranking apparently almost has become a part of folk culture. Yet this awareness has not been accompanied by any comparably large growth in class solidarity and collective class action. Attention and concern have remained largely anchored to status (ranking) rather than objective class position, to individual position and mobility rather than to class welfare and class conflict, to style of life rather than power. The traditional tendency persists: to see *rank orders of competitively achieving individuals* rather than *enduring organized social formations* based upon the distribution of economic and political power.[9]

Even a brief consideration of the causes contributing to awareness or lack of awareness of stratification shows that several quite different problems arise in considering the psychological reactions to the objective structure of stratification. First, to what extent do Americans *recognize* differences of income, wealth, safety, authority, and power? Second, what is the extent and kind of *awareness of classes as status groups*: do people recognize definite groupings of persons having a similar prestige rating, style of life, and in-group restrictions on social interaction? Third, is there real psychological *identification* with "one's class"—a sense of belonging to a solidary group of people having the same interests and values? Finally, what is the character and extent of *militant class ideologies* that define classes as struggle groups? The fact that these four questions, which concern four clearly different facets of "class consciousness," are often not distinguished in discussions of American stratification has led to unnecessary confusion.

Certain public opinion polls have been widely cited in an attempt to show that Americans predominantly think of themselves as middle class. The findings certainly show that Americans typically do not describe themselves as either "upper" or "lower" class *when explicitly asked to choose between these* terms and "middle class."[1] This reaction is not especially difficult to understand. To openly characterize oneself as upper class is widely felt in our society to be an offensive arrogation of privilege. On the other hand, the term "lower class" has acquired a connotation of moral opprobrium that describes far more than the bare fact of low economic level. Many Americans who will readily admit to being poor will consider it an insult to be called lower class.

So tenacious and deeply ingrained are the axioms of the equalitarian ethic that, as we have previously noted, there is considerable reluctance to discuss social stratification except in oblique and indirect fashion. Something real is being defended when wage workers refuse to accept the label "lower class": deference is real, and self-abnegation is real, and the workers' insistence upon social respect is a tangible influence in blunting and controlling the prestige claims of economically well-to-do groups.[2] It is broadly

---

[9] Compare the discussion by Robert M. MacIver and Charles H. Page, *Society* (New York: Holt, Rinehart & Winston, 1949), chap. 14.

[1] George Gallup and Saul F. Rae, *The Pulse of Democracy* (New York: Simon & Schuster, 1940), p. 169; *Fortune*, February, 1940.

[2] Lipset and Bendix, *op. cit.*, p. 111.

correct to say of American workers that they "do not want to be set off as a class apart [that is, as a prestige class], and if the agencies of public opinion were to attempt to set them off, the result would be nothing but resentment."[3]

The finding that three-fourths or more of a national cross section of the adult population label themselves as middle class is thus partly an artifact of the specific questions asked. Indeed, when "working class" is added to the list of choices, a rather different picture emerges. In the survey analyzed by Richard Centers, a national sample of white adult males were asked:[4] "If you were asked to use one of these four names for your social class, which would you say you belong in: the middle class, lower class, working class, or upper class?" The term "working class" was selected by fully half of those responding—a larger proportion than accepted the characterization of middle class (43 percent)—and there was a much closer correspondence between objective economic position and self-designation of class than in the *Fortune* and Gallup surveys cited above; in other words, the label "working class" is acceptable to what is objectively the working-class population, whereas "lower class" is not.

The meaning of the popular assertion that the United States has become a "middle-class country" is not self-evident. Certainly one can select an arbitrary division of the income distribution that would put most people in a broad middle range. Certainly most Americans think of themselves as "middle" rather than "upper" or "lower." A broadly similar respectable or comfortable style of life can be defined that characterizes a majority of families. But none of these things implies that middle-class persons dominantly influence major economic and political decisions nor even control the most important conditions of their own way of life.

The fact that there now is an enlarged middle-income stratum, having a broadly similar style of life, does not necessarily mean that class differences are disappearing or even being appreciably reduced. Not only are the poor still with us, but so also are the very rich. A generally rising level of formal education does not erase the continuing existence of very low and very high levels of education. Mass-produced automobiles are widely available— but a Jaguar is not a Chevrolet, nor does the driver of an eight-year-old Plymouth have any difficulty in recognizing a new Cadillac. The differences in income between persons of different educational levels appear to be increasing rather than decreasing. The income- and employment-gap between Negroes and whites is being maintained. Interpersonal relations across major categories of occupation and income may very well be decreasing. The most comprehensive recent study of differences in attitudes by educational levels concludes that such differences between high and low education have not decreased; differentiation by education is somewhat greater among younger than among older persons.[5]

[3] Jones, *Life, Liberty, and Property, op. cit.,* p. 349.

[4] Centers, *The Psychology of Social Classes, op. cit.,* p. 56.

[5] Norval D. Glenn, "The Trend in Differences in Attitudes and Behavior by Educational Level," *Sociology of Education,* 39, 3 (Summer 1966), 255–275. Because inequality in education has decreased, the total differentiation associated with educational levels may

The awareness of classes as status groupings (prestige classes) may be similarly characterized. *Individual differences in prestige* are typically recognized, often with remarkable precision and fidelity; but again, there is stubborn and widespread resistance to the notion that there are fixed prestige groups. Prestige groupings almost seem to be thought of as simple ratings of individuals or families on a scale of temporary competitive placement rather than as established ranks or definite layers in the social structure.[6] However, both the sensitivity to prestige ranking and the awareness of a *system* of prestige classes are highly variable among different portions of the population. It seems to be true, for example, that in relatively small communities, those groups considering themselves to be upper class see the whole community as systematically arranged into definite prestige strata, whereas at the lowest economic levels there is only a vague conception of a ranking system.[7] Warner indicates, for instance, that the lower-class person perceives class as a matter of wealth and power.[8]

Perception and awareness of prestige arrangements are affected not only by location in the class structure but also by mobility. In a local ranking system, the most definite and precise discriminations will typically be found either among the stable upper strata, where persons have had an opportunity to become thoroughly familiar with the entire structure and have had many occasions to develop awareness of class differences, or among those mobile persons who have in their own lives traversed a considerable portion of the prestige scale.[9] In general it seems that the finest distinctions are made in looking down upon the rank just below one's own or up to a position that is the object of immediate aspiration.

The large amount of vagueness and indeterminancy, especially in the great middle-class sector, is of great significance. In general, the very top and bottom strata are clearly recognized; but the intermediate gradations tend to be only loosely defined, and subdivisions of the large middle stratum have low social visibility.[1]

Because of the very nature of prestige classes, precise and stable discriminations can be maintained in a detailed way only within the confines

---

not have increased. But the findings are consistent with the view that "education is now a more important basis for the economic and cultural differentiation of a diminishing but still sizable lower segment, and of a growing, but still small, upper segment from the rest of the society" (p. 275).

[6] For vivid illustrations of this orientation among workers see Katherine Archibald, *Wartime Shipyard* (Berkeley: University of California Press, 1947).

[7] Cf. the studies of Warner, A. Davis, Useem, West, Hollingshead, and others, cited above.

[8] Warner, Meeker, and Eells, *Social Class in America, op. cit.*, p. 57.

[9] Cf. W. Lloyd Warner and Paul S. Lunt, *The Status System of a Modern Community* (New Haven, Conn.: Yale University Press, 1942), p. 44.

[1] Cf. the penetrating comment of Pfautz and Duncan: "The concept of 'closure,' which is crucial for the structure of status groups, would seem to have little meaning relative to the 'middle' classes; whereas the estate-tendencies at the extremes of the social class configuration as well as the 'communal' character of the upper-uppers and lower-lowers are obvious from the data at hand." Harold W. Pfautz and Otis D. Duncan, "A Critical Evaluation of Warner's Work in Community Stratification," *American Sociological Review*, 15, 2 (April 1950), 212.

of a community or other grouping small enough to be comprehended as a whole; and much of the research evidence on prestige classes has come from relatively small communities and groups—from a "Plainville" or "Elmtown" (Morris, Illinois) rather than from Detroit, Chicago, or Los Angeles. The large city is too complex, too mobile, too subject to change to permit the precise elaboration of ratings that can place every family in a village in an exactly defined niche.[2] Prestige stratification, in other words, is a different kind of system in different types of social structures within the United States. In the larger urban areas, the recognition of prestige differences becomes closely tied to the symbols of wealth and power; and only within the limited circles of more or less intimate association are more complex criteria employed and the finer distinctions drawn. The *total character* of the stratification system, therefore, varies according to the nature of the more inclusive social structure of which it is a part.

It follows from the preceding discussion that one type of class consciousness consists of an awareness of prestige rankings or the recognition of at least partly closed status-groupings sharing similar social ratings. This is *not* the same as class consciousness in the political or economic sense. The latter does not rest to anything like the same degree as the former upon intimate association, common culture, or homogeneity of social origins and current outlook. It consists of an awareness of similar economic and political interests; in its most fully developed form it is a belief in the identity of interest of all in one's own class and a conception of the class as a struggle group fighting for power against an opposing class or classes.[3] Similarity or identity of objective economic and political interests does not in itself necessarily lead to class consciousness, class identification, or class action. Full awareness of class interests, in this sense, is a highly sophisticated response, greatly dependent upon the perpetuation of a particular situation over such a period of time that an explanatory ideology can be developed, communicated, and widely accepted among people in similar political and economic circumstances. If there is to be collective class action oriented to class interests, it is of decisive importance, furthermore, that class be perceived as part of a *definite system of power*. Otherwise, similarity of con-

[2] In Minneapolis, over one-third of respondents either did not know their class, said there were no classes, or said they did not belong to any social class. Neal Gross, "Social Class Identification in the Urban Community," *American Sociological Review*, 18, 4 (August 1953), 398–404. Vagueness in images of stratification is reported by several other studies, for example, S. Stanfield Sargent, "Class and Class Consciousness in a California Town," *Social Problems*, 1, 1 (June 1953), 22–27; Gerhard E. Lenski, "American Social Classes: Statistical Strata or Social Groups?" *American Journal of Sociology*, LVIII, 2 (September 1952), 139–144.

[3] It is this type of class consciousness that is referred to in the following statement: "Highly competent leadership therefore seems to be required to *make a potential class aware of its existence*, by analyzing the totality of conditions which explain its self-identity." (Italics added.) Reprinted from D. Anderson and P. E. Davidson, *Ballots and the Democratic Class Struggle* (Stanford, Calif.: 1943), p. 252, with the permission of the authors and of the publishers, Stanford University Press. These discussions, of course, go back to the seminal distinction made by Marx between class *an sich* and class *für sich*; an enormous body of political and sociological commentary has developed around this distinction.

dition may lead to amorphous movements, made up of many isolated and limited struggles between classes, but not to a unitary class consciousness nor to the Marxian class struggle.

In particular, *militant* class consciousness cannot be adequately accounted for solely by objective current position in the stratification order. Other factors of substantial importance include irregularity of income and employment, sharp social differentiation and isolation of workers from other elements of the larger community, abrupt (collective) reversals of a previously improving economic situation, and recency of entrance into urban-industrial life. It may be hypothesized that the factors that accentuate class-conscious militance among industrial workers consist primarily of those conditions that (1) facilitate communication among similarly circumstanced workers and retard communication with persons in other strata, (2) render highly visible differences in income and style of life between workers and other strata, and (3) violate expectations or norms of fairness. The traditional radicalism of sailors, fishermen, stevedores, and lumberjacks, for instance, emerges under conditions of sharp distinctiveness in work and manner of living in combination with a high degree of isolation. The verbalized militancy of Detroit blue-collar workers is highest among Negroes who are Southern born and from farms, and among Polish-Americans among those born in Europe.[4] Migration involving social disruption and culture contrast possibly is influential also in helping to create class consciousness.

It seems plain that a high development of militant political and economic class consciousness does not exist in the United States. This conclusion is warranted in spite of several important indications of increased class awareness, notably the tendency of workers to gravitate toward political affiliations that partly express class interests, and the emergence of mass industrial unionization. Modern developments of this kind certainly represent mass action that is partly determined by recognition on the part of large numbers of individuals that they have economic and political interests in common. But there is as yet no real evidence that the middle and working classes contain a high proportion of persons who have developed a *systematic* conception of belonging to a definite class set against an opposing class.[5] The failure of communism to win any appreciable following in the American labor movement is by itself impressive testimony to the lack of militant class orientation. Unfortunately, we do not have the data necessary to say just *how much* of *what kind* of class consciousness is to be found among the various economic strata. It is quite possible that the small business elite of wealth and power is marked by a self-consciousness of class and of the broad power implications of its position. The same may well be

---

[4] John C. Leggett, "Uprootedness and Working-Class Consciousness," *American Journal of Sociology*, LXVIII, 6 (May 1963), 682–692.

[5] Archibald has observed that in a transient and uneducated group of wartime shipyard workers, resentment against wealthy, powerful, and educated groups did not "evolve into resentment against a distinct class of exploiters or expropriators. . . ." *Wartime Shipyard, op. cit.*, pp. 183–184.

true of some relatively small, well disciplined groups of industrial workers. On the other hand, the diverse, mobile, and unorganized middle strata show a notable unawareness of class[6] and certainly are very far from homogeneity of social perspectives.[7] Not only awareness of class but the very criteria and symbols of ranking are, as we have said, differently perceived from various locations in the structure. When a stratum has possessed wealth and its attendant advantages over a long period of time, especially in relatively stable communities, it tends to minimize the economic base of prestige-class distinctions and to lay stress upon manners, morality, ethnic or religious background, family history, and long residence in the community. It tends to look down upon the *nouveau riche* and, as Anderson aptly puts it, to be "conspicuously unostentatious in its manner and possessions."[8] On the other hand, people in the least privileged strata tend to see the upper portion of the structure largely in terms of wealth and power; and toward the possessors of economic power the less advantaged working groups hold complex and ambivalent attitudes. Disapproval of great wealth mingles with admiration of success and envy over its rewards. The degree to which differential reward is felt to form a *legitimate* order is always a crucial datum for diagnosing the stability of any social system.[9] Accordingly, this consideration of differing class perspectives raises the final question of this chapter: To what extent is American social stratification an integrated system, and how, short of perfect integration, can it exist as a working reality?

### Strains, Tensions, and Compensations

Like all other durable social arrangements, a continuing system of social stratification is maintained primarily by three sets of components: (1) the advantages it brings in interest gratification—its rewarding output to someone, (2) a consensus upon the beliefs, values, and norms that support it, and (3) the exercise of power.[1]

We have seen that there are great differences in the objective rewards received by various strata in our society. We know that elsewhere in the world, violent class struggle has driven societies and communities into sharply polarized camps, has led to civil war, has become the base and doctrine of vast political movements affecting most of the world. How is it possible that in the complex fabric of American society very different income-occupation strata and prestige classes can exist without severely dis-

---

[6] For example, see the suggestion: "Most class-conscious persons, it would seem, confine their thought of class to common modes of consumption, especially of the 'conspicuous' variety, paying little attention indeed to the economic base." Reprinted from D. Anderson and P. E. Davidson, *Ballots and the Democratic Class Struggle, op. cit.*, p. 251, with the permission of the authors and of the publishers, Stanford University Press.

[7] C. Wright Mills, *White Collar* (New York: Oxford University Press, 1951).

[8] Elin L. Anderson, *We Americans* (Cambridge, Mass.: Harvard University Press, 1937), p. 128.

[9] For a careful critique of studies of "class consciousness," see Gordon, *Social Class in American Sociology, op. cit.*, pp. 193–202.

[1] Wrong, *op. cit.*, p. 774.

abling conflicts? In the United States itself, clashes of interest between *economic* groupings have been frequent and often violent; some of these struggles—especially between industrial workers and their employers—have borne a definite "class" quality. Certainly, one cannot assume that our modern society is inevitably immune to class conflict. The stability of the stratification order cannot be taken for granted; rather, a primary problem is to explain specifically how the *relatively* low degree of tension and conflict in the American case has been possible in the past and to appraise the probability of a continuing peaceable order.

It is often overlooked that the very fact of social differentiation involving multiple statuses and multiple group-memberships necessarily means that total undivided loyalty to the largest social units is highly unlikely. Inevitably the subcollectivities are differently rewarded and differentially ranked; inevitably, the subunits of immediate interpersonal interaction become foci of emotional affiliation and social support and control for individuals. It follows that the collective interests of all subunits are never identical and sometimes are in opposition. Dissension and tensions, consequently, are inherent in organizations and societies.

Let us first ask what important foci of strain can be identified in the contemporary stratification order and then seek to discover what alleviating factors or compensations there may be. In the first place, awareness of actual inequalities in wealth and related objective advantages tend to be sharpened by the large and frequent fluctuations in economic conditions, especially since the society possesses no long-established aristocracy whose position could appear to be historically validated by usage and venerable tradition. Furthermore, American life has a public character; and wide publicity is given to luxury and conspicuous consumption by the wealthy. The conjunction of these factors with the equalitarian ideals of the culture gives power and wealth high social visibility and renders it difficult to establish differential privilege as an unquestioned prerogative of any special group or class. The main historic justifications for great wealth have seen wealth as the reward of effort, achievement, and the related virtues so familiar in the secular derivatives of Protestant ethics. But the old cultural axioms equating wealth and virtue were never completely immune to criticism and have become increasingly subject to skepticism and attack in the twentieth century. Among wage workers, there is a fairly widespread conviction that wealth is largely the result of inherited position, "pull" and "connections," or luck. Insofar as the basis of economic affluence is thought to be blind chance or the consequence of the principle "first come, first served," differentials of wealth may be tolerated and envied; but they are not likely to be admired as morally excellent. We have already noted that wealth or income does not correlate very precisely with socially valued accomplishments in the diverse fields of the occupational structure. Tensions arising from this source constitute another index of the value conflict engendered by the presence of imperfectly institutionalized economic power. For example, the seeming failure of many established upper-class groups in America to recognize that hazards to their long-time position may result from policies of ethnic, racial, and religious discrimination and exclusion[2] may give considerable hope and encouragement to all those who look with disfavor upon the successful establishment of aristocratic authority. For the ineptness of an establishment often is the best guarantee that its pretensions to moral leadership will not support its claims to direct the political and economic destiny of its society.

Of course, neither absolute inequalities nor even relative inequalities that lack full moral legitimation are uniformly associated with articulate mass resentment. Neither inequality nor injustice (as judged in a particular society) is, by itself, sufficient to produce mass rejection, protest, or revolt against particular stratification orders. To some degree, of course, these are perennial problems of all complex societies. The problems seem significant in the United States precisely because economic activity is so dominant a part of the society and because personal achievement is a central justification for differences in social rewards among men who have been encouraged by their culture to claim equality of opportunity.

Probably the most obvious focus of conflict in the American system is the clash between the principles of achieved status and status gained by birth or group membership. Belief in equality of opportunity, in free competitive placement, and in rewards somehow proportioned to the individual excellence of personal qualities and achievements conflicts with the tenacity of family and clique in perpetuating established position and differential opportunity; and patterns of discrimination and preference restrict the opportunities of persons in "minority groups," which altogether probably include more than one-third of the total population. On many fronts and in many guises this widely ramified conflict of normative standards and actual power groupings permeates the American scene. In its multiple extensions throughout the culture, it can also be said to be one of the main problems in integrating the values of the whole society.[3]

In the United States, both the objective stratification (of income, wealth, authority, and power) and the stratification of prestige ranking are closely connected with and influenced by racial and ethnic divisions. The most important and conspicuous case is that of the sharp differentials between black and white Americans. Since the late 1940's, Negro Americans have received in most years about one-half as much income per person as whites and have experienced about twice as much unemployment. As a consequence of past and current discrimination, Negro workers are concentrated in low income, insecure occupations, where little opportunity exists for overcoming the handicaps of low educational level, lack of skills, and problems of motivation. In a society experiencing long-term growth in levels of real income, the relative position of Negroes in income and occupation has not improved. The consequence is a widespread sense of deprivation and injustice.

[2] A performance described in some detail in Baltzell, *The Protestant Establishment, op. cit.*

[3] Cf. Robin M. Williams, Jr., with Edward A. Suchman and John P. Dean, *Strangers Next Door* (Englewood Cliffs, N.J.: Prentice-Hall, 1964), chap. 10.

*(handwritten margin notes: high aspirations discourages resignation withdrawal)*

A third primary area of strain, closely related to the two already mentioned, consists in the tendency to establish relatively high levels of aspiration at nearly all levels of the income-power hierarchies. The concentration of attention and effort upon secular success, the high evaluation of power, the belief in unlimited opportunity—these and similar influences tend to create a continuous upward pressure in the system and to discourage resignation, withdrawal, and apathy. The model American "has enough to hope for more"; and his culture, on the whole, continually reinforces his ambition without at the same time setting clear, customary limits to it. Obviously, these pressures do not affect all segments of the population equally but do constitute one of the features of American society that differentiates it from the major societies of Europe and Asia.[4] And insofar as there is this optimistic aspiration (whatever its precise empirical importance may be), the smooth working of the system is dependent upon very considerable opportunities for actual success among the highly motivated portions of middle and working strata. A sudden and severe blocking of mass ambitions in a society such as this would certainly have a very important effect upon the stability of the entire structure. By giving full weight to these features of American society, we may diagnose quite important strains in the system. Objective stratification is great and is subject to high social visibility. Value conflicts center upon the role of inherited or "unearned" wealth and of wealth obtained by noninstitutionalized means; and somewhat less obvious but still significant tensions are aroused by sensed discrepancies between reward and merit—as "merit" is culturally defined by the nominally dominant consensus. Notions of social justice are to an appreciable degree polarized into the camps of the "haves" and the "have-nots." And cleavage in the moral framework of the system is especially marked where the criteria of equal opportunity and personal achievement meet head-on with systems of ascribed status and preferential opportunity—most conspicuously in the case of ethnic, religious, or racial minorities.

All these elements exist in the broader context of a relatively secularized, ahistorical, and dynamic culture. To an impartial and detached observer the combination must appear to make a highly volatile social situation. That against such a background, and in an industrialized society, so little class conflict and so little political organization of workers has occurred is a fact so astonishing as to call for a far more comprehensive analysis than can be touched upon here. However, certain influences appear, even in a preliminary inspection, to help stabilize the existing stratification order. In briefest summary, these compensatory factors include at least the following:

*(handwritten margin note: why so little class conflict?)*

1. The high level of real income and the relatively wide distribution of a "comfort" level of living.
2. The actual incidence of upward mobility and the attendant hope of "getting ahead."

[4] Although the amount of certain kinds of vertical mobility may be much the same in highly industrialized nations, differences in values, beliefs, and mechanisms for handling strain may result in highly diverse consequences. Cf. Lipset and Bendix, *op. cit.*, p. 64.

3. The existence of a large middle-income, middle-prestige aggregate.
4. Widespread legal and political rights, nominally equalitarian.
5. The accessibility of public facilities and services.
6. The prevalence of equalitarian symbols and behavior patterns.
7. Intrastratum heterogeneity in culture.
8. Mutual insulation of prestige classes.
9. Participation in common organizations and activities.
10. Persistence of a complex body of beliefs and values that lends legitimacy to the going system.

Other restraining factors can undoubtedly be found, and the actual dynamic role of those listed is at present a matter of hypothesis rather than of fact. Nevertheless, our preceding analysis has suggested credible theoretical and factual grounds for thinking that these elements do play important parts in the real working equilibrium of stratification in America. At this point we can make only brief comments on each factor.

The high level of real income in the United States has been copiously documented: if America has not been the Eldorado it was thought to be by countless immigrants to its shores, it has, at any rate, produced a high level of material comfort for the great majority of the population. Although there are no precise measures of its importance, surely one of the most significant sources of acquiescence in the allocations of scarce values in the American case has been the rising levels of real income of the majority of the population. The shares are highly unequal, and we have seen that they are not becoming more evenly distributed; but they are cuts of a larger and larger pie. Over time, in short, the allocations have not represented a zero-sum game. Such participation in an expanding largesse apparently eases many (certainly not all) of the latent antagonisms of an inequalitarian order.

Among the most salient facts are these:

1. The absolute levels of income and wealth have increased greatly, so that the average level of living continues to rise. Per capita personal income in constant (1958) dollars rose from $1,646 in 1950 to $2,214 in 1965.[5]

2. Between 1947 and 1963, the proportion of families receiving incomes (in constant 1962 dollars) below $3,000 declined from 32 percent to 19 percent.[6]

3. In the highly technical field of historical income estimates, the experts disagree as to whether, or how much, inequality of incomes has changed in this century. Estimates vary depending upon whether averages refer to families, households, or unrelated individuals, upon how taxation is estimated, and so on. Kolko emphasizes the "hidden" and tax-free income of the very wealthy and believes that no lessening of inequality has occurred since 1910.[7] Herman Miller believes that such items as capital gains and

[5] United States Bureau of the Census, *Statistical Abstract of the United States: 1967* (88th Edition) (Washington, D.C.: Government Printing Office, 1967), Table 456, p. 321.
[6] Herman P. Miller, "Changes in the Number and Composition of the Poor," in Margaret S. Gordon (ed.), *Poverty in America* (San Francisco: Chandler, 1965), p. 89.
[7] Kolko, *Wealth and Power in America, op. cit.*, pp. 13–16; see also pp. 17–45.

undistributed profits (excluded from the census data) do not appreciably distort the real trends; and he estimates that the share of the top 5 percent of families and individuals decreased from 30 percent in 1929 to 20 percent in 1961.[8] However, he also points out that there has been no important change since World War II and that real poverty affects many millions of families at the other end of the scale.

4. It is not correct, although often publicly claimed, that in recent years a great "leveling up" of incomes has reduced inequality. The lower-income groups did not receive a larger share in the 1960's than in the 1940's; the gap between Negroes and whites probably widened and certainly did not narrow; differentials between occupational categories were stable or increasing.[9]

5. Low-income strata have small amounts and poor quality of housing, medical care, education. In 1965, when the median money income of *families* was $6,882, the lowest 20 percent of families received only 5 percent of the income.[1]

Although the material rewards of the system have often proved to be insecure and great enclaves of the population still do not share greatly in "the American standard of living," the real possibilities of acquiring greater income and prestige have reinforced efforts to strive within the system rather than to challenge it. These real possibilities—combined with the persistence of the attitudes of an earlier era—have led to the transfer of hope and ambition to the next generation. Belief in the American dream of upward mobility is resilient and thus far has been sufficiently reinforced by actual rises to stand as a prime support of adjustment to the existing situation.

It is true that in such a society positions of low income, social vulnerability, and low prestige typically are experienced by their occupants as depriving and frustrating. Yet such positions render hazardous the direct expression of resentment, rebellion, envy, or contempt for those better situated. Under these conditions and in a society in which the privileged strata are firmly in control and are supported and protected by a widely accepted set of ideologies, lower-strata persons may convert their alienative sentiments into attitudes that support the existing system[2]—either by devaluing that which they cannot have ("rich people aren't happy anyway"), by depoliticizing the problems ("it all depends on luck"), or by positively supporting the virtues of conformity.[3]

In all of these respects, the amorphous middle classes play a crucial part. Diverse in occupation and ambiguous in political orientation, various segments of the middle-income strata are linked by social origin, association,

[8] Miller, *Rich Man, Poor Man, op. cit.*, p. 35.

[9] *Ibid.*, pp. 37–55.

[1] United States Bureau of the Census, *Statistical Abstract of the United States: 1967, op. cit.*, Table 471, p. 333.

[2] See the striking data in Wilensky and Edwards, *op. cit.*

[3] We still need further empirical testing of the many stimulating insights available in these matters. See Max Scheler, *Ressentiment*, Lewis A. Coser (ed.), William W. Holdheim (trans.) (New York: Free Press, 1961).

and intermarriage to both the wage worker and the employer-executive strata. Permeated with the "central morality" analyzed by A. W. Jones, some parts of the middle groups lean now to one side and now to the other on issues of governmental policy and industrial organization. It is this middle aggregation that is often the solid core of reality behind the figment of "the public" to which both labor unions and management or employer groups sometimes appeal in times of industrial strife. Typically disliking extreme solutions, the middle strata tend to advocate compromising, middle-of-the-road policies. The old platitude that a strong middle class is a primary bulwark of social stability is not any the less valid for being commonplace; and any serious study of the American case is surely forced to impute a major role to these groups as a stabilizing "third party" between capitalist and proletariat.[4] It must be conceded also that the very vagueness of prestige-class distinctions within the middle-income levels, and between them and other portions of the hierarchy, is significant in blurring potential lines of identification and conflict. Furthermore, the middle strata exhibit enough examples of upward mobility to stand as a concrete symbol and embodiment of the reality of opportunity.

Turning now to the possible role of equal legal and political rights, one is confronted with complexities that defy brief analysis. On the one hand, nominally equal rights and obligations exist with respect to the franchise, political officeholding, military service, jury trial, and so forth, and conceivably encourage hope of more effective guarantees of equal opportunity; any "favoritism" shown the upper strata—less severe punishment for misdemeanors, less liability to the more dangerous and arduous military duties —might increase frustration and disillusionment. On the other hand, equalitarian political rights undoubtedly are apprehended by a high percentage of the American people as a real bar to status justice and the arbitrary exercise of economic and political power. Even as sheer creeds, these equalitarian rights have tremendous appeal.

We have no way at present of measuring precisely the distances between prestige-ranks, gradations of authority, or different styles of life. Yet the total array of data available to us concerning stratification in America leads almost irresistibly to the impression that sharp discontinuities are lessening in favor of a smooth series of overlapping levels in each of several scales. Individuals tend to deal with those who are just a little superior or inferior in authority; they compare themselves with others a step or two removed in prestige; they can always find nearby those with a little more or a little less education. Thus, adjacent pairs tend to be close in ranks; and the several ranked positions of a given person may be at rather different levels. When this finely grained pluralistic ranking is combined with considerable mobility, the whole system takes on qualities of looseness, tentativeness, and elasticity of evaluation.

[4] This is definitely *not* to say that American middle classes would play this role under any circumstances. Experience elsewhere would suggest that a suddenly impoverished and socially disorganized middle stratum may be a fertile source for aggressive political movements.

A major consequence of the extremely complex situation thus far described is a vagueness of class discriminations and a notable flexibility in certain types of interpersonal relations in which the exact determination of relative rank is a problem that does not need to be raised. Not only is this indeterminacy characteristic of many commercial facilities and services, but it is increasingly reinforced by public, governmental, and civic services and facilities that are either free or accessible at a nominal charge: libraries, parks, playgrounds, resorts and reserves, health services, educational facilities, and so on. In a society where so much of life is lived outside the home, the relative openness of so many areas of activity to a wide range of classes must be taken seriously as a mitigating factor in the impact of differential privilege and prestige distinctions.

The vagueness and flexibility of status discriminations in the special cases just mentioned point to a more fundamental basis for a low friction component in the American system. The society is characterized by a high ratio of secondary to primary social contacts; a very great deal of social interaction is casual and segmental—whether it be functionally specific economic transactions or the casual interaction of the audience or recreational crowd. And where social relations are highly segmental, or compartmentalized, they concern a limited area of activities and interests and very often can be insulated from any integral ranking of the person.[5] There is, accordingly, considerable leeway in ordinary life to avoid distinctions of station that engender hostility.

One striking and insufficiently analyzed fact about the nature of stratification in the modern urban setting is that interstrata relations tend to be *impersonal* and *categorical* rather than relations of *personalized superordination* and *subordination*. Under the feudal system of medieval Europe, the relation of individuals in lower strata to those above them were relations of personal dependence and obligation; one owed fealty to a *particular* lord, and one owed him the services and deferences in perpetuity, at least in theory. Furthermore, the bonds between superior and subordinate positions were *multiple* and *cumulative*: in one person were combined certain aspects of our modern tax collector, judge, policeman, landlord, employer, military chief, and, on occasion, religious leader. In a relatively static agrarian economy, with local production for local use and with low geographic mobility, the relations of social classes became rigidly stylized, person-to-person relations: stratification became an all-enveloping mode of actual social relations, affecting practically all of the individual's interests and values and, hence, was most closely related to his self-esteem. In contemporary America, on the contrary, many interstrata relations are either not sharply defined as invidious or else are peripheral to the individual's total activity and personality. The weight of authority and the exactions of deference tend to be diffused among a variety of specific statuses; the worker who has a subordinate role in the factory may still have in many instances opportunities

5 Lipset and Bendix, *Social Mobility in Industrial Society, op. cit.,* p. 111: "Americans may esteem the attainments of a man and recognize his high position, but they will not kowtow to him."

for superordinate status in off-job activities. The impersonality of authority, together with geographic and job mobility, tends to reduce the possibility of total personality involvement in particular hierarchical arrangements.

We have already noted the prevalence of "democratic" manners in inter-strata relations and have suggested that symbolic behavior of this sort must be given real weight as a factor of flexibility in the stratification scale. It may be, and probably is, of minor influence in comparison with the complex of opposite forces that create class-bounded interests, opportunities, and values; but it greatly reduces demands for deference and thereby makes it possible to an important degree for less privileged members of the society to avoid continual reminders of status differences in contexts where intense emotions might otherwise be aroused. It is our hypothesis, therefore, that equalitarian symbols and behavior patterns are not inconsequential illusions that simply mask the real class struggle, but rather that they have a tangible cushioning effect upon interpersonal relations between persons of different station in the stratification scale.[6]

Intrastratum heterogeneity in culture is of importance here because it reduces the potentiality of *class-structured collective action*, especially in labor organization and political action. Every main income or occupational category in American society is partially segmented by social categories attributed to real or assumed ethnic, religious, and racial differences. Industrial unionization has been retarded by such cleavages and distinctions among workers. As ethnic differences are gradually decreasing, they become less divisive, but for several generations they have worked against the development of a unitary labor union movement or a continuing political organization of workers. Cleavages centering around religious affiliations, ethnic backgrounds, and racial categories have been, in this sense, interchangeable with class cleavages. Whether the results may have been desirable or undesirable from other points of view is irrelevant to the effects in segmenting economically similar strata. Not only ethnic divisions but also other types of diversity—those of region, skill level, social origin—have contributed to the lack of a common culture among aggregates of persons having the same relation to the means of production.

In general, a threatened loss of established social position will arouse stronger resistance than the threatened loss of a prospective advantage, even a much greater advantage. Shifts in future potentialities are accordingly easier to bring about than re-allocations among claimants to present goods. Expanding economies, therefore, furnish the basis for much resolution of social oppositions through recentering of interests.

Beyond the early stages of factory industrialism, the more complex the technology (as indicated, for example, by level of education required to understand the basic processes and devices), the greater is likely to be the specialization. The greater the specialization, the finer the gradations of reward and recognition are likely to become. The finer the gradations, in

[6] Even though relatively high mobility occurs in spite of it, most countries of western Europe are generally conceded to emphasize differences of status more visibly and rigidly than is typical in the United States.

general, the less sharp the distinctions of prestige in adjacent positions. The less sharp the prestige distinctions, the less severe the opposition of strata. The less severe the opposition of strata, the less the collective solidarity. The less collective solidarity, the less the overt conflict of strata or classes. Hence given approximate equality of such relevant conditions as stability and absolute level of real income, the more complex the total technology of a society, the less likely it is to experience severe conflict.

Complex technology results from a large and sustained volume of innovations. Once under way such a system tends to produce continuing processes of rapid change. And the changes, in turn, produce a high rate of occupational mobility and, consequently, of stratification mobility.

Still another important mechanism affecting integration in modern industrial societies arises from the elaborate functional differentiation of activities, social positions, and collectivities. In general, it is likely that the greater the functional differentiation, the greater the range of talents and abilities that are socially recognized and rewarded.[7] The greater the functional differentiation also, the greater the number of separate ranking orders established in different collectivities. Thus, there is not only a proliferation of elites,[8] but also an exceedingly wide extension of relatively high levels of prestige in specialized activities and collectivities. The activities may be occupational or avocational (sports, arts, civic enterprises) and the "reference groups" which bestow recognition and acclaim are numerous and remarkably varied. One consequence is that a very high proportion of active adults can find themselves approved and respected in some important aspect of their lives.

The actual sociological character of a stratification system, it is now apparent, includes far more than either the objective distribution of scarce values or the institutionalized scale of social ranking.[9] This situation is clearly illustrated by the next factors to be considered, the mutual "insulation" of prestige classes, on the one hand, and the participation of differently evaluated individuals in common organizations and activities, on the other. Both must be discussed together because seemingly opposite tendencies here can in some respects have similar consequences. As a preceding discussion of intrastratum solidarity has shown, there are definite tendencies for intimate (primary) social interactions to be restricted to relations between persons of about the same economic level and/or prestige station. Cliques, friendships, visiting circles, and marriages all show this pattern. Insofar as they do,

---

[7] Kaare Svalastoga, *Social Differentiation* (New York: David McKay, 1965), p. 127: "Increasing functional differentiation implies that a wider range of talent may be rewarded. . . . In modern macrosocieties, the avenues to high social reward are typically manifold."

[8] Cf. Keller, *Beyond the Ruling Class, op. cit.*

[9] For instance, a high rate of individual social mobility does not of itself guarantee political stability and the acceptance of the existing institutional order. It may, on the contrary, lead to such high aspirations and strenuous competition as to produce large numbers of frustrated persons who readily accept radical or revolutionary solutions. The effects of social mobility in the United States depend upon a constellation of other factors which give mobility a meaning different from that which it may have in the newly industrializing countries of the world.

the most intimate and comprehensive social relations do not involve direct and continuing personal contacts with persons of widely dissimilar rank. Such insulation of social segments does, indeed, reduce opportunities for communication and value consensus in society as a whole. At the same time, at least in the short run, it establishes buffers and barriers to relationships that contain the possibility of serious conflict. To the extent that this insulation is a matter of mutual preference rather than categorical exclusion that is felt as stigmatic, it appears that the pattern helps stabilize the prestige-ranking system, in local communities, at least. Opposed to this insulation of strata is the crosscutting of class lines in organizations and activities of an impersonally specific nature, representing either *common* interests of the whole community or special interests that can be defined in such a way that class distinctions are largely irrelevant. Such activities and organizations are typically found in great variety in American urban communities; although research into their actual functions is largely lacking and greatly needed, it is probable that they contribute appreciably to the integration of the system.

### Extent of Integration of the System

A final and essential question that the sociologist is obliged to raise concerning any set of stratification arrangements is this: To what extent is there an integrated system? Many meanings can be given to the phrase "integrated system." For our purposes, a set of stratification arrangements will constitute an integrated system to the extent that the occupants of all positions evaluate both the principles of distribution and the actual distribution as "just," even though they may be dissatisfied with their own position. In overt behavior, this would mean that there are no important movements for political revolution or even for radical change in either the rules of the game or the existing differentials of privileges and rewards. In the fully integrated case, it would mean that even those of low position and those suffering loss of position would, nevertheless, defend the system and continue to conform to the institutional norms. No known society has had a perfectly integrated system. Clearly, however, willing acceptance and support is strong and widespread in some societies, whereas others maintain only a precarious domestic peace through extensive coercion; and some experience the upheavals of class warfare and revolution.

The notion of "distributive justice" is central to the description of integrated and nonintegrated stratification. Yet this is a peculiarly elusive and ambiguous concept that cannot be made to serve us well unless we can find in it a definiteness that permits its application to the real world. Some basic implications of the concept require comment.

First, there is no one substantive distribution of income, wealth, and other scarce and distributive values that is somehow objectively just in all societies. Highly inequalitarian arrangements have been regarded as ethically justified and have been strongly supported by a large proportion of the population in some cases. In others, much more equalitarian distributions have come to be regarded as morally outrageous and have been overthrown by force. It is not preordained what the proper allocations should be; and men in differing circumstances develop very different beliefs and values concerning this whole matter. Nor is it simply the case that deprived strata or individuals resent and rebel, whereas the more affluent or otherwise privileged always support the order that feeds them.[1] The single fact that best brings out the underlying complexity is that militant social protest most often comes not from those whose position is at the bottom of the heap but rather from those who have gained enough to hope for more but find their aspirations blocked by the established system.

In the second place, the allocation of the good things of this world among the members of a society can take place according to several disparate rules. The first and most elementary is in a sense not a rule at all— the simple fact of *power* to take and hold; although not a principle, the omnipresent exercise of power merges so imperceptibly into "legitimate authority" (as fear merges into respect, and hope of gain through the currying of favor transforms its guise into that of admiration) that we must acknowledge power as one of the important bases of distributive orders. Closely related, but distinct in several consequential ways, is the rule of *established precedent*, which may be roughly translated as "to him who hath, shall be given." This rule is more generally followed in our own society than is acknowledged by most apologists or defenders of the system. Indeed, major programs of the federal government have been organized on this basis.[2] A special variety of distribution by historical precedent is allocation on the basis of *categorical ascribed status*—race, religion, ethnic origin, birth as a citizen, and the like. A rigid aristocratic order of hereditary positions allocates privileges and rewards according to birth in certain kinship groups —as one English nobleman said, "with no nonsense about merit."

Still another rule of distribution is that of *patronage*, in the broadest sense of rewards to followers of a leader—of a political party, a religious grouping, a business enterprise, or any other social formation—in return for loyalty and support (rather than specific occupational achievement).

In open-class systems, a major principle of distribution is that of competitive *achievement*, in which rewards go to effective performance of valued activities.[3]

Allocations may be made according to some criterion of *need*, varying from a minimal standard of physical subsistence ("no one in America

---

[1] "Dissatisfaction with the system of privileges and rewards in a society is never felt in an even proportion to the degree of inequality to which its various members are subject." (W. G. Runciman, *Relative Deprivation and Social Justice: A Study of Attitudes to Social Inequality in Twentieth-Century England* (Berkeley and Los Angeles: University of California Press, 1966).

[2] Most subsidies, in the nature of the case, flow to groups and enterprises that already have preempted a place in the economy. During the New Deal era, the programs of the Agricultural Adjustment Administration allocated the permitted acreage for growing certain crops to individual farmers on the basis of their acreage in an earlier "base period." The result, of course, was to favor the larger, commercial farms.

[3] Categorical patronage and rewards for achievement often are combined. An especially clear and important example is that of various types of special benefits for veterans of military service.

should be allowed to starve") to complex conceptions of need based on age, sex, occupational requirements, or even personality characteristics.

In any society, unless a system of stratification is simply accepted in all of its historical concreteness, the existence of extreme privation and humiliation alongside vast opulence and enforced deference raises problems of justification. It is very doubtful, in fact, whether really extreme inequalities are ever enthusiastically endorsed by those who receive least. And if inequalities are to be accepted—no matter how reluctantly—as morally just and not merely inevitable, an ethical code that will answer to the problem is likely to be quite demanding in its requirements upon those whose portion of the scarce values is largest.[4]

Thus, we must return to the point suggested at the very beginning of this chapter: social stratification, so far as it is widely accepted, is part of the system of common values without which a society becomes a mere aggregate instead of a real system. No matter how unequal the distribution of social rights, no matter how differentiated the modes of living of various classes or status groupings, the *system* of stratification can be maintained on a largely voluntary basis so long as there is no widespread feeling that it violates grossly the *scale* of stratification (the morally justified criteria) and so long as there is a certain minimal belief in the legitimacy, or social validity, of the scale itself. Thus, there are two crucial questions to be asked in accounting for the stability or instability of any stratification order: (1) What consensus exists concerning a scale of stratification; is there substantial agreement *at all levels of the actual system* upon the criteria of position that should be acknowledged, accepted, and applied? (2) How closely does the actual stratification order follow the institutional standards, insofar as the latter exist? To ask these questions is to focus our attention upon the role of values and beliefs in supporting and perpetuating the institutional system or in corroding its ultimate basis. In contemporary America, a large body of systematic beliefs and values serves to explain and justify both the going *system* and the nominally dominant *scale*. The research evidence prerequisite to an adequate appraisal of possibly important changes in this "folk ideology"[5] does not yet exist.[6] But available studies seem sufficient to establish the presence of a pervasive, meaningfully interconnected set of doctrines that explain and justify the existing order. Into this category seem to fall (to take only a limited sample of items) belief in equality of opportunity and the correlated beliefs that tend to equate ability and reward, the popular prestige of economic success, and the whole complex that we call "individual responsibility." The total relevant belief-value system in its most fully developed form emerged out of the middle-class society of nineteenth-century America. In our culture, no institution can

---

[4] Compare this criterion, as suggested by Runciman (*op. cit.*, p. 273): ". . . the test of inequalities is whether they can be justified to the losers; and for the winners to be able to do this, they must be prepared, in principle, to change places."

[5] See Robert S. Lynd and Helen M. Lynd, *Middletown in Transition*, esp. pp. 408 ff.

[6] But the necessary work is under way; see Harold M. Hodges, *op. cit.*; Ephraim H. Mizruchi, *Success and Opportunity* (New York: Free Press, 1964).

long outlive *some* cultural rationale that can make its consequences seem just, or at the very least, inevitable. If, as seems to be the case, this "creed" has lost some of its power to monopolize attention and to motivate optimistic striving, it still commands the allegiance of enough middle- and upper-income people to constitute a stout support of the system. At the same time, another very different orientation appears to be replacing in appreciable measure the old work-virtue-reward complex among the wage-earner population. One central component—which, except quantitatively, is perhaps not so new as it appears—is an emphasis upon fortuitous success: the lucky break, the unexpected opportunity, the inspired idea, the winning number. The great cultural significance of a belief in luck as the avenue of success is that it decisively sunders reward from achievement and personal excellence. Chance is blind to moral worth and indifferent to striving; and if success and failure are thought to depend upon essentially accidental factors, neither the individual nor the social system itself can be perceived as the source of deprivation and malaise.

The questions suggested by these latter observations reach beyond the available data and raise basic issues of social policy. It will be enough if this exploration has suggested some of the major factors in the complex and changing sets of social processes we call stratification in the United States.

### SUGGESTED READINGS

BALTZELL, E. DIGBY. *Philadelphia Gentleman: The Making of a National Upper Class.* New York: Free Press, 1958. Exemplary monographic study. Shows how "class" emerges from "stratum." Careful and incisive use of historical materials.

BLAU, PETER M., and OTIS DUDLEY DUNCAN. *The American Occupational Structure.* New York: Wiley, 1967. Comprehensive and sophisticated analysis of national data. Unique. Indispensable for students who want to see how evidence and analysis differ from assumption and opinion.

BENDIX, REINHARD, and SEYMOUR MARTIN LIPSET (eds.). *Class, Status, and Power: Social Stratification in Comparative Perspective,* 2nd ed. New York: Free Press, 1966. Revised edition of a standard reader. Probably the best single reference for supplementary readings on the subject.

HODGES, HAROLD M. *Social Stratification: Class in America.* Cambridge, Mass.: Schenkman, 1964. Touches upon nearly every aspect of stratification. Especially good in description of the life styles of different strata and of subdivisions within them.

KELLER, SUZANNE. *Beyond the Ruling Class: Strategic Elites in Modern Society.* New York: Random House, 1963. Skillfully argues the thesis implied by the title. Rejects the model of a central elite or ruling class. Although the case may be pressed somewhat hard, the data and discussion are essential counterweights to overly simple interpretations of power and prestige.

KOLKO, GABRIEL. *Wealth and Power in America: An Analysis of Social Class and Income Distribution,* rev. ed. New York: Praeger, 1964. Severely critical of "optimistic" interpretations of data on wealth and income. Rejects claims of movement toward equalization.

LENSKI, GERHARD E. *Power and Privilege: A Theory of Social Stratification.* New York: McGraw-Hill, 1966. An interpretation of wide scope, stressing the part attributable to the exercise of power in the development of other types of inequalities.

MILLER, HERMAN P. *Rich Man, Poor Man.* New York: Crowell, 1964. Interestingly written popular presentation by an expert analyst of census data. Should be read in conjunction with Kolko's more radical critique.

PORTER, JOHN. *The Vertical Mosaic: An Analysis of Social Class and Power in Canada.* Toronto: University of Toronto, 1965. Highly useful for comparative study of our good neighbor to the North. This brilliant work shows how "ethnic" and "class" systems are interwoven in the social formations of national elites.

REISS, ALBERT J., JR., *et al. Occupations and Social Status.* New York: Free Press, 1962. "Hard" data and systematic analysis, giving well-grounded findings.

SVALASTOGA, KAARE. *Social Differentiation.* New York: David McKay, 1965. Tightly organized presentation of how stratification relates to differentiation. Clarifies several major areas of long and confused debate.

TUMIN, MELVIN M. *Social Stratification.* Englewood Cliffs, N.J.: Prentice-Hall, 1967. Brief, clear exposition of the fundamental issues and well-established generalizations. Incisive social commentary, closely related to research findings.

# American Economic Institutions

## THE NATURE OF ECONOMIC INSTITUTIONS

A merican economic institutions often have seemed the most conspicuous feature of the social structure; America is said to be above all a business civilization, impressive in its productivity, sometimes appalling in the violence of its economic fluctuations. The United States is a land of mass production; the assembly line is its symbol to the world. In an age of economic collectivism, it is widely regarded as the last major stronghold of "liberal capitalism."

The economic system has acquired such seeming independence from other areas of life that it often gives the appearance—partly illusory—of being self-generating and self-perpetuating. Economic activity has become so sharply differentiated from the containing social structure that it is deceptively easy to think of "purely economic" activity and to identify economic institutions with the common sense category "making a living." Yet from the accumulation of historical and anthropological knowledge about economic systems in widely different cultures we know that a sharp separation of "economy" from "society" is the exception rather than the rule. In nonliterate societies, production is typically for *use* rather than *sale*; and it is difficult to identify economic activity as something apart from family life, religion, magic, politics, ceremonial activities, and social relations generally; economic activity is embedded in and controlled by the society, even in a complex communal society such as existed in medieval Europe. In American society, on the other hand, the price-market system for a long time seemed to have been sundered from its social matrix, and, as Karl Polanyi expressed it, to have become an "autonomous zone" that tends to create "the delusion of economic determinism as a general law for all human society."[1]

What then do we mean by "economic"? What is an "economic institution"?

In all societies, men have wants that must be satisfied if life is to continue; and they have further wants, the satisfaction of which is an integral part of a meaningful way of life. In all societies, most able-bodied adults spent a large proportion of their time in making a living. Economic norms and values bulk large in any total social system. The facts of

---

[1] Karl Polanyi, "Our Obsolete Market Mentality," *Commentary*, 3, 2 (February 1947), 109–117; reprinted in Logan Wilson and William L. Kolb, *Sociological Analysis* (New York: Harcourt, Brace & World, 1949), pp. 557–567.

"need" and "preference" are intrinsic to man in society. Men "want" or "need"[2] some things more than others, but many of the things they want are not available in unlimited amount. Hence, scales of preference arise— value priorities and value hierarchies. This problem of choice-in-scarcity is the heart of the matter. *Some* values, such as those of religious devotion, group pride, community recreation, are inherently nondistributive; they are participated in rather than divided up. One person's enjoyment does not diminish another's participation in the same value complex—indeed, the value may *require* that others share it. But other values are distributive: they are divisible, and what one person appropriates diminishes what otherwise would be available to others.

Thus, human wants cannot all be satisfied. "Goods" are scarce. Even in a society of unlimited abundance of material goods, *time* would still be limited: so much time expended in securing one utility means that much less available to be spent in alternate ways. Every satisfaction of a want "costs something." The cost of a given resource in the production of a given utility is the sacrifice of its potential productivity in other possible applications. The basic economic problem, formally considered, is thus the allocation of scarce means to alternative ends.[3] Since no society has unlimited resources there will always be this central problem whether the economy is capitalistic, socialistic, communistic, or something else.

Economics as an analytic science deals systematically with the principles of rational allocation of scarce means for maximizing the satisfaction of wants, under various sets of formal assumptions about the social order. There are economic principles that apply to the isolated human individual apart from society ("Crusoe economics"); but it is the analysis of economic activity of functioning societies that is of use to the sociologist.[4] The usual types of formal economic analysis—whether classical, neoclassical, or Keynesian—presuppose the existence of a going social system that supplies the framework for economic activity. Increasingly, however, the modern emphasis upon "economics of development" and upon comparative studies of different regional, national, and international economic systems has

[2] The frequent use of quotation marks here is necessary: they are warning signals that all these words are full of ambiguities. In the socialized human being, "needs" are typically very far from being simple biological cravings.

[3] "An economic element enters in only insofar as the comparative scarcity of alternative means to a given end becomes relevant to the choice between them. This is always a consideration in addition to the technological, not in place of it. It means that the costs of use of a given means for a given end are considered. This, in turn, means that their comparative urgency for this and alternative ends becomes involved. Thus, the fundamental economic facts are scarcity, adaptation of means to alternative ends and cost." Talcott Parsons, *The Structure of Social Action* (New York: Free Press, 1949), p. 655.

[4] For a compact demonstration of such analysis, see Neil J. Smelser, *The Sociology of Economic Life* (Englewood Cliffs, N.J.: Prentice-Hall, 1963). Smelser defines economic sociology as "the application of the general frame of reference, variables, and explanatory models of sociology to that complex of activities concerned with the production, distribution, exchange, and consumption of scarce goods and services." (p. 32). For a well-known treatment by an economist see Paul A. Samuelson, *Economics: An Introductory Analysis*, 6th ed. (New York: McGraw-Hill, 1964).

brought variations in the cultural and social contexts into the center of thinking about economic change.

The great tradition of economic thought, beginning with Adam Smith and David Ricardo, postulated an abstract economic system in which the rational activity of men in the market generated a mechanism that could be visualized as completely self-contained and self-adjusting. This theory rested upon stringent, but often implicit and unrecognized, assumptions. It was forced to suppose that men are economically rational—that they try to put resources to the most productive use (that is, to the most profitable use) under changing costs and prices. A system of free competition—the "perfect system of natural liberty"—presupposes a price-market system in which each producing, selling, and buying unit is so small that in acting alone it cannot have an appreciable effect upon the market and in which the number of these units is indefinitely large. If the units of the system are to have independence, decisions of any one unit must be without effect upon the decisions occurring in other units. Under perfect competition, consumers have free choice of goods; and no producer controls more than a minute fraction of the output. Production responds to open-market demand rather than to direct order, and the interaction of an indefinite plurality of individuals each seeking to sell as dearly and buy as cheaply as possible has as its unintended by-product the maximization of utility of the whole aggregate. Assuming perfect mobility of the factors of production—capital, labor, managerial capacities, and so on—resources will shift out of any line of production less profitable than alternative uses of resources. Through the sensitive mechanism of prices competitively determined in the open market, every change in supply and demand is immediately transformed into decisions that continually "correct" the allocation of resources.

If this ideal system is to work, men must have knowledge adequate for economically rational action, and freedom and incentive to carry the action out. Even more important, the role of force and fraud in the allocation of goods must be minimal. There must be substantial equality of bargaining power, since any very great measure of inequality invites coercion. One may *trade*, or one may *take*; much of human history has been a story of the appropriation and use of goods through force rather than exchange—a long story of plunder, theft, piracy, extortion, tribute, brigandage, and the varied exactions of military conquest and rule. An orderly system of peaceable economic exchange can never safely be taken for granted as a universal human desire. On the contrary, economic activity by its very nature generates strong centrifugal tendencies toward breaking through social regulation, for economic relations always involve a measure of social distance and easily lead to acts of violence. When there is a well-established system of social norms regulating economic activity, these tendencies are inhibited, suppressed, or channelized within the framework of the larger value system of the society. But even in the most firmly established economic systems conflict easily emerges from economic dealings.[5] In the trivial case, the

5 Cf. Florian Znaniecki, *Social Actions* (New York: Holt, Rinehart & Winston, 1936), p. 593: "For trading arrangements to be safe, it is not enough for them to be objectively

outraged customer complains to or attacks the dealer who has "overcharged" or "cheated" him; in the wider arena, employers and employees resort to force and fraud, or nations fight rather than compete in the market. There is no guarantee in the nature of economic activity itself that it will fit into a larger system of values or of orderly social relations. Hence, institutional or normative regulation is just as "normal" and inevitable as in any other sectors of conduct.

The whole economic order, looked at sociologically, is a network of norms and expectancies—a web of "promises" as to the course that economic action will take or is supposed to take. Thus, in the United States, retail trade is typically carried on under a one-price system: the seller offers an item at a standard price, and the customer either buys or does not buy at that one price. There is little of the bargaining and haggling so characteristic of the market historically; the one-price system is a notable step toward impersonality in trade and stabilizes definite expectancies of behavior.[6] How strongly this whole pattern is invested with a socially normative quality may be seen in the moral indignation of the naïve American tourist in dealings with Italian taxicab drivers, Eastern traders, or their counterparts in his own culture. Even ordinary economic transactions continually deal with promises for the future. Currency consists of promises and is accepted in exchange as a matter of faith in its future redeemability in goods and services. When belief in redeemability disappears, as in periods of severe inflation or of serious social disorganization, the currency may become mere paper. Stocks and bonds are promises, as are checks, insurance policies, deeds, bills of sale, contracts. As Durkheim so cogently showed over fifty years ago, there is a noncontractual element in contract; the dependability of economic promises, the fulfillment of contracts, cannot be explained adequately on the basis of the immediate interests of the contracting parties.[7] A system of free contract could hardly function if every contract had to be enforced by private sanctions whenever the immediate interests of the contracting parties did not completely coincide.

The effect of social norms upon economic activity is further illustrated by the fact that in our free society no one is free to sell himself into slavery.[8] Economic pressures have often led to slavery, peonage, indenture systems, imprisonment for debt, and the like. There is certainly no immediate *economic* reason why the individual who has no values to offer in exchange except his own person should not sell himself as a slave.[9] Insofar as our

---

profitable to the parties: they must be subjected to specific positive norms which isolate them from extraneous sources of conflict, and prevent all conflicts that occur in the very process of bargaining from spreading beyond the trading situation." Reprinted by permission of Holt, Rinehart & Winston, Inc.

[6] The importance of the one-price system for our entire economy has been well stated in the report of the National Resources Committee, *The Structure of the American Economy*, Part I (Washington, D.C.: Government Printing Office, 1939), p. 98.

[7] Stewart Macaulay, "Non-contractual Relations in Business: A Preliminary Study," *American Sociological Review*, 28, 1 (February, 1963), 55–67.

[8] This way of putting the situation originally was suggested by lectures of Talcott Parsons at Harvard University.

[9] Nor are there immediate technical or economic reasons why opium should not be dis-

culture values personal freedom, it must erect institutional barriers that limit the encroachment of economic pressures. For instance, although the enforceability of private contracts is essential to the American economic system, contractual obligations are regularly set aside in bankruptcy proceedings. The laws and customs of bankruptcy provide for "wiping the slate clean," for the discharge of indebtedness through distribution of assets, even though the bankrupt individual or firm is able to meet far less than the full amount of indebtedness owed. Without this "abrogation of contract" the businessman could easily fall into life-long personal servitude to his creditors.

There is, then, no such thing as the "pure play of economic forces." Freedom of contract has basic institutional limitations. Similarly, freedom of consumer choice is confined to a culturally approved or tolerated range. "The determination of consumption is under the control of moral considerations, and it is consumption in turn which determines production and distribution; we would neither produce nor distribute what we did not wish to consume."[1]

The technically efficient means of securing goods through force and fraud are subject to continual normative regulation. And, indeed, the very character of men's so-called economic interests is not a constant feature of an invariant human nature but takes distinctive forms in different cultural settings. Not even economic rationality can be taken for granted as a fixed characteristic; rather, the kind and extent of economic rationality are dependent upon very complex conditions of the total social structure. For instance, American patterns of "business careers" would be impossible under such conditions of internal warfare and political instability as have prevailed in large portions of Asia during the twentieth century.

A market-price economy is a *cultural* fact. Goods might be distributed on the basis of power rather than exchange. Production might be carried on with forced labor or with labor bound to a particular social authority, or with the "contributed" effort of the family or other communal group. Not only compulsion but every form of traditionalized personal dependence and social immobility is a barrier to the operation of a true market economy.[2] As Weber has correctly insisted, economic activity is the "profane" activity par excellence and is universally felt to be inappropriate in primary "sacred" social relations. The commercialization of property and of labor, which was essential to the development of modern capitalism is, historically speaking, a recent and extreme development.

---

pensed over the soda fountains of American drugstores or hand grenades freely sold at the "Five and Ten." On purely economic grounds, any taste whatsoever may become the basis of production and trade. "Production," in the strictly economic sense, consists of supplying any good or service for which people will pay. And people often will pay for goods and services that threaten social order, safety, health and other valued conditions.

[1] James K. Feibleman, *The Institutions of Society* (London: Allen & Unwin, Ltd., 1956), p. 205.

[2] Znaniecki has analyzed some of the basic social reasons for the fact that "trading is known to be slow in appearing within collectivities whose participants are used to primary patterns of accommodation." *Op. cit.*, p. 589.

## TYPES OF SOCIAL MECHANISMS CONTROLLING ECONOMIC ACTIVITY

In some of the most abstract models of a laissez-faire economy, economic activity is considered to be primarily self-regulating—that is, noneconomic factors are considered formally irrelevant to the determination of the course of economic action. It is assumed that wants can be taken as constant or at least that economic activity does not itself change the character of wants. That the individual will pursue self-interest is taken as axiomatic. The role of social control is seen almost entirely as the limited intervention of the state to enforce contracts and to exercise police controls over force, fraud, and gross social disorder. In the main, any other ways in which social controls and noneconomic values might effect strictly economic behavior are not systematically taken into account and hence, by implication, are seen as irrelevant or of negligible importance.

Indeed, it is not easy to keep always clearly in view the fact that *every* aspect of economic activity is culturally defined and is both affected by and effects social interactions. This is true of production, saving, investment, entrepreneurship, management, labor, distribution, and consumption. Each of the main factors of production, conventionally labeled as land, capital, labor, and entrepreneurship, is subject to great variations in cultural definition and social regulation. For example, in the generic economic sense, what is "land?" It is a set of relatively fixed productive resources including physical land, other given physical resources, human knowledge and ability, and relatively stable values and generalized motivations relating to work, saving, and investment. Capital is likewise culturally defined, as resources readily available for production in varying quantities, depending greatly upon prospective rewards.[3] Labor, similarly, is the specific mobilizable effort of persons in relation to particular productive tasks; and entrepreneurship is the managerial and innovative parallel.

So long as economic analysis is clearly seen as a *partial* analysis of economic action and so long as its analytic assumptions are recognized as simplifying abstractions, it can be utilized as a profitable source of sociological knowledge. For example, one can make predictions as to what action would follow in particular situations *if* men were to follow the dictates of rational economic interest, *if* resources were perfectly mobile, *if* competition were completely free, and so on. Armed with these predictions, one can then compare them with the actual course of action, and the agreement or lack of agreement of the two will offer clues as to other important factors affecting behavior.[4] In many stock market transactions, for instance, or in the disappearance of an overvalued money according to Gresham's Law, or in the substitutability of competing commodities, actual behavior may

---

[3] However, there is in human social life an "inherent scarcity" that ultimately derives from our mortality and our limited capacities in relations to the indefinite expansiveness of our wants and aspirations.

[4] Cf. Max Weber, *The Theory of Social and Economic Organization*, A. M Henderson and Talcott Parsons (trans.) (New York: Oxford University Press, 1947), pp. 107 ff.

correspond rather closely to the predictions of the abstract economic analysis. But there will often be wide divergences between economic model and actual behavior; and it is precisely such divergences that frequently offer us fruitful insights.

Although all these qualifications are perfectly plain to the sophisticated student of economics, many of what are for economic science *methodological devices* (such as the useful analytic fiction of perfect mobility, or economic rationality) can become actual working assumptions of the larger culture. As implicit or explicit assumptions they can then make a real difference in the very character of the operating economic system. Such assumptions frequently become sufficiently explicit, systematic, repetitive, and widespread to constitute a large part of the explanatory and "justifying" creeds or ideologies of the system. It is roughly correct to say that the ideology of the early twentieth-century American business civilization included as basic tenets: belief that the greatest economic good of the society would be achieved through the unrestrained play of individual self-interest, faith in the sanctity of "private property;" belief in freedom of contract; the assumption that that economic order is best in which there is a minimum of state regulation; belief in the ability of a competitive market to maintain itself and to allocate the society's resources in the optimum manner. In their most clearly and fully developed forms, these conceptions, together with others congruent with them, were resolved into the picture of an automatically self-adjusting economy, composed of rational economic atoms, continually maximizing economic welfare through free competition. Only two types of mechanisms controlling economic activity were fully explicit: (1) the changing prices established in the open market, and (2) the limited "policing" functions of the political order.

Actually, the social controls of the economy are numerous and often far from self-evident.[5] First, the *market mechanism* itself is a control. Given a money economy and an organized market structure, the interdependent actions of numerous individuals and groups as they buy and sell change and readjust specific prices continually. And since every price is interdependent with other prices and is at the same time a cost to someone, the market mechanism constitutes in fact a vastly ramified impersonal system of controls over economic behavior. When the numbers of participating individuals and groups are large and when they are widely dispersed, this control is in the nature of an invisible "field structure:"[6] entirely impersonal forces seem to shape the ebb and flow of economic fluctuations; and it is difficult to identify, or assign responsibility to, any tangible agent or focus. Indeed, the market is highly sensitive as an allocative mechanism where it can operate freely within an accepted system of rules in the making of decisions concerning private goods. However, it is not capable of generating,

[5] A useful analysis of economic processes in their social context is given by Alfred Kuhn, *The Study of Society: A Unified Approach* (Homewood, Ill.: Richard D. Irwin and Dorsey Press, 1963), esp. Chaps. 31–39.

[6] This convenient term has been used by Karl Mannheim. See his *Man and Society in an Age of Reconstruction* (New York: Harcourt, Brace & World, 1940).

by itself, determinate decisions about public goods, or the relative quantities of private and public goods, or its own rules.[7]

It is through the institutional arrangements of the "free market" that the external control of production is effected in laissez-faire economy. There is an established, impersonal system of property and of exchange relations, not enforced *as a whole* by any one specific social authority, in terms of which decisions regarding economic production and exchange must take place. Yet, if the market mechanism is to be really free, there must be rules limiting compulsion, fraud, and collusion; prices must be determined by a "willing buyer and a willing seller." Competition without rules is inconceivable; nevertheless, the controls of the market system, once institutionalized, are relatively nonlocalized, impersonal, and nonspecific. The market-price mechanism is a "constraint" that may require drastic personal discipline and great modifications of individual behavior, yet these controls have long been regarded either as inevitable ("natural," an unchanging condition to which adjustment must be made), or as moral imperatives, or as both. So long and insofar as the undesired consequences of the system were viewed as outside the sphere of purposive social control, the constraints tended to be accepted with relatively little protest.

The "market" does not constitute an autonomous, inevitable, self-caused system, but is in its turn dependent on quite specific institutional structures. Thus, an enormous number of *specific cultural norms* that have binding and directing influence upon economic action constitute a second type of control. These norms are varied in object, content, and mode of influence or enforcement; they include statutory laws, common law, court decisions and interpretations, governmental regulations and policies, business codes, union rules, diffuse "customs," "trade practices," and many other varieties of normative standards that taken together make up a regulative framework without which a complex economic system is simply unthinkable.[8] The third type of control is the directive influence of *common cultural goals*, which may be collective aims such as military victory, or distributive goals such as profit making. At one time the economy may concentrate upon refrigerators and fashionable clothing; then, within a few months, the national resources are turned toward production of tanks and guns. Furthermore, the very constitution of economic "interests" and economic wants varies greatly not only from one culture to another but also in important ways from one historical period to another within the same culture. The productive surplus remaining after subsistence needs have been met may be invested in tools and factories—but it may be, and has been, used to construct magnificent cathedrals or used up in conspicuous

---

[7] Kuhn, *op. cit.*, p. 610.

[8] For some purposes, it would be important to make precise distinctions among a number of these specific types of norms. At this point, however, it is sufficient to establish only the broadest outlines of institutional patterning. The discussion of the above paragraph is concerned with "the canalizing action of laws, rules, and customs whereby the community shapes and molds and canalizes the actions of many separate individuals into co-ordinated form without the exercise of direct administrative control." National Resources Committee, *op. cit.*, p. 97.

consumption as part of a culturally stylized game of prestige. The ends for which wealth is sought vary greatly among known cultures: wealth may be a symbol of achievement, a means to power, a validation of social virtue; or it may be avoided on magical or religious grounds. Evidently, a significant part of the "controls" of economic action in every society lies in the dominant goals and interests; and consumer wants, saving and investment patterns, work incentives, and the whole pattern of allocation of resources are, in part, cultural variables, not deducible from intrinsic economic considerations alone.

When working at its highest effectiveness, the open market system is a remarkable social mechanism through which millions of separate decisions are translated into a coordinated flow of goods and services. Even under the ideal conditions of the "perfect market," however, the mechanism could not adequately reflect all crucial needs and preferences. It is not generally effective in dealing with negative wants—in preventing undesired conditions from arising. It is ill suited for long-time considerations of resource allocation and conservation; the unrestrained market often results in exhaustion of natural resources—the gutting of forests, soil, and oil and mineral deposits. Perhaps most important, the market does not automatically produce those highly important goods and services that are indivisible or are used in common (highways, national defense), or for which there is no individual price (local government services, public health facilities).

From a broader standpoint of ethical evaluation, the market system is open to the criticism that the allocations it establishes often do not meet various standards of justice. The market is perfectly capable of providing a profusion of mink coats while millions do not have adequate food or medical care. As Robert Heilbronner puts it: "The market is an assiduous servant of the wealthy consumer, but an indifferent servant of the poor one."[9]

A fourth type of controlling mechanism consists of *administrative* or *organizational coordination*, enforced by a definite and identifiable social organization, whether it be a factory, a corporation, a trade association, a labor union, a government bureau, or any other organized grouping. The dramatic expansion of controls of this kind during the past half-century is one of the outstanding social trends of the present era. In contrast to the constraints of the market, administrative controls tend to be localized, specific, and susceptible to interpretation in terms of personal or group "responsibility." It is one thing to see prosperity or economic disaster as the result of "the market" or "the business cycle;" quite another to see it as the responsibility of the AFL-CIO, U.S. Steel, the Department of Commerce, or "that man in the White House." The nature of these controls can be made to stand out in sharp relief if one contrasts the organization of agri-

[9] Robert L. Heilbronner, *The Making of Economic Society* (Englewood Cliffs, N.J.: Prentice-Hall, 1962), p. 229.

cultural production with that of large-scale industry in the period immediately prior to the advent of the New Deal in 1933. There were some 6 million essentially independent farm units reacting to the changing structure of prices and costs—typically small family enterprises, operating without any important *organizational* integration. With only minor exceptions, such as the chain farming carried on by certain commercial organizations, there were no administrative controls extending from one center to a number of producing units. Whereas much of large-scale industry in this period could be described as large systems of centralized control with relative "anarchy" between systems, agriculture presented a picture of many very much smaller control systems unconnected with one another save by diffuse cultural structures, including both the family system and the mechanism of the free market. Volume of production, time and place of production and sale, type and quality of commodity, allocation of productive resources—under the "liberal" system all were decided upon by large numbers of small producers acting independently. In modern, large-scale industry, on the other hand, a single corporate organization will control a large number of subsidiary units through an elaborate administrative network. Although the corporation as a whole is subject to the final test of profit and loss in the market, the allocation of resources within the organization itself is not necessarily dictated by "free market" principles. Control of behavior, and thus of economic decisions, within the large industrial enterprise or grouping of enterprises is *social* in nature: it is effected through established patterns of authority in an elaborate quasi-bureaucratic hierarchy, not through the impersonal pressures of the market. Furthermore, elaborate systems of *inter*corporate coordination have grown up, in the form of interlocking participation, common sources of financing, trade associations, "interest groupings," cartels, and so forth. Thus, there is a formal organization of, and concentration of economic control in, large-scale industry that contrasts sharply with the family-farm system of agriculture and perhaps even more sharply with the quasi-mythical portrait of an economy of individualistic competitive production.

Clarification concerning the main types of economic systems now present in industrialized societies may be provided by making broad distinctions (1) between private goods (which can be provided for and utilized by separate individuals) and public goods (which cannot be "divided up" among separate individuals) and (2) between production by private business and production by public agencies. Examples of private goods are: an automobile, a radio, a dinner, a house, a haircut, a job promotion. Examples of public goods are: national defense, sound currency, reduced air pollution, interstate highways. Combining the two classifications produces this scheme:[1]

[1] Adapted from Kuhn, *op. cit.*, pp. 559–560.

|  |  | Production carried out by: | |
|---|---|---|---|
|  |  | PUBLIC AGENCY | PRIVATE AGENCY |
|  | PUBLIC | Government | "Contract" or "delegated" production; quasi-public business; cooperatives.* |
| *Type of goods produced* |  |  |  |
|  | PRIVATE | "Socialism" | "Capitalism" |

\* We have no commonly used term for this type of production. Examples are provided by joint government-private corporations; military contracts; some aspects of communications (A.T.&T.).

If we classify utility-producing social units roughly into "public" and "private," we can then cross classify them by the kind of rights each may hold over "private" economic activity, such as rights to income *versus* rights to control the decisions made within the property-using enterprise. The result is as follows:

|  |  | *Type of rights held over "private" property* | |
|---|---|---|---|
|  |  | TO RECEIVE INCOME | TO CONTROL DECISIONS |
|  | "PRIVATE" | "Beneficent ownership" | Entrepreneurship; management |
| *Type of social unit* |  |  |  |
|  | "PUBLIC" | Taxation | Regulation |

The degree of what we have called "administrative" (or organizational) control is only *one* sign that the present American economy differs from that of "capitalistic" legend. Such scholars as Max Weber, Werner Sombart, Thorstein Veblen, John R. Commons, Goetz Briefs, and Emile Durkheim have repeatedly shown that the high development of certain capitalistic features in modern Western societies is a unique historical phenomenon resulting from an unusual combination of technical, political, and social conditions. Following Weber it can be said that a fully rationalized, capitalistic, free-market economy requires at least the following:[2]

1. Relatively complete separation of the *economic* uses of goods, services, human beings, and other means of production from all their other uses. For example, ownership of land as a transferable, alienable commodity is altogether different from feudal "ownership," which is inseparable from political authority (juridical, military, and so on). A house as a market good is separated from the social values and obligations attached to a "family homestead." Above all, the treatment of labor as a commodity necessitates separating economic considerations from traditional social obligations and ethical sentiments.

[2] For a more complete discussion see Parsons' introduction to *Theory of Social and Economic Organization*, esp. pp. 43–51.

2. Maximum concentration of rights over the nonhuman means of production in the hands of "owners."
3. The existence of formally free labor, which has no fixed right to a particular job. Workers are not bound by obligations of dependence to particular employers; conversely employers do not have inalienable duties to particular workers. Ideally, the workers cannot gain a livelihood from fixed property, for it would tend both to reduce mobility and to weaken the control of the employer.
4. Freedom of contract—the absence of a high degree of regulation of consumption, production, and prices. Within very wide institutional limits, the market mechanism is free to operate with a minimum of noneconomic "interferences."
5. A reasonably stable, or at least *predictable*, political order, including a calculable legal system and governmental administration. Authority for the enforcement of contracts is indispensable. The ideal political order is one that operates according to fixed, explicit rules, with a minimum of arbitrary authority, unpredictable change, and retroactive regulation.
6. A "formally rational" monetary system.
7. Some relatively high degree of control over the technical bases of production. Thus, it is a great advantage of the factory over the farm that it is not so subject to the vagaries of weather and other natural conditions. Similarly, a disciplined—that is, calculable—labor force is necessary for the maximum rationality of a capitalistic market economy.

Other conditions could be listed as significant bases for the type of economy under consideration—for instance, the separation of "household" from "business"—but those already mentioned are sufficient to underscore: *first*, the complexity of the institutional elements involved in economic activity; *second*, the interdependence of "economic" institutions with other parts of the social order; *third*, the frequently unrecognized existence of multiple control systems that are inevitable under *any* economic system.

## MAJOR STRUCTURAL CHARACTERISTICS OF THE AMERICAN ECONOMY

What are the *main* features of the institutional framework that surrounds economic activity in the United States? To answer this question we shall have to cut through the infinite detail of concrete facts to single out *dominant* features: for example, we shall devote little attention to agriculture and very small businesses, not because these are not important but because they are structurally less crucial than large industrial and financial organizations. Secondly, we shall have to distinguish between the cultural "theory" or ideology of the institutional system and the realistically effective goals and regulations.

In analyzing the American economy, it is vital to maintain an adequate sense of both continuity and change. To this end, we shall make frequent references to the history of various economic institutions. The period of the 1930's furnishes a particularly useful base line for many comparisons.

Although the American economic system has been greatly altered from the raw heyday of unrestrained corporate industrial concentration and expansion from, say 1890 to 1914, it is still anchored fundamentally to the institutions of the market and of profit-making property. Much talk of "social revolution" in connection with the New Deal and subsequent changes in governmental regulation ignores the fact that none of the politicoeconomic changes since 1932 has destroyed inequalities in income and wealth, or concentration of economic power, or the overwhelming emphasis upon profit making as the touchstone of the entire system. Business dominance of the society has become more mild mannered, less blatant, more indirect, more complex, and more skillful. But it has not been abolished or even seriously diminished with respect to the central institutions and the practical realities of power (the ability to control).

The central importance of different institutional arrangements for economic decision making renders the location of such power and authority one of the main marks for distinguishing types of economic orders.[3] A major shift in the location of decision-making powers means a change in the character of the system. The fact that in the United States the great majority of decisions concerning investment and production, as well as consumption, are made by individuals and officers of nongovernmental corporations marks the American economy as basically capitalistic. The growth of giant corporations has *centralized* the making of economic decisions, but it has not *socialized* it.[4]

### Summary of Characteristics

In this context, the sociologically significant features of the economic system can be summarized as follows:

1. It is an economy of mass production, operating under a factory system utilizing a highly developed technology. As one striking example, the aggregate horsepower per 100 production workers in manufacturing rose from 652 in 1939 to the staggering figure of 1,249 by 1962.
2. Industrial production is characterized by a minute specialization and division of labor.[5]
3. Industrial processes, tasks, and products are highly standardized.
4. That portentous social invention, the corporation, is the dominant form of organization of business enterprise.
5. Corporate ownership is widely *diffused*; production and control are highly *concentrated*. Ownership and management of corporations have become separated, with far-reaching consequences.

[3] Cf. William N. Loucks, *Comparative Economic Systems*, 7th ed. (New York: Harper & Row, 1965), p. 7.

[4] See, e.g., Edward S. Mason (ed.), *The Corporation in Modern Society* (Cambridge, Mass.: Harvard University Press, 1960).

[5] It is worth noting that the 1940 United States Census of Manufactures found it necessary to recognize 446 separate *industry* classifications, consolidated into 20 broad industrial groupings. As of the mid-1960's, there were 21,741 occupations, known under some 36,000 occupational titles. See United States Department of Labor, *Dictionary of Occupational Titles*, 3rd. ed. (Washington, D.C.: Government Printing Office, 1965).

6. There are very important systems of intercorporate coordination and control.
7. Large-scale units and administrative coordination lead to quasi-monopoly, "imperfect competition," and price rigidities.
8. Large scale labor unions play an important role, but unionization is stable or declining in many fields of employment.
9. Because of specialization of production, a highly developed monetary and credit system, and other factors, the various segments of the economy are closely interdependent; and changes in any one major portion of the system have complex repercussions elsewhere.
10. Central governments, both federal and state, intervene in economic activity on a wide scale through direct regulation and facilitation and through the indirect consequences of their other operations.
11. "Property rights" are in a state of rapid change; and the facts are radically different from those envisaged in popular ideologies and in certain important legal fictions.
12. The entire economy is subject to incessant development and innovation,[6] through factors ranging from the impact of inventions to the influence of international politics and war.
13. Governmental expenditures constitute a highly important sector of the economy.
14. There is widespread and increasing development of "social security"— over 50 million workers are potentially eligible for unemployment compensation, over 90 million have claims to federal old age insurance.

Such an economy is very different from nineteenth-century laissez-faire conceptions of the American system and cannot be described adequately by summary labels, such as "capitalism" or "corporacy." We must make a careful examination of the facts bearing on such outstanding characteristics as have just been outlined.

### The Dominance of the Corporation

Although sole proprietorships and partnerships are still numerous and vital in the economy—numbering over 10 million in 1964 and constituting nearly 90 percent of all firms—by far the most important form of business organization is the corporation. Items in point: (1) corporations account for 80 percent of *all business receipts;*[7] (2) of the *total national income* of $559 billion in 1965, 56 percent originated in corporate businesses—in contrast, for example, to the 12 percent constituted by general government;[8] (3) in 1966 the *total assets* of all nonfinancial corporations were estimated at $442 billion; in the preceding year, the assets of the 500 largest industrial corporations were $252 billion, well over half of the total.[9]

[6] The 1965 *Dictionary of Occupational Titles* lists 6,432 new jobs not described in the 1949 edition—although the total number of occupations actually was somewhat lower.
[7] United States Bureau of the Census, *Statistical Abstract of the United States: 1967*, Table 681 (Washington, D.C.: Government Printing Office, 1967), p. 484.
[8] *Ibid.*; calculated from Table 461, p. 324.
[9] *Ibid.*, derived from Tables 691–693, pp. 489–490.

Corporations dominate in utilities, communication, manufacturing, mining, transportation, and finance.[1] Even in wholesale and retail trade, over half the business is carried on by corporations. In agriculture, service trades, certain branches of construction, certain types of retail trade, and a few other relatively minor industries (such as manufacturing of women's clothing) corporations still do not predominate in production. But in the crucial heavy industries, such as steel, the corporation almost completely rules the field; and in the key sector of economic control represented by finance, corporations do more than 80 percent of the business. The corporation is thus the dominant institutional form of economic organization; and the modern period can be well characterized as an age of corporacy.[2]

Manufacturing in the United States is almost completely carried on under the corporate form of enterprise; even prior to World War II corporations accounted for nine-tenths of the total output in manufacturing. Furthermore, the very large concerns employ most of the workers. The long-term tendencies toward bigness continue; in manufacturing the share of the largest corporations has been increasing since World War II, as the following table shows.[3]

|  | Value added by manufacture, percentage accounted for by the: | |
| --- | --- | --- |
| YEAR | 50 LARGEST COMPANIES | 200 LARGEST COMPANIES |
| 1947 | 17 percent | 30 percent |
| 1958 | 23 | 38 |
| 1963 | 25 | 41 |

In 1963, the 50 largest manufacturing companies constituted just 1 percent of the number of establishments but produced 25 percent of the value of all shipments. The 200 largest concerns (just 3 percent of the total number) employed nearly a third of all workers in manufacturing and accounted for 42 percent of the value of shipments.[4] Thus, not only is this a corporate economy but also its center of gravity lies in the *large* corporation. With the concentration of economic activity in extremely large administrative structures, the corporation increasingly assumes powers and responsibilities

[1] William H. Husband and James C. Dockeray, *Modern Corporation Finance*, 5th ed. (Homewood, Ill.: Richard D. Irwin, 1962).

[2] David Lynch, *The Concentration of Economic Power* (New York: Columbia University Press, 1946), p. 9. This is a summary and analysis of materials produced by the investigations of the Temporary National Economic Committee. For later materials, see, Senate Subcommittee on Antitrust and Monopoly, "Administered Prices," a series of studies dating from 1957: e.g., Vol. 17, 85th Congress, 1st Session to 86th Congress, 2nd Session 1960 (Washington, D.C.: Government Printing Office, 1960).

[3] United States Bureau of the Census, *Statistical Abstract: 1967, op. cit.,* Table 1118, p. 750.

[4] *Ibid.,* Table 1119, p. 750.

that go beyond the merely "economic." For example, the American Telephone and Telegraph Company—the world's largest corporation nominally "private" in ownership—employs approximately 750,000 persons and has nearly 3 million stockholders. (The entire United States Post Office system in 1964 employed less than 600,000 persons). If we assume that each employee is a member of a nuclear family containing only two other persons and that the same is true of the nonemployee stockholders, the population with a highly immediate interest in A.T.&T. would be about 9 million persons. That giant of heavy industry, General Motors, employs well over a half-million persons (and has over 750,000 stockholders). In number of employees and wealth, our leading corporations rival sovereign political states.

*Industrial wealth and production are concentrated in relatively few large corporations.* The apparent degree of concentration varies somewhat, depending upon which of various possible indices are used to estimate it; but the central fact is quite clear. Even in the 1930's, for example, just 100 companies accounted for 32 percent of the total value of all products manufactured in the United States, and the percentage continues to rise. The amount of concentration differs, of course, in different industries. The landmark studies made by the Temporary National Economic Committee in the 1930's documented such variation.[5]

In certain industries a few very large producers account for the great bulk of the output. Thus, the four largest concerns in 1963 accounted for 79 percent of the value of shipments of motor vehicles and parts; four companies produced 67 percent of computers and related machines. The twenty largest concerns generated practically all of the production of aircraft (99 percent), tires and inner tubes (97 percent), computing and related devices (92 percent), motor vehicles and parts (90 percent), blast furnaces and steel mills (89 percent). Concentration of production is high also in aluminum, cigarettes, radio and TV receiving sets, petroleum refining, and some others.[6]

On the other hand, the industries having the highest concentration ratios (four companies accounting for 75 percent or more of the output) still represent only a small percentage of *total* manufacturing; and it does not appear that big business is rapidly increasing its share of the total market[7] even though mergers and consolidations continue to occur among large concerns. And a number of industries have low degrees of concentration, particularly those producing consumer goods. In the production of

[5] See Marshall E. Dimock and Howard K. Hyde, "Bureaucracy and Trusteeship in Large Corporations," *Monograph No. 11* (Washington, D.C.: Temporary National Economic Committee, 1940), pp. 4–5. (Hereafter cited as T.N.E.C. *Monograph No. 11*.) More recent studies give similar results, but not all indicate an increase in overall business concentration.

[6] See Table 1120, pp. 751–752 of United States Bureau of the Census, *Statistical Abstract of the United States: 1967, op. cit.*

[7] R. B. Heflebower, in Mason (ed.), *op cit.*, pp. 114 ff; Lintner holds that tangible assets of nonfinancial corporations do not now represent a substantially larger proportion of the national wealth than in the 1920's—roughly one-fourth in both periods—and the share of all tangible and intangible assets is only about one-fifth (Lintner, in Mason (ed.), *op. cit.*, pp. 173–174).

women's dresses, the largest four firms produce just 6 percent of the output; the largest twenty producers, only 14 percent.

The measurement of concentration of production is a difficult and highly technical problem in economic analysis; and this is not the place to explore its complexities. It is enough now merely to stress the fact that *large size does not necessarily mean monopoly*; it does not tell us directly how much concentrated economic or social control may exist. It does mean, however, that the social structure of very large economic organizations becomes a primary problem in the analysis of the total economic system in its social framework.

Large firms have grown more rapidly than the total economy. From 1947 to 1961, growth in number of corporations was nearly three times as rapid as growth in total number of firms. Corporations in 1947 were 7 percent of all firms and represented 69 percent of all private business receipts; by 1961, they were 11 percent of firms and received 77 percent of the receipts. And corporations are of much greater average size than other kinds of firms.[8] As of 1955, the 200 largest nonfinancial corporations owned nearly half of the total assets of some 435,000 nonfinancial companies. These holdings accounted for nearly one-fifth of the entire national reproducible tangible assets.[9]

There is no doubt at all, then, that the large corporation is of prime importance as a source of production and as a large-scale unit of social power. Nevertheless, as noted above, small economic enterprises predominate numerically. Most of the approximately 3 million farms in the United States are small family enterprises. In the nonagricultural industries, individuals and partnerships far outnumber corporations; there are in all about 6.7 million firms, whereas there are only 1.4 million corporations in the whole economy. Sole proprietorships, outside of agriculture, forestry, and fishing, numbered about 6 million in 1964. Partnerships, never a major form of business organization in this country, accounted for only a little over 900 thousand units. Politically and socially, these noncorporate entrepreneurial units are of considerable significance, as the discussion of social stratification in Chapter V has illustrated. But they are not the most important producers, nor do they wield central economic influence and control. The partnerships and individual proprietors are difficult to characterize. For example, very little evidence is available concerning the political attitudes and behavior or the class-linked ideologies of small businessmen in the United States.[1] There are a few bits of information that suggest that many feel hard pressed by the competition of "big business," feel antipathy

---

8 Anthony Downs, *Inside Bureaucracy* (Boston: Little, Brown, 1967), p. 255.

9 See these estimates in Gabriel Kolko, *Wealth and Power in America* (New York: Praeger, 1963), pp. 56–57.

1 John H. Bunzel, *The American Small Businessman* (New York: Alfred A. Knopf, 1962); Joel I. Nelson, "Participation and Integration: The Case of the Small Businessman," *American Sociological Review*, 33, 3 (June 1968), 427–438. Compare with Richard F. Hamilton, "The Behavior and Values of Skilled Workers," in Arthur Shostak and William Gomberg (eds.), *Blue-Collar World* (Englewood Cliffs, N.J.: Prentice-Hall, 1967).

for labor unions, and have little positive regard for governmental spending and the welfare state. It seems certain, however, that small businessmen constitute a most diverse population and that their social orientations vary greatly by income, ethnic origins, religious affiliation, and probably by type of business. These kinds of heterogeneity are superimposed upon the frequent economic marginality and structural ambiguity of small firms; the result is that whereas the small businessman may still serve to some extent as a "culture hero," his actual economic and political position often fails to fit the stereotype of sturdy independence and successful entrepreneurial initiative.

Corporations are not new. And there are fields in which they are not yet the dominant form of enterprise. But what is distinctive of the modern period is, first, the enormous extension and consolidation of the corporate system; second, its emergence (since the Civil War) in fields previously thought unsuitable for its extensive development (manufacturing and, increasingly though slowly, retail trade); third, the increasingly clear and marked development of certain internal corporate structures, above all the separation of ownership and management and the elaboration of hierarchical social structures.

It was clear to Berle and Means even in the 1930's[2] that a few huge corporate units rather than many small private enterprises form the core structure of American industry. In more recent years corporations have accounted for over 70 percent of the total value added by *all* business firms.[3] It is, therefore, even clearer today that any really serious attempt to understand the industrial system, the larger economic system, and indeed, the total social structure must grapple firmly with the nature of the corporation and its place in the network of economic institutions.

### Intercorporate Coordination

The extent of economic concentration is not adequately shown by data on the part played by individual corporations. In some fields, the number of important companies is so small as to suggest at once the possibility of monopolistic competition; but in most instances, the extent of centralized coordination will be understated unless we examine some of the numerous and intricate mechanisms whereby corporations are linked together into control systems of varying extent and unity. The following are among the more important:

1. Interlocking directorates;
2. Intercorporate stockholding;
3. Concentrated stock ownership by individuals or groups in several corporations;
4. Common servicing by large financial organizations; investment blocs;
5. Trade and business associations;

[2] A. A. Berle, Jr., and G. C. Means, *The Modern Corporation and Private Property* (New York: Macmillan, 1934) pp. 10–17.
[3] John Lintner, "The Financing of Corporations," in Edward S. Mason (ed.), *The Corporation in Modern Society*, op. cit.

6. Legal and contractual controls (utilized to coordinate subcontractors, retail outlets, patent controls, and so on;
7. Informal or tacit agreements and "understandings."

The establishment of *interlocking directorships* is an old method of achieving corporate integration. It does not necessarily lead to coordination: the directors in question may be inactive, or in a weak position on the boards of directors, or unable to exert a primary influence upon the managerial officers of the corporation.[4] The effectiveness of interlocks in achieving coordinated action has been much debated. There are some recent suggestions that the position of the management group in the large corporation may have weakened the influence of the board of directors. Also, interlocking directorships among competing companies are subject to legal discouragement under section 8 of the Clayton Act (1914), although this provision has proved to be considerably less than fully effective.[5] Certainly, however, the device is very common among noncompeting companies; and where extensive interlocks do exist, they help to form at least a certain "community of interest" that often may be expected to lead to substantial coordination and harmony of action.

*Intercorporate stockholding* is another type of link in the integration of clusters of corporate interests. Among the largest corporations a substantial number are tied to other large corporations by important stockholdings. The control potential of intercorporate stockholding is greatly increased when a number of corporations with similar interests converge upon a crucial "gateway" in an industry or group of industries. One of the clearest instances is the ownership of indispensable pipe line systems by a few of the large corporations in the petroleum industry.[6] Sometimes very wealthy *individuals or groups of individuals* can achieve substantial concentration of control through minority stockholdings in groups of companies—for example, the role of the Rockefeller family in several major oil producing companies.

*Financing organizations*, especially the large investment banks, play a strategic role in intercorporate coordination. To go back to the baseline period 1934–1939, the thirty-eight leading firms accounted for 91 percent of all securities handled. Although their "influence" or "control" is hard to measure exactly, the large financial organizations cannot fail to carry some degree of interest in and influence over the companies they serve. Furthermore, the financial companies themselves invest heavily in nonfinancial corporations. Life insurance companies, investment companies, and pension

[4] T.N.E.C. *Monograph No. 11*, p. 6.

[5] A Brookings Institution study called it "singularly ineffective." Leverett S. Lyon, Myron W. Watkins, and Victor Abramson, *Government and Economic Life*, Vol. I (Washington, D.C.: Brookings Institution, 1939), p. 289. On the other hand, Lynch (*The Concentration of Economic Power, op. cit.*, pp. 232–233) holds that the legislation has been effective, broadly speaking. Of course, enforcement of the Clayton Act has varied greatly at different times; one's judgment of its effectiveness in the present connection depends also in part upon an appraisal of the frequency of "dummy" directors and other informal means of circumventing the intent of the act.

[6] Cf. Lynch, *The Concentration of Economic Power, op. cit.*, p. 128.

funds increasingly have displaced individual investors as holders of corporate bonds. Furthermore, noninsured corporate pension funds hold a rapidly increasing proportion of common stocks, although, of course, this proportion will not continue to increase without limit. The important part played by nonindividual financial agencies of these kinds in both stock ownership and financing of long term corporate indebtedness tends to favor the large, well established corporations. It appears highly unlikely, however, that pension funds and similar fiduciary agencies will seek or gain effective control of large nonfinancial corporations in the foreseeable future.[7] Nevertheless, other concentrated gateways of finance help to maintain intercorporate linkage of the large industrial organizations.

Financial control of one kind or another is only one means, though an extremely important means, of intercorporate coordination. The *trade association* is another. The trade and business associations differ greatly among themselves in organization, aims, methods, and power; but they constitute in sum total a controlling system of real significance in various branches of industry and trade. There are several thousand of these national, state, and local associations. The business associations in banking, railroads, and electric power cover nine-tenths or more of the most important firms in their respective industries. The National Association of Manufacturers includes enterprises employing about one-third of the workers in manufacturing; and the officers and directors are drawn in considerable part from the largest corporations.

Among the varied activities of business and trade associations are gathering and disseminating information, developing and promulgating standards and policies, focusing attention upon and encouraging common action with regard to governmental policies, influencing public opinion, and establishing agreement on price and production levels.[8] Significant also are activities of a more diffuse and indirect character: for example, price-reporting systems can be effective indirect controls upon pricing policies. It is not possible to make any general appraisal of the importance of trade associations in price determination; but in some specific industries they appear to contribute to price leadership, collusion, resale price maintenance, and other patterns of unified action; in other industries, however, these consequences are lacking or minimal.

Certain other intercorporate linkages are maintained through *direct use of controls established by law*. Probably the most striking example is furnished by the so-called fair trade laws, which provide for price-maintenance contracts between manufacturers and retailers. Under the provisions of these laws—which exist in nearly all states—the manufacturer enters into a contract with a retailer stipulating the minimum resale price of a trademarked product; when any *one* such contract has been established, all other retailers in the state who have knowledge of the contract are bound by statute to hold to the minimum resale price established in the contract.

---

[7] Lintner, *op. cit.*, pp. 194–201.

[8] Alfred E. Kahn, "Cartels and Trade Associations," *International Encyclopedia of the Social Sciences*, Vol. 2 (New York: Macmillan and Free Press, 1968), pp. 320–325.

Prices are thus fixed "vertically," rather than horizontally through agreement among the retailers. If a particular retailer sells below the stipulated minimum, he is subject to a damage suit by other retailers or by the manufacturer.

This type of price agreement has had a complicated and stormy history, illustrating the instability of legal norms in this field. After having been held to be illegal, such agreements were later made possible by the Miller-Tydings Act of 1937 and by a Supreme Court decision of 1936, holding that the California and Illinois laws were not price-fixing acts. Later the Supreme Court held the fair trade contracts to be illegal, only to have the McGuire Act of 1952 reestablish and strengthen minimum-price agreements. Many retailers have defied the agreements, as the so-called discount houses demonstrate. The actual effect of the legislation, of course, is to permit manufacturers and dealers to fix prices at will. Unquestionably, such legal controls set into motion pressures toward further controls. Thus, as the editors of *Fortune* have cogently argued, the tendency in the fair-trade pricing of drugs is to set minimum prices that give a relatively high margin of profit in order to protect all retailers. The high profits then induce other types of retail outlets to stock drugs, and demands arise to restrict drug sales to druggists; the next step would be a system of restrictions on the number of druggists.[9] Although the resale price maintenance laws have not yet led to quota systems for entrance into the affected occupations, the "protectionist" principle embodied in such legislation is widespread in the present-day business community.

Practically any legal measure may become a part of the institutional framework of economic activity. Taxation, for instance, is not simply a neutral means of raising revenue; it is an instrument of public policy. The power to tax is the power to create or destroy, economically speaking. Tariffs, monetary policies, subventions have similar potential effects. In many instances, regulations and laws established and enforced for nominally non-economic reasons have important indirect economic consequences. A few illustrations will stand muster for a very numerous universe.

The manifest goal of building codes is to protect public health, safety, and convenience. In actual operation, some state and municipal codes minimize competition and protect favored positions among contractors and craft unions.[1] Likewise, sanitary regulations, inspection requirements, and safety provisions turn out with noteworthy frequency to be means of co-ordinating economic action or centralizing control. For example, the requirement that milk be pasteurized led quite directly to the growth of giant milk distributing firms, primarily because large capital is required for effective operation of pasteurizing plants. Or a given city may require that all milk sold there be from herds certified by municipal inspectors as free from tuberculosis. Suppose that the milk shed immediately surrounding the city is under severe competition from an out-of-state area with lower production

9 "The 'Fair' Trade Controversy," *Fortune* (April 1949), p. 76.

1 Cf. Thurman Arnold's comment that certain of these measures "are not building regulations but protective tariffs against other parts of the nation." *The Bottlenecks of Business* (New York: Reynal & Hitchcock, 1940), pp. 36–37.

costs, located a hundred miles away. If the municipal inspectors find it possible to inspect all dairy herds in the hinterland but never get around to the inspection of herds in the outside region, the local milk shed receives a noneconomic protection against the competition of the outer area. Many such trade barriers are established at the behest of, or with the acquiescence of, labor groups, farmers, and individual businessmen. They illustrate well how public regulatory action can become part of the interlocking structure of economic interests and organizations, corporate or otherwise.

Rarely are economic measures taken by government merely economic. They involve a complex political interaction in which popular beliefs and values about the "public interest" are utilized by pressure groups or politically strategic elements of the electorate. Thus, certain tariffs, which can be shown to reduce real national income, nevertheless are maintained. To abolish them would severely injure a small number of producers, whereas the larger total benefits would be spread thinly over a large number of unorganized consumers. A small number of highly interested, vigilant, and organized producers can thus completely outweigh a large aggregate of consumers to whom the possible gains are individually trivial.

A variety of control patterns has grown up and around *patent rights*. A sufficiently powerful and adept concern may "fence in" competitors by securing patents on all foreseeable improvements in machinery or techniques. The competing owner of a given patent can thus be prevented from improving his technical position and may even be completely immobilized from exploiting his primary patent by suits or the threat of suits for infringement of patent rights. When a new improvement is patented, the inventor or patent holder will find it difficult to sell his improvement except to the holder of the central complex of rights in the same field; the original patent controls can thus be further bulwarked by purchase of improvements made by others. In the entire process, the large-scale, well financed research and development arms of corporations obviously have great advantages.[2] Buying and suppressing an improved patent in order to protect the investment already made on the basis of an older patent,[3] making applications for patents in order to delay a competitive improvement, continuing and ingenious litigation against inventions seen as threats, litigation that may be so time consuming and expensive as to block effectively new competitive techniques or processes—all these devices enable dominant concerns or groups of concerns to maintain favorable positions.

Single inventions are often of maximum usefulness only when combined with other inventions. Often the patent rights to such complementary inventions will be in different hands; often also, patents may overlap in their claims. To meet these problems, systems have developed for cross licensing

[2] Cf. Lyon, Watkins, and Abramson, *Government and Economic Life, op. cit.*, pp. 138–139. The classic case of fencing-in is usually thought to be that of the Hartford-Empire Company in the glass container industry (cited on p. 138). See also the description in Lynch, *The Concentration of Economic Power, op. cit.*, pp. 273–279.

[3] Although a few dramatic cases of actual suppression of patents are on record, the practice probably is much less frequent and less important than popular belief would have it. After all, the major technical innovations of our times have been made by very large companies in strong market positions.

and for pooling of patents. In the automobile industry, there are provisions for interchange of patents on a royalty-free basis; and in many other instances pooling and cross licensing are common. It is difficult to weigh the effects of these arrangements: on the one hand, they undoubtedly facilitate technically useful combinations of patent rights; on the other, they are always potential sources of monopolistic control.

It is important to note the implications of the observation that patent rights constitute property. For this means that "property" as a set of actual valuable "things"—machines, buildings, railroads, land, blueprints, or technical data—is controlled by "property" as a set of socially enforceable rights. The *rights* often are held by individuals; much of the actual objects of value are controlled by large organizations and are not even capable of use by a single individual (for example, an automobile factory). At any rate, no matter what social evaluation may be assigned to them, these systems constitute still another example of specific institutionalized controls that extend among the organized enterprises of the business world.

## Imperfect Competition

A perfectly competitive economy is never found in any actual society, although it has been approximated in some portions of Western societies during the past three centuries. In general, it has been most closely approached during those periods in which agricultural societies have been becoming rapidly industrialized—when the basic character of the social structure has been changing, and traditional barriers and restraints have been dissolving. Then an economy subject to principles different from those guiding the environing social structure has arisen; and economic units, still small, have not yet become consolidated into new systems of *social* organization.

During most of the second half of the nineteenth century in the United States, conditions favored an approximation to a system of free competition. Both extractive and manufacturing industries were carried on by units small enough and independent enough to prevent any single one, or tightly organized combinations of them, from dominating the market. Fixed capital and overhead costs were small, so that direct costs took a determining role and entry into production was relatively easy for the small entrepreneur. As any student of economic history knows, earlier periods have witnessed recurring attempts to control production, prices, wages, and other economic variables by governmental edicts, guild regulations, and a variety of other forms of purposive control. What was new about so-called laissez-faire economies actually was not total lack of regulation but rather a certain kind of regulation that left wide scope for production and sale under competitive conditions.

The facts we have just reviewed, however, show that today competition in a free market has been partly replaced by a highly tangible web of financial and organizational controls. There are nodes or foci of concentrated production and centers of control in many crucial parts of the economic web, from which lines of control gradually fade out into areas of relatively free markets and independent production. Even within the corporate sector, an enormous flock of small companies contrast with the few giants that do most of the business.[4]

Where there is consolidated control, there is what economists call imperfect competition, whether monopoly, duopoly, oligopoly, or some intermediate shading of these.[5] In addition to the restrictions upon competition already discussed there are others arising from the "intrinsic" character of the present economic structure. The enormous capital investment now necessary in many industries eliminates or drastically limits the opportunities for new firms to enter the established field. Strategic control by existing large concerns over critical supplies of materials, techniques, or personnel has the same effect. Modern mass advertising tends to create extreme differentiation of products (even among those of essentially the same technical merits and cost) and thereby creates dealer and consumer preferences that militate against free entry of new competitors. When such "manufactured" patterns of preference are bolstered by resale price-maintenance systems, exclusive-dealer contracts, and similar devices, they take on added solidity as barriers. Even though the collaboration of big and small business often serves both well, at least in the short-run, there often are real and important conflicts of interest between large corporations and small businesses that act as suppliers or distributors. The classic instance perhaps is that of retail automobile dealers, who as relatively powerless satellites of the manufacturing giants often have been exposed to the immediate and unilateral exercise of corporate power.

There are, in addition, the increased possibilities of various kinds of informal agreements or "collusion" where a few great firms dominate a given field. Closely related, as to the effects upon the competitive system, are the widespread phenomena of price leadership, basing-point systems, and other versions of administered prices. Outside of some form of collusion or of governmental action, imperfect competition in general and administered prices in particular arise only when a few large producers supply a major portion of a given market; but as we have already seen, in a number of very important industries a few firms do so, and the decisions as to production and price made by any one producer cannot then be assumed to be independent of other producers. It is not easy to detect imperfect competition, and its incidence varies greatly from one portion of the economy to another. Sheer size of the leading concerns tells us very little, for giant companies may make a wide range of products and have little control of the

---

[4] Murray Gendell and Hans L. Zetterberg (eds.), *A Sociological Almanac for the United States*, 2nd ed. (Totowa, N.J.: Bedminster Press, 1963).

[5] Economic theories of imperfect competition are illustrated by such pioneering analyses as Edward A. Chamberlin, *Theory of Monopolistic Competition* (Cambridge, Mass.: Harvard University Press, 1933); Joan Robinson, *Economics of Imperfect Competition* (London: Macmillan & Company, Ltd., 1933). Important later works include Fritz Machlup, *The Political Economy of Monopoly* (Baltimore: Johns Hopkins Press, 1952); Joseph A. Schumpeter, *Capitalism, Socialism and Democracy*, 3rd ed. (New York: Harper & Row, 1950); Joe S. Bain, *Industrial Organization* (New York: Wiley, 1959). For additional bibliography see references in Henry William Spiegel, *Current Economic Problems*, 3rd ed. (Homewood, Ill.: Richard D. Irwin, 1961), pp. 387–389, 416–417.

market for any one of them. What is crucial is size *in relation to a particular market for a particular product*.[6] A small company store in an isolated mining town may have relatively more monopoly control in its local market than the largest wholesale distributor in the nation.

If prices are administered, they are administered *by* someone. A degree of market dominance sufficient to permit price administration on a national level is possibly only when economic enterprises are very large or held together into tight systems of control or agreement. And it surely can be expected that the norms and goals guiding the "control" groups in the large corporation in a position of monopoly, oligopoly, or price leadership will take into account more than short run profit. The impersonality and anonymity of the open market will diminish as tangible groups have to be considered, whether as opponents or "colleagues." Managers and directors will be increasingly moved by considerations of power, of institutional stability, and of the perpetuation of a given organizational pattern.

Imperfect competition and oligopoly occur not only in the conspicuous cases in the national market but also in local markets. The cement industry, with its relatively small firms and plants scattered across the country, at first glance might be expected to be highly competitive. But transportation costs are high, and any one local market is likely to be supplied by one firm or only a few; customers cannot easily go to other markets. If entry of new concerns is difficult, it will often happen that competition will be restricted in the interests of market stability and hoped-for price advantages. Where pure monopoly exists (extremely rare), the output will be lower and the price higher than under pure competition (also extremely rare). The most delicate and complex questions of social policy concern the endlessly varying "in-between" case of oligopoly.[7]

Free markets do not automatically maintain themselves. Economic combination is frequently at least as advantageous as individualistic competition. When, as in the present-day American business community, the term "price chiseler" becomes a popular epithet, business associations advocate a "live and let live" policy, and the word competition is coupled with "cutthroat," and when big business, small business, and labor groups are busy building a finer network of organization, then we begin to see a new cultural atmosphere surround the structure of economic life. At the same time, there are powerful forces working against the "closure" of the economic system by the growth of entrenched combinations and protected positions of special privilege. Technological innovation continues to go on at a rapid rate—creating new products, new forms of organizations, new consumer tastes, new structures of price and costs. In the American legal system, economic monopoly tends to be regarded as undesirable per se, and the law cannot be used (with some exceptions) to enforce monopolistic agreements. Cheap and rapid transportation and communication work against local

---

[6] And even complete control of a particular product or type of product will not have major economic consequences if the demand for the product is highly elastic, that is, falls or rises rapidly with price.

[7] Joel B. Dirlam and Alfred E. Kahn, *Fair Competition: The Law and Economics of Antitrust Policy* (Ithaca, N.Y.: Cornell University Press, 1954).

monopolies. Big companies often find it advantageous to deal in a wide variety of products rather than to concentrate on one. There are other factors. No "rule by monopoly" is in sight in the American economy.

### Other Barriers to a Perfect Market System

The ghost of the "economic man" has been repeatedly laid in recent years. Our previous discussion has perhaps suggested some of the specific reasons why he cannot exist. But there are others.

For economic man to function perfectly in a perfect market, resources, including labor, must be freely mobile. Labor is not freely mobile. Not only does it fail to shift from nation to nation as wage levels would dictate, but it is significantly immobile even within the borders of proverbially rootless America. For short-run periods each locality may be a quasi-independent labor market. Marked *regional* differences in wages persist over long periods. Agriculture tends to be chronically overblessed by available labor. Again, "free entry" into business is supposedly essential for a self-adjusting competitive system. New enterprises challenge the old in high-profit business, thus putting resources to most profitable use and preventing monopoly. Actually, of course, entry into occupations and economic enterprises, although free in form, is never unimpeded. First of all, and of prime importance, sufficient initial capital is difficult to raise. Small firms are in fact financed chiefly from personal savings and by loans from friends and relatives; and the larger new firms rely mainly upon savings of wealthy individuals. Very few new concerns are able to secure adequate bank loans or to sell sufficient securities on the public market.[8] Because the small firm does not have easy access to capital from the open capital markets, it is highly vulnerable to taxation or other measures that limit its capacity to secure such access.[9] In addition to patent controls previously discussed, exclusive-dealer contracts, price-decline guarantees, and long-term staggered contracts provide other barriers to free entry. Also, certain types of labor contracts and agreements operate to bar new firms from certain industries or localities. When a particular area or field is dominated by a few concerns, the aspiring newcomer may be met by a wide range of deterring actions, ranging from simple persuasion to threats, litigation, or violence. Financial controls are potentially important in checking very large new enterprises. A number of legal obstacles play a part—for instance, licensing provisions and franchises.

Finally, the organization of a national economy for military and other political ends is not compatible with laissez faire, nor with any completely "free" economic system. Even if the forms of market bargaining are preserved, the actual processes inevitably are changed. At the most obvious level, for example, it is highly understandable that large military contracts tend to go to large firms: during the period 1950–1956, for example, the one hundred companies receiving the largest contracts accounted for two-thirds of the dollars in defense contracts (and the ten largest contracts

---

[8] Alfred E. Oxenfelt, *New Firms and Free Enterprise* (Washington, D.C.: American Council on Public Affairs, 1943), pp. 146–160.

[9] Cf. Lewis H. Kimmel, *Taxes and Economic Incentives* (Washington, D.C.: Brookings Institution, 1950), pp. 35–36.

amounted to one-third).[1] War, preparation for war, the international commitments incurred in preparing for wars or striving to prevent them—these inevitably lead to drastic modifications of the competitive, open market system. Consumer wants are affected, and goods may be distributed by rationing rather than pricing. Resources, in men and capital, are allocated to ends quite different from those that would otherwise prevail. Explicit regulation grows.

Furthermore, the American system has come to be marked by a considerable amount of public enterprise, now widely accepted as legitimate and necessary. Particular proposals for expansion of public enterprise often do arouse controversy. But in every economy there are some goods and services that cannot be chosen by individuals in the market; these are public goods and services, the benefits of which are not subject to division into separable individual returns. Highways and streets, community sanitation, parks, control of pollution of the air, fire protection, and military defense are examples; these values cannot easily or effectively be provided by individual buying and selling in the open market. Imagine the consequences of competitive bidding for the services of fire-fighting companies. A pragmatic acceptance of "monopoly" is apparent in the treatment given "public utilities," for instance. Of course some services become public only after they cease to be lucrative for private entrepreneurs.

Thus, we see that our present economy is a congeries of control systems and that its "capitalism" is very different from that depicted in earlier ideology.[2] Nowhere is this fact more apparent than in the newer modes of corporate organization. If there can be said to be a "characteristic" unit in the system, it is the corporation, which accordingly deserves further attention.

## NATURE OF THE CORPORATION AND ITS ORGANIZATION

So far we have discussed the corporation more or less as if its nature could be taken for granted. Yet the deeper consequences of corporate organization are certainly not self-evident. The present-day corporation is more than a socially neutral mechanism for doing business: as Berle and Means have said, it "has attained a degree of prominence entitling it to be dealt with as a major social institution.[3] It is not surprising that debates concerning the role of the large corporation in our society reveal great diversity of conceptions and sharply conflicting criteria of evaluation. Some defenders of the corporate giants argue for the desirability of a benign "social responsibility:" the corporation would participate in the noneconomic affairs of local com-

[1] Carl Kaysen, "The Corporation: How Much Power? What Scope?" in Mason, *The Corporation in Modern Society, op. cit.*, p. 86.

[2] Indeed, in terms of the relations of the United States to many other nations, it may be unfortunate (i.e., misleading) to call the system "capitalism," so much does it differ (in productivity, distribution of wealth, governmental regulation, position of labor) from the early capitalism that so enraged Karl Marx, among others.

[3] Berle and Means, *op. cit.*, p. 1.

munities, and would guide its internal policies by considerations other than profit-maximization.[4] Other defenders praise the corporation just because it allegedly behaves very much as if guided solely by market considerations of maximum gain. Some of the critics produce the corresponding mirror images: the corporation is regarded as menacing because of its quasi-political power and enormous impact on community and family life, or it is condemned because it is seen as inevitably producing great social costs in its single-minded search for profits.

Corporations in the modern sense first arose in trading enterprises subject to great risks and requiring large amounts of capital. In America, a corporate charter was originally regarded as a contract between the state and the corporation for carrying on certain activities and was minutely scrutinized and rigidly protected. It was regarded as a special privilege, not as a "right;" and until well into the nineteenth century each charter usually required a special act of the state legislature.[5] Later, however, incorporation became simple and easy; and this loosening of the early rigid legal controls was of notable importance in the development of the modern structure.

It is often said that the most important feature of the corporation is the principle of limited liability. This feature is itself derived in our legal system from the more basic *right of the corporation to exist as an entity* apart from the individuals who are associated in the organization. The partnership is a cumbersome form of organization, especially for large businesses, because the partners retain their separate legal personalities and are individually held responsible for the entire enterprise. The corporate device at one stroke decisively cuts through the identification of concrete persons with the enterprise; thus, an abstract legal fiction can for many purposes operate with the unity of a private person.

The corporation is, then, a recognized legal entity having the rights of an individual to hold property, sue and be sued, enter into contracts, and otherwise conduct business in its own name. Although the corporation as such is fully liable for its financial obligations, the shareholders have only a liability limited to the amount of stock they hold. Through the right of the stockholder to transfer his shares, the total enterprise acquires continuity of existence. In actual practice it thus possesses institutional immortality; investors may change and personnel may come and go, but the corporation exists indefinitely, subject only to the necessities of the balance sheet and to charter renewals, which are usually granted. Unity, combined with limited liability, greatly facilitates the accumulation of large capital sums, increases the flexibility of financing, and allows diffusion of ownership; thousands of investors can contribute capital to a corporation that operates as a single unit.

In appraising the place and character of the large corporation in our economy, all roads start from the classic study of Berle and Means, published

---

[4] Norton E. Long has clearly described views of this kind. ("The Corporation, Its Satellites, and the Local Community," in Mason, *op. cit.*, p. 203).

[5] Berle and Means, *op. cit.*, pp. 129–130. The gradual loosening of the early detailed regulation is an illuminating chapter in the history of economic and social change in the United States.

in 1933. It still remains true, as that study held, that there is a crucial separation of actual control of the large corporation from the beneficient ownership (of rights to income) represented by the great bulk of the stockholders. Somewhat as the factory system brought large numbers of *workers* under unified direction and control, so the corporate system brought numerous bits of *wealth* together under a single management. The tremendous economic and social power of the large industrial corporation of our time represents the combination of these two features. It is difficult to realize what a basic change in the organization of society is thereby effected.[6]

The talk of the "new social responsibility" of the corporation must be largely discounted. Aside from the fact that much of the so-called social responsibility is an image created by the public relations departments of the corporations themselves, the fact is that the corporation is necessarily first and foremost committed to money making. If socially undesirable side effects ensue—water pollution, air pollution, racial ghettos, unemployment, poverty of the cast-off labor force—it is not expected that the corporation will rectify these consequences. In spite of the widespread impression that governmental regulation now effectively restrains the societal role of big business, the actual fact is that the large company is free to operate within very wide limits as it chooses. It can and does decide where to locate plants and offices, when and how to introduce new products or labor-displacing machines and processes, how many workers to employ, what dividends to declare, how high the salaries and benefits of executives shall be, how to dispose of its earnings.

Racial discrimination in employment in the United States probably could have been largely ended by now had the 200 largest corporations taken the lead during World War II or even as late as the Supreme Court's *Brown* decision in 1954. They did not elect to do so, and the massive consequences will continue to reverberate for years to come. The death of America's rivers and lakes is to an important extent the result of pollution from acids, oils, grease, sludge, and other industrial wastes, dumped into the waters as a means of cheap disposal. It is unnecessary to multiply examples of such social overhead costs, borne by the society as a whole (or by its less privileged members). The sum total of the pervasive impact of corporations' decisions far outrun either their willingness or their capacity to take full "social responsibility."

### Patterns of Control

If one could consider the corporation as if it were a political state, its citizens would be shares of stock rather than persons.[7] The share of stock is certainly one of the great social inventions of all time. By means of it great aggregates of concretely indivisible industrial goods can be divided into

---

[6] Berle and Means, *op. cit.*, p. vii: "It is the essence of revolutions of the more silent sort that they are unrecognized until they are far advanced."

[7] Wilbert E. Moore, *Industrial Relations and the Social Order*, (New York: Macmillan, 1946), p. 75: "Put in terms which are only slightly oversimplified, the corporation in legal theory is a fictional person whose behavior is determined by its elements which are pieces of paper."

small, uniform packages of rights to income and control, easily transferable, and hedged in against liability. The consequent dispersion of ownership, however, most definitely does not lead to a corresponding dispersion of direction and control of the corporation itself. On the contrary, the seeming paradox is that the more widely stock ownership is diffused, the more likely it is that effective control of business wealth will be concentrated. In a small or moderate-sized corporation, where there are only a few stockholders, ownership and management tend to be closely identified; not so in the very large corporations, which account for about one-half of the nation's industrial wealth. This is why it is so ambiguous to argue that the wealthy people no longer have the "ownership" of corporations, because stock in large corporations is so widely held. Common stock rights to dividends do not necessarily mean any control over corporation policies.

The roster of large corporations in the United States is rather stable, and the degree of concentration of economic activity in them has not changed greatly since the 1920's. In those industries where concentration is great— especially in public utilities, transportation, finance, manufacturing—monopolies or substantial degrees of oligopoly exist. Large size and oligopoly, together with relative independence of managers from close investor control, open up a range of managerial power not present in highly competitive markets.[8] In any case, the sheer size of the corporate giants gives wide social importance to decisions concerning pricing, product quality, technical research and innovation, plant location, investment, labor policies, relations with suppliers and distributors, advertising, and direct political influence.

An accurate one-sentence characterization of the ownership of corporations is that *investment ownership* is widely diffused whereas *control ownership* is highly concentrated.[9] The following salient facts summarize the pattern.

1. *Corporate shares are held by large numbers of individuals.* As of the end of 1937 it was estimated that about 8 to 9 million persons owned stock in corporations.[1] During the next three decades the total number of stockholders continued to increase, standing at 20 million in 1965.[2]

2. *Most shareholders own only a small number of shares.* Over 90 percent of the stockholders had net incomes of less than 5,000 dollars a year in 1937;[3] about one-half of all stockholders received less than one hundred dollars in dividends in that same year, and their aggregate dividends accounted for less than 5 percent of the total dividend income of individuals.[4]

---

[8] Carl Kaysen, in Mason, *op. cit.*, pp. 87–91.

[9] Moore, *op. cit.*, p. 77: "The concentration of economic *power* is in fact chiefly made possible by dispersion of capital ownership."

[1] Raymond W. Goldsmith, Rexford C. Parmelee, and others, "The Distribution of Ownership in the 200 Largest Nonfinancial Corporations," *Monograph No. 29* (Washington, D.C.: Temporary National Economic Committee, 1940), pp. 11–12.

[2] United States Bureau of the Census, *Statistical Abstract: 1967*, op. cit., Table 664, p. 471.

[3] L. H. Kimmel, *Share Ownership in the United States*, Brookings Institution (Washington, D.C., 1952), p. 10.

[4] *Ibid.*, p. 13.

A generation later, the much larger proportion of stockholders among American adults still was made up of small holders: on the average in 1962 each held only 3.4 shares (a figure less than that of a decade before).[5]

3. In spite of the dispersion of ownership indicated by the large number of shareholders, *stockholdings are actually highly concentrated among a relatively few persons.* The most recent studies indicate that there has been no important change in the distribution of holdings since the 1920's.[6]

4. Among the 200 largest nonfinancial corporations, Berle and Means showed that *the top 1 percent of shareholdings include approximately 60 percent of the common stock of these corporations.* This concentration of ownership in the very large corporation implies that a comparatively few shareholders have power over the investments of large numbers of small stockholders, who are typically passive and inarticulate in the direction of the corporation's affairs.

In only a few of our large corporations is absolute control wielded by individuals or family groups who own a majority of their shares. Ordinarily shareholding is so widely diffused that a minority bloc or "management" can achieve substantial control;[7] occasionally no one may have control— there may not be any one unitary locus of control that by itself dominates decisions.

Among the 200 largest nonfinancial corporations in the United States at the beginning of the 1930's, five major patterns of control could be distinguished, distributed as follows:[8] management group (44 percent); legal device (21 percent); minority stockholding bloc (23 percent); majority ownership (5 percent); and private ownership (6 percent). The companies in which control rested in the hands of persons or groups having a majority of the voting stock thus amounted to only 11 percent of all the giant corporations. Other studies have substantiated these general conclusions.[9]

For most of the corporate economy, the bulk of the stockholders have shifted to the status of mere investors. Control has moved into the hands of management and minority blocs; although the small stockholders are the great majority of all stockholders, they hold a rather insignificant proportion of the shares. Moreover, it appears that many of the directors of the very large corporations are also executive officers, and thereby actively engaged in management.[1] Importantly also, many managers own substantial amounts of stock, thereby retaining a very direct personal interest in profits

---

[5] Gendell and Zetterberg, *op. cit.*, p. 63.

[6] Robert J. Lampman, *The Share of Top Wealth-Holders in National Wealth, 1922–1956* (New York: National Bureau of Economic Research, 1962); Herman P. Miller, *Rich Man, Poor Man* (New York: Crowell, 1964); Gabriel Kolko, *Wealth and Power in America* (New York: Praeger, 1963).

[7] Berle and Means, *op. cit.*, pp. 80 ff.

[8] *Ibid.*, p. 94. Reprinted by permission of the Macmillan Company.

[9] See Robert A. Gordon, "Ownership by Management and Control Groups in the Large Corporation," *Quarterly Journal of Economics*, LII (May 1938), 367–400; Robert A. Gordon, *Business Leadership in the Large Corporation* (Washington, D.C.: Brookings Institution, 1945).

[1] See National Industrial Conference Board, *Corporate Directorship Practices*, Studies in Business Policy, No. 90 (New York: National Industrial Conference Board, 1959).

accruing to these holdings. Nearly half of the higher executives own stock.[2] All studies show high concentration of ownership.

Two crucial points emerge from the above facts: (1) to a large degree, ownership of stock has been divorced from control over the specific uses to which capital resources are to be put and from power over business policy;[3] (2) the dispersion of ownership is so far advanced that a further splintering of rights occurs in the form of management control. Note also that both the explicit law and usual judicial practice make it very difficult for the individual stockholder to successfully sue the corporation in which he holds stock for alleged fraud or other violations of fiduciary responsibility.

Thus, the governments of large corporations fall into three main types, representing successively greater separation of ownership from directing power. At one extreme is the comparatively rare "complete" ownership (the closed corporation) or majority control. At an intermediate point along the scale, there is "financial control"—a complex balance of power in which compact minority blocs of stockholdings or outside financial interests are the major influences in the central direction of the company. Finally, when ownership is so dispersed that no real financial control centers exist, the stockholders become pure investors and control devolves upon the officers and directors, who can then within very broad limits become self-directing and self-perpetuating. One fairly obvious possible result of such separation of decision makers from passive income-seekers would be increased reliance upon internal financing, divorcing the corporation from external capital markets. No clear trend in this direction has been observed, judging from the proportion of internal funds used to finance expansion in nonfinancial corporations or from dividend policies. Although there has been a decline in reliance upon new security issues (stocks, bonds, mortgages, and so on), corporations still rely heavily upon the external capital markets. Hence, the large corporation has not yet become a self-contained entity, unresponsive to its financial environment.[4]

Corporate control structure is often incredibly complex, shifting, and blurred; but we can see that at the very least it is now possible for persons to control a large business enterprise without having *any* appreciable ownership rights in the traditional sense. A new social type has been created: instead of the old captain of industry we have the professional salaried executive. The directors are elected by "the stockholders"—that is, by such groups as are able to mobilize effectively concentrated aggregates of voting power—and with the senior officers of the corporation they make up the main "management" group. This group is legally held in a "fiduciary" relationship to the body of stockholders; their position is one of trust and accountability; they are in theory bound to exercise "fidelity to the interest of

[2] Kolko, *op. cit.*, pp. 66–69.

[3] Joseph Livingston, *The American Stockholder* (Philadelphia: Lippincott, 1958).

[4] "Not only have nonfinancial corporations failed to encroach substantially upon the rest of the economy, but there has been no long-term trend upon reliance upon internal funds. . . . Corporations have not become free of the constraints of the capital market. We further find that profitability and the pressure of increasing sales are still the dominant determinants of investment outlays. . . ." (Lintner, *op. cit.*, p. 190).

the corporation" and to carry out their functions with "reasonable care and reasonable prudence."[5]

The exact legal meaning of this fiduciary status is extremely unclear at many points. An officer or director is not at liberty to use his position for personal gain at the expense of the corporation as a whole, but whether he is equally responsible to the *individual shareholders* is a question upon which legal precedents are divided. Corporations certainly do have internal sets of obligatory rules, authoritative decision-making, effective systems of command and of sanctions, and well-defined agencies of enforcement.[6] The most important decisions are made by small numbers of managers, often little constrained by any real countervailing power.[7] The wider social consequences may be enormous or trivial whether desirable or not. Whether automobiles are safe or unsafe, razor blades wear out quickly or slowly, industrial wastes are or are not poured into lakes, a local plant is closed or maintained in operation, or even whether a particular governing group in another country is supported or not—such decisions rarely are discussed in advance with the main body of stockholders and certainly not with a wider "electorate." In recent years, however, statutes and court decisions have tended to impose increasingly rigorous fiduciary standards upon management. Much of the talk of trusteeship, social responsibility, and the like is, of course, as yet largely sentimental rather than realistic; but it reflects the underlying structural changes that have separated financial "ownership" from controlling power and have catapulted management to a position of such autonomy as it now tends to hold.

### The Nature of Corporate Property

There has resulted the dissolution of the old atom of ownership into its component parts, control and beneficial ownership. This dissolution of the atom of property destroys the very foundation on which the economic order of the past three centuries has rested.[8]

The great development of the corporation signifies an entirely new system of property rights. Under the prior system of private and *individual* property, the entrepreneur was a clearly recognizable and dominant social type. An individual or group of partners both *owned* and *managed* the business; they advanced the capital, took the risks, made the managerial decisions—and incurred the penalties or reaped the rewards of the whole venture. In the closely held corporation, especially during its early development when the typical corporation was a pygmy by modern standards of

[5] Husband and Dockeray, *op. cit.*, p. 308. See Berle and Means, *op. cit.*, chaps. 5 and 6 and pp. 220 ff.

[6] "A mature political conception of the corporation must view it as a rationalized system for the accumulation, control, and administration of power. . . . The corporation is a body politic which exhibits describable characteristics common to all bodies politic." (Earl Latham, "The Body Politic of the Corporation," in Mason (ed.), *op. cit.*, p. 220.)

[7] For a naturalistic account of the behavior of the corporation man see Wilbert E. Moore, *The Conduct of the Corporation* (New York: Random House, 1962).

[8] A. A. Berle and G. C. Means, *The Modern Corporation and Private Property*, p. 8. Reprinted by permission of the Macmillan Company.

comparison, the stockholders really "owned the business." But in the large corporation of our time, "ownership" has become fragmented: it is simply one bundle of rights standing alongside other rights—the prerogatives of management, the intervention of government, the emerging status claims of labor. To understand the present economic system it becomes essential to look more closely into the meaning of property.

Property consists, first, not of *things*, but of *rights*; it is not a concrete object of reference but a socially recognized claim. The essence of property is *an institutionalized right* of persons or other *social units to scarce values*.[9] In our complex economy, many very important property rights concern such "intangibles" as trade-marks, patents, franchises, insurance, company good will,[1] even the right to a job. Second, property rights are always institutionally limited and regulated; for they establish schedules of *priority* for the use, transfer, or control of scarce values. In some property systems, various kinds of rights to the same concrete object (or "locus of value" as Moore terms it)[2] are diffused among several different parties. In America, however, the older conception of "private property" emphasized *concentration* of rights in the hands of an individual owner,[3] reserving to the society only such residual powers as the right of eminent domain and various particular uses of "police power." Ownership can refer thus either to (relatively) *unlimited rights* or to *unitary control*. Third, property may be held by individuals or by *other* social units—by governments, kinship units, churches, or other organized social entities. Property may be "private" in the sense of maximizing the bundle of rights assigned to a particular social unit, yet *nonindividual* in the locus of those rights. Finally, there is a broad distinction between rights of control and rights of beneficial ownership of property; for instance, one may control the uses of a good without enjoying the other values attached to it, or one may enjoy the fruits of a scarce value without having the right to determine the use to which it is put.[4]

What then are we to make of corporate property? We cannot here untangle the law of corporate property, but the main features have a certain sharp simplicity. If instead of asking "who owns the corporation" we ask "what *rights* are represented in corporate property," it is apparent that ownership of corporate property diverges in several important ways from unlimited ownership of individual private property. There are, first, *investment rights* of bondholders, creditors, and shareholders. In varying degrees, all of these owners are entitled under specified conditions to a return from funds they have placed at the disposal of the corporation. But they are not

---

[9] Wilbert E. Moore, "The Emergence of New Property Conceptions in America," *Journal of Legal and Political Sociology*, I, 3–4 (April 1943), 34–35.

[1] Among the assets of the Coca-Cola concern in 1952 were listed $41,440,683 for good will, trademarks, formulas, etc. (George Leland Bach, *Economics* (Englewood Cliffs, N.J.: Prentice-Hall, 1954), p. 236).

[2] *Op. cit.*, p. 37.

[3] It is partly because of this conception that "property" and "things" are so easily confused in our usual thinking.

[4] Cf. the related distinction between active property and passive property made by Berle and Means, *op. cit.*, pp. 346–347.

necessarily individual persons—they may be other corporate entities, or the corporation itself. It is therefore possible for ownership of a "private" corporation to be as nonindividualistic as government ownership. Second, the—by now proverbial—separation of investment rights from managerial control means, of course, that the stockholders do not have unlimited rights nor unitary control. Except for powerful minority-bloc stockholders the owner of a voting share turns over to the managerial group or other "control center" the actual disposition of his funds; and stockholders who *do* control the corporation have their powers by virtue, not of their stock, but of their position in the corporation power structure. The property represented by shares of stock is further limited by governmental regulation channelizing the uses of capital. It is potentially, and to some degree factually, limited by rights or quasi-rights of labor.

Thus, we have the "dissolution of the atom of property" referred to in the quotation at the head of this section. The label "private property" is a legal fiction of little help in determining what constitutes effective control of the productive apparatus of the society. Property is always a social fact and the real issues of public policy concern *what* control, by *whom*, for *what*, not whether or not property is to be regulated. For "property" means in part precisely the *exclusion of individuals from the use or enjoyment of certain scarce values except under specific conditions subject to the control of the property holder.* Rights belong to someone or some social entity, and they are only rights so long and to the extent that they are respected by others. Every property right therefore implies the duty of someone to respect that right, and every legitimized right of access to scarce values is at least potentially a form of property.[5] Corporate property is no exception and exists only so far as the dominant social consensus gives value and legitimacy to it.

### Internal Organization of the Corporation[6]

At this point it will be useful to review what has been discussed thus far. Beginning with a consideration of economic activity and economic institutions in general terms, we saw that normative regulation is a universal and indispensable property of economic systems just as it is of every other sector of social systems. We outlined certain dominant features of the American economy that seemed to be of special sociological interest, in particular, the dominance of corporate organization and the importance of large corporations. We then touched upon various types of intercorporate coordination and influence and arrived at the conception of a corporative *system* permeat-

[5] In the concise analysis by Max Weber, "property" was restricted to those appropriated rights that extend beyond the individual's lifetime and that are heritable. See the discussion by Parsons in *Theory of Social and Economic Organization, op. cit.,* pp. 40–41 and ff.

[6] In addition to sources already cited, useful references on this topic include: Chester I. Barnard, *The Functions of the Executive* (Cambridge, Mass.: Harvard University Press, 1938); Alvin W. Gouldner, *Patterns of Industrial Bureaucracy,* (New York: Free Press, 1954); Delbert C. Miller and William H. Form, *Industrial Sociology: The Sociology of Work Organizations,* 2nd ed. (New York: Harper & Row, 1964); Eugene V. Schneider, *Industrial Sociology* (New York: McGraw-Hill, 1957); William H. Whyte, Jr., *The Organization Man* (New York: Simon and Schuster, 1956); Theodore Caplow, *Sociology of Work* (Minneapolis: University of Minnesota Press, 1954).

ing the economy, especially in financial and industrial fields. Some of the many ways in which economic activity is controlled other than by the free market system were briefly reviewed. With this broad picture in mind we have returned to a closer inspection of control and ownership of the corporate unit itself.

We must now give brief attention to two other main aspects of corporate organization: (1) the internal differentiation of authority and function, and (2) labor relations. We may think of the corporate unit as a single plant or as a series of plants, offices, or stations under central management.

The corporation is a social organization—a system of human relations. The business corporation has profit making as its goal: it must meet the test of rational capital accounting or go out of business. Its means for attaining that end are its technical apparatus and materials, human labor, and "organization." We are interested in the social arrangements whereby the efforts of large numbers of persons are integrated toward corporate objectives.

Looked upon as a social organization, the corporation clearly embodies a system of power and authority. Not only may corporations be consequential for external political affairs, they are themselves "private governments."[7]

At the center (or, if you will, at the top) of the corporate organization is a small group of persons who by virtue of their formal office are given continuing responsibility and authority for forming and carrying out policies. They have great authority and overlook a wide range of general organizational problems. Frequently, they are salaried managers to whom has been delegated a large part of the powers nominally held by stockholders and directors. Usually, as we have seen, they also include representatives of financial control who are not employees of the corporation. The latter act as the mediating link between "outside" ownership, investment and creditor interests, and the internal body of the corporation as an operating unit.[8]

From the central control group the organization extends downward and outward through the progressive subdivision and delegation of *authority* and of *specialized functions*. What is commonly known as *"line"* organization is a hierarchy of positions that defines who will give and receive what orders, commands, and requests—invariably creating a hierarchy of prestige or rank. In principle, the subdelegation of authority can go on indefinitely, but there are always practical limitations. In very large organizations, the hierarchy tends to become cumbersome—the line of communication has a large number of transmission points, and a mass of detailed decisions converge upon the top positions; but this problem is partly avoided if each successively lower position in practice deals with questions of detail within the framework set by more general orders received from superordinate positions. A more difficult problem is presented by the many quite different areas of technical specialization that must be coordinated, and various "functional" schemes of organization in addition to, or in combination with, the line

[7] Richard Eells, *The Government of Corporations* (New York: Free Press, 1962).

[8] For simplicity, we are concentrating upon the industrial corporation, since it illustrates all the essential features of the fully developed corporate organization.

organization have developed in answer to it. Departmentalization represents only a slight departure—several functional areas may be mapped out and placed under subexecutives while otherwise straight-line authority delegation is practiced. Somewhat greater modification of the line structure leads to a line-staff scheme, in which technical specialists act as advisors at various levels but do not themselves hold authority. At the theoretical extreme, every office of authority would also be an office of specialized technical competence: the *technical hierarchy* and the *authority hierarchy* would coincide. However, this splintering of direction and control creates such numerous problems in organization that it is rarely approached in the industrial corporation. Instead, there typically emerges a basic line organization, which is then broken into functional branches and combined with a staff (technical) organization.

The internal differentiation of authority and of areas of competence in the large industrial corporation is highly developed. It is possible to identify six fairly distinct groups: (1) executives or top managers, (2) technical specialists, (3) junior line supervisors ("middle management"), (4) secretarial and clerical workers, (5) first-line supervisors (foremen), (6) shop and bench workers.[9] The whole structure exhibits regularities of belief and behavior that bear a remarkable resemblance to those of nonindustrial organizations of large size. In fact, what we have here is a particular subtype of bureaucratic social organization.

The notion of bureaucracy is an ideal type, which by definition never exactly fits any particular organizations. Organizations are not bureaucratic *or* nonbureaucratic; there are differing kinds and degrees of bureaucracy. It is an interesting commentary upon the importance of culturally standardized "blind spots" that many people still think of bureaucracy as confined to political government; but viewed as a descriptive label rather than as a curse word, it simply refers to the archetype of formal, functionally rational organizations that may be as diverse in other respects as schools, churches, universities, armies, and business enterprises. As an ideal type, bureaucracy is a formal order that coordinates the diverse but interdependent activities of persons into a definite organizational pattern. As described in detail by Max Weber and many others,[1] bureaucratic organization is defined by the following main characteristics:

---

9 Moore, *Industrial Relations, op. cit.*, p. 120. This is Moore's adaptation of the categories used by F. J. Roethlisberger.

1 All roads here start from Max Weber's *Wirtschaft und Gesellschaft* (Tubingen: J. C. B. Mohr, 1922), pp. 650–678. See also: Karl Mannheim, *Man and Society in an Age of Reconstruction* (New York: Harcourt, Brace & World, 1940), esp. pp. 46–49, 53–60, 319–325; Everett C. Hughes, "Institutional Office and the Person," *American Journal of Sociology*, XLIII, 3 (November 1937). The more recent literature is voluminous. For example: Peter M. Blau, *Bureaucracy in Modern Society* (New York: Random House, 1956); Reinhard Bendix, *Work and Authority in Industry* (New York: Wiley, 1956); Peter M. Blau and W. Richard Scott, *Formal Organizations* (San Francisco: Chandler, 1962); Michel Crozier, *The Bureaucratic Phenomenon* (Chicago: University of Chicago Press, 1964); Bertram M. Gross, *The Managing of Organizations*, Vols. I–II (New York: Free Press, 1964); James G. March and Herbert A. Simon, *Organizations* (New York: Wiley, 1958); Anthony Downs, *Inside Bureaucracy* (Boston: Little, Brown, 1967); Victor A. Thompson, *Modern Organization* (New York: Knopf, 1961).

*Characteristics of*
*Bureaucracy*

1. There is, typically, an explicit definition of official activities considered to inhere in specific statuses; areas of authority and competence tend to be formally specified.
2. There is a high degree of specialization of functions and duties.
3. Authority inheres in the *office* rather than in the person.
4. There is a clear separation between "private" or personal activities and the activities carried out within the organization or in its name. For instance, the officeholder must spend his entire working time in the service of the organization. There is, furthermore, a sharp distinction between his personal possessions and the goods of the organization; private budget and organizational budget are two different worlds.
5. The functioning of various offices within the organization is governed by generalized, abstract, but definite rules, which involve the categorizing of problems.
6. Procedure tends to be formal and impersonal, especially in dealings between superordinate and subordinate offices. Communications are recorded; forms of communication are stereotyped and ritualized; the intrusion of "personal" elements into organizational activities tends to be discouraged.
7. In an ideal bureaucracy, the selection of all except the highest policy-determining officials is by appointment (rather than election, inheritance, and so on) on the basis of technical competence.
8. Organization is hierarchical. Every office is a link in a chain of authority, and as a general rule, communications (orders, requests, information) pass through all the offices intermediate to the positions of the communicants.
9. The structure of offices is maintained by a relatively explicit and rigid discipline, as is shown by the imposition of various sanctions expected to encourage accuracy, caution, punctuality, methodical procedure, close coordination of activities.
10. A less essential but common characteristic of bureaucracy is provision for security of tenure among the officials—promotion by seniority, annual-wage plans, pensions, and fixed-tenure provisions that hold in the absence of quite gross negligence or misconduct.
11. There is a frequently noted tendency to maintain a body of "secrets of the office;" many organizational details are closely guarded against observation by outsiders.

These features have, of course, both "negative" and "positive" consequences. The alleged advantages include precision, reliability, functional rationality, accurate coordination of large systems of activity, and minimization of personal elements irrelevant to purposes of the organization. The disadvantages include tendencies toward ritualism, multiplication of procedures beyond the point of maximum efficiency, lack of adaptability to new situations, constricted and impoverished work-life, and excessive power striving.[2]

[2] Max Weber was overly impressed with the "positive" features. Modern studies show both the prevalence of deviations from the model he proposed and very important

A widespread development of bureaucratic structures has been a conspicuous feature of industrial societies during the past century. Since Weber's analysis, it has been recognized that bureaucracy is by no means limited to the state but is a prominent characteristic of the highly developed economic systems of modern nations. The "discovery" of bureaucracy has even led to claims that a revolutionary shift in power is occurring—not from the capitalists to the proletariat, but from the capitalists to the bureaucrats. This thesis contains unacceptable elements of exaggeration and oversimplification, but the tremendous growth in the social importance of bureaucracy cannot be doubted.

Our attention will be focused upon the *formal* organization. Recent research, it is true, has conclusively demonstrated the pervasiveness of *informal* organization that invariably accompanies the formal structure. It is simply not possible to predict behavior in any organization from its "blueprint" formal structure; and a major part of the management of an enterprise is necessarily devoted to understanding and dealing with groupings, relationships, sentiments, and practices that are not formalized or even explicit. Nevertheless, our present interest is primarily in the formal structure, partly because informal organization will be discussed in Chapter XII, and partly because the formal order is the indispensable framework that channelizes even the informal patterns.

Some of the most important features of bureaucracy appear to be inseparable from any large-scale organization. "Organization" means coordination and predictability. Where, as in the large industrial corporation, large numbers of people are simultaneously engaged in highly specialized activities focused upon a single objective, the "need for coordination" is enhanced while its attainment is rendered more difficult. With increasing size of organization, the diffuse and informal methods of communication and control that work well in small groups become increasingly hazardous and ineffective: coordination is hampered by overlapping authorities, gaps in communication, contradictory orders, and vague and shifting loci of responsibility. Sheer size of organization is enough to create *indirect* communication: face-to-face contact of all the communicating parties is impossible. As indirect lines of communication are set up, the formality of the organization is increased; for instance, communications must be authenticated when they pass between persons who have no direct contacts.

*Size* plus *specialization*, therefore, tend to produce bureaucracy. Specialization of function complicates the problem of coordination by necessitating both indirect communication and special coordinating centers.

The extent to which "economies of scale" give a competitive advantage to larger firms clearly varies among different types of businesses and lines of production. There is no doubt that there are limits to such economies—otherwise, we might expect to find corporations more gigantic than now exist—but real advantages often do accrue with larger size. In addition to

---

stressful and inefficient features in bureaucratic organization. For instance, the alleged "predictability" often holds only for those relatively high in the hierarchy, not for those subject to their often shifting and amorphous policies.

direct economies (derived from technological characteristics, greater bargaining power, efficiencies of specialization, and other similar factors), the larger corporations enjoy greater protection for regularized and stable administration.[3]

The modern industrial corporation tends to be bureaucratic not only because it is large and highly specialized but also because the workers are "separated from the means of production" and are dependent upon paid employment. Such is the case in American industry; and it is reinforced by the absentee ownership discussed above—ownership that necessitates delegation of authority from stockholders to directors and executives and from these to still other subordinate officers, with subsequent subdivision of authority and need for coordination. The existence of a "final control group" (whether "ownership" or "management") is thus crucial to hierarchical organization. If the organization were not responsible *as a whole* to some control group, there would not be the same pressure for unitary policy and control, and such coordination as remained could operate through the interaction of *functionally* specialized offices rather than through a chain of command. We could imagine, for instance, that a corporation holding all its own stock and manufacturing a single standardized product for an absolutely stable market might attain such equilibrium that there would hardly be a sharply graded hierarchy. But actually, the industrial corporation is responsible to control groups and typically produces several products for changing markets and with changing costs. The need for coordinated *changes* to meet new conditions pushes the organization toward hierarchy. Thus, the wider the extent of functional specialization, the more likely it is that authority will be vertically subdelegated.

The need for coordination arises whenever there are unlike activities carried on by different actors that are all necessary to attain a common objective. The existence of the need for coordination tends to increase the degree of centralization of authority. The existence of a common objective also favors centralized authority, however, through another set of processes —processes that at the same time work toward the development of a hierarchy of prestige. For individuals or collectivities that can promote the common objective by giving direction and advice create obligations among those thus helped, and the deference exacted by different "experts" and "authorities" typically forms a graded series.[4]

Bureaucratic formality arises partly from hierarchy itself. We already have seen that hierarchy involves differentiated functions, formal rules, and routines. But hierarchy further implies giving and receiving orders, with all the attendant possibilities of friction and conflict. By formality of procedure, "arbitrary" action can be limited, responsibility located and fixed, and personal involvement minimized. Furthermore, formality maintains verti-

---

[3] Oscar Grusky, "Corporate Size, Bureaucratization, and Managerial Succession," *American Journal of Sociology*, LXVII, 3 (November 1961), 267. Very large corporations, however, have higher frequencies of administration turnover ("succession") at top levels.

[4] Cf. Peter M. Blau, *Exchange and Power in Social Life* (New York: Wiley, 1964), p. 193.

cal "social distance" between statuses, so that very diverse and perhaps sharply incompatible persons can nevertheless interact sufficiently to fulfill their organizational functions. Formality, thus, not only "protects" the subordinates from arbitrariness but also supports the impersonal authority and prestige of the superiors and so helps maintain hierarchical control.

Of course, the corporation has both bureaucratic and nonbureaucratic features, and there is no doubt that in several important ways corporations are less bureaucratic than government agencies of similar size. Corporations are less likely to be tightly regulated by laws and written rules; a smaller proportion of the personnel are officials appointed on the basis of competitive formal tests of merit,[5] particularism is more prevalent, stable careers are perhaps somewhat less frequent, and it is likely that changes in procedures and structure are more frequent.

Every first-hand study of large economic enterprises documents not only the "informal" character of formally bureaucratic organizations, but also the power struggles, deviant behavior, and conflicts that do not appear in the structure of explicit goals and norms.[6] Also, in all except the very large and long-established quasi-public corporations, it is taken for granted that family connections and other nontechnical factors will be important in determining status and rewards within the organization; thus, what would be condemned as nepotism in the government corporation is "normal" in some business corporations—although the *larger* corporations show less nepotism and more universalism (less ethnic or racial discrimination) than is found in smaller concerns. Again, the business corporation has to show return on investment rather than simply stay within an appropriation. Finally, relations with employees, especially rank-and-file workers, obviously differ. (Corporate labor relations will be discussed in the next section.) Even with all these differences there is still an impressive similarity between the business corporation and governmental organizations of similar size. This similarity is significant, for it means much of "free enterprise" ideology is simply not applicable to most employees of large industrial corporations.

In the cultural theory of economic individualism, a person's rewards were earned by free competition in the market; effort and shrewdness were indexed by economic gain derived from a relatively impersonal process; personal success was not directly dependent upon a particular person's opinion of one's ability. Thus, if John Jones, merchant, was able to buy cheap and sell dear, he was an economic success, no matter how intensely he might be disliked by competitor Sam Smith. But if Sam Smith is a higher official in a corporate hierarchy, Jones' chances for promotion may not be unaffected by Smith's opinion of him on other than technical grounds. The banal example takes on significance when related to the dominance of the corporation; in established industries, the primary career-pattern is promo-

*[margin notes, handwritten:]*
*I in "Free Enterprise" Individual carves niche*
*I in corporation Individual is promoted within bureaucracy*

---

[5] It is not necessary to elaborate the fact that factors other than scores on official examinations are also important in government service.

[6] Melville Dalton, *Men Who Manage: Fusions of Feeling and Theory in Administration* (New York: Wiley, 1959).

tion in the *bureaucratic scale,* not competitive success as an individual entrepreneur. Therefore, every step up (or down) the ladder is dependent upon the decision of a particular superior office.[7] And positions may be assigned partly on the basis of class or ethnic background and family or clique affiliations. The corporation may develop informal groupings which act like "political machines" in rewarding members and excluding outsiders. At the logical extreme, membership in a particular informal group becomes a prerequisite for advancement. Though this extreme may not be reached in the large corporation—indeed, it is probably less important there than in small or medium-sized businesses—its institutional importance is difficult to overemphasize. Impersonal competitive placement in the open market employs universalistic norms, applying to individuals regardless of their particular group affiliations; *particularistic* norms, on the contrary, make group memberships and personal relations determine social position and economic reward. When business was small, outside regulation was minimal, and the market was competitive, the universal norms were continually reinforced by the character of day-to-day economic activity. In the large economic enterprise of today, however, universalistic standards depend upon deliberate policy. It is no longer even seemingly "automatic." Wherever the large corporation extends in American economic life, purposive control replaces the diffuse mechanisms of the market. *Cultural* structure becomes *social* organization, and this change is perhaps one of the deepest meanings of an age of corporateness.

The vertical organization of the large business concern in most cases manifests a fairly clear "breaking point" between the office and the shop—between the executive, clerical, staff, and supervisory force on the one hand and the rank-and-file workers on the other. Yet within both these broad divisions there is a continuous gradation of income, authority, and prestige. There is also both division and substantial overlapping in the social origins of those in the top and those in the intermediate ranks. For example, Warner and Abegglen have shown that just over one-half of major executives of corporations are sons of executives or business owners.[8] Greatly overrepresented are the sons of fathers in the professions and business; greatly underrepresented are sons of farmers and laborers. As compared with the study of Taussig and Joslyn (1928), the figures for the 1950's and 1960's show lessened recruitment from executive backgrounds and increased proportions from professions and other occupations. The many persons in intermediate levels constitute a significant portion of the new middle classes discussed in Chapter V. Obviously, these are "middle class" in a very different sense from the self-employed owners of small business that political rhetoric praises as the "backbone of the country." To place the white-collar employees of the new business bureaucracies in the same category as the old entrepreneurial groups obscures at least as much as it reveals. The salaried employee differs from the stereotyped "businessman" in life situation,

---

[7] Except, of course, as rights of promotion are limited by seniority provisions or other impersonal and automatic criteria.

[8] *Big Business Leaders in America, op. cit.*

avenue of success, discipline and self-direction, specific goals, and motivations. These are some results of the new modes of American economic organization.

### THE PROFIT MOTIVE

To understand the changing structure and actual modes of operation of the postindustrial American economy requires a close examination of the conventional wisdom which holds that something called the profit motive is the indispensable essence upon which the system rests. This is not merely a popular folk-belief. In an explicitly procapitalistic exposition, a standard textbook on comparative economic systems lists among the essential components of capitalism: the guidance of economic behavior by principles of maximizing gain, private property, inheritance of property, freedom of individual economic action, competition, and the "profit motive."[9] The ideal-typical model requires several modifications to fit modern developments. Even in the nineteenth century the significance of profit as a mainspring of economic activity was not total. An unknown but undoubtedly substantial amount of wealth in the United States has not come from entrepreneurial ingenuity in the pursuit of profits but rather from the "pure rent" accruing to persons who simply held on to inherited property that has increased in worth through population growth and general economic development. Care in choosing one's ancestors is hardly part of the profit motive, nor is the accident of birth in a period of economic escalation. Love of gain is not the profit motive, nor is it unique to capitalism.

Under the strict theory of private property and free competition, business takes all the profits it can get and bears all losses, even to the extent of complete failure. But in the present economy of huge interlocking units, it is very doubtful if any large sector of the economy will be allowed to collapse. The tremendous interdependence of the existing system is such that unchecked deflation quickly spreads cumulatively from one sector to another. Thus, in the Great Depression of the 1930's the threatened collapse of American agriculture had immediate and severe impacts upon life insurance companies and other large holders of farm mortgages, upon the agricultural implement industry and upon many other strategic industries. Total bankruptcy of the nation's railroads and airlines would drag along with it a host of indispensable financial organizations. Whatever the economic advantages of thoroughgoing depression in "purging" the economy, the main centers of political and social power are not likely to permit unrestrained losses so long as there is a going social order at all. The Great Depression reduced the real income per capita to somewhere near the level of 1900. No real revolution occurred. But any present-day government would certainly try every fiscal and regulatory measure at hand before permitting such a violent assault on living standards, vested interests, and general social morale.

Thus, the risk-taking functions of private business are being shifted

9 Loucks, *op. cit.*, pp. 22–40. In fact, the profit motive is said to be "the heart of the institutions of capitalism" (p. 40).

to the larger society through governmental intervention, with corresponding controls and limitations upon business, and the "profit motive" ceases to that extent to regulate economic activity. Correspondingly, subsidies and subventions and various kinds of politico-legal protections may reduce the incentives of profit in the full technical sense.

Otherwise, too, the profit motive has been radically transformed. Although business is expected to produce profit, it is no longer universally true that "profits are the reward of enterprise." The wage workers and salaried officialdom of a corporation are motivated by profits only indirectly, in that their jobs require continued solvency in the total enterprise. Insofar as the direct recipients of profits, the stockholders, do not manage the business, profits can not directly inspire effort and efficiency. Profit making is a second-order control so to speak, and may little "motivate" those actually operating the business. In a situation in which a few very large firms dominate a market, the really major decisions of managers will rarely be dictated by the immediate economic calculus alone. Of course, to say that considerations other than a strict interpretation of short-term profit enter into economic policies of corporations is not to say that profit ceases to be of great concern, nor is it to imply that corporation executives become economically irrational, whimsical, or sentimental. They do not. Indeed, the corporation has special facilities for securing and analyzing information and specialized norms of responsibility that tend to reinforce the norm of seeking rationally for some profit-maximization solution.[1] Also, a large proportion of major administrative officials in large corporations (nearly one-half in the 1950's), do themselves own stock; and many have holdings substantial enough to provide strong direct incentives to maximize returns. Nevertheless, most salaried employees in large corporations are far removed from the daily test of market profits. And in any case the separation of ownership from control shows that the "profit motive" is not a *motive* at all but an institutional goal; it is not a psychological state but a social condition. The fully developed corporate form today is likely to be manned by people with goals and incentives not so different from those of the personnel of nonprofit organizations. This fact is not envisaged in the traditional theories of property and economic incentives, and neither the law nor popular thought has yet come to terms with its implications.[2]

In the long run, an equally important development may prove to be the growth of flourishing nonprofit sectors of the economy. Much of the kind of excitement, prestige or glamour that attached to business entrepreneurship from the 1880's through the 1920's now is generated by activities in science, technology, education, and government, many of them carried out in nonprofit organizations. The "nonprofit" sector of the economy in-

[1] Thus, it may be argued that the corporation may be less likely than the individual entrepreneur to act in economic ignorance or to be swayed by personally idiosyncratic goals, values or interests.

[2] Cf. Moore's comment: "The ideology of 'free enterprise' is still widely expressed by corporation executives who are not in fact engaged in anything approaching free enterprise in the traditional sense, and is facilitated by judicial interpretation of corporate ownership of private property." "The Emergence of New Property Conceptions in America," *op. cit.*, p. 49.

cludes not only government at all levels, but a multitude of hospitals and other health-serving agencies, as well as organizations devoted to education, research, philanthropy, welfare services, and some cooperatives. This sector has grown rapidly in the years since World War II and now accounts for more than a third of all employment.[3] The possibility can now be seen that a future economy might center much less than now in manufacturing and commerce and much more in research, development, teaching, and direct services in medicine, recreation, art, social welfare, and the like.[4]

Corporate holdings of nonprofit agencies have been growing rapidly. Of the total stockholdings in all United States corporations in 1957, domestic individuals (excluding personal trust funds and nonprofit organizations) held 71 percent, "institutions" held 10 percent, and personal trust funds and nonprofit organization owned 16 percent.[5]

The increase of stock ownership by nonprofit organizations, and especially by the rapidly expanding pension funds, has been heralded as signifying a basic shift in the control of corporate property. But clearly, much depends upon how the votes attached to these stockholdings are used. In general, it would seem that the holdings of pension funds, universities, hospitals, professional associations, and the like, have not been used to challenge managerial control or to alter basically the policies of the profit-oriented corporations.

Many contemporary observers have been impressed with the similarities between large "private" corporations and large agencies of government. In both types of organizations there is a high development of bureaucracy; similar problems and procedures characterize management; and even the goals sought contain many similar elements. Both types are political in the sense of being concentrations of legitimized power. Yet a hard second look indicates that the differences that remain are vitally important. Contrary to many impressions, and to much "public relations" ideology, the large corporation has not "socialized itself," if by this phrase one means that it has ceased to seek profits aggressively or that in the absence of public negative sanctions it voluntarily refrains from profitable actions that have socially undesirable consequences. Also, in spite of all governmental regulation and influence, the private firm is far less subject to public supervision than are public agencies. It is impossible to avoid the recognition that managers of large corporate enterprises enjoy a very large scope of choice in making decisions that affect the entire economy, often with substantial political effects and with multiple impacts upon other aspects of the total society. The concentrated power of General Motors or U.S. Steel to set into motion an inflationary price-wage spiral, or to check an incipient recession by capital expansion, or to affect the national death rate—these are awesome powers that are little subject to any direct "democratic" con-

[3] Eli Ginzberg, Dale L. Hiestand, and Beatrice G. Reubens, *The Pluralistic Economy* (New York: McGraw-Hill, 1965).

[4] Cf. Robert L. Heilbronner, "The Future of Capitalism," *Commentary*, 41, 4 (April 1966), 23–35.

[5] Paul P. Harbrecht, *Pension Funds and Economic Power* (New York: Twentieth Century Fund, 1959).

trol. Whatever one may believe the "responsibility" of the large corporation should be, the actual existence of its enormous discretionary power is not in dispute: outside of government no other type of organization so decisively shapes modern American life.

## LABOR RELATIONS AND LABOR ORGANIZATIONS

Anything like a complete picture of American labor relations is too broad and complex to be given here.[6] We merely outline the basic institutional elements without descriptive detail, concentrating upon *industrial* labor, ignoring the migratory agricultural worker, the domestic service worker, the employee of the small shop, the remnants of independent crafts, and many others, important as they are. For most wage earners are employed in industry; there the crucial problems of power and conflict lie; and there the pattern is increasingly set for labor in other fields—for example, the rapidly growing service and clerical occupations are being increasingly mechanized and industrialized.

Early American labor relations developed in an economy with rich resources and scanty population; and these in combination with an open class-structure and a democratic political order have given a number of distinctive features to the American case.[7] The absence of feudal or other traditionalized social ties facilitated an early and thoroughgoing commercialization of labor. Labor became a market commodity in an individualistic economy. Unionism developed late, and against strong opposition. The extraordinary amount of violence accompanying the efforts of workers to organize has stamped labor-employer relations with a peculiarly American conflict-psychology. Yet the underlying dynamics of the labor movement are broadly similar to those of western Europe, reflecting similar institutional conditions.

As American industry developed and the wage earner became a factory "hand," labor relations became capitalistic market relations. Though ideology and law assumed equality of bargaining power, the individual worker was obviously not equal in bargaining power to his employer. The worker, personally free but propertyless,[8] was fully exposed to the insecurities of a fluctuating job market. As new large-scale industries built factories, the workers were recruited from European immigrants and American hinterlands. While industrialization was transforming American society

---

[6] For examples of recent works see Robert Dubin, *Working Union-Management Relations: The Sociology of Industrial Relations* (Englewood Cliffs, N.J.: Prentice-Hall, 1958); William H. Leiserson, *American Trade Union Democracy* (New York: Columbia University Press, 1959); Miller and Form, *op. cit.*; William H. Form and Delbert C. Miller, *Industry, Labor, and Community* (New York: Harper & Row, 1960).

[7] See the classic reference: John R. Commons, David J. Saposs, *et al.*, *History of Labour in the United States*, 4 vols. (New York: Macmillan, 1921–1935); cf. Maurice F. Neufeld, "The Sense of History and the Annals of Labor," *Reprint Series-No. 118* (Ithaca, N.Y.: New York State School of Industrial & Labor Relations at Cornell University, n.d.), pp. 1–13.

[8] As Briefs put it, his status became permanent but his job was not. Goetz A. Briefs, *The Proletariat* (New York: McGraw-Hill, 1937), chap. 3.

(from about 1880[9] to 1919), most workers were first-generation factory workers; their fathers had been farm people, and they entered industry as raw recruits for whom factory discipline was a sharp break with previous modes of life. Ethnic cleavages hampered coherent, united, and disciplined labor organization. Outside the skilled crafts and some occupations dominated by skilled European workers—for instance, brewing, the garment trades, and some portions of the coal mining industry—the labor force was constituted mainly of heterogeneous, unorganized, relatively unskilled workers without factory experience, who hoped soon to escape from wage work. They were spread over a vast territory, often disunited in creed and language, subject to incessant shifts in the labor market and rapid technological innovations. Their thinking was apt to be individualistic, stressing equality of opportunity, individual responsibility, and advancement through personal efforts. In the face of implacable resistance by employers, then, it is small wonder that unionism, especially industrial unionism, developed slowly and with great difficulty.[1] Although socialistic and syndicalistic movements did have some influence, most workers did not adapt a "radical" ideology.

These workers confronted a system in which employers were institutionally committed to treating labor as a commodity and were bound to accept no other obligations to the employee than paying wages.[2] In the pure type, capitalistic labor relations are segmental, not inclusive; only the cash nexus, the money wage, controls; the employee is free to quit his job and the employer is free to turn the worker out upon the streets; not personalized ties nor *noblesse oblige*, but the market bargain is the bond.

Now, economic relations as defined in this system are contractual, that is, segmental, limited, explicit, and formally voluntary. A contract is supposedly to the "interest" of all parties concerned, benefiting each; the obligations and rights are stated; and limitations are placed upon any attempt to broaden the stipulated terms. In all these particulars, contractual relations contrast sharply with kinship relations, friendships, and other "particularistic" relationships.

Being contractual, industrial employment establishes no nexus of common loyalties, interests, or obligations beyond the segmental, impersonal exchange of wages for services, impersonal in that no account is taken of values of individuals qua individuals. Impersonal relations thus depend upon limited "interests" such as economic exchange; and insofar as these interests are unstable, the relations based upon them will be transitory. In

---

9 After the first large craft union (the Knights of Labor, organized in 1869) had foundered on the rocks of a disastrous political effort, the American Federation of Labor dominated the labor movement from the late 1880's until the emergence of the CIO in the 1930's.

1 "Where no labor unions exist, where ethnic groups are strong and segregated, and where industrialism is just beginning, the social characteristics of employees count most heavily in shaping their economic destinies." (Miller and Form, *op. cit.*, pp. 441–442.)

2 Znaniecki, *op. cit.*, p. 615: "A perfect worker in the capitalistic enterprise is one who does exactly anything he is told to do, and does it for no other reason than because he is paid to do it."

our economy, mobility among jobs is high: for example, in the single year of 1955, 15 percent of all workers in industry changed jobs—representing over 10 million individual moves—and nearly half of these moves involved both a change in occupation and in industry.[3]

In strict capitalistic theory, the employer has no more right to expect "loyalty" from his employees than the latter have to expect security from him. This is an *institutional* fact, not a matter of the motives of particular individuals. In a dynamic economy, with technological change and short-term economic fluctuations, the contractual system of labor produces insecurity for the isolated individual worker. Just as any form of personal dependence is alien to contractual money-wage employment, so security of status has no institutional basis in the relations of workers to *particular* employers. In addition, the individual worker's bargaining power is strikingly unequal to his employer's. Without a mythical "natural identity of interests" between employer and employees, this weakness of bargaining power further contributes to the economic insecurity of the unorganized workers. Thus, unionization is not most prevalent among the poorest and most oppressed workers, who would seem to need it most as a means of amassing collective power for self-defense and for pursuit of advantage. The most deprived workers lack the economic and social resources to create, by themselves, the needed organization. Even within established unions, the most active workers tend to be those of higher socioeconomic standing.[4]

These basic characteristics of capitalistic labor systems are certainly not peculiar to the United States. However, other features of American labor relations do not have the same cross-cultural generality: the slow unionization, the prevalence of violence, the persistence of craft unionism and the lateness of industrial unionization, and the lack of "class consciousness" and political emphasis among labor. All these are interrelated. Thus, the open resources, expanding economy, and fluid class structure during the nineteenth century delayed the formation of a permanent wage-worker stratum. Ethnic and racial heterogeneity split labor. The lack of traditional solidarities and traditional ties to employers favored an individualistic, competitive outlook among workers as well as employers. In turn, the lack of labor solidarity minimized its political effectiveness and left the government—including the important judiciary—sympathetic to the needs and interests of business groups, with consequent further barriers to the organized articulation of labor's interests. Employers held what Laski calls "the atomic view of industrial power"[5]—the conception of a business as the unitary, private possession of its owners and managers and of the workers as "tools" having no claim or voice in determining the conditions of their work. Workers believed in (or at least hoped for) individual advancement, and held a strongly equalitarian creed. Both parties had a firm sense of their "rights,"

[3] Miller and Form, *op. cit.*, pp. 66–67.

[4] William Spinrad, "Correlates of Trade Union Participation," *American Sociological Review*, 25, 2 (April 1960), pp. 237–244.

[5] Harold J. Laski, *The American Democracy: A Commentary and Interpretation* (New York: Viking, 1948), p. 203.

and these rights were often incompatible. In this sense, labor relations were, and are, *moral* relations; and the bitterness and violence so common in American industrial history stem from conflicting values. To the clash of pecuniary interest has often been added a sense of moral outrage, for what is frequently thought to be at stake is an institutional principle—the "right of a man to run his own business as he sees fit," the "right of the worker to a decent wage," the claim of labor to have a voice in the internal affairs of the enterprise.

The United States, since its nineteenth-century experience with "radical" labor movements, has had no national *politically* radical unions. The older craft unions have remained thoroughly "businesslike." They fought to win members the right to bargain collectively and, then, the best pay and working conditions possible within the system—all this against formidable opposition. The labor-union movement developed by continual battle rather than peaceful expansion, yet the craft-type union has typically acted on "business principles;" it became another business enterprise, with labor as its product. Even the newer industrial unions have concentrated upon specific grievances and immediate tangible benefits rather than upon basic reshaping of the system.

The great diversity among organizations ordinarily lumped together as "labor unions" dictates caution in attempts to make generalizations about them and warns of the dangers of unwittingly being captured by stereotypes. Unions vary in internal structure: centralized or decentralized, hierarchical or not, bureaucratic or particularistic. They differ greatly in the scope of their activities and interests—from a narrow focus on bargaining for wages to a comprehensive social and political program. Some have an elaborate political or religious ideology; others strictly avoid any explicit ideological commitments.

There are local unions restricted to a single plant. There are craft unions that include only workers in particular occupations or groups of related occupations—electricians, plumbers, carpenters, and joiners. There are industrial unions that seek to include all occupations in a main industry—automobile manufacturing, steel. Finally, there are unions that attempt to organize workers in an entire geographic area, including diverse occupations and industries; perhaps the two closest approximations in recent American experience are represented by the Teamsters Union and District 50 of the United Mine Workers. Thus, unions have many different purposes and their activities have multiple consequences. When successful in bargaining they are "business" units, selling labor for maximum returns in wages and other economic benefits. They may enhance job-security, promote efficiency, retard technological change, restrict or expand opportunity for members of minority groups, influence elections and legislation, provide a sense of dignity and responsibility, reduce social conflict, enhance class solidarity.

When industrial unionism at long last was able to overcome the entrenched resistance of heavy industry in the 1930's, it did signalize an important change in several vital areas of the economy. Covering entire industries instead of specialized trades, the large industrial unions were able to bargain with the giant corporations.[6] Mass unionism is a reaction to mass industry and to the concentration of economic power in the large corporations and their interwoven communities-of-interest. It reflects the rise of a populous stratum of "permanent" industrial workers—fathers and sons of workers. Individually powerless, the industrial workers are powerful when welded into United Steelworkers of America, or United Automobile Workers, or United Mine Workers. When big business and big labor collide— as they must, for the sources of conflict are built into their institutions— the struggle tests our society's capacity to maintain a tightly articulated economy within the bounds of democracy. Opposition of interests, disagreement on issues, and overt conflict are not extraneous or accidental aspects of the modern industrial system. They are not primarily caused by bad men, misunderstanding, poor communication, or agitators. Nor would these oppositional processes disappear "if only techniques of better human relations were used." Opposition of interests is intrinsic to the institutional positions of employers and employees. (Of course, their mutual dependence is also built into the system). The labor market does not and cannot completely harmonize these interests under all circumstances.[7]

The conspicuous and often dramatic processes of contract negotiations and strikes and lockouts tend to monopolize public attention; consequently, the impression is created that "collective bargaining" consists exclusively of these processes. But the greater bulk of union-management relations inheres in the day-to-day bargaining over specific grievances and particular interpretations of the contract. It must be noted also that up until the last half-century, many strikes were ad hoc, spontaneous events that were not organized by unions at all. In the modern period, furthermore, even in times of greatest strike-activity, very little net working time is lost by strikes; and the most disruptive forms of strikes are exceedingly rare. The United States has never had a general strike; and even the agitational, quasi-political strike is almost unknown.

Popular impressions, strongly influenced by the reporting of the mass media, often suggest that strikes and collective bargaining are exclusively struggles over wages, hours, and fringe benefits. The implication is easily drawn that unions serve only to deal with these allocative problems. These impressions are misleading. There would be an important place for unions among our economic organizations even were wages and related matters not at issue. For the very first and most fundamental significance of the union is in its attainment of the right to protect its members against arbitrary

[6] Wilson and Kolb put the situation neatly in their statement that the unions become "rivals of the corporation for control of the labor market within the old institutional framework." *Op. cit.*, p. 554.

[7] "Basic to an understanding of industrial conflict is the realization that it is inevitable in highly industrialized societies which are not centrally and autocratically controlled." (Miller and Form, *op. cit.*, p. 369). On the other hand, the prominence of unions should not lead us to overlook the extent to which labor is still unorganized. For example, the 18 million union members in 1965 constituted less than one-third of the number of nonagricultural workers. The proportion unionized varies greatly from one locality to another, e.g., from over 50 percent in the State of Washington to less than 10 percent in North Carolina. Unions have been able to make only slow progress in the South.

disciplinary action, including capriciously punitive demotion and discharge. Only through a socially legitimated organization of workers has some modicum of lawlike procedures been developed, as over against the absolute "managerial prerogatives" of nineteenth and early twentieth-century industrialism.

The industrial worker and his union cannot be understood in strictly economic terms, nor in terms of a society of farmers, small businesses and independent craftsmen. He does not own the materials or machines he works with, nor control the conditions of his work. He is subject to the rigid and detailed discipline of mechanized, repetitive operations. Although the alleged loss of skills and "sentiments of workmanship" is probably overemphasized in our time, machine tending is the archetype of industrial work. The skills of the factory operative often become obsolete through further mechanization. If he dreams of individual achievement, the corporate hierarchy is, to say the least, not easily climbable. His stake in the job is in wages, not rewards of achievement "cumulative, unique, tangible and recognized."[8]

The existence of the unbelievably numerous and specific job classifications in many large industrial concerns—often with each having its own wage schedule and associated prerogatives—raises interesting and difficult questions concerning the sources and consequences of such detailed classifications and gradations. The direct technical advantage of specialization alone surely is an insufficient ground. The interests of workers in distinguishing themselves from those of lesser skill undoubtedly plays a part.[9] The existence of the system may help to reduce solidarity among workers and to channelize effort into individual advancement rather than collective action. In at least some instances, managements have regarded a detailed hierarchy of jobs as a system for enhancing control of the workers.

Active participation in labor unions does not appear to be a simple manifestation either of "alienation" or of radical views on labor-management relations. For example, in a study of four CIO industrial union locals, it was found that the more active members were the older workers, having greater seniority (and lower occupational aspirations); in three of the four cases, the active were no more likely than the inactive members to be hostile toward management.[1] The fact that workers may be generally accepting of or favorable to both employing company and the union has been shown in a study of packinghouse workers.[2] Of course, this does not necessarily mean that there is deep loyalty to either.

A work force that is socially homogeneous in ethnic and class origins,

[8] The quoted phrase is from a stimulating unpublished paper, "The Social Situations of Farmer and Factory Worker," by Nelson N. Foote.

[9] Workers often seem to be intensely concerned with wage differentials that appear exceedingly small to the outsider. Internecine struggles at this level would seem to be a source of disunity of which corporate managers are likely to be aware.

[1] Arnold S. Tannenbaum and Robert L. Kahn, *Participation in Union Locals* (Evanston, Ill.: Row, Peterson, 1958).

[2] Theodore V. Purcell, *Blue Collar Man: Patterns of Dual Allegiance in Industry* (Cambridge, Mass.: Harvard University Press, 1966).

that has a set of special skills and considerable control of its tasks, and that has extensive informal social interaction among its members while remaining isolated from other populations—such a work force is likely to have a high potential for group solidarity and disciplined collective action.[3] In contrast, a heterogenous, unskilled population in a situation of work and residence that retards intragroup communication is likely to be passive or apathetic, except for sporadic outbursts in times of sudden mass deprivation or frustration. Homogenous and highly isolated groups of workers, especially in dangerous occupations, often develop a high propensity to radical orientations and to strikes—a situation illustrated by loggers, longshoremen, and miners. Therefore, in stressing the basic conditions that are similar for the great bulk of employees, it is of course also important not to lose sight of the very great variations in different industries and occupations. Thus, skilled craftsmen with strong unions in a relatively prosperous and stable industry are likely to have high job satisfaction, a sense of a meaningful degree of control over the job, and considerable group solidarity. None of these characteristics is likely in industries where unionization is weak, skill levels low, work monotonous, and insecurity great. Alienation and dissatisfaction of workers, therefore, differ markedly among the diverse environments of our complex economic system.[4]

In a society in which there is much vague talk about "affluence" and "high-paid workers," it is important to realize that *objective* insecurity has not been abolished. Thus, the common impression that a high degree of economic security is afforded by "social welfare" provisions of state and federal government appears to be greatly inflated. For example, the proportion of those wage losses resulting from work-connected injuries that is actually covered by workmen's compensation has decreased markedly since 1939.[5]

Basic to the mid-century situation affecting American labor has been the persistence in periods of rising real income and intense business activity of chronic high-level unemployment (averaging 5 percent throughout the late 1950's and early 1960's). Technological displacement and changing job requirements have raised the question as to whether the "private" economy may be permanently unable or unwilling to employ certain kinds of workers at all. This in turn raises the possibility of a permanent "subproletariat," cut off from participation in the world of work. For example, the persistence during the early 1960's of unemployment rates of 25 percent or more among urban Negro youths was a social "danger signal," noted by social scientists, that received little public attention or action until highlighted by widespread urban riots which suggested that all might not be well in the affluent society.

[3] Cf. Leonard R. Sayles, *Behavior of Industrial Work Groups* (New York: Wiley, 1958).

[4] For specific analyses of some examples see Robert Blauner, *Alienation and Freedom: The Factory Worker and His Industry* (Chicago: University of Chicago Press, 1964). Contrary to some stereotyped assumptions, workers in the most highly automated setting did not show a severe degree of alienation.

[5] Department of Health, Education and Welfare, *Social Security Bulletin*, 29, 10 (October 1966), 25.

Significantly, out of insecurity and the recognition of a collective fate of limited opportunity, the unions have developed automatic standardized criteria for job holding and wage levels. Seniority,[6] for example, is a security device that sacrifices nominal opportunities for competitive advancement in favor of an impersonal safeguard against chance and favoritism in promotion, pay, discharge, and lay-offs.[7] Likewise "equal pay for equal work," so firmly embedded in industrial unionism, rules out not only age and sex but also ability, character, and "need" as criteria for rates of pay. The striving of industrial workers for stability and certainty is further shown by more sophisticated schemes, such as pensions, annual-wage plans, and union contracts that tie wage levels to a cost-of-living index. In this connection, it seems likely that much American popular thinking on questions of motivation of economic behavior may still reflect the overly simple assumptions of earlier generations' economists. This seems notably true of the assumption that "insecurity" is a necessary goad for work and saving. Actually, both common observation and some research findings suggest that assurance of some minimal level of economic security encourages rather than discourages economic effort.[8] For example, some realistic hope of economic security in old age apparently tends to promote additional saving for retirement. There is no evidence to support the idea that participation in social security and other public and private[9] retirement, insurance, and pension plans lessens other types of savings. On the contrary, such limited research data as have been analyzed suggest that such participation probably tends to stimulate additional efforts to provide for the future.

The worker's economic situation is most fully significant in its effects on *social* status. Unionism and efforts toward quasi-professional status for industrial work partly represent a reaction to the low social esteem of factory work both by the "general public" and by the workers themselves. One of our widest valid generalizations from experience is that human beings seek to lead meaningful and respected lives. The total situation of the factory worker deprives him of many of the supports for a sense of personal integrity —for instance, the impersonality of "being treated as a number," the degrading of skills, the opprobrium directed toward "labor," the insecurity of employment, the lack of personal involvement in the task, or of participation in decision making. These are not all the relevant conditions, nor do all apply to all workers. But, beyond question, deprivation of status and self-esteem has been prominent in industrial history in this and other countries. Unionism is one reaction to the threat not only to the worker's

---

[6] Philip Selznick and Howard Vollmer, "Rule of Law in Industry: Seniority Rights," *Industrial Relations*, 1, 3 (May 1962), 97–116.

[7] "In the typical factory situation, with very limited opportunities for promotion on the basis of work performance, the evaluation of merits is often a negligible item in the determination of the individual's career, being much outweighed by seniority, union activity, personal relations, and schooling." Theodore Caplow, *op. cit.*, p. 112.

[8] George Katona, *The Mass Consumption Society* (New York: McGraw-Hill, 1964).

[9] George Katona, *Private Pensions and Individual Saving* (Ann Arbor: University of Michigan Press, 1965).

economic security but also to his total social security. Labor-management strife is only partly "dividing the spoils"—important as that is. Workers are social beings (even as executives are); and threats to their wages, tenure, or control of their own destiny are not just segmental and peripheral threats but endanger the only life open to them. In response, they form not only unions but many other defenses, such as elaborate informal organizations and group solidarities within the plant.[1] However, under modern conditions involving various kinds of automation and cybernetic systems, it will not always be true that solidarities are generated on the job. Some types of industrial work are so organized as to practically prevent informal group formation, for example, the automobile assembly line.[2] Some research indicates that few industrial workers attach high evaluation to their work-connected social interaction.[3] But job satisfaction is a fact of central significance in the lives of many, and perhaps most workers; and the great majority in nearly all industries and occupations do not express active dissatisfaction with their jobs.[4]

Aside from their immediate meaning to workers on the job, unions are mainly significant in the larger structure of industry as foci of bargaining power and as potential sources of political power. As struggle groups, unions have used various modes of organization and strategic devices. Craft unions of highly skilled workers can restrict the production of new workers by apprentice, training, and licensing provisions. Another less rigorous method for fencing in a labor market is the closed shop, which makes union membership a condition of employment. Such protective devices as insurance, relief, and retirement funds both strengthen the worker and improve the union's support and striking power. Above all, of course, the unions have relied as a last resort upon direct action: the strike, the sympathetic strike, the boycott, or various other means of concerted pressure. In earlier periods, the United States experienced a relatively high level of strikes of extended duration. However, it has shared in the common tendency among Western nations for strikes to decline during the most recent decades.[5] For example,

[1] This aspect of the sociology of industrial relations has been much investigated in recent years. Its substantial importance can be recognized without allowing it to overshadow either the bedrock problem of power or the encompassing institutional framework. Representative works dealing with this field include: F. J. Roethlisberger, *Management and Morale* (Cambridge, Mass.: Harvard University Press, 1941); Elton Mayo, *The Human Problems of an Industrial Civilization* (New York: Macmillan, 1933); Thomas North Whitehead, *Leadership in a Free Society* (Cambridge, Mass.: Harvard University Press, 1936); William F. Whyte, *Men at Work* (Homewood, Ill.: Dorsey Press, 1961).

[2] C. R. Walter and R. H. Guest, *The Man on the Assembly Line* (Cambridge, Mass.: Harvard University Press, 1952).

[3] Robert Dubin, "Industrial Workers' Worlds: A Study of the Central Life Interests of Industrial Workers," *Social Problems*, 3, 3 (January 1956) 136.

[4] Robert Blauner, "Work Satisfaction and Industrial Trends in Modern Society," in Walter Galenson and Seymour Martin Lipset (eds.), *Labor and Trade Unionism* (New York: Wiley, 1960), pp. 339–360, esp. p. 353.

[5] See Arthur M. Ross and Paul T. Hartman, *Changing Patterns of Industrial Conflict* (New York, London: Wiley, 1960).

*progressive decrease in strikes*

the percentage of workers involved in any strike yearly declined from 12 percent in 1945 to 7 percent in 1950, and to 3 percent in 1965.[6]

*employer device*

*associations of employers*

*lock-out*

*armed force*

*strike-breakers*

*legal action*

*propaganda*

*company union*

Against the methods of struggle used by the workers, the employers have used a great variety of devices, diverse in form but alike in intent and consequence: employers' associations, lock-outs, armed force, strike-breakers, company unions, legal action, propaganda. Where compromise and conciliation end, industrial conflict begins; this conflict at times has been violent, and many of the social devices of war are familiar to the American industrial scene.

*union objectives*

*wages*

*working cond.*

*fringe benef*

*security*

*oth.*

*bargaining power*

Specific objectives sought at one time or another by unions include not only higher wages but union recognition, closed shop, safety regulations and devices, shorter hours, paid vacations, health insurance, retirement benefits, job security, seniority provisions, improved physical conditions of work, grievance procedures or change in wage differentials. Both unions and employers concern themselves not only with immediate issues but also with longer-term bargaining positions. The rather elusive concept of "bargaining power" may be made somewhat more concrete by examining the conditions that influence it. For example, the management of a company in a highly competitive industry has less bargaining power than the monopolistic concern—except at the point at which it can deny further union demands by inconvertible evidence that it could not survive competitively if the demands were to be met. Similarily, management has the bargaining advantage in periods of depression and high rates of unemployment. Highly skilled workers tend to have a strong bargaining position. The relative power of unions is diminished when the dominant political party is generally predisposed to favor business interests even in the absence of specific legislation restrictive of unions. Where unions have demonstrated an effective capacity to sustain punishing strikes, their bargaining position is strengthened.

*negotiators not free*

*subject to membership, gov. etc.*

The internal structures of unions and employing units are highly relevant to their capacities for sustained struggle. When managers and union officials negotiate, they do not meet as completely free agents. Managers are subject to the claims and demands of stockholders, trade associations, financial agencies, customers, suppliers, and governments. Union officials must take into account their national (international) officials, local union councils, other unions, "public" reactions, governments—and the possibility that their decisions will be rejected by the members of their own union.

*stockholders*

*overlap of political power*

It is never safe to ignore the role of power in economic action. The modern labor union movement makes increasing use of its political power to reach its objectives.[7] The destruction of independent labor organizations in totalitarian countries shows how all the effective weapons of the workers can be swept from their hands through political action. The newer industrial unions take a far more vigorous and broad interest in legislation

[6] United States Bureau of the Census, *Statistical Abstract of the United States: 1967*, *op. cit.*, Table 353, p. 248.

[7] For a general survey see Lloyd G. Reynolds, *Labor Economics and Labor Relations*, 3rd ed. (Englewood Cliffs, N.J.: Prentice-Hall, 1959); Walter Galenson and Seymour Martin Lipset (eds.), *Labor and Trade Unionism* (New York: Wiley, 1960).

and politics than did the older "business unionism," partly because their relations with the corporations are so important for social order and social integration that the power of government is bound to be invoked in cases of prolonged conflict.[8]

The confrontation of large corporation and organized workers is a central fact of our economic system that is altogether alien to the ideology of an atomistic, free enterprise system. None of the traditional concepts— "private property," capital, labor, enterprise, individualism—has its old meaning. A corporation is not an "individual," an assembly-line workman is not an independent craftsman. Yet for the foreseeable future the corporation and the union will occupy the center of the stage unless the third member of the case, government, takes over the full play.[9] The potential directions in which the economic order can move deserve close inspection, since a reconstitution of the criteria of economic morality and legitimacy is already well under way.

This problem is usually posed as a choice between "liberal capitalism," "communism," or "fascism," but our present analysis indicates that this way of seeing the problem is not analytically productive. Nineteenth-century model capitalism met an unrecognized demise some time ago, and not even artificial respiration seems to hold much promise of success at this late date. On the other hand, authentically totalitarian concepts seem so incongruent with the American needs and traditions that one must rationally doubt that they necessarily represent the "wave of the future."

The effects of unions upon wages undoubtedly vary in different industries and periods, and expert analysts disagree as to whether unions on the whole increase "labor's share" of national income. The weight of the evidence seems to favor the view that unions are able to exert some real influence in securing higher and more stable returns to their members than would otherwise prevail.[1] Nevertheless, the labor movement as a whole has experienced a cessation of growth, after its rapid expansion from the 1930's to mid-century.[2] Faced with extensive automation, the decline in unskilled occupations, the rising proportion of white-collar workers and of women employees, and other factors unfavorable to mass unionization of the older types, the unions confront new and complex problems. For the decade beginning in 1956, the absolute number of union members remained almost constant in a rapidly increasing total work force. Industrial unions actually lost membership in some cases, and few gains were made. Only a small proportion of the rapidly growing ranks of white-collar and technical employees became

[8] Ross and Hartman, *op. cit.*; Harold W. Davey, *et al.* (eds.), *New Dimensions in Collective Bargaining* (New York: Harper & Row, 1959).

[9] Dubin (*op. cit.*) has developed the concept of unions and managements as "antagonistic cooperators."

[1] See H. Gregg Lewis, *Unionism and Relative Wages in the United States* (Chicago: University of Chicago Press, 1963); Robert Ozanne, "Impact of Unions on Wage Levels and Income Distribution," *Quarterly Journal of Economics*, 73, 2 (May 1959), 177–196; A. M. Ross, *Trade Union Wage Policy*, (Berkeley: University of California Press, 1948).

[2] United States Bureau of the Census, *Statistical Abstract: 1967, op. cit.*, Table 349, p. 246.

organized. During the early 1960's, both the proportion of workers unionized and the absolute number of members decreased.[3] Nevertheless, it is not a foregone conclusion that white-collar workers will always be as much outside labor union ranks as in the past. The mechanization and automation of many clerical jobs and the routinized and impersonal character of the remaining tasks, together with lagging relative incomes, may induce white-collar workers to become increasingly receptive to unionization. Already the Retail Clerks International Association is one of the ten largest unions in the United States, with substantial concentrations of members among employees of the big food and drug chains.[4]

One view of modern occupations stresses the career of the individual within a specific organization. In this view the growth of large bureaucratic organizations makes promotion and security within a particular hierarchy increasingly crucial for careers. On the other hand, the growth of professional and technical occupations and of their occupational associations, as well as the existence of labor unions, suggests the possibility that the occupational grouping may be a more important source of control and advantage than the local business or governmental hierarchy. Both things do operate and are important; but their relative importance differs in various occupations and types of organizations. At the very least, these basic observations show that simplified notions of an inevitable and omnipresent absorption of work lives into the large bureaucracy are not justified.[5]

The larger implications of the trends reviewed have introduced confusion into received ideologies of both left and right. One important native brand of thinking blends the old economic individualism with the acceptance of bigness. It sees the importance of power, accepts the corporation as the locus of economic control, and envisages a society of large business units organized as hierarchies headed by a benevolent ("socially responsible") elite of managers. This nascent corporativism is as yet only vaguely formulated, but it probably represents the closest approximation to a native ideology contra the newly based claims and aspirations of unionized labor.

At the other extreme, there are various versions of "proletarian" ideologies, among which communism, however, is a minor item. But of more interest to us here are other solutions, between hierarchism of left and right, which do not envisage the destruction of democratic institutions. The professional business managers are beginning to accept notions of responsibility that allow labor an important measure of self-government. Similarly, the professional labor union administrator is increasingly willing to think of industrial and societal as well as labor problems. Many unions now press for efficiency in work, actively interest themselves in production problems,

---

[3] See the entire issue, "The Crisis in the American Trade-Union Movement," *The Annals of the American Academy of Political and Social Science*, 350 (November, 1963), esp. pp. 1–15.

[4] Michael Harrington, *The Retail Clerks* (New York: Wiley, 1962).

[5] One recent local study found no difference in patterns of occupational history between "corporate" and "local" enterprises, whereas type of occupation was strongly associated with "directed" or "undirected" careers. Cf. Joseph R. Gusfield, "Occupational Roles and Forms of Enterprise," *American Journal of Sociology*, LXVI, 6 (May 1961), 571–580.

and find substantial areas of common interest with managerial groups. The professionalization of the industrial workers themselves is of major importance to both developments. As workers advance in educational level, in security of employment and wage, in measure of respect, self-direction, and accountability accorded them in the general community, they become increasingly "professional" and not merely "workers." It is true that the degrading of skills through technological change is an obstacle to the development of an integral quasi-professional status for industrial labor; but the new technologies also require skilled workers to service the complex machines and processes. At the same time, the unions are becoming far more than fighting organizations or bargaining agencies. They increasingly provide educational programs, recreation, health services, aid in unemployment, illness, death. The new labor statesmen (Walter Reuther of United Automobile Workers is one of the clearest examples) recognize that continuing organizations must satisfy multiple interests.

It must be noted also that new procedures for resolving tension and conflict in industrial relations are contributing in a significant way to the formation of new institutional norms. Procedural devices have no magical properties and cannot create the illusion of harmony when real conflicts of interest are present. They can, however, ease communication, clarify expectations, and gradually contribute to a common set of codes and understandings. Much of the rawness, violence, and bitterness of industrial relations is traceable to the lack of just these codes.

The possibility remains, of course, that the industrial union will gradually harden into a self-perpetuating bureaucracy, so that the worker will be subject to two rigid hierarchies instead of one.[6] But both the corporation and the union have open to them the techniques and arts of group consultation and decision, of conference and discussion, of on-job training and upgrading by merit. To what extent such "democratic" flexibilities will actually prevail against the many forces tending toward hierarchy only the seer could say. It is clear, however, that one is not justified in assuming that size of organization is linearly related to such characteristics as hierarchy, centralization, formality, and democratic control. Various curvilinear relationships are conceivable and likely. For example, very small organizations may have to grow substantially before formality increases greatly. Or, beyond a certain very large size organizations may tend to decentralize some of the decision making and supervisory activities. Also, the character of the actual relationships referred to as "democratic control" may vary with size. Thus, William Faunce has shown for a sample of local unions of the United Automobile Workers that small locals are "more democratic" as judged by rates of member participation and turnover of leadership—but "less democratic" if judged by proportion of elections that were contested, presence of an "opposition party" on local issues, responsiveness of delegates to wishes of the members, and concern of delegates with accountability

[6] For an analysis of the factors working for and against democracy in unions, see Seymour Martin Lipset, "The Political Process in Trade Unions: A Theoretical Statement," in Morroe Berger, Theodore Abel, and Charles H. Page (eds.), *Freedom and Control in Modern Society* (New York: Van Nostrand, 1954).

to their electorate.[7] Thus, a distinction must be made between democratic procedures *within* local units and the degree to which local units are influential at the national level. In the U.A.W., at least, the larger locals are more likely than the smaller units to contribute to democratic processes in the national union, and the usual indicators of "democracy" in the small units are at best ambiguous and may be misleading. It is, of course, a basic fact that in large organizations of any kind only a small proportion of members will be active in leadership (decision making) and representative roles. But this fact in itself does not demonstrate an "iron law of oligarchy" nor render large size and lack of democracy inevitable partners.

## SECURITY, RIGIDITY, AND POSSIBLE NEW DIRECTIONS

This brief analysis of economic institutions necessarily has to leave out far more than it can even suggest. It would not be wise to end, however, without mentioning certain implicit problems raised by the presence of a "security psychology" in an age of corporacy. The following relevant facts seem to be well established.

1. Workers fear job scarcity or loss of accustomed levels of real income. They are sharply conscious of insecurity. They frequently strive for monopoly controls.

2. Managers and investors frequently, if not typically, act as nearly like monopolists as their control of a favored business situation permits.

3. Both labor and business interests are importantly *organized*. The economy is to a large extent an administered, organized system of massive units.[8]

4. The corporation and the union are in rivalry for the allegiance of the workers. Workers as such are not union inclined without question; more typically, they see themselves as being "bid for" by the union and the company; they constitute one corner of a triangle.[9]

5. The basic framework of labor relations is confused and changing—a "crisis conditioned, unformed institution"[1]—and the unsteadiness and

[7] William A. Faunce, "Size of Locals and Union Democracy," *American Journal of Sociology*, LXVIII, 3 (November 1962), 291–298. Articles dealing with formal organization constitute this entire issue of the Journal.

[8] Adolf A. Berle, Jr., *Power Without Property* (New York: Harper & Row, 1959).

[9] Lois R. Dean, "Union Activity and Dual Loyalty," *Industrial and Labor Relations Review*, VII, 4 (July 1954), 526–36. A minor and little known but interesting aspect of the labor union scene is the existence of a large number (possibly 1400) of small, single-firm, independent unions, with a total membership estimated as possibly around 400,000. Included are blue-collar industrial groups, white-collar clerical unions, and unions or guilds of professionals; in strength, organization and policies, they vary widely. A preliminary study is Arthur B. Shostak's *America's Forgotten Labor Organization* (Princeton, N.J.: Industrial Relations Section, Department of Economics, Princeton University, 1962).

[1] Benjamin M. Selekman, *Labor Relations and Human Relations* (New York: McGraw-Hill, 1947), p. v.

ambiguity of the legal and moral order open the door to the relatively free play of power and to all the suspicions, tensions, and recriminations that always arise from the exertion of power without consent.

Deep-seated forces are driving large groups of men into highly organized power units focused upon the advancement of partly disparate economic interests. Out of the clashes of these groups grow political pressures and state regulation. Unless the corporations and the unions can develop mutually acceptable relationships that prevent paralyzing conflict, increased government intervention is predictable. And in the American scene this intervention poses a deep conflict of values. The individualism of enterprise is disappearing into the corporation, the individualism of work into the discipline of the factory and the union. More and more, industrial relations concern masses, organizations, groups, and the differentiated statuses within these group entities, not the relations of a homogeneous aggregate of separate and equal individuals. The very real human beings who make up these social bodies have interests and values—desires for security, status, self-expression, autonomy, and recognition—that they can attain only through participation in collective action. Already workers in many instances have established something definitely resembling a "property right" in their jobs. The crucial question would seem to be whether and in what manner "security" can be attained—through relations to *particular employers*, to *unions*, or to *government*, or to some particular combination of these.

Already we have a widespread development of *status laws* in our economy: special legislation for farmers, industrialists, workers, and so on; special codes of rights and duties for different statuses and for differently situated groups. One conceivable course of development would be toward what might be termed a neofeudal restrictionism. This will be favored by every circumstance that either establishes fixed status prerogatives in the industrial system, or develops legal and customary supports of monopoly, or increases the dependence of the worker upon a particular employer. The last is especially important, for it offers the possibility of a true "road to serfdom."[2] Such dependence is reduced by all measures that promote free mobility. For instance, full portability of paid-in reserves in group pension and insurance plans facilitates mobility of university teachers under such plans as those of the Teachers Insurance and Annuity Association and the College Retirement Equities Fund.

If workers in their search for protection against economic vicissitudes were to succeed in "appropriating" their jobs from a particular employer, there would be two enormously significant side effects: first, every job opportunity thus appropriated would be withdrawn from the job market: it would truly become "private property;" second, the worker would be increasingly dependent upon a specific employer. Since all the advantages of

[2] Friedrich A. von Hayek in *The Road to Serfdom* (Chicago: University of Chicago Press, 1945) has argued that increased governmental intervention represents a new serfdom. It is definitely worth emphasizing that quasi-feudal structures would more easily be developed through paternal industrialism.

security and advancement would be bound up with this employer, the mobility of the worker would be diminished; nor is it to be supposed that employers would indefinitely accept duties toward a particular worker without demanding and getting rights of their own. The general tendency would be therefore toward establishing employer-employee relations marked by something close to "fealty" of the worker to the employer; faint analogues are presently found in the "loyalty to the firm" demanded in certain paternalistic companies. There would be a number of other rigidifying effects: stronger resistances to technological innovation, emphasis upon hierarchical and hereditary principles of industrial organization, and the freezing of existing geographic patterns of industry.[3]

Against the possibility of this sort of development in the American economy is ranged an impressive set of institutional and technical barriers. Only a few of the most important can be mentioned. In the first place, the total economy is subject to considerable instability and to powerful continued pressures for change (for example, international competition, the disruptions of war, the periodic imbalances of "trade cycles"). A rigid job-status regime requires a rather high degree of stability in techniques and in the total economy; thus, feudal economies are likely to be agrarian and localized. Second, the dual influences of government and the unions are already widespread and important; as they become firmly established, they limit the ability of particular employers and particular workers to form personalized and localized relationships. Third, the cultural values characteristic of workers, as of much of the whole society, induce a strong aversion to relations of personal dependence and paternal authority; this resistance has deep roots and a long historical background and is typically given up only under severe pressure. Thus, there are quite tangible legal barriers against many of the more extreme forms of personal dependence, "peonage," for instance. The highly developed money economy and the extreme commercialization of goods and services is a fourth inhibiting influence. Finally, the basic character of the business enterprise itself—the impersonal, deracinated corporate structure with its numerous nondirecting "owners" and its nonowning specialized managers and functionaries—does not offer any firm basis for particularized loyalty or dependence.[4] Besides, so long as labor is a cost to be minimized in an instable economy, the possibility of wholesale de-grading, shifting, and lay-offs will not be easily given up by business management.

What other lines of possible structural development are indicated by analysis? There is the pattern before us of "socialism" in Scandinavia and Great Britain, and of varying forms and degrees of communism, including Eastern European "compromise systems," and of Spanish and South Ameri-

[3] Lest these suggestions seem merely hypothetical, we may remind ourselves that many of the effects suggested are foreshadowed by the familiar one-industry town in which an employer attaches workers to the firm by benevolent "nepotism," seniority systems, health and welfare plans, home ownership, company unions, and other devices, "respectable" or not from the standpoint of union philosophies.

[4] Blauner, *op. cit.*; Melvin Seeman, "On the Personal Consequences of Alienation in Work," *American Sociological Review*, 32, 2 (April 1967), 273–285.

can versions of corporative states. In the earlier fascistic revolutions in Italy and Germany we have seen how the way for totalitarian control was prepared by industrial bureaucracy and cartels, so that a political coalition of disaffected social groupings—ranging from big industrialists and landed proprietors to peasants, conservative white-collar clerks, and workers—could simply take over a centralized, hierarchical administrative apparatus for new purposes, or for old purposes in new guises. In America, one might say, indeed, that to have "government take over business" would be equivalent in large part to having business take over the government, so powerful, organized, and interdependent are business structures and business interests and so inescapably intertwined are they with government.

Contrary to the views of some business spokesmen, the survival and welfare of "corporate capitalism" is inescapably dependent upon a strong central government. For some control of the business cycle is indispensable. And the possibility of a sufficient degree of control over the business cycle in a capitalistic system hinges upon the ability of the central government to influence decisions of investors and production managers. Since government in our society is the single largest recipient of income and the single largest spender, its theoretical potential to influence the economy is quite substantial. Whether it is, in fact, able to take the necessary actions is the crucial question. The means at its disposal are several: to increase or decrease taxes of various kinds, to increase or decrease the availability and cost of credit (primarily through changing the Federal Reserve discount rates), to issue or pay bonds, to increase or decrease direct governmental spendings for goods and services (based on borrowing or repayment of governmental obligations to banks), to increase or decrease reserve requirements of banks, and to use numerous less important specific devices. Most of the effective monetary and fiscal controls apparently can be invoked to check a threatened depression, although timing is an important problematic factor, and the existing controls are not claimed to be infallible. The most significant potential limitation in such "indirect management" of the economy is likely to appear in periods of increasing prosperity, approaching full use of resources. Such a situation is likely to create cumulative inflationary pressures that may make it politically difficult or impossible to impose the needed deflationary checks on the overactive system.

Some business ideologists still seem to maintain that competition in the present economy provides an automatically self-regulating system that maximizes economic welfare, without any central aid, regulation, or guidance.[5] It is hard to imagine an objective analysis of the actual operations of the system under which this view could be well supported; nevertheless, it continues to command considerable public deference.[6] Given the present in-

---

[5] For a detailed description of the ruling set of ideas and beliefs, see Francis X. Sutton, Seymour E. Harris, Carl Kaysen, and James Tobin, *The American Business Creed* (Cambridge, Mass.: Harvard University Press, 1956).

[6] A recent critical commentary upon the "free enterprise" ideology of our economy makes the acerb note that "the only existential meaning of *enterprise* is what businessmen generally happen to be doing at the moment, and *free* is merely the accompanying demand that they be left alone to do it." (David T. Bazelon, *The Paper Economy* (New York:

stitutions of property and authority, what actually could we expect from the formula "less government in business, more business in government"? Along this road probably would be met further restrictions of labor organizations, further development of bigness and centralization in business, and pervasive merging of economic and political power.

As the economy comes to be predominantly a system of large and interconnected organizations—corporations, trade associations, labor unions; financial companies (and trusts and pension funds), and government—the concentrations of power and influence tend to reduce "automatic" economic adjustments. As government, then, is called upon to supply indirect controls, the capacity of the increasingly "lumpy" and oligopolistic system to accept such controls will be tested. Such "acceptance" involves so-called self-restraint of private economic organizations upon the immediate pursuit of short-term gains. Whether the necessary forbearance can be developed will be decisive for the extent and character of future governmental intervention and, hence, for the basic institutions of property, contract, and the market.[7]

Different students of the American economy undoubtedly would not be in full agreement as to the most difficult "problems" for its future viability. Considerable support, however, could be found for each of the following: (1) control or resolution of conflicts that represent the breakdown of regularized relations of exchange (such conflicts disrupt production and create the possibility of cumulative disorder); (2) provision for absorption into productive and socially respected work of substantially all adults able to work and wishing to work; (3) allocation of adequate resources into socially desirable activities that will not be carried out by "private" enterprise acting solely in terms of profit—education, medical service, the arts, transportation facilities, scientific research; (4) avoidance of massive socially undesirable consequences, such as water and air pollution, arising as side effects of short-term profit seeking; (5) allocation of adequate resources to redress "inequities" regarded as unacceptable within the domestic population; (6) allocation of adequate resources to meet international responsibilities and obligations.

Obviously all of these represent value judgments, whether there is a given "problem" or not, and what is or is not "adequate." Clearly, however, the value judgments are problematic and clearly they are being made and will be made. Economic institutions of the future will be shaped not only by the structure of power and the satisfaction of economic interests but also by the conformity of the end effects of the system to normative expectations and demands.

---

Random House, 1963), p. 25.) However much as one might disagree with any of Bazelon's particular evaluations, the facts reviewed in this chapter adequately support his general view that the current popular image of the system corresponds very poorly with the actual situation.

[7] An economic textbook explicitly favorable to a capitalistic system soberly comments: "once a modern, fundamentally free-enterprise economy has spawned gigantic centers of economic power . . . the unassisted operation of competitive forces cannot be counted on satisfactorily to resolve conflicting interests" (Loucks, op. cit., p. 722).

Alternatively, should further extensions of governmental activity in economic life be accompanied by a really strong political labor movement, the existing structure of industry is capable of being turned in "socialistic" directions. For the foreseeable future, however, anything like real "nationalization" of industry is not to be expected from this source; it is not indicated by the intent of labor organizations, nor by their power to secure united political action, nor by the actual balance of powers that constitutes the American government-in-being.

The actual nature of the American economy and of the forces shaping the directions of its change cannot be neatly summarized by ideological labels. There is no easy escape from the laborious task of tracing concretely and in detail the norms and values and the real operating relationships of an economic structure that must seem excessively untidy to those who have become enamoured of simple and rigid formulas for complex and detailed problems. To repeat: this is an economy of giant corporations and giant unions. It is also an economy containing a diverse agricultural industry, organized in family enterprises, with an overlay of cooperative organizations and governmental regulation and assistance. It is also an economy containing many small businesses. And it is an economy in which a substantial segment of the population lives in poverty and shares a "culture of poverty" that increasingly evokes public concern and political attention. There is a very considerable measure of public ownership, municipal, state, and federal. Over this heterogeneous complex spreads an increasingly pervasive web of visible social controls and explicit regulation.[8] It is no longer even a slightly daring prophecy to say that no long-run diminution of the social control of economic affairs is in prospect. The hegemony of the market is past, the administered economy is here. The questions that remain can be squeezed into issues-in-principle and pressed to a conclusion in conflict and repression; but they can be subjected to reason, discussion, research, negotiation, and disciplined interplay of power within a morality that cuts across class-bounded moralities. We cannot say which roads will be taken nor impose further value judgments upon the attention of the reader. But we can see how thin is the line between "economic" and "political" activities and how questions of power unavoidably confront us at every turn. It is for this reason appropriate to turn now to consideration of political institutions in the United States.

### SUGGESTED READINGS

BENDIX, REINHARD. *Work and Authority in Industry.* New York: Wiley, 1956. Through the study of ideologies the author shows how the organizational structures of productive enterprises and of the larger social and political enterprises and of the larger social and political systems shape the values, beliefs, and imperative norms constitutive of economic institutions.

[8] Compare the comment of J. M. Clark, "we live in a society of organized pressure-groups, of commission-government, public utility regulation, antitrust action, farm price supports, social security, supervision of collective bargaining, and the kind of regional planning involved in the Tennessee Valley Authority." "America's Changing Capitalism: The Interplay of Politics and Economics," in Berger, Abel, and Page, *op. cit.,* p. 193.

BERLE, JR., ADOLF A., and GARDINER C. MEANS. *The Modern Corporation and Private Property*. New York: Macmillan, 1937. The classic reference on the subject—so often cited that many people may think they know it without ever having read it. They are mistaken; and it is as worth reading now as it was at the time of publication.

BLAUNER, ROBERT. *Alienation and Freedom: The Factory Worker and His Industry*. Chicago: University of Chicago Press, 1964. Comparative study of workers in different industries shows great differences in kind and extent of alienation and satisfaction. Decisive refutation of diffuse global assertions about "one-dimensional man." Retains and develops valid elements in concept of alienation.

CROZIER, MICHEL. *The Bureaucratic Phenomenon*. Chicago: University of Chicago Press, 1964. Influential study by an outstanding French sociologist. Develops a "crisis theory" of organizational change. Especially useful for ideas in comparative sociology of organization. Many insights applicable to large corporations.

LEISERSON, WILLIAM M. *American Trade Union Democracy*. New York: Columbia University Press, 1959. Authoritative discussion of structure and process in the organizations that illustrates how difficult and complex it is for the "labor movement" to be expressed in labor unions.

MASON, EDWARD S. (ed.). *The Corporation in Modern Society*. Cambridge, Mass.: Harvard University Press, 1960. Excellent collection of essays by eminent specialists. Especially pertinent for the present treatment are the chapters by Carl Kaysen, Earl Latham, John Lintner, and Norton E. Long.

MILLER, DELBERT C., and WILLIAM H. FORM. *Industrial Sociology: The Sociology of Work Organization*, 2nd ed. New York: Harper & Row, 1964. Widely used standard text in sociology of industrial organization. Contains extensive review and synthesis of research, together with well considered interpretative commentary.

MOORE, WILBERT E. *The Conduct of the Corporation*. New York: Random House, 1962. Distills vast amount of knowledge into clear exposition in nontechnical style. Wisdom, sprinkled lightly with irony, in naturalistic analysis of how men do, in fact, behave in corporate statuses.

SAMUELSON, PAUL A. *Economics: An Introductory Analysis*, 6th ed. New York: McGraw-Hill, 1964. A readable guide into the forest: the most widely used textbook in general introductory courses in economics. Look for the *implicit* sociology.

SMELSER, NEIL J. *The Sociology of Economic Life*. Englewood Cliffs, N.J.: Prentice-Hall, 1963. A tightly packed introduction to the *explicit* sociology, by a sociologist who knows his economics. Indispensable ideas for serious study.

WHYTE, WILLIAM FOOTE. *Men at Work*. Homewood, Ill.: Richard D. Irwin, 1961. Synthesis of long study and thought by a master of first-hand observation and systematic insight. Note the care with which Whyte relates generalizations to concrete situations.

# Political Institutions of the United States

*VII*

## THE NATURE OF POLITICAL INSTITUTIONS

I n any very complex society certain systems of cultural norms and social organization become sufficiently explicit and differentiated to be labeled as political. We then speak of government, the state, political parties, sovereignty. The apparent ease with which one can observe governmental organizations and political parties tends to give us an unwarranted assurance about these commonsense distinctions. What is ordinarily labeled political is by no means identical with the political elements in our society analytically considered. Therefore, we must make a brief analysis of the general problem of political power before turning to the specific American case.[1]

Just as all societies contain an economic sector, so all have a sector that may be regarded as political. We have seen that an "economy" is that subsystem of a total society which directly involves the production and distribution of scarce and transferable goods and services. It is usually said that the political arena concerns the acquisition and use of power. But control of economic goods seems to be potentially a source of power over persons, and much of the activities we customarily regard as political obviously have to do with the getting, allocating, producing, and using of economic utilities. In the United States today, as we have seen, the economic significance of governmental activity is very substantial;[2] and the realms of business firms and trade unions are permeated with the exercise of power and authority. What, then, should we seek out when we try to identify and understand political aspects of American society today?

Inherent in the association of human beings in society is the problem of regulating the power of some individuals or groups over others. The basic

[1] A useful sampling of general works dealing with the sociology of political behavior includes Bernard Berelson and Gary A. Steiner, *Human Behavior: An Inventory of Scientific Findings* (New York: Harcourt, Brace & World, 1964), pp. 417–436 and 443–449; Heinz Eulau, Samuel J. Eldersveld, and Morris Janowitz (eds.), *Political Behavior* (New York: Free Press, 1956); Seymour Martin Lipset, *Political Man* (New York: Doubleday, 1960); Lewis A. Coser (ed.), *Political Sociology* (New York: Harper & Row, 1966); Arnold M. Rose, *The Power Structure: Political Process in American Society* (New York: Oxford University Press, 1967).

[2] Cf. Eli Ginzberg, *et al.*, *The Pluralistic Economy* (New York: McGraw-Hill, 1965), p. 15: "More people are directly employed in government than in agriculture, mining, and construction combined. . . . In the decade 1950–1960, nine out of every ten new jobs added to the economy reflected, directly or indirectly, the activities of the not-for-profit sector."

231

political process is precisely the acquisition and exercise of power by certain individuals or groups over others; an abstract economics for the isolated individual is conceivable, if unimportant; but a similar political science is not.

Power, however, takes many specific forms. Fundamentally, there are three main ways in which some men control others. First, they may control the situation within which other people must act. Given such control, one may be able to use the *offer of advantage* or the *threat of disadvantage* to bring about desired action from others. Second, one may be able to change the way in which people perceive the situation. Thus, by supplying information one may induce recognition of new aspects of the situation, leading to a change in behavior. Third, under certain circumstances, one may control others by directly appealing to, or changing, their attitudes, values, or sentiments by persuasion and propaganda.

Politics is sometimes called the "engineering of consent." People are given information to affect their decisions; they are appealed to on the level of values and ethical norms; governments use a variety of rituals and ceremonies to symbolize and dramatize authority. There is also the persuasion of political reward, ranging from the ward leader's patronage or bribe to the offer of national economic advantage in world trade. And there is everywhere, after all, the use of coercive power—whether its role be large or small, overt or concealed, polite or brutal.

It is of little use to characterize the political process so broadly as to cover all conceivable modes of influencing behavior—to obscure by synthesis what must be separated by analysis. Our first central question thus becomes: What, in analytical terms, is essential to politics and the political? A formulation of considerable scientific usefulness regards the regulation of *coercive power* as the essential element. We may approach this formulation through a series of propositions:

1. *Social power* is the probability of the effective control of an individual or other social unit by another, regardless of the former's wishes. The actual *fact* of power can be taken quite apart from the various *bases* on which it may rest.

2. A particular variety of power is *coercive advantage*. Coercion is an effective threat of disadvantage to another unless he conforms, follows, obeys. "Illegitimate" coercion takes such forms as extortion, blackmail, and armed robbery. "Legitimate" coercion, by organized government, takes the form of fines, imprisonment, loss of civil rights, death, or other fates of greater or lesser punitiveness. Its "legitimacy" depends solely upon how the effective community under observation regards it. Much of the actual overt behavior of the officials of many governments in the world, present and past, has been indistinguishable from that which would otherwise be called "criminal," "antisocial" and the like. Indeed, by ordinary standards of what constitutes criminal behavior in most societies today, it is probably quite correct to say that persons in many high positions of political authority have been "criminals" more often than the people they have ruled.[3]

---

[3] See Pitirim A. Sorokin and Walter A. Lundeen, *Power and Morality: Who Shall Guard the Guardians?* (Boston: Porter Sargent, 1959).

*[margin: 3) uncontrolled coercive power = unstable phenomenon]*

3. Unregulated coercive power is always potentially disruptive of a social system. There is no assurance that it will be used in accordance with the major value systems of the society. Sheer naked force or the threat of such force is an inherently unstable phenomenon in social life and every continuing human group works out elaborate ways of controlling it.

*[margin: 4) Political institutions = norms regulating exercise of power]*

4. *Political institutions* are the complexes of norms regulating the acquisition and exercise of power by some individuals over others within a given territory, through social structures claiming a monopoly of ultimate authority.

*[margin: 5) STATE ≠ self-end ≠ (b) concentrated force ≠ (c) legitimate authority; structures = Monopoly of legitimate coercion (Government = group of persons manning state)]*

5. The most prominent political institution within our society is the *state*. It seems impossible to gain any clear notion of what the state might usefully mean by considering only the ends to which it is devoted. There is hardly any human interest that some political association that we would be forced to recognize as a state has not undertaken to further, hardly a collective activity for which some state at some time has not taken responsibility.[4] Nor is the state satisfactorily defined as the expression of concentrated force, for power and force are ubiquitous in associations and groups that are clearly not states. We might say that the state is an association to which a society attributes legitimate authority—but authority is also held by churches, families, clans, tribes, and many other diverse groupings. We are forced to define the state in terms both of the means most peculiar to it and of the (imputed) legitimacy of these means and the structure using them. Tentatively, then, we shall consider the state to be *the structure that successfully claims a monopoly over the legitimate use of coercion and physical force within a territory*.[5] The American state in this sense consists of all normative structures of this kind in our society. It is to be specifically distinguished from the *government*, which is the particular group of persons that at any given time mans the apparatus of the state. Government is the legitimate power-holding *group*; the state is the *structure* by which the group's activity is defined and regulated. A state may exist while particular governments rise and fall within it. The state is the form of which the government at any particular time is the operating embodiment.

Indeed, there is in the exercise of power and authority a "web of government," in Robert M. MacIver's suggestive phrase, that spreads throughout the entire society.[6] There is governing—the exercise of socially validated authority—in the family, in the school, in the economic enterprise, and in the religious group just as there is in the state itself. The state is but one of the relatively distinct institutionalized sectors of social life that becomes differentiated from the total community as a society becomes more complex. Neither state nor government is, or can be, coextensive with the total society.

*[margin: state ≠ coextensive with total society]*

---

[4] The diversity of the main types of activities now carried out by governments in the United States is conveniently suggested by the listing given in Austin Ranney, *The Governing of Men*, rev. ed. (New York: Holt, Rinehart & Winston, 1966), pp. 43–45; see also Ginzberg, *et al.*, *op. cit.*, chap. 3.

[5] In this as in most of the foregoing we are following Weber's formulations. Cf. H. H. Gerth and C. Wright Mills (trans. and eds.), *From Max Weber* (New York: Oxford University Press, 1946), pp. 77–78.

[6] R. M. MacIver, *The Web of Government* (New York: Macmillan, 1947).

*Basic Political Problem.*
*conflict over scarce values*

The basic political problem arises from the fact that in any aggregate of human beings seeking to attain goals, there is always the possibility of conflict. Persons want scarce values, and their efforts to acquire them may not leave "enough and as good" for others. As Thomas Hobbes clearly saw, if men are enough alike to have approximately equal capacities for desiring scarce values and if no bonds except the pursuit of immediate interests unite individuals, society becomes a normless jungle in which every man's hand is against his neighbor's.[7] Obviously, this portrait of society is not realistic, but suggests that in the immediate interests of discrete individuals there is no guarantee against conflict. It is difficult to find a real society in which there are no conflicts of interest, no competing loyalties, no disagreement concerning social rules. Even if the goals or ends of individuals are compatible, there is still the possibility of conflict over the means used. Above all, other human individuals are always potential means for the attainment of any one person's goals, and control of others is always a technically effective way of advancing interests that may be contrary to the interests of those controlled. Thus, there is always a "demand" for power. Like money, power is a "universal" means—it may be used in the service of a great variety of goals—and like money it is avidly sought. Its exercise can easily disrupt normative controls. Many men appear to find that having power is, to say the least, convenient. For some, it becomes a central and continuing goal. For a few, the desire for power becomes a total and insatiable preoccupation.[8]

There is, furthermore, a premium upon control of territory as well as people in political processes. For social aggregates necessarily occupy geographic territories, and the most destructive kind of conflict—physical violence—must occur within a definite place, although modern technology now makes possible the delivery of vast destruction across great distances. Sheer contiguity is of prime importance in the problems of power and conflict internal to a society.

Political authority would not be needed in a society in which the interests of individuals and groups were always compatible. Nor would it be needed if all men were saints—that is, if all consciences were clear, strong, and committed to the same values and norms enjoining beneficent treatment of others. Actual social life everywhere, however, is marked by oppositions of interests, by dissension, and by lack of perfectly internalized controls. Hence, neither mutual benevolence nor unaided conscience serves to harmonize the necessary social transactions of men.[9] And this crucial platitude holds,

[7] See the discussion of the Hobbesian dilemma in Talcott Parsons, *The Structure of Social Action* (New York: Free Press, 1949), pp. 89–102.

[8] In an era that has produced a Hitler and a Stalin, further examples may be unnecessary. Of the numerous instances scattered around the world in our times, perhaps a suitable prototype of the power-possessed dictator is supplied by Trujillo. See Robert D. Crassweller, *Trujillo: The Life and Times of a Caribbean Dictator* (New York: Macmillan, 1966). Some students of the use of terror might prefer to point to Duvalier of Haiti.

[9] Note Peter M. Blau's statement: "Without social norms prohibiting force and fraud, the trust required for social exchange would be jeopardized and social exchange could not serve as a self-regulating mechanism within these norms." *Exchange and Power in Social Life* (New York: Wiley, 1964), p. 255.

above all, for those who exercise concentrated power: if their actions are to harmonize with a system of values acceptable to those governed, the rulers must be constrained by rules that are enforced by definite social agents through definite, realistic social mechanisms. This means that power must be met by power and that if there are custodians who check other custodians, they must do so within the terms of *some* system of norms.

Conflicts disruptive of social order can be minimized in three ways: (1) by agreement upon common values that the members of the society can share; (2) by agreement upon the norms that will govern the means used to attain ends; (3) by the authorization of power to coerce, expel, or eliminate dissident and alienated elements of the social aggregate. Government rests upon all of these. Political authority, based upon a value consensus in the relevant social group, never lasts indefinitely without the backing of coercive power; but, on the other hand, political power without authority cannot maintain itself for long. Even the governing elite of a dictatorship that rules by terror must be held together by something other than coercion; and often sheer force is defeated by those apparently helpless against it.[1]

Indeed, "there is authority beyond the authority of government. There is a greater consensus without which the fundamental order of the community would fall apart,"[2] and, we may add, frequently does fall apart. Maintenance of political consensus is difficult; the task, incessant. Political views and dispositions toward political participation are learned, not just created *de novo* by the isolated individual. The study of political socialization, therefore, is essential for understanding maintenance and change in political systems and is one way of seeing how political institutions are related to other institutions, such as the family and education.[3] Thus, political authority cannot be understood exclusively as a matter of forms, procedures, constitutions, laws. All these may be full of effective social meanings; but they may be ritualistic pretensions, shadowy fictions.

Because spontaneous agreement is never complete, a primary task of all national governments is the regulation of the conflicting and divergent loyalties and interests that a nation as a *territorial* unit almost universally embraces. Indeed, it has even been held by some theorists that the state is itself simply a neutral reflection of an ever-shifting balance of power among diverse interests. To this conception belongs a doctrine that sees a system of checks and balances as a necessary base of the political order—a theory that has been particularly congenial to the pluralistic American society. The actual cultural heterogeneity of the society has made it extremely difficult to secure consensus upon *common* ends. At the same time, the political dominance of landed proprietors and commercial and business groupings through so much of national history easily combined with a philosophy of natural rights and laissez faire to produce effective agreement on broad

---

[1] Cf. Charles E. Merriam on the "Poverty of Power," in *Political Power* (New York: McGraw-Hill, 1934), chap. 6.

[2] MacIver, *op. cit.*, p. 85.

[3] Herbert Hyman, *Political Socialization: A Study in the Psychology of Political Behavior* (New York: Free Press, 1959).

*procedural* questions. If the positive common ends of the state could not be agreed upon, except within a highly limited scope, it was nevertheless possible to establish a framework of political *method* within which disagreements and conflicts could be resolved.

Agreement upon the procedures for acquiring and using power and for settling conflicts is not, however, necessarily an agreement upon form only. In democratic political orders, the procedures of governing and being governed acquire in marked degree the status of ends in their own right. For the essence of political democracy, one of its few dogmas, is that the policies of the government are continually subject to criticism and revision; the rulers are accountable to the electorate. Power can be acquired and exercised only within definite limitations. The problem of order in society has always been present, but has taken new forms in modern times. The difference between the state and the total social system has become clear. In modern, complex societies, conflict continuously occurs among individuals and groups, yet there is continuous effort to maintain legitimate authority and social consensus and cooperation.

The amoral Leviathan—the rule of untrammeled might—may be glorified by modern apostles of totalitarianism, but it is not a sociologically defensible description of states as they are; only under the most extreme conditions of social dislocation is it approximated. It is no accident that international politics is the area of governance where "rules of the game" are least honored and where coercion plays its most massive role: the absence of common values and norms that alone can keep conflicts of interests between nations within bounds contrasts strongly with the degree of normative order within national boundaries.

On the other hand, there is a common tendency, perhaps especially in American thought, to slur over or minimize the great historical significance of coercive power. The facts of how the strong tend to behave toward the weak are bitter medicine for a people who believe in the "consent of the governed." Undoubtedly the widespread use of force indicates that a society lacks integration of its value systems; the most stable order has least need for show of force. But equally certainly political institutions are not the result of a "social contract" of the individuals who make up the society or who did so at any time in the past: we must reject Locke along with Hobbes.

It is not, however, the "voluntary" or involuntary character of obedience (compliance) of the individual who is the immediate object of commands that distinguishes authority from power. Rather it is the legitimacy of the command—and a command may be legitimate even though the person to whom it is directed in any particular instance may not *willingly* comply. He may obey reluctantly and out of fear or calculation and still admit that the command is legitimate. And the command is still legitimate even if in the particular instance the recipient denies both its legitimacy and that of the issuing source so long as an effective consensus of *others* who are subject to the same source of commands accept it as legitimate. Authority grows out of norms accepted by a collectivity; the norms derive from joint dependence upon a source of power believed to be ultimately beneficial to that collectivity.[4] Once authority has been firmly established and exercised through definite social organizations, legitimacy may be and usually is transmitted as a matter of accepted practice through the choice of powerholders, effected by means of the institutions of authority themselves.[5]

The institutionalized political sector (system) of a society consists of an aggregate of organized sets of statuses and collectivities distinguishable by their primary specialization in the making and implementing of authoritative decisions of certain kinds, and in gaining and keeping access to the requisite power for doing these things. Among the main kinds of such political-authoritative decisions are the following:[6] (1) defining, establishing, and determining priority order among collective goals (moon rockets or public housing, guns or butter, new schools or supersonic aircraft); (2) allocating legitimized power, as well as more diffuse influence and prestige, to various individuals and collectivities within the society; (3) defining and exacting from various elements of the population the goods and services required to support the polity in its activities; (4) distributing various goods and services (including facilities, benefits, and rights) to individuals and collectivities, domestic and foreign; (5) organizing resources and activities for attainment of collective goals; (6) generating or organizing support for persons, parties, policies and other politically relevant social and cultural elements; (7) adjudicating conflicts and the application of rules to problematic cases.

*[handwritten margin note: main kinds of political decisions]*

The decisive points already suggested can be put briefly:

1. The political is the realm of power.
2. Power alone is not enough.
3. Regulated power, based on value consensus, is the core of *institutionalized* working politics. The legitimized coercive potential of the state is its most systematic expression. Obviously, there is also much power that is not legitimized.
4. The norms and values that constitute political institutions are not contractual in origin, nor do they simply represent domination by force.
5. The state can never be coextensive with the society; the political is always only one aspect of social control and social consensus.
6. Back of the formal structure of the state is always an informal pattern of operating practices and relationships, which may or may not correspond to the official pattern. Back of the operating government are the groups and interests that supply the dynamic element in politics.

In a period when states claim monolithic power, encompassing whole societies, it is necessary to emphasize that there are always definite limits to

[4] A point clearly analyzed in Peter M. Blau, "Critical Remarks on Weber's Theory of Authority," *The American Political Science Review,* LVII, 2 (June 1963), especially pp. 312–315.

[5] Cf. Adolf A. Berle, Jr., "The Laws of Power: An Approach to its Systematic Study," *Proceedings of the American Philosophical Society,* 111, 5 (October 16, 1967), 252.

[6] Cf. S. N. Eisenstadt, *The Political Systems of Empires: The Rise and Fall of Historical Bureaucratic Societies* (New York: Free Press, 1963), pp. 6–7.

the obedience that political authority can elicit. One of the first practical axioms of command is never to give an order that cannot or will not be obeyed; and even the most dictatorial authority discovers points beyond which it cannot go.[7] Even a legally all-powerful state is always hedged in and restricted to some degree by competing social authorities and the values they represent.

Some political power represents an authoritative mobilization that is mainly beneficent in terms of the goals and interests of those governed. This is "power-with." Some political power represents an authoritative distribution of scarce values in which some get more, some less in a zero-sum allocation. This is "power-over." And this distinction helps us to identify concrete instances in which particular governing bodies generate activities widely benefiting the population ruled or use their power to monopolize scarce values or skew the distribution strongly in favor of a relatively small portion of the total society.[8] The membership of a total political society, such as that of an empire or a modern nation-state, is uniquely diverse in its values and interests—a fact that follows from its territorial scope and non-voluntary nature. From these elementary facts follows the high likelihood of internal oppositions and conflicts—which in turn render highly probable the resort to "power over" in the form of authoritative resolutions of allocative problems. Only those who regard the sheer fact that there is some ultimate settlement of claims as an unmixed good will regard *all* governmental activity as a beneficial use of power-with.

The coercion exerted by the state in our society falls in three main areas. First is the broad category of "police power," the power to regulate without taking possession of property, believed necessary for maintaining internal peace and order and controlling aggression. Many other associations or other social units exercise legitimate coercion of various kinds;[9] but the state attempts to reserve to itself the peculiarly important sanctions of organized physical force, including the death penalty. Formerly its monopoly of physical force was far less complete—the state shared this sanction with the church and the family. Short of the dramatic means of inflicting imprisonment, death, and torture, the state may use its police and military forces to control movement and assembly; may control the flow of information to the public; may disseminate information and propaganda; may expel persons; may impose loss of citizenship. It requires various kinds of registration and

[7] This point has been elegantly developed by Robert M. MacIver in several major works, including *The Web of Government, op. cit.*, and *Power Transformed* (New York: Macmillan, 1964). See also Charles E. Merriam, *The Role of Politics in Social Change* (New York: New York University Press, 1936), pp. 83–87.

[8] A government may be "an unlimited-purpose, all-inclusive cooperative" or it may be a "sub-system . . . used by one segment of the population as a profit organization for its own benefit" (Alfred Kuhn, *The Study of Society: A Unified Approach* [Homewood, Ill.: Richard D. Irwin, 1963], p. 617).

[9] "The state can throw a man into prison. But an employer can take away his job. As the state can deprive a man of his life, the church can threaten his happiness for the future and make him extremely uneasy and unhappy while he lives. The state may tax, but the monopoly may raise prices and lower standards." Charles E. Merriam, *Public and Private Government* (New Haven, Conn.: Yale University Press, 1944), p. 9.

identification; it maintains elaborate records and systems of monitoring and surveillance.

Second is the taxing power. Although the citizen who pays taxes receives some public services supported from tax funds, he does not thus buy these services, for he is not free to decide whether or not to pay them. Taxes are levies we must pay even when we do not expect to benefit from the transaction. Furthermore, taxation readily lends itself to punitive ends. Indeed, the problems of taxation well illustrate both the power of the state and its limitations, and the dynamic forces and competing values back of policy determination. For taxes represent a mixture of voluntary contribution, payment for services, and legalized confiscation; of the three elements, the last bulks large, partly because behind the impersonal authority of the tax-collector are the differentiated interests that try to put the burden of taxation upon some other sector of the population. What is to be the incidence of property taxes, income taxes, corporate profits taxes, sales taxes? Because each type tends to bear most heavily upon particular groupings and because the most powerful blocs politically are not necessarily the largest numerically, it is highly probable that in our own society (as in many others) most citizens pay a large part of their taxes under some measure of compulsion.

Third is the monopoly of foreign relations and armed warfare; the state raises huge military forces that quite clearly could not be assembled on a voluntary basis, and it alone has the power to make war and agree to treaties.

Furthermore, the state dictates what persons may enter or leave its territory under what conditions. It also controls foreign trade through export and import regulations, financing, and tariffs. In the American case, there are several additional types of state coercion, including the right of eminent domain (the confiscation of certain kinds of property), jury duty, and others.

Obviously, the use of force has not been successfully confined to the government; force and the threat of force are potential in human relations of any kind and are by no means rare in actuality. Wherever cleavages of values are deep enough, the only arbiter may become violence. In the United States, we have had one revolution, one giant rebellion, a long series of smaller insurrections and riots (Whiskey Rebellion, Dorr War, Black Patch War, Colorado Mine War, the Great Riots, and so on), violent employer-labor relations, lynchings, race riots, and latter-day urban riots and quasi-insurrections. Consensus, compromise, consent—these are words for an integration of interests and values that does not come easily and cannot always be maintained.[1]

The primary practical test of authority is whether or not orders or demands directed to a particular individual or subcollectivity will be enforced, or at least "supported" by the effective "community" of *other* subordinates.[2] The test is *not* whether a particular individual "willingly" obeys; even in the most firmly established systems of authority he often obeys reluctantly and only under the threat of sanctions. The crucial test is whether or not the relevant third parties concur in the right of the authority to issue the orders

[1] On the above points see the classic analysis by V. O. Key, Jr. in *Politics, Parties and Pressure Groups* (New York: Crowell, 1942). chap. 22.
[2] Cf. Blau, *Exchange and Power in Social Life, op. cit.*, p. 212.

and to impose sanctions. It is not even essential that the particular orders and sanctions must be approved in each particular case—only that the disobeying agent will be disapproved for resisting. ("Mistakes may be made but the law must be obeyed.") The disapproval means that norms and values are being invoked. All authority rests in part on the principle of divide and rule.

A primary source of politics is the problem of order in society. In a small group in a stable environment, with a highly integrated value system, the problems of order may be so slight that the diffuse interaction of the whole grouping is sufficient to enforce norms and to contain whatever power striving might emerge under these conditions.[3] Political *organization* is lacking; and political institutions exist only in germ, diffused throughout the society and only indistinctly defined or recognized. Nevertheless, the political is always present, even if latent or covert; and with the development of any marked social differentiation or individualistic striving or cultural heterogeneity, definite and systematic institutional forms appear for the channeling and control of power. A definite state emerges with the establishment of a governing association having its own norms, especially those of the law.

If the polity consists of those aspects of social behavior that are primarily involved in the getting, using, and regulating of ultimately monopolistic power—especially of the use of force and the threat of force within a territorial society, it also *uses* the power it "has" or "represents" to attain goals. This means that the political system of a total society has responsibilities for the maintenance of that society in its environment. At a minimum such maintenance implies activities directed toward achieving major collective goals (for example, controlling economic depression or supplying public education), maintaining internal peace and order, and regulating foreign relations and protecting against attacks. Because of the extreme difficulty of accomplishing all these formidable tasks by consensus and rewards alone, the political system always uses *some* severe sanctions to maintain coercive controls.[4]

"Political" action in the broadest sense is thus primarily devoted to *control*. Although there is a political aspect in a great part of everyday interaction in small groups and local areas, the political comes most fully into its own in dealing with large scale and remote relationships and activities.[5]

The problem of social order is perhaps especially prominent in modern industrial societies, where demands upon the state are great and where several conditions weaken social consensus regarding the values, ends, and

[3] R. Lauriston Sharp, "People Without Politics: The Australian Yir Yoront," in Verne F. Ray (ed.), *Systems of Political Control and Bureaucracy in Human Societies*, Proceedings of the 1958 Annual Spring Meeting of the American Ethnological Society (Seattle, 1958), pp. 1–8.

[4] See Eisenstadt, *op. cit.*, pp. 5–8.

[5] McDonald even defines political phenomena as lying within the area of activities directed toward control of remote environments. In this view: "Polity is used to refer to the most comprehensive and inclusive unit which any individual regards himself as sharing with others who are unknown but determinate." Neil A. McDonald, *Politics: A Study of Control Behavior* (New Brunswick, N.J.: Rutgers University Press, 1965), p. 55.

*[handwritten: 4 conditions That weaken Social consensus today]*

rules of associational living. Among these conditions, four seem especially important. (1) The sharp internal differentiation of occupations and economic positions gives each special economic group and economic class its own social perspective and its own specific economic interests, both of which are often in deep opposition to those of other groups. (2) Because of international mobility, the political collectivity contains peoples of diverse cultures. Consensus is correspondingly difficult to achieve except in such highly abstract terms that apparent agreement may often fail in practice to avert serious tensions and cleavages. (3) The indirect and quasi-anonymous nature of many important activities, especially economic, removes them from direct, community wide surveillance and control. Adulterated food processed in one locality may be purchased by a buyer 3,000 miles away. (4) Rapid changes in social structures tend to unsettle convictions and bring norms into question; and it is correspondingly difficult for the individual to discern clear expectations that can guide his own behavior.

*[handwritten margin notes: 1) diversity occupation & econ. posi; 2) diversity Culture; 3) anonymous removed acts from community control; 4) rapid soc. pattern chan (bring quest. of norms)]*

The main kind of agreement upon values that remains possible is a consensus, not upon specific ends and particular actions, but upon relatively generalized principles, or upon inclusive and relatively unexplicit symbols.[6] The conspicuous place of coercive power in societies partly derives from the lack of consensus in such societies, partly from social differentiation, and partly from the lessened efficacy of interpersonal controls. As Blau points out, social approval tends to lose influence "because the multiplicity of groups and the possible mobility between them in complex societies enables deviants of nearly all sorts of escape from the impact of community disapproval by finding a subgroup of like-minded persons where they can find approval. Impersonal restraints are, therefore, of special importance in modern societies, and a basic source of impersonal restraint is power."[7]

*[handwritten margin notes: Possible consensus general prin.; use of pow. due to 1) lack of consensus; 2) social differentiation; 3) less interpersonal contact]*

In order to bring our discussion thus far to a focus, we have insisted (perhaps to the point of boredom) upon the central importance of coercion in identifying political phenomena. In addition, we have said that concrete political organizations (and especially governments) also engage in goal attainment that benefits individuals and collectivities. Difficult as it is to clearly see these two aspects simultaneously, both are intrinsic to governments-in-being. Political democracy, as understood in the United States, has not been thought to require centrally enforced unanimity on *specific* values and beliefs. Its great problem today is to reconcile the valued flexibilities and freedoms of its governing institutions with the pressures for consensus upon action in meeting crises. Thus, we must examine next the institutional framework with which American society confronts both the continuing and the newly emerging dilemmas of power in society.

*[handwritten margin note: summary]*

---

[6] The significance of this "attentuation of common values" was acutely seen by Emile Durkheim. Cf. Parsons, *Structure of Social Action*, pp. 323 ff.

[7] Blau, *Exchange and Power in Social Life*, *op. cit.*, p. 114.

THE STRUCTURE OF THE STATE
IN AMERICAN SOCIETY

Any summary description of a political system so complex as ours must be overly simple and incomplete. By listing, however, a few salient features of the dominant cultural structure, we can find convenient points for observing the system as a whole. At the level of *manifest* cultural norms, then, the American state is marked by these characteristics:

1. It is a limited constitutional democracy, republican in form.
2. It is a federal system; certain rights are reserved to the constituent states.
3. It is supposed to be a "government of laws rather than men;" there is great emphasis upon the written Constitution, which is interpreted by a judiciary of extraordinary powers.
4. The Constitution separates the governing powers and provides a complicated system of checks and balances.
5. The authority of power holders tends to be functionally specific and explicitly defined.
6. In theory, there is universal adult suffrage and the universal right to hold public office.
7. An extraordinary number of public offices are filled by popular election. The principal policy-forming officers are elected at regular and fairly frequent intervals.
8. The legal system explicitly lays down an elaborate system of civil rights for individuals.
9. Legislative bodies are typically bicameral; representation is based upon territory.
10. Certain of the above features lead to patterns of political behavior not provided for in the ideal patterns of the state—political parties and interest-group representation, for instance.
11. The formal structure of the state is derived in part from strictly *cultural* influences; ideas, ideologies and values supply the axiomatic "definitions of the situation" through which new or problematic political action is perceived at any given time—for example, ideas of natural law and the value and inviolability of the individual personality, the negative valuation of centralized authority, or the instrumental conception of government. On the other hand, political action, like all other social action, is not an automatic emanation of cultural values, ideas, or creeds; it is the action of concrete personalities motivated by goals and standards not deducible from laws, constitutions, and other formal elements of the state. Thus, our political institutions cannot be adequately understood without analyzing specific connections between them and other parts of the social structure.
12. In particular, the roles of economic interests, class structure, and ethnic groupings are crucial to the concrete political processes of our society.

As a new, revolutionary nation, the United States initially accepted a set of political principles and norms that went far toward institutionalizing

*Beginning of U.S.* → *Values:* universalism, achieved status, functional specificities
→ tolerated: particularism, ascribed status, diffuseness—esp
at local level

*The Structure of the State in American Society* 243

universalism, achieved status, and functional specificity. However, at the same time the actual governing system tolerated and supported ascribed status (notably slavery) and much particularism and diffuseness, especially at state and local levels, under the highly decentralized federal system.

*ad 2)* **The Federal System** *(subunits have power – so that no level of authority has right to pass on all gov. acts.)*

The American political structure is federal rather than unitary in form; that is, subunits of the state have powers such that no level of authority has the ultimate right to pass upon all governmental acts. The system is multi-centered, and the subordinate centers retain a marked degree of autonomy. It is the United States, not the United State. The structure of the central government is approximated on a smaller scale in each of the federated states, and each reserve some rights not subject to review by the central authority.[8] The federated system is marked by dual citizenship—a person is at the same time a citizen of the United States and of Nevada or Maine.[9] There is also a complete dual system of courts. The formal structure of federalism and the official forms of local government give little hint of the enormous variation in actual political structures and processes in different local areas—"varying from the narrowest oligarchy to the freest democracy, and from the most brutal tyranny to a near philosopher-king."[1]

*certain rights reserved to states*

*dual citizenship*

*dual court system*

*variation – practice – of local gov.*

In theory, the central government can exercise only those powers given to it by the written Constitution, whereas all other powers are reserved to the states; the nominal powers of the central government are thus strictly limited, leaving the states broad residual rights.[2] The central government cannot confer upon subordinate governments, or take away from them, functions and procedures. It cannot prescribe the official conduct of state or local officials. It cannot at will change the powers of state or local governing bodies. It cannot abolish states, counties, or other local units. No state may without its own consent be deprived of equal representation in the Senate. For a long time, the Bill of Rights, as it was interpreted by the courts, applied only to the *national* state. Limitations upon the invasion of individual rights by local and state governments and by private persons or organizations had to be sought mainly in the laws of the several states. In more recent years, the courts have read into the Fourteenth Amendment the limitations of the first ten amendments, and substantial areas of state action are now subject to the provisions of the Bill of Rights.

*– in theory central gov. limited*

*– recent years courts have applied Fed. constitution to areas beyond the of national jurisdiction*

Although the due process clause of the Fourteenth Amendment does not require the states to abide by every part of the federal Bill of Rights, the

---

[8] For example, the regulation of the suffrage, criminal law as applied by the state courts. See MacIver, *op. cit.*, pp. 160–161.

[9] The Constitution left many ambiguities and difficulties in the concept of citizenship. See John P. Roche, *The Early Development of United States Citizenship* (Ithaca, N.Y.: Cornell University Press, 1949).

[1] Norton E. Long, *The Polity* (Chicago: Rand McNally, 1962), p. 230; see also the portrait of local government given by Roscoe C. Martin, *Grass Roots* (New York: Harper & Row, 1965).

[2] Just the opposite principle is sometimes followed in federal unions, e.g., the initial structure of confederation in the Dominion of Canada.

Supreme Court has made it clear that the freedoms of speech and press, the right to counsel in capital cases, and several other rights must be respected by the states. Thus, the First Amendment, prohibiting an establishment of religion, does not apply to the states; but the Supreme Court has held that religious liberty is one of the rights protected by the Fourteenth Amendment against state action. Inherent in a system providing such an impressive amount of local legal autonomy are conflicts of authority and consequent pressures to establish a priority order for the laws and regulations established at the various levels of the structure.

*Federal system — one mark of pluralistic society*

The federal system, like the separation of powers and checks and balances to be discussed below, is a mark of the *pluralistic* nature of American society as a whole. In its origins, it reflected both the compromises with local vested interests and state autonomy and the distrust of strong centralized government that had been a characteristic of the national culture from colonial times. It seems curious to foreign observers that in certain sections or localities are permitted practices offensive to national majorities and damaging to the international relations and world position of the nation as a whole. In a federated nation with "regions as unlike as Norway and Andalusia"[3] what is "American" takes on rather different forms under the elastic formula of *e pluribus unum.* The institutions intended to limit governmental power, to diffuse authority, to control popular demands, to leave maximum power to private individuals and associations now struggle with the massive strains of industrial society and world power. The cultural heritage of political forms and creeds is molded and transmuted into new and often unrecognized directions as shifting but powerful interests contend within a changing social and moral framework.

*Conditions for success of democracy*

The conditions necessary for the successful operation of a democratic political system are more stringent than is perhaps generally realized. Political democracy requires: (1) a dependable agreement upon procedures for settling issues and resolving conflicts; (2) enough, but not too much, dissension and struggle for power to prevent the establishment of a monopolistic and self-perpetuating ruling group. Although these two minimal conditions are simple to state, they are difficult to achieve in practice, and they depend upon a very complicated and delicate balance within a social system.

It is within this formal system that the normative patterns now to be examined take on their limited but important causal role in the dynamics of the American social order.

### A "Government of Laws Rather than Men"

*(ad 3)*

*impersonal & universal rules*

This phrase represents a creed of the American political tradition. It suggests a state ordered by impersonal and universal rules, detached from the persons who govern and from the passions and foibles to which they may be heir. Back of the phrase is the Western legal and philosophic tradition of natural law, inherent rights, universalistic ethics, impersonal justice. Notwithstanding the extent to which the creed has not been practiced, the no-

---

[3] Dennis W. Brogan, *U.S.A.: An Outline of the Country, Its People and Institutions* (London: Oxford University Press, 1941), p. 9.

tion that laws bind those who make and execute them has been of first-rank importance in the shaping of our political institutions. But the sociologist must subject the notion to two major qualifications. First: the principle remains a mere creed unless there exist social bodies with the interest and the power to implement it. The entire conception of the rule of law has been elaborated as an ethical system in periods when nothing approximating an embodiment of it could be found in operating political associations. Second, laws are of different kinds; they differ as to source. There is the law of custom: the sanctioned, enforced rules that are never enacted or promulgated but that may form a regulative network more widespread and effective than edict or statute. There is common law, consisting of the accumulated decisions and opinions of the courts as they have interpreted custom and preceding court actions. There is administrative law, ground out as power holders devise rules to direct their own activities. What laws "stand above the state?"

We have seen that many of the important governmental norms are not matters of constitutional or enacted law. The extent to which custom rather than law "is the king of men," even with emphasis on a written constitution and a penchant for law making, can be easily documented. Congress ordinarily holds public sessions, but nothing in the Constitution says that it must. The Constitution implies that presidential electors are free agents, but the electoral college simply registers the popular vote and it would be thought outrageous for it to do otherwise. (The Constitution provides only that the President shall be chosen by electors to be selected in each state by the legislature in any manner it wishes. Popular election through parties was not expected, or desired, by the founding fathers.[4]) The Constitution specifies that representatives in the House must reside in the state they represent, but custom requires that they reside in the *district* they represent. The President's cabinet rests upon custom; so do political parties.

It appears that there are at least four main ways in which a government may rule by law. First, the power holders who make up the executive arm may be closely limited by rules, not of their own making. The discretion, the "arbitrary" personalized power, the "unending audacity" of the official may be checked. Second, it may be beyond the power of the legislature to remove certain rights; a fundamental law may be reserved as inviolate. Political democracy in the United States is a system in which the people cannot vote away their power to vote and in which any particular government can be turned out of office. Its essence is the permanent right to choose and dispose those who govern. Third, there may be an emphasis upon *cultural*

[4] The electoral college system means that the state-by state vote, and not just the national popular vote, determines the outcome of a presidential election. Thus, the electoral college is not without practical significance. In 1824, 1876, and 1888, the candidate who lost in the popular vote was made President. The system puts a premium on the capture of strategic states with large numbers of electoral votes, and thus places emphasis on a state-by-state campaign effort. One vote in the electoral college represents 75,000 votes in Alaska, but 393,000 in California. In attempting to judge the outcome of any particular national election it therefore is essential to know the direction of political preferences in each of the states. Neal R. Peirce, *The People's President: The Electoral College in American History and the Direct Vote* (New York: Simon and Schuster, 1968).

structure rather than *social* organization—upon the "rules of the game," rather than upon detailed supervision within a definite politically controlled organization. Specific actions may not be positively enjoined; rather, the limits of permissive action may be set. Finally, government by law may mean that the interpretation of law is monopolized by a group relatively independent of the legislature or executive. The existence of a separate legal tradition interpreted and enforced by such an independent body has been in fact a conspicuous and crucial feature of Anglo-American history. A judiciary not dependent upon any other *one* political authority is in a position to insist upon legal continuities and legal limits that would otherwise be subject to much greater pressure from the holders of legislative and executive authority.

"Government by law" in the United States, then, has tended to limit and define the areas of authority and competence of officials of the state. The individual is ruled by a number of different, and to some extent, competing authorities; the military officer can give orders legitimately only to his subordinates in the service, the policeman's reach is explicitly limited and circumscribed, the judge is not empowered to detect and prosecute as well as to render judgment. Of course, as we shall see, the actual behavior of officials rarely follows with exactness the formal categories laid down by law and other explicit regulations. Nevertheless, there is a great difference between latitude in interpretation or sub rosa evasion or violation of the institutional norms and a change in the formal institutional principles themselves. That authority is conceived in our culture as limited, functionally specific, and subject to law is of central importance.

Nevertheless, general "principles" and explicit legal provisions are almost never detailed enough to cover the problems raised in concrete situations. The "impersonal majesty of the law" must be filtered through lawyers, juries, judges, administrators. The practical meaning of a constitutional precept, statutory enactment, or common-law doctrine is never simply given but is always determined by interpretation. A crucial example is provided by the "due process" provisions of the Constitution (the Fifth and Fourteenth Amendments), which forbid Congress or the states to "deprive any person of life, liberty, or property without due process of law." Clearly, these clauses were intended to protect individuals or groups from unrestrained governmental action; but who is to decide what constitutes "due process of law?" As Edward S. Corwin has shown in a notable analysis, judicial interpretations, for most of the nineteenth century and the first three decades of the twentieth, turned "due process" into an elaborate bulwark of established property rights and used it as a means of blocking governmental action that might have curtailed the liberty of property in the interest of protecting or extending other liberties such as civil rights.[5]

Realistically, then, our legal system provides a government of laws only as a general framework, not as a fixed and determinate regulation of action in all its details. This framework remains, to be sure, a crucial factor in

[5] Edward S. Corwin, *Liberty Against Government* (Baton Rouge: University of Louisiana Press, 1948).

shaping political institutions. But the determination of what "the law" is, is as much a "political" act as any other in which social power is at stake— and may be no more or no less morally correct on that account. The relation between legal and moral norms is often subtle and complex, but legal prescriptions do in many instances give effective authority to moral dicta. Although the sheer existence of a legal norm is not enough to guarantee that it will influence judgments of morality, there is some evidence that the knowledge that certain conduct is forbidden by law is effective in changing moral judgments in the direction of conformity to the legal norms.[6] The importance of law is that it provides a relatively *explicit* and relatively *systematic* constellation of rules and that these rules are maintained by definite bodies of men who have an institutionalized interest in enforcing them.

### The Separation of Powers

The separation of powers in the American system is an example of a political device whose significance and functions are by no means identical with those commonly imputed to it. It is usually supposed that its prime *intent* as well as its actual *function* is simply to *limit* the power of the state by dispersing authority among legislative, executive, and judicial branches of the governing apparatus. Unquestionably, the Constitution was drafted with a vivid sense of the dangers of strong government. The popular will exerted through the legislature was perhaps as much feared, however, as was executive autocracy. The limitation of the state through the separation of its powers enabled centers of private power, especially in business, to act with a minimum of state intervention; at the same time basic changes in the political structure were rendered difficult from lack of authority sufficient to deal with the broader social and economic issues.[7] Thus, insofar as the separation of powers was actually instituted, the state was not only limited but also made relatively unresponsive to mass demands. The strict separation of powers originated in an era of the limited state, when detailed coordination of vast programs of centralized action was seldom necessary. The greatly augmented role of the "positive state" in modern times makes the literal rule an impediment to the prompt and effective accomplishment of many things commonly conceded to be desirable.

The separation of powers is real, as one can see by looking at the repeated struggles between the President and Congress, the Congress and the courts, the courts and the President. But it has never been so complete or clearly defined as the standard phrase might seem to indicate. In fact, from the very beginning of the republic, the principle was squarely contradicted by the doctrine of checks and balances. Since each major branch of the state is given the authority to check certain actions of another branch, each necessarily has some real power over the area of authority officially allocated to

[6] See Leonard Berkowitz and Nigel Walker, "Laws and Moral Judgments," *Sociometry*, 30, 4 (December 1967), 410–422.
[7] The most important economic and social forces of modern society extend far beyond regional and local bounds. Thus, the incorporation laws of the single small state of Delaware have had an enormous impact upon the *national* economic and political structure.

another. The Constitution itself, therefore, did not establish anything like a complete separation of powers.

First, the President has important constitutional controls over Congress. He has the power to veto legislation, and a veto can be overridden only by a two-thirds majority. He thus has not only the power to check legislative action but also a means of influencing the character of legislation before its passage. For the threat of veto can sometimes force the alteration of whole measures, or specific portions of them. The responsibility of the President to report to Congress on the state of the union and to recommend legislative action has provided the executive branch with an important legislative role. Successive Presidents—especially in periods of crisis—have taken the original vague authorization as the basis for submitting whole legislative programs to Congress; and as leaders of political parties and dispensers of patronage they have been able to put strong pressure upon legislators to vote in accordance with their recommendations. Equally important, the President possesses through legislative delegation a most impressive set of powers for "administrative action" that in intent and in consequence amounts to authority to legislate.

In addition to these highly important controls exerted directly through the office of President, the executive branch increasingly engages in an enormous amount of de facto legislation in the form of administrative orders, regulations, and rulings laid down by various departments, bureaus, commissions, and so on. Statutory law, like the provisions of the Constitution itself, is necessarily couched in terms too abstract and general to cover all the concrete problems raised by the attempt to apply it, and administrative rulings are forever modifying, extending, restricting, reinterpreting the intent of enactments. As the scope and complexity of executive action have expanded, the role of administrative discretion has inevitably had a corresponding development; and the rule making of the executive branch has become a substantial part of the legal order.[8] This function may be regarded as judicial if we remember that rule making is essentially what the courts do in rendering decisions upon problematic situations that have arisen under the law; it may be regarded as legislative if we remember that the rules laid down by the administrative body usually have the force of law, subject to the possibility of judicial review if challenged and, of course, to possible legislative retraction.

The growth of widely extended and highly complex administrative activities creates tendencies toward (1) the delegation of legislative powers to executive agencies, (2) an increased proportion of legislation initiated and influenced by executive agencies, (3) the increased role of governmental administrative agencies and their employees as "pressure groups," (4) di-

---

[8] "The theory that all legislative power must be exercised by the legislature is increasingly belied by the facts and reduced to the status of a legal fiction." J. Roland Pennock, *Administration and the Rule of Law* (New York: Farrar, Straus & Giroux, 1941), p. 60. For a detailed study of "political behavior" within new institutional frameworks see Philip Selznick, *TVA and the Grass Roots* (Berkeley and Los Angeles: University of California Press, 1949).

minished influence and prestige of legislative bodies. The separation of powers, more and more clearly, is a creed rather than a specific operating principle.

By virtue of a long series of "unplanned" changes, then, the executive bodies of the state have acquired vastly increased importance. In Chapter VI, we saw how the growth and internal differentiation of the business corporation can lead to the separation of ownership from control and to the growth of managerial power. In governmental bodies, the growth in volume, scope, and complexity of activities creates a similar transformation in which *residual power* gravitates to the *active* and *continuing* control centers of the executive agencies.

Thus, the executive legislates. On the other hand, the legislative branch shares the powers of the executive. The most conspicuous constitutional provision in this connection is the requirement that treaties be made with the advice and consent of the Senate. Furthermore, Congress has a clearly important control over executive performance through its control of appropriations: by withholding funds it can exert decisive influence upon specific executive actions. In recent years, congressional investigating committees have become another potent and spectacular legislative control upon the executive. Other informal types of legislative intervention in "executive" matters have developed. As many observers have pointed out, the main standing committees of Congress form a quasi-executive body. They do so much of the decisive work of Congress that they acquire a focal power not only in shaping legislation and in determining what measures will or will not be brought to a vote but also in influencing executive action. For the key officials of governmental agencies affected by a particular committee— military affairs, for instance—will be in frequent liaison with that body and will inevitably both influence and be influenced by it.

Of the three major branches of the state, the most nearly autonomous is the judiciary. Yet it is also the branch that most clearly intervenes to control actions in the areas of authority nominally reserved for the executive and the legislature. Through the process of judicial review, the courts are able to negate legislation and to disallow executive action at numerous crucial points. No act of the legislative branch is final until it has been passed upon by the courts, and in practice the anticipated reaction of the judiciary is bound to become an important factor in the shaping of legislation in the first place. Above all, any sharp departure from traditional conceptions is almost certain to raise the issue of constitutionality, as the series of Supreme Court decisions in the wake of the early New Deal so well demonstrated.

In the federal system of courts, the independence of the judiciary is supported in a very specific way by two provisions: (1) judges are not removable from office "during good behavior"—that is, short of the rare and difficult procedure of impeachment, they hold indefinite tenure; (2) salaries are not to be reduced during an incumbent's continuance in the office. Once appointed by the President and confirmed by the Senate, a federal judge therefore commands a considerable immunity to immediate extraneous pressures. The autonomy of judges in some state courts, however, is reduced by their popular election for short terms of office. Judges in these states are directly subject to most of the informal obligations, party considerations, and interest-group pressures that affect the elected legislator.

But purely formal considerations are enough to show that the independence even of the judiciary is also interdependence. The jurisdiction of the courts is always limited by the action of the legislative bodies, and the pronouncements of the courts are ineffectual except as they are supported and enforced by executive agencies. Judges themselves are either appointed or elected; the appointing authority is unlikely to ignore completely such considerations as the political affiliations and views on social issues of potential judges. Finally, long practice sanctions the power of legislative bodies to establish rules of procedure for judicial processes.

Because the major branches of the government are partly separated and yet highly interdependent, its structure is necessarily complex; there are many areas of overlapping authority, of ambiguous jurisdiction, of cross-purposes. The necessities of consultation and compromise produce large numbers of "tangent organizations" for liaison and mediation.

Since large-scale government actions only rarely fall completely within the authority of one branch of the state, and several centers of power must agree before the most important policies can be determined or carried out, policy is established after extensive deliberation and explicit consideration of a wide range of interests. On the other side of the coin, however, the separation of powers tends to make it difficult to arrive at clear decisions or to arrive at them quickly. Thus, there is a tendency to concentrate power in a single source when there is urgent pressure for rapid and consistent large-scale decisions illustrated by the increased power of the executive branch in periods of national crisis, especially war.[9]

### The Presidency

The presidential system in the American government gives the chief executive a position very different from that of a prime minister in a cabinet system. In Great Britain, for example, a cabinet composed of the heads of executive departments holds undivided party leadership and guides the legislative program as well. The Prime Minister as party leader must maintain his hold upon the party and upon the House of Commons in order to continue in office. The government may fall at any time if majority support of the cabinet fails. Through the close liaison of cabinet and Commons, a unified legislative-executive program is facilitated. Legislation is not subject to nullification by an independent judicial branch. In the American system, the basic separation of powers militates against common action by the President and Congress.[1]

The relations between the President and Congress are only to a small extent specified by law. Beyond some highly general assignments of authority, the Constitution itself gives little guidance. If the Constitution is

[9] See the extensive historical evidence in Clinton L. Rossiter, *Constitutional Dictatorship: Crisis Government in the Modern Democracies* (Princeton, N.J.: Princeton University Press, 1948).

[1] Although, as already noted, the separation of the two is by no means complete.

a model of brevity, it is also a document that is silent on many central problems of government-in-operation. The office of the President is therefore
left relatively open to the influence of noninstitutionalized forces: the personality of the incumbent, the shifting balance of party power, the presence
and character of domestic and international crises. In the presidency more
clearly than elsewhere in the federal structure, we can see the impact of great
forces focused through the personalities who have filled the office in crucial
periods: Washington, Lincoln, Wilson, Franklin Roosevelt. Since no clearly
defined institutional role has been provided for the extraordinary demands
forced upon the President in emergencies by the structure of the state, the
chief executive has been granted special powers in crisis that in the long run
have increased the authority and prestige of the office. Powers invoked in
war, revolution, and disaster have broadened from precedent to precedent,
particularly since the revocation of legislatively delegated authority would
require systematic planning that Congress has not often exercised. The delegation of powers has then frequently been left on the statute books. In the
second half of the twentieth century the President of the United States is
its chief legislator—both in proposing new laws to the Congress and in
directly "making law" by his executive actions, especially in foreign policy.
In the latter case, the President's exercise of power in times of crisis has
been termed "constitutional dictatorship." What must be added to this
characterization is that if international affairs are defined as a *continuous*
crisis, the constitutional dictatorship in that measure becomes continuous.

Because of these characteristics, the presidency provides a particularly
clear case study of the dynamics of political processes. The written Constitution together with the traditions and vested interests that have accumulated
around it seem to impose quite rigid barriers against the assumption of
emergency powers by the President. The whole weight of the legal forms is
toward the continuation of established patterns, short of the most drastic
emergencies such as actual military invasion or widespread rebellion; and
the United States has experienced relatively few and relatively slight deviations from constitutional forms in the presidency. On the other hand, each
major crisis has been accompanied by a drastic increase in the powers of the
President,[2] thus illustrating the principle that groups or social systems that
*are* going concerns typically react to grave external threat by an intensifica-
tion and concentration of authority.[3]

Although limited in authority, the presidency is far and above the most
potent focus of power in the federal system.[4] The President is chief executive. He also legislates: he may call special sessions of Congress; he must
inform it concerning the state of the union; he recommends measures; he
has the veto power; he is the leader of his party; he controls numerous appointments of interest to Congress; he has hundreds of other informal means

[2] Rossiter documents this point in detail in *Constitutional Dictatorship, op. cit.*, esp. pp.
215–220. The process ceases if a central polity cannot maintain a consensus on its own
legitimacy.

[3] Cf. Robin M. Williams, Jr., *The Reduction of Intergroup Tensions*, Bulletin No. 57
(New York: Social Science Research Council, 1947), p. 58.

[4] Long (*op. cit.*) calls the presidency an "elective monarchy."

of influencing legislation. Although opposition between Congress and the President is frequent and sometimes has the stuff of high drama, the less conspicuous but essentially important fact is that when the President and the majority of the Senate and House are of the same party, many of the legislators tend to welcome the active leadership of the President. Over the course of national history, the legislative functions of the presidency have increased greatly. Precedents have already been established[5] that indicate potentialities for even more sweeping presidential power, given combinations of such other factors as national crisis, strong party support, and a skillful and aggressive President. To the present time, however, the presidency is an *office*, not a position solely of personal leadership, nor of authority not bounded by constitutional rules.[6] In Weber's terminology, it is more nearly legal bureaucratic leadership than charismatic or traditional leadership.

## Constitutional Government and the Constitution

American political institutions grew out of deep aversions to *strong* government and to government of *undefined powers*, aversions that led to emphasis upon a written constitution, established as superior to the ordinary lawmaking process and subject to direct change only by special methods. But the written constitution is a special device rather than a defining criterion of the constitutional state. Constitutional states do not require written constitutions (nor must such states be democracies), but they require *a body of fundamental rules by which those who govern are themselves governed.* The rulers must be bound to a "legitimate order"—an established body of law, precedent, and custom—that they are considered to have no right to violate. They must derive their authority in the eyes of the governed from their position in this cultural structure and be restricted to acts this position authorizes. Constitutionalism implies government based on rules, precedent, principles. It stands in contrast to traditionalism, but also to the rule of the charismatic leader to whom is imputed (by his followers) an authority that is absolute, or at least indefinite, and that resides solely in the "magic" of the *person* who rules. Whether the personal ruler be "hero" or "opportunistic tyrant," he rules in himself and not as a constitutional officer.

It is decisive for a social order whether its political structure is one of *persons* or of *offices*. Constitutional government, when fully developed, achieves the separation of *government* from the *state;* of the person from the office he occupies. The separation is often less than complete but in large measure authority can be detached from specific persons and lodged in the impersonal structure of the state association. We can then see the phenomenon of the citizen who loathes a particular President but reveres the presidency, the many people who scorn the incumbent government but value the system under which it operates. The worth of political institutions is partly dissociated from the worth of individuals who represent them.

[5] *e.g.*, Lincoln's abrogation of the civil rights of citizens outside the zones of actual military operations.

[6] Mario Einaudi, *The Roosevelt Revolution* (New York: Harcourt, Brace & World, 1959).

Constitutional government requires that the state not be *identified with* the total society but be firmly subjected to *control by* it. For if state and government are subject to laws not of "their own devising" nor under their control, those laws must be derived from elsewhere in the larger community. There must be groups among the ruled that can resist effectively any pressure of government upon the normative boundaries.

The opposite side of the coin is the limitation of majority rule. Simple majority rule can just as easily lead to dictatorship as to democracy; men may vote away their right to choose their rulers. Democracy does *not* mean that what most of the people want always prevails. In a constitutional republic, civil liberties must be maintained; not so in a so-called "plebiscite democracy." Under the rules and values of the American system, we are not supposed to be free to throw away our freedom. In fact, of course, the possibility of a popular repudiation of representative democracy is always open and, therefore, conceivably could be taken.

The powers of the government of the United States are set by the somewhat elastic but definitely constricting bounds of a written constitution. Around that document has gradually accumulated a tremendous number of interpretations and commentaries, of court decisions, of beliefs and myths.[7] The Constitution enjoys a veneration that makes it a substantial barrier against sudden or far-reaching changes in the structure of the state. There is a "psychology of constitutionalism,"[8] a widespread conviction that the Constitution is sufficient to cover all emergencies, that deviations from its provisions are unnecessary and dangerous, that a breach of the Constitution would bring down the whole structure of ordered and lawful government.

When it was written, the Constitution was a drastic innovation, not only in its content but in its basic idea that the form of government could be purposively determined.[9] It was radical in the root sense of that word. Yet, in a similar sense, it has had conservative consequences. During the period of consolidation of authority and partial return to prerevolutionary conditions that always follows the instituting of a new state, the Constitution was one of the few symbols of national scope available to the loose federation of weak and disunited provinces. Furthermore, it has been a rallying point for conserving the political and civil liberties of individuals.[1] But it has been conservative in a more conventional sense, also, for it was actually adopted in a period of what was close to counterrevolution; and a major force in its drafting and adoption was the desire to insure internal stability and the

---

[7] Brogan (*op. cit.*, p. 30) is not greatly overstating the case when he says: "In most matters an irreverent people, the Americans are the most reverent people in the world in political matters. They regard the Constitution as sacred, as a national talisman. . . ."

[8] Rossiter, *op. cit.*, p. 211.

[9] Merriam, *The Role of Politics in Social Change, op. cit.*, p. 124: "It was the most monumental heresy of the eighteenth century and denounced by all but the revolutionaries of that day."

[1] Konvitz has distinguished *political rights*, such as the right to vote and hold office; *civil liberties*, such as those enumerated in the Bill of Rights; and *civil rights*, such as the right to employment and public access and accommodation without discrimination. Milton R. Konvitz, *The Constitution and Civil Rights* (New York: Columbia University Press, 1947), p. vii.

protection of property and trade.[2] Undoubtedly, the Constitution can be interpreted to conform to the interests of the more prosperous and propertied groups; and a stable legal order and venerated symbol of that order is advantageous to those interests.

This dual conservatism partly explains how it is that the Constitution can be defended with equal fervor by individuals whose motivations and interests are in most respects sharply opposed. The document has become almost a symbolic "sponge" that can absorb the allegiances of persons having amazingly diverse interests, values, ideas, political philosophies. Although the process by which this absorption occurs is not well understood (and is a research problem of first interest), its existence is probably of real importance to social stability. As with many other symbols of government, the very indefiniteness of the popularly imputed meanings facilitates a sense of order and integration not derivable from the specific applications of political doctrine.[3]

If, however, the Constitution is to provide guiding principles for the working legal order of the state, it must be specifically interpreted in order to resolve problems. And it is here that the document becomes a reality in substance rather than in symbol only. The Constitution-in-being is to a very large extent the aggregate of numerous definitions and interpretations by generations of legislators, lawyers, judges—and above all, by the Supreme Court.

### The Supreme Court

In the British system, from which the American state drew many of its own patterns, the courts do not have the power to declare *any* act of Parliament "unconstitutional"; fundamental constitutional law and ordinary or derivative law originate from the same source; there is no unitary written constitution. The constitution is what Parliament makes it.

In the American system, the courts have assumed and regularly exercise the power to declare constitutional or unconstitutional the acts of Congress, state legislatures, local governments, and executives at all levels. The final test of legal validity is the ruling of the Supreme Court. The Constitution is what the Court says it is.

The present extraordinary role of the Supreme Court was not envisioned in the formation of the republic. The powers now exercised are the outcome of a long development in which the authority of the Court was greatly extended, largely on its own initiative.[4] There were three crucial turning points in the process. The first is usually considered to be the action of the Court

[2] The classical reference is Charles A. Beard, *An Economic Interpretation of the Constitution of the United States* (New York: Macmillan, 1913).

[3] It has been suggested that the American Constitution had certain similarities to the British Crown as a point of anchorage for loyalties.

[4] Robert E. Cushman, "The Role of the Supreme Court in a Democratic Nation," reprinted in A. N. Christensen and E. M. Kirkpatrick (eds.), *The People, Politics, and the Politician* (New York: Henry Holt, 1941), pp. 562–576. A similar observation applies to the presidency. In both cases a basic question is suggested: What exactly is the *process* by which *new* authority is established? At the "growing points" of political authority we might look for clues for a more adequate theory of social change.

under Justice John Marshall in *Marbury v. Madison* (1803), when it refused to accept a scope of jurisdiction and declared its constitutional incapacity to take certain actions. The case did not establish the Court's power to declare legislative acts unconstitutional but only the Court's right to determine *its own* limits of jurisdiction under the Constitution. In the Dred Scott case (1857), the Court took the second decisive step in the extension of its own powers: it ruled upon the constitutionality of *congressional* action and thereby staked its claim to final review of legislative action. Finally, its interpretation and use of the doctrine of "due process of law" in the 1880's gave the Court the power to pass upon the *methods* by which governmental powers were used, as well as upon the substantive content of laws and regulations.

The power assumed by the Court to declare acts of the national legislature unconstitutional strikes many foreign observers as the most notable characteristic of the American state. Yet, as William Anderson has said, these decisions "are also only the most striking and dramatic examples of a regular judicial activity that runs from the very lowest courts up through the ranks to the highest court in the land."[5] In all these courts, the judges regularly pass upon complicated situations, full of gaps and apparent inconsistencies and ambiguities, and their decisions—quite apart from "integrity" or conscious bias—are necessarily affected by ideas and interests in no meaningful sense a part of law. That variation and instability in judicial decisions are very considerable is shown by differing opinions within the same court on a given case, different decisions by different courts on the same point of law, reversals of a court by itself at a later time. Any careful study of what the courts, including the Supreme Court, actually do shows that the process is not merely one of "discovering what the law is" but also of making and changing it.

What is so conspicuously true of the Supreme Court is a pervasive characteristic of the activity of judicial authorities at all levels. Only rarely is the law completely clear and specific. Typically the legal norms are open to a wide range of interpretations in particular cases—they do not merely permit the finding of "loopholes" but rather constitute a veritable "complex net of interconnected loopholes."[6] The judicial system is partly political throughout, that is, it uses a monopoly of legitimate force to impose decisions where specific consensus does not exist. Not only are legal rules often ambiguous but the "facts of the case" are typically open to multiple interpretations; and the different legal norms applicable to the instance at hand often are in opposition. Belief in the existence of a comprehensive set of clear and detailed legal rules unambiguously determining correct decisions may be a very useful social myth, but it is not an accurate representation of law in action.

[5] The author adds, "Sundays and holidays excepted, there is probably no day in any year when some court somewhere in the land is not holding some government to have acted unconstitutionally, or at least beyond its powers." William Anderson, *American Government* (New York: Henry Holt, 1942), p. 70.
[6] Bill J. Harrell, "The Problem of Order: Its Relevance to Law and Freedom," *Sociological Inquiry*, 37, 2 (Spring 1967), 224.

In the traditional conception of legal doctrine, the judges "declare" the law; they do not "make" it. Using well-tested rules, they engage in a highly technical task of determining what the law actually is, by inference and deduction from a large body of preexisting legislation and court decisions. In recent times, it has become evident that many decisions are not uniquely constrained by prior legal principles and decisions but rather represent, in part at least, *policy* decisions involving values, beliefs, and knowledge not intrinsic to the more narrowly conceived legal considerations at hand. In reaction against the earlier obviously unrealistic description of judicial process as completely objective, dispassionate, impartial, and quasi-mechanical, the newer naturalistic or relativistic views sometimes went to the other extreme of implying that decisions could be almost wholly interpreted as outcomes of pressures and preferences extraneous to pure legal considerations. Thus, judicial decision making could be seen as practically identical with legislating: both determine policies by choosing among interests and values.

In all broad judgments in constitutional law, the judges are constrained by statutory law, by prior court decisions and historical background, by logic, by considerations of social utility, and by considerations of general social philosophy. The *legal* constraints are clearly present, but they are not the only constraints. And when all the rules and other limitations have been taken into account, there frequently remains a considerable area of ambiguity and uncertainty left open for judgments in which informed and reasonable men may differ. In the very nature of the cases that finally "work their way up" to the Supreme Court, this area of problematic appraisal is especially wide. No wonder, therefore, that split votes are common. No peculiar personal biases nor hidden interests need be invoked—nor is it to be assumed that such decisions are "political" in any narrow or petty sense.[7]

In view of these facts, it is impressive that the courts, and especially the Supreme Court, are widely regarded as endowed with detachment and infallibility. And to the extent that this belief prevails, the stability of the state is supported through faith in the continuing judiciary.[8]

It is true, of course, that the Court itself is subject to important institutional restraints. Congress can pass new laws that contravene the effects of a Court decision, and in the long run the intent of Congress and prevailing public opinion do limit the action of the supreme judicial body. Still, even within such limitations, the Supreme Court stands in a focal position to decide conflicts among the states, between the states and the federal government, and among the branches of government. Its authority is not restricted to declaring legislation and executive practices unconstitutional; it can positively require governmental action, for example, to protect rights

---

7 As Paul A. Freund says: "The pursuit of justice, after all, is not necessarily easier than the pursuit of truth." ("Are the Justices Really Objective?" *Harvard Today* [Spring 1967], p. 26). See his *The Supreme Court of the United States* (Cleveland: World Publishing Company, 1961).

8 Note that in the national survey analyzed by North and Hatt the occupation of Supreme Court judge was popularly rated as the highest rank in a list of ninety occupations. See Albert J. Reiss, Jr., *et al.*, *Occupations and Social Status* (New York: Free Press, 1961).

of citizens. Under our system, the Court regularly, and necessarily, makes decisions that have the effect of new laws. It sometimes makes unpopular decisions, but over the years it continues to be a major source of stability in meeting the changing problems of government under new social and economic conditions.

### Legislative Bodies and Representation

Cynicism and disaffection sometimes are expressed concerning American political institutions because they do not provide for direct democracy in the details of governing. This populism easily turns into various notions of "plebiscite democracy" and mass action. But the direct rule of all the people is never found in any social groups save the smallest and most homogeneous and could not be the exclusive governing system of a large and complex modern nation. Political action through delegated authority is the only functionally feasible form of democracy in our present type of society.[9] Actually, of course, the legislative bodies of the nation in several respects more nearly represent "popular will" today than at earlier periods in our history, owing to such devices as the direct election of senators, and the recall, referendum, and initiative systems in various states. Also, beginning with the Supreme Court's decision in *Reynolds v. Sims* (1964), substantial movement has occurred in reapportioning state legislative districts to give equal representation to an equal number of people. The long-standing inequalities favoring small rural districts have been reduced, although not eliminated. Nevertheless, popular control of legislative bodies has been limited at both national and state levels by long terms of office and staggered terms for the upper house, preventing quick responses to popular will. The veto powers of the state and national executive and judiciary further weaken popular expression. Within the legislative bodies, a similar effect is also secured by the large majorities required for constitutional amendments. Other arrangements have the consequence of removing the members of legislative bodies themselves from direct popular control—the use of voice rather than roll-call voting, the disposal of legislation in the closed deliberations of legislative committees, control of nominations by a relatively small group of party leaders.[1] This representation is subject to popular control only intermittently and often only quite indirectly. Nevertheless, legislative bodies in the United States are composed of popularly elected and formally free representatives, sharing power with partly autonomous executive and judicial agencies.

It is of great importance that representation in all our legislative bodies is on a *territorial* basis and that the territorial units (states, districts, coun-

[9] This is not to say that direct democracy could not conceivably be instituted but only that it would require drastic sacrifices of other values. Cf. Grant McConnell, *Private Power and American Democracy* (New York: Knopf, 1966).

[1] However, the modern party convention and the direct primaries are probably more open to mass influence than were the earlier procedures of the legislative caucus, which prevailed until the 1820's. (V. O. Key, Jr., *Politics, Parties, and Pressure Groups* (New York: Crowell, 1942), pp. 361–373.) The history of the various nominating arrangements well illustrates how essentially the same processes can continue to operate through superficially very different political forms.

ties, wards), do not necessarily, nor even typically, correspond to real social groupings nor homogeneous interests. As a result (1) the representative does not represent a unified group; and (2) groups and interests are not given official representation by anyone entitled to act in their name but must find their own channels for influencing legislation. Consequently, legislators rarely know clearly or in detail what the "will" of their constituency is with regard to most of the specific issues of legislative action. The control of the voters as a whole is indirect; much of it occurs before a potential candidate is nominated. If his opinions diverge too far from the central views of the voters he will find it difficult to secure sufficient support to find a place on the ballot. Of course, the legislator who, once in office, steers an unpopular course may be defeated in a subsequent election—although this negative sanction is not easily predictable and is uncertain in its effect upon the legislator's stand on many particular issues.[2]

We all know that the national Congress and nearly all of the state legislatures are divided into upper and lower houses; but it is not self-evident how this system came to be or what consequences it may have. Bicameralism, like the separation of powers, was a device to limit governmental powers. Historically, it was the result of a compromise in the Constitutional Convention. There the representatives of the larger and more wealthy former colonies favored a national legislature made up of representatives apportioned to the states on the basis of population or taxable wealth. The smaller states favored a single chamber composed of representatives in equal number from each state. It was only after a bitter dispute that an upper house was established with fixed and equal representation by states and a lower house with representation by states in proportion to population. Since the Senate shared treaty making and appointive powers with the President, the smaller states were insured an authoritative voice in major national policies. Since the House was charged with the initiation of financial measures, the larger and wealthier states were given special weight in legislation affecting their economic interests. The familiar precedent of the British Parliament provided the broad outlines of the bicameral form, and the compromise concerning the basis of representation adapted it to the American situation. Once the national system had been established, it served in turn as a model for the individual states. Only the state of Nebraska now has a unicameral legislature. The bicameral system survives at the state level in spite of the fact that, contrary to common impression, the two chambers usually do not effectively "check" one another and in spite of much criticism on other grounds.[3]

In the national legislature, the power and prestige of the Senate as against the House rests upon definite and sociologically instructive grounds.

2 On all these matters, see V. O. Key, Jr., *Public Opinion and American Democracy* (New York: Knopf, 1962), esp. pp. 481–499. See also Malcolm E. Jewell and Samuel C. Patterson, *The Legislative Process in the United States* (New York: Random House, 1966).

3 Cf. Claudius O. Johnson, *Government in the United States*, 6th ed. (New York: Crowell, 1958), pp. 406–439; Belle Zeller (ed.), *American State Legislatures* (New York: Crowell, 1954).

The Senate is endowed by the Constitution with the treaty-making power, which it shares with the President, and therefore plays a central role in international relations; it likewise has the power to confirm or reject major appointments made by the President, and it is not slow to exercise this prerogative. Its small size as compared with the House makes possible greater freedom of debate and greater ease of interpersonal contact. The senators serve for long terms, and the security they gain upon election is conducive to independence of action.[4] Because of long tenure and control of appointments and other patronage,[5] senators are often able to build powerful state party organizations with which they can oppose the President or national party leadership. The Senate is often at variance with the President and with the House, partly because of overlapping terms of office. This device obviously contributes to the separation of powers, but by the same token it creates conflict within Congress itself.[6]

In Congress, as well as in the state legislatures, the legal forms of procedure are not definitive of the law-making process. Above all, the party machinery plays a primary role in shaping legislation and enforcing discipline. In each legislative body, an inner circle of leaders from each party attempts to give direction to party members; nearly all of the elaborate organization entailed is extralegal. Furthermore, legislative bodies are subdivided into numerous committees that act as sublegislatures—rules committees, steering committees, and a number of important standing committees. In these small groups much of national policy is made. One of the most interesting "unplanned" developments is the congressional committee of inquiry, a direct outgrowth of the separation of executive and legislative branches under a presidential form of government. Congress makes laws and appropriates funds for agencies over the specific operating practices of which it has little formal control. Unable to exercise the continuing surveillance of administrative action possible under a parliamentary government by reason of the presence of executives before the legislative body, Congress has developed this alternative method of overseeing administrative action.

The prevalence of the committee form of organization in legislatures reflects both the need for small working groups in deliberative bodies and the collegial nature of the larger organizations. Although there is a measure of hierarchy in the legislative branch—committee chairmen, speakers and presiding officers, party whips, and so on—a popularly elected body is always a "college" of approximate equals who must reach their decisions by discussion, negotiation, "pressure," and various informal arrangements, rather than by a strict chain of command.[7]

[4] Senators were chosen by the state legislatures until popular election was instituted by a constitutional amendment (the Seventeenth) in 1913.

[5] Through the extralegal custom of "senatorial courtesy," the Senate insures that appointments in any particular state that are objectionable to a senator from that state will not be confirmed.

[6] For a useful description of senatorial activities and careers see Donald R. Matthews, U.S. Senators and Their World (Chapel Hill: University of North Carolina Press, 1960).

[7] The relatively loose and slow-moving collegial organization tends to change under conditions of crisis. In emergencies legislatures tend to limit debate, to intensify and concentrate internal leadership, to delegate powers to executive agencies. The nominal form

Party membership alone is the most prominent factor associated with voting in the House, but even so, it accounts for only a small part of the total pattern. Representatives vary greatly in independence from party leadership and from state delegation influence.[8]

The extraordinary number of informal arrangements, committees, liaison agents, and so forth in our legislative bodies is favored by the large numbers of individuals involved, the deliberative nature of their tasks, and the lack of detailed legal definition adequate to specify necessary operating procedures; but it also derives from the separation of the legislative from the executive agencies. Congress has only indirect contact with the administrative departments, bureaus, commissions, and the like. Its members are subject to the pressures of groups in the specific districts or states that they represent, whereas the President is more nearly the focus of *national* problems and interests. The various particular executive agencies have their own organizational commitments, their vested interests, their special constituency pressing upon them to advance particular interests. Thus, the legislative and executive branches have different perspectives and interests; and there is no clear-cut constitutional channel for relating the two. Therefore, informal methods are largely used for executive-legislative communication and influence; and considerable tension between the two branches is frequent.

### Executive Agencies

Previous discussions of the separation of powers and of the presidency have already indicated some of the characteristics of the executive branches of the state. The over-all character of governmental administration in this country has been strongly influenced by the popular distrust of executive agencies, which are perennially seen as threats to "representative government;" the word "bureaucracy" is a prime political epithet. This attitude, founded in the early revolt against the executive authority of the British Crown, has been maintained in part by legislative and judicial attacks upon the executive arm as a competitor for power and prestige.

Yet generalized resistance to expansion of executive functions has not checked *specific* demands upon the state, having the cumulative effect of enormously increasing the amount and scope of administrative action, especially during the past half-century. Along with the sheer expansion—whether measured by personnel[9] or by expenditures—have gone tendencies toward (1) greater specialization of functions, both of agencies and of specific positions; (2) greater organizational complexity, both within particular agencies and among interdependent agencies; (3) greater professionalization

---

of Congress was about the same in 1933 as in 1925; yet the Hundred Days of the first New Deal Congress manifested a very different de facto organization and procedure.

8 For a detailed account of the remarkable complexity of Congressional voting, see David B. Truman, *The Congressional Party: A Case Study* (New York: Wiley, 1959).

9 However, paid civilian employees of the federal government in 1964 numbered only 2.5 million of a total employed population of about 70 million. Contrary to much popular belief, state and local governments have grown much faster in recent years than the civilian components of the federal establishment outside of the Department of Defense.

of officials, through training, permanence of office, and standardized technical qualifications; (4) elaboration of administrative rules and other bureaucratic characteristics; (5) political neutralization of the public employee; (6) growth of administrative discretion and the rule-making powers. Many of these so-called modern trends represent long standing and fundamental forces in our society.

We now have an enormous maze of interdependent and crisscrossing agencies, and the problems of coordination and control are correspondingly difficult. Inevitably, there is much overlapping of authority, with resulting interagency competition and defensiveness.[1] That these patterns are rooted in deep and persistent forces is indicated by the long history of successive administrative reorganizations at both federal and state levels that recurrently face the same essential problems.

These problems are primarily the outcomes of institutional structure not of particular personalities or political party affiliations of the officials. Much criticism has been leveled at the alleged waste or inefficiency entailed by a structure in which authority is so dispersed and central coordination is so tenuous. But, in any case, most Americans do not seem to think efficiency the highest value to be sought in government. The practice of rotating short-term elective offices, still common at state and local levels, is not efficient wherever either continuity of policy or specialized technical competence is of importance. The establishment of overlapping or conflicting executive agencies has been dictated not by considerations of over-all efficiency but by the desire to satisfy separate interests concerned with particular problems.

An apt illustration is provided by the office of state governor. In the early period of insistence upon separation of powers and of great distrust of governors, the state constitutions provided short terms and only very limited powers for governors. Although the passage of time has seen the growth of greater powers of the chief state executive, the office of governor generally still lacks any great measure of administrative control. The governor is in competition with other major elected officials; the officials and agencies he "supervises" are usually minutely bound by enacted regulations; he has little authority over local officials.

The separation of the chief executive positions from the legislative branch leads executive agencies to act very much like private pressure groups.[2] They seek to influence public opinion generally, to build up favorable attitudes in special publics, and to influence directly the legislature. They frequently propose, try to alter, or try to defeat legislation. They "lobby." They often act to an important degree as the "functional representatives" of special segments of the population—agriculture, labor, business interests. It is becoming increasingly clear that administration is never clearly nor wholly separated from legislation and hence always involves questions of politics and that government itself, in the form of these

[1] Illustrations are abundant, for example, the struggle over the establishment of a unified military department, the recurrent differences between the State Department and the military agencies over foreign policy.

[2] Key, *Politics, Parties and Pressure Groups, op. cit.*, pp. 175–189, 194–197

agencies, is thus becoming an increasingly important influence upon legislation and national policy. No matter how much some officials may seek to
pose all questions of policy as if they were only technical problems of ad
ministrative procedure, the cumulative effects of "interpretation" and "implementation" often are indistinguishable from statutory force. The recognition that administrators inevitably legislate in this sense when they make
binding policies that lead to enforceable rules is now widely accepted.
Since rules always affect power and "interests," administration always has a
problematic political aspect.

Furthermore, there are political problems, in a narrower meaning,
within both federal and state bureaucracies. Where some reasonably effective merit system is in operation, the lower ranks of the hierarchy are
filled by persons selected on the basis of examinations aimed at specific
vocational qualifications; but the upper policy-forming positions are usually
filled either by "political" appointees who do not make a career of government service[3] or by men who have demonstrated special competence outside of the system of qualifying examinations.[4] Department and bureau
chiefs are thus not infrequently opposed or circumvented by the permanent
staff. Rarely are the directing officials pure administrators who simply carry
out delegated policies; they are more nearly political strategists who for the
time being initiate and promote policies of the government in power. The
presidential cabinet is far from a perfect coordinating mechanism for such
officials, who tend to serve only so long as they agree with higher policies.
Such a structure is one source of difficulty in attempting to secure unified
policy on foreign and domestic problems.

We have now seen many instances of how artificial and misleading are
the labels "legislative" and "executive" if taken as literally descriptive. An
essential lesson, indeed, for the serious study of political institutions is that
the label does not necessarily describe the fact and that the only remedy is
attention to the details of actual behavior. Many contemporary organizations
and activities of the state defy conventional classification. The quasi-public
corporation, such as the Tennessee Valley Authority, is neither wholly
"government" nor wholly "business;" and its administrative problems could
be comprehended equally as well by either a business executive or a Washington bureau chief. Eighteenth-century labels cannot give us the key to
current social structures.

## THE POWER ELITE  (does it exist?)

Few subjects in the sociology of American life have aroused more interest
and controversy during the twentieth century than the question as to
whether a definite "power elite" or "ruling class" dominates crucial decisions

[3] Harold J. Laski, *The American Democracy* (New York: Viking, 1948), pp. 99–108,
notes the contrast with the British system.

[4] Persons who occupy the higher positions in the federal civil service are quite similar in
their middle- and upper-class backgrounds to top business executives (although the government workers more frequently have had graduate training). See W. Lloyd Warner,
*et al.*, *The American Federal Executive* (New Haven, Conn.: Yale University Press,
1963).

affecting the nation as a whole. One set of interpretations sees a relatively few strategic economic and political "command posts" from which most of the really important decisions are made. These positions are occupied by a loosely connected stratum of powerful or wealthy persons, who tend to interact with other members of the elites and to share common perspectives and goals. Although it is not explicitly held that there is any conspiracy or plot to control the society in the interest of a tightly-knit upper class, the effect of the alleged concentration of power is thought to be to create a small set of decision-makers who effectively direct societal policy, with little or no democratic responsibility toward the electorate as a whole.[5]

Now it is a verifiable and universal fact that at any particular time the *binding decisions directly affecting major lines of action of any national government will be made by a relatively small number of persons.* This fact is inevitable under any conceivably practicable form of the state for complex societies. It holds and must hold in genuine democracies, not just in "autocratic" states. It is a tendency that is accentuated by pressures for *quick* decisions on *complex* issues and is further favored by felt needs for some degree of secrecy and flexibility in such decisions. All these conditions are maximized in international relations, diplomatic negotiations, and military affairs.

The existence of concentrated decision making by itself definitely does not tell us whether or not there is a power elite, or if so, whether it is an elite responsible to and removed by "the people."[6] The crucial questions, rather, are these: (1) Is there a unitary elite, or a pluralistic set of elites? If the latter, how much consensus exists among the elites? (2) How are the decision makers chosen? (3) Do they operate in accordance with binding rules? If so, what are the sources of these rules? (4) Are the decision makers accountable to the governed? If so, how?

In the absence of quantitative data concerning constraints upon the decisions of power holders, it is possible for widely divergent views to be held by partisans of a "power elite" conception or a multi-influence conception of the power structure of American society. Certainly, Arnold Rose is correct in pointing to massive constraints at all levels upon the actions of elites—constraints derived from physical setting, resources, technology, institutional limits, values, political norms, and actions of counterelites.[7] Further, there is overwhelming evidence that the decision makers and those who influence their decisions at the national level are not by any stretch of the imagination a monolithic and continuing elite. What does have to be taken seriously are the specific forces and organizational channels that generate centralization or decentralization, "responsible" or "arbitrary" action, and the like.

Large-scale social structures in which the attainment of major goals

---

[5] This thesis is identified, above all, with the views of C. Wright Mills, *The Power Elite* (New York: Oxford University Press, 1956); and, for local communities, Floyd Hunter, *Community Power Structure* (Chapel Hill: University of North Carolina Press, 1952).
[6] Cf. Harold D. Lasswell, Daniel Lerner, and C. Easton Rothwell, *The Comparative Study of Elites* (Stanford, Calif.: Stanford University Press, 1952), pp. 7–8.
[7] Rose, *op. cit.*, pp. 18–19.

requires relatively close coordination (in time, space, phasing, sequence) of diverse subunits and types of activity develop a relatively high degree of centralized decision making and of hierarchical control. If goal attainment is, further, highly dependent upon rapid decisions and upon rapid, coordinated action to carry out the decisions, these tendencies will be greatly strengthened. If there are severe problems of dissension, opposition, and conflict within the organization, decision making tends to shift toward the upper (or central) parts of the hierarchy. Both rapidity of decision and internal conflict tend to produce secrecy; and severe external threat accelerates all of the above-mentioned developments.[8]

In the immediate future, the pressure of international situations alone will doubtless tend to tighten and unify administrative machinery and enhance the authority of the chief executive posts. Such developments represent modifications of the doctrines of federalism and separation of powers. Quite clearly also, the position of military agencies deserves attention, in view of events of recent history and in view of the long period of turbulence, in many parts of the world, that undoubtedly lies ahead.

### THE CIVIL AND THE MILITARY POWERS

Under the Constitution, Congress may not infringe "the right of the people to keep and bear arms" (Second Amendment). This provision has never been interpreted as a right of citizens to take up arms against the state; indeed, it succeeds the phrase "A well-regulated militia being necessary to the security of a free State. . . ." Early American leaders held that the maintenance and regulation of military forces was a crucial problem of all states and that the status of military agencies had peculiar significance to a political democracy; their concern is reflected in several major constitutional provisions.

In the formal structure of the American system, the military agencies are subdivisions of the executive branch, subject to certain checks by Congress. A civilian—the President—is commander in chief of the armed services, in war and peace, and in the past each main division of the military arm has been headed by a civilian. The official line of authority thus runs to a popularly elected chief executive. Congress is given control of appropriations, and the Constitution specifically limits any military appropriation to a term of two years. All military officers are nominally commissioned directly by the President; Congress is invested with the power to make "Rules for the Government and Regulation of the land and naval Forces" (Article I, Section 8). Finally, the power to declare war is assigned to the elected Congress, and the control of foreign policy is mainly vested in the President and the Senate.

Clearly the intent of the Constitution was to insure the supremacy of elective, civilian control over the armed forces of the national government.[9]

[8] For interesting hypotheses on these and related matters, see Anthony Downs, *Inside Bureaucracy* (Boston: Little, Brown, 1967), esp. Chaps. XII, XIII, and XV.
[9] "The founders of the American republic knew that again and again in the course of human affairs liberty has been destroyed by military dictatorships and in framing the

Similarly, in the various state constitutions there is usually some explicit statement that the military powers are subordinate to civil authority. (All the foregoing are official norms that do not completely correspond to the facts. As is commonly known, the civil heads of military departments have not been always able to control the military personnel.)

The one major exception to civil supremacy provided for by the federal Constitution authorizes Congress to suspend the privilege of habeas corpus during invasion or rebellion, when presumably the civil courts are unable to operate in normal fashion. Until recently the most dramatic instance of the suspending of habeas corpus was Lincoln's authorization of military arrests and trials of civilians outside the zone of military operations and in areas in which the civil courts were in operation. Although the Supreme Court ruled in *Ex parte Milligan* against the validity of the judgment of the military courts under these conditions, the possibility of military rule without the protections of civil procedures has remained. Indeed, World War II brought the forced removal of Japanese American citizens from the west coast; and the military rule of Hawaii again raised the constitutional question in a form similar to *Ex parte Milligan*. The Supreme Court held (in 1946) that the military courts have no jurisdiction over civilians in the areas where the usual civil courts are able to carry out their duties and where no immediate military danger exists,[1] thus once more affirming the principle of civil supremacy. But despite constitutions and statutes, military powers vastly increase during war; and the longer and more severe the conflict the greater the increase.

The relatively small and subordinate part played by military authority during most of national history is, of course, not explicable merely by the existence of constitutional provisions and paper barriers. For long periods no large standing military forces were necessary. Until recently, although the forms of large-scale military organization have been fully developed, the standing army has been small enough[2] to make military influence upon political forms slight except in periods of large-scale warfare.[3]

No one familiar with the history of the United States up to 1941 is likely to overlook the emphasis upon civilian control of military powers, or the lack of a larger standing military establishment, or the rapid demobilization after each war. Certainly, there is another story running concurrently—the protracted violence directed against the American Indians, the frequent use of military force to put down domestic disturbances, the massive fratricide of the 1860's, and the expansionistic military actions of the nineteenth and twentieth centuries.

Constitution they sought to establish firmly the supremacy of the President and Congress over the military arm of the Government." Charles A. Beard, *American Government and Politics*, 10th ed. (New York: Macmillan, 1949), p. 285.

[1] In *Duncan v. Kahanamoku*. See Rossiter, *op. cit.*, pp. 284–285.

[2] The entire regular Army of the United States consisted of about 165,000 men in 1940, on the brink of World War II.

[3] Bennett M. Rich, *The Presidents and Civil Disorder* (Washington, D.C.: The Brookings Institution, 1941).

*[margin: Militarization — un mean:]*

Yet, it has only been since World War II that one has had to think soberly about the possibility of a genuine militarization of American society. The ambiguous term "militarization" can refer to one or more of the following: (1) the continuous existence of large military forces in times of relative peace; (2) very long periods of partial mobilization of national resources and organizations for international struggle; (3) decisive importance of military considerations and military counsels and demands in decisions concerning a wide range of vital public policies; (4) the disappearance of even a limited degree of isolation from world politics; (5) increased influence of military activities upon other institutions and organizations of the domestic society.

*[margin: 7th Cent. — possibility of total war — shaped budget, ed. system, ec. activity]*

In the second half of the twentieth century, considerations arising from the possibility of total warfare (nuclear, chemical, biological, and so on) have decisively shaped the national budget, deeply affected the educational system, directly organized much economic activity. The effects on national policies are so profound as to raise the question of how far the society already may have moved toward a "garrison state"—that is "a state on a permanent war-footing, with the population in genuine fear of imminent conflict, so unlimited in its nature as to involve the total resources of the nation and so uncertain in its outcome as to necessitate the subordination of every consideration of democracy or warfare to 'military necessity.' "[4]

*[margin: endemic involvement in "police actions" — limited wars]*

Short of the garrison state, also, one can visualize a situation of endemic involvement in "police actions," counterinsurgency operations, and limited wars that would require a continuous partial mobilization and a corresponding military emphasis in national decision making.

*[margin: wars produce unexpected change]*

Consideration of many features of the military institutions of the nation does not require an analysis of the effects of war. But, of course, military organizations find their ultimate reason for being in the actual use of organized violence. And wars of all kinds are peculiarly productive of institutional change, including undesired and unpredictable consequences. The initial effects of mobilization are very different from the consequences of large-scale combat; and these are not identical with the later proximate outcomes of various kinds of "victory" or "defeat." Thus, the initial increase in societal stratification in periods of mobilization and early warfare as authority is centralized may eventually change into a "flat" system as a total concentration of power wipes out intermediate levels, reducing the masses to a common level.[5]

For the period since just after World War II, the increased importance of military activity is easily documented. In 1940, budget expenditures for

[4] Louis Smith, *American Democracy and Military Power: A Study of the Civil Control of the Military Power in the United States* (Chicago: University of Chicago Press, 1951), p. 7; cf. Harold D. Lasswell, *National Security and Individual Freedom* (New York: McGraw-Hill, 1950); Harold D. Lasswell, *The Civilian and the Military* (New York: Oxford University Press, 1956); John M. Swomley, Jr., *The Military Establishment* (Boston: Beacon Press, 1964); Irving Louis Horowitz, *The War Game* (New York: Ballantine Books, 1963); Burton M. Sapin and Richard C. Snyder, *The Role of the Military in American Foreign Policy* (Garden City, N.Y.: Doubleday, 1954).

[5] Cf. Stanislaw Andrezejewski, *Military Organization and Society* (London: Routledge and Kegan Paul, 1954).

Post WW II
Military Bud
(1940 - 17%
(1967 - 55%

national defense totalled $1.5 billion; in 1944, $76.8 billion; in 1957, $43.4
billion; in 1966, $57.7 billion. As a proportion of all federal government ex-
penditures, national defense accounted for 17 percent in 1940, 81 percent
in 1944, 63 percent in 1957, and about 55 percent in 1967.[6] Military personnel on active duty were 458,000 in 1940; 12 million in 1945; just under 1
million in 1957; and over 3 million in 1967.[7] The net growth is impressive.
Yet the enormous swings in size of the military establishment do not represent the behavior of a society bent upon a military way of life. Rather, the
fluctuations primarily reflect political estimates of the nature and extent
of external threats to national survival and "national interests."

A realistic analysis of political institutions must look closely at the organized management of violence. It would be folly to minimize the historical importance of sheer power in altering the distribution of other scarce
values and in shaping the basic framework of societies.[8] That importance is
so great that many have been tempted to generalize that political power,
resting on control of violence, has primacy over economic exchange and
other systems of reward and persuasion. Since 1945, however, the means of
violence have reached such levels of destructive potential that other approaches to the development of national influence may have risen in the
scale of effectiveness. Escalation of violence has an ultimate limit: total
mutual destruction.

There is no need to document for today's students of society the destructive potential of new technologies now in the possession of the great world
powers. There is clear evidence also of the greatly increased involvement of
military officers in the shaping and implementation of national policies.
The distinction between military and civilian matters has been reduced by
the permanent threat of Armageddon. This threat has increased the importance of deterring the use of absolute violence, not only through strictly
military capabilities but also through economic and political means; it has
widened the responsibilities and increased the prestige of military groups
and their leaders.[9]

At the same time, the prevalence in many nation-states since World
War II of internationally supported revolutionary movements, subversion,
terrorism, insurgency, insurrection, and guerrilla war has produced many

new levels
destructive po
military a
involved in
shaping policies
Threat of
Armageddon
- forces often
to avoid use
of absolute
violence

[6] United States Bureau of the Census, *Statistical Abstract of the United States: 1967,*
88th ed. (Washington, D.C.: Government Printing Office, 1967), p. 252.

[7] United States Bureau of the Census, *Historical Statistics of the United States* (Washington, D.C.: Government Printing Office, 1960), p. 736, and *ibid.,* p. 263.

[8] Cf. Alfred Vagts, *A History of Militarism* (New York: Meridian Books, 1959); Quincey
Wright, *A Study of War,* Vols. I–II (Chicago: University of Chicago Press, 1942);
Pitirim A. Sorokin, *Society, Culture and Personality* (New York: Harper & Row, 1947),
Chaps. 31–32; Hans Speier, *Social Order and the Risks of War* (New York: George W.
Stewart, 1952); Thomas C. Schelling, *Arms and Influence* (New Haven, Conn.: Yale
University Press, 1966).

[9] Cf. Morris Janowitz (with Lt. Col. Roger Little), *Sociology and the Military Establish-
ment,* rev. ed. (New York: Russell Sage Foundation, 1965); Morris Janowitz, *The
Professional Soldier* (New York: Free Press, 1960); Morris Janowitz (ed.), *The New
Military: Changing Patterns of Organization* (New York: Russell Sage Foundation, 1964);
Paul Y. Hammond, *Organizing for Defense: The American Military Establishment in the
Twentieth Century* (Princeton, N.J.: Princeton University Press, 1961).

situations in which deployment of maximum conventional force is difficult or impossible. Such situations typically are militarily chaotic and politically ambiguous, and show clearly that under these circumstances there are no such things as "purely military" decisions.[1]

Studies of the sociology of military affairs are few in number but have contributed greatly to knowledge of how different modern warfare and modern military organization are from the conventional stereotypes still common even among well-educated Americans.[2] Of course, it is part of the conventional wisdom to say that that military organization in many respects is practically the archetype of bureaucratic structures. The basic necessities of organization—if there is to be the centralized control of agencies concerned with the large-scale application of organized violence—make inevitable a substantial development of formalized, hierarchic, and coercive procedures. Military forces everywhere are managed in terms of authoritative rules applied to a membership largely involuntary in recruitment. The ultimate rationale of such organization is their potential commitment in combat; and at least those portions of the military organization likely to confront the life-and-death stress of combat simply cannot operate in the same way as universities or supermarkets. Nevertheless, as Morris Janowitz has shown, the modern American military establishment has been forced, or led, in the direction of greater flexibility and autonomy, greater decentralization of some kinds of decision making and greater emphasis upon positive incentives in addition to the disciplines of a punishment-centered hierarchy.[3]

It has been a deep conviction in our political thought that the existence in a nation of large military forces over a long period of time produces a segment of the population likely to be appreciably alienated from civil standards. The idea of a professional, permanent military establishment, in particular, raises the specter of an insulated, powerful, authoritarian and, ultimately, arrogant and politically ambitious social formation, which could someday become the master of a garrison state rather than the responsible instrument of a democratic polity. This consideration has been a major element in the American tradition favoring the temporary citizen-soldier.[4] But

---

[1] Cf. Janus K. Zawodny (ed.), *Unconvenitonal Warfare*, *The Annals*, 341 (May 1962); Harry Eckstein (ed.), *Internal War* (New York: Free Press, 1964); Samuel P. Huntington (ed.), *Changing Patterns of Military Politics* (New York: Free Press, 1967).

[2] See, for example, the works of Janowitz, *op. cit.*; Charles H. Coates and Roland J. Pellegrin, with Norman A. Hilmar, *Military Sociology: A Study of American Military Institutions and Military Life* (University Park, Md.: Social Science Press, 1966); Samuel A. Stouffer, *et al.*, *The American Soldier*, Vols. I–II (Princeton, N.J.: Princeton University Press, 1949); Albert D. Biderman, *March to Calumny* (New York: Macmillan, 1963); John W. Masland and Lawrence I. Radway, *Soldiers and Scholars: Military Education and National Policy* (Princeton, N.J.: Princeton University Press, 1957).

[3] For an authentic picture of combat "organization"—including the individual initiative and adaptability of the infantry soldier—see S. L. A. Marshall, *Men Against Fire* (New York: Morrow, 1947).

[4] Arthur A. Ekirch, Jr., *The Civilian and the Military* (New York: Oxford University Press, 1956), chap. XVII; Samuel P. Huntington, *The Soldier and the State* (Cambridge, Mass.: Harvard University Press, 1957).

the hasty large-scale mobilization of large forces and their equally hasty demobilization becomes increasingly inefficient and hazardous under the new conditions of military technology and international politics. Accordingly, the older policies come under increasing strain in a world of continuous revolution and insurgency, quasi-wars, large undeclared wars, and balance-of-terror politics.

## THE RIGHTS AND DUTIES OF CITIZENS

The relation of the individual to the state demonstrates the distinctive nature of the political monopoly of power. For the individual's allegiance to the state, unlike his membership in a labor union or a church, cannot easily be transferred; and he can resign from citizenship only at the cost of resigning from the whole society at the same time. That the status of citizen is a primary base for a series of other statuses is shown by the contemporary plight of large numbers of stateless persons who exist by sufferance within alien and often hostile nations or in international enclaves. In a world of nation-states each polity encompasses individuals as a totalistic, authoritative, and often awesome presence. Thus the state's monopoly of authority renders the rights and duties of citizens a matter of special interest to each individual—and to the sociology of political behavior.

In America, popular tradition has emphasized the *rights* of individual citizens against the state. Yet there must always be a duty wherever there is a right, for a right is meaningless unless someone has the duty to respect it. Our present concern is to discover the salient features of the normative reciprocities that define the statuses of citizens in relation to the American state.

Democracy cannot be identified with majority rule; the twentieth century has certainly furnished enough examples of dictatorial governments representing, or claiming to represent, substantial majorities of the population. Democracy is often thought to be a system in which minority elements are expected to acquiesce in any majority decision, but if so, the American system differs from it in two basic respects: (1) many of our political institutions check and limit direct majority rule; (2) a long list of rights are reserved to individuals, or more narrowly to citizens, as inviolable by ordinary legislative or executive action.

Such rights imply, of course, definite limits to majority rule and popular sovereignty. Unlimited popular sovereignty permits individuals no rights that the state is bound to recognize; the state is supposed to embody the people, and the representatives of the state are bound only by the expressed will of the electorate. The doctrine of unlimited popular sovereignty, at first glance so preeminently democratic, can thus quite easily justify absolutistic government. For majority rule is no guarantee of individual freedom; majorities can be as intolerant of dissent as any minority. The basic conception that the individual has rights the state must respect presupposes that the state is not coextensive with society but is only an institution within it.

*No rights are absolute*

In American constitutional law there are the well known formal provisions of the Bill of Rights and subsequent amendments.[5] In addition, a multitude of specific rights has been held to inhere either in citizenship in the United States or in citizenship in the separate states, or simply in residence within United States jurisdiction.[6] Yet none of these rights is absolute. Slavery and involuntary servitude are forbidden; but military service, jury duty, imprisonment for law violation, and various civil duties are compulsory. Compulsory sterilization and vaccination have been held by judicial decision as not violating personal liberty under the Fourteenth Amendment. Freedom of religion is guaranteed, but some laws are upheld that impose disadvantages or disabilities upon particular religious groups. Freedom of speech is a basic tenet of civil rights, but its specific interpretation always draws limits to permitted communication. Widespread use of wiretapping has been followed by employment of electronic devices that enable invasions of privacy without the physical intrusion of persons or devices into rooms or other enclosed places. Existing and prospective technology if fully and indiscriminately used by officials and by private organizations and individuals would render personal life transparent to malicious exploitation. It seems likely that in coming decades the legal definition and implementation of "rights of privacy" may be essential to meaningful survival of "freedom of speech." All rights are subject to complex variations in judicial interpretation and executive action; all have at some time been subjected to powerful demands for abrogation.

The federal government has only limited power to check state and local governments or private groups or individuals who may seek to deny these rights, except when such action falls within its express jurisdiction. The widespread denial of the suffrage and other rights of citizenship to Negroes for several generations is an example of how state and private action may nullify the seeming guarantees of the Constitution. With the passage and partial enforcement of the Civil Rights Acts of 1964 and 1965 such denials are being reduced and eliminated, locality by locality.

There is a sense in which the rights of free communication and free assembly are not privileges granted by the state but are conditions prerequisite for the existence of the state in the form of a constitutional democracy. Unrestrained freedom is, of course, impossible, for the freedom of one group or individual beyond certain limits infringes the freedom of others. Yet a very broad latitude for expression of opinion and for private action is a defining condition of a democratic system. These freedoms are difficult to establish and precarious to maintain.[7] Success seems to depend

---

5 Cf. the listings cited by Milton R. Konvitz, *The Constitution and Civil Rights* (New York: Columbia University Press, 1947), pp. 33–34; also, Milton R. Konvitz, *Expanding Liberties; Freedom's Gains in Postwar America* (New York: Viking, 1966).

6 A long series of court interpretations have had to deal with questions as to whether a given right applies to *citizens* only or to *individuals*, including aliens.

7 Our legal history is marked by a continuous and often disorderly battle between the protection of liberties under the due process rule, on the one side, and the vague "police power" applying to the health, safety, morals, and general welfare of the people, on the other.

upon (1) the absence of large groupings having basically incompatible values that could create fundamental cleavage of the social order; (2) relative absence of severe and long-continued external threats to the society; (3) division of social power among several different groups or strata so that no united minority (or majority) can seize power and suppress dissent. The interests and values that have become attached to inherited doctrines and political forms may also play a part in the American case.[8]

These considerations suggest a broader hypothesis. The rights (including immunities, privileges, liberties) of individuals within the political order depend, on the one hand, upon the widespread and ingrained value systems of the culture that live in individual personalities. Effective support of the principle that the governments, majorities, or private associations and individuals cannot violate certain rights of persons requires, at the least, conviction that value divergences are not so important as the worth attached to individual personality. The rights of individuals are never secure unless a large proportion of the population have real emotional reactions against violations of those rights. On the other hand, value consensus alone does not guarantee the preservation of rights. Those whose rights are violated must have the power to strike back; acquiescence in the violation of rights means that in the long run they will cease to exist.

Dissenters from popular views often are "troublesome" and "unpleasant" persons from the viewpoint of those whose values and beliefs are being challenged, often rudely. On their side, dissenters sometimes are highly intolerant of those who disagree with them, authoritarian in their self-convictions, and impatient with laws, procedures ("technicalities"), constitutions ("legalisms"), and orderly debate and negotiation. In situations of intense social controversy, therefore, those who speak for these procedural safeguards may become the target of all the contending partisans. In the heat of social battle, the importance in the longer run of a viable political center and associated neutral ground of basic rights may be forgotten.

In the United States, only a few organizations outside the judicial system itself devote major effort to defending and promoting the "Bill of Rights" freedoms. The best known private associations of this kind include the American Civil Liberties Union, American Veterans Committee, Anti-Defamation League of B'nai B'rith, National Association for the Advancement of Colored People, American Jewish Congress, and the National Council of Churches.

An example of how essential organized power is in establishing social rights is provided by the history of the "elementary" rights of the citizens in the United States to vote and to hold public office. Only after lengthy struggles were property qualifications dropped, certain religious qualifications removed, minority races and women enfranchised. A study of the history of these changes is rewarding in showing how far from automatic

[8] For example, groups that may have an immediate desire to suppress other groups may be deterred to some extent by allegiance to legal symbols that they hesitate to violate for fear of other repercussions.

they were, how intense and continued was the organized effort required to effect them, and how determined the opposition.

Thus, individual rights in the United States have had their source both in abstract ideal and concrete "necessities." A creed of democracy was developed in America upon conceptions of ethical equality that can be traced back in part to the universalistic ethics of the Judaic-Christian tradition, to Roman conceptions of universal law, and to the merging of the two in doctrines such as those of natural law and the social contract. It found a realistic social base in widespread economic and cultural opportunity, in the needs of a new state for mass support and armed service from the population at large, and in the lack of sharp class divisions. The absence of strong temporal powers of an established church favored doctrines of democracy and tolerance. These influences, although changed in some degree, continue and help to make it possible for many (not all) minorities to protect themselves and others from what they consider inequalitarian and arbitrary governmental actions.

The values and norms expressed in traditional political and civil rights are in every case the outgrowth of conflicts and struggles of the past. In society, unless there is a "problem," rules do not arise. Civil liberties and rights require rules for regulating the fiercest and most enduring conflicts, in which social status, personal reputation, indeed, life itself, are often at stake. Norms which can restrain such strong interests and prejudices are subject to incessant pressure; they do not maintain themselves automatically. Many object lessons on this theme have been provided in the years since the end of World War II. "McCarthyism"—so-called for the prominence of Senator Joseph McCarthy as a pursuer of alleged "radicals" in the early 1950's—was only one of many efforts to modify or destroy traditional safeguards for the individual. Actions ostensibly aimed at communism and subversion have violated long-standing rules concerning presumption of guilt, opportunity to know accusers and the nature of the charges, opportunity for rebuttal, the rights of witnesses, a hearing before an impartial judge, and many others.[9] Guilt by association, guilt by innuendo, and vague and indiscriminate charges (difficult to refute by evidence)[1] have been conspicuous in some congressional investigations and loyalty hearings. The criticism and protest aroused by these developments (as well as the struggles for power at high levels of the political structure, touched off by them) attest to the difficulty of sustaining agreement on basic questions of procedure in this matter.[2] Once again we see how the institutional regulation of power is a core problem of political systems.

[9] See the lucid summary of Robert E. Cushman, *Civil Liberties in the United States* (Ithaca, N.Y.: Cornell University Press, 1956), esp. pp. 177–205. This work contains an excellent bibliography.

[1] Cf. Daniel Bell (ed.), *The Radical Right* (Garden City, N.Y.: Doubleday, 1963); Samuel A. Stouffer, *Communism, Conformity and Civil Liberties* (Garden City, N.Y.: Doubleday, 1955); Edward Shils, *The Torment of Secrecy* (New York: Free Press, 1956).

[2] Cushman, *op. cit.*, p. 181: "Essential justice requires that a person not be punished for committing an offense so vaguely defined that a reasonable man could commit the crime without knowing it."

## POLITICAL PARTIES AND THE VOTERS

At the center of the web of government is the formal structure of the state, interlaced on the one side with ideas and value systems and on the other with the informal organization of governing as a concrete social process. Operating through, and in relation to, this whole structure are the millions of individuals and thousands of specific associations and groups that constitute the society as a whole. Between these individuals and groups and the state are the organized political parties, which in some respects are an extension of the governing association itself.[3] Political parties were not mentioned in the Constitution, and their later role was evidently unforeseen. The Constitution makers established a system of indirect election for crucial elective offices—senators were elected by the state legislatures, and the President was to be chosen by the electoral college, itself chosen by the state legislators. Not foreseen were the extension of suffrage, the growth of the party system, and the eventual change of the electoral college to a ceremonial body that merely transmits the results of the popular vote in each state.

But a mass of voters cannot elect representatives without some organization to propose candidates and focus political issues. Political parties are centrally important structures in many different types of politics; they are indispensable in the orderly operation of a representative type of democracy. In the United States parties began as purely "private" groupings, in response to the need for machinery to translate the popular will into the selection of governors. Gradually, parties came to be regarded as public or quasi-public agencies and their activities to be defined and regulated by law.

It is notoriously difficult to define just what is meant by "party." Groupings called parties are organized in widely different ways, use of a variety of methods, have different kinds of objectives. All parties have in common, however, the organized striving for control of the governing apparatus—they are continuing associations specifically organized to secure power over personnel and policies of the state.[4] They represent an open rather than a closed type of social relationship, and their immediate end is always the capture of power. Americans are accustomed to parties that (mainly) seek power through nonviolent means; and they take it for granted that a party defeated at the polls will accept the result more or less gracefully, or at least peacefully, and will simply bide its time to win victory in its turn by conventional methods. Parties in democracies are organized bodies that propose candidates and seek to win open elections as a means to control and use of the authority and facilities of the state. Typically, in relatively stable democracies the results of the elections are accepted without violent resistance by the defeated party, and the victors refrain from destruction

---

[3] The number of useful references is enormous. Any short list will seem biased. Works found particularly helpful for the present purposes included: Robert R. Alford, *Party and Society: The Anglo-American Democracies* (Chicago: Rand McNally, 1963); Maurice Duverger, *Political Parties* (New York: Wiley, 1954); see further references below.

[4] See Ranney, *The Governing of Men, op. cit.*, p. 332: "a democratic political party is an autonomous organized group that makes nominations and contests elections in the hope of eventually gaining and exercising control of the personnel and policies of government."

of their opponents. Quite obviously, however, there are parties that do not operate in this way. Americans are accustomed, furthermore, to parties that maintain themselves by voluntary recruitment and are not an official part of the administrative structure of the state; but the incorporation of the party as a closed group into the personnel of government, as in Soviet Russia or Nazi Germany, reminds us that very different arrangements are common elsewhere.

The United States is remarkable among the major societies of the modern world for the continuity and stability of a two-party system. Much effort has been devoted to explaining why political parties are strong in the United States and why the two-party system is maintained. The system of political democracy itself has been basic, but several more specific factors have been at work. The large number of elective officers running for relatively short terms makes it extremely difficult for the unorganized voters to select candidates; and the division of authority between federal and state governments, which makes it necessary to control both in order to carry out an effective national program, further strengthens the system. Established parties also tend to be perpetuated by the vested interests their presence has created and by the traditional loyalties they have attached. Furthermore, the separation of powers makes control of both the executive and the legislative branches especially important and thus impels those who wish power to consolidate their forces in a united organization.

In its historical origins, the two-party system was "in the culture," having been already well developed in Britain out of social class divisions. It has been favored by the presidential form of government, including the parallel system of governorships in the individual states. The separate and unitary executive cannot be divided up among a coalition of minor parties, as is possible with the cabinet of a parliamentary state.[5] A broad division of economic interests between agriculture on the one hand and trade, finance, and industry on the other helped for a long time to give added stability to the system. Once established, it created its own vested interests and cultural rationales. Furthermore, and of primary importance, the social order has been *relatively* free of the deep ethnic, religious, and class cleavages among politically effective portions of the population such as have produced a multitude of special-interest parties in Europe. Of course, a continuing two-party system is not unique to Anglo-American countries, being found also in such widely different nations as Turkey and Uruguay. However, the social structures and ideological conditions necessary for stable two-party systems have been relatively rare in the past, in spite of the enormous practical advantages of having basic political choices reduced to a selection between two organized groupings. Extreme social tension and conflict, even more than heterogeneity of interests and values, tends to disrupt a two-party system.[6] The most important support for the system in the political in-

[5] The presidential form is not essential to a two-party system, as the British case shows.
[6] As Duverger points out (*op. cit.*, pp. 214–215), a situation in which a strong totalitarian party seeks to destroy the established order is incompatible with such a system.

stitutions themselves undoubtedly lies in an electoral system in which victory may be attained by a simple majority voting in a single ballot.[7]

Many observers of American politics have criticized the party system because of the lack of clear party principles. From the Civil War until the New Deal, the two major parties often seemed to differ so little in policy and ideology as to constitute parties essentially organized around patronage. But, as often noted by political scientists, this very lack of sharply defined principles has been a source of stability in the system. Many of the attacks upon "lack of principle" seem to have assumed that the lack of sharp ideological boundaries between the Democratic and the Republican party is unique to the United States. What has been ignored by such observers is the fact that in other nations as well, different parties nominally based on the same ideology rarely conform neatly to a common set of clear principles. Different "socialist" parties within the same country act in very dissimilar ways, and the fact of great international differences in communist parties since the 1950's hardly requires documentation. The same label may cover highly unlike contents. In the American case, it certainly is true that each of the major parties is a complex and amorphous melange of diverse economic interests, religious groupings, ethnic stocks, and so forth, and thus must compromise and integrate numerous conflicts in order to gain national power. The struggle for power therefore concerns immediate problems; conflicts cannot be brought to the sharp definition of irreconcilable principle without destroying party unity. And this relatively easy-going and flexible situation is expressive, in its turn, of the broad value consensus of the society. Both major parties accept "political democracy" and a "capitalistic" economy, and their similarity is clearly shown by comparison with European parties of extreme right and extreme left. Since 1932, the Democratic party has had a special appeal to workers, and higher-income groups have been disproportionately in the Republican camp; but each party includes substantial numbers from every economic stratum. However, studies of voting behavior repeatedly have shown that socioeconomic position strongly correlates with party preferences. A comparative study of Australia, Canada, Great Britain, and the United States indicates that although both religious and regional cleavages are independently important in this country, class voting is present in all four cases and is not declining in any.[8]

Two features of our political institutions have worked against the development of class parties: first, territorial representation; second, the widening of the electorate to include nonpropertied sections of the population. The first creates the mechanical difficulty of finding, in a relatively fluid and heterogeneous society, districts in which one economic stratum is decisively and continually dominant.[9] The representatives may attempt

---

[7] *Ibid.*, pp. 217–228.

[8] Alford, *Party and Society, op. cit.*; Robert E. Lane, *Political Ideology: Why the American Common Man Believes What He Does* (New York: Free Press, 1962).

[9] Such dominance does occur. It is favored where a considerable proportion of the electorate is disenfranchised and where the masses are uneducated, poor, inarticulate, and divided by factionalism or lines of racial and ethnic cleavage. As Key has shown, parts of

to be the voice of particular classes, ethnic groupings, or other special interests within their district; but they may instead try to reconcile divergent and conflicting interests into some conception of the "general welfare" that guides their legislative activities. The second alternative, of course receives the highest nominal value in our culture; it is also in many ways the most difficult course. The "general welfare" is nebulous and finds few organized and politically potent groups to give it voice, whereas special and segmental interests are likely to be highly articulate and politically conscious. If parties corresponded closely to the interests of different economic strata, each stratum might receive unequivocal representation or be without any effective political influence, depending upon the shifting power balance of the various groupings. It is doubtful, however, whether parties organized strictly along the lines of economic class would be compatible with a true party system.[1] American political parties are full of temporary coalitions, decentralized power groupings, rapid changes in leadership, shifting lines of organization—all testimony to the pluralistic and flexible pattern of the underlying structure of values and interests and social collectivities. However, comparisons with "ideological" parties in other societies show that apparent doctrinal unity does not guarantee effective political cohesion— note the case of the French Radical Socialists characterized by Duverger as resembling "an incoherent agglomeration of associations linked by vague and variable bonds, resultant upon hidden intrigues, rivalries between cliques, struggles amongst factions and personalities."[2]

The extension of the suffrage has inhibited narrowly class bounded parties by making it necessary for the privileged strata to appeal to the masses of the voters. It has thereby helped to create parties (formally) based on issues. How important these tendencies are is a matter on which informed judgments differs, and there are those who view American parties as essentially screens hiding the underlying forces of narrow class interests; but it must be granted that the combination of territorial representation and mass electorate has muted the clash of organized class interests.

We have emphasized the two-party system, but other parties are not unimportant. Minor parties have seldom polled more than 5 percent of the popular vote, and their strength has typically been dispersed among a variety of small parties; but their total influence has been much greater than the electoral returns would suggest.[3] On several occasions, a third

---

the South are characterized by conditions that lead to the political dominance of a small, economically privileged minority. V. O. Key, Jr., with the assistance of Alexander Heard, *Southern Politics* (New York: Knopf, 1949), pp. 8–9, 17–18, 307–308.

[1] MacIver maintains that "any full identification of party and class is perilous to the democratic structure." *Op. cit.*, p. 211. See his whole discussion on pp. 208–224; cf. the conclusion of Seymour Martin Lipset, "Political Sociology" in Robert K. Merton, Leonard Broom, Leonard S. Cottrell, Jr. (eds.), *Sociology Today* (New York: Basic Books, 1959), p. 93.

[2] Duverger, *op. cit.*, p. 42.

[3] Key, *Politics, Parties and Pressure Groups, op. cit.*, pp. 273–274. The Progressives under the leadership of Theodore Roosevelt, in 1912, succeeded in capturing 27 percent of the total vote; there have been five other instances in which a minor party received 10 percent or more of the total vote. Louis H. Bean, *How to Predict Elections* (New York: Knopf,

party has seriously challenged the dominant parties—the Populists in 1892, the Bull Moosers in 1912, the Progressives in 1924, and the American Independent Party in 1968. The threat of strong third-party movements has undoubtedly been of importance in the incorporation of their demands into later policies of the major parties.[4] Minor parties rather clearly serve to crystallize and focus issues and grievances not being expressed through the traditional parties. When one of them establishes a territorial base by achieving control of state governments, it sometimes gains a bargaining position by holding a balance of power between the other parties. This situation is rare, however, and may not always be so effective as the alternative procedures of working as a cohesive faction within a major party, or of operating as a "pressure group,"[5] particularly since third-party challenges have been both rare and short lived.

A successfully functioning and stable democratic system probably cannot exist without a party system in which each party brackets a fairly wide segment of the various social strata and interest groupings. Otherwise, the tendency will be either toward unstable "coalition governments" or toward some form of more-or-less dictatorial system. Democratic systems must have considerable leeway for compromise. To the extent that each political party coincides with a unitary bloc of voters who are homogeneous in economic interests, religion, social status, and so on, the incentives for compromise are progressively reduced. A recurrent process, both at local and national levels, is the mobilization of previously apathetic citizens who with seeming abruptness turn out a mass protest vote against incumbent officials or issues favored by the perceived establishment. These "angry voters" may defeat a school-bond proposal, a fluoridation referendum, a school desegregation plan, or a powerful organization candidate.[6] The alienated and angry voter is both disaffected and mobilized; he uses the ballot as a vehicle of insult toward established authority; his vote is an expressive act and it is intended to injure.[7] When such voting becomes massive, polarized, and recurrent, the resulting sharp cleavages tend to drive the system toward conflicts so severe that democratic institutions may be tested beyond endurance.

In the modern period of intense nationalism and heightened social tension, public hostility toward the more extreme deviant parties takes on a quasi-religious character. The Communist party is, of course, the archheresy. Intolerance toward it, though bearing no close relation to the size of influ-

---

1948), p. 71. See John D. Hicks, *The Populist Revolt* (Minneapolis: University of Minnesota Press, 1931), esp. pp. 403 ff.

[4] For example, an impressive proportion of Populist demands, regarded as radical at the time, have been incorporated into later national and state legislation. See Hicks, *op. cit.,* esp. pp. 403 ff.

[5] On the above points see Key, *Politics, Parties and Pressure Groups, op. cit.,* pp. 287 ff.

[6] Murray B. Levin, *The Alienated Voter: Politics in Boston* (New York: Holt, Rinehart & Winston, 1960); Wayne E. Thompson and John E. Horton, "Political Alienation as a Force in Political Action," *Social Forces*, 38, 3 (March 1960), 190–195; Dwight G. Dean, "Alienation and Political Apathy," *ibid.,* pp. 185–189.

[7] For an excellent naturalistic portrayal of this political stance in another society (in which it is a much more common voting style) see Lawrence Wylie, *Village in the Vaucluse* (Cambridge, Mass.: Harvard University Press, 1957).

ence of the party, sometimes has threatened the tradition of toleration for other radical or unorthodox parties. A relatively new phenomenon of the 1960's was the appearance of a kind of diffuse "direct action" by elements objecting to national leadership and policies, the New Left, Student Power,[8] and Black Power movements. These movements first became a substantial political influence in the 1968 elections.

Major orientations to political parties, and to political events generally, differ greatly among various segments of the electorate and vary with changing historical circumstances. The most important of these orientations are (1) *traditional commitment* to a particular party, relatively regardless of immediate issues, personalities, or national events; (2) *"interest" politics*, in which considerations of individual and group advantage in wealth, income, power, and safety primarily determine behavior; (3) *ideological politics*, in which commitment to an organized set of beliefs and values is the overriding consideration; (4) *"status" politics*,[9] in which political behavior is importantly shaped by concern with social prestige, honor, or recognition, especially by anxiety about possible loss of privileged position. Partly overlapping with the politics or interests, ideology, and status is (5) *expressive politics*, representing the infusion into the political arena of behavior based on a great variety of affective states of discontent, hostility, suspicion, fear, affection, hope, and so on[1] regardless of origin or "intellectual" relevance.

Certainly, it is indisputable that each party includes highly diverse and often incompatible sectional interests; in Congress, Southern Democrats often have formed coalitions with conservative Northern and Western Republicans.[2] Indeed, the importance of such cross-party alliances is so conspicuous that it is sometimes said that there is a four-party system, in which the "liberal" and "conservative" wings of the two parties act as de facto parties. Mutual checkmate on crucial legislation often results.[3] Naturally enough, the organization of the parties on a local and state basis means that national organization and national issues tend to be considered in terms of their implications for state and local elections; in any particular geographic area, the party label may tell nothing as to the policies followed. No one would assume that "Democrat" in Mississippi means the same thing as "Democrat" in Michigan. This internal diversity is to some degree resolved or covered over during the actual campaign in national elections,[4] but in Congress and in state legislatures intraparty blocs of insurgents frequently function as loose subparties. National party control is often so weak that

8 "Students and Politics," *Daedalus* (Winter 1968), pp. 1–344.

9 Bell, *op. cit.*

1 See J. R. Gusfield, *Symbolic Crusade: Status Politics and the American Temperance Movement* (Urbana: University of Illinois Press, 1963).

2 This is not to say that either consensus or coalitions are to be taken for granted: the enormous tragedy of the Civil War stands as a sufficient reminder.

3 James MacGregor Burns, *The Deadlock of Democracy: Four-Party Politics in America* (Englewood Cliffs, N.J.: Prentice-Hall, 1963).

4 Not entirely or always—witness numerous third-party splits, e.g., Populism, Bull Moose, Dixiecrats, and the American Independent party in 1968.

elected representatives vote along the lines of particular interests represented among their constituents with great disregard for party regularity. Such extreme decentralization of control is a specific case of the principle that an organization or collectivity that cannot control the entrance and exit of members will always find it difficult to build a centralized and disciplined organization. The difficulties will be strongly accentuated if the central leadership has only limited and uncertain control of sanctions. The low cohesion of our national political parties partly derives from these two conditions—as well as from federalism and from the size and diversity of the total society.

### Party Organization

"Party membership" is an indefinite term because of the looseness of organization and the varying degrees of participation characteristic of our main parties. Does a party consist of all persons who vote its ticket in a particular election? Those who vote it regularly? Those who are registered and entitled to vote in its primary elections? Or those who actually do vote in the primaries? Or the active workers of the party? Or only the continuing leadership? In national elections as much as 30 to 40 percent of the qualified electorate does not vote, in local elections as much as 80 percent.[5] Probably not more than 10 percent of those who vote a party's ticket should be classed as active workers. The core of a party is quite small—the more or less continuously active leaders and officials, whose security and status are most closely bound up with the party's fortunes.

The formal organization of the major parties is built upon the small local units headed by precinct leaders ultimately responsible for getting out the vote. Through the thousands of these workers at the bottom of the national party hierarchy, the party must make its bid for power. Above the precinct comes the ward, which includes several precincts, and above this is the city or county unit. In each of the last a party committee attempts to guide and coordinate the political activities of the ward and precinct leaders. Within each state there is a state committee, and at the top of the structure is the national committee, composed of one man and one woman from each of the fifty states plus representatives from certain other areas. Members of the national committee are selected by the state delegates to the national party convention. The chairman of the national committee is named by the presidential nominee and has the responsibility of managing the national campaign. Around the chairman is built a small continuing staff that is greatly augmented during the course of the campaign itself.

In practice, however, this formal hierarchy does not accurately indicate the real pattern of organization and control. Great power may rest with leaders who occupy no official party position. Cliques and factions form at

[5] Key, *Politics, Parties and Pressure Groups, op. cit.*, p. 609. Useful references on historical background are Harold F. Gosnell, *Machine Politics: Chicago Model* (Chicago: University of Chicago Press, 1937); Edward M. Sait, *American Parties and Elections*, rev. ed. (New York: Appleton-Century-Crofts, 1939). Descriptions of more recent developments are given in references already cited, e.g., Key (*Public Opinion and American Democracy*, chap. 8), Alford, Duverger, and Burns.

all levels of the organization and contend with one another for power within the party. The nominally dominant national committee is often controlled by leaders at the lower levels of the hierarchy. And, of course, the parties do not have a system of expulsion of members—party irregularity is not strongly sanctionable in the case of the ordinary voter. It follows that a basic reason for the loose structure, decentralization, and ideological and programmatic vagueness that characterize American political parties is the absence of a clear and demanding criterion for membership.[6] Because any qualified voter can easily establish himself as a Democrat or Republican, or otherwise, solely by self-designation, those who vote in the party's primary elections in which candidates are chosen constitute a shifting population of diverse views, interests, and degrees of commitment and loyalty. Neither tight control of ideology nor strict discipline in following the party's leaders' directions can be established under these conditions.

The national parties as such nominate only the candidates for President and Vice-President. Senatorial candidates are named either by a state direct primary or by a state party convention; similarly, candidates for the House are selected by conventions or primary elections in the congressional districts. Central party leadership only very rarely is able to prevent nomination of a person supported by the local organization, even when the potential candidate has repudiated the national party platform and leadership.

The functioning party "machine" is thus a loose alliance of state and local organizations. The national chairman is able to exert unitary influence to any marked degree only during the national campaign. His control rests upon the common hope of victory, upon funds and services that can be made available to local organizations, and—when the party holds national power—upon patronage. But control is shared in an extremely complicated way by the President or presidential nominee, the national committee, members of the party in the national legislature, state and local "machines," and even extraparty groups and organizations.

Patronage, in one sense or another, is still an important basis for party discipline, although its role has been diminished by the growth of civil service systems, the increasing importance of federal jobs, the growth of professional social work and of insurance and pension plans, and the general shift toward more impersonal and centralized administration.[7] Since control of patronage is distributed among many different officials (such as the President, senators, state and local leaders), party organization cannot be a clear hierarchy but rather tends to take the form of a series of suborganizations centered around these various leaders.[8]

At the local level, informal personal ties and reciprocities of various kinds

---

[6] Duverger (*op. cit.*, p. 361) has gone so far as to say: "In fact the only real element of membership to be found in American parties consists in participation in the closed primaries, which can be compared with polls of the Belgian type."

[7] Theodore J. Lowi, *At the Pleasure of the Mayor: Patronage and Power in New York City, 1898–1958* (New York: Free Press, 1964).

[8] Again, a general principle: rigidly hierarchical organization finds its most reliable base in *appointment of personnel from above*. Where officials are elected, there is always the possibility that they will defy their "superiors" and appeal (sometimes successfully) to the electorate.

become more prominent in the maintenance of party organizations.[9] Kinship ties, personal friendship, the dispensing of small favors, local group identifications—these are the primary ingredients out of which the precinct leader builds a reliable bloc of votes that he can "deliver" as the basis of his power in the party. These blocs of votes are the unit cells that are massed into the solid core of party strength. In areas of stable social composition, except in periods of great social disturbance, the party leadership built upon such units is self-selecting and self-perpetuating.

In periods of social and economic stability, this type of organization gives the appearance of invulnerability; it survives numerous internal splits and changes in leadership and numerous "reform" attacks from the outside. Nevertheless, the system continues only under definite social conditions. It is at its strongest when political issues are few and trivial; any deep or revolutionary cleavage would go far to shatter the smooth operation of the established machines.

Many voters have overlapping group memberships or social identities that incline them in opposite directions on various issues; the resulting "cross pressures" tend to reduce extreme political partisanship. Furthermore, a great variety of interests is represented in a large number of organized groupings capable of making themselves felt at one or more of the numerous points of access to political influence and administrative decision making. Sharp political cleavage of massive party alignments is also minimized by the presence of many potentially strong but unorganized interests that could be inadvertently activated as politically potent groupings if existing "pressure groups" were to press their demands to the full. The threat of such activation of unorganized interests undoubtedly represents "shadow vetoes" in many political calculations. An additional factor in maintaining a relatively low level of extreme political partisanship, except in times of extreme depression or international frustration, is the existence of widespread satisfaction (sometimes called complacency) with the main political institutions and national social order. And, finally, of course, there is a very substantial consensus on major values and beliefs underlying many of the specific divergencies in particular interests.

The extent and kind of competitiveness between political parties varies greatly among the fifty states of the union. The degree of one-party monopoly or the extent of shifting of power from election to election is not necessarily the same for different national, state, and local contests—making simple generalizations unlikely. But the broad outlines of competitive or noncompetitive party politics do seem to be strongly influenced by two sets of factors. The first is the historically received institutional structure of party organization and state and local government; for example, the constitutional provisions in Virginia that make important local officials dependent upon the state government have been crucial in the power of the "Byrd machine" in that state, or the one-party system of many Southern

---

[9] Vivid documentation of local political organization is provided by William F. Whyte, *Street Corner Society* (Chicago: University of Chicago Press, 1943); see also Nathan Glazer and Daniel Patrick Moynihan, *Beyond the Melting Pot* (Cambridge, Mass.: M.I.T. Press and Harvard University Press, 1963).

states in the past. The second consists of the nonpolitical social structure and its geographic, technological, and economic bases. Party competitiveness tends to occur in states that are relatively wealthy and have well-educated populations.[1]

Parties, it is sometimes said, "express public opinion." At best this is a highly ambiguous statement; parties do not act upon diffusely held "raw" opinion but rather upon selected and weighted ("formed") opinion. The disparity between unformed mass opinion and party policies will be the greater in parties that are centralized, tightly organized, and committed to a systematic doctrine.[2]

Moreover, among the smaller political parties that have existed in this society, the American Communist party obviously warrants special attention. Even before extreme legal coercion was applied to it, the party was not able to secure a large following even from those segments of the population it regarded as best potential sources (industrial workers, immigrants, Negroes). Although it did acquire a majority of native-born members as a consequence of its efforts during the depression years of the 1930's, its greatest appeals appear to have been to persons already sensitized to a socialist ideology.[3] It is a basic generalization of political strategy that parties aiming at fundamental changes in the social system must develop strong organization and firm discipline. These conditions probably are favored by the requirement of an ideological commitment as a condition of party membership. Nevertheless, as such parties seek to permeate the electorate on a mass basis, they typically are forced to simplify and dilute the original doctrine.[4]

One must be very careful, however, to avoid exaggerating the similarity of the Republican and Democratic parties—a similarity that is partly stereotypic. American voters do not think the two identical nor do many of the contributors to campaign expenses. Even during periods of political conservatism and relative complacency, American voters in recent years have clearly distinguished between the two major parties, for example, regarding the Democrats as favoring greater governmental activity and as being the party of the workers rather than of the middle classes. During the 1950's, many persons voted for the Republican, Dwight D. Eisenhower, even while retaining a self-identification as Democrats and as working-class persons and while favoring social reforms that were rejected by the Republican candidate.[5] Yet they did not lose their class-connected preferences for "liberal" policies or for the Democratic party. Furthermore, as V. O. Key has demonstrated, the differences between the parties in views concerning

[1] Thomas W. Casstevens and Charles Press, "The Context of Democratic Competition in American State Politics," *American Journal of Sociology*, LXVIII, 5 (March 1963), 536–543.

[2] Duverger, *op. cit.*, p. 380.

[3] See Nathan Glazer, *The Social Basis of American Communism* (New York: Harcourt, Brace & World, 1961).

[4] Cf. Duverger's comments on the "doctrinal impoverishment" of Marxist parties during the last three decades in *op. cit.*, pp. 175–177.

[5] Heinz Eulau, *Class and Party in the Eisenhower Years: Class Roles and Perspectives in the 1952 and 1956 Elections* (New York: Free Press, 1962).

main national policies and problems become progressively greater as one moves up through the levels of the party organization from the individual voter to powerful national leaders.[6]

### The Voters and Voting Behavior[7]

American democracy is marked by a wide extension of the franchise; and a high value has been placed upon the voting privilege—at least until it has been won. The franchise is limited, of course, by voting qualifications, which in various jurisdictions include age, residence requirements, citizenship, literacy, tax payments, registration, and various special provisions such as the disenfranchisement of certain kinds of offenders against the law and of those "mentally incompetent."[8] Property qualifications for voting were common in the early republic (ten states required land ownership as a prerequisite for voting); and the right to hold public office was even more carefully restricted. Both voting and eligibility for public office seem to have been widely regarded as privileges granted by the state, not as rights automatically conferred by citizenship. For several decades after the revolution there was determined opposition to the removal of these qualifications;[9] and their absence in the national Constitution was not so much due to objections of political principle as to disagreements of the founders over the kind of property requirement that might be established. In many instances the essential effect of property qualification has been resecured in the states by alternative means such as stringent residence requirements, which tend to exclude mobile workers from the ballot, and educational requirements (directed against Negroes in the South); and for long periods in many states, and even now in some local areas, the lack of a really free and secret ballot placed many voters under the power of economically dominant individuals and groups. Formally free suffrage is, however, definitely the dominant ideal and widely found in actual practice.

The criteria of political participation are generally taken to be candidacy, office holding, voting, contributing funds to a party, soliciting votes, and the like. By such indicators, from 50 to 80 percent of adults are almost totally inactive, save in presidential elections. Over the years since World War I, between 50 and 60 percent of the electorate have voted in presidential elections. There is enormous variation among the states—for example, in the 1964 presidential election the percentage voting ranged from 77 percent

[6] V. O. Key, Jr., *Public Opinion and American Democracy* (New York: Knopf, 1961), chaps. 17 and 19.

[7] For important studies of this subject see, e.g., Angus Campbell, Philip E. Converse, Warren E. Miller and Donald E. Stokes, *The American Voter* (New York: Wiley, 1960); Eugene Burdick and Arthur J. Brodbeck, *American Voting Behavior* (New York: Free Press, 1959); Bernard R. Berelson, Paul F. Lazarsfeld, and William N. McPhee, *Voting: A Study of Opinion Formation in a Presidential Campaign* (Chicago: University of Chicago Press, 1954); Paul F. Lazarsfeld, Bernard Berelson, and Hazel Gaudet, *The People's Choice*, 2nd ed. (New York: Columbia University Press, 1948).

[8] During the Depression of the 1930's some interest groups even proposed to take away the voting rights from millions of people receiving public relief.

[9] See the review by J. Allen Smith, *The Growth and Decadence of Constitutional Government* (New York: Henry Holt, 1930), chap. 3.

in Utah to 38 percent in South Carolina and 33 percent in Mississippi. Overall, about one-third of the electorate failed to vote in recent presidential elections. Of these, at least one-half were blocked or deterred from voting by barriers imposed by the various states; racial discrimination still is a major factor.[1]

The use of the ballot varies greatly from one election to another.[2] The vote is heaviest in presidential elections and grows lighter in the successively more local contests. In purely local elections as few as one-fifth of the voters may make the effective political decisions. Key has suggested that the low participation in state and local elections probably increases the chances of control by a tight party organization.[3] At any rate, the extent of nonvoting documents the tendency for parties to be mainly constituted by a minority of active persons.

Yet the common indicators of political participation may overstate the inactivity or lack of involvement of the citizens: many overtly nonpolitical activities may convey essential political information and concerns to decision makers and may affect subsequent political events.[4] Voting is simply one, highly standardized activity among the several types of activity that make up political participation. At the most intensive end of the scale of participation are the activists, who expend substantial amounts of time, energy, or money in working for political ends in parties or pressure groups; by any useful criterion of "intensity" the activists constitute less than 2 to 3 percent of the electorate. Organizational *contributors* donate funds or give active assistance at certain times (during campaigns, legislative hearings); they may amount to 5 to 10 percent of the politically eligible adults. *Opinion leaders* show a high level of political awareness and information and discuss political matters with a circle of associates; perhaps up to 25 percent belong in this category. Those who do nothing more than *vote* typically account for somewhat more than half of the electorate in national elections, much less in local contests. *Nonvoting* persons who retain some minimal political interest may represent as much as 30 percent of qualified adults, whereas the completely uninformed and uninterested constitute somewhat less than 5 percent.[5]

Considerable evidence supports the following generalizations about some aspects of voting behavior.

1. Up until the civil rights movement of the 1960's, institutionalized disenfranchisement (resulting in poll taxes, literacy tests, and so forth)

---

[1] Robert K. Carr, Marver H. Bernstein, Donald H. Morrison, and Joseph E. McLean, *American Democracy in Theory and Practice*, 3rd ed. (New York: Holt, Rinehart and Winston, 1960), pp. 156–157; Angus Campbell, "Who Are the Non-Voters?" *New Society*, 68 (January 1964), 11–12.

[2] A concise summary is given by Richard M. Scammon, "Electoral Participation," *The Annals of the American Academy of Political and Social Science*, 371 (May 1967), 59–71.

[3] Key, *Politics, Parties and Pressure Groups, op. cit.*, pp. 608–609.

[4] Fred E. Katz and Fern V. Piret, "Circuitous Participation in Politics," *American Journal of Sociology*, LXIX, 4 (January 1964), 367–373.

[5] These estimates are slight modifications of those given in Robert E. Lane, *Political Life* (New York: Free Press, 1959), pp. 52–56.

prevented the voting of a high percentage of Negroes and many of the poorer whites in several Southern states. The changed political and cultural setting, dating from the massive legal changes of 1954–1965, has greatly weakened, although not totally removed, such systemic barriers to electoral participation.

2. Although aliens were permitted to vote rather generally until the 1920's, all noncitizens are now barred from the polls.

3. The general tendency is for older voters up to ages fifty-five through sixty to exercise the franchise proportionately more often than voters under thirty-five years of age.

4. Women are generally less likely than men to vote.

5. Persons in higher economic positions are more likely to vote than poorer people. Business and professional groups are especially likely to vote. Among workers, union members are more likely than nonmembers to vote.

6. Well-educated persons are more likely to vote than are persons with fewer years of school or college training.

7. A large proportion of nonvoters are characterized by political apathy —a kind of generalized indifference—and are not restrained by specific barriers. According to the data of one study, three-fourths of the nonvoters were so by deliberate decision; they intended in advance not to vote.[6] There is some evidence that political apathy tends to be most frequent among elements of the population that have been repeatedly blocked in their social and economic aspirations and those who in general constitute the least articulate and less advantaged portions of the community. Voting is most frequent among persons who are members of organized interest-groups and among those who are high participators in a variety of associations.

We must add that the idea that political apathy is always "bad" and full participation always "good" is subject to serious question. An extremely high level of political activity throughout a society is likely to signalize such serious cleavage and conflict as to foreshadow drastic political upheaval. This conclusion has been supported by an impressive body of research.[7]

8. Nonvoting would seem to be maximized, aside from barriers mentioned in points 1 and 2 above, when elections are frequent, ballots long and complex, registration procedures time consuming and difficult.

9. Voting is most widespread in times of social crisis.[8]

The findings of earlier studies of characteristics of voters and nonvoters were for the first time checked on a national scale by the Bureau of the Census by inclusion of questions on voting in its Current Population Survey in November 1964.[9] This vast survey verified the facts of higher proportions voting among men as compared with women, among middle-aged rather than the very elderly or the young, among white as compared with Negro citizens, among the better educated, among those with the higher incomes,

[6] Lazarsfeld, Berelson, and Gaudet, *op. cit.*, pp. 46–47.

[7] Cf. Lipset, "Political Sociology," *op. cit.*, p. 95.

[8] On most of the above points see Carr, *et al.*, *op. cit.*, pp. 159–160.

[9] See United States Bureau of the Census, Report No. 143, *Voter Participation in the National Election, November, 1964* (Washington, D.C.: Government Printing Office, 1965).

in the North rather than the South. It showed, in addition, that voting is generally higher in suburbs than in central cities and in urban than in rural areas; however, some rural states have high participation rates. Differences among religious affiliations are small and may be partly due to other factors; there are slight tendencies for Jews to vote most often, followed by Catholics and Protestants.

The main findings concerning party voting are the following:

1. A high proportion of voters regularly vote for the same party. The exact proportion varies from period to period and from one area to another but certainly has not dropped below one-half in any recent national election and probably has hovered around 70 to 80 percent for long periods.[1] Congressional districts tend to go consistently in favor of one of the parties over considerable periods: between 1946 and 1956, of the 435 districts represented in the House of Representatives, 185 were consistently Democratic and 169 were consistently Republican, while 81 (19 percent) shifted one or more times.[2]

2. "Traditional" voting is most marked in periods of relative stability and prosperity; and we cannot assume that it will necessarily continue to be of primary importance.

3. Indeed, the independent or shifting votes are numerous enough to make the margin of victory in many, if not most, elections. Hence, decisions on the basis of issues are potentially decisive, even when the majority of votes are "regular." Substantial proportions of voters split their tickets, that is, vote for some candidates of one party and some of another; in 1956, about 40 percent did so. Ticket splitters are either persons relatively indifferent to party identity or else highly interested but ambivalent about the issues, parties, and candidates.[3]

Most independent voters are not strongly committed to rational choice on the basis of clear political principles; all available studies show that the independents as compared with partisans are less interested in politics, less fully informed, less likely to vote at all, and less concerned about the outcomes of elections.

Studies of factors associated with party voting have supported these generalizations:

1. Voting against the party in power tends to increase in periods of economic adversity, but there are many possible offsetting factors.[4]

2. Although economic status alone is far from the determining factor in party affiliation or inclination, there has been for many years a marked

---

1 Lazarsfeld and associates (*op. cit.*) found in their study of the 1940 election in Sandusky, Ohio, that 77 percent of the voters voted as their parents and grandparents habitually had. See also the data cited in Key, *Politics, Parties, and Pressure Groups, op. cit.* More recent studies include: Berelson, Lazarsfeld, and McPhee, *op. cit.*; Angus Campbell, Gerald Gurin, and Warren E. Miller, *The Voter Decides* (New York: Row, Peterson, 1954). Over 200 generalizations from research on voting behavior are conveniently summarized in Berelson, *et al., op. cit.*, pp. 333–347.

2 Carr, *et al., op. cit.*, p. 167.

3 Ranney, *op. cit.*, p. 323 (citing Campbell and Miller).

4 The impressive regularity with which depressions result in the overthrow of the party in power has been shown in detail by Bean, *op. cit.*, chap. 6.

tendency for the wealthier groups to vote Republican, the poorer groups, Democratic. (There is an exception—much of the South, in which the Democratic party is eminently conservative.) In part such preferences result from early political socialization. Most Americans learn to prefer and to identify themselves with a political party early in life—in sharp contrast, for example, to the French situation in which few children (less than 30 percent) know the party affiliation of their father.[5]

3. In Northern and Western states, the highest percentage of Republican affiliation is found among persons who are high in socioeconomic status, Protestant, rural rather than urban, and identified with business rather than labor.

In terms of the processes of vote determination, research has revealed these regularities:

1. Changes in voting intentions during the course of a campaign lead to greater homogeneity within subgroups and consequently to a *polarization* of attitudes in the total community.

2. Stability of voting intentions appears to be a source of personal security in group contacts and is reinforced by interaction within politically homogeneous social circles.

3. Persons who change their voting intentions during the course of a campaign, and they are small in number, tend to be those who are either relatively little concerned with the outcome of the election or subject to contradictory group affiliations.

4. Face-to-face contacts in small groups are of primary importance both in reinforcing attitudes and in stimulating change.

5. Attention to political propaganda is selective; persons attend to those items toward which they are already favorably disposed; and a large proportion of those who are initially undecided emerge at the end of a campaign with a predictable stand. This process has been called activation.

6. Voters of definite early intention receive *reinforcement* of existing attitudes through arousal of interest and monopoly of attention.

7. The role of local party organization is, or may be, significant in all these processes but seems especially important in getting the nonvoter to vote and in activating the last-minute waverer. The proportion of conversions as a result of party activity seems to be quite small in most elections.

In general, the greater the amount of information the individual voter already has about relevant political matters, the more stable his political allegiances will be. On the other hand, the individuals having little information are least likely to be exposed to new information. Exposure thus interacts with amount of prior information—probably in such a way that the combination of moderate information and moderate exposure produces the greatest likelihood of change resulting from receiving new messages.[6]

The findings, just summarized, and many others not reviewed here,

---

[5] Philip Converse and Georges Dupeux, "Politicization of the Electorate in France and in the United States," *Public Opinion Quarterly*, XXVI, 1 (Spring 1962), 11–13.

[6] Philip E. Converse, "Information Flow and the Stability of Partisan Attitudes," in Angus Campbell, Philip Converse, Warren Miller, and Donald Stokes, *Elections and the Political Order* (New York: Wiley, 1966).

point to several conclusions anticipated in our previous analysis. (1) The immediate economic position of the voter cannot entirely explain the direction of his vote.[7] (2) Degree of interest in political affairs varies greatly among individuals and among different social strata and groupings. (3) Degree of interest and direction of voting are closely related to the group identifications and affiliations of individuals.[8] (4) Since group affiliations, in the aggregate, reflect the main institutional structures, election behavior is partly predictable in terms of basic social and cultural organization.

The major factors that have been shown to be associated with high or low political participation could be combined in extremely intricate patterns. Generalized socioeconomic status correlates strongly and positively with political interest, voting, and other political activity. High socioeconomic status, at the same time, is associated with a high level of organizational participation. High participation in nonpolitical associations, in turn, is associated with a high level of political activity. Various indexes of alienation are negatively associated with political activity; but political activity is correlated with both high socioeconomic position and organizational activity—both of which are negatively correlated with alienation. One of the few studies that has examined the network of partial associations among these factors finds that both socioeconomic status and organizational involvement relate positively to political activity with the other factor controlled.[9] On the other hand, when these factors are held constant, the association between alienation and political participation disappears, suggesting the possibility that most of the seeming effect of alienative attitudes is due to the fact that the most alienated are also lowest in socioeconomic position and general organizational participation.

Elections polarize the society into opposing camps. But the voting process is at the same time "a key mechanism of consensus in democratic society."[1] The peaceful acceptance of defeat at the polls is a striking demonstration of social cohesion. Because voters belong to different groups, are subject to cross pressures, and have overlapping interests and beliefs, they

[7] Both in the United States and elsewhere, "explanations" of voting solely in terms of class interests have sometimes been based on alleged facts that are not true. A remarkable instance is the stereotype or legend of the division of British voters in the nineteenth century along the lines of (Tory) landowners against (Liberal) capitalists. A recent re-study of the data shows that the fact was that men voted by trade and not by class. See John Russell Vincent, *Pollbooks: How Victorians Voted* (London: Cambridge University Press, 1967).

[8] For a striking demonstration of "ethnic" voting see the evidence concerning German-Americans in the 1940 elections in Bean, *op. cit.*, pp. 93–99. The same point is developed by Samuel Lubell, *The Future of American Politics* (New York: Harper & Row, 1952).

[9] William Erbe, "Social Involvement and Political Activity: A Replication and Elaboration," *American Sociological Review*, 29, 2 (April 1964), 198–215.

[1] Lipset, "Political Sociology," *op. cit.*, p. 92. Cf. Talcott Parsons, "Voting and the Equilibrium of the American Political System," in Eugene Burdick and Arthur Brodbeck (eds.), *Continuities of Social Research, III: The Studies of Voting Behavior* (New York: Free Press, 1958). Convincing evidence that voting in national elections during the 1950's reflected a high degree of consensus may be found in Berelson, *et al.*, *op. cit.*, and in Morris Janowitz and Dwaine Marvick, "Comparative Pressure and Democratic Consent," in Eulau, Eldersveld, and Janowitz, *op. cit.*

rarely agree in full with all the positions taken by the party with which they identify. Both major parties have to make concessions and compromises to gain the votes of their heterogeneous adherents. As conflicts are thus softened and diffused, the voting process helps to produce the political consent without which a viable political democracy would not be possible. Once again, however, this result will be found only when the initial dissensus, alienation, group antagonisms, and other disruptive factors are within limits —limits difficult to specify but certainly present.[2] In the United States the actual size of the "inert" and "alienated" population is unknown, but various studies of voluntary associations, political activity, and group memberships indicate that the proportion of the adult population that can be regarded as apolitical and disconnected from politically relevant groupings could not possibly be as much as 40 percent[3] and may well be as low as 25 percent.

## SOCIAL ORGANIZATION AND LOCAL POWER STRUCTURES

In making a formal analysis of power, one may sometimes forget that political behavior always occurs in specific, concrete social settings and is continuously affecting, and being affected by, social structures and processes that are not themselves political per se. And political processes are not, of course, merely the sum of separate acts of individual political atoms. Rather they are relational processes occurring in and among groups, communities, associations, organizations, and social movements. Only in societies in extreme states of disintegration and extreme crisis do we observe unmediated mass responses to political events—that is, the pluralistic reactions of large numbers of individuals who are wholly unconnected with one another save for a common political object of attention. Yet enough crucial cases of such mass politics have occurred to emphasize the necessity of appraising the possibility of such events in American society.[4]

As suggested above, a recurring theme in contemporary analyses of the structural contexts of political behavior concerns the degree to which political leaders and formal governmental agencies are connected with the electorate by a network of overlapping intermediary groups, associations, and relationships. One polar type of community is tightly interlaced with

[2] A large body of writings deals with these problems. Examples: William Kornhauser, *The Politics of Mass Society* (New York: Free Press, 1959); Joseph R. Gusfield, "Mass Society and Extremist Politics," *American Sociological Review*, 27, 1 (February 1962), 19–30; David E. Apter (ed.), *Ideology and Discontent* (New York: Free Press, 1964); Herbert McClosky, Paul J. Hoffman, and Rosemary O'Hara. "Issue, Conflict and Consensus Among Party Leaders and Followers," *The American Political Science Review*, LIV, 2 (June 1960), 406–427; Fritz Stern, *The Politics of Cultural Despair* (Berkeley and Los Angeles: University of California Press, 1961).

[3] Estimate by Rose, *op. cit.*, p. 20.

[4] Cf. Kornhauser, *op. cit.*, and other references cited in footnote 2 above. See also Scott Greer and Peter Orleans, "The Mass Society and the Parapolitical Structure," *American Sociological Review*, 27, 5 (October 1962), 634–646.

numerous overlapping linkages that extend from the top decision makers throughout the system to touch every member. At the other extreme, a detached elite operates vis-à-vis an unorganized mass. An intermediate form consists of a loosely connected congeries of diverse, independent subgroupings.[5]

Some observers, indeed, see the American case as one of mass society of a power elite *versus* alienated, apathetic but manipulable masses. Others stress the existence of a seamless web of politically relevant social formations intermediate between the individual citizen and the state. What does the evidence show? Since the national polity is built in part upon a system of territorial units and territorial representatives, an appropriate place to look first is the local community. Here the studies show great variations, but several of them point to the prevalence of an "in-between" set of community structures that transmits (and transforms) politically relevant expressions from individuals and subcollectivities to decision makers; such mediating social formations represent partially integrated structures but have certain "mass" characteristics. Thus, analyses of local referenda concerning fluoridation and school-bond issues show that rejection of the proposals is most likely when the community does not have a well-formed network between leaders and citizenry. The effect is especially marked when the community contains a large segment of persons in lower socioeconomic positions who do not participate in politically relevant associations, who rarely participate in political affairs, and who feel powerless and isolated from the channels of influence in the local power structure. Such voters, usually apathetic, often turn out a large negative vote in local referenda—partly as an expression of their disgruntled, frustrated, angry feelings toward an officialdom regarded as alien and unresponsive to their needs.[6] The evidence suggests that the more highly integrated communities tend to decide local issues by strong majorities and that the segments of the electorate most closely connected with the leadership are most likely to favor the type of referendum proposals here considered. In addition, however, the available studies indicate that other structural features are important: size of community, ethnic heterogeneity, relative size of the different social strata, and the presence or absence of social cleavages within the social and power elites.

The presence in a society of many protest movements, demonstrations, mass actions, riots and other forms of turbulence is usually seen in terms of conflict and disruption. At the same time, however, processes of opposition and conflict may contribute to the formation of new collectivities and the growth of new lines of solidarity. Thus the conditions suitable for diffuse, sporadic protest—marches, demonstrations, riots, and the like—may create the raw materials for more firmly organized and continuing protest movements. Such events, however, are not sufficient to insure a persistent and

[5] For illustrations in local communities, see Maurice Pinard, "Structural Attachments and Political Support in Urban Politics: The Case of Fluoridation Referendums," *American Journal of Sociology*, LXVIII, 5 (March 1963), 513–526.

[6] John E. Horton and Wayne E. Thompson, "Powerlessness and Political Negativism: A Study of Defeated Local Referendums," *American Journal of Sociology*, LXVII, 5 (March 1962), 485–493.

purposive organized effort. Both sociopsychological[7] and structural conditions affect the likelihood of the latter outcome. Sometimes the necessary organization is created in the very process of agitation, protest, and attack upon the existing power structure—as in the case of many successful subversive, guerrilla, insurrectionary, or revolutionary groupings. Much remains to be learned about the specific combinations of "structure" and "disorganization" that favor the several radically different political outcomes of situations of mass discontent.

Actual political structures and processes at the local level have been extensively studied in recent years; the very term "power structure" has become popular.[8] Although some studies draw sweeping conclusions from quite limited and particularized kinds of information (such as the reputational identification of leadership in a single community), the accumulating research shows how very complex the actual power relations are—as well as how difficult are the technical research problems of securing contextually valid data.[9] Over twenty local studies, published from 1928 to 1964, have presented data that were interpreted as evidence of "elite control." On the other hand, at least thirty-six other studies found evidence pointing to a pluralistic pattern or to the absence of a stable pattern of local power. Studies that relied upon the ratings by local informants of reputed influence (the "reputational method") found concentrated elites; those that studied decisions on specific issues or used other approaches tended to find pluralistic or dispersed power.

What are we to conclude? Which findings are valid? Undoubtedly both sets of data correspond to some actual situations; but neither is the whole truth, and either may lead to premature generalizations. The evidence presented is, at the least, adequate to show wide variability in the extent to which a single unified ruling elite, as over against various kinds of pluralistic aggregations of decision makers, actually exerts crucial local authority.[1]

---

[7] For example, belief in the possibility of substantially controlling one's own fate is a condition favoring willingness to participate in social protest movements. See Pearl Mayo Gore and Julian B. Rotter, "A Personality Correlate of Social Action," *Journal of Personality*, 31, 1 (March 1963), 58–64.

[8] Rose, *op. cit.*, pp. xiv–xv and chaps. I and VIII.

[9] John Walton, "Substance and Artifact: "The Current Status of Research on Community Power Structure," *American Journal of Sociology*, LXXI, 4 (January 1966), 430–438; John Walton, "Discipline, Method, and Community Power: A Note on Sociology of Knowledge," *American Sociological Review*, 31, 5 (October 1966), 684–689; M. Herbert Danzger, "Community Power Structure: Problems and Continuities," *American Sociological Review*, 29, 3 (October 1964), 707–717; Bert N. Adams, "Summaries and New Directions in Community Power Studies," *The American Sociologist*, 1, 4 (August 1966), 210–211.

[1] Compare the specific descriptions given in the following: Hunter, *op. cit.*; M. Kent Jennings, *Community Influentials: The Elites of Atlanta* (New York: Free Press, 1964); Robert A. Dahl, *Who Governs? Democracy and Power in an American City* (New Haven, Conn.; Yale University Press, 1961); Morris Janowitz (ed.), *Community Political Systems* (New York: Free Press, 1961); Robert E. Agger, Daniel Goldrich, Bert E. Swanson, *The Rulers and the Ruled: Political Power and Impotence in American Communities* (New York: Wiley, 1964); Edward C. Banfield and James Q. Wilson, *City Politics* (Cambridge, Mass.: M.I.T. Press and Harvard University Press, 1963); Roland L. Warren, *The Community in America* (Chicago: Rand McNally, 1963).

Also, the data deal with at least three different *kinds* of power: (1) potential power, residing in social position and in the control of resources and facilities; (2) generalized influence, that is, the demonstrated capacity to affect a wide range of decisions; (3) specific and active power—the overt, exerted ability to affect a particular decision. Any local community contains all three; the emphases and interrelations vary greatly in different localities; and the evidence does not justify the conclusion that a unified local establishment is the typical pattern.[2]

Many small and moderate-sized communities have a structure of power and leadership consisting of "a network of overlapping subgroups, some visible and some concealed,"[3] with some coordinating individual or cluster of individuals at the center. Variations among communities are to be expected in the extensiveness of such networks, the closeness of interconnections, their visibility, the degree of unanimity and coordination, and the durability of the structure across the range of issues and through time.[4]

INTEREST GROUPINGS

Our analysis of political behavior has moved through three main levels: first, the explicit cultural structure of the state—the relatively stable norms that guide the recurrent activities of governing; second, the less explicit norms of political practice or government-in-being; third, the structure of parties and the characteristics of voting behavior. Underlying these patterns are the strata, associations, groups, and other social units or categories of the total society, identifiable because they carry on activities that reflect various interests and values and express them in various symbols. It is, then, in these numerous crisscrossing groupings and their changing systems of values, beliefs, and interests that we must look for the bases of politics and governing, for the sources of the demands for power and of the acquiescence to authority. The structure of political institutions, it must be remembered, consists of repetitive behavior directed by enduring norms. Behavior is repetitive and norms are norms only as there is maintained a continuing set of beliefs, values, and interests among the individual members of the society. It is in this area, therefore, that we also must seek the dynamics of the political institutions, remembering always that social structure is constantly changing.

[2] See Rose's judicious appraisal, *op. cit.*, Chap. VIII.

[3] Charles M. Bonjean, "Community Leadership: A Case Study and Conceptual Refinement," *American Journal of Sociology*, LXVIII, 6 (May 1963), 680; See also Delbert C. Miller, "Town and Gown: The Power Structure of a University Town," *American Journal of Sociology*, LXVIII, 4 (January 1963), 432–443; Linton C. Freeman, *et al.*, *Local Community Leadership* (Syracuse, N.Y.: Syracuse University Press, 1960); Aaron Wildavsky, *Leadership in a Small Town* (Totowa, N.J.: Bedminster Press, 1964); Ritchie P. Lowry, *Who's Running This Town?* (New York: Harper & Row, 1965); Harold Kaplan, *Urban Renewal Politics: Slum Clearance in Newark* (New York: Columbia University Press, 1963).

[4] An important approach, showing how such variables as educational and socioeconomic levels of the population can affect decision-making processes is illustrated in Robert L. Crain and Donald B. Rosenthal, "Community Status as a Dimension of Local Decision-Making," *American Sociological Review*, 32, 6 (December 1967), 970–984.

Detailed analysis of so-called interest groups (or "pressure groups") in our society is available elsewhere,[5] and we can present here only a highly general overview of their nature and significance. The following generalizations seem to be true:

1. There is a prevalent interest-group conception of politics, as the "great game" of who gets what, when, and how.[6] Politics is seen as maneuver for advantage, and the state as a mediator among pressure groups.[7]

2. Economic specialization creates numerous specific interest groups in agriculture, industry, trade, finance, labor, professions.

3. Cultural diversity creates special groups working for the interests of (a) particular religious organizations; (b) ethnic or racial categories; (c) sectional or regional areas; and (d) a great variety of special causes, movements, and tastes, from antivivisectionists or vice crusaders to proponents of world government.

4. In short, the society is characterized by a large number of powerful interests, many of which are highly organized and highly skilled in the political arena. The actual diversity of concrete interests is so great that many different and useful listings of kinds of power groupings are possible, for example, one major survey and analysis has treated separately business, labor, agriculture, Negroes, public school teachers, intellectuals, the civil bureaucracy, and the military bureaucracy.[8]

5. Organized interests apparently propose most of the statutes passed by state legislatures and originate much legislation in Congress.

6. Organized interests maintain continuing relations with administrative agencies whose activities affect them.

7. Not all pressure groups work for the immediate self-interests of those they represent. There are disinterested interest groups whose objectives are not narrowly bound up with the wealth, power, prestige, or other distributive interests of their members.

8. Many interest groups are not only highly organized but also represent vast numbers of individuals or great aggregates of economic power.

9. Governmental action tends to pass over the least well organized seg-

5 Representative examples include Donald C. Blaisdell, "Economic Power and Political Pressures," *Monograph No. 26*, Temporary National Economic Committee (Washington, D.C.: Government Printing Office, 1941); Key, *Politics, Parties, and Pressure Groups, op. cit.*; Peter Odegard, *Pressure Politics, The Story of the Anti-Saloon League* (New York: Columbia University Press, 1928); John T. Salter, *Boss Rule: Portraits in City Politics* (New York: McGraw-Hill, 1935); Belle Zeller, *Pressure Politics in New York* (New York: Prentice-Hall, 1937); Bertram Gross, *The Legislative Struggle* (New York: McGraw-Hill, 1953); Andrew Hacker, *Politics and the Corporation* (New York: Fund for the Republic, 1958); Paul W. Cherington and Ralph L. Gillen, *The Business Representative in Washington* (Washington, D.C.: The Brookings Institution, 1962); Raymond A. Bauer, Ithiel de S. Pool, and Lewis A. Dexter, *American Business and Public Policy* (New York: Atherton Press, 1963).

6 Frank R. Kent, *The Great Game of Politics* (New York: Doubleday, 1923); Harold D. Lasswell, *Politics, Who Gets What, When, How* (New York: McGraw-Hill, 1936).

7 Cf. MacIver, *op. cit.*, pp. 219–220.

8 R. Joseph Monsen, Jr., and Mark W. Cannon, *The Makers of Public Policy: American Power Groups and Their Ideologies* (New York: McGraw-Hill, 1965). Compare Harmon Zeigler, *Interest Groups in American Society* (Englewood Cliffs, N.J.: Prentice-Hall, 1964).

ments of the public in favor of the aggressive group with a *specific* program. For example, in the political affairs of our large cities and metropolitan areas, many of the most important decisions are the outcomes of an "ecology of games"—of struggle, negotiation, and compromise among specialized interests that intersect in the same local setting. As Norton Long summarizes it: "The protagonists of things in particular are well organized and know what they are about; the protagonists of things in general are few, vague, and weak."[9]

10. Possibly, although not certainly, the marked articulation of pressure groups is a rigidifying influence upon the social order. It is so, by definition, to the extent that such groups are successful in gaining privilege.

What main categories of interests are important in the American political scene? The major groupings are unquestionably "economic," although not by any means always economic classes. First and foremost are the highly organized and economically powerful business associations, from which have developed many effective pressure groups. Among *general* organizations, the two outstanding instances, of course, are the National Association of Manufacturers and the Chamber of Commerce, with its more than 1,700 local units. Both organizations actively seek to influence governmental policy. Some of the most active business pressure groups, however, are specialized—for instance, the Committee of Utility Executives that fought the 1935 Public Utility Holding Company Act, or the numerous permanent trade associations. Business groups both favor and oppose particular legislation; but in recent years, their major emphasis has been upon blocking undesired action—opposing increased taxation, social security, extension of public regulation, and so on. The continued emphasis among many small businessmen upon the virtues of a decentralized economy with a minimum of governmental intervention is well known. However, small business is not politically united; and it is not clear that its alleged spokesmen are either representative or effective.[1] As a general rule, organizations purporting to represent business interests have favored state regulation rather than federal, apparently on the dual assumption that fifty states permit many delaying battles and that state regulation, when established, is easier than federal to deal with.

As a counterweight to business pressures stand the labor unions and their political-action adjuncts. Like business groups, the unions have contributed, although not so heavily, to campaign funds; they actively favor or oppose legislation; they propose laws; they exercise wide surveillance upon legislative action. As noted in Chapter VI, there are considerable differences in the orientation and tactics of the major unions. For many

[9] Long, *op. cit.*, p. 145.

[1] John H. Bunzel, *The American Small Businessman* (New York: Knopf, 1962); Harmon Zeigler, *The Politics of Small Business* (Washington, D.C.: Public Affairs Press, 1961). Studies by Richard F. Hamilton show considerable support among sales and clerical workers for "progressive" legislation and the expansion of governmental controls; see "The Marginal Middle Class: A Reconsideration," *American Sociological Review*, 31, 2 (April 1966), 192–199.

years the AFL opposed government interference in labor-management problems and only slowly modified this stand. Since it was in the main a loose federation of diverse craft-type unions, it was not always highly cohesive or united in policy. The CIO was characterized by a more systematic political consciousness and a greater willingness to enter directly into political campaigns. Today the combined AFL-CIO attempts to influence Congress and various state legislatures and interests itself in an imposing array of proposed legislation, ranging through specifically "labor" or "antilabor" bills to measures dealing with insurance, health, civil rights, immigration, and many other public issues.

Agriculture provides a third great aggregate of organized interests. Farm blocs have demonstrated themselves to be highly effective pressure organizations for many years, including the last three decades, a period when agriculture was becoming a less important part of the economy.[2] There are a number of major organizations: the American Farm Bureau Federation, the National Grange, and the Farmers Union, plus such compact and specialized agencies as the National Co-operative Milk Producers Federation. The legislative and administrative pressures for actions favorable to some agricultural interests, however, do not come solely from farmers and farm organizations.

To simply list "agriculture" as one of the major sectors from which organized political pressures develop may call up the image of the militant commercial farmer who has appeared in headlines in connection with congressional hearings or, more dramatically, in milk strikes and the like. Actually, much of the political power of agriculture derives from industries and other agencies whose fortunes are closely tied to those of farming.

Some of the organized professions are in part economic pressure groups, sufficiently distinct from labor, business, and agriculture to justify separate mention. Outstanding examples are the tightly organized and powerful American Medical Association[3] and the American Bar Association.

A variety of pressure groups exist that are organized around problems of ethnic, religious, and racial interests. There are the numerous neofascist and antiminority organizations, such as the Ku Klux Klan.[4] There are the "minority" organizations such as the National Association for the Advancement of Colored People and the various "hyphen-American" organizations. Al-

[2] This curious fact suggests a necessity for further study of why agriculture so seldom has been denounced as a "selfish interest." The pathos built up around farming and rural life in our national history apparently has much to do with the contrast between the reception of the demands of agricultural and of labor groups. See John Gaus and Leon Wolcott, *Public Administration and the United States Department of Agriculture* (Chicago: Public Administration Service, 1940), pp. 17 ff.

[3] Oliver Garceau, *The Political Life of the American Medical Association* (Cambridge, Mass.: Harvard University Press, 1941); George Rosen, *Madness in Society: Chapters in the Historical Sociology of Mental Illness* (Chicago: University of Chicago Press, 1968).

[4] See, for example, John M. Mecklin, *The Ku Klux Klan* (New York: Harcourt, Brace & World, 1924); Donald S. Strong, *Organized Anti-Semitism in America* (Washington, D.C.: American Council on Public Affairs, 1941); Leo Lowenthal and Norman Guterman, *Prophets of Deceit: A Study of the Techniques of the American Agitator* (New York: Harper & Row, 1949).

though not all of these act directly as pressure groups, they are seldom politically irrelevant. The same can be said for many organized religious bodies.

The organizations of military veterans, especially the American Legion, are well known. Commanding the presumption of a strong moral claim upon the society, veterans' organizations are typically able to work without concentrated opposition from other powerful pressure groups.[5] However, antiwar and antimilitary movements and organizations also have flourished at various times, for example, in the 1920's, just prior to American involvement in World War II, and during the 1960's.

In addition, there are a great many miscellaneous groups, varying greatly in importance and concerned with nearly every imaginable issue. Although many important organizations—such as the National Association of Manufacturers—do not report major expenditures for lobbying, the associations that do report (under the provisions of the Legislative Reorganization Act of 1946) often list large expenditures. Near the top of the list in recent years have been AFL-CIO unions, farm organizations, National Federation of Independent Businesses, American Legion, United States Savings and Loan League, American Medical Association, American Trucking Association, Association of American Railroads, International Brotherhood of Teamsters, National Education Association, and Co-ordinating Committee for Fundamental American Freedoms, Inc.[6]

Beyond the organized associations are broader and more diffuse alignments of interests such as those represented in rural-urban conflicts,[7] sectional or regional constellations, and interstate or interdistrict opposition.[8] These territorial alignments appear to be decreasing in importance, however, with the spread of urbanism and economic specialization and the increased ease of national communication and interregional mobility.

It is in the form of organized associations or groups that interests directly contend for power. Interest groups become pressure groups by exerting their influence at any level or in any branch or division of government. Their points of pressure are directed at whatever centers of power may be present.[9] This activity constitutes "lobbying." The older techniques of lobbying by outright or thinly concealed bribery and intimidation have tended to give way to other methods less vulnerable to public condemnation. The representatives of interest groups try to influence legislation both directly, by immediate contacts with legislative committees at formal hearings and in

---

[5] "In 1936 members of the House openly rejoiced that the three leading organizations of veterans had united on a bonus bill, a combination that made it possible for congressmen to please all. The entire membership of the Senate was present and voted on that bill—the first time in four years that such an attendance and vote were recorded." Johnson, *op. cit.*, p. 389.

[6] Rose, *op. cit.*, pp. 74–75.

[7] Concerned with such as issues as prohibition, taxation, daylight-saving time, and governmental subsidies.

[8] For example, the cotton South vs. the dairying North, the agricultural-debtor West vs. the industrial-financing East; "backcountry" vs. seaboard, upstate vs. downstate.

[9] Key, *Politics, Parties, and Pressure Groups, op. cit.*, p. 227: "Where power rests, there influence will be brought to bear."

personal conferences, and indirectly, by mobilizing support "back home," either by instigating petitions, letters, and so forth on a mass basis or by activating strategic individuals presumed to have influence with legislators. Practically every organized interest of any considerable importance has its representatives on duty at the key points of political authority. There are approximately 3,000 groups and persons registered under the federal Lobbying Act. Lobbying is a continuing and "normal" part of the governing process in America.

Attempts to regulate lobbying usually have not been directed at the *sources* of lobbying in powerful but not officially represented interests; rather they have sought to make lobbying public and in some measure accountable. Thus, many states require some registration of paid lobbyists and attempt to regulate the methods used in influencing legislation. The effectiveness of this type of regulation is doubtful both because of the vagueness of the legislation and the lack of rigorous enforcement. Indeed, lobbying seems to be increasingly a recognized means of functional representation of interests.[1] Lobbying could be abolished in the American system by providing official interest-group representation, or by organizing parties strictly along lines of special interests, or by other equally drastic action; but now pressure groups, operating as lobbies, make up a "third house" of our legislative bodies and are an inseparable part of the governing process.

The low repute of lobbying—like that of "politics" more generally[2]—is the result, in part, of "misplaced" norms; activities considered legitimate or even virtuous in business, for instance, are condemned in politics. The main alternative would be a system of functional (proportional) representation; but this on a national scale seems more likely to intensify rather than to diminish the clash of interest groups. Another alternative is the pulverization of private groups, leaving only isolated individuals outside of the organization of the state itself.[3]

Pressure groups are not unique to America nor to democracies. Even in the most rigid dictatorships, there are conflicts of interests, factions, pressures; and these may be all the more powerful for being concealed. What is characteristic of the United States is the relative openness of the whole process and the large number and variety of highly organized groupings.

None of the main classes of interests distinguished above are homogeneous or without sharp internal conflicts. In agriculture, there are Western

---

[1] See the statement of E. Pendleton Herring, "Lobby," *Encyclopaedia of the Social Sciences*, Vol. IX (New York: Macmillan, 1931), pp. 565–568. Herring called the lobby a "political institution."

[2] The generally acknowledged low repute of "politics" and the "politician" is documented by more systematic evidence. A nation-wide survey reported in 1946 that 65 percent of American adults said they would not want a son to go into politics as a life career, but 63 percent said they would want him to be a lawyer. The report comments: "That a certain stigma should be attached to politics in the eyes of the public, while the law is regarded as an upright and honorable calling, may seem paradoxical in view of the fact that the legal profession perhaps oftener than any other serves as a stepping stone to a political career." *Opinion News*, N.O.R.C., VII, 3 (August 6, 1946).

[3] A condition approached in Germany under Hitler and in the Soviet Union in the Stalinist years. For valuable evidence on the latter case see Alex Inkeles, *Public Opinion in Soviet Russia* (Cambridge, Mass.: Harvard University Press, 1950).

farmers, who may want federal reclamation of lands, versus their Eastern competitors, who either may not care or may oppose such a program; in industry there are the makers of steel and the users of steel; in labor there are diversities among the AFL-CIO, the railway brotherhoods, independent unions. *Any* group may become a pressure group—governmental agencies themselves can and do function as such.

As an outcome of an idealistic ideology in American culture that assumes the desirability of a perfect harmony of interests in society, one may observe a tendency to deprecate "mere compromise" (as over against "adherence to principle") in political affairs. But in their *allocative* aspects, political actions inherently and necessarily deal in compromises. Short of complete subjugation of opponents, there will always be cases in which there is no other way to resolve incompatible interests (and incongruent values and beliefs) at any particular time. Over longer periods, of course, values and interests may be changed; and it does happen that convergence and consensus are achieved on occasion. But with given values and interests, the choice often is between some measure of compromise and outright conflict. The problem of "balancing" or "equating" qualitatively diverse interests is not open to any easy process of calculation and trading. It is entirely possible to encounter situations in which *no* determinate social choice for the whole nation can be derived from the separate preferences of individuals and sub-collectivities. Although some of these "Arrow paradoxes"[4] can be solved in theory, the gaining of workable agreements must sometimes depend in part upon ignorance, vagueness, and uncertainty among some elements of the population concerning where their "best interests" lie, as well as upon the sheer complexity of the many, shifting trade-offs that are possible in legislative and administrative struggles.

The relation of interest groups to the state extends the pluralism and separation of powers into the institutions of the state itself. Theoretically, at least, the state is not identified with any particular segmental interest. As examples we have the separation of church and state, the ultimate political authority officially favoring no religious group; the limitation of direct governmental control of economic affairs; the lack of official representation of interest groups in legislatures; the absence of parties avowedly representing ethnic, racial, religious, or class groupings. The state is supposed to be the mediator and integrating focus for the numerous discrete interests of a differentiated society. Although this function is increasingly strained today, thus far the system has been elastic enough to survive quite revolutionary transformations of social structure.

In early America, property owners generally held the political power, and the main road to power was through the control of property. Many political thinkers wanted to restrict suffrage and eligibility for public office to those who had "a stake in the community." In our day, property and

---

[4] For an introduction to the possibilities of fascinating and challenging analyses in this complex field see the classic work: Kenneth J. Arrow, *Social Choice and Individual Values*, 2nd ed. (New York: Wiley, 1963); and James M. Buchanan and Gordon Tullock, *The Calculus of Consent: Logical Foundations of Constitutional Democracy* (Ann Arbor: University of Michigan Press, 1962).

power are increasingly divorced. Ownership of business does not necessarily mean economic power; and the politically powerful are not necessarily propertied. The power of management in the corporation and of the leaders of labor unions, farm organizations, business associations, and so on, derives, like political authority, from position in a functioning organization. The structure of power in the large economic organization is already somewhat similar to that of a "socialistic" order.

The historic association of property with power has now been shattered in country after country, most dramatically in the totalitarian regimes that have shown that *control* is what counts, not the form of property rights.[5] The National Socialists in Germany could leave the outward pattern of property largely intact while drastically amassing power—in the end practically depriving the nominal property owners of power. The lesson thus taught is reinforced by the experience of capitalistic countries, including the United States, in progressively divorcing control rights from ownership rights. The corporation has shown as decisively as the total dictatorship that individual ownership rights are no longer either a necessary or a sufficient condition for social power. Modern developments have made it increasingly plain that control is the central problem for economics as well as for politics and that the distinction between economic power and political power can become hazy indeed.

Conversely, one must agree with Weber that the political organization of national states already resembles what some forms of socialism advocate for economic organization. For, with nationalism, the local rulers and feudal estates "had been expropriated of their political means and had been displaced by the salaried officialdom of the modern bureaucratic state. The state had 'nationalized' the possession of arms and of administrative means."[6] In feudalism, economic power and political power were *merged*, but both were territorially and organizationally *diffused* rather than centralized. In a completely collectivistic society, however, the *anschluss* of economics and politics is not only complete but also it is centralized: state and economy become one, and under unitary direction—in contrast to democratic political orders in which there are *separate* economic and political elites supported by multiple and *different* interests.

Even with all the enormous consolidation of economic power in organized business and labor, the American economy still has competing, divergent, and conflicting interests;[7] consequently there is far from complete unity or centralization of economic power, and particular economic interests do not completely determine political policy. A similar granulation of political power is still characteristic. Of course, the "separation of powers" and "a system of checks and balances" cannot mean in the twentieth century what they did in the small agrarian republic of 1789; the great extension of

[5] Cf. Peter F. Drucker, *The Future of Industrial Man* (New York: John Day, 1942), esp. pp. 75 ff.

[6] Gerth and Mills, *op. cit.*, p. 49.

[7] Conflicting interests do not always neatly "balance out," although some tendency in that direction is argued by John K. Galbraith, *American Capitalism: The Concept of Contravailing Power*, rev. ed. (Boston: Houghton Mifflin, 1956).

the powers of the presidency, for example, is a consequence of the demands that wars and economic crises have made upon a governmental machine originally designed to disperse and limit both the power of officials and the voice of the people. Increasingly, therefore, the "compromise model" of interest-group politics fails to fit the realities of the later decades of the twentieth century. Some of the most fundamental decisions at the highest levels are those concerning foreign policy, where by no stretch of the imagination can the outcomes be said to represent a mere "balancing" of special demands of narrow interest groupings. Furthermore, a large and apparently increasing proportion of major policies are heavily influenced by technical, scientific, and administrative considerations that are either relatively independent of specific group pressures or are introduced at the behest of major executive agencies themselves or by committees of the Congress acting to *initiate* policy and not merely to respond to external demands.

## THE SYSTEM AS A WHOLE

Among the most striking differences that mark off major kinds of societies are their distinctive modes of arriving at, maintaining, or changing consensus. In highly organized, centralized hierarchical systems, consensus may be attained in a small subordinate grouping and then passed down through successive levels of authority and power, supplemented by mass communication. In a highly diffuse decentralized system, it is more likely that consensus will emerge, if it does, as a flexible and uneven growth that develops through "horizontal" communication and subsequent transmission to whatever central foci of decision making may exist. In large scale heterogeneous politics, there is always a multilevel system through which any societal agreement is reached. In one major type, the various subgroupings arrive at separate consensual views, which are then formed into new agreements by representatives at successively "higher" levels, culminating in national policy or ideology. If this ordered convergence is not provided for by the social structure (for example, the political party system), or fails by reason of excessive heterogeneity, any effort to arrive at a societal consensus may confront a multitude of "hardened" factional positions.

Time after time, the American polity has been confronted with deep clashes of ideologies and vested interests; and repeatedly the oppositions have been compromised or translated into a set of more tractable issues. The process failed in the Civil War, but even then the final conflict was repeatedly averted over a period of more than a full generation.[8] In the allocation and recentering of economic advantages and opportunities, many potentially savage confrontations have been moderated or resolved. A political style has developed that bears many resemblances to the model of bargaining in the marketplace. It has been based on the use of oppositions to create temporary clusters of unity and has sought to turn "issues of principle"

---

[8] The importance of the economic model for political process in the United States has been well argued by Peter F. Drucker, "On the Economic Basis of American Politics," *The Public Interest*, 10 (Winter 1968), 30–42.

into negotiable questions of relative advantage: as Peter Drucker says, "the mobilization of conflict to create unity, and the appeal to interest against the fanaticism of ideological faction."[9]

Repeatedly, then, in different aspects of American political institutions and political behavior a common pattern emerges: *the balancing of interests and compromising of conflicts through multiple power-centers, numerous separate channels of influence, and the subdivision of political authorities.* This kind of "political pluralism" is manifest in the federal system, with its complex division of authority among various levels of government; in the separation of powers and in the further subdivision of functionally specific authority within the major branches; in the loose "federal" organization of political parties, and in the system of territorial representation.[1] It reaches extreme development, with important side effects, in the politics of factionalism. In the "invisible government" it is manifest in the cross pressures of numerous interest groupings: diverse agricultural interests, manufacturing interests, separate business groupings, governmental officialdom, veterans, racial and ethnic minorities, religious groupings, geographic sections, professional associations, and so on. And, of course, the relative power of various segments, strata, and groupings is continually being increased or decreased by changes in the rules established and enforced through the legitimate authority of the government. The central problem of political decision making, therefore, is to find acceptable lines of action for the total collectivity in spite of diversity and opposition among the constituent parts of the relevant population.[2]

"Cultural pluralism" in the sense of freedom for diversity has been lauded in the United States. But the implicit assumption is that the diversity is not great enough to render a stable democratic order unworkable. Cultural *and* social pluralism in many societies means that the nation-state attempts to include sharply different ethnic and religious collectivities that may have few positive social bonds across lines of cleavage, being held together by economic links and political domination. This extreme kind of diversity-and-separation is most often found in large polities, with scattered populations, low urbanization, high illiteracy, and low per capita income.[3] But even in industrialized, literate, urban societies, polarization around differences in language, religion, and sectional interests can be highly disruptive, for example, the relationships between French-speaking and English-speaking populations in Canada, or the Flemings and Walloons in Belgium. In the United States, cultural assimilations of ethnic minorities

[9] *Ibid.*, p. 42.

[1] Cf. Key, *Politics, Parties and Pressure Groups, op. cit.*, p. 27: "The division of sectional interests into separate states probably contributes to national unity by splintering and weakening the potential strength of sectional drives."

[2] Kuhn, *op. cit.*, p. 634 says: "The basic problem is that of a huge cooperative whose sponsors must instruct the staff regarding goals, but in which the sponsors are much divided among themselves. The question is, which goals of which sponsors are to be adopted, in what proportion, and at whose expense."

[3] Marie R. Haug, "Social and Cultural Pluralism as a Concept in Social System Analysis," *American Journal of Sociology*, LXXIII, 3 (November 1967), 294–304.

into a "core culture" has gone quite far, although ethnic factors remain important. The great unresolved cleavage is the separatism imposed upon black Americans by discrimination and segregation.

To those who favor a unitary and centralized system of left or right the present structure of American political institutions is an anachronism. On the other hand, those who accept not only the fact but also the legitimacy of a plurality of value systems and specialized interests in modern political society, may accept American politics as a process of cross pressures, compromises, and the slow, uncertain, and uneven growth of consensus, which has to be rewon from time to time. In the latter case, there is little of the logical symmetry of consistent political creeds. The system is actually a congeries of continually changing subsystems; it is a multifaceted process rather than a unitary and fixed political mold.

On the other hand, the limited and fragmented state of the eighteenth century simply could not survive today. The eighteenth- and nineteenth-century philosophy of "boycotting government"[4] paralleled the conception of society as an aggregate of discrete individuals bound together in a system ruled by natural laws; within a framework of "natural justice" each individual acting in his own interests would contribute to the public good; it followed that the best government was that which governed the least. In fact, of course, the American state after 1791 was never so weak or limited as this political philosophy required, but it did leave extraordinary scope to private and decentralized power and to local autonomy. The "negative state" was functionally suited to a society of self-sufficient local areas and small-scale economic enterprises. Limited government was favored also by the infrequency of foreign wars and by economic opportunity coupled with a belief in self-reliance and self-confidence.

There has been much concern in American culture with "democracy" and "freedom." The present analysis concludes that the individual freedoms that apparently matter most in our culture depend not so much on political forms as on the basic social structure. Abundant experience shows that constitutions and bills of rights are not easily exportable to societies with radically different values. "Freedom," in one of its important meanings, is an attribute of social structure.[5] Requisite for maximal personal freedom are dispersion of power *and* limitation of both public and private power by rules that take their departure from a high evaluation of individual personality and consent. The political institutions dominant in our society require a tolerance of value diversities and conflicts of interests.

Perhaps increasingly, such institutions require sophisticated understanding. Where there are urgent demands for order and collective goal-attainment, there will be power seekers. When those who attain power are supported by consensus, political authority may be established. Consensus is always precarious, goal attainment is uncertain, collective ventures usually are hazardous. And where there is power, there is always the possible abuse

---

[4] The phrase is Merriman's. *The Role of Politics in Social Change, op. cit.,* chap. 10.

[5] See the stimulating analysis by Gerard de Gré: "Freedom and Social Structure," *American Sociological Review,* 11, 6 (October 1946), 530.

of power. For all these reasons, political problems are inescapable in human society. This chapter has tried to analyze only a few specific examples of these problems for one culture.

## SUGGESTED READINGS

ALFORD, ROBERT R. *Party and Society: The Anglo-American Democracies.* Chicago: Rand McNally, 1963. Important analysis of the political systems of Australia, Canada, Great Britain, and the United States. Uses opinion surveys, voting data, and many other sources of evidence. Gives particular emphasis to class bases of political cleavage, comparing class influences with those of region and religious background.

ALMOND, GABRIEL, and SIDNEY VERBA. *The Civic Culture.* Princeton, N.J.: Princeton University Press, 1965. Study of consensual bases of politics, using survey data, in Great Britain, West Germany, Italy, Mexico, and the United States. Demonstrates high level of political trust and commitment in the United States, contrary to some impressions but clear in *comparative* perspective.

BLAU, PETER M. *Exchange and Power in Social Life.* New York: Wiley, 1964. Elaboration of the idea that all social interactions may involve "exchange" —reward or penalty, advantage or disadvantage, credit or loss. Penetrating analysis of emergence of institutions and authority systems.

CAMPBELL, ANGUS, PHILLIP E. CONVERSE, WARREN E. MILLER, and DANIEL E. STOKES. *The American Voter.* New York: Wiley, 1960; and, by the same authors, *Elections and the Political Order.* New York: Wiley, 1966. Two landmark works in studies of voting behavior and its contexts. Although the institutional framework is taken as given rather than a problem to be explained, the unique data and many elegant analyses in these volumes deserve the most thoughtful attention.

DUZERGER, MAURICE. *Political Parties,* 2nd ed. New York: Wiley, 1959. An urbane and erudite interpretation. Historical and comparative approach helps place the American case in a clarifying perspective.

EULAU, HEINZ, SAMUEL J. ELDERSVELD, and MORRIS JANOWITZ (eds.). *Political Behavior.* New York: Free Press, 1956. Collection of useful essays. Interesting traces of the "Eisenhower years" in the tone or mood of several items, but much stands as valuable historical reference as well as contribution to generalizations about political behavior.

JANOWITZ, MORRIS. *The Professional Soldier.* New York: Free Press, 1960. Required reading for the citizen who wants to have an informed opinion on the significance of the military component in the future of our society. Stimulating analysis by one of the few American sociologists who has made a serious and continuing study of military affairs.

KEY, JR., V. O. *Public Opinion and American Democracy.* New York: Knopf, 1961. Likely to produce in the thoughtful student a series of instructive reflections upon participatory democracy. Key uses survey data as points of departure for incisive, often barbed, notes upon a wide range of political phenomena.

LIPSET, SEYMOUR MARTIN. *Political Man.* Garden City, N.Y.: Doubleday, 1959.

Well integrated set of studies and essays on fundamental problems by a well known political sociologist.

MACIVER, ROBERT M. *The Web of Government.* New York: Macmillan, 1947. Part of the mature wisdom of one of the great political sociologists of this century. Clear and judicious appraisal of basic elements of politics and governance.

ROSE, ARNOLD M. *The Power Structure: Political Process in American Society.* New York: Oxford University Press, 1967. Contains a dispassionate evaluation of polemics concerning "power structure," locally and nationally. Good sense and respect for facts—in contrast to dramatic claims of some of the popular "theories" here examined, especially notions of rule by conspiratorial power elites.

# American Education  *VIII*

## EDUCATION AS AN INSTITUTION

The student of social systems must grasp many interrelated processes simultaneously. "The state of the system as a whole," difficult as it is to comprehend or describe, is an important determinant of our understanding of the behavior of the distinguishable parts of the system. We have examined the family, the system of stratification, and the economic and political institutions. We turn now to another major and permanent institution—education.

Educational institutions derive from these two irreducible facts: (1) human culture is learned, not biologically inherited; (2) very young human beings are both plastic and incapable of survival, much less of developing social personalities, without adult care and teaching. The cultural heritage must be renewed for each generation; society is daily invaded by new "barbarians"[1] who have to learn thousands of specific skills, beliefs, knowledges, values, and norms if the culture is to have any continuity. A complex, technologically advanced society, greatly dependent upon science and rapidly changing, requires an elaborate system of instruction and indoctrination if it is not to regress to simpler levels—or to disintegrate in the face of the stresses to which all societies may be subjected.

In a broad sense, "education" is the totality of human teaching and learning. Even in the narrower sense of direct and intended instruction, it is an important aspect of many social actions not ordinarily thought of as "educational." Through most of history, and for very great numbers of the world's peoples today, education has not been provided by specialized personnel functioning in a separate organization but has been part of the ordinary routine of the society. Parents, elders, craftsmen, priests, warriors, and others, have instructed the young in the knowledge, skills, traditions, beliefs, and values of the particular social group. Indeed in all societies the ordinary day-to-day interaction of an individual with other individuals, from birth onward, continually "instructs" and reshapes his behavior. Everywhere, the child absorbs an enormous and complex range of cultural materials as a more or less unplanned, informal by-product of growing up in a family and community. And everywhere persons continue to learn as a result of their daily encounters with the world throughout life.[2]

---

[1] Cf. the striking statement by R. Pinot quoted in Pitirim A. Sorokin, *Contemporary Sociological Theories* (New York: Harper, 1928), p. 85.

[2] In a very real sense, "death" might be defined as the cessation of learning. In a world increasingly preoccupied with change, considerable attention is being paid to adult learning. See, for example, Orville G. Brim, Jr., and Stanton Wheeler, *Socialization After Childhood: Two Essays* (New York: Wiley, 1966).

Nevertheless, some formalized education is found in even the "simplest" cultures; if not schools in our sense, there are definitely institutionalized and systematic patterns of indoctrination and instruction—for instance, secret societies or initiation rites. In societies that like ours have highly developed occupational specialization and considerable general cultural heterogeneity, specialized agencies of education develop and elaborate their own norms and goals, their own specially trained and disciplined personnel. Education comes to be thought of as something one "gets," not the total experience of the whole personality.

Three main terms appear frequently in discussions of this subject: learning, education, and socialization. Often used interchangeably, they are not synonomous. "Learning" is the broadest concept, referring to any alteration in behavior (including all "mental" and "emotional" processes) consequent upon experience. "Socialization" refers to the learning of social behavior patterns and the cultural content involved in them. "Education" is a set of purposive processes aimed at inducing learning.

Within the broad rubric of education are several quite different processes. "Schooling" represents systematic teaching by a specialized agency, aimed at future activities of the pupils or students in settings outside that agency. "Training" is systematic teaching for special activities and roles within the type of settings in which the inculcated skills, knowledges, beliefs, and so on, will later be activated, or in specialized schools directly related to the anticipated activities. "Apprenticeship" is a special form of training in which the learner is expected to model his behavior directly upon that of persons already adept in the relevant performances. What is usually called liberal (or general) education exposes the student to a wide range of knowledge, evaluations, and direct or vicarious experience of a complex cultural heritage.

It is one of the distinguishing marks of modern secularized societies that education has been so removed from kinship and religious groupings. Although even in the United States organized religious bodies still conduct much educational activity and families do not always turn over their children to the school completely, or without reservations and emotional ambivalence, the degree of separation of formal education from family and church is extraordinarily extensive and sharp.

Educational influences operating directly upon the child include, of course, not only the socialization of family and playgroup and the formal instruction of the schools but also the enormously expanding impact of the mass media of communication—television, radio, books, magazines, the omnipresent flood of "comic books," movies, posters, and a great variety of public advertising. The social and psychological effects of the mass media have long been the objects of much attention and controversy. Although many critics and defenders of this or that medium or type of communication often show great persuasive gifts and appear to advance their views with much confidence, actual scientific demonstration of its alleged effects is still scarce and limited in scope. But the mass media do reach incredibly large audiences and saturate the environment of today's children, who on the average view television for at least twenty hours a week. And, of course, the media carry ideas, beliefs, symbols, knowledge, images of behavior, and pervasive styles of orienting oneself to other people that are often different from and in contradiction to the goals and standards of parents and of the schools.[3]

Furthermore, the reassuring note struck by many of the earlier studies—which suggested that the mass media had slight effects and at most merely accentuated the dispositions children already had—has been jarred by subsequent research. It now appears that the effect of endemic exposure to sight and sound of violence and sadistic behavior, for example, may be to weaken inhibitions and to encourage the acting out of such kinds of conduct.[4]

Although the present analysis must remain restricted largely to the schools and colleges, their power and significance must not be exaggerated. For much of the most vivid and enduring learning occurs outside of schools; and a sharp contradiction between academic instruction and other personal experience is often, and perhaps typically, resolved in favor of the latter.

At any rate, the possibility can no longer be minimized that in the long run mass communication will strongly affect basic modes of experiencing and behaving.

Education—including education by the mass media—is no more emotionally neutral than any other institution, and one must always remain aware of its dynamic elements and its "psychological" dimension. Of every educational situation it is important to ask:

1. *What* is being taught or learned? What content, intended and unintended, is being transferred?
2. *Who* is teaching? What are his or her position, derivation, and characteristics?
3. *How* is teaching being done? What are the organizing norms, the techniques, methods, interpersonal relations, and their consequences?

[3] Early studies dealt with motion pictures and radio. Examples include: Herbert Blumer, *Movies and Conduct* (New York: Macmillan, 1933); Paul F. Lazarsfeld and Patricia R. Kendall, *Radio Listening in America* (Englewood Cliffs, N.J.: Prentice-Hall, 1954); Robert K. Merton, *Mass Persuasion* (New York: Harper & Row, 1946). Later studies include Joseph T. Klapper, *The Effects of Mass Communication* (New York: Free Press, 1960); Lewis A. Dexter and David M. White (eds.), *People, Society, and Mass Communications* (New York: Free Press, 1964); Melvin L. De Fleur, *Theories of Mass Communication* (New York: McKay, 1966). (The estimate that children spend more than 20 hours per week in exposure to television is from De Fleur, p. 4.) It must be said, however, that the evidence does not seem to support the more sweeping claims for the influence—even apart from particular content—of the media, especially the popular work of Herbert Marshall McLuhan, *Understanding Media: The Extension of Man* (New York: McGraw-Hill, 1964) and, with Quentin Fiore, *The Medium Is the Massage* (New York: Random House, 1967).

[4] Leonard Berkowitz, *Aggression: A Social Psychological Analysis* (New York: McGraw-Hill, 1962); Leonard Berkowitz and Edna Rawlings, "Effects of Film Violence on Inhibitions Against Subsequent Aggression," *Journal of Abnormal and Social Psychology*, 66, 5 (May 1963), 405–412. See also summaries of research findings in Bernard Berelson and Gary A. Steiner, *Human Behavior* (New York: Harcourt, Brace & World, 1964), chap. 13; Wilbur Schramm, J. Lyle, and E. B. Parker, *Television in the Lives of Our Children* (Stanford, Calif.: Stanford University Press, 1961). Studies in England give results consistent with those reported in the United States. Cf. H. T. Himmelweit, A. N. Oppenheim, and P. Vince, *Television and the Child* (London: Oxford University Press, 1958).

4. To *whom* is the teaching directed?

The answers to these questions vary tremendously from one culture to another; and we shall soon inspect some of the ways in which our own culture contrasts with others.

The school is a definitely segregated social system, with its own patterns of authority and control, its distinctive groups and forms of organization, its special ceremonies and rituals, its peculiar language, its special norms and values.[5] To a large extent it is both a distinct social unit and a separate culture, depending upon the type of school. The homogeneity of the school culture and its unity and intensity of ingroup identification are usually greatest in schools that are simultaneously small, long established, maximally separated from the larger community, and relatively homogeneous as to the class, religious, and ethnic backgrounds of staff and students. These conditions are met in high degree in many wealthy private boarding schools, in certain established "prestige" colleges, and in some small rural schools. In the cities, on the other hand, many of the large public schools draw upon a heterogeneous student population and are unable to develop more than a highly formal unity.

The school as a social organization is split internally into many subgroups and subcategories. In the larger schools, the student population is divided into numerous cliques, gangs, and other informal and diffuse groupings; it is sharply age graded; it has many formal organizations and special extracurricular activities. The teaching staff is likewise organized into cliques and factions, and is graded into prestige ranks and placed in a hierarchy of authority; it may have its professional organizations or its teachers' union. Over teachers and students in the public schools is the authority of a principal, superintendent, or other executive officer. Behind the administrative authorities are the school boards. Operating at all these points, and at others, are the influences of parents and their organizations and of numerous special interests and groups from the larger society. The school is thus, like every other important social organization, both subject to forces arising outside itself and self-directing and self-activated.

The school comprises a complex system of reciprocal statuses and roles. The positions of teacher, student, parent, school administrator, board member, and so on are definitely institutionalized but not without tension and conflict. Parents and teachers seldom agree completely upon the standards by which the child is to be judged. Parents tend to see their children as members of the most intimate primary group, as projections of their own hopes and fears, as beings for whom they are accountable in the eyes of the community. Teachers tend to see the same children more impersonally and more nearly in terms of the school's requirements for discipline, control, scholastic achievements, or other special standards. Obviously, the schools

[5] A classic study: Willard Waller, *The Sociology of Teaching* (New York: Wiley, 1932), chaps. 2 and 9. In the more recent research, a highly intricate mapping of specific areas of autonomy and interdependence within the school and between the school and its environment has been partially accomplished. Cf. Fred E. Katz, "The School as a Complex Social Organizaiton," *Harvard Educational Review*, 34, 3 (Summer 1964), 428–455.

could not exist at all were these divergencies complete; but because school and family thus differ, an important degree of latent or overt conflict is built into the institutional situation itself.[6]

In our society much teaching is "ideational"—the teaching of ideas *about* activities rather than the demonstration of activities—and the young may be trained for future roles in which the teacher has himself had no direct experience. By contrast, in societies with a slight division of labor, "teaching" is carried on by persons who are themselves actively performing the roles into which they are inducting others. Such is the primeval teacher —the craftsman, soldier, priest, farmer, hunter, ruler—who trains others out of his own accumulated lore and experience. With the development of a more highly dynamic and differentiated society, however, the teacher who explains rather than demonstrates appears, at first usually in the priesthood, which has developed in all major societies with a written history. To transmit the sacred lore to new members of the priesthood there emerges the religious scholar and the sacred school.[7] With any advanced secularization of the culture, "schools" in the modern sense arise in two main ways: first, special branches of study become gradually separated from the sacred tradition; second, separate secular schools with their own lay teachers are established *de novo*.[8] As the society becomes more complex, the teacher becomes more specialized and less likely to *practice* his specialty; he becomes an expert or adviser.

Thus, the teacher emerges—and the secular school. What are the main outlines of the "separate culture" of a secular school system?[9] In the first place, the primary teacher-student relationship is one between those who wield institutional authority and those who are supposed to accept it. It is *also* mainly a relation between older and younger persons. Between teachers and students there will typically be differences in interests and values, in standards of conduct, and in the complexity of organization of perceptions and behavior. Schools in different cultures differ greatly in the kind and degree of teacher-student conflict and rigidity of discipline. Fragmentary evidence indicates that, in general, school discipline has been less severe and the teacher's role less authoritarian in the United States than in European countries.

The public, secular school of modern nations does not merely copy the culture of the local community in which it is located; it acts as a center for the diffusion of a much wider national and international culture. It often passes on new techniques, ideas, goals, and standards of conduct that differ appreciably from those current in the local area; and thus on occasion it comes into conflict with parents and with locally powerful individuals and groups. What it does in fact teach will typically represent a compromise be-

[6] The proliferation of parent-teacher organizations is partly a symptom of the tensions generated at the point of tangency between family and school.

[7] Florian Znaniecki, *The Social Role of the Man of Knowledge* (New York: Columbia University Press, 1940), chap. 3.

[8] *Ibid.*, p. 115.

[9] Here we borrow from Waller, *The Sociology of Teaching, op. cit.*, which contains insights concerning the sociology of education that even today have seldom been equaled.

tween these out-of-school influences and the professional and personal inclinations of the teachers. On the other hand the school's tendency to diffuse a wider culture can be highly significant on producing cultural homogeneity in complex societies.[1] The United States provides one of the greatest examples—its public schools played an enormous role in the "Americanization" of many millions of children of European immigrants.[2]

Perhaps the most crucial point about the separate culture of the school is precisely its separateness; for the fact that educational organizations are specialized and segmented parts of the society is both product and further cause of separateness and difference. Consider how remarkable is the central fact of a modern school system: from the age of six or less until late adolescence or early adulthood, children and youths are removed from a large part of most days of every year from the tutelage of family or church and from active participation in the ordinary activities of the wider society. Despite vocational training, "community-centered schools," "activity projects," and the like, the typical school is decisively separate from wider community activities.[3]

The school creates special attitudes in its teachers. For example, teachers are concerned to establish and maintain their authority; and they develop numerous social techniques to forestall threats to their authority. Parents always are a potential threat; and it is an unwritten rule in most public schools that the principal should support the teacher in cases of parental "interference" as well as in the teacher's dealing with children.[4] Similarly, the code holds that no teacher should criticize another before the pupils. Upon the teachers impinge not just the needs and demands of the pupils but the expectations and evaluations of other individuals and groupings in the wider community. The resulting "teacher morality" has much in common with the norms of other professions but shows understandably unique features. The teacher is expected to show "impartiality," to treat students with formal equality, and to maintain a certain impersonality or social distance in dealing with them.[5] He is not supposed to court popularity among

---

1 "Three conditions of our social order prompt expansion and proliferation in education: complexity, affluence, and danger." (Everett K. Wilson, *Sociology: Rules, Roles and Relationships* (Homewood, Ill.: Dorsey Press, 1966), p. 439.

2 Useful general works dealing with assimilation are Milton M. Gordon, *Assimilation in American Life* (New York: Oxford University Press, 1964); Oscar Handlin (ed.), "Ethnic Groups in American Life," *Daedalus* (Spring 1961); George E. Simpson and J. Milton Yinger, *Racial and Cultural Minorities*, 3rd ed. (New York: Harper & Row, 1965), esp. chaps. 20–21.

3 This is a descriptive, not an evaluative, statement. Some "separateness" is inevitable if there are to be schools at all.

4 "If the students find the principal a friendly court of appeal, it is much harder for the teacher to maintain control over them." Howard S. Becker, "The Teacher in the Authority System of the Public School," in Blaine E. Mercer and Edwin R. Carr (eds.), *Education and the Social Order* (New York: Holt, Rinehart and Winston, 1957), p. 354 ff.

5 The significance of these patterns has been analyzed only generally. One consequence is certainly to minimize personal attractions and antipathies that might be disruptive to learning; formality also insulates the teacher from direct personal vulnerability on matters outside his or her special institutional authority and competence. There are, quite cer-

the students. There are conventions of formality in teacher-teacher relations, especially in the presence of pupils. There is a code of workmanship—standards of proficiency and conscientiousness in doing one's job. Quite frequently the demands and expectations to which the teacher is exposed result in an emphasis upon punctuality, caution, and personal conformity beyond that found in the free professions or among business groups in the same communities. With increasing professionalism and unionization in an increasingly metropolitan society, however, the effective norms for personal behavior of teachers become more similar to those applied to other white-collar workers.

The students also inherit and develop a special culture. One of its prime components, in our public schools at least,[6] is group solidarity: the pupils are, for certain purposes, a group united *against* the school authorities. There is an injunction against "tattling" or "squealing" and disdain for the "teacher's pet." Students tend to establish with teachers the social distance that the teachers themselves feel an obligation to maintain. In their informal activities, students emphasize the hierarchy of age and make distinctions that seem incredibly fine to many adults. They demand exact conformity to the standards commonly shared at a particular age-grade level. They emphasize extracurricular activities and tend to deprecate "excessive" scholastic achievements.[7]

The above generalizations merely indicate a few of the relatively distinctive normative patterns of the school. The concrete norms vary, of course, through time and from one type of school to another; but we must pass over these variations at present.

We must not forget that educational institutions in *any* society are always affecting and being affected by other institutions. They are, for example, never really politically neutral; for seeming neutrality inescapably involves acceptance of the existing situation. It does not follow that education is not more "free" in some societies than in others, but educational systems cannot be fully understood without analyzing their specific interdependence with other components of the culture and the social system.

## PRINCIPAL CHARACTERISTICS OF AMERICAN EDUCATION[8]

### Unity and Diversity

In the United States there is no nation-wide system of schools under a central authority, nor is there any organized national enforcement of

---

tainly, other "functions." (Cf. Waller, *op. cit.*, chaps. 9, 10, and 14.) The norms of impartiality and formality are not, of course, invariant and are not always controlling. For further examples, see August B. Hollingshead, *Elmtown's Youth* (New York: Wiley, 1949), chap. 8.

6 The pattern probably has fairly wide cross-cultural application; but the differences commonly noted, between Germany and the United States for instance, are enough to warn against too ready generalization.

7 James S. Coleman, *The Adolescent Society* (New York: Free Press, 1961).

8 Basic references include Albert J. Reiss, Jr. (ed.), *Schools in a Changing Society* (New

standard curricula, organization, or methods.[9] Yet there is an "American system" clearly different from the educational institutions of many other cultures. Its unity is one of cultural themes and cultural structures rather than of centralized social organization. For we have one room rural schools and giant urban schools; those in affluent suburbs and those in the low-income areas; "progressive" schools and those that cling to the three R's; we have "colleges" that are trade schools and "colleges" in the tradition of the European universities. Standards vary, textbooks vary, controls vary, aims and methods vary. How can there be a "system" or "institution" in all this flux and variation?[1]

Education in this society remained highly decentralized in basic organization long after both the polity and giant economic enterprises had created strongly nucleated institutions. Yet an impressive degree of convergence in norms, goals, and operating procedures and practices was attained through a complex mesh of loosely coupled processes, organizations, and lines of communication.[2] These components include national recruitment of teachers, mobility of students, national markets for instructional materials, national examinations and scholarship and fellowship programs, major teacher training centers, rational organizations of educators and officials, accreditation associations, and professional associations and teachers unions.

As a set of organized movements from one "stage" of learning to another, the progression of the child through the American system of elementary and secondary schools and higher education is not really a single "ladder" but a set of overlapping and diverging pathways. Starting with nursery schools at ages three and four and merging into kindergartens at ages four and five, the child typically enters at age six into elementary (primary) school. Thereafter, he may continue through grade eight before going into a four year high school; or he may enter a combined junior-senior high school at the beginning of grade seven; or he may at that point move into a junior high school (grades seven through nine) and then to a senior

---

York: Free Press, 1966); Patricia Cayo Sexton, *The American School* (Englewood Cliffs, N.J.: Prentice-Hall, 1967); David Goslin, *The School in Contemporary Society* (Chicago: Scott, Foresman, 1965); Burton R. Clark, *Educating the Expert Society* (San Francisco: Chandler, 1962); Wilbur B. Brookover, *A Sociology of Education* (New York: American Book Company, 1955); A. H. Halsey, Jean Floud, and C. Arnold Anderson (eds.), *Education, Economy, and Society* (New York: Free Press, 1961); Robert J. Havighurst and Bernice L. Neugarten, *Society and Education* (Boston: Allyn and Bacon, 1957), esp. chaps. 7, 9, and 11.

9 "There is no American equivalent to the Ministry of Education found in many other Western societies." Neal Gross, "The Sociology of Education," in Robert K. Merton, Leonard Broom, Leonard S. Cottrell, Jr., *Sociology Today* (New York: Basic Books, 1959), p. 140.

1 "As one looks at the public school system of America, the first generalization one is tempted to make is that it is not a system at all and that no generalizations about it are true." Harold J. Laski, *The American Democracy* (New York: Viking, 1948), p. 328.

2 An incisive and important summary of this set of networks has been formulated by Sloan R. Wayland, "Structural Features of American Education as Basic Factors in Innovation," chap. 23 in Matthew B. Miles (ed.), *Innovation in Education* (New York: Bureau of Publications, Teachers College, Columbia University, 1964).

high school (grades ten through twelve). Beyond secondary school there are junior or community colleges, technical or vocational schools and institutes, general undergraduate colleges, and professional schools. Beyond the four-year college are many different kinds of graduate and professional training. Most of the public schools and colleges are paralleled by private or parochial organizations. In addition, the federal and state governments operate vast in-service training programs, as do industrial and business organizations. The total social structure of education in the United States, therefore, hardly can be said to exhibit a classic simplicity.

The unifying characteristics of American education are to be found not only in this complex aggregate of associations and groupings but also in common normative standards—conceptions of what education should be, its aims and functions. Yet even these show much diversity, as we shall see. Nevertheless, cultural themes, or the generalized assumptions and values[3] that can be inferred from the institutionalized norms, provide an appropriate point of departure. There is substantial evidence of institutional consistency and regularity, despite diversity.

### Faith in Education

The common cultural framework consists, first, in the widespread "faith in education," noted by both native and foreign observers as characteristic of the American scene for well over a century.[4] Yet there is also a strong tendency to deprecate the value of formal education. Education in general receives tremendous acclaim; education in particular is the object of widespread disaffection, criticism, and low esteem. To some Americans, however, education is a magic panacea,[5] the prime agency of progress; and America's faith in universal public education is its greatest asset. This faith is typically supported on two main grounds: first, that a democratic society requires an educated citizenry so that individuals may participate in the decisions of public policy; second, that education brings economic rewards and social advancement to the individual and strength and security to the national society.

Evidence of faith in education and the identification of education with the schools is not hard to find. American expenditures for education are impressive. There is the universality of compulsory attendance at elementary and secondary school and the very high attendance rates. There is the widespread "testimony," not merely of professional educators but of broad

---

[3] Counts speaks of "controlling ideas" and contrasts the systematic and consistent content of educational theories with the rough-hewn principles that have to be dug out from actual practice. George S. Counts, *The American Road to Culture, A Social Interpretation of Education in the United States* (New York: John Day, 1930), chap. 1, esp. pp. 3 and 7. The concept of "theme" has been developed by Morris E. Opler; see, for example: "Themes as Dynamic Forces in Culture," *The American Journal of Sociology,* LI, 3 (November 1945), pp. 198–206; "The Context of Themes," *American Anthropologist,* 51, 2 (April–June 1949), pp. 323–325.

[4] See Newton Edwards and Herman G. Richey, *The School in the American Social Order,* 2nd ed. (Boston: Houghton Mifflin, 1963), chap. 9.

[5] For a remarkable example, see Raymond M. Hughes and William H. Lancelot, *Education, America's Magic* (Ames: Iowa State College Press, 1946).

sectors of the population. There are richly endowed colleges and universities. The observant traveler finds that in the small American town the public school building dominates the scene much as the cathedral dominates the towns of Latin America and, formerly, much of Europe. On the other hand, a very large, although not exactly ascertainable, proportion of those Americans who profess enthusiasm for education are giving their support to a symbol or an ideal creed, not to the realities presented by schools. Organized education raises problems about the pay of teachers, the degree of equality of opportunity for students, the freedom of the teacher to pursue inquiry. Education-in-practice is frequently attacked as "too impractical," or as too expensive, or as corrosive of established beliefs and values, or as an incitement to discontent, or as too much concerned with irrelevancies or frills. On the other hand, to some of the most eloquent critics the schools seem to appear almost literally as "systems of involuntary servitude," in which young people are talked to *about* knowledges and skills they do not *now* use or need (but which they are told they will need in the future). The critics say that the relevance to the future of what is now being taught is highly doubtful at best and, therefore, cannot be clear or certain to the pupil. The curriculum is viewed as highly rigid, and the expected level and zone of performance as relatively low and narrow.[6] To the extent that these conditions prevail, motivation for learning may be expected to fall considerably short of a natural maximum.[7]

Faith in education is not universally shared, nor is it all of one piece. Its components deserve closer examination.

Much of this ambivalence reflects two contrasting attitudes: the practical interest in formal training as a means to occupational success, and the interest in the training of "the whole man"—the liberal-humanistic tradition with its stress upon the "social value of the mind disciplined by instruction to understand the world about it"[8] and upon intrinsic values in the cultural legacy. Education has been accepted by many not as an end in itself, but as a means to specific goals. The influence of older religious and classical education aiming to inculcate certain beliefs and values for their own sake never disappeared so completely from the American public school as some of the critics of education have believed—at the least the schools are expected, as Waller has said, to be "museums of virtue."[9] But the prac-

[6] Examples of such criticisms include: Paul Goodman, *Compulsory Mis-Education* (New York: Horizon Press, 1964); Edgar Z. Friedenberg, *Coming of Age in America: Growth and Acquiescence* (New York: Random House, 1965). See also, Harold Full (ed.), *Controversy in American Education* (New York: Macmillan, 1967); James B. Conant, *The American High School Today* (New York: McGraw-Hill, 1959); Martin Mayer, *The Schools* (New York: Harper & Row, 1961).

[7] Cf. Sarane S. Boocock and James S. Coleman, "Games with Simulated Environments in Learning," *Sociology of Education*, 39, 3 (Summer 1966), 215–217.

[8] Laski, *op. cit.*, p. 324.

[9] This happy phrase occurs on p. 34 of *The Sociology of Teaching, op. cit.* See also William W. Brickman and Stanley Lehrer (eds.), *Religion, Government and Education* (New York: Society for the Advancement of Education, 1963); Donald E. Boles, *The Bible, Religion, and the Public Schools* (Ames: Iowa State University Press, 1961); Robert Lee Collier, "Education, Religion, and the Kentucky Court of Appeals." *Bulletin*

tical and the liberal curricula have contended in the public school and the struggle has been intense, partly because different social groups have had different interests in the outcome.

Liberal education has seemed a suitable mark of "culture" and prestige to an economically secure elite (and to many who have aspired to join them); but it often has seemed immensely "impractical" to many farmers, self-made businessmen, and workers. Even when they have given it a certain deference as an esoteric, quasi-magical body of learning, they have had doubts concerning its value for their own children. Thus, education receives mass support; but the alleged faith in it is the resultant of complex and partly conflicting evaluations.

The creation of the public high school was largely a phenomenon of the period from 1890 to 1910; its establishment of a mass education, terminal program was practically complete by 1940. Since World War II, it has undergone a second great change: because of the rapid growth of college and university enrollment, it has become in great measure a mass college-preparatory organization. The transformation is peculiarly complex since the same system is expected to serve both the college bound and the terminal students, both of whom represent very large populations with differing expectations and claims. Furthermore, the system is now exposed to the evaluations and demands of a large proportion of parents who are themselves high school graduates or college trained and are highly articulate and often critical in their responses to the actions of the schools.[1]

*Mass Education*

In the United States we have *mass* education. Attendance in a tax supported public school system is compulsory.[2] Probably nowhere else has a society devoted so much of its time and resources to formal schooling. In 1966–1967 there were about 56,000,000 students, of whom about 6 million were in college. From generation to generation, since the middle of the nineteenth century, schools have multiplied, enrollment has grown, curricula have broadened and diversified, higher education has vastly expanded. The total result is something new under the sun.[3] As of the late 1960's, the proportion of the total population that was in some kind of "school" had increased to nearly 3 out of 10. Public school enrollment alone amounted to 46 million

---

of the *Bureau of School Services*, 33, 2 (Lexington: College of Education, University of Kentucky, 1960), pp. 181–182.

[1] Martin Trow, "The Second Transformation of American Secondary Education," *The International Journal of Comparative Sociology*, reprinted in Reinhard Bendix and Seymour Martin Lipset (ed.), *Class Status and Power* (New York: Free Press, 1966), pp. 437–449.

[2] The first compulsory school attendance law was established by Massachusetts in 1852; by 1918, all states had some legislation of this type. Edwards and Richey, *op. cit.*, p. 490.

[3] "In the United States over one fifth [in the early 1940's] of the people spend most of their waking hours as pupils in educational institutions. This situation is unique in human experience and, in fact, is without historical precedent in the nation." Paul H. Landis, *Population Problems* (New York: American Book Company, 1943) pp. 336, 337. As of the late 1960's, the proportion of the total population that was in some kind of "school" had increased to nearly 3 out of 10. Public school enrollment alone amounted to 46 million persons by 1967–1968.

persons by 1967–1968. Granted the notorious difficulties of any attempt to arrive at valid international comparisons, it is nevertheless clear that the United States, with a college enrollment equal to about 40 percent of its college-age population, has far and away the most massive program of higher education in the world.[4] Even if average achievement levels in some fields were to be lower here than in Britain, Europe, Japan, or the U.S.S.R. (and recent studies appear to demonstrate this in mathematics in elementary and secondary education), the net increment in knowledge and skills supplies an unprecedented cultural base. More than half of the adults in the United States in 1960 had at least ten years of formal education, and 16 percent had attended college. As of 1959, the percentage of the eligible age group completing secondary school was 65—as compared with 11 in France, 7 in the United Kingdom, and just under 7 in Italy. Of all persons of college-graduation age, the percentage attaining a first degree is 16.9 for the United States, as compared with 3.4 in France, 2.7 in West Germany, and 2.6 in Italy.[5] In 1965, 54 percent of high school graduates enrolled in college; in 1940, the comparable figure had been only 34 percent.[6]

In 1966, direct expenditures for education were 5.3 percent of the Gross National Product, amounting to just over 38 billion dollars; the rapidly accelerating federal expenditures alone accounted for 4.8 billion dollars.[7]

Our educational system has not just grown; it has exploded into a giant nationwide enterprise. It tends, furthermore, to have "mass" organization and practices. In the large urban schools, in the increasingly dominant consolidated school of the small town or rural area, and in the great metropolitan universities (though not in many experimental schools nor the many small schools and colleges), much of the organization and procedure is basically affected by the presumed necessity of "processing" great numbers of students through standardized stages.

Nearly all children of elementary school ages are enrolled—from six through thirteen years, 99 percent. Of youth aged fourteen to seventeen about 93 percent are still in school. And formal education increasingly extends into the higher age levels as college enrollments mount. Some effects of the long-time trends toward high education levels are already apparent. Less than 3 percent of the total population are illiterate; more than 75 percent of the appropriate age grouping graduate from high school.

The most important influences in the rise of universal public education include at least five that continue into the present. First, the early dominance of sectarian Protestantism in America, with its reliance upon individual access to religious truth as revealed in the Bible, was a real spur to elementary education. Many sects and denominations strongly encouraged

[4] The more highly restricted and selective systems of France and of the United Kingdom enroll, respectively, some 15 and 10 percent.

[5] Seymour E. Harris (ed.), *Education and Public Policy* (Berkeley: McCutchan Publishing Company, 1965), p. 8.

[6] Raymond W. Mack, *Transforming America* (New York: Random House, 1968), p. 54.

[7] Harris, *op. cit.*, p. 327.

their members to learn to read; many established schools and colleges. In more subtle ways, also, neo-Calvinistic movements created a predisposition toward formal education. The churches, at war among themselves, could well utilize literate defenders and argumentative skills; the school provided an agency for imposing upon the young the total discipline so important to the sterner branches of ascetic Protestantism; and the intellectual schematization of knowledge fitted the concept of an ordered and, for many sects, predestined world. A second major influence was the establishment of political democracy and the gradual widening of suffrage, which seemed to call for extension of educational opportunity to at least the politically responsible elements of the nation. Third, an awakening political consciousness, combined with extremely widespread and intense desires for upward social mobility, led the "common man," under upper-class leadership, to support the establishment of the great public school system. Fourth, after the emergence of complex, large-scale industry the needs of business for technicians and for literate, skilled workers gave further impetus to mass education. Finally, especially after the turn of the century, with the immigration of large numbers of non-English speaking people, the already established public schools were seized upon to "Americanize" foreigners and their children, to replace their Old World culture with some version of a new common culture. Thus, the United States, like modern dictatorships, though to far less degree and for different purposes, has relied upon state-supported, compulsory education to establish national unity.

A significant addition to American concepts of the place of education in national life is the development, out of social science research, of the concept of "human investment" in education.[8] From an older conventional point of view, expenditures for education were regarded merely as costs or consumption, as "expenses," just as one would conceive of funds spent for ice cream or clothing. But a wholly new set of implications were opened up as soon as the skills, knowledges, and motivations necessary for operating the economy are thought of as *capital*.[9] These qualities of human agents are then seen to be economic resources in the same sense as factory buildings, machines, roads, or industrial materials. Resources put into developing such characteristics through education, therefore, represent productive investments, not terminal consumption outlays. Economic analysis based on this concept show that, in fact, educational investments produce a high rate of return in economic growth. Although precise computations of quantitative effects obviously cannot be made from the historical data, a responsible analysis has indicated that the improvement through education in the quality of the labor force between 1929 and 1957 probably accounted for

[8] Studies in the economics of education are almost entirely a product of the years since 1955. See Mark Blaug, *Economics of Education, A Selected Annotated Bibliography* (Oxford, New York: Pergamon Press, 1966).

[9] Mary Jean Bowman, "The Human Investment Revolution in Economic Thought," *Sociology of Education*, 39, 2 (Spring 1966), 111–137. As this article points out, the basic idea goes back at least to Adam Smith but lay dormant until recently. T. W. Schultz was a major force in the new development. See his *The Economic Value of Education* (New York: Columbia University Press, 1963).

something like 23 percent of the growth rate of the total national income, or 42 percent of the growth per person employed.[1]

There are other influences; but those mentioned indicate what different forces have produced and now support the public schools. Many of them can be subsumed under widespread and long-enduring cultural themes—the high evaluation of children and youth, for instance, depending in part upon a belief in the future and in "progress." In fact this very capacity to mobilize the support of such multiple interests and values goes far to explain the wide popular base and continuing vitality of organized education.

### Mass Education

Let us summarize certain other important characteristics of American educational institutions:

1. The schools are still predominantly state controlled, although many are private (both secular and religious). In 1966, the percentage of pupils enrolled in private schools was just under 15 for the elementary level and secondary levels combined. Although slightly over a third of college enrollment is in privately controlled universities and colleges, the proportion is decreasing as the state university systems rapidly expand. A uniform education is formally available to all social and economic classes, although both its actual availability and quality are very strongly influenced by region, income, race, and residential location.

About half of the children of Catholic parents attend parochial schools, and the parochial system accounts for one of every seven children attending school. However, the percentage of Catholic children receiving parochial education through secondary school is decreasing; and the prospect is that a rapidly decreasing proportion will attend Catholic rather than secular colleges and universities.[2]

2. In the main, local and state governments control the school system. In the past, an extreme degree of local control has existed; at the present, some beginnings of a national set of standards are apparent, especially in the form of requirements related to racial desegregation as a condition for receiving federal fiscal aid.

3. The nominally supreme authority over the public schools is usually vested in officials either elected directly or appointed or elected by governors, legislatures, or boards that are themselves elected by popular vote.

4. At the local level, there is typically a marked, although decreasing, degree of autonomy for "lay" boards of control that represent influential segments of the community.

5. In the larger and more centralized school systems authority seems to be centered in the chief executive officer at each level of a firmly established hierarchy. Procedures are highly standardized.

[1] Harris, op. cit., p. 327. See Fritz Machlup, The Production and Distribution of Knowledge in the United States (Princeton, N.J.: Princeton University Press, 1962).

[2] See Robert Hassenger (ed.), The Shape of Catholic Higher Education (Chicago: University of Chicago Press, 1967); George N. Schuster, Catholic Education in a Changing World (New York: Holt, Rinehart & Winston, 1968); Christopher Jencks and David Riesman, The Academic Revolution (New York: Doubleday, 1968).

6. Students pass through a continuous series of stages from nursery school or kindergarten to the university, the stages usually unbroken by special selective examinations at any step until entrance into graduate or professional schools and often not then—in marked contrast to European systems generally.

7. There is on the whole one single system of elementary education, uniform for all who attend the public schools in contrast to the older European pattern in which pupils destined for secondary and higher education have been given separate and different treatment. (However, the European and American systems have been converging toward a common pattern in many respects, especially since World War II.)

8. There is an omnipresent "grading" system, which typically assigns quantitative scores for standardized competitive achievement.

9. Teacher-student relations are highly conventionalized but are on the whole more "informal" and equalitarian than in European systems.

### Financial Bases: Their Sociological Significance

1. The public school system is supported by general taxation and, with few exceptions, is free to all children.

2. Because the major incidence of taxation for the support of public schools falls upon real property, support of the schools typically arouses sporadic conflicts between large property holding groups and other elements of the community.

3. Because all are required to submit to taxes, yet members of some religious groups wish to maintain their own schools, questions of taxation easily become conflicts over general social policy and have, increasingly, taken on a political character.

### Cultural Themes

1. Emphasis is put upon the practical usefulness of formal education. Contemplative or speculative thought, art, and highly abstract theoretic work are relatively little valued.

2. Competitive success is stressed.

3. Continuous and widespread stress is put upon conformity to group standards, largely those of broadly middle-class strata.

4. Great attention is paid to the creed of democratic values, and teacher-student relations are supposed to be "democratic."

5. In practice public schools attempt to develop patriotic values and beliefs (the theme that Counts called "national solidarity").

These themes (or patterns of values) are summary descriptions of extremely complex tendencies in the whole culture. No one theme stands alone as clearly dominant; not only does each have its countertheme, but also each is at some limit checked and redefined by a constellation of other values. Furthermore, the identification and description of such generalized patterns of values requires, because of serious gaps in the evidence, a considerable measure of judgment based on a wide range of credible information rather than upon rigorously systematic data. Nevertheless, an examination of these themes even if brief and oversimplified, may be helpful in understanding educational institutions; such an examination will be made below.

## Public Control and "Secular" Instruction

The elementary and secondary schools are overwhelmingly public rather than private; although private-school enrollment has increased somewhat during recent years. In the colleges and universities, the long-run change has been toward state-supported centers. The principle of governmental responsibility for education has become firmly embedded in our contemporary culture, although only after a long struggle.

Since our political institutions separate church and state, government-controlled schools cannot in theory give "sectarian" instruction; although in practice, they are far from being completely secular. When the state school systems were established, most states contained several religious groupings, each intensely serious about its differences from the others but rarely dominant enough to get its own views adopted as school policy. The resulting compromise tended to make the public school a religiously neutral meeting ground for the community. Nevertheless, in the more rural areas, especially where a single denomination or aggregate of denominations monopolizes the allegiance of the community, religious rites and religious instruction in the schools are still common; and in many states, organized religious bodies attempt to influence the content of instruction and, in some instances, try to remove the barriers to religious teaching in publicly supported schools.[3] Furthermore, although secular control is very clearly supported in the legal systems of most states, the exact line at which instruction or observances become "religious" or "sectarian" is the subject of widely differing legal interpretations. In few parts of the nation can the schools be described as neutral toward religion. In addition, there is no doubt that gradual changes in law and practice have produced a trend that is strongly toward using public monies for support of religiously sponsored schools—although some of the aid is indirect and some (such as bus transportation or books) is defined as being "for the children" rather than "for the school."

### Equality of Opportunity

We saw in Chapter V that the educational system is one of the most important channels of vertical social mobility. Not only do the schools transmit the culture, they also winnow and sift the individuals who pass through them. As the day of the self-educated, self-made man passes in the United States, education becomes the ladder or escalator to white-collar, technical, managerial, and professional occupations. If there is to be even nominally free access to the better paid and prestige-carrying occupations, the necessary education must be open to all who have the capacities and

[3] See National Education Association of the United States, Research Division, "The State and Sectarian Education," *Research Bulletin*, XXIV, 1 (February 1946); W. Seward Salisbury, *Religion in American Culture* (Homewood, Ill.: Dorsey Press, 1964), chap. XIV; Full, *op. cit.*, pp. 298–324; Paul A. Freund and Robert Ulrich, *Religion and the Public Schools* (Cambridge, Mass.: Harvard University Press, 1965).

motivation to acquire it. The American system has gone very far in this direction.

Through high school, the public-school system is open to all students of defined ages, although many individuals leave school before reaching the legal age limit; and in a number of states the age of effective compulsory attendance is passed before high school graduation by a considerable proportion of the students. After high school, the economic status of the young person's family becomes more important than his academic abilities in determining whether he will secure a college education,[4] owing not only to the heavy expenses but also to the more subtle influences of class-typed goals and the expectations of teachers and others in the wider community. Insofar as the society maintains anything like its present family structure and systems of social stratification, some barriers of the latter type will remain; but economic barriers are being broken down by loan funds, scholarships, other forms of employment while in college, public aid to veterans, and tuition charges and fees in colleges supported by state and federal appropriations. Certainly the college is highly accessible and relatively inexpensive in comparison with the old continental universities. Though equality of opportunity for all who are equally gifted is not complete, it probably is greater than in any other nation. The trends are clear: the percentage of college-age youths actually enrolled in higher education has gone from 4 percent in 1900, to 12 percent in 1930, to 32 percent in 1955, and to over 40 percent in the late 1960's.

The most important and conspicuous exceptions to the actual openness of educational opportunity are two: (1) that brought about by racial segregation and discrimination; (2) persisting differentials associated with region, locality, and socioeconomic origins of pupils. Prior to the end of *legally established* racial segregation in the public schools, the dual educational systems of Southern and border states clearly did not provide opportunities equal to those of whites, although the differentials become progressively less over time. Prior to 1954, and partly in anticipation of possible Supreme Court action, the Southern states had been moving rapidly toward equalization of educational facilities for Negroes and whites. Expenditures per Negro pupil were only 43 percent of those for white pupils in 1940, but by 1952 they were 75 percent. The gap between salaries for white and Negro teachers had decreased, near equality had been reached in levels of training of teachers, in pupil-teacher ratios, in provision of bus transportation, and in length of school term. Nevertheless, very striking inequalities remained, especially in the Deep South. In other parts of the nation, although legalized segregation was rare, de facto separation was common; and in the great metropolitan areas of concentrated Negro population educational opportunities were obviously inferior to those available to white children living elsewhere.

Issues arising out of the presence of racial separation in the schools have brought clearly into focus several major clashes of values within the Ameri-

[4] Wilbur B. Brookover and David Gottlieb, *A Sociology of Education*, 2nd ed. (New York: American Book Company, 1964), Chap. 7.

can educational system. Supreme Court actions of 1954 and 1955 laid down the principle that racial segregation in the public school is "inherently unequal," denies the equal protection of the laws guaranteed by the Fourteenth Amendment, and hence is unconstitutional. The court directed that desegregation of the public schools be accomplished "with all deliberate speed." Although desegregation rather soon was accomplished on a large scale in areas bordering the South, (for example, Maryland, District of Columbia, Kentucky, West Virginia), strong resistance to compliance with the ruling of the Court developed in the Southern states.[5] Legislatures of eleven Southern states had passed over one hundred new prosegregation laws by 1957. Most of this legislation eventually was held to be unconstitutional, or proved to be ineffectual; but a "generation of litigation" ensued as various legal maneuvers and delaying tactics were employed in efforts to circumvent the intention of the Supreme Court.

In the confusion and conflict accompanying a major institutional change, some states even made provision for closing the public schools rather than complying with the legal requirement of desegregation; in some localities, public schools actually were closed in favor of hastily improvised private schools. The main tenor of court decisions is clearly opposed to these efforts to avoid desegregation by abolishing the public school system. Because of the strongly opposing forces at work in this situation, a long period of struggle and compromise has occurred; and many conflicts undoubtedly still remain to be experienced, especially in Northern metropolitan areas.

Even where no history of de jure segregation has existed, enormous concentrations of Negro population have developed in Northern and Western metropolitan areas—as a consequence of income differentials, social affiliations and preferences, and, above all, pervasive discrimination in employment and housing.[6] So long as these conditions exist, it is extremely difficult to provide equality of educational opportunity. Given the cultural and sociopsychological backgrounds, for example, the stigma of segregation, the fear and hostility caused by racial prejudice and discrimination—it is very unlikely that educational attainments can be maximized in schools attended solely or almost solely by Negro children.[7] Also, in the case of children from *all* racial and ethnic backgrounds—white, Negro, Spanish-speaking, Indian, or whatever—the sober possibility must be recognized that the multiple sources of low motivation, cognitive-conceptual deficits, and lack of learning skills among low income, culturally disadvantaged subpopulations, will, at best, be only very slowly overcome.[8] The effects of

[5] See the discussion in Simpson and Yinger, *op. cit.*, chaps. 19 and 20.

[6] The evidence is convincing that racial discrimination has been the major factor in generating the so-called "Negro ghetto." See Karl E. Taeuber and Alma F. Taeuber, *Negroes in Cities* (Chicago: Aldine Publishing Company, 1965).

[7] James S. Coleman, *et al.*, *Equality of Educational Opportunity* (Washington, D.C.: United States Office of Education, 1966); United States Commission on Civil Rights, *Racial Isolation in the Public Schools*, Vols. I–II (Washington, D.C.: Government Printing Office, 1967).

[8] See the revealing analysis of the interaction of such "background" factors with school environment in Edward L. McDill and James Coleman, "High School Social Status,

malnutrition, complications of pregnancy, and early childhood illnesses are widespread and important. The disadvantages of early socialization in the low income fatherless family are massive. Children bring accumulated deficits and tensions into the school; and the difficulties of adjustment and achievement of both Negroes and whites in integrated settings are, of course, very real.[9] Nevertheless, the overwhelming bulk of research findings and practical experiences point to the necessity of substantial integration of racial and ethnic subgroupings into the same schools if the difficulties are to be overcome.

Although the racial cleavages just reviewed obviously are at the center of the problem of "open opportunity," it is also evident that children from families in different income and occupational categories do not have fully equal opportunities. There is no need here to repeat the discussion of this matter in Chapter V above. However, it is important to note that sheer expansion in the proportion of children and youths reached by the educational system does not necessarily lessen differentials, by social class, in attendance or attainment. Between the 1850's and the 1930's in the United States the proportion of the population of secondary school age attending or enrolled in school increased from about 5 percent to 40 percent, whereas the socioeconomic composition of the school population remained essentially unchanged.[1] As the general level of education rises, the children of higher-income families still have a greater likelihood of attaining relatively advanced education.[2] Furthermore, the general increase in educational level tends to produce an increase in the educational requirements for employment, even in essentially manual occupations. Thus, a high school diploma may be required for entrance into a trade in which formerly a person could succeed without much formal preparation.

As the general level of formal education rises, it appears that the association of higher education with the better paid and more prestigious occupations is declining.[3] The increase in the educational attainments of the labor force is not primarily due to a shift into occupations that directly require higher levels of education as a specific necessity for required technical performance but represents rather a general upgrading across a wider range of occupations.[4]

It is essential to the understanding of the American educational system

---

College Plans, and Academic Achievement," *American Sociological Review*, 28, 6 (December 1963), 905–918.

[9] See the summary and evaluation of evidence by Urie Bronfenbrenner, "The Psychological Costs of Quality and Equality in Education," in Melvin M. Tumin and Marvin Bressler (eds.), *Conference on Quality and Equality in Education: The Proceedings* (Princeton, N.J.: Princeton University Press, 1966), pp. 2–11.

[1] C. Arnold Anderson, "Access to Higher Education and Economic Development," in Halsey, Floud, and Anderson, *op. cit.*

[2] This actually may be induced, in part, by the "guidance" of the schools themselves; see Aaron V. Cicourel and John I. Kituse, *The Educational Decision-Makers* (Indianapolis: Bobbs-Merrill, 1963).

[3] John K. Folger and Charles B. Nam, "Trends in Education in Relation to the Occupational Structure," *Sociology of Education*, 38, 1 (Fall 1964), 19–33.

[4] *Ibid.*, p. 33.

to see the reality of the differentials just discussed and to appraise their magnitude accurately. Nevertheless, for the long run, it is also essential to recognize that the principle of formal equality of opportunity is crucial for the potentialities of the institutional structure. Indeed, the agonizing quality of some of the issues we have surveyed stems directly from the clash between this principle and other cultural and social factors.

An educational system may follow the "Jeffersonian" model—it may open the race to everyone but eliminate all but the best from the final heats; or it may adopt the "Jacksonian" system and provide education at all levels for anyone. Recent trends in American education apparently have been mainly "Jacksonian," despite the fact that the schools and colleges are probably more important as selective agencies now than ever before. Universal public education has decreased the role of the family in training the child; changes in occupational and technological requirements have emphasized formal training; changes in the economic structure have increased the importance of education as a means of social mobility. Consequently, we find increased pressure to graduate all students from high school, to admit all high school graduates into college,[5] and to permit college students to continue in college as long as they wish.

In any competitive process, some "failures" occur. The degree of failure varies: many simply are less well rewarded than others, some are forced to drop out of the competition entirely. Competitive losses, apparently, typically bring some sense of frustration or deprivation. A high rate of severe failure in any competitive system where many of the losers have strongly hoped to win is likely to be stressful not only to individuals but also to the social arrangements that maintain the system. A system of mass competition may thereby be put under pressure to reduce stress in four primary ways: (1) by arranging for a large number of gradated successes and for many "consolation prizes," so that competitive loss at any stage may be experienced against the background of accumulated gain; (2) by providing alternative routes of achievement of lesser severity for those unable to survive the most intense levels of competition; (3) by a variety of persuasive and redefining efforts, directed toward inducing individuals to accept lowered or different aspirations ("counseling," "therapy," and so forth);[6] (4) by lowering standards—at the extreme, reducing the system to the "caucus race" in *Alice in Wonderland*, in which "all have won; and all shall have prizes."

The desire for education and the insistent demand for freely accessible schools and colleges owe much to the demand for equality of opportunity and to resistance to the development of a separate educated class. Americans generally use any term comparable to "intelligentsia" chiefly in irony

---

5 Some state universities are forbidden by law to refuse any applicant who can present evidence of graduation from an accepted high school in the state.

6 Burton R. Clark, *The Open-Door College: A Case Study* (New York: McGraw-Hill, 1960); and "The 'Cooling Out' Function in Higher Education," *American Journal of Sociology*, LXV, 6 (May 1960), 569–576. The rate of withdrawal at the college level is high: one study showed that in publicly controlled colleges, 47 percent of entering students had dropped out by the end of the second year. (Many, of course, reenter, somewhere, at a later time.)

or derogation, partly because of distrust of a class isolated from the larger whole by a different and "superior" mode of training. This attitude has been one of the foundations for the uniform system of public schools and helps to explain why that system has been so slow to give up college-preparatory curricula for the great majority of high-school students who do not go on to college. This insistence upon the same kind of education for everyone has continually conflicted with the Jeffersonian competitive-selection orientation. Both are authentically "American" and often are simultaneously held by the same people. In recent times, the movement for general education[7] has taken much of its strength from the former tradition.

However, in the development of vocational curricula, of junior high schools, of "community colleges" and junior colleges are tendencies toward the elaboration of different kinds of education for different types of students. Two of the crucial questions of social policy are (1) whether the student will be able to transfer from one type of curriculum to another,[8] (2) whether, and in what wise, *all* pupils are allowed to participate in a common educational culture.[9]

### State and Local Control

Until well into the twentieth century the financial support and the organization of the schools were overwhelmingly local, and there still is very little centralized direction typical of several secular school systems in continental Europe; for public education fell among the powers reserved to the several states, since it was not specifically delegated to the federal government by the Constitution, and the states have in general left much control to the local communities. Even in the late 1960's the total federal contribution to financing of public schools still amounted to less than 10 percent of the total cost. On the other hand, federal funds coming to the universities accounted for more than twenty-five percent of the outlays for higher education. Although the state and local systems have been highly autonomous—leading to such anomalies as the persistence of racially segregated schools long after national policy had become one of integration—the presence of relatively free national mobility and mass communication and of a common culture have led the various formally separate systems to move in similar directions, and the contemporary result certainly merits the name of a national system.

Most state school-systems are highly decentralized, with consequences too complex to be traced in detail here. Clearly, local autonomy has favored experiment with nearly every conceivable variation of organization, methods, goals, curricula, but it has also led to the uneven development of public-school systems and the very great disparities among states, among localities within states, and between rural and urban areas, in financial support, length

---

[7] Edwards and Richey, *op. cit.*, chap. 15; Report of the Harvard Committee, *General Education in a Free Society* (Cambridge, Mass.: 1945); Daniel Bell, *The Reforming of General Education* (New York: Columbia University Press, 1966).

[8] Malcolm S. Maclean, *Scholars, Workers, and Gentlemen* (Cambridge, Mass.: Harvard University Press, 1938).

[9] Report of the Harvard Committee, *op. cit.*

of school year, teacher training, and range and quality of the curriculum. Thus, per capita tax revenue in 1967, for example, ranged from $297 in Hawaii and $268 in Delaware down to $97 in New Hampshire and $95 in Nebraska.[1] Current expenditures per pupil for public schools varied from $918 in New York to $339 in Mississippi.[2] Average salaries of public school teachers (1967–1968) were $8,900 in California and $4,611 in Mississippi.[3]

Furthermore, decentralization has favored an extraordinary responsiveness of the school to local demands. The entire functioning of a school is greatly affected by the social characteristics of the population from which it draws its pupils. The teacher in a school drawing middle- and upper-class pupils inevitably has a role different from that of the teacher in a "slum" district. In the latter case, the teacher often has severe problems of discipline and confronts numerous instances of what are to him morally unacceptable behavior.[4] The school is supposed to be directly responsible to the people and the servant of their wishes, not the extension of the centralized authority of an inclusive church or state.[5]

Decentralization has several other consequences. For example, each area must compete for skilled teachers and administrators, who tend to flow to the wealthier systems—to the North and East, and within the states, to the cities and to the well supported, centralized rural systems. Insofar as this process gives "better" education to certain areas, it creates for them a competitive advantage; to him that has, more is given.

The details of the organizational structure of the various state systems vary, but a basic pattern has become typical. A state board or commission, nominally headed by a superintendent (or commissioner), may be vested in office either by direct popular election (most common), or by election by the legislature or the state board of education, or by appointment of the governor. Formerly, the state superstructure had very little real authority over the local systems; but today there are tendencies toward state centralization. The state agency influences local systems mainly through its power to allocate funds and set and enforce minimum standards. For example, the role of state as opposed to local or county financing has increased markedly in recent decades; the states' share of the total appropriations from tax receipts for public-school use increased from only 19.5 percent in 1931–1932 to 39.5 percent in 1955–1956.

At the grass-root level of city, county, or independent rural systems, the

---

[1] Research Division, "Rankings of the States, 1968," *Research Report 1968-R1* (Washington, D.C.: National Education Association, 1968), p. 39.

[2] *Ibid.*, p. 54 (with Alaska excluded).

[3] *Ibid.*, p. 22 (with Alaska excluded).

[4] For vivid examples see Howard S. Becker, "Social-Class Variations in the Teacher-Pupil Relationship," *Journal of Educational Sociology*, 25, 8 (April 1952), 451–465.

[5] Unlike European systems that were established by central governments, largely with explicit national ends in view. Paul Monroe has suggested that American schools were initially more nearly an outgrowth of "democracy" than of "nationalism." *Essays in Comparative Education* (New York: Teachers College, Columbia University, 1927). For recent comparisons, see John F. Cramer and George S. Browne, *Comparative Education* (New York: Harcourt, Brace & World, 1965); I. N. Thut and Don Adams, *Educational Patterns in Contemporary Societies* (New York: McGraw-Hill, 1964).

schools are governed by lay school boards or equivalent bodies. Until past mid-century such boards typically were composed mainly of persons from business and the professions and often representative of relatively conservative attitudes toward education.[6] Although only a few studies have been made, there is evidence that in urbanized areas in recent years, the school boards may be more heterogeneous and perhaps less conservative than was typically the case a generation ago.[7] Usually elected by the voters, their members may or may not represent the choice of a majority of the electorate.[8] In either case, however, the elected members keep the school program close to at least that segment of the community from which they come. In this sense the public schools are in high degree the product of the communities in which they are located.

The supervising agency in most states still has only a moderate degree of control of the local schools. Any major change has to diffuse through a multitude of discrete systems. Great variations in educational procedures and standards result, as is known by many battered college freshmen from inadequate schools. In our increasingly interdependent society centralization and standardization will doubtless grow.

## The Public School and the Community

The concrete focus of the system of elementary and secondary education is the school in the local community. The school, among other things, is a surrogate family, a center of cultural diffusion, a storage place for ideals. In the school, all other institutions converge. Through specific interpersonal relations there comes into the school the influences of family, class, church, business, government; the school is a knot in the web of community life. It is common, therefore, that American communities expect the school to play a part that will not modify the local culture greatly. Yet the teachers' training is presumed to make them different from the community. Hence, a problem arises: the teacher must be different yet not change anything in the culture; he must be a stranger, yet an ingroup member. Furthermore, the public school is a striking case of an organization staffed by trained people, who have been encouraged to regard themselves as professional workers, which is under the formal authority of laymen. Both the teachers and the public school administrators are involved in sets of roles in which they frequently confront incompatible expectations and demands. For example, a careful study of school superintendents showed a significant lack of agreement between superintendents and school-board members concerning the obligations of community members, professional educators, and teachers.[9]

[6] George S. Counts, "The Social Composition of Boards of Education," *School Review and Elementary School Journal: Supplementary Education Monographs*, No. 53 (1927); Hollingshead, *op. cit.*, pp. 123–142.

[7] Neal Gross, *Who Runs Our Schools?* (New York: Wiley, 1958); Brookover and Gottlieb, *op. cit.*, pp. 117–119.

[8] Cf. the reported situation in a small Midwestern town where popular apathy and technical maneuver combined to make the elections of the school board a ritual endorsement of a self-perpetuating group. Hollingshead, *op. cit.*, pp. 123–124.

[9] Neal Gross, Ward S. Mason, Alexander W. McEachern, *Explorations in Role Analysis: Studies of the School Superintendency Role* (New York: Wiley, 1958), chap. 8.

As already noted, teachers are often held to special standards of conformity and propriety; for there has been a close historic association between school and church in this country; and the latent social functions of the school are, in fact, similar in several respects to those of religious organizations. Willy-nilly the educator deals with values; he has exceptional opportunity to examine the unexamined axioms of the culture and interpret its crucial but vulnerable symbols. Since society is so largely equivalent to consensus, those who deal with values and beliefs as part of their occupational role—ministers, judges, writers, some artists, social scientists, teachers—touch upon the sensitive fringes of the bases of social order. In part for this reason, persons who deal with the beliefs and values that the community feels basic to its existence are the object of special surveillance and concern.

The roles of teachers are influenced by several rather more specific factors. About 70 percent of teachers in the elementary and secondary schools are women.[1] Although discrimination against married women as teachers—once common—has decreased rapidly, single women are still somewhat preferred. For a long time, over most of the United States, the typical public school teacher was "of native white stock, of rural or small-town origin, and from lower-middle-class homes."[2] Recruited in large numbers to meet the demands of a rapidly expanding school population, they have never had in any large proportion either the bargaining power of effective unions nor the quasi-monopoly controls over entrance into the occupation so consistently exercised by certain other professions. Wage or salary levels have been low in comparison with other professional or semiprofessional occupations requiring equivalent amounts of training. In spite of the verbal acclaim bestowed upon education, the teacher has not received a particularly high prestige rating. Yet, as demands for teachers mount, and the environing society changes, the status of the teacher may change. The percentage of teachers in public elementary and secondary schools who were men dropped from 43 percent in 1880 to 14 percent in 1920—but had climbed back to 25 percent by 1955. More recently, the somewhat enhanced prestige of teaching in at least some localities and the changing sources of recruitment have resulted in greater diversity of social and cultural characteristics among teachers.

Nevertheless, many of the long-standing problems remain. For example, the alternative occupational opportunities for male classroom teachers in secondary schools are sufficiently attractive to produce a high rate of turnover, with many such teachers moving into administrative positions within the educational system while others leave entirely. These competitive processes tend to remove from teaching some of the academically most competent, at the same time that the high school is being required to prepare for college a vastly increased proportion of its students and when revisions

1 United States Bureau of the Census, *Statistical Abstract of the United States: 1967,* 88th ed. (Washington, D.C.: Government Printing Office, 1967), p. 120.

2 Lloyd A. Cook, *Community Backgrounds of Education* (New York: McGraw-Hill, 1938), p. 300. Data on which these findings are based have been drawn from the studies of Evenden, Coffman, Moffett, and Kiely (cited by Cook, *op. cit.,* pp. 300–302).

of curricula and demands for "upgrading" of academic subject-matter are intensive and continuous.[3]

Social origins of teachers now vary greatly in different types of communities. In our large industrial cities, the composition of the teaching staff does not bear out traditional stereotypes. Rather, it is marked by great heterogeneity of origins—socioeconomic, religious, racial, and ethnic. In many urban areas the proportion from working-class origins exceeds the proportion from white-collar backgrounds.[4] As the public concern over education tests itself against the reality of taxes and the requirement for high standards in the face of rapidly expanding enrollments, revised conceptions of the teacher's status and roles may become effective.

The teacher transmits beliefs and values to the relatively unformed child, thus occupying a "triangular" relation between parent and child.[5] So long as the family is to any degree a solidary unit, it will not be a matter of indifference to parents how teachers influence their children; and cultural continuity from the viewpoint of the parents exists only to the extent that fathers and mothers can still communicate with their sons and daughters. Where the community is homogeneous in culture and the teacher is drawn from that same culture and thoroughly imbued with it, no particular acute problem arises. The teacher will be a fairly exact parent-surrogate, faithfully transmitting both the overt and covert content of the culture with a minimum of conflict. As the teacher, by training and background, diverges further from the local norms, friction grows.[6] Cultural heterogeneity of the community also creates problems; the teacher may then face divergent and often contradictory demands from different elements of the population. At the local level, severe tensions arise when the local community possesses a tightly unified culture and the teacher diverges greatly from it—as when urban, college trained, professional minded teachers are employed in stable rural or small-town school systems or when the white, middle-class teacher confronts the ghetto school. In these situations the teacher is a "stranger," not initially identified with any local ingroups, and by definition initially alienated, in the strict sense, from local groups and their standards.

In the early days of the public school system, in a rural and small-town atmosphere, the teacher was regarded practically as a hired adjunct to the families of the school district—and in fact, often received part of his or her

[3] Martin Trow in Bendix and Lipset, *op. cit.*, p. 445.

[4] Robert J. Havighurst and Bernice L. Neugarten, *Society and Education*, 2nd ed. (Boston: Allyn & Bacon, 1962), pp. 462–468; National Education Association, *Research Bulletin*, 41, 1 (February 1963), 26; William Wattenberg, *et al.*, "Social Origins of Teachers—Facts from a Northern Industrial City," in Lindley J. Stiles (ed.), *The Teacher's Role in American Society* (New York: Harper & Row, 1957).

[5] "The teacher conceives of herself as a professional with specialized training and knowledge in the field of her school activity: teaching and taking care of children. To her, the parent is a person who lacks such background and is therefore unable to understand her problems properly." (Howard S. Becker, "The Teacher in the Authority System of the Public School," in Mercer and Carr, *op. cit.*, p. 348).

[6] "there is frequently lack of consensus among teachers and pupils on the expectations they hold for incumbents of educational positions." (Gross, "The Sociology of Education" in Merton, *et al.*, *op. cit.*, p. 141.)

compensation as "room and board"—an arrangement that might involve staying in succession in the homes of various families in the locality. Only slowly did the status of teacher come to be a clearly separate and specialized office. In modern times, the quasi-professional or professional claims of the occupation have become increasingly effective. However, for many years after the large urban system had become highly bureaucratic in character, teachers continued to be regarded as individual practitioners rather than a collectivity of employees. Initially, teachers' associations were essentially petitioners to administrators and elected officials for changes in curricula, procedures, working conditions, or salaries. Increasingly, these organizations act as collective bargaining agencies and seek a greater part in determining educational policies.[7] As such organizations grow in size and in capacity for concerted action, the negotiations they precipitate seem destined to escalate from the local to the state level in an increasing proportion of instances.

It has been only in the second half of the twentieth century that teachers have developed large and militant enough organized efforts to be able seriously to challenge and negotiate with their employers. As organized negotiation has grown in importance, sharp controversy has developed around the different philosophies and strategies of the two main organizations: the National Education Association and the American Federation of Teachers. In the 1960's the long-standing competition of these organizations was given new vigor by the affiliation of the AFT with the Industrial Union Department of the AFL-CIO and by the spread of teachers' strikes to many large cities and to entire states. The NEA, a much larger organization, includes administrators and specialists as well as teachers and for many years emphasized "professionalism" rather than labor union tactics. The AFT is primarily made up of classroom teachers, is strongest in the larger metropolitan areas, and recognizes the right of local unions to strike and to engage in collective bargaining.[8] It seems apparent that even if there are marked differences between these organizations, the main thrust of impending changes in the educational system will be in the direction of more collective negotiations and stronger organizational effort among teachers. By the late 1960's, city-wide teachers' strikes had become common; and state-wide strikes (sometimes in the form of "mass resignations") were increasingly encountered. More and more teachers come from urban and working-class backgrounds and from among members of "disadvantaged" minorities (Negroes, Puerto Ricans, Mexican-Americans, and so forth).[9] Personalized ties with supervisors and with parents have become rare. Impersonality and specialization grow.

The sheer size of modern systems tends to produce some of these fea-

---

[7] Cf. Francis Keppel, *The Necessary Revolution in American Education* (New York: Harper & Row, 1966), p. 141; David A. Goslin, *op. cit.*, p. 135; Lesley H. Browder, *Teacher Unionism in America: A Descriptive Analysis of the Structure, Force, and Membership of the American Federation of Teachers* (Ed. D. dissertation, Cornell University, 1965), p. 12.

[8] Cf. Michael H. Moskow, "Teacher Organizations: An Analysis of the Issues," *Teachers College Record*, 66 (February 1965), 453–463.

[9] Cf. Brookover and Gottlieb, *op. cit.*, chaps. 11 and 12.

tures. The New York State Education Department supervises or otherwise deals with 4,000 public schools, 2,000 private schools, 230 colleges and universities and 400 libraries; it supervises administration of some $300 million in federal aid; it examines and licenses 22 professions. It has 3,300 employees (of whom 1,100 are professionals). It is administered by 5 associate directors, 15 assistant directors, 30 division directors and 56 bureau chiefs. It evidently is no longer an organization likely to encourage informality or the personalized style of the old "free professional."

### Internal Administration of the School

The administration of the public schools has been often and well described, and we will only briefly sketch its general outline. The principal or superintendent maintains his position in large part by balancing local power-groups. Under the shadow of the cost-conscious board of education, he must mediate between school and community. He is head of a formal structure but confronts the informal operating codes and subgroupings among teachers. The formal aspects of the school are generally most emphasized where its real social structure is least secure; there is then reliance on detailed textbooks rather than teachers, much protocol among the staff, much stereotyped conformity, elaboration of distance-stiffening social procedures in all interpersonal relations. There are strong tendencies to move all children along a defined path by uniform stages and with the same educational procedures. As the size of school units and systems increases, the centers of policy making move farther from the child; and considerations of administrative ease and of economy of money and effort then bulk large. On the whole, it appears that at all levels American education has increasingly adopted systems of administration similar to those of business and government. The rapid adoption of "scientific management," business principles, or models of efficiency based upon experience in factories, corporations, or operating units of government has led in many school systems to marked conflicts with other goals and values of the educational enterprise.[1] School administrators apparently find that only few of the situations with which they are confronted are without substantial ambiguity or clashing expectations and demands.[2]

And, of course, there are always the students, the ultimate raison d'être and presumed beneficiaries of the entire enterprise, but never merely clay for the potter. In any educational system there will be alienated and rebellious students: acceptance of the goals and normative demands and disciplines of educational organizations is no more to be taken for granted than in any other area of life. However, acceptance is eased when students have internalized the goals of scholastic achievement and are convinced that success in school will lead to desired rewards later on and when these orientations are approved, or at least tolerantly accepted, by their peers. To the

[1] Raymond E. Callahan, *Education and the Cult of Efficiency* (Chicago: University of Chicago Press, 1962).

[2] Neal Gross, *et al., op. cit.*; Melvin Seeman, *Social Status and Leadership: The Case of the School Executive*, Educational Research Monographs 35 (Columbus: Ohio State University, 1960).

extent that these conditions are not met, students may be expected to show alienative behavior,[3] ranging from diffuse inattention and restlessness to aggressive conduct and vandalism, truancy, dropping out, or organized protest.

In part a symptom of standardized administration is the practice of assigning quantitative and presumably interchangeable grades. Although there are signs of increasing dissatisfaction with these devices, they remain characteristic of American education generally. The grading system is convenient and economical. By reducing qualitative variation to differences that can be marked on a single quantitative scale, it provides impersonalized data for sorting individuals into the different educational channels. Once the examining and grading systems have solidified, any major change is rendered difficult by the inconvenience and confusion it is presumed to entail. Thus, we have an elaborate educational accounting system in which the units are courses and marks instead of dollars and cents. There is rather frequent criticism of it—for instance, that the grade tends to be confused with the learning it purports to mark or that the system induces excessive competition and anxiety.

## Federal Involvement in Education

State and local responsibility for education is still primary, but we must note the growing importance of federal agencies.[4] Land grants for education began in 1785, and the Morrill Act of 1862 gave specific support to state agricultural and mechanical colleges. Federal sources have subsidized vocational education, agricultural experiment stations, agricultural extension, veterans' education, and many other special types. Federal agencies have extensive in-service training programs and have connections with colleges and universities for both pre- and in-service personnel training. Both military and civil agencies operate colleges and universities or graduate schools.[5] Federal funds account for over one-fifth of national expenditures for education.

Federal expenditures for the direct support of education grew from $1.5 billion in 1955 to about $8.7 billion in 1966. There is no integrated federal program; diverse arrangements are made with other governments and with colleges and universities. Many agencies participate, with varied aims, organizations, fiscal bases, and legal positions. At least 200 recognizably separate programs are in operation, slanting into the state and local systems at various angles. Taking only programs of direct aid to education, there were, as of 1967, over 150 different federal programs, financed by more than

[3] Cf. Arthur L. Stinchcombe, *Rebellion in a High School* (Chicago: Quadrangle Books, 1965).

[4] Hollis P. Allen, *The Federal Government and Education* (New York: McGraw-Hill, 1950); Harold Orlans, *The Effects of Federal Programs on Higher Education* (Washington, D.C.: The Brookings Institution, 1962).

[5] Morris Janowitz, *The Professional Soldier* (New York: Free Press, 1960); John W. Masland and Lawrence I. Radway, *Soldiers and Scholars: Military Education and National Policy* (Princeton, N.J.: Princeton University Press, 1957).

300 separate appropriations and administered by some 21 federal departments and agencies.

Past federal programs have encouraged and indirectly guided education, with little direct and detailed control.[6] The strong fear of a centralized education program has been partly responsible for scattered and uncoordinated federal effort. Most national funds go to specialized education and not to a coherent general program. This arrangement seems to be what American society "desires," at least by default, although the resulting "imbalances" receive unfavorable comment.[7] Proposals for direct federal aid for general use in the schools have been made on many occasions but have met strong opposition.[8] Fear of federal control has been a factor. More important has been the issue of aid to private, especially parochial, schools; public opinion is deeply divided on this issue. Advocates of maximum separation of church and state interpret the First Amendment to prohibit any form of aid to religious organizations. Advocates of aid to parochial schools argue that the First Amendment does not preclude "nondiscriminatory" aid. Because these differing opinions are related to strong religious beliefs, no easy resolution of the question is likely; but the growing tendency to allocate state funds is obvious: for example, eighteen states use tax monies to support bus transportation for pupils in parochial schools; and the Federal Education Act of 1965, for the first time in American history, provided for both public and parochial schools support of library facilities, remedial services, textbook loan programs and "cultural" programs. The 1965 legislation providing federal aid to institutions of higher education— legislation sometimes compared in potential importance to the Morrill Act of 1862 that established the system of land-grant colleges—was enacted by Congress without serious public opposition, even though it made provision for religiously sponsored as well as public colleges and universities.

## Organized Interests and Education

The educational system is subject, of course, to attempted influence by organized associations of laymen, whose activities testify to a belief in its importance. The number of these organizations is uncalculated but extremely large and includes all major types of organized interests of our society. The larger and more effective include business, labor, patriotic, religious, benevolent, youth, citizen training, military, peace, fraternal, and political associations. There are prominority and antiminority groupings, associations of reactionary, conservative, liberal, and radical inclination. Each is devoted to its own version of the "American way of life," and few leave the schools to train youth without outside guidance. In general, these interests give full loyalty to the present social order. The larger and more

[6] The Smith-Hughes Act (1917) first gave a federal agency the right to accept or reject state programs (vocational education) through control of funds.

[7] Allen, *op. cit.*, pp. 289–291.

[8] Van Miller and Willard B. Spalding, *The Public Administration of American Schools* (Yonkers, N.Y.: World Book Company, 1952), pp. 134–142. (See also the second edition of this work, 1958.)

powerful of them are, of course, the more influential in the educational system; and they generally operate with slogans and programs couched in terms of patriotism, religion, free enterprise, and other reinforcing acknowledgments of faith.[9] The years immediately after the end of World War II brought many attempts to equate "loyalty" with "conformity"—two very different things.[1] On the other hand there have been conspicuous organized efforts to criticize and question foreign policy and national officials. Contrary to the views of many commentators at mid-century, dissent shows no sign of disappearing.

### CULTURAL THEMES

Having reviewed major characteristics of the organization of education, we turn now to treat briefly the principal cultural themes and values associated with education in the United States.

#### *Pragmatism and Practicality*   *( > Intellectuals )*

The epithets of a people hint at their basic value patterns. Among the favored terms of derogation applied by Americans to education we find "impracticality," "frills and fads," "long-haired professors," "theorizing," and so on through a long lexicon. The public that has supported organized secular education has not greatly tolerated learning for learning's sake nor "education for gentlemen"; historical erudition, Greek, Latin, and classic-humanistic learning have fared rather poorly in comparison with vocational and scientific training—from physics and chemistry to typing, cooking, or beekeeping. Modern American education is permeated with a very strong utilitarian and pragmatic emphasis. Its purpose is not thought to be the training of dilettantes nor well-rounded gentlemen of the aristocratic tradition. Education is not diversion or amusement; it is serious business, and the prime questions are: "What use is it?" "What can you *do* with it?"

Education in the United States has gained greatly in prestige and support in the years since World War II. Certainly the vastly augmented importance of the physical sciences and of technological specialties is evident on every hand. But these modern developments (greatly accelerated in the 1950's by the Soviet achievements in rocketry and space technology) have not done away with the continuing and recurrent devaluation of intellectual activities and intellectuals in general. Anti-intellectual currents, so strongly present among portions of the population in all periods of American history, often have drawn strength from democratic, antielitist sentiments of those who have seen "intellectuals" as part of a dominant political and economic stratum from which they feel excluded and alienated.[2]

---

[9] Among the many studies that attest this estimate see Bessie L. Pierce, *Citizens' Organizations and the Civic Training of Youth* (New York: Scribner, 1933).

[1] See the essay by Henry Steele Commager in Mercer and Carr, *op. cit.*, pp. 516–520.

[2] See Richard Hofstadter, *Anti-Intellectualism in American Life* (New York: Knopf, 1963); also, Christopher Lasch, *The New Radicalism in America 1889–1963: The Intellectual as a Social Type* (New York: Vintage Books, 1967), chap. 9.

### Individual Competition and Success

In the modern school or college teamwork is highly lauded, but in terms of sports rather than classwork. Stress on individual competitive success still typifies most of our higher educational system and is widespread in secondary schools.[3] The schools must be open to talent; all pupils must be motivated to succeed; the individual child or youth must sink or swim on his (alleged) own merits. Evidence of these attitudes includes indoctrination in the goals of success and in codes of competition, competitive grading, and "selling" education on its presumed money-value. Of course, group endeavor and social rewards for cooperation are not lacking in American education, but they have probably not rivaled the emphasis on competition. World events and the consequent domestic changes may, however, radically affect this particular value complex in our time. Increasing numbers of students and teachers advocate educational changes that reflect anti-individualistic, anticompetitive goals and values.

### Conformity

Much of what the school teaches is incidental to its explicit aims and goals. Perhaps few schools explicitly "indoctrinate for conformity," although "character development" and "education for citizenship" frequently are pseudonyms for instruction that in fact, if not in intent, produces generalized acquiescence to established authority and convention. But any education must educate for conformity to something.

Much of the conformity learned in American education seems overt and bare, and educators themselves often wonder to what extent it indexes a firm adherence to shared values. Whatever their psychological quality, however, *common* patterns of behavior and beliefs are greatly increased by the training offered by the schools. Comparative studies of the Soviet and American systems have suggested that the American versions of conformity tend to be linked to the theme of *individual* competition, whereas the Soviet schools strive to encourage *group* competition and collective responsibility. Of course, both systems necessarily stress individual accomplishment, but the American school emphasizes less collective responsibility and collective control.

### Democratic Creeds and Behavior

Early American education was strongly class limited; and the later public schools temporized between radically democratic notions and the rather different views of portions of the influential classes. (The creedal democracy of the textbooks took on new colorations during that long half-century from 1875 to the 1920's, when business power and prestige encouraged "business management" in the schools. Strict chain of command and unquestioning obedience of pupils pleased writers who admired business hierarchy.)[4] The ideals taught in the public schools have been largely "democratic," the

---

[3] Counts, again, presents a lucid account: *op. cit.*, chap. 5.

[4] Merle Curti, *The Social Ideas of American Educators* (New York: Scribner, 1935), pp. 230 ff.

teacher-pupil relation relatively informal, the peer-groups equalitarian; but the authority structure of the school has been, broadly speaking, less democratic than the creeds.

Some of the meanings of democracy as a value will be examined in Chapter XI. In education, evidences of democracy appear in the demand that everyone have the same access to education, in the creed of individual worth, in the pooling of diverse social classes in the schoolroom. A teacher is not supposed to comment on the humble or condemned origins of any student. If racial and other minority-group discrimination, or the limited communions of fraternity and sorority, or the aristocracy of got-here-first—if any of these prevail, as they often do, they do not constitute the standard of educational direction.[5]

In another aspect, the democratic theme found expression in the varied efforts of many educators to center the educational system upon the active potentialities of the individual children. Much misunderstood and given widely different interpretations, this general direction of movement—often called progressive education—profoundly affected the transition from the traditional rote learning to the procedures of modern schools.[6]

Under the stimulus of the civil rights movements of the 1950's and 1960's, and the general unrest and ferment centering upon racial and social-class differentials in educational attainment and opportunity, the entire educational system was subjected to intensive reexamination. Nationwide studies such as Project Talent, supported by the United States Office of Education, documented once more the fact that a substantial minority of high school seniors (15 to 34 percent) at various levels of above-average ability fail to enter college, primarily because of financial limitations.[7]

In the period since the U.S.S.R. orbited its first sputnik, the public school system has placed more emphasis upon science, mathematics, foreign languages, and basic reading and writing skills. New teaching methods and arrangements have been more widely introduced: team teaching, ungraded classes, homogenous groupings, teachers' aides, specialist teachers, audio-visual aids. Subjects formerly taught only in advanced grades have been moved back to earlier grades, and it appears that the amount of homework in many schools has increased sharply. Meanwhile, as the size of both local systems and of individual schools has increased, the organization has come to include increased specialization and increased reliance on formal procedures.[8] The greater use of counseling and guidance services, especially in the larger systems, has such far-reaching potential effects upon students and their later careers as to raise questions concerning the legitimate and

5 It is again necessary to note the continued existence of subsystems of ethnic and racial discrimination; see Chapters X and XI. See Keppel, *op. cit.*, pp. 31–49.

6 For an excellent appraisal of progressive education as a social movement, see Lawrence A. Cremin, *The Transformation of the School: Progressivism in American Education, 1876–1957* (New York: Knopf, 1964).

7 Keppel, *op. cit.*, chap. III.

8 National Educational Association, *The Principals Look at the Schools: A Status Study of Selected Institutional Practices* (Washington, D.C.: National Education Association, 1962).

desirable limits of the school's intervention into vocational plans and personality development.[9]

### Education in National Beliefs and Values

Education in all times and places seeks to induct the young into membership in the society—whether community, tribe, or nation. Whatever the effective intrasociety group that controls the educative agency, it will seek to give the students a common language, and a common set of ideas, beliefs, and values, although in modern times some educational programs have also sought to encourage students to learn about, and to appreciate positively, other cultures.

European educational systems generally have been national not only in organization but also in direction and content; and American education, though lacking central organization, also achieved substantial unity around a core of national values. Up to the university level, the history and culture of the United States receive the dominant attention; but world history and international materials also are included. In some schools, both public and private, highly sophisticated programs of cross-cultural studies have been developed. In all periods of national crisis, prior to the Vietnam conflict, educators in the public schools have supported national unity.[1] Whether in peace or war, the public schools have constituted a powerful, instrument of national solidarity.

### Uncertainty of Aims

There is, finally, uncertainty. In American education—as throughout the main societies of the world—old faiths and old cultural patterns have been shaken or dissolved. American education is stamped by variety, experiment, improvisation, eclecticism, and aversion to total planning. Yet, as noted before, there has been enough consensus to give a recognizable uniformity to a series of local systems across the nation.[2]

Critics of American education have commented on the outstanding lack of agreement concerning the ends that the schools should serve. Such agreement, however, requires a unified and stable society; and such a society we do not have. Short of forced unanimity, educational aims here are likely to retain much diversity, with only the gradual convergence produced by increased homogeneity in the whole culture.

The first great development in American educational institutions was the actual implementation of the idea of some kind of universal educational opportunity. Despite all the limitations we have noted, the achievement of this goal is well in sight. Equality of sheer access to some kind of higher education is increasingly being attained. More and more attention to the

[9] Cicourel and Kitsuse, *op. cit.*; Friedenberg, *op. cit.*

[1] Curti, *op. cit.*, pp. 542–544.

[2] "This uniformity stems from a variety of causes, prominent among which are recommendations of national organizations, statements by authorities, tradition, the concept of the 'American Dream,' and the remarkable ease with which ideas about education, as well as ideas about other questions are disseminated far and wide" (Mercer and Carr, *op. cit.*, p. 526).

quality of instruction and to the total effects upon students at all levels seems likely to produce further changes in goals, norms, organization, and procedures in the future. Studies of educational culture and social organization undoubtedly will prove, as time goes on, to be rich sources of findings concerning the relations between social structure and psychological processes. It is safe to assume that increasing research effort will be devoted to analysis of the varying effects upon *learning* that arise from different norms, statuses, organizational structures, groupings of students, academic disciplines, and procedures.[3] There has been and continues to be continuous critical examination of the efficacy and value of traditional classroom teaching and of other established arrangements. As alternatives are explored, it is likely that increased attention will be devoted to the search for differences between the social contexts that block, inhibit and "distort" intellectual and affective functioning and those that encourage and develop creativity and imagination.

### COLLEGES AND UNIVERSITIES

*Variety and Change*

A center of "higher learning" in America may be anything from a trade school to a university group occupied in the most highly developed research and scholarship. Here again we encounter enormous diversity and change. Like the secondary schools, colleges and universities are characterized by mass enrollments, a relatively open entrance basis, a multiplication of specialized courses of instruction, an emphasis upon practicality, a growing prominence of administrative standardization. The American universities are not purely "centers of higher learning;" they are also, in varying degrees and in varying ways, secondary schools, "social clubs," vocational preparatory schools, purveyors of mass athletics, military-training stations, research enterprises, museums, and reservoirs of consulting services.

The impact of massive world events of the last few decades has led to enormous changes in higher education. Alongside the established system of colleges and universities there have emerged numerous new community colleges, training programs in business and government (which extend to high levels of executive rank and competence), an extensive system of military education, and a great number and variety of programs in civilian adult education. According to authoritative estimates, the combined expenditures for educational programs operated by business and by military agencies already approach those of all colleges and universities. "Higher education" is no longer the exclusive province of the university.[4]

[3] See the summary of some presently available findings in Sarane S. Boocock, "Toward a Sociology of Learning: A Selective Review of Existing Research," *Sociology of Education*, 39, 1 (Winter 1966), pp. 1–45.

[4] "The number of students in business-sponsored educational programs now equals the total enrollment of all colleges and universities. Almost 90 percent of the 500 largest corporations have entered the field." The President's Commission on Education Beyond the High School, *Second Report to the President* (Washington, D.C.: Government Printing Office, 1957). p. 2.

The early colleges in America were mainly schools for the training of clergymen; ecclesiastical controls and theological emphasis characterized nearly all centers of higher learning until well into the nineteenth century. Secular instruction grew out of the gradual separation of special subjects from the older disciplines[5] and was encouraged by the substitution of businessmen and other lay persons for clergymen on the governing boards of the colleges and universities. Later on, wholly secular colleges and universities began to merge in great numbers, especially with the mushroom growth of state universities after 1870. Although the earlier theological tradition has left its stamp in many subtle ways upon the universities, the system of higher education is now dominantly secular, both in its control and in its curriculum.

### The University and the Society

Also, like the public schools, the colleges and universities tend to be controlled by a combination of business groups, political officials, and professional administrators. The governing boards of the larger private universities are heavily weighted with businessmen, and the objective dependence of the private university upon endowments undoubtedly has an influence upon the policies it follows.[6] Just as the privately endowed university seeks support from the wealthy, the state university has to deal with the politically powerful. In both instances, the American university has responded to social forces that impinge upon it from outside. In particular, from time to time many new subjects that are of interest and practical value to important segments of the population have been added to research and teaching programs; and the universities have vastly expanded their public service activities in consultation, publishing, and extension education. A very different response has been observed in those instances in which universities have bowed to pressure by avoiding controversial matters and by other constrictions of academic freedom. On the whole, however, freedom of research and teaching from gross interference has been maintained, especially in the more eminent universities. The rapid growth in public financing and control, together with strong pressures for "social involvement," suggest that the maintenance of a pluralistic system of mixed private and public support in which academic freedom and diversity of interests can flourish will not be easily accomplished.[7]

[5] Cf. the generic analysis of Znaniecki, *op. cit.*, and the important study by Logan Wilson, *The Academic Man* (New York: Oxford University Press, 1942). For sociological discussion of the special case of Catholic education, see John D. Donovan, *The Academic Man in the Catholic College* (New York: Sheed and Ward, 1964); Andrew M. Greeley, *Religion and Career* (New York: Sheed and Ward, 1963); Jencks and Riesman, *op. cit.*

[6] Although not now to the extent suggested by its caustic and perceptive critic, Thorstein Veblen in *The Higher Learning in America* (New York: Sagamore Press, 1957).

[7] See Richard Hofstadter and Walter P. Metzger, *The Development of Academic Freedom in the U.S.* (New York: Columbia University Press, 1955); Robert M. MacIver, *Academic Freedom in Our Time* (New York: Columbia University Press, 1955). One of the few systematic studies of the pressures for ideological orthodoxy during the early 1950's (the "McCarthy years") indicates that privately-financed colleges and universities received less pressure from trustees and political figures than did state-

Historical analysis suggests that the very rapid expansion and change in character of American universities was greatly facilitated by the absence of a single dominant university or of a fixed hierarchic order among them; the resulting decentralized competition favored innovation, variety, and eagerness to make recognized social contributions. In the United States, therefore, there has been an especially marked development of trends generally found in industrialized countries:

*Universities only a hundred years ago were exclusive academies of scholars pursuing privately their learned interests and instructing a small number of highly selected students who prepared to enter the civil service or one of the traditional professions, and in exceptional cases become scholars themselves. Today universities educate—in some countries—as much as a fourth to a third of all the young people in the appropriate age groups, and conduct research of vital importance for the survival or destruction of human society.*[8]

Today, the universities are the great repositories of science, so crucial to both peaceful and military technology; they are also one of the main custodians of universalism in ethics and the symbol and source of the professionalism that is increasingly influencing the social order.

Universities are deeply involved in the environing society through connections with all other major institutional sectors. First, and obviously, the universities take the sons and daughters of families to nurture and train—and to promote and graduate, or to eliminate from the competition; the events of admission or rejection to a desired college or university and of failure or successful graduation constitute major emotionally vital crises in millions of American families. And the universities are economic enterprises; they are paid purveyors of services, chiefly as they collect fees and tuition as charges for education. They contract and pay for goods and services. They often use large sums of public monies. As creators and disseminators of ideas and values they potentially affect the whole society. Their research has great economic value and is sometimes of crucial military significance. They are the objects of much political attention, and their students and faculties may play important political roles. They often support institutionalized religion; sometimes professors and students criticize and oppose it. They are custodians and practitioners of most of the "high culture" of the society in arts and letters. And they are major producers of recreation and ceremonial spectacles.

Universities are also inhabitants of local communities, where they maintain relations with other organizations and groups. The classic town-gown cleavage often persists today. The economic, political, and "cultural"

supported units and that the most successful resistance to political interference was in the high-quality private colleges and universities. Cf. Paul F. Lazarsfeld and Wagner Thielens, Jr., *The Academic Mind* (New York: Free Press, 1958). Further research, including cross-societal comparisons, would be quite valuable.

8 Joseph Ben-David and Abraham Zloczower, "Universities and Academic Systems in Modern Societies," *European Journal of Sociology*, III (1962), 45–84. Reprinted in abridged form in William J. Goode (ed.), *The Dynamics of Modern Society* (New York: Atherton Press, 1966), p. 359.

symbiosis of the university and its community is complex and sometimes precarious.[9]

Public reactions to higher education, thus, follow the general pattern found in the attitudes toward the public schools; but certain items have a different intensity and the total configuration is somewhat differently arranged. Main public attitudes include the following:

1. There is overwhelming generalized approval of college or university education, especially for boys. It is felt that the colleges generally do their work well.
2. College education is valued chiefly as a means to occupational success. Higher education is generally thought of as a weapon or tool in individual competition.
3. Correspondingly, relatively low (but increasing) value is attached to training in the arts, citizenship, "character development," and other indoctrinating, liberal, general, or humanistic studies. A liberal arts, or "cultural," education is more often approved for women than men.
4. Substantial minorities of the population have several important criticisms and fears, namely:
   a) A conception of higher education as impractical or as detached, isolated, or alienated from the viable values and concerns of the society;
   b) A fear of academic freedom; a hesitancy to endorse the full discussion of man and his problems—of religion, or communism, or foreign policy, for instance;
   c) Ambivalence toward the specialist and the scholar (frequently, an attitude of half-reluctant respect mingled with apprehension and hostility—shown, for instance, in the projective stereotype of the "diabolical scientist").

In several respects, then, many people in the society cannot seem to agree with the universities, yet cannot do without them. There appears, however, to be an increasing recognition of the need for intellectual leadership and an increasing awareness of the very narrow margin by which our society manages to produce the needed specialists and leaders.[1] Disparagement of intellectuals may not actually be analogous to a blind man beating his Seeing Eye dog.[2] But the crucial dependence of both the polity and the economy upon at least scientific and technological advance is increasingly acknowledged by the general public.

---

[9] Cf. Delbert C. Miller, "Town and Gown: The Power Structure of a University Town," *American Journal of Sociology*, LXVIII, 4 (January 1963), 432–443.

[1] Frederick Harbison and Charles Myers, *Education, Manpower, and Economic Growth: Strategies of Human Resource Development* (New York: McGraw-Hill, 1964); Robert H. Knapp and Joseph J. Greenbaum, *The Younger American Scholar: His Collegiate Origins* (Chicago: University of Chicago Press, 1953), pp. 93–100. (At that time, twenty-five universities produced 75 percent of doctorates awarded.)

[2] Ralph Ross and Ernest Van Den Haag, *The Fabric of Society* (New York: Harcourt, Brace & World, 1957), p. 386.

### University Organization

Uniformities in administrative structures and methods cannot be expected to extend to details among all the diverse types of colleges, research institutes, state universities, private universities, technical schools, and denominational colleges found in the United States. Yet a broadly common pattern can be discerned. It consists of the superimposition of a centralized quasi-bureaucratic organization upon the old "college" as a community of scholars and teachers. In the older tradition, the collegial organization was a loose association of individuals; departmental chairmen and deans tended to serve briefly and to hold a rather tenuous and uneasy authority. In the minds of the professors, the faculty and the university were synonymous. The internal hierarchy of the faculty tended to be one of academic prestige rather than administrative authority. The concept of individual and departmental autonomy was strong. As universities have become great centers of undergraduate teaching, however, the nonfaculty administrative organization has expanded rapidly; and authority has tended to move toward the president and the officials responsible directly to him. The administrative bureaucracy mediates between the university and the board of trustees (and through them to centers of power in the larger society) and tends to be acutely aware of the demands and criticisms of influential segments of the outside community. It is concerned with placating ruffled parents, raising funds, attracting students, increasing the renown of the organization, negotiating with governmental agencies, recruiting staff, planning facilities, and protecting the legal position and social legitimacy of the university. These are complex and difficult matters, often not well understood by either the more impatient of the students or the more insulated of the faculty. Because of the nature of its responsibilities, the pressures to which it is subject, and, possibly, some selectivity in its personnel, the administrative group differs in its interests, goals, and standards from the scientists, scholars, and teachers who make up the faculty. Tensions and misunderstandings are therefore common, and in some instances both severe and chronic.[3]

Unless a university faculty is made up of a mass of purely routine teachers, it has characteristics that militate against its development into a strictly hierarchial body along the lines of an army or a business corporation. Although the American university professor is typically dependent upon a fixed salary within a definite organization and hence does not operate with the autonomy of the free professional, he is still very far from being a strict "employee."[4] For the professor is a professional specialist doing work of a high order of complexity; and within his special field it is unlikely that persons "above" him in an administrative hierarchy will be competent to

---

[3] For the bitter flavor of the attitudes held by an iconoclastic scholar of an earlier era toward the administrative group, see Veblen, *op. cit.*, esp. pp. 220–224. Contrast the tone of this work with the orientations presented in Nevitt Sanford (ed.), *The American College* (New York: Wiley, 1962); and Jencks and Riesman, *op. cit.*

[4] Logan Wilson, *The Academic Man*, pp. 72–93; Robert S. Morison (ed.), *The Contemporary University: U.S.A.* (Boston: Houghton Mifflin, 1966); John J. Corson, *Governance of Colleges and Universities* (New York: McGraw Hill, 1960).

judge or supervise his work in any detail. The *technical* and the *administrative* hierarchies do not coincide. This fundamental basis for individual autonomy is reinforced by the long tradition of academic organization, extending back into medieval Europe, which emphasizes the governing of the university by collective action of a body of professional equals.

Modern university organization in the United States thus embodies a continuous struggle between the centralized-bureaucratic system and the diffused-collegial system.[5] Often the model of the business corporation has been so faithfully followed that the faculties have no real voice in the determination of policies or major administrative procedures; but many other universities, among them some of the most eminent, still provide for a considerable measure of faculty participation and control. Even so, however, faculties typically have no institutional channel for direct communication with the governing boards and little direct voice in the selection of the president;[6] and as universities have increased in size and complexity (the two traits are correlated but not identical), a large number of problems of finance, public relations, internal coordination, university-wide planning, and the like create strong pressures for delegation of responsibility to a non-faculty administrative group.[7] Informal and equalitarian relationships then tend to disappear in favor of hierarchy, formality, standardization. External political and financial pressures work even more unreservedly in the same direction. As a result the American university has moved far from the conception of a community of scholars.[8] It is not yet a rigidly hierarchical or centralized structure; and, indeed, it cannot be if it is to *create* as well as *disseminate* knowledge.

Under conditions of low mobility of faculty members and few attractive alternatives elsewhere, the older university often gravitated toward a system of local "baronies" or "feudal estates" in which department heads and deans exercised tight control over their underlings. Such control tends to disappear when the supply of well qualified faculty members is low relative to the effective demand.[9] Competitive bidding becomes brisk, mobility

---

[5] In the strict sense, total universities—even large ones—are not primarily bureaucracies, although they do contain bureaucratic parts or sectors. See Charles H. Page, "Bureaucracy and Higher Education," in Mercer and Carr, *op. cit.*; Neal Gross, "Organizational Lag in American Universities," *Harvard Educational Review*, 33, 2 (Winter 1963), 58–73; S. N. Eisenstadt, "Bureaucracy and Bureaucratization: A Trent Report and Bibliography," *Current Sociology*, 7, 2 (1958), pp. 117–119; Herbert Stroup, *Bureaucracy in Higher Education* (New York: Free Press, 1966).

[6] Wilson, *op. cit.*, pp. 76–79; MacIver, *op. cit.*

[7] It was Veblen's wry conclusion that most of these problems had been created by unnecessary expansion of administrative apparatus in the first place. His solution was simple and drastic: abolish the university presidency and the governing board. One does not have to accept his rather mordant evaluations to appreciate his sharp discernment of university structure. See *op. cit.*, chap. 8. For contrast, Paul Goodman, *The Community of Scholars* (New York: Random House, 1962).

[8] For a vivid picture of the older ideal-pattern see Carl Becker, *Cornell University: The Founders and Founding* (Ithaca, N.Y.: Cornell University Press, 1943), pp. 193–204.

[9] Theodore Caplow and Reece J. McGee, *The Academic Marketplace* (New York: Basic Books, 1958).

high, local dependence low. The dissatisfied professor simply moves to another position—at another university, or in government, or in business.[1] Under these conditions, the influence of the profession or discipline upon the individual faculty member tends to be great: his "standing" is potentially a national or international matter, not one of a local academic community,[2] and he is oriented to a national rather than a local "market."

American colleges and universities, like the secondary schools, are not tightly integrated into a common organization. The large numbers of individual units are marked by diversity, change, and experimentation. The interuniversity organizations provide some common direction, but in a loose and uneven way; and these organizations are themselves of widely different types. Some are organizations of professors, some of administrators, some of specific professions. Much flexibility and creativeness is thereby engendered, as well as much work at cross-purposes.

Relations among universities are often competitive. In the past the prestige of a particular university was widely felt to be enhanced by every increase in the size of its student body and the magnitude of its financial resources—and by the victories of its athletic teams. Such competitiveness may make some contribution to the universities' manifest aim—the transmission and creation of knowledge—even when the actual immediate goals of university administrators are to increase the wealth, size, and public renown of their institutions.[3] Budget increases do not automatically lead to better academic work, but they make it possible for *professional* opinion to exert pressure for better faculty and better facilities for research and teaching; and as students are better trained, there is created a more sophisticated body of alumni who make high academic standards a test of university prestige. As the old stereotype of the ivory tower fades in the face of realities, the actual attainments of faculty and students in scholarship, teaching, research, and public service become increasingly the criteria of evaluation.

### Students and the Undergraduate Culture

The special environment of college or university life develops, predictably enough, a distinctive culture.[4] The content of that culture changes through

---

[1] Rates of mobility are quite high, especially in smaller departments; mobility affects all ages and ranks. See Howard D. Marshall, *The Mobility of College Faculties* (New York: Pageant Press, 1964).

[2] John P. Millet, *The Academic Community* (New York: McGraw-Hill, 1962).

[3] A general principle is here illustrated: participants in systems of social action can contribute to achievement of the goals of the system without necessarily or even typically consciously working toward those goals. Indeed, the accomplishment of such goals appears to depend upon the mobilization of a variety of particularized goals that are seldom identical with the manifest ends of the total system.

[4] Walter L. Wallace, *Student Culture: Social Structure and Continuity in a Liberal Arts College* (Chicago: Aldine, 1966). Standardized research instruments have been developed to index the total environments of students and to describe subgroupings and subcultures within particular colleges or universities. See C. R. Pace, *The Influence of Academic and Student Subcultures in College and University Environments* (Los Angeles: University of California, 1965).

time—from the flapper and coonskin coat era, through the Great Depression[5] to the disruptions of wars, the impact of the civil rights movements of the late 1950's and early 1960's, the new Left of the 1960's. Yet continuities are not entirely lacking. In the coeducational university, the undergraduate student population is typically composed of young adults (mainly aged eighteen to twenty-three) of both sexes, the majority unmarried, separated from family and community of origin, culturally heterogeneous, living in a transitory world. There is a formal regulative university culture of rules and established traditions. There is an informal student culture with controlling norms on studying, dating, stratification, drinking, political activity, the questions of use of drugs, relations to the faculty and parents, and so on indefinitely. Students' standards and behavior are often contrary to official norms. Their special culture has continuity in spite of rapid turnover of personnel; each individual in going through college spans seven academic classes—his own, the three preceding, and the three following. The manifest aim of the students is to learn from formal instruction; what actually happens is a notably more complex matter.

Many colleges are custodial as well as educational; where this is the case, administrators spend much time dealing with or preventing breaches of the formal rules. The supervision, isolation, and control of masses of students to whom parents and others are not ready to give adult liberties and responsibilities is a task of real difficulty. In the intense group life of the campus undergraduates take on the codes and acquire the ideas about conduct that are most powerful in regulating their college life. The influences, of course, are received and responded to in a highly selective way. The magnitude of the effects upon students' attitudes and values to be expected from four years exposure to the college or university environment—after eighteen years of massive cumulative prior socialization—can be debated endlessly. Certainly, major changes are possible. On the other hand, the known resistance of personalities to changes contravening early socialization, the high degree of self-selectivity of attention and involvement, and the tendency for interpersonal relationships to be homogamous—all these argue against the likelihood of *major* changes among a *majority* of students. Clearly, however, the argument is likely to be inconclusive if couched in these highly general terms, even if recourse can be had to firm data. For the effects vary greatly not only with the initial characteristics of the entering student—his ability, his values, his aspirations, his major personality patterns, and his specific motivations—but also with differences in the educational milieu. The college or university to which he goes may be small or large, or gigantic;[6] it may dominate a small town or be inconspicuous in the metropolis; it may have a culturally homogeneous or heterogeneous student body, a faculty devoted to teaching or primarily committed to re-

[5] An illuminating portrait of the period just prior to World War II: E. Y. Hartshorne, "Undergraduate Society and College Culture," *American Sociological Review*, VIII, 3 (June 1943), pp. 321–332.

[6] Amos H. Hawley, Walter Boland, and Margaret Boland, "Population Size and Administration in Higher Education," *American Sociological Review*, 30, 2 (April 1965), 252–255.

search, a permissive or authoritarian system of regulation. It may encompass the student with an emphasis upon vocational preparation, or upon sociability and "well rounded" campus life, or upon broad liberal education, or upon intensive intellectual development. Its goals may be explicit and clear or unstated and ambiguous. Questions concerning the effects of higher education upon students, therefore, are most likely to receive sensible answers if they are specific questions.[7]

One point is evident from the studies already made: the peer groups developed in living- and study-units can very strongly influence academic performance and personal development. The power of peer groups may be expected to be maximal when the student freely choses to enter a group that for him has high prestige, when a high proportion of his total activities are related to the group, when the members hold similar values and beliefs, when the group is legitimized and supported by the normative authority of student leaders, faculty, and university administration. Small living-units having these characteristics are likely to elicit strong affective attachments, sensitivity to group opinions, and complex processes of interpersonal identification and differentiation. In units having a consistent set of aims upon which leaders agree, students tend to converge over time in many of their aspirations, values, and beliefs, although the effects are primarily within subgroups of highly involved students.[8]

Among the agencies of intensive peer group socialization and control, fraternities and sororities—where they still exist—seem especially likely to have strong effects because of selectivity, homogeneity, high involvement, strong sanctions, and a substantial degree of authoritative "indirect" control by alumni and the national organizations. Historically, these organizations have been important as agents of ethnic exclusiveness and ascribed status[9]—providing restricted group associations that tended to insure proper ethnic and class in-group marriages and promoted economic and political careers through advantageous access and sponsorship. Ethnic exclusiveness and out-group rejection often have been expressed in anti-Jewish attitudes.[1] Although both fraternities and sororities have moved toward lesser ethnic, religious, and racial exclusiveness, many still constitute closed, segmented units of the campus society that develop great ingroup solidarity, serve as

[7] Theodore N. Newcomb and Everett K. Wilson (eds.), *College Peer Groups: Problems and Prospects for Research* (Chicago: Aldine, 1966).

[8] See Rebecca Vreeland and Charles Bidwell, "Organizational Effects on Student Attitudes: A Study of the Harvard Houses," *Sociology of Education*, 38, 3 (Spring 1965), 233–250 (esp. pp. 241–248); and Rebecca Vreeland and Charles Bidwell, "Classifying University Departments: An Approach to the Analysis of Their Effects upon Undergraduates' Values and Attitudes," *Sociology of Education*, 39, 3 (Summer 1966), 237–254.

[9] There is a substantial literature on this point. For examples, Simon Marcson (ed.), Special Issue, "Segregation and Integration in College Fraternities," *Social Problems*, 2, 3 (January 1955); Bernard E. Segal, "Fraternities, Social Distance and Anti-Semitism," *Sociology of Education*, 38, 3 (Spring 1965), 251–264; John Finley Scott, "The American College Sorority: Its Role in Class and Ethnic Endogamy," *American Sociological Review*, 30, 4 (August 1965), 514–527.

[1] Segal, *op. cit.*, 259–262.

a mark of prestige, and train their members in orientations which in many cases may be appropriate to their later roles in business and professions. Students not belonging to these organizations often form their own, or participate in a rich collective life in various kinds of social movements, or find satisfying friendships in informal groupings; a considerable minority, however, become isolated or participate only in fleeting and chaotic social configurations.

The idea that peer groups exert strong influence upon educational aims and performance of college students is plausible; and much observation seems to support it. However, the more interesting questions concern not the presence of an influence but its exact character and differential impact upon various kinds of students under differing circumstances. For example, some data suggest (but have not "proved") that freshmen are relatively unaffected in their aspirations for advanced study by fellow freshmen but are quickly and substantially influenced by nonfreshmen. Also, as at least one study shows, the proportion who raise their aspirations during the early college experience are those with relatively poor academic records and low and uncertain occupational aims. Thus, peer-group influences may be maximal where aspirations are least firmly grounded in past performance or rational estimates of future prospects.[2] Such influences, in any event, are acting upon a person who brings into college a vast accumulation of beliefs and values from prior experience.[3] Much research, for a time, seemed to show that socioeconomic origins, although a strong factor in determining whether or not individuals went to college in the first place, were not highly correlated with likelihood of graduation among those who matriculated. Later studies raise the possibility that social origins and college graduation are in fact significantly related—especially among students of moderate performance in high school—if one includes a long enough period to take into account the dropouts who later return to complete their college careers.[4]

Among modern nations, the United States in the past was long regarded as unusual in the largely nonpolitical or apolitical orientation of its university students. Although the impression of quietism was exaggerated—witness the intense political activity of many students in the 1930's—it is true that student political involvement typically was low relative to that of many other societies.[5] With the widening of recruitment of both students and faculty and with the increased direct involvement of the university in the society around it, a marked increase in student "activism" emerged in

[2] Walter L. Wallace, "Peer Influences and Undergraduates' Aspirations," *Sociology of Education*, 38, 5 (Fall 1965), 375–392; also Wallace, *Student Culture, op. cit.*

[3] Paul Heist, "The Entering College Student—Background and Characteristics," *Review of Educational Research*, XXX, 4 (October 1960), 285–297.

[4] Bruce K. Eckland, "Social Class and College Graduation: Some Misconceptions Corrected," *American Journal of Sociology*, LXX, 1 (July 1964), 36–50. Compare with Dael Wolfe, *America's Resources of Specialized Talent* (New York: Harper & Row, 1954), pp. 160–163.

[5] Seymour Martin Lipset (ed.), "Student Politics," Special Issue of the *Comparative Education Review*, 10, 2 (June 1966).

the 1960's.[6] Many students of the New Left are marked by advocacy of direct mass action, an uncompromising idealism or romantic utopianism, an ahistorical immediacy, a disdain for calculation and compromise, and a tendency toward anti-intellectual orientation, in the sense of a rejection of "thought" in favor of "action." These characteristics, of course, were well-known marks of the European youth movements of the extreme Right of the 1920's and 1930's. Only some of the partisans of the New Left fit the description; but those who do have little in common with the disciplined political orientation of the left among earlier student generations. Others, however, do see beyond tactics to strategy and ideology, show an awareness of the uses of political rationality, and show a capacity for organization and sustained effort. Evidently, "student revolt" represents great diversity of values and social objectives.

From the substantial amount of information concerning the "activists" —those dissenters who join in collective action—we can piece together a composite portrait. On the whole—excepting for the moment the black student militants—the students who actively engage in collective dissent and protest are more likely than other students:

1. To come from families in middle and upper-middle income levels;
2. To come from minority racial, ethnic, and religious backgrounds;
3. To come from urban areas;
4. To enroll in liberal arts programs in social sciences and especially humanities;
5. To take as their role model and self-image the "intellectual" rather than "scientist," "professional," or "businessman";
6. To have less definite career plans and expectations;
7. To attend large, high-quality universities in metropolitan settings;
8. To be exposed to a high volume of political communication concerning national and international events and issues;
9. To be freshmen, sophomores, transfer students, or "perennial students;"
10. Perhaps most strikingly, to have parents who were and are radical or liberal and who in many cases support and encourage their activist offspring. As studies have shown among the Berkeley students, the active left does *not* primarily reflect discontinuity of generations nor alienation from parental values.[7]

---

[6] There is a large body of literature of very uneven quality. Cf. Michael V. Miller and Susan Gilmore (eds.), *Revolution at Berkeley* (New York: Dial Press, 1965); Seymour M. Lipset and Sheldon S. Wolin (eds.), *The Berkeley Student Revolt* (New York: Doubleday, 1965); Stanton M. Evans, *Revolt on Campus* (Chicago: Henry Regnery Company, 1961); "Students and Politics," *Daedalus*, 97, 1 (Winter 1968), entire issue, esp. Seymour Martin Lipset, "Students and Politics in Comparative Perspective," pp. 1–20, and Richard E. Peterson, "The Student Left in American Higher Education," pp. 293–317; Kenneth Keniston, *Young Radicals: Notes on Committed Youth* (New York: Harcourt, Brace & World, 1968).

[7] Jeanne H. Block, Norma Haan, and M. Brewster Smith, "Activism and Apathy in Contemporary Adolescents," in James F. Adams (ed.), *Contributions to the Understanding of Adolescence* (New York: Macmillan, 1967); Kenneth Keniston, *The Uncommitted* (New York: Dell, 1965).

Institutions of higher learning that twenty years ago enrolled very few students of low-income background and almost no black students now have substantial numbers of both and have increased also the religious and ethnic diversity of their student populations.

Black activists do not represent, of course, the same constellations of background characteristics or of central concerns as their white counterparts. They feel with special intensity that black people have been unjustly exploited, denied authentic identity, and blocked from rightful control of their own fate. The opening of opportunity for individual advancement and the weakening of "white-supremacy" domination tends to release suppressed hostility; and the spotty and variable character of whites' reactions elicits diffuse suspicion and militant "testing" behavior. More likely than whites in the same institutions to come from lower-income origins, they often find, or feel that they find, differences between white students and themselves in communicative styles, expressive behavior, tempo and phasing, and fundamental beliefs and values. Like some immigrants or refugees, they often recoil from the new environment, seeking solidarity and mutual defense and assertive power in all-black organizations and enclaves.

The high-quality preprofessional and professional institutions have few activists among their career oriented, highly selected, and very busy students. The low quality particularistic liberal arts colleges also produce few activists—although many alienated and apathetic conformists, collegiates and ritualists, and some hippies and delinquents. The vocational schools tend to attract students preoccupied with personal concerns and struggles. It is in the academic-intellectual centers that large numbers of intellectually active and "morally angry" students congregate.[8] Partly because of their family and peer-group experiences, many of these students are not disposed toward unquestioning acceptance of authority, some are disaffected, and a few are radically in opposition. Communicating their high expectations and demands, they stimulate one another in their moral indignation. A small proportion of highly active dissenters is able in many instances to mount dramatic confrontations with social authorities, who often react by rigidity, threats and punitive actions, and vacillating and poorly defined permissiveness. Much of the behavior of the so-called establishment, accordingly, exacerbates both realistic discontent and unrealistic, overdetermined attitudes toward order and authority.

The major targets of student dissent and collective protest often are characterized as the "power structure" and the "establishment"—that is, the main sources of authoritative decisions and influence, both in the society as a whole and within the universities. There are, of course, particular historical foci: the civil rights movement of the late 1950's and early 1960's contributed a background of moral and political concerns and dramatic instances of "nonviolent protest." The intense controversies aroused by American involvement in armed conflict in Vietnam provided

[8] "Attendance at university is stronger in pressing well-to-do students to a position to the left of their parents, than in moving those from less-privileged Democratic and liberal families to the right." Lipset, "Students and Politics in Comparative Perspective," *op. cit.*, p. 4.

a focus of special intensity, particularly in view of the potential impact of selective service on the student population. Although the specific issues change very rapidly, the challenge to established authority is a consistent theme. The more militant student leaders, far from taking "legitimacy" (in the sense explained in Chapter VII above) as a ground for acceptance of persons or organizations, often regard a successful challenge to the most firmly legitimized authority as especially praiseworthy. The most radical dissenters see the entire society as corrupt; for them the establishment as such is the enemy.

## Graduate Education

College graduation once marked the completion of formal education for that small fraction who thus joined the ranks of the diploma elite. But as college enrollments soared and the market demand for larger and larger numbers of highly trained persons increased, the proportion of graduates going into advanced training rose to levels that would have seemed quite unbelievable prior to mid-century. More and more, the undergraduate college or university becomes a preparation for graduate or professional education rather than a terminal phase. As of 1961, three-fourths of college seniors had some more or less serious plans for further training.[9]

Graduate education in the United States is usually dated from the program initiated at Johns Hopkins in 1876. Essentially early American graduate programs were modeled upon the prestigious German universities of that time and were established upon the base of undergraduate colleges primarily derived from British precedents. Both blueprints were soon modified, but the historical origins still are manifest in many traces.

Somewhat parallel to developments in the undergraduate colleges, so in graduate work, the original focus upon selection and training and socialization of elite cadres of scholars and teachers gave way to several very different kinds of advanced programs—professional schools, teacher-training colleges and departments, preparation of engineers and other technologists, training of scientists in research, and so on. As the society came to rely more and more upon very complex technology and systematically developed science, higher education became increasingly committed to technical and professional preparation.[1]

Politicomilitary and economic considerations after the 1940's created powerful pressures for greater attention and effort in research and research training in the physical sciences and technologies, with medical and life sciences following, and the social sciences and humanities occupying residual niches. At the same time, the vast increase in student enrollments at all levels generated strong demands for the preparation of teachers. The accelerating growth of knowledge—the "information explosion"—pressed upon the training capacities of the graduate schools, and their response accelerated the production and dissemination of knowledge. At the beginning of World

9 James A. Davis, *Great Aspirations: The Graduate School Plans of America's College Seniors* (Chicago: Aldine, 1964), p. 45.
1 Cf. Clark, *op. cit.*

War II, the graduate system was barely two generations old; within a few decades this infant set of institutions had become a central focus of the educational system and was radiating pervasive effects upon the entire society.[2] Widely accepted as indispensable, the graduate schools nevertheless (and necessarily) are subject to severe problems of priorities among fields and disciplines. Are the arts being neglected? Is it more important to have additional engineers to build advanced weapons-systems, or increased emphasis on research and training in the disciplines dealing with social conflict and social integration? How shall funds be allocated as between the preparation of teachers for urban schools and new equipment for research in nuclear physics? And even as the graduate school has been criticized during periods of warfare as inequitably sheltering some young men from military service, it has been asked to supply more well-qualified experts to man the intricate social and technological apparatus of modern civilization.

Formal education in our society often seems to the advocates of changes of various kinds to be primarily a stabilizing and conservative force, transmitting and reinforcing the *status quo ante*. Clearly, pressures are sometimes brought to bear upon educators to discourage criticism, or even analysis, of a very wide range of topics. Nevertheless, in the United States, education as a whole is much more dynamic than in many if not most societies about which we have any accurate knowledge on this point.

## CULTURAL GOALS AND EDUCATIONAL CREEDS

What goals can an educational system have? It can be directed toward (1) the absolute preservation of a static culture; (2) the production of a special ruling class, with virtues appropriate to the kind of authority exercised (Sparta, Rome, China); (3) the shaping of a "liberal" elite (Athens, England); (4) religious indoctrination (in part, medieval Europe, early New England, the nations and tribes of Islam); (5) the production of technologists—specialized workers, "useful" scholars, engineers, scientific technicians; (6) an inclusive humanistic training, intended to develop vocational competence, broad knowledge of culture, and motives for participating fully in the society.

No society ever focuses entirely on any one of these constructs. When we look closely at the special American case, however, it is possible to be more prosaic and more exact.

American education as a total configuration has aimed at the shared but competitive goals of individuals and groups, rather than at unitary collective ends. The cross-currents of different educational orientations are many, but some main directions are summed up in the perceptive title of Malcolm S. MacLean's *Scholars, Workers, and Gentlemen*. The earliest American

---

[2] Bernard Berelson, *Graduate Education in the United States* (New York: McGraw-Hill, 1960), pp. 38–39; John W. Gardner, *Excellence* (New York: Harper & Row, 1961); Oliver C. Carmichael, *Graduate Education: A Critique and a Program* (New York: Harper & Row, 1961).

schools at the elementary level aimed at the three R's and "moral instruction" and at the college level at the production either of clergymen and theologians or of "gentlemen" in the classic tradition.[3] The scholar of the older tradition was the highly selected and highly trained repository of the classic learning. His modern opposite number is the research scientist, for the old-style scholar has receded from the apex of the academic world. The scholar's education has never found a favorable context in American society, except when tied to the training of religious leaders. Neither a frontier society nor a business civilization values contemplation and detached intellectual activity above utilitarian activity. In the dominant cultural stereotype, the scholar is an "impractical" misfit.

The educational ideal of the gentleman, so strong in the English background, was cultivated for a time in the upper-class reaches of our society, especially in New England and the antebellum South. Many of the early political leaders of the nation were so educated. But as the whole culture became more and more preoccupied with technology and business, the rounded education originally developed for a social elite was increasingly overshadowed by vocational, professional, and scientific training. Furthermore, for a long time in our society there were very few "gentlemen" owing to the relative lack of an established aristocracy, the fluidity of social stratification, the preoccupation with business success, and the strong pressure of Jacksonian principles rooted in the political strength of an expanded electorate. In recent times, some of the old ideas of the gentleman's education have been revived. It even reappears in strangely streamlined fashion in new doctrines of "training for leadership." The newer versions of education for gentlemen are most characteristic of private preparatory schools and of the endowed "prestige" universities.

We have already seen enough of the cultural diversity and conflicting interests in the total society to indicate that organized education is not likely to show unity of objectives. Indeed, there have been times when many educators strove for something they thought to be complete value neutrality. During and immediately after World War II, however, a growing movement away from ethical neutrality and from a kind of eclectic factualism began to reach the proportions of a dominant trend among the theorists of education. The challenge of totalitarian systems provoked resurgence of emphasis upon education aimed at the development of particular values. Many educators have been questioning the exclusive stress upon "activity" and skills found in some schools. Educational philosophers again began to use freely words and phrases that had for a time seemed outmoded—"character," "moral values," and "the development of ethical judgment." As these emphases grew, they aroused old fears of indoctrination and rigidity. Hardly had these concerns been articulated when rebellion and activism challenged the boundaries of educational direction. Thus rapid shifts in attention and controversy come and go. Meanwhile, the long-term trends have steadily pointed toward the dominance of *expertness* as a central aim

[3] For a wonderful, not to say incredible, picture of the latter, see Daniel Defoe, *The Compleat English Gentleman*, D. Nutt (London, 1890).

of education in a society destined for yet a while to put much of its faith in science.

## SUGGESTED READINGS

BERELSON, BERNARD. *Graduate Education in the United States.* New York: McGraw-Hill, 1960. The most comprehensive general study up to 1960. Indispensable as reference and bench mark. Analysis anticipated many later developments.

BRIM, JR., ORVILLE G., and STANTON WHEELER. *Socialization after Childhood: Two Essays.* New York: Wiley, 1966. Focuses attention on the neglected area of transformations of adults through training, retraining, indoctrination, and other experiences. Gives special attention to postchildhood socialization into organizations.

BROOKOVER, WILBUR E., and DAVID GOTTLIEB. *A Sociology of Education,* 2nd ed. New York: American Book Company, 1964. Revision of a pioneering text. Good coverage of main topics.

CLARK, BURTON R. *Educating the Expert Society.* San Francisco: Chandler, 1962. Develops fruitful typology of colleges and universities and analyzes strains between the demands and opportunities of an "expert society" and of the students and the colleges.

COLEMAN, JAMES S. *The Adolescent Society.* New York: Free Press, 1961. Investigations of social pressures and patterns of conformity and value differentiation among high school students.

EDWARDS, NEWTON, and HERMAN J. RICHEY. *The School in the American Social Order,* 2nd ed. Boston: Houghton Mifflin, 1963. Widely used work in a revised edition. Provides a historical dimension and greater attention to educational content and the ideas back of policies than most general works about our schools.

GOSLIN, DAVID A. *The School in Contemporary Society.* Chicago: Scott, Foresman, 1965. Deals mainly with elementary and secondary education in the United States. Excellent analysis of the school as a subsystem of an environing society.

HOFSTADTER, RICHARD. *Anti-Intellectualism in American Life.* New York: Knopf, 1963. A study in depth of the persisting waves of anti-intellectualism and resentment of learned elites through national history. Traces many of the complex roots of this endemic feature of the society.

JENCKS, CHRISTOPHER, and DAVID RIESMAN. *The Academic Revolution.* Garden City, N.Y.: Doubleday, 1968. Highly informed and civilized commentary upon major changes—and resistance to changes—in American higher education.

LAZARSFELD, PAUL F., and WAGNER THIELENS, JR. *The Academic Mind.* New York: Free Press, 1958. A vivid documentation of sources of pressures for ideological conformity and sources of strength for academic freedom. The pressures change from time to time, but the generic problems are perennial.

SEXTON, PATRICIA CAYO. *The American School.* Englewood Cliffs, N.J.: Prentice-Hall, 1967. Brief and readable survey of main features of the school.

WALLACE, WALTER L. *Student Culture*. Chicago: Aldine Publishing Company, 1966. Excellent study of continuity and change in a liberal arts college. Shows how a diverse population of incoming students quickly comes to manifest many of the preexisting attitudes and values of the student "community." Raises interesting hypotheses concerning interpersonal influence and the social structure of student life.

# Religion in America

## INTRODUCTION: RELIGION AND SOCIETY

**A**ll societies have some system of beliefs and practices that may be termed religious. This is not an obvious or a simple generalization, for many societies do not have a religion in the sense directly familiar to most Americans. As we know, the political leaders of many nations profess and promote militant atheism. And were one to define religion in terms of certain kinds of supernatural beliefs, one would have to deny that Buddhism and Confucianism in their "classic" forms are religions. Nevertheless, substantial proportions of persons in all societies hold to "nonempirical beliefs" and carry out associated behavior marked by the qualities usually called religious. No society stops with the modes of meeting the recurrent and structurally important problems discussed previously—kinship, social stratification, economic activities, political processes, and education. It is within the remaining areas of social life that we must seek to identify religious phenomena; and, as in the case of institutions already discussed, we must locate the generic elements of the institution before describing the particular forms it assumes in America.

### Religion and Religious Institutions

The first problem is to find criteria that will make it possible to identify and describe religious institutions. Our immediate task is to understand what we mean precisely when we say that individuals accept or reject certain ideas or beliefs about the meaning of life, practice or fail to practice certain religious rituals, follow or do not follow certain rules of conduct sanctioned by religious authorities.

Until recent years, American social scientists had tended to neglect religion, for understandable if complex reasons. The neglect was serious because no society can be understood without also understanding its religion. We are not bound to give full credence to the assertion that we live in a secular world. An attempt to analyze American society without attention to religion would result in a queerly inaccurate reading of the system. Recent years have brought many evidences of renewed interest in the sociology of religion,[1] as well as a new awareness of the complexity

---

[1] Even casual observation is enough to alert the observer to the ubiquity of religious influences in American life: "Symbolic expressions of organized religion surround Americans. Communications are dated by the Christian calendar. Religious holidays are regularly celebrated. Coins and many postage stamps bear the slogan, 'In God We Trust.'

of specifying the functional place of religion in large-scale heterogeneous societies.[2]

Anyone who presumes to give a comprehensive formal definition of religion should realize that he necessarily is basing his characterization upon a poorly described, very small sample of unknown representiveness of the thousands of separate religions that have existed in this world. And, of course, the fact that something has been called "religious" does not necessarily make it so. There are very few kinds of human action that have not been involved in a religious context, including temple prostitution, holy wars, torture, executions, human sacrifice, self-mutilation, book-burnings, and many other acts not now usually regarded as intrinsic to or favored by religion.

It is so difficult to reduce religion to a general formal definition that the attempt may not be worth the effort; but we can at least circumscribe its area within the realm of the attitudes men take toward those entities and events that they interpret as being beyond the range of ordinary human understanding and control, sometimes including the sheer unavoidable awareness of "existence" or being. Religious attitudes are not identical with moral attitudes, which may refer to the secular world; although ethical concerns are important in some religions, they are minimal or secondary in others. Religions deal with ultimate human concerns—with the meaning of life and death and the cosmos. Men classify entities and events as sacred and profane, with many complicated intershadings between the two; the sacred is not necessarily a separate class of phenomena but is part of a continuum ranging from the purely technological through the conventional, aesthetic, and moral over to those orientations of high seriousness in which religion is to be found. Religions deal at some point with "sacred things" that are objects of nonempirical ideas and of intense moral respect. As Durkheim insisted, the quality of sacredness is "superimposed," not intrinsic to the objects, events, and entities to which sacredness is imputed.[3] There is nothing sacred about a wooden image; but to the believer an image of Christ is in another realm. There are many such crucial instances of the independence of sacredness from physical objects, for example, a rural schoolhouse is taken over for church services: local dances, once held in the same building, are then taboo.[4] Sacredness, like salvation, is not directly observable. Nevertheless, both make a *difference* in what people do and say: a man says he is "saved," and we can observe alterations in his conduct.

---

Political and legal oaths are sworn upon the Bible and in the name of God. Religious and pseudo-religious music and art are a significant part of the environment. Over a thousand places bear biblical names." (David O. Moberg, *The Church as a Social Institution; The Sociology of American Religion* (Englewood Cliffs, N.J.: Prentice-Hall, 1962), pp. 1–2).

2 Cf. Charles Y. Glock, "The Sociology of Religion," in Robert K. Merton, Leonard Broom, Leonard S. Cottrell, Jr. (eds.), *Sociology Today* (New York: Basic Books, 1959), pp. 153–155.

3 Emile Durkheim, *The Elementary Forms of the Religious Life*, J. W. Swain (trans.) (New York: Free Press, 1947). See the discussion of Durkheim in Talcott Parsons, *The Structure of Social Action* (New York: Free Press, 1949), chap. 11.

4 From an unpublished report by William G. Klein on a Kentucky mountain community.

At any given time religious ideas and beliefs at the most general level (conceptions of man, the physical universe, transcendental entities, ethics) provide an encompassing frame of reference within which social processes are defined. Many basic orienting conceptions are supplied also by philosophy, science, and humanistic knowledge and symbols. Historically, however, religious definitions of the universe have had special scope and importance—above all, in their transcendental elements. For the belief that there is a divine power or powers completely above man and nature provides a potential fulcrum *outside* the existing social system and its power structure; thus any human arrangement may become subject to criticism and accountability in terms of a higher power and the ethics believed to be supported by that power.[5] Similarly the idea that all men have a common origin in a divine creation and that they all partake of a divine prototype has always contained the possible implication that no man was without value and that no man was totally superior to others. Such fundamental orientations may serve, under special objective social conditions, as a basis for legitimate resistance to constituted authority and for the establishment and maintenance of limited authority, the "rule of law," and doctrines of individual political and civil rights.

For the empirical study of religion, Charles Glock's classification of aspects or dimensions of religious commitment is useful. He distinguishes the following components: (1) the *ritual* (or cultic) aspects that are involved in worship and organized participation; (2) the *creedal* (or ideological), concerning beliefs; (3) the *devotional* (experiential), involving private feelings or "experiences;" (4) the *cognitive* or intellectual aspect—knowledge about religion; (5) the *consequential*—the effects of religious commitment and practice upon other aspects of society, culture, and personality.[6] Defined in such a multidimensional way, religion evidently may be influential in the everyday social world or, by the same token, various aspects of religion may be affected by the other components of particular social contexts. For example, striking associations exist between definite social conditions and religious beliefs in so-called primitive societies. For a sample of fifty such societies, Guy Swanson shows that the conception of a high god is very strongly correlated with the presence of at least three levels of hierarchically ordered sovereign groupings, such as political kingdom, villages, kinship groups.[7] The direction of possible causation, of course, is not obvious in the correlation itself. Does belief in a high god tend to lead to a complex social hierarchy? Or does the social structure generate the conception of a single superordinate deity? Or are both phenomena the

[5] Herman Israel refers to "a transcendent metaphysical guide to propriety" ("Some Influences of Hebraic Culture on Modern Social Organization," *American Journal of Sociology*, LXXI, 4 (January 1966), 393).

[6] Charles Y. Glock, "On the Study of Religious Commitment," *Research Supplement to Religious Education* (July–August 1962), pp. 98–110. These distinctions are used in Charles Y. Glock and Rodney Stark, *Religion and Society in Tension* (Chicago: Rand-McNally, 1965).

[7] Guy E. Swanson, *The Birth of the Gods: The Origin of Primitive Beliefs* (Ann Arbor: University of Michigan Press, 1960).

results of some other factor or factors? Decisive direct evidence is not available. However, the total body of data suggests a tendency for the social structure in question to develop prior to the emergence of a high god or a monotheistic system. Experiencing the social facts of regularity of control, unity of authority, and symbolic focus of direction and protection, men may come to conceive of a larger, cosmic order. Struggling incessantly to comprehend and "come to terms with" the immediate and consequential universe around them, men may find that this social medium can supply the concepts and symbols by which they seek to represent the ultimate ground of being. In this interpretation, there is no necessary implication of a specific ontology, but there is a reasonably definite causal hypothesis.

As this example may suggest, religion means not merely the passive *acceptance* of beliefs but an active *commitment* to live by them. It is the deep involvement of the personality in the ultimate values and beliefs one feels compelled to take as given. Almost always it entails for the believer a sense of a power or powers in the universe greater than ordinary natural forces. Religion concerns the things that "really matter most:" the religious attitude is one of high seriousness, variously experienced as awe, devotion, reverence, supplication, wonder, exaltation, dread, thankfulness, and so on. Thus, rituals and ceremonies are considered by many religious bodies to have a sacramental quality that directly involves divine grace or favor. Other religious groupings regard certain rituals as only ordinances, symbolizing religious entities, conditions or events but not of direct divine efficacy. Still other groups restrict their "ritual" activity largely to ceremonies that encourage desirable conditions (mediation, fellowship) but are not believed to symbolize or express supernatural or transcendental or even sacred elements. Or, again, some religious groupings require that their members abstain from certain foods, drinks (members of some Protestant denominations are enjoined not to drink alcoholic beverages), drugs, condiments, and related substances. Members of the Church of Jesus Christ of the Latter-Day Saints may not use tobacco, alcoholic beverages, tea, or coffee. Orthodox Jews must observe elaborate dietary rules. Roman Catholics formerly abstained from meat on Fridays as a matter of obligation and still are encouraged to do so as a matter of individual conscience and piety.

Commitment to the norms of behavior prescribed in a religious system is not the same as orthodoxy of beliefs. Indeed, there are situations in which the extent of participation in the association of coreligionists is more predictive of norm conformity than is doctrinal conformity, as shown for instance by the fact that the "weak believer" who is actively engaged in the the religious community may show greater behavioral conformity than a "strong believer" who is relatively inactive.[8]

Men have beliefs that are nonempirical and cannot be tested by scientific

[8] For an interesting case in point (a study of a Mormon church), see John D. Photiadis, "Overt Conformity to Church Teaching as a Function of Religious Belief and Group Participation," *American Journal of Sociology*, LXX, 4 (January 1965), 423–428. Photiadis suggests that the introduction of multiple group-activities into church programs, far from necessarily being a sign of "secularization," may strengthen conformity by attaching individuals firmly to the group.

methods. *Some* beliefs and ideas are scientifically false, but everything that is not scientifically valid is not ignorance and error. If a man claims to have X-ray vision, we can test him and send him to a psychiatrist; but if he claims to have found salvation, we cannot in the same sense check his statement. Nor can we test the claim to the superiority of Buddhism over Christianity or the reverse as we can a claim regarding the relative candle power of two types of artillery flares.

Many religious beliefs and ideas fall in the vast heterogeneous category of the *non*scientific. They are not *un*scientific, because science cannot help in judging their validity. This obvious point is sometimes overlooked, with serious consequences to science itself. The present analysis attempts to be a scientific, sociological treatment, raising questions to which facts derived from observation can provide answers. When we analyze religious norms and values in terms of their functions for other aspects of the society, we are not concerned with the truth or validity of those norms and values. If we say that certain religious beliefs divert attention from social problems and thus facilitate acceptance of the social order, we should also remember that we can apply the same analysis to demonstrated scientific theories.

### Functional Contexts of Religion

Here we will give some attention to a so-called functional approach— involving appraisal of the causes and effects of a given social phenomenon in relation to the other social phenomena. For example, we will find evidence suggesting that particular religious orientations reduce anxiety in situations of stress. However, we do not wish to imply that the apparent consequences of particular religious variables could not result from other causes or that the functions we will discuss are all there are, or that certain values could not be achieved more readily by institutional changes.

In some systems, religion and social morality are inseparable; for the most part, this has been the case in Judaism and Christianity. In other instances, the emphasis upon individual salvation and mystical insight may be so strong that ethics in the ordinary sense takes a secondary and discon- nected place.[9] Nevertheless, every concrete religious system bears some relation to norms for social conduct. Every concrete religious system enjoins some norms of this nature. Thus, the *ethical norms* of Christianity and Judaism constitute a set of widely acknowledged standards supported by moral indignation against violations. Many religious norms, however, specify the relation of the believer to nonhuman or suprahuman entities. In a religion with a definite supernatural referent, the norms derived from rela- tion to the supernatural tend to extend into every area of behavior. Purely religious principles dealing with man's relation to religious entities comprise only a small part of the total religion. Religions also have normative *systems of ideas and beliefs* regarding, for example, the nature of man, the cosmos, supernatural entities. Religion is distinguished from other institutions by its central orientation to problems of meaning and its emphasis upon

[9] See J. Milton Yinger, *Religion, Society, and the Individual* (New York: Macmillan, 1957), pp. 25 ff.

ultimate ends of conduct. The body of cognitive ideas merges with myth on one side and with theology and philosophy on the other. Organized religions are characterized also by a *system of rituals* such as communion or baptism that are given their meaning by the beliefs and orientations. Another component is the *organized religious community*—which need not be a "church" in our sense; the religious community assumes many diverse forms and has many different types of leaders, such as priests, rabbis, or prophets. Religion is characterized by a large symbolic component arising from the "arbitrary" nature of religious referents, the complex relations of abstract beliefs to action, and from other important factors. Religious symbols have a wide range of referents—to external nature, to aspects of the social structure (father, king, lord, mother), to subjective conditions, to supernatural entities. There also is a proliferation of cross-symbol referents. Logical inconsistencies between beliefs can coexist without apparent difficulty—for instance, a person may believe that souls go directly to heaven, yet the ghosts are abroad on the earth.

Around the periphery of religion are numerous more or less closely related systems of art, literature, etiquette, recreation, and magic. The latter, for example, is ritual directed to empirical ends and is often marginal to religion; for instance, the use of prayer as a means of bringing rain to New York City in 1950.[1]

Why should men need religion? Among the existential sources which may plausibly be cited there are:[2]

1. *Uncertainty or contingency* in important events; often men are unable to predict or to count upon future conditions that are crucial to their life, safety, welfare and happiness. Life is uncertain.

2. *Ultimate powerlessness:* some of any person's desires to control his environment and himself are unattainable. Life is hazardous.

3. *Scarcity,* leading to frustration and deprivation; ultimately no one can have all his values attained or his wants satisfied. Men find themselves ignorant and dim of vision, weak, mortal, and deprived. Anyone is capable of imagining satisfactions he will never enjoy, projects he can never accomplish, values he will fail to express or exemplify—all dreams of omnipotence notwithstanding.

These three major types of basic life-circumstances appear to be those most often noted in expositions concerning the social and psychological settings of religious experience and behavior. It seems evident, however, that there are other existential bases of religious belief and activity, such as the importance and difficulty of social integration, including the control of strong "negative" emotions, and the need to express in a socially recognized and accepted way feelings of hope, joy, thankfulness, solidarity, and affirmations of society, values, and life itself. Security and a firm sense of identity conceivably may be enhanced by sacralization of norms and values.

---

[1] Note, however, that prayer is *supplication* to a higher power which may give or withhold the thing requested; magic is *manipulation,* and if the correct operations are performed, the intended result is supposed to follow.

[2] See the incisive discussion by N. J. Demerath, III, and Phillip E. Hammond, *Religion in Social Context: Tradition and Transition* (New York: Random House, 1969), chap. I.

Such sacralization may, on the other hand, exacerbate social conflict and encourage disabling rigidities in social systems.

Actual religious behavior represents a variety of fulfillments, escapes, aspirations, fears, and so on. The specific values and motives can be discovered only through an intensive analysis that will not be attempted here, since our concern is with general features of the human situation out of which religious institutions arise. In most general terms, religion provides men with a way of facing the problems of ultimate and unavoidable frustration, of "evil," and the generalized problem of meaning in some non-empirical sense, of finding some ultimate "why."

First, there is death. Of every ten persons born, ten die. As conscious beings, all men know that they must die and that every person they know and love must die. The sufferings and evils of the world bring dismay, grief, and anguish to most men at some time. As suicide demonstrates, some persons find life such an unbearable and endless torture that they destroy themselves. We cannot take for granted either the motivation of the individual to live out an integrated life or the capacity of group morale to sustain an integrated society. For man, mortality represents a fundamental and unavoidable frustration of deep desires and wishes. In the course of a normal lifespan every person loses by death persons of crucial emotional significance to him. People ask for a meaning that goes beyond medical or physiological explanations for support and reassurance in extremity.[3]

Unavoidable frustration arises also from imperfect or limited control of physical nature and of society. In our time, men ask whether the universe is basically safe for human manipulation. Every society raises such questions of meaning and develops some answers to them.

Then, there is the classic theological problem of evil. Not all religions contain a radical sense of evil; the "wrong" in some systems is just the inappropriate. Sin is apparently more culturally localized than guilt and shame. Whatever the case, men everywhere do have standards of conduct, the mark of being human. Yet everywhere standards are violated; everywhere, at some time, evil seems to prosper and flourish. In a very real sense, injustice is a universal human experience. This is so, surely, if "justice" is defined as identical treatment in terms of identical norms, for this often does not occur. It is so also if justice is defined as treatment according to norms established in the past, for these will be violated as social conditions change. We have already considered the possible abuses of power. And the old questions stand: Why does evil exist, why is there moral obligation, why must the good be destroyed? Religious institutions develop as *one* answer to the deepest human questionings; persons who have believed it possible to "abolish religion" have succeeded only in renaming it.

[3] Hints concerning important symbolic conflicts involved in ceremonies relating to death are given by Robert L. Fulton, "The Clergyman and the Funeral Director: A Study in Role Conflict," *Social Forces*, 39, 4 (May 1961), 317–323. Within a rather short period, the supervision of illness has been so much taken over by physicians and hospital personnel that much of the crucially important social and psychological setting of impending death is now in the hands of the secular custodians. See Barney G. Glaser and Anselm L. Strauss, *Awareness of Dying* (Chicago: Aldine, 1965).

There is another side to religion, more difficult to state. For religion is not solely a reaction to the frustrating and tragic aspects of the human condition. It can also represent a positive affirmation of the value of living, a faith in objective truth and goodness, a belief in the ultimate balancing of the cosmic scales. For many persons in all ages, this affirmation has sustained hope and energy not only in crises but in the "quiet desperation" so often confronted in daily life. For such persons, religion transforms death into life, sorrow into joy, incredible paradox into positive faith.

In one sense, the whole of Western civilization has the same religious orientation—it is transcendental and monotheistic with a universal ethic having supernatural sanction. American religion has other features in common with the religions of other Western societies; it is as American as the Hebrew writs or the Roman Church. Our discussion will deal with a few central elements common to Western religions and then touch on points distinctive to religion in the United States.

One other preliminary consideration must be made clear. Religious systems, as here defined represent at one and the same time complex cultural products, components of social interaction, and actual ingredients of living personalities. It would appear very unlikely, therefore, that any such system could be adequately understood—even in a limited, empirical, scientific sense—by some easy and simple formula such as "economic determinism" or "psychological projection." Rather we may anticipate that many of the phenomena of religion are subtle and are related to various social patterns in intricate combinations. There is no doubt, for example, that the influences of Judaic-Christian doctrines upon our total culture and society have been profound, but it is not self-evident how this result has come about. For example, the religious doctrine of the soul is so pervasive in Western conceptions of man that its full cultural significance is not always recognized and perhaps has never received the empirical analysis it deserves. The idea that man has a soul and that all souls are "equal before God" gives a distinctive basis for the ethical evaluation of individual personality. The idea of the worth, dignity, and inviolability of the individual unquestionably owes much to this belief, as do humanitarian ideals and various philosophies of human equality. Yet the original notion of equality here was not equality of rights but a common humility before the deity that proved historically to be compatible with rigid social hierarchy; a more radical concept of equality, however, was always latent in the system.

We can be sure that social action is never simply an emanation of religious ideas. Given a religious interest, however, the ideas *define* the situation—for example, whether there is salvation, and, if so, salvation for what and from what. Religion is always an interest, reciprocally related to an idea, that partly derives from and reacts back upon the "realistic" social situation. Thus, the Christian doctrine of the soul does not by itself lead to ethical equality; but it makes a *difference*, and the difference it makes is, in part, in the direction of high evaluation of the human individual qua individual.

The basic religious orientations of all Western societies are similar in their *unitary focus* and their *future orientation*. There is a single deity, and the universe is seen as moving toward a definite, ultimate end. Western religion has been chiefly monotheistic and eschatological; and although opposing tendencies—for example, impersonal pantheism and ideas of indefinitely recurring cycles—have arisen and remained in the Western tradition, they have never captured the culture.

In a sufficiently wide comparative perspective, it is very clear that Judaism and its Christian offspring have been dynamic, rather than passively receptive of the social order. Ascetic Protestantism and its "social gospel" offshoots have been particularly prone to social and political concerns; and even state-supported churches have always been somewhat unwilling to make unqualified submission to secular authorities. The great oriental religions—Confucianism, Hinduism, Buddhism, Taoism—have either stressed an ethic of orderly adaptation to a given secular world or a radical escape from or transcendence of the empirical world. On the one hand, there is the cultivated Confucian scholar and member of the gentry; on the other, the Buddhist mystic seeking nirvana. The Western traditions, although containing similar tendencies, have stressed an active mastery over the obstacles to religious fulfillment in society.[4]

What has just been said may seem to constitute a problem in the scientific understanding of religion, since both religion and magic receive greatest emphasis in situations of extreme stress.[5] Although intense interest in religion seems clearly associated with stress, it should be noted that not all such situations are resolved by religious formulations. Interest in religion is one of several responses to crisis, especially when nothing can be done to alter the threatening or depriving external situation. The fires of religion are apt to glow most intensely in the blast of collective terror, deprivation, and social disorganization. New religions, or at least new sects, commonly arise in such periods of social turmoil. The fervor of the martyrs, the passionate devotion of that "inner proletariat" that created a new world within the collapsing framework of Rome—these are not the characteristics of the sober, safe, respectable, careful, ritualistic heirs of the tradition.

Evidently both the social sources and the social consequences of religion vary in different societal contexts. The apparent variation is in part semantic: there is religion$_1$, religion$_2$, . . . religion$_3$. Established religions can tolerate considerable indifference. An organized religious body dependent upon and integrated within the social structure can deal more easily with passive conformity than with extreme piety. The militant advocate of the strictest interpretation of religious norms tends under such circumstances to be regarded as a fanatic and as disturbing the true sense of the established religion—no matter how necessary he may be to the continuation of the

---

[4] This orientation is strikingly different also from the this-worldly emphases of most known religions of preliterate societies. Cf. Robert N. Bellah, "Religious Evolution," *American Sociological Review*, 29, 3 (June 1964), 358–374. Neither magical nor supplicatory orientations involve the purposive obligation to remake the world of everyday life in conformity to a transcendent model.

[5] Note the significant, although limited, data from the experiences of American soldiers in World War II in Samuel A. Stouffer, *et al.*, *The American Soldier*, Vol. II (Princeton, N.J.: Princeton University Press, 1949), pp. 172–191.

fundamental tension from which the religion draws some of its compelling motives and values.

Each of the primary facets of religion—beliefs, values, norms, polity, rituals, community, participation, personal experience—in its turn reveals complexes of internal elements. Thus, for example, religious beliefs vary in their objects, in specific content, in fixity or dogmatic quality, in importance to individuals, in consistency, in degree of ambivalence, in extent of consensus, in explicitness, and in their modes of relations to other elements of total religious life. General sociological theory would lead us to expect systematic relations among these various aspects; and the small roster of relevant empirical studies supports this supposition. Thus, individuals who are orthodox in belief tend to regard their beliefs as highly important and to wish to convert others, whereas not only skeptics but also convinced atheists tend to attach less importance to their beliefs and to be less interested in persuading others to share their view.[6]

The *newly created religion* is specifically alienated from, and usually opposed to, the social order within which it emerges. It is, in fact, a danger to the established interests of the society, unless it can be used, as it often can, to divert disaffection away from direct attack upon the controlling centers of the secular order; observe how opposed to the whole existing society are the Jehovah's Witnesses and how weak is their political influence. The newly created sect most usually seeks to *withdraw* from the society rather than to attack it absolutely; but every deliberate alienation of this sort is a break in the social fabric that secular authorities are understandably reluctant to approve.

The *specific* content of religious systems does, of course, vary enormously. There are tangibly different social implications among possible concepts of the world; for example: (1) as an illusory, magic garden in which personalities consist of temporary and accidental aggregates of an eternal, impersonal world-stuff; (2) as planned by a single, rational, omnipotent deity and populated by minor replicas of him; (3) as a nurturing realm of numerous vague and benevolent spirits; (4) as a battleground of fierce and evil powers, warring eternally for glory and domination. Religious orientations toward the secular world range from uncompromising rejection to a kind of acceptance in which the sacred-secular distinction is hardly made. Similarly, the nature and extent of ritual and concrete symbolism vary widely, as do the ethics sanctioned by the religion proper, the attitude toward traditionalism, and the organization of the religious community. Conceptions of deity extend from highly anthropomorphic ideas, richly decorated by myth, to a transcendental orientation with very little intermediate symbolism.

Such radical variation is so well known that we can here dispense with documentation. It is enough for the moment to accept two basic points:

6 Snell Putney and Russell Middleton, "Dimensions and Correlates of Religious Ideologies," *Social Forces*, 39, 4 (May 1961), 288. This study (of a sample of 1,126 college students at thirteen colleges and universities) also shows that orthodox beliefs are associated with psychological authoritarianism, concern with social status, and political and economic conservatism.

one, *religion is a variable in human societies;* two, *differences in religion make a difference in social conduct.* Variations and changes in religious ideas and values are, by hypothesis, systematically related to variations and changes in other aspects of culture and society. It follows that religion can be treated as a real variable and can be brought within the framework of causal-functional analysis. It is not necessary to seek a universal definition of religion, since interest will be directed toward the influence upon behavior of *specific,* analytically different religions. For purposes of understanding American society, we do not have to deal with a religion undifferentiated from the intertwined matrix of communal life. Long ago in all Western societies, religion became a definite cultural precipitate, embodied in separate organizational forms and institutionally segregated. This fact offers a considerable convenience in analysis if we do not let it blind us to the more diffuse but very tangible operation of religious ideas and values.

This reference to causal-functional analysis requires a brief commentary, for "functionalism" has been the object of some controversy in the social sciences. Functional analysis as generally practiced is not a unitary approach or method but has two main forms. One type of functionalism is a particular kind of *causal* analysis: a given social fact is shown to have certain consequences; and these effects are defined in terms of maintenance or change of stated aspects of societies, cultures, and personalities. It differs from any other analysis of causes and effects (or, if one prefers, antecedents and consequences) only in specifying the outcomes in the context of preexisting structures. If it is said that the "function" of religious asceticism among Pentecostal Holiness sects is to divert attention from economic deprivation and political powerlessness, this would assert that the religious beliefs and practices in question actually do result in the lessening of these this-worldly concerns. Or, if the objective conditions of low income, insecurity, low education, and low social prestige are said to have the function of reducing capacities for political organization and to encourage an other-worldly orientation, the assertion is a causal one; and the "function" (consequence) is implicitly viewed from the standpoint of power structure and opposition of interests.

In the second form, functionalism does not deal directly with causes and consequences. Rather, it simply *describes* what activities are assigned to a particular structure, as when it is said that the function of the Supreme Court is to establish social policies when major legal doctrines are in conflict in particular cases. This is analogous to saying that the function of a carburetor is to mix explosive vapor for ignition in an internal-combustion motor—there is a structure designed to carry out or suitable for a specific activity or set of activities. In social analysis, the difficulties with this descriptive functionalism are that the same structures may carry out multiple activities, that the activities nominally assigned may not in fact take place and that other unassigned or even unrecognized activities can be occurring.

It therefore seems clear that it is almost impossible to avoid causal imputations in discussing functions. An insidious hazard of functional analysis is that antecedent-consequent relations will be asserted on the basis of plausibility, without rigorous attempts to verify the actual causal sequences. In this way, it is easy for hypotheses to take on the appearance of established generalizations.

The most difficult kind of functionalism is a causal analysis of processes maintaining steady states within *self-regulating systems*. The rigorous requirements of this type of analysis involve exact description of a bounded system, which includes a "negative feedback" cycle (somewhat analogous to the operation of a thermostat) such that deviations beyond some zone of acceptable values of a particular variable are reported to a control-source, which alters the conditions necessary to bring the system back within a zone of tolerance.[7] For most of the problems treated in this chapter, neither the methods of measurements nor the concrete data exist that would be required for this kind of functional analysis.

Primary emphases in many recent sociological interpretations have been upon the putative consequences of religious institutions in promoting social solidarity, reducing or controlling hostility and anxiety, maintaining morale and effort in the face of severe frustration and deprivation, and reinforcing social norms. There is adequate, although diffuse, evidence that these consequences do ensue for some individuals and collectivities practicing some religions under some circumstances. But surely the consequences listed do not *always* follow, and surely these "positive" outcomes are not the only effects of holding religious beliefs and carrying out practices religiously sanctioned. Anxiety may be reduced by belief in heaven—but also enormously instigated by genuine belief in a literal hell of everlasting fire. Common worship may reinforce solidarity among coreligionists but create sentiments of alienation, or even active hostility, toward those of other faiths. In short, religion may be disruptive as well as integrative, fearsome as well as comforting, destructive as well as supportive of morale and effort. Religion is more than and different from a do-it-yourself socioemotional repair kit; and plausible interpretations have no scientific claim until they have been tested against the recalcitrant evidence of actual behavior.

Fortunately, however, enough research has been accumulated—and critically reworked—to provide the foundations for a certain number of limited but important generalizations. Thus, insofar as religion does consist of a complex of ultimate value orientations, it can never be a neutral factor in social integration. Complex polities can and do contain different religions, but the operation of such systems is not likely to be the same as that of a political society in which a *common* religion prevails.

The possession of a common set of ideas, rituals, and symbols can supply an overarching sense of unity even in a society riddled with conflicts, for example, Europe in the late medieval period. The intense solidarity that is facilitated by religious unity, under certain objective conditions, can be reversed and the possibilities of intense conflict heightened when two interacting social systems possess radically different religious orientations

---

[7] Cf. Robert Zrown, *Explanation in Social Science* (Chicago: Aldine, 1963), esp. chaps. IX–XI; Walter Buckley, *Sociology and Modern Systems Theory* (Englewood Cliffs, N.J.: Prentice-Hall, 1967).

and are sharply opposed in such secular interests as wealth and power. Holy wars are not the gentlest of wars.

The actual social consequences of variations in religion can be briefly illustrated by the well-analyzed case provided by ascetic Protestantism[8] in its relation to economic institutions.[9] The hard core of the ascetic varieties of Protestantism was Calvinism; and from the latter developed a religious system that combined a transcendental interest with an attempt at active mastery of the secular world. The system emphasized an *active*, not a contemplative or ritualistic, attitude and contained a prominent element of rationality, both in its deep aversion to traditionalism (especially toward anything suggesting idolatry, magic, ritual, or mysticism) and in its attempt to make a rational system of ethics as a whole. The idea of a divine plan in nature helped prepare the way for the development of physical science.[1]

Broadly speaking, the doctrines of early ascetic Protestantism led toward making every man God's agent (a spiritually superior individual) and a laborer for the literal establishment of the kingdom of God on earth—in short, an ascetic living in the world rather than in the cloister. The early American Protestants tended to conceive of God as immediately and directly active in the world.[2] In their orientation, obedience to divine rulership was more emphasized than contemplation of divine perfection. All human institutions were imperfect; God alone was sovereign. It followed, among other things, that the power exercised by men was always subject to error and corruption and must be limited.[3] The organized church tended to be a disciplinary agent rather than a sacramental order; the individual was thought to have direct access to God, and his ethical responsibility was total; he was saved or damned absolutely; there was no avenue for relaxation of discipline. Prior Christian doctrines holding that specific good works and confession could absolve particular sins were in contrast to the neo-Calvinist insistence that one's works were signs of eternal grace or damnation.

Originally, the doctrines of predestination in Protestantism postulated an elite who were saved and others who were from the beginning condemned; there was no external signal to show the individual in which

[8] The standard starting point: Max Weber, *The Protestant Ethic and the Spirit of Capitalism*, Talcott Parsons (trans.) (New York: Scribner, 1958); Cf. Parsons, *The Structure of Social Action*, pp. 500–533. It is important to note that an adequate appraisal of the hypotheses sketched here must take into account the entire analysis of Weber's *Religions-soziologie*—of which the much-cited *Protestant Ethic* is only a fragment; see *The Sociology of Religion*, Ephraim Fischoff (trans.) (Boston: Beacon Press, 1963); *The Religion of China: Confucianism and Taoism*, Hans H. Gerth (trans. and ed.) (New York: Free Press, 1951) and *The Religion of India*, Hans H. Gerth and Don Martindale (trans. and eds.) (New York: Free Press, 1958).

[9] Demerath and Hammond, *op. cit.*, chap. III.

[1] Robert K. Merton, "Puritanism, Pietism, and Science," in *Social Theory and Social Structure*, rev. ed. (New York: Free Press, 1957), pp. 574–606.

[2] H. Richard Niebuhr, *The Kingdom of God in America* (New York: Harper & Row, 1959), pp. 19–24.

[3] *Ibid.*, pp. 78–79, "this doctrine . . . became a profound influence in American life, even when its sources were forgotten."

category he fell. This hard doctrine apparently did not lead to passivity: if one took it seriously, one also took one's religious responsibilities seriously. But the inner loneliness and insecurity occasioned by taking literally so bleak and inscrutable a theological position made it likely that the individual would look hard for some external sign that he could interpret as a sign of religious grace. As a result, various doctrines developed in which good works were held to be a sign of religious salvation.

These doctrines easily led to the justification of worldly prosperity on religious grounds, encouraging systematic and intensive economic activity.[4] It was a duty to be active in the calling God gave one in the secular world. All the virtues of sobriety, rationality, activity, frugality, impersonal devotion to a specific calling, and so on, so prominent in the total system, were congenial to successful business endeavor. Given the *objective possibility* of capitalistic enterprise, such a doctrine could actually motivate men to accumulate wealth on the basis of religious imperatives.

It is difficult to imagine a more appropriate example of how a religious position can support dynamic secular activity than that just sketched. Weber's thesis on the relation of the Protestant ethic to the development of modern capitalism may be criticized on other counts, but four points seem incontestable: (1) the religious ideas and values of ascetic Protestantism tally point for point with the ideas and motives "required" for disciplined, rationalized, persistent capitalistic effort; (2) Protestantism did precede the rise of capitalism in many areas (although not in others, such as northern Italy); (3) religious attitudes were only *one* of several primary causes for the development of capitalism, but were equally indispensable for the specific structure of the latter; (4) the specifically religious ideas evolved in a complex mutual interrelation between an environing social structure, a complex of religious *interests* (for instance, a sense of sin and a need for salvation), and other specifiable social elements.[5]

The above case, presented in compressed and highly simplified form, is one important example of how religious ideas can influence action. It is a hint rather than an analysis and, as Weber himself stated, tends to emphasize only one side of the causal chain. If we say the role of Protestantism in the development of capitalism illustrates the influence of religion on society, it may be advisable to consider briefly the opposition type of problem. For example, it is commonly observed that the membership of "emotional" sects in our society is largely (but not exclusively) drawn from socially marginal or disorganized populations, whereas the most prosperous,

4 Of course Protestantism is not the only religious system conducive to disciplined, "rational" economic activity. For instance, there are elements in the ethic of Zoroastrianism that appear to be conducive to economic acquisition, as well as to scientific and technical interests and achievements, in a manner very similar to those singled out in Weber's interpretation of Protestantism. See Robert E. Kennedy, Jr., "The Protestant Ethic and the Parsis," *American Journal of Sociology*, LXVIII, 1 (July 1962), 11–20.

5 Various criticisms of Weber's work, although useful in suggesting limits and qualifications and in detecting some errors in the data being used, have not refuted his basic position. For one not wholly successful attempt to reject the central argument see Kurt Samuelsson, *Religion and Economic Action*, E. Geoffrey French (trans.) (New York: Basic Books, 1961).

stable, and secure groupings tend to be characterized by formalistic religious practices and lack of overt fervor. Seriously deprived, frustrated, or oppressed groups, having no major realistic control of their situation, tend to produce sects and cults with a proliferation of emotional religious observances, especially if there is a free religious structure. The formal patterns of a universal established church can strongly inhibit and channelize such religious activity, born of desperation and alienation. Here, then, is an instance of the influence of society upon religion. Closer analysis will verify this supposition but will also show once again that the relation is reciprocal. Without some prior cultural definition of the situation in religious rather than in political or some other terms, the evangelical sect could not appear in the same way.

Let us be sure, however, that the limits and qualifications of these illustrative instances are emphasized. The whole "Protestant ethic thesis" often has been grossly misunderstood for failure to note the specific conditions under which it was alleged to hold. The so-called ascetic neo-Calvinistic ethic was only one of several major currents, even in early Protestantism. In the United States, almost from the beginning, there were sects and denominations that diverged radically from the doctrine of a predestinated religious elite of the "saved," embracing instead doctrines asserting the common availability of salvation through God's free offer of grace and the possibility of individual attainment of spiritual perfection.[6] Although many inconsistencies appeared in the various emerging theologies, the dual emphasis on "democracy of grace" and "achievement of perfection" constituted persistent, recurrent themes. The place of "works" versus "grace" as the basis for salvation has continued to be troublesome at all times. The inscrutable enigma of foreordained and selective salvation has not attracted the majority of Protestants. The doctrine of completely "free" and universal salvation is, no doubt, appealing to many; but other Protestants have felt that it fails to support religiously indispensable ethical disciplines. The doctrine of salvation through good works alone may provide strong incentives for right conduct but evidently conflicts with other central theological premises of many Protestant denominations. From these conflicting pressures, a resolution often found acceptable is the belief that religious grace is freely available through the basic choice of an act of faith and that good works, although not the ground of salvation, necessarily follow from the genuine commitment of the faithful.

So, even in the early phases of American history, there was not a single and clear Protestant belief-system or Protestant ethic. And in the contemporary society, the sheer diversity of creed and practice in the more than 200 denominations and sects commonly called "Protestant" defies brief summary. In theology, some "high church" denominations strongly resemble Catholicism; others are practically indistinguishable from Reform Judaism. Some groups emphasize ritual and sacraments (Lutheran and Episcopal);

---

[6] Doctrines of a "democracy" of salvation took two main forms. In Arminianism, it was held that God would not withhold his grace from those believers who made a genuine effort to follow God's will. In the more radical Antinomianism (*anti* = against; *nomus* = law), it was believed that God freely bestowed salvation upon all believers.

others essentially forbid ritual in any usual sense of the word. Some center all interests upon personal salvation in preparation for a life after death; others are eminently this-worldly in their concern with practical ethics, social policy, and psychological insights and adjustment. Some insist upon a detailed literal belief in a particular version of the Scriptures; others encourage relatively free interpretation, accept "symbolic" revisions of earlier doctrines, and accept scientific findings and historical criticism.

Finally, as Weber himself clearly saw, a religious orientation that profoundly affects other aspects of society in one historical period may not do so at a later point. For example, once a capitalistic economy has been established and has permeated the entire social order, followers of different religious orientations may fail to exhibit differences in economic behavior. Something of this kind apparently has happened in the United States. And as research evidence relating to the association between religious orientation and "worldly success" has mounted, the total portrait has become increasingly complex. For example, comparison of white Catholics and Protestants in Detroit shows higher occupational attainments among the latter,[7] although the highest Protestant category consists of the Episcopalians, who probably more than most other Protestants resemble Catholics in doctrine and practice.[8] Several other studies fail to find marked and consistent differences between Protestants and Catholics in aspirations or achievement motivation, occupational level, or in the aspirations of college graduates.[9]

Enough has perhaps been said to indicate the possibility that analysis of religious institutions is an extremely valuable approach to a diagnosis of the social system as a whole. The sociology of religion is not obsolete in this age of technology and science. There is no dialectic that makes it impossible to understand electronics without being an atheist; and the indications are that religious phenomena have causal significance in many important social processes—perhaps more than is commonly believed.

## DISTINCTIVE FEATURES OF AMERICAN RELIGIOUS INSTITUTIONS

Religious differences within Western cultures overlay a massive structure of common values and beliefs; Protestants, Catholics, and Jews can communicate within a shared cultural universe. As we have said, it is only in a detailed and relative sense that American religious institutions differ from

---

[7] Gerhard Lenski, *The Religious Factor* (Garden City, N.Y.: Doubleday, 1961).

[8] Albert Mayer and Harry Sharp, "Religious Preference and Worldly Success," *American Sociological Review*, 27, 2 (April 1962), 218–227.

[9] For example, Raymond W. Mack, Raymond J. Murphy, and Seymour Yellin, "The Protestant Ethic, Level of Aspiration, and Social Mobility: An Empirical Test," *American Sociological Review*, 21, 3 (June 1956), 295–300; Gerald Gurin, Joseph Veroff, and Sheila Feld, *Americans View Their Mental Health* (New York: Basic Books, 1960). Andrew M. Greeley, "Influence of the 'Religious Factor' on Career and Occupational Plans of College Graduates," *American Journal of Sociology*, 68, 6 (May 1963), 658–671, and Andrew M. Greeley, *Religion and Career* (New York: Sheed and Ward, 1963). (Caution in generalizing from the findings is desirable in view of the special population samples studied.)

their European counterparts; however, it is possible to outline certain characteristics that are relatively distinctive of religion in America. It is necessary here to omit most of the enormous accumulation of descriptive detail concerning organization, beliefs, and practices of specific religious collectivities in the United States. This massive factual background is readily available in textbooks and standard reference works.[1]

Major characteristics, most briefly, include the following:

GENERAL INSTITUTIONAL SYSTEM

1. The principle of separation of church and state is dominant; there is no established church.

2. Large numbers of diverse religious groupings coexist—ecclesia, denominations, sects, and many forms of cults, embodying various specific beliefs.

3. A relatively great degree of religious freedom exists; religious toleration is emphasized.

4. There are pervasive tendencies to emphasize the perfectibility of man and the possibility of human progress—in relative contrast to much of the nominally accepted theology and to the dominant themes of the European tradition.

5. There has been a comparatively far reaching secularization of beliefs, especially in Protestant groupings; an alienation from literal dogmas that predominated earlier; acceptance of religion on grounds of expediency; withdrawal from intense involvement in strictly religious problems and an associated interest in practical, secular activities carried on under church auspices.

6. There is a general doctrinal cleavage between the orthodox (fundamentalist) and "liberal" Christian beliefs, paralleled to some extent by a similar division in Judaism. This cleavage not only separates different denominations but is often an active problem *within* many of them.

7. Nonparticipation in organized religion is due mainly to indifference rather than to militant opposition.

RELIGIOUS ORGANIZATIONS

1. Religious bodies tend strongly toward local or congregational autonomy; even within relatively unified denominations there are powerful centrif-

[1] For reference, see James Ward Smith and A. Leland Jamison (eds.), *The Shaping of American Religion*, Vol. I, and *Religious Perspectives in American Culture*, Vol. II of *Religion in American Life*, Princeton Studies in American Civilization No. 5 (Princeton, N.J.: Princeton University Press, 1961). Also J. Paul Williams, *What Americans Believe and How They Worship* (New York: Harper & Row, 1962); Jerald C. Braver, *Protestantism in America*, rev. ed. (Philadelphia: Westminster Press, 1965); Frank S. Mead, *Handbook of Denominations in the United States*, 2nd ed. (New York: Abingdon Press, 1961). Among useful elementary texts and readers are Elizabeth K. Nottingham, *Religion and Society*, rev. ed. (New York: Random House, 1969); W. Seward Salisbury, *Religion in American Culture: A Sociological Interpretation* (Homewood, Ill.: Dorsey Press, 1964); David O. Moberg, *op. cit.*; Richard D. Knudten, *The Sociology of Religion: An Anthology* (New York: Appleton-Century-Crofts, 1967); Purnell Hardy Benson, *Religion in Contemporary Culture* (New York: Harper & Row, 1960); Thomas F. O'Dea, *The Sociology of Religion* (Englewood Cliffs, N.J.: Prentice-Hall, 1966); Demerath and Hammond, *op. cit.*, Part II.

ugal or secessionistic pressures. Protestant groups accent these features more than do Catholic groupings, but even the latter stand out in contrast to the European tradition.

2. Partly as a corollary of this trait, religious organizations tend to allow a relatively great role to lay leadership and to democratic control. Again, Protestantism gives the freest rein to these tendencies, but American Catholicism inclines more notably in this direction than does Catholicism in Europe or Latin America.

3. Evangelical activity, proselyting, missionary effort, and revivalism are strongly emphasized, partly as a consequence of religious freedom and the multitude of sectarian groupings.

4. Specific organizational forms vary greatly as do the activities of local congregations within a given denomination. The bare, sparse "services" of the small rural church stand in contrast to the multiple activities of the large, wealthy, secularized, urban establishment with its youth groups, dances, movies, athletic organizations, lectures, home services, bazaars and so forth.

5. Since there is no established church, religious organizations must depend for financial support upon formally voluntary contributions. An extensive *overt* commercialism has thus emerged—for example, business-like advertising, provision of what were formerly secular services and activities, and formally organized fund raising activities.

ORIENTATION TO THE SECULAR WORLD

1. Worldly success is widely and overtly approved—not condemned, ignored, or covertly sanctioned. This pattern is riddled with ambivalence, and it is difficult to speak of it without being misunderstood; but we will indicate more exactly later how ethical approval of secular success operates in its cultural setting.

2. Religious bodies tend generally to remain apart from those specific political struggles not impinging immediately upon their particular interests. Here again Catholicism on the whole differs from Protestantism, but American religious culture has mainly tended to eschew the age-old intimate relation between religion and state, church and rulers. Current indications are that this long-standing situation is undergoing considerable change. The line of separation between church and state is becoming less sharp, and the churches increasingly make public pronouncements on political issues and actively seek to influence legislation.[2]

3. No really important and militant anticlerical movement exists in the United States as yet, partly because, as we shall see, organized religion is relatively uninvolved in active politics, organized religious forces are dispersed, and there is an effective tradition of toleration. Furthermore, the lack of an established church has helped to prevent the identification of organized religion with the political and economic status quo.

4. As in all major civilizations, religion in America is characterized by

2 Leo Pfeffer, *Creeds in Competition: A Creative Force in American Culture* (New York: Harper & Row, 1958). See also Yinger, *op. cit.*, pp. 246–262; Luke E. Ebersole, *Church Lobbying in the Nation's Capitol* (New York: Macmillan, 1951).

a deep and enduring struggle among the main attitudes toward the secular world: active mastery, extreme devaluation and withdrawal, passive adaptation, and approval.

5. With some conspicuous exceptions, organized religion in the contemporary United States takes a conforming or conserving attitude toward the main features of the social order. Some religious leaders, however, are outspoken critics of economic and political policies and institutions, for example, of foreign policy and war, of racial segregation and discrimination, of concentration of power.

6. Modern American religion inclines generally toward a remarkable perfectionism and optimism in spite of nominal allegiance to a dominantly somber and pessimistic theology committed to doctrines of the evil nature of man, the corruption of the world, the tragedy of sin and ultimate damnation.[3]

7. No unequivocal cultural meaning can be attached to words such as "religious nonconformity" or "dissent" in America, for reasons given above. There simply is no church in the integral absolute sense familiar to Europeans from the Thames to the Danube, and hence there is not a unitary religious attitude toward the world of men and affairs.

Quite clearly, the above points touch only a few principal characteristics of American religion. The following consideration of the major features just outlined will also note briefly certain other patterns.

### Lack of an Established Church

The first clause of the Bill of Rights, prohibiting the establishment of a state church, simply legalized the social condition already existing in America. From the colonial beginnings, the immigrating population had a variegated religious composition—a sizable Catholic minority, a few Jews, and an enormously varied aggregate of dissenting Protestant sects. Perhaps much more significant, no single one, nor any practicable combination of these groups, was powerful enough to dominate the national government or to wield completely authoritative power in any one of the newly formed states. It was accordingly impossible to secure political consensus as to which *one* church should enjoy state establishment, and the strongly sectarian groups were certainly unwilling to see any rival receive such privileges.

Out of this heterogeneity, therefore, emerged the separation of church and state, which tended to produce further religious diversity. The taxgatherer was separated from the tithecollector, and the religious aspects of the total social structure barred both unitary church organization and any major state support of a particular religious body. The culture remained dominantly Protestant and overwhelmingly Christian; but politically supported religious monopoly was gone—a decisive departure from the European tradition. During the first century of the new nation, the well established or "conservative" denominations (Congregational, Presbyterian, Episcopal, Lutheran) diminished in relative influence in relation to the

[3] This tendency has been authentically discerned by William L. Sperry, *Religion in America* (New York, Macmillan, 1946), p. 15.

rapid growth of the "free grace," decentralized, individualistic denominations and sects, of which the largest were the Methodists and Baptists.

The single fact of the absence of an established church was therefore centrally important for the total character of religious institutions in this country.[4] It was both the product and the cause of denominationalism, with its attendant evangelism, and imposed on the churches the necessity of competitive financing through voluntary contributions. It also encouraged lay representation and control in church organization, as opposed to control by an ecclesiastical hierarchy, and facilitated local independence and secession tendencies in the individual denominations. It tended to reduce the symbolic reinforcement of mutually supportive political and religious authority by largely insulating religious from political organization. This eventually strongly encouraged jealous defensiveness among Protestant sects against the state. Although the Catholic churches (and to a lesser degree, the Lutheran denominations) have not held this attitude strongly, they also have been profoundly affected by lack of establishment.

No one church in American communities can speak for the entire people; as private associations all religious bodies are legally equal to each other. Although religious groupings throughout this society are stamped by recognizably "American" qualities, they are diverse, pluralistic, and incessantly changing.

As Sperry indicates, the United States as a total culture, permeated as it still is with Protestant views, does not understand the idea of a universal church;[5] it comprehends only the environing facts of numerous types of churches, cults, sects, denominations. Whatever unity there is in American religion is cultural rather than organizational, diffuse convergence rather than an authoritative and centrally controlled system of beliefs and symbols.

### Religious Freedom and Toleration[6]

Each dissenting group that came to colonial America wanted religious freedom for itself but was by no means prepared to grant religious liberty, or even toleration (a different concept), to all other sectarian movements. Freedom and toleration were only very gradually established in the face of the rival imperialism of sectarian groups, each holding staunchly to its own cherished version of the true faith and in most cases utterly impatient of dissent. In early New England it was a criminal offense to celebrate Christmas, and the death penalty could be evoked against Quakers and Catholics. Just before the revolution of 1776, any man in the colony of Virginia who denied the Trinity could be deprived of the custody of his own children.[7]

---

[4] Cf. Henry K. Rowe, *The History of Religion in the United States* (New York: Macmillan, 1924), pp. 52 ff.; Thomas C. Hall, *The Religious Background of American Culture* (Boston: Little, Brown, 1930); William W. Sweet, *The Story of Religion in America*, 2nd rev. ed. (New York: Harper & Row, 1950); Sperry, *op. cit.*

[5] Sperry, *op. cit.*, pp. 9–10.

[6] Convenient background sources: Hall, *op. cit.*, pp. 127–146, 264–266; Sperry, *op. cit.*, pp. 6 ff; M. Searle Bates, *Religious Liberty: An Inquiry* (New York: Harper & Row, 1945).

[7] Leo Pfeffer, *op. cit.*, p. 9.

And so it went. In the religious climate of early America, the fervent commitment to belief in the absolute sovereignty of a transcendental God did not encourage easy tolerance of dissent. Intolerance pervaded the early period of intense religious interest and internecine religious competition.[8] Orthodoxy was intense, group contrasts great. Aside from the early efforts of Roger Williams and the Calverts to establish toleration, there was no initial commitment to a religious freedom.[9]

Major factors in the rise of religious freedom and toleration include the following: (1) There was no cleavage between two or only a few opposing religious groupings but rather a fragmented diversity of numerous small sects; ingroup solidarity was diffused, and conflict could not be massive or unitary. (2) No one religious grouping had the opportunity to seize a dominant political position. (3) Due to the circumstances of settlement, there was no prior established church common to all the colonies[1] and, therefore, no common ecclesiastical interests in property, office, and institutional prestige. (4) Outside the solid centers of intense religious orthodoxy there was much public indifference to organized religion in the late eighteenth century; expanding economic and social opportunities tended to distract men from religion; many important political and intellectual leaders were thoroughly secular.[2] (5) The dissenting varieties of Protestantism had the incipient principle of toleration: since the individual believer had direct access to divine truth through the Bible, valid religious experience could be approached by divergent paths.[3] (7) Settlers were needed to provide labor, to aid in military security, and to increase capital gains; and the colonies accepting immigrants of various faiths could foresee tangible economic advantages. The factors named[4] are enough to indicate how power considerations, economic interest, religious organization, and creeds

[8] Men are always likely to be intolerant of opposition to their central ultimate values. In the formative period of the American political community, differences in formal religious beliefs and practices were widely interpreted as *ultimate* value differences.

[9] Salisbury, *op. cit.*, p. 35: "By the beginning of the eighteenth century there were only two colonies (Rhode Island and Pennsylvania) where Catholics enjoyed a large measure of civil rights. . . . the last political disabilities were not removed from the fundamental state laws until 1790 in South Carolina, 1798 in Georgia, 1806 in New York, 1818 in Connecticut, 1833 in Massachusetts, and 1835 in North Carolina." Political rights for Jews were not officially established in all states until 1868.

[1] Although most of the colonies did have some form of establishment, and some states persisted in it until the 1830's.

[2] The case of Thomas Jefferson is usually cited. However, George Washington was a deist and did not take communion, although he was not anticlerical and apparently was a dutiful vestryman in the Episcopal Church. (See Paul Boller, *George Washington and Religion*, Dallas: Southern Methodist University Press, 1963).

[3] For an excellent example see the account of the 1828 cleavage between orthodox and Hicksite factions of the Quakers: Robert W. Doherty, *The Hicksite Separation: A Sociological Analysis of Religious Schism in Early Nineteenth Century America* (New Brunswick, N.J.: Rutgers University Press, 1967).

[4] Other factors were the loose contacts with the parent organizations in Britain and on the Continent; the pressure of British proprietors to increase settlements; the fact that at the time of the revolution there were only a few thousand Catholics and a negligible number of Jews in the whole country.

converged to produce religious freedom—even though in a broad sense, "nobody intended it," a specific example of the fact that unforeseen and even unwanted consequences are common in collective social processes.

Religious liberty, once established as an official national doctrine, reinforced the continuing forces of a pluralistic society until the broad principle had worked deeply into the whole cultural fabric. Intolerance and conflict still occur in very substantial proportions, but they are opposed to, and not supported by, the dominant institutions.

The copresence of distinctively different religions in the same geographic area may result in antagonism and conflict or mutual accommodation. The followers of a particular faith have to "take seriously" the claims to religious validity and value of other religions only under those special social and cultural conditions that make intellectual elaboration a promising means of survival or expansion. One does not in the present sense "take seriously" the religion of an utterly alien people who are politically and economically separate and whose total culture is regarded as inferior. The necessity to justify a religious belief system appears to be strongly felt only when adherents of the differing faiths are present in the same society in substantial numbers, when at least one of the groups is actively proselytizing, and when the belief systems are similar enough to make conversion a reasonable possibility. These circumstances make it almost impossible to ignore the challenging belief system and very difficult to drive it out by force.[5] Yet it is a definite threat. Strong encouragement is thus created for "theology"— for the elaboration of beliefs, their systemization, and for the explication of creeds and symbolism. Beliefs then cease to be "primitive"—that is, held without awareness of the existence of and grounds for other beliefs. The more nearly alike in generalized social status the members of religious groupings are and the more plausible the opponent's arguments and appeals in terms of some of one's own basic beliefs and values, the more extensive and elaborate will be the theological development.

### Diversity of Religious Groupings

The Yearbook of American Churches for 1968 reported a total membership of 126 million persons in 241 religious bodies.[6] Major groupings include Buddhist, Old Catholic, Polish National Catholic and Armenian, Eastern Orthodox, Jewish, Roman Catholic, and Protestant. This great diversity has been encouraged by a cultural setting that has given free play to the (initially) dispersive tendencies of Protestantism and to leaders with new revelations—for example, Joseph Smith (Mormonism) and Mary Baker Eddy (Christian Science). Often the appearance of a new grouping, whether by schism or by separate genesis, has had only a secondary relation to strictly religious differences and has reflected instead secular differences such as national, racial, or class distinctions. One finds, for example, Swedish Lutherans and Norwegian Lutherans, Southern and Northern branches of

[5] However, some isolated sects and cults do manage overtly to ignore the outside challenge.
[6] Lauris B. Whitman (ed.), Yearbook of American Churches for 1968, 36th issue (New York: Council Press, 1968), p. 194. The Yearbook carefully points out the approximate nature of the available data.

several denominations—a residue of the Civil War—separate Negro denominations, fundamentalistic denominations, and expressive sects such as the Holy Roller groups.

The variety of groupings can only be fully appreciated by close study of individual denominations, sects, and cults. Yet even a running inspection of standard reference works gives convincing indications of the flavor of the diversity.[7] Thus, there are at least twenty-eight recognized separate associations or groupings of Baptists, including Free Will Baptists, Seventh Day Baptists, General Six-Principle Baptists, and Two-Secd-in-the-Spirit Predestinarian Baptists. There are twenty-five main bodies of Methodists. There is the American Carpatho-Russian Orthodox Greek Catholic Church. The lists include the Pentecostal Fire-Baptized Holiness Church, as well as the Krimmer Mennonite Brethren Conference, the Salvation Army, the Kadesh Church of Immanuel, and the Pillar of Fire. There are groups that practice foot washing and observe the Lord's Supper with unfermented grape juice and unleavened bread; those that prescribe distinctive clothing; those that "speak in unknown tongues." Many proselytizing groups are marked by strong convictions, intensive missionary and "witnessing" activity, and a high level of activity and involvement of laymen.

Most of the 241 denominations are quite small. Twenty-one denominations contain 90 percent of all members. Eighty-one religious bodies having 50,000 or more members account for 98 percent of church memberships whereas the remaining 2 percent is scattered through 160 groupings. The largest single organized church, the Roman Catholic, reported about 47 million members of a total reported church membership of 126 million, whereas the Protestant groupings accounted for somewhat more than another 70 million; and the number of Jewish persons was roughly estimated at 5.7 million.[8] However, the social importance of the smaller bodies is not adequately represented by their numerical standing, since the presence of so much diversity unquestionably strongly influences the total religious scene.

The formation of cults and sects constitutes a fascinating and important sociological problem; however, only a few points can be mentioned here. Cults and sects like other new religious movements are most likely to arise out of rapid social change, the disturbance of value systems, and conditions of religious liberty produced by religious heterogeneity. The genesis and continued survival of small schismatic sects is facilitated by the separation of church and state and the fact that congregational forms of church are well adapted to schism. The tightly knit sect is most likely to survive where there is sharp cultural isolation, frequently the result of a rural mode of life but also of systematic cultural barriers. Sects are developed by strata and

[7] Cf. the various issues of the *Yearbook of American Churches;* also, Frank S. Mead, *Handbook of Denominations in the United States, op. cit.* The latter contains an extensive bibliography, as does F. E. Mayer (revised by Arthur Carl Piepkorn), *The Religious Bodies of America* (St. Louis: Concordia Publishing House, 1961).

[8] Figures calculated from the 1968 *Yearbook, op. cit.,* pp. 195–207. All these data are highly approximate, and it is especially difficult to determine the number of persons actually active in the Jewish religious organizations. (Probably close to half of the persons reporting the Jewish faith are not active in a synagogue or temple.)

groups that are culturally marginal by reason of poverty, low social status, political domination by an alien culture, or, in some instances, ethnic and racial discrimination. Where there is marked social cleavage as between classes, nationalities, or races, sects expressing the separate aspirations of contending groups or strata tend to solidify the existing cleavages, although they may not enchance the power of the weaker groups.

However, the conventional distinctions between "church" and "sect" and "cult" are not adequate to characterize the main types of religious collectivities.[9] Several fairly large Protestant denominations with well-established organizations and complex and successful adaptations to the environing society nevertheless retain strong elements of the sect orientation. Among the conspicuous examples are the Society of Friends (Quakers), the Church of Jesus Christ of the Latter-Day Saints (Mormon), and the Disciples of Christ.[1]

Some denominations and sects of American Protestantism developed an extreme emphasis upon the spiritual freedom of the individual in all matters of religious faith and action and an extraordinary degree of autonomy of the local congregations from any kind of central authority. Under modern conditions, these conceptions tend to be strongly modified in actual practice when the religious body is large and is committed (by the very essentials of its faith) to extensive evangelical and missionary efforts.[2] Under these circumstances, central authority and extended formal organization tend to emerge as unintended and often unacknowledged by-products of such organizational "imperatives" of financing, coordination, interorganizational linkages, and maintenance of common purposes.

For over a century, the main denominational cleavages in the United States have not been based primarily upon doctrinal religious differences but upon political and economic alignments.[3] Lesser denominationalism appears to be the outcome of (1) major changes in religious value-belief systems (for example, a shift from theological to ethical interests, increased secularization); (2) the gradual blurring of ethnic and sectional divisions that have contributed so much to denominationalism; and (3) the convergence of common interests among Protestant bodies—in reaction to growing Catholic strength, to the felt dangers of secularization and of certain political movements, and to certain trends in ecclesiastical thought.[4]

[9] Benton Johnson, "On Church and Sect," *American Sociological Review*, 28, 4 (August 1963), 539–549.

[1] On the latter, Olive Read Whitley, *Trumpet Call of Reformation* (St. Louis: Tethany Press, 1959).

[2] Paul M. Harrison, *Authority and Power in the Free Church Tradition: A Social Case Study of the American Baptist Convention* (Princeton, N.J.: Princeton University Press, 1959).

[3] For landmark analyses of the various factors suggested above see Liston Pope, *Millhands and Preachers* (New Haven, Conn.: Yale University Press, 1942); H. Richard Niebuhr, *The Social Sources of Denominationalism* (New York: Holt, Rinehart & Winston, 1929); Sweet, *op. cit.*; Sperry, *op. cit.*; John B. Holt, "Holiness Religion: Cultural Shock and Social Reorganization," *American Sociological Review*, V, 5 (October 1940), 740–747.

[4] Among such trends: a sophisticated effort to state the central ethical contentions of

What Sperry has called the "religious fecundity" of our society is one of the dominant aspects of its religious history. The resulting mosaic of diverse religious bodies is an important and integral part of the loose, experimental, pluralistic motif running through the total pattern of American culture. Denominationalism and the multiplication of sects are intrinsic potentialities of a religious system emphasizing individual spiritual independence.[5] How much sectarianism actually occurs, however, depends upon the broader social context; and there are convincing indications that the environing structure of American society no longer supports the proliferation of denominations. For example, in 1962 the Lutheran Church of America was formed by a merger of the United Lutheran Church (2.5 million members) with the Augustana Lutheran (Swedish; 630 thousand members), the Finnish Evangelical Lutheran (36 thousand), and the American Evangelical Lutheran (Danish; 25 thousand members). Simultaneously, the American Lutheran Church was formed by merging the Evangelical Lutheran (Norwegian; over 1 million members) and the United Evangelical Lutheran (Danish; 67 thousand). These mergers index the fading away of formerly vital ethnic divisions.

Thus there are persistent movements for consolidation and federation among Protestant denominations.[6] Study and discussion are proceeding concerning possible organizational union of several large denominations representing distinctly different creeds and polities, including the United Presbyterian Church, the United Church of Christ, the Protestant Episcopal Church, the Methodist Church, the Disciples of Christ, the Evangelical United Brethren, and the African Methodist Episcopal Church. Should such a merger be effected it would combine in one body the sacramental-liturgical and the Bible-centered traditions, the hierarchical-priestly and the congregational-individualistic forms of organization. Already accomplished is the remarkable merger of the very different Congregational Christian and the Evangelical and Reformed Churches to form the United Church of Christ.

Among Protestant and Orthodox groupings the most substantial interdenominational organization is the National Council of the Churches of Christ in the U.S.A., which has over thirty of the larger denominations with about 42 million members. The more conservative Protestant bodies, including notably the Southern Baptist Church and the Missouri Synod, Lutheran Church, are not members. There are two main interdenominational bodies among the fundamentalist groupings.[7] The larger and less militant is the National Association of Evangelicals. The American Council of Christian Churches (which even declines to supply information for the *Yearbook of American Churches*) is a militant organization, strongly op-

---

Christianity and Judaism. In addition to the factors listed above, there are a number of less obvious causal conditions that could be given adequate treatment only in a monographic work.

[5] Rowe, *op. cit.*, pp. 52 ff.

[6] Nils Ehrenstrom and Walter C. Mueldcr (eds.), *Institutionalism and Church Unity* (New York: Association Press, 1963).

[7] See the discussion of "fundamentalism" on pp. 399–401 below.

posed to what it regards as the modernistic, pacifistic, procommunist, and pro-Catholic tendencies of the largest interdenominational organizations.[9]

Movement toward interfaith cooperation and unification, long limited to such inclusive organizations as the National Conference of Christians and Jews, received new impetus and specificity following the ecumenical emphasis of Vatican II, the great reorientation of the Roman Catholic Church under the leadership of Pope John XXIII.

The growing tendencies toward denominational mergers, interdenominational organization, interfaith cooperation, and ecumenical discussion and action—all these express both internal religious changes and changes in the social and cultural contexts. Some creedal differences formerly regarded as crucial are no longer thought to be of central importance; others have been dissolved, in effect, by reevaluation and interpretation. Some particular forms of organization and of ritual have become less sharply defined as sacrosanct barriers. At the same time, ethnic and sectional cleavages have lessened, rural-urban differences have diminished, and social class lines are less often invoked to separate denominations.

Even as the doctrinal and organizational scene is thus changing, both the prescriptions for behavior of religious leaders and their actual role-activities are also being altered. In comparison with the "traditional" statuses and roles of a half-century ago, the contemporary priest, minister, or rabbi is called upon to engage in a much wider range of activities; at the same time religious vocations are marked by more extensive specialization, as assistant pastors and lay specialists are added to provide services. The proliferation of activities—counselling, pastoral, educational, administrative, therapeutic, recreational—partly reflects the changing needs and demands of the laity and partly represents efforts to compensate for loss of earlier authority in the realms of belief and moral leadership.[1]

### Organizational Forms

The variety of systems of beliefs and values in American religious culture is paralleled by diversity in organizational norms. Three main ideal-types of church organization can be distinguished: the episcopal, the presbyterian, and the congregational. The essential differences can be suggested in an oversimplified way by saying that the center of gravity of the episcopal type is the ecclesiastical hierarchy; of the presbyterian, the constituent church bodies; of the congregational, the individual believer. The episcopal pattern is characterized by a definite ecclesiastical hierarchy having centralized control of appointments; church authority flows from the highest office down to the members. The prime example is the Roman Catholic Church, but many other religious bodies (Lutheran, Episcopal, Eastern Orthodox) are similarly organized. In a presbyterian structure, the church hierarchy is modified by lay representation in governing bodies, priestly rank is not strictly graded, and the individual *churches* are the units making up synods

[9] Moberg, *op. cit.*, pp. 261–264.
[1] Cf. James M. Gustafson, "The Clergy in the United States," *Daedalus*, 92, 4 (Fall 1963), 724–744; Sister Marie Augusta Neal, *Values and Interests in Social Change* (Englewood Cliffs, N.J.: Prentice-Hall, 1965).

and finally the denomination as a whole. The congregational denominations are rather loosely organized and go much further toward local autonomy and lay control; in the most extreme cases they have no formal priesthood or ministry and permit all members to act in this capacity—for example, the Society of Friends.

Falling somewhat outside of these three ideal-types are religious bodies such as the Salvation Army with its quasi-military structure, as well as many groups that are simply amorphous and shifting clusters of adherents who follow some charismatic leader. Scattered through certain urban areas (for example Detroit, Los Angeles) and culturally marginal rural localities, one finds a variety of small "congregations" led by lay preachers who claim authority by revelation rather than by investment from an established denomination or sect.

Religious groups tend to vary in their attitude toward the social order in a manner partly manifest in the forms of their organizations. (1) The established church—the ecclesia—claims authority over all or nearly all members of a given society, often extending across national political boundaries; it is typically accommodated to the existing social order, sometimes holding political authority itself or, at least, actively supporting secular authority.[2] (2) The *sect* is a religious protest group that tries to insulate itself from the larger society or, failing that, attacks the secular order. (3) The *established sect* has a well-defined polity and stable relationships with other religious groupings and secular authorities but retains a keen sense of separate belief and distinctive mission. (4) The *denomination* is a tamed sect that has made its peace with other religious groupings and either supports or tolerates the mundane society. (5) *Cults* are loose, personalized groupings, tending mainly, although not universally, to withdraw from and deprecate secular activities.

The ecclesia is characteristic of societies having a relatively stable and unified ruling group and has its greatest strength in societies of an isolated-sacred type. Sects and denominations emerge as societies develop a complex associational structure. Cults occur most frequently in highly differentiated and fragmented societies, especially in urban civilizations marked by a high degree of anomie (normlessness). America has been prolific of cults and sects, some of which have been militantly reformist, others quietistic; some have voiced an eschatological pessimism about man and society.[3]

### Indifference and Opposition toward Organized Religion

In America there is no sharp division between those within the religious fold and those outside it, as there tends to be in Europe.[4] It is extremely

---

[2] A more complete classification would include the "universal church"—an even more inclusive and firmly established organization than the ecclesia.

[3] Bryan R. Wilson, *Sects and Society* (Berkeley and Los Angeles: University of California Press, 1961); Elmer T. Clark, *The Small Sect in America*, rev. ed. (New York: Abingdon-Cokesbury, 1949); Allan W. Eister, *Drawing-Room Conversation* (Durham, N.C.: Duke University Press, 1950); Leon Festinger, Henry W. Riecken, and Stanley Schachter, *When Prophecy Fails* (Minneapolis: University of Minnesota Press, 1956).

[4] Sperry, *op. cit.*, pp. 19–21.

difficult, in fact, to determine just how many members the churches have, since no clear boundary marks off members from those who participate without formal membership. Militant secular opposition rarely occurs in America.[5] Anticlericalism is typically mild or individualized, and many persons not adhering to churches take an active positive interest in religious ideas and values: the fringe of sympathetic bystanders is very large.

Disaffection with religion in this country generally takes the form of indifference rather than opposition. Churches die of gradual social anemia rather than of violent illness. Perhaps the nearest approach to an anticlerical movement consists of nativist agitation directed against Catholicism, but even here no recent groups or organizations have acquired a definite focus or established a real united front. The numerous cross-cleavages in American religion tend to diffuse conflict at the same time that they partially prevent the churches from having a concentrated social or political impact.

### Secularization

Much has been said about the secularizing tendencies in our culture. Although adequate research is badly needed on this matter, the following observations seem well supported in a general way. It is variously noted that much of religion has become a matter of private ethical convictions, that the churches are active in secular affairs,[6] that religious observances have been losing their supernatural or other-worldly character. It is said that religion in America tends to be religion at a very low temperature. Men of religious convictions note with concern the fraying of the Christian (and Judaic) tradition as a new generation emerges, having little training in, or attachment to, religious doctrine, and wonder if the "moral capital" of the past is being dissipated. Many observers comment critically upon the "fragmentation" of religious organization and upon the allegedly corrosive effects of the multiplicity of belief systems.

On the other hand, the evidence already reviewed shows that militant anticlericalism is lacking, that church membership is large, and that, in some areas, fervent sects are continually arising. We know further that religion is given continued public and political approval, that "Godless" is a powerful epithet, that the nonadherents of the churches nevertheless tend to regard religion as vaguely "a good thing,"[7] and that recent and continuing world crises appear to have been associated with increased interest in certain aspects of religion. Over the course of national history, the proportion of the population affiliated with organized religion certainly has increased greatly. Membership apparently continued to increase in the mid-century decades. And, according to testimony gathered in repeated polls by the American Institute of Public Opinion, church attendance by adults rose slightly during the

---

[5] On the difficulties confronted by organized irreligion, see N. J. Demerath, III, and Victor Thiessen, "On Spitting Against the Wind: Organizational Precariousness and American Irreligion," *American Journal of Sociology*, LXXXI, 6 (May 1966), 674–687.

[6] "Activism" is often applied to American religion as a term of reproach by European churchmen.

[7] In Sperry's delightful phrase, these are the people who are "imperfectly irreligious." *Op. cit.*, p. 256.

1950's and declined slightly during the 1960's, showing no marked upward or downward trend over a period of nearly twenty years; in 1966, 44 percent of the sample reported attendance during the week preceding the interview.[8]

As popularly used the term "secularization" often refers to changes in ethical rules or specific norms of behavior: thus, the relaxation of a rule against drinking of alcoholic beverages or lessened requirements for attendance at worship services may be called secularization. "Secularization," however, surely means more than the mere fact of a change in rules or customary practice. The opposite of secularization presumably is sacralization, a process whereby things formerly religiously neutral or profane come to have the quality of being set apart as nonutilitarian objects of attitudes of serious respect, awe, or reverence. The whole of life may be permeated with sacredness; but the existence of numerous norms of proper conduct does not automatically imply that any of them have a genuinely religious significance. If religion in the broadest sense centers in a deeply serious—even if in some way "joyful"—concern with the ultimate ends of existence, then the essential quality of secularization might be the replacement of such central concern with the immediacies of instrumental tasks and goals, of hedonic gratifications, and of social relationships of low intensity and slight commitment.

How, then, can we appraise secularization in American culture? These propositions are ventured: (1) Interest in religion is a drastically changing variable, linked with such factors as social stress, attacks upon religion, degree of mass involvement in other types of values. (2) No clear permanent trend in secularization in all aspects of life has been conclusively established. (3) Present tendencies include continued vitality of sect-making elements, slow erosion of religious beliefs in sophisticated strata, pressures toward revived concern among the bulk of the population. Neither intense mass religiosity nor complete secularism appears to be permanent historical possibilities. America is not irreligious, but a whole configuration of forces has pressed in the direction of a slow but pervasive withdrawal of attention and affect from the organized traditional religions. It is frequently suggested that modern nationalistic values and practices are in some way a secular counterpart of traditional religion. Much of the personality identification and involvement once centered in the churches appears now to flow into various types of private, personal relations, or into nationalistic or other secular "religions." Within organized religion, the older symbols of sin, repentance, heaven, hell, salvation, and associated beliefs have slowly receded in favor of emphases on fellowship, ethics, humanitarianism, and civic concern.[9] The great religious holy days have become, more and more, simply "holidays."[1]

---

[8] *Yearbook of American Churches for 1968, op. cit.*, p. 228.

[9] Benjamin Franklin Crawford, *Changing Conceptions of Religion as Revealed in One Hundred Years of Methodist Hymnology* (2 vols.) (Carnegie, Pa.: Carnegie Church Press, 1938). See the basic discussion in O'Dea, *op. cit.*, pp. 86–97.

[1] James H. Barnett, *The American Christmas: A Study in National Culture* (New York: Macmillan, 1954); Mark Benney, *et al.*, "Christmas in an Apartment Hotel." *American Journal of Sociology*, LXV, 3 (November 1959), 233–240; James H. Barnett, "The

The pattern of secularization in the United States contrasts sharply with that found in Western Europe and Great Britain.[2] In both the latter cases, membership and attendance have declined; and in the continental countries militant secularist and anticlerical movements have been prominent. In the United States, the formally secular nature of the state, from the very first, meant that political opposition need not carry religious implications; and political liberalism or radicalism did not have to be antireligious. Secularization in American society could occur quietly, almost imperceptibly, and at no point has seemed to represent an irreversible step.

A broad hypothesis, worthy of intensive study, is that the main result of modern secularization of organized religion is the destruction of the belief in a transcendental being, which removes both the supernatural sanctions for our ethical system and a central value focus for the established beliefs.[3] In any event, it might be said that ethics tends to replace a transcendental deity. We have no systematic empirical evidence as to whether, to any degree, an intense belief in a deity to whom the individual is in some sense personally accountable provides both an active tension and a unifying symbolic focus for values and beliefs; nor do we know how such a religious conviction affects tangible social relations.[4] Nevertheless, the widespread loss of a belief in a transcendental God would be the most far-reaching aspect of secularization—deeper in its long-range implications than disaffection from any particular organized religion. In a period of history when many theologians have discussed the decline of traditional forms of faith in terms of "de-Christianization" or the "death of God," the search for new foundations of theism is intensive.[5]

Much of the criticism of religious life in the years since World War II has not involved a direct challenge to values espoused by or identified with religious faiths but rather has centered upon the alleged failure of organized religion to advocate and practice its own main ideals effectively. In particular, many critics accuse organized religion of capitulating to the secular status quo, of having become a comfortable and respectable mode of adjustment to the existing state of society.[6] Of course, every collectivity or individual that in any way alleviates social distress without changing

Easter Festival: A Study in Cultural Change," *American Sociological Review*, 14, 1 (February 1949), 62–70.

2 An excellent brief analysis: Bryan R. Wilson, *Religion in Secular Society: A Sociological Comment* (London: C. A. Watts & Co., Ltd., 1966), pp. 86–102.

3 For an incisive evaluation of major theological developments in modern Christianity, see John Macquarrie, *Principles of Christian Theology* (New York: Scribner, 1966).

4 For example, there has been some disciplined speculation to the effect that a certain ethical universalism, combined with "impersonalism" in social relations, results from neo-Calvinistic religious beliefs in which duty to God takes the central place and other human beings become means to the glory of the deity.

5 See, for example, Leslie Dewart, *The Future of Belief: Theism in a World Come of Age* (New York: Herder & Herder, 1966).

6 Charles Y. Glock, Benjamin B. Ringer, and Earl R. Babbie, *To Comfort and to Challenge: A Dilemma of the Contemporary Church* (Berkeley and Los Angeles: University of California Press, 1967), pp. 2–7.

the sources thereof—or which aids individuals to make psychological adjustments to frustration, deprivation, value contradictions and the like—obviously may be charged with helping to maintain an undesirable state of society. This is the case in those activities of organized religion which are alleged to aid individuals to accept an unjust or ineffective set of societal arrangements.[7]

In general, the available data do indeed suggest that religious involvement is greater among persons whose needs for comfort and support are greater and whose nonreligious resources for coping with strain and distress are relatively small. For example, Glock's study found that persons in positions offering little prestige or social deference and approval—the elderly, the familyless, women, parishioners of relatively low socioeconomic status—were more likely to be highly involved in church life than their less deprived counterparts.[8]

In any complex religious organization, there are likely to be differences in the belief system as it is formulated and understood at "high" levels—by officials, theologians, seminary teachers, and publicists—and the popular, grass-roots, everyday beliefs of the bulk of adherents. Ethical imperatives seen by leaders may not be regarded as relevant by the bulk of adherents. A related finding from a study of members of the Protestant Episcopal Church is that the extent of religious involvement is not correlated with attitudes toward whether or not the church should actively challenge social ills and injustices. However, the more actively involved members show a "religiocentric commitment" which emphasizes individual faith and regeneration and tends to regard more direct social action by the church as inappropriate or superfluous.[9]

However, were participation in organized religion *primarily* a matter of the more objectively economically deprived elements of a society seeking emotional solace or other-worldly compensations, one would expect greatest participation among those of lowest socioeconomic position. In the United States, on the contrary, the lower strata participate less. Nor is this explained simply by a generally lower level of participation in organizations: differences in religious activity between blue-collar and white-collar strata remain when participation in other organizations is held constant. However, there is evidence that sectarian religiosity and organized political or economic action may represent alternative responses to economic deprivation.[1]

[7] See any sampling of these commentaries: Peter L. Berger, *The Noise of Solemn Assemblies* (Garden City, N.Y.: Doubleday, 1961), and *The Precarious Vision* (Garden City, N.Y.: Doubleday, 1961); Pierre Berton, *The Comfortable Pew* (Toronto: McClelland and Stewart, 1965); Harvey Cox, *The Secular City* (New York: Macmillan, 1965); Martin Marty, *The New Shape of American Religion* (New York: Harper & Row, 1959); Gibson Winter, *The Suburban Captivity of the Churches* (New York: Macmillan, 1962).

[8] Glock, *et al., op. cit.*, p. 205.

[9] Glock, *et al., op. cit.*, chap. 6; see p. 172: "people are motivated to become deeply involved in a church out of primarily personal concerns; for example, the feeling of deprived status in the secular society."

[1] Cf. Rodney Stark, "Class, Radicalism, and Religious Involvement in Great Britain," *American Sociological Review*, 29, 5 (October 1964), 698–706.

Yet, even in "postindustrial" America, the tendency of low-income strata to favor sectlike religious organizations as well as their strong tendency to embrace fundamentalism continue to be prominent in Protestantism.[2]

Participants in the Pentecostal sects and denominations tend to be persons of low education and low income, in less prestigious occupations, migrants rather than settled residents, with few organizational memberships, and poorly integrated into stable social groups outside the family. This generalization, supported by several studies in the United States, is consistent with findings concerning similar religious movements among American Indians, in Melanesia, and in the Middle East. Yet the exact sources and consequences of these facts are not self-evident. The usual description of the Holiness sects emphasizes their fundamentalism, otherworldly orientation, emphasis on personal salvation, emotionally expressive religious services, esoteric beliefs, and "legalistic" ascetic moral codes.[3] It is commonly thought that one of the main social consequences of these sects is to promote acceptance of culturally marginal and economically deprived social positions.[4] The consequences of the ascetic commitments and religious disciplines of these groups, however, may not be fully caught in such formulations; worthy of future study is the idea that the sects in question may also inculcate and reinforce values of self-direction and achievement.[5] From the accumulated studies now in hand it is plain that much progress has been made in analyzing the sociocultural correlates of differences in religious affiliation, belief, and practice. For all the increased empirical evidence that has been accumulated, however, the challenge of unexplained variations remains great. Thus, when we know that "fundamentalist" beliefs in the Southern Appalachians are more prevalent in rural than in urban areas, among the less educated, and among the lower socioeconomic strata, it is still necessary to explain why the general level of acceptance is so high in all subgroupings.[6] For this demonstration, a wider and yet precise comparative analysis is needed—and thus far, lacking.

### The "Return to Religion"

To many observers during the 1950's it seemed that the long-time trend toward secularization in American culture had been reversed. Even allowing for unreliability and error in the statistics, there were evidences of increased church membership and participation.[7] Public piety was widespread;

---

[2] N. J. Demerath, III, *Social Class in American Protestantism* (Chicago: Rand-McNally, 1965).

[3] Benton Johnson, "Do Holiness Sects Socialize in Dominant Values?" *Social Forces*, 39, 4 (May 1961), 309–316.

[4] Pope, *op. cit.*; John B. Holt, *op. cit.*

[5] Johnson, *op. cit.*

[6] Thomas R. Ford, "Status, Residence, and Fundamentalist Religious Beliefs in the Southern Appalachians," *Social Forces*, 39, 1 (October 1960), 41–49.

[7] Thomas Ford Hoult, *The Sociology of Religion* (New York: Dryden Press, 1958), chap. 5.

political leaders still used the language of religion.[8] The mass media gave much attention to religious topics. Although church attendance and membership are very imperfect indexes of religious involvement, the data do show substantial increases, both over the long run and in recent decades. Church membership as a percentage of total population went from 49 in 1940 to 64 in 1965; attendance increased from 37 percent in 1940 to 49 in 1958 and then decreased to 44 in 1965. However, there is a long-time trend of declining ratios of clergymen to population; and financial contributions have not increased proportionately with income.

Yet, much disagreement exists as to the meaning of these changes. For one thing, the "religion" to which many people have returned itself may be highly secularized—a vague belief in the goodness of religion, or of "the American way of life," or a kind of spiritual tranquilizer, or a recipe for easily attained "peace of mind." No one knows how deeply religious the new participants are. It seems certain, however, that in Protestant and Jewish groups much of the content of present-day religious activity and thought would have been regarded as secular ("worldly") even a half century ago.[9] In its optimism and its stress on social and psychological adjustment, the alleged revival of religion still embodies some of the long-standing features of religion in America described in earlier pages.

Furthermore, fluctuations in interest and participation are not new in American religious life. Waves of revivalism and religious awakenings have recurred from the early eighteenth century down to the present.[1] After the decades of low interest and participation the Great Awakening associated with the name of George Whitefield prevailed for a generation after 1725. Another such period extended over a period of about forty years from 1795. In the last quarter of the nineteenth century and extending down to the eve of World War I, a succession of revivalistic ministers (for example, Dwight L. Moody and Billy Sunday) reacted against modernizing tendencies in Protestantism and brought "old-fashioned religion" to an industrializing society. Newer forms of revivalism continue in the second half of the twentieth century, as exemplified by Billy Graham.[2]

There is no convincing evidence of a mass revival of supernatural beliefs, or of intense commitment to the search for salvation as the primary goal of life, or the infusion of religion into all aspects of daily living. Thus,

[8] By now it is generally forgotten that none of the first seven Presidents of the United States was formally a member of a church. (See Pfeffer, *op. cit.*, p. 29.) On the lack of religious participation and commitment at the time of the founding of the republic, see Gustav A. Koch, *Republican Religion: The American Revolution and the Cult of Reason* (New York: Henry Holt, 1933).

[9] "even apart from profound change of doctrine or faith, there has been an accommodation in religious conduct and activities to the forces and inventions of secular life to such a degree that the practical meaning and influence of religion has been revolutionized." Herbert W. Schneider, *Religion in Twentieth Century America* (Cambridge, Mass.: Harvard University Press, 1952), p. 12.

[1] Whitney R. Cross, *The Burned-Over District: The Social and Intellectual History of Enthusiastic Religion in Western New York, 1800–1850* (Ithaca, N.Y.: Cornell University Press, 1950), esp. pp. 1–30.

[2] William G. McLaughlin, Jr., *Modern Revivalism: Charles Grandison Finney to Billy Graham* (New York: Ronald Press, 1959).

the so-called revival of religion in recent years has been marked by a strongly instrumental emphasis: religious belief and practice is advocated because it promotes family unity, or mental health, or social conformity, or national loyalty. At the same time, much vagueness is found as to just what it means to "be religious," a vagueness tending toward eclecticism concerning specific creeds. Often, it seems, such mild commitment and formless beliefs would hardly appear to devout and fervent believers as "religion" at all.

Yet this description fits only the more liberal or secularized main-line denominations; and some of the most rapidly growing denominations hold firmly to specific traditional creeds or else claim a return to original Christian beliefs. Overall, the great majority of Americans hold to conservative or fundamentalistic beliefs; a very crude estimate would suggest that at least two-thirds of church members would fall on the religiously conservative side.

The "new denominationalism," as Glock and Stark have termed it, consists of the clustering of major Protestant denominations according to degree of acceptance of traditional central beliefs: the existence of God, the divinity of Jesus, life after death, faith versus works as bases for salvation, and the like. At one extreme are the fundamentalist groupings in which nearly all members express firm belief in central orthodox beliefs; these include the Southern Baptists (the largest single Protestant denomination), the Missouri Synod Lutherans, and most of the small sects. Somewhat less frequent adherence to orthodoxy is found in the conservative denominations such as the American Baptists and the American Lutherans. Still more secularized or liberal are the Disciples of Christ and the Presbyterians. Finally, there are the liberal denominations—primarily Congregational, Episcopalian, and Methodist—in which a majority of the members do not testify to firm belief in the main traditional doctrines.[3]

### Optimistic Beliefs

The reciprocal relation between specifically religious beliefs and other elements of the culture is exemplified by the changing nature of basic concepts of man and society held in American religious groups. What has seemed to some commentators to be a peculiar kind of secularization really is a reflection of very early theological formulations. How is one to understand the fact that despite a theology, inherited from Europe, that stressed original sin, the innate depravity of man, and the evils of the world and the flesh, our religious culture rapidly became permeated with an optimistic view of the perfectibility of man and his institutions? For three centuries there has been a seeming tendency to give lip service to pessimistic religious doctrines while avoiding their (apparent) behavioral implications. The resolute self-confidence and optimism so often noted in American history derived partly from religious ideas and values; but its main roots were apparently in other portions of the culture and in the objective situation of a

---

[3] See the summary presented in Charles Y. Glock and Rodney Stark, "Is There an American Protestantism?" *Trans-Action*, 3, 1 (November–December 1965), 8–13 and 48–49. The full study is reported in *Religion and Society in Tension* (Chicago: Rand-McNally, 1965).

wealthy, strong, and expanding society. But this interpretation of the development would be much too superficial, for there has been also a continuing "optimistic" source in the religious traditions themselves—specifically in the powerful ideal of establishing the kingdom of God on earth
through a "blessed community" of religiously motivated men. Recurrently
expressed from the time of the Massachusetts Bay Colony, through aboli-
tionism, the social gospel, and various movements for social reforms, this
idea continues to operate as a "hidden agenda" behind many activities that
have a surface appearance of secular optimism. In the modern period the
social activism of the churches incorporates a recognition of some of the
complexity and resistance of opposing forces.

Nor are such doctrinal sources of faith in social improvement confined
to the oldest Protestant denominations. In fact, two of the denominations
that are comparatively recent in origin and completely native to the American scene—Christian Science and the Church of Jesus Christ of the Latter-
Day Saints—are both resolutely optimistic (in very different ways) in viewing the human condition and man's power to affect his own destiny. The
doctrines of the Mormon Church contain strong emphases upon active
achievement and self-improvement, stressing mastery of self and the external world.[4] Spiritual development is progressive and unceasing. Men are
free agents, and their development depends upon knowledge and discipline.
Every man has the potentialities of "becoming like God." High evaluation
of education and recreation follow from the basic doctrines. The theology
decisively rejects any doctrine of original sin and regards men as wholly
free to choose good or evil. There is universal resurrection after death—
unconditional redemption—for all living creatures. Beyond this general
salvation, there are degrees of exalted immortality, achieved by degrees of
performance in earthly life.

Of course, the original religious presuppositions with their intellectual
demands and their calls for disciplined effort often are lost in the popu-
larization of optimistic faith. Calls to diluted and "easy" optimism—
along with exhortations couched in activistic, pragmatic, and individualistic
terms—are conspicuous in popular religious inspirational literature, in
which religion is credited with great efficacy in obtaining worldly success
and personal emotional security.[5] Nevertheless, it is significant that even
among the most sophisticated theological spokesmen, a period of pessimistic
adaptation in mid-century was followed by efforts to formulate a "theology
of hope." We have yet to witness a basically nonaffirmative religion.

### Political Orientation

Religion may be regarded by members of some societies as one among
several institutionalized sectors, and not necessarily the most important. Or

[4] Thomas O'Dea, *The Mormons* (Chicago: University of Chicago Press, 1957). For a
more detailed historical account: Leonard J. Arrington, *Great Basin Kingdom: An Economic History of the Latter-Day Saints, 1830–1900* (Cambridge, Mass.: Harvard University Press, 1958).

[5] See description of the content of forty-six best-selling inspirational books (1875–1955)
in Louis Schneider and Sanford M. Dornbusch, *Popular Religion: Inspirational Books in
America* (Chicago: University of Chicago Press, 1958).

it may be regarded as the center, the source, the criterion for all other institutions. Certainly the Western religious tradition has contained the central idea of religion as "beyond culture," as a source illuminating, transforming, and judging the entire secular culture. Although this claim to a unique position has weakened, it remains true that Judaic-Christian ethical standards could hardly be promulgated by the churches without any reference to political issues and events; and the churches, as a whole, have always insisted upon the right, at least, to make moral judgments about the social order. In making these judgments, the churches, because of the principle of separation, become outside critics or proponents—"friends of the court"—rather than integral components of the system of secular authority. Nearly every variant group and stratum in the society has had the support of some church or sect that interpreted Christian doctrine in the light of that group's needs and interests. The political position of the churches, especially perhaps of the Protestant denominations, has varied accordingly and has changed drastically over the course of time. The separatist tradition has encouraged political neutrality—for example, "preachers should not meddle in politics"—and the divided political allegiances of the members of most large denominations has worked against partisan (party) endorsement by the organized religious bodies. Yet by serving as public forums and pressure groups the churches have a political weight important enough to be a tangible factor in the calculations of practicing politicians.[6]

The political thought of the churches has been strongly shaped by the class affiliations of the membership, by economic and political pressures, by the changing dominant interests and values of the wider secular culture.[7] There was a long period lasting into the fourth quarter of the nineteenth century when the main, although not the only, pattern of organized religion was to support doctrines of laissez faire and sanctity of property. Wealth was regarded as a reward of moral virtue; social rewards and deprivations were believed part of a divine plan. This relatively unified outlook began to crumble in the 1880's and 1890's. The evangelical equalitarian element, always germinal in Western religions, then came increasingly to the fore, notably in the social gospel.[8] Although not a direct political movement, the "liberal" formulations of the social gospel helped to prepare the way for new concepts of the social responsibilities of the state in the twentieth century.

Thus, religious beliefs and values, although molded by nonreligious forces, have their own inner dynamics. It seems to be impossible to predict

---

[6] Political involvement of organized religious groups appears to be increasing. See Yinger, *op. cit.*, chap. 9; Hoult, *op. cit.*, chap. 9.

[7] For an excellent detailed account of this, see Henry F. May, *Protestant Churches and Industrial America* (New York: Harper & Row, 1949). The backgrounds of neo-orthodox positions are specified by Donald B. Myers, *The Protestant Search for Political Realism, 1919–1941* (Berkeley: University of California Press, 1960).

[8] Note also the rise of Christian socialism in this period; as represented by such leaders as Wendell Phillips, W. D. P. Bliss, and George D. Herron. See J. Dombrowski, *The Early Days of Christian Socialism in America* (New York: Columbia University Press, 1936).

in accurate detail the political thought of the churches from a knowledge of the most immediate economic and political interests of their constituents.

In the study of human behavior, some of the most obvious errors are the most seductive. Nothing is easier than to ascertain the nominal membership of individuals in different religious groupings—and then to attribute the most diverse behavioral patterns to these differing religious affiliations. Thus, it has been said on the basis of certain limited data, Catholics are low in educational aspirations, or Protestants emphasize deferred gratification, or Jews are political liberals—all by implication, because of differences in religious faith. But the most elementary sociological considerations would immediately call for testing such generalizations by examining the other major group memberships and statuses of the populations in question —socioeconomic position, rural or urban origin and residence, region of the country, ethnic or racial category, educational level or background, and so on. Should differences associated with religious membership continue to hold when such other factors are taken into account, a more refined analysis would then extend to the specific beliefs and practices of individuals. It might turn out, for instance, that certain nonreligious differences are closely associated with orthodox beliefs but not with amount of interaction with coreligionists, whereas other differences correlate strongly with frequency of religious participation but hardly at all with religious doctrines held. In this case, one has at least the beginning of a genuine analysis; and the more nearly one can by refined statistical methods and study designs separate the covariation of social phenomena with *different* components of religion, the better the possibility of strong inferences about what causes what.

### A Note on Catholic and Protestant Orientations

We have emphasized the fact that, from a wide comparative perspective, the main branches of the Judaic-Christian tradition have many important beliefs and values in common. There are, however, perceptible disagreements in American culture, constituting the immediate source or symbol of appreciable tension between different religious groups. Tension over real differences in values and beliefs is usually compounded with other sources of cleavage: class and ethnic affiliations, economic competition, "projective" antipathies, and others.[9] We are not concerned here with intergroup relations but with certain salient differences in *institutional* beliefs and practices.

One can speak here of *tendencies* only; not all members or officials even of the relatively unified Roman Catholic Church agree about all the matters mentioned below.[1] Still, certain differences in beliefs, implied values, ritual

[9] For certain analytic hypotheses on these problems see Robin M. Williams, Jr., *The Reduction of Intergroup Tensions* (New York: Social Science Research Council, 1947), pp. 51 ff, and *Strangers Next Door* (Englewood Cliffs, N.J.: Prentice-Hall, 1964), chap. 10.

[1] A common Protestant stereotype of the Catholic organization as a completely rigid hierarchy, with detailed control over the beliefs and actions of every parishioner, is highly exaggerated. The church claims ultimate authority and stands absolutely on certain dogmas but is highly elastic in many matters falling outside of the inner core of doctrine

practices, and form of organization are clearly present as social tendencies, rather than as either-or contrasts. American Catholicism, of course, retains the absolute conviction that *specific* doctrines are vitally important and that a vague belief in a generalized religion is not enough. The church holds that its faith is the one true faith and on the basis of this premise has in the past held positions, for example, concerning interfaith cooperation, rather different from that of many Protestants. Since the great "renewal" set in motion by the Second Vatican Council in 1963–1965, many elements within the church have moved strongly toward interfaith cooperation and ecumenical emphases.[2] Some changes have also occurred in church polity, lessening somewhat the contrast between the Catholic organization and the presbyterian and congregational forms within which most Protestants participate. The norms of organization are closely tied to differences in the basic cultural definition of the church; in the one case, it is regarded as divinely instituted; in the other, as a human device for collaboration in religious affairs. On the one hand, Church officials are conceived to be vice-regents of the deity; on the other, respect for ministers tends to be more strongly tempered with a view of them as fallible humans, imperfectly seeking religious truth. Although some important Protestant denominations are liturgical, most of them tend to minimize rituals and church symbolisms. In the Roman Catholic Church there are the seven sacraments of baptism, Holy Eucharist, penance, confirmation, matrimony, holy orders, and extreme unction. Members are bound by the Ten Commandments, and by six obligatory rules (precepts) concerning attendance at Mass, confession, communion, fasting and abstinence, contributions to the church, and obedience to marriage laws. In addition the moral teachings of the church are specific and elaborate, extending into every major area of life. Protestants generally accept only baptism and communion as obligatory sacraments, although marriage partakes of the same quality. Moral rules differ considerably among denominations, ranging from vague general principles to lists of highly specific prohibitions and prescriptions.

Catholic and Protestant groups also differ broadly in the emphasis laid on the individual person as over against the corporate body. Under medieval Catholicism, the individualistic implications of the Christian emphasis on the salvation of the individual were largely neutralized by the role of the church as the supreme earthly repository of divine authority and salvation. The individual had access to the deity only through the church hierarchy, a disciplined religious group controlling dogma, creed, and ritual, and suppressing dissenters or incorporating them into various special religious orders. Although not promulgated until the late nineteenth century (1870), the doctrine of Papal infallibility in matters of faith and morals emphasized the contrast with Protestantism.

In Protestantism, on the other hand, the Scriptures became the touch-

and ritual. The common Catholic stereotypes of Protestantism also have their factual defects, of course.

[2] For an illuminating study of attitudes among Roman Catholic priests toward change, see Sister Marie Augusta, Neal, S.N.D., *Values and Interests in Social Change* (Englewood Cliffs, N.J.: Prentice-Hall, 1965).

stone of orthodoxy; and since there was no universal church to decide between differing interpretations, the individual had to judge for himself. "In the last analysis . . . the emphasis was not on the preservation of a tradition of values *common* to the members of the community, even to all Christians, but on the safeguarding of the freedom of conscience of the individual in his *differences* from others. . . ."[3] The doctrine of free access of the individual to religious salvation thus contained an inherent centrifugal element. One consequence was the multiplication of denominations and sects as diverse doctrinal interpretations emerged.

It is probably fruitless to speculate upon what eventual limits may be revealed in the various movements toward cooperation among and consolidation of religious groupings. There is abundant evidence of many convergences in ritual and polity, and in the nonreligious social and cultural characteristics of several of the largest Protestant denominations, and between these bodies and the Roman Catholic church. Furthermore, some formerly crucial differences in moral teachings appear to be moving toward workable resolutions, and even some creedal differences may turn out to be subordinate to acceptable common reformulations.[4] However, there is no indication at all that certain dogmas now regarded by the bodies holding them as absolutely definitive of central religious truth are open to such reconsideration. As Father Gustave Weigel put it, on these matters, "the Protestant is not yet ripe for conversion nor will the Catholic ever be."[5] Although it does not necessarily constitute an unbridgeable difference, Marianism—adoration of or devotion to the Madonna—is an example of Catholic belief and practice not shared by nonliturgical Protestants, rarely well understood by them, and not accepted when understood.

Participation in the public activities of organized religion is greatest among Catholics and least among Jews, with Protestants falling in between. (Because much of Jewish religious observance centers in the home and because Protestant and Catholic groupings differ greatly in the obligatory quality of participation, these differences do not necessarily accurately reflect "involvement" or commitment.) Among Protestants, participation is greater among women than among men; it is greater for children and older people than for young adults. Participation is greater in those social positions where we would expect "religious need" to be greatest, for instance, among widows and the aged,[6] but this tendency is counteracted to some extent by factors making for high general participation in organiza-

---

[3] Parsons, *op. cit.*, p. 54.

[4] A common Bible, acceptable to Catholics and Protestants, is now mentioned by religious scholars as a definite and fairly early possibility. See Walter M. Abbott, S.J., "The Ecumenical Movement in America: 1990," *Catholic Mind*, LXIII, 1196.

[5] Quoted in Salisbury, *op. cit.*, p. 278. Original citation: "Catholic and Protestant: End of a War?" *Thought*, XXXIII, 130 (Autumn 1958), 383.

[6] "From the psychological point of view, then, religion has its greatest relevance to the points of maximum strain and tension in human life as well as to positive affirmations of faith in life, often in the face of these strains." Talcott Parsons, *Religious Perspectives of College Teaching in Sociology and Social Psychology* (New Haven, Conn.: The Edward W. Hazen Foundation, n. d.), p. 15.

tions, such as stable residence and middle-class position.[7] The total rate of participation clearly depends also upon the obligatory norms and organization of the religious bodies. The Catholic Church goes further in requiring total commitment to specific doctrines and rituals. The clarity of requirements and the definiteness of authority in the Roman Catholic bodies contrasts with the diffuse organization and varied theology often found among the many Protestant denominations.

We have pointed to sources of unity and of accommodation among the major religious bodies. It is essential to add that different religious groupings do take opposing stands on important social questions. Their opposition is not a mere matter of ignorance and prejudice.

Relations among members and leaders of religious groupings in the United States often are competitive, sometimes cooperative; only rarely in recent decades, however, have there been sizeable conflicts in which the effort has been made to displace a rival totally from competition. Nevertheless, numerous instances continually arise in which the direct opposition of faith groupings results in what Salisbury calls contravention—the actions of one grouping in protesting or advancing its own beliefs, values, and interests result in the blocking of others in the pursuit of their religious or secular goals.[8]

It is a familiar fact that there are radical divergences among the major value-orientations distinctive of the various organized faith groupings in the United States. A partial list of the more important of such divergences that may become involved in interreligious opposition or strife includes the following:

1. Whether there is a sharp distinction between a religious and a secular realm.
2. Whether religion is regarded as one among many of the interests of men or as something that pervades or dominates all aspects of behavior and experience.
3. Whether all religions are considered to have some validity, as "ways" or "paths" toward an ultimate reality or whether only one specific religion is true and all others are in error or positively sinful.
4. Whether authentic, valid religious status can be established solely through individual experience or only through the medium of a divinely established organization.
5. Orientations toward both secular and religious authority; evaluation of discipline.
6. Whether major stress is placed upon the religious organization ("church") as a community of individual believers, or as a disciplinary agency, or as a sacramental order.

[7] Berelson and Steiner, *Human Behavior, op. cit.*, pp. 392–393. Compare the findings for Great Britain: Michael Argyle, *Religious Behavior* (New York: Free Press, 1959). Also W. Seward Salisbury, *op. cit.*, pp. 85–90.

[8] Salisbury, *op. cit.*, pp. 254–269; John J. Kane, *Catholic-Protestant Conflicts in America* (Chicago: Henry Regnery Company, 1955); Kenneth Underwood, *Protestant and Catholic* (Boston: Beacon Press, 1957).

7. Whether the individual's particular religious orientation and affiliation are accepted as a matter of choice or election or as given.
8. The evaluation of individual religious questioning and speculation.
9. Whether social morality is deemed impossible without commitment to organized religion or without faith in the deity.
10. Whether the existing social order is to be attacked as evil, shunned, tolerated, supported, or reformed; whether organized religion should seek to influence "secular" social action, and if so, how.
11. Estimation and evaluation of the scope, quality, and potentialities of human intelligence and rationality.
12. The evaluation of science.
13. Whether human nature is considered to be basically evil, good, mixed, or neutral.
14. Estimation and evaluation of the possibilities of human improvement: the perfectibility of man versus the conception of man as a creature inherently weak, fallible, and prone to error and evil.
15. The scope and quality of personal responsibility for conduct, total culpability versus environmental extenuation.
16. Whether asceticism is positively or negatively valued.
17. Orientation toward suffering and punishment.
18. Orientation to religion as a means of "therapy" or "adjustment"; religious commitment as a solution for personal difficulties or for social, economic, and political problems.
19. Estimation and evaluation of the possibilities and means of resolving conflicts arising from differing religious views.
20. Evaluation of religious heterogeneity, religious "liberty," and "toleration;" approval of sectarian diversity versus ecumenical movements.

This listing could be extended to include such important additional matters as conflicts of religious and secular assumptions concerning value priorities and hierarchies, or the use of religion to promote and obtain non-religious goals. Even this limited inventory is enough, however, to suggest in a fairly special way that divergent value orientations, associated with particular faith groupings, contribute directly to interreligious dissension in matters of public social policy and personal social conduct. Note again that this implies that interreligious conflict is not merely a matter of "prejudice." We are here confronted with real differences in the values to which people are, or may be, deeply committed.[9]

Many early Protestant groups stressed a doctrine of total, integral religious responsibility of the individual. Sin was no longer regarded as an isolated act that could be wiped out by specific amends, confession, or ritual absolution. If one takes seriously the most rigorous Protestant concepts, then the soul is saved or damned as a whole; and specific repentances alone are no guarantee of salvation. This concept of religious personality

[9] Robin M. Williams, Jr., "Religion, Value-orientations, and Intergroup Conflict," *The Journal of Social Issues*, XII, 3 (1956), 16–17. Reprinted by permission of The Society for the Psychological Study of Social Issues.

requires a rigorous discipline of all activities during the total life-span of the person. Rousseau had this necessity in mind when he said that Protestantism, in attempting to escape from the monastery, had instead made every man a monk; that is, that the "heroic" discipline formerly reserved for the religious elect was now doctrinally obligatory for everyone.

The Reformation was individualistic in still another sense. When religious salvation was a *strongly desired goal*, the emphasis on the direct relation between the individual and God tended to deemphasize the personal relations of individuals to others, either singly or corporatively. In the ideal-typical case, the relation to the Deity was thus literally all-important; other individuals were important only insofar as they affected in turn one's own relation to the Deity. Thus, to the degree that the doctrine was accepted in actual fact, social relations became indirect and instrumental in a unique way. They were relations *through* the common object of religious attention and devotion; they were instrumental in the measure that other persons were means or hindrances to one's own salvation.

Undoubtedly the rigor of this ideal-typical position has been greatly relaxed in modern times; and it is entirely possible that the mass of Protestants never fully accepted the sterner theological formulations of it. However, many Protestants do differ from the Catholic position in the respects suggested above. Broad analyses of historical and statistical data—such as the works of Weber and Troeltsch—have supplied some highly illuminating clues as to the significance of these differences in religious value-orientations for social conduct. More precise analysis now awaits further research and theoretical development.[1]

The part played by religious background in occupational values and motivation—a question of incessant concern since Weber's *The Protestant Ethic* posed the issues sharply—has been the object of several important studies. Gerhard Lenski suggested in a study of a Detroit sample that Catholics in comparison with Protestants are likely to show less "economic rationality" and to be disinclined to enter scientific careers.[2] In contrast, Andrew Greeley's analysis of a national sample of college graduates finds that Catholics are as likely as Protestants to plan a research career. Although Catholics are most likely to choose careers in a large company, whereas Jews tend to choose law and medicine and Protestants to choose education as an occupation, the data do not show that Catholics are any less interested than Protestants in making money, on the one hand, or in scientific pursuits, on the other. For this highly educated population, then, differences associated with religious background do not suggest a marked concentration of "Protestant ethic" characteristics among Protestants.[3]

It must be said, however, that for the most part, the data and the debates over research dealing with Catholic-Protestant differences in social

[1] The above sketch of certain aspects of Protestant and Catholic orientation is, of course, highly selective and is formulated in ideal-typical terms, having no pretension to completeness. It simply suggests once more how certain connections between religious phenomena and the social structure can be posed for empirical research.

[2] Cf. Lenski, *op. cit.*

[3] Greeley, *op. cit.*

mobility and achievement values have not actually borne directly on the issues raised so long ago by Max Weber. It is not surprising that as Catholics, Jews, and Protestants of various kinds have been exposed over a long period to many common conditions and influences in American life, many of the social and cultural differences originally associated with religious affiliation have been reduced. Differences have not been eliminated —for example, Catholics tend more often than Protestants to define life satisfactions in religious terms and certainly to view the clergy in a radically different way.

It is precisely the highly diffuse embeddedness of intrinsic religion in pervasive and enduring sets of social relationships that so complicates analysis of the connections between "religion" and "society." For the *associational* involvement of members of religious groupings in the specifically organized corporate activities of worship may be either dominant or subordinate in relation to communal involvement in informal interactions with coreligionists. More specifically, the influence of religious beliefs, values, and practices upon various aspects of social behavior is always compounded with two other large categories of influence: (1) the formal and informal group memberships and attendant personal relationships that grow up primarily as a consequence of membership in a particular faith or sectarian grouping; (2) the historically associated social and cultural characteristics of members of particular religious grouping (low or high socioeconomic position, urban or rural concentration, ethnic origin)— characteristics that may or may not be causally connected with the *content* of religious belief and practices. This situation calls for care and sophistication in sociological analysis. If one finds, for example, that Protestants more frequently than Catholics have higher income and occupational standing, and more formal education,[4] it clearly will not do simply to assume that strictly religious elements somehow account for the differences. Analytic caution is further called for by the enormous variations within "Protestantism"—theologically and socially there are vast differences between Unitarians and Presbyterians and Baptists and Pentecostal Holiness adherents. In a study of the population of Detroit, Mayer and Sharp found that on a scale of economic and social achievements Jews and Episcopalians were at the top, whereas Catholics were matched by the small Protestant sects, and Baptists fell at the bottom of the rankings. *Average* differences among the three main faiths, therefore, may conceal as much as they reveal. On the other hand, when Mayer and Sharp attempt to equate roughly the various religious groupings, for such ascribed "handicaps" as rural origin, foreign background, and extent of experience in Detroit, the main differences in achievement remain. In view of the seemingly contradictory findings of some other studies,[5] however, these results can not be taken as conclusive. They do suggest that the *total complex* of factors associated with being Catholic or Baptist is conducive to low economic

[4] Mayer and Sharp, *op. cit.* See the major interpretative analysis of Detroit data in Lenski, *op. cit.*

[5] Seymour Martin Lipset and Reinhard Bendix, *Social Mobility in Industrial Society* (Berkeley: University of California Press, 1959); Mack, Murphy, and Yellin, *op. cit.*

standing in contrast to being Episcopalian, Jewish, Calvinist, or semi-Christian (Unitarian).

### And the Case of Judaism

The three main divisions within Judaism—Orthodox, Conservative, and Reform—are products of a complicated history of adjustments and resistances to the new conditions encountered by this ancient faith in American society. In spite of considerable prejudice and discrimination, the environing society has generally been one of religious freedom. In the absence of the constraints of the ghetto, Jews rapidly assimilated many of the behavior patterns and beliefs and values of the dominant Protestant society. As they moved up the socioeconomic scale, the detailed rituals and taboos of Orthodoxy became less compelling and less attractive. Secularism made heavy inroads. The Reform movement attempted to retain the identity of an ethnic church while adapting drastically to the American environment. It carried forward trends, which had already begun in Europe, toward modification of dietary rules (*Kashrut*), changes in the "decorum" of synagogue services and in forms of worship. Family pews replaced the traditional segregated seating of men and women; "American"-style sermons became more common. Orthodoxy meanwhile struggled to preserve the sacred tradition in its fullness. Conservative Judaism came into being as a "middle way," modifying forms of worship and organization while holding to what were regarded as the essential religious beliefs.[6] It aims to be thoroughly "American" but to retain a distinct *religious* identity, even as assimilation gradually erases ethnic distinctiveness. Many of the changes in forms of worship represented responses to felt dissonance with middle-class Protestant values and practices. The strains were numerous and specific; for example, the traditional position of women under Orthodoxy was felt to violate middle-class norms of sex equality; as male participation declined, under the impact of secularization, the religious role of women became more crucial; the end result was a greatly changed role for women in the Reform and Conservative movements.

In its organization Judaism is highly decentralized. Although there are many superordinate Jewish organizations of a primarily secular and ethnic character, the basic unit of religious organization is the congregation of the local synagogue or temple. This characteristic seems congruent both with the strong sense of community obligation in the tradition and with the emphasis upon the unique religious responsibility of the individual. Orthodox Judaism has no doctrine of "salvation by faith" or "free grace"; one is religiously correct by following a prescribed total way of life, as defined by 613 precepts concerning prayers, holy days, dietary practices, dress, and numerous details of daily behavior.[7]

Judaism centers around the Torah (the first five books of the Scripture),

---

[6] Nathan Glazer, *American Judaism* (Chicago: University of Chicago Press, 1957); Marshall Sklare, *Conservative Judaism: An American Religious Movement* (New York: Free Press, 1955); Yinger, *op. cit.*, pp. 287–293.

[7] A convenient brief description of Judaism is Chapter VII of Salisbury, *op. cit.*, pp. 138–156.

which in a narrative of events from the creation of the world to the death of Moses lays down ethical precepts, ritual forms, laws, doctrines concerning the nature of God, and the conceptions of the community of believers. The extended Talmudic developments and commentaries upon the basic texts represent an enormous historical record of reflection upon nearly every aspect of religious life and ethical doctrine. Partly because of the stress upon detailed law and ethical precepts, Judaism has emphasized knowledge and learning and in later times has not regarded dogmatic and specific creeds as matters of obligatory faith.[8] It has permitted a considerable degree of speculation and of diversity of interpretations. Just the opposite holds for its ethical system; it has elaborated a highly complex system of specific prescriptions for moral behavior.

The social outcomes of the religious tradition include a stress upon philanthropy (derived from *Zedakeh*—charity as social justice), rational mastery of the world and of human impulses (alcoholism and juvenile delinquency are infrequent among nonsecularized Jews), close family ties and community life, respect for intellectual activity, high concern with social justice, strong group consciousness, and a conception of the good life as one of moderation, not extreme self-denial.[9] The doctrines interpose no bar to interfaith cooperation, and Jewish leaders have entered readily into such organizations as the National Conference of Christians and Jews.

### Fundamentalist-Modernist Cleavages

Generalized characterizations—those treating American religious culture "as a whole"—are necessarily inaccurate in detail. They are subject, also, to a less obvious but more serious difficulty, namely, the tendency to distortion arising from overemphasis upon dominant or striking features. Three historical generalizations concerning religion in America deserve reexamination in the light of these considerations: (1) that the society has been primarily influenced by Protestant Christianity, (2) that the dominant types of Protestant denominations have represented the "ascetic" Protestant ethic described by Weber, (3) that something called "fundamentalism" is a single homogeneous religious position. Preceding sections of this chapter have touched upon the first two points; we turn now to the third.

From the very beginnings in colonial America[1] Protestant bodies tended to divide along the great cleavage of salvation by "grace" or "faith" alone versus salvation regarded as an outcome of, or else as signalized by, some

---

[8] This refers to the main thrust of Judaism in twentieth-century America. We are aware that some forms of orthodoxy could be more puritan than the Puritans, and just as dogmatic or authoritative. Yet there was always the religious scholar, whose work might or might not be consistent with the ideas received from the past.

[9] "In probably no other American subculture is so high a value placed upon learning and intellectuality, or upon the helping of the poor by the rich and the weak by the strong, or upon living a good life upon earth in full use of one's body." Lawrence H. Fuchs, "Sources of Jewish Internationalism and Liberalism," in Marshall Sklare (ed.), *The Jews: Social Patterns of an American Group* (New York: Free Press, 1958), p. 599.

[1] Emery Battis, *Saints and Sectaries: Anne Hutchinson and the Antinomian Controversy in the Massachusetts Bay Colony* (Chapel Hill: University of North Carolina Press, 1962).

form of "good works." At the antinomian extremes, the state of religious grace was divorced from rules of conduct.

For purposes of comparison in the preceding sections we formulated a historic ideal-type of one major Protestant orientation. It has been abundantly shown, however, that "Protestant" is a label covering a heterogeneous assemblage of organizations and of systems of belief and practice that would require volumes for any detailed analysis. Here we shall be content with the convenie..t example provided by fundamentalism versus modernism (or liberalism), a division that cuts its way across the total pattern of religion in America. In broadest outline, the Fundamentalist position stresses otherworldly concerns rather than social issues. Fundamentalism has the greatest strength in rural areas, especially in the South. It represents past Protestant orthodoxy, often supported by groups that have been increasingly assaulted by rapid change and by insecurity-engendering cultural influences, but also strongly held by very large numbers of economically prosperous and socially stable persons. It has shown great tenacity in relatively well educated urban populations in those regions and areas in which it had prevailed prior to urbanization.

It is estimated that more than 5 million persons belong to the strictly fundamentalistic groupings that emphasize commitment to what they define as the original, pure Christian doctrines, based upon the infallible teachings of the Bible. Many individuals and groups formerly labeled as fundamentalists now prefer to be known as Conservatives. Whatever the name, however, the basic position characterizing them is an acceptance of religious revelation, apart from science and fallible human reason; a belief in the absolute accuracy and unchangeable truth of the original divinely inspired Bible; belief in a distinct supernatural order; acceptance of Jesus as the Christ who brings salvation; belief in resurrection and an afterlife in Heaven or Hell.[2]

Within Protestant Fundamentalism are two major groupings of denominations and sects: (1) the highly articulate exponents of "original" fundamentalism represented by the American Council of Christian Churches; (2) the more moderate and conciliatory churches, organized as the National Association of Evangelicals, which has encouraged such movements as Youth for Christ and the Inter-Varsity Christian Fellowship.[3] The American Council has been militantly opposed to any form of ecumenicalism or "modernism," to neoorthodoxy, and to alleged radicalism among the churches affiliated with the National Council of Churches of Christ in America.

Contrary to what might seem to be an "obvious" implication, religious fundamentalism does not necessarily or invariably lead to conservative or reactionary political positions. Especially in lower socioeconomic strata, fundamentalism often is associated with a nonpolitical (apolitical)

[2] Salisbury, *op. cit.*, pp. 121–122, 267–269; Moberg, *op. cit.*, pp. 280–294; Glock and Stark, "Is There an American Protestantism?" *op. cit.*, pp. 8–13, 48–49.

[3] Louis Gasper, *The Fundamentalist Movement* (Paris and the Hague: Mouton & Company, 1962).

orientation in which only individualized, strictly religious questions are of interest.[4]

The modernist or "liberal" movements deviate from the position just sketched in their attempts to reconcile their beliefs with the findings of science and of history and to apply Christian doctrines to modern social problems. The broad inclination of modernism toward ethics rather than salvation and toward rationalism rather than traditional beliefs has apparently appealed to the relatively secularized elements of Protestantism, especially to socially and economically secure urban groups.

Several branches of modern Protestantism have come to a reluctant and often painful acceptance of historical criticism, evolutionary views, and to qualified and partial acceptance of birth control and divorce. Doctrines of predestination and election have diminished in acceptance; sin and salvation are less emphasized; social and ethical concerns have become more prominent. Yet countercurrents are also present as in a renewed note of pessimism and disillusionment concerning man and society,[5] especially in "neoorthodoxy."[6] Even while a book called *The Power of Positive Thinking* is bought by more than a million people, the more sophisticated Protestant theologians are wrestling anew with the problems of tragedy, evil, and weakness in human life and seek religious affirmations adequate to the "problems of meaning" in modern times.

Thus, the "cult of reassurance" is widely popular among secularized and anxious adherents—the marginally religious—who return to the churches. The spiritual emphasis of neoorthodoxy, on the other hand, has been largely confined to small numbers of theological thinkers.

These doctrinal cleavages represent different transformations of religious ideas and beliefs as these have interacted with secular thought and have been remolded by theological analysis of prior positions; at the same time, the objective social situations of believers have encouraged modifications in the typical religious positions of different classes, ethnic groups, and the like. At the present time, Protestant fundamentalism is largely carried by sects or denominations holding the allegiance of groups that are defensive against secularism and the social and cultural changes of the new metropolitan society.

In these compressed pages we have neglected (or left with only passing mention) a great many important aspects of our religious institutions—notably, the processes of development from sect to denomination, the major doctrinal positions within Protestantism (for example, the marginal case of Lutheranism), and the more exact evidence on the social correlates of different religious systems. We have attempted only an elementary sketch of the most central and distinctive norms and values in the major re-

[4] Howard Elinson, "The Implications of Pentecostal Religion for Intellectualism, Politics, and Race Relations," *American Journal of Sociology*, LXX, 4 (January 1965), 403–415.

[5] See, for example, Thomas Hamilton, "Social Optimism and Pessimism in American Protestantism," *Public Opinion Quarterly*, VI, 2 (Summer 1942), 280–283.

[6] Cf. Yinger, *op. cit.*, pp. 276–282.

ligious traditions of our society and will now turn to a broader consideration of the interrelations of religion with certain other institutions.

## RELATIONS OF RELIGION TO OTHER INSTITUTIONS

Because of its crucial position in the total value-integration of a society, religion has widely ramified relations with other institutions. For example, a religious system may strongly support the family—sanction marriages, supervise child care, ritualize bereavements; or, require celibacy or the severance of family ties. Either way, however, the two institutions are not mutually indifferent. It has been indicated that the attitudes of religious bodies toward the state range from the ready acceptance of certain ecclesia-like organizations to the radical antipathy of a sect such as the Jehovah's Witnesses.[7] Generalizations here are subject to considerable hazard; it is only by specifying *different* religious orientations that precision can be introduced into the analysis. Most of the assertions to be made in this section refer, explicitly or implicitly, to particular types of religious orientations or organizations. The following propositions are representative of descriptive generalizations that are current in discussions of the social role of religion in America.

### Social Stratification

Local religious groupings in the United States tend to be sharply segregated along lines of social stratification; this applies also, to a less extreme degree, to larger groupings (sects and even whole denominations). Of course, the relationships between social class and religious participation are complex. The higher the average stratification level in a denomination, the lower the average attendance of its members. On the other hand, *within* each denomination, the higher the position of individuals, the higher also is their rate of participation in the church. Thus, interdenominational comparisons show a negative correlation, but intradenominational analysis shows a positive association between social class and participation.[8]

### Political Activity

At least nominal public acceptance of religion tends to be a prerequisite to political success and to a lesser degree to business success in the smaller communities.

Multiplicity of religious affiliations of the political electorate, under the two-party system, encourages sectarian neutrality of the parties. This is expressed in selection of candidates of various numerically important faiths,

[7] Herbert H. Stroup, *The Jehovah's Witnesses* (New York: Columbia University Press, 1945), esp. pp. 147–168; Marley Cole, *Jehovah's Witnesses* (New York: Vantage Press, 1955).

[8] Harry C. Dillingham, "Protestant Religion and Social Status," *American Journal of Sociology*, LXX, 4 (January 1965), 416–422; Bernard Lazerwitz, "Some Factors Associated with Variations in Church Attendance," *Social Forces*, 39, 4 (May 1961), 301–309.

in avoidance of controversial statements of religious issues, and in many other ways.

Confirmation of the fact that organized religious bodies continue the tendency to express views supportive of the existing social order and inconsistent with drastic political revision of it may be found in many studies.[9] Yet, we must repeat, the inferences to be drawn from these findings are not self-evident. For one thing, religiously based beliefs and values may enter into political behavior, not as a matter of simple "expression" of such orientations but as part of a complex interaction with degree of involvement in religious activity and with socioeconomic status. One suggestive study, for example, shows that both "fundamentalism" and high socioeconomic position tend to go with Republican voting; but since fundamentalism is most frequent in lower strata, the apparent effects of "religious involvement" and "class" tend to be offsetting. However, a maximum "conservative" influence seems to occur in a Southern city in which major denominations of the middle-class population are themselves fundamentalist.[1]

It may seem obvious that political and religious realms of authority would often turn out to be mutually supportive, that is, that there would be a "natural" tendency for established political and economic power to favor stability in the organized religious system.[2] But the facts of dissent, social activism, and prophetic criticism of the status quo must be kept in view. Also, the hazards of unjustified inferences are increased if correlations between religious affiliation and other social phenomena are interpreted without direct analysis of the actual beliefs of adherents of the religious body in question. Thus, it may be observed that members of fundamentalist Protestant denominations in the South tend to be racial segregationists, Republican voters in 1962, and conservative in political and economic matters. It does not necessarily follow, however, that their *religious* beliefs led to these correlates. Fundamentalism, indeed, may lead to opposition to racial segregation and to apolitical withdrawal rather than right-wing political activity.[3]

### Education

Organized religious groups are generally concerned over the presumed secularizing influences of public education and strive with widely varying intensity and success to promote or supply religious instruction. With in-

[9] Cf. Glock and Stark, *Religion and Society in Tension, op. cit.*, pp. 191–200, 225. Even the alleged "radical" theology of Protestant neoorthodoxy turns out, upon close analysis, to represent a churchly, socially conservative force. (Toyomasa Fusé, "Universalistic Religion and Particularistic Social Order: A Study in Protestant Theological Strategy," paper in press, January 1967, pp. 1–20).

[1] Benton Johnson, "Ascetic Protestantism and Political Preference in the Deep South," *American Journal of Sociology*, LXIX, 4 (January 1964), 359–366.

[2] Peter L. Berger and Thomas Luckmann, *The Social Construction of Reality: A Treatise in the Sociology of Knowledge* (Garden City, N.Y.: Doubleday, 1966), p. 113; see in this connection Alfred Balk, *The Religion Business* (Richmond, Va.: John Knox Press, 1968).

[3] Cf. Howard Elinson, *op. cit.*, pp. 403–415.

creasing frequency, issues arise concerning the role of parochial schools, the issue of state support, the infusion of religious instruction and religious symbols into the public schools.

The teachings of religious organizations have been reexamined from time to time with a view to understanding possible effects upon intergroup relations. It seems clear that even when religious or racial prejudices are explicitly rejected, many of the materials used in religious education in the past have held the potential of contributing to negative intergroup stereotypes.[4] On the other hand, religious considerations clearly contribute to movements for social reform emanating from colleges and universities, often influenced by members of the campus clergy. The well-educated professional religious leaders—priests, rabbis, ministers, teachers—often are far more "liberal" or "radical" than the majority of members of religious organizations.

## Family

Even though civil marriages are everywhere legal, the great majority of American marriages are performed by religious officials; the church is still felt necessary to give ceremonial sanction to the family.

## Economic Activity

In most of the important religious groupings, the churches have advanced doctrines approving of business activity and established economic structure. These ideas, however, have involved considerable ethical tension, and there is a persistent tendency to demand that economic actions conform to religiously sanctioned norms.

## General

The intense pragmatism of American culture is exemplified in religious themes stressing the value of religion as a means to morality, peace and order, and worldly success. There is a marked tendency to regard religion as good because it is useful in furthering other major values—in other words, to reverse the ends-means relation implied in the conception of religion as the ultimate value in experience.

These are a few examples of descriptive generalizations. Before continuing we must distinguish between religion *as a system of ideas and value orientations* and organized religion as the *formal structure of the community of participants.* We should not confuse intrinsic religion as a cultural fact with the churches that partly express it socially. For example, there are religious ideas and values in our culture that are socially far more dynamic than those typically advanced by the well-established churches.[5]

[4] See for example: Bernhard E. Olson, *Faith and Prejudice: Intergroup Problems in Protestant Curricula* (New Haven, Conn.: Yale University Press, 1963); Edward H. Flannery, *The Anguish of the Jews* (New York: Macmillan, 1964); Charles Y. Glock and Rodney Stark, *Christian Beliefs and Anti-Semitism* (New York: Harper & Row, 1966); Walter M. Abbott (ed.), *The Documents of Vatican II,* (New York: The American Press, 1966).

[5] Proof of this rests not only on logical or semantic considerations but also on the clear tendency for new sects periodically to draw the more radical implications.

Furthermore, the relation of religious ideas and value orientations to specific social action is always complex and at least in our culture is typically loose and unstable for several reasons: (1) strict interpretation of Judaic-Christian ideas imposes very stringent requirements upon conduct that conflict with many other values and interests; (2) because of the non-empirical referents of religions systems, their social implications are peculiarly subject to arbitrary variation, and widely different definitions of a situation can be and are drawn from the same basic beliefs; (3) religious idea-value systems often influence conduct, not as exact definitions of expected behavior but as diffuse symbolic configurations having a tendency to spread and thereby lend sanctity or legitimacy to a range of diverse social practices and structures. Thus, we can take it as a postulate that no major institution is completely unaffected by religion. For instance, religious ideas and motivations played an important part in the rise of modern science, currently regarded by some people as the archenemy of religion.

As we noted earlier, every concrete religious grouping makes a tacit or avowed choice among these radically different possible orientations to the secular world: (1) militant attack upon it, (2) withdrawal or escape from it. (3) tolerance toward it, (4) active support of it. Within each of these four modes of approach there exist numerous qualitative variations; for example, withdrawal may mean escape from evil, or it may mean a positive and confident movement into experiences felt as superior to the ephemeral events of secular life. In this respect, as in many others, there are *varieties* of religious experience. There is always a certain tension between religious values—those concerned with "sacred things"—and considerations involving secular power of the religious organization. A religious organization never represents only a purely religious set of values and ideas—the latter appear to be phenomena of personal experience that are not fully compatible with the inevitable compromises of a continuing organization. To the degree that a religious movement succeeds in its *religious* mission, it gains converts and adherents. As it does this, it necessarily becomes a force in the secular world of the here-and-now; it gains wealth and political influence; it becomes deeply involved in the world. We can make the imprecise but valuable generalization that, where religious liberty prevails, the orientation of an organized religious body is strongly affected by the realistic social positions of its constituency—for example, secure groups that are well satisfied with the distribution of social rewards generally support religious organizations that approve of and reinforce the secular order; deprived and disaffected populations without effective political power tend toward sectarian withdrawal from an evil world; similar populations that see a realistic hope of social power tend to develop sects or movements aimed at attack upon or reform of the society.[6] We can leave aside here the situation under an inclusive established church.

One of the most important findings that can be drawn from the analysis thus far is this: *American religious organizations are highly segregated from*

---

[6] It must be stressed that religious movements constitute only one of several possible kinds of collective action in response to the indicated conditions.

*other institutionalized structures.* It is perfectly true that *norms* having religious referents and sanctions run through a wide variety of activities outside of organized religious bodies. But the very fact that religion in our culture is so frequently equated with the churches is a telling indication of the compartmentalization of religious norms. Religious ideas, symbols, beliefs, values have become firmly solidified in definite social organizations having their own specialized personnel, symbols of separate identity, special channels of communications, and segregated group affiliations. In addition, the separation of church and state has tended to isolate the churches from political power and from educational influence. These factors and the fragmentation of religious organization have made it possible for secular powers to force the churches quite generally into neutrality, isolation, or "bystander" support with reference to other institutions. The churches have often been told to "stay out of politics" (or, business affairs) and have sometimes heeded the admonition. The public generally assigns organized religion a special, circumscribed place as the repository of values that are inherently of the highest good, but that should be safely insulated and restricted to ceremonial occasions ("Sunday religion") so that they cannot interfere too much with the ordinary business of the society. This tendency may be given radically different evaluations: it may be called "religiosity" rather than religion, with Harold J. Laski,[7] or "traditional" rather than "intrinsic" religion, with J. Milton Yinger,[8] or it may be highly approved. We are not concerned here with these questions of value, but wish only to point out the relatively circumscribed and separate position of organized religion. Although there now seems to be some movement toward a closer involvement of religious organizations in the wider life of the society, it is still generally true, as Christian Gauss has said, that religion does not "permeate and inform" the other phases of our culture to the extent characteristic of earlier centuries.[9]

Although only a judgment, the opinion may be ventured that in the late nineteenth century the ascetic Protestantism that gave moral and symbolic reinforcement to economic pursuits and nationalistic aspirations lost a large part of its dynamic quality. With the rise of social protest movements in the early twentieth century, a number of religious groups reasserted their role as ethical critics of the society; but because most of the activities associated with the social gospel were utopian and unorganized, their social influence was diffused and indirect,[1] although in the long run substantial. Although there is a prophetic and radically ethical strain in the basic religious

[7] Harold J. Laski, *The American Democracy* (New York: Viking, 1948), pp. 320–321.

[8] J. Milton Yinger, *Religion in the Struggle for Power* (Durham, N.C.: Duke University Press, 1946), pp. 6–11.

[9] Cf. the pertinent remarks of Constantine Panunzio, *Major Social Institutions* (New York: Macmillan, 1939), chap. 19 and pp. 498–499, with the appraisal made nearly three decades later by Glock and Stark, *Religion and Society in Tension, op. cit.,* p. 184: "Looking at American society as a whole, however, organized religion at present is neither a prominent witness to its own value system nor a major focal point around which ultimate commitments to norms, values, and beliefs are formed."

[1] Yinger, *Religion in the Struggle for Power, op. cit.,* pp. 135–138. Chapter 5 of this work is a valuable treatment of the relation of the churches to economic issues.

tradition, the corporate actions of the major churches appear to have been mainly shaped by external forces rather than by the immanent development of religious value-orientations. This fact has led to the continual emergence of lower-class sects, alienated from the established denominations; it has meant that the churches have usually followed rather than led social change. As Yinger has well emphasized, religion is one among many of the interests of men and organized religion is one among many of the groupings sharing social power. Organized religions, once firmly established, typically resist change in their own doctrines and polity, as well as in secular affairs having religious relevance. This tendency, of course, is not confined to America or the West. Indeed, Judaic-Christian systems have inclined far more to social innovation than other major world religions.[2]

In the above paragraph we explicitly restricted the generalizations to the major churches that include the majority of church members and in any short-term perspective represent the preponderant social power of organized religion. However, a minority in most denominations does not sanction the status quo; and in the sects there is still more frequent expression of radically ethical positions. If the sects are often otherworldly and to that extent direct men's interests away from social issues and problems, it remains true that sects and sectarians represent the modern analogues to the ancient movements of ethical prophecy; they perpetuate the "explosive element"[3] in the tradition. Some organized churches so stress faith, ritual, and worldly unconcern or obedience to constituted secular authority that their main social effect probably is to help stabilize existing secular arrangements. It would be a gratuitous error, however, to accept this relatively simple relationship as definitive of the social place of institutional religion. There are limits defined by religious idea-value systems beyond which even the most conservative churches will not readily acquiesce to secular powers; and the small ethical sects (and analogous subgroupings within larger bodies) serve both as stimulus to less innovative churches and as curators of uncompromising religious ethics.

## RELIGION AND THE STRUCTURE
## OF AMERICAN SOCIETY

With its mosaic of organizations and beliefs, American religion is at one with the inveterate cultural pluralism that, at least up to now, has been one of the most outstanding traits of this society. The weakened place of the church as the intermediary to the Deity has contributed to sectarian divisions, and the very form of organization of many Protestant churches has reinforced pluralistic tendencies. Nearly one third of all church members belong to congregational bodies whose loose organization and strong local autonomy seem to represent sheer anarchy to Europeans steeped in the tradition of the universal church. The organizational structure of the

---

[2] It remains true that all organized religion is beset by the tendency toward absolutizing what is transient and local in the name of the enduring and universal.

[3] *Ibid.*, p. 226.

churches, therefore, resembles the diffuse and decentralized institutions of kinship, stratification, and education more than it does the economic and political systems. American religion for all its diversity demonstrates, with regard to cultural themes, the tendencies toward individualism, pragmatic emphasis, and ethical and humanitarian concerns[4] encountered in several other phases of the culture.

A society's common-value system—its "moral solidarity"—is always correlated with and to a degree dependent upon a shared religious orientation; more precisely, among the common values of a society are those of "intrinsic" religion, characterized by nonempirical referents and moral respect. This particular class of values is reciprocally related to other values current in the society. Now, social tension and struggle arise from two broad types of dividing factors. First, there are the differences in "interests" centered around scarce and divisible values: mainly power, prestige, and wealth —corresponding to the institutions of government and politics, social stratification, and economics. So far as a society focuses attention and effort upon the divisive "intermediate values," other things remaining the same, it will decrease its internal cohesion or solidarity.[5] But there is another type of social cleavage based upon incompatibility of ultimate values—say, between a devout Quaker and a storm trooper—in which differences go far beyond any question of immediate instrumental values. Where the members of a social aggregate hold ultimate convictions in common, there is a cohesion capable of overriding otherwise disruptive conflicts over scarce means-values. On the other hand, it equally follows that when such a solidary grouping is faced with another grouping similarly committed to a different common-value system there is increased likelihood of severe conflict. Our society places great emphasis upon the competitive institutions; the past devaluation of shared collective aims and the stress upon interests that set group against group and individual against individual has produced obvious strains on consensus. In addition, there are many ethnic and other cultural differences. The mere fact of such internal diversity does not necessarily diminish social stability—many societies have been both stable and integrated over long periods while maintaining great intrasocietal differentiation. What appears to be especially crucial in the American situation is the fact that so few cultural differences are stable, rationalized, and taken for granted.

At the most abstract level of values and symbols, there is enough commonality in America for religion to be on the whole a unifying factor, especially when there is awareness of radically different orientations elsewhere. Nevertheless, the great variation in specific religious beliefs and practices has very important divisive implications. Even the most general and universally acknowledged religious principles have variant results in practice. For instance, all our major religious bodies officially sanction a universalistic ethic and doctrines of religious equality; insofar as these

---

[4] As contrasted with transcendental problems, on the one hand, or ritualistic concentration on the other.

[5] Our statement here has to be carefully guarded because the concrete results are highly variable in different cultural contexts.

principles are believed in, it would seem a priori that they should mitigate tensions concerning social stratification, both by softening the asperities of invidious comparison and by providing religious "compensations" for lower strata. It is equally plausible a priori to suppose that such doctrines could lead to increased resentment by making social inequalities harder to endure. The potential consequences are not always the actual consequences. It must be noted, in addition, that the conditions of social life set limits to what religion can demand or do, *if* society is to continue. We need not go so far as the obvious case of universal religious celibacy to find examples: self-mortification carried to such extremes as to threaten social survival; food taboos leading to excessive malnutrition; "take no thought for the morrow," carried to the point of lack of responsibility for the care of one's children; "fanatical" demands for conformity, leading to conflict and persecution. The present survey indicates that the strictly religious interests of the churches, although they have an independent role in society, are in America often subordinated to other institutionalized interests.[6]

The questions raised by religious diversity concern the future development of American social structure as a total system. The consequences of religious liberty are here fully at hand, regardless of one's evaluation of them. It can be said on strictly empirical grounds that religious toleration, in a broad sense, is essential for the continuation of the most distinctive aspects of the institutional structure. The suppression of any important existing religious group, for example, would unquestionably deal a serious blow to the whole system, with extremely deep, complex, and far-reaching repercussions. The religious conflicts moving partly beneath the surface are to an important extent checked and blunted by diversity and freedom. It is commonplace to say that no one is tolerant of ultimate values differing radically from his own, and there is truth in this statement even though its essential terms are all ambiguous. Religious toleration in this society can be interpreted, at least in part, as a sign that the crucial values of the system are no longer couched in a religious framework. However, more basically, "free" institutions and groups can arise only under conditions of considerable social heterogeneity in interests and values. Critical social thought, invention, and innovative behavior, "secularization," a limited government founded on impersonal universal law—all these are fundamentally dependent upon the existence of varied groups within the area of interaction of a given society. Once secularization has gained momentum—after arising in the interstices of a complex structure—it in turn constitutes a dynamic tendency toward further secularization, up to a point determined by complex functional limitations, whose specification cannot be taken up here.

A homogeneous society will be a "sacred" society, marked by an absolute value-system and intolerance of deviant behavior. In a situation involving many contending groups (classes, religious groups, ethnic groups, and so on), there are strong pressures toward secularization. These can be clearly

---

[6] "Subordinated" here obviously represents a very complicated estimate. The above statement may be taken as the author's considered judgment rather than as an attempt at scientific generalization.

seen in the interplay of multiple attacks and counterattacks and in the emergence of defenses, rationalizations, accommodations, and philosophies of compromise and toleration that are found in such situations.[7] The breach of monopolistic control of thought and valuation that occurred with the disintegration of the medieval church opened the way to these developments in religion. The contact of varying and conflicting social perspectives and belief systems of differently situated groups and strata worked toward both relativism of values and toward a certain kind of intellectual objectivity. In the culture of the United States we find a massive laboratory in which to observe these developments.

In an age of localism, internal cleavages among religious groupings in the United States could be partly neutralized by geographic insulation. Now that no important group is really isolated from others, a different basis of relationship is inevitable. For all the specific religious differences found in the culture, the total scene is still one of relative peace.[8] This result depends upon an implicit value-consensus in which religious differences are subsidiary to the values of religious liberty. This consensus, in turn, is not a mystical emanation, but is maintained by a number of quite specific conditions and mechanisms—for example, the pluralistic power-balance, the vested interests of established religious organization, particular features of the political structure (such as the two-party system and constitutionalism as mediated through the judiciary). In the last analysis, however, none of these conditions, singly or in combination, is sufficient to explain the place of religious institutions; and we come back once more to the existence of a residual common-value element that provides the indispensable meanings and rationales for the complex and unusual structure.

### SUGGESTED READINGS

ARGYLE, MICHAEL. *Religious Behavior*. New York: Free Press, 1959. Concise summary and synthesis of research. Useful comparative data for U.S.A. and Great Britain.

BALK, ALFRED. *The Religion Business*. Richmond, Va.: John Knox Press, 1968. Highly readable short account of the little-known facts about the massive economic importance of organized (and tax-exempt) religion in the United States.

BERELSON, BERNARD, and GARY T. STEINER. *Human Behavior*. New York: Harcourt, Brace & World, 1964, pp. 417–436, 443–449. Catalogue of empirical generalizations. Useful as reference and as challenge to more systematic formulations.

[7] These processes have been sketched by students of the sociology of knowledge. Cf. Karl Mannheim, *Ideology and Utopia* (New York: Harcourt, Brace & World, 1936), pp. 5–20, 250–256; *Man and Society in an Age of Reconstruction*, Edward Shils (trans.) (London: Harcourt, Brace & World, 1940); pp. 79–107.

[8] The importance of anti-Protestant, anti-Catholic, and anti-Judaic currents is recognized. Still, these have not recently led to overt conflict on anything approaching the scale often recorded in other societies; and it is not to be assumed that *religious* differences alone account for that conflict which does exist.

DEMERATH, N. J., III, and PHILLIP E. HAMMOND. *Religion in Social Context: Tradition and Transition.* New York: Random House, 1968. Exceptionally clear and concise survey of sociology of religion, ranging from the classical literature to detailed research on contemporary American religion.

DURKHEIM, EMILE. *The Elementary Forms of the Religious Life,* J. W. Swain (trans.). New York: Free Press, 1947. One of the few really great classics in sociology of religion. Raised fundamental issues that still challenge research today.

GLOCK, CHARLES Y., and RODNEY STARK. *Religion and Society in Tension.* Chicago: Rand-McNally, 1966. A series of essays dealing with the theme of the strains between intrinsic religion and the sociocultural setting in which it finds expression—and frustration. Soundly based in the extensive empirical studies carried out by the authors.

HARRISON, PAUL M. *Authority and Power in the Free Church Tradition: A Social Case Study of the American Baptist Convention.* Princeton, N.J.: Princeton University Press, 1959. A study with profound implications. Shows how centralization and formalization of organization developed in a religious body with doctrines directly antithetical to these developments. A remarkable analysis of a strategic case for understanding the dilemmas of organized religion "in the world."

LENSKI, GERHARD. *The Religious Factor.* Garden City, N.Y.: Doubleday, 1961. Based on analysis of survey data from Detroit but generates findings of general significance. Statistical analysis documents contemporary importance of religious background and affiliation.

MAY, HENRY F. *Protestant Churches and Industrial America.* New York: Harper & Row, 1949. Admirable historical study, tracing the mutual influence of received religious traditions and ideas as over against the explosive social changes of the nineteenth century. Essential for an adequate understanding of the social gospel components in modern Protestantism.

O'DEA, THOMAS. *The Sociology of Religion.* Englewood Cliffs, N.J.: Prentice-Hall, 1966. Presents a lucid synthesis of the field. Noteworthy for the author's analysis of the "dilemmas of institutionalization" and for the probing discussion of secularization and sacralization within organized religious groupings.

SKLARE, MARSHALL. *Conservative Judaism: An American Religious Movement.* New York: Free Press, 1955. A book which foreshadowed many later interpretations. Traces in detail the influences, both external and internal to the religious tradition, which led to this uniquely American form of Judaism.

SWANSON, GUY E. *The Birth of the Gods: The Origin of Primitive Beliefs.* Ann Arbor: University of Michigan Press, 1960. Analysis of fifty societies, relating religious beliefs and practices to other aspects of the social context. Adds empirical weight to some of Durkheim's hypotheses.

SWEET, WILLIAM W. *The Story of Religion in America,* 2nd rev. ed. New York: Harper & Row, 1950. Provides keen historical depth for present-day analysis. A rich storehouse of keen observations, basic facts, and many illuminating insights.

WEBER, MAX. *The Protestant Ethic and the Spirit of Capitalism,* Talcott Parsons (trans.). New York: Scribner, 1928. Undoubtedly the most influential single work in sociology of religion. Endlessly debated, often "refuted," perennially rediscovered. Has limitations that Weber may have understood more clearly than some of his critics. A "must" reading.

WEBER, MAX. *The Sociology of Religion,* Ephraim Fischoff (trans.). Boston: Beacon Press, 1963. Selections of major portions of Weber's monumental, unfinished writings on the topic. Show the depth and complexity of his thought and help to place the thesis of *The Protestant Ethic* in context adequate to dispel many simplistic criticisms.

WILSON, BRYAN R. *Religion in Secular Society: A Sociological Comment.* London: C. A. Watts & Company, 1966. Special interest attaches to Chapter 6, a comparison of secularism in Britain and America; but the entire work is a graceful and clear account of a difficult subject.

YINGER, J. MILTON. *Religion, Society, and the Individual.* New York: Macmillan, 1957. Contains both a collection of readings and the author's mature thought on most of the basic issues in the empirical study of religion in its social context.

# *Institutional Variation and the Evasion of Normative Patterns*

X

## INTRODUCTION

With the discussion of religion, we complete our selective outline of major institutional structures. In the interests of brevity we have omitted many normative systems, for example, those involved in language, law, recreation, art, and expressive culture generally. However, a minimum sample of functionally crucial norms has revealed certain clues as to the dynamic interrelations of institutions in the society as a whole. We have also observed ambiguities in norms, conflicts of institutions, and variations in nominally accepted standards; but the preceding discussions probably have made institutional systems seem more rigid and clear than is justified by the concrete facts.

The institutionalized norms of social conduct never fully define concrete action. A norm is a standard (not necessarily explicit) for the course that action *should* follow, not a description of the action that actually occurs. Social action, on the other hand, is always specific and situation bound: it is action here and now—under particular circumstances of time and place, of particular configurations of values, interests, knowledges, and powers. It is affected by a variety of nonnormative conditions that limit or facilitate the actions prescribed. As was shown in Chapter III, many norms are so highly generalized that their specific implications for action can be drawn only imperfectly by a long process of cultural accretion; and many others seem to make demands upon conduct that are extremely difficult to meet in practice.

If we compare institutions to a skeleton, or to the girders of a building, or to a "grid" across the social fabric, we do not intend that such statements be taken literally. An institutional norm is not a point or a line, but a *zone:* typically, a norm is subject to appreciable variations in perception and application, even under highly favorable circumstances. There is usually a "permissive" zone of variation around even the most specific and strongly supported norms; certain kinds and degrees of overconformity and of underconformity are expected and tolerated. The ambiguities and variability of norms are important but difficult to recognize because of our persistent tendency to think of institutions as solid and well-articulated entities. Even in a highly unified culture, different portions of the normative structure always manifest a wide range of obligatoriness, explicitness, and specificity. After all, so-called deviant behavior still is—for the most part

—social behavior; and in any event it comes to be *defined* as deviant by social acts, that is, the labeling of the questionable conduct, by others, as outside the bounds of the ordinary, normal, or proper. This classification is made effective by the imposition of sanctions upon the person regarded as the author of the offending acts. Deviance, therefore, is always the outcome of interaction—it is in this sense "created by society"—and is of varying kinds.[1]

Shading off from the level of the most obligatory norms are norms of lesser definiteness held with lesser firmness, as shown for instance by vagueness of definition and by lesser severity of penalties for violations—for example, the conventional or preferred patterns of etiquette and fashion. All these are still parts of the manifest—"public," "official"—cultural structure; they are real prescriptions as to the course action is supposed to follow; but the extent of consensus and the severity of sanctions are lower than for institutions—"there is no disputing with tastes." As Robert MacIver has said: "Society does not need common rules for everything." Our own society has many areas of relative indifference or quite vague definition. Any widely applicable norm necessarily covers a variety of concrete situations, where it engages in action along with other norms. Hence, there is a certain variability that is intrinsic to institutions as well as to other normative patterns.

We have seen that one of the important defining characteristics of culture is that it contains systems of normative regulation of conduct. Inherent in the social interaction of people everywhere is the formal necessity for regularized expectations of others' conduct; and stable expectations can be built up only on the basis of some actual regularity. As any given aggregate of human individuals continues to interact under relatively constant external conditions over a period of time, most of the major life-situations become structured in terms of mutual expectancies for conforming patterns of behavior, some of which become morally obligatory because of their functional importance *for the society's value system.* The norms having this quality are linked together into the clusters or complexes we have termed "institutions."

Now it is conceivable that a culture could be so well integrated that (1) its basic normative patterns would remain stable over very long periods of time and (2) that at any given time deviations from conformity to the norms would be slight and rare. Among the gross conditions conducive to this stability and conformity are such elements as a small population with stable birth and death rates, adjusted to a stable physical milieu, and isolated from other cultures. It is possible that the members of such a society would eventually work out behavior regularities and normative structures so well adjusted to individual needs and to the exigencies of social organization that violations of institutional norms would be exceedingly rare and there would be a high degree of consistency of behavior with its ideal patterns and neat interlocking of norm with norm throughout the culture.

[1] Howard S. Becker, *Outsiders: Studies in the Sociology of Deviance* (New York: Free Press, 1963).

In actual fact, we do not know of any large-scale societies in which such perfect integration has been achieved.[2] Every modern society that is at all complex carries a culture in which there are very many important strains and "inconsistencies." With increasing size and complexity of the society, subcultures appear, carried by relatively autonomous groups or strata within the larger society. Within a given political entity, such as a nation, the differentiation of groups may proceed to such a degree that we have to be quite cautious in speaking of *a* culture at all; we may find only a tenuous linking together of a congeries of groups each with its own comparatively distinct value-system, its special problems, its distinctive social perspectives. Often, territorially adjacent groups living under the same larger political structure subscribe to opposing values and follow antithetical norms in important areas of life. A morally obligatory norm in one group may be merely tolerated in another and thoroughly disapproved in still another. For purposes of sociological analysis there then arises the very tangible question as to what a "deviation from the norms" is as over against "a tolerated pattern of evasion," or a distinct "subculture."[3] Thus, in a society of unprecedent social exposure and incessant public and private discussion of sexual behavior, the general fact is no longer even slightly newsworthy that such behavior often deviates widely from publicly accepted norms, or that the "rules of the game" are often seen as vague, ambiguous, contradictory or lacking entirely.[4] Since public morality, however, still can bring catastrophic sanctions down upon persons from respectable social circles unfortunate enough to be discovered in disavowed conduct, extensive concealment and evasion is the frequent accompaniment of unconventionality.[5]

Much of the apparent inconsistency in American culture is nothing more or less than the hallmark of a society with marked internal social differentiation. It is not difficult to see that a Mexican American village in Arizona is different from a town in the backcountry of New Hampshire. The two communities differ appreciably in language, in religion, in many other of the major institutional frameworks. They have in common an allegiance to the same national authority with respect to certain impersonal rights and obligations (voting, taxes, military service), and they share certain very broad cultural values. The fact that the two communities

[2] Not even the early Americans of New England escape from this generalization. See the evidence and analysis in Kai T. Erikson, *Wayward Puritans: A Study in the Sociology of Deviance* (New York: Wiley, 1966).

[3] Cf. Marshall Clinard, *Sociology of Deviant Behavior* (New York: Holt, Rinehart and Winston, 1957), pp. 9–16; Irving Spergel, *Racketville, Slumtown, Haulburg: An Exploratory Study of Delinquent Subcultures* (Chicago: University of Chicago Press, 1964).

[4] See the unusual study of upper middle-class "preachment, practice, and pretense" by John F. Cuber and Peggy B. Harroff, *The Significant Americans: A Study of Sexual Behavior Among the Affluent* (New York: Appleton-Century-Crofts, 1966).

[5] Abortion is the prototype; 99 percent of the 1 million induced abortions each year are performed outside hospitals and are, therefore, "outside the law." See: David T. Smith (ed.), *Abortion and the Law* (Cleveland: The Press of Case Western Reserve University, 1967); also, Edwin M. Schur, *Crimes Without Victims—Deviant Behavior and Public Policy: Abortion, Homosexuality, Drug Addiction* (Englewood Cliffs, N.J.: Prentice-Hall, 1965).

represent subcultures is, however, unmistakable. But it is equally clear that this situation does not necessarily constitute any particular problem for the society as a whole so long as the two groups are not in direct interaction and do not directly confront one another's differing orientations. The same holds for other types of groups or social categories—racial divisions, social classes, specific occupational groups, and so on—so long as there is mutual insulation. The fact that a *total* society contains a great number of diverse patterns of behavior does not allow us to infer that it automatically thereby affords *specific individuals* a wide range of choice among variants. For the diversity may represent primarily different sets of norms, values, and beliefs, each of which is obligatory within certain subcultures—ethnic, class, religious, racial, regional, local, and so on. The total range of behavior for "Americans" is very great—but the permissible and possible range is far less for a low-income white, female, Baptist living in a small town in Texas than for a member of the Jet Set. And so for each other segment. Each separate grouping remains separate, at least to the extent of restricting its contacts with other groupings to impersonal, functionally specific relations. Thus, although the total larger society may be very diverse internally, and may form only a loosely integrated system, within each subculture there may be high integration of institutions and close conformity of individuals to the patterns sanctioned by their own group.

The possibilities for the smooth functioning of such a "mosaic" society are not, to say the least, very great in the modern world. Diverse subcultures have been linked together through the extraordinary development of transportation and communication, occasioning widespread mutual awareness of other groups and their cultures, as well as much direct personal contact. This awareness of differing or similar values and specific patterns of conduct is rarely a matter of emotional neutrality; the presence of conflicting normative standards is typically not taken in a purely "factual" way, but on the contrary produces some degree of social tension. When originally segmental groups interact with others and begin to lose their closed, quasi-autonomous character, what were at first *conflicts between the standards of different groups* tend to become *intrapersonality conflicts* for the individual. It is in part through this specific dynamic mechanism that a "strain for consistency" is set up in the total culture.

Problems of interinstitutional conflict, therefore, become very real and concrete when seen in terms of the typical *personal* dilemmas involved. The "relation of Church and State" is an abstract formula that may embrace the problems of a conscientious objector—or of a group confronted with secular school requirements contrary to their religious beliefs. The tensions between family institutions and the economic order are observable in such specific cases as the disruption of family groups through unemployment. Thus, the collision of semiautonomous institutional systems is a major area in which the student of society must look for sources of deviant behavior patterns and for change in the normative patterns themselves.

The most general conditions for a high degree of conformity among institutional norms have already been suggested—basically, conditions that make it possible for conformity to produce conformity. When in any group or social system there is high consensus on the *standards* of conduct, ordinary social interaction continually reinforces conformity by precept, example, approval (respect, affection) and a great variety of complex and often unconscious mechanisms. Behavior is incessantly and subtly corrected by the responses of others; firmly interdependent expectations are integrated into mutually supporting self–other patterns. Incipient nonconformity is subject to immediate and unanimous attempts at control, and overt nonconformity occasions reaffirmation of the threatened norm through disapproval and the imposition of sanctions.

To summarize the points thus far discussed:

1. Even within a relatively unified and stable culture there is some normative variability because of the *generalized nature of norms* vis-à-vis the specific situations of action, because of the *causal role of nonnormative conditions* and because of *individual differences in perception and interpretation.*[6] It is a fact that in many instances nominally accepted norms are too difficult or stringent for full conformity.
2. Many societies contain appreciably different subcultures. American society is a conspicuous case. Much deviation from allegedly universal norms represents a clash of subcultures. As subcultures interpenetrate, some of these conflicts become intrapersonality conflicts.
3. In a society possessing high normative consensus, interactive processes control and reinforce conforming behavior in such a way as to redirect incipient violations.

In the United States, nonconformity to nominally accepted norms partakes, of course, of the intrinsic sources of ambiguity and deviation found in all cultures, as well as of the differing standards of relatively separate subcultures.[7] Also, a relatively high rate of certain types of nonconformity is expectable because of rapid social change. Another specific set of factors working in the same direction is found in the often-noted tendency in our culture to establish legal or other official regulation that is manifestly contrary to widely accepted practice. This is in part traceable to a moral-ritual attitude toward law—that law should set up ideal norms "to educate the people," even though strict enforcement is impracticable. Laws often more nearly represent expressions of sentiment than realistic means for direct regulation of behavior: by "passing a law" certain values or ideals can be affirmed without seriously affecting social practice. Furthermore, as we saw in Chapter VII, much legislation is the work of small but powerful pressure-groups whose wishes may diverge quite widely from those of the majority.[8]

[6] These differences are accepted here as given facts; to explain them is a major task for psychology and social psychology.
[7] The extreme complexities of both deviance and control are well illustrated in Howard S. Becker (ed.), *The Other Side: Perspective on Deviance* (New York: Free Press, 1964).
[8] For relevant analyses see Edwin M. Schur, *Law and Society: A Sociological View* (New York: Random House, 1968), chap. 4; Gresham M. Sykes, *Crime and Society* (New York: Random House, 1968).

Certainly many social norms, including laws, are widely accepted as reasonable and gratifying solutions to problems of communication (language; agreement upon signals and codes), of coordination (traffic rules; "first come, first served"), and of many other quasi-technical social arrangements. However, the most strongly institutionalized norms represent relatively enduring settlements of opposition and conflict. They are solidified resolutions of interpersonal and intergroup demands, claims, and struggles. Where there is no inclination toward violation of a rule, an obligatory norm typically does not appear. Institutional norms are those that forbid people from doing things they otherwise would be disposed to do, and urge them on to carry out activities they otherwise would not be spontaneously moved to do in just the way required.

If these observations are correct, a tendency to violate socially obligatory norms may be posited as inherent in organized human life. There are, of course, some obligatory rules that command general voluntary acceptance and conformity, by reason of convenience and facilitation of desired ends—rules of etiquette and convention, technical procedures useful in efficient goal attainment, and the like. But even these on occasion are felt by some persons as impediments or annoyances and are resisted.

Further, in the particular instance of American culture, there is no doubt that many of the most highly approved modes of behavior are strongly task centered and success centered. Emphasis on the goals of wealth, power, and prestige creates a "bombardment of interests" that tends to break down the restraining power of the institutionalized definitions of appropriate means to reach the cultural goals. As the extreme example, the emphasis upon "getting yours" in terms of individual success becomes so great that "anything goes"—action escapes from all normative regulation except the tests of technical efficiency in reaching the prized goals. Insofar as social rewards come solely or chiefly from the achievement of goals rather than from conformity to the rules of the game, there is a long-run pressure toward high rates of individual deviation and nonconformity.

Any individual relates himself to whatever norms he takes to be generally accepted in his society in one of the following ways: (1) He accepts them as morally binding upon his own conduct as well as upon that of others—for example, he conforms in the absence of external sanctions; he feels guilt or shame if he deviates; he actively advocates, defends, or enforces the norms. (2) He accepts the norms only as *conditions* that he takes into account because of the extraneous rewards or penalties attached; conformity and nonconformity are appraised in utilitarian terms. (3) He decisively rejects the norms per se, either by withdrawal or active attack.

Full conformity throughout a society or group is dependent upon the actors' having adequate *knowledge of the norms*, an *identification with them*, and *support and reinforcement* from other persons. Both normative consensus and individual conformity can be maintained only by incessant effort and active social evaluation. Even under the most stable conditions of high cultural integration, the smooth flow of conduct along group-sanctioned channels is only seemingly automatic; and modern societies have shown the possibilities for virtually complete dissolution of entire institutional systems. Such dissolution seems generally to involve both a gradual loss of motivation (the spread of apathy) and a high rate of contranormative behavior. Open violation of a norm, strongly supported by most of the community, is simply "crime" or "misbehavior;" but if a large number of individuals commit such violations, the norm itself becomes problematical —the situation either is approaching a split into subcultures, with different standards, or the norm is losing its controlling authority generally. The fact that norms are often vague and are not all felt as equally obligatory or real must be reemphasized when we use terms such as "evasion," "deviation," or "violation." All cultures have numerous alternatives and flexibilities in their effective norms; in the small and allegedly "simple" societies in which many theorists have professed to see the ironclad mold of clear and unbending custom, modern anthropology is demonstrating a degree of flux and variability not so different from our own society. The exemption of violators of norms from punishment often occurs on grounds of "extenuating circumstances." These circumstances vary greatly from group to group and situation to situation—including such conditions as intention ("I didn't mean to"), mood, provocation, alcohol, fatigue, hunger, conflicting obligations. There are "ideal" norms, and then there are "latent" (covert or unrecognized) norms shading over into sub rosa practices and countermores patterns. In addition there is differentiation of norms, by age, sex, class, and so on. It is important not to mistake differentiation or permissible variation for evasion or violation.

Of course, the definition of evasion or deviance by persons actually involved in the situations in question varies from one position to another. What the prosecuting attorney calls a violation may be regarded as a customary shading of a technical rule by a business executive. Also, of course, deviance and evasion occur among those charged with enforcing rules as well as among persons subject to their authority. The enforcement of building or housing codes in our cities furnishes numerous excellent examples. Housing codes and zoning rules allow much room for discretionary judgment in enforcement, and officials come under great pressures to evade the letter of the law on some occasions. The result, frequently, is selective and differential enforcement.[9]

We are interested here in a still more complicated situation, namely, one where a publicly accepted norm is covertly violated on a large scale, with the tacit acceptance or even approval of the same society or group, at least so long as violation is concealed. *Public* violation, on the other hand, is often felt to require punishment, even when private evasion and violation are prevalent and widely recognized. It is not always simple to determine whether one is observing *evasion* of a norm actually expected to guide real

[9] Scott Greer, *Urban Renewal and American Cities* (Indianapolis: Bobbs-Merrill, 1965), p. 49: "In short, the process of code enforcement creates severe strains upon the city agencies responsible. They modify these strains through (1) selective enforcement by areas within the city, and (2) the use of different standards for different kinds of people, neighborhoods, and housing."

behavior or simply an *alternative norm,* widely accepted or acquiesced in, although rated in public estimation as lower in cultural value than the ideal but nominal standards.[1] Frequently, a manifest institutional pattern seems symbiotically related to an opposing pattern that is also accepted. Thus, a strong patriarchal family system, giving women a markedly subordinate status and enforcing rigorous feminine chastity, frequently occurs along with a highly developed system of prostitution. Or again, bureaucratic organizations require that requests or orders must be recorded in writing and passed along all steps in an administrative hierarchy; but this rule typically is accompanied by an informal system of off-the-record communication and action, operating without official sanction. Such patterns may be as normative as the manifest rules and may even be essential to the attainment of the major values being sought in the system.

Perhaps the most interesting example of apparently counterinstitutional patterns is found in those not infrequent instances in which individuals are punished precisely because they *fully* carry out the prescriptions of a moral code—even when the code is nominally and publicly placed at the apex of culturally approved values. Sometimes these heroic individuals are regarded as "saints;" but they are also regarded, in certain circumstances, as "fanatics," "trouble makers," "subversive"—the person who takes literally religious injunctions against killing and refuses military service, for instance, or the zealous proponent of absolute truth who refuses to tell conventional "white lies," or the minister who insists upon a literal implementation of brotherly love in intercultural and interracial relations. Thus, established institutions may thrive upon a relatively large amount of passive conformity and discreet deviation, but are often allergic to full and energetic conformity to their more "utopian" norms.

In summary, within any given social aggregate, variations in normatively oriented behavior may represent (1) rebellion against the norms, (2) anomic withdrawal of supports, (3) personal or idiosyncratic interpretations, (4) subcultural differences, (5) alternative patterns within the same subculture, (6) regularized evasion (or violation) of utopian and heroic standards or of norms expected to control actual behavior.[2] Analysis of each of these variations is necessary for a full picture of the state of a social system.[3] For the time being it seems most illuminating to concentrate upon patterns of regularized evasion.

The typical situation producing large-scale patterned evasion of nominally dominant norms appears as follows:

[1] Morris E. Opler, "Cultural Alternatives and Educational Theory," *Harvard Educational Review,* XVII, 1 (Winter 1947), 28–44.

[2] Once again it must be emphasized that these types of situations are not confined to our own society nor even to complex modern societies. Anthropological research shows numerous examples in preliterate societies. As James S. Slotkin has said, there frequently is "a customary way of not conforming to custom; . . ." See his *Social Anthropology* (New York: Macmillan, 1950), pp. 81 ff.

[3] For further distinctions and analysis see the articles by Robert Dubin; Richard A. Cloward, Robert K. Merton, Dorothy L. Meier, and Wendell Bell; Gwynn Nettler, John I. Kituse, and David C. Dietrick; and Harold L. Wilensky and Hugh Edwards in *American Sociological Review,* 24, 2 (April 1959).

1. For "reasons" functionally important to the social structure and the main value-systems, a certain activity, thing, or belief is prohibited and widely condemned.
2. But a large proportion of the socially powerful, and otherwise function-ally essential, members of the relevant adult population demand the prohibited element.
3. Normative consensus is insufficient to prevent this demand from arising or to deter considerable numbers of individuals from catering to it.
4. But consensus is great enough to prevent a public repudiation of the norm itself. [This fact derives from (1) above.]
5. Many of those who violate or evade the norm hold "essential"[4] status in the social system; there is accordingly a strong resistance to wholesale punishment. [See (2) above.]
6. Hence, the situation is handled by: (a) public affirmation of the norm; (b) covert acceptance of widespread violation and evasion; (c) periodic token or "ritualistic" punishment, or punishment of those whose arrears unavoidably become public.

No comprehensive analysis or systematic comparison of data along these lines is available for American society as a whole. Some rather important evidence can be assembled, however, by examination of a few strategically chosen situations.

## SPECIFIC EXAMPLES OF PATTERNED EVASION

The following more-or-less random listing of a few well-known examples of established modes of contravening norms usually thought of as "dominant" in our society will serve as preliminary orientation to our present problem:

1. Prohibition vs. the bootlegging and speak-easy industry, prior to repeal of the Eighteenth Amendment; organized gambling.
2. Impersonal, disinterested governmental services vs. political graft, "fix-ing," "status justice."
3. Family mores vs. prostitution.
4. Classroom honesty vs. accepted patterns of "cribbing."
5. Promotion by technical competence vs. nepotism, racial discrimination (as seen, for example, in the systematic evasion of civil-service laws).
6. Universalistic legal justice vs. white-collar crime, the public defender system, bias in jury selection, racial discrimination.
7. Prescribed patterns of sexual behavior vs. the patterns revealed by studies of actual behavior.
8. Legal rules regarding divorce vs. court practice ("void" divorces, the "alimony racket").
9. Professional codes vs. such practices as fee splitting among doctors,

---

4 The quotation marks here signalize a question-begging adjective.

violations of state and federal statutes and administrative regulations by retail pharmacists,[5] ambulance-chasing among lawyers.[6]
10. Ethical concepts of truth vs. some advertising, financial transactions ("business is business").

The items named are diverse enough to illustrate how very different concrete problems contain common factors. We will now describe some of these cases briefly.

Civil-service laws or merit systems are widespread in American governments. These systems were established after long effort and many struggles, often against the overt or covert opposition of legislators and political leaders. Merit provisions manifest the high value placed upon universalistic standards of achievement and reward in the occupational structure and have been widely acclaimed as major reforms. However, numerous evasions of the manifest intent of civil-service laws have long existed.[7] The basic legislation itself is sometimes very limited in applicability. For example, it may exempt all important officials (such as department heads) from civil-service regulation, together with their immediate staffs; it may exempt the great mass of unskilled and semiskilled workers—often the majority of the governmental employees. Similar effects are secured by the device of non-competitive examinations. Biased grading of examinations sometimes occurs. An important evasion is the large-scale use of "temporary" (exempt) appointments that are repeatedly renewed. A still more involved device is that of appointing employees under exempt job-classifications but utilizing them for duties nominally attached to nonexempt positions, leaving the latter jobs unfilled. There is also the practice of contracting for services from private business rather than directly employing the necessary personnel. This practice has been extended to using vouchers for materials to pay for contracted services. It is sometimes possible to control the merit commissions, which are appointed to administer the law, by control of their membership, for example, by appointment of "right guys" who operate behind the respectable facade provided by "honest but ineffective" members. The entire merit system may be sabotaged by deliberately inadequate appropriations for enforcement and administration. This is not quite so obvious, perhaps, as the outright abolition of classified jobs and the reassignment of these tasks to "politically" appointed personnel under different labels; but it appears to be of comparable effectiveness.

Norms of proper performance in important work-roles often are selectively applied and circumvented by elaborate systems of group-sanctioned violations and evasion. One case, so perfectly illustrative of the conditions

---

[5] Earl R. Quinny, "Occupational Structure and Criminal Behavior: Prescription Violation by Retail Pharmacists," *Social Problems*, 11, 2 (Fall 1963), 179–185. Retail pharmacists are both businessmen and licensed professionals; violators of rules governing prescriptions tend to define their roles in "business" terms.

[6] Kenneth J. Reichstein, "Ambulance Chasing: A Case Study of Deviance and Control Within the Legal Profession," *Social Problems*, 13, 1 (Summer 1965), 3–17.

[7] V. O. Key, Jr., "Methods of Evasion of Civil Service Laws," *The Southwestern Social Science Quarterly*, XV, 4 (March 1935), 337–347.

we have specified as to serve as a model, has been reported from a study of normative conformity and deviance in an aircraft factory. Assembly-line fabrication of airplane wings was carried out with considerable sense of urgency—a production chart was the test of effectiveness. In bolting pre-formed plates to the wings, workers often found that alignment was dis-torted, preventing quick placement of bolts. A hard-steel cutting instrument —the tap—could be used to form a new alignment by cutting new threads. But this procedure destroyed the effectiveness of "stop-nuts" designed to lock bolts into the wing plates so that the bolts could not be dislodged by vibration in flight. Because of the obvious danger to the finished aircraft and to any persons involved in its flights, the use of the tap was the most serious crime of workmanship conceivable in the plant, particularly since it could also be an illegal method of concealing structural defects. But at least one-half of the workers owned a tap; senior mechanics often possessed four or five, of varying sizes; new workers were taught how to use the tap— "with discretion"—and foremen warned them "not to get caught using a tap." Workers apprehended for the first time in using the tap were given ceremonial reprimands by inspectors and foremen. The emphasis was upon *discreet usage*, employing the tap in only a minority of instances and those cases in which production would be seriously slowed by following correct procedures. Workers and foremen rationalized use of the tap by regarding quality control as the responsibility of the inspectors charged with maintain-ing Air Force standards. Given the pressures for rapid production, the use of the tap was imperative, even though it was a "crime" apart from the semi-covert system that both supported and regulated its use.[8]

Turning to an example taken from a different context, divorce law and its practice is instructive. A principle of American law is that divorce cannot be based upon mutual agreement: this would be collusion, a specific bar to absolute divorce. Actually, however, it has been estimated that over 90 percent of divorces in the United States are in fact divorces by mutual agreement; most proceedings are not contested, and decrees are very rarely challenged. Further, divorces are regularly granted by states lacking legal jurisdiction to issue the decree.[9] The ordinary Reno divorce is usually treated as valid, even though it is "void" in the dominant legal theory that requires bona fide residence in the state granting the divorce. Although the courts are able to find legal doctrines to justify their refusal to treat these divorces as void, the law as written doctrine differs obviously from the law as practiced by the courts—an instance of dead-letter law, systematically circumvented by the courts themselves in response to social pressure. There is also the well-known and widespread evasion of laws concerning the

[8] This account summarizes only part of the context, which should be studied in its en-tirety: Joseph Bensman and Israel Gerver, "Crime and Punishment in the Factory: The Function of Deviancy in Maintaining the Social System," *American Sociological Review*, 28, 4 (August 1963), 588–598.
[9] Fowler V. Harper, "The Myth of the Void Divorce," *Law and Contemporary Prob-lems*, 2, 3 (June 1935), pp. 337–341, 344, 346–347; Nelson M. Blake, *The Road to Reno* (New York: Macmillan, 1962); Irving Mandell, *The Law of Marriage and Divorce* (New York: Oceana Publications, 1958), chaps. 1–5; and publications cited in Chapter IV.

"grounds" for divorce. For many years New York State required unilateral proof of adultery; and for those willing to accept a judicial record of this offense divorce was otherwise relatively easy and quite binding. A thriving "industry" emerged for fabricating evidence of adultery; the legions of professional corespondents, private detectives, cameramen, and informers were the overt symptoms of a *system* for evading the legal norms.

"Political corruption" is so widespread and persistent as to be a "normal" process in many communities. Political parties want votes and the funds necessary to get votes; business groups want protection and privilege; quasi-criminal and criminal elements of the community want immunity. These highly specific wants represent strong interests and tangible advantages. Organized prostitution, gambling, and narcotics, for example, are big industries, supplying products for which there is a heavy demand but which are publicly disapproved; the underworld is thereby vulnerable and at the same time able to pay well for the privilege of systematically violating the law. On the other hand, the mass of those voters who disapprove of political corruption is often apathetic about the (largely unnoticed) day-by-day alliance of business, government, and crime.[1] Politics is a relatively minor and episodic interest with them—whereas to the practicing politician it is a full-time way of life, to the businessman it is a crucial factor in operations, and to the gang leader or captain of organized illicit business it is a matter of survival. As a matter of fact, of all known crimes against property, only about 20 to 25 percent result in an arrest (and fewer still in a conviction).[2] On a purely actuarial basis, a well informed and skillful member of an organized group devoted to theft (in one form or another) has a very high probability of escaping penalty. Consequently, many persons evidently find that crime does pay.

If highly attractive goods and services for which there is a strong and widespread desire can be produced profitably, but are prohibited by law from being produced or offered for sale, several consequences are inevitable. One is that persons without a firm commitment to law observance will find illicit transaction tempting, either as sellers or as buyers. Another result is that an appreciable proportion of law-enforcement officials will sometimes stop short of fully rigorous enforcement in the face of much participation in and tacit acceptance of the illegal traffic by otherwise law-abiding people. It is quite predictable also that satisfied "customers" will not report to the officials those who purvey such illicit satisfactions to them and that even the disgruntled buyers will rarely place themselves in further jeopardy by reporting their own complicity. Because the illegal purveying to widespread private demand is likely to be lucrative, the business operators will be willing to pay well and to render important favors of one kind or another in return for protection from interference by the guardians of the law. At the same

---

[1] Useful background information has been interpreted by The President's Commission on Law Enforcement and Administration of Justice, *The Challenge of Crime in a Free Society* (Washington, D.C.: Government Printing Office, 1967).

[2] See Department of Justice, *Uniform Crime Reports—1966* (Washington, D.C.: Government Printing Office, 1967), pp. 102–104.

time, competition and rivalry among the illegal operators will tend to be controlled by extralegal or illegal means, thus creating a secondary system of predatory crime, especially organized coercion, and violence.[3]

Organized crime in the United States is a modified free enterprise system—a set of business firms organized for illegal purposes or using illegal methods but organized much as legal businesses are and, indeed, often carrying on regular transactions with the latter. Extensive illicit organization is found in the gambling industries, the illegal lotteries ("policy" or "numbers" rackets). narcotics traffic, prostitution, vending machines, and even the rubbish- or garbage-carting business.[4] Organized crime is big business, and it continues to thrive decade after decade. Supplying demanded goods and services,[5] intimidating or killing troublesome customers or rivals, building alliances with "legitimate" local economic and political power-groupings, relying upon public indifference and complicity—in such ways organized crime has become an established feature of national life.

Commodore Vanderbilt is credited with the vehement rhetorical question as to whether anyone supposed that a railroad could be operated in accordance with the laws. He referred to a legitimate industry. In the highly organized illicit business built up under the direction of Al Capone, there was order and conformity, but only because of the latent structure of legally forbidden but widely accepted practices. Capone is said to have protested, almost plaintively, after his conviction for income-tax evasion[6] that all he had ever done was to supply beer and whisky to "our best people." Back of organized crime is an elaborate network of connections with the police, the courts, and legitimate business.[7] Especially interesting are the situations in which, externally, the law takes its course and the larger community sees a ceremonial reaffirmation of its institutional rules—as during prohibition, when, on periodic "round-up days," mass arrests were made, the offenders given nominal fines or sentences, and permitted to return

[3] Cf. Elmer H. Johnson, *Crime, Correction, and Society*, rev. ed. (Homewood, Ill.: Dorsey Press, 1968), chap. 9; Gus W. Tyler, *Organized Crime in America* (Ann Arbor: University of Michigan Press, 1962).

[4] See Gus Tyler (ed.), "Combating Organized Crime," *The Annals*, 347 (May 1963), esp. articles by Thorsten Sellin, Alvin J. T. Zumbrun, and Eliot H. Lumbard.

[5] Thus, "society has made a place for La Cosa Nostra by demanding illicit gambling, alcohol, and narcotics; usurious loans; and a cheap supply of labor . . ." (Donald R. Cressey, *Theft of the Nation: The Structure and Operations of Organized Crime in America* (New York: Harper & Row, 1969), pp. 72–73. In the special issue of *The Annals* "Combating Crime," Vol. 374 (November 1967), Lloyd E. Ohlin and Henry S. Ruth, Jr. (eds.) see also the article by Henry S. Ruth, Jr., "Why Organized Crime Thrives;" by John A. Gardiner, "Public Attitudes Toward Gambling and Corruption;" and by Richard H. Blum, "Drugs, Behavior, and Crime."

[6] Not for bootlegging, destruction of property, extortion, purveying of commercialized vice, etc.

[7] It is instructive to compare the authoritative study, *The Illinois Crime Survey*, published in 1929, with the report of the President's Commission on Law Enforcement and the Administration of Justice, *Task Force Report: Organized Crime* (Washington, D.C.: Government Printing Office, 1967). The striking similarity of the *basic* patterns reported is eloquent evidence of the deeply embedded character of the symbiosis of "illegal" and "legal" groups and organizations.

to business.[8] The objective effect upon the liquor industry was equivalent to that of a license-fee system. However, public reaction to this system differs sharply from the reaction to "bribes" paid to policemen or judges in order to attain the same end. In both cases, the law violator stays in business at a price; but the latter practice is culturally registered as a law violation, the first is a ceremonial affirmation tending to assimilate or obscure the covert pattern of evasion. The same pattern of ritualistic law "enforcement" is often found in commercialized "vice," where recurrent raids are widely dramatized and have some real effect in dispersing and concealing organized prostitution and even reducing its prevalence but do not succeed in suppressing continuous evasion.[9] Here also the covert pattern has extensions into the political system (elected officials, party leaders, police, the courts) and into legitimate business—real estate, for instance.

The resolution of conflicting values and interests need not be covert or informal. The state of Mississippi has provided a fascinating example in its 1944 statute imposing a tax on sales prohibited by law. The state had long before prohibited the sale of alcoholic beverages, and prohibitionist sentiment blocked repeal. But many citizens wished to drink. The demand was met by products imported from neighboring areas. The wholesale suppliers reported to the Mississippi state government the names of buyers and the amount purchased. In the heyday of this arrangement more than 1,000 persons held federal liquor dealer licenses. The state collected its tax, while agencies charged with enforcing prohibition did not need to have any official knowledge of the transaction. Prohibition was thus nominally upheld, drinkers had their potions, and substantial tax revenues augmented the state's treasury.[1] Such public forthrightness is rare. This uniquely explicit arrangement finally came to an (official) end in 1966 with the repeal of statewide prohibition.

Any serious study of these matters shows why the waves of reform so often break upon the reefs of those established evasions that often seem to be "secondary institutions." The existence of a continuing relationship between organized crime and the governmental structure depends not only upon subcultural differentiation and the convergent interests of personnel in the two structures but also upon the supporting portion of the overtly legal business system and upon the fact that many of the end products of crime are in great demand by considerable numbers of the outwardly law-abiding population.

Reform that attempts simply to suppress these patterns, or to deal only with the "supply" side of the equation, is not likely to be successful. Realistic

---

[8] The theoretical significance of this case was first called to the writer's attention by Robert K. Merton.

[9] Compare the conclusions of the following: Walter C. Reckless, *Vice in Chicago* (Chicago: University of Chicago Press, 1933); Kingsley Davis, "The Sociology of Prostitution," *American Sociological Review*, 2, 5 (October 1937); Illinois Association for Criminal Justice, *The Illinois Crime Survey* (Chicago, 1929), pp. 845–863.

[1] See the lively account by David L. Cohn, "A Little Prohibition in Mississippi," *The Atlantic*, 203, 6 (June 1959), 57–59.

social action will have to take into account (1) the pervasive vested interests in institutionalized evasion and violation; (2) the existence of a "demand"—not confined to the *declassé* portions of society—for illicit activities and products; (3) the partial dependence of patterned evasion upon the particular nature of the dominant institutions. Thus, we might postulate a situation in which persons lacking in technical competence and administrative integrity are elected to offices of great community responsibility at salaries considerably below the going rate in private business. Let us suppose also that the majority of the population tends to deprecate "politics" and is apathetic about the government; at the same time, the government requires many services and products from private business, and the latter is subject to inspection and regulation. If, furthermore, the norms of business-government relations are ill defined and a case of "graft" is exposed, a frequent public reaction is to "kick the rascals out," without altering the basic structural situation.[2] When considering reform it is always relevant to appraise the total consequences (What will the proposed alterations cost, in the broadest sense?).

Efforts to control crime and systemic evasion through detection and punishment of individual law-violators completely by-pass the organizational and institutional arrangements that typically are the more important determinants of the *rate* of crime. Much could be learned about problems of controlling crime from a genuine analysis of the strategic economic and social features of illegal markets, criminal business organization, and criminal "trade practices." Criminal businesses fall into several distinct types: black market operations (selling commodities and services illegally), racketeering—both criminal monopoly and extortion, black-market monopoly (for example, narcotics), and cartels (collusive price-fixing maintained by criminal action). Outright and rigid prohibitions (against "drugs", abortion, gambling) create a situation in which only those who are willing to be criminals can compete and under some conditions may generate centralized large-scale criminal organizations. These results probably would be regarded by most law-abiding citizens as fairly heavy social costs. Since the usual legal and punitive means employed in the past show no indication of ever "abolishing" such consequences, a more sophisticated analysis of the contributory conditions might suggest strategies that in combination would be more effective in reducing undesired consequences.[3]

Many of the cases examined so far have been instances in which the manifest, official norms apparently enjoy substantial popular support— that is, the norms are really expected to control behavior. In certain other instances there seems to be a larger utopian component in the norms that

[2] Few have surpassed Lincoln Steffens in grasping the intertwined causative factors in this type of situation. His insights are still fresh. Cf. *The Autobiography of Lincoln Steffens* (New York: Harcourt, Brace & World, 1931), esp. pp. 215–238, 407–415, 464–469. One is sometimes tempted to agree that the more things change the more they remain the same. Steffens would find few surprises today.

[3] Cf. Thomas C. Schelling, "Economics and the Underworld," *Harvard Today* (Spring 1967), p. 28.

are circumvented. As we have observed, a norm is, by definition, seldom perfectly actualized.[4] If the publicly avowed standards are highly generalized and conflict simultaneously with strong interests and tacitly accepted values and operating rules, what then emerges is typically not considered an "evasion;" rather, there is an abstract creed, given great symbolic importance but culturally insulated from operating practice. For example, a policeman is supposedly an impartial instrument for law enforcement. However, quite aside from criminal connivance, the policeman usually has a wide range of discretion in when, how, and upon whom he will visit sanctions.[5] He may show "favoritism"—or he may show kindness, take intentions and extenuating circumstances into account. In the rarefied principle of the legal system, a man is always regarded as innocent until proven guilty. Yet American policemen not infrequently shoot and kill fleeing suspects, even when the suspected violation is minor; and spokesmen for the police fight vigorously any effort to establish civilian review boards to monitor alleged injustice or brutality in law enforcement. In the case of the prosecuting attorney, the decision to prosecute, the severity of the charges, and numerous other crucial matters clearly involve extralegal considerations in many instances. In any event, however, the official is expected to give public and ceremonial expression to the impartiality of the law.

The American jury system is a venerated institution: not only is the right to trial by jury written into the Constitution, but its importance in a democratic system of values is generally taken for granted. Nevertheless, the jury system often becomes a means whereby skillful or powerful law violators escape punishment; and the system of selection and trial procedure goes far to prevent jurors from playing the ideal role culturally attributed to them.[6] It has been shown (for example by the Ruth Commission in Pennsylvania) that jurors are frequently ignorant of essential facts and of legal terminology, that cases are sometimes decided without an understanding of the charges or even without knowledge of which case is being passed upon. The important point here is that the jury may absorb a large part of the "blame" for seeming miscarriages of justice, whereas the abstract symbols and the creedal norms of the law remain unscathed. The full functional significance of this pattern has yet to be adequately analyzed.

Circumvention of norms is not confined to crime and "disreputable" behavior; it is common to find within a particular ingroup regularized systems of conduct that are contrary to publicly voiced standards that have the position of "mores." In the field of education, the importance of "connections" in academic placements in the period immediately before World

---

[4] In the case of a society committed to extremely "high" standards, those that for any reason are difficult of attainment, much of the dynamism of the social system seems attributable to a continuing tension between ideal norms and situational realities.

[5] Michael Banton, *The Policeman in the Community* (New York: Basic Books, 1964); O. W. Wilson, *Police Administration* (New York: McGraw-Hill, 1963); Jerome Skolnick, *Justice Without Trial* (New York: Wiley, 1966).

[6] Harry L. Kalvern, Jr. and Hans Zeisel, *The American Jury* (Boston: Little, Brown, 1966).

War II has been pointed out by Logan Wilson, who shows that much favoritism was due to technical and institutional barriers to free, impersonal competition;[7] in addition, the norms of "impartial appointment on the basis of merit" were sometimes violated because of personal ties, internal university politics, and so on. Collegiate athletics periodically gives us examples of evasion or outright violation of rules concerning payment of players. In the business world, strong tendencies to violate governmental regulations were revealed by the extensive black-market (and "gray-market") operations on the part of "respectable" businesses during World War II.[8] More than 200,000 firms received penalties. The number of border-line evasions must have been much larger. Similar practices are revealed from time to time in ordinary business affairs.[9]

A final illustration may indicate how this type of analysis applies to large-scale social problems. Intergroup relations oriented to "racial" distinctions constitute a chronic and serious problem in the United States. The problem, however, exists in different forms in different groups and localities; and the normative regulation of interracial behavior occurs in a number of very different ways. In some areas, especially in rural portions of the Deep South, tension and conflict arise largely from the efforts of the white population to maintain castelike controls and privileges. The problem there can be analyzed as a clash of subcultures, each relatively unified as to the rightness of its standards. Gunnar Myrdal's thesis of an "American dilemma"[1] in which white people are torn between their creeds and their specific operating practices would not apply to the case in which the dominant whites feel little value-conflict in supporting inequalitarian, discriminatory patterns. For example, the legal doctrine of "equal but separate" public services for whites and Negroes in many areas is largely a cultural fiction: national law requires open access, some localities insist upon segregation and castelike prerogatives, and the unequal and separate facilities result. The specific evidence of normative conflict is that there is at least an *awareness* of different standards and an attempt to justify the local system. One can move through many intermediate types of such situations to something very close to "institutionalized" evasion in many Northern cities. In New York State, for example, it is illegal to refuse service to Negroes in commercial establishments. There is enough social consensus to support the passage of such legislation; there is considerable public disapproval of discrimination; many white people feel uneasy or guilty when they act in ways defined as "discriminatory" or "prejudiced." Yet there are well-marked

---

[7] Logan Wilson, *The Academic Man* (New York, Oxford University Press, 1942), pp. 50–51, 54–56. See also A. B. Hollingshead, "Ingroup Membership and Academic Selection," *American Sociological Review*, 3, 6 (December 1938), 826–833.

[8] Marshall B. Clinard, *The Black Market* (New York: Holt, Rinehart & Winston, 1952), p. 39; Edwin H. Sutherland, *White-Collar Crime* (New York: Holt, Rinehart & Winston, 1961.)

[9] John G. Fuller, *The Gentlemen Conspirators* (New York: Grove Press, 1962); Frank Gibney, *The Operators* (New York: Harper & Row, 1960); Donald R. Cressey, *Other People's Money* (New York: Free Press, 1953).

[1] Gunnar Myrdal, with the assistance of Richard Sterner and Arnold Rose, *An American Dilemma*, 2 vols. (New York: Harper & Row, 1944).

patterns of informal segregation, and the legal barriers against discrimination are often evaded. For example, restaurants have developed very elaborate devices of evasion such as the "freeze-out," in which service is delayed on various pretexts for an intolerable length of time, or the "friendly brush-off"—an appeal to the Negro patron to leave "because the other customers will object"—or the "rough house" pattern of cold food, overcharges, spilled soup, or brusque service.[2] These acts are often performed by persons professing belief in equal rights. Patterned evasions are, probably typically, the products of specific, recurring *situations* in which immediate interests, group stereotypes, and interpersonal ties and expectations take precedence over the more abstract ideal norms.[3] Quite clearly, many of the specific situations that emerge are so delicately balanced that an apparently trivial factor can move the pattern decisively over to either the discriminatory or the nondiscriminatory mode.

The consequences of the widespread and dramatic exposure of such covert systems of institutional evasion deserve analysis on a scale far beyond what has been done to date. It seems to be generally assumed that public exposure of violations of norms strengthens consensus and the commitment to the dominant institutions. This assumption is sometimes true, but in other cases the disclosure may actually weaken support of the nominal institutional regulation by changing expectations (the realization that many others share the practice) and by activating interests and values previously defined as forbidden.

The considerations just reviewed indicate why a sociological analysis cannot stop with treatment of the manifest institutional structure. The manifest norms must be known; but an understanding of violation, variation, and evasion is equally necessary, both for science and for social action. Culture and society are always changing; and the first tiny breaches of normative structure are to be carefully watched in any attempt to comprehend the sources of social change.

Because previous chapters have so closely focused upon the main institutions of the society, it is especially necessary here to stress the relation of individuals to their institutions. No one lives in a culture as a whole. We live in particular segments of the total culture—in a particular family, class, school, church, and so on. What we directly experience is always a variant of the patterns discernible by external scientific abstraction; and each of us has countless occasions for idiosyncratic interpretation of norms. The most

---

2 Cf. Robin M. Williams, Jr., with the assistance of John P. Dean and Edward A. Suchman, *Strangers Next Door* (Englewood Cliffs, N.J.: Prentice-Hall, 1964), chaps. 6 and 9.

3 Cf. Myrdal, *op. cit.*, p. xliii. " 'The American Dilemma,' referred to in the title of this book, is the . . . conflict between, on the one hand, the valuations preserved on the general plane, which we shall call the 'American Creed,' where the American thinks, talks, and acts under the influence of high national and Christian precepts, and on the other hand, the valuations on specific planes of individual and group living, where personal and local interest; economic, social and sexual jealousies; considerations of community prestige and conformity; group prejudice against particular persons or types of people; and all sorts of miscellaneous wants, impulses, and habits dominate his outlook." Our analysis would add to this the points outlined on pp. 429–430 above.

complete description of institutional norms would still not tell us exactly how to act in specific situations. It is, therefore, not a source of wonder that there is variation, evasion, and complex change in institutions; it is at least equally remarkable how much regularity, conformity, and predictability do exist.

## CULTURAL FICTIONS

Implicit in the foregoing discussion are distinctions among various levels of "reality" in the normative definition and regulation of conduct. In some cases, cultural blueprint and typical behavior are so congruent that either one can be predicted from the other with a low margin of error; however, we have seen instances in which stated norms and observed behavior differ widely.[4] Regularized evasions sometimes are a means to fill a gap between norm and action; in other cases, they resolve the clash of two or more norms which carry conflicting behavioral requirements.

When behavior is defined within a group or community as "bad," "abnormal," "deviant," and the like, the usual commonsense assumption seems to be that the consequences of such behavior (and the evaluation and labeling of it) are wholly disruptive or damaging to "the social order." In our analysis, we have tried to appraise the validity of three rather different points: (1) that crime and deviant behavior often are inevitable consequences of dominant values, institutions, and social structures within a given society; (2) that much deviant behavior represents *organized* evasion of norms; and (3) that systemic evasion may have the consequence of permitting continuance of norms and social structures that otherwise could not be maintained. Although these assertions are imprecise, their validity in a broad sense seems reasonably well certified by observation and experiment. A further clarification has been provided by the recognition that deviance may be either rejected or accepted and that in either case, the consequence may be either to strengthen or to weaken the group or social system,[5] depending upon the specific conditions. An indiscriminate tolerance of deviance can lead to normative chaos and group disintegration. But an overly rigid, global, and diffuse demand for strict behavioral and ideological conformity can cause excessive social cleavage and fragmentation and can choke off the sources of creative problem-solving innovations. Conversely, what might be described as "functionally selective" rejection of deviant behavior can strengthen sentiments of conformity and solidarity, clarify norms, and reinforce commitment to maintenance of the system. There are even instances in which acceptance of the deviance may strengthen the social unit's capacity to survive and to satisfy its members' needs. Of course, it is not necessary to elaborate upon the parallel fact that much nonconformity is immensely destructive *in terms of existing values*, without any apparent or immediate gain to offset the damage. One must add, how-

[4] For one more instance, not often recognized, see: Leon J. Friedman, *Virgin Wives: A Study of Unconsummated Marriages* (Springfield: Charles C. Thomas, 1962).

[5] Lewis A. Coser, "Some Functions of Deviant Behavior and Normative Flexibility," *American Journal of Sociology*, LXVIII, 2 (September 1962), 172–181.

ever, that only rarely is there any objective technique for measuring "damage" or "gain"—even when the values at stake are clear.

We come now to a still different phenomenon, that of "cultural fictions."[6] A cultural fiction exists whenever there is a cultural description, explanation, or normative prescription that is both *generally accepted as a norm* and *typically followed* in conduct but is at the same time markedly at variance with the subjective conceptions or inclinations of participants in the pattern or with certain objective scientific knowledges. Many so-called fictions are simply "arbitrary" from the standpoint of any particular individual—although *not* necessarily so from the perspective of the functional needs within a society having a particular set of value orientations,[7] for example, language, methods of measuring space and time, numerous minor social usages, the elaboration of etiquette. Many, if not most, cultural norms are not rigidly anchored in the nature of man as a biological organism nor in the nature of the physical environment. To take one of James Woodard's deliberately commonplace examples, there would not seem to be any biological or physical factors that would indicate a fork as the suitable instrument for eating peas—a spoon would seem to be more efficient and possibly more adaptive biologically. The prescribed usage is in this sense arbitrary, although agreement upon any one procedure does provide predictability and to this extent facilitates social interaction.[8] Clearly identifiable cultural fictions occur when private affective and perceptual responses do not correspond to the overt pattern; for example, the chief executive expresses deep regret over the resignation of a subordinate when it is clearly understood that everyone was elated to see the event accomplished. Such conventional forms of expression and interaction are pervasive even in a society so loosely organized and informal as the United States.

When conventional forms are consistently practiced by all members of a social group, they typically evoke sentiments felt to be consistent with the outward pattern of conduct. They are not then "mere forms" but actually define the individual's conception of proper and desirable behavior; the individual "really feels" and "wants to act" as the convention dictates he should. Conventions supported by such psychological involvement are not fictional except in the sense that all social norms and values are fictional because they are validated by consensus and practice rather than by realities independent of the social system.

There is a "front stage" and a "back stage" in all, or nearly all, social behavior—an organized presentation to other persons that differs from

---

[6] "Fiction" here has no ontological significance; it is used only as a convenient descriptive term, to be understood in the sense indicated by the discussion to follow.

[7] This section originally was stimulated by the analysis of James W. Woodard, "The Role of Fictions in Cultural Organization," *Transactions of the New York Academy of Sciences*, Series II, VI, 8 (June 1944), 311–344. Our treatment, however, does not intend to treat as "fiction" all social practices that cannot be given a "scientific" rationale.

[8] Woodard says that in this example there is an implicit fiction. We prefer here to say that it is an "arbitrary" usage and to reserve the term "fiction" for instances of divergence between cultural norm and the actors' private perceptions and evaluations of the situation.

the total mélange of action elements that press for overt expression. What goes on back of the stage ordinarily is kept well concealed from the spectators—much as the diners in fashionable restaurants often are saved from traumatic disillusionment by being out of view of what is happening back in the kitchens. In ordinary person-to-person exchanges, the externalized social self that is presented to others often differs greatly from the total sociopsychological self, of which it is a highly selective expression.[9]

To the degree that the "as if" conventions serve to limit and define spontaneous personal responses, they facilitate social interaction of various kinds. Even when unguided private sentiments are such as would disrupt interaction, a common orientation to conventional forms provides the minimal predictability necessary to continued participation. Stereotyped behavior (including statements of sentiment, feeling, value) becomes "fictional" only when the *culturally ascribed meaning* of the behavior is in opposition to the *privately held meanings actually operative* in the situation. In extreme instances it is possible to identify a very complex structure of "fictions:" individual A and individual B may each be aware they are using fictional forms and that the other individual is also aware that they are and yet continue to act conventionally. As Woodard suggests, formality (conventionalization, protocol) tends to be at a maximum when *it is important that interaction occur,* there are *few and weak positive ties* between the participants, and the interaction involves relatively *severe conflicts of interests or values.*[1] Examples include diplomatic convention, military courtesy, much of etiquette, academic decorum, judicial procedures. In our own society, as in others, it continually happens that certain beliefs are expressed, values stated, assumptions accepted, actions performed when the participants in the pattern themselves recognize fictional elements in what they are saying or doing. In a great many of these patterns, not "hypocrisy" but functional deviousness[2] is perhaps the most meaningful characterization of the situation.

The degree of "reality" or "fictionality" of social events varies greatly: outright lie or deception; errors or mistakes; staged illusions; playing of a part; conventional fictions; fully committed action, involving a person's deepest convictions. At one extreme, the actor knowingly states or implies by his other behavior something contrary to fact. At the other extreme, the person would not wish to act in any other way than he is acting; and his overt behavior corresponds, in some strong sense, to the total integrated self. In between are many complex combinations of selectivity, commitment, involvement, intensity, illusion, and deception. The fictional ele-

[9] Understanding of the detailed processes involved has been advanced by the work of Erving Goffman in *The Presentation of the Self in Every-Day Life* (Edinburgh: University of Edinburgh, Social Sciences Research Centre, 1956); *Behavior in Public Places: Notes on the Social Organization of Gatherings* (New York: Free Press, 1963); *Encounters: Two Studies in the Sociology of Interaction* (Indianapolis: Bobbs-Merrill, 1961); and *Interaction Ritual* (Garden City, N.Y.: Doubleday, 1967).

[1] Woodard, *op. cit.,* pp. 326–332.

[2] *Ibid.,* p. 329. See also Wilbert E. Moore and Melvin M. Tumin, "Some Social Functions of Ignorance," *American Sociological Review,* 14, 6 (December 1949), 787–795, esp. p. 791.

ments often are not at all immediately obvious, either psychologically or socially.

Much deviance may be "masked" by being considered accidental. For example, an unknown but substantial proportion of "accidental" deaths and injuries are outcomes of destructive tendencies—in particular, many automobile accidents clearly represent suicidal or homicidal attempts, although this is often not self-evident nor easy to prove. Fatalities on the streets and highways of the United States—now occurring at fantastic figures of over 50,000 per year—exceed those from military losses in all of the nation's wars, yet seem to be rarely protested, are rarely regarded as avoidable, and seldom are defined as the expectable outcome of deviant or antisocial motivations. Driving under the influence of alcohol is so clearly an extreme hazard that one must wonder why the possible connections between aggressive or destructive urges, subsequent drinking, and consequent death or mayhem on the road are so systematically ignored or minimized. Certainly some automobile "accidents" combine suicide and murder.

Many commonly accepted beliefs concerning deviant behavior are either contrary to fact or their truth is not demonstrable. "Crime does not pay" is often cited as a reinforcement of conformity; but it seldom added that only one-fourth to one-third of major crimes are solved by the police.[3] The degree of infallibility imputed to doctors, judges, or political leaders may not always be based on a detached appraisal of performance. Where it is vital to have confidence, we often act "as if" our beliefs were more secure than we inwardly feel them to be.

Perhaps the phrase "cultural fictions" seems to imply too harsh a judgment of the validity of many social beliefs to which it might be applied. Perhaps "ideology" would fit better as a label for sets of ideas and beliefs that purport to explain and justify existing social and cultural conditions. Ideologies flourish at points of actual or potential conflict of interests, of inconsistencies of beliefs and values, of discrepancies between norms and practice. The elaboration of an ideology is a sign that tells us to expect some underlying strain or tension. It is, therefore, to be expected that ideologies will grow in profusion around questions of the distribution of rights and privileges as over against deprivations, obligations, and sacrifices. Why should some be wealthy and others poor? Why should some young men be sent into combat while others safely complete their preparation for a professional or business career? Why should some pay a much larger proportion than others of their income in taxes?

Ideological luxuriance surrounds the subject of taxation in our society.[4] Different groups and strata pay very different amounts and proportions of their income in taxes; the tax structure is studded with special dispensa-

[3] Herbert A. Bloch and Frank T. Flynn, *Delinquency: The Juvenile Offender in America Today* (New York: Random House, 1956), p. 253. Many victims do not report crimes against them—from 11 percent of automobile thefts to 90 percent of alleged consumer frauds (Johnson, *op. cit.*, pp. 28–30).

[4] See Louis Eisenstein, *The Ideologies of Taxation* (New York: Ronald Press, 1961), in which a tax lawyer wittily exposes the vast amount of mythic discourse and emotionally charged political rationalizations that "justify" the distribution of the burdens of taxation.

tions, such as, the exemption from taxation of interest on state and local bonds, special (favorable) treatment of capital gains, large allowances for depletion of oil and gas, and special provisions for reductions of taxable income in very high income brackets (income-splitting, exemption of expense accounts, business perquisites). Since the structure as a whole conforms to no consistent principle and since strong interests and divergent values are persistently involved, the ideological descriptions rarely correspond neatly with the actual situations.

If cultural definitions are to be socially effective, however, they must be invested with some kind of reality by the society's members, and the pressure to accept fully the definitions and prescriptions becomes the more intense the greater the stress and the higher the ranking of the values involved in any particular case. One can arrange cultural items in continuous gradients, from usages and conventions practiced by individuals who accept them as necessary or expedient fictions over to the abiding beliefs and values not regarded as in any sense fictional. Hence, the determination of just what is a cultural fiction (and in what sense) is rarely even so apparently easy as in the case of the peas-and-fork example. When the culture bearers themselves are *not* aware of any "as if" element in their practices or beliefs, is there ever any basis for imputing such an element to their behavior? To many people in America the large corporation represents "private property" —they attach to corporate organizations the values and symbols historically associated with the control of property by individual entrepreneurs. Is this belief-value complex a cultural fiction or not? The answer appears to be yes but no: it is not a fiction to those Americans who hold the view, but it is a fiction if one compares the modern corporation to private property as defined in earlier periods of history. It is only in this limited sense that scientific analysis is justified in describing this cultural orientation as partly fictional. And this example, perhaps, has already implied that cultural patterns are especially likely to be perceived as fictional—both by participants and by analytical observers—when (1) beliefs or value orientations conflict,[5] or (2) "creeds" enjoin beliefs without modeling the conduct required for their effective operation ("lip service"),[6] or (3) certain practices and beliefs have ceased to command personal commitment or involvement from large numbers of people. Examples under each of these categories can be described in our own society. Thus, when we find verbal assent to creeds of democracy and equality existing alongside racial discrimination, the sources of seeming contradiction include elements of direct value conflict—and the "fictional" appearance of the creedal beliefs may not be apprehended by persons caught in the cross pressure.[7] Out of such conflicts there emerge,

[5] Under definable conditions this produces what Kenneth Burke terms "perspective by incongruity"—*Permanence and Change* (New York: New Republic, 1936), Part II, esp. pp. 118 ff. Note in our modern society (just prior to World War II) the vogue of semantics and psychoanalysis, the development of relativistic thought, the prevalence of "debunking." And note also the very different developments that were then associated with war and politico-ideological conflict.

[6] Really a special case of (1).

[7] Self-conscious and deliberate use of a normative façade to conceal radically antithetical values does occur, of course. But it is easy to overestimate its importance. As Machiavelli

under differing conditions, the victory of one set of values, a compromise, or a new synthesis or mutation. On the other hand, cultural fictions often represent the more subtle processes of "loss of conviction,"[8] expressed in the language of psychology as withdrawal of affect, or loss of identification and involvement. In the latter case, change in the main institutions and systems of belief derives more immediately from slow attrition than from revolutionary attack. Value orientations retain effective regulatory power in conduct only to the extent that they are actually practiced—that is, defended when attacked, used as referents for concrete action, affirmed in social interaction. Only those orientations that are strongly invested with attention and effort escape the museum of cultural fictions.

## CONCLUSION AND IMPLICATIONS

It has been repeatedly stressed in this chapter that social norms vary considerably in the way individuals conceive of and conform to them. In addition, we suggested the crucial point, in connection with cultural fictions, that shared assumptions and expectations can play an essential part in behavior, even when regarded by the actors as fictional or when so described by external analysis.[9] Recent empirical studies investigating the variability of norms and their modification under situational cross pressures seem to support the lines of analysis followed here. Thus, Samuel Stouffer suggests: "It may be precisely the ranges of permissible behavior which most need examination if we are to make progress in this realm which is so central in social science. For it may be the very existence of some flexibility or social slippage—but not too much—which makes behavior in groups possible."[1] Institutional flexibility, within limits, appears to be a necessary condition for the functioning of social systems. Moreover, some evasions and violations of particular given cultural rules seem clearly "functional" for the maintenance of *other* cultural structures in the same society.[2] Thus in the end the subject matter of the present discussion resolves itself into questions of values and value priorities. All that social science, as science, can do is to analyze the conditions which are causal in the appearance of deviant behavior, institutionalized evasion, cultural fictions—and normative change. We have not

---

long ago understood, it is very difficult for men to be consistently and thoroughly "bad" and hypocritical at the same time.

[8] Cf. Archibald MacLeish, "The American State of Mind," *The American Scholar*, XIX, 4 (Autumn 1950).

[9] Cf. Gustav Ichheiser, "Misunderstandings in Human Relations: A Study in False Social Perception," *American Journal of Sociology*, LV, 2, Part 2 (September 1949), pp. 1–70. See esp. p. 44: "For it is in the nature of human relations that their basic assumptions and expectations have to be accepted as valid even if at times these are much at variance with the facts which they allegedly represent. Otherwise a predictable functioning of social relations would not be possible, and society, as we know it, could not exist."

[1] Samuel A. Stouffer, "An Analysis of Conflicting Social Norms," *American Sociological Review*, XIV, 6 (December 1949), 707–717.

[2] The *literal* enforcement of every norm subscribed to by the members of American communities would certainly produce tensions on a scale so enormous as to challenge imagination.

undertaken to judge—either to condone or to condemn—the observed patterns. Whatever the analysis may have left undone, it has quite forcibly confronted us with the basic question of the role of *values* in the functioning of social systems. To this question the following chapter will be devoted.

## SUGGESTED READINGS

BECKER, HOWARD S. (ed.). *Outsiders: Studies in the Sociology of Deviance*. New York: Free Press, 1963. Lively and informative collection of essays by authors who know their materials well. Raises important questions of social policy in the course of presenting data and explanatory discussion.

CLINARD, MARSHALL. *Sociology of Deviant Behavior*, rev. ed. New York: Holt, Rinehart & Winston, 1963. A widely used and excellent textbook. Relates its discussion to critically selected research.

COHEN, ALBERT K. *Deviance and Control*. Englewood Cliffs, N.J.: Prentice-Hall, 1966. Reviewed for Chapter XIV below. Excellent high-level introduction to its subject.

ERIKSON, KAI T. *Wayward Puritans: A Study in the Sociology of Deviance*. New York: Wiley, 1966. The Puritans were not always so "puritan"—nor were they so prone as often believed to inflict harsh and relentless punishment. In this clearly written book, the Puritans of New England serve as exemplars of generic processes of deviance and control. Presents an ingenious theory relating kind and amount of deviance to the character of the boundaries of the effective social "community."

GOFFMAN, ERVING. *The Presentation of the Self in Everyday Life*. Edinburgh: University of Edinburgh, 1956. Highly influential work. Exceptionally penetrating discussion of the "stage management" involved in ordinary social interaction.

JOHNSON, ELMER H. *Crime, Correction, and Society*, rev. ed. Homewood, Ill.: Dorsey Press, 1968, esp. chap. 9. Careful synoptic treatment of sociological aspects of crime and of efforts to control and penalize deviance. Good coverage of the literature.

STEFFENS, LINCOLN. *The Autobiography of Lincoln Steffens*. New York: Harcourt, Brace, 1931. Vivid, sensitive portrayal of the ambiguities and paradoxes of deviance, punishment, evasion, conformity, respectability, and power. For those who mistakenly think that present society is unusually hypocritical: read and reflect again.

WILLIAMS, ROBIN M., JR. with the assistance of JOHN P. DEAN and EDWARD A. SUCHMAN. *Strangers Next Door*. Englewood Cliffs, N.J.: Prentice-Hall, 1964, chaps. 6 and 9. Extensive surveys and intensive observations showing the clashing expectations, beliefs, values, and interests that generate variability of behavior, unstable norms, and patterned evasions. Analyzes sources of strain and conflict, foreshadowing the dramatic changes in black-white relations in the 1960's.

# Values in American Society

## XI

## AN ANALYSIS OF VALUES AND VALUE-ORIENTATIONS

### Why Study Values?

I n sketching the main outlines of the ordered institutional life of the United States our focus has been upon recurring ideal patterns—and those systematic deviations that are sufficiently persistent, uniform, and enduring to be thought of as *structure* in a large and heterogeneous society. The analysis began with the institutionalized and conventional prescriptions for approved conduct. These ideal patterns were shown to be inferences from observations of behavior, but analytically different from the total behavior taken at a commonsense level of observation. Our second level of analysis therefore had to concern itself with actual regularities in behavior—not just with norms, standards, and orientations but with the interaction in which norms are imperfectly actualized.

This step-by-step analysis has traced a part of the most obvious structural framework of the American social order. Even this limited degree of analysis required a rather sharp focus upon certain portions of society and accordingly a systematic neglect of others. In short, to gain insight into the structural elements of norms and social organization we have deliberately put on "blinders" to shut out other observations. This process is legitimate, indeed unavoidable, in any systematic examination of a social system; but we must not stop with our first approximation.

Our next step is to describe the major patterns of *values* that can be identified in American society. Of course, "American values" are not values necessarily exclusive to, or even peculiar to, the United States, nor do all Americans share them. We wish to discover the extent to which any particular value or value complex is in fact present in this society.

There are, however, important grounds for expecting American culture to be characterized by a value system appreciably different from other cultures. Most obvious perhaps is the different environment—different location, physical surroundings, climate, resources, and so on. Equally impressive are the many diverse cultural strains and the subsequent crosscultural contacts within the American aggregate. Aside from these, and from any possible genetic selectivity, we know that a society separated from others by spatial and sociopolitical barriers will, over a period of time, develop a relatively distinctive culture.

The data cited in following pages indicate that in a broad comparative view, American culture does bear out this proposition. The real problem, however, is to identify and appraise the value patterns that are relatively most distinctive and important.

We cannot, however, proceed to identify these patterns without first seeing how the concept of social institutions involves the concept of value. For the individual facing his culture, institutions are a sort of map or "blueprint" of the main outlines and contours of expected and obligatory conduct. Institutionalized rules at any given time in a particular culture implicitly say: "These and these are the things that are expected, these and these are the probable consequences of conformity and nonconformity." Social norms are the rules for the game of life. But rules ultimately make no sense unless they guide men in reaching goals that are valid and valuable for the human beings who make rules, enforce them, resist them. Looking at institutions from the outside, as impartial observers, we see them as sets of norms by which people are able to know what is expected and required. In addition to this function of *orientation*, institutions represent *internalized values* that are felt as binding for the personality—conscience, life goals, preferred subjective states of various kinds. Institutions get inside us. We come to feel that an obligation is *ours*, not just an arbitrary, imposed rule. We come to accept as valuable and right, for us, some of the standards of conduct and goals of effort that are held by our parents, our peers, or others with whom we identify or wish to emulate. Of course, institutions are not *identical with* values; institutions are more specific than the values to be found in them, and the same basic value may be found in several different institutions and may remain relatively constant through a variety of changes in particular institutional norms. Nevertheless, the continued existence of any particular system of institutions depends in great part upon the extent to which the pattern contains values actually invested with affect and meaning for the participants. Thus, institutions typically are both "facts of the external world" that the individual must take into account and value patterns within the personality. Every act, or failure to act, in the interdependent web of sociocultural life has consequences; institutions and the values they represent are continually being reinforced, maintained, changed, or destroyed by the shifting patterns of human thought and action. "Stability" of culture is, therefore, a dynamic process in which a delicately balanced system of values is maintained.

Americans currently face a period in which few institutions, beliefs, or values can any longer be taken for granted. All are under strain; all are challenged. Basic transformations of man and society are now underway, and many vital choices of values must be made.

## What Is Meant by Value?

It is essential for *this* analysis that we secure a clear conception of what values are and of how we may recognize and analyze their role in a system of motivated social action. We are concerned with values as observable variables in human conduct, not with an appraisal of various values as being better or worse than others, nor with the meaning and ontological status of value as a concept, however important these problems may be. For our purposes, we must seek a conception of value that can be referred to definite evidence.

A common notion is that value refers to any aspect of a situation, event, or object that is invested with a *preferential interest* as being "good," "bad," "desirable," and the like. This conception is not enough for present purposes. Any formal definition of value is likely to be too general to be of great use to a sociological analysis, and a certain kind of general definition seems to involve an inevitable circularity—to define value as "interest," for example, is only another way of saying value. It is enough here if we circumscribe the boundaries of value. What are experienced by individuals as values have these qualities: (1) They have a conceptual element—they are more than pure sensations, emotions, reflexes, or so-called needs. Values are abstractions drawn from the flux of the individual's immediate experience. (2) They are affectively charged: they represent actual or potential emotional mobilization. (3) Values are not the concrete goals of action, but rather the *criteria* by which goals are chosen. (4) Values are important, not "trivial" or of slight concern. (Although this statement is circular, it suggests the possibility of studying values through the study of choices.)

Clearly, there are often intense and widespread *interests* that are both ethically disapproved and held to be inimical to group welfare—murder or vice for example. On the other hand, we easily recognize values that are at the same time interests or desires of individuals, objects of ethical approval, and approved as conducive to group welfare: for example, personal honesty or a happy monogamous marriage. Furthermore, there are the dramatic and often tragic situations in which an ethical value is in conflict with a current social value—the situation, for instance, of the conscientious objector in time of war.

In the consideration of values, a useful point of departure lies in the elementary facts of *preference* and *selection*. Men prefer some things to others; they select particular objects and courses of action from a range of possibilities present in a situation. *Some* human behavior, at least, is purposive: people can and do state their goals in advance and can then be observed to act as if they were in fact pursuing those ends. Objects, events, experiences are desired and sought out, or are eschewed or avoided. Men are not creatures of indifference; the world is not emotionally neutral for us, nor are all things equally desired or esteemed. Accepting this, we must still be careful to see the highly consequential distinction between "value" in the sense of an *evaluation* of an object of regard, on the one hand, and the *standards* by which such evaluations are made, on the other. We find it natural to say such things as, "Americans place a high value upon education," "that certainly was a worthwhile experience," "he is a most valuable member of our organization," or "political democracy is the best form of government." These are evaluations *of* objects as when it is said: "The value placed upon 'future success' has receded in favor of 'respectable and stable security' seen in shorter time range."[1] It is precisely the fact of placing a

[1] Clyde Kluckhohn, "Have There Been Discernible Shifts in American Values During the Past Generation?" in Elting E. Morison (ed.), *The American Style* (New York: Harper & Row, 1958), p. 204.

value *on* something to which we often are referring in ordinary speech when we use the term "value." On the other hand, we frequently find ourselves using the same word to refer to the *standards* by which evaluations are made and in terms of which choices and evaluations are defended and justified, to ourselves and others. As Clyde Kluckhohn has noted, there is a basic distinction between "that which is desired" and "that which is desirable" (worthy of being desired, properly the object of desire). Values in the sense of standards are "conceptions of the desirable." They are criteria for deciding what we should want. What these standards are is not immediately given to us by knowing the goals men seek, the ideologies they profess, or the gross preferences they exhibit in their conduct.[2] To know that a man seeks, say, money or success tells us next to nothing about the *criteria* in terms of which these goals are judged worthwhile.

Empirically considered, value is not an all-or-none matter, but a continuum.[3] At one pole, we find those moral values that are true matters of conscience. Values of this order are present when the individual who violates them shows a reaction of strong guilt or overwhelming shame and the group imposes strong censure upon the offender or when the person who acts in accord with an accepted standard of evaluation experiences gratification, a clear conscience, and an enhanced self-image and is rewarded and honored by his fellows. Such moral values are the core of the individual's internalized conscience. They also define the central institutional structure of the society—although the accepted mores do not necessarily coincide with the "highest" social ethics and the ethical position of any given individual may not be identical with either the mores or the highest ethics. From the point on the value continuum at which the moral quality is emphasized, values shade off into those evoking less intense guilt or shame and less severe social sanctions, for example, esthetic standards, conventional proprieties, and simple norms of expediency or technical efficiency. Only careful research testing can establish the position of any "alleged" value along this continuum in the actual functioning of a society.

Values are manifest in human behavior, but not all behavior shows forth values; physiological activities are not values, nor are sheer reflex acts. On the other hand, a disinterested moral judgment of a governmental policy is clearly an evaluative act. Between such widely separated cases lie numerous activities of appraisal, preference, and selection: interests, aversions, attractions, desires, wants, needs, choices, likes, affections, pleasures, duties, moral obligations, and many others. To consider all selective behavior as "valuing" is to broaden the term beyond any analytical usefulness. To narrow the meaning of value to "moral value" is to constrict its scope so

[2] It is clear also from the foregoing that values are not identical with "motives" or "needs" of individual personalities. Things, processes, events, and the symbols designating them are valuable only in relation to the preferences of sentient actors; therefore, as Charles Morris says, the values attributed to objects are "objectively relative," inhering in a relation between properties of the object and preferences of the valuing subject. See his *Signification and Significance: A Study of the Relation of Signs and Values* (Cambridge, Mass.: Harvard University Press, 1964).

[3] For an excellent philosophical analysis see Stephen C. Pepper, *The Sources of Value* (Berkeley and Los Angeles: University of California Press, 1958).

narrowly as to necessitate numerous ad hoc extensions for dealing with matters which we are forced to recognize as value laden.

In view of these considerations, we here define values as those *conceptions of desirable states of affairs* that are utilized in selective conduct as *criteria* for preference or choice or as *justifications* for proposed or actual behavior. Values are closely related, conceptually and empirically, to social norms; but norms are the more specific, concrete, situation-bound specifications; values are the criteria by which norms themselves may be and are judged. Values are not the same as needs, desires, or motives, for everyone at some time has desires that he judges negatively, and one may evaluate highly, for others, a condition he himself does not desire to attain or experience. There would be no human values were men not energetic organisms; but "energy" alone cannot generate the standards we call values. The remarkable thing is, rather, that values can steer or canalize or actually define powerful needs and gratifications in ways far removed from primary biological promptings.[4]

Of course, values are not just "given" independently of the whole nexus of biological, demographic, ecological, physical, psychological, and social factors that enter into the direct causation of behavior. Values have causes. At times, and in some circumstances, the area of free play for values as determinants of behavior may be very greatly limited. Nevertheless, once value standards have been developed, there seems to be no ground to deny, in principle, that they may in their turn become causes of behavior. The matter cannot simply be decided a priori by a simple fiat or act of will of the student of human conduct.

And, again, of course, values emerge in the experience of people in evaluating objects of desire; hence, values are to be found in the relation between a human actor and the objects that are of concern to him.[5] Our treatment will have to neglect esthetic and expressive values in the interest of describing those values (and beliefs) that most clearly characterize the main institutions of the society. For this purpose, we do not need to argue the ancient questions concerning the objectivity of values or their quality of absoluteness or lack of it. Our basic questions are (1) what, in fact, are the conceptions of the desirable to be found in this society and (2) what does the presence of these values tell us about the actual functioning of the social system? It will be necessary to deal with some clusters of belief-and-value that are diffuse and vague, as well as with highly generalized and explicit value-orientations. Throughout we must be watchful to distinguish

[4] This section is adapted from the article, "Values" by this author in *International Encyclopedia of the Social Sciences*, Vol. 16 (New York: Macmillan and Free Press, 1968), pp. 283–287. Of course, it is quite legitimate to define values in terms more restrictive than those used here; one may prefer to consider only moral values, or to reserve the word values for "satisfactions that are self-sufficient," as suggested by Harold Fallding, "A Proposal for the Empirical Study of Values," *American Sociological Review*, 30, 2 (April 1965), pp. 223–233.

[5] Cf. Clyde Kluckhohn, "Values and Value-orientations in the Theory of Action: An Exploration in Definition and Classification," in Talcott Parsons and Edward A. Shils (eds.), *Toward a General Theory of Action* (Cambridge, Mass.: Harvard University Press, 1951), pp. 388–433.

values, as criteria, from the evaluations of social conditions and processes; it is hoped that the context of the discussion will keep us on the right path.

Values and beliefs are related but not identical. *Beliefs* have primarily an existential reference: they concern what the believer takes as reality— the properties of and relationships among entities and processes. Beliefs are true or false, valid or invalid, or not testable. There is in beliefs *as such* no criterion of good or bad, only "is" or "is not" (in some sense and in some degree). The standards involved are cognitive. Valid cognitive beliefs constitute knowledge. Knowledge, error, and untestable beliefs comprise the storehouse of cognitive culture.

Concretely, beliefs usually involve a normative (evaluative) aspect in addition to the evaluation of them as valid or invalid; that is, the belief itself is either desirable or undesirable on grounds other than its cognitive correctness, or it refers to a state of affairs that is thus desirable or undesirable.

Evaluative beliefs concerning desirable social states represent applications of cognitive, cathectic (affective), and evaluative standards to real or imagined social relationships, units, and processes. When such beliefs fall together into relatively coherent and relatively stable clusterings, such organized aggregates of beliefs and values may be termed *ideologies*. A "justifying" ideology says "Here is an existing set of desirable social arrangements." A "radical" or "utopian" ideology says, "Here is a good future state of affairs that should replace the present one." Ideologies have been highly salient, to say the least, in this century of continuous revolution.

Institutions are organized sets of widely accepted and strongly supported obligatory norms. Obligatory norms tend to be clustered into statuses; and interrelated sets of statuses are organized around main foci of values and interests in recurrent situations, for example, birth of children, allocation of scarce means, and use of power. These organized networks of statuses constitute the main structures of kinship, social stratification, economy, polity, education, religion, and recreation.

Obviously, a description of any total society must deal with beliefs, ideologies, norms, and institutions, as well as the values that are here the main focus of attention.

Values concern the goals or ends of action and are, as well, components in the selection of adequate means.[6] Even insofar as choice is not deliberate or conscious, all action nevertheless is of one kind rather than another. Some balancing of alternatives must occur whenever alternatives exist. Since acts, including failures to act, typically involve a renunciation of other possible courses of behavior, every act "costs something." In this sense, values and their arrangement into hierarchies are defined by choices.

When we say that a person "puts a high value" on something, what do we mean? We seem to mean that the person is willing to expend effort or make sacrifices to attain or maintain a certain identifiable state of affairs. To "put a high value on education," for example, may mean such behavior

---

[6] Cf. further analysis of the implications of this statement in the author's "Individual and Group Values," *The Annals*, 371 (May 1967), 20–37.

as long and arduous study, the sacrifice of money that could have been spent for other purposes, the acceptance of deprivation with regard to many attractive immediate gratifications. Since the human life-span is not infinite, all such expenditures of time involve the sacrifice of alternative uses. In this sense, the choice of values involves an "economy" of human energy.

At first glance, then, the criterion of *choice* seems to provide an adequate way of defining values empirically. We reason that any choice involves a renunciation of other values: the choice of A over B, B over C, and so on, would thus define a hierarchy of values.[7] If we look for crucial situations of choice and systematically record typical modes of choosing, we can then characterize the dominant and subsidiary goals and, eventually, the standards of value by which selections are ordered in any given group or situation. Linton reports that among the Comanche Indians of the plains, when the camp was raided by an enemy group, a man was supposed to save his mother-in-law before attempting to escape himself or save his property. In so far as this ideal pattern was actually carried out, it evidently represented some guiding principle as to the priority of values in that culture. To take a different illustration, a Chinese son in the old tradition would have been expected to save his father from danger before helping himself or his brother. There are many such examples of crucial choices; and, indeed, our unreflective sense of values is to an important extent compounded from observing, hearing about, and participating in exactly this way in the various kinds of choices within situations set for us by the surrounding culture.

Data on choices may be derived from direct observation of spontaneous behavior, from testimony of witnesses, from self-reporting, and from various indirect evidences. Thus, for example, in a society with a highly developed money economy, much can be learned about the patterns of general values from the patterns of money expenditure, since money is a particular measure of economic "value"—that is, of value in exchange. The study of family budgets, general patterns of consumer expenditure, public expenditures, the flow of the national income, and so on, is subject to interpretation in these terms. If we know that at a given level of income, rural families invest a larger proportion of their net income than do urban families, whereas urban families are more likely to put their funds into present consumption, we can immediately begin to raise questions as to the respective evaluation of, say, security or current enjoyment by the two groups.

An important difficulty in using choices as indices of values lies in the gross quality of concrete choices. The so-called simple choices of everyday life typically concern selection among *complexes* of values. To study for tomorrow's class rather than to go to the theater in the company of friends —neither course taken purely as behavior in itself indicates a value. The value-considerations may be standards of positive intellectual interest, of achievement, of sociability, esthetic values, and so on indefinitely—not isolated values, but interconnected systems of values. Yet we do have evidence that cultural standardization so defines and limits choices that we can

[7] For a difficult but promising philosophical analysis of direct relevance, see Georg H. von Wright, *The Logic of Preference* (Edinburgh: Edinburgh University Press, 1963).

expect to find in any given group or social system a regularity of choices in recurrent situations that under systematic study reveals a pattern of values.

Another possible test for the existence of values is to observe *directions of interest*. To what do people "pay attention?" We may study a society in which literature and other arts are permeated with an otherworldly emphasis. We may find on every hand, in the conversation and daily activities of the people, a preoccupation with transcendental or supernatural formulations of life problems. A first approximation might justify the statement that such a society is marked by a strongly religious value-system, subject to further testing from other sources of evidence.

We may also secure evidence on values by focusing upon what people say their values are. We find, in fact, that a great deal of verbalization consists in the explicit avowal or disavowal of certain values. *This* is said to be good, *that* bad; this is desirable, that undesirable; this is worth working or fighting for, that is worthless. Thus, the Westminster Assembly said: "Man's chief end is to glorify God and enjoy Him forever." This statement appears to represent a value system rather different from that indexed by: "Man is the measure of all things." The explicit statements of value positions are, of course, not completely reliable. They may represent "mere lip service," largely divorced from realistic conduct. No student of human conduct can accept uncritically, as final evidence, people's testimony as to their own values. Yet actions may deceive as well as words, and there seems no reason for always giving one precedence over the other.

Even when not explicitly stated, values can often be inferred directly from verbal materials. In argument, for instance, the statements arousing "heat," emotion, and so on, are clues to values. In assertion and counter-assertion, there frequently emerges level after level of favorable or unfavorable reactions—a "regress" that in certain cases can be followed back to certain irreducible or ultimate values.[8]

Verbal materials may also be analyzed by more complex methods going beyond the explicit, manifest, or apparent content. Systematic attention should be given to those implicit premises necessary for a meaningful account of (to "make sense of") explicit statements. It is commonly observed, for example, that what is *not* said is often more significant than what is said, reminding us again that the things in a culture that are most completely taken for granted typically turn out to be of fundamental importance in that culture.[9]

The material thus uncovered or reconstructed does not, of course, consist wholly of values, but includes "beliefs" and other cognitive elements.

[8] "Ultimate" or "irreducible" here refers only to the fact that a point may be reached at which a *basis for discussion no longer exists*; that is, there is an incompatibility of bias that cannot be resolved. We do not wish at this time to go into any broader questions as to what ultimate values may mean, except to point out that value positions that appear irrevocably incompatible are sometimes subject to redefinition that discloses a deeper agreement.

[9] Much of the work of psychiatrists and clinical psychologists, and much of psychological testing (for example, the use of projective techniques), is directed to the discovery of meaning, beliefs, and values that are not readily made explicit by the person himself. A variety of experimental techniques can be employed, also, in the study of values.

In its most simple and somewhat misleading formulation, a belief is a conviction that something is real, whereas a value is a standard of preference. Thus, a man may *believe* (that is, say he believes) that there is life after death; but this statement tells us nothing directly as to whether immortality is for him a positive or a negative value, or a matter of indifference. Two people both may have believed that Mussolini "made the trains run on time," but for one this belief signified approval of Italian Fascism, whereas for the other it indicated the "false efficiency" of a system violating basic human values in other respects. Although beliefs are often opportunistic in shaping themselves to interests, the relation is reciprocal and sometimes allows a considerable degree of independent variation. Otherwise stated, value relates closely to cognition; but the perception of what is supposed to exist is distinct from the subject's bias of favor or disfavor toward this supposed reality and from the standards he uses to defend his evaluation.

For purposes of social analysis, one great advantage of testimony, or of verbalization in general, is its capacity to reflect subtle shadings of values. This quality probably accounts for the common dissatisfaction with descriptions of behavior that neglect the reasons people give for their conduct. For it is in explanations and reasons that we often discover the significant value predicates that uncover the normative regularities behind seemingly varied actions.

Still another source of evidence is found by observing the reward-punishment system of a group or society, noting the incidence of *social sanctions*. What behavior is rewarded and praised? What is censured, disapproved, and punished? How great are the rewards and how severe the penalties? Under what circumstances is a given act, ordinarily disapproved, held excusable? What priority of values is involved in the "disapproved act" *versus* "extenuating circumstances?" What are the relatively stable and the relatively unstable elements in a series of related situations? When conduct must resolve two or more mutually incompatible value elements, how does the effective community react?

Chapter III suggested that observation of sanctions is a most useful way to detect the normative structure of a society. We can now reexamine the same data to track down more accurately the value elements in particular norms. Recalling that a norm specifies what action should be carried out in a given situation and how the action should be performed, let us look for the implicit values. The parental dictum "You should wash your hands before meals" is a norm; and the "should" indicates "it is a good thing to do this." This statement may carry an implicit syllogism—for example, dirty hands carry germs, germs are a hazard to health, health is desirable, therefore the rule. Or, considerations of social conformity may be involved ("what would the guests think"), or esthetic elements (dirty hands are ugly), and so on. On the conscious level, of course, such a normative statement may be largely unrationalized and taken as unproblematic in itself.

Suppose we assert that cleanliness is a major focus of value in American society. We could establish or refute such a statement by recording the following types of observations: (1) In this society, people often choose between activities that promote cleanliness and other types of activity (for example, cleaning house *versus* going to church or enjoying leisure). A great deal of time and effort is lavished on washing hands, taking baths, preparing clean clothes, scrubbing and sweeping, collecting and disposing of trash, and so on. (2) Newspapers and magazines devote much space to news, articles, and advertising dealing with cleanliness and ways of promoting it in various areas of life. (3) Comments asserting or implying a bias in favor of cleanliness are extremely common, not only in response to direct questioning but also in the form of unprompted statements. (4) Analysis of a wide sampling of spoken and written materials reveals an extraordinary number of instances that assume "cleanliness is desirable" as an implicit concept underlying the assertions. (Thus, in the frequent articles on new housekeeping methods there are many that never make the value statements directly.) (5) Children are approved and otherwise rewarded for cleanly behavior, but meet frowns, censorious speech, minor deprivations, and physical chastisement for certain violations of this pattern. Although the rewards and penalties may be less obvious in later life, adults, too, face sanctions for conduct disregarding this value.

Putting all these lines of evidence together and assuming for illustrative purposes that no important contrary facts are found, we can say that cleanliness is definitely a positively valued condition in American society, or in whatever segment of that society we may have in view. However, in a sense it is arbitrary to formulate cleanliness as the complex that is to be termed a value. One might conveniently and legitimately go beyond this formulation to a concept of some more generalized value—for example, orderliness or personal self-discipline—provided only that other evidence and convenience in analysis warrant the more inclusive description. There may be many levels of generality that can be identified in this way, depending upon the nature of the data and upon the purposes of analysis.

This much detail concerning possible approaches to the empirical study of values in society seems essential in order to underline the nature of the present analysis. Starting with the initial location of value in a relation of a person to an object of interest, the sources of evidence mentioned above indicate just so many "operational definitions" of value: value as *overt choice or preference,* as *attention or emphasis,* as *statement* or *assertion,* as *implicit premise,* as a referent of *social sanctions.* These various evidences are "pointers" that say "this is what is meant." Not all are of equal usefulness for every purpose, but all are useful. When used in combination, these several different approximations gain reliability in so far as they are mutually consistent.

The inventory of values held by a particular person or shared within a population are not jumbled together in a completely random assortment.[1]

[1] It should be noted at this point that "group value" is an ambiguous term that may refer either to (a) a similar or like goal, as when "getting ahead" (as individuals) represents a value complex held by all individuals throughout a group or (b) a desired state for the group taken collectively (as military security may be so regarded). A "group goal" we may define as a future state of affairs intended to be reached by collective action. Thus, a group goal is *not* necessarily identical, or even congruent, with the values, motives, or goals of individual members considered distributively. See the discussion in Robert M.

Rather, they are assembled into organized sets or systems, to an important extent. Although compartmentalization of subsets does occur, as well as disconnectedness of unit values, the total evidence of patterned aggregation is quite convincing. Further, many different individuals hold the same values; and this sharedness also exhibits orderliness, for example, high intercorrelations of certain values and subsets of them. Therefore, societies may be characterized by value distributions and by the arrangements of subsystems of values in different portions of the social structure.[2]

## WHAT ARE "DOMINANT VALUES"?

Upon leaving the United States after an extended visit, Sir William Beveridge observed that there were "six Americas in search of a faith." In a social order of the flux, variety, and groping suggested by this statement, can anything be said as to its hierarchy of values? Are there any focal values that can be held to be "dominant" in the American scene? Which values are *common* (shared), which are intense, or less intense, which are persistent or transitory, which take precedence over others? To be at all specific about the structure of American value-systems, some concrete tests of value dominance are obviously needed.

Dominant and subordinate values *for a group or social system as a whole* can be roughly ordered to these criteria:

1. *Extensiveness* of the value in the total activity of the system. What proportion of a population and of its activities manifest the value?
2. *Duration* of the value. Has it been persistently important over a considerable period of time?[3]
3. *Intensity* with which the value is sought or maintained, as shown by: effort, crucial choices, verbal affirmation, and by reactions to threats to the value—for example, promptness, certainty, and severity of sanctions.
4. *Prestige of value carriers*—that is, of persons, objects, or organizations considered to be bearers of the value. Culture heroes, for example, are significant indexes of values of high generality and esteem.

The application of these criteria may be illustrated by the complex we call democracy. Let us, purely for purposes of convenient demonstration, define democracy as a combination of (1) high evaluation of individual persons apart from their extrinsic characteristics or positions, (2) elective rather than appointive or hereditary choice of leaders, (3) reliance upon discussion and group consensus in determination of collective policy, (4) reservation of certain minimal social rights on an equal basis to all group members. How would we, then, test the hypotheses (1) that democracy is or is

---

MacIver and Charles H. Page, *Society* (New York: Holt, Rinehart & Winston, 1949), pp. 32 ff.

[2] This paragraph is from the author's "Individual and Group Values," *op. cit.*, p. 27.

[3] Or has it been thought important through time by the population in question? Not antiquity as objective fact but antiquity as belief may be the more significant factor. This observation was suggested to the writer by R. Lauriston Sharp.

not highly valued in America and (2) that democracy does or does not occupy a dominant position in the value hierarchy?

The first step is to secure evidence as to the prevalence of democracy in the various institutions and subcultures of the society. To what extent is there democracy in family, education, religious group, stratification system, government, economic system? At once we are aware of great variation among and within the several institutional sectors. There are, for example, democratic and nondemocratic family institutions. The criteria of democracy are met in full in some sectors of our political system, hardly at all in others. In the economic system, democratic organization is rare—hierarchy, subordination, and direction by authority are more usual.

As we take systematic inventory in this way, we find emerging from the mass of detail a pattern indicating that democracy is a widespread focus of positive evaluation in America. In comparative and historical perspective, the test of extensiveness shows a more pervasive emphasis on democracy in this society than in many other major systems; and examination of the historical record for the United States certainly shows a persistence through time of democratic values. However, there have been complex and often contradictory variations in this persistence in different periods and in different sectors of the society, and the specific meanings of democracy have changed in important ways. For instance, we have seen many manifestations of a tendency toward political democracy—such as the removal of property restrictions on voting and eligibility to office, the extension of the franchise to women, and the rapid extension of political rights and liberties and civil rights and protections to racial minorities in the generation following World War II;[4] on the other hand, certain invasions of previously established rights—for example, the internment of Japanese-American citizens during World War II, or the abuses of congressional investigating powers during the period of McCarthyism in the late 1940's and early 1950's. The more completely history is analyzed, the greater is our awareness both of the persistence of democratic values and of the inadequacy of summary characterizations of the culture as a whole. Attempts to estimate the *intensity* with which democratic values are affirmed, defended, sought, and maintained or the prestige accorded to democratic and nondemocratic culture bearers reveal similar complexity and variation.

Let us assume, however, that we have all the data specified earlier as requirements for determining the position of a value in a society. From these materials we can presumably say that value X is actually an operative value in the culture, and we can specify with some accuracy its place in the value hierarchy. We do not yet, however, have all the information needed for a definitive analysis of the part played by value X in the social system as a whole. For we have not yet faced the thorny problems posed by differing levels of valuation, differing degrees of ritualism or realism, and various types and degrees of value integration.

These levels of valuation of course represent analytic distinctions that

---

[4] For a review, see Milton R. Konvitz, *Expanding Liberties: Freedom's Gains in Postwar America* (New York: Viking, 1966).

overlap and crisscross in concrete experience. For example, the objects and events that are valued, typically are valued *both* as ends and as means to further ends. Likewise, the same value may have both ritualistic and non-ritualistic modalities; or it may be the object of lip-service, only, in one context and the focus of intense total behavioral involvement in another. Such complexities and variations, however, constitute questions of fact rather than of the scheme of analysis, which concerns us at the moment.

As the discussion of democracy shows, again, the generalized value-orientations that may lie behind specific institutional arrangements are not easily disentangled. Just what standards of value are used for evaluating "democracy" as good or bad? The answer is not obvious and it is complicated by the fact that such relatively specific *evaluations* represent a mixture of values, as such, together with knowledge, cognitive beliefs, and a wide variety of other factors peculiar to the actual social situations in which we look for evidence of values. We cannot remind ourselves too often that values are not identical with institutions—and assuredly not identical with all behavior. It is perfectly possible for men who hold the value orientation "all men should have maximum freedom to develop their personal potentialities" to approve of great restrictions on personal freedom in a situation of military crisis—not because freedom is not still a value for them, but because other vital considerations are involved. Abstract cultural values are never apparent in pure form in actual behavior: they are always "situationally specified."

### WHAT ARE VALUE SYSTEMS?

It is clear that in our society the range of interests, beliefs, values, knowledge, and so on is so great that precise and detailed characterizations can be done only for carefully delimited segments of the society. Any attempt to delineate a national character or typical American values or a national basic personality type is extremely hazardous, not only because of serious gaps in the requisite data but also because of the enormous value-diversity of the nation. This diversity we know to be so marked that a common core of values which could be said to hold for the whole population would probably be quite highly generalized. Furthermore, values change through time, rendering any static cross-section inventory subject to periodic reappraisal.

These considerations explain why the present chapter speaks of American value-*systems* rather than of American values. Certain common values and symbols may be of great importance in national integration, but we cannot be certain without further evidence. On the other hand, there are sound reasons for seeking value systems rather than discrete and isolated values. We might conceivably find that there are in fact no systems deserving the name; but the search for systems will keep us looking for relationships and interconnections, consistencies and inconsistencies and hence help us to see form, order, and equilibrium where these actually appear.

"System" here refers to some determinate arrangement of parts or entities—to a set of relationships that is more than a chance ordering of parts —which has a boundary, internal ordering, and some qualities of unity. To speak of value systems is, then, to imply that values are not simply distributed at random but are instead interdependent, arranged in a pattern, and subject to reciprocal or mutual variation.[5]

In describing value systems in American society we are mainly concerned with the distinctive elements of these systems, and not with "universal" features shared by the human species as a whole. For example, we will give comparatively little attention to the biogenic "drives" or "needs" such as hunger, thirst, sex, activity, rest, and the like.[6] However important, this substratum of behavior is generic and subcultural; it does not specifically explain problems that are definitely sociogenic or cultural. All human beings know hunger; but hunger alone will not explain a Minnesota wheat farm, a culturally induced aversion to milk, or a social premium on dinner at the Waldorf Astoria. Similarly, we shall have little to say about such social virtues as bravery, honesty, or loyalty in their most general aspects. Of course, we shall deal with certain universal social values such as those involved in social status or in ethnocentrism; but our prime concern will be not with the universality of these abstract patterns, but with their particular form and content in this particular culture.

## THE PROBLEMS OF CONSISTENCY, INTEGRATION, AND LEVELS OF VALUATION

Even the brief illustrative material so far considered suggests that American society does not have a completely consistent and integrated value-structure.[7] We do not find a neatly unified "ethos" or an irresistible "strain toward consistency." Rather, the total society is characterized by diversity and change in values. Complex division of labor, regional variations, ethnic heterogeneity, and the proliferation of specialized institutions and organizations all tend to insulate differing values from one another.[8] Much potential conflict and strain, as well as much potential integration, is thereby avoided. Yet such insulation is itself peculiarly difficult to maintain in the American social order. For one of the most important features of that order is its delicate interdependence, especially in its economic and political structure. Because of this fundamental interdependence, individuals and groups hold-

[5] James H. Tufts, *America's Social Morality* (New York: Holt, Rinehart & Winston, 1933), p. 24: "In studying the character of a group or of a people it is in point to look not only at this and that detail of conduct-business, politics, crime, philanthropy, vice— but also at the main end or ends, if there be such, which the group more or less consciously pursues." And Kluckhohn, in Parsons and Shils, *op. cit.*, p. 409: "There is a group at any given point in their histories."

[6] For a brief summary of social psychological theory in this area, see Roger Brown, *Social Psychology* (New York: Free Press, 1965).

[7] "A simple society with a culture all its own and with no disturbing contacts with the outside enjoys a success in conditioning its members no modern society can expect." Ralph 'philosophy' behind the way of life of every individual and of every relatively homogenous Linton, *The Study of Man* (New York: Appleton-Century-Crofts, 1936), p. 110.

[8] For a brilliant and sensitive sketch of one of the most important variants of the dominant value-patterns within American society, see W. J. Cash, *The Mind of the South* (New York: Knopf, 1941). Compare with David Bertelson, *The Lazy South* (New York: Oxford University Press, 1967).

ing different and often incompatible values not only become aware of one another but often interact directly. Millions of contact points involving problems of values are created in economic dealings, political activity, education, and other major areas of life. Simultaneously, mass communication creates gigantic magnetic fields of common and conflicting items of knowledge, judgments, beliefs, and values.

There are limits—although rather wide ones—to the degree of incompatibility of beliefs and values that can exist in cultures or in individuals short of the disappearance of a meaningful system. Clashes of value become crucial for social organization when they emerge in those areas of person-to-person interaction that are essential to the maintenance of the system—for example, in family life or in work relations. Persistent value-conflicts in these areas will lead, variously, to personal disorganization, to the emergence of insulating social mechanisms, or to the disruption of the system of interaction. Similarly, in mass behavior, persistent and widespread value-tension leads to political struggle, schismatic cleavages, or the segregation of various groupings into a kind of mosaic society.

In America, the whole problem presented by different levels of valuation has been emphasized by hundreds of studies and investigations, especially since Gunnar Myrdal's formulation of the hiatus between the values of the American Creed and the operative values of the society.[9] The nominally dominant ideals of our society, for instance, would open opportunities for economic gain to all technically qualified persons irrespective of class, family membership, creed, ethnic or racial stock, religion, or other particularistic considerations—and such has been the main tenor of the law, in spite of many exceptions. "Fair play" is often cited as a national virtue. Pronouncements of culture heroes, high officials, and other leaders have overwhelmingly emphasized a universal right to employment and other economic opportunities. Much of this ideal, however, has not become an integral part of daily life; there is a gap between culture and society marked by a lack of emotional commitment to this traditional value. Yet the power of the ethic of universalism has been demonstrated at the national level in recent major actions intended to reduce racial discrimination. Total abolition of "racism" as a historically received doctrine came to be demanded during the widespread urban turbulence of the 1960's.

## MAJOR VALUE ORIENTATIONS IN AMERICA

We can now outline certain major value-configurations in American culture. For convenience, we will proceed by abstracting certain dominant themes from the many important regional, class, and other intracultural

[9] Gunnar Myrdal, with the assistance of Richard Sterner and Arnold Rose, *An American Dilemma*, Vols. I–II (New York: Harper & Row, 1944); see esp. Vol. I, p. xliii. For later summaries of research see George E. Simpson and J. Milton Yinger, *Racial and Cultural Minorities*, 3rd ed. (New York: Harper & Row, 1965); Robin M. Williams, Jr., with the assistance of John P. Dean and Edward A. Suchman, *Strangers Next Door* (Englewood Cliffs, N.J.: Prentice-Hall, 1964); *Report of the National Advisory Commission on Civil Disorders* (New York: Bantam Books, 1968).

variations. The simplified picture that results will, of course, be inaccurate in every concrete detail—it will be a series of ideal types, subject to numerous exceptions. Nevertheless, these abstracted patterns will serve as working models against which variations and contradictions can be more clearly seen; the value configurations thus identified will represent *tendencies* only, but they will bring out certain regularities that would not otherwise be easily seen. At a first approximation, we can use these tentative formulations in each instance as test cases. For each alleged value-pattern let us ask: Is it actually an important value in American society? How do we know whether it is or not? Where does it stand in relation to other values? Within the total society, what groups or subcultures are the main bearers of the value, and what groups or subcultures are indifferent or opposed? How do the mutually supporting or antagonistic value-systems work toward or against the integration of the culture as a whole?

Such systematic questioning will help us avoid naïve acceptance or rejection of the broad descriptive generalizations that follow. Reasonably adequate documentation is provided in the references cited, but limited space makes it impossible to present here anything like the full evidence pro and con. However, the entire preceding analysis should be considered in reaching conclusions.

We will list a value or theme frequently observed in the American scene, cite a few illustrations, and comment briefly upon the nature and significance of the alleged value-pattern. Nearly every statement will bring up unsolved problems and gaps in existing knowledge, but some firm knowledge we do have. Many major themes in American culture have been identified. From them, we may secure clues concerning values themselves. Thus, for example, several recurrent themes stand out in Lee Coleman's compilation of "American traits," based on comprehensive sampling of the literature from early times down to 1940. Traits imputed to American society in all major historical periods included: associational activity, democracy, and belief and faith in it; belief in the equality of all as a fact and as a right; freedom of the individual in ideal and in fact; disregard of law— "direct action;" local government; practicality; prosperity and general material well-being; puritanism; emphasis on religion, and its great influence in national life; uniformity and conformity.[1] Coleman's analysis showed that nearly every conceivable value or trait had at one time or another been imputed to American culture by authoritative observers. At the same time, his "lexicographic analysis" did demonstrate a very substantial core of agreement that appears to reflect real and important value-constellations— different writers often formulate broadly the same values in different terms. Our own discussion of certain prominent clusterings of values and beliefs now follows. Only after these rather specific materials have been reviewed in some detail will we attempt to state what appear to be the most pervasive generalized value-orientations, which constitute a systemic base for the

[1] Lee Coleman, "What Is American: A Study of Alleged American Traits," *Social Forces*, XIX, 4 (May 1941), 498; for a more recent and comprehensive discussion, see Seymour Martin Lipset, *The First New Nation* (New York: Basic Books, 1963); also, Bertram M. Gross (ed.), *A Great Society?* (New York: Basic Books, 1968), esp. chaps. 2, 6, 7, and 10.

more particularized themes now to be examined.[2] At the end of this chapter we shall state the most basic and most abstract value-orientations which are especially marked in the United States. But these high-order patterns cannot be laid down beforehand; they can be stated only after a detailed examination of the concrete themes (value-belief complexes) revealed by a critical examination of the evidence. In most of what follows, therefore, we shall not be dealing with values, but rather with the *evaluations* in which values can be discovered.

### *"Achievement" and "Success"*

First, American culture is marked by a central stress upon personal achievement, especially secular occupational achievement.[3] The "success story" and the respect accorded to the self-made man are distinctly American, if anything is. Our society has been highly competitive—a society in which ascribed status in the form of fixed, hereditary social stratification has been minimized. It has endorsed Horatio Alger and has glorified the rail splitter who becomes President:

*Periodic public opinion polls are not needed to justify the selection of Abe Lincoln as the culture hero who most fully embodies the cardinal American virtues. . . . Even the inevitable schoolboy knows that Lincoln was thrifty, hard-working, eager for knowledge, ambitious, devoted to the rights of the average man, and eminently successful, in climbing the ladder of opportunity from the lowermost rung of laborer to the respectable heights of merchant and lawyer.[4]*

Emphasis upon achievement must be distinguished from the broader valuation of personal excellence. All societies have standards of character and proficiency, and accord rewards to those best meeting whatever standards are most highly appraised, whether of military prowess, ritual knowledge, asceticism, piety, or whatnot. The comparatively striking feature of American culture is its tendency to identify standards of personal excel-

---

[2] We will try to state simply the involved theoretic issues in this approach: (1) We do not find factual evidence to justify us in "deducing" particular value-complexes from more abstract value-orientations that might be set up a priori. It seems safer to infer the more general from the more particular; we wish an anchor in demonstrable facts. (2) On the other hand, people do learn values from numerous specific experiences; and these learned criteria do become generalized, emotionally important, and shared. (3) Hence, we do not reject the idea that there is a relatively stable, shared set of values of high generality, (4) But it is necessary to demonstrate whether this is, or is not, the case.

[3] Earlier insights and hypotheses in this matter were developed and given imaginative research expression by David C. McClelland, *The Achieving Society* (New York: Van Nostrand, 1961). McClelland suggests, on the basis of historical data, that a protracted rise in "need for achievement" *precedes* periods of sustained economic growth and that long-term declines in need for achievement precede lengthy periods of economic stagnation or decline. Summaries and interpretations of research on achievement motivation contain much material relevant to achievement values; see, for example, Bernard Rosen, *et al.* (eds.), *Achievement in American Society* (Cambridge, Mass.: Schenkman, 1967); Brown, *op. cit.*, chap. 9. See also Michael McGiffert (ed.), *The Character of Americans* (Homewood, Ill.: Dorsey Press, 1964), chaps. V and VI.

[4] Robert K. Merton, "The Self-Fulfilling Prophecy," *The Antioch Review* (Summer 1948), p. 199.

lence with competitive occupational achievement.[5] In the pure type, the value attached to achievement does not comprehend the person as a whole but only his accomplishments, emphasizing the objective results of his activity. Because of the preoccupation with business, the most conspicuous achievements have been those centered in business enterprise. We can say, with Harold Laski and many others, that the "values of the business-man" dominate and permeate national life. Yet achievement has never been completely identified with sheer business success; for example, such an assumption does not account for the respect and privilege accorded to the professions. Seen in the context of other major value themes,[6] business success seems to be a dominant focus, but not the dominant value-pattern, in American society. Increasingly, its position has to be shared with professional, political, military, artistic, and other types of achievement.

However, as already noted, economic success has been so heavily stressed in certain parts of our society as to impose a widespread and persistent strain upon institutional regulation of means used to attain this goal. At the extreme, only questions of technical effectiveness enter into the choice of means—thus, the "Robber Barons," "business is business," and much organized crime, vice, and racketeering. Perhaps the apogee of largely unrestrained economic acquisition was reached in the period of "business baroque" from about 1890 to 1912, when the leaders of business "exulted openly in power and riches, won by national centralization."[7]

Research evidence is not fully adequate for an accurate appraisal of the extent to which success rather than achievement has moved to the center of the values of our culture. Although we shall argue below that achievement is still a major value—a central criterion of desirability—there is a considerable amount of evidence indicating that explicit emphasis upon achievement has been declining during recent decades.[8] Whereas achievement refers to

[5] For other cross-cultural perspectives, see Don Martindale (ed.), "National Character in the Perspective of the Social Sciences," *The Annals*, 370 (March 1967), 1–163; Robert M. Marsh, *Comparative Sociology* (New York: Harcourt, Brace & World, 1967).

[6] The so-called success philosophy attains its full cultural meaning only along with a particular kind of moral individualism. See John F. Cuber and Robert A. Harper, *Problems of American Society* (New York: Holt, Rinehart & Winston, 1951), p. 356: "The basic premise of this philosophy is that individuals, not classes, are the real competing units. A man is said to reap his reward by his 'own' efforts, skills, and perseverance."

[7] Miriam Beard: *A History of the Business Man* (New York: Macmillan, 1938), p. 641. For a similar period in the ancient world see Gilbert Murray, *Five Stages of Greek Religion* (New York: Columbia University Press, 1925).

[8] This general idea had been persuasively presented by David Riesman, with Ruel Denney and Nathan Glazer, *The Lonely Crowd* (New Haven, Conn.: Yale University Press, 1950) and then by William H. Whyte, *The Organization Man* (New York: Anchor Books, 1956). For examples of the later scattered but often ingenious studies see: Richard DeCharms and Gerald H. Moeller, "Values Expressed in American Children's Readers: 1800–1950," *Journal of Abnormal and Social Psychology*, LXIV (February 1962), 136–142; Murray A. Straus and Lawrence J. Houghton, "Achievement, Affiliation, and Co-operation Values as Clues to Trends in American Rural Society, 1924–1958," *Rural Sociology*, 25, 4 (December 1960), 394–403; S. M. Dornbusch and L. C. Hickman, "Other-Directedness in Consumer-Goods Advertising: A Test of Riesman's Historical Theory," *Social Forces*, 38, 2 (December 1959), 99–102.

valued accomplishments, success lays the emphasis upon rewards. Amoral success striving may not have gone to the lengths suggested by some observers, but the important point is that once success goals are divorced from the ultimate values of society, the way is opened for a corrosion of regulative norms.[9] In the United States, the available evidence suggests that, even though success is often regarded as an end in itself and sometimes there is almost no positive relation between success and moral virtue, yet the success pattern is still linked to achievement, achievement is still associated with work, and work is still invested with an almost organic complex of ethical values. Thus, success is still not a primary criterion of value in its own right but rather a derivative reward *for* active, instrumental performance. There is growing evidence that performance in consumption is partly replacing performance in work: how one spends his income, rather than what he did to earn it appears increasingly to be a mark of "achievement."[1] Nevertheless, as Dixon Wecter has suggested, the American heroes are not merely successful—they must be successful within a certain ethical framework: they must be, or appear to be, "self-respecting, decent, honorable, with a sense of fair play; no Machiavelli nor Mussolini need apply."[2] The belief that virtue will be rewarded and that success attends upon effort dies hard; and in our culture failure is still more likely to be charged to defect of character than to blind fate, capricious accident, or impersonalized social and economic forces; and the wealthy and powerful still either desire or find it expedient to justify their position in the name of "service" and "stewardship." One need not be immediately persuaded by the intellectually fashionable cynicism which holds that all such defensive rationalizations are simply false. Achievement in valued activities may be alternatively formulated as contribution to societal welfare, if one can prove that the valued activities do contribute to a common good. This hypothesis obviously is not always defensible, for it is clear that some achievements may benefit small portions of the population while having a strongly negative effect upon others. Nevertheless, it is likely that an accurate accounting, could it be made, would show that many valued achievements do represent net increments to welfare—although, of course, there need be no one-to-one relation between degree of achievement and contribution to a common good, no matter how defined.

The dimensions of success values may perhaps be clarified by an examination of the place of wealth and its attainment in the culture. Many

[9] A pioneering exploration pointing to some of the more important personality strains engendered by high levels of aspiration in a competitive order was the work of Karen Horney; see, for example, *The Neurotic Personality of Our Time* (New York: Norton, 1937). We already have reviewed the general problem of deviant behavior.

[1] See, for example: Eli Chinoy, *Automobile Workers and the American Dream* (Garden City, N.Y.: Doubleday, 1955); David Riesman, "The Suburban Sadness," in William M. Dobriner (ed.), *The Suburban Community* (New York: Putnam, 1958).

[2] Dixon Wecter, *The Hero in America* (New York: Scribner, 1941), p. 482. (This comment has to be qualified to take into account a Huey Long and an Al Capone, as well as the hero worship of the movie stars or television favorites who are presented as living in opulent success as the result of luck or "personality"—unrelated to traditional moral virtues.)

foreign and native observers have viewed American society as grossly acquisitive and materialistic, as naïvely impressed by bigness, speed, wealth, and power. Such a view is entirely too simple. For one thing, the theme of achievement unlimited is not limited to economic prowess or acquisition. In hundreds of complex forms it is pervasive in American *expressive* culture, where emphasis on the vision of the future produces impatience with the imperfect present and striving toward a salvation yet to be attained.[3] Furthermore, it is not self-evident that "materialism" is the essential component even in Americans' attitudes toward money.

We may begin by eliminating any interpretation such as "of course money is wanted because it is the universal agency for satisfying any desires that can be met by purchasable goods."[4] For many profitable activities are socially condemned and not widely carried on; and people strive intensely for wealth long after their basic physical needs have been met or even after they have achieved nearly every conceivable means for satisfying their desires. Santayana's insight has more accurately indicated the central historic function of money in the American value system: "It is the symbol and measure he (the American) has at hand for success, intelligence, and power; but as to money itself he makes, loses, spends and gives it away with a very light heart."[5] In a society of relatively high social mobility, in which position in the scale of social stratification basically depends upon occupational achievement, wealth is one of the few obvious signs of one's place in the hierarchy. Achievement is difficult to index, in a highly complex society of diverse occupations, because of the great differences in abilities and effort required for success in various fields. At the same time, the central type of achievement is in business, manufacturing, commerce, finance; and since traditionalized social hierarchies, fixed estates, and established symbols of hereditary rank have had only a rudimentary development, there is a strong tendency to use money as a symbol of success. Money comes to be valued not only for itself and for the goods it will buy, but as symbolic evidence of success and, thereby, of personal worth.

Much the same type of analysis applies to the so-called American love of bigness. It is said that Americans are impressed by size qua size; "bigger and better" is a childish love of quantity as such. Actually the important thing is that "better" is presumed to be *implied* by "bigger." Things are good not so much because they are big, but because goodness is assumed

---

[3] Robert N. Wilson, "Fitzgerald at Icarus," *Antioch Review* (Winter 1958); see this theme in a newer mode in Norman Podhoretz, *Making It* (New York: Random House, 1967).

[4] The American sociologist Charles Horton Cooley pointed out as long ago as the turn of the century that "wealth as an object of ambition and a measure of success owes its ascendency to its social implications, and the pursuit of it is by no means a proof of materialism or sensuality. . . . The fact that a man desires it, throws little or no light upon the real object of his ambition." *Sociological Theory and Social Research* (New York: Holt, Rinehart & Winston, 1930), p. 222; the quotation is from the essay "Personal Competition," which first appeared as an article in 1899.

[5] George Santayana, *Character and Opinion in the United States* (New York: Scribner, 1920), p. 185. Cf. Geoffrey Gorer, *The American People* (New York: Norton, 1948), p. 177: "It can be said that, as a general rule, the acquisition of money is very important to Americans, but its retention relatively unimportant."

and bigness therefore means more of something already considered valuable. Again Santayana has well expressed the essential point: "Respect for quantity is accordingly more than the childish joy and wonder at bigness; it is the fisherman's joy in a big haul, the good uses of which he can take for granted."[6] Unquestionably, we are dealing here with a culture that values action and the mastery of the physical world;[7] and its whole history has been, in the main, an experience of expansionism and mastery: increasing population, increasing territory, increased levels of living, and so on. Given the definition of such things as good, respect for quantity directly follows.

It is obvious that one may hold achievement as a value without having a high level of motivation to achieve; for example, many persons who acknowledge high occupational achievement as a desirable state are not effectively motivated to do the things required for such achievement. Nevertheless, a rather high positive correlation exists. It is accordingly relevant that a number of studies report especially strong achievement motivation among executives and managers;[8] persons in both managerial and professional occupations more often than persons in other occupations give high ratings to the importance of achievement and accomplishment in their jobs.[9]

### *"Activity" and "Work"*

In the United States is to be found what is almost the ideal type of a culture that stresses activity; it is no accident that the business so characteristic of the culture can also be spelled "busyness." Although there clearly is exaggeration implied in Laski's flat statement that few Americans "find it easy to be happy unless they are doing something,"[1] we know that a notable series of observers have overwhelmingly agreed that America is the land of haste and bustle, of strenuous competition, of "ceaseless activity and agitation."[2] In this culture the individual tends to "face outward"—to be interested in making things happen in the external world. In ideal type, he seeks to dominate the world of nature, to subdue and exploit the physical world around him. This pattern, which forms a *leit motif* in American history, may be explained historically, of course, as developing out of religious tradition, frontier experience,[3] ceaseless change, vast opportunity, and fluid

---

[6] Santayana, *op. cit.*, p. 182.

[7] Cf. Harold J. Laski, *The American Democracy* (New York: Viking, 1948), p. 42: "No attempt to grasp the nature of the American spirit can be complete which does not emphasize the degree to which action is of its essence."

[8] Victor H. Vroom, *Motivation in Management* (New York: American Foundation for Management Research, 1965), pp. 15–20.

[9] Nancy C. Morse and R. S. Weiss, "The Function and Meaning of Work and the Job," *American Sociological Review*, 20, 2 (April 1955), 191–198.

[1] Laski, *op. cit.*, p. 15.

[2] See the summary in Lee Coleman, "What is American?" *op. cit.*, pp. 492–499; also, Henry Steele Commager, *America in Perspective* (New York: Random House, 1947), p. xii.

[3] Cf. Constance Rourke's characterization of the man of the frontier: "Strength was his obsession—size, scale, power: he seemed obliged to shout their symbols as if after all he were not wholly secure in their possession." *American Humor: A Study of the National Character* (New York: Harcourt, Brace & World, 1931), p. 36.

social structure. Whatever its sources, the sheer fact of this emphasis on "action" is enough for present purposes.

Directed and disciplined activity in a regular occupation is a particular form of this basic orientation. If Justice Holmes could say that the purpose of life "is to function," the resonance his words aroused applied particularly to *work* in a full time vocation. This high evaluation of work has been called typical of the culture by many students of the American scene.

A strong emphasis upon disciplined productive activity was to be expected in America during the first two centuries in which value systems were being generalized out of experience. Work was required for *group* survival along the moving frontier from the first settlements until the continent had been won. The rule "he who does not work shall not eat" expressed the deadly struggles of the early settlement period. To this compulsion was added the dawning sense of the rich rewards to be had in a land of relatively unappropriated resources. Furthermore, the population was mainly recruited initially from the working classes of Britain and Europe;[4] except in a few areas of the South and New England, there was no aristocratic class to give prestige to leisure and to stigmatize manual labor and trade. Finally, there was the influence of the so-called Puritan tradition—that is, of all those varieties of Protestantism in which secular occupational activity was invested with religious sanction and in which successful works became a sign of grace. This "metaphysical drive to work"[5] permeated the older agrarian culture of this country[6] and exists today in practically the original quasi-religious form in some rural areas and among other subgroupings that have not yet fully assimilated the more recent cult of success and conspicuous consumption. The emphasis on work is strong in some professional and executive circles. Even in leisure and expressive behavior, the purposive and obligatory emphases often persist.[7]

It is important to note, however, that a marked drive actively to *shape* and *control* the world—in contrast to passivity or sheer adaptation—apparently antedates both the specific "achievement" and "work" values. Several European societies long before the industrial era showed this strong urge to have dominion over the external world. Modern forms of achievement through work represent only one of many routes to active mastery. Of course, the *desire* for such mastery has been widespread in many societies, Western and non-Western. Even so-called doctrines of fatalism do not

---

[4] Max Savelle, *Seeds of Liberty* (New York: Knopf, 1948), p. 219. "From the beginning, America was made up of what they call in England the middle and laboring classes, and it has always remained so. This is, in fact, one of the important points about it." (James Truslow Adams, *The American: The Making of a New Man* [New York: Scribner, 1943], p. 49).

[5] The phrase used by Goetz Briefs, *The Proletariat* (New York: McGraw-Hill, 1937).

[6] For a clear description see James M. Williams, *Our Rural Heritage* (New York: Knopf, 1925). Suggestive data, showing the persistence of the older patterns among rural and low-income urban population, are given by John P. Clark and Eugene P. Wenninger, "Goal Orientations and Illegal Behavior Among Juveniles," *Social Forces*, 42, 1 (October 1963), 49–59.

[7] Cf. Lionel S. Lewis and Dennis Brisset, "Sex as Work: A Study of Avocational Counseling," *Social Problems*, 15, 1 (Summer 1967), 8–15.

seem to prevent men in nearly all cultures from acting positively to control the conditions of life.[8] However, the strength of the commitment to the criterion of activity does appear extraordinarily great in the American instance.

In the American case the emphasis upon work as an end in itself represented a convergence of factors all operating in one direction—a mutual reinforcement of self-interest, social recognition, and ethical and religious precepts; "work" therefore became a value incorporated into the ego ideal of the representative personality types of the culture, and often approached the intensity of a true matter of conscience. If distinctive foci of values can be found in this complicated culture, it seems that one should look into the strong positive appreciation of the support for *worldly, instrumental activism*.[9] From this emphasis follows the stress upon universal standards of performance. And this in turn (logically and in fact) implies a concern with universalizing opportunity for performance to a high degree, and with encouraging the maintenance of the full capacities of individuals for valued performance. So it is that efforts to improve health conditions and extend educational opportunities are often approved on these grounds.[1] Consistent with the main values also are the high evaluations placed upon teamwork and upon executive or managerial roles, the approval of technology (as "control of the world"), and the distinctive form of individualism in which the emphasis is upon permissiveness for a wide variety of achievements.

Although, as later discussion will show, work as an end in itself has lost some of its earlier potency, it is still important to remember that it has formed one of the core elements in the historic culture. It was, however, closely linked to an agrarian social structure in which the independent farmer and the small businessman were representative social types.[2] In such a society, work was embedded in the wider meanings attached to these statuses. As the social structure has become more and more differentiated, as manual labor has lost its connection with the control of private property, and as differentials of wealth and power have become crystallized, work as such has been devalued. The focus of positive valuation is now shifting to certain patterns of achievement and success, and beyond these, to consumption and expressive values.[3]

However, it is easy to exaggerate the magnitude of the changes. In mid-

[8] Cf. the special issue, "Fatalism in Asia: Old Myths and New Realities," *Anthropological Quarterly*, 39, 3 (July 1966), esp. the summary statement on page 252.

[9] Talcott Parsons, *The Social System* (New York: Free Press, 1959), pp. 180–200.

[1] Notice how often public support for "health and welfare" measures is sought on the ground that we are "wasting our human resources" if we do not support efforts to increase capacities for performance.

[2] High evaluation of work certainly was not universal. Cf. Bertelson, *op. cit.*, for discussion of colonial and antebellum Southerners' attitudes toward work.

[3] Leo Lowenthal (ed.), *Literature, Popular Culture, and Society* (Englewood Cliffs, N.J.: Prentice-Hall, 1961); the alleged virtues of "leisure" are now extolled, with obvious ambivalence, in many learned discussions; see, for example, *Leisure in America: Blessing or Curse?*, Monograph No. 4 (Philadelphia: American Academy of Political and Social Science, April 1964), esp. pp. 30–41.

century, about 80 percent of persons in the labor force testify that they would continue to work even if they had the means to support their present mode of life without working.[4] Work often involves a desired and desirable expenditure of energy, a means of controlling and expressing strong affective states, a means of helping other people, a context of sociability, an avenue for gaining recognition—not to mention its instrumental rewards in money or power. Thus work represents a cluster of moral and affective conditions of great attractiveness for many people; and involuntary idleness often constitutes a severely threatening and damaging social condition.[5]

When work is highly involving and gratifying, producing a sense of autonomy and consummation, it shades over imperceptibly into "play." From being a constrictive *instrumental* activity, unsatisfying in itself and carried on only as a means to future satisfaction, it can become an *expressive* activity, in which the doing is its own reward. In the neo-Calvinistic orientation work conceived as a means of religious discipline often seems to have generated a considerable measure of value autonomy and of consummatory gratification. In the age of the assembly line, work increasingly tended to become divorced from any larger set of meanings and values other than as sheer instrumentality. It is now possible to see that under conditions of high productivity and increased leisure, work might gain a new and greater autonomy as a major arena of value realization and personality-expression, overcoming some kinds of "alienation."

### "Moral Orientation"

A third major value-configuration relates to a particular type of ethical quality in the total cultural orientation. Authoritative observers from abroad from Tocqueville, through Bryce, Siegfried, and others, down to recent studies have agreed on at least one point: Americans tend to "see the world in moral terms." They do not mean mere conformity to the detailed prescriptions of a particular moral code, but rather to a systematic moral orientation by which conduct is *judged*. It is asserted that the quasi-mythical figure, the "typical American," thinks in terms of right or wrong, good or bad, ethical or unethical. This attitude goes beyond questions of expediency or immediate utility—and beyond purely traditional or customary criteria of behavior—to test conduct against some systematic ethical principles. For example, Margaret Mead cites the prototypic query of a student who asked whether we *ought* to have a conscience.[6] And Myrdal says explicitly: "The conflict in the American concept of law and order is only one side of the 'moral overstrain' of the nation. America believes in and

---

[4] Nancy C. Morse and R. S. Weiss, *op. cit.*; Victor H. Vroom, *Work and Motivation* (New York: Wiley, 1964).

[5] Cf. the review of evidence in Vroom, *Work and Motivation, op. cit.*, pp. 30–45. It may be recalled that Sigmund Freud held that major keys to mental health were to be found in two areas of productivity: love and work.

[6] Margaret Mead, *And Keep Your Powder Dry* (New York: Morrow, 1942), chap. 6. Compare Robert Blauner, *Alienation and Freedom: The Factory Worker and His Industry* (Chicago: University of Chicago Press, 1964), and Daniel Bell, *Work and Its Discontents* (Boston: Beacon Press, 1956).

aspires to something much higher than its plane of actual life."[7] The presence of an element of moral overstrain in our culture seems to be established. This has a wide range of consequences, including ritualism, vacillating or compensatory behavior, "split between theory and practice," so-called "hypocrisy" (note the repeated charge of radical youth in the late 1960's), and so on. Individuals facing severe tension between their incorporated ethics and current social "realities" may resolve the conflict by developing a militant reform mentality[8] or becoming "cynical"—we often suspect that the self-styled cynic is a highly moral person who is reacting to loss of faith in the efficacy of his code. Often also those who radically reject the present society are objecting to the incomplete realization of that same society's ideals.

The central themes of morality in America have undoubtedly had a common base and unified direction, derived from Judaic-Christian ethics. Of special importance has been the so-called Puritan ethic. Beginning as a rigidly theocratic system, it has gone through drastic modifications. At first it was markedly averse to traditionalistic forms and uncompromising toward the profane world. When works came to be interpreted as a sign of grace assuring salvation, it turned to a morality in which economic success became prima facie evidence of moral correctness. In Laski's words:

*What begins as a theocratic principle ends by becoming a tradition that it is not very easy to distinguish from utilitarianism. . . . To work hard, to lead an orderly life, to have a name for integrity and fair dealing, not to spend one's substance in reckless display, to have the resolution to carry out the purposes you undertake— it is, roughly, to an ethic such as this that the religion of America had been shaped when the basic tradition was formed.[9]*

Clearly this generalization applies to only one major aspect of a much more complex orientation, as noted in Chapter IX on religious institutions.

### *"Humanitarian Mores"*

We shall use the term "humanitarianism" to refer to another important value cluster in American society, meaning by it emphasis upon any type of disinterested concern and helpfulness, including personal kindliness, aid and comfort, spontaneous aid in mass disasters, as well as the more impersonal patterns of organized philanthropy. Do these things represent important values in America?

It is easy to amass contrary evidence. We could cite the expulsion and

---

[7] Myrdal, *et al., op. cit.,* Vol. I, p. 21. This phrase, however, is a question-begging formulation, as we shall see in more detail later. "Overstrain" is itself a value-laden concept. However, it does suggest a strong tension between nominally dominant ethical principles and the pragmatic codes and exigencies of actual social life.

[8] Thus Harold D. Lasswell has suggested that anxiety resulting from the severe conscience assumed to be typical of much of middle-class America often leads to the attempt to enforce moralistic legislation upon others: "Emotional fixation upon the unqualified reaffirmation of 'principles' is one result of the anxieties generated by the threatened conscience." *World Politics and Personal Insecurity* (New York: McGraw-Hill, 1935), p. 226.

[9] Laski, *op. cit.,* p. 27.

extermination of the Indians, slavery, the sweatshop pattern in industry, and a long catalog of child labor, lynching, vigilantes, and social callousness in many forms. Probably few peoples have so copiously documented and analyzed what they themselves consider to be the "bad" aspects of their history—a revealing fact in itself, for it was broadly the same culture that produced the behavior and then pronounced it undesirable or wrong. Even so, the evidences of humanitarian values meet all our tests for a major value. For one thing it is striking that failure to follow the standards of concern and helpfulness have not been defended as legitimate in themselves; they have been interpreted as *deviance from* a criterion that is not basically challenged or "justified" in terms of other, allegedly more vital values. Certain patterns of mutual helpfulness and generosity were already apparent in colonial America, despite the stern theology and stringently disciplined individualism, and have persisted to an important extent down to the present time.

Of course, it is only in a wide comparative perspective that the importance of the humanitarian mores can clearly be seen. In the past, there has been a frequent tendency to hope for the triumph of the underdog, to show a quick, impulsive sympathy for people who are in distress "by no fault of their own;" to feel anger at the overbearing individual group, or nation; to take pride in America as a haven for the downtrodden and oppressed.[1] The proverbial generosity of American people toward other societies facing mass disaster—for example, earthquakes, floods, fire, famine—has elements of exaggeration and myth; but it does index a real and persistent theme broadly based on religious or quasi-religious ideas of brotherhood, even though it has often been overridden by dividing interests and competing values. The enormous range of relatively disinterested humanitarian activities in America—the commonplace United Fund, the "service club" activities, the public welfare agencies, the numerous private philanthropies, and so on[2]—stands in striking contrast to the treatment meted out to "the poor" and the "sturdy beggars" in many other parts of Western society within the past two centuries.

As always, however, this value pattern does not stand alone but is reinforced and complemented, or checked and limited, by other values. Humanitarianism is closely related to the cluster of values implicit in the conception of a progressing equalitarian democracy. In the form of what might be called pseudo-humanitarian philanthropy, on the other hand, the pattern sometimes has lent itself to the justification of economic inequalities. Throughout American history, the humanitarian theme has

---

[1] As in many other instances, the orientation has been changing and there are indications that the welcoming symbolism of the Statue of Liberty has lost much of its appeal for a world power in a time of international tension and crisis. Once again we must remind ourselves that values are subject to fluctuations and trends. Cf. Tufts, *America's Social Morality, op. cit.,* p. 35: "To speak of any single interest or end, as though the mind of the people were one and were settled upon the same objective throughout a period, is to assume too much unity and stability."

[2] The phenomenon of the "volunteer worker" is further evidence. There may be as many as a third of the adult population of the United States who give unpaid help to various religious, social, political, civic, and service organizations.

clashed in a variety of ways with the conception of rugged individualism. Vernon L. Parrington has compactly summarized for an early period the conflict that still remains a prominent element in the shaping of the total value system:

*At the beginning of our national existence two rival philosophies contended for supremacy in America: the humanitarian philosophy of the French Enlightenment, based on the conception of human perfectibility and postulating as its objective an equalitarian democracy in which the political state should function as the servant to the common well-being; and the English philosophy of laissez faire, based on the assumed universality of the acquisitive instinct and postulating a social order answering the needs of an abstract "economic man," in which the state should function in the interest of trade.*[3]

As a general principle, humanitarianism appears as axiomatic in many public statements. It is said in an authoritative report on alcoholism, for example: "A basic belief of our civilization is that suffering should be relieved, regardless of the person, his contribution to society, or the manner in which the suffering was brought about."[4] Yet aid to persons in distress often involves a severe clash of values and beliefs as "generosity" is checked by various conceptions of "justice" and "moral responsibility." Thus, the House of Representatives in 1967 passed legislation, later revoked in part, that limited federal contributions for families with dependent children in which the father is absent. Although the small children who could not be aided can hardly be said to be responsible for choosing their fathers, evidently the Representatives who voted for the bill wished to bring negative sanctions to bear upon mothers of illegitimate children and upon fathers who are not supporting their children. In a similar vein, some proposed medicare legislation would have denied hospital and supplementary insurance benefits to members of certain proscribed organizations or to persons who have been convicted of specified criminal offenses. Thus a kind of punitive moral orientation comes into opposition with those forms of humanitarianism that do not make aid contingent upon the moral performance of the person in need.

### Efficiency and Practicality

American emphasis upon *efficiency* has consistently impressed outside observers. The Germans even coined the term *Fordismus* to refer to the standardization, mass production, and "streamlined" efficiency of American industrialism personified on the continent by the name of Ford. "Efficient" is a word of high praise in a society that has long emphasized adaptability, technological innovation, economic expansion, up-to-dateness, practicality, expediency, "getting things done." The mere listing of these words and phrases serves to bring out the multiple extensions of efficiency as a standard against which activity is judged. Such a standard is premised in the first

[3] Vernon L. Parrington, *Main Currents in American Thought*, Book III (New York: Harcourt, Brace & World, 1930), p. xxiii.

[4] Thomas F. A. Plant, *Alcohol Problems: A Report to the Nation by the Cooperative Commission on the Study of Alcoholism* (New York: Oxford University Press, 1967), p. 33.

place upon the active orientation to the world of the here and now, so characteristic of our culture. As we have emphasized, this crucially important canalization of interest at once sets this society apart from societies placing greater emphasis upon esthetic, contemplative, ritualistic, mystical, or otherworldly concerns.

That being active is emphasized, however, tells us nothing about the kind of activity sanctioned. Even a culture centering its interest upon purposive technical mastery of its physical environment (and, to some degree, of its social problems also) might conceivably act in relatively traditionalistic ways. The Western world generally, however, has tended to unite activity and substantive rationality, focusing upon a choice of the most effective means for a given end. Since systematic wealth-getting, technological achievement, and productive organization of effort have been strongly sanctioned, pressure has been created to search for "better methods," with the result that America epitomizes high regard for efficiency in techniques. In this kind of social climate, there is high sensitivity to such epithets as "backward," "inefficient," "useless." "Technical values" are greatly appreciated; especially in skilled trades, technical, quasi-professional, and professional vocations there is systematic indoctrination in the standards of "doing a good job"—the difference between a skilled and an unskilled performance. Despite the continual pressure of pecuniary or profit-making considerations, the values of good technical performance certainly have a measure of independent influence.

It is, of course, difficult to find direct evidence that would permit appraisal of the relative magnitude of technical (workmanship) values as over against economic efficiency (profit making) criteria. Without doubt the two sets of standards quite often are in direct opposition; and the ideals of craftsmanship and good engineering often give way to planned obsolescence, unsafe products, and shoddy materials.

The elevation of sheer technique into something closely approaching a value in its own right involves the familiar tendency to turn means values into goal values through a gradual withdrawal of attention and affect from the original ends—a development that is reenforced in so far as immediate interests and short-run goals are stressed. A culture that in the first place tends toward an ahistorical and utilitarian orientation will be especially likely to encourage just those behavior patterns in which technical efficiency can become valued for its own sake.[5]

Although efficiency can and has become in this way a standard for evaluation, in certain areas of our culture it is a derivation rather than a basic theme. In economic activities and other fields that have acquired considerable autonomy apart from the ultimate-value systems of the society, the stress upon efficiency is a complex derivation from the values attached to action, to material comfort, and perhaps especially, to mastery over nature and disorder. For efficiency—like cleanliness, work, and systematic-

---

[5] American critics of this tendency have not been lacking. Especially noteworthy is Thorstein Veblen, *The Theory of the Leisure Class* (New York: Macmillan, 1899), and *The Theory of Business Enterprise* (New York: Scribner, 1904); see David Riesman, *Thorstein Veblen: A Critical Interpretation* (New York: Scribner, 1953).

universal ethics—is a *discipline*; and its meaning depends finally upon the broader meanings of the primary "orderliness" that underlies it.

Emphasis upon efficiency is obviously related to the high place accorded science (especially as translated into technology) and to the overweening importance attributed to practicality. One of the blackest public curse-words we have is "impractical"—in the culture at large, the practical man is the good man, an embodiment of a major value. Although we could trace this interrelated set of attitudes back to the frontier tradition, there are more immediate influences in the contemporary culture contributing to its survival. "Practical" orientation is basically short-range adjustment to immediate situations. The practical man concentrates upon goals attainable in the given situation and solves immediate problems as they arise, leaving to others the more abstract and long-range problems. Thus it seems clear that practicality as a positive value involves very important presuppositions as to other values. For instance, it typically assumes the worth of the basic social order within which action occurs. It characteristically rests on a whole set of implicit premises, among which are the stress on *activity* and *rationality* already mentioned above.

New meanings of the theme of efficiency undoubtedly are developing. "Efficiency" often has been applied to actions that really represent the single-minded attainment of a goal or accomplishment of a task, with minimal attention to attendant costs, injuries, or disruptions outside the narrow zone of immediate attention. Thus, it may be "efficient" to dump industrial wastes into streams and lakes or to fill the air with cumulatively noxious chemical effluviants. Such so-called social costs may be *negative goods*—they may subtract from the positive sum of available satisfactions in a community or society. Much efficiency within individual social units (families, firms, organizations) is attained by highly rational calculations within a limited sphere of relevance—a meticulous process that often contrasts starkly with total disregard of negative "side-effects" or "by-products."

Standards of pure efficiency can of course apply to any kind of human behavior; there is a technique for mysticism as well as a technique for producing automobiles. However, there is nothing practical, in the American meaning, in a dominant concern with purely esthetic or intellectual interests, nor in veneration of the past; asceticism, philosophic withdrawal, pessimistic quietism have never very long or very greatly stamped the American ethos; such tendencies have been confined to depressed or oppressed cultural enclaves, to small sectarian movements, or to individuals alienated from the main currents of national life.[6] In part this view of practicality lies back of the attitude caricatured in Henry Ford's dictum: "History is bunk." Americans have been called, not with entire justification, a people without a sense of history; but it is significant that they generally have not been overly troubled by such comments.[7]

6 In more recent years, various antiefficiency and antirational themes have found favor among "hippies" and substantial numbers of other youths.

7 The idea that America is a civilization without a history is, in fact, largely an illusion of observers who have not understood the basic world-view of the culture, especially its future orientation.

The practicality theme represents at least three quite different although closely related dimensions: (1) the nature of the immediate ends for activity; (2) the guiding criteria for arranging ends into a hierarchy of value; (3) the implicit conceptual framework—the absolute social logics—within which values are perceived. With respect to the sanctioned immediate ends of conduct, we have already seen a convergence upon the goals of certain kinds of success. Practicality as to concrete goals of actions correspondingly has meant the canalizing of action in the service of those specific life-models most highly approved in the general culture—broadly speaking, rational, strenuous, competitive striving for personal validation through occupational success. In so far as this definition of the situation has been accepted, only those things have been considered practical that contributed to this end. Second, as a guiding principle for arranging value priorities, practicality represents a particular form of what Max Weber called *Zweckrationalität* as over against *Wertrationalität*—the rational weighting of values in a pluralistic framework rather than overwhelming concern with a single value or end. In the latter case, all other considerations except the achievement of that end become irrelevant; in prototype this is the stand of the political and religious fanatic, the insatiable hedonist, the monomaniacal economic man. American standards of practicality seem to have led mainly in the direction of a multifaceted balancing of values.

Finally, practicality affects the conceptual schemes (explicit and implicit) that broadly characterize the culture. Even American philosophy displays a practical and critical cast and has been in various ways pragmatic, instrumental, relativistic.[8] Of course, consistency among various evaluative standards may be studied at any level of explicitness and in any aspect of behavior; but the really generic values are likely to be detectable not only in everyday routines but also in highly abstract cultural products. Accordingly, it seems to add force to the above observations to note that throughout the last half-century most of the really influential thinkers in American philosophy and philosophy of history have not been idealists, monists, or absolutists but rather have been pragmatists, relativists, or pluralists in many diverse ways.[9]

Thus, the theme of practicality points us again to activistic, rational, and secular (but "ethical") emphases of the culture; at the same time, it hints of possible tendencies toward the dissipation of the content of "ultimate" values in favor of immediate adaptability to immediate interests

[8] Charles A. Beard and Mary R. Beard, *The American Spirit* (New York: Macmillan, 1942), pp. 661–670; among numerous present-day examples note the striking case of philosophy of art: "The trend toward broadening the scope of aesthetics, making it more descriptive and empirical in aim and method, is part of a larger trend in American thought away from metaphysical idealism and dualism and toward a more naturalistic orientation . . . The trend . . . (the so-called 'twilight of the absolute,' which seems new and revolutionary to some French writers) has long prevailed in the United States" (Thomas Munro, "Recent Developments in Aesthetics in America," *ACLS Newsletter*, XV, 2 (February 1964), pp. 2–3.)

[9] Cf. John H. Randall, Jr., *Nature and Historical Experience* (New York: Columbia University Press, 1958), p. 30.

and satisfactions. As a highly derivative pattern, practicality does not provide in itself any sure anchorage for continuing organization and integration of individual activity. It is not a basic value. In common with the emphasis on *procedure* in American concepts of freedom and democracy, the emphasis upon practicality indicates a society that has tended to take for granted the implicit value framework within which practical action acquires meaning and rationale.

### "Progress"

From the society's earliest formation as a distinct national entity there has been a diffuse constellation of beliefs and attitudes that may be called the cult of progress. This broad theme has no unitary value such as would tangibly regulate specific individual behavior but is rather a certain "set" toward life that has permeated a wide range of behavior patterns. Various aspects of this complex are those allegedly typical American traits discussed earlier—"optimism," an emphasis upon the future rather than the past or present, "boosterism," receptivity to change, faith in the perfectibility of the common man. At least in the enterprising middle classes, progress has been a prime article of faith. Our rich vocabulary of epithets ("backward," "outmoded," "old-fashioned," "stagnant," and the like) can be understood *as epithets* only against the unquestioning assumption that the new is the better—that "forward" is better than "backward."

From Tocqueville to Laski, inquiring foreign observers have been impressed with the faith in progress and the high evaluation of the future in the United States as contrasted with Europe. Americans have felt their present to be better than their past and have felt adequate to deal with a future that will be still better. "Throughout their history Americans have insisted that the best was yet to be. . . . The American knew that nothing was impossible in his brave new world. . . . Progress was not, to him, a mere philosophical ideal but a commonplace of experience. . . ."[1]

The importance of the idea of progress is in part brought out by the examples of contrasting societies in which it has been, or is, absent. As John B. Bury has shown in a classic work,[2] the concept of progress has emerged only recently in history. For example, the ancient Greeks apparently believed in eternally recurring cycles, or else placed the Golden Age in the past. Medieval times tended to devalue radically the life of the present in favor of a static conception of society as far less significant than the supernatural world and the afterlife. Only with the breakdown of the feudal order and the emergence of a new society in western Europe did the idea become established that human nature is subject to continuous improvement and that society as a whole is inevitably moving toward a better order of life. This orientation, at first largely restricted to small circles of intellectuals in Europe, was made to order for the formative years of the United States. In the beginning America was promise, rather than past; hope, rather than accomplishment. For a long period the promise was

---

[1] Henry Steele Commager (ed.), *America in Perspective* (New York: Random House, 1947), pp. xi and xiv.

[2] John B. Bury, *The Idea of Progress* (New York: Macmillan, 1932).

kept and the hope was fulfilled to a remarkable degree. Belief in progress involves acceptance of changes, the idea that changes are tending in a definite direction, and the belief that the direction is good. To generations of Americans all three components seemed verified: things were changing, they were moving in a central direction, they were getting better.

In the form in which it had been molded by the Enlightenment, progress was conceived as the beneficent unfolding of man's capacities for reason and goodness. In the course of its later development, however, the idea picked up dominant overtones of Social Darwinism ("the survival of the fittest") at about the same time that its application was being more and more restricted to economic and technological realms. By the late nineteenth century, the concept had been largely assimilated to the values of a complex and expanding industrial order. Progress could now become a slogan to defend the course of technological innovation and economic rationalization and concentration. If small entrepreneurs, farmers, or urban workers felt economic distress, their condition could be considered a regrettable but necessary and temporary by-product of the triumphant march of progress. Progress became identified with "free private enterprise," in fact, at a time when the individual entrepreneur was already clearly certain to be supplemented by vast economic organizations the development of which was to change the traditional laissez-faire concepts of "private property" and "economic freedom."

The assumption that wants or needs always outrun available means was basic to the popular concept of irreducible economic scarcity as the basis of free-market systems. From this premise followed a belief in the positive value of ever-increasing quantities of goods and services, as illustrated in the dogma that ever increasing per capita gross national product is the touchstone of progress toward "abundance."

*Material Comfort*

In the 1920's during the triumph of the so-called new era (of permanent prosperity), a highly critical French observer could say of Americans that they "consider it only natural that their slightest whim should be gratified."[3] Even during this period there were millions of Americans who would have considered themselves fortunate to secure basic necessities for nutrition and shelter; yet notwithstanding its exaggeration, André Siegfried's comment points attention to the value placed upon a *high level of material comfort.* Even before World War II, the United States undoubtedly had one of the highest material levels of living in the world, as judged by such criteria as adequacy of nutrition, medical care, facilities for shelter, transportation and communication, and so on.

The fact that material comfort undoubtedly is highly approved and sought after in the culture tells us very little in itself about what specific values are involved; the "American standard of living" has its undertones and overtones of meanings—from nationalistic identification to symbol of success, competence, and power and from a token of moral excellence to

[3] André Siegfried, *America Comes of Age* (New York: Harcourt, Brace & World, 1927).

something very close to a terminal goal at the level of hedonistic gratification.

There is some criticism to the effect that passive gratification elements in American society have become increasingly prominent in recent decades. The most obvious although probably not the most important index of this trend is provided by commercial advertising that emphasizes comfort and effortless gratification: eat this, chew this, drink that; take a vacation; be catered to; and so on. The major focus is upon receiving, looking at, being stimulated, in short, maximum pleasurable sensation with minimum effort or activity. Television and motion pictures are perhaps the clearest examples. "Spectator" sports fit the same pattern—huge audiences watch others perform. Even more striking is the emergence of a set of "drug cultures" in which involvement in the main activities of the preexisting society is minimized in favor of chemically induced psychological states. A more general shift toward a "fun morality" (rather than self-denial or "puritanism") is shown by sophisticated content-analysis of popular fiction.[4]

The gratification motif appears in mass entertainment with all the clarity of a caricature.[5] For motion pictures. Dorothy Jones's early analysis of a hundred films (appearing in 1941–1942) already showed a predominance of the "happy ending"—at the end of the picture, about 60 percent of all major characters were indulged with respect to all of their wants.[6] Analysis of popular theater offerings in the United States and Germany over several decades prior to the Hitler era showed that the dramas on the American stage much more often stressed personalized goals, romantic love, and the happy rather than tragic ending.[7] Leo Lowenthal's study of biographies appearing in two mass circulation magazines from 1901–1941 suggests that there has thus been a shift from the "idols of production" to the "idols of consumption"—from attention focused on substantial achievement in social organization and economic production to the people who embellish leisure time. Furthermore, in their content the more recent

[4] Martin U. Martel and George J. McCall, "Reality-Orientation and the Pleasure Principle: A Study of American Mass-Periodical Fiction (1890–1955)," in Lewis A. Dexter and David M. White (eds.), *People, Society, and Mass Communications* (New York: Free Press, 1964), pp. 283–334. Similarly a content analysis of best-seller novels for 1900–1904 and 1946–1950 showed that "the writers of popular fiction presented alcohol in positive rather than negative terms, and the tendency to see drinking as supportive and good increased during the half-century span." (Harold W. Pfautz, "The Image of Alcohol in Popular Fiction: 1900–1904 and 1946–1950," *Quarterly Journal of Studies on Alcohol*, 23, 1 (March 1962), 146.)

[5] For summaries of research see Sebastian de Grazia, *Of Time, Work, and Leisure* (New York: Twentieth Century Fund, 1962); Joffre Dumazedier, *Toward a Society of Leisure* (New York: Free Press, 1967); Harold L. Wilensky, "Mass Society and Mass Culture: Interdependence or Independence," *American Sociological Review*, 29, 2 (April 1964), 173–197.

[6] Dorothy B. Jones, "Quantitative Analysis of Motion Picture Content," *Public Opinion Quarterly*, VI, 3 (Fall 1942), 411–428; see Martha Wolfenstein and Nathan Leites, *Movies: A Psychological Study* (New York: Free Press, 1950).

[7] Donald V. McGranahan and Ivor Wayne, "German and American Traits Reflected in Popular Dramas," *Human Relations*, I (August 1948), 429–455; see also Patrick Johns-Heine and Hans H. Gerth, "Values in Mass Periodical Fiction, 1921–1940," *Public Opinion Quarterly*, 13, 1 (Spring 1949), 105–113.

biographies emphasized the private lives and consumption of the subjects. "It is neither a world of 'doers' nor a world of 'doing' for which the biological curiosity of a mass public is evoked. . . . instead of the 'givers' we are faced with the 'takers.' "[8]

Of course, a certain kind of "materialism" may emerge in a society, even though it is not initially a primary criterion of desirability—in the sense that the sheer availability of creature comforts and the incessant advertising used to sell them creates a social pressure to concentrate effort and attention upon them.[9] It is in this derivative way that an economy of affluence may drain away energy and commitment from values that stand higher in the nominal hierarchy of preferences.

But what if desires for goods and services are not, in fact, unlimited? What, indeed, if the wants for the kinds of goods and services that can be sold at a price turn out to be quite definitely satiable, under social and cultural conditions now emerging and in prospect? Values are not independent of beliefs, and beliefs are not completely immune to the facts of new experience. Beyond the level of biologically essential subsistence, what will be considered as "adequacy," "comfort," or "affluence" is normatively defined in a great variety of ways; and *material* goods may be *negatively* valued. As needs or desires or wants for food, drink, shelter, clothing, temperature control, physical protection, and sexual gratification are well met, the proliferation of desires may move into other consummatory activities, many of which are not closely dependent upon "material things" and many of which also are not supplied for a price in the market—social interaction and friendship, affection, creative work, art, recreation, religious expression. The satisfaction of such desires will still be "economic"—but in many cases only in the sense that the requisite activities require time and energy that is thereby withdrawn from *production* of physical objects and physical services or from the *consumption* of such goods and services.

The American experience gives some support to the hypothesis that in so far as a group or society is able to attain a high plane of material comfort, it will tend increasingly to emphasize the "hedonistic values," unless checked by internal social danger or outside threat. Apparently, at least in Western societies, the objective opportunity to secure material comforts elicits, in the long run, a desire for them. Once a high standard of living has been enjoyed, however, it is extremely difficult to reduce the level of sensation.[1] As new wants emerge and are satisfied over a period of time, they become accepted, "normal," and in this process they at the same time come to be felt as rights to which one has a moral claim. When the level of material

---

[8] Leo Lowenthal, "Biographies in Popular Magazines," in Paul F. Lazarsfeld and Frank N. Stanton (eds.), *Radio Research, 1942–1943* (New York: Duell, Sloan and Pearce, 1944), p. 527.

[9] And the continuous "teaching" of the mass media permeates the society. Here one simply has to refer to Marshall McLuhan, *Understanding Media* (New York: McGraw-Hill, 1964).

[1] For a vast documentation of the idea that the modern era has a "Sensate" culture see Pitirim A. Sorokin, *Social and Cultural Dynamics*, 4 vols. (New York: American Book Company, 1937–1941), and, in briefer form, *Society, Culture, and Personality* (Durham, N.C.: Duke University Press, 1943), esp. Part Seven.

comfort of a whole people has been rising over a considerable period of time, it will be reduced only reluctantly even under the duress of great social emergency.

But the picture just sketched is highly incomplete. First, it does not take into account the large amount of participation in active sports, the vast activity of vacation travel, or the millions of home workshops and the popularity of "do-it-yourself" hobbies. Nor does it give enough weight to the millions of amateur painters, actors, writers, and other artists. One must remember also the large audiences who actively appreciate serious concerts and the theater. (Americans spend more money for admissions to concerts than to baseball games.) Although passive entertainment predominates, it has not displaced the active and purposive use of leisure time. Second, the newer emphasis upon consumption and leisure does not necessarily indicate a basic change in values. There certainly is more leisure time and there are more consumer goods and services available to the American people than ever before. And, although the evidence is impressionistic, there probably is some real alteration in the emphasis upon and arrangement of traditional evaluations, for example, a lessened evaluation of asceticism, coupled with a lessened future-time orientation, leads to the enjoyment of leisure without the guilt and ambivalence it carried in a "puritan" ethos.[2] In the absence of convincing data, however, it is best to hold open the possibility that new patterns of consumption and leisure actually are being assimilated to older values, for instance, "consumption" may be interpreted both as reward for achievement and as a kind of achievement itself; the use of "gadgets" may merely confirm the value of instrumental activity; and recreation may be evaluated as a means for maintaining the capacity for work and achievement. The conclusion that "material comfort" leads to loss of high evaluation of disciplined endeavor would be premature. There is substantial evidence, for example, that professional values in work—including intellectual and expressive interests—have tangible trade-off weights as measured against money income in the market.[3]

### Equality

The avowal of "equality," and often its practice as well, has been a persistent theme through most of American history. Even modern economic organization, which in many ways epitomizes inequality,[4] has stressed "equality of opportunity." Yet few other value complexes are more subject to strain in modern times.

The United States began its independent political existence as a congeries of societies, which in the main had broken sharply with the traditions

[2] Clyde Kluckhohn, "Have There Been Discernible Shifts in American Values During the Past Generation?" in Elting E. Morison (ed.), *The American Style* (New York: Harper & Row, 1958), p. 204.

[3] John F. March, Jr., and Frank P. Stafford, "The Effect of Values on Pecuniary Behavior: The Case of Academicians," *American Sociological Review*, 32, 5 (October 1967), 740–754. Data are from self-administered questionnaires from 51,505 persons in professional, technical, and kindred occupations.

[4] Note how far the ideology of communist countries is from indicating the actual hierarchy of industrial organization there.

of social deference and with the hierarchical social structures that still characterized Britain and Europe. The generalization has its exceptions. New England was originally ruled by an elite of the religiously elect. Remnants of feudal land customs had persisted for a time in various areas in such forms as quitrents and primogeniture. Indentured servitude and imprisonment for debt had represented direct transmissions of neofeudal practices. But in general all individual arrangements embodying traditional social inequalities were dissolving. In retrospect, as always, this result now seems to have been inevitable. Actually, it was the consequence of a highly complex constellation of factors. There was the laxity of political control by England partly as a result of the distance from Britain and Europe. Also, only a small number of the colonists had been aristocrats, whereas the majority was of middle- and lower-class origins, and many of them rejected the class distinctions of their parent society. Mass accessibility to abundant resources made it seem possible for "anyone to become a king on his own" and thus helped to dissolve old hierarchies and social forms through movement, acquisition, and independence. The potential equality of all sorts and manners of men was encouraged by such ideological factors as the deeply individualistic tendencies in Protestantism, as well as by philosophical and political ideas that worked in the same direction. (Locke and the French nationalists, for instance, affected not only the founding fathers but much wider circles of eighteenth-century America.)

Other factors encouraging the emergence of equality as a value may be left aside for present purposes.[5] It will suffice here to see that this society in its formative periods was one that could, and wished to, break with its hierarchical tradition and that this break was favored by fundamental objective and ideological conditions. Thus, until the late nineteenth century, America was able to develop without having to face widespread conflict between the principle of equality and the principles of achievement and freedom. In this remarkable historical experience, through generation after generation, the values of equality were crystallized and elaborated. People saw the disappearance of primogeniture, the abolition of indentured servitude, of imprisonment for debt, of slavery, of property qualifications for voting and public office; there was provision for the common man to acquire a stake in the land and to secure a free public education; women gained one legal right after another; and even discriminations against minorities were sharply challenged time after time.

However, as Tocqueville saw more than a century ago, America had to face sooner or later a conflict of values that he described as a contradiction between the principle of freedom and the principle of equality. For instance, the cumulative effect of freedom to pursue individual advantage, given the opportunities and institutional framework of nineteenth-century America, was to destroy equality of condition. The liberty of which Tocqueville spoke was a freedom from feudal or mercantilistic restraints on the economic individualism so congenial to the early American situation. But this

[5] For example, the influence of geographic mobility, mutual dependence under frontier conditions, the lack of a complex division of labor, and highly developed urban life.

freedom could only lead under the historical circumstances to the emergence of what he called a manufacturing aristocracy, an outcome far from the perfect commonwealth of equal citizens that some idealizers of a yeoman republic desired. Not only did the specific conditions of American life accentuate the tension of equality versus liberty, but also the very attempt to blend Locke and Rousseau was intrinsically difficult.[6] Both liberty and equality are authentic and historically inseparable parts of Western democratic tradition, but for all their affinity their union has often posed perplexing dilemmas.

Already it becomes plain that the meanings of equality are various and that it does not help us very much to characterize a society as simply equalitarian or the reverse. Modern America, of course, shows inequalities of wealth, power, and prestige; and there is far from being perfect equality of opportunity to acquire these things. As Henry Alonzo Myers has eloquently indicated, men are not in fact equal in any specific ability or capacity;[7] in a complex and heterogeneous society they are likely to have very unequal access to scarce goods. The extent of the so-called objective or material inequalities, however, is itself in part a function of the basic value-system.[8]

A thorough-going insistence on equality is not likely to stop with the demand that ascribed barriers to opportunity be removed—rather it tends to go on to claim that "what men are entitled to by right is not the partial amelioration of their inequalities but the full, equal realization of their capacities."[9] Taken literally, this sort of demand goes to the very bases of our social system and would require truly radical changes to be actualized.

If equality is a basic value in our society, it must meet our operational tests: (1) the individual must feel guilt, shame, or ego deflation when he acts in inequalitarian ways and (2) there must be sanctions supported by the effective community for conformity or nonconformity. The extensiveness of these reactions must be weighed against parallel responses to any behavior manifesting hierarchical principles of human relations. Although no such quantitative assessment can be made from the available evidence, it is nevertheless clear that inequalities, hierarchical emphases, and various kinds of discriminations are common in American life. Taken as a whole

---

[6] "From its very beginning the theory of democracy linked together the two ideals of liberty and equality, and quite early it became apparent that these two would not unite as easily as the democrats of Thomas Jefferson's generation had hoped." (George H. Sabine, "The Two Democratic Traditions," *The Philosophical Review*, LXI, 4 (October 1952), 451–452. This basic linkage, involving at the same time a permanent opposition, is a major theme of Lipset's *The First New Nation, op. cit.*, in the form of "achievement" versus "equalitarianism."

[7] Henry Alonzo Myers, *Are Men Equal?* (New York: Putnam, 1945). The author, however, argues cogently for intrinsic equality as a central element in the American ethos.

[8] When the modern proponents of "inevitable inequality" argue that greatly unequal rewards are *necessary* in order to get the most *important* social functions performed, it is seldom noticed that the question of necessity is being begged along with the question of importance.

[9] Richard Lichtman, "Toward Community: A Criticism of Contemporary Capitalism," *Occasional Paper* of the Center for the Study of Democratic Institutions of the Fund for the Republic (Santa Barbara, Calif.: 1966), p. 45.

America appears to present a highly confused situation in which conflicts and compromises are accompanied by myths, legends, and conventional fictions until the main value directions become difficult to trace. Much of the seeming complexity, however, does not really concern basic value-orientations but rather represents either deviance or, at least equally important, different restrictions of the value in different *social roles and situations*. Certainly the relationship between a police officer and the automobile driver to whom he gives a traffic ticket is not "equalitarian." But this is a narrowly limited and defined relationship in a specific situation; the police officer has no generalized superiority over the hapless motorist in other roles and situations.

The problems can be grasped more readily if we differentiate among the several senses in which equality may be a value. It is useful, as we saw in Chapter V, to distinguish between intrinsic and extrinsic valuations. Extrinsic valuations are those judgments of value that depend upon generalized social categories and external symbols of status such as sex, age, nationality, occupation, rank, income, wealth, medals, race, authority. Intrinsic valuation has to do with the immediately personal qualities of the individual apart from any categorical social attributes; and its presence is demonstrated whenever one person feels an obligation to treat another person as—in any degree—an end in himself rather than purely as a means. To put it negatively, the person is given an intrinsic value when we feel guilt or shame if we do not act with some regard for his presumed human sensibilities, regardless of his categorical social status or group membership. Whenever such intrinsic valuation is at work, it constitutes a "floor" below which the person cannot be devalued or degraded—a guarantee of minimal equality.[1] Extrinsic valuations focus upon what a person *has*; intrinsic valuation concerns what the person is as an individual. It is obvious that the two imputations of value often do not coincide, as when we say that a man "doesn't deserve his rank" or "he may have a million dollars but he isn't worth two cents as a man."

At the level of explicit doctrine, intrinsic equality is widespread in American culture, both in the form of a specifically religious conception (the equality of souls before God, the divine nature within every person, and so on) and in the more secularized formulations that attribute an irreducible quantum of value to every person: "a man's a man for all that," "after all they are human beings," or the categorical imperative to "treat others as ends rather than means." At the level of overt interpersonal relations, adherence to a sense of intrinsic human value is discernible in a wide variety of specific behaviors—perhaps most obviously in "democratic manners." America has always impressed observers from more rigid and hierarchical societies as being marked by an extraordinary informality, directness, and lack of status consciousness in person-to-person contacts. This general openness of social relations can only be maintained in a culture in which intrinsic personal value is a widespread and effective assumption.

[1] Compare Lipset, *op. cit.*, p. 2 with the comments of John Porter on Canadian society in *The Vertical Mosaic* (Toronto: University of Toronto Press, 1965), p. 366.

In more concrete terms, equality is exhibited in the way individuals actually *relate* to others in ordinary interpersonal activities. Are individuals in American culture typically related to others by superordination and subordination, or are interpersonal relations typically horizontal? The answer to so sweeping a question can be built up only by induction from the enormous variety of social rules actually existing in our society; a definitive analysis must wait upon a great amount of further systematic research. However, much of the evidence in the preceding chapters on the major institutions is relevant here: we have seen, for example, how the central family-type emphasizes equality of in-law families and how the relations of husband-wife, parent-child, and sibling-sibling tend to be nonauthoritarian and nonhierarchical modes. In examining educational organization, it was suggested that, in spite of definite hierarchical emphases, the teacher-student relation in America is less rigid, formal, and authoritarian than in analogous European situations. On the other hand, we have seen much evidence of strongly hierarchical and authoritarian emphases, especially in large-scale economic and political organizations. And running through the whole society is the salient thread of nonequalitarian beliefs and practices concerning interpersonal relations with persons of a different racial or ethnic grouping. Nevertheless, in our provisional appraisal equality rather than hierarchy seems on the whole characteristic of concrete social relations—although perhaps more clearly at the level of the *goals and standards* of conduct than in the uneven compromises of going practice. As Professor Sabine puts it: "The demand that men of differing position shall meet on terms of mutual respect and self-respect has been and will continue to be a recurring demand made in the name of democracy."[2] On this point, something approaching a crucial "experiment of nature" is available to us in the reactions of American soldiers to military life in World War II. Military organization is the example par excellence of hierarchy. In World War II, the vast majority of American soldiers accepted the necessity of war and the legitimacy of military authority. Yet, as hundreds of specific studies showed, these same soldiers complained of the unequal privileges of officers and enlisted men and the insistence upon detailed observance of rituals and subordination and deference. It was clear also that one of the strongest forces that kept men working and fighting as organized groups was loyalty to their comrades and equals and that "teamwork" (the term is significant) rather than psychological dependence upon authority figures was the crux of the American version of military morale.[3]

A second major type of equality consists of specific formal rights and obligations. In the United States the strain toward equality of legal rights for all citizens or even residents has been strong and continuing. Formally equal civil rights—from military service to voting, from public education to taxation—represent not only freedom but also equality. In the sense of freedom these rights may be said to guarantee every individual a certain

[2] Sabine, *op. cit.*, p. 473.

[3] See the findings presented in Samuel A. Stouffer, *et al.*, *The American Soldier*, Vols. I and II (Princeton, N.J.: Princeton University Press, 1949), especially chaps. 6, 8, 9, and 10 of Vol. I, and chaps. 3, 6, and 7 of Vol. II.

openness in his life-space.[4] It is in this equality of specified rights that the second major theme of American equality has developed, rather than in doctrines of equal individual potentialities, achievements, or rewards.

The third type of equality is substantive equality of social and, above all, economic rewards. Here it seems quite clear that the principles of economic freedom and individual achievement have strongly dominated principles of equality. The reigning conception has been that of *equality of opportunity* rather than *equality of condition*. Concessions toward substantive equality of condition—for example, the income tax in so far as it is graduated—have not leveled difference in wealth; and the upper and middle classes of the society continually have insisted upon a moral claim to the existing differentials. It is quite striking that one of the earliest and most widespread reactions to Marxism, as popularly understood, was to select precisely the idea of "equal distribution of wealth" as the target of censure and moral outrage.

Every principle of equality is subject to its sharpest violation in the case of minority groups, especially Negro, or black, Americans. Few other aspects of our society are so well documented as this one. The multiple value-conflicts involved are combined with structural sources of conflict (political, stratification, economic, ecological) into a uniquely intractable source of societal tension—and of pressures toward social change.[5]

In widest perspective it appears that the inequalities in American culture that are felt to contravene equality values most severely are of two kinds: first, the denial of nominally universal rights of citizenship and violations of nominally universal rules of impersonal justice; second, the denial of opportunities for achievement in the formally open competitive order. It is certainly true that American culture has never found it overly difficult to tolerate great differences in certain types of individual privileges or rewards. Where rewards have been seen as consequences of achievement—including the successful acceptance of responsibility and exercise of authority—inequality of reward tends to be accepted as legitimate.[6] Where control of facilities is regarded as necessary for performance of valued functions, as in the case of the capable business executive or military leaders, resentment is minimized. The tautology that inequality is not resented unless considered to be undeserved takes on an important meaning as soon as we are able to specify what "undeserved" actually means. By and large in the United States, it has meant *categorical* privileges—rewards not earned by effort and achieve-

[4] Jane Cassels Record and Wilson Record, "Ideological Forces and the Negro Protest," *The Annals*, 357 (January 1965), 89–96. Although the case is overstated in some respects, an effective argument has been developed by John P. Roche for the thesis that both "equality" and "freedom" have gained important legal reinforcement and social support during the last half-century. See John Roche, *The Quest for the Dream* (New York: Macmillan, 1963).

[5] Cf. Chapter V. See also Robin Williams, *op. cit.*, esp. chap. 10; Robert Penn Warren, *Who Speaks for the Negro?* (New York: Vintage Books, 1966); Lewis Killian, *The Impossible Revolution?* (New York: Random House, 1968).

[6] Cf. David M. Potter, *People of Plenty* (Chicago: University of Chicago Press, 1954), pp. 90–91. "Equality of opportunity," as Potter observes, originally meant emancipation from fixed, ascribed status; its other face, therefore, was freedom.

ment (including moral achievement) within the basic institutional rules for fair competition. Here is the core of "the American tradition" of equality. The dominant cultural value is not an undifferentiated and undiscriminating equalitarianism, but rather a two-sided emphasis upon basic social rights and upon equality of opportunity. And there is clear evidence that, in spite of all exceptions and contradictions, the great majority of Americans in recent times have felt that the society actually does provide equality of rights. Especially widespread in the United States is the expectation of universal enforcement of regulations and basic equality of treatment from governmental officials. More than eight of every ten persons (about the same as in Britain) expect equality of treatment from governmental bureaucracy and the police—in contrast to just over fifty percent in Italy or even less in Mexico.[7]

These general views have been independently examined in comparative analyses by S. M. Lipset and by John Porter, among others.[8] Beyond question American political patterns, as well as all other institutional sectors, have been profoundly affected by the fundamental and continual opposition between achievement values and equality values. Equality is a "charter-value," being deeply involved in the initial political legitimization of the nation;[9] competitive achievement may be less formally accredited but is even more pervasively elaborated as a primary, axiomatic referent for evaluation.

It is important to note the role of this value complex in the periodic resurgence of native, homespun "radicalism" in America. The historical record indicates that the demand for equality of traditional rights and equality of economic opportunity has not, in the main, grown out of imported ideologies, but has emerged from the received traditions. The long ground-swell of the populist movement[1] in the late nineteenth century provides a good example of how American movements for economic reform, at least until the depression of the 1930's, have been essentially the attempt of the "little man," and especially of the farming population, to check the power of "big business." These movements never really challenged in any thoroughgoing way the concepts of private (individual) property and free enterprise; rather, they represented the counterattack of the old style private (individual and familial) property and the free (small, independent, competitive) enterprise against the emerging forces of large-scale, corporate property and large-scale industrial, financial, and commercial combinations.[2]

---

[7] Gabriel A. Almond and Sidney Verba, *The Civic Culture* (Princeton, N.J.: Princeton University Press, 1963), p. 108.

[8] Lipset, *op. cit.*, especially chaps. 5 and 7; Porter, *op. cit.*, esp. chap. 12; see also Clinton Rossiter, *Conservatism in America* (New York: Vintage Books, 1962), pp. 201–202.

[9] "In the United States there is a utopian image which slowly over time bends intractable social patterns in the direction of equality, but a Canadian counterpart of this image is difficult to find." Porter, *op. cit.*, p. 366.

[1] An excellent source on this important phase of American history is John D. Hicks, *The Populist Revolt* (Minneapolis: University of Minnesota Press, 1931).

[2] See the discussion in Henry Bamford Parkes, *The American Experience* (New York: Knopf, 1947), chap. 13. For example: "The antitrust laws were peculiarly American and were a product of the agrarian tradition; they had no parallel in Europe" (p. 292).

It has been part of the fundamental pathos of American culture to believe that virtue should and will be rewarded—and more particularly that such economic virtues as hard work, frugality, and prudence should receive a proportionate reward. The axiomatic value of this moral equation has been closely linked with the premise that everyone (at least, all in "one's own" group) has an equal right to fundamental opportunities. Without question, this whole principle is currently undergoing severe strain and extensive redefinition. Further discussion of these changes must be deferred to Chapter XIV; the essential present point is that values of equality in the received American culture of the modern period have centered around the dual themes of civil rights and economic opportunity. It is quite unlikely that in the last quarter of the twentieth century these historically powerful components of "equality" will be enough to sustain the political integration of disaffected American minorities. The demand for various kinds of substantive equalities—amounting to categorical and preferential status in the view of many white, middle-income persons—has become a political reality.

For most of America's history, the definitions of equality in substantive terms were politically unacceptable. Only after the 1950's did the persistence of relative poverty and the growth of massive turbulence among low-income black Americans begin to lend serious force to the conception of a universal minimal level of living. The older criterion of equality of opportunity not only permitted but demanded great emphasis upon liberty of action;[3] the newer inclination pointed toward increased public controls in the interests of a redistributive political economy. Apart from real or imagined oppositions of immediate economic and political interests, the questions of public policy that have been called forth by the "revolution of rising expectations" clearly involve genuine clashes of basic values.

### Freedom

We need no research to tell us that the verbal affirmation of the value of freedom is widespread and persistent.[4] We very much need sophisticated research to enable us to understand what this fact signifies. The widespread positive reaction to the symbolic value of the word is illustrated in many ways. For example, public opinion polls show that freedom in general, or in some specific application, such as freedom of the press or of worship, is most often mentioned as the greatest advantage of the American form of government.[5]

That something real in actual social relations lies behind the word freedom cannot be doubted. Yet the reality is not in the unconditional listing

---

[3] Potter, *op. cit.*, p. 96.

[4] Savelle's conclusion from his study of the eighteenth century is: "Thus the great common denominator of American social thinking was the ideal of social freedom—freedom to rise, that is—individualism, and social fluidity. If the Americans still believed in aristocracy, it was now, in theory at least, predominantly . . . based upon the ideal of an aristocracy of merit, of individual worth." Max Savelle, *Seeds of Liberty* (New York: Knopf, 1948), p. 280.

[5] See *Opinion News*, VIII, 6 (March 18, 1947); Almond and Verba, *op. cit.*, pp. 102, 185; V. O. Key, Jr., *Public Opinion and American Democracy* (New York: Knopf, 1961), pp. 39–50 and chap. 21.

of categorical freedoms, for it can quickly be shown that actual social life and "unconditional freedom" are contradictions in terms. Furthermore, what are restraints from one point of view may be rights or "privileges" from another, as when a person wants "to do his duty" (and finds it to his advantage to do so).

American conceptions of freedom mainly stem from an orientation that characterized European thought for several centuries; freedom is compatible with causality and determinism; it does not mean uncaused behavior but rather behavior that is not subject to restraints that are in some sense external and arbitrary. In this view, although behavior is always determined— that is, influenced, caused, or conditioned—it is nevertheless possible to give a definite meaning to the statement that it may also be "free." All life in society involves the limitation of behavior not only by the physical world, including the limitations of the human body and mind, but also by reciprocal rights and obligations among persons; every social group furthermore must cope with problems of authority and power. What, then, is to be said of the American emphasis on freedom?

The historical context of freedom as a value pattern in our culture begins with the centuries-long process whereby area after area of life was removed from the web of interlocking controls of feudal Europe. With the rise of nation-states and of urban life and with the expansion of industry and trade, the settled, hierarchical society of Europe moved into an unprecedented colonizing phase. The American colonies were one result, and in them the trend toward emancipation was intensified. At one point it might be a struggle against quitrents; at another, restiveness under mercantilistic restraints; still elsewhere, a revolt against an established religious hierarchy. Always the demand was for freedom *from* some existing restraint. That the major American freedoms were in this sense negative does not mean, of course, that they were not also positive: they were rights to *do*, by the same token that they were rights to be protected from restraint. Nevertheless, the historical process left its mark in a culturally standardized way of thought and evaluation—a tendency to think of rights rather than duties, a suspicion of established (especially personal) authority, a distrust of central government, a deep aversion to acceptance of obviously coercive restraint through visible social organization. At the time in which the primary political and economic structure of the new society was laid down, the great threat to freedom was perceived as coming from the centralized, absolutistic state; and the obvious course seemed to be to erect every possible barrier to centralized governmental control. The main import of the doctrine of checks and balances was to prevent the central state as much as possible from undertaking any positive action beyond a very few carefully defined areas of authority. Such a view of government reflected a society in which the politically effective elements of the community wanted above all to have "room" to make their own decisions,[6] to develop their

[6] For most of the national history down to the 1950's these elements were primarily within the white population. Only recently has the value of freedom been *fully* confronted in relation to black Americans. It has not been easy to discard the effects of a history of categorical subordination and discrimination with reference to a substantial racial minority.

own spheres of social power, to escape from the surveillance of kings and ministers of state. This particular sort of freedom was premised on a sweeping faith: the confidence of the individual in his own competence and mastery.

It is thus in the peculiar features of the concept of freedom to which value is attached in America that our present interest centers. We know, for instance, that when both American leaders and the leaders of the Soviet Union say they value "freedom," the words do not carry identical value loadings. The differences cannot be wholly explained either as special pleading or as simple ignorance, and examination of the variation between the two orientations may help to clarify the American case. Broadly speaking, the Soviet conception of freedom emphasizes security in the sense of rights to employment, medical care, economic support, education, and cultural participation *within* an accepted framework set by the neo-Marxist state. In this system, many of the liberties prized in Anglo-American culture were regarded as irrelevant if not meaningless, at least through the end of the Stalinist era. On the other hand, American spokesmen emphasize freedom of speech and assembly, a multiparty, representative political system, private enterprise, freedom to change residence and employment.

The above contrasts, stated in oversimplified form, serve to pose more sharply the problem of what "freedom" it is that is valued in American society. In the historically developed orientation—which may no longer exist in the same form—the central principles seem reasonably clear. A major implicit cultural premise in the dominant valuation of freedom has been *the equating of "freedom" with control by diffuse cultural structure rather than by a definite social organization.* Thus, it has seemed to make a great difference whether the individual receives a certain income or has a certain type of occupation as a result of an apparently impersonal, anonymous, diffuse, competitive process, as against "being forced" to accept that employment or remuneration by law or by the command of a visible social authority. A foreclosed mortgage has been culturally defined in a radically different way from governmental confiscation of the same property. To be tied to a given locality by diffuse cultural pressure and lack of economic opportunity is regarded as a kind of constraint quite different from such controls as a police order or a governmental regulation.

Upon this kind of axiomatic base, American culture has tended to identify a very great variety of forms of personal dependence as lack of freedom. To "work under a boss" was not so long ago regarded as a loss of freedom. The widespread reluctance to take employment as a domestic servant and the low evaluation attached to this type of occupation appear to reflect in part the same complex. One of the earliest and most persistent criticisms of American society by aristocratically minded foreign observers

---

The value-conflicts have been more complex than generally realized even by some careful scholars. Cf. Stanley M. Elkins, *Slavery: A Problem in American Institutional and Intellectual Life* (Chicago: University of Chicago Press, 1959)—a work that builds upon Frank Tannenbaum, *Slave and Citizen: The Negro in the Americas* (New York: Knopf, 1947). Both these works have been given penetrating criticism by David B. Davis, *The Problem of Slavery in Western Culture* (Ithaca, N.Y.: Cornell University Press, 1966).

has concerned the absence of a docile serving-class and the impertinence of the "lower orders."[7]

The underlying psychological constellation in traditional American attitudes toward freedom thus seems to be a posture of self-confidence and expansiveness, coupled with a tendency to reject all absolute claims to personal authority. This syndrome permeates relations of parents and children, men and women, employers and employees, the citizen and *Monsieur le Bureau*. In this sense the American conception of freedom is clearly that of Locke rather than of Rousseau, of the protection of particular liberties and the tolerance of disagreement rather than the homogenization of private groups and individuals into an omnipotent general will.[8] Not "plebiscite democracy" but "inalienable rights" reflects the central value. In either case, however, there is an explosive utopianism implicit in the American vision of freedom.

Viewed in these terms, the theme of freedom is far broader than any particular institutional sector of the society. It rests in the last analysis upon an even more basic conception of the individual as an integral agent, relatively autonomous and morally responsible. (See the section on "Individual Personality" that follows.) Above all, a sociological analysis must make explicit the difference between *freedom as a value* and the *particular historical definitions of freedom in terms of special institutional forms.*[9] Liberty in America began as a release from certain political restraints; the economic liberty thus secured was eventually accompanied in its turn by discords and dislocations in the social structure. In our day the greatest threats to freedom, conceived in liberal democratic terms, appear in economic dislocation and class conflict. The reaction to this situation has given us a "welfare state" in which freedom is no longer so clearly tied to a social system of private property and inactive government. The necessary implications for freedom as a value are by no means wholly clear; it is patent, however, that the dated and localized definition of freedom as practically synonymous with eighteenth-century economic philosophies is no longer accepted by the great majority of people in our society.

The core meaning of this shift can perhaps be illustrated by a glance at the so-called laissez-faire economics, which was so much more than either laissez faire or economics; it constituted, in fact, a whole system of social philosophy, an elaborate and interconnected set of social values and beliefs. The conception of man around which the doctrine centered was that of the discrete human atom, calculating his economic self-interest and acting "rationally" in the unlimited pursuit of gain. The "perfect system of natural liberty," suitable to this concept, would guarantee the sanctity of contracts,

---

[7] Charles A. Beard and Mary R. Beard, *The American Spirit* (New York: Macmillan, 1942), p. 488.

[8] "The absolutely sovereign and omnicompetent state is the logical correlate of a society, which consists of atomic individuals." Sabine, *op. cit.*, p. 467.

[9] Fred Somkin, *Unquiet Eagle: Memory and Desire in the Idea of American Freedom, 1815–1860* (Ithaca, N.Y.: Cornell University Press, 1967). This study shows the power of the belief in American freedom, along with the deep tensions it implied, and contained, and produced.

the stability of media of exchange, and the rights of private property. In such a system, so its proponents believed, "when men are free from all governmental interference, virtue finds its tangible reward in wealth and vice its penalty in economic failure."[1] In this way religious axioms were assimilated to the theory of universal social good through economic competition. Support of such a system, under a political democracy, was sought through an additional doctrine, which in this case held that the economically successful are fittest because this very success attests to their moral superiority. Freedom then becomes the economic freedom of the entrepreneur, and democracy becomes a form of government giving maximum protection of property rights. Progress becomes technological advance and economic expansion. Individualism is equated with the right of the individual to use his property as he sees fit, within very broad limits, and to compete freely with others. Society is a neo-Darwinian jungle in which only the fittest *should* survive; and the fittest are those who can win out by intelligence, industry, or ruthlessness.

This "organic" cluster of doctrines has foundered against twentieth-century realities. Because the cultural definition of freedom has changed and because the threats to freedom are now apprehended in different quarters it is easy to assume that the emergence of the welfare state signalizes our departure on a "road to serfdom." We suggest that the status of freedom *as value* must not be prejudged because of changing social mechanisms. Freedom inheres in the *relationships* between an individual and other individuals and groups. It exists to the degree that individuals are enabled to make the choices they wish to make, with minimal use of coercion and minimal infringement of the "spontaneous" actions of others. So long as American society safeguards the right of the individual to a wide range of moral autonomy in decision making, so long as the representative character structure of the culture retains a conscience that is more than simple group conformity—so long will freedom be a major value. Emphatically, institutional forms are not unimportant; but their significance must be found by specific analysis, not by uncritical prejudgment.

Recent changes in the direction of equality through governmental action have sometimes been interpreted as a reduction in freedom. Assuredly the balance between the two is debatable. But it is oversimplification to regard graduated income taxes, or increased equality of income, or legal bars to racial discrimination and segregation merely as restrictions upon the wealthy or the racially prejudiced. A certain equality of rights is essential to fair bargaining, workable compromises, and mutual respect—all vital ingredients of freedom. Equality and freedom are necessary the one to the other, and neither can be pressed to extremes without damage to the other. David Potter has gone precisely to the heart of this complex matter in his analysis of how an emphasis upon equality in the sense of universal human dignity led to denial that intrinsic differences in human worth correspond to differences in social rank—and how this resulted in

---

[1] Myers, *op. cit.*, p. 140. The passage cited is a paraphrase of certain of the doctrines of William Graham Sumner.

"the rejection of authority . . . [as] the most pronounced of all the concrete expressions of American beliefs in equality."[2]

### External Conformity[3]

Even as early as the 1830's, Tocqueville commented on the necessity of safeguards against a possible "tyranny of the majority" in America and thought that public compulsion had already penetrated into private affairs in a censorious way not usual in the France of his day. Nearly a century later Siegfried, another and more critical Frenchman, visualized America as a land of vast uniformity in speech, manners, housing, dress, recreation, and politically expressed ideas. In 1948, Laski pointed to an "amazing uniformity" of values, thought that "business *mores*" had permeated the culture, and tried to show that "the American spirit required that the limits of uniformity be drawn with a certain tautness."[4] Many Europeans in the period prior to World War II had thought American conformity-behavior to have a certain harried, compulsive quality and had referred to standardization, "flatness," and lack of individuality in comparison with the continent. In the period between 1920 and World War II European observers seem to have been especially (and overly) impressed with conformity themes in America. Thus, Richard Muller-Freienfels, in a book published in 1929, stated, "Distance, uniqueness, and originality are European values, which are foreign to the American. His values are the very reverse of these: adherence to type, agreement, similarity."[5]

These appraisals—which in fact have often been biased and exaggerated —come as something of a shock to a people that has made much of individual initiative, the rights of the individual, personal independence, "rugged individualism." Yet it should be no surprise that an intensely active, democratic society should define tolerance of individual nonconformity largely in terms of sanctioning technological and economic innovation.[6] In the field of so-called personal morals, the culture is one in which there is a tendency to legislate conformity—a tendency acted out again and again from the early "blue laws" to prohibition and the Hays Office. In the field of intellectual heterodoxy, although the United States has produced a

[2] David M. Potter, "Individuality and Conformity," in McGiffert, *op. cit.*, p. 241.

[3] A spate of concerns about conformity during the 1950's is indicated by the popularity of such works as: Riesman, *et al.*, *The Lonely Crowd, op. cit.*; William H. Whyte, Jr., *The Organization Man* (New York: Simon and Schuster, 1956); Vance Packard, *The Status Seekers* (New York: David McKay, 1959). Numerous other writings, as well as the mass media, gave attention to the topic. One even suspects that many Americans at that time were trying to find out how much they ought to avoid conformity in order to conform with an acceptable norm of nonconformity.

[4] Laski, *op. cit.*, pp. 49–51.

[5] Richard Muller-Freienfels, *Mysteries of the Soul*, Bernard Miall (trans.) (London: Allen and Unwin, 1929). This view has been common among those who feel that if industry turns out standardized goods for a mass market it follows that the whole culture is "standardized."

[6] Cf. Lipset, *op. cit.*, p. 132: "Other-direction, or to put it less dramatically, sensitivity to the opinions of others, is an epiphenomenon of the American equalitarian ethos, of the opportunities for rapid status mobility, *and* of the general growth of an urban, bureaucratic society."

Thoreau, a Henry George, its freethinkers and dissenters, a considered judgment would be that really radical nonconformity in speculative thought has not been outstanding, at least in comparison with other countries of Western culture. American "individualism," taken in broadest terms, has consisted mainly of a rejection of the state and impatience with restraints upon economic activity; it has not tended to set the autonomous individual up in rebellion against his social group. In a "nation of joiners,"[7] individualism tends to be a matter of "group individualism," of the particularized behavior of subcultures.

Men universally seek the approval of *some* of their fellows and therefore try to be "successful" by some shared standards of achievement or conformity. This characteristic is the outcome of universal requirements of group life and of the basic nature of the socialization process; otherwise stated, conformity and the desire for social approval are formal qualities that are part of the very definition of society. In this sense, conformity is not a *value* at all but simply an end product of other values and the necessary adjustments entailed by life in groups.

Our real interest is knowing how rigid the conformity is and what specific content defines conformity or success in a particular group or culture. There are societies in which conformity may be a matter of proficiency in religious ritual, others in which it consists of exemplifying warrior virtues, others in which esthetic activities are the measure.[8] Similarly, in all societies men tend to conform to the groups with which they are most deeply identified; but both the degree of conformity and its kind differ greatly in various cultures. In short, conformity can be treated as a value only insofar as *sheer adherence to group patterns* is actually divorced from the content and implications of those patterns. This is rare.[9] It is only among a people who have lost the capacity for autonomous value-decisions that the sheer conformity of a goose-step order can approach a terminal goal. By and large, American conformity has rarely had the latter quality for an extended period, although other directed as well as instrumental conformity has been widespread from early times.[1]

It is useful to examine American conformity emphases for the light they may throw upon other dimensions of the value system. Several gen-

[7] This catch phrase is misleading. The United States exhibits a vast amount of organizational activity, but most Americans participate in very few voluntary organizations; see Chapter XII.

[8] "A few hundred years ago it seemed the most natural thing in the world to the ambitious among our ancestors, to sell off their property, raise a company and set off to the Holy Land to rescue it from the infidels. This is incomprehensible to us, but we see nothing strange in a man of ambition and imagination devoting a lifetime of strenuous endeavor to the making of tubs or the organized slaughter of hogs." Cooley, *op. cit.*, p. 225.

[9] Sabine (*op. cit.*, p. 471) goes so far as to say: "Every society depends upon and exacts some kind and degree of conformity, and different cultures support widely different systems of status, but no culture reduces its members to automata or fails to acknowledge that self-respect is both a genuine good and a powerful human motive."

[1] Cf. Seymour Martin Lipset and Leo Lowenthal (eds.), *Culture and Social Character* (New York: Free Press, 1961). Note the contrasts of American vs. Nazi German school song books in Hans Sebald, "Studying National Character Through Comparative Content Analysis", *Social Forces*, 30, 4 (May 1962), 318–322.

eral sociological hypotheses are relevant to this examination. We know that a functioning group or society that feels threatened from the outside tends to tighten social controls over behavior involving the group's solidarity and striking power. Wars supply the most dramatic examples, but the political "witch hunts" in periods of international tension are equally in point.[2] We know further that a group ridden by internal insecurities and tensions will, under certain conditions that need not be specified here, tend to raise its threshold of toleration for nonconformity: "The looser the package, the tighter must be the string"—if the package is to hold together at all.[3]

Some preoccupation with external conformity is to be expected in a society in which upward social mobility is highly prized and frequently achieved. The competitive striving of an upwardly mobile group in a society organized around the economic enterprise requires stringent discipline over the expression of sexual and aggressive impulses, over patterns of consumption, over the uses of time and resources. In this aspect, conformity is derivative from equality of opportunity in conjunction with success striving.[4] Furthermore, an emphasis upon external conformity easily develops out of the premise of basic human equality: if all are equal, then all have an equal right to judge their fellows and to regulate their conduct according to commonly accepted standards; some such cultural equation has been widely accepted in the broad middle classes of American society. The exceptions to the pattern occur in those classes and groups in which special license follows from exclusion of the group from the application of principles of equality (for example, the very rich, certain déclassé strata, and so on).

Interestingly enough, the very heterogeneity of American culture tends to produce a stress upon external conformity. Given the varied cultural backgrounds of the population and the desire that the various groups should continue to live together in the same society, conformity in externals becomes a sort of "social currency" making it possible to continue the society in spite of many clashes of interests and basic values. If it is gradually learned that the exhibition of cultural differences—whether they be of dress, or language, or religious faith, or political philosophy—seems to lead to friction in interpersonal relationships or even to public disturbances, a whole series of complex adjustments are set in motion. Among the possible responses to such a situation is the practice of withdrawing tension-producing items from general social circulation: for example, one finds popular maxims such as "never argue about religion or politics." The individual comes to

---

[2] Samuel A. Stouffer, *Communism, Conformity, and Civil Liberties* (Garden City, N.Y.: Doubleday, 1955).

[3] Milton Rokeach, *The Open and Closed Mind* (New York: Basic Books, 1960); Eric Hoffer, *The True Believer* (New York: Harper & Row, 1951).

[4] And yet, the child-rearing values of middle-class Americans are more *child-centered* (rather than adult-centered) and more likely to encourage *self-direction* (rather than conformity to external prescriptions) than are the corresponding values of either American working-class parents or of parents in Italy. See Melvin L. Kohn, "Social Class and Parental Values," *American Journal of Sociology*, LXIV, 4 (January 1959), 337–351; Leonard I. Pearlin and Melvin L. Kohn, "Social Class, Occupation and Parental Values: A Cross-National Study," *American Sociological Review*, 31, 4 (August 1966), 466–488.

reserve controversial matters to an intimate social circle of like-minded persons; public discourse and behavior are correspondingly more highly standardized. An elaborate social currency develops; set conversation-pieces, clichés, and standardized public opinions that can be passed smoothly along the channels of social interaction almost as a counterpart to the flow of money in the exchange economy.

The economic system itself contributes to the conformity theme in two other main respects. First, the high degree of specialization of economic roles in a highly developed money economy means that much social interaction is functionally specific, impersonal, transitory, and frequently laden with clashes of immediate economic interests. These are precisely the kinds of conditions most likely to produce conventionalized or stereotyped behavior.[5] Second, the relations of economic dependence of the individual upon other persons or groups are often such as to permit stringent conformity demands.

By definition, if people felt strongly enough in opposition to any of these pressures and were at the same time not strongly inhibited by the negative sanctions that could be brought to bear on their opposition, the agreement on procedural rules of the game would evaporate. And indeed, it is among elements of the population that are simultaneously alienated and relatively resistant to conventional sanctions that the nonconformity of dissent—to the point of widespread "disorder" and violence—has emerged among Negroes, college and university students of draft age, and a great variety of youthful "drop-outs." There are some scattered data which suggest the possibility that the main historic values that centered upon traditional moral orientations and instrumental activism—as well as upon group-conformity and loyalty—are most prevalent in rural areas, low-income populations, and entrepreneurial occupations, suggesting that current changes in social structure may be working to reduce the dominance of the older values.[6]

### Science and Secular Rationality

It has become a commonplace observation that the application of science and related secular rational approaches have transformed the external conditions of American culture along with many other major cultures of the world.[7] Applied science is highly esteemed as a tool for controlling nature. Significant here is the interest in order, control, and calculability—

---

[5] Cf. James W. Woodard, "The Role of Fictions in Cultural Life," in *Transactions of the New York Academy of Sciences* (1944). Interesting enough is the research finding that the proportion of respondents who choose any given item in a personality test to describe themselves is a direct function of the *independently rated* "social desirability" of the attribute described in the item. See the definitive study: Allen Edwards, *The Social Desirability Variable in Personality Assessment and Research* (New York: Dryden Press, 1957).

[6] See, for example, Clark and Wenninger, *op. cit.*

[7] Compare the statement of a prominent physicist: "Our culture has the outstanding property of striving to convert all experience into rational scientific knowledge"—Henry Margenau, "Western Culture and Scientific Method," in Lyman Bryson, Louis Finkelstein, and Robert M. MacIver (eds.), *Conflicts of Power in Modern Culture* (New York: Seventh Symposium of the Conference on Science, Philosophy and Religion, 1948), p. 16.

the passion of an engineering civilization. This interest is congruent with the externalized orientation that we have already met in several previous guises; historically it is linked also to the fundamental assumption of an ordered universe in which rational human beings can continually improve their situation and themselves.

But the prime quality of "science" is not in its applications but in its basic method of approaching problems—a way of thought and a set of procedures for interpreting experience. We need only mention the long history of the "warfare of science and theology" in order to suggest the conflicts of belief and value that have accompanied the rise of science. However, it may be well to remember that the anti-evolution trials occurred only a few decades ago and that popular attitudes toward science still contain strong ambivalences. The caricature of the "diabolical scientist" coexists with the stereotype of the benevolent laboratory magician. Faith in science is a faith; its continued existence is dependent upon other convictions, and these other convictions are interdependent with the real social structure. Science is a particular manifestation of the rational-theoretic theme, which F. S. C. Northrop among others regards as a distinguishing feature of our entire culture.[8] It is this ordering and stabilizing component that links science to the broader tendency in our culture to translate experience into systematic abstract concepts—to transform the fleeting, confused flow of immediate experience into standardized categories that permit, and in part create, prediction and control. Thus, science, socially considered, is above all a *discipline*, as Max Weber has so eloquently shown.[9] Our main interest here is accordingly to ask: a discipline for what?

Very broadly, emphasis upon science in America has reflected the values of the rationalistic-individualistic tradition. Science is disciplined, rational, functional, active; it requires systematic diligence and honesty; it is congruent with the "means" emphasis of the culture—the focus of interest upon pragmatism and efficiency and the tendency to minimize absolutes and ultimates. The applications of science profusely reward the strivings for self-externalizing mastery of the environment. We think it fair to say that science is at root fully compatible with a culture orientation that attempts to deny frustration and refuses to accept the idea of a fundamentally unreasonable and capricious world.

In recent years, certain social scientists have held that science is "morally neutral." If they mean merely that science cannot allow its findings to be distorted by value presuppositions extraneous to its accepted methods and models of proof, then these statements are acceptable. But it must be quite obvious that the findings of science will often have important value implications. It must be clear that the problems chosen for study are, or may be, selected in part on the basis of nonscientific values. Finally, the existence of basic theoretic science and the free exercise of scientific method presuppose

---

[8] F. S. C. Northrop, *The Meeting of East and West* (New York: Macmillan, 1946).

[9] Especially in his "Science as a Vocation," in H. H. Gerth and C. Wright Mills (trans. and eds.), *From Max Weber: Essays in Sociology* (New York: Oxford University Press, 1946), pp. 128 ff.

a definite social structure and system of values.[1] Honesty and clarity are not just luxury virtues in science; on the contrary, they are essential defining characteristics.[2] The same can be said for the faith in the order of nature and the faith in human reason—these are elements of a definite credo, manifesting values that are widely assaulted in the contemporary world. Their preservation in America apparently depends upon the continued and adequate functioning of an orderly, pluralistic society.

### Nationalism-Patriotism

In every society we find men participating in certain groups to which they feel they owe loyalty and with which they identify themselves; and we find other groups identified as outgroups toward which the individual feels estrangement, sense of difference, or enmity. This distinction, in small, localistic nonliterate societies, is often so sharp that others are not considered "men." Analogous situations exist in the so-called complex civilizations, perhaps most strikingly in the denial of a common humanity to the enemy in time of war. Such intergroup cleavages involve that scaling of values called ethnocentrism, that is, the diffuse value-attitude making one's own group the point of reference for judging all others. All known societies are to some extent ethnocentric; individuals everywhere tend to give a preferential value to their own culture. Strictly speaking, ethnocentrism applies to every distinctive group from the smallest clique to the largest civilization. Today, however, the sentiments attached to the nation-state have overwhelming importance; and nationalistic feelings seem the prime example of ethnocentric values. For this reason, it is particularly important to examine the place of nationalistic or patriotic evaluations in the social systems of America. As in the case of conformity, nationalism is not a single, clear value-orientation, used in making judgments of desirability, but rather a complex set of evaluations and beliefs. We are dealing here with a diffuse and extremely complex phenomenon and can do no more than to suggest a few very elementary points.

First, we distinguish between two polar types of nationalistic values that are inextricably mingled in concrete situations. The first type may be described as undifferentiated or totalistic nationalism, demanding total and unquestioning allegiance to national symbols and slogans and tending to make "Americanism" a rigid orthodoxy. Criticisms of any features of American life are close to treason, and "un-American" is the epithet for any deviation from a rigid, although vaguely defined, cult of conformity. The quasi-religious character of this complex is manifest in its creedal emphasis, its concern with ritual and symbolism, its elaboration of dogma and its correlative "inquisitions." The contrasting ideal type of national-patriotic orientation tends to place less emphasis upon undifferentiated loyalty, rather con-

[1] There are societies in which it has been held that biological theories must conform to political doctrine.

[2] A valuable analysis of the institutionalization of values in relation to the control of deviant behavior in scientific work is given in Robert K. Merton, "Priorities in Scientific Discovery: A Chapter in the Sociology of Science," *American Sociological Review*, 22, 6 (December 1957), 635–659.

ceiving of patriotism as loyalty to national institutions and symbols because and in so far as they *represent* values that are the primary objects of allegiance. Thus, "America" may be felt as worthy of loyalty because it is considered to embody or to stand for political democracy, respect for individual personality, a high standard of living, freedom of worship, or any other important value. This pluralistic patriotism usually presupposes basic acceptance of the nation-state as a framework of allegiance; but it does not preclude critical appraisal of men, events, or policies in value terms broader than those of in-group loyalty as such.

The basic tension between these contrasting orientations[3] is compactly summarized by the fact that a legislative group concerned with "un-American" activities can itself be condemned as un-American.

A third orientation only became a serious possibility during the intense domestic discord concerning the conflict in Vietnam in the 1960's. That possibility is the outright rejection of national policies and of the moral and legal claims of the national government upon its citizens—to the point of refusing to serve in the armed forces, of actual migration to other countries, and of the renunciation of American citizenship. Should such activities become sufficiently widespread, it would follow that the nation-state would be unable to maintain any military commitments abroad and would therefore presumably cease to function as a world power. Of course it is likely that a large number of the most militant objectors held that in the Vietnam conflict the American government could no longer legitimately demand compliance, because its policies in this instance allegedly had departed from such central values as democracy, freedom, and humanitarianism. Opposition to military service and to other prescriptions of legal authority then could be defended either in terms of individual conscience or the pluralistic patriotism described above.

Nationalism in the modern sense is, of course, a relatively recent development in Western history. In the case of American nationalism, it is clear that the early colonists for a long time thought of themselves as Englishmen (or Germans, Swiss, French) rather than "Americans." Even after the establishment of the new nation it was not uncommon to find that "my country" might as well mean Dinwiddie county, Virginia, or the State of Vermont, as the nation taken as a whole.[4] It took the Civil War and a whole series of subsequent developments[5] really to displace provincial patriotism in favor of national feeling.

3 Cf. Savelle, *op. cit.*, "The split in nationalistic pride between those who glorify the melting-pot and those who fear the un-American activities of foreigners whose ideals do not exactly coincide with their own is no new thing; it has apparently been one of the dialectical strains within American nationalistic feeling almost from the beginning."

4 Merle Curti, *The Roots of American Loyalty* (New York: Columbia University Press, 1946). chap. I. Even in World War II, an appreciated chord was struck by the Secretary of the Navy when he told a Texas gathering that he had been assured that Texas would not make a separate peace.

5 For example, modern methods of communication and transportation which break down the barriers between local communities. It may be added that modern nationalism has emerged concurrently with the dramatic weakening of family and other *gemeinschaftliche* structures; and there may be definite functional connections between these two developments.

An important component of American nationalistic values is that a generalized sense of fulfillment and confident hope had been built into the culture for a period of over two centuries; and even the shocks of recent depressions, wars, and other deep crises have not dissipated the widespread satisfaction of a people who feel that the country "has been good to them." Indeed, in some respects World War II and its immediate aftermath seemed to reinforce this attitude by producing a vivid sense of social and economic conditions in other areas of the world. Bearing on this point, roughly comparable public opinion polls in a number of countries, taken immediately after World War II, showed that only in Australia (itself also a "colonial" nation) did so small a proportion of the people as in the United States in the immediate postwar years express any desire to live in another nation.[6] It would be a mistake, moreover, to suppose that such positive attachment to one's own society is merely the complacency of the well fed. It is a much more value-laden sentiment of favorable appraisal of the society's basic institutions. Indeed, one of the most striking characteristics of American national pride is its overwhelming preoccupation with political institutions. In a survey of five national samples of adults, the question was asked, "Speaking generally, what are the things about this country that you are most proud of?" The percentages who volunteered comments on government or political institutions were: Italy, 3; Germany, 7; Mexico, 30; United Kingdom, 46; United States, 85.[7]

This sense of satisfaction incorporates supposedly *universal* values. A purely tribal patriotism conceives of its culture as having a unique destiny and does not think of extending its values to the rest of mankind. But American nationalism, like the religions that have contributed so heavily to the culture, involves the idea that elements of the American way of life should be widely adopted elsewhere.[8] This secular counterpart of the missionary spirit is both an index of the strength of nationalistic feeling and a potent source of misunderstanding and resentment in international affairs. In peace as well as in war, many citizens have believed that the United States must have a mission as a crusader for righteousness.[9] Other peoples have not always regarded the matter in that light. It may be an eventual historical irony that this moral sense, turned back in criticism upon the national state, could reverse its original meaning and direction.

The universalistic elements in national feeling, however, have conflicted with certain kinds of expansionism, on the one hand, and tendencies toward isolationism and national autarchy on the other. American expansionism in its earliest phases was undertaken by the pioneer, the speculator, the trader, and the missionary, and aimed at the possession of the land, chiefly

[6] Surveys by International Gallup Polls, reported in *Opinion News* (June 15, 1948), National Opinion Research Center, University of Chicago.

[7] Almond and Verba, *op. cit.*, p. 102.

[8] Concerning the very tangible influence of a moralistic orientation, with its attendant "sense of mission," upon America's role in world affairs, see Chapter 14 of Parkes, *op. cit.*

[9] This is abundantly documented in many studies. See, for example, Curti, *op. cit.*, pp. 48 ff.; F. H. Hartmann, *The Relations of Nations* (New York: Macmillan, 1957), pp. 610–611

through purchase, rather than at the conquest and the rule of alien peoples. It was only toward the close of the nineteenth century when the economic exploration of our own backwoods was nearing completion that chauvinism of an expansionist turn became widespread.[1]

On the other hand, autarchic nationalism goes back to the very beginnings of the republic. A sense of alienation from Europe, a "belief in the degradation of the Old World and the mounting fame of America . . ." (Curti), was common even before the revolution. The entire socioeconomic situation of early America encouraged turning attention away from Europe and the past and toward the mastery of the new continent. Thanks in large part to geographic position—and the British Navy—nineteenth-century United States could with impunity make a slogan of the doctrine of no entangling alliances. The isolationism that began as a matter of necessity and historic accident became a positive virtue throughout a good part of the nineteenth century. Although the old-style isolationism has been rendered objectively impossible by World War II, the Cold War, and subsequent international involvement, some of the values it symbolized remain active in the current scene. Illustrating the complex possibilities of redefinition of values is the turning  of "moral perfectionism" from a *support* of national involvement in international responsibility from about 1945 to 1965 to an antimilitary, antinationalistic demand that the United States cease "trying to be the world's policeman."

Perhaps the most important sociological generalization that can be invoked here is that intense nationalistic conflict will always have drastic consequences for the value systems of a democratic society. In particular, it inevitably brings in its train a large military establishment—and a centralization of social power. The modern state in time of war must by its own terms of existence have centralized control of production; it must regulate consumption: there is actually no more infallible prescription for the destruction of laissez faire, the free market and the individual entrepreneur. To sustain limited wars in the nuclear age, furthermore, requires a steadiness of long-range purposes and a widespread popular commitment to collective goals that appear difficult to attain in an affluent, individualistic social democracy.

## Democracy

Like freedom or progress, democracy in American culture is a highly complex and derivative theme. The nation that fought a great war under the slogan of making the world safe for democracy lives under a constitution that contains no direct reference to democracy; the democracy of the founding fathers is not that of twentieth-century industrial society; the meaning of democracy is one thing to the advocate of black power and another to the Ku Klux Klan. Here again the cultural meanings of a value theme and its actual role in social structure are full of complex variations, conflicts, and shadings through time and from one part of the society to another at a given

[1] Adams, *op. cit.*, pp. 304 ff. and 346 ff.; Miriam Beard, *op. cit.*, chaps. 24 and 25; Curti, *op. cit.*, p. 6; Wallace Evan Davies, *Patriotism on Parade* (Cambridge, Mass.: Harvard University Press, 1955).

time. Furthermore, the content of democracy is in considerable part subsumed under other value complexes discussed elsewhere in this chapter: for example, freedom, equality, humanitarianism; and in any case, a reference to democracy does not denote a clear, unitary value but a multiple nexus of more specific beliefs and primary values.[2] Nevertheless, no matter how elaborately qualified, the sheer prevalence of culturally sanctioned attention to something called democracy forces us to include it in our listing of major value-themes.[3]

Along with majority rule, representative institutions, and the rejection of the monarchical and aristocratic principles under which the society began, early American democracy stressed the reservation of certain "inalienable rights" as unalterable by majority rule.[4] Basically, this sort of democracy rested upon the implicit belief in natural law, as opposed to personal rule, and in the moral autonomy of the individual. The actual shape of the democratic credo was a synthesis of clashing ideologies; but it was the insistence of the average citizen upon equality of political rights that actually forced the Bill of Rights into the Constitution. Major themes in the gradual crystallization of the main democratic creed thus included equality of certain formal rights and formal equality of opportunity, a faith in the rule of impersonal law, optimistic rationalism, and ethical individualism. As already suggested in the discussion of freedom, the theme of democracy was, concretely, an agreement upon *procedure* in distributing power and in settling conflicts. Liberal democracy, American model, arose in reaction to an epoch in which the great threats to security and freedom were seen in strong, autocratic, central government. The new system was devised in such a way as to limit and check centralized governmental power and to establish an ordered pattern for agreeing to disagree. Such a pluralistic view of social power was clear and explicit on questions of procedure, although it left the common ends of the society largely undefined.

Gabriel Almond and Sidney Verba have concluded that the United States has a "participant civic culture," marked by active participation, a sense of civic obligation, social trust, a sense of political competence, emotional involvement in political campaigns, and pride in the political system. The "imbalances" in this pattern, they suggest,[5] derive from the great emphasis on participation coupled with distrust of central authority—a tendency we would be inclined to call "activistic populism."[6] Given the continuous emphasis upon democracy and the strong background of moral

2 See Seymour Martin Lipset, "The Value Patterns of Democracy: A Case Study in Comparative Analysis," *American Sociological Review*, 28, 4 (August 1963), 515–531.

3 It is sufficient to note that Coleman (*op. cit.*, p. 498) found that democracy is one of the few "national traits" mentioned by observers in all major historical periods.

4 Adams, *op. cit.*, p. 258.

5 Almond and Verba, *op. cit.*, pp. 440–441.

6 Americans—even more than British citizens—believe that individuals should participate actively in the public affairs of their communities—in sharp contrast to the attitudes found in Italy. Furthermore, Americans tend to feel a sense of political potency, believing that they can influence both local and national government. (*Ibid.*, pp. 170–172 and 184–185.)

absolutism, disaffection with national leaders and policies easily takes the form of an assertion of the moral omnipotence of popular action. Moralistic activism, in turn, may come to be felt as an end in itself—requiring no positive programs or intellectual justification. At this extreme, of course, left and right become blurred in an amorphous actionism. Whether widespread dissent of this character can be sustained within a democratic set of procedures remains an open question.

In a culture that strongly emphasizes universalistic norms and an active, instrumental approach to life, the stress upon individual achievement, especially in business occupations, tends to direct attention and energy away from collective goals, as well as away from expressive and contemplative concerns. Although these emphases are changing, they have thus far been strong enough to lend a distinctive quality to this innovative, flexible, open-ended system.

As can be seen, the theme of democracy has converged with those of equality and freedom; and all three have been interpreted and reinterpreted along with the moralistic optimism of the doctrines of progress. Our previous surveys have shown some of the complicated deviations and conflicts within these orientations; the present section is briefly handled because of the overlapping of democracy with other themes. The cumulative review of major value-orientations seems more and more clearly to point to one central constellation that gives coherence to a wide range of others, including democracy. This nuclear or focal theme we shall call the value of individual personality. In one aspect, its relation to democracy has been given a classic statement by Carl Becker:

> Its [modern liberal democracy's] fundamental assumption is the worth and dignity and creative capacity of the individual, so that the chief aim of government is the maximum of individual self-direction, the chief means to that end the minimum of compulsion by the state. Ideally considered means and ends are conjoined in the concept of freedom: freedom of thought, so that the truth may prevail: freedom of occupation, so that careers may be open to talent; freedom of self-government, so that no one may be compelled against his will.[7]

Thus, insofar as majority rule and conditional and limited authority based upon uncoerced consensus and universalistic rules[8] are highly evaluated in the culture, the main American concepts of democracy are consistent with a particular set of value postulates concerning the nature and significance of the individual in society. The hypothesis that respect for and trust in individuals as persons is closely connected with libertarian political beliefs

---

[7] Carl Becker, *Modern Democracy* (New Haven, Conn.: Yale University Press, 1941), p. 27.

[8] "In most other countries, naturalization is a privilege granted administratively and sometimes capriciously without reference to clearly defined standards of eligibility uniformly applied to all applicants. In the United States, legally admitted immigrants are entitled to naturalization regardless of origin, income, occupation, wealth, or other socioeconomic characteristics if they meet other specified requirements." (Leo Grebler, "The Naturalization of Mexican Immigrants in the United States," *The International Migration Review*, I (New Series, No. 1) (Fall 1966), 17.

and with faith in democratic processes was formulated in the first edition of this work, without access to data adequate to appraise its validity. More recently, a substantial number of studies have shown that there is in fact such a relationship. A generalized "faith in people" strongly correlates with liberal-democratic political views.[9]

### Individual Personality

Writing in 1897, Émile Durkheim incisively described a pattern of value in Western civilization that he called the cult of individual personality.[1] Basically this cult sets a high value on the unique development of each individual personality and is correspondingly averse to invasion of individual integrity; to be a person is to be independent, responsible, and self-respecting, and thereby to be worthy of concern and respect in one's own right. To be a person, in this sense, is to be an autonomous and responsible agent, not merely a reflection of external pressures, and to have an internal center of gravity, a set of standards, and a conviction of personal worth. Above all, the individual is not considered to be released from all sociocultural controls. As Parsons has put it: "This is not a matter simply of freeing the individual from ethical restraints imposed by society, it is a matter of the imposition of a different *kind* of restraint. Individuality is a product of a certain social state. . . ."[2] Not the unrestrained biologic human being, but the ethical, decision making, unitary social personality is the object of this cult of the individual. What is positively valued in the tradition now under examination, in other words, is not just any kind of personality whatsoever, but rather a certain kind of individual.

The personality that is the object of high value in this particular tradition is something of intrinsic worth, not valued simply as a member of a group nor as a means to some ulterior end. This orientation to the person, it must be repeated, is the product of a definite social situation. There is no real paradox in saying that individuality can be a social product and a common social value; the development of individual personality is a *shared value* rather than a *collective end* in a group or social system. The emergence and maintenance of this state, however, is intimately related to other aspects of the society. To maintain a high evaluation of individual personality in this peculiar sense is surely a difficult and precarious feat, for there are factors inherent in society that continually threaten the value. The crucial fact in this connection is that other persons are always potential tools or threats in relation to the attainment of any one individual's separate interests; control over others is always a potentially efficient means to securing one's individual desires. There is always some measure of this centrifugal bombardment of interest that creates pressures toward "using" other people

[9] Rose K. Goldsen, *et al.*, *What College Students Think* (Princeton, N.J.: Van Nostrand, 1960), pp. 133–152; Morris Rosenberg, "Misanthropy and Political Ideology," *American Sociological Review*, 21, 6 (December 1956), 690–695; Almond and Verba, *op. cit.*, pp. 266–270, 284–287.

[1] *Le suicide*, Book III (Paris: 1897; new ed., Paris: F. Alcan, 1930), chap. I.

[2] Parsons, *The Structure of Social Action* (New York: Free Press, 1949), pp. 333–334.

in an essentially amoral utilitarian fashion. Under certain social conditions, the integrity of the individual *qua* personality, thus, may largely disappear. Slaves in the ancient world were not persons in the modern meaning. The fate of the laboring population during certain phases of the Industrial Revolution further illustrates how strong interests sometimes break through protective values centering around the person. A high valuation of the individual in the present sense is difficult to maintain under conditions of great social stress, crisis, and privation—in war, famine, natural disaster, revolution, plague, and the like. In general, whenever great urgency is felt for the accomplishment of a collective task, requiring coordination, speed, and great differentials of sacrifice, there is a tendency to regard individuals as tools rather than values in themselves. Militaristic societies often tend to exalt the collectivity over the individual, and for functionally understandable reasons. Similarly, an overwhelming stress upon profit making in organized economic enterprises quite obviously would tend toward an impatience with individual scruples, needs, and peculiarities and toward a calculating, impersonal use of others solely as a means toward the dominant end. In our own society the pressures and ambivalences involved in the valuation of individual personality are highlighted by the specific case of respect for freedom of conscience in religious matters.

We have said that the value of individual personality has been important in the received tradition of America, but that it is subject to very powerful contravening influences. What evidences are there as to its actual place in the total culture? In the first place, we note a large number of important legal provisions that appear to have as *part* of their function the protection of personal freedom or the physical or social integrity of the person; to mention a few—illegality of slavery and peonage (note that a person cannot even voluntarily sell himself as a slave); illegality of imprisonment for debt, and provision for bankruptcy proceedings (in this context, also, a limitation on economic rights in the interests of personal freedom); prohibitions against personal defamation (libel and slander); prohibition of "improper search and seizure;" prohibition of "cruel and unusual punishment;" right of habeas corpus, and so on. Perhaps the most striking instance of the lengths to which the law has gone in the attempt to preserve the person from attack is found in the definition of suicide as a crime. The free individual in our society is not free to take his own life because of the axiomatic value that he is not presumed to have the right to destroy.[3] A number of facts already cited in preceding pages also may be taken as evidence of the value attached to the interpersonality. So, for example, the presumed universal and impersonal system of legal justice not only reflects equality and democracy but also, at what is probably a still more basic level, the concept of a universal worth, a claim for consideration, simply because one is an individual. "Status justice," graded according to external criteria of rank, birth, and so on, is in principle radically incompatible with this orientation. Similarly, humanitarian practices may be inter-

[3] The contrast with the traditional Japanese hara-kiri or Hindu suttee is striking evidence of the basic nature of the value-belief complex we are examining.

preted as partly expressive of concern for personality as a value, whatever *other* values and specific interests may be involved.[4] Still another, and crucially important, datum is found in the religious doctrine of the soul—that every human being has an immortal soul and is by the same token invested with the value imputed to the soul.

The reality of the value of individualism in our culture is observed not only in derivative forms such as manifest ideology, law, and formalized behavior patterns but also at the level of implicit assumptions and unconscious practices. For example, it is typical of the culture that the question as to whether there is actually such an entity as "the individual," "self," or "ego" is usually not even thought of, and if raised, is greeted with surprise or shock.[5] *Of course* individuals exist, of course they have separate individual needs and rights. As Dorothy Lee says:

*The value of individualism is axiomatically assumed. . . . A newborn infant must become individuated, must be taught physical and emotional self-dependence; we assume, in fact, that he has a separate identity which he must be helped to recognize. . . . The need for privacy is an imperative one in our society, recognized by official bodies such as state welfare groups and the Department of Labor. And it is part of a system which stems from and expresses our basic values.[6]*

Nevertheless, it is not at all easy to define objective and comparable measures of this value that would enable us to compare different parts of the population or different historical periods. The "value of individual personality" as impressionistically conceived represents an extremely complex cluster of more specific desirable states or conditions, such as uniqueness, self-direction, autonomy of choice, self-regulation, emotional independence, spontaneity, privacy, respect for other persons, defense of the self, and many others. It follows that future studies that seek adequate empirical indicators of changes and variations in this value complex probably will require whole "families" of indices or "surrogates" of these standards of desirability in human conduct. Yet there seems no reason to doubt that a society that draws up a declaration of rights for children, that is appalled by self-immolation of the individual for the group, that perceives groups as aggregates of cooperating but separate individuals—that such a

---

[4] Again the general principle is illustrated by the fact that any concrete social behavior typically is multivalued; the referents of value can be disentangled only through painstaking analysis. Although the necessary research largely still remains to be done, sufficiently precise and comprehensive studies would probably show trace lines of this value in exceedingly diverse manifestations. To what extent is the practice of tipping resisted because of "degrading" implications? Is there repugnance to cremation of the dead because it is felt to be a symbolic dissolution of the concept of the individual? Is the value of individual personality an important factor in resistance to sterilization legislation—or to legalization of euthanasia?

[5] The deep-seated quality of these assumptions is acknowledged even by critics who repudiate them and who seek to introduce radically different conceptions and values. For example, a popular writer who advocates views adapted from Eastern philosophies, especially Zen Buddhism, well illustrates the point: Alan Watts, *The Book* (New York: Pantheon Books, 1966).

[6] Dorothy Lee, "Are Basic Needs Ultimate?" *Journal of Abnormal and Social Psychology*, XLIII, 3 (July 1948), 393–394.

society incorporates the value of the individual at the deepest levels of its unconscious presuppositions. As a matter of fact, the sociologically alert student is likely to guess at once that so pervasive a theme is maintained by quite special modes of child training and basic socialization; the hypothesis would be that this value complex is embedded in the central affective-cognitive structure of the representative personalities of the culture.

As in every other theme we have examined, this value is not universally accepted; nor is it maintained without effort. To take only one example, the component of privacy is now affected by the rapid development of technologies of surveillance and detection—wiretapping, miniature radio transmitters, distant-listening devices, spike microphones, telescopic cameras, peephole gadgets, concealed recorders, and so on and on. The security of the individual against unwanted observation and disclosure has become problematic.[7] Widespread use of eavesdropping and other intrusive methods have been reported; these practices allegedly are used by private detective agencies, industrial investigations, the Internal Revenue Service, the police, the Federal Bureau of Investigation, and many other governmental and corporate agencies, as well as by individuals seeking to breach the privacy of others.[8]

### Racism and Related Group-Superiority Themes

The commitment of large segments of American society to doctrines stressing the value and dignity of the individual has been real, deep, and widespread. The same can be said of the principles of equality, of humanitarian values, of political freedoms, and so on through the list of "publicly dominant" value patterns already listed. Once full weight has been given to all these "rational-humane" values in the received traditions of the society, it must be recognized at the same time that the values of the creed have continually struggled against pervasive and powerful countercurrents of valuation. One of the chief conflicts, and in many ways the most important conflict, has centered around those diverse patterns that have as their common element *the ascription of value and privilege to individuals on the basis of race or particularistic group membership* according to birth in a particular ethnic group, social class, or related social category.

Racialistic doctrines were first given widespread currency and intellectual elaboration in the slavery controversy during the decades immediately prior to the Civil War. The value anomalies into which the proslavery position led,[9] in a culture so strongly stressing an individualistic religion and a democratic political system, gradually produced an explicit system of

---

[7] "The right of privacy is among the most important of all rights, as it is the most neglected and the most attacked in our time." Thomas I. Cook, "Individual Liberty Today: Challenge and Prospect," in Morroe Berger, Theodore Abel, Charles H. Page (eds.), *Freedom and Control in Modern Society* (New York: Van Nostrand, 1954), p. 190. By permission of Van Nostrand Reinhold Company, a division of Litton Educational Publishing Inc., Litton Industries, Princeton, N.J., 1954.

[8] Cf. Edward V. Long, *The Intruders: The Invasion of Privacy by Government and Industry* (New York: Praeger, 1967).

[9] Wilbert E. Moore and Robin M. Williams, Jr., "Stratification in the Ante-Bellum South," *American Sociological Review*, 7, 3 (June 1942), 343–351.

thought that relied upon assumptions of biological superiority to buttress the existing system of power and privilege.[1]

Space forbids anything like full documentation of the pervasiveness of organic (or more narrowly, racist) orientations in our society. Adequate evidence is to be found in works already cited. It is enough to say that categorical discriminations are still widespread in established practice, and until past midcentury often were crystallized into whole systems of legislation. It is not necessary here to explore the fears, vested interests, and multiple sociopsychological sources of the superiority-exclusiveness theme indicated by these legal acts. We must agree with Morris Opler,[2] however, that these facts reflect a view of society that in its extreme forms implicitly rejects "freedom" and individual ethical responsibility, certain conceptions of progress, and rational mastery of culture. Thus, the organic-racist view of man—insofar as its logical implications are actually worked out in human relations—stands in sharp opposition to most of the value orientations already reviewed. If a society begins with the premise that the human nature of individuals is biologically fixed and that different physical types or "races" are innately superior or inferior, then the unlimited development of this theme will make meaningless, or positively evil, the values of equality, democracy, freedom, rationality, progress (in the sense of human improvement through learning), humanitarianism, individual achievement linked with moral autonomy, and the central values of personality. The ultimate logical outgrowth of complete organicism is an exclusionistic society, rigidly organized in a static hierarchy.

It becomes apparent that a very important part of the conflict of value systems in the United States can be economically summarized in terms of tension between *values centering around the concept of the responsible individual personality versus values organized around categorical organic conceptions.*

Without doubt, group discrimination and racism are deviant themes, contrary to the *main* thrust of American society. But the sharp conflicts and agonizing dilemmas they occasion require us to make explicit the bases of the ideological conflict.[3] No permanent resolution of the tensions—both intergroup and intragroup—is possible short of the repudiation of the entire theme of racial superiority and inferiority. Recognition of achieve-

---

[1] "The race dogma is nearly the only way out for a people so moralistically equalitarian, if it is not prepared to live up to its faith." Myrdal, *et al., op. cit.,* Vol. I, p. 89; cf. Thomas F. Gossett, *Race: The History of an Idea in America* (Dallas: Southern Methodist University Press, 1963); William R. Stanton, *The Leopard's Spots* (Chicago: University of Chicago Press, 1960); Louis L. Snyder, *The Idea of Racialism* (Princeton, N.J.: Van Nostrand, 1962). Contrast with "Statement on race and racial prejudice" (Paris: United Nations Educational, Scientific and Cultural Organization, 1967).

[2] Morris E. Opler, "Cultural and Organic Conceptions in Contemporary World-History," *American Anthropologist,* XLVI, 4 (October–December 1944), 448–449; see also Pierre van den Berghe, *Race and Racism* (New York: Wiley, 1967).

[3] The fantastic complexity of evaluative disagreements concerning public policies in this area involves differences in values, beliefs, facts, interpretations, expectations—as well as numerous misunderstandings. For a remarkable case in point, see Lee Rainwater and William L. Yancey, *The Moynihan Report and the Politics of Controversy* (Cambridge, Mass.: The M.I.T. Press, 1967).

ment and respect for personality and moral character must be individual, not categorical, if such evaluations are not to arouse conflict in a society with the value-patterns described in these pages. The rapid decline in racist beliefs among white people from the 1940's on suggests the possibility that greater consistency in the belief system may result from the disintegration of nineteenth-century racial ideology. The movement to sweep away legally enforced segregation and public discrimination, which started in the 1930's, led to an established *national* policy of nondiscrimination by the time of the passage of the 1964 Civil Rights Act. Note also that in the year 1965 Congress passed drastic amendments to the basic immigration laws, ending restrictions based on ancestry and place of birth: the amendments stipulated that prospective immigrants should not be discriminated against "because of race, sex, nationality, place of birth, or place of residence."[4]

### CONCLUSION

This rather lengthy and schematic review has not done justice to any one theme, but perhaps it at least has placed before us a range of important value-positions current in our society and suggested their complex interrelations. It must always be kept in mind that these themes, values, and systems of belief do *not operate as single and separate units* but *are in continually shifting and recombining configurations* marked by very complex interpenetration, conflict, and reformulation. Furthermore, our descriptive scheme that necessitated separate isolation and labeling of themes must not be allowed to leave the impression—to repeat an earlier caution—that values are disembodied elements which somehow function apart from concrete social relations and personalities. Although values *are* abstractions, everything described in this chapter must be capable of observation, in some sense, in the behavior of real personalities and in actual social structure, or else we have mistaken fancy for fact. Let us repeat: values emerge from the fundamental experiences of men, and are, therefore, subject to all the external conditions of that experience; but values also constitute, in their turn, real—not epiphenomenal—determinants of social behavior. Let us also reiterate that any identifiable value's influence is altered not only by variations in (nonvalue) conditions but also by the configuration of other values that is present. Thus in one situation value X may be supported by compatible value Y; in another instance opposed by incompatible value Z; in a third case, X occurs in the presence of Y (positive) and Z (negative). No simple "adding up" of isolated values will give more than a stereotypic distortion of the actual processes of value realization, value blockage, and value change. We may sometimes yearn for simple generalizations in this field, but it would be no service to pretend that any exist. The universe of values is intractably pluralistic.

Furthermore, anything approaching an "adequate" analysis of the full context of each value we have studied may well be beyond the capacities

[4] D. G. Benn, "The New U.S.A. Immigration Law," *International Migration*, 3, 3 (1965), 99–107.

of any living individual or intellectual discipline. For major themes have intricate relationships with numerous other themes and are embedded in subtle and often inaccessible social processes. Thus, we would suppose that intensive comparative study of complex historical materials, as well as of contemporary surveys, observations, and experiments, will be necessary before we gain a satisfactory appraisal of the theme of "active mastery" in our culture. In its most explicit and highly elaborated forms, this theme involves a sharp separation of man from nature on the one hand, and of the human from the divine on the other. In this view, however, man is the child of God, or carries a divine spark or divine mandate. Set over against the world, he is above all "lesser creatures." He has a special charter to occupy the earth and to "have dominion over" both inanimate nature and other living things. Cut off from the omnipotence and omniscience attributed to the active source of creation, he strives to attain infinite powers—immortality, perfect goodness, total control. Actual personal commitment to this Faustian or Promethean world view would define a *doing* orientation to life. And the tangible expression of such a will to *do* and to master must be concentrated purposiveness in task-like activity. Such activity necessarily would tend to have a highly selective "single minded" quality.

Fortunately, such elaborate specification is not essential for some approximate and provisional understanding of the total set of major value-themes current in American society. Perhaps the total picture may be clarified by a summary classification. In the first place, there are the quasi-values or *gratifications*, taken at a hedonic or physiological level, implicit in the entire analysis and especially important in the section on "material comfort." Second, we may identify the *instrumental interests* or means values, for example, wealth, power, work, efficiency. Although these interests may become values in themselves, it is convenient to consider them primarily as instrumental to the achievement of other values. Third, we have the *formal-universalistic values of Western tradition:* rationalism, impersonal justice and universalistic ethics, achievement, democracy, equality, freedom, certain religious values, value of individual personality. Fourth, there is a class of *particularistic, segmental, or localistic evaluations* that are best exemplified in racist-ethnic superiority doctrines and in some (not all) aspects of nationalism.

Running through these patterns of interests and values are certain still more general "dimensions" or "orientations" that are not typically explicit but must be identified by highly abstract inference. Because of this abstract quality, the inadequacy of the data, and the removal from observed phenomena by several stages of inference, the statement of such basic dimensions is a difficult undertaking and the following propositions must be taken as suggestive rather than definitive.[5]

1. American culture is organized around the attempt at *active mastery* rather than *passive acceptance*. Into this dimension falls the low toler-

[5] In the nature of the case, anyone—including the author—can think of numerous exceptions to each of these generalized formulations, as well as widespread *alternative* themes.

ance of frustration; the refusal to accept ascetic renunciation; the positive encouragement of desire; the stress on power; the approval of ego assertion, and so on.

2. It tends to be interested in the *external world* of things and events, of the palpable and immediate, rather than in the inner experience of meaning and affect. Its genius is manipulative rather than contemplative.

3. Its world-view tends to be *open* rather than closed: it emphasizes change, flux, movement; its central personality types are adaptive, accessible, outgoing, and assimilative.

4. In wide historical and comparative perspective, the culture places its primary faith in *rationalism* as opposed to *traditionalism*; it deemphasizes the past, orients strongly to the future, does not accept things just because they have been done before.

5. Closely related to the above is the dimension of *orderliness* rather than unsystematic ad hoc acceptance of transitory experience. (This emphasis is most marked in the urban middle classes.)

6. With conspicuous deviations, a main theme is a *universalistic* rather than a *particularistic* ethic.

7. In interpersonal relations, the weight of the value system is on the side of *"horizontal"* rather than *"vertical"* emphases: peer relations, not superordinate-subordinate relations; equality rather than hierarchy.

8. Subject to increased strains and modifications, the received culture emphasizes *individual personality* rather than group identity and responsibility.

In broadest outline, then, American society is characterized by a basic moral orientation, involving emphases on active, instrumental mastery of the world in accordance with universalistic standards of performance. It is a pluralistic system, in which it is not easy to secure unitary commitment to collective goals. It permits a wide range of goals for achievement. If one were to guess, it might be said that its greatest vulnerabilities as a survival system lie not in external threats or even its inner conflicts, but in the possibility of shapelessness and loss of common energizing goals or of sufficient commitment to cope adequately with societal concerns as such. This closing comment, however, is intended to raise a question, not to state a conclusion.

**SUGGESTED READINGS**

ALMOND, GABRIEL A., and SIDNEY VERBA. *The Civic Culture.* Princeton, N.J.: Princeton University Press, 1963. One of the few sources of systematic data permitting cross-national comparisons. Demonstrates clearly some of the distinctive assumptions and evaluative criteria manifest in political attitudes and behavior in the United States.

CURTI, MERLE. *The Roots of American Loyalty.* New York: Russell & Russell, 1946. Provides essential sense of context and development in orientations to nationalism and patriotism. Represents the kind of history that helps to free the reader from the blindness of being entrapped in the present moment.

GROSS, BERTRAM M. (ed.). *A Great Society?* New York: Basic Books, 1968. Uneven but stimulating collection of essays, ranging over most of the changes and dilemmas of values in the third quarter of the twentieth century.

KEY, V. O., JR. *Public Opinion and American Democracy.* New York: Knopf, 1961. Already suggested as reading useful for study of political institutions and political processes; but may be read with profit as a unique exercise in keen interpretation of nonobvious vectors in value orientations.

KONVITZ, MILTON R. *Expanding Liberties: Freedom's Gains in Postwar America.* New York: Viking, 1966. Sets the record straight by scholarly and judicious exposition of the major movement to establish and expand universalism and equality of opportunity in law and public policy in the first two decades after World War II.

LIPSET, SEYMOUR MARTIN. *The First New Nation.* New York: Basic Books, 1963. Integrated set of essays, making major use of the concept of values. Especially productive discussion of the theories of achievement and equality.

MARX, LEO. *The Machine in the Garden.* New York: Oxford University Press, 1964. Fascinating attempt to show how technology and industrialism were assimilated to a tradition of pastoral virtues.

MYRDAL, GUNNAR, *et al. An American Dilemma,* 2 vols. New York: Harper & Row, 1944. Like many other "monumental" or "classic" works, cited perhaps more often than read with care. Vastly illuminating as a bench-mark study and as guide to identification of enduring complex dynamics in values in the United States.

PARKES, HENRY BAMFORD. *The American Experience.* New York: Vintage Books, 1959, chaps. 13–14. Good example of skillful use of historical data to construct synoptic account of main values and beliefs.

PEPPER, STEPHEN C. *The Sources of Value.* Berkeley and Los Angeles: University of California Press, 1958. Philosophical analysis in terms of a "naturalistic" theory of value. Remarkably productive of ideas suitable for empirical testing in sociological studies of values.

RIESMAN, DAVID, with the assistance of RUEL DENNEY and NATHAN GLAZER. *The Lonely Crowd.* New Haven, Conn.: Yale University Press, 1950. One of the most widely read books in sociology. Highly stimulating and perceptive. Even its errors are instructive, and it stands up well under repeated readings.

ROKEACH, MILTON. *Beliefs, Attitudes, and Values: A Theory of Organization and Change.* San Francisco, Calif.: Jossey-Bass, 1968. Advocates clear distinctions of beliefs, attitudes, and values, and development of systematic research-based theory of values. Presents experimental data and provocative hypotheses.

SANFORD, CHARLES L. *The Quest for Paradise.* Urbana, Ill.: University of Illinois Press, 1961. Insightful discussion of how the images and themes of expansion and active mastery have contrasted with visions of redemption through primitivistic withdrawal.

WESTIN, ALAN F. *Privacy and Freedom.* New York: Atheneum Press, 1967. Thoughtful exploration of value problems raised by modern methods of surveillance, monitoring, interrogation, and required disclosures of information. Discusses possible systems of protecting privacy. Gives less attention to questioning why it is that the same society that so emphasizes privacy is marked by extensive interest in opportunities in self-disclosure as well as in voyeuristic access and public disclosure of "secret" information about persons.

# Social Organization in the United States

## THE NATURE OF SOCIAL ORGANIZATION

Up to now we have been concerned mainly with the major institutional norms and salient value themes of American society. Not so much has been said about the actual social *interactions* and social *relations* that constitute the society as distinguished from the culture.[1] As Chapters X and XI have suggested, however, social life is not a simple emanation or reflection of broad cultural norms. The script for a drama is not the play as it is enacted; the musical score is not the symphony as the orchestra renders it. Culture consists of norms, values, beliefs, and the like. Social organization consists of interactions. The present chapter will focus upon the web of recurring social interactions in which cultural norms and values are ceaselessly being actualized, modified, evaded, or contravened—and in which new norms and values are created from time to time.

There are two main ways to distinguish cultural structure from social organization. The principal distinction has been implicit in the whole preceding discussion: cultural structure has been conceived as a series of norms or ideal patterns to which people are oriented. The cultural web of shared norms, goals, and values is *one* of the major determinants of social action. However, the interactions of persons in specific situations seldom perfectly follow the cultural blueprint—if, indeed, there is a clear or unified cultural prescription at all. Furthermore, much patterning is not directly regulated by cultural norms. Thus, for example, in complex formal organizations one continually encounters beliefs and values as well as informal social structures that are not prescribed by the organization itself and, even more striking, patterns of behavior that are not prescribed by any well-established traditional norms.[2]

A second distinction, partly overlapping the first, is based upon *the degree to which norms are enforced by explicitly designated agents,* whether these be individual positions or organized groups. Cultural

[1] Among many useful general works on social organization: Scott Greer, *Social Organization* (New York: Random House, 1955); Amitai Etzioni, *Modern Organizations* (Englewood Cliffs, N.J.: Prentice-Hall, 1964); Theodore Caplow, *Principles of Organization* (New York: Harcourt, Brace & World, 1964); James G. March (ed.), *Handbook of Organizations* (Chicago: Rand McNally, 1965); Robert Presthus, *The Organizational Society* (New York: Knopf, 1962).

[2] Alvin W. Gouldner, "Organizational Analysis," in Robert K. Merton, Leonard Broom, Leonard S. Cottrell, Jr. (eds.), *Sociology Today* (New York: Basic Books, 1959), pp. 410–412.

regulation occurs when normative standards are maintained by the diffuse action of the whole social group—as in a small rural community or a group of close friends. Sanctions are meted out on the basis of a diffuse consensus; no particular individual or group is clearly responsible for maintaining the accepted patterns or for enforcing the rules of the game. On the other hand, a great many values and norms are specifically allocated to particular functionaries for enforcement, fostering, and support. To the degree that regulation is thus focalized, it is sometimes said that "cultural structure" passes over into "social organization." This is another way of saying that diffuse, informal social organization is transformed into more highly structured organization. Of course, we are dealing with continuous gradations rather than sharp dichotomies. Nevertheless, it is a great aid to clarity if we hold continually in mind the primary division: on the one hand, a *cultural structure* (language, art, belief systems and ideas, various other symbols and symbol systems, norms of all kinds); on the other hand, *ongoing interactions*, regularized by mutual expectancies and concerns of the participants. It is in the immediate person-to-person relations that much of culture acquires meaning and affective value, and in them the individual anchors his perceptions and his personality organization.

Social organization refers to human action insofar as the actor takes into account the actions of others. As persons interact, mutual expectations and concerns arise; and as interaction continues over time, more-or-less definite *patterns* emerge. At the level of elementary social routines there is much social action that might be called recurrent aggregative behavior. It does not have the elaborate and well-bounded character of social groups or formal organizations, nor does it show the fluidity of collective behavior such as crowds, riots, crazes, panics, and the like. Rather, recurrent aggregative behavior is found in routinely repeated situations, in which endlessly varied sets of individuals react in a similar manner to standardized circumstances, for example, assemblies of persons in vehicles of public transportation.[3] The obvious regularities of overt action in such situations are based on established expectancies. In the absence of such expectancies, the simplest interactions become confusing: two people come face to face around a street corner and teeter back and forth erratically in the effort to structure the manner of passing. If there is a definite expectancy—that each will go to his right side of the sidewalk, or any other easily signaled rule—the actual course of action has a radically different quality. The *minimal* specification of social organization would thus run: it is that state of interaction in which the actions of any one participant are to an appreciable degree determined by his orientation to the behavior of other participants.

Social organization does not appear all at once: it develops through time. Groups have histories. All social structures have developed out of nonstructures, as mere aggregates gradually transform themselves into

[3] Morris Davis and Sol Levine, "Toward a Sociology of Public Transit," *Social Problems*, 15, 1 (Summer 1967), 84–91.

definite social groups or collectivities. The emergence of organization means that norms arise and consensus develops; it also means that internal differentiation occurs (leadership, hierarchy, cliques, sociometric clusterings). The sociopsychological processes of perception, motivation, and evaluation that are necessarily involved are intricate.[4] Organization may be quite temporary—as in the patterned interaction of a street crowd—or relatively permanent, as in religious, political, or familial groupings. The patterning of action may be formal, rigid, and explicit, or it may be flexible, vague, and implicit. In any case, the generic quality in which we are interested is the property of *recurrence*: the fact that interactions become predictable, that is, patterned, through participants' becoming aware of each other's behavior. Organization in this sense operates quite as clearly in a friendship as in an industrial corporation. Organization is a "special density of interaction," to use Chester I. Barnard's phrase, and its basic identifying mark is that participants come to act in regularized ways through meaningful apprehension of what others have done, are doing, and are likely to do.

Whenever a given interaction pattern is repeated often enough to give rise to relatively stable expectancies among the actors, we call it a *social relation*. There may be an appreciable degree of diffuse organization in a social aggregate, without the specificity and continuing structure of social relations. Like organization, however, a social relation is not an all-or-none matter: it always exists in some *degree*. At what level of structuring and permanence we decide to attach the label is largely a matter of convenience for various specific kinds of analysis.

In the fully developed case, social relations are clearly guided by culturally stylized rights and obligations shared by the participants. Conduct is defined and shaped by a definite system of institutional norms, for example, family relations or the social systems of organized religious bodies. From such definite and elaborated systems one can move along in a continuum over to the limiting cases in which interaction occurs without mutually shared codes of conduct. Strictly speaking, any frequently recurring social relation will be one in which *some* concepts of rights and duties will come to be shared. The cultural regulation may be so rudimentary and superficial, however, that we find it more useful to speak of various kinds of *collective behavior* in which social relations are relatively unstructured by cultural norms.[5] The extreme case here is the transitory and amorphous *public* that momentarily crystallizes around a political issue, acts upon it, and then dissolves to reform into a succession of other publics. Certain types of *crowds* (casual street gatherings, masses at sports events) also illustrate the situation of patterned interaction not closely canalized by norms of obligation and privilege linked to that interaction. Still a third variety of interaction falling outside the category "social relations" as defined above consists of the numerous *situational fields* in which people are thrown

[4] See the detailed study of the spontaneous development of social structure in a previously unacquainted student population: Theodore M. Newcomb, *The Acquaintance Process* (New York: Holt, Rinehart & Winston, 1961).
[5] Ralph H. Turner and Lewis M. Killian, *Collective Behavior* (Englewood Cliffs, N.J.: Prentice-Hall, 1957).

together in relatively unstructured, new or ad hoc situations that are not yet clearly defined or regulated culturally. Fourth is the area of mass communication and those kinds of "mass" behavior that are marked by common responses to separately received messages. Much of this one way, pluralistic action is pseudosocial or parasocial; but it may nevertheless have tremendous effects upon an entire society.[6]

"Social group" is one of those treacherous terms with an apparently simple commonsense connotation that conceals ambiguities. As a crude first approximation, a group may be described as a given aggregate of persons playing interrelated roles and recognized by themselves or others as a unit of interaction.[7] The simplest operational index of a group is *the presence of relatively high interaction rates* among the members,[8] but this criterion is not sufficient to distinguish a group from an organization or a relation. A social group is one form of organization and it *contains* social relations. It seems best, then, to reserve the term for those interacting aggregates of persons in which the participants regard themselves, for certain purposes, as a unit of solidarity possessing similar or shared interests, values, or behavior patterns that set them off from other groups. A well tested and generally accepted classification of groups is still to be developed, although several useful typologies are rather widely used. The main variables that will have to be incorporated in any comprehensive classification are being explored—for example, behavior in groups clearly depends greatly upon the extent to which a common or collective goal exists and, if so, what kind of goal. It seems that task centered, or instrumental, groups differ profoundly from those that primarily emphasize pure sociability, or discussion of ideas. It is unlikely also that principles of behavior derived from studies of task-oriented groups can be applied without modification to groupings that are primarily organized around the acceptance and promotion of definite ideologies (especially political and religious beliefs).[9]

Another dimension of groups is illuminated by analyzing informal social interaction as a series of *exchanges of values*; from these exchanges there

[6] Melvin L. DeFleur, *Theories of Mass Communication* (New York: David McKay, 1966), p. xiv: "The modern urban industrial society could not exist as a social system without mass communication. It has become a deeply established part of every major social institution—political, economic, religious, educational, and familial—as these sociocultural patterns have taken shape in the advanced societies of the world."

[7] A closely related index is the degree to which the aggregate is a closed system of interpersonal preferences or choices.

[8] For the extensive research literature on small groups and the problem of cohesion see A. Paul Hare, Edgar F. Borgatta, Robert F. Bales (eds.), *Small Groups: Studies in Social Interaction*, rev. ed. (New York: Knopf, 1965); Dorwin Cartwright and Alvin F. Zander (eds.), *Group Dynamics: Research and Theory*, 2nd ed. (Evanston, Ill.: Row, Peterson, 1960); A. Paul Hare, *Handbook of Small Group Research* (New York: Free Press, 1962); Bernard Berelson and Gary A. Steiner, *Human Behavior* (New York: Harcourt, Brace & World, 1964); John W. Thibaut and Harold H. Kelley, *The Social Psychology of Groups* (New York: Wiley, 1959); Theodore M. Mills, *The Sociology of Small Groups* (Englewood Cliffs, N.J.: Prentice-Hall, 1967).

[9] See Vladimir C. Nahirny, "Some Observations on Ideological Groups," *American Journal of Sociology*, LXVII, 4 (January 1962), 397–405.

develop net products of personal "social credit" in terms of approval, respect, prestige and power. Assuming rational calculations and a lack of institutionalized statuses, the interacting parties will seek to spend social credit in exchanges that increase their power in later exchanges.[1] The nature of such exchanges, however, is basically affected once norms attached to definite statuses enter into the situation. Norms—for instance, those incumbent upon married partners—may set limits for exchange loss such that the person who gives most freely of affection and commitment does not thereby lose "bargaining power" in future exchanges.[2] Similarly, a professor may repeatedly help a student with advice and information without thereby placing the student in a position of *personal* social indebtedness; because it is the professor's duty to render such aid, the student is free to accept it as his due.

Groups taken purely as social exchange systems would be characterized by a "unique, terminable-at-will, equal-authority relationship."[3] Actual enduring groups typically are not pure exchange systems, but rather have normative, coercive, and noncalculative aspects. The difference between a *social group*—as one form of social organization—and an *institutional structure* is vividly suggested by the case of a specific family group whose members disperse geographically when the children grow up. The institutions of kinship are still there—individuals know the generally expected and obligatory norms and could fairly readily be reactivated to practice them—but a real interacting group may almost, or completely, cease to exist.

A group differs from a mere aggregate of unrelated individuals in so far as there is both *interaction* in terms of relatively stabilized roles *and* a sense of group identity. A company of raw recruits turns into a group as there emerges a recurrent network of role-patterned relations, together with an awareness of difference from other social aggregates. Our observational tests for the presence of a group thus include (1) observation of frequency of interactions and (2) testimony and other evidence of recognition of group identity. A third avenue of study is the observation of *social sanctions*. It may be taken as an identifying criterion that no organized group exists without a viable system of positive and negative sanctions that both reflect and help to maintain regularized patterns of behavior. Numerous regularities have been discovered in well-structured groups and organizations; for example, given an established organization that is actively functioning, there is a high likelihood that:

1. Members will overestimate its prestige relative to other organizations of the same type.

[1] George Caspar Homans, *Social Behavior: Its Elementary Forms* (New York: Harcourt, Brace & World, 1961), and *Sentiments and Activities* (New York: Free Press, 1962). For reviews of Homans' works see the entire issue of *Sociological Inquiry*, XXXIV, 2 (Spring 1964); also, *American Journal of Sociology*, LXVII, 4 (January 1962), 454–461.

[2] Peter M. Blau, *Exchange and Power in Social Life* (New York: Wiley, 1964).

[3] Alfred Kuhn, *The Study of Society* (Homewood, Ill.: Richard D. Irwin, 1963), p. 416.

2. An outside threat will be met by increased solidarity, increased centralization and lowered toleration of deviance.[4]
3. An "increase in interaction between unequals, when the amount of joint activity remains unchanged, leads to a decrease of the superiors' power."[5]
4. Participants will become emotionally involved in primary groups.[6]

To understand *concretely* what occurs in the behavior of people in groups, it is necessary to take into account a great deal more than the sheer *pattern* of interaction. The total behavior includes as formal and invariant aspects at least the following:

1. Two or more persons playing interrelated roles in recurrent activities; to the degree that the group comprises a social system, the performance of these roles is directed and regulated by culturally sanctioned goals and means;
2. Certain cultural goals emerging as group objectives; these need not be highly explicit or identical with the goals and motives of individuals comprising the group's population;
3. Culturally approved means—that is, normatively regulated ways of acting in relation to cultural goals;
4. Sanctions—the patterned rewards and penalties already mentioned as a diagnostic sign marking the presence of a functioning social aggregate.

Knowing only these characteristics of a given group it will be possible to make many useful predictions about it. In fact, accurate information on these four points may be sufficient for numerous practical purposes of personal orientation or social management. Where more specific and detailed description or prediction is desired, it is necessary to supplement the first approximation by a study of the unique constellation of interacting personalities. The more specific our relation to the group becomes, the more important it is to know this peculiar configuration in its entirety. In this respect, it is correct to support the commonsense hunch that intensive firsthand acquaintance with a group supplies knowledge not attainable in any other way. Furthermore, dynamic predictions about a group probably will always be greatly improved by intensive data on the specific personalities involved—over and above the stylized roles typically assigned in the group interactional process.

## MAIN TYPES OF SOCIAL ORGANIZATION

Even on the basis of the very broad distinctions presented in the preceding section it is possible to begin developing descriptive hypotheses about social organization in the United States. The nation's great individual mobility and cultural heterogeneity alone suggest that this is a society broadly charac-

[4] Caplow, *op. cit.*, p. 2.
[5] *Ibid.*, p. 8.
[6] *Ibid.*, p. 18.

terized by *relative instability of social relations, rapid emergence and dissolution of social groups,* and *relatively great importance of collective behavior in the total system.* As considerable evidence shows, these depictions are valid as descriptions of modal tendencies, of course, with proper detailed qualifications. However, to go much beyond such statements requires further analytical breakdown of the phenomena of social organization. In view of the form in which most of the available data are cast, it seems appropriate to work with fairly concrete *types* of social organization, used as first approximations to the reality that we wish to understand.[7] Whenever possible, the attempt will be made to show what meaningful variables can be isolated from these relatively crude classifications.

Sociological studies have developed a large number of typologies of social organization. Although diverse in content, in level or kind of abstraction, and in systematic quality, certain lines of distinction have recurred time and again under superficially different labels.[8] In spite of various discrepancies and ambiguities, most attempts at classification draw a primary line of distinction between *societies* and *associations.* As Wilson and Kolb have stated it:

*A society is a social group within which the members share the basic elements and conditions of a common life. It is an inclusive group encompassing other social groups and relations. . . . An association, on the other hand, is much more limited in scope. It is organized around a limited set of interests or values which people believe they can enjoy through concerted action.*[9]

Either societies or associations may be made up of few or many subgroupings, linked together in greater or lesser degree. In the case of total, inclusive societies type concepts, such as *Gemeinschaft* (community) and *Gesellschaft* (association), are necessarily quite general, serving however, the indispensable function of locating in the larger social framework the particular types of social relations, social systems, groups, associations, or communities that we may wish to study in detail. Such inclusive types must be employed with full awareness that they are ideal types and therefore will *never* fit exactly any particular society. Instead they represent logical extremes, against which the characteristics of any particular society can be brought out in sharp relief.

Consideration of the known societies of the world, past and present,

[7] D. S. Pugh, D. J. Hickson, C. L. Hinings, K. M. Macdonald, C. Turner, and T. Lupton, "A Conceptual Scheme for Organizational Analysis," *Administrative Science Quarterly,* 8 (December 1963), 289–315. This article proposes a classification based on six elements: specialization, standardization, formalization, centralization, configuration, and flexibility.

[8] One of the most persistent central themes has been the distinction between sacred and secular social structures. Certain aspects of this dichotomy run through the work of nearly every outstanding theory of society. Durkheim spoke of organic versus mechanical solidarity; Tönnies worked out the parallel distinction between *Gemeinschaft* (community) and *Gesellschaft* (association); Maine referred to a society of status versus a society of contract; Sorokin contrasted ideational and sensate systems; Cooley emphasized primary groups; MacIver developed the community-association contrast.

[9] Logan Wilson and William L. Kolb, *Sociological Analysis* (New York: Harcourt, Brace & World, 1949), p. 267.

indicates that many approximate the model of folk or simple communal societies. These are usually relatively small and stable systems, economically self-sufficient, marked by absence of elaborate division of labor or highly differentiated associations; the whole unit is held together by rather rigid codes and value systems, enforced through diffuse pressure and mediated through a society-wide network of interpersonal relations. Many other societies have retained the unity and rigidity or stability of the folk society to a high degree but have developed a fairly elaborate division of labor, complex social stratification and political systems, and differentiated and highly organized religious groupings. These complex communal societies have existed in the form of feudal orders, as in medieval Europe and in certain periods of Chinese history, in the caste society of India, and in many of the larger nonliterate sòcieties studied in modern times. On the other hand, the Western history in which American society has had its being has been stamped for centuries by the unprecedented development of associational modes of organization. By briefly examining the polar types of communal and associational societies we will find paths into the analysis of other and more specific types of organization.[1]

*Communal and Associational Societies: Gemeinschaft and Gesellschaft*

As noted above, the ideal types of communal and associational societies are only approximated in particular local communities or national societies. The prototype of the communal society is the isolated rural community (whether primitive or part of a modern nation); that of the associational society is the rapidly changing, specialized, segmented, and impersonalized urban center. Of course, New York or Chicago are associational aggregates only in part; and our El Cerritos, "Plainvilles," and Appalachian rural neighborhoods contain associational elements even within a broadly communal context.

Although jarring and shattering effects of rapid urbanization upon large masses of immigrants and rural migrants may be exaggerated in the historical and sociological literature, there was a solid reality behind the image of mobility, anonymity, heterogeneity, isolation, and *anomie* of the nineteenth and early twentieth century American cities. But international immigration has become tightly controlled, urban patterns have widely diffused, real incomes and educational levels have risen, social services have increased. Many such stabilizing and adjustive changes have reduced the gaps between many ethnic and occupational segments. Much evidence now points to the widespread existence in metropolitan areas of *both* associational membership and involvement in networks of kinsmen and friends on the part

[1] The most comprehensive scheme for describing total social systems is found in the works of Talcott Parsons, especially *The Social System* (New York: Free Press, 1951). See also Talcott Parsons and Neil J. Smelser, *Economy and Society* (New York: Free Press, 1956); and Talcott Parsons, *Societies: Evolutionary and Comparative Perspectives* (Englewood Cliffs, N.J.: Prentice-Hall, 1966). The distinction between communal and associational relations was elaborately developed and applied by Robert M. MacIver in a series of works extending from *Community: A Sociological Study* (London: Macmillan, 1917) through Robert M. MacIver and Charles H. Page, *Society* (New York: Holt, Rinehart and Winston, 1949).

of many—perhaps a majority—of the adult population in metropolitan areas.[2]

Thus, what starts out as a broad classification of total communities or societies turns out, upon closer inspection, to imply a more specific classification of social relationships. The associational society has a large number and variety of specific associations, a loose articulation of the component units of the social structure, and few universally practiced behavioral codes; it gives an important place to law and administrative controls. The communal society, in pure type, would show relatively slow social change; few specialized, free-standing associations; rigid coordination or integration of subunits; many universally accepted values, goals, and norms of conduct; relative lack of specialized and impersonal mechanisms of social control.

Perhaps the central characteristic of associational relations is that they are instrumental in the service of further relatively definite interests. Insofar as relations are associational, they are precisely instruments, a means in the pursuit of ends; not the ends themselves. This instrumental character of associational relations is exemplified in various processes of political bargaining and maneuver and in a wide range of relations primarily oriented to economic exchange and economic power. In communal relations, on the contrary, the main emphasis is upon the relation itself and the personalities and other values directly activated in it.

Communal relations are likely to stress diffuse attitudes (for example, respect, affection, loyalty, and so on) rather than rationally instrumental actions. Associational relations typically imply separateness of interacting persons, whereas in communal relations it is presupposed that the participants are linked together by many common activities and values. Closely related is the specificity of associational relations; typically they are narrowly and explicitly defined and restricted to a specific interest or life area. The prototype is the narrowly contractual relation of buyer and seller in an open market exchange transaction, in which everything is formally irrelevant to the relation except considerations of price, quantity, and quality of the goods being exchanged. The rights and obligations of the parties are specific and definite—neither more nor less than explicitly agreed upon for the specific occasion—and the establishment of any particular associational relation does not imply any *other* social relations between the participants. If the employee wishes to claim additional wages on the ground that he "needs it more" than the employer, there is nothing in the employer-employee relation itself that supports his claim. On the other hand, an identical claim by one's parents or other close relatives has an exactly opposite import; in this case, the burden of proof is shifted to the individual who wishes to deny a claim or refuse an obligation—one turns down his brother's request for a loan on grounds of some other and "higher" communal obligation. This

---

[2] For examples, see: Herbert J. Gans, *The Urban Villagers: Group and Class in the Life of Italian-Americans* (New York: Free Press, 1962); Herbert J. Gans, *The Levittowners* (New York: Pantheon Books, 1967); Aida K. Tomah, "Informal Group Participation and Residential Patterns," *American Journal of Sociology,* LXX, 1 (July 1964), 28–35; Wendell Bell and Marion Boat, "Urban Neighborhoods and Informal Social Relations," *American Journal of Sociology,* LXII, 4 (January 1957), 391–398.

indefiniteness of the common activities and ends is associated with the important part played by various kinds of symbolism in communal relations. The drudgery of household tasks has one meaning when the tasks are performed as employee and another when performed by a wife as part of her family role. In associational relations, the major emphasis tends to center upon objective rights and overt performance; in communal relations, the stress moves toward questions of meaning, intent, motive, and feeling.

Implied in the schematic description given thus far is the tendency to define associational relations as emotionally neutral, or at least to consider the feelings of the participants as formally irrelevant. The proverbial impersonality of large-scale, specialized associations reflects a task-centered or function-oriented mode of organization in which certain specific activities are supposed to go on irrespective of the subjective sentiments of the participants.

On the other hand, primary group solidarity often is said to be favored by "homogeneity"—and indeed there is overwhelming evidence that certain kinds of primary group solidarities are favored by homogeneity of age, sex, ethnic characteristics, socioeconomic position, and value patterns, for example, in work groups and in neighborhood cliques. But solidarity is also favored by interdependence in goal attainment and by complementarity of capacities, favoring mutual gratification; and both of these conditions imply a certain heterogeneity. There is no real paradox here. Solidarity through homogeneity is likely to be favored when the group's members carry out similar tasks or where task interdependence does not require cultural differentiation—as in assembly-line operations—or when the group coheres around expressive activities. Solidarity through heterogeneity probably takes a larger place when differences in status enhance mutual gains under conditions in which the group's survival and welfare are highly dependent upon cooperation among specialists. "Solidarity," therefore, may develop from both communal and associational bases.

It is clear that concrete social relations will seldom if ever embody in pure form the whole complex of characteristics included in either of the two types. Each of the characteristics is a variable that will be found in greater or lesser degree and in combination with other variables. We regard concrete social relations, therefore, as the point of intersection of readings on all the variables in combination; in any one such cluster we will often find high development of certain associational elements along with high development of one or more communal features, or the reverse. For example, a doctor-patient relationship may turn out to be highly specific, limited, rational, and impersonal—however, we may find that the doctor, instead of pursuing his own immediate self-interest, is treating the patient's welfare as an end in itself. But, again, if the ideal types are used cautiously as a means of analysis they will be highly useful in diagnosing any social structure. Their function in this respect is perhaps similar to the stain that a biologist applies to bring out features of a cell structure he wishes to observe. Such a classification can help us to formulate certain conditional—"if and when"—predictions or generalizations about contemporary social structures. In particular, our ideal types direct attention toward consequences and correlates of an extreme development of instrumental social relations.

We already know that the modern industrialized society of America is conspicuous for the development of highly specialized economic activities, of widespread commercialization of practices and activities, of large-scale political and economic structures, of high geographic mobility, of numerous special-interest groups. If, and to the degree that, the social relations emerging in such a context generally become instrumental in the service of specialized interests, we may expect the correlative conditions to develop that are now to be sketched. Limiting our view for the moment to conditions prevailing in economic and political sectors of our large urban centers —that is, to those parts of American society in which highly developed associational relations are most frequent and in which they set the *dominant* pattern—we find many trace lines left by communal reactions to instrumental human relations.

We have seen that when social organization becomes solely a matter of association in the service of specific impersonal but individualized goals, then by definition the situation is one of a manipulative attitude toward persons. Now an individual who thus manipulated all his human relations would be the logical extreme of what psychiatry calls the psychopathic personality—a person to whom all others appear simply as means to his private goals—and a social aggregate operating toward others solely in this way would be the distilled essence of the interest group. Obviously few individuals or groupings develop associational patterns to these extremes; and if they did, we should not have a society in any historical sense of the term. Nevertheless, it is not difficult to cite many examples in which a recognizable approximation to the pure type does exist. Certain kinds of advertising and propaganda and the attempted manipulation of legislation by pressure groups certainly qualify as cases in point. The management of large bodies of men for military purposes necessarily will often be strongly marked by impersonal and instrumental patterns.

Much seemingly communal behavior has come to be regarded widely as pseudo-Gemeinschaft; the favorite popular sterotype is that of the baby-kissing politician, but many other gestures supposedly symbolizing friendship or solidarity are met with the skeptical query, "What is he trying to sell?" (or "put over"), "Wonder what he's after?" In reaction to sensed manipulation (real or imagined), there has developed a pervasive tendency to resist the acceptance of statements at their face value.

To meet a situation in which the areas of good faith in social relations are uncertain or importantly deficient, many individuals permanently reduce their expectations as to the sincerity of others, systematically discounting in advance the apparent motives and claims of other persons. The "put-on" is a ritualization of distrust. So thoroughly has this skepticism permeated our urban society that large numbers of persons question their own statements. The classic phrase here is the well-known preface, "I may be rationalizing, but. . . ."[3]

[3] See Robert K. Merton, "The Sociology of Knowledge," Chapter 13 in Georges Gurvitch and Wilbert E. Moore (eds.), *Twentieth Century Sociology* (New York: The Philosophical Library, 1945).

The above observations suggest that in our complex social structure there will be many intrusions of Gesellschaft elements into relations traditionally defined as communal, and the reverse. For instance, the functioning of bureaucratic organizations typically shows some tension as a result of Gemeinschaft importations that run counter to the formal structure—in one direction, nepotism; in another, the expectation of or demand for *personalized* behavior when impersonal-categorical treatment is the organizational norm. Such "misplaced" relations and expectations are perennial sources of administrative problems.

The Gemeinschaft-Gesellschaft classification is a useful orientation device. It is not a theory of social organization and can become misleading if used indiscriminately. For purposes of the present chapter, this particular typology is a way of focusing upon very broad tendencies in the society as a whole, for example, the shift from rural modes of life or the functional specificity of economic relations. For a more specific examination of the structure of associations and groups, we will find it convenient to utilize the notions of *formal* and *informal* organization.

### Formal and Informal Organization

Sociological analysis must continually guard against the common tendency to think of organization solely in terms of *formal* organization. As has been emphasized already, the reality is that we have a continuum from extremely formalized and persisting structures over to transitory, informal, or even unrecognized clusters of interaction. To focus solely upon the more formal structures is to miss some of the most important things to which we need to orient ourselves in our society.

What, then, is formal organization and what is its relation to informal organization? These questions can best be approached by examining a few simple but basic propositions about behavior in social aggregates. First, it is known that *the behavior of individuals in association with others exhibits a number of emergent properties, not predictable from knowledge of the participants taken separately.* Second, among the emergent properties of behavior in interaction is the *fact that an aggregate of persons that, for whatever causes, remains in meaningful interaction for any considerable period will develop regularized patterns of interpersonal conduct.* Leaving its genesis to one side, we simply can take this spontaneous tendency toward structuring as a fundamental empirical regularity, holding for hostile and discordant interactions (guards and prisoners, for example) just as for positive relations.[4] Third, *every formal organization that continues for any considerable period develops an informal organization alongside the formal*

[4] In the spectrum of organizations, an extreme position is occupied by those that totally segregate, encompass and regulate the lives of their members (inmates)—those termed by Goffman "total institutions"—including prisons, monasteries, hospitals, convents, concentration camps, some utopian religious communities, reformatories, boarding schools, sanatoria, many nursing homes, and homes for the elderly. See: Erving Goffman, *Asylums* (Garden City, N.Y.: Doubleday, 1961); Gresham M. Sykes, *Society of Captives* (Princeton, N.J.: Princeton University Press, 1958); Richard A. Cloward, *et al.* (eds.), *Theoretical Studies in Social Organization of the Prison* (New York: Social Science Research Council, 1960).

*one.*[5] (For the moment let us defer asking what "formal" means.) The presence of informal organization is, in principle, easily demonstrable by fairly crude observation. In a certain college classroom, the teacher never assigns seats and roll call is never taken: there is no official or even explicit specification of seating arrangements. Yet within a few weeks the amorphous aggregate has become patterned; with high regularity the same individuals occupy the same seats day after day—an informal organization has emerged. This sort of spontaneous structuring, although at a rudimentary level, contains the basic elements upon which even the most elaborate organizational systems are built. Note also that this informal organization arose within and is added to the more generalized cultural patterning of appropriate classroom conduct.

One of the by now classic illustrations of the emergence of informal organization within a formal structure is provided by the studies of Western Electric workers summarized by Roethlisberger and Dickson.[6] Investigations of factors affecting production had shown that output variations could not be accounted for by physical factors of lighting, rest periods, and the like, and had located the source of increased production in the social atmosphere of the work situation. It was quickly demonstrated that the formal organization of the factory was not predictive of workers' behavior. The official group leader was observed to act in many instances as a representative of the workers rather than management. Furthermore, output records showed an amazingly constant rate of production. Individuals were punished by their associates for exceeding the production norm accepted by the group; and still more significantly, such imposition of sanctions was accepted by the recipients. All these clues clearly pointed to an informal organization, different from and even counter to the formal patterns. Through the network of interpersonal relations in the work group, it represented a powerful controlling force, but one that was largely unadmitted and unrecognized by the participants or their nominal supervisors. Thus, if we consider a formally organized group to be one in which the members interact as occupants of explicitly defined and interrelated roles, performing prescribed functions, we can predict that continuing formal groupings will quickly develop an informal organization, simply as a by-product of action directed toward the formal objectives of the organization. The explicit roles of the formal structure will be modified by the emergence of an informal sociometric pattern of interpersonal relations, attractions, and repulsions. Lines of communication emerge outside the official structure. Subgroupings develop their particularized interests and loyalties, their partly divergent

[5] Cf. Chester I. Barnard, *The Functions of the Executive* (Cambridge, Mass.: Harvard University Press, 1938), chap. 9; Wilbert E. Moore, *Industrial Relations and the Social Order*, rev. ed. (New York: Macmillan, 1951), chap. 15; Fritz J. Roethlisberger and William J. Dickson, *Management and the Worker* (Cambridge, Mass.: Harvard University Press, 1939).

[6] *Ibid.*, pp. 522 ff. For critical reexamination of these studies, see Alex Carey, "The Hawthorne Studies: A Radical Criticism," *American Sociological Review*, 32, 3 (June 1967), 403–416; Henry Landsberger, *Hawthorne Revisited*, IX (Ithaca, N.Y.: Cornell Studies in Industrial and Labor Relations, 1958).

purposes.[7] The interpersonal and subgroup networks of informal character built up their own understandings, procedures, goals—sometimes emerging with relatively distinctive cultures different from the formal patterning.[8]

Many analyses of bureaucracies have stressed the constraining influence of formal rules. However, an old if neglected insight is that rules can protect subordinates from arbitrary actions of administrative superiors. A recent study has shown in two government-controlled organizations in France that the subordinates gain much freedom and security by relying upon the rules, whereas the higher officials are much more exposed to criticism and attack. Michel Crozier also shows how the bureaucratic setting encourages mutual solidarity and support among peers in the junior ranks, where impersonal authority, a sense of distance from the top, and an objective, recognized common fate facilitate joint action and group goals.[9]

Even if an organization, once established, were to be a completely closed system, one still would observe differing structures, processes, and outcomes that would arise from differing initial inputs and from the varying combinations and consequent products these would generate through time. Conversely, initially homogeneous organizations would come to vary as they confront differing external demands, opportunities, and threats from the environment. Actual organizations are shaped by both sets of influences. Many so-called theoretical controversies in attempts to explain organizational behavior arise from selective attention to one or the other. What may be an ideal system from an internal ("human relations") standpoint— democratic, permissive, consensual, flexible—may have very low survival capacity in an extremely severe environment. Or, hierarchical forms, developed when personnel were sharply divided into social classes, may be inefficient and conflict engendering when the members of the organization come to be recruited from a relatively equalitarian and affluent society.[1]

Because of the multiple sources of variation, even structurally identical organizations carrying out the same tasks under similar external conditions may come to differ greatly in their actual modes of operation.[2] Ultimately, of course, the tests of organizational success are severe—the organization may be utterly destroyed. But, even so, there often is a very great range of acceptable performance. And "in the short run and for small increments

---

[7] The importance of latent organization—as well as its inevitability—has been well stated by Philip Selznick, *TVA and the Grass Roots; A Study in the Sociology of Formal Organization* (Berkeley and Los Angeles: University of California Press, 1949), p. 255.

[8] Cf. Gouldner, *op. cit.*, p. 412, on "latent identities" (sex, age, ethnic membership, etc.).

[9] Michel Crozier, *The Bureaucratic Phenomenon: An Examination of Bureaucracy in Modern Organizations and its Cultural Setting in France* (Chicago: The University of Chicago Press, 1964).

[1] It has been suggested that as modern large-scale organizations "become larger, richer, and more specialized, they seem to move from a broad-based pyramidal structure toward a diamond-shaped structure, having the bulk of membership concentrated in the middle levels." (Caplow, *op. cit.*, p. 58.)

[2] See the striking case reported by Peter M. Blau, *The Dynamics of Bureaucracy* (Chicago: University of Chicago Press, 1955), pp. 53 ff.

... there is only a slight relationship between the effectiveness of the total organization and any one of its components."[3]

Around the central fact of the inevitable emergence of informal organization within the formal structures, several other predictabilities emerge:

1. The major factors in the *immediate* causation of behavior must be present in the unit of interaction, which always has its informal aspects. This means that any larger organizational structure determines behavior only as its forces are transmitted to individuals in the small units of immediate personal relations.
2. In all large-scale formal organizations: (a) *informal subunits* arise and command their own segmental loyalties; (b) hence, the coordination of subunits becomes an important problem for the organization as a whole; (c) the segmentation of both formal and informal organizations creates special problems of communication.
3. There is a high probability that as a formal organization continues to function, the latent goal of *perpetuating the organization* will emerge as a major concern of organizational leaders.
4. All other things being equal, the larger the numbers of individuals and subgroups to be coordinated within a single organization, the more likely it is that the structure will become formalized; more specifically, that action will be increasingly oriented to explicit and impersonal rules.[4]
5. With increasing complexity of any given type of organization (especially those organizations oriented to action rather than to deliberation, consultation, and so on) there is a tendency for the structure to assume a hierarchical form.

These propositions already suggest that the concept of formality may involve a number of different dimensions. Formal organizations are characterized by a high *degree of repetitiveness* (stereotyping) in the behavior of the participants; but this is not a sufficient criterion, for many informal groups exhibit the same characteristics. Nor is it enough to point to the *rigidity of the regulative norms,* nor to the *severity of sanctions,* nor to the existence of *specialized roles.* All these phenomena are found in structures no one would consider formal. In combination with the above variables, however, three other items serve to define what we recognize as formal organization, namely: the *explicit* nature of organizational norms, a marked degree of *impersonality* (stress upon detachment rather than emotional involvement), and a relatively great emphasis upon well-defined patterns of *deference and social distance* between the occupants of hierarchically ordered positions.

Formal organizations are named and recognized units that have definite boundaries: it usually is clear who is a member and who is not, as well as

---

[3] Caplow, *op. cit.,* p. 167.

[4] Size is roughly correlated with structural complexity. Even in a structurally simple group or organization, however, the addition of members rapidly produces changes in the internal patterns.

when one has come "inside" or remains "outside." There are clearly patterned sets of internal relationships, guided by many explicit norms. Some
collective purposes, goals, or tasks are publicly defined. Organizations,
however, rarely have only one clear and commonly accepted collective goal.[5]

These defining variables are intercorrelated—they tend to move together—but each has a considerable range of independent variation. In
general we would hypothesize that formality, as the composite of the values
of this cluster of variables, will be maximized when (1) the activity of large
numbers of individuals is being directed toward a common collective goal;[6]
(2) the organization includes many highly specialized roles; (3) the participants are culturally heterogeneous (in addition to their differentiated
organizational positions); (4) the goals of the organization are considered
highly important, tangible, and urgent ("required" coordination + speed
= increased emphasis upon formal structure). The most important formal
structures in our society are large-scale organizations, built upon minute
specialization in the performance of tangible tasks and directed toward a
common but complex goal that requires an elaborate coordination of activity. The extensive coordinative system depends upon a high order of predictability that is typically sought, in turn, by the standardization of artifacts, techniques, procedures—and social roles.[7] The greater the pressure
for *precise* and *rapid* coordination, the greater the tendency toward explicit
regulation, hierarchy, and impersonality. The greater the differentiation of
interests, privileges, and functions among numerous specialized positions,
the greater the possibility of attenuated value-consensus; and hence, within
limits, the more tendency to stress explicit deference-patterns.[8]

The pure type of formal organization would be a depersonalized structure of explicitly defined and regulated statuses. We do not find the ideal
type, but we can observe fairly close approximations to it. The kind and
degree of formality clearly depends in part upon the particular goals of
the organization. Formality is also related to the external and internal stress
to which the organization is exposed: the military protocol of peace time is
drastically modified in an active combat operation.[9] And both goals and
stress are interdependent with the degree and kind of value consensus exist-

[5] See, for example, R. M. Cyert and J. G. March, *The Behavioral Theory of the Firm*
(Englewood Cliffs, N.J.: Prentice-Hall, 1963), p. 28; J. D. Thompson and W. J.
McEwen, "Organizational Goals and Environment: Goal-Setting as an Interaction Proc-
ess," *American Sociological Review*, 23, 1 (February 1958), 23–31.

[6] Note an additional definition of formal organization as "any social group engaged in pur-
suing explicit announced empirical objectives through manifestly coordinated effort. . . ."
(Stanley H. Udy, Jr., "Administrative Rationality, Social Setting, and Organizational
Development," *American Journal of Sociology*, LXVIII, 3 (November 1962), 299.

[7] Compare this abstract formulation with the known characteristics of the U.S. automobile industry, or with those of a modern army. For the latter case: Samuel A. Stouffer,
*et al.*, *The American Soldier*, Vol. II (Princeton, N.J.: Princeton University Press, 1949),
pp. 76–149, and Vol. I, pp. 362–429.

[8] Cf. C. H. Page, "Bureaucracy's Other Face," in Peter I. Rose (ed.), *The Study of
Society* (New York: Random House, 1967), pp. 258–268.

[9] This correlate is not *inevitable*, but it is a frequent tendency.

ing within the organization: a highly unified group is not so likely to maximize formal structure as is a discordant aggregate.[1]

It is impossible here to go into a number of fundamental questions raised by these introductory considerations. Under what specific circumstances, for example, may we expect centralization of control, or decentralization; explicitness of norms; rigidity or flexibility of organizational rules; impersonal or personalistic norms; hierarchy or democracy? Available data and theories lead us to suspect that *centralized control* will be maximal in formal organizations when rapid action is, for any reason, regarded as imperative and when the organization is thought (by its members) to be threatened as a whole by external groups. Organizational norms apparently are the more likely to be *explicit* the larger the number of individuals, the longer and more complex the channels of communication, the more varied the interests and values of the participating members. Norms tend to become explicit also in situations of change and crisis—for example, in newly formed associations. It seems to be a fact that the social groupings in which implicit-personalized norms are most prominent tend to be long established and nonspecialized.

In general, the internal characteristics of organizations vary as the external demands ("pressures") and opportunities vary. An environment that exposes different parts of an organization to highly diverse pressures tends to encourage decentralized authority, high participation of the organization's members, and emphasis on internal communication.[2] On the other hand, concentrated central authority in task-centered organizations is favored by recurrent situations in which successful goal-attainment is very uncertain, failure will be catastrophic (extremely damaging and irreversible), and close coordination of effort in space and time is essential. Symphony orchestras that depend on voluntary donations for financial support meet these conditions. So do military forces in combat, where there is the additional pressure created by reluctance and ambivalent motivation of members.[3]

A strong combination of forces within formal organizations tends to create internal pressures for growth; and growth eventually creates counterforces. The outcomes of such dynamic cross-pressures vary with the initial structure of organizational control and the character of intraunit communication, the resources available, and a large number of other factors.[4] Not surprisingly, therefore, organizations that are called bureaucratic always

[1] In all the tentative generalizations suggested in this chapter we have to add the mental reservation, "within a broadly similar culture." For example, there is no guarantee that the formalities of Chinese or Japanese culture follow the same predictive principles.

[2] Richard L. Simpson and William H. Gulley, "Goals, Environmental Pressures, and Organizational Characteristics," *American Sociological Review*, 27, 3 (June 1962), 344–351.

[3] The complicated interplay of forces affecting the military authority system is clearly sketched in Morris Janowitz, with Roger Little, *Sociology and the Military Establishment*, rev. ed. (New York: Russell Sage Foundation, 1965), esp. chaps. 2, 4, and 5. Highly useful for study of formal organizations more generally is James G. March and Herbert A. Simon, *Organizations* (New York: Wiley, 1958).

[4] For a stimulating array of hypotheses see Anthony Downs, *Inside Bureaucracy* (Boston: Little, Brown, 1967).

have nonbureaucratic features. In short, large scale, complex, formal organizations do not fit a single model. The classic bureaucracy is approximated most closely in organizations that for one reason or another require close coordination of relatively routinized activities by a single center of power. Other organizations that deal with highly varied and changing processes, products, or situations—especially those that primarily work with interpersonal relations—are likely to move toward decentralized decision making, less rigid hierarchy, less impersonality, less sharp demarcation of areas of authority, and less emphasis upon strict obedience to uniform rules. Many large organizations in economic, political, educational, and other fields now combine in complex ways the features of these two extreme types.[5] (The next section of this chapter provides a few additional clues as to the incidence and sources of variation in the formal elements of social organization in the United States.)

Aside from broad ideal-types (Gemeinschaft, formal organization, and so on) against which any particular social structures can be scanned and analyzed, a large number of more specific classifications are available. The latter have been constructed from various combinations of diverse criteria; to illustrate with only a few, typologies of groups and associations have been presented, including one or more of the following variables:

1. *Duration:* "temporary" or "permanent."
2. *Size:* "large" or "small."
3. *Complexity:* inclusion of subunits and complexity of linkages among them.
4. *Criterion of membership:* voluntary or involuntary.
5. *Accessibility:* open or closed.
6. *Scope of interests, values, or goals:* "interest-group association" versus inclusive community.[6]
7. *Type of control structure:* hierarchical versus equalitarian.
8. *Centralization of authority:* focused or diffuse.

It is sufficient for present purposes if we recognize the large amount of taxonomic work that has been done on social organization without going into details not essential for the immediate task at hand. Our major concern is with the most general characteristics of the organizational forms of point-to-point interaction,[7] with special attention to those features outlined in preceding pages.

[5] Eugene Litwak, "Models of Bureaucracy Which Permit Conflict," *American Journal of Sociology*, LXVII, 2 (September 1961), 177–184.

[6] Roland L. Warren, *The Community in America* (Chicago: Rand McNally, 1963); Irwin T. Sanders, *The Community: An Introduction to a Social System* (New York: Ronald Press, 1966); Roland L. Warren (ed.), *Perspectives on the American Community* (Chicago: Rand McNally, 1966); MacIver and Page, *op. cit.*, chaps. 1, 2, 17.

[7] It is recognized that there is also organization resulting from the orientation of nominally separate individuals to similar diffuse influences—for example, what Mannheim calls unorganized masses, field structures (commerce, propaganda publics), situations, social mechanisms (division of labor, patterns of competition). Karl Mannheim, *Man and Society in an Age of Reconstruction* (New York: Harcourt, Brace & World, 1940).

## GENERAL CHARACTERISTICS OF SOCIAL ORGANIZATION IN THE UNITED STATES

Viewing American social structure from a highly general perspective, the following features stand out as of special diagnostic importance:

1. Stable groups and associations with marked Gemeinschaftliche characteristics are subject to marked strains. Examples include divorce and family instability, comparative weakness of neighborhoods and other locality groups, permeability and instability of many ethnic communities. However, as noted in earlier chapters, many groupings of this type have shown great tenacity and resilience under stress. In addition to the persistence of some ethnic collectivities in modified forms, one must note the great and continuing importance of religious affiliations and organized religion. Extended kinship ties have not disappeared and often play a part in social organization far greater than that envisaged in the image of modern urbanized society as a disconnected aggregate of alienated individuals. The support and control encountered by the individual in his occupational activities must not be summarily discounted. And the tremendous development of a great variety of voluntary special-interest associations further restrains us from a too-precipitous or unqualified diagnosis of *anomie*.[8]

2. There is an enormous proliferation of formally organized special-interest associations of the most diverse kinds. Specialized associations have multiplied, whereas the parts played by traditionalized groupings based on proximity, diffuse common values, and direct and inclusive personal relations have diminished.

3. Large scale, centralized formal organizations occupy a very significant and increasingly strategic position in the total social structure.

4. Many groups and associations are highly transitory; both the birth rates and death rates of organizations are high; there is much shifting of individuals among organizations and sets of social relations.

5. Considerable portions of the social structure are marked by ephemeral, impersonal, segmental relations, corresponding to slight development of inclusive groups.[9] Examples include bohemias, recreational patterns, migratory populations; in a different way, mobile and competitive occupational situations.

6. As an aspect of specialized *associations*, there is high specialization of social *roles*; individuals frequently play several different and segmental roles. Otherwise stated, there is marked compartmentalization of social activities—in particular, a radical separation of occupational activity from other life areas.

7. Local communities are highly open to chains of interaction initiated at far-removed centers of organization; they are also comparatively permeable to strangers.

---

[8] Adapted from the author's "Friendship and Social Values in a Suburban Community: An Exploratory Study," *The Pacific Sociological Review*, 2, 1 (Spring 1959), 4.

[9] "Casual fluidity is the 'American way' and by long habituation 'feels right.' " Robert S. Lynd, *Knowledge for What?* (Princeton, N.J.: Princeton University Press, 1939), p. 63.

8. Multiplication of specialized formal associations, especially of the centralized, hierarchical types, leads to development of numerous mediating, coordinating, or tangential organizations; for example, coordinating committees, clearing-house organizations; councils; multiplication of offices and associations charged with mediating and coordinating tasks; federated associations.

9. More generally, both the total social structure *and* the internal structures of large formal organizations are highly complex: in the latter, numerous specialized statuses are arranged in intricate systems within systems; in the former, varied groups, communities, and associations are interrelated in extended networks, chains, and subsidiary social systems.

10. There is a varying but substantial amount of collective behavior manifesting social unrest—ranging from diffuse expressive violence to organized political movements, including riots, boycotts, demonstrations, marches, strikes, forcible seizure of buildings and persons, obstruction of access to public facilities, and a variety of threatening actions. Such widespread activism often reflects a pervasive alienation from the main institutions and legitimizing values and beliefs of the national society and of its political system. Social conflicts are severe and frequent as counter-forces are activated.

11. Massive and rapid communication increasingly conveys a continuous stream of highly selected but diverse information to all parts of the society.

12. There probably is an increasing proportion of individual persons and organizations that is subject to "overloads" of both information and of requirements for making decisions; such literal overloading takes two main forms: (a) repeated and frequent incompatibility of demands upon decision makers and (b) the impossibility of acquiring, organizing, and using the needed information in the actual time available.

13. Emerging from the conditions listed above is a condition of ultra-organization in which many social actors are simultaneously members of many collectivities, but at different times shift memberships rapidly,[1] and in which any particular organization maintains relationships with a large and continually changing set of groups and organizations.

### The Role of Primary Groups

It first has to be emphasized that great interstitial areas of the society lie on the margins of organization strictly conceived. In this twilight zone of semi-structured interaction belong the casual crowds and audiences of metropolitan life—aggregates held together in highly transitory contacts by momentary polarization around a similar or shared interest of some kind. Here also are many of the unstable interactions of unattached persons living outside organized groups; thus, high rates of mobility and ethnic heterogeneity characterize cities with high crime rates and low rates of voluntary contribution to "welfare" agencies.[2]

[1] For example, the high turnover of professional and managerial workers; cf. Caplow, *op. cit.*, p. 245.

[2] Robert C. Angell, *The Moral Integration of American Cities* (Chicago: University of Chicago Press, 1951).

As has so often been pointed out, American society is not marked by a high development of traditionalized groupings based on proximity, direct personal relations, and the intimate sharing of common values.[3] Small stable primary groups have been the building blocks of human societies over most of the world in all past history. The family, the neighborhood, the village or commune, the local community are the basic units upon which more elaborate and indirect social structures are erected. In the United States, these small units of intensive continuing personal interaction have been considerably attenuated by forces arising in the whole process of industrialization and urbanization. With high mobility, in a secularized, economically oriented culture, the local groups and family units take a less prominent place in the total social structure. Correlatively, increased importance attaches to organizations that are nonlocal and indirect. Nevertheless, it remains true that the various types of localistic primary groups are basic to the organization of American, as to any other, society. First are the millions of immediate-family units, each a cluster of intensive interaction. No one has counted the thousands of neighborhoods that still constitute vital social units for millions of people—even, contrary to some impressions, in the supposedly impersonal maelstrom of the great cities.[4] Running through local social structures are numerous play groups, cliques, visiting circles, friendship constellations, and diffuse interpersonal attachments giving body and texture to the more formalized structures. Closely analogous groupings exist in the form of work groups, religious units, small groupings of interaction in schools—in short, within all large-scale formal organizations.

Thus we have, on the one hand, the diffuse relations and groupings of local neighborhoods and communities, of cliques and friendships, of work and play groups; on the other side, the more highly structured communal social systems of families, churches, social classes, minority groupings (in part), and various so-called fraternal or "social" organizations. Much is retained of Gemeinschaft-like structure.

Yet these groupings have been overshadowed by other forms of interaction. We have been considering groups that are (1) *durable*, that is, persisting in the face of such factors as external stress, shifting individual motives, segmental disadvantages, changes in membership, (2) manifesting high *continuity* of person-to-person relations—the same persons interact together over extended periods *and* with the expectation of continued interaction,

[3] Cf. Robert C. Angell, *The Integration of American Society* (New York: McGraw-Hill, 1941), esp. chap. 2.

[4] Author's note: This statement in the original edition ran contrary to many then-current stereotypes. Research during the subsequent years now permits us to document the point. In addition to the references cited in Chapter 4, see Morris Axelrod, "Urban Structure and Social Participation," *American Sociological Review*, 21, 1 (February 1956), 14–18; Basil G. Zimmer, "Participation of Migrants in Urban Structures," *American Sociological Review*, 20, 2 (April 1955), 218–224; Donald L. Foley, "The Use of Local Facilities in a Metropolis," *The American Journal of Sociology*, LVI, 3 (November 1950), 238–246; Wendell Bell and Maryanne T. Force, "Urban Neighborhood Types and Participation in Formal Associations," *American Sociological Review*, 21, 1 (February 1956), 25–34; Gans, *op. cit.*; Eugene Litwak, "Voluntary Associations and Neighborhood Cohesion," *American Sociological Review*, 26, 2 (April 1961), 258–271.

(3) including an *extensive range* of activities, accounting for a high proportion of each member's total activities and interests, (4) tending toward diffuse, *nonspecific norms* of right and obligation.

We have suggested that these organic, or more broadly Gemeinschaft-like, groupings are relatively weak in American society. The basis for this diagnosis is not obvious, nor to be taken for granted. Let us attempt to appraise it. "Weakness" we can define to mean (sociologically) relatively slight development of the four characteristics just listed, for a high proportion of all social interactions; or (psychologically) slight involvement of individuals in such groupings. Types of these groupings include: stable locality groups, families, community churches or religious orders, highly developed and enduring occupational associations and work groups. Specific evidences of the attenuation of these groupings include:

1. High rates of population mobility, disruptive of locality groups; low development of traditional patterns of solidarity—for example, work exchange, community mutual-aid patterns.[5]
2. Extremely high divorce rates; prevalence of migration from area of residence of parental family; discontinuity of generations; low interaction-rates in extended kinship circles; relatively great functional specificity in intrafamilial relations; high proportion of extrafamilial activities.[6]
3. Considerable secularization of organized religion; mobility of members; nonparticipation in churches.
4. High mortality of small business concerns; rapid shifts in industries and jobs; great geographic mobility of labor; functional specificity of occupations.

To these must be added (5) the increased centralization of relatively impersonal large-scale political and economic associations and (6) the presence of interstitial social zones in which many individuals are isolated from continuing interaction with a meaningful circle of close associates.

Every tendency just mentioned can be questioned, of course, by citing contrary facts. As Albert J. Reiss points out: "It was formerly taken for granted that neighborhood life is at a 'minimum' in cities except in ethnic areas and among children. Recent studies . . . have questioned this general assumption . . . pointing to data on close interpersonal relations in many urban neighborhoods."[7] The weighting of the opposing lines of evidence

---

[5] Partial functional equivalents in social service agencies and the like represent different group structures.

[6] Changes in family relations in middle-class populations clearly seem to form one of the major preconditions for both "alienation" and "activism" among youth. See David L. Westby and Richard G. Braungart, "Class and Politics in the Family Backgrounds of Student Political Activists," *American Sociological Review*, 31, 5 (October 1966), 690–692; Kenneth Keniston, *The Uncommitted: Alienated Youth in American Society* (New York: Harcourt, Brace & World, 1965); and Kenneth Keniston, *The New Radicals: Notes on Committed Youth* (New York: Harcourt, Brace & World, 1968); Erik H. Erikson, *Identity: Youth and Crisis* (New York: Norton, 1968).

[7] Paul K. Hatt and Albert J. Reiss, Jr. (eds.), *Cities and Society: The Revised Reader in Urban Sociology* (New York, Free Press, 1957), p. 9. See, for example, Donald L. Foley,

is a complex judgmental process and depends in part upon the standard of comparison or base-line chosen. Also, the extent to which lessened familism is directly associated with participation in voluntary associations is confounded with differences associated with rural-urban residence, ethnic membership, socioeconomic position, and religious affiliations. In general, participation in voluntary associations is highest among persons of higher education or occupational level and in urban areas.[8] All in all, however, it is the present thesis that in contrast to American society in previous generations there has been a definite over-all decrease in the proportion of social organization contained within organic groupings. This change undoubtedly has profound social and psychological implications in many different ways;[9] for example, the great current emphasis on security can hardly be understood apart from the loss of stable group support for many individuals—it is certainly far more than a purely economic development. We should recognize, at the same time, that familism and localism are extremely tough strands in the social fabric; and primary groups still form the basic network of social structure. It begins to appear likely that much of the often-noted "disorganization" of city life may be a transitional by-product of rapid urban growth, and may not be intrinsic to the urban setting.

### Proliferation of Formal Associations

The United States has long been characterized as "a nation of joiners," a happy hunting ground for "organizers," "promoters," and the like. It is said that American individualism is "group individualism."[1] As long ago as the 1830's, that extraordinary observer Alexis de Tocqueville remarked: "In no country in the world has the principle of association been more successfully used, or more unsparingly applied to a multitude of different objects, than in America."[2] A long line of other perceptive foreign observers have also commented on the extraordinary role of private associations organized around special interests. It is the formal, named, openly proclaimed voluntary association that is conspicuous in the United States; its purposes are typically assumed to be legitimate and openly declared. In other societies, "voluntary associations" may have a different character; for example, highly informal voluntary associations, often with sub rosa activities and purposes,

---

*Neighbors or Urbanites? The Study of a Rochester Residential District* (Rochester, N.Y.: University of Rochester Press, 1952).

[8] When these factors are controlled, some data show no relationship between kinship participation and membership in voluntary associations.

[9] "From the psychological standpoint, the key to the understanding of well integrated organic societies is to be found in the fact that in these societies the collective impulses and wishes are absorbed by the smaller groups of which they are composed. These smaller groups then canalize and direct their energies toward their own particular ends." Karl Mannheim, *op. cit.*, p. 62.

[1] Angell, *op. cit.*, p. 3: "So significant has become the role of free-standing groups in contemporary life that one is tempted to say that our society is characterized by group individualism." For a similar comment see Charles W. Ferguson, *Fifty Million Brothers* (New York: Farrar, Straus and Giroux, 1937), p. 12.

[2] Alexis de Tocqueville, *Democracy in America: The Republic of the United States of America and its Political Institutions* (New York: Barnes, 1877), Part I, p. 204.

appear to be very numerous in France, although formal associations seem fewer than in the America case.[3] In any case, the contemporary United States contains an enormous number of formal organizations of the most diverse kinds.[4]

As an exhibit in point, here is a brief list of organizations taken, partly at random and partly with malice aforethought, from the *World Almanac:*[5]

1. Aaron Burr Association
2. American Legion
3. American Swedish Historical Foundation
4. Appalachian Mountain Club
5. Chinese Women's Association, Inc.
6. Commercial Law League of America
7. Cooperative League of the U.S.A.
8. Daughters of the Cincinnati
9. Elks, Benevolent and Protective Order of
10. Horseshoe Pitchers Association of America
11. Iceland Veterans
12. Nut Growers Association, Northern
13. Paper Institute, American
14. Speech Association of America
15. Woman's Christian Temperance Union, National
16. Zonta International

The variety of voluntary special interest associations suggested by this sampling is documented by numerous community studies. Warner and Lunt were able to identify 899 associations in a city of approximately 17,000 people and to find for study 357 relatively permanent and important associations. The groupings studied were composed of 12,876 memberships held by 6,874 individuals.[6]

Comparison of several national societies, however, shows that the United States is not alone in having numerous and diverse voluntary associations. Membership in such organizations is associated with urban life, urbanization of rural areas, and relatively high economic and educational levels; but

[3] Jesse R. Pitts, "The Family and Peer Groups," in William J. Goode (ed.), *The Dynamics of Modern Society* (New York: Atherton Press, 1966), pp. 39–41.

[4] For a collection of articles on voluntary associations, see Nicholas Babchuk and Charles K. Warriner (eds.), "Signposts in the Study of Voluntary Groups," in *Sociological Inquiry*, 35, 2 (Spring 1965), 135–240.

[5] *The World Almanac and Book of Facts, 1968* (New York: Doubleday, 1968), pp. 639–654. The total includes over 1,000 organizations under the heading "Associations and Societies in the United States." Presumably this sample is highly selective, including only those considered important enough for listing in a very compact reference volume. See also Gale Research Company, *Encyclopedia of Associations, Vol. I: National Organizations of the United States,* 5th ed. (Detroit: 1968), in which the sheer listing of over 12,000 active associations requires nearly one thousand large double-columned pages (pp. 15–1003).

[6] W. Lloyd Warner and Paul S. Lunt, *The Social Life of a Modern Community* (New Haven, Conn.: Yale University Press, 1941), pp. 303 and 320. See the whole of chap. 16, "The Formal and Informal Associations of Yankee City."

large numbers of them have been reported in such diverse nations as Japan, Thailand, West Germany, Nigeria, Israel, and Ghana.[7] Moreover, the actual prevalence of membership and participation must not be exaggerated by implication. Some national surveys have shown that nearly half of American families report no membership in voluntary associations.[8] According to David Sills' authoritative summary, inactive memberships probably are underreported and participation is overreported; he estimates that among American adults, some nominal membership in one or more voluntary, part-time, special-interest organizations is very prevalent (possibly as high as 75 percent) but active participation characterizes only a small minority (possibly as low as 20 percent).[9] Formally organized special-interest associations are most highly developed in urban areas but have increasingly pervaded the open country as well.[1] The range of interests represented by these associations is impressive, and the variety of structures is correspondingly great. The private, voluntary, special-interest associations include benevolent and philanthropic groupings, fraternal orders, clubs, educational organizations, economic associations, special occupational groupings, and so on through numerous special categories. In preceding chapters, we have already observed the multiplicity of religious denominations, of political pressure groups, of education-related associations. The pattern of multiple associations cuts across the major institutions and laces together the partly differentiated groups and strata of local communities.

Even a casual sampling of data on such associations will lend body to the above statements. Thus, according to their own reports at the end of 1960, the major fraternal orders in the United States claimed a total membership of about 12 million persons—a sharp decrease from the 20 million of the 1940's.[2] As of the 1960's, there were over 4,000 chapters of

[7] See the comprehensive treatment of the state of knowledge on this topic in David L. Sills, "Voluntary Associations: Sociological Aspects," *International Encyclopedia of the Social Sciences*, Volume 16 (New York: Free Press, 1968), pp. 362–379. Sills points out that by "voluntary associations" we generally mean spare time, participatory, non-state, common interest, purposive organizations, most of whose members are unpaid volunteers.

[8] C. R. Wright and H. H. Hyman, "Voluntary Association Memberships of American Adults: Evidence from National Sample Surveys," *American Sociological Review*, 23, 3 (June 1958), 286.

[9] Cf. Sills, *op. cit.*, p. 365.

[1] A study of an upstate New York rural community covering an area with a population of 4,000 revealed 129 formal organizations—James E. White, "Theory and Method for Research in Community Leadership," *American Sociological Review*, 15, 1 (February 1950), 55. Cf. F. A. Bushee, "Social Organizations in a Small City," *American Journal of Sociology*, LI, 3 (November 1945); Mirra Komarovsky, "The Voluntary Associations of Urban Dwellers," *American Sociological Review*, 11, 6 (December 1946).

[2] See "Fraternal Orders," *Collier's Encyclopedia*, 1966 ed., Vol. 10, and compare with "Fraternal Orders," *Encyclopaedia of the Social Sciences*, Vol. VI, and "Masonry," *ibid.*, Vol. X. For the earlier period, note the comment of Ferguson, *Fifty Million Brothers*, p. 35. "American secret and nonliturgical societies are in many respects singular. Whatever may be true of the rest of the world or of past history, we present an array of orders altogether baffling. . . ." *Op. cit.*, p. 5.

national college fraternities and more than 2,500 sorority chapters.[3] The distinctive "service clubs" (Rotary, Kiwanis, Lions, Civitans, Optimists, and so on) cover the nation, with some unit in practically every urban center and in many rural areas.

Among special women's organizations, the General Federation of Women's Clubs includes 15,000 member organizations (state, national, and international affiliates) claiming 11 million individual members.[4]

There are large organizations of veterans of military service—the American Legion, the Veterans of Foreign Wars, the Disabled American Veterans, and the American Veterans of World War II and Korea. In addition, there are many smaller and more specific groups—more than 500 of these organizations are active enough to hold annual reunions.[5]

In rural areas, the American Farm Bureau Federation with its affiliated cooperatives has 1,500,000 members; the National Grange lists approximately 850,000 dues-paying members; the 4-H clubs enrolled in 1954 about 2 million youths.[6]

By 1960, the A.F.L.-C.I.O., composed of many national and international unions and organizing committees, with state, county, and local union councils and hundreds of local industrial unions, had about 14 million members.[7]

As a further indication of the organizational profusion of a society of great specialization in sciences and technologies, note the existence of more than 800 membership societies devoted to a particular scientific or technical discipline.[8]

And so it goes.[9] These associations, note, are in addition to the elaborate formal organization represented by business enterprises, foundations, and many other forms of private associations.

But what does this proliferation of associations mean? What are the sources and implications of such a conspicuous and pervasive patterning of social structure? There is first of all the elementary and crucial fact of a

[3] "Greek Letter Societies and College Fraternities," *Encyclopedia Americana,* 1967 ed., Vol. 13. There were some 60 national fraternities, 36 national sororities, more than 100 professional fraternities, and about 40 honor and recognition societies. See also W. R. Baird, *Manual of American College Fraternities,* 18th ed., by John Robson (ed.) (Menasha, Wis.: George Banta Company, 1968).

[4] "Club," *Encyclopedia Americana,* 1967 ed., Vol. 7, p. 137.

[5] "Veterans' Organizations," *Encyclopedia Americana,* 1967 ed., Vol. 28.

[6] "American Farm Bureau Federation," *Encyclopedia Britannica,* 1968 ed., Vol. 1; "Grange," *Encyclopedia Americana,* Vol. 13; "Four-H Clubs," *ibid.,* Vol. 11.

[7] "American Federation of Labor-Congress of Industrial Organizations," *Encyclopedia Britannica,* 1968 ed., Vol. 1.

[8] National Academy of Sciences, *Scientific and Technical Societies of the United States,* 8th ed. (Washington, D.C.: National Academy of Sciences Printing and Publishing Office, 1968).

[9] Probably very few Americans are aware of the existence of the Halibut Fisherman's Wives Association, which received some public attention in Seattle in 1966 for its part in controversies over the extension of the twelve-mile fishing limits for waters off the coast of the United States.

*permissive power-situation.* The American political system not only tolerates but encourages private groupings. No totalitarian order can or will tolerate such widespread diversity of private associations relatively independent of the formal structure of the state. The situation in the United States is obviously not one of complete freedom of association—the history of the labor movement is alone enough to disabuse us of that impression—but the main long-run tendency has been to permit very great latitude to quite diverse associations.[1]

A permissive governmental policy, based on a pluralistic power structure, makes *possible* the developments of interest here; but it is not enough. There must also be forces creating associations—"demands" for interaction not met by other forms of social structure. Why do we have so many formal associations when for most human beings in all past societies the full activities of life were sufficiently encompassed by the family, the work group, and the local community? The asking of this question itself suggests one element of an answer: the special-interest association and the formalized congeniality grouping partly replace the void left by the *dissolution of older patterns of group interaction* and partly represent the vast growth of specialization, together with mobility and affluence. As urbanization has advanced in a mobile, industrial order, the old social units have been reduced in importance. But the demand for stable group support and association has not diminished correspondingly.[2] The massive spread of suburbanization in the post-World War II years marked a new phase in American group life in which casual amiability is emphasized in informal social relations among near dwellers who are not neighbors in the traditional rural sense.[3] This line of analysis is useful, but does not constitute an adequate explanation. For example, it does not appear that people join special-interest associations *because* they lack primary-group ties; the evidence rather points in the other direction: people who have primary group memberships are more likely to be members and to be high participators in voluntary associations.[4]

[1] For example, "The phenomenal growth of fraternal orders throughout the English-speaking world since the middle of the last century has been associated with the development of democratic institutions and the consequent freedom to form voluntary associations for the promotion of common interests."—Frank H. Hankins, "Fraternal Orders," *Encyclopaedia of the Social Services,* Vol. VI, p. 423. The relative decline in the importance of such organizations since World War II perhaps is one reason for the omission of any article on the topic in the newer *International Encyclopaedia of the Social Sciences* (1968).

[2] Cf. Maurice R. Stein, *The Eclipse of Community: An Interpretation of American Studies* (Princeton, N.J.: Princeton University Press, 1960), and Charles F. Marden, *Rotary and Its Brothers* (Princeton, N.J.: Princeton University Press, 1935). Marden implies that the service clubs represent, in part, reactions to the change from rural and village society to the urban situation of relatively great impersonality, competition, and psychosocial isolation.

[3] Robert C. Wood, *Suburbia: Its People and Its Politics* (Boston: Houghton Mifflin, 1959); Bennett M. Berger, *Working-Class Suburb* (Los Angeles: University of California Press, 1960); S. D. Clark, *The Suburban Society* (Toronto: University of Toronto Press, 1966); William M. Dobriner (ed.), *The Suburban Community* (New York: Putnam, 1958)

[4] Sills, *op. cit.,* p. 373.

The situation is, rather, that the traditional diffuse-ascribed groupings are wholly inadequate to express the interests and facilitate the goals of the diverse people of a rapidly changing society with elaborate division of labor.

For example, the incidence of different types of associations and other groupings in various social strata suggests the sources from which they derive. In culturally marginal or uprooted populations in the lower-income levels, it is the fraternal order, the religious cult or sect, or occasionally the union in which common support and defense is sought. In the top-income levels, the prestige association is the form assumed by formalized congeniality groupings, although there is extensive participation in other voluntary private associations, based on considerations of civic duty, or prestige and economic advantage. It is in the broad middle classes that one finds the great development of private associations organized in the name of fraternal, civic, service, benevolent, educational, and recreational purposes.[5] Many of these associations exhibit familistic and communal symbols, and creeds that seem to contrast markedly with the competitive, functionally specific relations so highly emphasized in middle-class business and professional occupations.

More broadly, the multiplication of associations is an outgrowth of cultural diversity and occupational differentiation, as like-circumstanced individuals seek to interact with one another and to combine in the pursuit of specialized interests common to a particular segment of the population. The tendency to form associations around special interests represents also the dominantly activistic bent of American culture.

The voluntary fraternal or civic associations apparently serve a variety of functions for different individuals and groupings. These associations sometimes constitute an avenue for advancing the economic interests of individuals, through the opportunities provided for personal acquaintance, knowledge of business opportunities, and the like; and for the young professional or businessman membership may be a *sine qua non* for success in some local communities. Certain organizations appeal to members as a badge of respectability or symbol of prestige. Many (overtly noneconomic) associations become means of economic and political control by particular groups and individuals over others. We have already suggested that such associations to some extent provide belongingness and a sense of community to many individuals having few stable and secure affectional or status bonds. The conspicuousness of benevolent and service motifs in these organizations further hints that they may provide ritual alleviation of anxieties and hostilities and guilts aroused in the area of competitive occupational life. But these are questions of social psychology that we must leave aside with this mention. We can be sure, however, that multiple motives are involved

5 See Murray Hausknecht, *The Joiners* (New York: Bedminster Press, 1962). Cf. Elizabeth Bott, *Family and Social Network* (London: Tavistock Publications, 1957), p. 86: "Voluntary associations appear to thrive best in areas where people are similar in social status but do not know one another well; the common activity gives people an opportunity to get to know one another better."

and that the nominal aims of these organizations do not fully describe their consequences.[6]

Returning to structural matters, we are again reminded that associational proliferation is, up to a very high level, generative of further associations. Specifically, as the number of separate groups and associations increases within the same general community, the number of points at which two or more organizations impinge upon the same interest or simultaneously affect the same individuals will increase. Each point of intersection creates a need for regularizing the tangential interaction.[7] Thus, both the family and the school converge upon the child, and the Parent-Teacher Association mediates the triangular relation; or, the multiplication of benevolent, civic, and youth-training associations creates pressures that lead to a united fund or community chests, councils, coordinating agencies, and so on. In some American communities, the large number of formally organized groups and associations appears to have reached practically the upper limit in their demands for participation—a limit imposed by sheer paucity of time, short of obliterating the basic institutions and informal groupings. This is the familiar picture of so-called overorganization in many local areas, a condition which would have been unthinkable in the old-fashioned rural community. Further, the existence of competition and conflict among organizations itself often generates still more associational activity and the elaboration of group structures.[8]

## Some Characteristics of Large-Scale Formal Organizations[9]

Although the total society shows a loose articulation of exceedingly diverse associations and groups, many of its component organizations have become very large, complex, and tightly structured. Although the over-all pattern is still pluralistic—with many relatively autonomous crisscrossing groupings— certain centers of organization have come to represent foci of centralized control over highly formalized structures. Centralization and bureaucratization of organized controls are not confined to the new leviathan of modern government but are also characteristic of corporate business, of large labor unions, and of many other associations. Thus, even at the level of the local

6 David L. Sills, *The Volunteers* (New York: Free Press, 1957) gives a rich case study of the maintenance of local volunteer participation in the activities of the National Foundation for Infantile Paralysis.

7 Cf. Eliot D. Chapple and Carleton S. Coon, *Principles of Anthropology* (New York: Holt, Rinehart & Winston, 1942), pp. 337–338, 418–425.

8 Arnold M. Rose, "Voluntary Associations Under Conditions of Competition and Conflict," *Social Forces*, 34, 2 (December 1955), 160.

9 Available references on this subject are numerous and will not be cited at all the points at which they apply. For the general characteristics of bureaucracy, see the references listed in Chapter VI and the following: Michel Crozier, *The Bureaucratic Phenomenon* (Chicago: University of Chicago Press, 1964); March (ed.), *op. cit.*; Downs, *op. cit.*; Etzioni, *op. cit.*; Victor A. Thompson, *Modern Organization, A General Theory* (New York: Knopf, 1961); Bertram M. Gross, *The Managing of Organizations*, Vols. I–II (New York: Free Press, 1964); Morris Janowitz, *The Professional Soldier* (New York: Free Press, 1960); Amitai Etzioni (ed.), *Complex Organizations: A Sociological Reader* (New York: Holt, Rinehart & Winston, 1961); March and Simon, *op. cit.*

community the ubiquitous United Fund or Community Chest is one of the clearest homely examples of the degree to which the practices of large scale formal organizations have permeated the voluntary private associations.

The prevalence of large-scale associations is so obvious, and has been so copiously documented in previous chapters (especially VI and VII), that it is not necessary to present additional evidence here. The role played in the whole society by large formal organizations has enormously increased during the last fifty years. Massive administrative units and combinations of units are the order of the day in business, labor, government, and increasingly in education, religion, philanthropy, and other fields. These formal organizations constitute a giant superstructure upon the organic groupings, continuing from earlier times. The disintegration of the latter's localistic mode of social organization is accompanied by large-scale bureaucratization *and* by the growth of noninstitutional collective behavior. Americans may still talk in nostalgic terms of village and country life, but they must learn somehow to live with the large formal association. It becomes correspondingly important to understand the structure and functioning of the latter.

"Organizations" can be usefully defined in many different ways. Of basic importance, however, is the distinction between formal, goal oriented organizations and other kinds of collectivities, such as communities, social classes, ethnic groupings, and congeniality circles and cliques. Organizations have a high degree of identity boundedness and definiteness of structure: for example, they have a name and a distinctive set of symbols; definite criteria of membership; established goals; definite procedures of recruitment, promotion, and demotion, and of expulsion and retirement.[1]

Both the internal structure and functioning of an organization and its relations with its environment are affected by the *goals of the organization as a unit*. Granted, such goals are often vague, multiple, complex, and difficult to identify objectively and clearly. Nevertheless, unit goals do exist; they differ among concrete types of organizations (factories, universities, prisons, armies, mental hospitals, research laboratories); and the existence of different goals will have consequences for behavior even within organizations of the same general type. An illustration is found in the contrast between the goals of custodial control and care versus rehabilitative treatment in organizations dealing with incarcerated juvenile delinquents. Organizations primarily committed to the custodial emphasis tend to have a relatively simple and centralized control-structure.[2] Those that focus upon remedial treatment have more complex departmental structures involving a greater sharing of executive power. (Once such basic patterns are estab-

[1] Caplow, *op. cit.*

[2] Mayer N. Zald, "Organizational Control Structures in Five Correctional Institutions," *American Journal of Sociology*, LXVIII, 3 (November 1962), 335–345. Delegation of control in treatment-oriented organizations is encouraged not only by needs for autonomy and initiative but also by the superintendent's exposure to greater external demands, especially in securing financial support and in explaining and justifying the emphasis upon treatment.

lished, it is likely that they, in turn, help to determine the future goal-emphasis of the organization.)

Goal-attaining organizations in the real world always operate in uncertain and imperfectly known environments, in which obtaining additional information is costly. Those who make decisions concerning the functioning of the organization have limited time and limited capacities to process information. Decision makers have multiple goals and are moved by personal interests as well as by organizational objectives and norms.[3] To the external observer lacking detailed acquaintance with the everyday realities, many organizations may at first present the appearance of smooth, almost automatic, functioning. Typically, the appearance is deceptive. Most organizations run on blood, sweat, and tears. "Trouble" is an endemic condition. It is not entirely frivolous to suggest that the first law of the functioning of large, complex organizations is "If anything can go wrong, it will."[4]

So long as one concentrates attention primarily upon voluntary associations, it is possible to acknowledge the existence of power and authority without giving them any high priority in analysis. For the members of voluntary associations are able, by definition, to leave the organization at any time when better alternatives appear—and any undesired imposition of power will increase the attractiveness of alternatives. However, when one turns to large-scale, goal oriented organizations, especially in economic and political fields, the facts of power and authority inevitably become centrally important for our understanding of how such organizations operate. It is not possible to imagine such organizations functioning under actual conditions (rather than in an abstract, simplified model) without the exercise of power and the development of legitimized authority. The conditions necessary for spontaneous coordination are much too stringent.[5] Furthermore, much social organization involves discordant and antagonistic relationships and strong elements of coercion; but it is no less "social" or "organized" by reason of its abrasive, tense, or power-oriented qualities.[6]

A large number of cumulated studies indicate that definite characteristics appear as a formal organization reaches a certain level of size and complexity. Insofar as the organization is, for any reason, structured to *act as a unit*, there must be some central directing focus.[7] Whether the officials at the

---

[3] Downs, *op. cit.*, pp. 2–3.

[4] The second law comes into play when there is excessive tinkering with the structure in efforts to stop things from going wrong, namely, "If you reorganize often enough, you will destroy the whole enterprise."

[5] Cf. Renate Mayntz, "The Study of Organizations," *Current Sociology*, XIII, 3 (1964), 115: "To control organizational activities merely by impersonal rules so that nobody ever has to give an order which others must obey would be possible only under a series of unrealistic assumptions, *e.g.*, goal consensus, goal stability, the absence of motives for members to disobey rules, and a maximum of information on the consequences of alternative modes of action."

[6] Prisons are not typically regarded as pleasant settings for interaction, and their nominal efforts toward "rehabilitation" often are ineffective. But they always have an elaborate social structure. See Cloward, *et al.*, *op. cit.*

[7] It does not always have to act as a unit. Indeed, the parts of complex organizations always have some independence (functional autonomy) and defend themselves against extreme

directing center be elected or appointed, and regardless of how democratically derived may be the decisions they announce or execute, the unitary action of the organization must be taken through an extended chain of delegated authority and activity. The larger the organization and the more specialized its subunits and individual roles, the larger the number of intermediaries between the center of authority and the mass of the members.[8] Organizational complexity on a large scale is typically associated with "bureaucratic" characteristics, as previously noted in Chapters VI and VII.

Of course, size alone does not permit us to infer a great deal about other characteristics of an organization. It is the interaction between size and other major features of organizations that produces the most interesting relationships.[9] Thus, large size *in combination* with complexity of division of labor in interdependent activities and with urgency of coordination in both time and space favors centralization of control; but large size of a total organization made up of many relatively self-contained units operating under highly variable local conditions may be quite compatible with extensive decentralization of decision making. Large organizations often are highly formalized; but they need not be if other effective mechanisms of social control are present, for example, a high level of professionalization.[1]

A specific example of the untrustworthy character of the conventional wisdom concerning bureaucracies is the sweeping generalization that the size of the administration staff increases disproportionately with growth in size.[2] Some research, indeed, has found that larger organizations have a greater percentage of staff explicitly designated as administrative.[3] Other studies (of a different kind of organization) show that larger organizations have a smaller proportion of workers in administrative tasks.[4] Still other research shows a curvilinear relationship—as size increases, the percentage of personnel in administration at first goes up rapidly, then levels off and decreases.[5] These results are no longer surprising, for neither size nor com-

centralization of control and decision making. See the discussion by Gouldner, *op. cit.*, pp. 419–426.

[8] George C. Homans, *The Human Group* (New York: Harcourt, Brace & World, 1950), p. 406, states this generalization in a somewhat different form.

[9] Theodore R. Anderson and Seymour Warkov, "Organizational Size and Functional Complexity: A Study of Administration in Hospitals," *American Sociological Review*, 26, 1 (February 1961), 23–28.

[1] Richard H. Hall, J. Eugene Haas, and Norman J. Johnson, "Organizational Size, Complexity, and Formalization," *American Sociological Review*, 32, 6 (December 1967), pp. 903–912.

[2] Cf. the quasi-serious formulation of C. Northcote Parkinson, *Parkinson's Law* (Boston: Houghton Mifflin, 1957), pp. 2–13.

[3] F. C. Terrien and D. C. Mills, "The Effects of Changing Size Upon the Internal Structure of an Organization," *American Sociological Review*, 20, 1 (February 1955), pp. 11–14.

[4] Anderson and Warkov, *op. cit.*; Reinhard Bendix, *Work and Authority in Industry* (New York: Wiley, 1956), p. 222.

[5] Amos Hawley, Walter Boland, and Margaret Boland, "Population Size and Administration in Institutions of Higher Education," *American Sociological Review*, 30, 2 (April 1965), 252–255; Eugene Haas, Richard Hall, and Norman Johnson, "The Size of the

plexity is a sufficient condition for predicting either formalization or relative size of administrative components. Both of the latter are affected directly by needs for coordination and servicing of the internal units of the organization, by diversity of organizational tasks, by skill levels and other characteristics of the workers, and by the technologies of communication, information processing, and social control—for example, computers and other electronic equipment,[6] committees, and formal codes of procedures.

Although many organizations do not seem to be greatly affected by the technology of their operations, this situation may appear to be so only because attention is focused on organizations using a similar technology or upon organizations that in fact do not employ specialized technologies that have any very important structural consequences.[7] But if an organization concentrates upon production of commodities or services that requires extensive equipment and technical processing procedures, technology may indeed make a difference. Research on industrial organizations has begun to produce promising indications that "technology" is crucially tied together with the *character of the product*, on the one hand, and the *structure of organization*, on the other. Specifically, there are important differences among organizations that produce goods or services (1) in small batches of individual, custom-made units, or (2) in large batches of standardized units (assembly, mass production), or (3) in a continuous flow (sequential processes, integrated to produce a single homogeneous item, such as gasoline, together with by-products). Organizations differ in structure among these three types. For example, the distinction between informal and formal organization is highly important in mass production organizations but not in firms or plants devoted to either unit or process production. Mass production firms continually face incompatibilities between requirements of technical coordination and needs for social integration; these conflicts are less crucial in the other two types of organization. In the highly integrated processing firms, the technical organization of work (supervision, control, phasing) is practically dictated by the sheer engineering of the facilities; not so in the unit production firms, where production is nonroutine and social and technical requirements must be continually reappraised.[8] And these developments have other complicated effects; for instance, as organizations increasingly have to rely upon technical experts for many essential aspects of their operations, potential conflicts emerge between those who hold organizational *authority* and those who have *expert knowledge*; the hierarchy of technical competence does not coincide with the hierarchy of ordering and supervising.[9] This is not to say that the conflicts are insoluble. In fact,

Supportive Component in Organizations: A Multi-organizational Analysis," *Social Forces*, 42, 1 (October 1963), 9–17.

[6] Robert Boguslaw, *The New Utopians: A Study of System Design and Social Change* (Englewood Cliffs, N.J.: Prentice-Hall, 1965).

[7] Stanley H. Udy, *Organization of Work* (New Haven, Conn.: Human Relations Area Files Press, 1959), esp. chap. 4. Udy distinguishes four kinds of production organizations: familial, custodial, contractual, and voluntary.

[8] Joan Woodward, *Industrial Organization: Theory and Practice* (London: Oxford University Press, 1965).

[9] Thompson, *op. cit.*

the ultimate decisions almost always are promulgated by the nonspecialists; but the orders and prescriptions often will have been primarily influenced by the experts.

To the degree that organizations operate in terms of explicit, general rules and regulations, another set of consequences follows: internally, the explicit definition of operating procedures maximizes the interchangeability of personnel and helps to insure certain gross predictabilities of behavior. Similarly, the formalization of office, including the definition of responsibilities, reduces the likelihood of interpersonal conflicts by furnishing unequivocal standards for determining jurisdiction. A system of rules often protects subordinates from arbitrary personal actions on the part of superior officials; such a system also may help to inhibit the development of segmental cliques and political machines within the organization. Any particular social structure is likely to have multiple functions rather than a single consequence. In the present case, it is likely that the same rules that protect subordinates and minimize cliques *also* operate to enhance the possibilities of *centralized* control, e.g., by making rewards contingent upon the rule-making authority rather than the subordinate official.

To release a large organization from the canalizing and restraining effects of a system of formal rules would be, in general, to open the door to widespread particularistic influences (favoritism and so forth) and to court the risk of internal schism and disintegration. On the other side, an impersonal system of generalized rules seems to have widely noted negative consequences, for example, red tape.[1] Categorical rules, in the nature of the case, do not allow for the full complexity of specific situations—it is precisely one of their main functions to reduce variation, flexibility, extenuating circumstances, and the like. This normative rigidity is a perennial problem in the relations of the organization to its public of customers, clients, or citizens. For to the individual facing the organization at its contact edge his own unique needs and circumstances are of paramount interest, whereas to the organizational official the situation is a case to be dealt with in terms of explicit general rules. The resentment of the citizen, client, or customer at "bureaucratic arrogance" is often the expectable consequence of these clashing perspectives, which in their turn are related to and in part derived from the basic structural situation.[2]

The impersonal-categorical structure of the large business or governmental organization thus continually produces the possibility of clashing norms and expectations at its outer edges. Internally, much the same type of problem arises. Many of the personnel (a significantly neutral word) enter the organization with values and expectations functionally appropriate to

[1] In a study of 150 formal organizations in nonindustrial societies, strictly "bureaucratic" characteristics were found to be *negatively* associated with "rational" characteristics. (Stanley H. Udy, Jr., "Bureaucracy and 'Rationality' in Weber's Organization Theory: An Empirical Study," *American Sociological Review*, 24, 6 (December 1959), 791–797.

[2] Problems of individual differences and individual motivation are not unimportant. It is a plausible hypothesis, for example, that individuals who are markedly insecure in their own personalities and group relations are especially prone as officials to rely upon the "letter of the law." For some suggestions on this point see Morris Rosenberg, "The Social Roots of Formalism," *Journal of Social Issues*, V, 1 (Winter 1949).

the intimate, diffuse, personalized relations of primary groups. If the organization emphasizes functionally specific, depersonalized behavior, such individuals tend initially to react in a personal, overly affective manner to situations in which the norms of the organization call for specific, impersonal, disinterested action. Nominally institutionalized sanctions, for instance, are perceived as friendly gestures, favoritism, dislike, insult.[3] The truly bureaucratic structure finds any high level of overtly affective personal relations disturbing. On the other hand, just to the degree that the organization *is* impersonal, it probably tends to produce anxiety and other tensions among its members—especially new personnel and individuals at the subordinate levels of administrative hierarchies.[4]

There are, of course, other problems—from the standpoint of the administrative center of the large organization—that arise from basic regularities of group process. Each subunit of interpersonal interaction tends to become a psychological reference group for its participants. It is accordingly not uncommon that loyalties to the subunit take precedence over the goals and norms officially dominant for the organization as a whole. Hence, a recurrent task of centralized administration is that of diagnosing and treating "excessive" segmentation of the organization. Again, there are multiple implications. Segmentation is often associated with power aggrandizement by officials, that is, empire building. Or the subgroup becomes a powerful source of resistance to technological and organizational changes initiated outside the group. It is quite possible that much of the administrative shifting of personnel and dissolution and regrouping of units, so common in large organizations, has as one effect the atomizing of solidary internal segments representing potential threats to unitary control.

Autonomy of subunits may be defined as independence from control by other parts of the organization (singly or in combination). A *completely* independent unit would not be a "part" of an organization; but short of that limit, there are widely different degrees of independence and control. Fred Katz has proposed the following propositions concerning the factor making for subunit autonomy:

1. The *"greater the degree of specialized knowledge and skills required of the occupant of a position, the greater the degree of autonomy that accrues to the position; . . ."*[5]
2. The *"accomplishment of functional contributions to a system requires a degree of autonomy from that system."*[6]

[3] And, of course, this meaning may on occasion actually be imputed to the act by all parties concerned.

[4] Not all the characteristics found in actual bureaucracies are distinctive to them. Such features as formal rationality, limited objectives, functional specificity (segmental participation), performance (achievement) emphasis, and compensatory rewards are not peculiar to bureaucracies. Most nearly definitive of bureaucracy are hierarchical structure of authority, specialized administrative staff, and rewards differentiated by office or rank. Cf. Udy, *op. cit.*, pp. 791–795.

[5] Fred E. Katz, *Autonomy and Organization: The Limits of Social Control* (New York: Random House, 1968), p. 21. (Italics in original).

[6] *Ibid.*, p. 23.

3. Prescriptions concerning expected behavior are less specific and comprehensive, leaving more scope for autonomy, among elite or "top" members of organizations.[7]

4. In relations between clients and professionals, *"if an asymmetrical relationship is to persist under noncoercive conditions,* a degree of autonomy must be *guaranteed for the person in the weaker role."*[8]

5. Demonstrated or presumed loyalty or involvement creates a basis for autonomy: *"an actor's strong commitment to an organization and its goals tends to be accompanied by autonomy privileges."*[9]

6. Different *kinds* of autonomy and control develop from different sources of financial support and legitimizing authority; the patterns are quite complex.[1]

Because of specialization, unit segmentation, and extended lines of indirect communication, every large organization encounters significant problems of communication. The difficulties are enhanced in some respects, insofar as the structure of offices is rigidly hierarchical, the opportunities for promotion are slight, and the personnel at various levels are recruited from different social origins. In passing through several intermediate links, communications are typically subject to reformulation and distortion; experienced administrators can almost always point to instances in which the original communication has arrived at its destination in scarcely recognizable form.

In a very large organization that is marked at the same time by a high degree of functional specialization and great internal complexity, the sheer problem of coordination of activity toward a common end becomes enormously difficult. The problem has recently appeared in perhaps its most obviously dramatic form in the organization of government for dealing with world problems; but the complexity of the coordinative problems of a large corporation, a large university, or a single governmental department are sufficient to tax, and sometimes overtax, the knowledge and ingenuity of those responsible for planning and administration. The forces making for bigness and centralization are more easily seen than those leading back to new forms of decentralization. Yet centralization has its limits; and the decentralization of rule making and decision-making authority offers real advantages in many large-scale organizations.[2] We do not believe that there is an inherent trend toward ever larger and more centralized organization which can proceed without limit.

Relationships between and among organizations—just as among social positions and other subunits—are not free to vary randomly or haphazardly. Social relationships are "constrained." The constraints arise from environ-

---

[7] *Ibid.,* p. 24.
[8] *Ibid.,* p. 28.
[9] *Ibid.,* p. 35.
[1] *Ibid.,* pp. 152–155.
[2] On this problem, one should consult, in its entirety, the work of Herbert A. Simon, *Administrative Behavior: A Study of Decision-making Processes in Administration Organization,* 2nd ed. (New York: Macmillan, 1957).

mental barriers, threats, and opportunities. They also derive from scarcity of time, energy, and other resources and facilities relative to tasks. In addition, relationships are subject to constraints of congruity, that is, the compatibility of various combinations of positions. Not all combinations are equally compatible in terms of consistency of the beliefs and evaluations involved, nor in efficiency in goal attainment, nor in specific norms applicable to incumbents of the particular positions in question.

To the extent that these assumptions are justified, we must predict that many conceivable combinations of positions and relationships will never, or only very rarely, occur or be repeated. Other combinations will be found with a frequency very much greater than expected by chance alone. And if there is in fact such definite clustering of positions and relationships the recurring sets must follow definite "rules" or "pathways" of patterning.[3] Similarly, there must be very intricate problems, worthy of close study, in the relationships *among*—and not merely within—organizations.[4]

We need not go into the numerous specialized problems of the giant association: provision for the regularized handling of dissatisfactions: the phenomena of "telephone diplomacy," interstatus antagonisms, "buffer states;" problems of recruitment, selection, training, promotion, and demotion; and so on. Enough has been said to suggest one of our main points: that the large-scale formal structure by its very form creates a wide range of social problems and challenges not likely to be easily solved by automatic processes or common-sense notions. Even at a quasi-technical level ("social engineering") an understanding of these structures requires a range of complex social knowledge still not fully appreciated even among executives. And the problems of social organization are never merely technical, no matter how much the administrators seek to turn all questions of policy into questions of procedure. Instead, the questions of organizational structure and process are always value laden; they always raise ethical issues. Thus there is meaning in the platitude that wisdom as well as knowledge is implicated in action in this field.

Two comments remain to be added concerning the place of large-scale organizations in the society as a whole. First, as the size and power of organizational units increase, *the consequences of decisions increasingly outrun the limits of the unit in which they originate.* As the chains of interaction and interdependence become longer and more intricate, actions taken at centralized decision-points have far-flung repercussions. No set of administrators, no matter how wise and conscientious, can make decisions which take into account anything like the full consequences of those decisions. As more and more of the social structure is aggregated or polarized

[3] Cf. Dorrian Apple Sweetser, "Path Consistency in Directed Graphs and Social Structure," *American Journal of Sociology*, LXXIII, 3 (November 1967), 287–293; also, Morris F. Friedell, "Organizations as Semi-Lattices," *American Sociological Review*, 32, 1 (February 1967), 46–54.

[4] William M. Evan, "The Organization-Set: Toward a Theory of Interorganizational Relations," in James D. Thompson (ed.), *Approaches to Organizational Design* (Pittsburgh, Pa.: University of Pittsburgh Press, 1966), pp. 173–191; William M. Evan and John A. MacDougall, "Interorganizational Conflict: A Labor-Management Bargaining Experiment," *Journal of Conflict Resolution*, XI, 4 (December 1967), 398–413.

into a relatively few giant associations, furthermore, each set of decisions elicits massive adjustments *en bloc* on the part of other large bodies affected by the act of any one of them. In an age of localism and small groups, the unforeseen consequences of organized actions had a limited impact on the wider society and often were in a sense self-corrective in the short run because of the immediacy of the consequences. The policy decisions of a major corporation or labor union have consequences not only affecting vast numbers of individuals but also evoking secondary and tertiary adjustments over a long time-span. Thus, the collective action of the large organization is increasingly freighted with a public interest in the widest sense of the term.

A second implication seems of great importance in the whole problem of societal integration in the United States, as well as in other industrialized areas of the world. With the development of huge formal organizations, especially in economic and political fields, the dissatisfactions and frustrations incident to life in society become, at least potentially, subject to *generalized* imputations of responsibility. An American farmer faced by drought and Indian raids in 1790 was in no position to perceive his plight as the consequence of a definite social structure. A Detroit worker in our day knows the name of the company for which he works, can identify the union to which he belongs, is likely to have some opinion of labor legislation and in some measure to be accustomed to praising or blaming highly visible social structures and their leadership. From the imputation of responsibility to a *specific* large-scale corporation, union, or political organization, it is not too difficult to define the situation in terms of an entire social system. It is noteworthy that political programs aimed at basic social change generally stress a systematic and total view of the sources of frustration. We are not saying that this stress necessarily occurs but only that the modern social structure provides a screen highly receptive to such projections of responsibility—for good or ill. In short, the increased centralization and formalization of our social structure vastly increases the likelihood that any major change will become a *political* problem. There are currently many voices raised to ask that the large organization be "humanized"—given flexibility, and brought into line with the values presumably basic for the individuals it affects. Other elements of the American population seem committed to maximum development of the formalized aspects of the large association. Whatever value position the student of these problems may take, it is apparent that we have only begun to acquire the needed knowledge of the structures and processes implicated in these problems.

### The Individual and Social Organization in American Society

What does this provisional diagnosis of American social structure signify in terms of the individual persons whose repeated actions constitute that structure? Very briefly, we will collate certain observations already implicit in the preceding analysis.

The institutions of a society confront the individual in the form of *statuses*—established positions, culturally defined in terms of socially recognized and enforced rights and obligations, and subject to common evaluation by the group. The social organization appears to the individual as a set of *roles*, partly corresponding to the statuses and partly a matter of incipient, latent, or noninstitutionalized regularities in individual conduct.

The most general function of social organization from the standpoint of the individual is that of providing predictability in interpersonal relations. Individual conduct can be organized only if there is some minimal regularity in the behavior of others. Otherwise, there can be no recurrent social referents for behavior and no such thing as adjustment, because the very social ground upon which the person stands provides no stability.[5] Some of the consequences of low predictability may be observed among "marginal men," adolescents, delinquents, divorced persons, expatriates and displaced peoples, organizational staffs subjected to drastic changes in policy, and, quite generally, in uprooted and socially mobile populations.[6] Rapid and important shifts in the social organization *to which the individual is oriented* —and especially in those specific groupings in which his basic role-involvements and sense of membership have previously been established—typically result in marked personal *dis*-orientations, manifest in erratic behavior and evidences of affective disturbance. These consequences are of varying duration, intensity, and qualitative nature in different group contexts but appear in some form and measure whenever individuals are repeatedly subjected to unpredicted variations in the structure of the social field that go beyond the zone of expectable instability established by past experience. At the extreme, one quite literally does not know what to expect. If such dissolution of the social pattern involves values central to the person's self-identity, the shattering of stable social expectations seems catastrophic for personality integration. If these processes were to become general in a given population, *common* orientation would disappear, and with it society properly speaking.

Bureaucracy has become a special object of criticism and active protest by alienated youths and the new left, in America as well as in many other countries. Many college age youths, including both political activists and "flower children," have criticized established large-scale organizations as a major evil. For many, the "solution" is an anarchistic community, in which love and consensus will obviate any enforcement of rules or centralization of control. Other critics, even if less optimistic concerning the prospects for spontaneous cooperation, have serious doubts about the human value of the large complex organizations that permeate our society. Yet few specific proposals for alternative social arrangements have found any widespread assent.

In the second half of the twentieth century, the classic sociological ideas of normlessness—Durkheim's *anomie*—and of alienation (developed especially from Hegel, Marx and their followers) have become part of the

[5] The solidity of social organization is a primary factor in the development of personality and in the determination of specific behavior. This crucial point has been developed by numerous investigators.

[6] Not *all* the characteristics of these categories, of course, are attributable to instability or to changes in group membership.

everyday culture. College students self-consciously talk of their "identity crises."[7] Youthful spokesmen among black Americans urge a new "racial identity," some finding it in a sense of positive identification with historic accomplishments and states of being attained within the mainstream of Western culture; others seek a sense of continuity with Africa or identify with world-wide revolutionary forces. Both the students and the black militants have engaged in large-scale violent demonstrations. Meanwhile, massive rioting repeatedly has swept across the great cities of the North and West. Social divisiveness and great turbulence continue to exist amid a society of high standards and levels of material comfort and of personal safety and opportunity.

Over against a portrait of *anomie* and much collective behavior we may contrast, first, the stable, traditionalized, social structures that in some respects provide high predictability and relatively rigid expectations. The price paid for this situation includes, among other things, lack of social mobility and of latitude for individual variation and spontaneity.

Then there are, second, the centralized systems illustrated in the national state or, on a lesser scale, in the large economic organization. At the extreme, again, such structures assimilate into a pattern of discipline and hierarchy the major constituent groupings of the society. And this too has its costs.

In the present American case, the total social structure is, on the surface, paradoxical. On the one hand, the large numbers of industrial workers or employees of business or governmental organizations spend a major part of their lives in relatively rigid and explicitly regulated group contexts. This is the "discipline of the job"—a phenomenon so massive that only anthropological and historical contrasts enable us to become sensitive to its place as a central radix of social organization in America. Similarly, the formalized control-systems of government interlace the society—from the local police to the F.B.I. and loyalty commissions, from the parking meter to the immigration station. On the other side, we are confronted with numerous evidences of instability and rapid change in the personal relations and group memberships of individuals, not only in the casual flux of urban recreation and in formalized special-interest associations and "social" groupings but also in marriage and the family, in residence groups, and in class-typed social circles. It seems, therefore, that outside the sway of the relatively rigid and centralized association, very large areas of life are characterized by shifting and comparatively formless interaction.

Between the chaos of fragmented diversity or of anomic atomization of social relationships and the enforced unity of a totalitarian order lies the ground of enduring groups and relationships that provide security adequate for individual gratifications and achievements and flexibility sufficient to allow adaptation to changing conditions. The implied golden mean can be clearly defined, but its attainment is rare and precarious in any society.

We cannot here essay anything like a comprehensive appraisal of the

---

[7] Which is not to say that those who so speak always understand the real meaning of the phrase; cf. Erikson, *op. cit.*

character of "mass behavior" as over against formalized organizations. We merely make the observation that the consequences of apparent instability and rapid change in social structure do *not* seem to carry the disorganizing impact in American society that would be anticipated from the observed experience of Gemeinschaftliche societies undergoing analogous instability. (This would be true at least up to the point at which violence, and reactions to it, might so disrupt the society as to render its delicate and largely unrecognized adjustive procedures ineffective.) *If* this judgment is correct, and to the degree that it is, one clue to an explanation would seem to lie in the presence in this society of numerous well elaborated patterns for coping with both social instability and changes in group memberships. To take only one prominent example, the whole system of vertical occupational mobility confronts the mobile individual with countless shifts in expectations and often with real and emotionally important changes in personality models, group memberships, and group identification. Withal, the *pattern* of mobility is expectable and expected. And—at least in the upward direction—there appear to be rather elaborate stylized mechanisms of withdrawal, alienation, entrance, and assimilation as the individual passes from one context to another. Analogous patterns seem to exist for the transitions of residential mobility. The very casualness, specificity, and impersonality of public contacts, we suggest, tends to insulate individuals from many conceivably traumatic consequences of unpredictability and misplaced expectations. Rigidity or flexibility, stability or change, predictability or its lack—these are, after all, *relative* notions. The most important fact, within quite wide limits, may not be the absolute amount of instability or change, but the *range of the expectable zone of variation.* Insofar as individuals in our society have been prepared to discount a marked degree of change and variation, their reduced expectations of permanence and stability permit acceptance and support of a society of "becoming" rather than "being."

## SUGGESTED READINGS

CAPLOW, THEODORE. *Principles of Organization.* New York: Harcourt, Brace & World, 1964. Treats organizations as a clearly bounded subset of systems. Particularly notable are the use of explicit models in predicting organizational behavior and the attempt to state relations among variables in the form of principles.

ETZIONI, AMITAI. *Modern Organizations.* Englewood Cliffs, N.J.: Prentice-Hall, 1964. Brief review of concepts and hypotheses dealing with complex formal organizations, drawing heavily from the author's own research. Uses typologies and several original conceptual distinctions.

HARE, A. PAUL, EDGAR F. BORGATTA, ROBERT F. BALES (eds.). *Small Groups: Studies in Social Interaction,* rev. ed. New York: Knopf, 1965. Careful selection of representative work on major topics in this field. Provides a solid basis for understanding the challenges to research, and anchors theory in dependable findings.

MARCH, JAMES G. (ed.). *Handbook of Organizations.* Chicago: Rand McNally, 1965. Wide-ranging collection of contributions from many of the best studies of organizations. Stimulating, informative. Best read in moderate-sized portions.

MILLS, THEODORE M. *The Sociology of Small Groups.* Englewood Cliffs, N.J.: Prentice-Hall, 1967. Distinctive in its approach but appreciative of the main stream of research. Clearly written. Likely to stimulate further thought about what goes on in "small groups."

THIBAUT, JOHN W., and HAROLD H. KELLEY. *The Social Psychology of Groups.* New York: Wiley, 1959. A seminal book, deserving of renewed attention. High ratio of ideas to pages. Clear grasp of structural properties of groups. Presents powerful hypotheses concerning basic sources of norms and other structural emergents of processes of interaction.

# Interrelations of Major Institutions and Social Groupings

## INTRODUCTION: SOME GENERAL CONSIDERATIONS

In the foregoing chapters, some attention necessarily has been given to the relations among various partially autonomous institutions; and it has been necessary from time to time to allude to social and cultural changes. But, in the interest of clarity, the analysis concentrated on one thing at a time and proceeded as if structure were a fixed state rather than a continually moving pattern, in order to arrive at a first approximation. We must now focus more sharply on the massive problem of institutional interrelationships. Our present questions are of this order: How are institution A and institution B connected? How does group X relate to group Y? How is norm 1 linked to norm 2, and this to still others? And what more extended and complex systems of interrelations exist, and how is it that the whole sociocultural structure operates as a going concern?

We are in this way returning to the primary question raised at the beginning of this book: How is it possible that more than 200 million human beings constitute a political entity and, in considerable measure, a recognizable culture? We cannot hope here to fully answer such a question but only to extend our understanding somewhat by systematic consideration of the problems involved.[1]

We will begin with a few quite general propositions:

1. *Both institutions and groups can be treated as systems.* A system is a definite arrangement of parts having boundaries and unity or cohesion, resisting external forces, and persisting through time. In this sense, the concept is used as in the physical sciences; and the facts of human behavior are conceptualized as a series of systems: personalities, relationships, groups, associations, institutions, societies, cultures.[2] Using systems

---

[1] Let us assert, once more, the great value of *comparative* studies—both of particular kinds of institutions and organizations and of total societies. See the author's "Recent Developments in Research on Social Institutions," *The Annals of the American Academy of Political and Social Science,* 374 (November 1967), 171–184; Robert Marsh, *Comparative Sociology* (New York: Harcourt, Brace & World, 1967); Richard L. Merrit and Stein Rokkan (eds.), *Comparing Nations: The Use of Quantitative Data in Cross-National Research* (New Haven: Yale University Press, 1966).

[2] Precedents for this approach are numerous, and the basic ideas have a very long history. Analysis focused on systemic connections among the components of total societies has

analysis, we can say that the family institution resists external forces (recognizing the elliptical nature of the statement, since concretely it is the individual *as a participant in* the institutional pattern who resists), or that an "economically rational" governmental policy is resisted because it "encroaches upon the rights of business," and so on. Such statements, of course, involve a very high order of abstraction and must be rigorously inspected; however, the emergent properties of groups and institutions are sufficiently well demonstrated to justify their analysis as real systems.

2. Institutions *are not completely separate or autonomous systems but show multiple interconnections and mutual dependencies.* Thus, the total society is constituted of various subsystems and their reciprocal linkages. Of course, not *all* structures or elements of any particular society are interrelated, and the existing interconnections vary tremendously in kind and importance; however, the search for interrelationships has already yielded enough knowledge to demonstrate the scientific value of treating a society as a system composed of multiple subsystems.

3. In any society, *the main institutions do not exhibit the qualities of a system in equal measure.* Where social patterning has developed to the point at which subsystems of institutionalized behavior are identifiable at all—and we know of no continuing societies so "simple" that this is impossible—some institutions will be more segregated, self-contained, outwardly resistant, and so on, than others. This has been demonstrated, if crudely, in studies indicating that cultural diffusion and social change are initially absorbed by the least structured portions of institutional systems. Thus, when Western industrialism and constitutional forms of government came to Japan in the nineteenth century, the results broadly taken, were (1) an assimilation of "capitalism" to the family system (rather than, as in the United States, an adaptation of the family *to* the economic institutions); (2) constitutional government took on strongly feudalistic features at the local level and a highly hierarchical centralized structure, organized on the principle of group responsibility, at the national level.[3] Speaking loosely

---

been much emphasized in the most recent decades. Examples go back to the brief discussion of "integration" in Ralph Linton's *The Study of Man* (New York: Appleton-Century-Crofts, 1936), chap. 20 and Robert M. MacIver's *Society* (New York: Long and Smith, 1931), chaps. 10–12; see also Robert M. MacIver and Charles H. Page, *Society* (New York: Holt, Rinehart and Winston, 1949), chaps. 18–20. It is pointed out by Eliot D. Chapple and Carleton S. Coon that functional interdependence can be demonstrated only from observation of systems undergoing *change*. *Principles of Anthropology* (New York: Holt, Rinehart & Winston, 1942), p. 462. Pitirim A. Sorokin, *Society, Culture, and Personality* (New York: Harper & Row, 1947) continually emphasizes the idea of interconnected systems in both the social and cultural fields. From a radically different perspective, George C. Homans analyzes the small group as a system in *The Human Group* (New York: Harcourt, Brace & World, 1950). Major attention to system problems characterizes the many works of Talcott Parsons, e.g., *The Social System* (New York: Free Press, 1951); *Societies* (Englewood Cliffs, N.J.: Prentice-Hall, 1966). Books explicitly concerned with the concept of social systems are numerous; note such different examples as: Charles P. Loomis, *Social Systems, Essays on Their Persistence and Change* (Princeton, N.J.: Van Nostrand, 1960); Walter Buckley, *Sociology and Modern Systems Theory* (Englewood Cliffs, N.J.: Prentice-Hall, 1967).

3 Morris E. Opler, "Japan: The West of the East?" *Patterns for Modern Living, Division 3, Cultural Patterns* (Chicago: The Delphian Society, 1950); John F. Embree, *The*

but not incorrectly, we would regard this as a case in which the combined kinship-stratification systems proved to be more rigid than the indicated economic and political arrangements.

4. Contrary to all theoretical systems that posit the universal dominance of a particular institution, for example, the economic, *the central or leading institution(s) varies from society to society in a given period, and from one period to another in a given society.* Further, there may not in fact be any one clearly dominant institutional system. The easy literary labeling of whole epochs, itself in part a culture-bound product of Western history, can create the impression that one era or society is wholly "religious," another overwhelmingly "economic," but this is an imposed, poetic unity, not a description of the actual multiplicity of institutional systems and group contexts.

It is as easy to state the logical and operational criteria for establishing the degree to which one institution predominates in a society as it is difficult to find the required data. A first approach to the problem is the controlled observation of *change.* If we find that changes in institution A are invariably followed by important changes in institutions B . . . n but that changes in institutions B . . . n are followed by few or insignificant changes in institution A, then A is presumably a "prime mover" or dominant vector in the social system. Such a clear-cut situation does not exist empirically, but *degrees of variation* in several interconnected institutions are, in principle, subject to observations testing such causal salience according to the model just outlined. A second and more specific procedure for appraising dominance consists of systematic observation of what occurs when *various sets* of *institutional norms conflict* in particular situations. If particular norms, conceived as part of institution A, always or in some preponderant proportion take precedence over the *other* norms, this is a test of the extent to which one institutional complex is more predictive of behavior than others.[4] This abstract statement is translatable into terms as specific as whether an American businessman renounces the purchase of a new car in order to give aid to a needy relative, a religious body, or to reinvest in his business. When value conflicts and value priorities entail definitely institutionalized norms of social relations, we are following the shorthand practice of speaking in terms of conflicts and compatibilities of institutions. The next section will confront some of the specific senses in which institutions are related; here it is enough to emphasize that accuracy on this subject requires that *specified* normative systems, not "institutions

---

*Japanese Nation* (New York: Farrar, Straus & Giroux, 1945); George B. Sansom, *Japan: A Short Cultural History*, 2nd ed. (New York: Appleton-Century-Crofts, 1943); Charles B. Fahs, *Japanese Government: Recent Trends in Scope and Operation* (New York: Institute of Pacific Relations, 1940); Robert Bellah, *Tokugawa Religion* (New York: Free Press, 1957); James G. Abegglen, *The Japanese Factory* (New York: Free Press, 1958); Kunio Odaka, "The Middle Classes in Japan," in Reinhard Bendix and Seymour Martin Lipset (eds.), *Class, Status, and Power*, 2nd ed. (New York: Free Press, 1966), pp. 541–555.

[4] For an example of the use of highly informed judgments in making such diagnosis: Robert L. Heilbronner, "The Future of Capitalism," *Commentary*, 4, 4 (April 1966), 23–35.

in general," be kept clearly in view. Even so, it is by no means simple to determine when certain norms are, or are not, "compatible." For one thing, the content accessible at a commonsense level quite often conceals and is at variance with less obvious functional patterns, for example, the way nepotism in government becomes loyalty in the family. Again, a particular norm or value does not have an absolute meaning in social action but depends upon *relations in a context,* for example, occupational duties that might seem *a priori* to be incompatible with stable family life can be transvalued as part of a total scheme of living, so that "job" and "home" do not compete but rather mutually reinforce a pattern of activity which is valued *as a whole.* Furthermore, institutional patterns that seem logically in conflict are very often not involved in the same specific roles, groups, or situations, so that social action results in little or no conflict: for example, the same groups may hold simultaneously that government should stay out of business, protect the home market, force the "chislers" to maintain prices, and regulate the labor unions.

From these considerations, another general rule can be derived: *institutional interrelations can be deduced only to a very limited and uncertain extent from the apparent content of cultural norms.* Therefore, before high-level generalizations can be derived in this area, specific norms and values must be empirically traced through specific social roles and social groups.[5] Fortunately, a rapidly increasing accumulation of studies represents deliberate attempts to analyze a well-defined *point of intersection* of major institutions. For instance, many studies show that social class background is strongly related to pupils' performance in school; a comparative study of five nations finds that authoritarian patterns of parental dominance are negatively associated with the likelihood that children will continue their education into secondary school;[6] a comparison of twelve nations indicates that neither the large size of a society nor of its markets will produce a high degree of division of labor unless there is a relatively high development of technology.[7]

We are beginning to see specific attempts to estimate at least the *direction* and *relative magnitude* of total clusters of effects flowing from one institutional context to another. Thus, although it has been repeatedly shown that both educational level and occupation are strongly related to certain value-patterns, a recent study suggests that the effect of education is indirect: education is highly correlated with occupational level, and occupation is closely related to values.[8] Within the same occupational category,

---

[5] For this reason, the title of the present chapter brackets together institutions and social groupings.

[6] Glen H. Elder, Jr., "Family Structure and Educational Attainment: A Cross-National Analysis," *American Sociological Review,* 30, 1 (February 1965), 81–96.

[7] Jack P. Gibbs and Harley L. Browning, "The Division of Labor, Technology, and the Organization of Production in Twelve Countries," *American Sociological Review,* 31, 1 (February 1966), 81–92.

[8] Leonard I. Pearlin and Melvin L. Kohn, "Social Class, Occupation, and Parental Values: A Cross-National Study," *American Sociological Review,* 31, 4 (August 1966), 466–479.

however, education is only weakly associated with values, whereas, at any educational level, occupation strongly relates to values. The authors infer that it is occupational position rather than education which accounts for most of the variation in fathers' values.[9]

In many instances we will be able to infer highly important relations between institutions simply from the sheer facts of exchange or flow of resources or information. A notable case in point is the relationship between the political and the kinship sectors in American society through the Social Security programs: by means of Old Age, Survivors, Disability, and Health Insurance the federal government conveys "transfer" and "saving" payments to millions of families.[1] Although the exact effects upon living arrangements, authority patterns, and other aspects of intrakinship relations are not fully known, it is clear that important effects must exist.

The general question thus raised is How are the various institutions and correlative social structures connected with one another?

## HOW INSTITUTIONS ARE INTERRELATED

If the assumptions stated in the preceding section are to be useful for the empirical study of society, we must be able to specify the modes of interrelation in a testable form. If institutions are systems, causally or functionally connected with other systems, we must specify the mechanisms of linkage.

To begin with, we may set up the model of a social system in which institutions are not embodied in clearly defined associations or groups but are merely norm complexes to which the behavior of all members of the society is oriented. In such a case, to put it somewhat oversimply, institutions would be *facts of culture and of personality*, not *differentiated social structures* within the society. There would be definite norms, and these would be institutional, in our sense, but they would neither be labeled as separate institutions nor carried in special organizations. No actual society is so little differentiated. Even in small nonliterate groups, subsisting by gathering and hunting, there is some organizational precipitate of institutional norms, such as a more or less autonomous family structure, or a shaman, or a rudimentary chieftainship. In reference to such societies, however, it is initially difficult to think of institutional interrelations because the connections appear almost selfevident. The members of the society may not and usually do not think of separate religious, familial, economic, or political activities; they simply carry out their daily activities, that we, as outside observers see as a web of behavior controlled by norms that we would call institutional. In the course of a lifetime, any particular individual

---

[9] *Ibid.*, p. 478.

[1] See Leonore A. Epstein and Janet H. Murray, *The Aged Population of the United States*, U.S. Department of Health, Education, and Welfare, Research Report No. 19 (Washington, D.C.: Government Printing Office, 1967). Basic current data are published monthly in the *Social Security Bulletin*; for example, in January 1968 the total number of beneficiaries under OASDI was 23.8 million.

will participate in all these nonnucleated[2] institutions; for the most part there are no specialized personnel to maintain specific institutional subsystems. To the degree that this is the situation, *interinstitutional* relations are largely synonymous with *intrapersonality* adjustments: the integration of institutions occurs through the mechanisms of personalities. This does not imply that all personalities are alike, even in the most simple societies; on the contrary, the range of personality differences always is substantial. The point is, rather, that the relations among institutions are mediated by intrapsychic means, not structurally. In his various statuses the individual functions in terms of ideas, beliefs, values, and norms defining his relations to other persons; and his total activity, therefore, requires the resolution of conflicting norms or beliefs that may occur in specific situations; any "strain for consistency," however, would be the adjustment of individual actors scattered through the system as a whole.

However, this model of a society with unspecialized institutions does not fit actual cases; even at a tribal level, societies exhibit considerable specialization of institutions. Certain activities are segregated and responsibility for them assigned to chiefs, medicine men, and so on; and specialized norms develop to regulate these statuses. Each of these normative subsystems as they develop in a small society may be represented by only a few persons or a single person. In a larger society with more definite specialization, such status systems typically become the basis for definite organizations composed of specially designated personnel. Whenever specialization appears, relations between institutions become relations of groups, organizations, or social categories *mediated through the direct person-to-person interaction of individuals occupying differentiated statuses.* This is a mode of connection very familiar to us—the minister consults the mayor, the parent interacts with the teacher, the banker talks with the legislator. Back of the interacting principals are the respective "constituencies" (parishioners, or family members, or voters, and so on) who comprise reference groups for the institutional representatives. Of course, the intrapersonality adjustments continue, and remain important, at this level of structural segregation also.[3] The new element here is the direct interrelation of specialized roles, representing partly autonomous normative systems.[4]

An obvious secondary elaboration of this pattern is the development of chains of mediated interaction—from institution A to B, and thence to C and D—as when the minister intercedes with the judge on the behalf of a youthful offender to have the latter remanded to the school, which in turn

2 The term is from F. Stuart Chapin, *Contemporary American Institutions* (New York: Harper & Row, 1935); see esp. pp. 13 ff. We are here borrowing the term for a more restricted usage.

3 This is demonstrated by studies of personality in relation to culture and social system. For example: Daniel R. Miller and Guy E. Swanson, *The Changing American Parent* (New York: Wiley, 1958); John J. Honigmann, *Culture and Personality* (New York: Harper & Row, 1954); J. W. Whiting and I. L. Child, *Child Training and Personality* (New Haven, Conn.: Yale University Press, 1953); Talcott Parsons and Robert F. Bales, *Family, Socialization, and Interaction Process* (New York: Free Press, 1955).

4 Theodore D. Kemper, "Third Party Penetration of Local Social Systems," *Sociometry*, 31, 1 (March 1968), 1–29.

deals with the family. Various still more complicated structural variations arise out of such mediated or tangential relations. Thus, the Supreme Court in our political system is a complex mediating agency that deals with problems involving every major institution of the society.

What we are directly observing here is still the concrete behavior of individual persons, from which, we must remember, institutions are abstracted—just as personality systems or groups are inferred from similarly concrete behavior. These abstracted systems are not arbitrary; they are necessary to account for observed properties of conduct. Here, as always, we are interested in *differences*: what difference does it make if institutional norm complexes are, or are not, incorporated into separate systems of social organization;[5] and, if there are relatively autonomous institutional systems, what relations subsist among them? For example, it can be noted quickly that an outstanding feature of modern American society is the extraordinarily sharp separation of institutions, at the *social* level. Each institutional cluster in our society *tends* to be segregated from others and to involve distinctive statuses occupied by specialized personnel. The common tendency to equate religion with the church, education with the school, politics with government is partly based on the recognition of such distinct systems of activities, beliefs, knowledges, values, and symbols. *One* aspect of this differentiation and segregation is that individuals are involved in multiple statuses and multiple group memberships; we are thus familiar with role segmentation and also with the fairly common situations in which there is some type of conflict of roles or group memberships. Another feature of the situation is perhaps less often noted in its full significance, namely, the orientation of individuals in one status or group to *other* statuses or groups, as with the orientation of the teacher *as educator* to the parent *qua* parent. Even the most highly specialized statuses are not related only to similar statuses but to different statuses located in separate groups or associations. Under certain conditions, those occupying a similar status may form an organization that interacts *as a system* with a body whose members are persons holding a polar status in a two-sided relation: for example, workers who comprise a labor union which deals with employers. Group relations carried on by "representatives" have special characteristics, differing from those of informal person-to-person interactions. And in a highly complex structure, there is still another organizational level comprised of mediating and coordinating systems, represented by role specialists in their own partly independent groups or associations.

The intention here is to treat institutions as main structural components of social systems and to regard a social system as a network of "flows" or "exchanges" among social units. Institutions define the units of the system, the channels of influence, and the rules of allocation and decision. The

[5] For clarity, we must avoid the confusion of identifying *institutions* (as distinctive normative-sets) with *organizations* (as bounded clusterings of interactions). For example, one should read Buckley (*op. cit.*) in full awareness that the book essentially equates the concept "institution" with "large-scale" organization (e.g., pp. 128–129). Here we are concerned primarily with studies that analyze normative systems, whether or not the obligatory norms are specific to any concrete group or large-scale organization.

units among which interactions occur are concretely specifiable as, for example, individuals, households, labor unions, business firms, churches, schools, voluntary associations, delinquent and criminal gangs, and units of government. The flows consist of (1) consummatory goods and services, (2) instrumental goods and services, (3) personnel, and (4) "messages." For many purposes, it is useful to analyze aggregative as well as unit-to-unit flows; the former may have properties not easily detectable at the levels of the concrete unit.[6] In addition to the immediate influences arising from direct communication from one institutional sector to another, there are complex or indirect-mediated influences. Thus, a particular political system may so affect adult members of the society that they are led or instigated to use certain methods of child rearing rather than others; these childhood disciplines in turn, may generate belief and attitude conducive to acceptance of one type of religious belief system rather than some other type. For instance, there is some evidence indicating that societies with beliefs in aggressive supernatural beings are more likely than those with beliefs in benevolent deities or spirits to have punitive or hurtful practices of treating infants and are also more likely to reward their children for self-reliance and independence and to punish for the absence of behavior having these qualities.[7] Although the direction of causation is not given by the mere fact of correlation, there are many macroscopic studies in which the *fact* of interinstitutional connections is clearly demonstrated. Thus, as we may recall from Chapter IX, Swanson's study showed that a belief system containing a high god almost always appears in societies having four or more levels of "sovereign groups."[8] The same author subsequently has strongly reinforced the hypothesis that the political system affects the religious system: in forty-one European societies, the religious changes of the Reformation (from 1490 to 1780) universally found acceptance in societies with prior political regimes in which authority derived from compromises among interest groupings or from a limited or "balanced" central regime; societies with a strong centralized monarchy or governing elite almost always remained Catholic.[9]

As the cultural fact of institutionalization is translated into special areas of organized interaction, the *organization* (the church, capitalistic enterprise, and so on) may develop considerable autonomy in relation to the values and norms of other institutionalized organizations; and this development, indeed, has taken place on a vast scale in the United States.[1] With

[6] Williams, "Recent Developments in Research on Social Institutions," *op. cit.*, p. 172.

[7] William W. Lambert, Leigh Minturn Triandis, and Margery Wolf, "Some Correlates of Beliefs in the Malevolence and Benevolence of Supernatural Beings: A Cross-Societal Study," *Journal of Abnormal and Social Psychology*, 58, 2 (March 1959), 162–169.

[8] Guy E. Swanson, *The Birth of the Gods* (Ann Arbor: University of Michigan Press, 1960).

[9] Guy Edward Swanson, *Religion and Regime* (Ann Arbor: University of Michigan Press, 1967).

[1] As Chapter VI indicated, a crucial instance was the partial "escape" in periods of laissez faire of economic activity from the control systems of local community, church, and government.

the growth in scale of the whole society, there have been general tendencies for those organized structures to become larger, more complex, more centralized in control. As this occurs, in such a highly interdependent society, the numerous interactions of large and elaborately organized systems frequently lead to "institutional imperialism" as one system seems to "encroach" upon another.

It has been shown, then, that institutions may be interconnected through *intrapersonality responses* to different norms and values, through the *direct interaction of role specialists*, through *mediated relations* involving several institutions[2] and through *indirect effects* resulting from impacts upon personality functioning.

American society has gone very far in the creating of definite organizations with specialized personnel to carry on activities culturally assigned to the institutional areas broadly distinguished in earlier chapters. The general significance of this process is that *different individuals* and *different organizations* are the prime carriers of the various sets of norms which otherwise would be partial systems of the same personalities or overlapping roles in a relatively undifferentiated community. Perhaps it could be shown that kinship and social stratification are, in the present sense, the least specialized institutions, since they are relatively diffuse, nonnucleated systems, permeating a very wide range of actions; but even in these two cases there are many areas of relatively sharp separation and insulation.

"Strains" in the interrelations of institutions appear as: (1) intrapersonality conflicts resulting from incompatible roles and statuses and from incompatible role-sets and status-sets,[3] and the resulting responses to these conflicts; (2) social conflict, either of *associations* or "communal" groups (for example, ethnic groupings). These conflicts, as a matter of fact, furnish some of the clearest indications that we actually are dealing with real systems.[4]

Finally, institutions are related through processes not involving person-to-person interaction, either directly or through specialized representatives. These are the processes Karl Mannheim designates as "field structures:" recurring mass influences transmitted through the society as segmental reactions of individuals to common stimuli: mass propaganda, changes in interest rates or wages, unemployment. These diffusely received influences are highly relevant to institutional stability *and* to institutional change. *In present-day society, a great deal of the linkage between and among institutional sectors is mediated through mass communication.* Leaders and spokes-

[2] In these terms, a "simple" society would be defined as one in which unmediated relations dominated.

[3] Two theoretical treatments provide an excellent basis for analysis of these matters: William J. Goode. "A Theory of Role Strain," *American Sociological Review*, 25, 4 (August 1960), 483–496; Robert K. Merton, "The Role Set: Problems in Sociological Theory," *The British Journal of Sociology*, VIII, 2 (June 1957), 106–120.

[4] For the specific complex interplay of communal and associational elements in struggles at the local level see Robert L. Crain, *et al.*, *The Politics of School Desegregation: Comparative Case Studies of Community Structure and Policy Making* (Chicago: Aldine, 1968).

men in government, business,[5] unions, education, or religion explain and persuade through television, radio, advertisements, and mass-circulation newspapers, magazines, books, pamphlets, and so on. The received messages flow along the interconnected pathways of primary groups and leadership patterns.[6]

These five patterns seem to be the most important forms of institutional linkage and reciprocal effect. We will now illustrate how the approach suggested here may be applied—in studies of kinship, political and economic institutions, and science and education in relation to the polity—to the contemporary American scene. The treatment is necessarily excursive since rigorous analysis would require a synthesis of basic research beyond the scope of this book.

### SELECTED CASE STUDIES OF INSTITUTIONAL INTERRELATIONS

*Case #1: Kinship in the Web of Institutions*

Several suggestions as to the place of kinship relations and family groups in the society have already been advanced (especially in Chapters IV and V). For example, there is the proposition that our industrial and commercial order, with its great specialization and rapid change, favors the small, isolated, discontinuous, nuclear family of neolocal residence. By the same token, this type of family system is encouraged by high rates of vertical social mobility.

The converse propositions also hold. Thus, a system of strong extended kinship relations may be expected to be a partial barrier to the free mobility of labor and economic resources from one geographic area or line of production to another. And the greater the importance of kinship in the total social structure[7] the more likely it is that social strata will be rigid and social mobility low. Such a society will also tend to be traditionalistic in other major respects, for example, in religion, education, government, and to deemphasize and resist social change. At the same time, the larger the areas of social relations defined in terms of kinship, the more likely it is that the dominant norms in *other* institutions will be particularistic rather than uni-

---

5 For an analysis of the statements of business leaders, see Francis X. Sutton, Seymour Harris, Carl Kaysen, and James Tobin, *The American Business Creed* (Cambridge, Mass.: Harvard University Press, 1956).

6 John W. Riley, Jr. and Matilda White Riley, "Mass Communication and the Social System," in Robert K. Merton, Leonard Broom, Leonard S. Cottrell, Jr. (eds.), *Sociology Today* (New York: Basic Books, 1959), pp. 537–578; Bernard Berelson and Gary A. Steiner, *Human Behavior* (New York: Harcourt, Brace & World, 1964), pp. 527–585; Lewis Anthony Dexter and David Manning White (eds.), *People, Society, and Mass Communications* (New York: Free Press, 1964), esp. pp. 29–201 and 337–409.

7 By "greater importance" we mean: a higher proportion of individual interactions with persons who are "relatives," or otherwise stated, a higher percentage of all social relations which are culturally defined by the facts of marriage and descent. There are other useful operational indexes, such as inventories of choice behavior, of expressed norms, of patterns of mutual aid among relatives, of legal priorities, of occupational apprenticeship in family contexts. For useful research findings, see Bert N. Adams, *Kinship in an Urban Setting* (Chicago: Markham, 1968), esp. pp. 30–32, 131–134, 176–178.

versalistic: the stranger will tend to be outside the sphere of morality, unless he can be assimilated to a kinship status; law and justice will tend to be conceived in terms of *particular* statuses; an especially sharp distinction is likely between ingroups and outgroups. It is also less likely that other types of relations, for example, economic, will be functionally specific—as it is sometimes said, kinship is fundamentally opposed to contract. Or, to turn to political structures, such societies appear especially likely to have hierarchical governing structures built upon local segmental groups. On the other side, the lack of a strong centralized government is often associated with marked development of family authority and with a salient role for kinship in the regulative order of the entire society.[8] Where kinship groups are strong, extended, and stable in dominantly rural societies, we often find that the organization of the state is a sort of film on the surface of the society, failing to penetrate directly to the mass of individuals. One notes also that modern revolutionary totalitarian movements seem initially to invade the family in many respects, for example, encouraging children to inform on their parents.

Part of the much discussed "invasion" of the family unit by other parts of the society is the redefinition of family values and norms themselves as a consequence of recurrent—often nearly continuous—exposure to standards of consumption purveyed by the mass media; standards of physical and mental health and of child rearing and marital relations espoused by physicians, nurses, teachers, social workers, dieticians, and other professional workers; standards of intergenerational relations produced in peer groups of youths; and so on. As Otto Pollak puts it: *"The function which truly has been taken away from the family by other institutions is not education, health care, or homemaking, but the autonomy of setting its own standards."*[9]

These illustrations indicate that the place of kinship in American social structure is actually a special case of interrelations requiring wider examination. The important question for the study of the total ramifications of kinship can be put specifically: How and to what extent is the fact of relation by birth or marriage socially utilized in defining and regulating activities outside the immediate system of the family itself? From this way of raising the problem there follow innumerable further and more specific questions. For example:

Who "owns" property? Who transmits it to whom, and how?

Who or what cares for and supports dependent persons, the very young, the aged, the ill, the disabled?

Who nurtures, supports, disciplines, instructs, and provides models for children, adolescents, and young adults?

[8] Cf. Carle C. Zimmerman, *Family and Civilization* (New York: Harper & Row, 1947), p. 14: "The abundance of law and order agencies and the multiplicity of external bonds holding societies together during the periods of statute law and strongly developed central governments made the internal cohesion of family groups less and less necessary as a unified social force."

[9] Otto Pollak, "The Outlook for the American Family," *Journal of Marriage and the Family*, 29, 1 (February 1967), 194.

Where, how, and by whom are religious rites performed? Is there other domestic religious observance?

What is the part of kinship units in economic production?

To what extent and how is kinship a criterion for or advantage in securing political power?

To what extent is trade divorced from kinship ties and obligations?

How permeable, and in what respects, is the family unit to actions of persons outside the kinship status-system?

To continue with the last question, we have previously diagnosed the modal American family type as permeable to external influences, both culturally and in actual interaction patterns. As will be recalled, the legal order penetrates into family solidarity by a vast number of provisions which assign *individual*, not family group, responsibilities and rights, as, for example, in limiting parents' rights to control and discipline children.

From similar indications we have concluded that the kinship system plays a *relatively* dependent part in the total institutional structure, especially as related to the economic and political areas. It is perhaps in these areas that we have the most convenient access to further clues as to dynamic interconnections.

Kinship plays into the economic structure, in the first place, through *occupation*. By definition, kinship is particularistic in its basic pattern; it is the basic area of status ascription and the primary orientation is to "*who you are*," not what you are or can do. In contrast, the occupational structure in our society is much more universalistic—the central criteria concern abilities and capacities and achievements, rather than status tests (family membership; who needs the job, and so on). From these two propositions, it follows that since an emphasis upon occupation as a primary determinant of social station necessarily implies a lessened role for kinship, a reduction in the size and scope of the basic family unit becomes a meaningful consequence of our elaborately differentiated occupational structure. This has just been stated as a formal deduction from the definitions given. But much evidence supports the conclusion that the small-family system results in part from competitive occupational placement in a dynamic economy, as when economic changes force families to disperse. Competitive occupational placement seems to strain family solidarity, creating pressures both toward reduction in size and toward insulating certain family roles from the competitive matrix.[1] The absence of the worker from home and family during his occupational activity—or, more drastic, his absence through desertion occasioned by unemployment or partial employment—has as one consequence for family structure the mother-centered pattern of child training and the lack of an occupational apprenticeship of sons to the father. Whatever degree of father-son discontinuity is thus introduced is reinforced by rapid changes in occupational opportunity (as well as by the pattern of upward social mobility). Still more generally, the removal of economic production from the home radically affects the total pattern of family rela-

[1] See the more detailed discussion in Chapter IV.

tions. It would seem that the most important fact is not the loss of economic functions as such but the reduction in intrafamily interaction centered upon purposeful common goals and involving numerous shared understandings, expectations, disciplines, and affective patterns. As has already been noted, another factor here is the functionless place of many aged persons in the family system, due in part to the demand for relatively young workers.

The instability of the economic system has periodically subjected family solidarity to severe strains. But here we note that the same mass impact, for example, unemployment, is *not* followed by a simple and undifferentiated change in family units. The limited available evidence indicates that unemployment intensifies the previously established latent structure of the family unit; that is, strongly solidary families tend to retain their unity best, disunited families become more disunited.[2] In any case, a major alteration in economic opportunity, for urban workers without property, sets off changes in the balance of reciprocal roles and expectations within the family unit.[3]

Family structure is always one of a mutually dependent set of variables in the concrete character of an economic situation. For example, in some parts of the Southern Appalachians a family system developed, through the nineteenth and early twentieth centuries, in which extended kin relations were strong, intergeneration continuity was relatively great, sex roles well defined, birth rates high. Under conditions of limited agricultural resources, comparatively limited emigration, and the dominance of the principle of equality of siblings in inheritance, the initial result was a rapid parcelization of the land. As the family system was perpetuated—in isolation from deviant cultural patterns—the subdivision of farms reached a stage at which steeper and less productive lands were cleared for cultivation. With the existing technology, this led to severe soil erosion and other depletions of agricultural resources. This threat to the standard of living developed during a period of lessened cultural isolation, which made for awareness of outside employment opportunities, as well as of new market goods obtainable only through money expenditures. One consequence of all these factors was an increase in migration of young people from the area. Migration, in turn, reacted back upon the family in a number of ways, for example, youth-parent conflict, the development of something like a system of ultimogeniture. Without following the complex sequence further, this case points to the kinds of data needed to analyze the dynamics of social interdependence in reasonably specific terms.

Kinship ties, like many other forms of established social relations, can constitute a very definite obstacle to the economic rationalization of production, as when, in some cases, family rights and obligations have so penetrated business enterprises that inefficient relatives may be given crucial jobs, or capital needed for technological changes may be siphoned off into

[2] Mirra Komarovsky, *The Unemployed Man and His Family* (New York: Dryden Press, 1940), pp. xii, 24 ff.

[3] Cf. E. Wight Bakke, *The Unemployed Man* (New York: Dutton, 1934) and, by the same author, *Citizens Without Work* (New Haven, Conn.: Yale University Press, 1940), esp. chaps. 8–9; Mirra Komarovsky, *Blue Collar Marriage* (New York: Random House, 1962), chap. 13.

consumption within the extended family. We have already suggested that values or obligations developed in the family can retard economically adjustive mobility. Perhaps the most striking fact about the American situation, however, is precisely the relatively slight role of familial institutions in these respects.[4] Although, as noted in Chapter IV, kinship linkages remain important in urban America, the "linkages" often are quite loose and flexible. In a study of kin networks in a small Southern city, Bert Adams found that less than 6 percent of the sample population had received help from relatives in getting started occupationally.[5] At the same time, awareness of specific secondary relatives was present in 90 percent of the cases; and the kin of orientation are objects of continued contact, concern, ritual, enjoyment, and occasional exchange or aid. But kin relationships constitute open and changeable networks rather than firm and fixed groups; and economic-occupational values typically have priority over familistic values in "altering subjective relations between the kin of orientation."[6]

We also know that the family group is a basic medium for the actual definition of economic "needs" and "motives." Thus, it is now certain that older theories that found the key to economic incentive in some sort of egoistic self-interest are quite inadequate: men, in our society as well as in others, typically work not merely for themselves but for an actual or potential family group. The task alone does not supply the incentives for work. The values, and correlative disciplines, involved in family living are different from those of nonfamily living. This is manifest in different consumption and saving patterns: and *different* family structures similarily carry variant economic implications. In the inadequately charted field of the economics of consumption, the peculiarities of American family systems may eventually find a very tangible place. One may note such possible clues as the individualization of buying and consumption, the role of women as purchasers, the partial replacement of familial activities in the home by commercialized recreation, the budgetary and market implications of status patterns, the shifts in demand schedules with those changes in the demographic situation resulting from changes in family norms.

To continue following kinship through the institutional systems of the society, let us examine briefly a few of the more obvious connections between family and political structures. The first salient point here is that our political norms *tend* to eliminate kinship as a direct basis for political power. Not ascribed status, but elective or appointive office is the dominant institutional mode,[7] for example, the commonplace rules against nepotism. However,

---

[4] An important exception is the part played by kinship units in the control and transmission of great wealth.

[5] Adams, *op. cit.*, p. 132. "The general picture is . . . [that] the more active and apparently satisfactory relations between the kin of orientation are predicated upon a minimum of direct involvement—as kin—in other societal systems."

[6] *Ibid.*, p. 174.

[7] Elements of ascription, of course, affect the achievement of political power, chiefly through the role of the family in fixing membership in ethnic, racial, or religious categories. However, this is by no means a simple case of kinship ascription—note, for instance that the distinctions in question are *categorical* rather than a matter of specific family

we have seen that while, at first glance, our culture seems to insulate government from family, the reverse is not true—the state intervenes on a large scale in the regulation of the family. Nor is the family system completely passive in the face of governmental claims—witness the interesting case in which the military establishment rescinded a new policy of bringing back to the United States the family dependents of servicemen stationed in other countries. The policy was established for economic and political reasons—to check the outflow of dollars—but the possible political impact of the "moral outrage" summoned up by the threatened disruption of family units proved too high a cost.[8]

The federal, state, and local governments of the United States exercise legal or administrative controls over an extraordinary range of matters directly related to marriage, family, and kinship. Consider this small sample: regulation of sexual relations, qualifications for marriage, control of juvenile delinquency, divorce and separation, abortion, birth control, adoption, education, inheritance, health, illegitimacy, economic support of dependent kin, employment of children and women, insurance and retirement, military conscription, tax exemptions, and family allowances. Each of these areas is rich in controversy and clash of values, and the changing emphases in law and governmental practice with regard to support, guidance, control, and protection of familial autonomy reflect incessant and often dramatic struggles.[9]

At the basic level of personality formation, the family unit is itself a miniature government, as Robert MacIver, Charles Merriam, Harold Lasswell, and others have pointedly reminded us. The primary conceptions of authority and patterns of response to authority are initially established in parent-child relations. All parents everywhere must, by virtue of their status, demand some conformity from young children. The way in which the child responds to parental authority supplies the base upon which successively modified reactions to authority and power relations are later developed. This does not imply a mechanical or automatic "carry-over." The notion that adult responses to political figures are simple *recapitulations* of childhood relations to parents or siblings is contradicted by the impressive evidence for the situational determination of conduct. The American family system tends, broadly, to minimize parental coercion and unquestioning obedience and to stress sibling equality. To *the degree that* this is the case, the familial norms would seem to be congruent with a democratic political system.[1] A comparative perspective wide enough to include China, Japan,

lines and that even the present factual situation is very far from complete institutionalization.

[8] Cf. Eugene Litwak, "Extended Kin Relations in an Industrial Democratic Society," in Ethel Shanas and Gordon F. Streib (eds.), *Social Structure and the Family: Generational Relations* (Englewood Cliffs, N.J.: Prentice-Hall, 1965), pp. 306–307.

[9] Cf. Samuel Mencher, "Social Authority and the Family," *Journal of Marriage and the Family*, 29, 1 (February 1967), 164–192. "Although there still remains sensitivity to the autonomy of the family, there has been a great growth of state authority in the affairs of the family during the past half-century" (p. 129).

[1] *But* note that the basic form of the American state was laid down in a period when family structure was much more "patriarchal" than now.

and Germany raises the hypothesis that the dominant family patterns in our society are relatively unfavorable to coercive authority. In urban, middle-class families there are widespread patterns of child training that seem to encourage the questioning of suggestions or commands: the child comes to ask "why" rather than to comply "because Father says so." At the same time, it is likely that the infrequent use of coercive authority by parents makes it seem all the more arbitrary when it does occur. Whether or not such "permissive" child-rearing is consistent with later willingness to accept as necessary the existence of political authority and the use of military force is a question of social and sociological importance.

The foregoing discussion may be described as disciplined speculation, recording at the level of hypothesis this sampling of possible intrapersonality connections between family institutions and political authority, in the absence of evidence needed to support more systematic analysis.

The relations between kinship and social stratification cannot here receive much analysis beyond that given in earlier chapters. We have indicated that kinship can affect stratification positions at the one extreme by defining the actual *unit* of ranking in the stratification order; but, on the other hand, it may be given little weight as a criterion of stratification position. To the degree that kinship is minimized in the determination of ranking, the way is opened for development of stratification systems in which position is based upon the achievements and qualities of individuals.[2]

The most obvious—and most crucial—connection between kinship and stratification, as institutional systems, is to be seen at the point of intergeneration transmission of position. The central fact here is that *insofar as family membership is a direct criterion of class position the whole effect is to perpetuate indefinitely the status quo ante;* where family determines class the result is to freeze the stratification system into a rigid mold. Conversely, a system of stratification based solely upon personal achievement would be incompatible with the family as we know it. For then there could be no hereditary transmission of status, and kinship groups would have to become atomized in this aspect. To the extent that family groups are social units they usually generate forces tending toward the use of kinship as an institutionalized criterion of position in the stratification scale. In American society the relatively slight emphasis on kinship as a criterion of class position militates against family continuity—and thereby is functional for a mobile open-class system stressing personal achievement as a primary criterion. In this aspect, the "weakness" so often deplored in the American kinship institutions is integrative with the cultural principles of upward social mobility through individual occupational achievement. This is another way of saying that a kinship system with strong intergeneration continuity would be incompatible with the fluidity of social classes that has been one of the remarkable features of America in the past. The one large-scale exception to the principle of individual achievement as the basis for ranking is that

2 It is *not* inevitable that low stress on kinship will lead to an individualistic system of stratification. At least in the short run it is possible that membership in nonkinship groups (for example, political party organizations, cliques, etc.) could be utilized for the assignation of status, relatively apart from personal qualities and achievements of individuals.

of position assigned or ascribed on the basis of membership in a distinctive racial or ethnic group. The significant consequence here is precisely the tension, conflict, and moral unease that this kind of ascribed status arouses in our society—striking evidence of the difficulty of integrating an open-class system with the use of particularistic criteria of stratification.

## Case #2: Economic and Political Institutions—the Problem of Control

Here we confront an area of clamor and the clash of arms. There is a "Marxian" definition, and a "Fascist" definition, and a variety of other views that clearly go beyond causal analysis to evaluate the ends or values to be served by economic and political arrangements. Here we will assume both that certain ends are attainable under all of the currently controversial systems and that some ends that are attainable under one system are not in others. Our task is not to evaluate these alternatives but to seek additional clarification of the evolving structural alignments in the American case. In a field where so much ideological conflict and confusion exist it may be useful to make quite explicit the elementary propositions from which we start:

1. Political power and economic activity are universal institutional systems, and the two are never completely independent.
2. Political authority never includes all social power, and nominally economic relations always have power implications.
3. Both political and economic institutions are affected by other institutions and operate within a wider societal framework.
4. Some normative definition and regulation of economic activity is present in every society; social controversy arises over the amount and kind of regulation—it is not a simple matter of "regimentation" versus "freedom."

During recent decades there has been an apparently widespread belief that governmental intervention is a recent innovation in American life. Although the nature and extent of the state's role in economic affairs has certainly changed drastically, even since World War I, the belief that governmental intervention—whether support or regulation—is really new is an illusion. The governments of large and complex social orders have always actively dealt with economic behavior.[3] Inevitably, under any set of conditions yet known to history, the role of the state tends to become larger as the economic system becomes more complex. The more specialization of production, the more *interdependent* an economy becomes. And the larger the units of economic production and exchange, under conditions of great specialization and technological complexity, the more crucial this interde-

---

[3] "There has never been in the history of civilized nations an economic system in which governments were not used to regulate individual action and to carry on certain economic activities directly, and it is equally true that there has never been an economic system in which some reliance was not placed on the initiative of private individuals." Leverett S. Lyon, Myron W. Watkins, and Victor Abramson, *Government and Economic Life*, Vol. I (Washington, D.C.: The Brookings Institution, 1939), p. 11.

pendence is for the integration of the whole society. No state—whatever political label it may wear—can or will ignore this fact.

In present circumstances the *political* implications of economic activity have become increasingly evident. The interpenetration and mutual relations of economic activity and political power extend into levels that are not easily visible and can only be discerned by analysis of great difficulty and complexity, requiring, among other things, initial care in the specification of concepts. In Chapter VI, it was found convenient to treat economic institutions as those interrelated clusters of normative rules and values that most directly govern the allocation of scarce means to alternative ends. Action is purely economic action insofar as it is guided by the attempt to maximize utility by applying given resources to those uses costing least in terms of their returns.

It is useful to follow Max Weber in distinguishing *economic* action, in the above sense, from *economically relevant* action and from *economically conditioned* action.

Much economically relevant behavior is not directly concerned with the production of utilities for exchange nor with the exchange process, for example, the use of time for noneconomic ends, such as recreational or religious activities that reduce the resources of a group or society for the production of economic utilities. A widely different case consists of the use of force or coercion for the direct acquisition of utilities: robbery, piracy, war booty, reparations, and the like. Although these types of activities certainly have been of enormous relevance to the total picture of economic production and distribution, they are not economic actions per se. Another example here is the allocation of economic resources to political or more broadly societal ends, with relatively little consideration to ordinary criteria of cost; instead the main guiding norm may be whether this use of resources is likely to insure a given social end, such as military victory, at whatever cost.

Economically conditioned activity is also guided, in the main, by noneconomic goals and norms, although economic considerations appreciably affect the course of action. The character of the music produced in a particular society will be affected by the economic bases for composing and playing music. The religious activity of an economically deprived stratum is not likely to be identical with that of privileged groups. Similarly, the family, recreation, war, and innumerable other sociocultural phenomena are not concretely economic activities; but all are potentially subject to variation because of economic factors playing through the total situation.

If we accept the convention of restricting *economic* activity to the peaceable allocation of scarce utilities to alternative ends and maintain the broad distinction between this and economically *relevant* and *conditioned* activities, we have a convenient base for examining the relation between the economic sector and the political institutions of a society. It is easy to see that the vegetable pushcart vendor is doing something different from the policeman who demands to see his peddler's license; but it is very important to see precisely what the difference is, why it occurs, and what its implications are as the scale of action and organization widens into the entire social order.

We have found the central elements of political activity in the acquisition and use of power and have seen this aspect of action emerge whenever a plurality of human beings are interacting. But the capacity to control actions of others may be fairly evenly diffused throughout a society or group, or it may be highly concentrated into one or a few strategic foci. In considering *political* power we have concentrated upon the institutional regulation of power that successfully claims legitimacy in the ultimately monopolistic use of coercion within a given territory, and especially upon the state as the association exercising this sort of power. Within the associations and groups that make up the apparatus of the state, legitimated authority eventuates in imperative control (Weber):[4] the probability that a specific command will be obeyed by a given group of persons. This is the form of authority most obvious to common sense—but it is clear that imperative control is not confined to government but resides also in the parent's rule in the family, the employer's command of employees, the priest's orders to the religious follower, and so on. Imperative control is most highly formalized and clearly defined in certain types of *corporate groups*—groups in which social relationships (1) are closed to outsiders (or else restricted as to admission by specific rules) and in which (2) group norms are enforced by specific individuals who are charged with this enforcement as their regular function in the group.[5]

From these distinctions several significant conclusions follow:

1. Insofar as individuals or associations engaged in overtly economic activities are able to exert power over others, their character becomes increasingly governmental. One can imagine, for example, that one giant corporation came to control all manufacturing in the United States. How far would this be from a state?

2. The *internal* regulation of large economic associations involves authority and imperative control exercised in ways similar to those prevailing in administrative units that are popularly thought of as government rather than business. There is always the possibility that imperative control within the economic enterprise will be at least as rigid and severe as its opposite number in the governmental agency. The question cannot safely be prejudged.

3. Even on purely theoretical grounds, it can be predicted that much political activity will be economically relevant; that much will be economically conditioned; and there is no *a priori* reason to suppose that the state may not engage in strictly economic activities. The mere existence of a specialized state means the appropriation of considerable amounts of economic utilities, which are thereby withdrawn from other potential pro-

---

[4] Max Weber, *The Theory of Social and Economic Organization*, A. M. Henderson and Talcott Parsons (trans.) (New York: Oxford University Press, 1947), pp. 152–157.

[5] Weber goes on to say that a system of order that governs corporate actions *as such* is administrative. A system that governs action outside the corporate group is then termed regulative. This will be an important point for the present discussion. *Ibid.*, pp. 150–152.

ductive uses. It is not inconceivable that large standing military forces, extensive bureaucracies, and other social apparatus relevant to war can immobilize the productive surplus of a society.

Perhaps these considerations are enough to suggest that questions centering upon economic freedom and governmental intervention are likely to be greatly confused and blurred unless certain crucial distinctions are made. The more important points may be put in the form of questions, to be answered in any analysis of the total social system:

1. *How much* power from *any quarter* is being exercised upon individuals in the society?
2. How intense is this type of control? What sanctions are utilized, and with what institutionalized regulation? At what point does taxation become confiscation, or monopoly prices lead to expropriation of the small entrepreneur, or punitive law become arbitrary persecution?
3. Is power concentrated or diffused within the social order? To what degree does any one institutionalized association or group have a monopoly of power? Is the society characterized by a pluralistic or monolithic power structure?
4. How is power distributed among the various institutional sectors? What belongs to church, to family, to industry, to labor, to the state, to something else?
5. To what extent is power institutionally regulated? This is another way of asking: To what extent has power been transmuted into legitimate authority? Still more specifically, to what degree is control exercised according to reasonably predictable universalized rules?

As we have seen, the forces that shaped nineteenth-century America led to the development of a limited state that was ideally to intervene as little as possible in the free play of competitively determined economic decisions being made by large numbers of formally free workers and enterprisers selling their services or goods in the open market. The state was to have a restricted and clearly defined zone of authority. It was to be a regulative rather than an administrative order, in Weber's sense. The economic arena was visualized as sharply separate from government and as a nearly autonomous self-adjusting order.

Even while these conceptions were being systematized the real structure of American society moved rapidly to the point of negating many of the basic conditions upon which the old-style economy had rested. As the economic structure shifted toward large-scale corporative organization, the relation of government and business became a persistent focus of political tension. Stripped down to essentials, this became a running conflict over the question whether *specific* powers of various kinds were to be lodged in the corporation, the labor organization, or the state. After a period of unprecedented lack of governmental control over economic life, recent decades have shown a world-wide shift toward concentration of economic control in the state. In the United States, there had been a period of at least fifty years (say, from 1880 to 1930) when one might say that there was government of a highly imperative kind within the enterprise or firm but relative anarchy between firms. Aside from certain state regulations and aids to be mentioned later, the control of the *total* economy was a diffuse *cultural* control, not the explicit regulation of a *definite social organization*. The great development of our day is the centralization of structure, both of business and labor organization and of the state; and this increasingly means that economic problems become political problems. It was one of the curious blind spots of laissez-faire theories that they failed to see how liberal capitalism depended upon a high degree of stability in the political-legal system. This very special economic system is severely strained in any society continually upset by political upheavals, or subject to unpredictable reversals of basic social rules, or to major shifts in the politically oriented allocation of resources.[6]

We are now in a position to attempt a highly condensed diagnosis of the present American situation in somewhat more specific terms. Concretely, business and government are interrelated at thousands of specific points. In the first place, the organizations and personnel of the state operate in numerous ways to *facilitate* or *implement* economic activity. Among the more important forms of implementation are:[7]

(1) Development of corporation law making possible limited liability and extended life for business enterprises; (2) provision for bankruptcy and reorganization of business enterprises; (3) provision and operation of patent laws; (4) providing standard coinage, suppressing counterfeiting, maintaining redemption of currency; (5) support and regulation of banking, for example, chartering, inspection, deposit insurance; (6) regulation of stock and commodity exchange mechanisms; (7) provision of facilities, procedures, and regulations for adjusting management-labor disputes; (8) supplying essential standards: monetary standards, weights and measures, physical composition and performance of materials and products;[8] (9) undertaking research and disseminating the findings, for example, by the Bureau of Mines, Department of Agriculture, Public Health Service, National Bureau of Standards, military agencies, Weather Bureau; (10) collecting and disseminating information; for *producers and distributors*, for example, by the Departments of Commerce, State, Agriculture; on *employment*, for example, by the United States Employment Service, Bureau of Labor Statistics; for *consumers*, by the Bureau of Standards, Public Health

---

[6] It may have been some such considerations as these which led Herbert Spencer to equate "industrial society" and peace. If industrial society—by which he meant capitalism —does not insure peace, it can at least be said that liberal capitalism is highly vulnerable to the effects of war.

[7] We borrow freely here from the presentation of Lyon, Watkins, and Abramson (*op. cit.*), drawing especially on Vol. I, pp. 41–390.

[8] For example, note this highly abbreviated list of selected early statutes: Food and Drug Act (1906 and 1938), Meat Inspection Act (1907), Cotton Futures Act (1914), Commodity Exchange Act (1936), Grain Standards Act (1916), Tobacco Inspection Act (1935), Perishable Commodities Act (1930)—or even the Standard Apple Barrel Act of 1912.

Service, Bureau of Home Economics; for *investors*, by the Securities and Exchange Commission.

One could continue at great length to list the specific supportive activities of the state, at all levels, in facilitating the functioning of the economic system—even aside from such obvious activities as the enforcement of property and contract norms and the provision of direct subsidies, tariffs, and a favorable legal framework. Many of the present services of the state to business represent the expansion to new functions as they have become important as a result of changes in the economic system itself. To take item (10) above for illustration: governmental information and statistical services were established to help the individual or small organization to secure the information necessary for rational economic decisions. This had become more difficult as the economy became more complex, shifting and interdependent and the market area widened. Again, the establishment and enforcement of technical standards through the state is an economically relevant activity of an importance greater than is usually recognized.[9] For mass production in a highly specialized and interdependent economy it is essential to have a high degree of standardization of weights, measures, qualities, specifications. The wider the market and the greater the technical complexity of production and distribution, the more dependent is smooth economic adjustment upon technical precision and upon uniformity of goods—materials, tools, devices, components.

In the above respect, then, the state serves as standard setter and facilitating mechanism for economic action. This is one economically relevant aspect of our political structure.

The second major area of political-economic relations is the *regulation* of economic activities. This permanent and inescapable aspect of governing seems to be widely regarded in the United States both as a new development and as a *limitation* upon the activity of the businessman. Realistically, however (1) the state has always been important in the regulation of the American economy; (2) much state regulation has been the direct result of demands for regulation from the business community itself; (3) much regulation is positive in its consequences both for the profitability of particular activities and for the economy as a whole. In particular, it is essential to recognize the extent to which the state has exerted itself to *maintain competition*.[1] Free markets, we remember, do not maintain themselves. Although the Sherman Antitrust Act (1890) was followed by the greatest period of industrial combination in the national history, a long series of later legislative actions and judicial decisions shows continued efforts to maintain a competitive situation.

A major activity of American governments is the *regulation of the plane or mode of economic competition* through the establishment and enforce-

---

[9] It is not inevitable that the state will be the agency for establishment and maintenance of such standards—the task can be, and is in part, performed by private organizations, for example, trade associations. For various definite reasons, however, the state is likely to play a major part in this field.

[1] Again we are referring to distinctions made by Lyon, Watkins, and Abramson, *op. cit.*, Vol. I, chap. 3.

ment of standards of market conduct. Many of these standards are very old, having been derived in large part from British common law, for example, prohibitions against misrepresentation of one's products as those of another's, misappropriation of trade secrets, inducing breach of contract, malicious interference or molestation.[2] These common-law standards were not under the charge of public officials, and required that a plaintiff prove malice in the action of the accused. As statutory legislation developed, these limitations were partly overcome. Administrative regulation, such as that exercised by the Federal Trade Commission, is now directed against the misbranding of products; the misrepresentation of effects, of geographical origin, of value; the simulation of trademarks and names. Special regulation of specific industries proscribes "deceptive practices" (Food and Drug Act); or requires that certain information be disclosed (obligatory grading of products, labeling of food and drugs, certain financial information concerning market securities); or it maintains minimum standards of quality or composition, for example, control of animal diseases and insect pests, composition and quality of seeds.

In the present period of American history, the reader of this book will not require any extended reminder that the state plays a major part in the *regulation of collective action of workers.* The basic labor law of the United States was initially built upon the common-law doctrines concerning "conspiracy" and "restraint of trade." The old conceptions of conspiracy as used by the courts represented strong barriers to unionization. Deriving from the doctrines regarding restraint of trade, the Supreme Court decision in the famous Danbury Hatters case (1908) held organized labor activity illegal if it retarded the "free flow of commerce between the states," even if the means used were otherwise lawful.

To these barriers to workers' concerted action, there was added the effective use of court injunctions.[3] Only with the New Deal in the 1930's was organized labor given legal means to carry on large-scale collective bargaining effectively. This development was in part reversed by later legislation.

Among the most important general implications emerging from our brief review are the following: (1) The central political authority has continuously had a crucial part in establishing and maintaining a stabilizing framework of rules for economic activity. (2) Much of the regulation has been indispensable to the orderly fulfillment of economic interests. (3) Economic interests and economic conflicts produce incessant political struggles. The concept of the state as umpire in the economic field is undergoing drastic modification, both because of international pressures and because of internal changes. Instead of a clearcut capitalism of small independent units, there is a "mixed" economy including small proprietors (retail trade, agriculture, etc.), small corporations, large corporations, cooperatives, quasi-

[2] Specific categories of action falling under this heading: attacks on the reputation of a competitor, disparaging a competitor's product or impugning his credit worthiness, making spurious threats of litigation, intimidating employees or customers. (*Ibid.,* pp. 312 ff.)
[3] These developments largely nullified the hopes of those who had regarded the Clayton Act (1914) as the "Magna Carta of Labor."

public nonprofit enterprises (educational, research, medical, etc.), traditional governmental enterprises (post office), government corporations. Due to war and the threat of war, the ends of economic production depend greatly upon political ends and wider social considerations. Quite aside from military impacts on production and allocation,[4] the normal operation of the civil economy increasingly depends upon an extensive and intricate set of activities of political agencies.

The economic system is now so thoroughly intermeshed with government that a return to the limited state of 1900 would require virtually complete reorganization of *both* systems. The emergence of a "welfare" state reflects, in part, the new political participation of labor; and this in turn derives from mass industrialism in the context of democratic political institutions. But the great expansion of governmental activities in such fields as social security does not make any less important the continuing supportive, facilitating, and regulative functions that will be carried out in some form under *any* political system in an industrial society.

Many other important governmental activities cannot be described in the present brief discussion. Government fiscal policy, for instance, is so important in our present society that it deserves full analysis as a sociological no less than an economic problem. The same is true of the political determination of the distribution of the national income—through taxation, tariffs, direct production of goods and services, contracts with nongovernmental businesses, and so on. Government itself is now a major segment of the whole economy. Governmental activities, together with other not-for-profit components (hospitals, universities, foundations, cooperatives) generate a contribution amounting to not less than one-quarter of the gross national product; and possibly as much as two-fifths of all employment is accounted for by the not-for-profit sector of the economy.[5]

In view of the thousands of points of connection between the political and economic orders, there is room for much disagreement as to the most important general features of the present American case. Certainly, however, one of the most significant developments is the widespread movement toward an *administrative* rather than a regulative order,[6] or as we have said earlier, a shift from diffuse cultural structure to definite social organization. This development is occurring within business and labor as well as in the relations between government and economic organizations. The signs are

[4] Although economists may disagree about the specific effects of particular programs of defense or military spending, it seems clear that—on strictly *economic* grounds—neither war nor peacetime defense expenditures are necessary for full employment and a high level of economic activity in the United States. (Cf. Paul A. Samuelson, *Economics*, 6th ed. (New York: McGraw-Hill, 1964), pp. 785–786.

[5] Eli Ginzberg, *et al.*, *The Pluralistic Economy* (New York: McGraw-Hill, 1965), p. 193.

[6] In the same sense suggested by Weber in *The Theory of Social and Economic Organization*, *op. cit.*, pp. 150 ff. A regulative political system fixes and supports the canalizing rules for economic units but does not set the ends of economic activity nor lay down positive and mandatory courses of action. In a purely administrative order, both the economic ends and the details of action are established within a definite administrative staff that has the power to make its decisions mandatory.

numerous: large corporations, trade associations, unions, governmental organizations, price agreements, price controls, administrative allocation, and "rationing" of goods. The watchwords are centralization and administrative coordination. However, these tendencies are not all-encompassing, nor do they invariably represent rigidity or constriction of the action of individuals or small groups. Yet the shift toward an administrative order is undoubtedly a central fact of the times. The crucial question is whether, and how, a pluralistic power system can be maintained under the new structural conditions. In particular, the student of social policy will now be led to consider what specific arrangements may facilitate or prevent the coalescing of economic and political elites[7] or how crucial collective goals may be attained under alternative mixtures of private and public enterprise.

## Case #3: Science, Education, and Polity

We have noted at several points that the different major institutional sectors represent different degrees and kinds of social organization. Strongly nucleated and centralized forms of organization are conspicuous in the polity and the economy. Smaller units and more diffuse and varied linkages characterize the religious and educational sectors, although both are moving rapidly toward larger units and greater centralism. Highly diffuse and nonnucleated are the "organizations" associated with stratification and, especially, with kinship.

It has become a widespread usage to speak of "science as an institution"[8] or of "the institutions of science"—sometimes with the qualification that science is considered a nascent or emergent set of institutions. Certainly by the criteria used in the present study, the sciences constitute a definite institutional sector of the total sociocultural system. Of course, they are highly derivative institutions, having emerged only recently in the history of even the most elaborately differentiated societies. Even the early technology of the Industrial Revolution was not based so much on prior scientific principles as upon discoveries and inventions growing rather directly out of the arts of craftsmanship and the ad hoc solution of practical problems. For much of the period of scientific development from 1650 to the time of World War I, applied technology and basic scientific theory were only loosely connected and technology often moved ahead without benefit of scientific principles.[9]

[7] One might think, for instance, of the professionalization of both labor and management; of the educational system (both in its selective function and in its research and teaching functions). Cf. the discussion and references in Chapters V and VI.

[8] Note these examples: Frank E. Hartung, "Science as an Institution," *Philosophy of Science*, 18, 1 (January 1951), 35–54; Gerard DeGré, *Science as a Social Institution* (New York: Random House, 1955); Don K. Price, *The Scientific Estate* (Cambridge, Mass.: Harvard University Press, 1965); Norman Kaplan (ed.), *Science and Society* (Chicago: Rand McNally, 1965); Warren O. Hagstrom, *The Scientific Community* (New York: Basic Books, 1965); Norman W. Storer, *The Social System of Science* (New York: Holt, Rinehart & Winston, 1966). An important committee of scientists has described science as "one of the institutions of society." (American Association for the Advancement of Science Committee on Science in the Promotion of Human Welfare, "Science and Human Welfare," *Science*, CXXXII (July 8, 1960), 68–73.)

[9] See H. Butterfield, *The Origins of Modern Science, 1300–1800* (New York: Macmillan,

Yet in modern times, systematic science has transformed crucial aspects of human life both through new conceptions of the nature of man and the universe and through technological applications in fields as diverse as communication, nuclear energy, plant and animal breeding, medicine, and social organization and management.[1] Because of the unforeseen, indirect, and widespread social effects of scientific work, the "institutions of science" have become primary sources of social and cultural change in all other institutions.

Is there a single definable entity or system in what we call "science"— is there *Science* with a capital letter, or only *sciences?* The answer depends solely upon how specific we wish a definition to be, for there are some characteristics common to all science[2]—physical, biological, and social— and yet every new specialty shows unique features. The sciences consist of organized bodies of knowledge—data and interpretations—concerning an empirical world; but they include also nondemonstrable beliefs or assumptions. Sciences, as working disciplines, have elaborate sets of technical and conventional norms; and they also are guided by genuinely obligatory rules, which, in effect, define what a scientist must do to be a scientist, and must not do. To the extent that there exist such socially enforceable and enforced norms, marked by high consensus and strong sanctions—to just that extent, the *sciences* are institutions. To the extent that there is important commonality in these norms across substantive fields, we may speak of the *institution* of *science.*

"Science" as a *product* of social life is a part of culture: its knowledge, beliefs, symbols, artifacts, rituals, norms, and values are cultural products, as much as language, art, law, or soothsaying. "Science" as a set of *processes* is a kind of social action; scientific investigation represents a highly complex type of social activity. Like all other social action, it is oriented to norms, guided by goals and sanctions, embedded in groups and relationships. It exemplifies several important types of cultural change, including both the continuous, small, accretive processes and the systemic, radical changes of fundamental assumptions and strategies (Thomas Kuhn's "paradigms").[3]

These considerations are crucial for analyzing the relations of science to other institutions. In terms of cultural effects, scientific values, symbols, and modes of thought have spread pervasively into every other sector, in-

---

1957); note the eloquent statement of I. I. Rabi in Aaron W. Warner, Dean Morse, and Alfred S. Eichner (eds.), *The Impact of Science on Technology* (New York: Columbia University Press, 1965), pp. 13–15.

[1] Merton estimates that 90–95 percent of all the behavioral scientists who have ever lived are alive today. Robert K. Merton, "The Mosaic of Behavioral Sciences," in Bernard Berelson (ed.), *The Behavioral Sciences Today* (New York: Harper & Row, 1964), p. 249.

[2] See Chapter XI, pp. 487–9 above. Merton identifies four central common value-imperatives: universalism, disinterestedness, communalism of findings, and systematic skepticism. (Robert K. Merton, *Social Theory and Social Structure* (New York: Free Press, 1957), esp. pp. 553–561.) Clearly, research in many industrial and military contexts does not fully abide by some of these canons.

[3] Thomas S. Kuhn, *The Structure of Scientific Revolutions* (Chicago: University of Chicago Press, 1963).

cluding even religion[4] and family systems. In terms of social organization and lines of communication and control, "science" primarily represents a *point of intersection of other institutions*—above all, of education, polity, and economic institutions. Yet, beyond question, there is a real sense in which scientific norms and goals have become an autonomous source of major social and cultural influences.

Let us begin by reviewing a few main facts indicative of the twentieth-century "explosion of science"—a recent period in which all curves of growth in science, for a time, were exponential. During the period 1954–1966 the gross national product slightly more than doubled—from $365 million to $740 million. Meanwhile total expenditures for education (excluding capital outlays) tripled, rising from about $11 billion in 1954 to about $37 billion in 1966. And during the same years total funds for research and development increased over four times; and federal funds increased by a factor of five. Total national expenditures for research and development activities rose from $5.2 billion in 1953 to about $24 billion in 1967. Funds for basic research, as distinguished from applied research or technological development of devices and process, rose from $0.5 billion in 1953 to $3.2 billion in 1966.[5]

Although from the beginning of the nation's existence, science and technology have had connections and reciprocal influence with government and political activity, a new phase began with the end of World War II. The necessary concern of the national government with nuclear weapons and atomic energy provided the locus from which the physical sciences[6] suddenly entered the political arena—first as advocates and consumers of vast federal expenditures for research and, second, as advisers, advocates, and decision makers in crucial areas of political policy. Because of high bargaining power, validated performance, and effective organization, a relatively small population of scientists (a few hundred at most) were able so to influence legislation and executive action as to create the tremendous and very rapid growth of "Big Science, the independent, semiautonomous subculture of pure and applied research, supported by taxation but ultimately accountable only to itself."[7] In a world of apocalyptic fears—symbolized by the bomb—and of great expectations and demands dependent upon technological advances, the high status and opulence accorded science by gov-

---

[4] Cf. the classic statement of a popular but one-sided view: Andrew D. White, *A History of the Warfare of Science with Religion* (New York: D. Appleton, 1899). Cf. John G. Gerstner, "The Science Religion Conflict—Its True Laws," in John C. Monsma (ed.), *Science and Religion* (New York: Putnam, 1962), pp. 61–71; Merton, *op. cit.*, Talcott Parsons, *The Social System, op. cit.*, pp. 326–383.

[5] National Science Foundation, "National Patterns of R & D Resources; Funds & Manpower in the United States, 1963–68," *NSF* 67-7 (Washington, D.C.: Government Printing Office, 1967), pp. 22–26.

[6] The life sciences played a secondary part—although there was rapid growth in the National Institutes of Health. The social sciences were practically ignored for a long while; and as late as 1967 the social sciences accounted for only about 4 percent of federal research obligations.

[7] Eric Larrabee, "Science and the Common Reader," *Commentary*, 41, 6 (June 1966), 44. Allocations of national resources for science, of course, actually are "ultimately" political—as Larrabee is at pains to make clear (p. 46).

574   Interrelations of Major Institutions and Social Groupings

ernment may indeed appear to establish "the scientific estate" as a permanent extraconstitutional center of ruling power.[8] The close connection of science and engineering with military technology developed simultaneously with the close supervision by government of firms producing weaponry and other military equipment and supplies.[9]

Both in governmental units and in industrial and business establishments the institutional norms of science are represented by scientific professional and technical associations and by the more diffuse network of publications and personal relationships among scientists. These norms sometimes coincide with the demands of political and economic consumers of scientific findings; this happy case is most common when governmental or business agencies subsidize "pure research," without the expectation of an immediate and predictable output. The more usual circumstance is some tension or struggle as a consequence of goals and norms that differ as between science and the political and economic sectors.[1] Representative clashes include the emphasis in science upon full publication to insure open criticism versus military or industrial secrecy; the tentative and qualified character of many research findings versus the demand for quick practical applications; the institutionalized skepticism of the research worker versus the pressure of the employing agency to claim success for its programs.

A rapidly growing section of professional workers consists of scientists in industrial organizations; in this setting the norms of scientific work and the goals of scientists are often brought out in sharp relief when they come into conflict or manifest cross-purposes with the goals and rules of the industrial enterprise. Tensions, strains, and conflicts may arise concerning goals, social controls, incentives, and responsibilities. There often is a tendency for the industrial concern to press the research scientist for quick results in the search for new or improved products and processes; and this pressure may run counter to the scientist's concern for elaborate replication, rigorous proof, and theoretical relevance. The effort of management to exert detailed control may offend the scientist's standards of autonomy and initiative. The company may wish to minimize the scientist's involvement in outside professional activities and to rely upon incentives of pay and promotion within the firm; the scientist often is strongly oriented to professional recognition and peer-group approval of his work. The industrial

[8] Meanwhile the popular prestige of scientific occupations had increased—in contrast to stability or slight decreases in most other occupational categories studied; see Robert W. Hodge, Paul M. Siegel, and Peter H. Rossi, "Occupational Prestige in the United States, 1925–63," American Journal of Sociology, LXX, 2 (September 1964), 286–302, esp. p. 300.

[9] Price, op. cit., pp. 38–43. (As of 1967, the federal expenditures for research and development were about $15 billion. Three agencies accounted for 86 percent of this total: Department of Defense, National Aeronautics and Space Administration, and Atomic Energy Commission).

[1] See Simon Marcson, The Scientist in American Industry: Some Organizational Determinants in Manpower Utilization (New York: Harper & Row, 1960); William Kornhauser, Scientists in Industry: Conflict and Accommodation (Berkeley: University of California Press, 1962); Anselm L. Strauss and Lee Rainwater, The Professional Scientist: A Study of American Scientists (Chicago: Aldine, 1963); Norman Kaplan, "Professional Scientists in Industry: An Essay Review," Social Problems, 3, 1 (Summer 1965), 88–97.

organization often seeks to make the scientist responsible for "practical results;" the scientist may reply that creativity cannot be thus confined or dictated.

As the expenditures of the federal government for research and development (R & D) reached the level of some $15 billion annually in the mid-1960's, it had become obvious that the major economic impact of federally supported research and development upon regions and localities made it an item of substantial political importance. Even the relatively small part of R & D funds going to universities—in 1965, $1.3 billion or 9 percent of the total—is large enough to raise questions of geographic distribution: the point was made with some emphasis by President Johnson's memorandum of September 1965 to the heads of departments and agencies indicating that the distribution of research funds to universities should be such as to increase the number of institutions "capable of performing research of high quality." Extensive Senate hearings during the late 1960's, conducted by the Subcommittee on Government Research, produced extensive testimony concerning the issues involved in "equitable distribution" of research funds.

For the universities, the size and character of federal support has become a central factor in budgeting and in educational policy: as early as 1953, universities and colleges were receiving one-half of their funds for basic research from federal agencies; and by the mid-1960's the figure had risen to about two-thirds.[2] Although there is little evidence that federal agencies have sought improperly to control academic affairs or educational policies, it is clear that large-scale federal grants and contracts affect the allocation of effort within universities and are bound to raise complex and delicate questions concerning institutional boundaries and modes of government-university relationships.[3]

This brief sketch must stand merely as an opening to the fascinating world of the ramified connections of science with thousands of specific norms and social activities and relationships.[4] It must be noted, nevertheless, that reciprocal influences of science and other institutions are not limited to the direct-massive types just illustrated but include highly indirect and pervasive effects. For example, it is plausible to suppose that the institutionalization of science contributes to the further professionalization of occupations. And the increasing importance of the professions, in a society so heavily committed to physical science and industrial and military tech-

[2] National Science Foundation, *op. cit.*, pp. 7–8.

[3] Issues of freedom and objectivity are especially prominent in areas of highly important and urgent potential application. See Don K. Price, *Government and Science: Their Dynamic Relations in American Democracy* (New York: New York University Press, 1954); Paul F. Lazarsfeld and Wagner Thielens, Jr., *The Academic Mind* (New York: Free Press, 1958); Walter Gellhorn, *Security, Loyalty, and Science* (Ithaca, N.Y.: Cornell University Press, 1950).

[4] For materials, in addition to sources already noted, see Bernard Barber, "Sociology of Science: A Trend Report and Bibliography," *Current Sociology*, V, 2 (1956), 91–153; Bernard Barber and Walter Hirsch (eds.), *The Sociology of Science* (New York: Free Press, 1962); Walter Hirsch, *Scientists in American Society* (New York: Random House, 1968).

nology, holds up the model of professionalism to persons in many other occupations. Particularly likely to be emulated are the professions' claims to have special autonomy (self-regulation), to enjoy social honor, and to define the conditions of entrance into and modes of practice of the occupation. More and more occupational groupings seek to convince the general public and governmental authorities that they deserve these privileges because of their ethical standards, their willingness to give service, and their base in special (scientific or technical) knowledge.[5] As the advantages of professionalism become more widely appreciated, there is an understandable tendency for these claims to be made on behalf of occupations that have only slight warrant by the rigorous standards of traditional professions.

Still more indirect and diffuse are the influences of science as a system of beliefs and ideas, a style of thought and action, a basic orientation to the world.[6] For all the ambivalence that science arouses, it is increasingly a touchstone for judgments in determining and evaluating both public and private policies, in spite of its avowedly value-free position. The very effectiveness of scientific procedures in discovering "how things work" sometimes leads to ill-formed beliefs about its capacities for selecting goals and providing criteria for value choices. At the very least, however, the vast growth of science—physical, biological, psychological, and social—tends to permeate the social system with unprecedented inputs of reliable and systematic information. This fact alone opens up new and profound aspects of societal change and societal self-guidance and control.[7]

Even the short survey undertaken here indicates how demanding a full analysis of the societal system would be, but also suggests how very rewarding it would be also. Eventually much of the necessary work will require quantitative data, exact models, and computerized processing of the information.[8] In macrosociology it is essential to deal with aggregative data in which the phenomena in which we are interested are not localized in any one definite social organization or even a large set of such organizations or groups. Rather, the pattern of behavior we wish to study—whether it be social mobility, mass violence, mutual aid in crisis, or whatever—is dispersed widely through the social structure. It may be manifest in millions of families, or workgroups, or business firms, or appear in rapidly changing interstitial collectivities and social movements. The "units" which then can serve us in tracing large-scale processes necessarily become institutions—or some other categorizing of equivalent scope.

[5] See Everett C. Hughes, "Professions," *Daedalus*, 92, 4 (Fall 1963), 655–668.

[6] Cf. Alfred North Whitehead's comment that science rests on "the inexpugnable belief that every detailed occurrence can be correlated with its antecedents in a perfectly definite manner, exemplifying general principles." *Science and the Modern World* (New York: Mentor Book, 1956), p. 13.

[7] Cf. the two issues of *The Annals* on "Social Indicators" (May and September 1967); Amitai Etzioni, *The Active Society* (New York: Free Press, 1968). The crucial place of "information" (or cybernetic control) in the development of social systems is becoming increasingly clear.

[8] Exploratory studies of this kind have begun, e.g., Guy H. Orcutt, *et al.*, *Microanalysis of Socioeconomic Systems: A Simulation Study* (New York: Harper & Row, 1961).

The challenge of these conceptions is enormous. Note what is involved in even the most simple inventory of structural—let alone processual—relations among major institutions. If each of the institutional sectors we have described in this work is taken only in one-to-one relations with the others, we have the following matrix:

| Institutional Sectors: (a) | KINSHIP | SOCIAL STRATIFICATION | ECONOMY | POLITY | EDUCATION AND SCIENCE | RELIGION |
|---|---|---|---|---|---|---|
| KINSHIP | — | $1_a$ | $2_a$ | $3_a$ | $4_a$ | $5_a$ |
| STRATIFICATION | $1_b$ | — | $6_a$ | $7_a$ | $8_a$ | $9_a$ |
| ECONOMY | $2_b$ | $6_b$ | — | $10_a$ | $11_a$ | $12_a$ |
| POLITY | $3_b$ | $7_b$ | $10_b$ | — | $13_a$ | $14_a$ |
| EDUCATION & SCIENCE | $4_b$ | $8_b$ | $11_b$ | $13_b$ | — | $15_a$ |
| RELIGION | $5_b$ | $9_b$ | $12_b$ | $14_b$ | $15_b$ | — |

*Institutional Sectors: (b)*

If horizontal entries in the top-right portion of the table, noted as $1_a$ to $15_a$, are considered to represent analyses of the influences flowing from institutions listed in the left-hand margin, then the vertical entries, $1_b$ to $15_b$, would represent the reverse flows. Therefore, thirty main kinds of studies are required merely to inventory the first-order relations. And, of course, some of the analyses of greatest practical interest and value must deal with three or more relations simultaneously: education-religion-polity or family-economy-stratification-polity (illustrated by public measures to create employment for low-income families). To gain real causal or predictive understanding of how social systems are maintained and are changed requires specific and systematic analysis of networks of such relationships.

A few examples may serve to give greater meaning to these points. Innovations in methods of analysis are making possible new understandings of relationships between aggregated societal conditions, such as occupational position of the urban poor and prior social processes. Thus, O. D. Duncan has utilized a "cohort" analysis of changes in education to show that educational attainment depends less strongly upon either family size (number of siblings) or the presence of both parents than it does upon prior educational attainment and occupational category of the head of the family.[9] In a quite different area of analysis, when we view institutions as organized, dynamic sets of relatively stable but continually changing norms, we are led to seek carefully for any work dealing directly with norms—their origins and formation, their maintenance, their organization into sets and subsets, their modification and displacement. The growing interest of some students of institutional relations in legal codes opens up the possibility of showing

[9] Otis Dudley Duncan, "Discrimination Against Negroes," *The Annals*, 371 (May 1967), 85–103.

direct effects of specific norms upon defined institutionalized behavior,[1] for instance, of "welfare" legislation upon family stability.[2] Studies of crises bring out in clear view priorities of norms and group obligations and loyalties. "The prominence of family-related roles in postdisaster behavior has been repeatedly shown. Survivors immediately turn their anxiety toward the possible fate of their families; even officials with well-defined community rescue roles find these in severe and occasionally hopeless conflict with their felt responsibilities as fathers and husbands."[3]

To put the whole matter of analysis in compact form: institutional interrelations are best studied by comparable observations, at two or more points in time, of changes in flows of information, resources, or personnel among normatively differentiated social units. Extended to strategic parts of an entire society, such analysis will show the dynamic complexity of a society in being. By doing this it will avoid the misleading simplicity of much popular diagnosis and commentary on American society, at home and abroad. For those who value a closer approach to the real world, this effect would be a signal gain.

## SUGGESTED READINGS

ADAMS, BERT N. *Kinship in an Urban Setting*. Chicago: Markham Publishing Company, 1968. Good example of illuminating monographic study. Close analysis of information from survey of families throws new light on controversies concerning extent and kinds of linkages among kin-related nuclear families.

BARBER, BERNARD, and WALTER HIRSCH (eds.). *The Sociology of Science*. New York: Free Press, 1962. Solid and stimulating collection of essays. Surveys the main studies, illustrating both the internal organization and modes of functioning of science and its multiple connections with other institutional sectors.

BERELSON, BERNARD, and GARY A. STEINER. *Human Behavior*. New York: Harcourt, Brace & World, 1964, chaps. 13–14. Once again, consultation of this reference book is a valuable way of orienting oneself to a minimal set of empirical findings.

EISENSTADT, S. N. *The Political Systems of Empires: The Rise and Fall of the Historical Bureaucratic Societies*. New York: Free Press, 1963. Impressive analysis of the intricate interplay of political changes with structures and processes in kinship groupings, territorial communities, ethnic and religious

[1] Jack P. Gibbs, "The Sociology of Law and Normative Phenomena," *American Sociological Review*, 31, 3 (June 1966), 315–325.

[2] It was not until 1962, nearly three decades after the initiation of public programs of aid to dependent children, that the assistance was made available to families in economic need because of the unemployment of the father, present in the home. The change was made by reason of increasing assertions that earlier regulations encouraged desertion or other forms of family breakup. See Nathan E. Cohen and Maurice F. Connery, "Government Policy and the Family," *Journal of Marriage and the Family*, 29, 1 (February 1967), 10.

[3] George W. Baker and Dwight W. Chapman (eds.), *Man and Society in Disaster* (New York: Basic Books, 1962), p. 16.

collectivities, stratification segments, urban groupings, and others. Shows the enormous importance of control of mobile resources and of the symbols of authority.

MARSH, ROBERT. *Comparative Sociology*. New York: Harcourt, Brace & World, 1967. Comparative studies must take into account interrelations of items being compared across societal boundaries. Marsh's work contains excellent illustrations of how the relationships between factors or variables may be affected by "context"—that is, an interdependent set of other variables.

MERTON, ROBERT K. *Social Theory and Social Structure*. New York: Free Press, 1957. This collection of elegant essays illustrates throughout a mode of thinking that continually searches out linkages and interactions among the components of social systems.

PARSONS, TALCOTT. *Societies: Evolutionary and Comparative Perspectives*. Englewood Cliffs, N.J.: Prentice-Hall, 1966. The leading structural-functional theorist in American society advances a neoevolutionary interpretation of large-scale social change. Drawing upon extensive comparisons of historical materials, this work sketches a series of processes leading to hypothetically invariant sequences of change. Equilibrium and disequilibrium among components of social systems as key conceptions.

PRICE, DON K. *The Scientific Estate*. Cambridge, Mass.: Harvard University Press, 1965. Knowledgeable interpretation of the rise of big science and the emergence of an inner network of physical scientists and technologists who strongly influence many governmental policies and administrative decisions.

SWANSON, GUY EDWARD. *Religion and Regime*. Ann Arbor: University of Michigan Press, 1967. Uses European historical data in an elaborate and careful study of the relationship between type of political system and receptivity to the Protestant Reformation. Shows a remarkable consistency between the two orders of events.

# The Integration of American Society

# XIV

## INTEGRATION AND CHANGE IN SOCIAL SYSTEMS

N̲o society as a going concern is adequately defined by its institutions alone. Institutions constitute only the most definite systems of statuses that define expected, permissible, and obligatory interpersonal relations. But there are the additional facts of normative variability and evasion, of deviation or violation, of nonsocial factors in the situation, of relations to other societies, of noninstitutional aspects of the culture. Moreover, every society contains oppositions of interests, differences of beliefs, clashes of values, and greater or lesser amounts of overt social conflict. Finally, every society continuously undergoes some change—slow or fast, small or great, superficial or profound. No reader of these pages who has reached this point will be under any illusions that "American society" is a unitary unchanging monolith of perfect consensus.

The interrelations of the institutions reviewed in previous chapters are only one aspect of the problem of social integration. Some studies are restricted to "the influence of the increasing differentiation of groups."[1] In other instances, the problem of integration is discussed from the standpoint of class struggle, race relations, political federalism, alienation, anomie, divorce, suicide, "our schizoid culture," an alleged "American character," mass society, almost ad infinitum. Evidently a term that has been turned to so many uses is sufficiently protean to require handling with care. One way to exercise such care is first to see what integration is *not*.

For sociological purposes, "integration" is not a term to be used to convey a *concealed* value-judgment.[2] When we say that one society is highly integrated and that another is loosely integrated, we do not necessarily imply that one is "better" than the other, any more than we would mean that one biological organism was better than the other because its parts were more closely interdependent. Although *social* integration represents phenomena of a quite different order than do biological organisms, there likewise occur societies in which the constituent elements are, in some real sense, mutually consistent or causally related; and there are societies loosely held together or abounding in inconsistencies. On

---

[1] Robert C. Angell, *The Integration of American Society* (New York: McGraw-Hill, 1941), p. 6. Angell's analysis, however, actually deals at length with the commonality of values and norms, or lack thereof, in a wide range of social structures.

[2] Although, of course, *some* values are always *implied* in the selection of the problem itself.

the other hand, if one is repelled by the term integration, because of fears concerning the prospects for freedom and spontaneity in individual life, it may be equally useful to recall that the freest and most creative persons are not those who give greatest rein to impulses dissociated from continuing social relations to other individuals. Many persons have found that the chaotic expression of fragmentary impulses is not freedom but psychological slavery. These problems of valuation are not intrinsic to the concept of integration as a descriptive or analytic term.

Second, social integration is not to be identified with the inclusiveness of highly formalized social organization. Some of the most highly integrated societies appear to have a rather slight development of formal associational structures. On the other hand, what seems on the surface to be a thoroughly integrated group or society with a developed formal organization often turns out to be a system largely organized through the coercive power of a small subgroup.

Third, integration, in the present context, refers to a property of societies that can be identified by definite, publicly communicable signs and then shown to vary in relation to other properties or conditions. It is *not*, therefore, considered to be a quality that can only be apprehended by direct intuition.

Fourth, the integration of a society is not indexed by the mere coexistence of certain items in the same geographic area or political unit. As Sorokin has cogently insisted,[3] neither *spatial adjacency* nor the association of cultural items through a *common external factor*, such as climate or geographic conditions, tells us anything about causal or functional integration or about integration at the level of meaning. Sheer physical proximity does permit interaction through which a common life can be developed, but there are too many instances of social conflict between, or estrangement of, geographically adjacent or intermingled populations for us to expect that proximity will necessarily increase the likelihood of integration. The same consideration applies to the common influence of other nonsocial factors: climate, geography, or physical heritage may lead to similarity of behavior, but the similarity may or may not be integrative.

Finally, integration does not mean homogeneity, or identity in all respects throughout a society. A completely homogeneous society would be, in fact, a completely unstructured "field," with nothing to give it momentum or direction. Only where there is first differentiation can there be integration: this is as true of sociocultural systems as of any others. Children and adults differ, men and women differ, teachers and students differ—and it is the essence of their integrated roles that they are different. Societies are not integrated by being internally undifferentiated, and the cultural commonality necessary to their continued existence must be detected on a level far

---

[3] For a conveniently concise statement of his position, see Pitirim A. Sorokin, "Forms and Problems of Culture-integration and Methods of Their Study," *Rural Sociology*, I, 2 (June 1936), 128–141. Sorokin makes the important point that not all the co-existing elements in a given area or social aggregate are connected either causally or meaningfully. Contrary to all theories that postulate that every item of a culture must be interrelated, the fact is that many items are essentially unrelated.

removed from complete unanimity in every area of activity, belief, and value.[4]

### Cultural and Social Integration

To what may "societal integration" refer? The answer is, to any category of culture or society; in the *culture*, to interests, values, norms, beliefs, symbols and to various systems and subsystems of these; in the *society*, to collectivities, groups, associations, communities, and other units of interaction. The integration of a culture is related to but not identical with the integration of a group or society. Overtly regularized and orderly interaction not infrequently occurs between individuals having relatively few beliefs and values in common. We find many examples of a broadly common culture extending over a large number of local groups or even major political entities that are either not interacting or else are in open conflict. Or, there may be an apparently unitary culture with respect to some elements (say, a religious system, or a common set of political institutions), but with great internal differentiation along lines of class and caste, or in other respects. The daily operation of a differentiated social system requires an elaborate cultural coding of social positions and identities; of who is to do what, when, where, and how; of rights, obligations, duties, privileges, immunities, disabilities; of areas of privacy and open access; of trust and vigilance. This kind of detailed mapping of the ordinary interactions that constitute a social system in being is so complex as to defy full comprehension by anyone. A substantial degree of such coding, however, is indispensable to anything that could be called "integration."

Social integration is not identical with cultural integration nor with personality integration, but may be closely related to both. Cultural integration has to do with the relationships among assemblages of beliefs, knowledge, values, norms, and symbols of many different kinds. Well-integrated cultures show pattern consistencies and pattern congruities, although these do not necessarily entail a single focus or a single theme or "principle." (In fact, different cultures show greatly varying emphases on the very desirability of "consistency.")

The integration of personalities represents a third distinct set of exigencies relating to the management of needs and motives and to the highly complex psychological processes of individual persons. A society is possible in which most individuals are well integrated as personalities although subcollectivities are in severe conflict or the effectiveness of collective goal-attainment is low because of poor coordination of effort.

These three systems—social, cultural, psychological—are intricately connected; but aspects of each may vary to some extent independently of the other systems. Our primary attention here, of course, is upon social integration.

We should distinguish between the sheer fact of *cohesion* of a social

[4] Cf. Angell, *The Integration of American Society*, pp. 19–20: "A sense of moral community does not require people to think alike on all issues. . . . The crucial question is . . . whether they concur in the ultimate values to be realized."

aggregate on the one hand, and the *integration* that occurs through shared values and beliefs. Factual cohesion refers merely to a human aggregate whose members interact without a disabling degree of overt conflict, regardless of the conditions upon which this state of affairs may depend.[5] There is a rather wide range within which an important degree of cohesion, in the sense of coordinated activity, can be maintained by coercion, the effective threat of the few over the many. Our liberal cultural bias should not lead us to suppose that all overt cohesion rests on consensus or voluntary participation.[6]

Much of the coordination of human actions derives from interdependent interests in the utilization of scarce and divisible values. In pure type, we would here visualize a social aggregate held together solely by a convergence of individual interests. Collective ends would consist only of those necessary to the achievement of separate individual ends. In one direction the prototype is economic exchange between persons of radically different culture; in another, the interdependence of fate in the face of a common danger. Some human interests in subsistence and safety are so nearly universal as to be a major factor in the cohesion of all major human aggregates. Further, once a marked division of labor has arisen from any source, the sheer interdependence of individual interests militates against the disruption of a society, in so far as individuals recognize that interdependence.

In actual societies, however, neither coercive power nor interdependence of separate interests exists in isolation from the sharing of common goals and other normative elements—for example, cognitive standards, symbols, rules, values. At this level, the term "integration" refers to something beyond causal regularity or coordination. Integration is more than a balance-of-power situation or a symbiotic interdependence. Modern sociology seeks to find this something else by investigating the extent and kind of common-value orientations in a social system. A basic postulate is that the integration of a society can be defined in terms of the sharing of common prescriptions and proscriptions for conduct, belief, valuation. This has been expressed from time to time in various ways: that a society is a human aggregate possessing a common ultimate-value system; that a society is integrated to the degree that conformity is voluntary; that society is possible because people share "a common world of experience." It seems securely established that (1) the continuing operation of any social aggregate does depend upon

[5] Even this statement about minimal regularity presupposes some criteria for appraising what is to be considered conflict or orderliness. From the standpoint of a purely *causal* analysis any social activity is presumably orderly, in the sense of being caused, even though it may represent normative chaos.

[6] It is often supposed, for example, that enduring systems of caste are fully accepted at all levels. But note this appraisal: "Caste systems are always in disequilibrium . . . characterized not by consensus but by conformity. They are maintained not by agreement but by sanctions. When change occurs it is quickly rationalized in order to maintain the system and the myth of its stability. That social order prevails most of the time does not mean that those who comprise the system willingly accept their position within it any more than it means that it is static." Gerald D. Berreman, "Stratification, Pluralism and Interaction: A Comparative Analysis of Caste," in A.V.S. de Reuck and Julie Knight (eds.), *Ciba Foundation Symposium on Caste and Race: Comparative Approaches* (London: J. & A. Churchill, 1967), pp. 67–68.

a minimal sharing of normative orientations; (2) the extent and kind of *common* orientation varies enormously among known societies; (3) integration at this level requires highly specific processes and cannot be taken for granted as belonging to the nature of human association. Integration of societies cannot be adequately explained by reducing the problem to biological and physical factors. Large and complex social aggregates that can operate as real social systems certainly do not have to have a complete sharing of all values throughout the population. Institutionalized tolerance and a minimal development of "good manners" go a long way, even in the absence of either collective goals or high value-consensus in other regards. Yet, "some manner and degree of interpersonal consensus is a necessary condition for social organization at any level of complexity."[7] Since societies are neither held together on the basis of a rationalistic "social contract," nor are they purely congeries of power systems, it is in the residual area of the sharing of a common culture that the sociological explanation of integration must center. This is a hard-won insight in the history of thought about society, and its importance must be emphasized. At the same time "the sharing of a common culture" remains a vague and unproductive cliché unless it can be specified what is shared, to what extent, and through what structures or processes.

Furthermore, social organizations and the entailed commitments of their members may produce results not at all directly predictable from the values held by the individuals involved. As Lipset points out, for example, there was strong opposition in the early 1950's to Senator Joseph McCarthy among Southern Democrats whose political party commitments overrode any possible ideological sympathies.[8] That highly differentiated societies may have greater difficulty than less differentiated societies in securing conformity to a uniform set of norms need not be true by definition; but even if nontruistic, the generalization is not very surprising or instructive. Less obvious and more interesting is the complex hypothesis developed by James G. March and supported by his analysis data from fifteen societies. As further elaborated by Robert Marsh: "the more differentiated the society, the less likely that its subsystems will be autonomous, the less manipulatory potential the group will have over its members, and the greater the amount of deviance from group norms will be."[9]

### The Concept of Social System

Whether or not any particular society constitutes a "system" is an empirical question about which argument is largely fruitless: not debate but the facts of the case will enable us to appraise the extent to which systemic qualities are present. Various societies, groups, or organizations will be more or less

[7] Theodore M. Newcomb, "The Study of Consensus," in Robert K. Merton, Leonard Broom, Leonard S. Cottrell, Jr. (eds.), *Sociology Today* (New York: Basic Books, 1959), p. 277.

[8] Seymour Martin Lipset, "Democracy and Working Class Authoritarianism," *American Sociological Review*, 24, 4 (August 1959), 484.

[9] Robert Marsh, *Comparative Sociology* (New York: Harcourt, Brace & World, 1967), p. 144.

systemic, and in differing ways.[1] It may be argued that modern industrial or postindustrial societies are so disorderly, conflictful, changing, and loosely articulated that one should not attempt to analyze them as systems. Against this view, two considerations seem decisive. First, to reject systems analysis out of hand is to prejudge an issue that can only be decided by empirical test. Whether such analysis is or is not sufficiently informative to be worthwhile can be known only when serious efforts have been made, using the best available techniques, concepts, and data. Second, the global question, Are societies systems? is too gross to elicit a very useful answer. For the obvious answer is both yes and no—some parts of actual societies are closely interconnected and behave in systemlike ways; others are unconnected or related in an erratic, unpredictable fashion. The interesting and potentially vital question is, rather, What *portions* of given concrete societies (or, if one prefers, sociocultural congeries) have *what kinds* of connections with other portions; and to *what extent* and *how* does the whole complex exhibit the qualities of a system? When the major airlines and the machinists' union together generate a protracted strike, the event immediately affects business firms, families, government, professional associations, and many other specific social structures. Eventually the central government is "forced" to take some kind of authoritative action. When the major steel manufacturers raise prices in a period of growing inflationary pressure, economic analysis can show an elaborate network of tangible ramifications, perhaps extending to partial destruction of savings and pensions of retired persons. Raising the academic requirements for college entrance immediately affects secondary schools. And so on. But some parts of American society are very little affected by processes occurring in other parts. (Decisions concerning federal support of scientific research presumably are not greatly influenced by changes in courtship practices in rural North Dakota.)

Contrary to some formulations, then, we do not define a *social system* as an ongoing equilibrium, for this characterization might seem to imply more stability and orderliness than the facts show. We do regard social systems (including inclusive societies such as modern nation-states) as relatively enduring sets of interrelated institutions that provide recurrent patterns for survival and reproduction of given human populations. Many such systems are highly open and responsive in relation to their environments. Social systems consist of continuous and intermittent communicative acts between persons, these acts being to an important degree recurrently predictable to the actors, partly by reason of common orientation to knowledge, beliefs, values, and norms drawn from a shared culture. In a fully interdependent social system every set of acts between any set of actors affects, and is affected by, every other set of acts; and all sets are influenced by the total system. Such a completely articulated system is a limiting case, closely approximated only in relatively small-scale segmental networks of interaction. Total societies are partially articulated systems in which some subsystems may be highly interdependent (a tightly linked economy or a

[1] For an eloquent appreciation of this point, see Pitirim A. Sorokin, *Sociological Theories of Today* (New York: Harper & Row, 1966), pp. 133–154.

centralized and bureaucratized polity), whereas others are only loosely connected by low rates of interaction, with many discontinuities or gaps.[2]

Communication flows, or exchanges of symbols or messages, persons, goods, services, or money constitute actual or potential influences upon behavior. The stability or instability, change or maintenance-of-state, of a social system is an outcome of the numerous, continuous, and continuing "transactions" among its constituent units. Among the causes of any complex unit of social behavior, therefore, is always some preceding social event. Such events are not random but rather are "constrained"—not only by physical, biological, and biopsychic factors but also by systemic social structures. Although the social constraints are "channelizing" rather than "determining," that is, they allow much scope for the operation of other causes, they do give direction to both processes of system change and of maintenance or restoration of preexisting social conditions. *Integration, therefore, is as much a dynamic process as is change.*

For a highly differentiated, structurally complex national social system, the requirements for effective political integration appear to be more stringent than commonly realized.[3] As specialized statuses and subcollectivities multiply, the number of connections of interdependence grows rapidly. But the process of differentiation tends to remove more and more relationships from ascribed and particularistic structures, to increase mobility, to generate divergencies of interests, to multiply certain kinds of differences in beliefs and values.[4] Means of exchange must be generalized, as by money or credit; and the same process must occur in values, together with a respecification of norms applicable to differentiated subunits. The differentiated system tends, then, to be both *diverse* and *dynamic*; it changes rapidly and is distinctive in the prominence of what might be called heat-and-light variables—money, mobility, competition, energy consumption, rapid communication, and the like. Such an energetic and complex system is a tricky mechanism, especially because it necessarily depends upon very large-scale coordination of numerous diverse activities. The extreme interdependence means that localized disruptions can quickly spread their effects throughout the system. *Such systems are greatly dependent upon procedural agreement,* for divergences and oppositions of interests and values are endemic, and effective functioning is highly vulnerable to the concerted action of relatively small collectivities. In the absence of *known agreement*[5] upon principles or

2 "We can best look at modern society as a loose collection of overlapping communities of work, religion and ethnicity, race, class, and locality held together mainly by economic interdependence, by legal, military, and political institutions, and by the media of mass communication and entertainment."—Harold L. Wilensky, "Class, Class Consciousness, and American Workers," in William Haber (ed.), *Labor in a Changing America* (New York: Basic Books, Inc., 1966), p. 44.

3 Cf. Talcott Parsons, *Societies: Evolutionary and Comparative Perspectives* (Englewood Cliffs, N.J.: Prentice-Hall, 1966), pp. 22–29.

4 Useful for comparison with the American case is the excellent study by Harry Eckstein, *Division and Cohesion in Democracy: A Study of Norway* (Princeton, N.J.: Princeton University Press, 1966).

5 Thomas J. Scheff, "Toward a Sociological Model of Consensus," *American Sociological Review*, 32, 1 (February 1967), 32–46. An actual operative consensus may require both

rules of procedure for coping with substantive disagreements and conflicts, the tendency is (1) for disruptive confrontations to increase, (2) for resolutions of conflict to be forced to higher levels of the power-authority system. High incidence of punishing social disruption, therefore, always contains the potential of leading toward a centralized-repressive solution. This possibility is also favored by the "utopian" intransigence of some advocates of change, in conjunction with the "fundamentalistic" intransigence of elements of the population who feel most threatened.[6]

Furthermore, by reason of very complex processes that cannot be detailed here, the differentiated-interdependent society always has great difficulty in excluding from full participation and reward any sizable segment of the people on grounds of ascribed status.[7]

The actual operation of a society as an objectively possible system, to repeat, depends upon the multiple interaction of a series of factors. Here we shall treat only a few aspects of the whole complex problem, without presuming that these represent either the specificity or the completeness required for a comprehensive analysis of the American situation.

The solution to problems of integration is only one of the requirements for viable societies. Total social systems can be destroyed. This means that a given society can lose its sociocultural autonomy and be turned into a different *type* or at the extreme that its people or its culture or both can be destroyed. To understand integration, it may be useful to examine the possible modes by which a particular system can cease to exist:

1. By *overwhelming conquest*: Carthage, Tasmania, many tribal peoples; a twentieth-century nightmare of nuclear or "special weapons" warfare.
2. By *loss of commitment*: alienation, "failure of nerve," withdrawal of energy and motivation, loss of faith.
3. By *internal conflict*: sufficiently severe and massive polarization or fragmentation, based on opposition of interests and values and the inadequacies of coping mechanisms to deal with conflict.
4. By cumulative *ineffectiveness in goal attainment*.
5. By failure to prevent *progressive loss in adaptive capacities*.

Aside from overwhelming conquest, the other possibilities correspond to the four system-problems outlined by Talcott Parsons: all societies must have *generalized* capacities to cope with the environment (adaptive sector), must achieve particular goals (*goal-attainment* sector), must somehow manage internal relationships among subcollectivities (*integration* sector), and

---

agreement and awareness of the agreement and awareness of this awareness in self and others.

[6] E.g., "To the fundamentalist, the demand for greater generality in evaluative standards appears to be a demand to abandon the 'real' commitments. Very severe conflicts often crystallize about such issues." (Parsons, *op. cit.*, p. 23.)

[7] The author has tried in several studies to analyze the reasons for this. See, e.g., *Strangers Next Door* (Englewood Cliffs, N.J.: Prentice-Hall, 1964), chap. 10; "Social Change and Social Conflict: Race Relations in the United States, 1944–1964," *Sociological Inquiry*, 35, 1 (Winter 1965), 8–25.

must maintain a cultural system and provide for an acceptable demand-gratification exchange with personality systems (*pattern-maintenance and tension-management* sector). The crucial point is that each set of system problems requires scarce resources and not all can receive full treatment at any given time. Yet neglect of one sector will in time always have "negative" effects upon one or more of the others. Extreme emphasis on pattern maintenance may produce rigidities, such as a frozen political ideology that prevents needed actions in international relations, that interfere with effective adaptation to a changed external environment. Relentless devotion to adaptation may seriously affect integration, as in the case of forced capital accumulation and industrialization during the Stalinist era in the U.S.S.R. A society or a group may pour so much of its energy and other resources into social integration—illustrated by concentration on social rituals—as to radically reduce its capacities to attain technical, economic, or political goals. And, finally, an extremely task-centered system, driving hard to attain particular goals one after another, may wreak havoc with distributive justice and generate serious social cleavages and conflicts before effective counter-measures can be mobilized. The growth of metropolitan areas in the United States in recent decades has produced numerous illustrations.

Integration is a concept derived by high-order abstraction, removed by several steps from the numerous concrete observations to which it is ultimately anchored. Accordingly, in what follows we will continually refer to the more detailed analyses and data already presented. In some aspects, *every* preceding chapter has dealt with problems of societal integration. The present task is thus largely one of rearranging old facts in somewhat different patterns.

## FACTORS IN THE COHESION OF AMERICAN SOCIETY

Whatever integration may exist in the United States is quite obviously not the integration of a small, stable society in which a common set of detailed standards and goals is shared by practically all members. Nor is it the integration of a society permeated with the sense of a long, slow-growing common history. Indeed, this country constitutes something close to a crucial experiment concerning the consequences of sociocultural diversity in modern mass society. Its continued existence under essentially the same form of government through so many years when the crash of falling states has echoed through the world demonstrates, at the least, that complete cultural homogeneity is not a functional necessity for *that* much stability.

If we examine the *general* bases of social cohesion—those applicable to any society—a great many different lists can be derived, each useful in terms of a certain set of data and a certain conceptual scheme. Here we shall not seek a highly refined set of analytic variables but shall work with a provisional and rather crude set of factors. The discussion will proceed in terms of these items: (1) mutual dependence and individual gains; (2) mechanisms and techniques of coordination and integration; (3) external pressures; (4) common value-orientations; (5) the unity of diversity: overlapping identities and multigroup membership.

These categories have all the disadvantages of remaining fairly close to a common-sense level, but the advantage of tying the discussion down to practically important structures and processes that have already received a fair amount of attention in social science research.

### Mutual Dependence and Individual Gains

Let us begin by considering the place of individual gains, or the congruity and interdependence of interests. Quite aside from a community of ultimate values, it is the present contention that a major part of the cohesion of this society derives from a community of interest—that is, the *sharing* of an agreement that permits widespread satisfaction of *separate* interests to attain economic goals and any other scarce, divisible values. Congruity of interests refers to the situation in which individuals continue to interact and to avoid conflict on the basis of the gains each anticipates from perpetuation of the social framework essential to interaction. Thus, individuals mutually antagonistic in other respects often collaborate in the pursuit of their separate interests in income, power, safety, or prestige; or class-conscious industrialists and workers maintain relationships because of their economic interdependence. There is some base of value consensus in such collaboration, but it is so limited that one had best speak of dependence and interests rather than values.[8]

Recognition of the role of common normative orientation does not mean the underestimation of the importance of mutual dependence and tangible gains of individuals. Under conditions of expanding economic opportunity, peoples of very diverse cultures have acted in America almost as if they had a tacit agreement to minimize their differences while exploiting the abundant resources. This historical "agreement," of course, implied *some* value consensus and aided the development of a broader common orientation. But for several generations strong immediate incentives for the acceptance of existing institutions, especially of property and government, were provided by widespread opportunities for economic acquisition and by a rising material level of living. Almost all classes participated in these gains, although by no means to the same extent. A major key to understanding the particular ways in which American society has avoided violent and disjunctive political changes in the twentieth century lies in the remarkable configuration of "middle-class" interests and values.[9]

[8] "Where primitive societies are fragile and tightly integrated around a common core of shared values, industrial societies are more loosely textured. They can contain within themselves all sorts of conflicts and divergent philosophies; integration is not related to a single centre but to a variety of regional, ethnic, class, and minority loyalties. This is why industrial societies can absorb changes, whether planned or not, so much more quickly and easily."—Michael Banton, *Roles: An Introduction to the Study of Social Relations* (New York: Basic Books, 1965), p. 53.

[9] For evidence on the complexity of this configuration, however, see Harold L. Wilensky, "Mass Society and Mass Culture: Interdependence or Independence," *American Sociological Review*, 29, 2 (April 1964), 173–197.

Because the basic value-system allowed and encouraged it—because the economic and political institutions and the basic resources favored it—there has come to pass a society in which the majority of the people do not feel unjustly deprived or oppressed.[1] Many of these same people are accustomed to deferred gratification, indirect procedures for maximizing welfare, relatively complex weighing of public issues, daily practice in compromise and self-control. In such a context the advantages of enough social stability to permit the continued flow of numerous gratifications are apparent to many citizens of the commonwealth.

Let us note once more that we are not referring to "crass hedonism" or "materialism." The presence of many complementary and mutually facilitating interests is an indispensable factor in the peaceful operation of any society. The source of order in the "interdependence of interests" is not superficial or secondary but profound and basic.[2] Life itself, and all that life and the security for living can mean, depend upon some such ordering. Many things essential for life and for a measure of security arise from cooperation and exchange. Exchange rests upon the likelihood that men, on the average, will prefer a diversity of goods and services to a single good or service. As F. Y. Edgeworth's first law has it, "if an individual is indifferent as between two bundles of commodities then he will prefer any average of these two bundles to either one of them."[3] It follows that if exchange is possible, trading will make everyone better off. At the same time, any cooperation in production will make it possible to reap advantages of specialization, economies of scale, and other facilitation of want satisfaction within the cooperating population. A society with an effective set of cooperative and exchange relationships has the potential of cumulative increase in total goods and services, resulting in higher average rewards across the whole population.

Yet, the existence of these conditions does not in itself ensure an acceptable *allocation* of rewards and averages to all elements of the society. A principle of distributive justice is not given by the sheer facts of production and exchange. Of course, as has been noted in Chapter V, inequality of reward does not by itself produce social cleavage and upheaval. It bears repeating that drastic concerted action to transform a social system seems usually to come from *powerful* groupings that feel their *legitimate aspirations systematically blocked* or their vested positions drastically threatened. This is a prime storm signal. We have previously surveyed evidence pointing to a high level of wants and aspirations in our society, as well as to con-

[1] The evidence for this is very clear—in spite of the prominence of conflict and of strident social criticism. Cf. Gabriel Almond and Sidney Verba. *The Civic Culture* (Princeton, N.J.: Princeton University Press, 1963); V. O. Key, Jr., *Public Opinion and American Democracy* (New York: Knopf, 1961), esp. pp. 40 ff., and many other sources reviewed in Chapters V, VII, and XI above.

[2] John S. Chipman, "The Meaning and Nature of Equilibrium," in *Functionalism in the Social Sciences*, Monograph 5 (Philadelphia: The American Academy of Political and Social Science, 1965), pp. 35–64.

[3] *Ibid.*, p. 42.

siderable awareness of differential rewards. The central value-orientations of the society include a large component of divisive goals and a relatively low development of diffuse-participative values. At the same time, class cleavage has been, on the whole, less sharp than in several other industrialized nations; for example, there is less "class" voting than in either Australia or Great Britain.[4]

On the basis of certain commonsense assumptions, the pattern of social mobility in the United States might seem especially conducive to a general sense of satisfaction and distributive justice—for it has high rates of upward mobility, low rates of downward mobility.[5] Furthermore, those who gain the top levels tend to retain their eminence; and this stable elite might be expected to invite emulation and to serve as a steadying force in a fluid society. Furthermore, there has been a long-time trend for average levels of living to increase. Yet neither rising levels of real income nor the participation of increasing proportions of the population in styles of life formerly reserved for a much smaller elite of high prestige necessarily presage increased consensus or political integration. Crucial conditional factors are: whether the stimulation of wants outpaces the rise in available goods and services; how uneven the changes are in the distribution among various social categories of the population; how consistent the changes are with dominant conceptions of distributive justice.

A social system that appeals for allegiance solely on the basis of its ability to deliver economic goods to the individual is on precarious ground in the modern world. Adherence to social institutions can never be exclusively the result of a cold-blooded calculation of specific individual advantages in acquiring scarce values. At the very least, an additional element of legitimacy is involved. It is perhaps especially crucial in a social system like that of the United States that differential rewards be apportioned both according to a *common set of standards of legitimacy* and to the *effective distribution of social power*. In this way, even a consideration of such factors as the material level of living and the distribution of income forces one eventually back to a common value factor. At *some* point, operating integration does depend upon consensus.

This matter should be examined carefully. "Consensus," as ascertained from the separately expressed orientations of individuals, may represent either (1) similarity or homogeneity of views, or (2) the belief ("perception") that others hold a certain orientation. These two aspects have been characterized by Theodore Newcomb as "homogeneity of orientation" as over against "perceived consensus." There may be a high level of actual substantive agreement that is not clearly or accurately estimated, and people may believe that nearly everyone else holds to a view which in fact most others reject. At any specific time, therefore, one of four types of consensus situations may exist:

[4] As noted in Chapter V; see Robert R. Alford, *Party and Society* (Chicago: Rand McNally, 1963).

[5] Works by Lipset and Bendix and by S. M. Miller, as synthesized by Marsh, *op. cit.*, pp. 163–168.

| | | PERCEIVED CONSENSUS: BELIEF THAT OTHERS HOLD A CERTAIN ORIENTATION | |
|---|---|---|---|
| | | *Present* | *Absent* |
| HOMOGENEITY OF ORIENTATION (SUBSTANTIVE CONSENSUS) | *Present* | Recognized pluralistic consensus | Unrecognized pluralistic consensus |
| | *Absent* | "Pluralistic ignorance"; spurious consensus | Manifest absence of agreement |

This is a cross-sectional, static image of consensus. When the growth of agreement is followed as a process through time, successive levels of substantive agreement and shared awareness of agreement can "leapfrog" to the limiting case of 100 percent identity of views, in which all individuals believe that all others hold identical views, that everybody believes that all others believe this, and that everyone is aware that all believe that all others believe that everyone holds the same orientation. At this level the consensus will appear to everyone as complete and unalterable; it will be perceived not as contrived or as a pluralistic achievement but rather as intrinsic, given, in the nature of things. At some point such awareness of awareness of agreement can come to seem supraindividual and wholly irresistible.[6] Such seamless and all-enveloping consensus is extremely rare in complex societies undergoing rapid change. And attenuated consensus opens the possibility that existing allocations may be defined as "arbitrary," thus encouraging increased resort to direct use of power, especially coercive power.

### Mechanisms and Techniques of Coordination and Integration

It thereby becomes evident that the factors that explain the emergence or development of a certain social system are not necessarily the same as those that maintain it once it is fully established. A particular kind of capitalistic economic order developed in the United States through complex historical sequences. Once developed, it contained constraining elements, relatively independent of the particular values and motivations of any one individual or partial segment of the system, for example, the necessity of making profits in business, the dependence of the propertyless worker upon wages. Around the established structures a variety of vested interests cohere. That is, these interests carry an element of customary rightness or

6 Scheff, *op. cit.*, pp. 34–36; also, Peter L. Berger and Thomas Luckmann, *The Social Construction of Reality: A Treatise in the Sociology of Knowledge* (Garden City, N.Y.: Doubleday, 1966), p. 28.

moral claim. Therefore, vested interests always resist change in greater degree than do those interests related to temporary advantage and immediate or prospective gain. To this source of stability is added the interdependence of interests involved in an operating system that insures existing arrangements against sudden or fundamental alteration unless drastic maladjustments occur. The primary implication for the American situation seems to be that the continuation of the given economic and political structure requires that a "stake in the system" be widely held. Otherwise, the rigidity of vested interests in opposition to the claims and aspirations of nonvested interests is likely to place severe and increasing strains upon ultimate societal consensus. Goetz Briefs[7] has pointedly characterized as the "adventure of capitalism" the attempt to operate a social system in which large numbers of workers are propertyless and insecure but at the same time are personally free citizens of a democratic state. When we discussed social stratification and the role of interest groups in politics, we saw the possibly disruptive consequences of the erosion of consensus in a society of marked economic cleavages. Interests alone are not enough, and mutual dependence through the division of labor is not enough. For these factors to contribute to cohesion, two additional elements appear essential, as *minimal* conditions: (1) congruent interests and dependencies must be linked together, and disruptive interests insulated from one another, through definite social structures; (2) there must be *procedural* agreement as to the rules under which interests may be pursued. Under the latter heading, for instance, falls the acquiescence of losers in political elections. Under the former condition must be included all those structural arrangements and techniques of action that articulate interdependence and block conflictful interactions. Such arrangements we may call mechanisms of cohesion, if it is understood that the phrase does not connote automatism but is being used merely to indicate structural or technical factors as distinct from other elements of societal equilibrium.

Among the mechanisms of cohesion is one that at first glance may seem wholly divisive in its implications. It consists of various types of *isolation,* or *insulation, of groups and statuses from other groups or statuses.* Individuals occupying certain statuses simply do not directly interact with persons in certain other statuses, or interact only minimally and in rigidly circumscribed patterns. A "map" of the interaction patterns of most American communities would unquestionably show definite clusters of frequent interaction, separated from other clusters by social voids only lightly bridged by a few individuals. We have already commented on the numerous small groups and "nodes" of interaction that form in large formal organizations.

Yet, how could common understandings and common values develop under conditions of group isolation and status separation? Where is integration in a mosaic of inwardly focused social segments? The answer is that group separation is not a road to convergence upon a common-value system in anything except a procedural sense—say, an implicit agreement to differ

---

[7] See the provocative Chapter 13 of Goetz Briefs, *The Proletariat* (New York: McGraw-Hill, 1937), pp. 237–267.

and to remain separate. However, if groups differ radically in their values and interests, a mutually accepted insulation is one, if not necessarily the best, mechanism for at least the temporary avoidance of overt friction. The remedy can also cause the disease: groups that initially share the same values, or have the bases for developing a fundamental commonality, will gradually diverge from one another insofar as they cease to interact meaningfully and share in common experience; the more indirect and abstract the communication, the more the mutual orientation in terms of generalized stereotypes and the less the ability of each person fully to "take the role of the other." The basic problems are clearly evident in the case of black and white Americans, as well as in the separate world of the very poor, whatever their ethnic membership.

Consensus and empathy are not characteristic products of distance and insulation. Above all, there is a crucial difference between isolation resulting from *mutual preferences* of individuals to associate with a certain in-group and the separation resulting from *categorical exclusion*.

There are two major types of social insulation. One is true isolation—a lack of interaction. This occurs by virtue of physical separation of communities, within each of which people work out long-time interpersonal relations with others; it occurs by reason of systematic withdrawal from participation—as in upper-class exclusive clubs, or in the defense-avoidance behavior of repeatedly rebuffed groups, or in patterns of residential segregation, and so on. The second type of insulation involves direct, person-to-person interaction but consists of formalized and limited patterns of relationships such as the constrained interaction of superiors and subordinates in rigidly hierarchical organizations or the etiquette of many functionally specific occupational roles. Such insulation is attained by numerous specific devices. It may or may not be equally accepted by the parties to the relationship. Often the relation is one of subordination-superordination, involving differential privileges defended by the one party and resented by the other. Where the relation is not too markedly asymmetrical in this respect, the formalized insulation of roles and of groups sometimes permits limited interaction between persons who would come into conflict in a more inclusive and personalized relation.

Much of the separation of true *groups* in our society is basically a matter of the preferential association of persons within a broadly similar culture who share special activities and values: the occupational group, the congeniality circle, and the like. This preferential association is not necessarily rigidly exclusive, and the groups thus formed often absorb new members and shed old ones with considerable facility. In some large-scale instances, however, the separation of *groups* is preceded by, and is dependent upon, the segregation of inclusive social *categories*: "Negroes" (or "black Americans" or "Afro-Americans"), Mexicans, Indians, Protestants, Catholics, Southerners, and so on.[8] In these cases, individuals are assigned to gen-

---

8 The very use of terms here is problematical. A generation ago the words "colored" or "black" were considered derogatory or gauche by white and black intellectuals, and "Negro" or "Negro American" was favored. The rejection by the Black Muslims of "Negro" prefigured the shift to emphasis upon the positive evaluation of blackness:

eralized categories cutting across interacting groups, occupational statuses, and concrete communities.

In American society, the existence of conspicuous social categories and statuses is rendered salient not only by the sharp awareness of discriminatory patterns but also by the very high level of mass demands for affluence, power, and recognition. Where equality of opportunity plus social recognition and acceptance are not fully offered, the result is severe tension and, increasingly, overt conflict.

Mechanisms of cohesion operate at all levels of the social structure, from the relationship of the individual in the smallest group to the political coordination of a nation or nations. To participate in groups that provide regularized expectations seems to be a necessary condition for the organization of personalities as unitary systems. Thus, the behavioral integration of the individual is in large measure an outcome of the integration of the groups in which he is involved. A situation in which individuals can find no stable group to which they may belong leaves the personality without the continual *reinforcement* of patterned behavior that seems essential to meaningfully integrated conduct. The discomforts and frustrations of the anomic situation—of the unsupported individuals in the midst of the "lonely crowd"—are real, and result from real causes. We cannot deal here with the psychological complexities presumed in these statements. We can safely assume that there is a need for interaction, no matter how complex its sources, and that for this reason group participation necessarily means a process of reciprocal control among individuals. Put in commonsense terms, this means that individuals give up a considerable degree of autonomy and renounce many nonconforming tendencies in seeking group membership.

It is in this context that the condition of the primary group in American society may be seen in something like an adequate perspective. The millions of "special areas of density" of interaction—in families, work groups, congeniality groups, neighborhoods, and so on—are still the basic matrices in which psychological security and behavioral consistency are anchored.

Social systems contain four main levels of structure: (1) the "primary" or "technical," (2) the managerial; (3) the "institutional," and (4) the "societal."[9] At the primary level, units of the social structure are engaged in physical production (farms, factories), or carrying out administrative decisions made at higher levels (industrial work group, army platoon), or in integrating individuals and groups (extended family), or in maintaining

"black is beautiful." And "black separatism" as it emerged in the 1960's in the United States clearly represented a partly purposive process of ethnogenesis—of the creation of a new social identity through dramatized common aims, activities, and reconceived past. See Stokely Carmichael and Charles V. Hamilton, *Black Power: The Politics of Liberation in America* (New York: Random House, 1967); Gary T. Marx, *Protest and Prejudice* (New York: Harper & Row, 1967); Robert Penn Warren, *Who Speaks for the Negro?* (New York: Vintage Books, 1966); Talcott Parsons and Kenneth B. Clark (eds.), *The Negro American* (Boston: Houghton Mifflin, 1966); *The Autobiography of Malcolm X*, with introduction by M. S. Handler (New York: Grove Press, 1965); Lewis M. Killian, *The Impossible Revolution? Black Power and the American Dream* (New York: Random House, 1968).

[9] Talcott Parsons, "General Theory in Sociology," in Merton, Broom, and Cottrell, *op. cit.*, pp. 5 ff.

and modifying motives, values, beliefs, and other cultural elements (modification of formal roles in small groups). Above the primary level, managerial roles and structures are concerned with the regulation and disposal of the primary level's output, with securing and allocating necessary facilities, and controlling and supervising the primary units, as in the relation of a business firm to one of its factories.

The *institutional* level of organization, in a sense "encompasses" the primary and managerial levels; it consists of the structures by which such a unit as a business firm or a university is linked into and partly controlled by other parts of the system. Thus, a board of trustees defines limits for the activity of the organization, helps to legitimize it in the community, and to some extent coordinates its activity with that of other managerial units. A variety of forms, including voluntary associations, exists at this level. Finally, all these types of units coexist in the same society and mutually affect one another. The *societal* level is the zone in which the adjustment, mediation, compromise, and regulation of conflicts among institutional units take place. This is the realm of national (or international) political institutions.

In the preceding chapter we dealt with connections and exchanges among institutional sectors. Positive articulations of this kind add to the network of integrative bonds. The maintenance of boundaries and separations may also be an essential aspect of societal integration; this is another way of saying that encroachments and disruptive interferences are thereby reduced. As Lewis Coser has argued in some detail, many social conflicts are integrative not only within solidary collectivities but also across the contending units by reason of boundary defining and relationship-defining effects.[1] Short of specification through direct conflict the primary modes by which separation of two institutional sectors may be maintained are basic but simple and clear:

1. The requirement that *different* personnel act in *representative* roles, for example, that a religious leader may not simultaneously speak for the state.
2. Different *sources of financial support*.
3. Separate *lines of authority*, defining areas of autonomy (the policeman does not give orders to the teacher in the schoolroom).
4. Different and separate *programs of socialization and indoctrination* (the factory does not give religious instruction).
5. Different *symbols* of identity and meaning.
6. Different *means of social control* (compulsion, persuasion, reward); typically all are used in all sectors, but there is specialization of emphasis as in compulsion for the state, reward in the economy, indoctrination in religion and family.

Various examples of lack of one or more of these conditions may be recalled from earlier discussions.

[1] Lewis A. Coser, *Continuities in the Study of Social Conflict* (New York: Free Press, 1967).

Above the small groups and unit organizations are layers upon layers of more extensive organization. Individuals frequently participate in a number of different groups or associations; and the smaller groups are in various ways linked by communication, representation, and chain interaction into larger unities. If the struggle of a large union with the representatives of management in an entire industry may disrupt a larger system of coordination from time to time, it nevertheless represents enormously complex coordination within each of the contending aggregates. In all the major nucleated institutions, the total aggregate of individuals does not participate *directly* in the higher foci of control and communication but is linked together by systems of representation or imperative control. As larger and larger systems of organization have spread across our society, the roles of the nodal control points and centers of communication have become increasingly greater and increasingly invested with a public interest. Every major action at these centers of linkage throws up a moving wave of tangential effects through a labyrinth of channels. At the levels at which separate systems of interaction, imbued with different values and interests, come into contact, coordination is achieved (if at all) through processes of negotiation, compromise, and so on, or by reference to still *other* systems. In situations of impasse, there is either the intervention of a higher authority, as when the state enters industrial disputes, or representatives of the different parties appeal to some larger public. In these ways, every long-continued struggle of large organizations tends to spread in widening circles; and cumulative "resonance" is a definite possibility unless there are definite ways by which negative feedback can occur, so that the appropriate (relevant) points of decision making can be apprised of the nature and magnitude of the "distress" or "demand" signals and their probable secondary reverberations.

Under such circumstances, the cohesion of the society as a whole depends more and more obviously upon the sheer availability of *knowledge* and *techniques* for dealing with the problems of tension and conflict in intergroup and interorganizational relations. This factor is somewhat neglected in analyses of societal cohesion, but its importance seems evident from our present analysis of American society. In a discussion focusing so much upon common-value factors, it is necessary to emphasize that cohesion in such a society is in part a strictly technical problem. The knowledges and skills adequate to the affairs of a localistic republic are simply not sufficient for the organizational demands of our present system. In recent decades, the social sciences have begun to make new attacks on the relevant problems with new research methods and increasingly sophisticated theories. We have also seen the emergence of a small but important corps of specially trained and skilled practitioners—social workers, psychiatrists and psychologists, anthropologists, economic analysts, statisticians, labor-and-management specialists, and so on. The number of skilled and motivated practitioners is still very small, and there are vast dark continents in which they can find little certified knowledge for their use. However, some useful foundations have been laid.

Differences of values and oppositions of interests are intrinsic and "normal" in nearly all differentiated collectivities.[2] Integrated functioning is always a problematic achievement, having continuously to be renewed. As a routine fact of experience also, actual rivalries and conflicts are frequent in most social systems. Many such oppositions are resolved only through the elimination, defeat, or withdrawal of one party from the confrontation. Others, however, are resolved through processes that result in compromise, agreement, new alignments, transformation of issues, and other genuinely integrative outcomes. The procedures, techniques, or social devices used in such processes are accordingly of great interest.

In the very broad sense just suggested, techniques and mechanisms of resolution of opposition and conflict include appeals to law and judicial process, mediation, arbitration, delegated negotiation (as in collective bargaining), appeals to mutually accepted "third parties," authoritative appeals to superordinate values and goals,[3] devices for avoiding premature commitments (straw votes, discussion of agenda, advisory opinions, informal mediation), procedures for delay and exploration (studies, commissions, investigations, "cooling off" periods), coöptation of dissidents or opponents, and many others.[4] The similarily diverse strategies and tactics include diversification or the widening of the area of issues, programming negotiations to deal first with least difficult disagreements, prompt dispersal of crowds, emphasizing initially the need for objective fact-finding, seeking new allies, focusing attention on specific issues rather than persons or abstract ideologies.

No magic is to be attributed to any of these mechanisms and techiques. Nevertheless, all together, the knowledges and skills of tension management and conflict resolution surely are of substantial importance in the achievement of integrated social arrangements.

With reference to "mechanisms and techniques" it should be noted that mass communication is an essential factor in the present state of cohesion of American society. The relatively standardized body of information and value stimuli to which great numbers of people are being exposed is a pervasive factor in common responses to national and world events.[5] Whether the net effects will be integrative or disintegrative can not be asserted in general terms; the effects vary greatly under different conditions.

[2] Some of the basic conditions producing this situation are suggested by the following: Philip Selznick, "Foundations of the Theory of Organizations," in Amitai Etzioni (ed.), *Complex Organizations* (New York: Holt, Rinehart & Winston, 1961), pp. 21–22; Alvin W. Gouldner, "Reciprocity and Autonomy in Functional Theory," in Llewellyn Gross (ed.), *Symposium on Sociological Theory* (Evanston, Ill.: Row, Peterson, 1959); Wilbert E. Moore, "A Reconsideration of Theories of Social Change," *American Sociological Review*, 25, 6 (December 1960), 814; Alvin L. Bertrand, "The Stress-Strain Element of Social Systems: A Micro Theory of Conflict and Change," *Social Forces*, 42, 1 (October 1963), 1–9.

[3] *"social solidarity among individuals or groups is enhanced by recognition of the sharing of a positive and noncompetitive regard for a common object of concern."*—Williams, *Strangers Next Door, op. cit.*, p. 390. See the whole of Chapter X of this work.

[4] James Coleman, *Community Conflict* (New York: Free Press, 1957).

[5] See Karl Mannheim, *Man and Society in an Age of Reconstruction* (New York: Harcourt, Brace & World, 1950), esp. pp. 129 ff. and 256–259; Melvin C. DeFleur, "Mass Communication and Social Change," *Social Forces*, 44, 3 (March 1966), 314–326.

Without communication there is no society. This truism becomes important when we attempt to give it a specific application. In the case of national societies, it calls attention to the enormous differences in total functioning that can be caused by differences in the extensiveness, speed, ease, and accuracy of communication among the various parts of the society. Quick and full communication obviously is not a sufficient condition for societal integration, and it can be disruptive rather than integrative under some conditions, but it is a facilitating condition for *social* integration of a complex national society.[6]

The United States has possessed two great internal communicative advantages. Due to a series of special conditions, a single language has retained dominance as the medium for public discourse, and the great majority of persons who do not have English as the mother tongue are bilingual. Second, the whole society is permeated with multiple systems of fast and technically reliable means for disseminating messages.

### External Pressures

Communication is closely related to the complex processes often characterized as *reactions to external pressures*. We have spoken earlier of the unifying consequences of external threat upon functioning groups and social systems. The specific processes involved here are becoming more exactly known, although they are still imperfectly understood.[7] In our day, of course, the prime pressure is war and the threat of war.[8] The large amount of voluntary effort and sacrifice elicited by World War II, for instance, is documentation of a body of sentiment without which the enormous mobilization of global conflict would be unthinkable. It may be that the mood of the men who fought that war was more nearly that of Greek tragedy than "high-strung patriotic emotion,"[9] but it is plain that the impact of war galvanized into concerted action a wide range of previously discordant segments of the society. There was the typical centralization of authority, increase in centralized regulation, increase of intolerance toward "deviants." A previously diffuse ethnocentrism was structured and directed. As the war continued, those who felt their sacrifices to be great pressed to have others "do their part." For large sectors of the population, there were many

---

[6] This is not to underestimate the remarkable versatility and ingenuity often shown in overcoming language barriers among people who wish to communicate. Cf. Einar Haugen, "Semicommunication: The Language Gap in Scandinavia," *Sociological Inquiry*, 36, 2 (Spring 1966), 280.

[7] See Otto Klineberg, *Tensions Affecting International Understanding*, Bulletin 62 (New York: Social Science Research Council, 1950); Kenneth E. Boulding, *Conflict and Defense* (New York: Harper & Row, 1962); J. K. Zawodny (ed.), *Man and International Relations*, Vols. I–II (San Francisco: Chandler, 1966); Thomas C. Schelling, *The Strategy of Conflict* (Cambridge, Mass.: Harvard University Press, 1960).

[8] Lest there be misunderstanding, war is not necessary to integration, and the ultimate consequences of war may be very different indeed from its proximate effects.

[9] The phrase is from Hugo Munsterberg, *American Patriotism and Other Social Studies* (New York: Moffat, Yard, 1913), p. 5. For extensive data on the attitudes of American troops see Samuel Stouffer, *et al.*, *The American Soldier* (Princeton, N.J.: Princeton University Press, 1949), Vol. I, chap. 9 and Vol. II, chaps. 3 and 12.

immediate gains in income, prestige, and power. Meanwhile, great numbers of individuals continued with their accustomed tasks in terms of previously established motives, expectations, and goals. As the war continued there was, at least for those in military services, a growth of common experiences —no matter how unpleasant or frightful at the time—which in the end left a new residue of shared values and traditions. The cohesive effect of World War II seems beyond doubt. But that was a war which the American people generally accepted as unavoidable and as directed against governments whose policies were clearly the negation of central values of many Americans.

External conflicts that do not initially have a rationale that gains such acceptance, on the other hand, have deeply divisive effects to the extent that the warfare is (a) not quickly or clearly successful, (b) ambiguous or abhorrent in its perceived value-implications. To many Americans, the conflict of the 1960's in Vietnam was such a divisive war. In an affluent social democracy it is probably always difficult for a government to evoke unity for costly warfare fought for abstract, remote, and complex objectives, or to convince the potential fighters that the far-off danger is real.

Up to the present era, wars have been fought primarily as acts of collective desperation or as more or less calculated zero-sum games of a high-status struggle for scarce values. They most definitely cannot be regarded as sheer expressions of "irrational aggression." (The psychological states of men in modern battle have very little in common with the motivations, or aims, of those who made the decisions to send them there; and neither is very close to the vicarious onlookers in the civilian population.) Far from being an automatic expression of aggressive needs, modern war, waged by a democratic polity, requires a degree of consensus and mobilization of resources and energies that is difficult to effect and is problematical in consequences.

### Common-Value Orientations

Finally, it cannot be too strongly emphasized that the fact of integration of value standards does not rest on deductions from speculative theory but is an observable condition that has already been roughly indexed in some situations by empirical research. For example, studies of American troops in Europe toward the end of World War II showed high consensus upon the evaluation of "combat credit" as a basis for determining the order of release of men from the Army.[1] The agreement extended to men in non-combat duties who were going against their own self-interest in advocating full combat credit for front-line troops only. Although most soldiers testified to a desire to return to civilian life as soon as possible, over 70 percent of men in rear-area units voted full combat credit to front-line troops and only 15 percent claimed that men in the rear-area Army and corps headquarters should receive similar credit. In this case, clearly, standards of fairness and

[1] See the data and the description of the social context in Stouffer, *op. cit.*, Vol. II, pp. 62–64.

"rational appraisal" took precedence over self-interested claims. Without some such process, the operation of a highly differentiated social system without widespread recourse to force is not conceivable.

We can see again how the integration of social systems, large and small, is not a matter of everyone's doing or saying the same things but of the *functionally strategic* convergence of the *standards* by which conduct is evaluated. It was once believed that Catholics and Protestants could not live together in the same society. They do so live in American society (and elsewhere) by reason not only of mutual insulation, and not only by virtue of the diminished intensity of traditional religious values, but also by increased sharing of a vast body of nonreligious norms and goals. To those who conceive of society as an organism, it must seem incredible that a system so heterogeneous as American society can exist and function. The marked differentiation of economic levels and prestige classes has sometimes been taken to presage class conflict and basic alteration of the society. In such cases, a commonly neglected factor is the cohesion represented by common-value orientations extending across the many lines of social and cultural differences. Some of these common orientations are in the nature of generalized creeds: explicit, publicly communicated statements of principle that seem to serve as referents for a great variety of activities. A number of such orientations were reviewed in Chapter XI, where we also saw that value uniformities are not confined to the explicit creeds of democracy, individualism, equality, and so on. There are also implicit common themes of great importance—for example, the high evaluation of activity, the stress upon conformity, the assumption that "like should associate with like," the agreement upon procedures for handling conflicts. Common-value orientations at this level do not imply agreement upon the detailed norms regulating specific behavior patterns; in the latter category there is surely great diversity, but the diversity is to a large extent assimilated by the *belief* that there is consensus upon ultimate principles that supply the generalized meanings for conduct. It is extremely important also that many of the implicit understandings that make society possible are not just *implicit* but are also resistant to statement: it is as if there is a tacit agreement not to express or to become aware of what would be dysfunctional. We greatly need careful research in this area, for observation already shows the existence of a mass of specific devices for thus suppressing disruptive elements. We suspect that a study of areas of blocked communication would often reveal conflicts that remain nondisabling only so long as they are kept from overt crystallization. The present suggestion is only that, beyond relatively conscious avoidance of conflict, there are complex latent systems of compartmentalization and insulation that are largely unrecognized but that have great functional significance. It has been indicated previously that a great deal of the "flatness" of American public discourse is probably due to the search for noncontroversial conversational pieces; if so, the implicit premise is that agreement should take priority over difference. Indeed, it is a legitimate hypothesis that one of the most pervasive and deep-rooted elements of cohesion in the heterogeneity of America is the incessant strain toward overt agreement, toward a unified public morality, signalized by external conformity.

All this most definitely does not mean that effective social cohesion is always enhanced by reliance upon value consensus. A collectivity that depends primarily upon ideology rather than interdependence will be highly vulnerable to new stresses caused by changes in survival conditions. Preoccupation with value consensus may divert attention and effort away from urgent immediate problems of realistic adaptation, and at the same time encourage dissension, defection, and schism.[2]

A common value-system, therefore, is not enough. The delicate coordination of activities required under conditions of present urbanized society highlights the inadequacy of "common values" for social integration. Vivid illustrations are provided by mass behavior in disaster. Under the impact of mass disaster from earthquakes, fire, flood, storm, or explosion, certain aspects of social structures and processes stand out in a way not observed under conditions of normal routine. Such catastrophes show clearly that chaos can result from highly responsible behavior. Individuals' first sense of duty is to their immediate family; and thousands of uncoordinated efforts to locate and help family and friends can be severely maladaptive for the total community. Highly disciplined organizations accustomed to crisis provide the best examples of coordinated rather than merely concerted responses to needs. Uncoordinated helpfulness can bring results either tragic or ludicrous or both, as in the case of the Dutch village whose repeated broadcasts for a surgeon and cattle fodder brought on the following day no less than six surgeons and ten tons of cattle feed.[3] Even more incapacitating is "convergence behavior" in which would-be helpers, along with "sightseers" and others variously motivated, jam transportation and communication channels and in other ways impede purposive coordinated activity. The studies of disasters repeatedly underline the crucial importance of communication, trained personnel, means of coordination, and reliable organization.

The social structures of modern urban societies are possible only by the articulation of *congruent expectations* in the interactions of *diversely motivated* actors, organized into linkages among a very large number of diverse subsystems. For most of these interactions, it suffices if people know enough to synchronize actions in time and space and to perform specific acts upon proper signals. But it is crucial that the coordination does take place.

We are thus continually being reminded that "consensus" is not a self-evident concept. For instance, people may agree on the terms upon which they will disagree. However conflictful, this makes for a clean argument. *Cognitive* consensus is the basis for debate, acceptable value-dissonance, and the tremendously important, ordinary agreements-to-disagree that

---

[2] These possibilities are beautifully illustrated by the analysis of Phillip E. Hammond, "The Migrating Sect: An Illustration from Early Norwegian Immigration," *Social Forces*, 41, 3 (March 1963), 275–283.

[3] Allen H. Barton, "The Emergency Social System," in George W. Baker and Dwight W. Chapman (eds.), *Man and Society in Disaster* (New York: Basic Books, 1960), p. 250.

should never be underestimated. After all, the "friendly enemy" is a familiar and important social type.

In a great many social processes, the consensus required for workable interdependence and continued orderly interaction is primarily a matter of implicit agreement to accept the right of others to keep on doing whatever they are doing. Consensus may refer to many quite different elements of culture, personality, society, or the physical world:

1. Knowledge, the "facts of the case," how things work.
2. Beliefs, cognitive conceptions of reality, empirical or nonempirical.
3. Meanings, of codes or symbols.
4. Values, conceptions of the desirable.
5. Goals, objects of attainment.
6. Means, judgments of effectiveness of instrumentalities or modes of attaining goals.
7. Norms, rules for acceptable behavior.
8. Styles, or particular modes or ways of acting.

Consensus may be located or have its relevance in many different kinds of social units—friendship pairs, social circles, families, work groups, military formations, communities, churches, political parties, strata or classes, racial categories, labor unions, business firms, nations, coalitions of nations. The extent and kind of agreement needed obviously varies greatly in different kinds of collectivities.[4]

It is hoped that certain features of our analysis have by now become repetitious, for it is by systematic reexamination that we have our best hope of understanding the daily miracle of society-in-being. This is our rationale, at least, for returning once more to the role of *common symbols* in American society. It is perhaps true that no one is yet able to demonstrate scientifically precisely what this role is. At least one provisional hypothesis, however, is sufficiently impressive to be mentioned here. Most crudely put, it is that many of the most important symbols of national unity have so little specific ideological content that they create a common allegiance by being all things to all men.[5] "Everybody" gives allegiance to the flag, reveres the Constitution, and the Supreme Court, and knows that George Washington was an embodiment of national virtues. Unless the symbols have to be interpreted in terms of *specific* actions and values, they can constitute an overarching set of referents for enormously varied orientations throughout the society. We will seriously misunderstand the fact that human behavior is symbolic if we look exclusively at the "apparent content" of creeds and icons. It is being suggested here that, within wide limits, precisely the amorphous, protean, and unstructured nature of the most inclusive societal symbols gives them their enormously powerful capacity for *defining as com-*

[4] Contrary to the fears characteristic of a certain kind of romantic liberalism, comprehensive and well-organized systems of thought and analysis do not necessarily either reflect or lead to tightly controlled economic and political systems.

[5] For a suggestive example of symbolic variation see Edgar A. Schuler, "V for Victory: A Study in Symbolic Social Control," *Journal of Social Psychology*, XII, second half (May 1944), 283–299.

*mon* that which, from other points of view, is different or even incompatible.[6]

An important specific example of symbolic integration is afforded by the behavior of American political leaders. The role once attached to leaders of organized religion who were expected to fuse in their activities the common symbols of society has to a large extent devolved upon political figures. The high governmental official is expected to stand as a symbol of the whole community and to deal with and integrate very diverse interests and values, and partly for this reason alone, he participates in and endorses the legitimacy of many different, sometimes even radically incompatible, groups and activities. In the realm of symbols no less than in the compromising of interests, political institutions form the prime focus of cohesion in the United States. The government is increasingly the focus of power struggle and certainly could not survive in a democratic form without some compensating development of integrative patterns. The high development of national symbols, and the association of them with the top governmental offices, seems clearly to be one such reaction to the disruptive struggles of interest groupings.

In our efforts to understand conflict and integration, consensus and dissensus, cohesion and disruption, we must use special care to avoid the *aggregative fallacy*. This fallacy has a long history of insidious influence in Western social thought. It consists of analyzing macrosocial processes on the basis of the unwarranted assumption that structurally complex large-scale phenomena may be understood and predicted simply by adding up or extrapolating the regularities observed in small groups and other structurally simple collectivities. In an extreme form, the fallacy produces a caricature of society as "small groups writ large," thus ignoring the enormous differences introduced by successive levels of organization and successive complications of communication. A nation is not a neighborhood; a factory is not a sociability circle; a dyad in the laboratory is not an infantry division in combat. Undoubtedly there are regularities which hold at every level of organization. But, equally, each new type of context produces new combinations of factors and each level of organization manifests patterns not found at less complex levels.

Basic understanding of how societies function requires a clear grasp of the essential differences between the processes of direct interpersonal communication and exchange in small groups and sets, on the one hand, and, on the other, the processes of indirect, macroscopic interaction among collectivities that are subunits of more complex structures. In the latter case the value consensus needed for interaction differs from that of the primary level. It is more often explicit, it more often relies upon generalized symbols, and it is expressed in formalized media of exchange. Means of authenticating identity and authority similarly differ. The part played by "idiosyncrasies" and particular motives of individuals lessens. Behavior is more strongly affected by institutional norms and long-term exchange balances

[6] However, not all the consequences of this kind of consensus will be considered desirable by everyone.

rather than by immediate gratifications and specific interpersonal reciprocities. The *structural* complexities of the macrostructure are multiplied far beyond the possibilities at the small-group level. Interpersonal approval and disapproval became less effective as sanctions, and extrinsic rewards and coercion bulk larger in social control.[7]

Of course, there are many already known connections between micro-level processes and integration or disintegration in the larger societal systems; and it is likely that numerous other linkages will be discovered as research continues. For example, the establishment of values as strong internalized controls of personality functioning and social behavior apparently requires the early identification of the child with one or more nurturing adults.[8] Failure of such identification seems to result in later difficulty in maintaining stable interpersonal relations or firm commitments to "principles." Widespread withdrawal of parents or equivalent functionaries from nurturance and guidance conceivably could produce a massive failure by a new generation to support the main institutions and survival activities of a whole society; and this certainly would produce crucial economic and political upheavals. Short of such speculative scenarios, the present work has reviewed numerous human instances of micro-macro linkages in every institutional sector.

An important difference between Western industrialized societies and the developing or underdeveloped areas today appears to be the clear relationship in the latter between political and economic determinants of class position and social mobility. In Western nations, and certainly in the United States, there has been very substantial opportunity for attainment of relatively high social position on the basis of business success. In many of the developing nations, social rank and upward mobility (and often income and wealth as well) tend more to be determined by political power or education or a combination of the two, as in attainment of position in the central governmental bureaucracy.[9] The consequence is that the middle classes in industrialized societies have been more largely recruited through economic channels and have been less preoccupied with the acquisition and maintenance of political position. Thus, the relative autonomy of the economic sector has highly important consequences for the system of social stratification.

In societies of highly developed functional differentiation, an important mode of integration is the presence of communication from one institution in the normal activities of other institutions. The greater the extent to which any one institution is thus reflected in the processes of socialization and social control in all of the other institutions, the greater is likely to be the

[7] See the clear statements on all this in Peter H. Blau, *Exchange and Power in Social Life* (New York: Wiley, 1964), pp. 24–31.

[8] "Identification" may be of several radically different kinds, ranging from a smooth, non-stressful and emotionally warm process to the tense, desperate incorporation called "identification with the aggressor."

[9] Cf. Bert F. Hoselitz, "Advanced and Underdeveloped Countries: A Study in Development Contrasts," in William B. Hamilton (ed.), *The Transfer of Institutions* (Durham, N.C.: Duke University Press, 1964), pp. 46–49.

integration of that institution with the others. A prominent example in the United States, as in many other industrialized nation-states, is the extent to which political information, beliefs, and values "penetrate and affect the socialization processes of other social systems, such as the family and the church, so that they introduce general citizenship content into their socialization processes."[1] In our society, not only family and church but also school, labor union, business firm, and even stratification structures (such as "prestige" clubs) are often penetrated by political content.

### The Unity of Diversity

A return to a small, simple, and strictly limited state in America would involve such a pyramid of improbabilities that we might as well call it impossible. If this be granted, the central role of government raises anew the eternal question: Who has custody of the custodians? Who watches the watchers? The classic American answer seems to have been *other* custodians. The attempt has been to counter the irresponsibility of any absolute power by separate authorities, systems of checks, referrals of policy to public consent, interplay of interests—in short, the whole pattern of pluralistic balance. Enough has already been said of the consequences and limits of this pattern under current conditions. The problem does serve, however, to point to a source of cohesion not yet mentioned: *the unity coming directly from diversity.* There is no real paradox here. One outcome of diversity in this society is a multiple overlapping of groups and social categories that blurs considerably the sharp edges of potential cleavage—for example, the "cross-pressures" that operate upon individuals whose different membership and reference groups pull them toward different political alignments or the internal heterogeneity of the major political parties. Without these relatively fluid, crisscrossing allegiances it seems highly probable that conflict would be increased, assuming that class differentiation did not diminish. American society is simply riddled with cleavages. The remarkable phenomenon is the extent to which the various differences "cancel out"—are noncumulative in their incidence. There is this much realistic sociological meaning in *e pluribus unum.*[2]

The problem of value integration occurs as a problem of *meaning*—either of the actually apprehended meanings, or of the conceivable meanings that can be revealed by analysis. It also poses itself as a *causal* problem of the effects of various combinations of and alterations in values; it may be analyzed as a *functional* problem of the interconnected consequences of

[1] Gabriel A. Almond, "A Functional Approach to Comparative Politics," in Gabriel A. Almond and J. S. Coleman (eds.), *The Politics of Developing Areas* (Princeton, N.J.: Princeton University Press, 1960), p. 5.

[2] Cf. Robin M. Williams, Jr., *The Reduction of Intergroup Tensions* (New York: Social Science Research Council, 1947), p. 59, for the hypothesis that "a society riven by many minor cleavages is in less danger of open mass conflict than a society with only one or a few cleavages." This long-lived proposition has appeared again and again in social science writings, impressing itself on observers in many different contexts. Cf. Max Gluckman, *Custom and Conflict in Africa* (New York: Barnes and Noble, 1964), pp. 2 ff.; Lewis A. Coser, *Continuities in the Study of Social Conflict* (New York: Free Press, 1967), pp. 1–11.

different value-belief phenomena *for* selectively ordered aspects of society, culture, and personality. Our present analysis has almost wholly eschewed consideration of integration at the level of meaning. Because the materials are enormously complex and the available studies are quite rudimentary, an adequate treatment of meaningful coherence in American culture probably will have to wait for some time.[3] Here we have sought to avoid imposing external judgments regarding consistency or inconsistency in the interest of focusing upon the most definite and clearly identifiable institutional structures. It will be noted that as a consequence the present chapter concentrates largely upon the formal aspects of integration rather than upon the content of values and interests.

## CONFLICT AND INTEGRATION

There is no automatic guarantee, to be sure, that diversity of oppositions will result in societal harmony.[4] Indeed, American history is studded with violent polarizations in which opposition of interests, beliefs, and values could not be contained within the available framework of peaceful resolution. It was a violent revolution that established the nation; a ferocious Civil War nearly destroyed it; and there was chronic warfare with the American Indians down to nearly the end of the nineteenth century. In addition, there is a long roll-call of riots, mob violence, strikes accompanied by violence, mass demonstrations, and other outbreaks.[5] Concrete examples of widespread recurrent disagreement, oppositions, and conflicts within American society since mid-century include community strife concerning fluoridation of water supplies,[6] financing of schools, racial discrimination, educational desegregation, the military draft, the war in Vietnam, interreligious relations, management-union struggles,[7] political ideology. Not every disagreement or opposition is conflict. Several critical inventories of

[3] This type of analysis, in any case, goes far beyond the bounds of any one discipline; it has to be achieved by a synthesis of the approaches and findings of the behavioral sciences together with major contributions from philosophy.

[4] Both consensus and opposition (including violent opposition) are part of the "normal" functioning reality of most societies. Cf. the author's "Some Further Comments on Chronic Controversies," *American Journal of Sociology*, LXXI, 6 (May 1966), 717–721.

[5] Cf. references in Williams, *The Reduction of Intergroup Tensions, op. cit.*, p. 4; Alfred M. Lee and Norman D. Humphrey, *Race Riot* (New York: Dryden Press, 1943); Arthur I. Waskow, *From Race Riot to Sit-In, 1919 and the 1960's* (Garden City, N.Y.: Doubleday, 1966); Stanley Lieberson and Arnold R. Silverman, "The Precipitants and Underlying Conditions of Race Riots," *American Sociological Review*, 30, 6 (December 1965), 887–898; *Report of the National Advisory Commission on Civil Disorders* (New York: Bantam Books, 1968).

[6] There is an extensive research literature on this one matter alone, e.g., Bernard and Judith Mausner, "A Study of the Anti-Scientific Attitude," *Scientific American*, 192, 2 (February 1955), 35–39; Benjamin D. Paul, William A. Gamson, S. Stephen Kegeles (eds.), "Trigger for Community Conflicts: The Case of Fluoridation," *The Journal of Conflict Resolution*, XVII, 4 (1961), 1–81; William Gamson, *Power and Discontent* (Homewood, Ill.: Dorsey Press, 1968), pp. 147–149.

[7] Ralf Dahrendorf, *Class and Class Conflict in Industrial Society* (Stanford, Calif.: Stanford University Press, 1959).

research-based knowledge about social conflict[8] have reiterated from time to time the need to carefully restrict the meaning of the term "conflict." Conflict proper is *not* competition, rivalry, opposition of interests, differences in belief, misunderstanding, hostility, tension, social cleavage, dislike, or aggressiveness. Conflict is an overt process of social interaction, involving two or more social units, in which at least one party seeks to destroy, injure, thwart, or otherwise block or harm the other, against opposition or resistance.[9]

What are the relationships between processes of integration and processes of conflict? As a matter of definition, a specific conflict, while in process, is a negation of integration at that particular time and in that particular context. Yet the conflict may be resolved in such a way that future integration is enhanced, and the failure of an incipient conflict may result in perpetuation or accentuation of malintegrative conditions. Conflict may increase in-group solidarity in each of the contending collectivities, clarify group boundaries and the social and psychological identity of individuals, rectify or block injustices, inhibit aggrandizement. In short, under *some* conditions, some kinds of conflicts have outcomes that may be regarded as "desirable" in terms of various widely approved values. In other instances, conflict eventuates in vast suffering, societal disruption, and the creation of long-enduring animosities and vengeful policies. The sheer fact of "conflict" does not carry with it an invariant set of value-implications.

Much conflict is highly gratifying to many of the participants and to onlookers as well. This is apparent in structured, recurrent "contests" or "oppositions" such as elections, sports, debates, even strikes. It also applies in the more deadly affairs of riots, rebellions, and wars. The gratifications often come from instrumental gains: wages, profits, markets, access to other scarce values. But there are also often consummatory rewards—self-aggrandizement, revenge, social approval, sex, love, a good conscience, or the sheer expression of values—or of hatred. Unless we recognize that conflict often is rewarding, we will be unable to approach an understanding of its prevalence and persistence.[1]

Existing compilations contain a great many useful empirical generalizations and hypotheses applicable to conflict, conflict-resolution, and integration in the United States. For example:

*The larger the number of conflicts in any particular context, the less likely that any one will become all-inclusive with respect to persons, groups, energies, and resources.*[2]

[8] Examples: Arnold M. Rose, *Studies in Reduction of Prejudice* (Chicago: American Council on Race Relations, 1947); Williams, *The Reduction of Intergroup Tensions*, *op. cit.*, esp. pp. 52–77, "Racial and Cultural Relations," in Joseph B. Gittler (ed.). *Review of Sociology* (New York: Wiley, 1957), pp. 423–464; Raymond W. Mack and Richard C. Snyder, "The Analysis of Social Conflict—Toward an Overview and Synthesis," *Journal of Conflict Resolution*, I, 2 (June 1957), 212–248.

[9] Mack and Snyder, *op. cit.*, pp. 217–219.

[1] Coser, *op. cit.*; also Lewis A. Coser, *The Functions of Social Conflict* (New York: Free Press, 1956).

[2] Mack and Snyder, *op. cit.*, p. 237.

*Conflicts between collectivities within a national society are least likely to develop or to become intense when the members of each potentially conflicting unit are subject to cross-pressures of interests and reference-groups with regard to the divisive issues.*[3]

*Conflicts between collectivities within a national society are least likely to develop or to become intense when resources to resolve the issues or gratify the interests occasioning opposition are relatively abundant, and when the contending units share a large number of congruent or supportive values and interests.*[4]

Agreement or disagreement upon the desirability or propriety of some particular norm is not the same as consensus or dissensus concerning the legitimacy or validity of the rule.[5] As we have seen repeatedly in preceding chapters, a very considerable amount of disagreement is normal in the United States concerning particular laws, rules, policies, and other decisions binding upon collectivities. Disagreements of this kind do not seriously threaten the *constitutive* consensus of the society unless they become so intense and the opposing claims so divergent that the institutional procedures for resolving opposition come to be regarded as unjust and, then, as illegitimate. If this happens, and to the degree that it develops, the fundamental basis of voluntary social order is brought into question; at the extreme, there will be violent revolution and the forcible imposition of a new order.

## INTEGRATION, ANOMIE, AND ALIENATION

"American culture" and "American society" are concepts ultimately referable to regularities observed in the behavior of individuals, each of whom experiences society as consisting largely of the regularities he encounters in the behavior of a relatively small circle of other persons. To the degree that regularity disappears in that circle, the individual is in a normless situation, no matter how firm and consistent normative regulation may be elsewhere in the society. This is *anomie* at the concrete level of its impact upon specific persons. Few facts are so important in analyzing a society as those concerning the stability of normative patterns in the basic units of person-to-person interaction. Thus, divorce, extremely high mobility, and other forms of small-group dissolution provide clues to the total state of the social system. In day-to-day social life, what really matters most immediately to the individual is what he can count upon from his network of personal relationships—in terms of financial aid if needed, care in illness or other crisis, emotional support, permissiveness, constraint, and guidance. Both the *level of gratifications* and the *stand-by reliability* of each man's personal community are crucial for his experience of social order and disorder, free-

---

[3] Suggested by propositions 18 and 47, *ibid.*

[4] Suggested by propositions 47 and 48, *ibid.*

[5] Note the concise analysis in Albert K. Cohen, *Deviance and Control* (Englewood Cliffs, N.J.: Prentice-Hall, 1966), pp. 16–18, and this comment: "In a heterogeneous, rapidly changing society, there are few rules whose validity somebody does not deny and whose application is not regarded as an illegitimate attempt on the part of some to enforce their predilections on others" (p. 19).

dom and restraint, security and insecurity.[6] Of course, the social network around each individual is in turn greatly dependent upon the surrounding social system.

The condition in which individual persons confront a world only weakly and poorly defined or controlled by norms, found in all societies, is one of several major forms of departure from logically ideal congruity and smooth functioning. We may distinguish the following types of "disjunctions" and "failures" in the total action systems of a society:[7]

1. *Cultural:* lack of logical or aesthetic congruity; lack of normative consistency; disruptions of meaning.
2. *Cultural-social boundary:* (a) failure of cultural norms, values, beliefs, symbols to control behavior; (b) failure of social interaction to support and maintain cultural patterns.
3. *Social:* conflict; lack of coordination or articulation; failure of predictability; generation of noxious reactions in the social and physical environments.
4. *Social-personality boundary:* (a) "social overload"—excessive demands and stresses upon personality arising from the system (or "lack of system") of social interactions and relationships; lack of support and guidance; inadequate gratification and freedom; (b) deviant behavior, arising from intrapersonality tensions or deficiencies; lack of commitment; withdrawal of support and participation.
5. *Personality:* disabling neuroses and psychoses.
6. *Personality-organism boundary:* (a) organismic deficiencies and malfunctioning (chronic disease, genetic defects); (b) psychosomatic disease or disorder.

Anomie in the classic Durkheimian sense cuts across at least the second, third, and fourth of these types of disjunction and may be analyzed in the form of various breakdowns in the wider normative definitions to which immediate behavior in the small situation is oriented. One of the most interesting aspects of anomie at this macroscopic level is the problem of the stress placed upon cultural goals as over against institutionalized means. This mode of stating the problem is contained in a well-known analysis by Robert K. Merton so germane to the present chapter that we recapitulate its main points. Merton's analysis[8] proceeds through the following steps, among others:

1. Deviant, nonconforming behavior is not predictable on a biological basis; the *rate* of deviance varies in different social structures, and is in part the result of definite social pressures toward nonconformity.

[6] For a comparative perspective, see Jules Henry, "The Personal Community and Its Invariant Properties," *American Anthropologist*, 60, 5 (October 1958), 827–831.

[7] Talcott Parsons, "An Approach to Psychological Theory in Terms of the Theory of Action," in Sigmund Koch (ed.), *Psychology: A Science*, Vol. III (New York: McGraw-Hill, 1959), pp. 612–711.

[8] Robert K. Merton, "Social Structure and Anomie: Revisions and Extensions," in *Social Theory and Social Structure* (New York: Free Press, 1957), pp. 131–194.

2. In the cultural regulation of behavior there are both legitimated *goals* and *institutionalized norms* defining prescribed or proscribed means for attaining the goals.
3. Cultural goals and the regulation of means have a range of independent variation; goals may be so stressed that normative regulation practically disappears, or the goal may be lost in an emphasis on the means-norms.
4. In American culture there is very great emphasis upon monetary success; this emphasis is systematically inculcated and reinforced; and the goal is held out to all classes of the society. There is not "a corresponding emphasis upon the legitimate avenues on which to march toward this goal."
5. Innovative or deviant responses are expected to occur at different rates in various subgroups or strata of the society. For example, stress on innovation in upper economic strata leads to "white-collar crime" and sharp business practice; in lower strata, to racketeering and petty crime. Ritualism—a way of reducing level of aspiration—is expectable on a considerable scale in the respectable lower-middle strata.
6. A wide variety of beliefs and symbols in American society have the presumed function, insofar as they are effective, of defining frustrations in individual or nonsocial terms. This is the "conservative counter-myth" as against the mythology of rebellion, which attributes mass frustration to the status quo system and proposes an alternative system.
7. Conformity is the dominant response in the context of the success pattern. But the value placed upon competitive success produces a strain toward deviant behavior. For the system to be stable, rewards at all positions in the scale must be proportioned to support the rules of the game and not just victory in the struggle. In the American system, *alternative* goals means schemes remove some of the disruptive potential of the primary stress on monetary success, for example, subcultural emphases upon nonmonetary success goals.

Recall the evidence that in American society high aspirations are stimulated by indoctrination, by public example, by successive experience, and by popular mythology. No neat correspondence is to be expected between such aspirations and actual opportunities, either on the average or in *every stratum and subcollectivity.* Further, the goals are often vague and the successes and rewards of other persons easily become objects of luxuriant fantasy, far removed from the actual conditions; and these tendencies are accentuated by rapid change. The dysfunction of high and indefinite aspirations and limited opportunities often occurs concurrently with heterogeneity of norms and high rates of "deviant" success. Thus, modern metropolitan United States might be expected to have a relatively high incidence of weak and erratic normative controls. As a consequence of anomie—the full or partial breakdown of social standards—many individuals respond by attitudes of *alienation* and *anomia.*[9] The absence of reliable conformity to

[9] Robert K. Merton, "Anomie, Anomia, and Social Interaction: Contexts of Deviant Behavior," in Marshall B. Clinard (ed.), *Anomie and Deviant Behavior* (New York: Free Press, 1964), pp. 213–242, esp. pp. 217–230.

consensual standards creates a social condition; the responses to it include feelings of powerlessness, meaninglessness, distrust, cynicism, futility, depression, diffuse hostility, hopelessness.[1]

Merton's analysis thus takes *one* aspect of normative regulation and opens up possible lines of analysis for showing the differing consequences of different means-ends emphases in variously situated groups and strata in a culture with a modal emphasis upon continuous active striving for success in a competitive occupational system. The analysis helps to specify how normative regulation can be weakened or dissolved by a strong "bombardment of interests" directed toward any scarce distributive value whatsoever. In a society so goal centered as we have found America to be, a primary type of anomie is the corrosion of institutional norms by activistic emphases on scarce goals.

But this type of anomic condition is not the only one important for contemporary society.[2] We should not overlook the fact that rejection of norms and goals includes the phenomenon of cultural apathy with respect to standards of conduct. Qualitatively different aspects of the latter condition are variously connoted by terms such as indifference, cynicism, moral fatigue, disenchantment, withdrawal of affect, opportunism. One prominent type of apathy is the loss of involvement in a previously sought cultural goal, such as occurs when continued striving results in persistent and seemingly unavoidable frustration.[3] The loss of central life-goals leaves the individual in a social vacuum, without focal direction or meaning. But another crucial kind of apathy seems to emerge from conditions of great normative complexity and/or rapid change, when individuals are pulled this way and that by numerous conflicting norms and goals, until the person is literally disoriented and demoralized, unable to secure a firm commitment to a set of norms that he can feel as self-consistent. Under certain conditions, not yet understood, the result is a kind of "resignation from responsibility:" a discounting of principled conduct, a lack of concern for the maintenance of a moral community. It seems that this lostness is *one* of the basic conditions out of which some types of political totalitarianism emerge. The individual renounces moral autonomy and is subjected to an external discipline.[4]

---

[1] *Anomia* is a psychological condition, consisting of attitudes of despair, depression, and the like. *Anomie* is the social condition of normlessness—which often leads to the individual's reaction of anomia.

[2] Anomie is of course a matter of degree, and to characterize a situation as anomic is to assume some standard of adequate normative development. This may be an empirical standard, for example, derived from eixsting modal definitions of the culture under study, or a hypothetical standard, for example, derived from an abstract model of a perfectly integrated system. For a clarifying analysis see Bruce P. Dohrenwend, "Egoism, Altruism, Anomie, and Fatalism: A Conceptual Analysis of Durkheim's Types," *American Sociological Review*, 24, 4 (August 1959), 466–473.

[3] For example, the apathy accompanying enduring and hopeless unemployment. Cf. B. Zawadzki and Paul F. Lazarsfeld, "The Psychological Consequences of Unemployment," *Journal of Social Psychology*, VI, 2 (May 1935); also the previously cited works of E. Wight Bakke.

[4] Note that a rigidly authoritarian system, if it is total, in its turn destroys individual ethical autonomy. The essence of the situation is in the familiar "we were only carrying out orders." (Of course the "orders" may be the implicit compulsions of a "participatory democracy.")

Widespread normative apathy, however, seems to generate several kinds of counterreaction—above all, the rise of leaders interested in mass power, and the simultaneous demands for conformity on the part of those who feel threatened. If these tendencies are combined with external political and military threats, real or presumed, one may expect an especially strong movement toward rigid formulae of conformity and security. If Americans are to meet the coming years with some continuity of institutional principles, an understanding of reactions to anomie may help in acquiring perspective on the problems of the day.

If anomie is a *social* condition, it must refer to lack of realistic, socially supported norms that actually define and regulate particular kinds of actions. The indexes that should be used to identify and appraise anomie include a variety of measures of agreement upon and conformity with social rules. The *psychological* conditions of anomia cannot be measured by the same indicators; their appropriate indexes are responses indicative of beliefs, values, and feelings directed toward or concerned with norms, normlessness, social authority, conformity or nonconformity, and the like.[5] An increasingly sophisticated body of research has demonstrated many connections between both the social and the psychological conditions and important patterns of overt and covert behavior, including schizophrenia, racial and ethnic discrimination and prejudice, voting behavior, suicide, alcoholism, authoritarianism, juvenile delinquency of certain kinds, social participation (friendships, voluntary associations).[6] Anomia itself has been shown to be strongly related to lack of success or opportunity to attain important life-goals: persons most blocked or deprived by reason of old age, low education, low income and occupational position, physical disabilities, social isolation, categorical discrimination, and similar disadvantages or barriers are most likely to express anomia.[7]

Much remains to be discovered about the processes by which the social inequalities found in all complex societies come to be accepted (when this does occur): how ambitions are limited, achievements overvalued, defeats redefined, and how resentments come to be suppressed, modified, redirected, contained, or muted. Although an unknown continent here exists, some present insights give promise of leading to greater knowledge. It seems likely, for example, that the potential for resentment sufficiently massive and focused to provide a firm basis for effective political action against

[5] The most frequently used research device is Srole's opinion scale of anomia, which characterizes the condition as consisting of the belief that community leaders are indifferent, that little of value can be accomplished, that the world holds little promise for one's children, that one's own goals are not being attained, and that one's fellows can not be counted upon for concern and help. See Leo Srole, "Social Integration and Certain Corollaries: An Exploratory Study," *American Sociological Review*, 21, 6 (December 1956), 709–716.

[6] See the elaborate summary: Stephen Cole and Harriet Zuckerman, "Appendix: Inventory of Empirical and Theoretical Studies of Anomie," in Clinard, *op. cit.*, pp. 243–311.

[7] For illustrative data: Dorothy L. Meier and Wendell Bell, "Anomia and Differential Access to the Achievement of Life Goals," *American Sociological Review*, 24, 2 (April 1959), 189–202.

inequalities is greatly reduced in stable societies by the continuous pre-occupation of individuals with the most immediately perceived differentials. Since the differentials most directly and vividly experienced tend to be those of "adjacent" social ranks or strata, the foci of both aspiration and resentment tend to be constricted and specific. As W. G. Runciman has suggested: "Most people's lives are governed more by the resentment of narrow inequalities, the cultivation of modest ambitions and the preserva-tion of small differentials than by attitudes to public policy or the social structure as such."[8]

In modern social commentaries, the highly fashionable omnibus term "alienation" has become encrusted with so many vague connotations as to be practically useless for exact description; it has been taken to refer to generalized despair, sense of powerlessness, rage, meaninglessness, norm-lessness, isolation, self-estrangement, and possibly other conditions or atti-tudes.[9] In various ways all of these disaffected orientations are relevant to the study of social integration. But it is essential to make the distinctions clearly, and to deal with one thing at a time.

The feeling of powerlessness often is alleged to be common in modern society, as a reaction to the centralization of economic and political de-cision-making and to lack of effective personal involvement in organizations "intermediate between the family and the state." Fortunately some in-formative research is available to partially test this large allegation. One of the mitigating influences against a sense of powerlessness usually is said to be participation in organizations. A study in Columbus, Ohio, shows that persons belonging to labor unions or business or professional associations are significantly less likely than unorganized workers to express feelings of powerlessness (with the exception of white-collar workers who do not aspire to upward social mobility).[1] The data show that the feeling of lacking power to influence events is not merely a reflection of socioeconomic status or of generalized despair.

An additional central facet of normative problems in our society is, of course, the whole pattern of group solidarity and conflict, which has been treated extensively in this book and elsewhere. It is enough to note here one possible connection between anomic conditions and problems of inter-group, or intercategory, relations. If individuals feel that the normative structure upon which their psychological security depends is threatened by forces they cannot identify or understand, they frequently exhibit an in-creased intolerance of ambiguity or differences in social relations. This is

[8] W. G. Runciman, *Relative Deprivation and Social Justice* (Berkeley and Los Angeles: University of California Press, 1966), p. 285.

[9] Melvin Seeman, "On the Meaning of Alienation," *American Sociological Review*, 24, 6 (December 1959), 783–791; Dwight G. Dean, "Alienation: Its Meaning and Measure-ment," *American Sociological Review*, 26, 5 (October 1961), 753–758; Robert Blauner, *Alienation and Freedom* (Chicago: University of Chicago Press, 1964), esp. chaps. 2 and 8.

[1] Arthur G. Neal and Melvin Seeman, "Organizations and Powerlessness," *American Sociological Review*, 29, 2 (April 1964), 216–226; Blauner, *op. cit.*

a context highly favorable to rigidly categorical definition of outgroups. If the outgroups are external to the society, one consequence is to minimize internal differences, for example, through the sense of national membership by contrast to others. But this sort of integration through heightened emphasis upon categorical group membership gives only a precarious unity; and in net balance, it seems unlikely that this will be the *main* dynamism of social cohesion in America. The institutional precipitate of the most enduring values is perhaps deeper and more commonly held than many "leaders of the people" seem to believe.

All enduring social relationships not based exclusively on coercion involve a substantial amount of "faith" or "trust." Much of the regularity of a going society rests upon a vast substratum of implicit trust—that within some acceptable zone of likelihood and accuracy persons are what they appear to be, that promises will be kept and commitments fulfilled, that allegations are factually correct, that extremely destructive acts will not be committed without apparent reason or without forewarning indications, that political authorities will act in the interest of attaining consensually validated collective goals.[2] A society in which trust has disappeared is no longer a viable society: to destroy trust is to subvert, in the literal sense of undermining the foundations.[3] Confidence in the reliability of behavior, in the veracity of statements, and in some meaningful sincerity of expressed intentions and evaluations is a boundary condition of social integration.

Finally, we must always remind ourselves of the obvious point: *integration as a continuously problematic social achievement is relative to the standards by which people judge their society and their own life in it.* American culture contains a set of extraordinarily demanding criteria that can be invoked by critics and advocates of social change. With increased prosperity, health, security, education, and with increased sociopolitical awareness, many people expect and demand that "the society" provide not only political rights and liberties, not only civil rights, not only protection against poverty and ill health, but also a high degree of personal control and personal freedom and even a secure sense of personal identity and a "meaningful life." If such demands are made in sufficiently extreme terms, no society could conceivably meet them in full; but the existing social system may still be rejected on grounds of its failure to meet ideal criteria. Although we are now on highly speculative ground, it may well be that a certain compassion for human imperfection and a modicum of tolerance for social error and ineffectiveness are still necessary for the maintenance of any society as it copes with uncertainty and change.

### A Note on the Problem of Indexes

We need not emphasize the fact that variation and individual differences in values and beliefs are not to be confused with *anomie*. No one individual

---

[2] On political trust: Gamson, *op. cit.*, pp. 39–58. Gamson clearly shows that distrust is a narrower concept than alienation.

[3] For an excellent description of certain kinds of political subversion see Russell Rhyne, "Patterns of Subversion by Violence," *The Annals*, 341 (May 1962), 65–73.

ever experiences or knows the complete range of the value orientations current in his society; and some idiosyncratic variation always occurs. Nor can anomie be inferred from the simultaneous existence of apparently conflicting cultural orientations; the conflict may not be registered by the population, or it may be resolved or rationalized in some wider value-belief complex, or the differing orientations may be insulated between noninteracting groups. Partly for these reasons, anomie as a social condition has to be defined independently of the psychological states thought to accompany normlessness and normative conflict. Conflict of norms, for instance, is an important fact only when two or more normative standards enjoin actions that cannot be carried out by the same person in the same situation. Conflict or congruity may be taken as the independent variable—as a *cultural* fact to be defined by a stated degree of consensus in the group or society being examined. The *behavioral outcome* is the dependent variable. The intervening variable consists of the *psychological state* of individuals—for example, their anxiety or feelings of frustration. The basic model for explanatory purposes is: normative situation → psychological state → behavioral item or sequence.[4] The problem is to show how a defined *normative structure* is associated with or followed by *certain patterns of conduct* (or lack of pattern) and then to relate the two via psychological variables.

A possible model for developing indices of integration or anomie would then be as follows: first, we establish the existence of a widely accepted norm; the research techniques here range from public opinion surveys to detailed observation and interviewing. If possible we also establish indications of intensity of responses, for example, by the severity of sanctions evoked by violation. In both aspects we build up the generalized indices in terms of specific pieces of *behavior*—having children, going to college, saving money, committing suicide, voting, and so on—selecting the items of behavior on the basis of the commonly imputed meanings discoverable in the culture. Thus the commonly listed "social problems" in the United States represent the judgment of someone that an existing social condition is contrary to some norm, such as crime and delinquency, divorce and desertion, suicide, and so on. For example, *given* a widespread and intense conviction that suicide is undesirable or wrong or sinful, a high suicide rate becomes an index of malintegration; and by reason of the connection between loss of definite normative structure and some types of suicide, it becomes a partial index of anomie.[5]

The magnitude and incidence of riots and other forms of collective turbulence and violence are obvious indicators of breaks in integration.

[4] Strictly speaking, of course, the arrows should be written ↔: the relations are reciprocal.

[5] The common impression that personal and social disorganization have increased greatly in American society over the decades of the twentieth century is difficult to support by hard facts. The overall suicide rate was only very slightly higher in 1960 than in 1900. See Louis I. Dublin, *Suicide: A Sociological and Statistical Study* (New York: Ronald Press, 1963); Andrew F. Henry and James E. Short, *Suicide and Homicide: Some Economic, Sociological and Psychological Aspects of Aggression* (New York: Free Press, 1954); Jack P. Gibbs and Walter T. Martin, *Status Integration and Suicide* (Eugene: University of Oregon Press, 1964); and Robert Hagedorn and Sanford Labovitz, "A Note on Status Integration and Suicide," *Social Problems*, 14, 1 (Summer 1966), 79–84.

However, highly sophisticated measurement and techniques of analysis are required to extract the most useful information from such events.[6]

Trends in indicators must be examined with great care and skepticism. Thus, contrary to many assertions, the scanty data available suggest that rates of psychosis in large urban centers were as high a century ago as they are today.[7] Conclusions based on apparent trends in reported rates of crime and juvenile delinquency are subject to fearful hazards arising from changing definitions, completeness of reporting, methods of law enforcement, and other factors.

By selective attention to mobility, heterogeneity, urbanism, social leveling, and mass communication, many critics of modern industrial society derive an image of a rootless and manipulable population that is volatile in ideology, vulnerable to propaganda, escapist and privatized in leisure-time activities, and increasingly without high standards of taste in art and recreation. This description has been shown to be overly diffuse and exaggerated. The United States is a prime case of high industrialization, mobility, and "massification." Yet it retains high religious-group participation, associational activity, effective family organization, and an impressive amount of locality social ties and associations. Social structure is very far from being "dissolved." Yet the exposure to mass media is not exaggerated by the critics: about 80 percent of the population spend four hours or more a day viewing television or listening to radio; in nine of every ten homes there is a television set in operation for five or six hours a day.[8]

Other examples could be described at great length. But the moral is simple: global impressionistic judgments of the state of integration of a whole society are likely to be quite untrustworthy. A scientifically defensible description of the integration of a group or society can only be built up by critical assembly of many items of laboriously derived information. It is one thing to be able to suggest appealing—or alarming—insights, quite another, to analyze the specific conditions and consequences of social integration and disintegration.

## SUGGESTED READINGS

BAKER, GEORGE W., and DWIGHT W. CHAPMAN (eds.). *Man and Society in Disaster*. New York: Basic Books, 1960. Description and interpretation of social behavior under extreme conditions, including examples of "emergency social systems" that operate in crises when usual functioning is severely disrupted.

BLAU, PETER M. *Exchange and Power in Social Life*. New York: Wiley, 1964. Already reviewed in connection with Chapter VII. Relevant here as conceptual analysis of processes by which "equilibrium bargains" are found,

[6] Cf. Milton Bloombaum, "The Conditions Underlying Race Riots as Portrayed by Multi-dimensional Scalogram Analysis," *American Sociological Review*, 33, I (February 1968), pp. 76–91.

[7] Herbert Goldhammer and Andrew W. Marshall, *Psychosis and Civilization* (New York: Free Press, 1953).

[8] Wilensky, *op. cit.*

norms are established, and a spreading network of consensual authority may become accepted.

COHEN, ALBERT K. *Deviance and Control.* Englewood Cliffs, N.J.: Prentice-Hall, 1966. Problems of integration and change at the level of relatively small-scale, chronic types of normative deviation, violation, and rebellion. Critical and sophisticated approach, going beyond the conventional wisdom.

COSER, LEWIS A. *Continuities in the Study of Social Conflict.* New York: Free Press, 1967, Part I and chap. 10. A sane and insightful treatment of the moot topics of conflict and violence. Shows how conflict may represent either disintegrative or integrative processes, depending upon specific conditions and upon the scope of the collectivity under consideration.

GAMSON, WILLIAM. *Power and Discontent.* Homewood, Ill.: Dorsey Press, 1968. Succinct formulation of crucial issues and hypotheses. Generates new perspectives by treating its topic in terms of a gamelike model of authorities and those reacting to authorities.

MALCOLM X. *The Autobiography of Malcolm X*, with introduction by M. S. Handler. New York: Grove Press, 1965. The illuminating saga of a remarkable man who experienced and in several ways resolved and eventually transcended some of the most agonizing conflicts and dilemmas of the modern world.

MARX, GARY T. *Protest and Prejudice.* New York: Harper & Row, 1967. Skillful presentation of national survey data on attitudes and opinions of black Americans in a period of turmoil. The findings may be surprising.

MERTON, ROBERT K. *Social Theory and Social Structure.* New York: Free Press, 1957, pp. 131–194. Contains the classic essay on social structure and anomie that has given direction to a whole generation of thought on problems of conformity, dissent, and innovation.

PARSONS, TALCOTT. "An Approach to Psychological Theory in Terms of the Theory of Action," in Sigmund Koch (ed.), *Psychology: A Science*, Vol. III. New York: McGraw-Hill, 1959, pp. 612–711. Ideas enough for a generation of research. Contains highly important clues as to levels and types of integration—psychosomatic, psychological, social, and cultural. Requires careful and thoughtful reading to see the implications of its sophisticated theoretical formulations.

RUNCIMAN, W. G. *Relative Deprivation and Social Justice.* Berkeley: University of California Press, 1966. Based on data from England and Wales, but highly relevant to the American case—or, indeed, to any other society. Confronts the basic problem of differential responses to various actual inequalities—and the far-from-perfect correlation between "injustice" and "sense of grievance."

STOUFFER, SAMUEL A., *et al.*, *The American Soldier.* Princeton, N.J.: Princeton University Press, 1949, Vol. I, chap. 9, and Vol. II, chaps. 3 and 12. Illuminates processes of integration under conditions of inequality and extreme stress. Analyses of massive data from soldiers in World War II, both in training in the states and overseas and in combat.

WILLIAMS, ROBIN M. JR., with the assistance of JOHN P. DEAN and EDWARD A. SUCHMAN. *Strangers Next Door.* Englewood Cliffs, N.J.: Prentice-Hall,

1964, chaps. 7–10. Summary volume reporting results of the Cornell Studies in Intergroup Relations. From a focus on ethnic relations and prejudice and discrimination, the analysis eventually moves into the generic problem of integration of a complex multigroup society.

# Social and Cultural Change

## XV

A REVIEW

**W**e have now analyzed some main components of the structures and processes that, taken together, constitute "American society." We have seen that this national society is a highly dynamic and differentiated social system, operating in terms of very complex cultural inputs and demanding great amounts of both human and nonhuman energies. We have seen also that the total society is socially and culturally heterogeneous in many respects. We have emphasized the great extent to which it is subject to strain, deviance, tension, dissensus, and conflict, while at the same time we have surveyed the impressive evidences of structure and continuity.

Institutions have not been conceived here as fixed, static entities but as recurring processes—as moving sets of statuses and relationships among statuses. Institutional norms—the "atoms" or "genes" of our analysis —similarly have been regarded as rules that represent the outcomes of bargains, the resolutions of conflicts, the clarifications of ambiguities, the stabilization of competition, the consensual efforts to control power, the agreements to facilitate goal attainment. Many such rules are long-lived; many are redefined or abolished after a relatively short time. Thus, both stability and change may be observed all around us in the very core of social structure. Although there is great variation in the speed with which each of the numerous aspects of sociocultural systems changes, no alert student of American society is likely to overlook or underestimate the prevalence of change. Indeed, the characteristic preoccupation of our times with change is more likely to lead us to exaggerate the changefulness of the twentieth century in comparison with earlier times. Our present social world does move at an unprecedented rate; but very few historical societies ever have been static for very long.[1]

This book has chosen to focus initially upon structure rather than process, on the premise that before we can most effectively study change it is useful to see what it is that changes. Yet we have been continually aware that it is not possible realistically to deal with any important aspect of American society or culture without considerable attention to changes and trends. Structure in the sociocultural world is the changing fixity of a

---

[1] "The speed of contemporary change is not totally illusory but it can be exaggerated as when we pass a much slower-moving auto on the road and it seems to be standing still." Wilbert E. Moore, *Social Change* (Englewood Cliffs, N.J.: Prentice-Hall, 1963), p. 1.

continuous process, like the contours of a whirlpool in a rapidly moving stream. A stable society is not necessarily *uneventful,* so long as the events occur in a recurrent normative framework. Social motion does not always mean social change. Change occurs when there is a shift in pattern, when new relationships emerge, new standards and goals become shared.[2] It is not necessarily social change if an individual meets a situation new to him nor if individuals vary in their behavior in given types of situations—only when the difference is shared and endures long enough to be recognizable as a new structure can we say that the culture or the society has changed. We can imagine a society with many meaningful events, rich in zest and drama, in which people over long periods live by essentially the same codes, have the same ideas and beliefs, and handle life crises by established patterns. We stress this point because of a tendency in modern American thought to equate social stability with a dull, monotonous routine.

Every preceding chapter has reported social and cultural changes, and at many points explanatory interpretations have been presented. It would be unnecessarily repetitious to review that material here. This chapter, therefore, is restricted to a highly selective commentary upon a relatively few patterns of change that we regard as especially important socially and that are apt illustrations of interesting lines of development in social science.

## SOME GENERAL THEORIES

In line with distinctions used throughout this volume, it is convenient to discriminate between cultural change and social change. The first has to do with changes in systems of ideas of various kinds, in beliefs, in values and norms; included also in this category are changes in the technical apparatus used for dealing with the physical world. On the other hand, *social* change refers to shifts in the ongoing interaction patterns of person-to-person relationships. In treating both categories of change, a sociological analysis gains in power as it is able to specify how and where the change occurs—in what areas of social structure, in what specific items, at what rates, through what processes. To give only one example, it makes a great difference whether the political history of a people is that of shifts in ruling elites, that occur largely independently of the masses (palace revolutions, *coups d'état,* and so on) or whether political changes directly involve major portions of the population and affect basic social structures other than the state itself.

The analysis of long-range social change is assuredly one of the most difficult aspects of the scientific study of societies. Nevertheless, much valuable monographic work has accumulated during the past three generations; and many errors and inadequacies of earlier theories have been eliminated. We are now able to renounce a large part of the sweeping theories of a Comte

---

[2] Karl Mannheim, *Ideology and Utopia* (New York: Harcourt, Brace & World, 1936), p. 75: "By social stability we do not mean uneventfulness or the personal security of individuals, but rather the relative fixity of the existing total social structure, which guarantees the stability of the dominant values and ideas."

or a Spencer, and to counsel ourselves to the disciplined patience necessary for the construction of more limited but more solidly grounded descriptions and explanations. It is a major gain, furthermore, that we can now definitely discount all theories reducing the explanation of social and cultural change to a single factor.

If we look for sources of change that permit scientific treatment, we can identify several classes of factors of the sort that served as prime movers in the earlier reductionist theories. First, there is the physical environment, in so far as it is analytically independent of human activity. No one doubts the concrete importance for human action of climate, topography, resources, location, and so on; but it can be easily shown that vast social changes occur without change in physical conditions. Likewise, granting that the biological nature of men must never be overlooked, it is not through any known alterations in that nature that we can explain the enormous and rapid changes of modern societies. In short, we do not see how one can explain a variable by a constant. If on this basis one rejects geographic or biological determinism, there is left the residual area of culture and society itself. Here again, one encounters monofactorial explanations—economic determinism, idealistic emanationism, the great man theory of history, and so on.[3] Without taking space here to support the contention, it is the present view that all these—including Marxism—are demonstrably and seriously inadequate and misleading. What are here called reductionistic explanations have in common the attempt to eliminate men's ideas and values as real causal variables—to regard them as reflections of some more basic condition. On the other hand, the present view is that *Das Kapital* has not been without influence on human history and that Einstein's $E = MC^2$ likewise has made a difference, *and* that in neither of these illustrative events have subsequent developments been simple reflections of a single underlying factor.[4] Conversely, neither the present tide of world communism nor atomic weapons are emanations of the ideas to which we conventionally trace them for purposes of punctuating the continuous stream of history. In short, the explicit position of our analysis is that sociocultural factors must be treated as primary variables in explaining change, not merely for methodological convenience but because ideas and value orientations cannot be reduced to lower orders of complexity without serious loss in understanding and predictive power. One compact way of summarizing the whole point is to say our theories of social change will make an important difference in the way in which we orient ourselves and hence in the way we will act.[5]

[3] All these closed systems are literally pseudoscientific. But this does not imply that the remedy is an indiscriminate electism nor the easy evasion of the problem through a meaningless multiple factor approach which is unable to specify whether one thing is more important than another.

[4] Cf: "We are made by what we have made. We project our ideas into the world of reality, and when they have taken shape and form, they shape and form us by their reaction upon us. A nation makes a system of law and government, and that system, in its measure, makes the character of that nation. We build more greatly than we know; and our acts have consequences beyond our intentions."—Ernest Barker, *National Character* (London: Methuen, 1927), p. 4.

[5] Extreme reductionism, if really taken seriously, would have us leave the crucial determination of events to those who have *other* convictions.

All too briefly, certain of the most general factors in change may be summarized as follows:

1. Changes in physical environment or biological nature, not due to the agency of cultural factors—for example, natural catastrophes, climatic changes, human genetic changes, development of new diseases.
2. Frequency and character of intercultural contact—for example, invasion, conquest, migration, trade.
3. The complexity of a given culture and social structure—for example, differentiation of subcultures, of statuses and roles.
4. The type of value orientations present in the total system, for example, the relative emphasis upon tradition or innovation, upon otherworldly or this-worldly interests. Generalizing, a portion of sociocultural changes are derived from processes internal to the system being examined.
5. Within any given sociocultural system, certain changes emerge from the unanticipated consequences of purposive social action—for example, the secularization of a religious tradition through following out its own precepts or the precipitation of an unintended war.
6. Idiosyncratic and creative variations in individual behavior arising both from various difficulties in conformity to norms and from certain sources of indeterminancy and spontaneity in the social development of the individual human being.

No one of these types of factors operates as a single or isolated influence. Rather, each produces its effects in continuous interaction with the others. Rapid individual upward social mobility evenly distributed across ethnic and social groupings may produce extensive cultural assimilation and political consensus; equally rapid average mobility that leaves some groupings far below others may have the effect of increasing cultural cleavage and political dissensus. In a society with a low degree of division of labor and with high consensus, social differentiation of occupations and economic organizations may result in increased productive efficiency and in greater capacity for collective action because of heightened interdependence. Under conditions of a high degree of division of labor and low value-consensus, further social differentiation may produce social conflicts and frictions that hamper efficiency and interfere with efforts to project and attain collective goals.

Social change as a *historic* process is irreversible and concretely unique. The search for genetic or sequential explanations of change therefore leads to an infinite regression: event *A* was preceded by events *B* . . . n, and so back toward some first cause. It follows that in the attempt to establish any type of predictive generalization, the diffuse historic reality must be analyzed into repeatable categories that can be systematically related as interacting variables. This has been implicit in the whole of the present analysis; and it applies specifically to the problem of integration in change. Every social system is a *functioning* entity, with interdependent structures (kinship, political associations, and so on) and processes (for example, social mobility), that maintains a definite autonomy from its environment and from other social systems. The fact that American society differs from the Indian societies that once existed in the same geographic area, and from its European origins, is partly the result of such relative independence.[6] The total structure of the American system up to now has been relatively favorable to social change. The social structure has been relatively free from rigidly vested status systems. The culture has been marked by strongly rationalistic elements, by an orientation away from traditionalism and toward adaptability and ingenuity in meeting new situations. Internal heterogeneity has made for an extraordinary mingling of cultures in a mobile society undergoing rapid urbanization and industrialization. The cultural focus on business activity and technological development has opened up wide segments of the system to especially rapid change.[7] The outwardly spiraling impact of scientific discovery and technological innovation, made possible by a definite and unusual cultural context, is too familiar to require description here.[8] The general picture has been one of extremely rapid advances in the application of scientific knowledge to the manipulation of physical and biological structures and processes. The social changes *partly* attributable to these developments range from the demographic revolution occasioned by lowered death rates and (more directly) lowered birth rates, to the mechanization and specialization of work, to the mobility and anonymity of urban life, to possible indirect repercussions upon primary value-orientations.

The central fact in the social history of the United States, almost to the present century, was that Americans were busy at the task of opening up the social order to the relatively unrestrained interplay of private economic competition and cultural diversities. The counterpoising fact is the transformation of the basic trends as the society has become an urban, industrial world-power, and as the international scene has changed, and as world-wide changes affect both the external and the internal operation of the nation as a society and as a polity. In the world as a whole, the end of World War II marked a new epoch, marked by the end of old-style empires, the emergence of large numbers of new nations, vast political instability, great shifts in

[6] This is probably the place to note that any projections as to the future of American society that anyone might wish to make from the present analysis cannot assume that internal changes in an interdependent world will continue to occur with the same autonomy as in the past.

[7] The "culture lag" theories, made explicit in the work of William F. Ogburn (and based in part on the earlier ideas of Thorstein Veblen and Karl Marx) maintains that technological change leads and that other changes follow. In American society, the valid element in these theories is found in the fact that the culture has been characterized by a value system that made it possible for economic and technological activities to change rapidly and hence to take on special causal significance. In other societies and in other times, the role of technology in social change is definitely minor.

[8] For the descriptions of the astonishing technological change in American agriculture, see Carl C. Taylor, *et al.*, *Rural Life in the United States* (New York: Knopf, 1949), esp. chap. 30; Lee Taylor and Arthur R. Jones, Jr., *Rural Life and Urbanized Society* (New York: Oxford University Press, 1964), chaps. 9–15; Alvin L. Bertrand (ed.), *Rural Sociology: An Analysis of Contemporary Rural Life* (New York: McGraw-Hill, 1958), chaps. 24–26.

international power and international alignments, intense demands for "modernization" and "economic growth," new dimensions of military potential for destruction, and staggering rates of growth in population. According to estimates by the United Nations, present rates of fertility would produce a world population of 7.5 billion by the year 2000, and even a substantial decrease in birth rates would leave 6.1 billion.[9]

The major trends of social and cultural development in the world include several that have been unilinear for a very long time: the growth of population, the increase of societal scale, the size of organizations, the volume of long-distance communication and transportation, the destructive capacity of weapons, the speed and range of vehicles, the cumulation of scientific knowledge and of technology, and the specialization of social statuses. *None of these trends can continue indefinitely in the same direction at the same rate.* For example, present rates of population growth continually extended would quickly leave no spot of ground for standing room. Extrapolation of past rates of increase in the number of scientists would soon outrun the total population.[1] *Rates* of growth eventually must decline; and absolute upper limits will in some cases be reached relatively soon as historical time goes, that is, in a century or less. Thus, many of the "unlinear" trend-lines we now see will turn out to be logistic, or "S-shaped" curves.

### TRENDS — PAST AND CURRENT

In the America of the late twentieth-century, there are already many signs that some long-run trends are beginning to level off or change direction. This appears to be a "watershed" era. We live at the beginning of the end of a long period in which many social changes cumulatively moved in a similar direction, a direction of increased scale, increasing specialization, increasing complexity of social structure, increasing inequalities, increasing energy-levels based on using up minerals, increasing anomie, decreased kinship ties, increasing secularization, sharpening of distinctions between work and leisure and between "private" and "public" arenas of life. Many of these trends already have slowed, and others have reversed. Bigness and complexity of social organizations in certain cases are beginning to approach upper limits. Inequalities in stratification systems have passed their maximum. Kinship and other particularistic-diffuse social patterns are reasserted in modified forms. "Work" and "leisure" promise to become more alike. The increasing pollution and noxious contamination of the biophysical environment conceivably could continue to be tolerated; but unquestioned acceptance of despoilation of the biosphere seems unlikely in the future.

[9] "None of these totals provides a basis for much optimism about the population outlook, and therefore, the outlook for economic development or for peace during the remainder of this century." Philip M. Hauser, "Family Planning and Population Programs: A Book Review Article," *Demography,* 4, 1 (1967), 411.

[1] Cf. Don K. Price, *Government and Science* (New York: New York University Press, 1954), p. 113.

The trend toward occupational specialization continues; but its virtues are now open to some critical inspection, and its limits may not be indefinitely far away.

At the level of fairly concrete descriptive generalizations, a number of important changes in American society over the last half-century can be stated simply:

1. Urbanization.
2. Continuing and increasing geographic mobility of the population.
3. Industrialization, and decline in agriculture as proportion of work force.
4. Mechanization, automation, cybernation.
5. Rising real per capita product.
6. Increase in life expectancy; control of communicable diseases.
7. Rising levels of education; growth in scientific and technical knowledge.
8. Occupational specialization.
9. Increase in occupations dealing with services and in clerical, technical, and professional pursuits.
10. Spread of mass communication.
11. Specialization of family activities ("functions"); decreased importance of kinship in total social structure.
12. Specialization and secularization in religious organization.
13. Decrease in ethnic nationality and religious cleavages; greater salience of ethnic-racial claims and conflicts.
14. Increase in universalism and equality in national economic and political sectors.
15. Growth in scope and activity of central polity.
16. Growth in scale and centralized direction of economic enterprises and related organizations.
17. Interpenetration of economic and governmental norms, exchanges, relationships.

Without adding further to what could easily become a very long list indeed, let us move to a more general level.

In terms of actual social organization, the following trends have been observable over relatively extended periods: (1) reduced autonomy and cohesion of small locality groupings; (2) increase in number and relative importance of voluntary special-interest formal organizations; (3) diminished clarity and exclusiveness of ethnic groupings based on national origins; (4) increased importance of mass publics and mass communication; (5) growth in number and importance of large-scale, complex formal organizations; (6) centralization of control and communication within large-scale organizations; (7) penetration of local communities and kinship groupings by formal, centralized agencies of control and communication.[2]

2 Portions of the following are adapted from the author's "American Society in Transition: Trends and Emerging Developments in Social and Cultural Systems," in James H. Copp (ed.), *Our Changing Rural Society: Perspectives and Trends* (Ames: Iowa State University Press, 1964), pp. 3–38.

These changes in social organization have moved the system as a whole in the direction of *greater interdependence, centralization, formality, and impersonality*. As we become more and more dependent upon "society-in-general" we are less and less dependent upon any particular individual persons. In terms of Parsons' pattern variables, the main movements have been toward emphases upon universalism, neutrality, and functional specificity.[3]

As specialization and centralization have developed, *objective* interdependence has grown. Tighter and tighter causal connections link together the components of the societal system; failures of synchronization or coordination are not locally absorbed but tend to be transmitted to all parts of the system. This property seems evident from all the facts at hand. Much less obvious, and much less well supported by objective data, are the concurrent changes in personal-social relationships. On the whole, it seems plausible to suppose that there is a long-run tendency to reduce the area of particularistic, diffuse, and affective relations. In a certain sense this represents a "depersonalization" of social structure.[4] It is not reasonable to suppose that this trend, if it does exist, can proceed without limit. Nor is it likely that it can be adequately compensated for by the parasocial communication of the mass media and the one-way personalization of public figures in government or in the world of sports and entertainment.

With the growth of interdependence, small communities have come increasingly under the influence of forces originating outside the local area: economic changes, mass media, migration of population, political influences, and extra-local organizations. Decreasing localism shows itself in many forms. A well known, but striking, example is the continuous decrease in the number of public school districts—for example, from 127,000 in 1932 to 49,000 in 1958—while public school enrollment was increasing from 26.5 million to 39.4 million. Never before in history have so many local areas been so permeable to external forces.[5]

Were it possible to make a systematic comparison of all major aspects of American social life in 1900 and in the 1960's, we would probably find a consistent decrease in the sharpness of differentiation between and among major social statuses, categories, and collectivities. Rural-urban differences clearly are less. Class differentials are less obvious or sharp. Occupational status differences are blurred, especially between manual and nonmanual jobs. Ethnic distinctions, on the whole, have faded. And the ways of life

[3] The conflicting emphases, of course, are always present in some important degree. Space limits forbid discussion here of the very complicated shifts in the achievement-ascription and self-collectivity variables, as well as in the "adaptive structures" thereby generated.

[4] Such depersonalization has been deplored by many social critics—writers who deal with the search for a new basis for a "sense of community" (from T. S. Eliot to Robert Nisbet), commentators who call for the humanization of urban life (Lewis Mumford), neo-Thomist philosophers, the communitarian movements among youths, and a great variety of more technical and analytic spokesmen.

[5] And countermovements have appeared, as in the case of demands for local control of schools. Controversy over relations of teachers to a local board in the Ocean Hill-Brownsville district in 1968 led to a strike by New York City teachers, closing the nation's largest school system for a lengthy period.

of blacks and whites probably are increasingly similar, although the remaining differences are all the more sharply salient.

Developments in social organization in the United States suggest the possibilities that the greater the similarity of conditions in different geographic regions and the greater the sociocultural homogeneity of the population, the greater the likelihood of society-wide organizations, and the greater the likelihood that decision making will be successfully centralized within these organizations. At the same time, the greater the perceived threat to the nation as a whole in the field of international relations, the greater the tendency to centralize decision-making in the national polity.[6]

American *culture* probably is becoming more uniform, even though its *social* structure is increasingly differentiated. But this broad generalization must not obscure the numerous divergencies and discontinuities, which are both results and causes of rapid sociocultural changes, for example, rural-urban differences in attitudes toward racial desegregation, class differences in political tolerance or in attitudes toward education. Regional cultural distinctiveness, in spite of temporary resurgence in situations of conflict, probably has diminished only slowly, and definitely not in all aspects.[7] Under conditions of strain induced by rapid change, "nativistic" and "fundamentalistic" reactions are frequent.

The long-term movement toward the dominance of large-scale formal organizations (General Motors, Department of Defense, AFL-CIO, National Broadcasting Company, Federal Bureau of Investigation, and so on) is perhaps the most conspicuous single trend in the social structures of the twentieth century. That such organizations may develop strong pressures for discipline, coordination, and generalized conformity is well known. Deserving of more intensive study are the conditions within large organizations, which permit or encourage flexibility, initiative, and freedom. We already know that in *some* instances, as organizations become more highly differentiated and complex, organizational controls over individuals tend to become less rigid and punitive and to leave larger scope for self-direction and for collaborative participation in the making of decisions. Especially to the extent that specialized roles involve special competencies, not easily reducible to routine, the motivation and understanding of the individual become more important; and the necessary initiative and adaptability are not easily secured by primary reliance upon formal rules supported by negative sanctions. On the whole, also, the processes of differentiation of statuses, organizations, and collectivities have reduced the *ascriptive* components of social structure and, in this sense, have increased the potential range of choices of role occupants. The widening of range of choice is another way

---

[6] Richard A. Schermerhorn, *Society and Power* (New York: Random House, 1961), p. 94: "The organizational drift from local to national scope has led to increased decision making in central headquarters; this is true of both large-scale corporations and unions. Similarly the increase of federal functions and controls in government has progressively narrowed the choices of local officials and leaders."

[7] Analysis of more than forty national surveys of public opinion throws doubt upon the assumption of decreasing cultural differences among geographic regions. See Norval D. Glenn and J. L. Simmons, "Are Regional Cultural Differences Diminishing?" *Public Opinion Quarterly*, 31 (Summer 1967), 176–193.

of saying "increased variety of statuses and roles;" it is, of course, also true that any *one* status may be highly specialized and limited (for instance, machine tender).

Along with the growth of large-scale formal organizations and the multiplication of special-interest associations, contemporary urban society is marked by a considerable amount of crowd behavior, mass behavior, and formation of transitory publics and of more enduring social movements. The sociological image of mass society must not be overdrawn, for stable group structures canalize much of the collective responses to common stimuli. Nevertheless, rapidly changing collective responses are intrinsic to the mobile, commercialized urban social systems. Such systems also usually generate much highly variable and deviant forms of behavior.

As we have seen, social and cultural changes derive from multiple causes; and no simple *a priori* formula can explain them. At the same time, some positive theoretical conclusions have been reached, which are consistent with the data reviewed in this book. Although a conception of "technological" or "economic" factors as prime movers in social change is not acceptable, a chastened notion of "instrumental action" must be given an important place in any theory of change in modern societies. Thus, *given* an emphasis upon efficient means-ends adaptation, technological and economic innovations, accepted because of instrumental effectiveness, bring in their wake complex effects upon other parts of the social system. "Technology" did not cause the current development of suburban communities, but suburbia would not have been possible without modern technology. Again, technological and economic developments have greatly enlarged the volume of business and size of market required for rural trade centers in the United States and have made it difficult for the smaller centers to supply some of the essential services now demanded by the rural population. Scientific and technological developments in medicine and nutrition are bringing world-wide demographic changes of the greatest importance. The growth of cities creates greater social mobility through development of complex division of labor, creation of new occupational opportunities, and differential birth rates. In addition, the urban culture and social system enhance knowledge of opportunities, increase the possibilities of education, give rise to aspirations and the social skills to implement ambitions, and increase the likelihood of some kinds of social unrest.

The point is that technological and economic developments can attain, and have actually attained, under some social and cultural circumstances, a limited but important causal autonomy. This does *not* mean that "material" factors become the source of change. Modern technology derives from a vast fund of knowledge and ideas, and from a peculiar set of beliefs, interests, and values. But it is *through* technology, applied primarily in the service of economic and political organizations, that these cultural elements become dynamic in the social system. In general, American society in the twentieth century has shown great innovativeness in technical and economic sectors and in certain kinds of collective goal-attainment, such as health services, military operations, and education. So long as changes of this kind did not directly and obviously threaten internal order and solidarity, or markedly reduce capacity for adaptive flexibility in dealing with the physical environment and external relations with other societies, the negative consequences —whatever they might be—could be absorbed by the less resistant, less "powerful" parts of the societal community. The "readjustments" could be made by local communities, by farmers, by small businesses, by voluntary associations, by families, by low-income strata, by the politically inarticulate. The centers of activity pressing for innovation and growth in scale and complexity did not directly receive "negative feedback," rather they were rewarded by income, wealth, power, authority, deference, esteem, and sense of expressing and creating high values.

## THE FACTORS SUPPORTING CHANGE IN AMERICA

The high degree of mobility and flexibility at the level of microstructures (small groups, families, business firms) in this society has tended to support the developments we have sketched. For a social system can effectively continue while containing a very great amount of stress, strain, tension, and maladaptation if these conditions affect individuals or subcollectivities *that separately have access to acceptable alternatives*—another job, a different organization or group, another recreational pattern, or even a more understanding friend. High geographic and social mobility may minimize change *of* the system by maximizing small-scale adjustments *to* it. The larger structure remains intact precisely because of the numerous small adaptations going on in its more "plastic" subcomponents.[8]

Such diffuse absorption of change, however, cannot proceed indefinitely. For the disruptive consequences that eventually accumulate in certain parts of the population in a metropolitan society come to have high visibility and are likely to stimulate collective actions for more basic change in the allocations of rewards or in the rules of the societal community.

Every society must allocate energies and other resources among the competing demands for (1) generalized adaptive capacities, (2) particularized goal-attainments, (3) social integration, (4) maintenance and creation of cultural patterns. Very broadly, the main emphases in American society for several generations have been in the adaptive and goal-attainment sectors, centering in the economy and the polity. The highly energetic activities in these areas have produced massive unintended and undesired consequences: air and water pollution, traffic congestion, racial ghettos, urban sprawl, and many kinds of "crowding" and interference effects. These conditions result when the individual social units (individual persons, business concerns, etc.) are free to carry on activities that give the actor large short-run rewards and only small negative feedback but that result in *collective* accumulation of conditions which are noxious, frustrating, or deprivational to large numbers of people.

A main direction of change for a long time in many societies, and very

8 If fully successful, such processes would produce a condition of ultrastability of the macrostructures.

strongly so in the United States, has been toward greater *differentiation:* an increase in the number of *"structurally distinct and functionally specialized units in a society."*[9] Such differentiation applies both to statuses and to collectivities. One result is greater complexity—larger numbers of qualitatively distinct relationships and sequences among different kinds of units. Another result is the attentuation of simple consensus among homogeneous groups and new problems of integration through more inclusive symbols and values and through a more differentiated structure of norms and of organizational linkages.

A viable modern society must be capable of sustaining continuity through continuous and important changes in its technological apparatus and procedures, in its economy, and in its polity. What conditions could make possible such a remarkable feat? Probably the most important condition is basic consensus upon (1) a relatively few highly generalized cultural *value-orientations* and (2) generalized *procedures* for establishing norms, resolving conflicts, and determining collective goals. The more differentiated the system, the less it can rely upon either a detailed substantive consensus or a fixed social structure. It can achieve *continuity* (stability of boundaries and synchronization of changes) only through numerous rapid *changes;* and these must be kept in close enough coordination with prior values and norms to avoid "ungovernable" fundamentalistic and utopian reactions that would polarize the society and result in basic discontinuity in its main institutions.

There is, of course, never any automatic guarantee that such continuity will be sustained. Even the most stable social system in action represents a moving series of equilibria of contingency—a problematic and continuously changing set of relationships with an environment and among the subcomponents of the system itself. The "relationships" in question can be defined as inputs and outputs—flows of energy, resources, information, personnel. For the initial system to remain stable, the kinds of flows and their magnitudes must remain within *some* limits. Even if the limits are often difficult to specify, one can easily see that an industrial nation cannot remain unchanged if 90 percent of its physical scientists and engineers emigrate in a single year nor if it receives in a single year an influx of ethnically distinct refugees equal to one-half the receiving population.

Therefore, the magnitude of changes *in* the system that can be handled without change *of* the system is finite. Furthermore, a social system is in one aspect an information-generating agency; and any system that develops new information is bound to change to some extent—and it is inevitable that some of the change will be unpredictable.[1]

In terms of dominant value-orientations, the most striking *generalized*

[9] Robert Marsh, *Comparative Sociology* (New York: Harcourt, Brace & World, 1967), p. 31. Marsh computes an index of differentiation (based on percentage of males in non-agricultural occupations and gross energy consumption per capita) according to which the United States is the most highly differentiated national society. Its index score of 109 may be compared with Sweden's 63, Italy's 41, the U.S.S.R.'s 41, Turkey's 24, and Mainland China's 13.

[1] Otherwise we would now know everything that will be known later.

characteristic of this social system is the primacy of mastery or success across a wide range of situations and goals, with the second priority the attainment of particular focal objectives. That is, the society has been primarily committed, on the whole, to an *adaptive* emphasis on instrumental mastery; it has invested its resources and energies very heavily in acquiring wealth, skill, knowledge, power—"instruments" useful in attaining many different kinds of goals.[2] Secondarily, it has taken the option of concentrating upon particular *goal-attainments*. Probably one can safely generalize that the society's emphasis upon *integrative* values has ranked third, rather far down the line, and that *pattern maintenance* has been in last place.

Any collectivity with this rank ordering of values will be especially likely to exhibit rapid change. Both the adaptive and the goal-attainment emphases are high-energy options, involving directed and concentrated efforts to alter physical, biological, cultural, and social environments. A plurality of diverse instrumental activities is certain to create strains in social relationships, including the solidarity of collectivities,[3] and to impose difficult demands upon pattern-maintenance (socialization, culture storage and arrangement, symbolization, maintaining congruent patterns). Thus, certain processes of social change are generated quite directly by the basic characteristics of our economy: for example, improvements in technology adopted in the interests of profit making tend to increase the marginal productivity of capital relative to that of labor and thereby provide strong incentives for the substitution of capital for labor in production.

In any system of relatively high differentiation—one with marked occupational specialization and of many specialized collectivities in economic, religious, political, military, and educational areas—there will be differences in rewards, in control of facilities, and in characteristic interests generated by occupational experiences. These differences will lead to differences in associational patterns; and the two sets of influences will combine to produce shared subsets of values and beliefs.

Accordingly, institutionalization of the total system will never be complete, and will always involve some social tension and conflict and some psychological ambivalence. To say that a social system is made up of sets of institutionalized patterns of interaction, therefore, is not to say that it is necessarily stable and certainly not that it is uniform or static.

Undoubtedly, the most comprehensive kind of sociocultural change is a shift in a major pattern of values or value orientations. There is a sense in

2 A factor analysis of 236 variables for 82 nations has shown that some 40 percent of the original variance is associated with 3 practically uncorrelated indicators: size, wealth, and main political orientation. The single factor most predictive of all other characteristics of a national society is its gross national product. See Jack Sawyer, "Dimensions of Nations: Size, Wealth, and Politics," *American Journal of Sociology*, 73, 2 (September 1967), 145–172.

3 Cf. S. N. Eisenstadt, "Institutionalization and Change," *American Sociological Review*, 29, 2 (April 1964), 235–247. An active society continually reallocates facilities and rewards, with differential effects upon different subcollectivities and with incessant shifts in power among such collectivities. These and other related processes are likely to produce much strain and consequent "irrational" reactions. See Talcott Parsons, *Structure and Process in Modern Societies* (New York: Free Press, 1960), chaps. 6–7.

which this is true by definition: if values are generalized criteria of desirability, a basically different set of values (or of emphases and relationships within a given set) necessarily represents a pervasive reordering of social behavior. However, the important nontruistic proposition is that once a new value-pattern has come to be accepted as so fully legitimate that the burden of proof is simply assumed to be on the advocate of an opposing pattern, then the dominant pattern continues to attract additional adherents and to extend its coverage into more and more activities across all institutional sectors.

On the other hand, it would seem that in cycles or sequences of change, the value-patterns—say, individualistic achievement—usually will change only after predisposing changes have taken place in at least the reward-deprivation levels (for instance, through mass unemployment) and in allocations (such as a shift from small business to large corporations)—resulting in various kinds of frustrations and in a challenge to some important collectivities within the society.

The resistance of value patterns to changes in social conditions is illustrated by the defensive rigidity of many white Americans in holding to conceptions of categorical group-superiority in the face of massive changes in educational levels, occupations, aspirations, and political importance of black Americans during the middle decades of this century.

Changes in social structure during the twentieth century certainly have been accompanied by shifts, perhaps less easily discernible, in value orientations. Even though the United States of today has a recognizable continuity with the new nation of 1776, it cannot be said that the dominant beliefs and values are identical; and it is difficult to state in any brief or precise way just what the changes have been. The following appraisals of outstanding shifts in value orientations therefore stand as *questions* or as judgments of a very broad and complex character.

First, we must ask: in what respect or in what ways may values and value orientations conceivably change? Although the following inventory is incomplete, values and beliefs may be transformed in the following modes:[4]

1. Creation: A new evaluative criterion or belief is developed out of new experience and becomes effective, at some level, in regulating behavior.
2. Relatively sudden destruction: Although extremely rare, there are some instances in which there is a quick extinction of a previously accepted value.
3. Attenuation: Slow diminution of the intensity of affect and commitment; decrease in interest and attention, as fewer and fewer persons promote, support, teach, or defend the belief or value orientation.
4. Extension: Application to objects and events in addition to those included in the original sphere of relevance.
5. Elaboration: The value or belief is progressively rationalized, symbolized, dramatized, documented and otherwise made more complex or more embedded in its sociocultural context.
6. Specification: A generalized orientation increasingly is defined in terms of a variety of particular contexts, resulting in modifications and restrictions.

[4] The passages following (to page 634) are taken from the author's "Individual and Group Values," *The Annals*, 371 (May 1967), 29–31.

In the United States it seems that "freedom" is not now felt to be violated by compulsory vaccination, compulsory school attendance, or peacetime military conscription.

7. Limitation: It would be a limiting case if any given value—in confronting other values—were not altered at all; generally there is some change even if only in the direction of absolutism. A frequent outcome, however, is that a particular value comes to be bounded or limited by the recognized claims of other values. Thus, we have noted that in American democratic creeds and practices, it has always been necessary to accommodate a persisting strain between *freedom* and *equality:* each is necessary for the democratic position, but neither can be pushed to extremes without negating the other.

8. Explication: In the form of folk virtues, values are typically implicit— indeed, often altogether inaccessible to explicit formulation by their bearers. At the opposite extreme, highly systematic explications of values are formulated in creedal or philosophical systems. In American society there is a vast accumulation of explicit value statements. Scattered evidence suggests increasingly explicit affirmation of major values. Such explication seems to be favored by rapid changes in specific social conditions and norms as well as by direct challenges to the standards themselves, for example, the attacks of totalitarian political movements.

9. Consistency: A concern with consistency itself represents a distinctive value position. Greater systematic explicitness at the level of national political assertions and mass-media creeds almost certainly increases a sense of "contradiction," "inconsistency," and "hypocrisy" when viewed against some of the daily realities of behavior; examples include equality vs. freedom, and humanitarianism vs. achievement.[5]

10. Intensity (absolutism, centrality): A value initially accepted as one among many standards, say, humanitarianism, may become so intensely held and promoted as to become the center of life. A value such as "personal achievement," formerly the focus of many other criteria, may lose its central intellectual and emotional *raison d'être,* become relativized and recede into the ranks of the ordinary criteria of daily life.

A society in which the store of knowledge concerning the consequences of action is large and is rapidly increasing is a society in which received norms and their "justifying" values will be increasingly subjected to questioning and reformulation. As our knowledge concerning the consequences of racial segregation has exposed effects upon education, employment, income, family life, crime, and intergroup hostility and conflict, value conflicts have been revealed, and some have been sharpened. As we learn more about the consequences of different kinds of childhood discipline upon personality development, pressures are generated to reevaluate punitive measures, permissiveness, and so on.

It is likely that in the United States over the last three decades there has developed an increase in the positive evaluation of *cognitive* criteria for judging both individual conduct and collective policy and practice. As levels of formal education rise—both on the average and with respect to the proportion of persons mastering high levels of knowledge and conceptual skills

---

[5] Awareness of inconsistencies between traditional beliefs and values and new knowledge may lead to change. Cf. Herbert H. Hyman and Paul B. Sheatsley, "Attitudes toward Desegregation," *Scientific American,* 211 (July 1964), 16–23.

—and as societal processes inexorably call attention to interdependence of consequences of social actions, the disregard of facts and causal reasoning is likely to be increasingly regarded as a *moral* fault. This tentative prediction is not intended to be an expression of wish fulfillment. Rather we believe that the indicated direction of value movement already is objectively present, as suggested by the increased part played in legislative, administrative, and even judicial decisions by relatively systematic attention to cognitive considerations as to both "the facts of the case" and to causes and consequences—with regard to military strategy and tactics, welfare policies, penal and correctional practices (rehabilitation, the death penalty), effectiveness of educational and therapeutic practices, economic policies, transportation, urban development, environmental pollution, and many other areas. Obviously, this is not to say that "rationality" (however conceived) is necessarily increasing, nor that attempted solutions to problems are necessarily increasingly "adequate," whatever that might mean. It is only to suggest as worthy of further definition and study the proposition that a "knowledgeable society"[6] will increasingly give a positive evaluation of knowledge—up to some limit not yet closely approached.

As shown in Chapter XI, it is possible to make gross estimates of at least the direction of change during this century in main patterns of value. See page 636 for a tabular summary:[7]

In terms of these broad estimates, during the period from around 1900 up to the end of World War II, the major thrust was in the direction of further positive development of the themes analyzed. Since 1945, however, there is a suggestion of lessened emphasis on activity and achievement, some disillusionment concerning "progress," and some loss in humanitarianism under the exigencies of war. The available information is highly imprecise, and these changes should not be overemphasized; on net balance, during the last half-century the conclusion probably has to be "the same main values—only more so." The changes that have occurred are clearly important, but for the most part they grow directly out of elements already present at the beginning of the period of review. Yet changes there certainly are. The main directions evidently are from instrumental to consummatory values, from achievement to expressiveness, from competitive individualism to categorical emphases on status, dignity, recognition, and the like.

In the present study we have worked as best we might with bits and pieces of evidence as to changes in values and in consensus regarding them. It is our definite impression that the unity of American value-systems has been commonly underestimated. It is our hypothesis that commonality of values is, more than generally recognized, a matter of belief that there is consensus, not that there is agreement upon the detailed content of every norm and value. The conformity so often criticized in American life has not usually been seen in its functional significance as a pervasive signaling of a shared culture. Furthermore, all the diversity of America that can be shown

[6] Robert E. Lane, "The Decline of Politics and Ideology in a Knowledgeable Society," *American Sociological Review*, 31 (October 1966), 649–662.

[7] Williams, "Individual and Group Values," *op. cit.*, p. 36.

| VALUE-BELIEF COMPLEXES | directions of change— period (approximate)* | |
|---|---|---|
| | 1900–1945 | 1945–1966 |
| Activity | Indeterminate | — |
| Work | — | — |
| Achievement | — | + (post-Sputnik I) |
| Success | + | + |
| Material comfort | + | + |
| Humanitarianism (domestic) | + | + |
| Humanitarianism (war) | + | — |
| "Absolute" moral orientation | — | Indeterminate |
| Practicality | + | — |
| Efficiency | + | — |
| Science and secular rationality | + | + |
| Progress | + | — |
| Freedom | Indeterminate | — |
| Equality | + | + |
| Democracy | + | Indeterminate |
| Conformity (to social pressure) | + | + |
| Individual personality | + | Indeterminate |
| Nationalism | + | — to + |
| Racism—group superiority | — | — |
| **Totals** | | |
| Increase | 13 | 8 |
| No change or indeterminate | 2 | 3 |
| Decrease | 4 | 8 |

* (—) is decrease; (+) is increase.

by a detached analysis is probably not so generally perceived by the majority of the people. In spite of many changes and of some quite severe value-conflicts, this analysis suggests, there are substantial common themes and basic cultural axioms.

There is a real toughness in the cohesion of this society, but the strains are great. The main value-problems center upon (1) *value opposition,* as in racial cleavages, student protests and radical movements, and struggles for economic equality; (2) *value withdrawal,* as in the "dropout" and "hippie" populations, or in other modes of "opting out" of the mainline society; (3) *value priorities,* where collectivity goals and public concerns may receive slight attention or commitments of resources or where no stable or clear ordering of claims can be achieved. These three problems are those of conflict, of alienation, and of anomie—the latter in the special form of social aimlessness and cultural shapelessness.

Perhaps the most important questions concerning value orientations in our society are three. First, to what extent are the traditional orientations becoming more, or less, the object of intense commitment of strong personal involvement? Otherwise stated, how much do Americans value the values they seem to claim? It is clear that no new major creeds as yet command widespread public allegiance. The language of values now current would have been understandable prior to the twentieth century. But we have also to ask—and cannot answer, by evidence, because no one knows what it is crucial to know here—how intense and firm is the commitment to the value-belief systems commonly believed most characteristic of the culture.

The second question brings us again to the problem of integration: To what extent and in what ways is the consensual basis of social cohesion changing? That is, in what wise is there more or less agreement upon common values? Where is consensus weakening, and where is it being strengthened? What new syntheses and emergents can be discerned? How is it possible to meet the claims of distributive justice and retain other main values? Can value oppositions be sufficiently tolerated to avoid destruction of freedom but not so much as to perpetuate unnecessary inconsistencies?

The third question extends the problem of integration in change beyond the permeable boundaries of American society: How far and how solidly can the value orientations herein described or suggested be extended *and* modified in a larger commonality?

To the first question—value commitment—we can bring only a composite impression, suggestive rather than definitive. It is that a period of progressive disillusionment and attenuation of commitment to "principled" value orientation, perhaps most marked from the early 1920's to World War II—which we noted in the 1960 edition of this work as "drawing to a close"—ended in the 1960's. What new cycles will ensue no one can confidently say.

The last question concerns by implication the capacity of the American people to understand *other* cultures and to work with others to create collaboratively a manageable common core of those intercultural values that seem a prerequisite to common survival. It would be a fault not to raise this question. And it would be both impossible and presumptuous here to pronounce dicta concerning it. More than enough pronouncements are continually made every day.

At the very end of this long study, however, it should be declared that we have not found ground in the evidence, hypotheses, and theories reviewed in this volume for concluding that the future of American society has a single clear direction, fully determined by the basic processes and structures now present. Diversity and alternative lines of development have not been eliminated by "inherent necessities" of the present social order. This is not to say that the proximate future is wholly unpredictable and indeterminate. Existing structures and processes constitute restraints, guiding influences, and facilitating inducements. The future will not be whimsical. But the elements that enter into the developments now under way are numerous; and their potential combinations, generating new possibilities, are incalculable but extremely large.

American society, therefore, has before it a large number of objectively possible futures. It is not inevitably predestined to become a monolithic industrial-military order; nor a pluralistic, equalitarian democracy; nor a chaotic, alienated mass society; nor a rigid centralized security society. Its creative options are many.[8] Indeed, to the extent that it succeeds in establishing reliable control over the main adaptative and goal-attainment problems, without exhausting its energies, it may open up possibilities as yet unimagined for innovations in the areas of social relationships and in expressive and consummatory activities.

This work is being closed with questions, not answers; with new searches, not closed systems of interpretation. This approach is believed to be in the spirit of science. It is also believed to be in accord with the historic meaning of American society—a society that has hoped to be, above all, the society of possibility.

## SUGGESTED READINGS

BUCKLEY, WALTER. *Sociology and Modern Systems Theory.* Englewood Cliffs, N.J.: Prentice-Hall, 1967. Important discussion of "morphogenic" processes and clear exposition of different types of equilibria and of change. Overly critical of intellectual predecessors but stimulating positive contributions.

ETZIONI, AMITAI. *The Active Society.* New York: Free Press, 1968. Subtitled "A Theory of Societal and Political Processes," this book examines the possibilities of self-conscious guidance of total societies. Defining an active society as one that controls the conditions of its functioning in terms of normative guidelines, the analysis proposes methods of self-transforming control.

HAGEN, EVERETT E. *On the Theory of Social Change.* Homewood, Ill.: Dorsey Press, 1962. Provocative exposition of a bold thesis relating changes in social status to child-rearing practices, leading to changes in aspirations and motivation, and eventually to entrepreneurial or other innovative

---

[8] Cf. Amitai Etzioni, "Toward a Theory of Societal Guidance," *American Journal of Sociology,* 73, 2 (September 1967), 173–187.

activity. Speculative, but fruitful of important hypotheses. Shows critical inadequacy of many conceptions of "economic development."

MANNHEIM, KARL. *Man and Society in an Age of Reconstruction.* London: Routledge & Kegan Paul, 1940. Because Mannheim thought deeply about really important matters, this work has enduring relevance. Many of his penetrating observations are valid clues to patterns of change extending toward the year 2000.

MOORE, WILBERT E. *Social Change.* Englewood Cliffs, N.J.: Prentice-Hall, 1963. Reviewed for Chapter II above. Should be carefully reexamined at this point. See also by the same author, *Order and Change.* New York: Wiley, 1967.

SMELSER, NEIL J. *Theory of Collective Behavior.* New York: Free Press, 1962. Multifactor model of change. Collective outbursts and movements interpreted as outcome of a necessary sequence of social and psychological processes.

SOROKIN, PITIRIM A. *Social and Cultural Dynamics.* 4 vols. New York: American Book Company, 1937–1941. Monumental, erudite, and opinionated overview of historical fluctuations in art, science, ethics, law, social relationships and collectivities, war, and revolution. Develops cyclical theory of history —ideational, idealistic, and sensate phases. Sees our culture as late sensate.

# Index

## N A M E S

Abbott, Walter M., 393, 404
Abegglen, James C., 137, 207, 549
Abel, Theodore, 223, 229, 498
Abramson, Victor, 184, 187, 563 ff.
Ackerman, Charles, 93
Adamic, Louis, 13
Adams, Bert N., 291, 556, 560, 578
Adams, Don, 326
Adams, James F., 348
Adams, James Truslow, 8, 459, 493, 592
Agger, Robert E., 291
Albrecht, R., 83
Alford, Robert R., 125, 273 ff.
Allen, Hollis P., 332, 333
Allport, Floyd H., 41
Almond, Gabriel A., 303, 478, 479, 491 ff., 590, 606
Anderson, C. Arnold, 312, 323
Anderson, Dewey, 123, 134, 136 ff.
Anderson, Elin L., 151
Anderson, Theodore R., 536
Anderson, William, 255
Andrezejewski, Stanislaw, 266
Angell, Robert C., 524 ff., 580, 582
Anshen, Ruth, 50, 59, 77, 85
Apter, David E., 289
Argyle, Michael, 394, 410
Archibald, Katherine, 148, 150
Arnold, Thurman, 186
Arrington, Leonard J., 389
Arrow, Kenneth J., 298
Axelrod, Morris, 525
Ayoub, Millicent R., 70

Babbie, Earl R., 384
Babchuk, Nicholas, 528
Bach, George Leland, 199
Bain, Joe S., 189
Baird, W. R., 530
Baker, George W., 578, 602, 617
Bakke, E. Wight, 559, 612
Bales, Robert F., 60, 508, 545, 552
Balk, Alfred, 403, 410
Baltzell, E. Digby, 104, 128, 137, 153, 164
Banfield, Edward C., 291
Banton, Michael, 428, 589
Barker, Bernard, 137, 575, 578

Barker, Ernest, 622
Barnard, Chester I., 200, 517
Barnett, James H., 383, 384
Barton, Allen H., 602
Bates, M. Searle, 374
Battis, Emery, 399
Bauer, Raymond A., 293
Bazelon, David T., 227, 228
Bean, Louis, 276, 286, 288
Beard, Charles A., 254, 265, 467, 482
Beard, Mary R., 467, 482
Beard, Miriam, 455, 492
Becker, Carl, 343, 494
Becker, Howard S., 310, 326, 329, 414, 417, 437
Bell, Daniel, 272, 278, 325, 461
Bell, Robert R., 88, 91
Bell, Wendell, 420, 513, 525, 613
Bellah, Robert N., 363, 549
Ben-David, Joseph, 340
Bendix, Reinhard, 51, 95 ff., 132 ff., 202, 315, 329, 397, 536, 549, 591
Benn, D. G., 500
Benney, Mark, 383
Benoit-Smullyan, Emile, 109
Bensman, Joseph, 423
Benson, Purnell Hardy, 371
Berelson, Bernard, 231, 283 ff., 351 ff., 394, 410, 508, 556 ff.
Berger, Bennett M., 531
Berger, Morroe, 223, 229, 498
Berger, Peter L., 385, 403, 592
Berkowitz, Leonard, 247, 307
Berle, Adolph A., Jr., 183, 192 ff., 224, 230, 237
Bernard, Jessie, 51, 55, 74, 97
Bernstein, Marver H., 284n
Berreman, Gerald D., 110, 583
Bertelson, David, 451, 460
Berton, Pierre, 385
Bertrand, Alvin L., 598, 624
Beshers, James M., 142
Biddle, Bruce J., 43, 45
Biderman, Albert D., 268
Bidwell, Charles, 346
Blaisdell, Donald C., 293
Blake, Nelson M., 423
Blau, Peter M., 138, 164, 202, 205, 234 ff., 303, 509, 518, 605, 617
Blaug, Mark, 317
Blauner, Robert, 86, 217 ff., 461, 614
Bliss, W. D. P., 390

Bloch, Herbert A., 434
Block, Jeanne H., 348
Bloombaum, Milton, 617
Blum, Richard H., 425
Blumer, Herbert, 307
Boat, Marion, 513
Bogue, Donald J., 120, 128
Boguslaw, Robert, 537
Boland, Margaret, 345, 536
Boland, Walter, 345, 536
Boles, Donald E., 314
Boller, Paul, 375
Bonjean, Charles M., 292
Boocock, Sarane S., 314, 338
Borgatta, Edgar F., 508, 545
Bott, Elizabeth, 40, 59, 71, 83, 532
Bottomore, T. B., 105
Boulding, Kenneth, 599
Bowman, Mary Jean, 317
Bradshaw, Benjamin S., 142
Brainerd, Carol P., 134
Braungart, Richard G., 526
Braver, Jerald C., 371
Bredemeier, Harry C., 142
Brenner, Robert H., 120
Bressler, Marvin, 323
Brickman, William W., 314
Briefs, Goetz, 176, 211, 459, 593
Brim, Orville G., Jr., 305, 353
Brisset, Dennis, 459
Brodbeck, Arthur J., 283, 288
Brogan, Dennis W., 244, 253
Brofenbrenner, Urie, 78, 323
Brookover, Wilbur B., 312, 321, 327
Broom, Leonard, 91, 103, 276, 312 ff., 505 ff.
Browder, Lesley H., 330
Brown, Julia S., 49
Brown, Roger, 451
Brown, Robert, 366
Browne, George S., 326
Browning, Harley L., 550
Bryson, Lyman, 487
Buchanan, James M., 298
Buckley, Walter, 39, 366, 548, 553, 638
Bunzel, John H., 182, 294
Bushee, F. A., 529
Burchinal, Lee, 62
Burdick, Eugene, 283, 288
Burke, Kenneth, 435
Burns, James MacGregor, 278
Bury, John B., 468
Butterfield, H., 571

*i*

Calhoun, Arthur W., 77
Callahan, Raymond E., 331
Campbell, Angus, 283, 284, 285, 287, 303
Cannon, Mark W., 293
Caplow, Theodore, 200, 342, 505, 510 ff.
Caplowitz, David, 120
Capone, Al, 456
Carey, Alex, 517
Carlin, Jerome E., 127
Carmichael, Stokely, 595
Carmichael, Oliver C., 351
Carr, Edwin R., 310, 329, 337, 343
Carr, Robert K., 284, 285, 286
Cartwright, Dorwin, 508
Cash, W. J., 451
Casstevens, Thomas W., 282
Cattell, Raymond B., 109
Catton, William R., Jr., 92
Centers, Richard, 124, 147
Cervantes, Lucius F., 93
Chamberlain, Edward A., 189
Chapin, F. Stuart, 39, 552
Chapman, Dwight W., 578, 602, 617
Chapple, Eliot D., 533, 548
Child, Irving L., 552
Cherington, Paul W., 293
Chinoy, Eli, 456
Chipman, John S., 590
Christensen, A. N., 254
Christensen, Harold T., 97
Cicourel, Aaron V., 323, 337
Clark, Burton R., 312, 324, 350, 353
Clark, Elmer T., 381
Clark, J. M., 229
Clark, John P., 459, 487
Clark, Kenneth B., 595
Clark, S. D., 531
Clinard, Marshall B., 123, 415, 429, 437
Cloward, Richard A., 420, 516, 535
Coates, Charles H., 268
Cohen, Albert K., 122, 437, 609, 618
Cohen, Nathan E., 578
Cohn, David L., 426
Cole, Marley, 402
Cole, Stephen, 613
Coleman, A. Lee, 453, 458, 593
Coleman, James, 29, 311, 314, 322, 353, 598
Coleman, J. S., 606
Collier, Robert Lee, 314
Collver, Andrew, 66
Commager, Henry Steele, 458, 468
Commons, John R., 176, 211
Conant, James B., 314
Connery, Maurice F., 578
Converse, Philip E., 283, 287, 303
Cook, Lloyd A., 328
Cook, Thomas I., 498
Cooley, Charles Horton, 457, 485, 511

Coon, Carleton S., 533, 548
Copp, James H., 626
Corson, John J., 342
Corwin, Edward S., 246
Coser, Lewis A., 120, 121, 156, 231, 431, 596, 606 ff.
Cottrell, Leonard S., Jr., 91, 276, 312, 356, 505, 556, 584
Counts, George S., 313, 319, 327, 335
Cox, Edward B., 119
Cox, Harvey, 385
Crain, Robert L., 292, 555
Cramer, John F., 326
Crassweller, Robert D., 234
Crawford, Benjamin Franklin, 383
Cremin, Lawrence A., 336
Cressey, Donald R., 425, 429
Crevecoeur, Jean, 13
Cross, Whitney R., 387
Crozier, Michel, 202, 230, 518, 533
Cuber, John F., 88, 415, 455
Cumming, Elaine, 93
Curti, Merle, 335, 337, 490, 491, 492, 502
Curtis, Richard F., 141
Cushman, Robert E., 254, 272
Cyert, R. M., 520

Dahl, Robert A., 291
Dahrendorf, Ralf, 100, 607
Dalton, Melville, 206
Danzger, M. Herbert, 291
Davey, Harold W., 221
Davidson, Percey E., 123, 134 ff.
Davies, Wallace Evan, 492
Davis, Allison, 78, 103, 148
Davis, David B., 481
Davis, James A., 350
Davis, Kingsley, 54, 87, 103, 112, 142, 426
Davis, Morris, 506
Day, Lincoln, 96
Dean, Dwight G., 277, 614
Dean, John P., 153, 430, 437, 452
Dean, Lois R., 224
DeCharms, Richard, 455
Deeg, Maethel E., 126
DeFleur, Melvin L., 307, 508, 598
Defoe, Daniel, 352
Degler, Carl N., 71
de Grazia, Sebastian, 470
DeGré, Gerard, 571
Demerath, N. J., III, 358, 367 ff., 411
Denney, Reuel, 455, 484, 503
de Reuck, A. V. S., 110, 583
Dewart, Leslie, 384
Dexter, Lewis A., 293, 307, 470, 556
Dickson, William S., 517
Dietrick, David C., 420
Dimock, Marshall E., 181
Dinkel, Robert M., 84
Dirlan, Joel B., 190
Dobriner, William M., 456, 531
Dockeray, James C., 180, 198

Dodge, Norton T., 73
Doherty, Robert W., 375
Dohrenwend, Bruce P., 612
Dombrowski, J., 390
Donovan, John D., 339
Doolittle, James, 145
Dornbusch, Sanford M., 389, 455
Dotson, Floyd, 83
Downs, Anthony, 182, 202, 264, 521, 533, 535
Drucker, Peter F., 299, 300, 301
Dubin, Robert, 211, 219, 221, 420
Dublin, Louis I., 616
Dumazedier, Joffre, 470
Duncan, Otis Dudley, 117, 134 ff., 164, 577
Duniway, Benjamin C., 54, 72
Dupeux, Georges, 287
Durkheim, Emile, 176, 241, 356, 411, 495, 511
Duverger, Maurice, 273 ff.

Ebersole, Luke E., 372
Eckland, Bruce K., 347
Eckstein, Harry, 268, 586
Edwards, Allen, 487
Edwards, Hugh, 126, 156, 420
Edwards, Newton, 313, 325, 353
Eells, Kenneth, 106, 148
Eells, Richard, 201
Ehrman, Winston, 92
Ehrenstrom, Nils, 379
Eichner, Alfred S., 572
Einaudi, Mario, 252
Eisenstadt, S. N., 87 ff., 237, 240, 343, 578, 632
Eisenstein, Louis, 434
Eister, Allan W., 381
Ekirch, Arthur A., Jr., 268
Elder, Glen H., Jr., 80, 550
Eldersveld, Sammuel J., 231, 288, 303
Elinson, Howard, 401, 403
Eliot, T. S., 627
Elkin, Frederick, 90
Elkins, Stanley M., 481
Embree, John F., 548
Epperson, D. C., 90
Epstein, Leonore A., 551
Erbe, William, 288
Ericson, Martha C., 78
Erikson, Erik, 90, 526, 544
Erikson, Kai T., 415, 437
Etzioni, Amitai, 505, 533, 545, 576, 598, 638
Eulau, Heinz, 231, 282, 288, 303
Evan, William M., 541
Evans, Stanton M., 348

Fahs, Charles B., 549
Falding, Harold, 442
Faunce, William A., 224
Feibleman, James K., 170
Feld, Sheila, 370
Ferguson, Charles W., **527, 529**
Festinger, Leon, 381
Finkelstein, Louis, 487

Fiore, Quentin, 307
Firth, Raymond, 83
Fischoff, Ephraim, 367
Fishbein, Morris, 54
Freedman, Maurice, 48, 57, 73, 95
Freedman, Ronald, 14, 17, 18
Freeman, Linton C., 292
Freeman, Mervin M., 88
Flannery, Edward H., 404
Flexner, Eleanor, 71
Floud, Jean, 312, 323
Flynn, Frank T., 434
Foley, Donald L., 525, 526
Folger, John K., 323
Foote, Nelson N., 216
Force, Maryanne T., 525
Ford, Thomas R., 386
Form, William H., 109, 128, 134, 200, 211 ff., 230
French, E. Geoffrey, 368
Freud, Sigmund, 50
Freund, Paul A., 256, 320
Friedenberg, Edgar Z., 314
Friedell, Morris F., 541
Friedman, Leon J., 431
Fuchs, Lawrence H., 399
Full, Harold, 314
Fuller, John G., 429
Fuller, Lon L., 31
Fulton, Robert L., 361
Furstenberg, Frank F., 67
Fusé, Toyomasa, 403

Galbraith, John K., 299
Galenson, Walter, 219, 220
Gallagher, Art, Jr., 141
Gallup, George, 146, 491
Gamson, William, 607, 615, 618
Gans, Herbert, 513, 525
Garceau, Oliver, 295
Gardiner, John A., 425
Gardner, Borleigh B., 78
Gardner, John W., 351
Gardner, Mary R., 78
Gasper, Louis, 400
Gaudet, Hazel, 283, 286
Gaus, John, 295
Gellhorn, Walter, 575
Gendell, Murray, 11, 12, 189, 196
Gerstner, John G., 573
Gerth, Hans H., 144, 233, 299, 367, 470, 488
Gerver, Israel, 423
Gibbs, Jack, 33, 34, 36, 550, 578, 616
Gibney, Frank, 429
Gibson, Duane, 16
Gilmore, Susan, 348
Gillen, Ralph L., 293
Ginzberg, Eli, 210, 231, 570
Gittler, Joseph B., vii
Glaser, Barney G., 361
Glazer, Nathan, 13, 65, 281, 398, 455, 484, 503
Glenn, Norval D., 131, 147, 628
Glick, Paul C., 85
Glock, Charles Y., 356, 357,

384 ff., 400 ff.
Gluckman, Max, 606
Goffman, Erving, 433, 437, 516
Goldenweiser, Alexander, 26
Goldhammer, Herbert, 617
Goldrich, Daniel, 291
Goldsen, Rose K., 495
Goldsmith, Raymond W., 195
Gomberg, William, 182
Goode, William, Jr., 37, 42, 51, 57, 67, 91 ff., 133, 340, 528, 555
Goodman, Paul, 314, 343
Goodsell, Willystine, 77
Gordon, Margaret S., 155
Gordon, Milton, 13, 65, 144, 310
Gordon, Robert A., 196
Gore, Pearl Mayo, 291
Gorer, Geoffrey, 80, 457
Goslin, David A., 312, 330, 353
Gosnell, Harold F., 279
Gossett, Thomas F., 499
Gottlieb, David, 87, 321, 327, 330, 353
Gottman, Jean, 14, 19
Goudsblom, Johan, 67
Gouldner, Alvin W., 200, 505, 518, 536, 598
Grebler, Leo, 494
Greeley, Andrew M., 339, 370, 397
Green, Arnold W., 78, 79
Greenbaum, Joseph J., 341
Greenfield, Sidney M., 66
Greer, Scott, 289, 419, 505
Gross, Bertram M., 202, 293, 453, 503, 533
Gross, Llewellyn, 598
Gross, Neal, 44, 45, 149, 312 ff., 343
Grusky, Oscar, 205
Guest, R. H., 219
Gulley, William H., 521
Gurin, Gerald, 370
Gurvitch, Georges, 515
Gusfield, Joseph R., 222, 278, 289
Gustafson, James M., 380
Guterman, Norman, 295
Guttman, Louis, 108, 139

Haas, J. Eugene, 536
Haber, William, 586
Hacker, Andrew, 293
Hagedorn, Robert, 616
Hagen, Everett E., 638
Hagstrom, Warren O., 571
Hall, Richard H., 536
Hall, Thomas C., 374
Haller, Archibald O., 107
Halsey, A. H., 312, 323
Hamilton, Charles V., 595
Hamilton, Richard F., 182, 294
Hamilton, Thomas, 401
Hamilton, William B., 605
Hammond, Phillip E., 358, 367, 371, 411, 602
Hammond, Paul Y., 267
Handler, M. S., 595
Handlin, Oscar, 310

Hankins, Frank H., 531
Harbison, Frederick, 341
Harbrecht, Paul P., 210
Hare, A. Paul, 508, 545
Harper, Fowler V., 423
Harper, Robert A., 455
Harrell, Bill J., 255
Harrison, Paul M., 378, 411
Harrington, Michael, 120, 222
Harris, Seymour E., 227, 316, 318, 556
Harroff, Peggy B., 88, 415
Hartley, Eugene L., 78
Hartman, Paul T., 219, 221
Hartmann, F. H., 491
Hartmann, George W., 124
Hartshorne, E. Y., 345
Hartung, Frank E., 571
Hassenger, Robert, 318
Hatt, Paul K., 108, 126, 526
Haug, Marie R., 301
Haugen, Einar, 599
Hauser, Philip M., 19, 624
Hausknecht, Murray, 532
Havighurst, Robert J., 78, 314, 329
Hawley, Amos, 14, 345, 536
Heard, Alexander, 276
Heflebower, R. B., 181
Heilbronner, Robert L., 174, 210, 549
Heist, Paul, 347
Henderson, A. M., 171, 565
Henry, Andrew F., 616
Henry, Jules, 610
Herring, E. Pendleton, 297
Herron, George D., 390
Hickman, L. C., 455
Hicks, John D., 277, 478
Hickson, D. J., 511
Hiestand, Dale L., 210
Hiller, E. T., 111, 113
Hilmar, Norman A., 268
Himmelweit, H. T., 307
Hinings, C. L., 511
Hirsch, Walter, 575
Hodge, Robert W., 109, 117, 134, 143, 574
Hodges, Harold M., 105, 122, 125, 163, 164
Hoffer, Eric, 486
Hoffman, Paul J., 289
Hofstadter, Richard, 334, 339, 353
Holdheim, William W., 156
Hollingshead, August B., 123, 141, 148, 311, 326, 327, 429
Holt, John B., 378, 386
Holtzman, Abraham, 86
Homans, George C., 41, 46, 56, 60, 509, 536, 548
Honigmann, John J., 552
Horney, Karen, 456
Horowitz, Irving Louis, 266
Horton, John E., 277, 290
Hoselitz, Bert F., 605
Houghton, Lawrence J., 455
Hoult, Thomas Ford, 122, 386, 390
Hsu, Francis L. K., 85

Hughes, Everett C., 202, 576
Hughes, Raymond M., 313
Humphrey, Norman D., 607
Hunter, Floyd, 263, 291
Huntington, Samuel P., 268
Hurlbut, John B., 70, 74
Husband, William H., 180, 198
Hyde, Howard K., 181
Hyman, Herbert H., 125, 235, 529, 634

Ichheiser, Gustav, 436
Inkeles, Alex, 12, 107, 115, 297
Ishwaran, K., 67
Israel, Herman, 357

Jacobs, James Ripley, 7
Jacobson, Paul H., 94, 97
Jahoda, Marie, 90
Jamison, A. Leland, 371
Janowitz, Morris, 231, 267 ff., 303, 332, 521, 533
Jefferson, Thomas, 8, 474
Jencks, Christopher, 318, 353
Jennings, M. Kent, 291
Jewell, Malcolm E., 258
Johns-Heine, Patrick, 470
Johnson, Benton, 378, 386, 403
Johnson, Claudius O., 258, 295
Johnson, Elmer H., 425, 437
Johnson, Norman J., 536
Jones, Alfred Winslow, 124, 125, 147
Jones, Arthur R., Jr., 624
Jones, Dorothy B., 470
Joslyn, C. S., 136, 207
Justice, Department of, 424

Kahl, Joseph A., 122
Kahn, Alfred E., 185, 190
Kahn, Robert L., 216
Kalvern, Harry, Jr., 428
Kane, John J., 394
Kaplan, Harold, 292
Kaplan, Norman, 571, 574
Katona, George, 218
Katz, Fred E., 284, 308, 539, 540
Kaufman, Harold F., 141
Kaysen, Carl, 192, 195, 227
Kegeles, S. Stephen, 607
Keller, Suzanne, 125, 137, 140, 160, 164
Kelley, Harold H., 46, 508, 546
Kemper, Theodore D., 552
Kendall, Patricia R., 307
Keniston, Kenneth, 87, 348, 526
Kennedy, Robert E., Jr., 368
Kennedy, Ruby Jo, 54
Kephart, William M., 94, 97
Keppel, Francis, 330, 336
Kent, Frank R., 293
Key, V. O., Jr., 239, 257 ff., 301, 303, 422, 479, 503, 590
Killian, Lewis A., 477, 507, 595
Kimmel, Lewis H., 191, 195
Kirk, H. David, 70
Kirkpatrick, E. M., 254

Kituse, John I., 323, 337, 420
Klapp, Orrin E., 44
Klapper, Joseph T., 307
Klein, Viola, 71
Klein, William G., 356
Klineberg, Otto, 599
Kluckhohn, Clyde, 440, 442, 472
Kluckhohn, Florence Rockwood, 129
Knapp, Robert H., 341
Knight, Julia, 110, 583
Knupfer, Genevieve, 122
Knudten, Richard D., 371
Koch, Gustav A., 387
Kohn, Hans, 10
Kohn, Melvin L., 78, 135, 486, 550, 551
Kolb, William L., 166, 215, 511
Kolko, Gabriel, 118 ff., 155, 164, 182 ff.
Komarovsky, Mirra, 51, 61, 98, 122, 529, 559
Konvitz, Milton, 253, 270, 449, 503
Kornhauser, Arthur, 124
Kornhauser, William, 289, 574
Kriesberg, Louis, 108
Kroeber, A. L., 39
Kuhn, Alfred, 172 ff., 238, 301, 509
Kuhn, Thomas S., 572
Kuznets, Simon, 118

Labovitz, Sanford, 616
Lambert, William W., 554
Lampman, Robert J., 118, 119, 196
Lancelot, William H., 313
Landecker, Werner S., 127
Landis, Paul H., 315
Landsberger, Henry, 517
Lane, Robert E., 275, 284, 635
Lang, Olga, 85
Larrabee, Eric, 573
Lasch, Christopher, 334
Laski, Harold, 213, 262, 312, 314, 406, 458, 462, 484
Lasswell, Harold D., 263, 293, 462
Lasswell, Thomas E., 130
Latham, Earl, 198
Laumann, Edward O., 108, 139, 141, 142
Lazarsfeld, Paul F., 283 ff., 307, 340, 353, 471, 575, 612
Lazerwitz, Bernard, 402
Lee, Alfred M., 607
Lee, Dorothy, 497
Leggett, John C., 150
Lehmann, H. C., 128
Lehrer, Stanley, 314
Leierson, William H., 211, 230
Leites, Nathan, 470
Lenski, Gerhard E., 101, 149, 165, 370, 396, 397, 411
Lerner, Daniel, 263, 266
Levi-Strauss, Claude, 23
Levin, Harry, 81
Levin, Murray B., 277

Levine, Sol, 506
Levy, Marion J., Jr., 142
Lewin, Kurt, 77
Lewis, David M., 107
Lewis, David T., 14, 16, 17, 18, 19, 20, 117
Lewis, Gordon F., 138
Lewis, H. Gregg, 221
Lewis, Lionel S., 56, 459
Lieberson, Stanley, 13, 19, 607
Lichtman, Richard, 474
Linter, John, 181, 183, 185, 197, 451, 548
Linton, Ralph, 26, 29, 46, 49, 59, 76, 113
Lipset, Seymour Martin, 51, 95, 102 ff., 125 ff., 146, 154, 158, 164, 219 ff., 276, 285, 288, 303, 315, 329, 347 ff., 453, 474 ff., 503 ff.
Little, Roger, 267, 521
Litwak, Eugene, 62, 65, 522, 525, 561
Livingston, Joseph, 197
Long, Huey, 456
Long, Edward V., 498
Long, Norton E., 193, 243, 251
Loomis, Charles P., 548
Loucks, William N., 178, 208, 228
Lowenthal, Leo, 295, 460, 471, 485
Lowi, Theodore J., 280
Lowry, Ritchie P., 292
Lubell, Samuel, 288
Luckmann, Thomas, 403, 592
Lundberg, Ferdinand, 140
Lundeen, Walter A., 232
Lunt, Paul S., 106, 128, 139, 148, 528
Lupton, T., 511
Lyle, J., 307
Lynch, David, 180, 184, 187
Lynd, Helen M., 128, 163
Lynd, Robert S., 128, 163, 523
Lyon, Leverett S., 184, 187, 563, 567, 568, 569

Macaulay, Stewart, 169
Maccoby, Eleanor E., 76, 78, 81
MacDonald, K. M., 511
MacDougall, John A., 541
Machiavelli, Niccolo, 435, 436
Machlup, Fritz, 189, 318
MacIver, Robert M., 26, 146, 233 ff., 339, 343 ff., 487, 511 ff.
Mack, Raymond W., 316, 370, 608, 609
MacLean, Malcolm S., 325
MacLeish, Archibald, 436
Macquarrie, John, 384
Maine, Henry S., 511
Mandelbaum, David F., 50, 59
Mandell, Irving, 423
Mangus, A. R., 94
Mannheim, Karl, 172, 202, 410, 522, 527, 598, 621, 639
Marcson, Simon, 346, 574
March, James G., 46, 202,

505 ff., 545
March, John F., Jr., 472
Marden, Charles F., 531
Margenau, Henry, 487
Marsh, Robert M., 19, 455, 547, 579 ff., 631
Marshall, Andrew W., 617
Marshall, Howard D., 344
Marshall, S. L. A., 268
Martel, Martin U., 470
Martin, Roscoe C., 243
Martin, Walter T., 616
Martindale, Don, 367, 455
Marty, Martin, 385
Marvick, Dwaine, 288
Marx, Gary T., 595, 618
Marx, Karl, 105, 106, 149, 192, 624
Marx, Leo, 503
Masland, John W., 268, 332
Mason, Edward S., 178 ff., 192 ff., 230
Mason, Ward S., 44, 45, 327
Matthews, Donald R., 137, 259
Mausner, Bernard, 607
Mausner, Judith, 607
May, Henry F., 390, 411
Mayer, Albert, 370, 397
Mayer, Albert J., 122
Mayer, F. E., 377
Mayer, Kurt B., 138
Mayer, Martin, 314
Mayntz, Renate, 535
Mayo, Elton, 219
McCall, George J., 25, 470
McClelland, David C., 454
McConnell, Grant, 257
McClosky, Herbert, 289
McDill, Edward L., 322
McDonald, Neil A., 240
McEachern, Alexander W., 44, 45, 327
McEwen, W. J., 520
McGee, Reece J., 343
McGiffert, Michael, 454
McGranahan, Donald V., 470
McKenzie, R. D., 14
McLean, Joseph E., 284
McLaughlin, William G., Jr., 387
McLuhan, Herbert Marshall, 307, 471
McPhee, William, 283
Mead, Frank S., 371, 377
Mead, Margaret, 57, 461
Means, G. C., 183, 192 ff., 230
Mecklin, John M., 295
Meeker, Marchia, 106, 148
Meier, Dorothy L., 420, 613
Mencher, Samuel, 561
Mercer, Blaine E., 310, 329, 337, 343
Merriam, Charles E., 22, 235, 238, 253, 302
Merritt, Richard L., 19, 547
Merton, Robert K., 44, 91, 94, 276, 307 ff., 356, 367, 420 ff., 505, 515, 555, 556, 572 ff., 610 ff.
Metzger, Walter P., 339

Miall, Bernard, 484
Middleton, Russell, 49, 364
Miles, Matthew B., 312
Miller, Daniel R., 50, 552
Miller, Delbert C., 200, 211 ff., 230, 292, 341
Miller, Herman P., 115 ff., 155 ff., 196
Miller, Michael V., 348
Miller, Van, 333
Miller, Warren E., 283, 285, 287, 303
Millet, John P., 344
Mills, C. Wright, 104, 133 ff., 233, 263, 299, 488
Mills, D. C., 536
Mills, Theodore M., 508, 546
Mizruchi, Ephraim H., 163
Moberg, David O., 356, 371, 380
Moeller, Gerald H., 455
Moore, Wilbert E., 66, 114 ff., 194 ff., 202, 209, 230, 433, 498, 515, 517, 598 ff.
Monroe, Paul, 326
Monsen, R. Joseph, Jr., 293
Monsma, John C., 573
Morison, Elting E., 440, 472
Morison, Robert S., 342
Morris, Charles, 441
Morris, Richard T., 31, 103, 109
Morrison, Donald H., 284
Morse, Dean, 572
Morse, Nancy C., 458, 461
Moskow, Michael H., 330
Moynihan, Daniel Patrick, 13, 65, 281, 499
Muelder, Walter C., 379
Muller-Freienfels, Richard, 484
Mumford, Lewis, 627
Munro, Thomas, 467
Munsterberg, Hugo, 599
Murdock, George P., 49, 59, 63, 96, 98
Murphy, Raymond J., 109, 370
Murray, Gilbert, 455
Murray, Janet H., 551
Musgrove, F., 87
Myers, Charles, 341
Myers, Donald B., 390
Myers, Henry Alonzo, 474, 483
Myrdal, Gunnar, 123, 429, 430, 452, 462, 499, 503

Nahirny, Vladimir, 508
Nam, Charles B., 91, 143, 323
Neal, Arthur G., 614
Neal, Marie Augusta, 380, 392
Nelson, Joel I., 63, 182
Nettler, Gwynn, 420
Neufeld, Maurice F., 211
Neugarten, Bernice L., 87, 312, 329
Newcomb, Theodore M., 78, 124, 346, 507, 584
Niebuhr, H. Richard, 367, 378
Nisbet, Robert A., 94
North, Cecil C., 83, 108, 126, 128
Northrop, F. S. C., 488
Nottingham, Elizabeth K., 371

Odaka, Kunio, 549
O'Dea, Thomas F., 371, 383, 389, 411
Odegard, Peter, 293
Ogburn, William F., 624
O'Hara, Rosemary, 289
Ohlin, Lloyd E., 425
Olson, Bernhard F., 404
Opler, Morris, 313, 420, 499, 548
Oppenheim, A. N., 307
Orcutt, Guy H., 576
Orlans, Harold, 332
Orleans, Peter, 289
Orshansky, Mollie, 121
Owsley Frank L., 114
Oxenfelt, Alfred E., 191
Ozanne, Robert, 221

Pace, C. R., 344
Packard, Vance, 484
Page, Charles H., 223 ff., 343, 448, 498, 512 ff.
Palmer, Gladys L., 134
Panunzio, Constantine, 406
Parker, E. G., 307
Parkes, Henry Bamford, 478, 491, 503
Parkinson, C. Northcote, 536
Parmelee, Rexford C., 195
Parrington, Vernon L., 464
Parsons, Talcott, 39, 46, 56 ff., 76, 102, 111, 167 ff., 200, 234, 241, 288, 356, 367, 393, 442, 460, 495, 512, 548 ff., 610, 618, 632
Paul, Benjamin D., 607
Pearlin, Leonard I., 78, 135, 486, 550, 551
Peirce, Neal R., 245
Pellegrin, Roland J., 268
Pennok, J. Roland, 248
Pepper, Stephen C., 441, 503
Petersen, William, 19, 20
Peterson, Donald G., 126
Peterson, Richard E., 348
Petterson, Samuel C., 258
Pfautz, Harold W., 148, 470
Pfeffer, Leo, 372, 374
Phillips, Wendell, 390
Photiadis, John D., 358
Piepkorn, Arthur Carl, 377
Pierce, Bessie L., 334
Pinard, Maurice, 290
Pinot, R., 305
Piret, Fern V., 284
Pitts, Jesse R., 528
Plant, Thomas F. A., 464
Podhoretz, Norman, 457
Polanyi, Karl, 166
Pollak, Otto, 557
Pool, Ithiel de S., 293
Pope, Liston, 378, 386
Porter, John, 122, 165, 475, 478
Potter, David M., 477, 478, 484
Powers, Mary G., 143
Press, Charles, 282
Presthus, Robert, 505
Price, Don K., 571 ff., 624
Pugh, D. S., 511
Purcell, Theodore V., 216

Putney, Snell, 364

Quinny, Earl R., 422

Rabi, I. I., 572
Radway, Lawrence I., 268, 332
Rae, Saul F., 146
Rainwater, Lee, 50, 61, 98, 499, 574
Ramsey, Charles, 87
Randall, John H., Jr., 467
Ranney, Austin, 233, 273, 286
Rawlings, Edna, 307
Ray, Verne F., 240
Reckless, Walter C., 426
Record, Jane Cassels, 477
Redfield, Margaret Parle, 56, 76
Reeves, Jon, 87
Remmers, H. H., 90
Reichstein, Kenneth J., 422
Reid, Otto M., 84
Reiss, Albert J., Jr., 117, 165, 256, 311, 526
Reiss, Ira L., 88, 92
Reissman, Leonard, 122
Reubens, Beatrice G., 210
Reynolds, Lloyd G., 220
Rhyne, Russell, 615
Ricardo, David, 168
Rich, Bennett M., 265
Richey, Herman G., 313, 325, 353
Riecken, Henry W., 381
Riesman, David, 318, 353, 455, 456, 465, 484, 503
Riley, John W., Jr., 556
Riley, Matilda White, 556
Ringer, Benjamin B., 384
Robson, John, 530
Robinson, Joan, 189
Roche, John P., 243, 477
Rodman, Hyman, 74
Roethlisberger, Fritz J., 219, 517
Rogoff, Natalie, 138
Rokeach, Milton, 486, 503
Rokkan, Stein, 19, 547
Rose, Arnold M., 123, 231, 263, 289 ff., 429, 452, 533, 608
Rose, Peter I., 520
Rosen, Bernard C., 135, 454
Rosen, George, 295
Rosenberg, Morris, 80, 495, 538
Rosenthal, Donald B., 292
Ross, Arthur M., 219, 221
Ross, Ralph, 133, 341
Rossi, Alice S., 58, 69
Rossi, Peter H., 107, 109, 117, 122, 574
Rossiter, Clinton, 250, 251, 253, 478
Rosten, Leo, 132
Rothwell, C. Easton, 263
Rotter, Julian B., 291
Rourke, Constance, 458
Rowe, Henry K., 374, 379
Runciman, W. G., 112, 162, 163, 614, 618

Russett, Bruce M., 9, 10, 20
Ruth, Henry S., Jr., 425

Sabine, George H., 474, 476, 482, 485
Sait, Edward M., 279
Salisbury, W. Seward, 320, 371 ff., 393 ff.
Salter, John T., 293
Samuelson, Paul A., 167, 230, 570
Samuelsson, Kurt, 368
Sanders, Irwin T., 522
Sanford, Charles L., 503
Sanford, Nevitt, 90, 342
Sansom, George B., 549
Santayana, George, 457, 458
Sapin, Burton M., 266
Saposs, David J., 211
Sargent, S. Stanfield, 149
Savelle, Max, 459, 479, 490
Sawyer, Jack, 632
Sayles, Leonard R., 217
Scammon, Richard M., 284
Schachter, Stanley, 381
Scheff, Thomas J., 34, 586, 591
Scheler, Max, 156
Schelling, Thomas C., 267, 427, 599
Schermerhorn, Richard A., 628
Schneider, David M., 56, 60, 93
Schneider, Eugene V., 200
Schneider, Herbert W., 387
Schneider, Louis, 389
Schnore, Leo, 15, 19
Scott, John Finley, 346
Scott, W. Richard, 202
Schramm, Wilbur, 307
Schultz, T. W., 317
Schumpeter, Joseph A., 189
Schur, Edwin M., 415, 417
Schuster, George N., 318
Sears, Robert, 78, 81
Sebald, Hans, 485
Seeman, Melvin, 226, 331, 614
Segal, Bernard E., 346
Selekman, Benjamin M., 224
Selznick, Philip, 103, 218, 248, 518, 598
Sewell, William H., 79
Sexton, Patricia Cayo, 312, 353
Shanas, Ethel, 62, 98, 561
Sharp, Harry, 370, 397
Sharp, R. Lauriston, 240
Sheatsley, Paul B., 634
Sherrington, C. S., 22
Shils, Edward, 272, 442
Short, James E., 616
Shostak, Arthur B., 182, 224
Shuler, Edgar A., 603
Sibley, Elbridge, 135
Siegel, Paul M., 109, 117, 574
Siegfried, Andre, 469
Sills, David L., 529, 531, 533
Silverman, Arnold R., 607
Simon, Herbert A., 202, 521, 533, 540
Simmons, J. L., 25, 628
Simpson, George E., 13, 51, 310,

322, 452
Simpson, Richard L., 521
Sklare, Marshall, 398, 399, 411
Skolnick, Jerome, 428
Slater, Carol, 72
Slotkin, James S., 420
Smelser, Neil J., 167, 230, 512, 638
Smircich, R. J., 92
Smith, Adam, 168, 317
Smith, David T., 415
Smith, J. Allen, 283
Smith, James Ward, 371
Smith, Louis, 266
Smith, Page, 13
Smith, Richard Austin, 137
Smith, T. Lynn, 17
Snyder, Louis L., 499
Snyder, Richard C., 266, 608, 609
Sombart, Werner, 176
Somkin, Fred, 482
Sorokin, Pitirim A., 11, 26, 37, 39, 46, 127 ff., 232, 267, 305, 471, 511, 548, 581, 585, 639
Spalding, Willard B., 333
Speier, Hans, 102, 103, 267
Spencer, Herbert, 567
Spengler, Joseph J., 18
Spergel, Irving, 415
Sperry, William L., 373, 374, 378, 381, 382
Spinrad, William, 213*n*
Spregel, Henry William, 189
Srole, Leo, 128, 613
Stafford, Frank P., 472
Stanton, Frank N., 471
Stanton, William R., 499
Stark, Rodney, 357, 385, 388, 400 ff.
Steffens, Lincoln, 427, 437
Stein, Maurice R., 531
Steiner, Gary A., 231, 307, 394, 410, 508, 556, 578
Stern, Bernhard, 77
Stern, Fritz, 289
Sterner, Richard, 23, 429, 452
Stiles, Lindley J., 329
Stinchcombe, Arthur L., 332
Stokes, Donald E., 283, 287, 303
Storer, Norman W., 571
Straus, Murray A., 455
Strauss, Anselm L., 361, 574
Streib, Gordon F., 62, 83, 84, 85, 98, 561
Strong, Donald S., 295
Stroup, Herbert, 343, 402
Stouffer, Samuel A., 144, 268, 272, 363, 436, 476, 486, 520, 599, 600, 618
Suchman, Edward A., 153, 430, 437, 452
Sumner, William Graham, 483
Sussman, Marvin, 62
Sutherland, Edwin H., 123, 429
Sutton, Francis X., 227, 556
Svalastoga, Kaare, 160, 165
Swain, J. W., 356
Swanson, Bert E., 291
Swanson, Guy E., 50, 357, 411,

552, 554, 579
Sweet, William W., 374, 378, 411
Sweetser, Dorrian Apple, 541
Swomley, John M., Jr., 266
Sykes, Gresham M., 417, 516

Taeuber, Alma F., 20, 322
Taeuber, Karl E., 20, 322
Tangent, Pierre, 123, 129
Tannenbaum, Arnold S., 216
Tannenbaum, Frank, 481
Tarver, James D., 67
Taussig, F. W., 136, 207
Taylor, Carl C., 624
Taylor, Lee, 624
Tenhouten, Warren, 87
Terrien, F. C., 536
Thibaut, John W., 46, 508, 546
Thielens, wagner, Jr., 340, 575
Thiessen, Victor, 382
Thomlinson, Ralph, 94
Thomas, Edwin J., 43, 45
Thomas, R. Murray, 107
Thompson, Edgar T., 103
Thompson, J. D., 520, 541
Thompson, Victor A., 202, 533, 537
Thompson, Warren S., 14 ff., 117
Thompson, Wayne E., 87, 277, 290
Thut, I. N., 326
Tobin, James, 227, 556
Toby, Jackson, 34
Tocqueville, Alexis de, 527
Tomah, Aida K., 513
Tönnis, Ferdinand, 511
Triandis, Leigh Minturn, 554
Trow, Martin, 315, 329
Truman, David B., 260
Tufts, James H., 451, 463
Tullock, Gordon, 298
Tumin, Melvin M., 100, 165, 323, 433
Turner, C., 511
Turner, Frederick Jackson, 6
Turner, Ralph H., 77, 507
Tyler, Gus W., 425
Tylor, Edward Burnett, 26

Udy, Stanley H., Jr., 520, 537, 538, 539
Ulrich, Robert, 320
Underwood, Kenneth, 394
United States Department of Labor, 178
Useem, John, 16, 123, 129, 148
Useem, Ruth Hill, 16, 123, 129, 148

Vagts, Alfred, 267
van den Berghe, Pierre, 499
van den Haag, Ernest, 133, 341

Veblen, Thorstein, 176, 339, 342, 343, 465, 624
Verba, Sidney, 303, 478 ff., 491 ff., 590
Vernier, Chester G., 52 ff., 70 ff.
Veroff, Joseph, 370
Vince, P., 307
Vincent, John Russell, 288
Vollmer, Howard, 218
von Hayek, Friedrich A., 225
von Wright, Georg H., 444
Vreeland, Rebecca, 346
Vroom, Victor H., 458, 461

Walker, Nigel, 247
Wallace, Samuel E., 120, 128
Wallace, Walter L., 344, 347, 354
Waller, Willard, 58, 308, 309, 311, 314, 354
Wallerstein, James S., 123
Walter, C. R., 219
Walton, John, 291
Warkov, Seymour, 536
Warner, Aaron W., 572
Warner, W. Lloyd, 103 ff., 137, 139, 148, 207, 262, 528
Warren, Neil, 90
Warren, Robert Penn, 477, 595
Warren, Roland L., 291, 522
Warriner, Charles K., 528
Watkins, Myron W., 184, 187, 563 ff.
Waskow, Arthur I., 607
Wattenberg, William, 329
Watts, Alan, 497
Wayland, Sloan R., 312
Wayne, Ivor, 470
Weber, Max, 144, 171, 176, 200 ff., 367, 369, 411, 412, 488, 565, 570
Wecter, Dixon, 456
Weigel, Gustave, 393
Weiss, R. S., 458, 461
Welch, Maryon K., 109
Weller, Fred A., 52, 56
Wenninger, Eugene P., 459, 487
West, James (pseudonym), see Withers, Carl
Westby, David L., 526
Westin, Alan F., 503
Westley, William A., 90
Westoff, Charles F., 17
Wheeler, Stanton, 305, 353
White, Andrew D., 573
White, David M., 307, 470, 556
White, James E., 529
Whitehead, Alfred North, 576
Whitehead, Thomas North, 219
Whiting, J. W., 552
Whitman, Lauris B., 376
Whitley, Olive Read, 378
Whyte, William Foote, 219, 230, 281

Whyte, William H., Jr., 200, 455, 484
Wildavsky, Aaron, 292
Wilensky, Harold L., 126, 156, 420, 470, 586, 589, 617
Williams, James M., 459
Williams, J. Paul, 371
Williams, Robin M., Jr., 114, 121, 151, 251, 391, 395, 430 ff., 523, 547 ff., 606 ff., 633, 635
Willmott, Peter, 65
Wilson, Bryan R., 381, 384, 412
Wilson, Everett K., 131, 310, 346
Wilson, James Q., 291
Wilson, Logan, 166, 215, 339 ff., 429, 511
Wilson, O. W., 428
Wilson, Robert N., 457
Winter, Gibson, 385
Withers, Carl, 112, 127, 141, 148
Witty, P. A., 128
Wolcott, Leon, 295
Wolf, Margery, 554
Wolfenstein, Martha, 470
Wolfle, Dael, 347
Wolin, Sheldon S., 348
Wood, Robert C., 531
Woodard, James W., 432, 433, 487
Woodward, Joan, 537
Wright, C. R., 529
Wright, Quincey, 267
Wrong, Dennis H., 101, 151
Wyle, Clement J., 123
Wylie, Lawrence, 277
Wylie, Philip, 80

X, Malcolm, 618

Yellin, Seymour, 370
Yinger, J. Milton, 13, 51, 310, 322, 359, 372, 390 ff.
Young, Frank W., 50
Young, Michael, 65

Zald, Mayer N., 534
Zander, Alvin F., 508
Zawadzki, B., 612
Zawodny, Janus K., 268, 599
Zeigler, Harmon, 293, 294
Zeisel, Hans, 428
Zelditch, Morris, 60
Zeller, Belle, 258, 293
Zetterberg, Hans L., 11, 12, 189, 196
Zimmer, Basil, 525
Zimmerman, Carle C., xiii, 93, 557
Zloczower, Abraham, 340
Znaniecki, Florian, 168 ff., 212, 309, 339
Zuckerman, Harriet, 613

# SUBJECTS

achievement, value of, 454–8
activity in America, 458–61
adolescence, *see* youth
administrative (organizational) control, 174–7
AFL-CIO, politics and the, 294–6, 530
aggregative fallacy, 604
agencies, governmental, 260–2
agriculture: technology and, 10; pressure groups, 295–8
alienation, 543–4
Americanism, *see* nationalism
anomie: portrait of, 543–4; in American society, 609–17
associational society (Gesellschaft): definition of, 511–13; urban centers as prototypes of, 512; characteristics of, 513–14; in America, 515–16
associations: membership in, in upper income strata, 122; business and trade, 185; formal, proliferation of, 527–33
attitudes, intrastrata differences in, 123–26
authority, as criterion in stratification, 105, 111

beliefs: defined, 27; interstrata differences in, 106–10; education in, 334–7; as distinguished from values, 443
Bill of Rights, 243, 252, 373
birth rates, 17, 18
black Americans, *see* Negroes
black-market operations, 427, 429
Black Power, 595
Buddhism, 363
bureaucracy: in business, 202–8; in government, 260–2, 268; in American social organization, 533–45

Calvinism, 367
Caste: characteristics of, 100; interactional definition of, 111*n*; defined, 113
Catholic Church: American features of, 372, 374; membership of, 377; nativistic movements against, 382; characteristic beliefs and practices of, 391–4
Catholics, 373, 374, 375*n*, 393, 396–7
change, *see* social change
checks and balances in government, 244, 247–50
children: equality of siblings, 68–69; status and roles of, 77–83
Christianity, 329, 359, 363, 371, 390
church: distinctive features of in U.S., 379–82; separation of state and, 371, 373–4; organizational forms of, 371–2, 380–1; political neutrality, 389–91; *see also* religion
cities, growth of, 14, 15
civil rights, 477–9
civil-service laws, evasion of, 421–2
CIO, 212, 216
citizens, rights and duties of, 269–72
class, *see* social stratification
class conflict, 99–100, 124–5, 149–52, 159–60, 162–4
class consciousness, 105–6, 125–6, 128, 143–51; Marxian concept of, 143, 150; factors affecting, 145–51
cohesion of society, 582–3; factors in, 588–607

collective behavior, 507, 534, 629
colleges, 338–50
communal society (*Gemeinschaft*), 511; rural community as prototype of, 512; characteristics of, 513–14
competition, imperfect, 188–92
conflict: escalation of, 587; techniques for resolving, 235, 597–8; and integration, 600, 607–9
conformity: nature of, 30–1; conditions favoring, 414, 416–19; as value, 484–7; and deviance, 610–11
Confucianism, 363
conscientious objectors, 440
consensus: on norms, 52–53; political, 239–41; procedural, 586–7; types of, 591–2; complexity of, 602–4; and societal continuity, 631
Constitution, U.S., 242–3, 230, 231, 232, 252–4
constitutional government, 252–4
corporations: dominance of, 179–83; intercorporate coordination, 183–8; nature of, 192–4; control of, 194–8; property in, 198–200; internal organization of, 200–08
corruption, political, 384–5, 421, 424–5
crime, organized, 418, 425–7, 455
cults, 364, 371, 377–8
culture: defined, 25–6; normative aspects of, 27–8; transmission of, 28, 31; characteristics of, 98; undergraduate, 344–50
cultural change, 620, 622–5, 628–9, 631–8
cultural fictions, 431–6
cultural goals, in economic action 173–4
cultural integration, 582
cultural norms: defined, 28–9; dimensions of variation in, 30–1; distribution of, 30; enforcement of, 30–2; explicitness of, 36; specificity of, 36; in economic action, 173; character of, 413–14; variation in, 413–19; evasion of, 419–31; "cultural fictious," 431–6; values represented by, 435–6, 443; *see also* institutions

death rates, 18, 19
death, religion and, 361
democracy: rights of citizens and, 269–72; education and, 335–7; as a dominant American value, 448–9, 492–5
differentiation, trend toward, 630–1
descent in American kinship system, 56, 57–8
directorates, interlocking, 184
divorce: American legal view of, 52–4; reasons for prevalence of, 94–6; legal rules of, versus practice, 421, 423–4
dominant institution, criteria of, 549–50
Dred Scott case, 255
"due process of law," 246
*Duncan v. Kahanamoku*, 265

economic action, concept of, 564
economic institutions: nature of, 166–70; and controlling social mechanisms, 171–7; structural features of, 177–9; instability of, 166; control of, 173; religion and, 367–9, 372; and political controls, 225–9, 563–71; *see also* corporations; labor organizations

economic systems, types of, 175–7
ecumenicalism, 379–80, 392–3
education: as institution, 305–11; American, characteristics of, 311–32; federal involvement in, 332–3; interest groups and, 333–4; cultural themes of, 310–12, 319–20, 334–8; "higher," 338–51; cultural goals of, 351–3, 362; *see also* schools; teachers
efficiency, 464–6
elders, in the family, 83–7
elections, *see* voters and voting
electoral college, 245
equality: of educational opportunity, 319–25; as American value, 472-9
estates, 113–14
evangelism, 350, 361, 374
evil, religion and, 361
executive branch of government: powers and duties of, 248–9; agencies of the, 260–2
exogamy, 50

fair trade laws, 185–6
family: bases for analysis of, 47–51; American legal norms of, 51–6; defining features of, 56–68; equality patterns in, 68–70; women and men in the, 70–7; children in the, 77–83; elders in the, 83–7; youth, 87–90; romantic love and the, 90–2; stability and instability of the, 92–7; religion and, 362; *see also* kinship system
family units, nuclear vs. extended, 61–8
federal government: nature of system, 243–50; separation of powers in, 244, 247–50; the Presidency, 250-2; the Supreme Court, 244, 254–7; legislative bodies, 248–9, 257–60; civil and military powers of, 264–9
formal organization: informal vs., 516–21; characteristics of, 519–22; problems of, 537–41
formality, 516–21; and stratification, 130
freedom: religious, 371, 374–6; as American value, 438, 479–84; personal, protection of, 483, 496–8
functionalism, 365–6
Fundamentalism, religious, 399–401
*Gesellschaft, see* associational society
*Gemeinschaft, see* communal society
geographic factors in American society, 6–10
government: and facilitation of economic activity, 567–8; and regulation of economic activity, 567–71; *see also*, political institutions; state, the American
"government of laws," 244–7

"hedonistic values," 469–70
Hinduism, 363
housing codes, evasion of, 419
humanitarianism, 462–4
husband: and wife, equality of, 69; status of, 69; role of, 69–70

immigration, 13
impersonal relations: between social strata, 158–9; in associational society, 513–16
incest taboo, 49–51, 60
indexes: of anomie, 616–17; of integration, 616–17
individual, social organization and the, 542–5
individual personality, 495–8

industrial relations, 211–24
informal organization, formal vs., 45, 516–21
in-laws, "equality" of, 68
institutions: norms of a society, 33–7; defined, 37; examples of, 38–9; institutional norms, character of, 52–3; interrelations of, 547–78; *see also* economic institutions; education; family; political institutions; religion; social stratification
integration of society: meaning of, 580–4; in America, 588–607; and mutual dependence, 589–90; mechanisms of, 592–9; and external pressures, 599–600; and common value-orientations, 600–6; and diversity, 606–7; and conflict, 607–9; and anomie, 609–17; and alienation, 614–15
intercorporate stockholding, 184
interdependence and societal integration, 589–90
interest groupings: and the political system, 292; and education, 333–4
interlocking directorates, 184
interrelations of institutions: modes of, 551–6; and mass communication, 555; strains in, 555; kinship, 556-63; economic and political, 563–71; science, education, and polity, 571–6; in total social system, 576–8
isolationism, 492

Jews, 370, 373, 375n, 376–7, 380, 393, 397
Judaic-Christian doctrines, influence of, 362, 407
Judaism, 359, 363, 369, 391, 398–9
judicial branch of government, 254–7
jury system, 428

kinship and other institutions, 556–63; economy, 557–60; occupations, 558; polity, 560–2; stratification, 100, 111, 113, 136–43, 562–3
kinship system: defined, 47; structural features, 56–60; and social stratification, 100, 111, 113, 136–43; relation to other institutions, 556–63
knowledge defined, 27

labor organizations, 214–22, 223–9
laissez-faire economy, 168, 173, 191
law, family, 45, 51–5
law-norms, 37n
learning, 306
legal rights, and social class, 118–20, 123, 155, 157
legislative bodies: control of, 257–60; representation in, 257–8
legislative branch of government, 248–9
life expectancy, 18
lobbying, 296–7

*Marbury v. Madison*, 255
marriage: statistics on, 16; family law and, 53–5; mate selection for, 58–9; husband-wife equalities in, 59; patterns of class boundaries and, 124–9
market mechanism as economic institution, 172–3
market system, perfect, barriers to, 191–2
mass media as educational influence, 306–7
material comfort, value placed on, 469–72
"McCarthyism," 272, 449

military powers of federal government, 264–9
military organization, stratification of, 144–5
mobility of population, 11, 15–16; effect of on kinship, 59
modernism, 399–401
moral orientation, 461–2
mortality rates, 18, 19
motion pictures, 470

nationalism, 489–92
natural resources, *see* resources
Negroes (black Americans): voting rights, 283–5; educational opportunities, 319–25; discrimination against, 421–2, 498–9; as a "category," 594–5
nepotism, 421
New Deal, 162, 178
norms: defined, 28; character of, 29–36, 39, 413–19; *see also* cultural norms; institutions
norms: variation in, 413–14, 436; evasion of, 419–31

occupations, 106; and stratification, 106–10, 116–17, 121; prestige of, 108–10; intergeneration transmission of, 131–8
oligopoly, 189–90
open-class system, 100, 113–14
organizations, large, problems of, 537–41

patent rights, 187–8
patriotism, 489–92; *see* nationalism
patronage, 280
pluralism, political and cultural, 301–2
police power, 238
political authority 233–40; distinguished from power, 236–7
political institutions: nature of, 231–40; of the American structure, 242–72; political parties, 273–83; interest groupings, 292–300; pattern of, in U.S., 300–3, 563–71; and economic institutions, 563–71
political parties, 273–83
politics: social class and, 149–52, 156; religion and, 389–91, 400–1
population: growth of, 12, 13; heterogeneity of, 13; urban, 13, 14, 15; mobility of, 15, 16; age distribution of, 16; proportion married in the, 16; educational status of the, 19
poverty: "rediscovery of," 120–3; and taxation, 119–20
power: as criterion for stratification, 105, 111; interstrata differences, 122–3; as index of strata, 127; coercive, 232–4; *see also* political institutions
power elite, 262–4, 290
power structures, local, 289–92
practicality, emphasis upon, 310, 467–8
Presidency, 250–2, 235–8
pressure groups, *see* interest groupings
primary groups, role of, in U.S., 524–7
privacy, 497–8
professional codes, evasion of, 421–2
profit motive, 208–11
progress, 468–9
prohibition, 421, 426
prosperity, 11*n*, 154–6, 166
prostitution, 421

"Protestant Ethic," 367–70, 396–400
Protestantism: ascetic, 363, 367; characteristics of, 367–70; American features of, 376–82; diversity in, 376–82; organizational forms of, 380–1; political orientations of, 390; and Catholicism, 391–8; fundamentalism and modernism in, 399–403
Puritanism, 459, 462

racial and ethnic relations, 121, 139–40, 153
racial discrimination: in employment, 194; in education, 321–3; as value-problem, 421, 429–30, 498–9
racism, 498–9
radicalism, 478–9
ranking: intrinsic and extrinsic, 111–13; congruity of, 142–3; *see* social stratification
religion: in the schools, 320, 333; influence of on American society, 355–6, 404–10; problem of definition, 355–6; aspects of, 357–9; functional contexts of, 359–70; features of American, 370–99; freedom of, 371, 374–6; diversity of groupings, 376–80; organized, indifference and opposition to, 381–2; secularization of, 371, 382–6; "return to," 386–7; fundamentalist-modernist cleavages in, 399–402; and other institutions, 357–8, 385–6, 402–7, 554; in American social structure, 407–10; and common values, 408–10; *see also* church
religious ethics, change in, 383–4
religious participation, 372, 382, 385–8, 393–4
resources: land, 8; minerals, 8; technological, 10–12
revivalism, 372
rights and duties of citizens, 269–72
riots: urban, 121, 217, 239; labor, 239
role, definitions of, 43
Roman Catholic Church, *see* Catholic Church
rules of residence, effects of, on kinship, 59

sanctions, 33–5
science, 353, 487–9, 571–6
schools: as social system, 308–11; organization of, 311–13; control of, 325–7; financial bases, 319; religious instruction in, 320, 333; equality of opportunity in, 319–25; racial segregation issue, 321–3; administration of, 331–2; individual competition in, 319, 324; *see also* education; teachers
sects, religious, 364, 371, 377–9
secularization, 371, 382–6
separation of powers in federal government, 244, 247–50
sexual behavior: restraints upon, 48–9; patterns of, 421
Sherman Antitrust Act, 568
sibling equality in American family, 68–9
situational field, 507–8
slavery, 7, 481, 496
social categories, separation of, 594
social change: integration and, 580, 585–6; in America, 620–38; theories of, 621–5; as trends, 625–30; and technology, 629–30; factors supporting, 630–8; in values, 632–8
social class, defined, 113
social differentiation: distinguished from stratification, 101; and extrinsic ranking, 112
social group: defined, 45; formal, 45; informal,

45; nature of, 508–10

social identities as types or categories, 43–4

social integration, *see* integration of society

social mobility: intergenerational, 131–8; career, 133–4

social organization: concept of, 44; informal, 45; nature of, 505–7; types of, 510–22; characteristics of, in U.S., 523–45; primary group in, 524–33; formal associations in, 527–33; large organizations in, 533–42; the individual and, 542–5; changes in, 626–9

social sanctions, 33, 34, 35, 446

social stratification: defined, 100–2; varieties of ranking in, 102–6; segmental, 103, 129–30; Marxian analysis of, 105–6, criteria for, 110–13; ideal types of, 113–14; ideology of, 114–15; and income and wealth, 115–20; and social participation, 122; variations in, 126–31; interstrata interaction, 138–42; awareness of, 143–51; strains, tensions, and compensations, 151–61; integration of system of, 161–4

social system: concept of, 584–8; levels of structure in, 595–6; change in, 631

sociocultural regulation, diverse levels of, 39–40

state, the, defined, 233

state, the American: characteristics of, 242; structure of, 242–72; rights and duties of citizens in, 269–72; separation of church and, 371, 373–4

status defined, 42–3

status consistency, *see* ranking, congruity of

stockholding, intercorporate, 184

stratification, *see* social stratification

stratum solidarity, 138–42

structure, social 23–4; cultural, 44

subcultures, 415–16, 419, 430–1

success, value of, 455–6

Supreme Court, U.S., 244, 254–7

systems: concept of, 24, 25; groups and institutions as, 547–9

tariffs, 186

taxation, 186

taxing power, 239

teachers, 308–11, 327–31

technological resources, 10–12

technology, 469; defined, 27

Tennessee Valley Authority, 229, 262

territory, control of, 234, 257–8

trade associations, 185

transportation facilities, 11, 18

undergraduate culture, 344–50

unions, labor, 174, 214–23

universities, 338–51; university organization, 342–4

urbanization, 13–15

valuation, levels of, 449–50, 452

value-orientations, major, in America, 452–502

value systems, 450–1

values: defined 27, 442; education in, 314, 319, 329, 337, 351–3; concept of, 436–48; group, 447; dominant, 448–50; integration (consistency) of, 451–2; change in, 632–8

voters and voting, 283–89

veterans, organizations of, 530

violence in employer-employee relations, 211

wealth, attitudes toward, 456–7

women, roles of, 70–7

work, valuation of, 459–61

youth, position and role performances of, 87–90

zoning rules, evasion of, 419

# About the Author

Robin M. Williams, Jr. is Henry Scarborough Professor of Social Science and a member of the Department of Sociology at Cornell University. He received his undergraduate and M.S. degrees from North Carolina State University and his Ph.D. from Harvard University. Since coming to Cornell in 1946 he has taught and lectured at many other universities in the United States and abroad.

Professor Williams is a past president of the American Sociological Association, the Sociological Research Association, and the Eastern Sociological Association. He has served also as secretary of the American Sociological Association. In addition, he has been a consultant or research advisor to several federal, state, and private organizations.

Concerned primarily in his research and teaching with the fields of intergroup relations, institutional analysis, and theory of social organization and change, he has written *The Reduction of Intergroup Tensions* (1947), *American Society* (1951, 1960), and *Strangers Next Door* (1964); co-authored *What College Students Think* (1960) and *The American Soldier*, Volumes I and II (1949); and edited (with Margaret W. Ryan) *Schools in Transition* (1954).

# A note on the type

This book was set on the Linotype in ELECTRA, a type face
designed by W. A. Dwiggins. The Electra face is a simple
and readable type suitable for printing books by present-
day processes. It is not based on any historical model,
and hence does not echo any particular time or fashion.

This book was composed, printed and bound by The Book
Press, Brattleboro, Vermont. Typography by Jack
Ribik. Binding design by Muriel Nasser.